COMPLETE

CONTRACT

TEXT, CASES, AND MA

CW01496954

COMPLETE

CONTRACT LAW
TEXT, CASES, AND MATERIALS

André Naidoo

Senior Lecturer, De Montfort University

OXFORD
UNIVERSITY PRESS

OXFORD
UNIVERSITY PRESS

Great Clarendon Street, Oxford, OX2 6DP,
United Kingdom

Oxford University Press is a department of the University of Oxford.
It furthers the University's objective of excellence in research, scholarship,
and education by publishing worldwide. Oxford is a registered trade mark of
Oxford University Press in the UK and in certain other countries

Published in the United States of America by Oxford University Press
198 Madison Avenue, New York, NY 10016, United States of America

British Library Cataloguing in Publication Data

Data available

Library of Congress Control Number: 2020950906

ISBN 978–0–19–874986–8

Printed in Great Britain by
Bell & Bain Ltd., Glasgow

Preface

Contract law has the luxury of being enjoyable, logical and intriguing. In addition, as consumers we enter contracts routinely, often without a second thought, and that makes the subject very relatable. With its common law origin, contract law is based mainly on case law and, fortunately, most of the judgments are engaging and inspiring. I also like to think that contract law comes from a happy place; after all, contracts are about bringing people together. And, while it is typical for criminal law to dominate novels and TV shows, the hit series Suits is a welcome step in the right direction.

Those studying a major law subject like contract law currently benefit from a genuine range of different books. These range from those written by experienced lecturers right through to books written by those who have contributed to the development of the law and the shape of the subject. All of the books have their special qualities and the wide range reflects the diverse needs of law courses and students.

The aim of Complete Contract Law is to provide students with a comprehensive yet accessible study aid that contributes to the existing range. As a text, cases and materials book, it provides explanatory text but also extracts from the significant cases and relevant legislation to enhance the reader's understanding of the principles and the scope of their application. Along with an accessible narrative, the book makes use of pedagogical features that you can find out about in the Guide to the Book. One new feature I have employed is the Guided Case Reading feature. This presents the larger or pleasantly challenging case extracts with supportive annotations, directing the reader to the key themes to focus on and easing them into the task of understanding judgments fully. It is hoped that the reader will feel supported throughout in the development of their knowledge and understanding of the subject.

Of course, a book of this type relies on the efforts, skills and knowledge of many others to whom I owe a debt of gratitude. Starting with the immensely helpful team at OUP, I would like to thank Helen Swann for her initial work in taking the book proposal forward and also for her editorial support, suggestions, and general management throughout as the Senior Commissioning Editor. In addition, I had the benefit of the following development editors: Nicola Hartley, Alexandra McGregor, Stephanie Southall (who deserves an award for securing the most initial draft chapters from me), Natasha Ellis-Knight and Livy Watson (to whom I am also grateful for her help in developing the initial format of the Guided Case Reading feature). I am particularly grateful for their support and patience in the light of my inability to meet most of the agreed deadlines—to the extent that I can no longer recall the original date for completion!

Beyond the OUP team, I owe a significant debt of thanks to David McGrogan (Northumbria University) for allowing this book to benefit from his comments and ideas resulting from his detailed and skilful editorial contribution. I am also grateful to Omar Madhloom (University of Bristol) for his helpful comments and suggestions on a number of draft chapters.

I would also like to thank the many anonymous reviewers who took the time to evaluate my rough draft chapters to provide both positive comments and constructive criticism to inform the level and content of the book.

Finally, I would like to extend my thanks to the following colleagues for their encouragement and support during my career: Professor Chris Willett (University of Essex), and from my own law school, Kevin Bampton during his time as my Head of School, Professor David Oughton (now retired), Debra Brown and David Hodgkinson. Finally, I would like to express my thanks to the great Professor Michael Furmston (who sadly passed away last year) for encouraging me to take on a project of this type.

Acknowledgements

Grateful acknowledgement is made to all the authors and publishers of copyright material that appears in this book, and in particular to the following for permission to reprint material from the sources indicated.

Incorporated Council of Law Reporting: extracts from the *Law Reports: Appeal Cases* (AC), *Chancery* (Ch), *King's Bench Division* (KB), *Queen's Bench Division* (QB), and *Weekly Law Reports* (WLR).

LexisNexis: extract from ***All England Reports* (All ER)** © **LexisNexis:** *CTN Cash and Carry v Gallaher Ltd* [1994] 4 All ER 714, Court of Appeal; and extracts from ***Butterworths*™ *Law Reports of the Commonwealth* (LCR):** *Chwee Kin Keong v Digilandmall.com Pte* [2004] SGHC 71; [2005] 2 LRC 28, Singapore High Court. Reproduced by permission of RELX (UK) Limited, trading as LexisNexis.

Every effort has been made to trace and contact copyright holders prior to publication. If notified the publisher will undertake to rectify any errors or omissions at the earliest opportunity.

Guide to using the book and online resources

Complete Contract Law: Text, Cases, and Materials includes a number of features that have been carefully designed to enrich your learning and help you along as you develop your understanding of contract law.

You will find further support on the book's online resources, at **www.oup.com/uk/naidoo1e/**

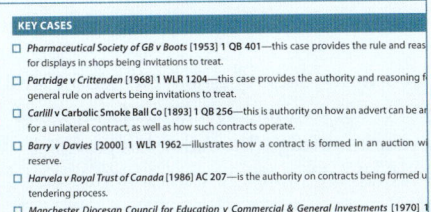

Learning Objectives Each chapter begins by listing in brief what you should have learned by the end of the chapter, to help structure your learning.

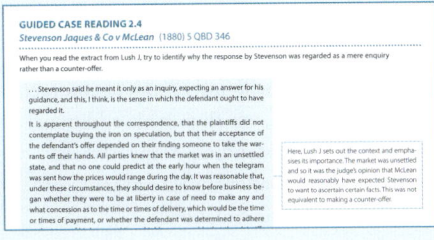

Key cases and materials Cases play an integral role in the development of contract law, so it is important to read case judgments in order to fully understand the subject. This book includes extracts from a wide range of cases and legislation, which complement the author's explanations.

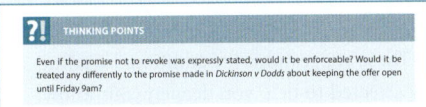

Guided case reading This unique feature focuses on the most important cases in each chapter, providing detailed annotations to support your understanding of the points made and develop your independent case reading skills.

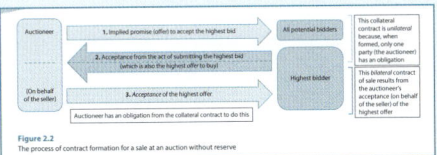

Thinking points Thinking points throughout the text help you to engage actively with the issues and develop your critical thinking.

Diagrams Diagrams appear at key points throughout the book, helping to make important and challenging points as clear as possible.

KEY POINTS

■ An offer for a unilateral contract can be ended if the intention to revoke it is communicated before performance of the act of acceptance has started.

■ If performance has started, the offer becomes irrevocable but will only result in a contract when performance is complete.

■ Revocation should be communicated in a manner that has an equivalent effect to the one used to make the offer.

Key points Key point features summarise and reiterate the most important information throughout, to help you identify and absorb these crucial points of law.

→ **CROSS-REFERENCE**
for the formation of contracts in the context of automated machines see 3.4.

contract would be the acceptance for the shop's separate (prop second contract, the shop would be under an obligation to give other terms are satisfied.

A display of goods in a vending machine should be regarded of the machine. This is based on the reasoning of Lord Denning [1971] 2 QB 163 which concerned an automated ticket machine

Cross references These helpful notes make navigation quick and easy by pointing you to a different section or chapter where a topic is discussed in more detail.

Here we address a common negotiating device for businesses Businesses often need to buy a major item like a special piece of service like the construction of a new building. Shopping around suitable party to do the work can be very time consuming. An alte the business and invite others to submit a **tender** for the work. For ous building companies might be invited to send in their best quo

tender
is a bid to buy or sell something and is usually classed as an offer.

The tendering process is seen as a fair way to find a party to con compete for the contract and are given an equal chance of succeed tendering process is used so much by public sector bodies when t business from the private sector. A familiar example is the Natio process was used to find a company to run it.

Definitions Key terms are highlighted and defined in the margin, for ease of reference.

QUESTIONS

1. What is the basis for the general rules making adverts and displays in a shop invitations to trea do those rules continue to be suitable in the modern day?

2. Getz 1 Ltd attend an auction advertised as 'without reserve' to buy some of the famous early puters on display. When the bidding starts for an Apple III (1980) computer, Getz 1 Ltd's bid of is the highest. However, the auctioneer decides that the price is too low and withdraws the Does Getz 1 Ltd have a contract and are they entitled to the Apple III?

3. 'The way contracts are formed using the competitive tendering is fair and reflects the reaso expectations of the parties.'
Discuss.

4. XS Pizza Ltd emails everyone on its mailing list offering a free pizza to anyone that wears its p tional T shirt in public for the entire day (9am to 9pm). Tosi queues to collect her T shirt at 9a

End of chapter questions These questions provide the ideal opportunity for you to test your understanding of a topic and practise applying your knowledge. The author has provided answer guidance in the book's online resources, so you can check your thinking.

1. Zara visits her local supermarket. She takes several items from the shelves and places them in her shopping basket before placing the basket of items in front of Zak, the cashier, at the checkout, ready to pay. Which **one** of the following statements **most accurately** describes the normal process of contract formation in this situation?

○ The display of items is an offer and Zara accepted that offer by placing the items into the shopping basket.

○ Zara made an offer by placing the items into her shopping basket and Zak will have accepted that offer when he passes the items over the barcode reader.

○ Zara made an offer by taking the items to the checkout and Zak will have accepted that offer when he passes the items over the barcode reader.

○ The display of items is an offer and Zara accepted that offer when she took the items to the checkout.

○ The display of items is an invitation to treat and Zak will make an offer when he passes the items over the barcode reader.

Multiple choice questions You will find a bank of contract law MCQs on the online resources, which provide additional opportunities to check your understanding. Many of these questions include scenarios which allow further practice of applying your knowledge to realistic situations.

FURTHER READING

Graw, 'Puff, Pepsi and "That Plane" – The John Leonard Saga' (2000) 15 JCL 281.
An interesting article about adverts and offers for unilateral contracts.

Jackson, 'Offer and Acceptance in the Supermarket' (1979) 129 NLJ 775.
A short article on contract formation in basic supermarkets like those from the 1970s.

Scott, 'The auction house: with or without reserve?' [2001] LMCLQ 334.
A useful short case note analysing *Barry v Davies*.

Simpson, 'Quackery and Contract Law: Carlill v Carbolic Smoke Ball Company (1893)' in Leadi Cases in the Common Law (OUP) 1995, p. 259.
This chapter provides a detailed analysis of *Carlill v Carbolic Smoke Ball Co* in its historical background and its significance in

Further reading These suggestions for additional reading have been carefully selected to help you deepen your knowledge of the subject.

Good faith

Implied terms of good faith and relational contracts

The facts in *Essex CC v UBB Waste (Essex) Ltd* [2020] EWHC 1581 (TCC) concerned a 25-year contract for the design, construction, financing, commissioning, operation and maintenance of a mechanical biological waste treatment plant to process household waste. One question which arose was whether the contract was a so-called relational contract which contained an implied obligation of good faith. In addressing this question, Pepperall J referred (at [105]) to the non-exhaustive list of nine factors identified by Fraser J in *Bates v Post Office (No. 3)* [2019] EWHC 606 (QB) and explained (at [106]): 'While this is a useful approach, it must be kept firmly in mind that these nine factors do not fall to be construed like the words of a statute, rather they are helpful indicia of a relational contract. Indeed, Fraser J no doubt had this very much in mind in his comments at [726]'.

Updates to the law Visit the online resources to stay up to date with key developments in case law and legislation.

Summary Contents

Summary Contents

Detailed contents

PART 3 ENFORCEMENT OF THE CONTRACT

PART 4 FACTORS THAT CAN END THE CONTRACT

Table of cases

Table of legislation

Table of Statutory Instruments

Rules

European Union Legislation Directives

Regulations

Introduction to the Study of Contract Law

1

LEARNING OBJECTIVES

By the end of this chapter you should be able to:

- understand the shape and use of contract law;
- appreciate the classic model of contract law and the gradual move away from it;
- understand how case law principles are applied;
- explain the role and significance of good faith in the performance of relational contracts.

INTRODUCTION

This chapter provides an essential basic overview of contract law and its application. The aim is to provide enough context to serve as a foundation for the understanding of the legal principles covered by the subsequent chapters. Knowing the shape of an area of law, what it is about, and its sources are always important steps before studying individual substantive topics. Equally, it is important to know the basic role of the legal rules and principles, as well as the approach adopted by the courts when applying them.

1.1 What Is a Contract?

Before studying the law relating to contracts, it is important to have an idea about what a contract is and the form that a contract can take. It might be surprising to learn that there is no legislative or case law definition of a contract. The absence of such a formal legal definition suggests that there is no need for one in practice, but various legal scholars have attempted to define what a contract is. According to Treitel on The Law of Contract (now by E. Peel, 14th edition, Sweet & Maxwell (2015)):

> A contract is an agreement giving rise to obligations which are enforced or recognised by law. The factor which distinguishes contractual from other legal obligations is that they are based on the agreement of the contracting parties.

This definition is a useful starting point. By addressing what it includes, we will see the criteria that need to be met in order for a contract to be created. The wide scope of the definition, resulting from what it carefully does not include, reflects the wide range of contracts that exist.

1.1.1 A 'Legally Enforceable' Agreement

We can see that on a basic level, a contract is simply a type of agreement, but it can be distinguished from any other agreement by the fact that it is *legally* enforceable. This status of being legally enforceable means that, in theory, if a party to the contract fails to perform its obligations, the other party could enforce the agreement in a court and be awarded compensation for losses resulting from the failure to perform. We will see that an agreement is typically formed by one party making an offer which is then accepted by the other. For the agreement to be legally enforceable, there are two requirements. First, it must appear that the parties intended for the agreement to be legally enforceable. The second requirement is known as 'consideration' and requires the agreement to reflect an exchange of value between the parties.

1.1.2 The Absence of a Prescribed Format

Ordinarily, there is no requirement that a contract must take a specific format or be presented in a certain way. It might be easy to think of contracts as detailed formal documents with a special legal significance. The common image of a contract is a document made up of several pages using formal legal language that only lawyers understand. Perhaps it requires the signatures of the parties and maybe an old wax seal with a unique stamp. An alternative common image of a contract is one negotiated aggressively by lawyers, drafted and then presented in a corporate folder to be signed. The reality of contracts is very different. Generally, contracts do not have to be presented in a particular way, they can be oral—based on what two people say to each other—and such an agreement is as enforceable as a written contract. Of course, it is necessary to be able to prove what was said and agreed, and this involves giving testimony in court for a judge to weigh alongside other evidence and rule on what was said. But once an oral contract is proven, it is as enforceable as a written one. A contract could even be expressed as a few sentences on a paper napkin or as a sequence of text messages.

The absence of set formalities or format requirements for contracts represents a general position rather than an absolute one because there are some exceptions where legislation does require formalities. A contract in the form of a deed is often associated with the transfer or sale of real property rights like the ownership of a house or land. The Law of Property (Miscellaneous Provisions) Act 1989 requires a **deed** to be a written document that describes itself as a deed; it has to be signed by the party making it and witnessed by two people who also sign. Contractual parties sometimes choose to enter a contract in the form of a deed. One reason for doing so is to avoid the requirement of an exchange of value that applies to ordinary contracts. However, beyond the use of deeds, generally there is no set format for a contract.

deed
is a legal instrument that is described as a deed, and is signed and witnessed, usually to pass on rights.

1.1.3 The Diversity of Contracts

The general absence of a set format for contracts helps to explain why contracts are so diverse. To appreciate the diversity of contracts, we only have to think about the contracts that we have entered into as consumers. You might have entered into a range of written contracts in the form of actual documents, which is typical when arranging accommodation, insurance or a mobile phone plan. These might well have been entered into online, starting with a digital document that can then be printed. You will certainly have entered into many less formal but equally important everyday contracts. When we buy online or even download an app, we enter into a contract which is available on screen, with notice of the terms and our agreement to them being signified by clicking a box confirming that the terms have been read. Each time we go out and buy from a shop we are entering an oral contract, whether we are buying an expensive PC tablet or a pack of sweets. For each transaction, there is a contract with the shop which is enforceable for up to six years. The receipt is just one form of evidence that the transaction took place rather than the contract itself, because as we will see, such a contract is formed before the receipt is issued. The same applies to the snacks or drinks we buy from vending machines; for each transaction we have a contract with the supplier that runs the machine. We enter into a contract every time we buy a train or bus ticket, and each time we hire a taxi or order a takeaway. Just like the contract from a shop purchase, the contract in all these situations is not in a physical or tangible form, but it does exist and, just like the contracts we enter with a shop, it will have terms.

1.1.4 The Sources of Contract Terms

All contracts have terms, and it is the terms that represent the content of the agreement. These terms create obligations and rights, usually for both parties. When buying from a shop we are promising to pay a price for the goods and, if agreed, that price becomes a term of the sales contract. In return for the payment, the shop will be seen as having promised to give ownership of the goods to the buyer. Of course, in the everyday shop purchase, the obligations and rights are not actually discussed. Instead, they are expressed by the conduct of the parties and the price is expressed on a tag or label. In addition, there might be terms displayed inside shops and a common example is a term allowing you to return items later if you change your mind. You might be familiar with some shops stating that you have 30 days to return goods for any reason, which is particularly useful when buying clothing that you have not tried on. Ordinarily, a shop is under no legal obligation to allow a refund just because you have changed your mind or the clothes do not fit, because you and the shop have a contract. However, shops compete with each other for customers and do so not just on the basis of quality and price, but also on the terms they use. By displaying that customers have such a right, the wording becomes an expressed term of the sales contract, giving customers a *contractual* right to return the goods within the period specified.

While express terms are important, everyday contracts consist of much more. Alongside the express terms, we often have terms that are implied by legislation or the courts. Such terms are assumed to be part of the contract automatically and there is no need for the parties to state or agree on them. A good example of legislation implying terms is the Consumer Rights Act 2015. It implies a range of useful terms into our consumer contracts, including a term requiring the goods to be of satisfactory quality. This means the seller is in breach of that term if the goods are sufficiently defective, and such a breach results in a range of possible remedies under the Act. The consumer could end the contract for a refund or, alternatively, have a repair or a replacement. In some circumstances, the consumer could be entitled to a price reduction.

While parties will often seek to enforce a particular term or range of terms within the contract, it is possible for a party to have enforceable rights that exist outside of the contract, and that is our next point.

1.1.5 Freestanding Rights from Legislation

In addition to the express and implied terms of a contract, a party to a contract might benefit from separate additional rights arising from legislation, such as those from The Consumer Contracts (Information, Cancellation and Additional Charges) Regulations 2013. In the context of distance sales, like those made online or over the phone, the Regulations give consumers the right to cancel the sales contract within fourteen days. Such a right is not implied into the contract and is instead a free-standing right from a rule of law.

1.2 The Shape of Contract Law

As with any subject we study, it is useful to have an overview of its general shape before commencing, so that the topics are not viewed in isolation. This section provides that brief overview. In the mid-twentieth century contract law books by Treitel and by Cheshire and Fifoot contributed significantly to the knowledge of contract law. Just like the earlier treatises by Anson (1879) and Pollock (1875), these later books influenced the development of the law, with judgments regularly citing their opinions. Today, the structure of contract law set out by Anson and developed by Treitel and Cheshire and Fifoot continues to be replicated by current textbooks in some way.

1.2.1 Topics Concerning the Existence of a Contract

The common starting point is the law relating to the formation of contracts, beginning with agreement. This is about how the courts determine if the parties to a dispute have an agreement. Such disputes typically arise where one party argues that there has been a breach of contract and the other argues that there was never an agreement, and therefore never a contract to breach. The normal rule is that an agreement consists of an offer by one party that was accepted by the other. Both aspects—the offer and the acceptance—raise a range of issues. For example, did a particular proposal that was accepted actually amount to an offer under the law? Even where it did amount to an offer, it might be that the offer was ended before the purported acceptance took place. Further issues arise in relation to acceptance. It might be that not enough was done for acceptance to have taken place, such as the wrong method of acceptance being used or the method adopted being too late to be effective. We explore the law relating to offer in Chapter 2 and the law relating to acceptance in Chapter 3.

Even where the existence of an agreement is obvious, a party might argue that the agreement is not enforceable and therefore not a contract. This might be based on there being no intention to enter a legal relationship, and we will see that the courts have developed strong presumptions to determine whether such an intention exists. For example, if the agreement is a social arrangement like two friends agreeing to meet at the cinema, then it will be presumed that their agreement was not intended to result in a legal relationship. In contrast, when a consumer buys from a trader or when two businesses enter an agreement, it is presumed that a legal relationship was intended. A related issue is whether the agreement is certain enough. If there are important matters that have been left out of an agreement or important terms that are vague, it might be held that it was too uncertain to be enforced. Likewise, such uncertainty could be taken as an indication that the parties did not intend to have a legal relationship. We explore both the law relating to intention to enter a legal relationship and certainty in Chapter 4.

A further general requirement for an agreement to be enforceable, and therefore a contract, is known as consideration, and this is the subject of Chapter 5. Essentially, the agreement has to represent the model of a bargain, which involves an exchange (or a promise of an exchange) of one thing of value in return for another. If an agreement requires one party to give something to the other (or promise to do so) without the other doing anything in return, then that is simply a gift rather than a contract (unless the agreement is expressed as a deed).

The issue of parties having the capacity to enter into a contract is less prominent now and so this is addressed in the online resources for this book.

KEY POINTS

A contract is a legally enforceable agreement and requires the following:

- an agreement between the parties, usually indicated by the acceptance of an offer;
- it must appear that the parties intended to enter a legal relationship and the terms must be sufficiently certain;
- the agreement must represent an exchange of value between the parties, known as consideration.

1.2.2 Topics Concerning the Content of a Contract, Performance, and Breach

The terms represent the parties' obligations to be performed. A great number of contract disputes, particularly between businesses, arise because one party argues that a term has been breached and the other party disagrees. Such disputes are often resolved by the courts interpreting the relevant term, and the proper approach for courts to take in doing so has been a significant issue in more recent cases.

Alternatively, such disagreements might be based on one party arguing that there was no such term to breach, which then brings us to the law relating to the sources of contract terms. Terms can be expressed by the parties in a number of ways and there is case law concerning when an oral statement amounts to a term of a contract, as well as how oral statements can be added to terms that have been expressed in writing. Similarly, there are cases concerning how written statements can be incorporated into oral contracts.

Beyond express terms there are also implied terms. We will see that terms can be implied into contracts by rules from legislation. In addition, there are circumstances when the courts can imply a term into a particular disputed contract, and also circumstances where the courts can imply a term into all contracts of a certain type. We will examine the law relating to the sources of contract terms and the methods used to interpret express terms in Chapter 6.

Another key issue regarding the terms of contracts is how terms are regulated by the common law and legislation, and that is the subject of Chapter 7. This concerns the extent to which the courts and legislation can protect parties from unfair terms. We will see that from an early stage, businesses had the freedom to add terms to exclude or limit their own liability for a breach of contract and even liability for their own negligence. As an example, consider booking at a salon to have your hair dyed blue. If the treatment results in your hair being a different colour, then ordinarily the salon would be in breach and liable to compensate you for the loss caused by the breach. However, what if contract terms state that the salon will not be liable for loss caused by errors in hair colouring? Such a term attempts to exclude liability for the salon's breach. We will see that the courts developed limited ways to reduce the effectiveness of such terms and then, later, legislation was introduced to regulate their use. The most significant legislative control was based on an EU directive on unfair terms in consumer contracts which has been firmly incorporated into UK law.

The terms represent the parties' obligations to be performed. When a party refuses to perform its side of a contract, there is a clear breach, and potential disputes can arise over the options of the innocent party. Can they treat the contract as one that they can end following the breach? Can the innocent party choose to continue to perform its obligations and then sue for the agreed price due under the contract? Alternatively, a dispute can arise where a party is in breach by performing their obligations badly. While the innocent party will be entitled to compensation for loss resulting from the breach, the question might arise as to whether the innocent party can treat the contract as having ended. The relevant case law on such disputes is the subject of Chapter 8.

KEY POINTS

- It is common for contract disputes to be focussed on the terms of the contract.
- There is law relating to the interpretation of terms, the sources of terms, and how certain terms can be challenged.
- There are legal rules on what is required for performance of a contract and the options following a breach.

1.2.3 Topics Concerning the Remedies

Chapters 9, 10 and 11 are concerned with remedies following a breach. We will see in Chapter 9 that the primary remedy is in the form of compensatory damages. The idea is that parties creating a contract do so with an expectation that performance will put them in a certain position. Following a breach, the compensation is aimed at protecting that expectation by putting the innocent party (financially) in the position they should have been in, had the contract been performed. A particular issue is the type of losses that can result in compensation. For example, the traditional law focussed on the recovery of financial loss but then later developments recognised that in certain consumer contracts there could be compensation for non-financial loss, such as where a breach causes a loss of enjoyment or disappointment.

Chapter 10 explores the rules limiting the award of compensation and a major limit, which is known as the remoteness rule. The idea is that the party in breach should only be liable for the risk of loss that was deemed to be accepted when the contract was created. It means that parties in breach are not expected to compensate for *all* of the losses resulting from their breach. Instead, they are only liable for losses that would have been reasonably foreseen (at the time of making the contract) as a likely consequence of a breach. Another limit is the duty to mitigate, which means a party cannot expect compensation after unreasonably increasing its losses, and should take reasonable steps to reduce the losses suffered following a breach. Any unreasonable increase in loss, or loss that could have been reduced, will not be recoverable.

Chapter 11 then turns to the non-compensatory remedies, which are exceptional. We will see that in the highly unusual case of *Attorney-General v Blake* [2001] 1 AC 268, the House of Lords awarded damages that were not compensating for loss, but were in fact awarding the profit gained by the party in breach as a result of the breach. Such an approach is very rare because it is not based on established contract law principles and is more like the remedy used in the law of unjust enrichment. The less exceptional remedies from equity, in the form of injunction and specific performance, are also addressed, as well as the performance-based remedies found in the Consumer Rights Act 2015.

Chapter 12 is concerned with the availability of remedies for parties other than those that created the contract. It focusses on the extent to which such third parties can enforce a contract. An example would be when a contract is made by two parties to transfer goods to another (third) party. If the transfer does not take place, that third party will want to enforce the contract. There is legislation in the form of the Contracts (Rights of Third Parties) Act 1999 that gives third parties the rights to enforce contracts in certain circumstances. When the Act does not apply, there are some common law cases with limited mechanisms which remain relevant.

KEY POINTS

- The primary remedy following a breach is compensatory damages and the amount awarded will be limited by the remoteness principle and where relevant, the duty to mitigate.
- Non-compensatory damages are exceptional, as are the remedies from equity.
- In certain circumstances, it is possible for a contract to be enforced by a third party.

1.2.4 Topics Concerning the Ways to Escape from a Contract

Having covered the law associated with contract formation and contractual rights and remedies, we turn to the ways in which a party can escape a contract, starting with the vitiating factors. The term 'vitiating factors' refers to things done before the contract was created that undermine the consent of one party. This can then result in that party having the limited option of rendering the contract void. Typically, the vitiating factors come in the form of wrongdoing by one party, and the relevant law is distinct from topics covered in previous chapters because it does not concern rights arising from the contract. Instead, since the wrongdoing is based on something done before the contract was created, other areas of law are relied upon. We begin with law of misrepresentation in Chapter 13, which is the law relating to contracts entered into as a result of a false statement by one party. We will see that not all false statements can be relied upon to end a contract, but for those that are successful the contract might be ended by rescission, a remedy developed from equity. In addition, damages awards for resulting losses are based on the type of action brought, which depends on the type of false statement. Depending on the circumstances and what can be proven, a claimant might have to rely on the tort of deceit or the tort of negligence. In other circumstances the claimant could rely on the Misrepresentation Act 1967 for damages.

The second vitiating factor of duress is the subject of Chapter 14. A lot of the principles and scope of this area have developed in more recent years. Initially it was concerned with a party entering into a contract following a threat to their life by the other party, but it is now much wider, and covers threats amounting to illegitimate pressure generally. Just like with misrepresentation, there is pre-contractual wrongdoing that undermines the consent to the agreement and so the remedy of rescission applies.

A related area of law, but one which was developed initially by the courts of equity, is undue influence, and that is the subject of Chapter 15. Undue influence is concerned with a more subtle type of pressure, often arising from a relationship where one party has a dominant position over the other. In such cases there is no threat from the dominant party but, instead, it is in a position of influence that has been abused. An extreme example would be a transaction between a religious leader and his or her disciple. If a gift or contract cannot be explained by ordinary motives in such a relationship, the influence would be undue and therefore wrong. This can then result in the contract being rescinded. A key issue in this area arose from the many cases concerning wives who had entered into contracts with banks consenting for the matrimonial home to be used as security to support a loan for the husband's business. Following the failure of the husband to repay the loan, the banks took action to take possession of the homes and then the wives argued that they entered the relevant contracts following undue influence by the dominant husband. The courts then developed a way to enable the wives (and anyone in a non-commercial relationship with the party benefiting from the loan) to end the contract in certain circumstances. The chapter also addresses the limited principles associated with the exploitation of weakness.

The two other significant ways of escaping a contract are known as frustration and mistake, and unlike the vitiating factors of misrepresentation, duress and undue influence, these are not concerned with wrongdoing. The law relating to frustration of contracts is covered by Chapter 16, and concerns circumstances in which an event outside the control of the parties makes performance of a contract impossible. We will see that the grounds for frustration are very limited but, if they can be established, the contract is ended automatically. The cases are usually based on a dispute arising from one party claiming there was a breach of contract, and the other arguing that the contract was frustrated. A successful action results in financial adjustments based on the powers the courts have from the Law Reform (Frustrated Contracts) Act 1943.

Finally, Chapter 17 is concerned with contracts entered into as a result of a mistake. Again, successful actions are exceptional but the impact of a such an action is significant because the contract is made void from the start, as if it had never existed. A significant part of this area concerns mistakes that are made that prevent an agreement being formed known as an 'agreement mistake'. Such mistakes are discovered later, after the parties think a contract exists, with the party that made the mistake then arguing that the contract is void. The key issue in agreement mistakes is about where one party appears to make a mistake as to the identity of the other party and such an issue relates to misrepresentation too. For that reason, it can be much easier to understand after the law of misrepresentation has been covered.

The remaining significant part of mistake is known as 'common mistake'. This is where the agreement was made by both parties mistakenly relying on the existence of a state of affairs that did not actually exist at the time of creating the contract. A simple example would be a contract between an agent and promotor for a particular famous music artist to perform, with neither party realising that the music artist had already passed away. In such a case, performance of the contract was always impossible. In contrast, frustration applies when performance becomes impossible *after* the contract was entered, for example if the music artist passed away sometime after the contract was made. For this reason, it is often said that common mistake is about 'initial impossibility' and frustration is about 'subsequent impossibility'. The later cases on common mistake are heavily influenced by the more established principles of frustration, and so that is why mistake follows the chapter on frustration.

The issue of illegality and contracts that are contrary to public policy is covered in the online resources.

KEY POINTS

- Pre-contractual wrongdoing such as misrepresentation, duress and undue influence are vitiating factors that impair the consent to the contract. They can result in the contract being rendered void.
- A party can also escape from the contract following an agreement mistake or a mistake that made the contract impossible to perform from the start.
- A contract can also be ended on the basis of frustration which is where the performance of the contract becomes impossible.
- The principles of mistake and frustration are exceptional.

1.3 The Parties' Intentions

Throughout any book on contract law, there will be references to what the parties to a contract intended. Our starting point is that a contract is treated as an expression of what the parties intend to do. When a dispute arises—for example, when the parties argue about whether or not a contract exists or about the meaning of a particular term—it is for the courts to interpret and apply what the parties intended and that is done using a range of rules developed from the cases. It is important to appreciate how the courts work out what was intended by the parties.

1.3.1 The Objective Approach

Generally, when the courts determine what the parties intended, they are not concerned with what is called a *subjective* approach, meaning an approach that looks into what was actually in the minds of the parties at the time. Instead, the courts adopt an *objective* approach, focussing on what the parties *appeared* to intend based on factors such as what they said and did in the context of the circumstances, what we can describe as the parties' **apparent intentions**. In the context of a dispute about whether or not a contract exists, Lord Denning MR in *Storer v Manchester City Council* [1974] 1 WLR 1403 explained:

apparent intention describes what a party appeared to intend.

> In contracts you do not look into the actual intent in a man's mind. You look at what he said and did. A contract is formed when there is, to all outward appearances, a contract. A man cannot get out of a contract by saying: "I did not intend to contract" if by his words he has done so.

From this comment, we can see that the objective approach could result in a contract being created even if one of the parties had no actual intention to enter into a contract at that stage. What matters is what the parties *appeared* to have intended, and that is why we can participate in many transactions without realising that contracts have been formed. A more detailed statement relating to not only the formation of an agreement but also the need for an intention to enter a legal relationship was made in *RTS Flexible Systems Ltd v Molkerei Alois Muller GmbH & Co KG* [2010] UKSC 14, where Lord Clarke observed:

> [45]The general principles are not in doubt. Whether there is a binding contract between the parties and, if so, upon what terms depends upon what they have agreed. It depends not upon their subjective state of mind, but upon a consideration of what was communicated between them by words

or conduct, and whether that leads objectively to a conclusion that they intended to create legal relations and had agreed upon all the terms which they regarded or the law requires as essential for the formation of legally binding relations.

The objective approach makes a great deal of sense both from the perspective of the contractual parties and also the courts. When a party appears to intend to enter into a contract, the other party can go about their business knowing that a contract exists. If a subjective approach was applied based on the actual intention of parties, it would mean that a party could do everything to make it look like they were entering into a contract, only to claim later that this was the last thing on their mind. Essentially, there would be no point in entering into a contract without some sort of mind-reading ability. Such a subjective approach would take away the security and business certainty that contracts are created to reflect. It would also result in the case law being of little value because it would not be possible to say that acting in a certain way or saying certain things will or will not result in a contract.

?! THINKING POINTS

What motivates parties to enter contracts in the first place?

In contrast, the objective approach of focussing on what was said and done has the advantage of providing more certainty for parties and predictability in the cases.

1.3.2 The Perspective of the Reasonable Person

The process to determine the apparent intention of a party cannot be based on the personal (subjective) opinion of the judge deciding the case. Instead, the assessment should be based on a uniform standard or perspective that judges use and that parties can rely on. The objective perspective used by the common law is that of the 'reasonable person'. On that point, in *Trentham (G Percy) Ltd v Archital Luxfer Ltd* [1993] 1 Lloyd's Rep. 25, Steyn LJ (as he then was) observed that the 'governing criterion is the reasonable expectations of honest men'. In its simplest form, it refers to what the reasonable person in the position of the parties would have intended. The case concerned two businesses, and so when Steyn LJ referred to the way in which apparent intentions are determined or measured, he said that 'the yardstick is the reasonable expectations of sensible businessmen'.

Clearly, the way particular facts might be viewed and interpreted by the reasonable person is not an exact science and so there is scope for judges to bring in certain qualities. An example would be the traditional recognition that the reasonable person can read English, a point discussed at 6.2.3. The wide scope can also be used to reflect a degree of fairness; for example, we will see at 6.2.6 that the reasonable person expects terms that are unusual or impose a heavy burden to be expressed in a prominent way. This practice and ability of the courts to use the standards of the reasonable person to pursue certain objectives is captured by Lord Radcliffe's description of the reasonable person as 'no more than the anthropomorphic conception of justice' (*Davis Contractors Ltd. v Fareham Urban District Council* [1956] A.C. 696). Put another way, the objective standard of the reasonable person can be used as a tool to enable judges to deliver the right result.

While the common law has developed using the objective standard of the reasonable person, it is not the only standard to be applied in contact law. Consumer rights legislation aimed to reflect rights found in EU law often makes use of a more protective perspective of the 'average consumer', and some examples of this are discussed at 7.7.8 and 15.12.

The reliance on the general objective approach is not confined to disputes about whether a contract was created. It has a much wider application covering all aspects of contract law that are determined by the parties' intentions. A significant example is the interpretation of contract terms, a process often referred to as the 'construction' of the contract. Construction in this sense is necessary when the courts are faced, as they frequently are, with disputes over the meaning of terms and whether or not there has been a breach. The approach taken is discussed in detail in 6.4, but, briefly, the overall approach to construction was explained by Lord Clarke (for the Supreme Court) in *Rainy Sky SA v Kookmin Bank* [2011] UKSC 50 in the following way:

> [21]. . .[T]he exercise of construction is essentially one unitary exercise in which the court must consider the language used and ascertain what a reasonable person, that is a person who has all the background knowledge which would reasonably have been available to the parties in the situation in which they were at the time of the contract, would have understood the parties to have meant.

Again, we can see the standard of the reasonable person as a point of reference to apply an objective assessment to resolve a dispute.

1.3.3 Residual Subjectivity

Finally, on this issue of the parties' intentions, it should be appreciated that there are some limited exceptions to the objective approach. In some instances, particularly in the context of contracts being created following a mistake, the subjective knowledge of a party can be relevant. However, as explained in 17.4, objective evidence has to be used to determine what a party a knew.

KEY POINTS

- The parties' intentions are determined by an objective approach which results in more certainty and predictability.
- Generally, the standard of objectivity to be applied is that of the reasonable person in the position of the parties.

1.4 Contract Law as a Foundational Subject

In the real world, there are many types of contracts because different sectors of business use certain contracts tailored for their needs. There are contracts used in employment, shipping, insurance, the sale of goods or services between businesses, leases, the transfer of intellectual property like music copyright, and those used in the building industry. There are many more examples, including those used by public bodies. All such contracts are highly specialised, and contract lawyers practising in certain areas of law will have expertise in their own types of contracts. Such expertise is necessary because there will be either specific laws or practical issues that will be relevant to that type of contract. As an example, we can take the familiar context of an employment contract. Over the years there has been a great deal of legislation concerning such contracts, mainly concerning the rights of employees. To understand employment contracts, it is necessary to know about the rights arising from the specific legislation too. The same can be said about many other types of contracts, and no single textbook can detail comprehensively the law relating to all of these types of contracts, and no contract law course or module could do so either. For that reason, a common question is whether there really is a law of *contract* or if there are separate laws of *contracts*. Certainly, it is more convenient to study the specialised aspects of the law on contracts in distinct modules like land law, consumer law, commercial law and employment law. This means that the study of what we call contract law is not about such specialised contracts. Instead, contract law is about the foundational principles applicable to contracts generally, making it an essential starting point.

1.5 The Legal Sources of Contract Law

Unlike many other jurisdictions with their civil codes, the contract law of England and Wales is not found in the form of a comprehensive legislative rule book. Instead, contract law was developed by the common law, and while today there is a lot of legislation applicable to specific contracts like employment contracts, (foundational) contract law remains mostly case law based. It is useful to understand how the case law basis directs our focus when studying contract law as well as the different sources of contract law that have to be taken into account.

1.5.1 The Common Law Origin of Contract Law

We will see that there are some very old cases that are of relevance to the subject of contract law, some from as far back as the sixteenth century, but at that time, these cases were not understood to be representing 'contract law'. Instead, these cases resulted from the old system of relying on an action of *assumpsit* (which is Latin for 'he has undertaken') to enforce informal agreements (as opposed to agreements made using a deed). A distinct law of contract was only recognised by the first book on general principles of contact law by Leake in 1867, though this was framed in the more limited context of what has to be proven in court and the defences to be used. That was then followed by the highly influential treatises on contract law by Pollock (1875) and Anson (1879). These significant treatises pulled together many cases to represent certain legal principles specific to contracts and provided the necessary theoretical framework for those principles. Essentially, they defined the shape of contract law.

→ **CROSS-REFERENCE**
For the definition of a deed see 1.1.

Most of the early original case law developed out of disputes between businesses. The result of the cases would have been important for the parties, but for us, the real significance of the cases lies in the reasoning behind the decisions of the courts. This reasoning forms the basis of precedent, in other words, the rule represented by the case (known as the *ratio decidendi*) which is then binding on lower courts. It will then be the rule to be applied in the future when other parties have a dispute over the same issue. The rule might apply to disputes over something different if the reasoning can be extended to cover it. Likewise, the rule will not apply if a new case is said to be too different for the reasoning to hold. Beyond the immediate reasoning of a case, there are often additional opinions expressed by judges (*obiter dicta*) which are not binding, but can be so influential that they become part of the reasoning in a later case. Likewise, the courts of England and Wales could be influenced by the reasoning adopted by other common law jurisdictions like those of Canada and Australia. This process using binding precedent and influential authorities is how our common law develops and why judgments from the cases are so important. They enable us to have a more accurate understanding of what rule is represented by a case as well as the potential scope of the rule. It is for that reason that this book has extracts from the main judgments along with an explanation of them.

1.5.2 The Role of Principles from Equity

References to the 'common law' often include contract-related case law principles as well as the relevant principles developed originally by the courts of equity. In that wider context, the 'common law' means law that is distinct from areas governed by legislation. Alternatively, reference to the 'common law' principles can be used to distinguish them from equity. A detailed account of the development and operation of the courts of equity is not necessary here, but it is useful to have a very basic awareness of the jurisdiction represented by equity because of its role (albeit a fairly limited one) in contract law.

Before the Judicature Act 1875, there were common law courts and courts of equity. The common law courts adopted a rigid, more predictable approach to their cases, but such an approach sometimes led to unfair results. The remedy following disputes was in the form of compensatory damages. In contrast, the courts of equity involved decisions by the Chancellor on behalf of the King, and cases were decided initially with the use of a great deal of discretion, based on fairness and good conscience.

Such an approach was flexible and therefore unpredictable, though in later years it became increasingly rule-based and more rigid. Remedies like specific performance, which orders a party to perform, or injunctions ordering a party not to do something, were developed by the courts of equity. The Judicature Act 1975 fused the common law courts and courts of equity into a single court system, essentially with the common law courts administering equity. However, the laws remained separate so that common law remedies resulted from common law actions and equitable remedies resulted from equitable actions. We will see that in some instances, the remedies from equity might be sought by a claimant rather than damages. In addition, we will see that in some cases, the principles of equity have been developed and applied to recognise obligations where the common law was unable to do so. Among lawyers, the judgment of Denning J (as he then was) in *Central Properties Trust v High Trees House Ltd* [1947] KB 130 is a famous example of such an approach, and we will look at this at 5.11.

1.5.3 The Use of Tort and Unjust Enrichment

Even as a foundational subject, the law of contract consists of more than just common law contract principles, principles from equity and some relevant legislation. It interacts with, and makes use of other areas of common law, in particular the law of tort and what has become known as the law of unjust enrichment. It is generally accepted that the laws of contract, tort and unjust enrichment represent a wider private law of obligations. They are all concerned with the law regarding rights and obligations between private parties such as individuals and businesses, in contrast to public law, which is concerned with the relationship between private parties and the state.

A great deal can be said about the distinction between contact, tort and unjust enrichment, but for our purposes, a basic brief account is sufficient. The main way to distinguish contract law from the others is based on contract law being concerned mainly with obligations within an agreement between parties. In contrast, the obligations from tort and unjust enrichment are imposed by rules of law. Alternatively, the three areas of law can be distinguished based on the traditional aims of their remedies following a breach of the obligations. Traditionally, following a breach of contract, damages are compensatory and aim to put the innocent party financially in the position they would have been in had the contract been performed. Following a breach of an obligation from a tort like the tort of negligence, the damages are also compensatory but are aimed to put the innocent party in the position they were in before the harm or loss occurred. Finally, following unjust enrichment, like when a party is paid money by accident, the remedy is restitutionary in that it reverses the unjust enrichment.

While these types of private law obligations are commonly studied as separate areas and are represented by a range of distinct books, even the foundational law of contract shows some overlap. The overlap is particularly apparent in the context of misrepresentation, discussed in Chapter 13, which relies on torts such as deceit (fraud) and negligence. Likewise, in the context of remedies, the restitutionary remedy from unjust enrichment (discussed at 11.4) is often relevant when a court finds that there was never a contract formed in the first place (typically where it is decided that there was never an agreement in the first place). Consequently, the law of contract's non-legislative sources are common law cases concerning contracts, principles from equity, and some aspects of tort and unjust enrichment.

1.5.4 Legislation and EU Law

It can be said that the law of contract is mainly—rather than exclusively—common law based, because there is also legislation that applies in certain circumstances. Some of the legislation originates from the UK Parliament, and was passed in order to address a gap in the common law or resolve a problem that had developed within the common law. We will see that some legislation was passed to impose into contracts additional obligations, the most prominent examples being the Sale of Goods Act 1979 and the Consumer Rights Act 2015. Related to obligations, the Unfair Contract

Terms Act 1977 restricts the use of terms that exclude or limit liability in commercial contracts, and a wider level of protection is provided for consumers by the Consumer Rights Act 2015. We also have legislation on enforcement in the form of the Contracts (Rights of Third Parties) Act 1999, which aims to solve a specific common law problem and allows for contracts to be enforced by a party other than those that created the contract. In the context of remedies, the Misrepresentation Act 1967 provides some rules on remedies where contracts have resulted from certain types of false statements. Likewise, the Law Reform (Frustrated Contracts) Act 1943 provides for financial adjustments between the parties when a contract has become impossible to perform. There are other examples, but these are the main instances of legislation relevant to foundational contract law and they all serve to improve upon the common law position or solve a problem that arose within the common law.

Beyond the types of legislation addressed earlier, it is important to appreciate that there are also legislative provisions and statutory instruments that are based on EU law. During the period when the UK was a full member of the EU, the EU passed legislation in the form of **directives** which contain rights and obligations which the national law of Member States must give effect to. Such directives were wide-ranging, covering environmental obligations through to rights relating to equality, employment and consumers. It is the directives on consumer rights that made EU law a further source of contract law.

Just like directives on other areas, the directives on consumer rights resulted in national laws aimed at providing some uniformity among Member States on certain legal issues. Such uniformity has been underpinned by both demand and supply-side rationales. Put simply, a high level of consumer protection that is adopted by all Member States leads to consumer confidence in cross-border purchases. Without such uniformity, it is thought that consumers would be discouraged from buying goods and services from sellers in other Member States. The different consumer rights among Member States would then amount to a barrier to cross-border trade and undermine a fundamental aim of the single market represented by the EU. On the supply side, uniformity creates a level playing field for business traders because they will all have the same obligations and proportionate costs. Without such uniformity, businesses in states with a low level of consumer protection will have lower costs. Essentially, they would be trading using a state advantage rather than competing on their own merits and, again, that would result in a barrier to cross-border trade. As a result of EU directives, there are a range of consumer rights in UK legislation and statutory instruments, and many relate to the consumer contract. Perhaps the most significant for contract law is Part 2 of the Consumer Rights Act 2015 which is the most recent version of the legislation implementing Directive 93/13/EEC on unfair terms in consumer contracts. Part 1 of the Act also represents the rights from Directive 99/44/EC on certain aspects of the sale of consumer goods and associated guarantees. We will also see that there is UK legislation implementing the rights and obligations from various other directives on issues like distance sales (as opposed to sales in a shop), e-commerce, and unfair commercial practices such as pressure selling and false advertising.

The crucial point about the EU law relating to contracts is that it is given effect in current UK legislation and therefore represents a part of English contract law. The UK withdrawal from the EU (commonly known as Brexit) did not remove the legislation that resulted from being a member of the EU. Even though many of the statutory instruments refer to an EU obligation as their basis, they still remain in force because the European Union (Withdrawal) Act 2018 provides that the national law based on EU law remains in force. This measure was necessary to ensure that the law remained certain and had no gaps immediately following the UK withdrawal from the EU.

directive
is a form of EU legislation that instructs Member States to give effect to certain laws by a certain date to achieve a particular objective.

KEY POINTS

- Contract law is mainly common law-based and makes use of principles from equity, tort, and unjust enrichment.
- The legislation that applies to contracts exists to either solve a problem with the common law or to initially implement EU objectives.

1.6 The Application and Role of Contract Law

Legislation will dictate how its own rules apply, but the general application and role of contract law, particularly in the context of the common law, is not so clear-cut. For example, does contract law consist of rules that are imposed on all parties to a contract? At the other extreme, do the rules simply represent a default position that applies when it is not clear what the parties appeared to intend? The answer enables us to understand *how* to apply the rules.

1.6.1 The Classical Model of Contract Law

The general starting point is often referred to as the 'classical view', 'classical theory' or 'classical model' of contract law. This is used to explain the early, traditional operation of contract law. However, we will see that many old cases reflecting such a model continue to represent the current position on a particular issue. Furthermore, when judges develop the law so that it moves away from the values of the classical model, they sometimes use the language of the classical model to give the appearance of remaining faithful to it. This is partly a result of judicial precedent but also a result of an unwillingness on the part of many judges to be seen as creating new rules off-the-cuff, or what is sometimes called 'legislating from the bench' by American commentators. And undoubtedly, some judges generally favour the understanding of the law of contract which the classical model enshrined. The point is that a basic awareness of this model helps us to understand the approach of the courts in the earlier cases as well as the approach some modern judges purport to adopt.

The classical model of contract law is generally based on cases from the late eighteenth century and the nineteenth century. It required contracts to reflect an exchange of value and the focus was on what the parties agreed at the time of creating the contract. It was also underpinned by what is called 'freedom of contract' as well as the 'sanctity of contracts'.

1.6.1.1 Freedom of Contract and the Sanctity of Contract

Freedom of contract represents the idea that parties are free to choose to enter contracts and also have the freedom to determine their terms. The sanctity of contract refers to the courts enforcing what the parties have agreed. These combined elements meant that if the contract turned out to be very one-sided or even unfair, it would be enforced and the law would not intervene as long as the contract was created freely. In other words, if a party did not like the terms, then they should not have entered into the contract.

It is generally accepted that this notion of contractual freedom was influenced by the '*laissez-faire*' economics of the time. *Laissez-faire* is a French term that literally translates as 'allow to do', and broadly signifies a 'policy of leaving things to take their own course, without interfering' (Oxford English Dictionary). In the economic context, this meant that businesses were given the freedom to be regulated by the market forces of supply and demand and there was very little intervention by the state. This was seen as enabling the growth of businesses, industrialisation, and the creation of wealth. The concept of *laissez-faire* is consistent with the idea of contractual relationships being regulated by what the parties agreed rather than having state rules in the form of legislation and case law to regulate such relationships. It was generally believed that the courts' enforcement of what was agreed had the merit of producing legal certainty for the parties. They would not have to worry about legal rules interfering with their agreed obligations and rights. Once a clear agreement was made, the parties could rely on those terms to be enforced and could then weigh the financial risks represented by such contracts. The idea of enforcing what was agreed (irrespective of how one sided the contract might be) is consistent with the assumption underlying the classical model, that parties are individualistic and are only concerned with their own competing self-interest, much like gaming as a single player against another.

The classical model was also probably based on an assumption that parties are of equal bargaining strength, which means they are equally informed about the law and equal in their ability to negotiate to protect their own interests. In reality, the parties often had no such equality and, certainly in the context of consumers and employees, there was no real ability to negotiate terms, and therefore no true freedom of contract for both parties. Furthermore, parties would often have no real choice but to contract with a particular supplier where that supplier was the only one. The increased use of stand-ard terms by businesses in the same sector had the same effect, whereby the customers would have no choice but to accept those terms. That point was emphasised by Lord Reid in *Suisse Atlantique SA v Rotterdamsche Kolen Centrale NV* [1967] 1 AC 361 in the context of terms excluding liability:

Probably the most objectionable are found in the complex standard conditions which are now so common. In the ordinary way the customer has no time to read them, and if he did read them he would probably not understand them, and if he did understand and object to any of them, he would generally be told he could take it or leave it, and if he then went to another supplier the result would be the same. Freedom to contract must surely imply some choice or room for bargaining.

1.6.1.2 The Move Away from the Classical Model

Even by the late nineteenth century, freedom of contact was being limited by the courts, and their use of implied terms is just one example, though these were implied to reflect what the parties appeared to intend. Likewise, trends towards more state intervention resulted in legislation on tenancies, pay-ments and lending. The first Sale of Goods Act from 1893 implied terms into sales contracts, though these could be contractually excluded by the parties.

By the mid-twentieth century there was more judicial criticism of freedom of contract, mainly in the context of consumer contracts, with the point by Lord Reid in the *Suisse Atlantique case* being just one example. Some judges, while criticised for their judicial activism, began to do more to reflect principles of reasonableness and, in some instances, fairness. This could be achieved using the scope of the objective approach to claim that such developments were within the par-ties' apparent intentions. Such an approach reflects the contract philosophy that Professors Adams and Brownsword identified as 'consumer welfarism' in their leading work on contract theory ('The Ideologies of Contract' (1987) 7 LS 205). More recently, there has been a move away from the literal interpretation of contracts which was embedded in the classical model to an approach based on the context of the contract.

Along with more intervention by the courts, the last quarter of the twentieth century is associated with a trend towards more intervention from Parliament in the form of legislation serving to limit freedom of contract. Most notable developments include the Unfair Contract Terms Act 1977, which limited the use of certain terms, and the significant limit on contractual terms which came from the UK implementing EU legislation to protect consumers from unfair terms (initially in 1994 before moving to Part 2 of the Consumer Rights Act 2015). Likewise, there are statutory instruments providing rights to consumers in relation to distance sales as well as unfair commercial practices. Equality legislation also serves to limit contractual freedom by preventing suppliers from discriminating against buyers on any of the protected grounds (e.g. age, disability, gender, gender reassignment, marriage and civil partnership, pregnancy and maternity, race (including nationality), religion or belief, sexual orientation, etc). This is all in addition to the legislation applicable to specialised contracts, for example, employment contracts and contracts relating to financial services.

The intervention by the courts and Parliament represents a modern contract law that is clearly distinct from the classical model. However, we have to appreciate that the values of that model are still used to explain a great number of cases. These cases might be old cases representing the current position or recent cases based on older precedents. Even modern cases regularly adopt an approach reflecting values from the classical model, particularly where the parties are large businesses. We will see that a lot of cases can be explained using such values. For example, there are recent cases where the courts continue to refer to the need to ensure certainty rather than impose standards of reasonableness. Likewise, there are many cases where the courts emphasise that that law will not interfere with bad bargains (bad deals) freely made. Such cases reflect what Professors Adams and Brownsword identified as the contract philosophy of 'market individualism' that encourages competitive trading underpinned by freedom of contract and self-interest.

Perhaps a more fundamental factor which we will see throughout the topics covered is the court's emphasis on applying what the parties intended so that, generally, a lot of contract law continues to be led by what appeared to be agreed rather than by legal rules imposed on the parties. The practical significance of this is important to our basic understanding of contract law. Essentially, it means that the (foundational) law applicable to contracts is not a set of rules or instructions on how to draft a contract. Likewise, it cannot be said that contract law is a set of rules that parties and lawyers must follow whenever a contract is made or performed. Instead, we will see that, following a dispute, generally the courts will work out what the parties appeared to have intended and then give effect to that intention. This task will often require the courts to interpret the terms of the contract and the conduct of the parties. Such an approach makes sense given that a contract is an expression of the parties' intentions. By adopting this approach over time, a significant body of rules has resulted. But the crucial point here is that the case law largely represents rules that apply when the parties have not been clear enough and comprehensive about what they intended. Consequently, in many instances, if it is obvious that the parties intended to enter into a contract and the contract terms are clear and obvious about all aspects of the relationship, then no case law will apply. If there is some disputed aspect that is unclear or not covered by the terms, then the courts will apply a rule from the case law to decide what appeared to be intended in the circumstances. With that in mind, a lot of contract law can be viewed as a set of default rules that apply when there is a dispute.

We will see that there are some exceptions to the focus on the parties' intentions, where a rule exists and operates irrespective of what the parties intended. Some of these derive from the case law, with one example being the requirement of a contract to involve an exchange of value or the promise of such an exchange. This is known as the requirement of consideration and is detailed in Chapter 5. In addition to the case law exceptions, the rules from legislation are often rules that are imposed on the parties. The legislation that applies to consumer contracts, like the Consumer Rights Act 2015, is a good example. Beyond the case law and legislative exceptions, there are many cases indicating that judges sometimes impose a standard of reasonableness or fairness when 'interpreting' what the parties 'intended'. When doing so, the cases reflect a modern contract law approach that makes use of greater intervention, but under the guise of giving effect to what the parties intended. Furthermore, some leading commentators have argued that judges *should* impose certain protective standards of fair dealing and good faith into the contractual relationship when resolving a dispute. Many have even argued that the common law approach should be replaced with a comprehensive contract code like those used in civil law jurisdictions. Such a code could represent requirements and rules for contracts that are applied to give effect to values like fair dealing and good faith.

KEY POINTS

- Under the classical model, disputes were resolved based on what the parties agreed at the time of contracting only.
- Such intentions were assessed on the assumption of freedom of contract, the sanctity of contract and parties being self-interested market actors.
- Later cases show a more interventionist approach in which rules or standards were imposed.
- Many cases are still explained by the values of the classical model.
- A lot of contract law can be described as default rules that only apply when the parties have not been clear enough about their intentions.

1.6.2 Relational Contracts

One key element of the classical model is that disputes are resolved by focussing on what was agreed *at the time* the contract was made. The problem is that with long-term contracts (e.g. franchise agreements and contracts for a large-scale construction and so forth), the parties will often need to make adjustments and co-operate more to fulfil the aims of their contract. The classical tradition of simply resolving disputes could then been seen as inadequate. Focussing on the express rights and obligations that were agreed long ago enables parties to rely on technical breaches to disrupt the contract. An alternative theory of 'relational contracts' was put forward by scholars in the US, most notably in the published work of Professor MacNeil, and by UK-based scholars such as Professor Hugh Collins and Professor David Campbell. A detailed account of relational contract theory is more appropriate for specialised academic work, but it is useful for us to have a very basic idea of the position of relational contracts, as this constitutes an important contract law development.

Relational contract theory treats long-term contracts as a means to achieve the parties' common commercial objectives. The focus is then on the parties' continuing relationship goals rather than the specific rights and obligations arising from the contractual document. Such an approach would then mean that there are additional obligations of co-operation and even good faith. The forward-thinking theory of relational contracts remained no more than a theory in English law until *Yam Seng Pte v International Trade Corp* [2013] EWHC 111 (QB). In this case, Leggatt J (as he then was) acknowledged relational contract theory as the basis for implying a term imposing a duty of good faith. According to Leggatt J, relational contracts were longer-term contracts requiring:

→ CROSS-REFERENCE
For more detail on the duty of good faith see 1.5.3.

> [142]. . .[A] high degree of communication, cooperation, and predictable performance based on mutual trust and confidence and involved expectations of loyalty which are not legislated for in the express terms of the contract but are implicit in the parties' understanding. . .

This approach of implying a term of good faith into relational contracts was then adopted and approved by a number of first instance decisions of the High Court. While the appeal courts have not assessed the obligations arising from a relational contract, the Court of Appeal has acknowledged the existence of such contracts. An example is *Amey Birmingham Highways Ltd v Birmingham City Council* [2018] EWCA Civ 264, where Jackson LJ explained:

→ CROSS-REFERENCE
For the cases recognising relational contracts as a basis for implying a term of good faith see 1.5.3.

> [92]. . . In recent years there has been much academic literature on relational contracts and on the question whether they are subject to special rules. See, for example, Professor Hugh Collins' paper 'Is a relational contract a legal concept?' in Contracts in Commercial Law (Degeling and others, Thomson Reuters 2016). . .
>
> [93]. . . Any relational contract of this character is likely to be of massive length, containing many infelicities and oddities. Both parties should adopt a reasonable approach in accordance with what

> is obviously the long-term purpose of the contract. They should not be latching onto the infelicities and oddities, in order to disrupt the project and maximise their own gain.

The recent recognition of relational contracts in English law is a very significant shift away from the traditional approach grounded in the classical model of contract law. It means that the courts will continue to rely on the what the parties agreed at the time of the contract (a classical model approach), but in certain long-term contracts, they might impose additional co-operation obligations on the parties. The emerging guidance from subsequent High Court cases shows that the parties' apparent intentions in relational contracts can be used as a framework to impose cooperation obligations such as those of good faith and fair dealing, and that is our next topic.

1.6.3 Good Faith and Fair Dealing

Principles of fair dealing and good faith (both represented by 'good faith') can be viewed as values of modern contract law that sit at the opposite end of the spectrum to the classical model of contract and are well established in civil law jurisdictions and the US. Such values are said to require standards of commercial decency and reasonableness, and are therefore not easy to define. Typically, good faith is associated with openness and honesty between the parties in their negotiations, and cooperation and honesty during performance of the contract. For an example of an obligation of good faith during negotiations, consider the negotiations before creating a contract for a building project. If the obligation applied, it might be breached if the project owner had no genuine intention to enter a contract with a builder they were negotiating with, and was only negotiating to put more pressure on another, preferred builder to enter a contract for the same project. In the context of the performance of a contact that has been agreed, an obligation of good faith could be breached if the project owner deliberately made it difficult for the builder to perform in order to encourage them to quit and pave the way for cheaper builders to take over. The principle of good faith is therefore inconsistent with the assumption of the classical model that parties are individualistic and that the contract represents their self-interest only.

Good faith has been a major subject of academic writing and debate, with entire books devoted to it. The debate and analysis of the principle is far beyond the scope of this book, but it is useful to have an introductory appreciation of good faith as a key theme among academics that has gained some limited judicial support in the recent case law.

1.6.3.1 The 'Traditional' Position in England and Wales

The starting point is the traditional position that the contract law of England and Wales has no *general principle* of good faith. In contrast, most civil law jurisdictions have a general principle of good faith, and in some other common law jurisdictions, a good faith obligation is implied into all contracts. With that in mind, Leggatt J observed that English law was 'swimming against the tide' (*Yam Seng Pte Ltd v International Trade Corporation Ltd* [2013] EWHC 111).

While there is no general principle of good faith, it is a concept that has a role in specific circumstances. A key example that we will see in 7.7.5 is the requirement of good faith in the assessment of unfair terms in consumer contracts. That assessment is now in the Consumer Rights Act 2015 but was originally from a statutory instrument from 1994 giving force to the provisions of a directive from EU law. Likewise, good faith is a concept used in the Commercial Agents (Council Directive) Regulations 1993, again implementing a directive from EU law.

Beyond the legislation giving effect to requirements from EU law, the example of insurance contracts shows us that good faith was not completely alien to the traditional common law of England and Wales. In *Carter v Boehm* (1766) 3 Burr 1905, which concerned an insurance contract, Lord Mansfield famously recognised a mutual duty of utmost good faith. This duty required a high degree of openness during negotiations in the form of an obligation on each party to reveal information that the other party would regard as important when deciding to enter into a contract. This was quickly limited by later cases to a duty that applied to insurance contracts only and was later codified into section 17 of the Marine Insurance Act 1906. In recent years, this good faith duty has been replaced for the purposes of consumer insurance contracts by the Consumer Insurance (Disclosure and Representations) Act 2012 and its effect was modified for the purposes of commercial insurance contracts by the Insurance Act 2015. However, beyond this specific instance of insurance contracts, the common law of England and Wales has not adopted a general duty of good faith (i.e. a duty of good faith that applies to all contracts generally).

1.6.3.2 The Rejection of a General Duty of Good Faith

The courts of England and Wales have resisted suggestions that there should be a general duty of good faith. The reluctance to adopt such a general principle is often attributed to good faith being perceived as something that would cause uncertainty, even though it is well established and appears to work in other jurisdictions. Furthermore, it is seen as being inconsistent with the classical tradition of treating parties as self-interested rather than having objectives based on co-operation, a point that was observed by Lord Ackner in the House of Lords case of *Walford v Miles* [1992] 2 AC 128:

➜ CROSS-REFERENCE
On the rejection of a pre-contractual obligation to negotiate in good faith see 4.5.1.

> However the concept of a duty to carry on negotiations in good faith is inherently repugnant to the adversarial position of the parties when involved in negotiations. Each party to the negotiations is entitled to pursue his (or her) own interest, so long as he avoids making misrepresentations.

Some judges have shown an appreciation of good faith but expressed that it was not necessary in English law, the most notable being the following observation by the influential Bingham LJ (as he then was) in the Court of Appeal case *Interfoto Picture Library Ltd v Stiletto Visual Programmes Ltd* [1989] 1 QB 433. Having referred to the existence of good faith and fair dealing in many civil law jurisdictions, Bingham LJ turned to explain how the common law deals with problems with unfairness:

> English law has, characteristically, committed itself to no such overriding principle but has developed piecemeal solutions in response to demonstrated problems of unfairness. Many examples could be given. Thus equity has intervened to strike down unconscionable bargains. Parliament has stepped in to regulate the imposition of exemption clauses and the form of certain hire-purchase agreements. The common law also has made its contribution, by holding that certain classes of contract require the utmost good faith, by treating as irrecoverable what purport to be agreed estimates of damage but are in truth a disguised penalty for breach, and in many other ways.

The approach of dealing with issues of unfairness using 'piecemeal' on-demand solutions results in the development of exceptions to the general rules, but only as and when they are needed to resolve a dispute. Such a reactive approach is very different from having a 'top down' general principle of good faith.

The absence of a general principle of good faith does not mean that the courts have no experience with the concept of good faith. Increasingly, commercial parties include an obligation to act in good faith during the performance of their contracts. When a dispute arises, the courts will need to interpret this obligation to determine if it has been breached. However, in such instances the courts have based their interpretation on the way the good faith obligation was intended to be defined by the parties, using the specific wording, and wider context of the particular contract. In doing so, cases like *Mid Essex Hospital Services NHS Trust v Compass Group UK and Ireland Ltd* [2013] EWCA Civ 200 and *Health & Case Management Ltd v The Physiotherapy Network Ltd* [2018] EWHC 869 show different standards of co-operation in performance resulting from terms including an express reference to good faith. This is because the obligation of good faith would have been unique to these cases, based on their own facts.

1.6.3.3 The Recent Recognition of Good Faith in Performance

Perhaps the most notable development in recent years has been the emerging judicial support for an implied term of good faith in performance. In *Yam Seng Pte Ltd v International Trade Corporation Ltd* [2013] EWHC 111 (Comm) Leggatt J set out the basis for a good faith obligation being an implied term in relational commercial contracts. The case concerned a 30-month contract for the distribution of Manchester United branded toiletries. After classing the contract as relational, it was held that there had been a breach of an *implied* term to act in good faith. According to Leggatt J, such a term would be breached by conduct that would be 'regarded as commercially unacceptable by reasonable and honest people', and was implied based on the parties' apparent intentions and the context of the contract. The imposition of this duty was justified as being consistent with the contract in the following way:

→ CROSS-REFERENCE
On relational contracts generally see 1.6.2.

> [148]. . .[I]ts recognition is not an illegitimate restriction on the freedom of the parties to pursue their own interests. The essence of contracting is that the parties bind themselves in order to co-operate to their mutual benefit. The obligations which they undertake include those which are implicit in their agreement as well as those which they have made explicit.

Accordingly, this duty was not inconsistent with the assumption of parties being self-interested, and was simply a reflection of that quality. In effect, the context of the contract showed that it was in the parties' (self-)interest to cooperate.

Subsequently, in *Bristol Groundschool Ltd v Intelligent Data Capture Ltd* [2014] EWHC 2145, Richard Spearman QC (sitting as a deputy judge) recognised an implied term to act in good faith because the contract, which was for the development of computer-based pilot training materials, was within what Leggatt J identified as the relational sphere. A more limited supporting observation was made by Beatson LJ in *Globe Motors v TWR Lucas Verity Electric Steering Ltd* [2016] EWCA Civ 396, to the effect that courts might be more willing to imply such a term into relational contracts.

There was some doubt about the legal basis used in these cases to imply the relevant term. As we will see in 6.5.3–6.5.8, judges cannot imply a term whenever they want to. Instead, the common law has developed certain tests to be satisfied as the legal basis for implying terms. The approach adopted by Leggatt J (in the *Yam Seng case*) reflected the modified test developed by the highly influential Lord Hoffman in *Attorney-General of Belize v Belize Telecom* [2009] UKPC 10. That test linked the process of implying a term with the interpretation of contracts, but was subsequently met with disapproval by the Supreme Court in *Marks & Spencer plc v BNP Paribas Securities Services Trust Co (Jersey) Ltd* [2015] UKSC 72

→ CROSS-REFERENCE
For the discussion of Lord Hoffman's basis for implying terms and its subsequent rejection see 6.5.5.

However, the doubt that emerged over the legal basis for Leggatt J's judgment was short lived. Following the *Marks & Spencer* case, courts have continued to show approval for implying a term of good faith into relational contracts, which suggests it can be done using the traditional legal basis for implying terms. In *Al Nehayan v Kent* [2018] EWHC 333 (Comm), Leggatt LJ identified a contract intended to be a long-term collaboration as 'relational' and implied a term of good faith as essential to the parties' reasonable expectations. Likewise, in *Bates v Post Office Ltd* [2019] EWHC 606 (QB), based on the *Yam Seng* case, Fraser J classed the contract as relational and implied a number of good faith obligations. In doing so, the judge emphasised that good faith included more than a requirement to act honestly, and also included duty of fidelity or loyalty to the aims of the contract. At the same time, the duty does not require a party to treat their interests as secondary to those of the other party, a point made by Leggatt LJ in *Al Nehayan v Kent*.

?!   THINKING POINTS

Should an obligation of good faith be implied into all relational contracts?

Bates v Post office concerned a new computer payments system that the Post Office imposed on so-called Sub-Postmasters and Postmistresses along with a contract. The contract stated that any discrepancies between the payments by the sub-post offices and what the computer system recognised would be deemed to be the fault of the sub-post offices. When discrepancies arose, the Post Office claimed the monetary difference from the sub-post offices and ignored evidence showing faults with its own computer system. Fraser J went so far as to say that the ignorance of the computer errors was the '21st-century equivalent to maintaining that the earth was flat'. By recognising that the obligation to act in good faith went beyond a mere requirement of honesty, he held that the Post office were in breach for a range of different conduct. This included their failure to co-operate and investigate the discrepancies, through to the absence of providing training and support.

The approach of Fraser J in *Bates v Post Office* was cited with approval and applied by Andrew Hochhauser QC (sitting as a Deputy Judge) in *SPI North Limited v Swiss Post International (UK) Limited* [2019] EWHC 2004 (Ch) and also by Teare J in *New Balance Athletics Inc v Liverpool Football Club and Athletic Grounds Ltd* [2019] EWHC 2837 (Comm). Other cases have shown approval of a good faith obligation being implied into relational contracts, but have been unable to do so on the facts based on the limits of the approach adopted by Leggatt J in *Yam Seng*. In *UTB LLC v Sheffield United Ltd* [2019] EWHC 2322 (Ch), Fancourt J cited the judgment of Leggatt J with approval and identified the contract in the investments and shareholders' agreement in the case as relational. However, Fancourt J was unable to imply a term of good faith because the parties had a very detailed, professionally drafted contract which created a strong inference that the parties did not intend anything more than what was expressed in it. The same approach was adopted by Judge Pelling QC in *TAQA Bratani Ltd v Rockrose UKC58 LLC* [2020] EWHC 58 (Comm). These cases reflect the initial point made by Leggatt J in *Yam Seng* that the implied term of good faith in relational contracts is not absolute. Instead, such a term will not be implied when the conduct of the parties is effectively 'legislated for in the express terms'.

Importantly, the recent cases show clear approval for the approach adopted by Leggatt J in *Yam Seng*, and demonstrate that it survives the confirmation of the traditional tests for implying a term by the Supreme Court in *Marks & Spencer*. Perhaps the most important points are that, collectively, the cases not only show an acceptance of the concept of relational contracts, but also an acceptance of good faith in contract law, certainly in the context of relational contracts.

KEY POINTS

- The recent recognition of relational contracts is a significant departure from the classical approach of focussing on what was agreed at the time of contracting.
- The recent cases show that an obligation of good faith is implied into relational contracts unless it appears to be excluded by the parties, either expressly from the terms or impliedly from the circumstances. This also represents a further shift away from the classical model.

CHAPTER SUMMARY

- A contract is an agreement made with intention that it will be legally enforceable.
- Contract law concerns issues regarding the formation of contracts; the sources, interpretation and regulation of terms; when a breach takes place and the resulting consequences; and ways to escape a contract through vitiating factors, mistake, or frustration.
- The parties' intentions are determined using an objective approach based on the standard of the reasonable person.
- A lot of contract law can be understood as default rules to apply when the parties have not been clear enough about their intentions.

■ The law of contract concerns foundational principles and mainly consists of common law rules. Principles from equity, tort, and unjust enrichment can also be relevant.

■ Many cases still give effect to the values of the classical model, which is based on the freedom and sanctity of contract, and a view that contracting parties are self-interested. Later cases show a trend away from the classical model to a more interventionist one.

■ The most significant recent development away from the classical model is the recognition of relational contracts and an implied obligation to act in good faith.

KEY CASES

☐ *Yam Seng Pte Ltd v International Trade Corporation Ltd* [2013] EWHC 111 (Comm)—represents the initial authority recognising relational contracts and how a duty to act in good faith can be implied.

☐ *Bates v Post Office Ltd* [2019] EWHC 606 (QB)—A recent application of *Yam Seng* that confirms a duty to act in good faith that is wider than honesty.

QUESTIONS

1. Explain the objective approach to contract law and how it can be used as a basis for legal development.

2. Explain the classical model of contract law and the trend towards a modern contract law.

3. Explain the extent to which the common law of England and Wales reflects a duty of good faith in the performance of contracts.

 For answer guidance to these questions please visit the online resources at www .oup.com/uk/naidoo1e/, where you will also find multiple choice questions to check your understanding of key concepts.

FURTHER READING

The references to further reading are intended to assist with any further research into points addressed in this chapter. As a list, it is longer than those in subsequent chapters because of the wide range of themes that an introduction to contract law raises.

Adams & Brownsword, 'The Ideologies of Contract' (1987) 7(2) LS 205.
A leading contribution to modern contract theory that identifies two philosophies of consumer welfarism and market individualism reflected in modern contract law. It is long but very clear.

Atiyah, The Rise and Fall of Freedom of Contract (OUP) 1979.
This is a book written by one of the most significant legal commentators of the twentieth century and is seen as a major contribution to the higher-level understanding of contract law. Freedom of contract is traced with the wider social, political, and economic background along with theories underpinning contract law.

Collins, 'Is a relational contract a legal concept?' in Dedeling, Edelman, and Goudkamp (eds) Contract in Commercial Law (Thomson Reuters) 2016.
This is a detailed, authoritative chapter on the significance of relational contracts as a distinct type of contract attracting different rules.

Saintier, 'The elusive notion of good faith in the performance of a contract: why still a bête noire for the civil and the common law?' [2017] JBL 441.
A clear and detailed assessment of good faith in performance that compares the English common law with the civil law of approach in France. It is particularly useful for the way in which duty is defined.

Smith, 'Contract Theory' (Clarendon Law Series) 2004 (Also available in Oxford Scholarship Online)

A clear and detailed book that identifies and evaluates the various theories underpinning the common law of contract. It is an excellent way to explore the different academic views.

Steyn, 'Contract law: fulfilling the reasonable expectations of honest men' (1997) 113 LQR 433.

This is by Lord Steyn, a significant and inspiring judicial contributor to the development of modern contract law. The opinions from this article have been cited in judgments and it is a highly recommended read.

Whittaker, 'The proposed "Common European Sales Law": legal framework and the agreement of the parties' (2012) 75 MLR 578.

This is very useful for an understanding of the EU initiative to have a common sales law.

Willett, 'Re-theorising consumer law' (2018) 77(1) CLJ 179.

A detailed and clear evaluation of the current theoretical model underpinning consumer contract law that suggests an alternative framework.

PART 1

Creating the Contract

Agreement Part I: Offer

2

LEARNING OBJECTIVES

By the end of this chapter you should be able to:

- understand how the objective approach to contract, based on the *apparent intentions* of the parties, applies to the creation of a contract
- assess proposals for a sale to work out if they are likely to be an offer
- analyse the way contracts are formed in alternative sales methods such as auctions and the tendering process
- evaluate the different ways an offer can come to an end

INTRODUCTION

We saw in Chapter 1 that the main ingredient for a contract is the appearance of an agreement. We also saw that such an agreement is formed by one party making an *offer* (the offeror) which is then *accepted* by another (the offeree). Though these requirements seem simple enough, it is possible for disputes to focus on the existence of an agreement. The practical context of such disputes typically starts with one party arguing that the other is in breach of contract. The other party then argues that there was never an agreement in the first place and, therefore, no contract to breach.

Cases dealing with such disputes have enabled the courts to develop a range of principles in order to work out whether or not an agreement exists. This chapter focusses on the principles relating to offers. We will look closely at a range of proposals such as those made through adverts, displays of goods and negotiations, to see the extent to which they can be treated as offers. We will then move on to explore when offers are made in auction sales and the tendering process. Finally, we will see how offers can be brought to an end.

The second part of agreement is the law relating to acceptance, which is explained in Chapter 3.

2.1 Offers and Invitations to Treat

Our starting point is to look at what is meant by an 'offer'. An offer can be defined as a proposal to enter a contract on certain terms made with the intention that it will be legally enforceable when it is accepted. Such an offer can be made to a particular party, to a defined group of parties, or even to the general public. There is no requirement for an offer to be in writing and so an offer can be oral, or even implied from the conduct of a party. What matters is that *objectively*, there appears to be an offer. If the proposal is not seen as an offer, it will be classed as an *invitation to treat*, as shown in Figure 2.1.

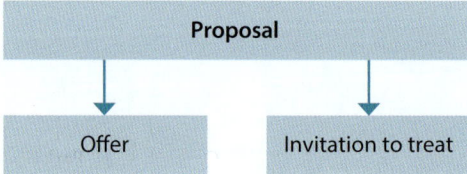

Figure 2.1
The legal status of a proposal to sell

invitation to treat
is a proposal that invites others to negotiate or make an offer.

An **invitation to treat** is a quaint term that is not part of our everyday language but it continues to be used in contract law. The term is used to describe a proposal that invites others to negotiate or make an offer.

Since an invitation to treat simply invites others to negotiate or make an offer, it cannot be 'accepted' and no agreement can therefore result from it. If there is no actual offer, then there is nothing to accept at that stage. This means that it is very important to know when a proposal is an offer, rather than a mere invitation to treat.

The courts decide the status of a proposal based on the *apparent intention* of the party making the proposal. This is based on the relevant facts such as the words used, the conduct of the parties and the surrounding circumstances. The point can be illustrated by the House of Lords case of *Gibson v Manchester City Council* [1979] 1 WLR 294. The case concerned a letter from the Council to its tenants stating that it '*may be prepared to sell*' its council houses to existing tenants. A form was included for each tenant to make a formal application to buy the house that they were renting. This form was completed by Gibson and returned. However, following local elections, the new council stopped the sale of council houses. Gibson then claimed he already had a contract to buy the council house that he was renting, meaning that the council would be in breach of contract if it cancelled the arrangement. With some sympathy for the claimant (and the 350 tenants in the same position), the House of Lords decided that the letter was not an offer. It meant that filling-out the form did not result in a contract. The reasoning is neatly captured by the following comment by Lord Russell:

vendor
is a more formal term for a seller, and is commonly used to describe a seller of property.

> My Lords, I cannot bring myself to accept that a letter which says that the possible **vendor** "May be prepared to sell the house to you" can be regarded as an offer to sell capable of acceptance so as to constitute a contract. The language simply does not permit such a **construction**.

construction
means interpretation, i.e. the meaning of words.

The point here is that the wording of the letter did not show an *apparent intention* by the Council to make an *offer* to sell. Using the words 'may be prepared to sell' showed that there was no definite intention to make a legal offer. That language was viewed as being too vague. It appeared to say that the council was thinking of selling rather than making an actual offer to sell. This meant that the letter simply indicated an intention to enter negotiations.

Of course, in everyday situations many proposals are made in a range of different ways. Obvious examples for consumers include adverts and displays of priced goods in shops. These types of proposals, along with those more familiar to businesses, have been considered in case law and are explained later. We will see that proposals made in certain everyday situations are usually regarded as invitations to treat. However, it is important to remember that these cases are laying down no more than a default presumption. It may be that in a particular situation, something which is usually found to be an invitation to treat (like an advert) may be an offer. This will be the result when there is a clear *apparent intention* for an offer to be made.

KEY POINTS

■ If the intended effect of the proposal is obvious from the start using clear, definite wording—i.e. if it is clear from the language used that an offer has (or has not) been made—then no dispute will arise about the status of the proposal.

2.2 Displays of Goods in Shops

A display of (priced) goods in a shop is certainly a proposal for a sale, but what is the status of such a proposal? Is it an offer to sell to customers? Alternatively, is it simply inviting customers to make an offer to buy the goods? In *Fisher v Bell* [1961] 1 QB 394, Lord Parker CJ referred to the status of displays as a well-established principle in the following way:

> It is perfectly clear that according to the ordinary law of contract the display of an article with a price on it in a shop window is merely an invitation to treat. It is in no sense an offer for sale the acceptance of which constitutes a contract. That is clearly the general law of the country.

The comment expresses the status of displays with absolute certainty. Such a proposal is not offering to sell the goods to customers. Instead, it is inviting customers to make an offer to buy the goods. The case concerned the Restrictions on Offensive Weapons Act 1959, s.1 (1). This Act stated that an offence would be committed where a person 'offers for sale' certain prohibited weapons. The question was whether the offence had been committed by the owner of a shop displaying a flick-knife with a price tag in the window. On the basis that an ordinary display is not a contractual *offer*, it was decided that no offence could have been committed. In response to the case, s. 1(1) of the Act was amended in 1961 to include 'exposure' for sale. That way a display of goods like the one in *Fisher v Bell* would then be covered by the offence.

The case is traditional authority for the status of shop displays. However, it does not explain the *reasoning* behind the principle. In addition, it expresses the principle as a rule rather than a starting point or presumption. In order to understand that reasoning, it is necessary to address the earlier case law.

2.2.1 Background to the Traditional Position

The traditional position is that, generally, a display of goods is an invitation to treat rather than an offer to sell. This seems to have developed from early cases like *Timothy v Simpson* (1834) 6 C & P 499, a case that, like *Fisher v Bell*, concerned a criminal matter. It concerned a violent incident in a shop after a customer refused to leave the premises in protest at being quoted a higher price for an item than the one which was displayed in the window. The court held in effect that there was no freestanding right for a customer to make a purchase at the stated price, but it did not come to this conclusion on a contractual analysis. It simply stated that a shop has a right to refuse to sell an item and eject a trespasser. This early attitude was explained by Professor Winfield in 'Some Aspects of Offer and Acceptance' (1939) 55 LQR 499:

> . . . [A] more natural interpretation of the display of goods in a shop with a marked price on them would be that the shopkeeper impliedly reserves to himself a right of selecting his customer. A shop is a place for bargaining, not for compulsory sales . . . If the display were an offer, then the shopkeeper might be forced to contract with his worst enemy, his greatest trade rival, a reeling drunkard or a ragged and verminous tramp.

This observation suggests that the early case law established a right for shops to choose who could buy their goods. To decide otherwise would result in what Professor Winfield described as compulsory sales, because the shop would be under an obligation to sell to anyone wishing to buy. That would include people that the owner of the shop did not want to sell to. This is the basic principle which the law seeks to effect. It was later put on a more formal contractual footing by coming to the conclusion, as in *Fisher v Bell*, that a shopkeeper does not make an offer in displaying goods, but is rather inviting the customer to make an offer (which the shopkeeper is then entitled to reject). If it were the other way round and displaying goods in a shop constituted an offer, then any customer could simply 'accept' that offer and claim compulsory entitlement to the goods, undermining the very principle on which the law is based.

The early cases relate to the traditional shop where customers would enter and tell the shopkeeper what they wanted. The shopkeeper would then find the goods and present them to the customer. Shopping today is generally modelled on customers selecting the goods in the shop and then presenting them to a cashier or self-serve till.

2.2.2 Displays in Ordinary Shops Today

The status of displays in the shops we know today was addressed by the Court of Appeal in *Pharmaceutical Society of Great Britain v Boots Cash Chemists (Southern) Ltd* [1953] 1 QB 401. The case concerned the Pharmacy and Poisons Act 1933 s.18 (1). The Act required the *sale* of certain products to be supervised by a registered pharmacist. The point of *sale* would be the point where a contract is formed between the shop and the customer. The Pharmaceutical Society argued that the display of goods on the shelves amounted to an offer to sell. It then argued that acceptance took place when a customer selected a product and placed it in their basket. On that basis, it was argued that a contract was formed when the customer took the item off the shelf and put it in their basket. Boots only had a registered pharmacist near the till rather than at every shelf, and so the Court of Appeal had to decide if this meant a registered pharmacist was supervising 'sales' for the purposes of s. 18(1) of the Act.

The Court of Appeal agreed with the earlier decision of Lord Goddard CJ and rejected the Pharmaceutical Society's argument. According to the decision, Boots had indeed complied with the Act by having a registered pharmacist at the till, which was the point of sale. The case remains good authority for the rule that an ordinary display in a shop is just an invitation to treat rather than an offer. The reasoning was explained by Somervell LJ in the following way:

> Is a contract to be regarded as being completed when the article is put into the receptacle, or is this to be regarded as a more organised way of doing what is done already in many types of shops—and a bookseller is perhaps the best example—namely, enabling customers to have free access to what is in the shop, to look at the different articles, and then, ultimately, having got the ones which they wish to buy, to come up to the assistant saying 'I want this'? The assistant in 999 times out of 1,000 says 'That is all right,' and the money passes and the transaction is completed. I agree with what the Lord Chief Justice has said, and with the reasons which he has given for his conclusion, that in the case of an ordinary shop, although goods are displayed and it is intended that customers should go and choose what they want, the contract is not completed until, the customer having indicated the articles which he needs, the shopkeeper, or someone on his behalf, accepts that offer. Then the contract is completed. I can see no reason at all, that being clearly the normal position, for drawing any different implication as a result of this layout.
>
> The Lord Chief Justice, I think, expressed one of the most formidable difficulties in the way of the plaintiffs' contention when he pointed out that if the plaintiffs are right, once an article has been placed in the receptacle the customer himself is bound and would have no right, without paying for the first article, to substitute an article which he saw later of a similar kind and which he perhaps preferred. I can see no reason for implying from this self-service arrangement any implication other than that which the Lord Chief Justice found in it, namely, that it is a convenient method of enabling customers to see what there is and choose, and possibly put back and substitute, articles which they wish to have, and then to go up to the cashier and offer to buy what they have so far chosen. On that conclusion the case fails, because it is admitted that there was supervision in the sense required by the Act and at the appropriate moment of time. For these reasons, in my opinion, the appeal should be dismissed.

The decision makes it clear that the display in a shop of priced goods is not an offer by the shop to sell the goods. Instead, the proposal in the form of a display is an invitation to treat. The customer then chooses the items and then offers to buy them. The reasoning focussed on the fact that a customer would want to have the ability to pick up items and then change their mind and return them to the shelf. Somervell LJ made no reference to the need for a seller to be able to refuse a sale. However, that reason was addressed by Lord Goddard CJ in the first instance decision and the judgment of Somervell LJ in the Court of Appeal agreed with the judgment of Lord Goddard CJ. In combination the two judgments produce the desirable outcome, which is that sellers are protected in being able to choose who they sell goods to, and purchasers are protected from the risk of accidentally accepting and remain able to change their mind until their purchases are definitively completed.

The existence of an offer is based on what appears to be intended. The decision in *Pharmaceutical Society of GB v Boots* means that the seller does not show an apparent intention to make an offer just by displaying goods because of the inconvenience it would impose on both the seller and customers.

KEY POINTS

A display of goods in a shop is not an offer to sell. Instead, it is an invitation to treat. The customer makes an offer to buy by taking an item to the till and making the offer of payment.

This means that a customer has no *contractual* right to buy goods at the price displayed. For an example of the practical significance of this, consider an Apple i-Pad in an ordinary display with a price of £7.99. That display is an invitation to treat, so when you try to pay £7.99 for the product, you are simply *offering* to pay £7.99. The store could then kindly accept your offer or, it could reject your offer and tell you that if you want it, you'll have to pay £799.00. This is a result of the case law rule on ordinary displays. It may not reflect the actual expectations of customers, but it does serve to protect shops from the risks of having the wrong price displayed. This does not mean that shops can routinely mis-price their goods to tempt you in. If a shop has been misleading consumers with incorrect prices it could be prosecuted under the Consumer Protection from Unfair Trading Regulations 2008, SI 2008/1277. Originally these Regulations were enforced by Trading Standards. But following amendment in 2014 (the Consumer Protection (Amendment) Regulations 2014, SI 2014/870), private enforcement by consumers has been made possible.

To reject the argument by the Pharmaceutical Society, the judgment of the Court of Appeal only had to show that the contract was not formed at the shelves. The case does not tell us precisely *how* the offer is made because there was no need to, and there remains a lack of clarity about this. It might be that the customer makes an offer by simply presenting the goods at the till based on the price displayed. But consider the use of barcode scanners. Is the price displayed on the screen after scanning what the customer is offering to pay, or is it simply an indication of what the shop is willing to accept? Furthermore, the *Boots* case provides no guidance on how the shop accepts the offer or precisely when acceptance takes place. Surprisingly, these questions remain unanswered, a point that was echoed by Lindsay J in *Debenhams Retail plc v The Commissioners of Customs & Excise* [2005] EWHC 1540. In the judgment, it was observed that while a contract was formed at the till, the precise way in which it was formed was 'uncertain'.

 THINKING POINTS

Based on the way we buy goods in a supermarket, when do you think offer and acceptance take place?

2.2.3 Displays Making an Offer

So far, we have looked at cases about the ordinary display of priced goods, but these do not create an absolute rule for all displays of goods. We saw at 1.3 that in contract law, the courts generally enforce the parties' *apparent intentions*. It means that the decisions on displays are based on a presumption of intention, i.e. that the seller could not have intended to have made an offer just from displaying priced goods. It does not mean that displays can never amount to offers. Instead, from an objective perspective, if there is a clear intention for a display to be an offer, then it ought to be treated as one.

There is no case law directly on the point, but familiar promotions using phrases such as 'special offer' or 'buy one get one free' will not on their own make the display in question an offer to sell. Consider a display of goods with such wording followed by terms explaining that the promotion applies 'while stock lasts' along with a date for when the promotion expires. In such circumstances, it would appear that the shop is making some kind of offer. But is this wording sufficient to turn the display into an offer to sell? Such wording will be seen as the shop making a separate offer, one that is accepted by the customer completing the purchase of the goods. The shop is effectively saying: 'if you enter a contract for a particular item, then you can have another for free'. But the display in itself will still only be an invitation to treat. It would still be for the customer to make the offer to buy. Acceptance by the shop would then result in a contract in the usual way, and the creation of this contract would be the acceptance for the shop's separate (promotional) offer. Under this resulting second contract, the shop would be under an obligation to give the free item to the customer if any other terms are satisfied.

→ CROSS-REFERENCE
for the formation of
contracts in the context
of automated machines
see 3.4.

A display of goods in a vending machine should be regarded as an offer by the owner or operator of the machine. This is based on the reasoning of Lord Denning MR in *Thornton v Shoe Lane Parking* [1971] 2 QB 163 which concerned an automated ticket machine at a car park.

2.3 Advertisements

Adverts are another type of proposal commonly found in newspapers, magazines, journals, and flyers; or on the radio, television, websites, social media and so on. Normally, (just like shop displays) adverts are not offers and instead, they are classed as invitations to treat. Again, the rule is based on *apparent intentions* to the effect that objectively, the advertiser could not have intended to have made an offer.

2.3.1 The Rule on Ordinary Adverts

The rule on ordinary adverts is clear from *Partridge v Crittenden* [1968] 1 WLR 1204. The case concerned the Protection of Wild Birds Act 1954, s. 6(1). Under this section, a criminal offence would be committed where a person 'offers for sale' certain wild birds. The seller, Partridge, had placed the following advert in a journal: 'Quality British ABCR . . . Bramblefinch cocks, Bramblefinch hens, 25s each'. The Court of Appeal had to decide if placing the advert was a criminal offence. It confirmed that since an advert is an invitation to treat (rather than an offer), no offence had been committed. The main judgment was delivered by Lord Parker CJ who explained the rule for adverts in the following way:

> I think that when one is dealing with advertisements and circulars, unless they indeed come from manufacturers, there is business sense in their being construed as invitations to treat and not offers for sale. In a very different context Lord Herschell in *Grainger & Son v Gough (Surveyor of Taxes)* ([1896] AC 325 at p. 334), said this in dealing with a price-list . . .
>
> "The transmission of such a price-list does not amount to an offer to supply an unlimited quantity of the wine described at the price named, so that as soon as an order is given there is a binding contract to supply that quantity. If it were so, the merchant might find himself involved in any number of contractual obligations to supply wine of a particular description which he would be quite unable to carry out, his stock of wine of that description being necessarily limited."
>
> It seems to me accordingly that not only is that the law, but common sense supports it.

The reference to Lord Herschell's judgment in *Grainger v Gough* is significant for addressing the practical consequences of sellers having limited stock. If adverts were always classed as offers, sellers would have a contract with all the buyers who communicated their acceptance. Consequently, the seller would be liable for non-delivery where there is not enough stock to meet the orders contracted for. Treating an advert as an offer therefore presents a serious risk to the seller. On that basis, the reasonable person would presume that an advertiser did not intend to make an offer.

While this reasoning is well established, it is easy to question if it was really necessary. After all, if adverts were presumed to be offers, it could be implied that the offers expire when the stock has run out. Such an approach would protect the seller from the limited stock problem.

 THINKING POINTS

Does the rule making adverts an invitation to treat protect sellers at the expense of the reasonable expectations of consumers?

The limited stock problem is the key factor in the judicial reasoning behind the rule on ordinary adverts. However, there are practical 'common sense' reasons to support the rule. Adverts are often vague and leave out the less important information about the goods. This means there is room for discussion or negotiation about what is being proposed. In such circumstances, it could be argued that the advert was not intended to be an offer. In addition, the rule on ordinary adverts allows the advertiser to check that the other party is capable of performing their obligations. One example is the fact that a seller can check that the buyer has the ability to pay before entering the contract. Also, if it is assumed that sellers displaying goods in a shop want the right to refuse customers, surely the same can be assumed for those that advertise their goods. The rule allows a seller to choose who they want to sell to.

→ CROSS-REFERENCE
The issue of uncertainty is explained in Chapter 4.

KEY POINTS

Generally, adverts are not classed as offers. Instead they are invitations to treat.

2.3.2 Adverts Making an Offer

The rule on adverts is based on a presumption that an offer is not intended. It follows that an advert will be treated as an offer if (objectively) it shows a clear intention to be an offer. An early example of such an advert can be seen in the famous case of *Carlill v Carbolic Smoke Ball Co* [1893] 1 QB 256.

In *Carlill*, the defendant company placed an advert in a number of journals for their carbolic smoke ball. The advert was a response to the flu pandemic and it claimed that the smoke ball would cure as well as prevent the catching of the flu, colds and various other diseases. Contrary to these claims, the device just puffed-out acidic smoke that would make the user's nose run. The advert promised £100 as a reward to anyone that contracted the flu having used the smoke ball as directed. It even stated that £1000 had been deposited in a bank to show the manufacturer's sincerity. Mrs Carlill had used the smoke ball as directed and contracted the flu. She then claimed £100 but the Company refused to pay.

At first instance, Hawkins J found in favour of Mrs Carlill. This decision was on the basis that a contract existed between Mrs Carlill and the Company. As a result, the Company had a contractual obligation to pay her. The Company then appealed to the Court of Appeal and put forward a range of arguments. However, these arguments were rejected unanimously by the Court of Appeal and the original decision was upheld.

Essentially, the company made three key arguments:

- that there was no offer;
- if there was an offer, then there was no acceptance and therefore no agreement; and,
- if there was an agreement, it was not legally enforceable.

We are concerned with the first argument about whether or not an offer was made and we can explore this using the relevant extracts from the judgment of Bowen LJ.

GUIDED CASE READING 2.1
Carlill v Carbolic Smoke Ball Co [1893] 1 QB 256

When you read the following extracts from the judgment of Bowen LJ, try to identify:

- The reasons relied upon by the Company to argue that the advert was not an offer.
- Why these reasons were rejected.

I am of the same opinion. We were asked to say that this document was a contract too vague to be enforced.

The first observation which arises is that the document itself is not a contract at all, it is only an offer made to the public. The defendants contend next, that it is an offer the terms of which are too vague to be treated as a definite offer, inasmuch as there is no limit of time fixed for the catching of the influenza, and it cannot be supposed that the advertisers seriously meant to promise to pay money to every person who catches the influenza at any time after the inhaling of the smoke ball. It was urged also, that if you look at this document you will find much vagueness as to the persons with whom the contract was intended to be made—that, in the first place, its terms are wide enough to include persons who may have used the smoke ball before the advertisement was issued; at all events, that it is an offer to the world in general, and, also, that it is unreasonable to suppose it to be a definite offer, because nobody in their senses would contract themselves out of the opportunity of checking the experiment which was going to be made at their own expense. It is also contended that the advertisement is rather in the nature of a **puff** or a proclamation than a promise or offer intended to mature into a contract when accepted. But the main point seems to be that the vagueness of the document shews that no contract whatever was intended. It seems to me that in order to arrive at a right conclusion we must read this advertisement in its plain meaning, as the public would understand it. It was intended to be issued to the public and to be read by the public.

> Here, Bowen LJ addresses the Company's argument that they had not made an offer because the advertisement was not clear. A crucial element in determining if an offer has been made is its clarity. If a proposal is not clear, then it will not show an intention to be bound. Bowen LJ indicates that he considers this to be the crux of the case, and not another reason advanced by the Company, which was that their advertisement was only promotional material and not therefore taken seriously by potential customers.

puff or puffery

is the old way of describing sales hype that no reasonable person would take seriously (e.g. 'The best grime album in the world, ever!').

How would an ordinary person reading this document construe it? It was intended unquestionably to have some effect, and I think the effect which it was intended to have, was to make people use the smoke ball, because the suggestions and allegations which it contains are directed immediately to the use of the smoke ball as distinct from the purchase of it. It did not follow that the smoke ball was to be purchased from the defendants directly, or even from agents of theirs directly. The intention was that the circulation of the smoke ball should be promoted, and that the use of it should be increased. The advertisement begins by saying that a reward will be paid by the Carbolic Smoke Ball Company to any person who contracts the increasing epidemic

> For Bowen LJ, adverts are directed at the public and so the relevant point to consider was how the public would have construed the advert. This represented the main test to be applied.

after using the ball. It has been said that the words do not apply only to persons who contract the epidemic after the publication of the advertisement, but include persons who had previously contracted the influenza. I cannot so read the advertisement. It is written in colloquial and popular language, and I think that it is equivalent to this: '100*l*. will be paid to any person who shall contract the increasing epidemic after having used the carbolic smoke ball three times daily for two weeks'. And it seems to me that the way in which the public would read it would be this, that if anybody, after the advertisement was published, used three times daily for two weeks the carbolic smoke ball, and then caught cold, he would be entitled to the reward. Then again it was said: 'How long is this protection to endure? Is it to go on forever, or for what limit of time?' . . . I think, more probably, it means that the smoke ball will be a protection while it is in use. That seems to me the way in which an ordinary person would understand an advertisement about medicine, and about a specific against influenza. It could not be supposed that after you have left off using it you are still to be protected forever, as if there was to be a stamp set upon your forehead that you were never to catch influenza because you had once used the carbolic smoke ball. I think the immunity is to last during the use of the ball. That is the way in which I should naturally read it, and it seems to me that the subsequent language of the advertisement supports that construction. It says: 'During the last epidemic of influenza many thousand carbolic smoke balls were sold, and in no ascertained case was the disease contracted by those using' (not 'who had used') 'the carbolic smoke ball,' and it concludes with saying that one smoke ball will last a family several months (which imports that it is to be efficacious while it is being used), and that the ball can be refilled at a cost of 5*s*. I, therefore, have myself no hesitation in saying that I think, on the construction of this advertisement, the protection was to [endure] during the time that the carbolic smoke ball was being used . . .

Was it intended that the 100*l*. should, if the conditions were fulfilled, be paid? The advertisement says that 1000*l*. is lodged at the bank for the purpose. Therefore, it cannot be said that the statement that 100*l*. would be paid was intended to be a mere puff. I think it was intended to be understood by the public as an offer which was to be acted upon.

But it was said there was no check on the part of the persons who issued the advertisement, and that it would be an insensate thing to promise 100*l*. to a person who used the smoke ball unless you could check or superintend his manner of using it. The answer to that argument seems to me to be that if a person chooses to make extravagant promises of this kind he probably does so because it pays him to make them, and, if he has made them, the extravagance of the promises is no reason in law why he should not be bound by them.

It was also said that the contract is made with all the world—that is, with everybody; and that you cannot contract with everybody. It is not a contract made with all the world. There is the fallacy of the argument. It is an offer made to all the world; and why should not an offer be made to all the world which is to ripen into a contract with anybody who comes forward and performs the condition? It is an offer to become liable to any one who, before it is retracted, performs the condition, and, although the offer is made to the world, the contract is made with that limited portion of the public who come forward and perform the condition on the faith of the advertisement.

Bowen LJ here shows that the basic terms of the proposal were clearly stated and would be readily understood by members of the public to have a particular meaning. They would understand it to mean that if they used the product as prescribed and then contracted the flu, they would have a right to the reward of £100.

He then goes on to indicate that the advert was not vague just because it did not state how long the protection from the product would last. Instead, the duration of protection could be implied as lasting during use. He places a strong emphasis on how the public would 'naturally' read the wording.

Bowen LJ then addresses the Company's argument that the public would not take the advert seriously and would regard it as a 'mere puff'. The fact that the advert referred to the £1000 in the bank meant that the argument could be rejected easily. He adds the important point, which English judges have tended to state very forcefully, that it is the responsibility of contracting parties to make sure they do not fall into 'bad bargains'. It was, in short, the Company's own fault for making an 'extravagant promise', and that it found itself bound into an undesirable contract.

Here Bowen LJ rejects the argument that an offer to the world would lead to a contract with the world which is impossible. Instead, such an offer would result in a contract with those that performed the conditions of acceptance only.

In summary, then, the Company had argued that the advert could not be an offer because it was too vague; because it was a 'mere puff' and would have been understood by the public as not to be taken seriously; and because one could not 'make a contract with the world' through an advertisement. Bowen LJ dismissed all these arguments. The advert had been clearly worded, would be understood by the public to be a genuine proposal rather than 'mere puff', and could be capable of forming contracts with anybody fulfilling the conditions. These were buying the smoke ball and using it as directed, and catching the flu. Because Mrs Carlill had done this, she had met the requirements stated in the advert. She had thus 'accepted' the offer stated in it.

It was made clear from the rest of the judgment (and that of Lindley LJ) that the advert was an offer for a **unilateral contract**. To accept the offer, all Mrs Carlill had to do was perform the conditions stated in the offer. Therefore, on the facts, once she used the smoke ball as directed and contracted the flu, a contract existed. In that resulting contract, it was only the Company that had an obligation to perform (i.e. the obligation to pay). The resulting unilateral contract can be contrasted with the more typical **bilateral contract** under which both parties are under an obligation to perform. For an example, consider a contract for the sale of goods which requires the seller to transfer ownership of the goods and for the buyer to make the payment.

> **contract is unilateral** when only one party has an obligation to perform.

> **contract is bilateral** when both parties have an obligation to perform.

?!   THINKING POINTS

What wording could have been added to the advert to prevent it being an offer?

An advert for goods was also held to be an offer in the US case *Lefkowitz v Great Minneapolis Stores* (1957) 86 NW 2d 689 (Supreme Court of Minnesota). Being an American case, the decision is not binding on English courts, but it is generally held to be indicative of the approach English courts would, and should, take in similar circumstances. Here the defendant advertised in a newspaper three fur coats worth $100 for a price of $1 each, adding 'Saturday 9am sharp' and 'First come first served'. The claimant was the first into the shop and tried to buy a coat for $1 but was refused on the basis that he was a man and the coats were for women. The case turned on the status of the advert and it was held that the advert showed a clear intention to be an offer. The wording used was firm and precise. It made clear that the shopkeeper intended to form a contract to sell a fur coat for $1 to the first three people arriving on or after 9am on the Saturday in question. The claimant had been one of those people. In addition, there was no limited stock problem because the advert made clear there were only three items and it was a matter of 'first come, first served'. These factors help to demonstrate there was an intention to make an offer.

The *Carlill* case was applied by the Court of Appeal in *Bowerman v ABTA* [1996] CLC 451. This was about a notice by ABTA (the Association of British Travel Agents) displayed in a travel agent's shop. The notice made it clear that by buying a holiday from a travel agent that was an ABTA member, the customer would have the benefit of insurance provided by ABTA against the financial failure of that travel agent. Following *Carlill*, the Court of Appeal construed the notice as it would be understood by an ordinary member of the public. On that basis, it was an offer which would be accepted by performance, i.e. the customer buying a holiday from the travel agent who was a member of ABTA.

KEY POINTS

An advert can be an offer if it shows an intention to be an offer.

2.4 Websites and E-commerce

The basic principles concerning offers and invitations to treat can be applied to on-line shopping. When images of goods are displayed on a webpage with a price, it will be treated in the same way as a display in a shop. It will be presumed to be a mere invitation to treat rather than an offer just like in the *Boots* case. Likewise, if a webpage displays an ordinary advert, it will be presumed to be an invitation to treat just like in *Partridge v Crittenden*. On the other hand, if the wording on the webpage shows a clear intention to be an offer then it will be treated as such, just like the advert in the *Carlill* case.

The Electronic Commerce (EC Directive) Regulations 2002 also contains rules relating to website sales. Regulation 12 states that generally an 'order may be but need not be a contractual offer'. That does not seem clear, but it simply means that a buyer might make an offer by placing an order depending on the nature of the website. Regulations 9(c) and 11(1)(b) impose an obligation on the trader to allow a prospective buyer a clear opportunity to correct any input errors before placing an order. Reg. 12 adds that for these purposes, an order is a contractual offer. Consequently, it is the buyer that makes the offer by completing the order. However, the terms of the website will state what is required for the order to be complete.

Over the years, there have been a number of widely publicised reports of pricing mistakes on retail websites:

- In 2016 computer manufacturer HP listed a laptop for £1.58 reduced from £2378.
- In 2014 DIY store Screwfix Direct listed all products at £34.99. This resulted in many customers placing orders including one for a sit-on lawn mower worth £1599.
- In 2012 the Argos displayed a Nokia Lumia smartphone for £199.99 instead of £449.99.
- In 2011 Currys listed a Samsung Galaxy Netbook for £22 instead of £229.
- In 1999 Argos listed a Sony TV for £2.99 rather than £299.

In these main examples, there was nothing to indicate an intention to make an offer. So, in each instance, the seller was able to cancel the orders and argue that the advert was simply an invitation to treat. On that basis, potential buyers could not insist on paying the price displayed.

Even if there was an *apparent intention* to make an offer, the seller might be able to avoid selling goods for the price displayed. If a price looks like an obvious mistake, then a resulting contract might be unenforceable.

→ CROSS-REFERENCE
For the case law on such mistakes see 17.4.1.

THINKING POINTS

Out of the previous examples, which prices do you think should be regarded as obvious mistakes?

Perhaps the most significant way in which on-line sellers can protect themselves is through the use of their contractual terms. Often, before payment is required, websites will ask the customer to tick a box agreeing to the seller's terms in order to continue. Some buyers might just tick the box without reading the terms; after all, these terms are usually very detailed and lengthy. Ticking the box to agree to the terms (before the contract is complete) means that the terms are part of the contract when it is created. If you read the terms from most on-line sellers, you will see that they actually state when an offer is made and when acceptance of an offer takes place. When terms are agreed in this way, they represent an obvious indication of the parties' intentions.

→ CROSS-REFERENCE
The validity of certain contract terms can be challenged using legislation. This is detailed in 7.7.

If the relevant terms are clear, then a contract is formed when the terms say so. Of course, the same can be done in a supermarket or any other shop. Detailed terms could be displayed stating precisely when the contract is formed, but it is not practical or necessary for shops to do so. In contrast, a webpage can have lots of terms and not allow the transaction to proceed without the buyer indicating their agreement to the terms. It is also important to appreciate that on-line sellers have a need for terms specifying when contracts are formed because more can go wrong. There can be technical problems resulting in a lost connection during a transaction; and mistakes can be made on the prices displayed, or the discounts applied at checkout. For such reasons, sellers will often specify that the contract is formed once the goods are dispatched (sent).

2.5 Auction Sales

As consumers, we are very familiar with the use of on-line auction sites. These are simply on-line versions of the traditional auctions which buyers attend and in which they actually see the goods to be sold. Such traditional auctions continue to be significant, particularly for the sale of antiques and memorabilia, old cars, houses and cattle. Just like with on-line auctions, buyers submit bids and the successful bid results in a contract. To establish how such a contract is formed, the courts have analysed the traditional auction process in terms of offer and acceptance.

2.5.1 How Contracts Are Made at Auctions Where Goods Have a Minimum Price

It was established at an early stage that an advert for an auction is not an offer to hold it. *Harris v Nickerson* (1873) LR 8 QB 286 concerned an advert for an auction to be held for furniture and building materials. Harris went to the auction but the goods described in the advert had been withdrawn. Harris then sued for his wasted time and expense in attending the auction. He argued that by attending, he accepted an offer and so there was a contract to hold the auction for the items advertised. This argument was rejected firmly by the court because it would be extremely inconvenient and risky for the auctioneer to be liable to anyone that attended. This can be explained on the basis of *apparent intentions*: the auctioneer could not have intended to have made an offer given the risks of doing so.

The auctioneers' request for bids at the start of an auction is not an offer. Instead it is merely an invitation for bids from potential buyers (*Payne* v *Cave* (1789) 100 ER 502). The bids from the potential buyers are the offers in an ordinary auction.

2.5.2 How Contracts Are Made at Auctions without a Minimum Price

Some auctions are described as auctions 'without reserve'. This means that the goods have no minimum (i.e. reserve) price and will be sold automatically to the highest bidder. In *Warlow v Harrison* (1859) 1 E & E 309 the court stated that an advertisement of an auction 'without reserve' is an offer to sell to the highest *bona fide* bidder. A seller bidding on their own goods to stop them being sold is not a *bona fide* bidder.

The comment from *Warlow v Harrison* was *obiter* (rather than the *ratio* of the case) and therefore not binding but it was the basis for the decision in *Barry v Davies* [2000] 1 WLR 1962. This case concerned an advert for an auction *without reserve* for two engine analyser machines worth £14,000 each. The claimant submitted a bid of £200 for each item. There were no further bids, so the auctioneer withdrew the goods which were later sold to another buyer. The claimant then brought a damages claim on the basis that he had a contract for the machines. The Court of Appeal upheld the trial judge decision and found in favour of the claimant bidder. The main judgment by Sir Murray Stuart-Smith is a good example of how *obiter* can turn into the binding *ratio* of a case, but also, it explained how a contract is formed in an auction without reserve in the following way:

bona fide
is a Latin term meaning 'good faith'. In this context it refers to a genuine bidder.

➔ CROSS-REFERENCE
Obiter dictum and its use along with the *ratio decidendi* were explained in 1.5.1.

. . .

The judge held that it would be the general and reasonable expectation of persons attending at an auction sale without reserve that the highest bidder would and should be entitled to the lot for which he bids. Such an outcome was in his view fair and logical. As a matter of law he held that there was a **collateral contract** between the auctioneer and the highest bidder constituted by an offer by the auctioneer to sell to the highest bidder which was accepted when the bid was made. In so doing he followed the views of the majority of the Court of Exchequer Chamber in *Warlow v. Harrison* (1859) 1 E. & E. 309. . . Although therefore the decision of the majority is not strictly binding, it was the reasoned judgment of the majority and is entitled to very great respect. . . there was a separate collateral contract with the auctioneer; there is no reason why such a contract should not exist. . .

In *Harris v. Nickerson* (1873) L.R. 8 Q.B. 286 . . . The claim was rejected by the Court of Queen's Bench. In the course of his judgment Blackburn J. said, at p. 288:

"in the case of *Warlow v. Harrison*, 1 E. & E. 309, 314, 318, the opinion of the majority of the judges in the Exchequer Chamber appears to have been that an action would lie for not knocking down the lot to the highest *bona fide* bidder when the sale was advertised as without reserve; in such a case it may be that there is a contract to sell to the highest bidder, and that if the owner bids there is a breach of the contract. . ." And Quain J. said, L.R. 8 Q.B. 286, 289:

"When a sale is advertised as without reserve, and a lot is put up and bid for, there is ground for saying, as was said in *Warlow v. Harrison*, 1 E. & E. 309, 314, that a contract is entered into between the auctioneer and the highest *bona fide* bidder. . ."

In *Johnston v. Boyes* [1899] 2 Ch. 73, 77 Cozens-Hardy J. also accepted the majority view in *Warlow's* case as being good law. . . So far as textbook writers are concerned both Chitty on Contracts , 28th ed. (1999), vol. 1, p. 94, para. 2–010 and Benjamin's Sale of Goods , 5th ed. (1997), p. 107, para. 2–005 adopt the view expressed by the majority of the court in *Warlow's* case.

> **collateral contract** is a secondary contract that is separate to the main contract of sale.

We can see in the main judgment by Sir Murray Stuart-Smith how the *obiter dicta* from *Warlow v Harrison* becomes the basis for the binding authority on how contracts are made in auctions without reserve in the decision in *Barry v Davis*. To summarise, first, it is important to appreciate how the actual sales contract is formed. That is the contract which entitles the successful bidder to own the goods in return for paying the price. Technically, that contract is between the bidder as the buyer and the owner of the goods as the seller, but in practice, it is made between the bidder and the auctioneer who is acting on behalf of the seller (as the seller's agent). In terms of offer and acceptance, the bid is the offer to buy the goods at the price indicated in the bid. The auctioneer then creates the sales contract by accepting the bid. This sales contract is then the ultimate aim of the auction.

In an auction without reserve, the auctioneer also makes an implied promise (an offer) to accept the highest (genuine) bid (i.e. the highest offer for a sales contract). Such acceptance then creates a sales contract with that bidder for the price indicated by that bid. It is an implied promise by the auctioneer because the words 'without reserve' are taken to mean that there is no minimum price and therefore that the highest bid will be successful.

As illustrated in Figure 2.2, this implied promise (which is an offer) is then accepted by the act of submitting the highest genuine bid. This act of submitting the highest bid results in a separate collateral (secondary) contract between the bidder and the auctioneer. Under this collateral contract, the auctioneer is under an obligation to accept the highest offer (the highest bid) to create a contract of sale with that bidder. In such circumstances, if the auctioneer does not like the value of the bids and decides to withdraw the goods, the auctioneer would be in breach of the collateral contract it has with the highest bidder. If the highest bidder does not pay for the goods following the auctioneer's acceptance, the bidder is in breach of the main sales contract.

Just like the cases on adverts and displays, the cases on auctions are based on the courts' interpretation of the *apparent intentions* of the parties. The cases do not *impose* rules on the nature of the agreement. Consequently, if an auctioneer does not want the bids to be treated as acceptance of an offer, the terms of the offer could say so clearly along with how the contract is to be formed. That is often the case with on-line auctions. They have terms stating when and how the contract is to be formed, and generally under

Figure 2.2
The process of contract formation for a sale at an auction without reserve

these terms bids do not result in a contract between the bidder and the auction platform. Instead, they just result in a contract between the bidder and the seller. The intention expressed in the terms would then be followed by a court in any dispute. Alternatively, if the terms of an on-line or traditional auction do not state clearly how the contract is to be formed, then the case law described earlier will apply.

KEY POINTS

- Ordinarily, in an auction, the bids are offers that are accepted or rejected by the auctioneer.
- In auctions advertised as being 'without reserve,' the auctioneer is promising (offering) that the highest genuine bidder will be successful. The highest bid is then accepted by the auctioneer (on behalf of the seller) to form a contract of sale.

2.6 The Tendering Process

Here we address a common negotiating device for businesses and how it results in a contract. Businesses often need to buy a major item like a special piece of machinery or they want a major service like the construction of a new building. Shopping around to find the best price or the most suitable party to do the work can be very time consuming. An alternative is to publicise the needs of the business and invite others to submit a **tender** for the work. For example, for a new building, various building companies might be invited to send in their best quote hoping to get the job.

    The tendering process is seen as a fair way to find a party to contract with. The idea is that parties compete for the contract and are given an equal chance of succeeding. It is for these reasons that the tendering process is used so much by public sector bodies when they are looking to contract with a business from the private sector. A familiar example is the National Lottery, for which a tendering process was used to find a company to run it.

tender

is a bid to buy or sell something and is usually classed as an offer.

2.6.1 How the Contract Is Made in the Tendering Process

Normally, the request for tenders is treated as an invitation to treat rather than an offer. It is then the individual tenders that represent offers (*Spencer* v *Harding* (1870) LR 5 CP 561). The party that invited the tenders will then accept or reject them. However, the position is different in cases where the request for tenders indicates that the most competitive tender will be successful. In *Spencer* v *Harding* it was stated (*obiter*) that in such situations, the request amounts to an offer to contract with the party that submits the most competitive tender. That is very similar to the approach in *Carlill* and *Barry v Davies* because the offer is accepted by performance (i.e. the act of submitting a tender).

A case directly concerning this point is *Harvela Investments v Royal Trust Company of Canada* [1986] AC 207. We will see that this also featured a problem resulting from the use of what is called a 'referential' bid. That is a bid that can only be worked out by referring to another bid.

In *Harvela Investments v Royal Trust Company of Canada*, the defendant invited tenders for the purchase of a bundle of shares. The invitation was sent to both the claimant (Harvela) and Sir Leonard Outerbridge. It said that the defendant would 'accept the highest offer'. The claimant submitted a tender of C$2,175,000 but Outerbridge tendered a bid of C$2,100,000 or C$101,000 above the highest tender. The additional bid of C$101,000 above the highest tender is an example of a referential bid. The defendant then confirmed the sale with Outerbridge. In response, the claimant brought an action arguing that it had submitted the highest valid tender. This argument was based on the idea that only fixed bids (i.e. tenders for a fixed amount) should be valid and that the referential bid should not count. The House of Lords agreed and held that the defendant was in breach of a contract with Harvela.

The judgment by Lord Diplock explains how a contract is formed when the party inviting tenders states that the best tender will succeed. We shall go through the extract of the relevant part of the judgment together.

GUIDED CASE READING 2.2
Harvela Investments Ltd v Royal Trust Company of Canada (C.I.) Ltd [1986] AC 207

When reading the extract of Lord Diplock's judgment, try to identify how the contract was formed.

. . .

The construction question turns upon the wording of the telex of 15 September 1981 referred to by Lord Templeman as 'the invitation' and addressed to both Harvela and Sir Leonard. It was not a mere invitation to negotiate for the sale of the shares in Harvey & Co. Ltd. of which the vendors were the registered owners . . .

> Lord Diplock referred to the telex inviting tenders and observed that it was not an invitation to treat, but an offer.

Its legal nature was that of a unilateral or 'if' contract, or rather of two unilateral contracts in identical terms to one of which the vendors and Harvela were the parties as **promisor** and promisee respectively, while to the other the vendors were promisor and Sir Leonard was promisee. Such unilateral contracts were made at the time when the invitation was received by the promisee to whom it was addressed by the vendors; under neither of them did the promisee, Harvela and Sir Leonard respectively, assume any legal obligation to anyone to do or refrain from doing anything.

> Here, he goes on to reason that the offer was for a unilateral contract, rather like in the case of *Carlill*. One was made by the vendors (the 'promisor') to Harvela (as a 'promisee'), and one by the vendors to Outerbridge (as the other 'promisee'). Just as Mrs Carlill had no obligation to use the smoke ball or catch the flu, here there was no obligation for Harvela or Outerbridge to submit a bid.

promisor
is a party making a promise. A 'promisee' is the party that the promise was made to.

The vendors, on the other hand, did assume a legal obligation to the promisee under each contract. That obligation was conditional upon the happening, after the unilateral contract had been made, of an event which was specified in the invitation; the obligation was to enter into a **synallagmatic contract** to sell the shares to the promisee, the terms of such synallagmatic contract being also set out in the invitation.

> However, once they had submitted bids, the vendors had an obligation under its contracts with both bidders to then enter into a further bilateral contract with the highest bidder (that is, a contract in which the vendor provided the shares and the buyer provided the money).

synallagmatic contract
is another way of referring to a bilateral contract where both parties have obligations to perform.

By committing itself to contract with the highest tender, the defendant (vendor) made an offer for a unilateral contract to both parties (the potential buyers). The bids (tenders sent by the potential buyers) then resulted in unilateral contracts with both parties, as shown in Figure 2.3. In other words, the act of submitting a tender was acceptance which resulted in both potential buyers having their own unilateral contract with the seller. Under each of these unilateral contracts, the seller was under an obligation to enter an ordinary (bilateral) contract of sale with the buyer that submitted the highest bid.

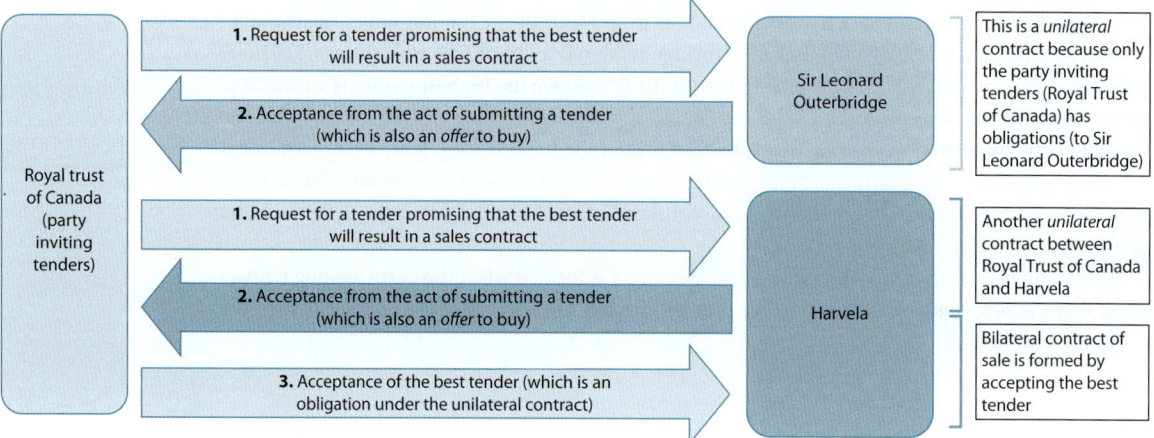

Figure 2.3
The contract formation process in *Harvela* following the House of Lords decision

This approach of having unilateral contracts with all of the parties might appear overcomplicated. It is tempting to think that a more straight-forward alternative would be to say that an offer is made to both parties, but is accepted by the act of submitting the best tender. However, the approach by Lord Diplock in *Harvela* has an important advantage. By recognising a unilateral contract with each party, it means that the party inviting the tenders can owe enforceable obligations to each of the other parties during the process. An example would be an obligation to consider all of the tenders. Such an obligation would only be enforceable if it was contractual, and that would therefore require a contract with each party involved. This was the approach applied by the Court of Appeal in *Blackpool & Fylde Aero Club Ltd v Blackpool Borough Council* [1990] 1 WLR 1195.

The unilateral contract in *Harvela* was from an *express* promise. In *Blackpool & Fylde Aero Club Ltd v Blackpool Borough Council* [1990] 1 WLR 1195, the Court of Appeal recognised a unilateral contract from an *implied* promise. Tenders were invited by the Council-run airport to bid for the right to operate pleasure flights, and while the claimants submitted a bid before the deadline, it was overlooked by the Council. The Court of Appeal held that the invitation had an implied promise to consider all of the tenders received by the deadline. This implied promise was seen as reflecting the *apparent intention* of the Council. When the tenders were submitted, it resulted in unilateral contracts with the Council and each bidder (based on the approach from *Harvela*). Each of these contracts contained an implied obligation to consider the specific bid provided it was received by the deadline. The failure to consider the tender from the claimants was therefore a breach of the relevant unilateral contract.

2.6.2 The Effectiveness of Referential Bids

The remaining issue in the *Harvela* case was the question of who submitted the highest bid. This turned on whether the referential bid was a valid one. On this point, Lord Templeman explained four problems with the use of referential bids:

■ The referential bid can only be quantified if there is a fixed bid to base it on. What if there is no such fixed bid?

- The use of a referential bid means that one party never has the chance of winning. Yet the whole purpose of the tendering process with confidential bids is that all parties have an equal chance of winning.

- The purpose of the process is for each party to submit their best bid. Yet with referential bidding this may not come to light.

- If two parties submit referential bids, the results could be 'bizarre'. Depending on the figures, it could result in the highest bid being lower than Harvela's fixed bid!

According to Lord Templeman, these problems meant that there was an *apparent intention* that referential bids were to be excluded. Of course, if a party making the offer shows a clear intention to allow referential bids, then their use would be valid assuming there are terms stating how the referential bids are to be assessed.

?! THINKING POINTS

Do the cases on displays, adverts, auctions, and tenders encourage parties to make their intentions more obvious?

2.7 Termination of an Offer

When an offer is accepted and it results in an agreement, the original offer no longer exists. However, before this time, an offer might come to an end (i.e. be terminated) by:

- lapse of time;
- revocation by the party making the offer;
- rejection by the party that the offer is made to;
- death of a party (in some cases).

2.7.1 Lapse of Time

If an offer specifies a time limit within which it must be accepted, then acceptance must be within that time limit. Once the stated time limit passes, the offer will no longer exist. This is simply the effect of the intention expressed in the offer. But what if no time limit is specified? In such circumstances, the offer will end after a *reasonable* period of time, with what is *reasonable* depending on the circumstances.

In *Ramsgate Victoria Hotel Co v Montefiore* (1866) LR 1 Ex 109, an offer to buy shares was deemed to have lapsed in the four months it took for the offeree to decide to accept. Shares are price sensitive and are typically bought and sold quickly. These factors meant that the offer would 'reasonably' lapse within a short timeframe.

?! THINKING POINTS

Can you list any factors that might be relevant to how long an offer should last?

The reason *why* an offer can terminate after a reasonable period of time was explained in *Manchester Diocesan Council for Education v Commercial & General Investments* [1970] 1 WLR 241.

GUIDED CASE READING 2.3

Manchester Diocesan Council for Education v Commercial & General Investments Ltd [1970] 1 WLR 241

When reading the extract of the judgment by Buckley J, try to identify:

- The basis of each possible reason why an offer with no deadline terminates after a reasonable period of time.
- The basis of Buckley J's preference for one reason and the rejection of the other.

. . . There appear to me to be two possible views on methods of approaching the problem. First, it may be said that by implication the offer is made upon terms that, if it is not accepted within a reasonable time, it must be treated as withdrawn. Alternatively, it may be said that, if the offeree does not accept the offer within a reasonable time, he must be treated as having refused it. On either view the offer would cease to be a live one upon the expiration of what, in the circumstances of the particular case, should be regarded as a reasonable time for acceptance. The first of these alternatives involves implying a term that if the offer is not accepted within a reasonable time, it shall be treated as withdrawn or lapsing at the end of that period, if it has not then been accepted: the second is based upon an inference to be drawn from the conduct of the offeree, that is, that having failed to accept the offer within a reasonable time he has manifested an intention to refuse it. If in the first alternative the time which the offeror is to be treated as having set for acceptance is to be such a time as is reasonable at the date of the offer, what is reasonable must depend on circumstances then existing and reasonably likely to arise during the continuance of the offer; but it would be not unlikely that the offeror and offeree would make different assessments of what would be reasonable, even if, as might quite possibly not be the case, they based those judgments on identical known and anticipated circumstances. No doubt a court could resolve any dispute about this, but this approach clearly involves a certain degree of uncertainty about the precise terms of the offer. If, on the other hand, the time which the offeror is to be treated as having set for acceptance is to be such a time as turns out to be reasonable in the light of circumstances then existing and of circumstances arising thereafter during the continuance of the offer, whether foreseeable or not, an additional element of uncertainty is introduced.

> Buckley J identified two possible ways to explain why an offer can terminate after a reasonable period of time.
>
> The first possibility was that it is implied by the offer that it will end after a reasonable period.
>
> The second is based on what can be inferred by the offeree's conduct, i.e. by not responding for a reasonable period, the offeree has rejected the offer. In both instances, the question is simply what would count as a 'reasonable' period of time. But as Buckley J went on to explain, this may very well differ depending on the approach used.

> In the first alternative, what is 'reasonable' will have to be assessed at the time the offer was made, because the offer itself is held to imply the relevant term. This will lead to uncertainty because there will be differing perceptions about what is 'reasonable', and it will not be clear how changes in circumstances subsequent to the making of the offer should figure in that calculation. In other words, it involves considerable speculation.

The second alternative, on the other hand, involves simply an objective assessment of facts and the determination of the question whether on the facts the offeree should, in fairness to both parties, be regarded as having refused the offer.

> The second alternative is much more certain and straightforward because it is a matter of deciding what is fair based on an objective assessment of what has actually taken place. Here, there is no speculation because it is just a question of what has happened.

It does not seem to me that either party is in greater need of protection by the law in this respect than the other. Until his offer has been accepted it is open to the offeror at any time to withdraw it or to put a limit on the time for acceptance. On the other hand, the offeree can at any time refuse the offer or, unless he has been guilty of unreasonable delay, accept it. Neither party is at a disadvantage. Unless authority constrains me to do otherwise, I am strongly disposed to prefer the second alternative to the first.

> This led Buckley J to decide that the second alternative was preferable in the absence of any particular injustice or imbalance of power between the parties.

While it was recognised that an offer with no deadline will end after a reasonable period of time, there was no authority to explain why. Buckley identified two possible ways to explain why such offers will end after a reasonable period. The first possibility was that it is implied in the offer that it will end after a reasonable period. That involves implying such a term into the offer and Buckley J referred to the uncertainty involved in working out what period was intended by the offeror. It would involve assessing the offer at the time it was made and considering the circumstances at that time as well as those that seemed likely to happen. It was observed there was a good chance that the parties would disagree about what period would be implied by the offer. On that basis, it was said that the first (offeror-led) possibility would result in uncertainty.

The alternative, second possibility for the offer terminating after a reasonable period was offeree-led. It was suggested that after failing to accept during such a period, it could be inferred that the offeree had rejected the offer. The period is then worked out based on the circumstances and conduct of the offeree. This involves an objective assessment and would not result in the same uncertainty that the first possibility would cause. For that reason, Buckley J expressed a clear preference for the second possibility as the most workable option.

KEY POINTS

An offer without a deadline ends after a reasonable period when it can be inferred that the offeree has rejected the offer.

2.7.2 Revocation of an Offer

An offer can be withdrawn (revoked) by the offeror if the following requirements are met:

- Revocation must be communicated to the offeree.
- The communication must be *before* acceptance takes place.

For revocation to be communicated, it must be received. In addition, it is not enough for the offeror to act inconsistently with the offer, for example by selling the goods elsewhere. The revocation rule can be illustrated by the case of *Byrne v Van Tienhoven* (1880) 5 CPD 344. The (defendant) seller posted an offer to sell 1000 boxes of tin plates to the (claimant) buyer on 1st October. On 8th October, the seller posted a letter revoking the offer. On 11th October, the buyer received the offer and telegraphed his acceptance. On 20th October, the letter of revocation was received by the buyer. The buyer then brought an action for breach of contract. It was held that the revocation was too late. It had been communicated (since the letter of revocation has been received) but this was not before acceptance, which had took place on 11th October.

What if the revocation is *received* but not *read* or is received outside business hours? In *The Brimnes Tenax Steamship Co. Ltd. v The Brimnes (Owners)* [1975] QB 929, revocation of an offer was sent via telex, an early variant of the fax machine. Edmund Davies LJ stated:

> [Counsel for the ship owner]. . .submits that, by leaving the telex machine working, the charterers in effect represented that any message so transmitted to them during ordinary business hours would. . .be dealt with promptly. . .I respectfully agree.

Because the telex machine was on, messages received would be effective from that point. That meant that, as long as the revocation was received, it could be assumed objectively that it had been read. This gets around the potential problem of parties claiming that they have not read a communication that was received and hence that the revocation was not communicated. The message arrived during ordinary business hours and so it can be assumed by default that it was read on receipt. As a result, we can say that ordinarily, it is enough for a message to be *received* rather than *read*. In Chapter 3 we will see similar comments relating to when acceptance is effective.

➜ CROSS-REFERENCE
On acceptance being received outside business hours see 3.2.3.

The reference to 'during business hours' suggests that ordinarily, messages received outside office hours should be effective from the next working day. In other words, the revocation will be *received* when it is likely to have been read.

2.7.2.1 Revocation Communicated by a Third Party

Although revocation must normally be communicated *to* the offeree, it does not have be communicated *by* the offeror. In other words, an offer can be revoked by a third party (a third party is someone other than the offeror or offeree, or the parties to the contract).

The case of *Dickinson v Dodds* (1876) 2 Ch D 463 is the authority for revocation by a third party. In this case, on Wednesday (10th June 1874) Dodds delivered to Dickinson a written offer to sell a property. The letter stated that the offer would remain open until Friday 9am (i.e. 12th June). On the Thursday afternoon, Dickinson was informed by his agent, Mr Berry, that Dodds was offering the property to another buyer, Mr Allan. In fact, on that afternoon the property was sold to Mr Allan. At around 7am Friday, Dickinson then had a letter of acceptance handed to Dodds. Dodds refused to take it on the basis that the property had been sold. Dickinson then claimed that he had a contract and sued for breach. The Court of Appeal held that there was no contract because Dickinson had notice from a third party, i.e. his agent, that the offer had been revoked. According to Mellish LJ, all that mattered was that the offeree had 'notice in some way' that the offer had been withdrawn.

The fact that the offer stated it would remain open until 9am Friday did not make a difference. It was observed that such a promise was not enforceable because Dickinson had not given consideration (something of value) in return, to make the promise enforceable. The issue of consideration is covered in Chapter 5. But for our purposes at this stage, the promise to keep an offer open until Friday 9am was no different to saying: 'I promise to keep the offer open until 9am Friday, but I might revoke it earlier.'

2.7.2.2 Revocation of an Offer for a Unilateral Contract

We have seen already that for revocation to be valid, it must be communicated to the offeree. In the content of an offer to the world (like that in *Carlill*), direct communication to an offeree is not possible because there is no way of knowing who has seen the offer. However, it is still possible to revoke an offer for a unilateral contract. There is no direct English case on this, but the English courts would probably take the same approach as the US Supreme Court in *Shuey v US* (1875) 92 US 73. In this case, in April 1865, the Secretary for War used a newspaper to offer a reward for information leading to the arrest of an accomplice of the man who assassinated President Lincoln. In November, the President issued a revocation of the offer. In 1866, unaware of the revocation, the claimant provided the information and claimed the reward. Mr Justice Strong giving the opinion of the court stated that the offer could be revoked through the same channel in which it was made with the same 'notoriety'. He went on to state that the public should know that the offer could be revoked in such a way.

The point from *Shuey* is that an offer for a unilateral contract can be revoked in a way that is objectively capable of reaching those who might have seen the offer. That can be done by communicating revocation in manner that is equivalent to the one used to make the offer. This is why reference was made to the method and level of publicity. Consider an offer made on a TV advert during a popular late-night show. It is very unlikely that such an offer could be successfully revoked during the 6am news broadcast on the following morning. Such an attempt to revoke would have no real chance of reaching the same kind of audience. Likewise, it might not be possible to revoke the offer by placing a notification in the morning newspaper. However, the method used does not have to be *precisely* the same as the method used for making the offer. An offer might be made through a TV advert directing people to a website, for instance. In such circumstances, revocation communicated through that website might be sufficient.

Another problem with the revocation of an offer for a unilateral contract relates to *when* revocation can be effective. An offer cannot be withdrawn once it has been accepted. However, acceptance of an offer for a unilateral contract requires the offeree to do something, and the contract is only formed when that act has been completed in full. Does that mean the offer can be revoked at any time up the point when the act has been completed? Such a strict application of the traditional requirements for revocation could be very unfair to an offeree who has already started to perform the required act and has spent money and time doing so.

An example would be an offer to pay £1000 to the winner of the local marathon. Acceptance (and therefore a contract) would only take place by completing the required act, in this case, by winning the race. During the race, in the final mile, the offeror appears on a scooter and uses a loud hailer to announce that the offer has been revoked. If the traditional rule was applied strictly, the revocation would be effective because it was communicated before acceptance. But clearly this would be unfair towards all the participants in the race, who would have wasted a great deal of time and energy for no purpose. This potential for unfairness creates the need for a modified revocation requirement in the context of offers for a unilateral contract.

The first case to confirm an alternative approach was *Errington v Errington* [1952] 1 KB 290. In this case, a father had bought a house for his son and daughter-in-law. He promised them that if they paid off the mortgage, he would sign the house over to them. The couple started to make payments and then the father died. In his will, he left the house to his widow who attempted to obtain possession of the house. A question for the Court of Appeal was whether the father's offer could be revoked once performance of acceptance (the payments by the couple) had begun. It was decided that once performance starts, the offer cannot be revoked. On this point in the main judgment, Denning LJ observed:

> The father's promise was a unilateral contract - a promise of the house in return for their act of paying the instalments. It could not be revoked by him once the couple entered on performance of the act, but it would cease to bind him if they left it incomplete and unperformed, which they have not done. If that was the position during the father's lifetime, so it must be after his death.

Denning LJ stated that the offer for a unilateral contract cannot be revoked if performance of the required act has started. It does not mean that the offer has been accepted at that point. Such acceptance only happens when the act has been completed. Instead, the offer is irrevocable and cannot be withdrawn. If the act is not completed, then there is no contract. One difficulty with the comment by Denning LJ is that it is not based on any authority. However, it was cited with approval by Longmore LJ in *Soulsbury v Soulsbury* [2007] EWCA Civ 969 which then gives his comments more weight.

While Denning LJ felt that the father's promise was *irrevocable* once performance commenced, His Lordship did not explain why. In *Daulia Ltd v Four Millbank Nominees* [1978] Ch 231, Goff LJ delivered the following *obiter* comment adopting the same approach as Denning LJ, but he also set out a basis or mechanism for such an approach. On this issue, Goff LJ began by making it clear that a contract only exists once the required act has been completed:

> Whilst I think the true view of a unilateral contract must in general be that the offeror is entitled to require full performance of the condition which he has imposed and short of that he is not bound, that must be subject to one important qualification, which stems from the fact that there must be an implied obligation on the part of the offeror not to prevent the condition becoming satisfied, which obligation it seems to me must arise as soon as the offeree starts to perform. Until then the offeror can revoke the whole thing, but once the offeree has embarked on performance it is too late for the offeror to revoke his offer

The comment supports the idea that once an offeree starts the required act, the offeror cannot revoke the offer. It also shows that the limit on the offeror's ability to revoke the offer is from an implied term in the offer. In other words, it is implied in the offer that it will not be revoked once performance starts. This is another rule that is based on what appears to be intended in such circumstances. So, if the offer actually states that it can be revoked right up to the point when the act is completed, then that express intention would have to be followed.

?!   THINKING POINTS

Even if the promise not to revoke was expressly stated, would it be enforceable? Would it be treated any differently to the promise made in *Dickinson v Dodds* about keeping the offer open until Friday 9am?

A good alternative way of explaining *why* an offer for a unilateral contract is irrevocable once performance starts is the 'double offer theory'. This was suggested by McGovney, in 'irrevocable offers' (1914) 27 Harv. LR 644. The idea is that the offer for a unilateral contract really consists of two offers. There is the *principle offer* which is the reward in return for completed performance. In addition, there is an implied *collateral (secondary) offer* to keep the *principle offer* open once performance has started. This *collateral offer* is accepted by performance being started and creates a *collateral contract*. It means that if there is an attempt to revoke during performance, the performing party can sue for breach of the *collateral contract* and be awarded damages.

KEY POINTS

■ An offer for a unilateral contract can be ended if the intention to revoke it is communicated before performance of the act of acceptance has started.
■ If performance has started, the offer becomes irrevocable but will only result in a contract when performance is complete.
■ Revocation should be communicated in a manner that has an equivalent effect to the one used to make the offer.

2.7.3 Rejection: Refusal and Counter-offer

Rejection of an offer by the offeree terminates the offer. This means once the offeree has rejected the offer, the offeree cannot later try to accept the offer, because it will no longer exist. To reject an offer, the offeree could simply communicate their refusal. Alternatively, the offeree might try to change the terms of the offer. When an offeree responds with new terms, it is called a 'counter-offer' and is as much a rejection of the original offer as a refusal.

The main authority on the effect of a counter-offer is *Hyde v Wrench* (1840) 3 Beav 334. In this case, Wrench offered to sell his farm to Hyde for £1000. Hyde responded by saying he would give £950 for the farm and Wrench refused. Hyde then said that he accepted the original offer of £1000 for the farm. When Wrench refused to carry out the transaction, Hyde brought an action to force the sale. It was held that the counter-offer of £950 had terminated the original offer and hence there was no offer left to accept. Hyde could not unilaterally re-invoke the original offer and accept it. The counter-offer had then been rejected and so there was no contract.

It can be said that a counter-offer shows an objective intention to reject the offer. The offeree is saying 'no' to the original offer, but in a different way. Based on that reasoning, it might be possible for the offeree to keep an offer alive by adding that the response it not a rejection, but is simply an enquiry.

KEY POINTS

If the offeree responds with changed terms it is usually taken to be a rejection of the offer which then terminates the offer. The simplest way to think about this is that if a proposal is given in response to an offer which implies a rejection of the original terms, it is a counter-offer.

A counter-offer should not be confused with a mere enquiry or request for information. A request for information will not terminate the offer, and the offeree might therefore still be able to accept. In *Stevenson v McLean* (1880) 5 QBD 346, McLean had the titles to quantities of iron to sell. They contacted Stevenson who was in the business of buying iron to sell to others and asked Stevenson to find a buyer. McLean then offered Stevenson the iron at 40s per ton. In response, Stevenson telegraphed 'Please wire whether you would accept forty for delivery over two months, or if not, longest limit you would give'. When this was received, McLean sold the iron to another party and sent a telegram to inform Stevenson of the sale. Before this telegram from McLean was received, Stevenson telegraphed their acceptance. It was held that there was no counter-offer by Stevenson; instead the response to the offer was just an enquiry. This meant that the offer had not been terminated and had therefore been accepted by Stevenson's final telegraph.

Whether a response by the offeree is a counter-offer or a mere enquiry depends on the facts and circumstances indicating what the offeree's intention appears to be. It is useful to read the relevant extract of the judgment by Lush J in *Stevenson v McLean* to see the significance of such facts and circumstances.

GUIDED CASE READING 2.4
Stevenson Jaques & Co v McLean (1880) 5 QBD 346

When you read the extract from Lush J, try to identify why the response by Stevenson was regarded as a mere enquiry rather than a counter-offer.

> . . . Stevenson said he meant it only as an inquiry, expecting an answer for his guidance, and this, I think, is the sense in which the defendant ought to have regarded it.
>
> It is apparent throughout the correspondence, that the plaintiffs did not contemplate buying the iron on speculation, but that their acceptance of the defendant's offer depended on their finding someone to take the warrants off their hands. All parties knew that the market was in an unsettled state, and that no one could predict at the early hour when the telegram was sent how the prices would range during the day. It was reasonable that, under these circumstances, they should desire to know before business began whether they were to be at liberty in case of need to make any and what concession as to the time or times of delivery, which would be the time or times of payment, or whether the defendant was determined to adhere to the terms of his letter; and it was highly unreasonable that the plaintiffs should have intended to close the negotiation while it was uncertain whether they could find a buyer or not, having the whole of the business hours of the day to look for one.

Here, Lush J sets out the context and emphasises its importance. The market was unsettled and so it was the judge's opinion that McLean would reasonably have expected Stevenson to want to ascertain certain facts. This was not equivalent to making a counter-offer.

> Then, again, the form of the telegram is one of inquiry. It is not 'I offer forty for delivery over two months,' which would have likened the case to *Hyde v. Wrench*, where one party offered his estate for 1000l., and the other answered by offering 950l. Lord Langdale, in that case, held that after the 950l. had been refused, the party offering it could not, by then agreeing to the original proposal, claim the estate, for the negotiation was at an end by the refusal of his counter proposal. Here there is no counter proposal. The words are, 'Please wire whether you would accept forty for delivery over two months, or, if not, the longest limit you would give'. There is nothing specific by way of offer or rejection, but a mere inquiry, which should have been answered and not treated as a rejection of the offer. This ground of objection therefore fails.

Here, Lush J turned to the actual content of the telegram itself and made clear that it was not specific enough to amount to an offer in itself. The implication is that it was not clear enough to indicate an intention to be bound, and hence was not in itself an offer. This meant it could not be a counter-offer.

From the extract of the judgment, we can see that there were two related factors that made the response by Stevenson a mere enquiry rather than a counter-offer. First, the circumstances surrounding the market and the parties. Stevenson (the buyer) was in the business of buying iron to sell to others and that is why Stevenson was asked to find a buyer. It was also known that Stevenson would not accept the offer until he had found a buyer. Furthermore, it was known that the iron market was 'unsettled' with prices changing by the day. That meant it was known that Stevenson would have to negotiate with other potential buyers on terms such as the delivery period. The point is that in such circumstances, it would be reasonably expected that Stevenson would make enquires about what compromises could be made in order to be in a position to accept.

➡ CROSS-REFERENCE

The offer/counter-offer process in the context of businesses using standard form contracts is detailed at 3.6.1.

The second related factor that made the response an enquiry was the language. Stevenson was not putting forward a new offer. Instead, the telegraph was worded as an enquiry. The approach in this case shows that there may be a fine line between a counter-offer and a mere enquiry. A response to an offer needs to be assessed in the context of the *apparent intention* of the parties and is based on the context. It means that for something to be a counter-offer, we need to see (from an objective perspective) an intention to reject the original offer.

In some cases, the 'language of an enquiry' alone might not be enough. For example, consider *Hyde v Wrench*. What if Hyde asked 'will you accept £950, or, if not, then what price below £1000 would you allow?' it is likely that such a response will appear as a counter-offer (i.e. an intention to reject). It is worded as an enquiry, but it is in effect declaring that the price of £1000 is not acceptable and must be lower. In other words, it shows no intention to be bound by the original terms stated.

KEY POINTS

An enquiry seeking flexibility in the terms of an offer might keep the offer alive, if in the circumstances such an effect is reflected by the apparent intention of the parties.

2.7.4 Death of the Offeror or Offeree

There is no clear authority on how the death of a party could end an offer. In *Dickinson v Dodds*, Mellish LJ stated (*obiter*) 'that, if a man who makes an offer dies, the offer cannot be accepted after he is dead'. This makes sense in the context of an offer to provide a personal service of some sort that can only be done by the offeror. The same can apply to an offeree who has been offered a payment to perform a personal service. An example may be a cooking lesson by a particular celebrity chef, or a training session by a particular sportsperson. In *Reynolds v Atherton* (1921) 125 LT 690 Warrington LJ stated:

> I think it would be more accurate to say that, the offer having been made to a living person who ceases to be a living person before the offer is accepted, there is no longer an offer at all. The offer is not intended to be made to a dead person or to his executers, and the offer ceases to be an offer capable of acceptance.

estate

is everything that a person owned at the time of death and is controlled by an 'executor' or administrator on behalf of the deceased person.

Again, we can see the logic here *if* the offer assumes the existence of the offeror or offeree. Otherwise, if performance can be completed by the executors of an **estate**, then the offer should remain open to be accepted.

CHAPTER SUMMARY

■ For an offer to be made there must be an *apparent intention* to make one.

■ Ordinary displays of priced goods are regarded as invitations to treat, which customers make an offer to buy.

■ Ordinary adverts are regarded as invitations to treat, but one can be an offer if there is an *apparent intention* to make one.

■ An auction 'without reserve' will ordinarily amount to an offer for a unilateral contract to sell to the highest bidder.

■ Ordinarily, an invitation for tenders is an invitation to treat and each tender is an offer.

■ When an invitation for tenders says that the most competitive tender will result in a contract, it will be treated as an offer for a unilateral contract under which the best tender will be accepted.

■ Offers can be ended by lapse, revocation, rejection and (possibly) death.

■ If there is no deadline, the offer will lapse after a reasonable period of time as the offeree is taken to have rejected the offer by not responding.

■ An offer can be revoked as long as the revocation is communicated to the offeree before acceptance takes place.

■ Revocation does not have to be communicated *by* the offeror.

■ An offer for a unilateral contract cannot be revoked once the offeree starts to perform the act of acceptance.

■ A counter-offer is a form of rejection and therefore terminates an offer, but a mere enquiry may not be a counter-offer and so the original offer remains to be accepted.

KEY CASES

☐ *Pharmaceutical Society of GB v Boots* [1953] 1 QB 401—this case provides the rule and reasoning for displays in shops being invitations to treat.

☐ *Partridge v Crittenden* [1968] 1 WLR 1204—this case provides the authority and reasoning for the general rule on adverts being invitations to treat.

☐ *Carlill v Carbolic Smoke Ball Co* [1893] 1 QB 256—this is authority on how an advert can be an offer for a unilateral contract, as well as how such contracts operate.

☐ *Barry v Davies* [2000] 1 WLR 1962—illustrates how a contract is formed in an auction without reserve.

☐ *Harvela v Royal Trust of Canada* [1986] AC 207—is the authority on contracts being formed using a tendering process.

☐ *Manchester Diocesan Council for Education v Commercial & General Investments* [1970] 1 WLR 241—provides the explanation for why an offer with no deadline terminates after a reasonable period.

☐ *Byrne v Van Tienhoven* (1880) 5 CPD 344—represents the general requirements for revocation of an offer.

☐ *Soulsbury v Soulsbury* [2007] EWCA Civ 969—represents the latest authority on revocation of an offer for a unilateral contract.

☐ *Hyde v Wrench* (1840) 3 Beav 334—represents the well-established effect of a counter-offer.

☐ *Stevenson v McLean* (1880) 5 QBD 346—shows how an enquiry could keep the offer alive.

QUESTIONS

1. What is the basis for the general rules making adverts and displays in a shop invitations to treat, and do those rules continue to be suitable in the modern day?

2. Getz 1 Ltd attend an auction advertised as 'without reserve' to buy some of the famous early computers on display. When the bidding starts for an Apple III (1980) computer, Getz 1 Ltd's bid of £4000 is the highest. However, the auctioneer decides that the price is too low and withdraws the item. Does Getz 1 Ltd have a contract and are they entitled to the Apple III?

3. 'The way contracts are formed using the competitive tendering is fair and reflects the reasonable expectations of the parties.'

   Discuss.

4. XS Pizza Ltd emails everyone on its mailing list offering a free pizza to anyone that wears its promotional T shirt in public for the entire day (9am to 9pm). Tosi queues to collect her T shirt at 9am. She wears it all day, takes photos and returns to XS Pizza at 9pm. She is told that the offer was withdrawn on its Facebook page at 1pm. Is Tosi entitled to the free pizza?

 For answer guidance to these questions please visit the online resources at www .oup.com/uk/naidoo1e/, where you will also find multiple choice questions to check your understanding of key concepts.

FURTHER READING

Graw, 'Puff, Pepsi and "That Plane" – The John Leonard Saga' (2000) 15 JCL 281.
An interesting article about adverts and offers for unilateral contracts.

Jackson, 'Offer and Acceptance in the Supermarket' (1979) 129 NLJ 775.
A short article on contract formation in basic supermarkets like those from the 1970s.

Scott, 'The auction house: with or without reserve?' [2001] LMCLQ 334.
A useful short case note analysing *Barry v Davies*.

Simpson, 'Quackery and Contract Law: Carlill v Carbolic Smoke Ball Company (1893)' in Leading Cases in the Common Law (OUP) 1995, p. 259.
This chapter provides a detailed analysis of *Carlill v Carbolic Smoke Ball Co* in its historical background and its significance in the history of contract law.

Agreement Part II: Acceptance

3

LEARNING OBJECTIVES

By the end of this chapter you should be able to:

- understand what is required for valid acceptance;
- apply the rules on when acceptance takes place;
- analyse the problems associated with acceptance by email;
- evaluate the court's approach to the 'battle of the forms' where each party tries to rely on its own standard terms to govern their relationship.

INTRODUCTION

As we saw in Chapter 2, acceptance of an offer will result in an agreement. It means that in a dispute about the existence of a contract, whether or not acceptance took place may be a significant issue. The practical context of such disputes is simple. Typically, the offeree responds intending to accept an offer and create a contract. The offeror then denies that a contract exists, often because they have found a better deal elsewhere. To justify this, the offeror might then argue that not enough was done for acceptance to take place. Such arguments have resulted in a lot of interesting case law on what is required for acceptance.

In this chapter, we look at the key cases and principles relating to acceptance. We begin by considering the law concerning what is sufficient for acceptance. Next, we explore the rules concerning *when* acceptance is communicated. The chapter then turns to the use of standard pre-drafted terms used by businesses to form an agreement. This is a significant issue that is often referred to as the 'battle of the forms'. Finally, we consider the extent to which both offer and acceptance are necessary for an agreement to exist.

3.1 Valid Acceptance

The first issue we need to consider in relation to acceptance is what is required for it to be valid. This is often referred to as the 'fact of acceptance'. The question is whether the offeree has done enough to demonstrate an intention to accept the offer and create an agreement. We will see that this requires:

- complete agreement to the terms of the offer;
- compliance with any requirements regarding the method of acceptance;
- the acceptance to have been made in response to the offer.

Let's address these issues in turn.

3.1.1 Complete Agreement to the Terms of the Offer

➜ CROSS-REFERENCE
To remind yourself of the effect of a counter-offer see 2.7.3.

Essentially, for acceptance to be valid, the offeree has to agree to the terms of the offer. The offeree cannot change the terms or add to them. In Chapter 2 we saw that if the offeree responds with new terms, it might be treated as a counter-offer. Likewise, a response that says 'I accept' but then includes a change to the terms could also be considered to be a counter-offer (*Northland Airlines Ltd v Dennis Ferranti Meters Ltd* [1970] 114 Sol Jo 845). Such responses do not show an intention to accept the terms of the offer.

Valid acceptance does not have to take place using precisely the same terms as the offer. What matters is that the offeree has shown an intention to agree to all of the terms. It means that if an acceptance simply expresses a term that was implied by the offer anyway, then acceptance will be valid and the communication will not be held to have been a counter-offer.

3.1.2 Where a Method of Acceptance Is Specified

When we think of an offer having terms, the obvious ones that come to mind are those relating to the actual deal, for example, the relevant goods or services and the price. However, the terms of an offer will often go further and specify *how* acceptance should take place. An example would be an offer stating that acceptance should be by email. It is not necessary for an offer to specify a method for acceptance. But if a method is specified, then in principle, such a requirement should be followed for acceptance to be valid. After all, such an approach is consistent with the need for complete agreement with the offer. However, we will see from the cases that it is very important to look at the *way* a method is specified. The wording used in the offer will determine if the method must be followed for acceptance to be valid.

➜ CROSS-REFERENCE
For more detail on the tendering process see 2.6.

In *Manchester Diocesan Council of Education v Commercial & General Investments* [1970] 1 WLR 241 school premises were being sold using a tendering process. The claimant seller created a form to be used by any parties submitting a tender and the form contained terms. Condition 4 of the terms stated that the seller should send its letter of acceptance to the address in the buyer's tender (meaning that in every tender, each of which was an offer, it was a stipulation that communication of acceptance should be performed in this way). In September, the seller sent a letter of acceptance to the successful buyer. This acceptance should have been sent to the buyer's company address, because that was the address stated in the buyer's tender. Instead, it was sent to the buyer's company surveyor, who had been involved in the earlier negotiation process. In December, having had no response, the seller wrote to the buyer's solicitors asking for confirmation that a contract existed. In January, the solicitors replied saying they were unable to confirm that a contract existed. This is because the buyer had not received the letter of acceptance, which had been sent to the wrong address. In response, the seller immediately sent a letter of acceptance to the address of the buyer's company but the buyer informed them that it was too late to accept their offer.

Buckley J held that the first letter of acceptance was valid and so a contract existed when that letter was received by the offeror. The specified method of acceptance was not followed, but it did not matter because the wording did not make the method 'the sole permitted method of communicating an acceptance'. The judgment provides some useful guidance on the effect of making a specified method of acceptance compulsory, and the extent to which an alternative method can be used when the offer does not make the specified method compulsory. Buckley J's guidance is detailed in the following extract from the judgment:

> It may be that an offeror, who by the terms of his offer insists upon acceptance in a particular manner, is entitled to insist that he is not bound unless acceptance is effected or communicated in that precise

way, although it seems probable that, even so, if the other party communicates his acceptance in some other way, the offeror may by conduct or otherwise waive his right to insist upon the prescribed method of acceptance. Where, however, the offeror has prescribed a particular method of acceptance, but not in terms insisting that only acceptance in that mode shall be binding, I am of opinion that acceptance communicated to the offeror by any other mode which is no less advantageous to him will conclude the contract. Thus in *Tinn v. Hoffman & Co.* (1873) 29 L.T. 271, where acceptance was requested by return of post, Honeyman J. said, at p. 274:

"That does not mean exclusively a reply by letter by return of post, but you may reply by telegram or by verbal message or by any means not later than a letter written by return of post."

If an offeror intends that he shall be bound only if his offer is accepted in some particular manner, it must be for him to make this clear. Condition 4 in the present case has not, in my judgment, this effect.

Moreover, the inclusion of condition 4 in the defendant's offer was at the instance of the plaintiff, who framed the conditions and the form of tender. It should not, I think, be regarded as a condition or stipulation imposed by the defendant as offeror upon the plaintiff as offeree, but as a term introduced into the bargain by the plaintiff and presumably considered by the plaintiff as being in some way for the protection or benefit of the plaintiff. It would consequently be a term strict compliance with which the plaintiff could waive, provided the defendant was not adversely affected. The plaintiff did not take advantage of the condition which would have resulted in a contract being formed as soon as a letter of acceptance complying with the condition was posted, but adopted another course, which could only result in a contract when the plaintiff's acceptance was actually communicated to the defendant.

Buckley J's reasoning and opinions provide us with some useful guidance on specified methods of acceptance. It tells us that the way a method is specified is very important. If it is specified with wording that shows a clear intention that only one method of acceptance is to be used, then acceptance must take place by that method. If a different method is used, the offeror is not bound by it and there is no agreement. Essentially, in these circumstances, the offeror can ignore the attempted acceptance that uses the wrong method. However, while the offeree is bound to use the stipulated method, the offeror is not. He or she can deem acceptance to be valid even if it is not compliant with the stipulated method. An offeror might receive an acceptance through a different method but then choose to go ahead with the transaction anyway if the terms are favourable. Buckley J only said that he felt this was 'probable'. There was no authority to support his view, but it just made sense. After all, it would be strange if an offeror could not allow an alternative method to form a contract, if he or she is happy to do so. It would undermine the principle of freedom of contract to suggest otherwise. Of course, this part of the judgment is *obiter dicta* and therefore not binding. However, such an option is commercially pragmatic and therefore probably the approach that would be taken if ever a ruling was required on the matter.

The rest of the extract is about the use of an alternative method when the specified method is not compulsory. In these circumstances, the alternative method can result in a contract once it is 'communicated' to the offeror. However, it is important to appreciate that the alternative method has to be 'no less advantageous' for the offeror as the one suggested. That means from the offeror's position, the alternative must be just as good as the specified method and not put the offeror in a worse position. In practice this means that the alternative must not impose greater costs or inconvenience on the offeror. If the offer requests that an email be used to communicate acceptance, for instance, but is not absolutely clear in its language, the court might decide that a letter is not a suitable alternative because the information in it is not capable of being processed electronically and hence is more time consuming to handle.

Just like the cases covered in Chapter 2, the decision of Buckley J reflects the *apparent intentions* of the parties. Since the wording of the offer did not show a clear intention to make the method of acceptance compulsory, it showed an intention to allow for alternative equivalent methods.

→ CROSS-REFERENCE
For the law on when acceptance is communicated see 3.2.

KEY POINTS

■ If a method of acceptance is specified, it will only be compulsory if it clearly indicates that only that method is valid.

■ If this is not the case, an alternative can be used as long as it is no less advantageous to the offeror.

The reasoning of Buckley J in *Manchester Diocesan Council of Education v Commercial & General Investments* was applied by the Court of Appeal in *Yates Building Company Ltd v R J Pulleyn & Sons (York) Ltd* [1976] 1 EGLR 157. The case concerned an offer that was in the form of an option to purchase property. This option was made by the seller (Pulleyn) to Yates. The option stated it was exercisable by 'notice in writing', adding 'such notice to be sent by registered or recorded delivery post', but the buyer, Yates, sent the notice (i.e. acceptance) by ordinary post. The seller then acknowledged receipt of the notice but said that it was not valid acceptance because ordinary post was used. The Court of Appeal held that the notice given was valid acceptance. Lord Denning MR (with whom Orr LJ and Scarman LJ agreed) reasoned that the specified method was not worded as a compulsory requirement. In addition, ordinary post was no less advantageous to the seller because the seller had received the notice in writing on time. Lord Denning also observed that registered or recorded post had been specified in order to protect the buyer because it would give the buyer proof that the acceptance had been delivered. On that basis, Lord Denning stated that the buyer could waive the protection and take the risk of the seller denying that the notice was received.

?! THINKING POINTS

Can you identify any circumstances where the use of ordinary post in *Yates v Pulleyn* could have been less advantageous to the seller?

The cases show that it is important to be clear when specifying a method of acceptance. In *Siemans Hearing instruments Ltd v Friends Life Ltd* [2014] EWCA Civ 382, a lease contract referred to a right that could be exercised by giving notice, which 'must' take a very specific form. The use of the word 'must' was enough for the Court of Appeal to treat the specified method as compulsory. This is because it is difficult to construe the word 'must' as meaning anything other than that only the specified method could be used. In other cases, with different terms and different facts, more might be required to make such an intention obvious.

3.1.3 Acceptance Must Be in Response to the Offer

In ordinary bilateral situations (where both parties have obligations), the accepting party would be responding to an offer. However, the position concerning an offer for a unilateral contract (where only one party has obligations) is not so simple. You will recall that such offers are accepted by another party performing the act of acceptance specified in the offer. But what if a person completes the required act without being aware of the offer? A common example is the offer of a reward for the return of a lost dog. You might simply recognise the dog and return it without knowing about the offer. We will now see that in order for an act to count as acceptance of a unilateral offer, it must have been performed in response to that offer.

In *R v Clarke* (1927) 40 CLR 227 (Aust), following the murder of two police officers, the Government of Western Australia offered a reward for information leading to the arrest and conviction of the murderers. Clarke was not one of the murderers, but was arrested and charged for the crime. He then gave information which led to the conviction of the murderers. When he claimed the reward, it was

→ CROSS-REFERENCE
For an example of a unilateral contract see the *Carlill case* at 2.3.2.

refused, so he sued the government. During the hearing, he admitted that he gave the information to protect himself, without thinking about the reward. The court then held that he was not entitled to the reward because his performance was not acceptance.

The judges based their decisions on the idea that Clarke was not acting in reliance on the offer—which is another way of saying that he would have given the information anyway, even in the absence of the reward. Since it was something he would have done anyway, he was not carrying out the act in exchange for the reward but for unrelated reasons, and this meant there was no true agreement.

One of the judges, Higgins J observed that ordinarily it could have been presumed that Clarke acted in response to the offer by giving the information, but such a presumption was rebutted by the fact that Clarke admitted that he was not acting in response to the reward when he gave the information. Clearly, then, evidence also matters. Ordinarily, if you return a lost dog without ever knowing of the existence of a reward, it would appear that you have acted in response to the offer, and it could then be assumed that the owner would give you the reward. If, however, it is somehow proven that you did not know of the existence of the reward, your performance would not be treated as acceptance because it would not in response to the offer.

THINKING POINTS

- Is it fair that a helpful citizen who returns a dog without knowledge of a reward will not have a contract for the reward, even though the act that the offeror was willing to pay for has been performed?
- As a justification for the rule, can you think of circumstances where performance of a required act might result in a contract where both parties have obligations?

R v Clarke is a puzzling case in some respects because it is difficult to reconcile with the decision in *Carlill*. The reason why Mrs Carlill started using the smoke ball was to avoid the flu. Since that was the case, can it realistically be said that she was performing that act in exchange for the reward? It could reasonably have been argued that, like Clarke, she would have used the smoke ball anyway, and hence there was no true exchange. Another problem is that there is a case in English law with striking similarities to *Clarke*, but in which the court came to the opposite conclusion. In *Williams v Carwardine* (1833) 4 B & Ad 421, an offer of a reward was made in return for information leading to the arrest and conviction of a murderer. Mrs Carwardine gave the information and said she did so to 'ease her conscience and in the hope of divine forgiveness'. In other words, just like Clarke, she presumably would have given the information anyway irrespective of the existence of the reward, but the court held that she was entitled to the reward. The court in *Clarke* attempted to reconcile these problems by suggesting that because Clarke was particularly firm about having no intention to claim the reward (he said that 'When I gave evidence in the criminal court I had no intention of claiming the reward'), then it was implicit there was definitely no intention to contract. But it is also hard to avoid the conclusion that the court in Western Australia was simply trying to find any reason to justify not giving Clarke a reward—because while he had not been directly involved in the murders in question, he was an associate of the actual murderers, and had been engaged in illegal activity with them. But there does seem to be general acceptance that there must at least have been some knowledge of the existence of the offer in the mind of the person carrying out the stipulated act in order for it to qualify as acceptance.

KEY POINTS

The acceptance must be in *response* to the offer.

3.2 Communication of Acceptance

Another important issue in the topic of acceptance is the question of exactly *when* the acceptance is effective. This is important because it is the point in time when a contract is formed. At that stage, it is not possible to withdraw the offer because it no longer exists—the contract takes over and of course, the obligations under the contract are enforceable. We will see that the apparent intention of the offeror can dictate what is required for acceptance to be communicated. An example would be an offer that states that acceptance must be by email and is only effective once the message is received in the offeror's inbox. In such a case, the acceptance will only be 'communicated' once it is actually in the offeror's inbox. The problem is that offers do not always show such a clear intention about when acceptance will be deemed to be effective. Consequently, the case law has developed a number of rules to help the courts identify what must have been intended. We will address application of these rules in turn.

➡ **CROSS-REFERENCE**

For an example of the importance of timing of acceptance and revocation, see *Byrne v Van Tienhoven* at 2.7.2.

3.2.1 The General Rule on Communication of Acceptance

On the issue of when acceptance takes place, there is a general rule that acceptance is effective once it is 'communicated'. This requires the acceptance to be *received* and means that the offeror ought to know when a contract is formed. Without this general rule, the offeror could end up having a contract without knowing, and it is assumed that this is something no offeror would intend.

KEY POINTS

The general rule is that acceptance is valid when it is communicated (received).

With face-to-face dealings it is obvious when the acceptance is communicated, and no issues arise. Communication is *instantaneous* in that once the offeree indicates their acceptance, the other party will be aware of it immediately. However, since other forms of communication are instantaneous but without a face-to-face component, the courts have had to develop guidance for when there is acceptance by an instantaneous method of communication. Much of this guidance developed from disputes that took place many years ago. This means that the cases are about methods of communication that are outdated, like the use of telex, which as we have seen was an early forerunner of the fax. However, the principles developed for these outdated methods will be relevant when the courts are faced with disputes over the more familiar, modern methods of communication like emails.

➡ **CROSS-REFERENCE**

Modern methods of e-commerce, such as email and websites, are explained in 3.5.

3.2.2 Instantaneous Communication and the General Rule

We already know that the general rule requires acceptance to be communicated, and therefore that acceptance is effective when it is received. This applies to what are said to be 'instantaneous' communication methods. Such instantaneous methods tend to be direct, such that the parties readily know whether acceptance has been communicated or not. In other words, 'instantaneous' methods are those which take place directly, as in face-to-face dealing, for example on the telephone.

Despite its age and therefore its focus on telephone and telex methods, the Court of Appeal case of *Entores Ltd v Miles Far East Corporation* [1955] 2 QB 327 provides some useful guidance on the application of the general rule to instantaneous methods of communication. In this case, a Dutch company sent its acceptance to a company based in England. This acceptance was in the form of a telex. Following a dispute, the English company wanted to bring an action for breach of contract, and at that point a question arose as to whether the English courts had jurisdiction to initiate the action. The applicable jurisdiction would be determined on the basis of where the contract was formed, so the Court of Appeal had to work out when (and therefore where) acceptance took place. If it took place when the telex was sent, the contract would have been formed in the Netherlands. If it took place when the telex was received, it would have been formed in England. It was held that since the telex was a form of instantaneous communication, the general rule applied. This meant that acceptance took place when the telex was received in England, so that was where the contract was formed.

In the main judgment, Denning LJ explained the position with regards to instantaneous communication and went on to comment on the position when things go wrong with the method of communication.

GUIDED CASE READING 3.1
Entores Ltd v Miles Far East Corporation [1955] 2 QB 327

As you read this extract, try to see how Denning LJ uses the fault of the parties and the control they have to work out their responsibilities.

. . . [T]here is no clear rule about contracts made by telephone or by Telex. Communications by these means are virtually instantaneous . . .	Denning LJ begins with the central problem, that English law had not yet established clear rules on the formation of contracts by instantaneous forms of communication (which, although not exactly new, had only recently become widespread).
The problem can only be solved by going in stages. Let me first consider a case where two people make a contract by word of mouth in the presence of one another. Suppose, for instance, that I shout an offer to a man across a river or a courtyard but I do not hear his reply because it is drowned by an aircraft flying overhead. There is no contract at that moment. If he wishes to make a contract, he must wait till the aircraft is gone and then shout back his acceptance so that I can hear what he says. Not until I have his answer am I bound . . .	
Now take a case where two people make a contract by telephone. Suppose, for instance, that I make an offer to a man by telephone and, in the middle of his reply, the line goes 'dead' so that I do not hear his words of acceptance. There is no contract at that moment. The other man may not know the precise moment when the line failed. But he will know that the telephone conversation was abruptly broken off: because people usually say something to signify the end of the conversation. If he wishes to make a contract, he must therefore get through again so as to make sure that I heard. Suppose next, that the line does not go dead, but it is nevertheless so indistinct that I do not catch what he says and I ask him to repeat it. He then repeats it and I hear his acceptance. The contract is made, not on the first time when I do not hear, but only the second time when I do hear. If he does not repeat it, there is no contract. The contract is only complete when I have his answer accepting the offer.	He reasons by analogy. First, he chooses the example of two people having a face-to-face conversation. If one person makes an offer and the other replies with an acceptance knowing that it might not have been heard, there cannot be a contract at that point in time. In these circumstances it would only be right for the person accepting the offer to make sure that he spoke again and this time was heard. Only then would there be a contract.
Lastly, take the Telex. Suppose a clerk in a London office taps out on the teleprinter an offer which is immediately recorded on a teleprinter in a Manchester office, and a clerk at that end taps out an acceptance. If the line goes dead in the middle of the sentence of acceptance, the teleprinter motor will stop. There is then obviously no contract. The clerk at Manchester must get through again and send his complete sentence. But it may happen that the line does not go dead, yet the message does not get through to London. Thus the clerk at Manchester may tap out his message of acceptance and it will not be recorded in London because the ink at the London end fails, or something of that kind. In that case, the Manchester clerk will not know of the failure but the	Denning LJ then uses a similar analogy—that of a telephone conversation. If one party makes an offer and the line then goes dead just as the other is in the process of saying they accept, so that the offeree cannot be sure the offeror has heard the acceptance, there cannot be a contract. It is for the person who is trying to accept, to redial and make sure that the acceptance is heard.

London clerk will know of it and will immediately send back a message 'not receiving'. Then, when the fault is rectified, the Manchester clerk will repeat his message. Only then is there a contract. If he does not repeat it, there is no contract. It is not until his message is received that the contract is complete.

In all the instances I have taken so far, the man who sends the message of acceptance knows that it has not been received or he has reason to know it. So he must repeat it. But, suppose that he does not know that his message did not get home. He thinks it has. This may happen if the listener on the telephone does not catch the words of acceptance, but nevertheless does not trouble to ask for them to be repeated: or the ink on the teleprinter fails at the receiving end, but the clerk does not ask for the message to be repeated: so that the man who sends an acceptance reasonably believes that his message has been received. The offeror in such circumstances is clearly bound, because he will be estopped from saying that he did not receive the message of acceptance. It is his own fault that he did not get it. But if there should be a case where the offeror without any fault on his part does not receive the message of acceptance—yet the sender of it reasonably believes it has got home when it has not—then I think there is no contract.

My conclusion is, that the rule about instantaneous communications between the parties is [that the] contract is only complete when the acceptance is received by the offeror: and the contract is made at the place where the acceptance is received . . .

. . . Applying the principles which I have stated, I think that the contract in this case was made in London where the acceptance was received. It was, therefore, a proper case for service out of the jurisdiction.

> The reasoning from these two analogies was then applied to the telex. If an offeree sends an acceptance to the offeror and the line goes dead half way through, the offeree would know that the message might not have been received. Again, it is for the offeree to make sure acceptance is received.

> However, Denning LJ does add the important caveat here that this may not be the case if acceptance is not communicated due to fault of the offeror. If the offeror did not receive a message of acceptance because he had failed to replace the ink in the machine, for example, and then did not notify the offeree that this had happened, the court may well hold that acceptance was in fact communicated, as the offeree would have done all that could be fairly required.

> The inescapable conclusion for Denning LJ, then, is that in general a contract is formed on receipt of the acceptance when an instantaneous form of communication is being used. This meant the contract was formed on the telex's arrival in England and hence English law applied to it.

The essence of Denning LJ's approach, then, is that the risk of the message not being received generally falls on the offeree. The offeree is usually in a position to make sure that the acceptance is received because, after all, it is the offeree who is actually sending the communication. The offeror may be entirely in ignorance about it. Moreover, the offeror is in a position of weakness by generally not knowing of the existence of a communication of acceptance, until it is received. The offeree on the other hand chooses the time to communicate the acceptance. For these reasons it is right that the offeree bears the risk of a message not being received. It must be remembered, though, that this is a general rule and if it is the offeror's own fault that the message is not received, then it is the offeror who bears the risk of non-delivery.

The same general rule that applies to acceptance by instantaneous communication methods like phone and telex was applied to the use of fax in *JSC Zestafoni Nikoladze Ferroalloy Plant v Ronly Holdings Ltd* [2004] EWCA 245. The extension of the rule to faxes makes sense because a fax is like a telephone call; the only difference is that the message is printed on paper by a machine rather than being in the form of sound through a phone speaker. If the fax transmission has not connected, the sender will know to try again.

?! THINKING POINTS

Given the reasoning used to apply the general rule to phones, telex and fax, do you think the same should apply to instant messaging platforms like Messenger and WhatsApp? It is useful to consider how these methods allow us to know when a message is sent, received, and possibly when the message has been read.

On the facts of *Entores*, the telex had been received by the offeror. That means Denning LJ's comments on what happens if the acceptance is not received were not essential to the decision. Consequently, these comments were *obiter* and not strictly binding. However, they are highly persuasive and regarded as representing the correct legal position. They were subsequently followed by the House of Lords in *Brinkibon Ltd v Stahag Stahl und Stahlwarenhandelsgesellschaft G.m.b.H.* [1983] 2 AC 34 (the '*Brinkibon*' case). The issue in this case was very similar to that of *Entores*. A contract had been formed using telex messages between London and Vienna. The House of Lords had to work out if the English courts had jurisdiction to initiate a claim for breach of contract. To do so, they had to work out where the contract was formed and that was based on when acceptance took place. Having decided that acceptance was from a telex sent from London to Vienna, it was held that the contract was formed in Vienna. This outcome was based on the general rule being applied to the use of telex.

Lord Fraser approved of the approach in *Entores* and added some useful guidance on the parties' responsibilities when using instantaneous communication. The first point was about the rule in practice:

> I have reached the opinion that, on balance, an acceptance sent by telex directly from the acceptor's office to the offeror's office should be treated as if it were an instantaneous communication . . . like a telephone conversation. One reason is that the decision to that effect in *Entores v. Miles Far East Corporation*. . . seems to have worked without leading to serious difficulty or complaint from the business community.

The point here is that the rule on acceptance by instantaneous communication is consistent with the expectations of those in business. Lord Fraser then addressed the responsibilities of the offeror:

> Secondly, once the message has been received on the offeror's telex machine, it is not unreasonable to treat it as delivered to the principal offeror, because it is his responsibility to arrange for prompt handling of messages within his own office.

The next point was about the responsibility of the offeree:

> Thirdly, a party (the acceptor) who tries to send a message by telex can generally tell if his message has not been received on the other party's (the offeror's) machine, whereas the offeror, of course, will not know if an unsuccessful attempt has been made to send an acceptance to him. It is therefore convenient that the acceptor, being in the better position, should have the responsibility of ensuring that his message is received.

Based on the opinion from Lord Fraser the following points can be made:

- The offeree will generally know if the message has been received, and so the offeree has to ensure that the message is received by the offeror's machine.
- When the message is received by the machine, acceptance is effective at that point. The offeree has done all that it can.
- If the message is not read by the offeror or is not printed by the machine, that is the fault of the offeror. The message is classed as being communicated and so acceptance is effective at that point.
- This approach seems to reflect the expectations of businesses.

The guidance from Lord Fraser's opinion is based on the same principles as the comments by Denning LJ in *Entores*. The risk of a message not being received or read is placed on the party at fault. That fault is based on the level of control the parties have in the communication process. But it is important to remember that the guidance from Denning LJ and Lord Fraser applies when the offeror has not been clear enough about when acceptance is to be effective. An offeror can circumvent the guidance by stating clearly when acceptance will be effective. In other words, an offeror can get around the guidance by showing a clear intention for acceptance to be effective at a particular time only. An extreme example would be where it is stated in the offer that acceptance is effective only after the message has been actually read.

KEY POINTS

When the general rule applies, acceptance is effective when it is received and capable of being read.

3.2.3 Where the Instantaneous Method Is Received Outside Office Hours

The guidance from the cases covered so far applies to acceptance that is equivalent to a face-to-face transaction. But what if a message is sent outside office hours? It seems that such acceptance would be effective when it can be reasonably expected to be communicated. Usually, that would be the start of the next working day. The point was made in *Tenax Steamship Co v Owners of the Motor Vessel Brimnes (The Brimnes)* [1975] QB 929 and *Schelde Delta Shipping BV v Astarte Shipping BV (The Pamela)* [1995] 2 Lloyds Rep. 249. Whilst both cases involved a withdrawal notice (revocation) sent by telex rather than acceptance, there is no reason to think that the same approach would not apply to acceptance. It is important to consider the factual background of each case because that is useful to work out the *apparent intentions* of the parties. For example, an offeree might know from previous dealings that an offeror never does business on a Friday. In such circumstances, acceptance received by a voice mail at 10pm Thursday night might be effective at the usual start of business on the following Monday.

In the *Brinkibon* case, Lord Wilberforce expressed an important opinion about instantaneous communication which included a reference messages sent outside of office hours. It is useful to read the relevant extract because it provides judges with flexibility and has been cited in later cases:

> Since 1955 the use of telex communication has been greatly expanded, and there are many variants on it. The senders and recipients may not be the principals to the contemplated contract. They may be servants or agents with limited authority. The message may not reach, or be intended to reach, the designated recipient immediately: messages may be sent out of office hours, or at night, with the intention, or upon the assumption, that they will be read at a later time. There may be some error or default at the recipient's end which prevents receipt at the time contemplated and believed in by the sender. The message may have been sent and/or received through machines operated by third persons. And many other variations may occur. No universal rule can cover all such cases: they must be resolved by reference to the intentions of the parties, by sound business practice and in some cases by a judgment where the risks should lie.

Essentially, Lord Wilberforce observed that the set-up used for the instantaneous communication could vary. On that basis, it was not possible to have one single, fixed rule. Instead, some cases would have to be resolved using the 'intentions of the parties', 'sound business practice' and a decision on 'where the risks should lie'. It is convenient to have clear rules, but it is important for judges to have the flexibility to deal with more complicated arrangements for communication. Factors like the fault of the parties and at what stage each party had control would be relevant to working out where the risks should lie.

So far, we have looked at the general rule that acceptance is valid from the time it is communicated to the offeror. Ordinarily, that means the agreement would be formed when the offeror *receives* the acceptance. However, there are exceptions to this general rule, and they are explained at 3.3. The chapter then turns to vending machines and more familiar, modern methods such as websites and email. In particular, we look at whether the general rule or an exception should apply to acceptance by email.

3.3 Communication of Acceptance: Exceptions to the General Rule

Since the general rule is that acceptance is effective once it is communicated (i.e. received), any exception to the rule would mean that a contract is formed without acceptance being received by the offeror. The first exception is known as the 'postal rule'. When this applies, the letter of acceptance is valid at the time it is posted (the time it is sent). Another exception is where the offeror waives the need for acceptance to be communicated. When that happens, a contract can be formed without any communication of acceptance. The third exception is acceptance by conduct. Here a contract can be formed because the conduct of the offeree indicates acceptance. This conduct may be sufficient even though there has been no actual communication of a statement confirming acceptance. The law relating to these exceptions is detailed in turn.

3.3.1 Acceptance by Post

Ordinarily acceptance by post is effective when it is *sent* rather than when it is received. In such circumstances, the contract is formed before the letter of acceptance is received. This means that a contract is formed without the offeror knowing about it until later. In a dispute, it would be for the claimant offeree to prove when the acceptance was posted. That can be done by using the Post Office and asking for 'proof of postage' at the time. Alternatively, the claimant could persuade a judge of the time of posting using testimony of the circumstances existing at the time of posting.

While the exception concerning the use of the post is often referred to as the 'postal rule', it is important to appreciate that it is not an absolute rule that applies whenever there is acceptance by post. Instead, it only applies when the parties are not clear about *when* they intend acceptance by post to be effective. For that reason, the post rule operates more like a default presumption. We will start by addressing the basis of the postal rule before turning to when it applies, and then how it can be set aside.

3.3.1.1 The Basis of the 'Post Rule'

The case of *Adams v Lindsell* (1818) 1 B & Ald 681 is often cited as authority for the post rule. It was even the case Lord Wilberforce cited when he referred to acceptance by post in the *Brinkibon* case. In *Adams v Lindsell*, Lindsell (the seller) posted a letter offering wool to Adams (the buyer) on 2nd September. The letter stated 'receiving your answer in course of post' (meaning by return of post). This offer was wrongly addressed and delayed, so it was received by Adams on 5th September. Adams then posted his acceptance the same day. Unaware of the delay, Lindsell in the meantime sold the wool to another party. This prompted Adams to sue for breach on the basis that he had accepted the offer and therefore had a contract. The court had to determine if acceptance had taken place and held that the acceptance by post was effective at the time it was posted. That meant a contract was formed on 5th September and Lindsell was liable for breach having sold the wool to another party. Interestingly, the report for the case does not refer to the application of a 'postal rule' or presumption. It seems more likely that the court ruled on the basis that Lindsell had been negligent in putting the wrong address on the offer that he posted, and therefore it was his own fault that there had been a delay in the communication of acceptance. In other words, it appears to be the type of scenario which Denning LJ was talking about in *Entores* in which acceptance is held to have been communicated if the offeree has done all that can be reasonably expected in the circumstances. However, in later cases the rule crystallised that acceptance by post is effective at the time of posting by default.

The case of *Household Fire Insurance v Grant* (1879) 4 Ex D 216 shows that even if the letter of acceptance never arrives (through no fault of the offeree), it is still effective from the time of posting. In this case Thesiger LJ in the Court of Appeal explained the rule and gave reasons for it, and so it is useful for us to go through the relevant part of the judgment.

GUIDED CASE READING 3.2
Household Fire and Carriage Accident Insurance (Limited) v Grant   (1879) 4 Ex D 216

When reading the extract of the judgment by Thesiger LJ, try to identify the reasons given to justify the postal rule.

. . . I see no better mode than that of treating the Post Office as the agent of both parties, and it was so considered by Lord Romilly, MR, in *Hebb's Case* (1867) Law Rep 4 Eq at p. 12 when in the course of his judgment, he said: '*Dunlop v Higgins* (1848) 1 HL Cas 381 decides that the posting of a letter accepting an offer constitutes a binding contract, but the reason of that is, that the Post Office is the common agent of both parties.' . . . But if the Post Office be such a common agent, then it seems to me to follow that, as soon as the letter of acceptance is delivered to the Post Office, the contract is made as complete and final and absolutely binding as if the acceptor had put his letter into the hands of a messenger, sent by the offeror himself as his agent, to deliver the offer and receive the acceptance.

[The judgment referring to other judicial statements indicating that the contract is formed when the letter is posted and then continued]

. . . The acceptor in posting the letter has, to use the language of Lord Blackburn, in *Brogden v Metropolitan Rail Co* (1877) 2 App Cas 666 at 691, 'put it out of his control, and done an extraneous act which clenches the matter, and shows beyond all doubt that each side is bound'. How then can a casualty in the post, whether resulting in delay, which in commercial transactions is often as bad as no delivery, or in non-delivery, unbind the parties or unmake the contract? To me it appears that in practice a contract complete upon the acceptance of an offer being posted, but liable to be put an end to by an accident in the post, would be more mischievous than a contract only binding upon the parties to it upon the acceptance actually reaching the offeror, and I can see no principle of law from which such an anomalous contract can be deduced.

There is no doubt that the implication of a complete, final, and absolutely binding contract being formed as soon as the acceptance of an offer is posted, may in some cases lead to inconvenience and hardship. But such there must be at times in any view of the law. It is impossible in transactions which pass between parties at a distance, and have to be carried on through the medium of correspondence, to adjust conflicting rights between innocent parties so as to make the consequences of mistake on the part of a mutual agent fall equally upon the shoulders of both. At the same time I am not prepared to admit that the implication in question will lead to any great or general inconvenience or hardship. An offeror, if he chooses, may always make the formation of the contract which he proposes dependent upon the actual communication to himself of the acceptance. If he trusts to the post, he trusts to a means of communication which as a rule does not fail, and if no answer to his offer is received by him, and the matter is of importance to him, he can make inquiries of the person to whom his offer was addressed.

Here Thesiger LJ sets out the orthodox reason for the existence of the postal rule, found in previous case law. This is that the Post Office is a 'common agent' for both parties. An agent means, in effect, an official representative. By handing the letter to the Post Office to deliver to the offeror, the offeree is in effect giving it to the official representative of the offeror, and that is the same thing ultimately as simply giving it to offeror. Since this is the case, posting the letter is in itself communication of acceptance.

Having established this, Thesiger LJ was then to decide what would happen in the case of a delay or non-delivery. He concluded that the worst outcome would be if this resulted in the cancellation of the contract (the contract having been formed as soon as the letter was posted). Note also that Thesiger LJ did entertain the possibility that the contract could be held not binding until the letter was received—that is, following the general rule for communication of acceptance. But the weight of precedent meant he could not take this possibility seriously.

Thesiger LJ recognised that the post rule could cause some inconvenience and hardship for the offeror, because it might mean not knowing whether acceptance had taken place (as in the case of *Adams v Lindsell*, for instance). But this was acceptable, because when the post was being used one party would always have to bear the risk of delay or non-delivery. It had to be one or the other.

An important caveat was added here, however, which is that if the offeror does not want to bear the risk of delay or non-delivery, the terms in the offer could specify that acceptance will only be communicated by post when the letter is received. The implication seems to be that the offeror has control over the wording of the offer and so the offeror is responsible for leaving the fate of the contract in the hands of the Post Office.

On the other hand, if the contract is not finally concluded except in the event of the acceptance actually reaching the offeror, the door would be opened to the perpetration of much fraud, and, putting aside this consideration, considerable delay in commercial transactions, in which dispatch is, as a rule, of the greatest consequence, would be occasioned, for the acceptor would never be entirely safe in acting upon his acceptance until he had received notice that his letter of acceptance had reached its destination.

Another final justification for the postal rule is added here. This is that, if acceptance by post was only communicated on receipt as a general rule, an offeror could always deny receipt of the letter in order to escape a contract. This would mean that the person accepting the contract could never be entirely sure whether to act, without confirmation from the offeror that the letter had definitely been received. This would cause unnecessary delays. The suggestion is that the postal rule is simply a more efficient default rule than the alternative.

The judgment indicates that when post is a permitted method of acceptance, it is effective once the letter is posted. The previous authority stated that the Post Office could be seen as an agent for both parties. On that basis, posting the letter would be equivalent to handing it to a person acting as an authorised representative of the offeror. In such circumstances, posting the letter would be equivalent to handing it to the offeror.

Thesiger LJ observed that acceptance at the time of posting has less scope for abuse than if acceptance by post had to be received. If it did have to be received, the problem is that offerors might deny that the letter had arrived. After all, the use of post does not give the parties the same degree of knowledge that the communication has or has not been received. Such an approach would make doing business by post very difficult and risky.

A further justification of the 'postal rule' related to the risks associated with post such as letters getting lost or delayed. According to Thesiger LJ, it is not possible for both parties to take responsibility for such risks. The postal rule puts the risk on the offeror, who may end up having a contract in ignorance of its existence because of a lost or delayed letter. There is no risk on the offeree because once the letter is posted, the offeree has the certainty of knowing that the contract has been formed. This was considered fair because it is the offeror that has allowed acceptance by post in the first place. More importantly, the offeror has the opportunity to be protected from the risks of post by stating that the acceptance must be received. On that basis, if the opportunity for such protection is not taken, it can be fairly said that it appears that the offeror intended to bear the risks of post.

3.3.1.2 The Requirements for the 'Post Rule' to Apply

The act of posting a letter of acceptance is sufficient for acceptance to be effective. Once posted, the letter is then in the control and authority of the post office. In *Re London & Northern Bank ex parte Jones* [1900] 1 Ch 220, it was held that ordinarily, the act of handing a letter to a postman would not be sufficient. It was observed that the relevant Post Office rules meant that a postman was not authorised to receive letters in that way. Consequently, by handing the letter to the postman, the letter was not in the control and authority of the Post Office. Cozens-Hardy J, delivering his judgment, even said that without Post Office authorisation, he could not 'regard the postman as anything better than a boy messenger' of the offeree.

While the postal rule became well established as a rule of convenience, it became seen as an outdated principle, developed when post was perceived as fast and reliable. However, it has not been overruled or rejected. Instead, cases show the courts acknowledging limits on its application. An important limit comes from *Henthorn v Fraser* [1892] 2 Ch 27 where it was shown that the postal rule only applies when it is reasonable to use the post.

In this case, Henthorn was handed an offer to buy some houses. The next day the offer was revoked using a letter by post which arrived at 5pm. However, Henthorn had already posted his acceptance, at 3.50pm. It arrived outside office hours and was opened the following morning. The question was whether the acceptance was effective before the revocation. It was held that the acceptance was effective when it was posted and so a contract existed at that point. Lord Herschell acknowledged authority to support the rule on acceptance by post. His Lordship then explained when the rule applies:

> Where the circumstances are such that it must have been within the contemplation of the parties that, according to the ordinary usages of mankind, the post might be used as a means of communicating the acceptance of an offer, the acceptance is complete as soon as it is posted.

The two parties were on opposite sides of the River Mersey, in Liverpool and Birkenhead respectively, and so it had been reasonably 'within their contemplation' to use the post to communicate acceptance—even though the offer was initially given in person. This comment means that for acceptance to be effective on posting, it must be a method that the parties would have (objectively) expected. That would be when the use of post is expressly permitted or, alternatively, where its use is either implied by the offeror, or implied from the circumstances as it was here.

 THINKING POINTS

In what circumstances would it not be reasonable to use the post to communicate acceptance?

3.3.1.3 Exclusion of the Postal Rule

The offeror can state that the acceptance by post must be received in order to be effective. In doing so, the offeror is expressing an intention to avoid the risks of using the post and place the risks on the offeree. The case of *Holwell Securities v Hughes* [1974] 1 WLR 155 is the main authority for this point. It concerned an option to purchase (the offer) which was 'exercisable by notice in writing'. The posted letter of acceptance had been correctly addressed and paid for, but it never arrived. The Court of Appeal held that the acceptance was not effective because the postal rule did not apply. As a result, there was no contract. It is useful to read the relevant parts of the judgments to appreciate the limits to the application of the post rule.

GUIDED CASE READING 3.3
Holwell Securities Ltd v Hughes [1974] 1 WLR 155

The following extracts are from the judgments by Russell LJ and Lawton LJ. When reading these:

- try to identify the reasons why the post rule did not apply. These represent limits on the application of the rule;
- try to find anything that suggests a negative attitude towards the use of the post rule.

We start with the lead judgment by Russell LJ (with whom Buckley LJ agreed):

> [The postal rule was acknowledged as an exception to the general rule. It was then observed that on the facts of the case, the parties would have expected the acceptance to be sent by post. Russell LJ then continued]
>
> But that is not and cannot be the end of the matter. In any case, before one can find that the basic principle of the need for communication of acceptance to the offeror is displaced by this artificial concept of communication by the act of posting, it is necessary that the offer is in its terms consistent with such displacement and not one which by its terms points rather in the direction of actual communication . . .

Russell LJ here makes clear that the wording of the offer has to be consistent with the 'artificial' concept of the postal rule in order for that rule to apply. This suggests that, while the postal rule is often said to be a default position, it is actually an exception to the principle that acceptance must be communicated to the offeror in order for a contract to be created.

The relevant language here is, 'The said option shall be exercised by notice in writing to the intending vendor . . .', a very common phrase in an option agreement. There is, of course, nothing in that phrase to suggest that the notification to the defendant could not be made by post. But the requirement of 'notice . . . to,' in my judgment, is language which should be taken expressly to assert the ordinary situation in law that acceptance requires to be communicated or notified to the offeror, and is inconsistent with the theory that acceptance can be constituted by the act of posting . . .

It is of course true that the instrument could have been differently worded. An option to purchase within a period given for value has the characteristic of an offer that cannot be withdrawn. The instrument might have said 'The offer constituted by this option may be accepted in writing within six months' in which case no doubt the posting would have sufficed to form the contract. But that language was not used, and, as indicated, in my judgment, the language used prevents that legal outcome. Under this head of the case hypothetical problems were canvassed to suggest difficulties in the way of that conclusion. What if the letter had been delivered through the letter-box of the house in due time, but the defendant had either deliberately or fortuitously not been there to receive it before the option period expired? This does not persuade me that the artificial posting rule is here applicable. The answer might well be that in the circumstances the defendant had impliedly invited communication by use of an orifice in his front door designed to receive communications.

We can now turn to the other judgment, which was delivered by Lawton LJ:

. . . Does the rule apply in all cases where one party makes an offer which both he and the person with whom he was dealing must have expected the post to be used as a means of accepting it? In my judgment, it does not. First, it does not apply when the express terms of the offer specify that the acceptance must reach the offeror . . . Secondly, it probably does not operate if its application would produce manifest inconvenience and absurdity. This is the opinion set out in Cheshire and Fifoot, *Law of Contract*, 3rd ed. (1952), p. 43. It was the opinion of Lord Bramwell as is seen by his judgment in *British & American Telegraph Co. v. Colson* (1871) L.R. 6 Exch. 108 . . . The illustrations of inconvenience and absurdity which Lord Bramwell gave are as apt today as they were then. Is a stockbroker who is holding shares to the orders of his client liable in damages because he did not sell in a falling market in accordance with the instructions in a letter which was posted but never received? . . . [W]ould a young soldier ordered overseas have been bound in contract to marry a girl to whom he had proposed by letter, asking her to let him have an answer before he left and she had replied affirmatively in good time but the letter had never reached him? In my judgment, the factors of inconvenience and absurdity are but illustrations of a wider principle, namely, that the rule does not apply if, having regard to all the circumstances, including the nature of the subject matter under consideration, the negotiating parties cannot have intended that there should be a binding agreement until the party accepting an offer or exercising an option had in fact communicated the acceptance or exercise to the other. In my judgment, when this principle is applied to the facts of this case it becomes clear that the parties cannot have intended that the posting of a letter should constitute the exercise of the option.

Here, Russell LJ compares two potential wordings of an option agreement like the one in question. The document said that the option could be exercised by 'notice in writing to' the vendor. This implied that the vendor must actually receive notice for it to be effective. This would mean the postal rule should not apply. If on the other hand it had said the offer could be 'accepted in writing' within a certain time period, this would suggest that the offer was a 'firm' one which could be accepted by the act of writing the notice and sending it, which would mean the postal rule should apply. Note the practical consideration underpinning his reasoning: an offeror can revoke an offer right up until receipt of acceptance if the postal rule does not apply. This is important when time is of the essence (as it was in this case) and this consideration also clearly influenced Russell LJ's decision.

Russell LJ emphasises here the objective nature of legal reasoning. Saying that the offer must be 'received' does not literally mean it has to have been actually received. It is sufficient if it can be reasonably said to have been received, i.e. by being put through the offeror's letterbox (the 'orifice' in the front door). Once that has been done, whether the letter is actually picked up and read is the offeror's own responsibility.

Lawton LJ emphasised practical considerations: the postal rule should not apply if it would produce 'manifest inconvenience and absurdity'. Certainly, everybody can agree that no rule should apply if it would have those effects. The question is where the line lies between 'inconvenience and absurdity' and a reasonable application of the rule.

Here, Lawton LJ makes clear that this line lies close to what is reasonable than what is 'inconvenient and absurd'. What matters is what the parties appeared to have intended. If it objectively seems that they would not have intended the postal rule to apply, then it will not.

Both judges demonstrated a little hostility towards the post rule. That is understandable given that by the time of the case, the rule appeared outdated and did not exist in jurisdictions outside of the common law. Russell LJ appeared eager not to allow it to apply and labelled it an 'artificial concept'. Lawton LJ also seemed to be implying that it was very easy for the postal rule to be deemed inconvenient and absurd. The effect of the judgment is that the rule can be ignored where it is commercially convenient to do so. That is consistent with the early opinion by Thesiger LJ in *Household Fire Insurance v Grant*. That opinion viewed the post rule as a rule of convenience. It was a way to allocate the risk of post when the parties have not indicated when acceptance should be effective.

The limits recognised in *Holwell v Hughes* go beyond the requirement that it must be reasonable to use the post. That requirement is just about the use of post being expected or contemplated by the parties. Both judgments recognised that even if it is reasonable to post acceptance, the application of the postal rule can be expressly or impliedly excluded. Table 3.1 summarises the requirements for the postal rule to apply.

Table 3.1

A summary of the requirements for the postal rule to apply

It must be reasonable to use the post	*Henthorn v Fraser* [1892]
The acceptance must be in the control and authority of the Post Office	*Re, London & Northern Bank ex parte Jones* [1900]
The postal rule can be displaced by contrary intention (i.e. it can be expressly or impliedly excluded)	*Holwell v Hughes* [1974]

3.3.2 Where the Offeror Waives the Need for Communication of Acceptance

Another exception to the rule requiring acceptance to be communicated is where the offeror indicates that there is no need for acceptance to be communicated. We will see that this can work well in the context of an offer for a unilateral contract. However, if the requirement is set aside in the context of bilateral contract, it can result in a serious problem. We will address each of these circumstances in turn.

3.3.2.1 Waiving the Requirement to Communicate Acceptance: Unilateral Contracts

➜ CROSS-REFERENCE
For the detail of *Carlill v Carbolic Smoke Ball Co* see 2.3.2.

A well-established example of an offer for a unilateral contract setting aside the need to communicate acceptance is the *Carlill* case. In that case, the Court of Appeal made it clear that the offer *impliedly* waived (set aside) any need for the offeror to be notified of the acceptance. On that point, Bowen LJ stated: '. . .as notification of acceptance is required for the benefit of the person who makes the offer, the person who makes the offer may dispense with notice to himself'. That meant that Mrs Carlill did not have to tell the Smoke Ball Company that she was accepting the offer. This would presumably meant writing to them to let them know that she intended to use the smoke ball as directed in the hope of not catching the flu, which would clearly have been absurd. Instead, to accept the offer she simply had to complete the relevant act.

The point is that when communication of acceptance is only for the benefit of the offeror, he or she can set the requirement aside. This is workable in unilateral contract situations because if a contract is formed, the offeror is the only party with an obligation. Consequently, the offeror is the only one to benefit from notice of acceptance because he or she will then know that there is a contractual obligation to perform. So, if the offeror wants to take that chance of not knowing, then he or she has the freedom to not require notice of acceptance. The requirement is then impliedly waived by the offer.

The position of the offeree is very different. He or she would have acted in response to the offer in order to receive some sort of benefit. By doing what was required by the offer, the offeree will know if the contract has been formed. Therefore, an additional requirement for notice of acceptance does not provide any benefit to the offeree. It follows that the absence of such a requirement will not have a negative impact or impose a disadvantage on the offeree. There was no disadvantage to Mrs Carlill in there being no requirement to notify the Smoke Ball Company of her acceptance, for example. For that reason, it is workable for the offeror to have the freedom to set aside the requirement for communicated of acceptance.

The comment from Bowen LJ was applied more recently in *Dresdner Kleinwort Ltd v Attrill* [2013] EWCA Civ 394. This case concerned a commercial bank that announced an intention to separate its investment division from its banking division. This was the first step to selling or closing the investment division. To encourage staff to remain at the bank, the bank announced to its staff that they would receive a guaranteed employment bonus. Later, the bank decided not to pay the bonus and so 104 employees brought an action for it. During the resulting case, the bank put forward a range of arguments to justify their refusal. One of these arguments was that if the announcement was an offer, there was no communication of acceptance from the staff. Relying on the comment by Bowen LJ in *Carlill*, Elias LJ stated that in the circumstances, nobody would expect that they have to actually communicate acceptance. The announcement did not impose an obligation or disadvantage on the employees. It was therefore implied that everyone that could benefit from the promise, had accepted. He added that individual acceptance was inconsistent with the nature of the promise by the bank. It was 'wholly unrealistic' to assume the bank intended to pay only those who had communicated acceptance and to exclude the other staff.

KEY POINTS

Generally, when there is an offer for a unilateral contract, it will imply that there is no need to provide notification of acceptance. Performance of the required act will result in a contract.

It is important to appreciate the significance of the basis for notification being impliedly waived. The wording and the type of offer might show an intention to waive the need for notification. However, the offer could actually state that notification of acceptance *is* necessary in order to accept. Such a clear expression of an intention to require notification will mean that the offer can only be accepted if notification is provided. In practice, such an expression would make the requirement part of the act of acceptance to be performed.

3.3.2.2 Waiving the Requirement to Communicate Acceptance: Bilateral Contracts (the Rule on 'Acceptance by Silence')

In contrast to the position with unilateral contracts, the requirement to communicate acceptance is very important to the offeree in ordinary bilateral contracts (where both parties have an obligation). Consider an offer to buy your phone for £10 which states that to accept, you are simply to do nothing and not respond. Such an offer is setting aside the requirement for your acceptance to be communicated. That might sound convenient, but there would be serious consequences if acceptance were to result from doing nothing. It would be possible for an offeror to impose a contract on an offeree. If we go back to the phone example, what if you are unable to communicate an intention to reject the offer? Perhaps you did not see the offer because it was emailed to you and you have not had a chance to check your inbox. If your silence (i.e. your doing nothing in response) were to result in a contract, you would be under a contractual obligation to sell your phone at such a low price. So in bilateral situations, the requirement for acceptance to be communicated serves to protect the offeree. For that reason, there has to be a limit on when the offeror can set aside the requirement of acceptance to be communicated.

Felthouse v Bindley (1862) 11 CB NS 869 is often cited as the key case dealing with acceptance by silence. In the case, a nephew (John Felthouse) intended to sell his horse to his uncle (Paul Felthouse).

There was a query over the price so the uncle wrote to his nephew stating 'If I hear no more about him, I consider the horse mine at £30 15s'. The nephew did not reply. Six weeks later at an auction selling the nephew's farming stock, the horse was included in the stock to be sold. The nephew had told the auctioneer (Bindley) not to sell the horse because it had been sold already. Unfortunately, in spite of this, the auctioneer accidently sold the horse. He even wrote to the nephew to apologise for the mistake. The uncle believed he had been the owner of the horse before the auction took place. On that basis, he sued the auctioneer in **conversion**. This action would only succeed if the uncle actually owned the horse before it was sold at the auction. According to the court, no contract for the horse was formed between the uncle and the nephew. It meant that the uncle was never the owner and so his action against the auctioneer failed.

conversion
is a tort imposing liability for dealing with goods in a way that it is inconsistent with the rights of the real owner.

In the main judgment, Willes J explained that the uncle had made an offer to buy the horse but there had been no acceptance by the nephew. It was acknowledged that the nephew intended for the horse to be sold at the price stated in the offer. However, the nephew had not communicated this intention to the uncle. It was also observed that the uncle had no right to impose on the nephew the sale of the horse. The case is sometimes criticised because on the facts, it was clear that the nephew thought he had a contract with his uncle. That is the reason why he told the auctioneer not to sell the horse. It seems he was happy to form a contract by not responding to the offer. However, the offer required acceptance from silence, or more accurately, inaction (i.e. doing nothing). If it were possible to form contracts in this way, there would be situations where sales are imposed. In addition, allowing acceptance by silence or inaction would result in a great deal of uncertainty. Ordinarily, it would be difficult to know if the silence was an indication of acceptance or simply a result of the offeree forgetting to respond.

KEY POINTS

Silence (i.e. doing nothing) will not be enough to accept an offer even if the offer stipulates it will.

The basic rule on acceptance by silence from *Felthouse v Bindley* is echoed in the legislation relating to inertia selling. This is where a business sends unrequested goods and then requires payment unless the goods are returned by a certain date. The Unsolicited Goods and Services Act 1971 introduced protection to those that received such goods by allowing the goods to be treated as gifts. This legislation remains in place to protect businesses from inertia selling. The protection for consumers is now found in the Consumer Protection from Unfair Trading Regulations 2008. Regulation 27A makes such goods unconditional gifts to consumers. In addition, it is an offence under the 2008 Regulations for a business to demand payment from a consumer for goods that have not been requested by the consumer.

Felthouse v Bindley has been taken to represent a general principle against acceptance by silence or inaction. Even in the context of a unilateral contract, there might not be express notification of acceptance but at least there is positive action from the offeree's performance of the requested act. It seems however that the rule against acceptance by silence or inaction is not absolute. In *Allied Marine Transport Ltd v Vale Do Rio Doce Navegaçao SA, The Leonidas D* [1985] 2 All ER 796, Goff LJ indicated that there could be 'special circumstances' where acceptance by silence or inaction could take place. These 'special circumstances' were not explained. However, it is not difficult to imagine circumstances where an offeree should not be allowed to rely on *Felthouse v Bindley* to deny that a contract exists. An example could be where there is a well-established course of previous dealings between parties in which they perform contracts based on the silence of the offeree. In such circumstances, it would be very difficult for the offeree to suddenly rely on *Felthouse v Bindley* without giving prior notice.

Another example is the one suggested by Peter-Gibson LJ in *Re Selectmove* [1995] 1 WLR 474 in an *obiter* comment:

> Where the offeree himself indicates that an offer is to be taken as accepted if he does not indicate to the contrary by an ascertainable time, he is undertaking to speak if he does not want an agreement to be concluded. I see no reason in principle why that should not be an exceptional circumstance such that the offer can be accepted by silence. But it is unnecessary to express a concluded view on this point.

This suggests that acceptance by silence could work if the offeree has committed itself to only communicate a rejection of the offer. Presumably, it would have to be shown that the offeror is also happy with the arrangement. The comments from both Goff LJ and Peter-Gibson LJ show that there is some support for an exception to the rule against acceptance by silence. However, such comments have not been taken further to firmly establish such an exception.

3.3.3 Acceptance by Conduct

While silence is not enough to accept an offer, it is possible to accept an offer by conduct rather than an express statement. This is another exception to the general rule requiring acceptance to be communicated. Such acceptance by conduct is well established as demonstrated in the House of Lords case of *Alexander Brogden v Metropolitan Railway Co* (1877) 2 App Cas 666. In this case, Brogden Co had supplied coal to a railway company for years without a formal written contract. They decided to formalise their arrangement and so the railway company sent a draft contract to the head of Brogden Co, Alexander Brogden. He filled in the contract, marked it at the bottom as 'approved' and returned it to the railway company. This draft contract was simply placed in a drawer by the railway company. The railway company then made orders for Brogden's coal and were supplied the coal based on the terms of the draft, for two years. When there was a disagreement, Brogden denied that a contract existed since the draft was not formalised.

Lord Blackburn explained that placing the draft contract in the drawer was not sufficient to create the contract. The first draft was an offer to Brogden. By completing it and adding further detail, Brogden made a counter-offer. Even if the railway company believed it had accepted the terms of the draft (the counter-offer), it still had not indicated its acceptance at that stage. However, acceptance was indicated later by the conduct of the railway company. Interestingly, the House of Lords did not identify precisely when acceptance took place. It seems that acceptance took place either when the first order was made or when the coal was supplied. What mattered here was that the conduct of the railway company showed an intention to accept the terms of the draft agreement, because it had continued to trade with Brogden's for a lengthy period apparently on the basis of there being a contract.

Based on the idea of acceptance by conduct, in principle an offer to supply goods could be accepted by the other party using them. Similarly, an offer to buy goods could be accepted by despatching them in response. Such action should be taken to indicate an intention to accept the offer. It follows that if an offer states that express notification of acceptance is required, then this will serve to exclude acceptance by conduct.

3.4 Automated Ticket and Vending Machines

As consumers, we are very familiar with automated ticket and vending machines. Often, we are faced with an automated ticket machine in a car park or a railway station. Vending machines are often in public places as a convenient way to buy a drink or snack. There is no doubt that each purchase results in a contract between the buyer and the business running the machine. But at what point does acceptance take place?

The case of *Thornton v Shoe Lane Parking* [1971] 2 QB 163, is the main authority on the formation of such contracts. It concerned a contract made using a ticket machine in a car park. In the main judgment, Lord Denning MR took the opportunity to comment on *when* and *how* such a contract is formed:

> The customer pays his money and gets a ticket. He cannot refuse it. He cannot get his money back. He may protest to the machine, even swear at it. But it will remain unmoved. He is committed beyond recall. He was committed at the very moment when he put his money into the machine. The contract was

concluded at that time. It can be translated into offer and acceptance in the following way: the offer is made when the proprietor of the machine holds it out as being ready to receive the money. The acceptance takes place when the customer puts his money into the slot. The terms of the offer are contained in the notice placed on or near the machine stating what is offered for the money. The customer is bound by those terms as long as they are sufficiently brought to his notice before-hand, but not otherwise. He is not bound by the terms printed on the ticket if they differ from the notice, because the ticket comes too late.

In this comment, Lord Denning identified the moment when the customer is committed as the point at which a contract is formed. That point is when the money is inserted because after that there is nothing left to do and no way to reverse the payment. His Lordship then worked backwards from that point to frame the transaction in terms of offer and acceptance. As the final act, paying had to be acceptance. That meant the offer had to be the machine standing there with its terms displayed nearby.

This analysis works for transactions that use the process described by Lord Denning, and it generally reflects the process used by most machines today. Consider a vending machine or even a car park 'pay and display' machine. They will require you to make a selection and then insert your money or payment card. After doing so, you might be able to eject money or press cancel after enter entering your PIN. But if you do not do that and instead, simply press a button to confirm the transaction, you are committed at that point and you cannot undo your action. Your final act would therefore be acceptance. It is therefore possible to apply Lord Denning's analysis in *Thornton* straightforwardly to vending machines allowing payment by credit or debit card.

The wide scope of the analysis by Lord Denning is illustrated by *R (on the application of Software Solutions Partners Ltd) v Revenue and Customs Commissioners* [2007] EWHC 971 (Admin). In that case, the analysis was applied to a computer system used by insurance brokers to place insurance cover. Kenneth Parker QC (sitting as a Deputy High Court Judge) observed that once the broker typed the details into a programme set up by the insurer, the broker was committed and could not change his mind, and that had to constitute acceptance and therefore was the moment the contract was formed.

?! THINKING POINTS

At what point is the contract formed when you stop at an entry barrier at a car park, press a button to be issued with a ticket before being allowed in to park and then pay later when you return to exit the car park?

3.5 Acceptance for Contracts Made through E-commerce, Websites, and Email

Given the everyday use of email and websites to enter contracts of sale, it may be surprising to learn that there are no clear, default rules on *when* such contracts are formed. We know that there is always a possibility of an electronic message being delayed or never arriving. We are relying on independent internet service providers to reroute such messages and provide a secure connection. Parties to a transaction have no control over the mechanics of a message going from one computer to another. In addition, most consumers and businesses are not familiar with the mechanics and technical journey of a message. We just click a button and expect the process to work. Such unfamiliarity with the mechanics of sending messages along with the lack of control and the risks of failure encourage businesses to routinely protect themselves. They usually do so by stating clearly in their terms when the contract is to be formed. The inclusion of such an express intention means there is no need for there to be a dispute about when acceptance was effective. The intention expressed in the terms will dictate the outcome. That might well be the reason why the courts of England and Wales have not had devise a rule to apply to acceptance using a website or email. The courts would only be required to do so if the time of acceptance is an issue in a dispute regarding such an agreement and the parties have not expressed an intention about when the contract is to be formed. Of course, this is not to suggest that such a case could never arise. If it did, the question would be what default rule could apply. We will now explore the possible rules that could apply to email and then to websites.

3.5.1 Acceptance by Email

Due to its ease and speed, email has largely replaced the traditional letter for negotiating and contract making. Contracts by email could involve sending a draft agreement as an attachment which is then completed and returned as an attachment. Alternatively, parties could simply use ordinary email messages to form a contract. Often, contracts formed by email involve both attachments and the use of additional email messages.

When email became a widely used method of communication, it started some debate over the rules that could apply. The main question related to *when* acceptance by email should be effective. Should the post rule apply so that the acceptance is effective when sent? Alternatively, should email acceptance by valid when received? Academic opinion favours the application of the general rule which requires the acceptance to be received (e.g. Donal Nolan, 'Offer and Acceptance in the Electronic Age' in Contract Formation and Parties (A Burrows and E Peel, eds, 2010) at 61). This approach has gained some judicial support in recent years too.

In *Thomas v BPE Solicitors* [2010] EWHC 306, it was argued by one party that the 'postal rule' applied to email acceptance. This was rejected by Blair J who expressed an opinion in favour of the general rule. The opinion also acknowledged that there could be serious difficulties in determining when the email is deemed to be received. The point did not matter on the facts because the email had been received. However, Blair J cited the comment by Lord Wilberforce in *Brinkibon* that addressed different circumstances and said that no universal rule can apply and that decisions have to be made based on 'the intentions of the parties, by sound business practice, and in some cases a judgment where the risks should lie'.

The most detailed judicial opinion on the use of email is from the High Court of Singapore in *Chwee Kin Keong v Digilandmall.com Pte* [2004] SGHC 71. While this is from a different jurisdiction, contract law in Singapore is based on the common law of England and Wales. This means it can be used as persuasive authority. The extract of the judgment provides a detailed account of the arguments and this makes it very useful.

GUIDED CASE READING 3.4
Chwee Kin Keong and Others v Digilandmall.com Pte Ltd [2004] SGHC 71

When you read the extract by Rajah JC try to identify:

- the reasons why the postal rule might apply to email acceptance;
- the reasons why the general rule might apply to email acceptance.

[97] . . . When considering the appropriate rule to apply, it stands to reason that as between sender and receiver, the party who selects the means of communication should bear the consequences of any unexpected events. An e-mail, while bearing some similarity to a postal communication, is in some aspects fundamentally different. Furthermore, unlike a fax or a telephone call, it is not instantaneous. E-mails are processed through servers, routers and internet service providers. Different protocols may result in messages arriving in an incomprehensible form. Arrival can also be immaterial unless a recipient accesses the e-mail, but in this respect e-mail does not really differ from mail that has to be opened. Certain internet service providers provide the technology to inform a sender that a message has not been properly routed. Others do not.

Here Rajah JC sets out the basic problem with emails when it comes to the traditional rules, because it is not easy to classify them as instantaneous or not. Emails are much faster than the post, but are not quite instantaneous and are reliant on an intermediary (the ISP) which resembles the Post Office. This means that an argument could be made that the postal rule would be suitable to use with emailed acceptances. On the other hand, emails are to all intents and purposes instantaneous and very reliable, which would suggest that the rule of receipt should be used.

[98] Once an offer is sent over the internet the sender loses control over the route and delivery time of the message. In that sense, it is akin to ordinary posting. Notwithstanding some real differences with posting, it could be argued cogently that the postal rule should apply to e-mail acceptances; in other words, that the acceptance is made the instant the offer is sent . . . acceptance would be effective the moment the offer enters that node of the network outside the control of the originator. There are, however, other sound reasons to argue against such a rule in favour of the recipient rule. It should be noted that while the common law jurisdictions continue to wrestle over this vexed issue, most civil law jurisdictions lean towards the recipient rule. In support of the latter it might be argued that, unlike a posting, e-mail communication takes place in a relatively short time frame. The recipient rule is therefore more convenient and relevant in the context of both instantaneous or near instantaneous communications. Notwithstanding occasional failure, most e-mails arrive sooner rather than later.

> Note also that Rajah JC begins this analysis by emphasising a factor which was used to justify the postal rule in earlier cases which we have discussed: namely, that since the offeror will typically be the one deciding on the means of communication and should therefore bear the risk of things going wrong as a general rule.

[99] Like the somewhat arbitrary selection of the postal rule for ordinary mail, in the ultimate analysis a default rule should be implemented for certainty, while accepting that such a rule should be applied flexibly to minimise unjustness . . . In the absence of proper and full arguments on the issue of which rule is to be preferred, I do not think it is appropriate for me to give any definitive views in these proceedings on this very important issue . . .

[Rajah JC then referred to the Vienna Convention on International Sales 1980 and continued]

> Ultimately, though, Rajah JC concludes this part of the analysis by saying that the justifications for one or other rule are not as important as simply having a default which is relatively certain. The implication is that it does not particularly matter what the rule is, as long as it is applied consistently so that people know what it is and can act accordingly.

[100] . . . It appears that in Convention transactions, the receipt rule applies unless there is a contrary intention. Offer and acceptances have to 'reach' an intended recipient to be effective. It can be persuasively argued that e-mails involving transactions embraced by the Convention are only effective on reaching the recipient. If this rule applies to international sales, is it sensible to have a different rule for domestic sales?

[101] The applicable rules in relation to transactions over the worldwide web appear to be clearer and less controversial. Transactions over websites are almost invariably instantaneous and/or interactive. The sender will usually receive a prompt response. The recipient rule appears to be the logical default rule . . .

[The many causes of email faults were addressed to show that any rule would have to deal with complicated possibilities]

> He finishes by considering the rules set out in the Vienna Convention on International Sales 1980, which the UK and Singapore are not parties to but which are widely used elsewhere. He also considers other online transactions not carried out by email, and then finally looked at some of the other factors that would need to be considered. Ultimately, which he does not come out and say so explicitly, the inference is that, since it does not really matter which rule is used as long as it is certain, it is probably best to have a default rule that is consistent with the international rules—i.e. the rule of receipt, which is to say the general rule, rather than the postal rule.

[103] The amalgam of factors a court will have to consider in risk allocation ought to include:

(a) the need to observe the principle of upholding rather than destroying contracts,

(b) the need to facilitate the transacting of electronic commerce and

(c) the need to reach commercially sensible solutions while respecting traditional principles applicable to instances of genuine error or mistake.

It is essential that the law be perceived as embodying rationality and fairness while respecting the commercial imperative of certainty.

This detailed opinion on acceptance by email shows why there has been debate over what rules should apply. Rajah JC did not express a clear opinion about which rule should apply to email, but in the end his judgment did hint that the general rule is the better option.

The opinion recognised some good reasons supporting the general rule requiring the email to be received. This was based on the way email usually operates, giving the sender the chance to know if the message has been received. In addition, Rajah JC referred to the benefit of being consistent with other jurisdictions that generally require acceptance to be received. However, the issue of *when* an email is *received* can be complicated. Lord Fraser in *Brinkibon* observed that the telex is communicated when it is received by the machine. At that point, a failure to read it is the fault of the offeror. The problem with email is that the message could be received by the final server but not be accessible to the recipient. If the server is in the control of the offeror it is no different to the telex point made by Lord Fraser. However, it is equally possible that the offeror has no influence or control over the final server because it is operated by an independent third party.

While judicial opinion appears to prefer to treat email as instantaneous communication, the legal position remains uncertain. For that reason, parties using email should make it clear when acceptance will be treated as effective. In doing so, the parties are allocating the risks and responsibilities between themselves and should therefore have no need to resort to litigation.

3.5.2 Websites

Consumers are increasingly buying goods over the internet using websites or apps. So, we need to consider which acceptance rule applies. We know from 2.4 that adverts on websites are generally invitations to treat and so the customer makes the offer by placing their order. In *Chwee Kin Keong v Digilandmall.com*, Rajah JC suggested that when purchases are made on websites communication should be regarded as instantaneous and hence acceptance will be effective when received.

There is some legislation that applies to websites rather than emails—the Electronic Commerce Regulations 2002. Unfortunately, the Regulations are not very helpful on the issue of contract formation as they do not define precisely when contracts are formed. That being said, there are some relevant obligations and rules:

> Regulation 11(1) refers to recipients (buyers) placing an order and states that the seller must:
>
> (a) acknowledge receipt of the order to the recipient of the service without undue delay and by electronic means. . .
>
> Regulation 11(2) adds:
>
> (a) the order and the acknowledgement of receipt will be deemed to be received when the parties to whom they are addressed are able to access them. . .

These rules *always* apply to consumer sales, but if the sale is between two businesses, they have the freedom to agree their own terms. Based on Regulation 11, it is sometimes said that acceptance takes place when the buyer actually receives the acknowledgment of the order being received. After all, the 'order' would usually be the offer. However, the Regulation only refers to orders and the acknowledgement of receiving an order. There is no specific reference to acceptance or when the contract is formed. In fact, it is possible for a business to comply with these rules and still state in their standard terms that the contract is actually formed when the goods are dispatched. In such circumstances, the sending of the goods would constitute acceptance.

As far as websites are concerned, it could be said that there is no longer a need for the law to develop specific rules on when the contract is formed.

- Regulation 9 states that traders must clearly indicate to customers the procedure for creating the contract.
- Regulation 11(1)(b) imposes an obligation on traders to give the customer an effective means of identifying and correcting input errors before placing the order.

These rules mean that there should be no mistakes by the buyer (or any that the buyer can complain of) and the contract is made based on the express terms required by the Regulation 9. As a result, there is no need for a general rule to establish the parties' *apparent intentions*. Instead, their apparent intentions are identified by the express terms of the contract.

3.6 Beyond the Traditional Application of Offer and Acceptance

Having explored the rules on acceptance, we can turn to two important contexts of contract formation, both of which present a challenge to the strict (traditional) application of offer and acceptance. They are important because they reflect the reality of business practice. The first is known as the 'battle of forms', wherein parties try to form an agreement based on their own conflicting sets of standard terms. The other issue is about the recognition of agreements where there is no clear offer or acceptance. Each will be addressed in turn.

3.6.1 The 'Battle of Forms' Context

It is common practice for a business to have its own printed standard terms for the contracts they are likely to enter. These documents detail the standard terms that the business always wants in its contracts. The idea is that these documents or forms are then filled in by another party to create a contract. If the other party (the offeree) signs the standard form without altering it, then there is no doubt that a contract had been formed. Such a contract will be based on the terms contained in the offeror's standard form. It is easy to see the commercial convenience of using such standard forms rather than having a lawyer draft a new contract every time one is needed.

Unfortunately, the use of such documents is far from convenient when two parties have their own standard form and expect their own form to create the contract. Here, an offer is made using the offeror's standard form. The offeree then indicates 'acceptance' through its own standard form, which has different terms. On a strict traditional analysis, there would be no contract because the offeree's response would be treated as a counter-offer. However, in such cases, the parties often behave as if a contract has been formed. Both parties carry on and perform what they believe to be the contract. At a later stage when a dispute arises, the courts have to determine if the parties have a contract and if they do, whether it is on the offeror's terms or the offeree's terms. There are only two cases that discuss this issue, and they favour what has become known as 'the last shot theory'. This is that the contract terms are based on the last set of terms to be put forward.

3.6.2 The Traditional Approach—the Last Shot Theory

The main case on this so called 'battle of forms' is *Butler Machine Tool Co Ltd v Ex-Cell-O Corporation (England) Ltd* [1979] 1 WLR 401. In the case, the claimant seller used its standard form to offer a machine tool to the defendant buyer for £75,535. This offer by the seller was issued on 23rd May 1969 and the terms included a price variation clause. The clause meant that the price could change according to any increase in the costs of production. These terms also stated that the seller's standard terms prevailed over the buyer's terms. On the 27th May, the buyer responded to the offer by placing an order, but did so using their own standard form which referred to a fixed price. At the bottom, there was a tear-off slip for the seller to sign which stated: '. . .we (i.e. the seller) accept this order on the terms and conditions stated. . .' (i.e. on the buyer's terms). On 5th June, the seller signed the tear-off slip. This was then sent with a note stating that the order 'is being entered in accordance with our revised quotation of 23 May'. By the time of the delivery, the seller demanded more money based on the price variation clause and the buyer refused to pay.

Following the dispute and resulting first instance decision in favour of the seller, the Court of Appeal had to decide which terms the parties were bound by (if at all). It was held that there was a contract and that it was based on the buyer's terms. The judgments of Bridge LJ and Lawton LJ represent the majority reasoning, and their approach is represented by Figure 3.1. Both judgments classed the letter on 23rd as an offer by the seller and the response by the buyer was a counter-offer. This counter-offer was then accepted by the seller when it signed and returned the tear off slip which acknowledged the contract on the buyer's terms. The note added with the return of the tear-off slip referring to the 'quotation' and terms of the 23rd was regarded in both judgments as no more than a reference to the basic price and the description of the goods. In effect, the buyer had the 'last shot' here, meaning the last set of terms on which there appeared to be agreement (because the buyer had signed and returned the slip) and so the buyer's terms prevailed.

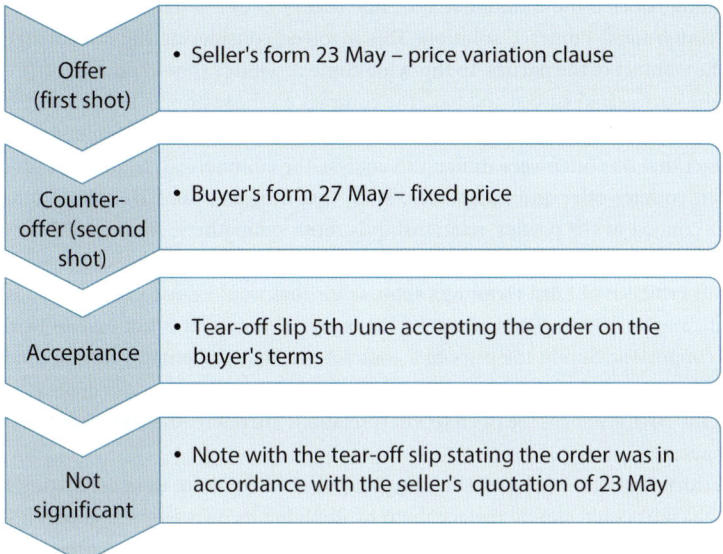

Figure 3.1
The approach of the majority in *Butler Machine Tool v Ex-cell-o* [1979]

The reasoning adopted by the majority was traditional as it was based on traditional principles of offer and counter-offer. It has the appearance of certainty in that you look for the last-shot of terms before acceptance. However, it can be criticised because it could be based on an artificial and arbitrary classification of what the parties did. Consider the fact that in the case, the acceptance of the last shot was the signing of the tear-off slip. However, what of the note that accompanied the slip? This was not interpreted as a shot, but why not? According to the majority it was not significant and as Lawton LJ observed, the note 'disappeared from the story'. Such a conclusion could undermine the certainty that is supposed to be reflected by the traditional principles.

It might appear that the traditional approach results in inefficient transactions because it encourages parties to have the last shot. In doing so, it could result in a long sequence where each set of terms is sent and re-sent until there is an act of acceptance. But that criticism is not a realistic one. It does not reflect how businesses usually enter contracts. Usually, there is no team of lawyers competing with another team to submit the last shot. Instead, there are sales agents and administrative staff. They attach their standard terms every time they communicate about a potential transaction. These standard form terms have been drafted or approved by a lawyer some time ago. It is unlikely that the staff using the forms pay attention to what their own terms say! It is only when a dispute arises that the courts have to make sense of the contractual relationship.

KEY POINTS

Generally, when businesses use their own standard forms, the contract is based on the last set of terms put forward before an act of acceptance.

3.6.3 The 'Compromise Contract' Suggested by Lord Denning MR

The other judgment in *Butler* was delivered by Lord Denning MR. His Lordship also decided in favour of the buyer but used different reasoning. Of course, it is minority reasoning and is therefore not binding. However, it is very important because it lays the potential foundation for a flexible approach that could be developed by later cases.

Lord Denning rejected the traditional 'last shot' theory as out of date and preferred to use what he called a 'compromise contract' solution. This involved considering the documents as a whole, along with the conduct of the parties. In this wide context, a judge should then identify the 'material points' that the parties had agreed and base the contract on those points. If there were any conflicting terms these would be replaced by terms implied by the court. This has the merit of flexibility and reflects the fact that it is often very difficult to analyse the commercial negotiation process in clear terms of offer, counter-offer and acceptance. With that in mind, Lord Denning's approach based on the wider context of the parties' relationship is more sympathetic to the reality of commercial transactions.

The obvious criticism of Lord Denning's approach is that would cause uncertainty for businesses. First, the outcome turns on what is meant by the 'material points'. It is not easy to work out which points are so important. Surely, the price in a contract is a 'material point', yet from the judgment, it seems that the price variation clause might not have been. Secondly, the wider context of the parties' conduct and the circumstances are open to interpretation. Therefore, the wider context creates more scope for disputes.

Another criticism is that Lord Denning suggested that where there were conflicting terms in the two forms, the court could simply replace them by implying its own terms instead. This would give the judge a great deal of discretion to essentially make an agreement for the parties rather than give effect to their intentions. For this reason many traditional theorists about contract law would recoil from Lord Denning's approach.

→ CROSS-REFERENCE

For an example of Lord Denning encouraging terms to be more prominent see 6.2.6.

Interestingly, Lord Denning observed that in some cases, the battle is won by the party that gets the 'blow in first'. This is an *obiter* comment suggesting a first-shot theory. It was based on the idea that if a response makes a fundamental change to the first terms, that change should be sufficiently noticeable. It should not be hidden in small print. If the change lacks sufficient prominence, then according to Lord Denning's comment, it may not be effective and so the terms shot first should govern the contract. This approach reflects Lord Denning's attempts to make contracts more transparent and open (with no hidden clauses).

3.6.4 Alternative Suggestions

Professor Adams, (Adams, 'Battle of forms' (1979) 95 LQR 481), observed that 'any attempt to formulate a tidy set of answers to the problems raised by the production line contracts (meaning "battle of the forms" scenarios) is likely to be futile'. He suggested that each case should be dealt with on its own facts to produce fair results. He also observed that sometimes the fairest result would be to say that neither sets of terms apply and then apportion compensation under principles of reliance and restitution. In other words, one option is to decide there is no contract. Then, as a remedy, the parties' pre-contractual position can be restored, and compensation paid based on the costs the parties have incurred in relying on statements made during negotiations. This was the remedy adopted by Goff J in *British Steel Corporation v Cleveland Bridge and Engineering Co Ltd* [1984] 1 All ER 504. The case was about work done in response to a **letter of intent** rather than a 'battle of forms' but it does present an additional solution. A further suggestion by Professor Adams is to allow any previous course of dealings to indicate that the parties are operating under a particular set of terms. Of course, that relies on

letter of intent

is a document showing an intention to enter a contract later.

the existence of previous dealings on consistent terms. But if such a course of dealing exists, it could go some way to show what the parties appear to intend in their most recent dealings.

3.6.5 The Most Recent Significant Case on the 'Battle of Forms'

The most recent significant case on the battle of forms is *Tekdata Interconnections Ltd v Amphenol Ltd* [2009] EWCA Civ 1209. It concerned a long-term contractual relationship between the parties. During this relationship, the buyer would send orders with its own terms. The seller would then acknowledge the order, but would also add that the seller's terms applied. This would be followed by performance by the parties. The dispute arose because the buyer claimed there was a breach. The seller then tried to rely on their terms, which exempted them from liability. Therefore, it was necessary for the court to determine which terms applied.

The traditional approach would suggest that the seller had the last shot because acceptance by conduct followed each time. However, the first instance judge (Simon Brown QC) did not apply the traditional approach based on offer and acceptance. Instead, the wider approach suggested by Lord Denning in *Butler* was applied. From this wider context, it was decided that the parties must have intended to be bound by the buyer's terms. However, the Court of Appeal applied the traditional analysis and held that the contract was based on the seller's terms. It is useful to view an extract of the main points from the judgments.

GUIDED CASE READING 3.6
Tekdata Interconnections Ltd v Amphenol Ltd [2009] EWCA Civ 1209

When you read the extracts from Longmore LJ and Dyson LJ try to identify:

▪ their views on the limits of the traditional approach;
▪ the extent to which they leave open the possibility of Lord Denning's approach being applied in the future.

Longmore LJ:

[The argument from the respondent that *Butler Machine Tools v Excello*, is not authority for abandoning the traditional approach was addressed. Longmore LJ then continued]

11. I agree with [Counsel for the respondent's] submissions on the aspect of the case, while accepting that, as Lord Denning said, there will be cases when one must glean from documents passing between the parties and from their conduct whether agreement has been reached. The way in which I would put it is to say that the traditional offer and acceptance analysis must be adopted unless the documents passing between the parties and their conduct show that their common intention was that some other terms were intended to prevail.

[the decision of the judge at first instance was analysed]

20. In paras 2-110 and 111 of *Chitty on Contracts* (30th ed.) Professor Sir Guenther Treitel points out that the traditional offer and acceptance analysis is not always without its difficulties . . . he cites the words of Lord Denning MR in *Butler* and his similar words in the earlier case of *Gibson v Manchester City Council* [1978] 1 WLR 520, 523. He then says of these comments 'But such an outright rejection of the traditional analysis is open to the objection that it provides too little guidance for the courts (or their parties or their legal advisers) in determining whether an agreement has been reached' and I might add 'on what terms' . . .

> Here Longmore LJ emphasises one of the foundational principles of English contract law—that ultimately what matters is the parties'intentions. If they appeared to have a common intention that some set of terms should prevail, then that must be given effect—even if it does not seem that those terms are clearly identifiable in the sense of there being an offer which has been accepted. But it is clear that this is only likely to be a very rare occurrence and courts will proceed with caution—not least because departing from the traditional approach will cause uncertainty.

So, although I am not saying that the context of a long-term relationship and the conduct of the parties can never be so strong as to displace the result which a traditional offer and acceptance analysis would dictate, I do not consider the circumstances are sufficiently strong to do so in this present case. Indeed I think it will always be difficult to displace the traditional analysis, in a battle of forms case, unless it can be said there was a clear course of dealing between the parties. That was never proved.

Dyson LJ:

22. I agree with the judgment of Longmore LJ.

23. The so-called 'last shot' doctrine has been explained in *Chitty on Contracts* (30th edition) at para 2-037 as meaning that where conflicting communications are exchanged, each is a counter-offer, so that if a contract results at all (eg from an acceptance by conduct) it must be on the terms of the final document in the series leading to the conclusion of the contract.

This doctrine has been criticised in *Anson's Law of Contract* (28th edition) at p. 39 as depending on chance and being potentially arbitrary as well as on the ground that, unless and until the counter-offer is accepted, there is no contract even though both buyer and seller may firmly believe that a contract has been made.

25. In my judgment, it is not possible to lay down a general rule that will apply in all cases where there is a battle of the forms. It always depends on an assessment of what the parties must objectively be taken to have intended. But where the facts are no more complicated than that A makes an offer on its conditions and B accepts that offer on its conditions and, without more, performance follows, it seems to me that the correct analysis is what Longmore LJ has described as the 'traditional offer and acceptance analysis', ie that there is a contract on B's conditions. I accept that this analysis is not without its difficulties . . . I also accept the force of the criticisms made in *Anson*. But the rules which govern the formation of contracts have been long established and they are grounded in the concepts of offer and acceptance. So long as that continues to be the case, it seems to me that the general rule should be that the traditional offer and acceptance analysis is to be applied in battle of the forms cases. That has the great merit of providing a degree of certainty which is both desirable and necessary in order to promote effective commercial relationships.

[Pill LJ delivered a judgment that agreed with both Dyson LJ and Longmore LJ]

> One possible example of a circumstance in which departing from the traditional model may be justified is said to be the example of a long-term relationship where there has been a consistent course of dealings (as Professor Adams had suggested). In those circumstances, terms which were previously agreed and used over that course of dealings might be preferred. But the existence of such a course of dealings must be proved, and here it was not.

> For Dyson LJ there were clear problems with the traditional 'last shot' doctrine, as identified in textbooks. And he agrees that there cannot be a general rule that will apply in absolutely all cases of 'the battle of forms'. But he also adopts a conservative position that certainty should prevail and that therefore it is preferable for the traditional approach to be used unless there a good reason not to do so.

Both judgments agree that on the whole that it is best for the law to be predictable and certain, because that is in the end more important for businesses and lawyers. This means that the traditional approach should be used, although it cannot be insisted on where there is a very good reason not to (as when there is apparent clear contradictory intention by the parties).

?! THINKING POINTS

Why do you think Longmore LJ felt the need to acknowledge Lord Denning's approach and the use of previous dealings as a possibility?

The approach of Lord Denning in *Butler* as acknowledged in *Tekdata* is part of a much wider issue on agreement about whether the offer and acceptance analysis are always necessary. We will address the basics of this issue at 3.6.6.

3.6.6 Is the Use of Offer and Acceptance Always Necessary?

The early cases in our two chapters on agreement show that an agreement is founded on finding an offer, and the acceptance of it. And, indeed, most contracts can be formed through offer and acceptance. In addition, in most cases where there is no offer or no acceptance, it is obvious that there is no agreement. The problem is that in some cases, the existence of an agreement is obvious, yet it might be impossible or too artificial to identify a clear offer or acceptance. This raises a question about the role of offer and acceptance. Are offer and acceptance required as a rule, and if so, what is the extent of the rule? Alternatively, are offer and acceptance just tools that are used by courts for convenience?

In *New Zealand Shipping Co. Ltd v A M Satterthwaite & Co. Ltd, The Eurymedon* [1975] AC 154, Lord Wilberforce addressed the limits of using offer and acceptance as strict requirements.

> It is only the precise analysis of this complex of relations into the classical offer and acceptance, with identifiable consideration, that seems to present difficulty, but this same difficulty exists in many situations of daily life, e.g. sales at auction; supermarket purchases; boarding an omnibus; purchasing a train ticket; tenders for the supply of goods; offers of rewards; acceptance by post; warranties of authority by agents; manufacturers' guarantees; gratuitous bailments; bankers' commercial credits. These are all examples which show that English law, having committed itself to a rather technical and schematic doctrine of contract, in application takes a practical approach, often at the cost of forcing the facts to fit uneasily into the marked slots of offer, acceptance and consideration.

The statement is very important because it is from an influential Law Lord and challenges the absolute use of offer and acceptance. It recognises that the traditional requirements of offer and acceptance result can in a technical approach. This technical approach is difficult to apply to certain situations where it is obvious that a contract exists. It can result in an artificial analysis, because the facts are being forced into terms of offer and acceptance in order to recognise a contract that clearly exists. One of the examples mentioned was the case of supermarket purchases. We know that a purchase results in a contract between the supermarket and the buyer. We know that the goods displayed are generally an invitation to treat. But it is not clear how the offer is made and precisely when acceptance takes place. Using offer and acceptance in such a situation is rather artificial. After all, do customers really intend to make the shop an offer? Does the person at the checkout think they are accepting an offer or simply offering to sell?

> ➔ CROSS-REFERENCE
> For a discussion of the issues of contract formation in supermarkets see 2.2.2.

The comment by Lord Wilberforce was cited by Lord Denning MR to justify a wider contextual approach to the 'battle of forms' problem in *Butler*. Lord Denning MR also applied this approach earlier in the Court of Appeal case of *Gibson v Manchester City Council* [1978] 1 WLR 520 stating:

> . . . To my mind it is a mistake to think that all contracts can be analysed into the form of offer and acceptance. I know in some of the text books it has been the custom to do so: but, as I understand the law, there is no need to look for a strict offer and acceptance. You should look at the correspondence as a whole and at the conduct of the parties and see therefrom whether the parties have come to an agreement on everything that was material. If by their correspondence and their conduct you can see an agreement on all material terms—which was intended thenceforward to be binding—then there is a binding contract in law even though all the formalities have not been gone through: see *Brogden v. Metropolitan Railway Co.* (1877) 2 App.Cas. 666.

> It seems to me that on the correspondence I have read—and, I may add, on what happened after—the parties had come to an agreement in the matter which they intended to be binding.

Lord Denning was not simply observing that the offer and acceptance analysis can be overly technical and artificial. The comment was going much further to suggest that there was no need to look for offer and acceptance to ascertain the apparent intentions of the parties. From Lord Denning's perspective, the use of offer and acceptance were at best, judicial tools used for convenience. The House of Lords did not approve of the approach adopted by Lord Denning and overruled the Court of Appeal decision. In the House of Lords decision ([1979] 1 WLR 294), the significant comment on the role of offer and acceptance came from Lord Diplock who observed:

> My Lords, there may be certain types of contract, though I think they are exceptional, which do not fit easily into the normal analysis of a contract as being constituted by offer and acceptance; but a contract alleged to have been made by an exchange of correspondence between the parties in which the successive communications other than the first are in reply to one another is not one of these. I can see no reason in the instant case for departing from the traditional approach of looking at the handful of documents relied on as constituting the contract sued on and seeing whether on their true construction there is to be found in them a contractual offer . . . and an acceptance of that offer . . . I venture to think that it was by departing from this traditional approach that the majority of the Court of Appeal was led into error.

Here Lord Diplock explained that the Court of Appeal should have framed the dealings between the parties in terms of offer and acceptance. So, unlike the Court of Appeal, the House of Lords applied the traditional analysis. In doing so, it found that there was no contract because there was no offer or acceptance. The result of the case emphasises the importance of the traditional analysis as a rule rather than a tool for convenience. But what is the extent of the rule?

Lord Diplock's comment recognises there are limits to analyses based on offer and acceptance. His Lordship acknowledged that the analysis does not work well with certain contracts, but these are 'exceptional'. The traditional offer and acceptance analysis is therefore the *normal* rule. Such an approach might result in facts being forced so as to make the analysis of offer and acceptance work, but it results in more certainty for businesses. Without it, the existence of a contract would be disputed more often. In other words, the traditional approach as the normal rule allows for more certainty and results in fewer disputes. Even when there is a dispute, the normal rule means that lawyers can point to the existence of an offer that was accepted or the clear absence of either requirement. This means that more disputes can be resolved out of court through negotiation because one party will know it is in a weak position and the other will know it is in a strong position. In contrast, if establishing that there has been an agreement is based on views about the parties' conduct and the wider context, both sides would have good arguments. This would result in more disputes being taken to the courts—an option that should be viewed as the last resort.

Overall, the importance of certainty means that the courts are keen to require identification of offer and acceptance, even if the application to certain case facts seems artificial. At the same time, the courts do not want to be inflexible. Consequently, the courts see there is merit in acknowledging that in exceptional circumstances, there could be an agreement established on the basis of the parties' intentions indicated by the wider circumstances and by their conduct. Judges should not set aside the traditional analysis in the way that Lord Denning did so easily. Instead, the routine starting point—the *normal* rule—is the traditional analysis based on offer and acceptance.

CHAPTER SUMMARY

- There must be complete assent with the terms of the offer. Otherwise, the response will be seen as a counter-offer.
- Where an offer has an essential requirement relating to acceptance (like the method of acceptance) then it must be followed. However, equivalent alternatives might be permitted if the offeror has not done enough to make the requirement essential.
- Acceptance must be in response to an offer, but the motive for accepting is not relevant.
- The general rule is that acceptance is effective once it has been communicated (received). Exceptions to the rule include:

  - The postal rule, under which mailed acceptance is effective when sent, but it must be reasonable to use the post and the rule must not be expressly or impliedly excluded by the offeror.
  - Where communication of acceptance is waived by the offeror, although acceptance by silence (inaction) is generally not permitted.
  - Acceptance by conduct, which takes place when the offeree has acted in a way that indicates an intention to accept.

- Automated ticket and vending machines present an offer so that acceptance takes place when the customer is committed—like when payment is made.
- Emailed acceptance and the use of websites to communicate acceptance are likely to operate on the basis of the general rule.
- The traditional analysis based on offer and acceptance will be applied to 'battle of forms' cases. In exceptional cases courts may look to the wider context in such cases to identify the terms of an agreement.
- There is scope for exceptional cases to recognise an agreement in the absence of offer and acceptance using the wider context, but this will be rare.

KEY CASES

- *Manchester Diocesan Council of Education v Commercial & General Investments* [1970] 1 WLR 241—provides the rule on the use of alternative methods of acceptance.
- *R v Clarke* (1927) 40 CLR 227 (Aust)—provides authority that acceptance must be in response to an offer.
- *Entores Ltd v Miles Far East Corporation* [1955] 2 QB 327—provides reasoning for the application of the general rule to instantaneous communication.
- *Household Fire Insurance v Grant* (1879) 4 Ex D 216—provides authority for the post rule and its reasoning.
- *Holwell Securities v Hughes* [1974] 1 WLR 155—confirms the limits and exclusion of the post rule.
- *Felthouse v Bindley* (1862) 142 ER 1037—represents the rule on acceptance by silence (inaction).
- *Tekdata Interconnections Ltd v Amphenol Ltd* [2009] EWCA Civ 1209—shows how the courts approach the 'battle of forms'.

QUESTIONS

1. On Monday, Gamer Phones (Retail) Ltd received a brochure from Smart-Tech Manufacturing Ltd. It offered a 30% discount on all smart phones for all orders placed by 5pm Friday using the pre-paid envelope. Pawel, the manager of Gamer Phones, completed the order form and posted it on the

Wednesday. Due to a disruption to the post, the order was received on the Saturday. Is Pawel entitled to the discount?

2. Daisy is a seller of high-performance cars. She received a written offer from a buyer for the purchase of her Audi RS7 for £50,000. The offer stated that if Daisy did not reply within two weeks, it would be presumed that Daisy has accepted the offer. She did not reply within that period. Is Daisy under an obligation to sell the car for £50,000?

3. 'The rule of receipt (the general rule) should apply to emailed acceptance'. Critically discuss.

4. Critically evaluate the way the courts have responded to the 'battle of forms'.

 For answer guidance to these questions please visit the online resources at www .oup.com/uk/naidoo1e/, where you will also find multiple choice questions to check your understanding of key concepts.

FURTHER READING

Morgan, 'Battle of the Forms: Restating the Orthodox' (2010) 69 Cambridge Law Review 230.
This is a useful short case note on the significance of *Tekdata Interconnections Ltd v Amphenol Ltd* [2009].

Nolan, 'Offer and Acceptance in the Electronic Age' in A Burrows and E Peel (eds), Contract Formation and Parties (2010) OUP at 61.
A very detailed analysis of the how the law could apply to the formation of contracts by email.

Certainty and the Intention to Enter a Legal Relationship

4

LEARNING OBJECTIVES

By the end of this chapter you should be able to:

- explain the requirements of, and the close relationship between, certainty and intention to enter a legal relationship;
- understand the role of the courts and the factual assessment that is applied to work out if the agreement is a contract;
- evaluate the position on agreements to negotiate a contract;
- apply the presumptions relating to intention in the context of domestic/social agreements and business agreements.

INTRODUCTION

The previous chapters explained the law that applies to the creation of an agreement. But a *contract* is more than just an agreement; it is a *legally enforceable* agreement. To be legally enforceable, a number of requirements have to be met. First, the agreement must be certain enough so that it is capable of being enforced (the certainty requirement). Secondly, it must appear that the parties intended to enter or create a legal relationship (the intention requirement). A third requirement that generally applies is that the parties must provide sufficient consideration (the consideration requirement).

Many cases raise an issue of certainty, or intention or both. Disputes about these requirements can arise in a range of circumstances. Typically, one party claims that there has been a breach, and the other then argues that their agreement is too *vague* or *incomplete* to be a contract. Alternatively, that other party might argue that there was no intention to enter a legal relationship and the agreement was just a friendly or familial one.

In this chapter we will explore the basic law on the certainty and intention requirements. We begin briefly with the relationship between the requirements. We will then turn to the detail relating to the certainty requirement before moving on to the intention requirement. The requirement for consideration is much more complicated and needs to be treated separately in its own right. It is detailed in Chapter 5.

4.1 The Relationship between Certainty and Intention

From a practical perspective, an agreement that is uncertain would be unenforceable because it would not be possible to define the parties' obligations. Such uncertainty can result from terms being vague or the agreement being incomplete. Alternatively, even if the terms are clear and complete, it might be argued that in the circumstances, there was no intention to enter a legal relationship. In other words, the parties could make a clear agreement, but it still might appear that there was no intention for it to be enforceable in the courts. While each of these issues are enough to prevent an agreement being enforceable as a contract, in practice they often overlap.

The basic requirement of certainty as well its relationship with intention was mentioned by Leggatt J in *Blue v Ashley* [2017] EWHC 1928 (Comm) in the following way:

> [61] Vagueness in what is said or omission of important terms may be grounds for concluding that no agreement has been reached at all or for concluding that, although an agreement has been reached, it is not intended to be legally binding. But certainty and completeness of terms is also an independent requirement of a contract. Thus, even where it is apparent that the parties have made an agreement which is intended to be legally binding, the court may conclude that the agreement is too uncertain or incomplete to be enforceable-for example, where it lacks an essential term which the court cannot supply for the parties.

The comment acknowledges that both vague terms or incomplete agreements can indicate that there was no intention for a legal relationship. It also recognises that certainty is a distinct requirement. This means that if the agreement is too vague or incomplete, it will not be enforceable as a contract, even if there was a clear intention for the agreement to be legally enforceable. That will be the case when it is just not possible to define what was agreed.

For convenience, we will address the issues of certainty and intention in turn, but in doing so, we will keep in mind that in practice they often overlap.

4.2 The Certainty Requirement and the Role of the Courts

The obligations agreed in a contract must be sufficiently certain to be enforceable, but sometimes agreements have terms that are vague because of the language used. For example, the language might be ambiguous, such that it is capable of more than one meaning. Likewise, an agreement could be uncertain because the parties have deliberately left out an important term. That might seem a little strange, but usually in practice parties want to enter a contract to start trading quickly. To do so, they might leave out certain terms for them to be decided at a later date. This is especially likely where a contract is made by business people rather than lawyers. This point was acknowledged by Lord Wright in *Hillas & Co Ltd v Arcos Ltd* [1932] All ER Rep 494, wherein His Lordship observed of the agreement that:

> [It] cannot be regarded as other than inartistic, and may appear repellent to the trained sense of an equity draftsman. But it is clear that the parties both intended to make a contract and thought they had done so. Business men often record the most important agreements in crude and summary fashion; modes of expression sufficient and clear to them in the course of their business may appear to those unfamiliar with the business far from complete or precise.

This comment is applicable to many agreements. Business people enter agreements that may seem clear to them at the time. However, to the trained eye of an expert lawyer, such agreements may be incomplete or lack the precision needed to identify clear obligations to enforce. Such agreements may be so incomplete or vague that a court may view them as negotiations rather than final contracts.

When parties find themselves in a dispute about vague or missing terms, the court will have to assess the agreement to work out if it is a contract. It might be possible to interpret the terms in a way that defines the obligations so that it is possible for either party to enforce them. The interpretation carried out by the court is an objective one. It should be based on the language of the agreement and facts from the surrounding circumstances. These might include what was done in previous dealings, or even the accepted practice in the relevant trade. Whatever factors are relevant, it is important to appreciate that it is not for judges to simply rewrite contracts. Instead, it is the role of the court to interpret the agreement based on the parties' apparent intentions.

The decisions in the cases tend to be fact-specific. After all, each agreement has its own wording. In addition, the relevance of previous dealings and what is understood in the trade will vary among the cases. This means that this area of law does not give us a clear set of rules on *when* terms will be deemed too vague or *when* agreements will be deemed incomplete. Instead, we focus on the approach of the courts and the factors relevant to their approach.

It is possible however to identify a few very general principles. On the issue of terms being clear, in *Scammell and Nephew Ltd v Ouston* [1941] AC 251, Viscount Maugham observed that:

> …[I]n order to constitute a valid contract the parties must so express themselves that their meaning can be determined with a reasonable degree of certainty.

So, a contract has to be workable and does not have to be *absolutely* clear and certain. Instead, it just needs to be *sufficiently* certain from an objective perspective. That means it has to be possible to identify the obligations to be enforced.

Another general principle is that judges will lean towards deciding that a contract exists, rather than deciding that no contract was formed. Some judges might adopt a very generous approach to their interpretation, so that they 'fill in the gaps' a little too easily. In doing so, their interpretation gets dangerously close to re-writing the agreement. In contrast, some judges might be very cautious or strict and decide that no contract exists. However, it seems that generally, judges try to recognise that a contract has been made, all else considered. Lord Wright in *Hillas v Arcos*, for instance, after noting that businesspeople often enter into crude and imprecise agreements, went on to say:

> It is accordingly the duty of the court to construe such documents fairly and broadly, without being too astute or subtle in finding defects
> …[E]ven if the construction of the words used may be difficult, that is not a reason for holding them too ambiguous or uncertain to be enforced, if the fair meaning of the parties can be extracted

The comments encourage judges to interpret terms (or construe agreements) so as to recognise that a contract exists, but to do so in a balanced way. They should not go out of their way to find faults with the wording, but also not be too quick to overlook such faults.

In the same case, Lord Tomlin echoed this point by stating:

> …[T]he problem for a court of construction must always be so to balance matters that, without violation of essential principle, the dealings of men may as far as possible be treated as effective, and that the law may not incur the reproach of being the destroyer of bargains.

This statement indicates that where possible, the courts should try to interpret vague terms to work out the intended meaning. The aim is to try to recognise the agreement that the parties thought they had. To be too strict would mean destroying bargains, which would have a damaging effect on commerce. But this must be done without rewriting the agreement because that would be a 'violation of essential principle'—namely that the court is not there to make an agreement for the parties, but simply to enforce what they have agreed.

More recently in *Durham Tees Valley Airport Ltd v bmibaby Ltd* [2010] EWCA Civ 485, Toulson LJ encouraged judges to uphold contracts as far as it is possible to do so by stating:

> Where parties intend to create a contractual obligation, the court will try to give it legal effect. The court will only hold that the contract, or some part of it, is **void for uncertainty**, if it is legally or practically impossible to give to the agreement (or that part of it) any sensible content.

void for uncertainty means that the agreement is not a contract.

Suggesting that judges should try to uphold the agreements as contracts unless it is practically impossible appears to go much further than the comments made in the older cases. This increased willingness to make sense of the agreement and try to recognise the contract intended was acknowledged more recently in *Blue v Ashley* [2017] where Leggatt J stated:

> The courts are, however, reluctant to conclude that what the parties intended to be a legally binding agreement is too uncertain to be of contractual effect and such a conclusion is very much a last resort.

Overall, then, courts will err on the side of holding that an enforceable contract exists, with the current judicial attitude appearing to be even stronger in this regard.

So far, we have simply looked at the cause of the uncertainty problem and the role of the courts. Having done so, it is now useful to turn to some key cases to see the approach taken by the courts. We will start with the category of vague agreements.

4.3 Vague Agreements

Agreements can be vague where the terms relating to important issues are capable of different meanings. It is then for the courts to try to identify what meaning was intended by the parties. Here we will examine some of the main factors used by the courts to achieve this.

4.3.1 The Facts Surrounding the Agreement

A useful example of the relevance of surrounding facts is *Hillas & Co Ltd v Arcos Ltd* [1932] All ER Rep 494. The claimant buyers were large timber merchants based in Hull. They had an agreement to buy '22,000 standards of softwood goods of fair specification over the season 1930'. Clause 9 of the included conditions gave the buyers an option to buy from the sellers '100,000 standards for delivery during 1931'. The option to buy did not refer to the size, quality or type of timber to be supplied. When the claimant buyer chose to exercise the option, the seller was unable to supply the goods. This was because they had sold their stock to another party. The claimant then sued for breach of the option contract. In response, the seller argued that the option agreement only referred to '100,000 standards'. It added nothing about the specification. According to the seller, that description was too vague to be a contract and required further detail to become enforceable. This defence was rejected by the House of Lords, and it was held that the option resulted in a complete contract. The term used in the earlier performed agreement to buy 22,000 standards ('of softwood goods of fair specification') was implied into the option contract.

In the reasoning, Lord Tomlin stated that the term in the option, referring to '100,000 standards', was extremely vague and did not even refer to timber as the product. But the question was whether the option had an identifiable meaning that was intended by the parties. On this, it was observed that the parties were very familiar with the Russian softwood trade. They had carried out the sale of the 22,000 standards without a problem because the description of the wood for that contract was clear enough for the parties. In the circumstances, it was implied that the same description would have been intended for the option contract. That made the option sufficiently certain to be a binding contract as soon as it was exercised by the buyer.

KEY POINTS

If the parties have had previous dealings, it might be possible to say that the terms used in those dealings are implied in a later agreement that is vague.

Hillas v Arcos is a good example of how the surrounding facts can be used to work out what a vague term was intended to mean. The House of Lords developed a way of finding the meaning based on the terms of the first transaction. It is useful to contrast this with another House of Lords case, *Scammell and Nephew Ltd v Ouston* [1941] 1 AC 251.

The case concerned an agreement to buy a new van. The buyer (Ouston) and seller (Scammell) agreed a price and that the buyer's old van would be used in part exchange. They also agreed that the remaining amount due would be on hire-purchase terms over two years.

However, before any hire-purchase terms were agreed, the seller refused to continue. The buyer then took action for breach of contract. In response, the seller argued that the agreement was too uncertain to be a contract and so there was no contract to breach. This argument was based on the fact that the hire-purchase terms had not been worked out and agreed. The House of Lords upheld this argument and decided that there was no contract.

The lead judgment by Viscount Maugham began by stating that contracts must be expressed with a *reasonable* degree of certainty. His Lordship then turned to the parties' reference to 'hire-purchase terms' and the different options that could have been intended. It was observed that the arrangement could be from the seller directly to the buyer. That would mean that the seller would be paid in instalments with interest. Alternatively, if a finance company was involved, the seller would be paid in full by the company. The buyer would then have to pay a larger sum to the finance company by instalments along with interest. Since there was nothing to indicate which arrangement appeared to be intended, it was therefore not possible to identify the rights and obligations of the parties resulting from their agreement.

Furthermore, while the parties had referred to a two-year period, nothing was said about the interest payable and what rights the owner had if instalments were not paid on time. This would not have been a major problem if there were standard terms used in the trade. Such standard terms could be implied by the court on the basis that such terms must have been intended. However, the judgment observed that it was common knowledge that terms varied a great deal in the industry. Reference was made to terms relating to the quality of the goods, obligations to provide repairs, and the common use of unfair terms imposed on buyers, which is why the Hire-Purchase Act 1938 was enacted.

Essentially, the reference to 'hire-purchase' terms was too uncertain for the agreement to be a contract. There was no way of knowing what type of hire-purchase arrangement the parties might have intended. In addition, they had not even agreed the important matters that are usually covered in hire-purchase agreements. Consequently, based on an objective assessment of the facts, the House of Lords agreed it was not possible to define the important rights and obligations of the parties. On that basis, there was no contract.

hire-purchase
is where a buyer takes possession of the goods and pays the price by instalments. Once the payments are complete, ownership passes to the buyer.

?! THINKING POINTS

Might the result have been different if the parties had had regular previous dealings with consistent hire-purchase arrangements and terms?

4.3.2 The Significance of Performance

If the parties have already started to perform their purported obligations, then it is more likely that a contract will be recognised. This makes sense, because if the parties are actually performing what they must consider to be the obligations they owe to each other, then it is difficult to say that the agreement was too vague to be performed. On this point, in *Trentham (G.Percy) Ltd v Archital Luxfer Ltd* [1993] 1 Lloyd's Rep 25, Steyn LJ observed:

> The fact that the transaction was performed on both sides will often make it unrealistic to argue that there was no intention to enter into legal relations. It will often make it difficult to submit that the contract is void for vagueness or uncertainty. Specifically, the fact that the transaction is executed makes it easier to imply a term resolving any uncertainty, or, alternatively, it may make it possible to treat a matter not finalised in negotiations as inessential.

According to this statement, if there has been performance (i.e. there has been an 'executed' agreement) it can indicate that the parties did intend to have a contract. Such performance also means it is less likely that the agreement will be construed as having been too vague because it has actually been performed. If the parties were able to perform, the agreement was surely not all that unclear. Similarly, any gaps in the agreement can be filled-in by implying a term that reflects the aspects of performance accepted by the parties. Finally, vague terms (or terms that were left to be completed later) could be removed as unnecessary because they did not cause a problem with performance.

KEY POINTS

If the parties have performed their agreement, it is *more likely* that the court will say it was certain enough to have been a contract.

Performance of an agreement only means there is a greater *chance* of a court deciding that the agreement is clear enough. It is possible for a court to decide that the agreement is too uncertain, even though there has been some performance by the parties. A good example is *British Steel Corporation v Cleveland Bridge & Engineering Co. Ltd* [1984] 1 All ER 504. In this case, negotiations took so long that British Steel commenced performance of its obligations, delivering consignments of steel nodes to Cleveland Bridge, expecting to finalise a contract later. However, the parties had failed to agree on a number of points—crucially, these included liability for late delivery and progress payments—and so they never did finalise the agreement. A dispute arose about late delivery of the nodes and their consignments being delivered in the wrong order. Goff J was unable to find a contract because too much had been left out—most notably the two terms which would have provided a resolution to the dispute.

Both the *Trentham* and *British Steel* cases were addressed by Lord Clarke in *RTS Flexible Systems Ltd v Molkerei Alois Müller GmbH & Co* [2010] UKSC 14. His Lordship referred to the factual nature of the cases to explain the view of Steyn LJ in *Trentham* and the result in *British Steel*. Steyn LJ in *Trentham* said performance was a good indication of a contact. In *British Steel*, there was no contract even though there had been performance. But, in *British Steel*, the parties had not agreed on the very important terms. According to Lord Clarke, a failure to agree on the very important terms limits the significance of performance.

The distinction made by Lord Clarke was reflected on more recently by the Supreme Court in *Wells v Devani* [2019] UKSC 4. In this case, the trial judge accepted that an oral contract existed between a developer of flats (Wells) and the claimant estate agent (Devani) who found a buyer for some of the flats. It was also accepted from their conversations that Devani was to receive a 2% commission. However, one of the arguments Wells put forward was that the agreement was uncertain because nothing was said about what would trigger the payment of the commission. Was it payable on finding a buyer; the exchange of contracts; or when the sale was completed? In the Court of Appeal, Lewison LJ found that the event triggering payment was of critical importance and, therefore, that the contract was incomplete. However, on this point, Lord Kitchen's lead judgment relied on *Scammel v Ouston* in stating:

> But the courts are reluctant to find an agreement is too vague or uncertain to be enforced where it is found that the parties had the intention of being contractually bound and have acted on their agreement.

Lord Kitchen then agreed that the trigger for payment was of 'critical importance' but it did not prevent a contract. Instead, based on the facts it was enough that a reasonable person would understand that payment was to be made on completion of the sale. This is what would be 'naturally understood'. On that basis, the agent was entitled to a commission since the sale had been completed.

KEY POINTS

- Performance can indicate that a contract exists, but if the important terms have not been expressed, then a contract is less likely to be held to have been made.
- It might be possible to say that the (unexpressed) important terms have been agreed, if it is clear what the parties must have intended on that issue.

4.3.3 Meaningless Terms Can Be Ignored

We have already seen that vague terms can mean that an agreement is not enforceable as a contract. But what if the vague term is not about something that's important to the agreement? It would seem very formal to allow the vagueness of a very minor term to prevent the entire agreement being enforceable. The solution is a straightforward one. When a vague term relates to something unimportant or inessential, it is possible for a judge to say that the term is meaningless and can be ignored. This has the same effect as removing the term from the contract.

Authority allowing meaningless terms to be ignored is found in *Nicolene Ltd v Simmonds* [1953] 1 QB 543. This case concerned a contract for the sale of steel bars. The (claimant) buyer made an offer by sending a letter ordering the goods. The (defendant) seller accepted using a letter adding that 'the usual conditions of acceptance apply'. The buyer then confirmed, by informing the seller where to deliver the goods. When the goods were not delivered, the buyer claimed damages for breach of contract. At first instance, the judge awarded damages to the buyer, so the seller then appealed. He argued that the 'usual conditions' term had no meaning because there were no 'usual conditions' between the parties. According to the seller, this meant that the agreement was too vague to be enforceable. In the Court of Appeal, the seller's argument was rejected. The reasoning was based on the term being meaningless and, on that basis, it could be ignored. Denning LJ explained when a term is likely to be considered meaningless along with reasons why such a term should be ignored, in the following way:

> In my opinion a distinction must be drawn between a clause which is meaningless and a clause which is yet to be agreed. A clause which is meaningless can often be ignored, whilst still leaving the contract good; whereas a clause which has yet to be agreed may mean that there is no contract at all, because the parties have not agreed on all the essential terms. I take it to be clear law that if one of the parties to a contract inserts into it an exempting condition in his own favour, which the other side agrees, and it afterwards turns out that that condition is meaningless, or what comes to the same thing, that it is so ambiguous that no ascertainable meaning can be given to it, that does not mean that the whole contract is a nullity. It only means that the exempting condition is a nullity and must be rejected. It would be strange indeed if a party could escape from every one of his obligations by inserting a meaningless exception from some of them…
>
> In the present case there was nothing yet to be agreed. There was nothing left to further negotiation. All that happened was that the parties agreed that "the usual conditions of acceptance apply." That clause was so vague and uncertain as to be incapable of any precise meaning. It is clearly severable from the rest of the contract. It can be rejected without impairing the sense or reasonableness of the contract as a whole, and it should be so rejected. The contract should be held good and the clause ignored. The parties themselves treated the contract as subsisting. They regarded it as creating binding obligations between them; and it would be most unfortunate if the law should say otherwise. You would find defaulters all scanning their contracts to find some meaningless clause on which to ride free.
> …The sentence is meaningless and must be ignored, but the contract, nevertheless, remains good.

The judgment shows that if a term is vague and relates to an important or essential issue, then it cannot be ignored. Instead, it means that the parties still have to agree on that issue. On that basis, there is no contract because it would not be workable without that term being agreed. *Scammell v Ouston* as an example of this. There, the reference to 'hire-purchase terms' related to an essential issue (the entire way in which payment would be made) and so the term could not be ignored. It was something essential that was *to be* agreed.

In contrast, in *Nicolene v Simmonds*, Denning LJ observed that the term was so vague that it could not be defined. For all practical purposes, it was meaningless. It did not relate to anything essential and it was clear that even without the term, the agreement was complete and workable. On that basis, the term was removable ('severable') because the contract would exist and work without it. The approach of ignoring or removing a meaningless term was justified on the basis that a party should not be able to rely on their own poor drafting to escape a contract (or deliberately insert meaningless terms into an agreement as a way of escaping liability if things go awry).

The judgment also emphasised the parties' intentions, and how maintaining the contract was consistent with those intentions—objectively assessed. The parties had both acted in such a way that each would reasonably have expected each other to perform their obligations. Of course, if the parties act like they have a contract, it does not mean there definitely is one. The *British Steel* case is an extreme example of that point. However, courts will attempt to give effect to the parties' apparent intentions if it is at all possible to do so.

→ CROSS-REFERENCE
For the facts of *Scammell v Ouston* see 4.3.1.

KEY POINTS

Whether a term is capable of being ignored is based on the fact of the case. In some cases, the vague term will be classed as meaningless and to be ignored. In others cases, if it relates to something important, it will be classed as something that remains to be agreed.

4.4 Incomplete Agreements

Sometimes parties enter an agreement but leave out something important to be decided later. It might be surprising to learn that parties sometimes even leave the price to be decided later, and that this has been the subject of some important cases. This might be because the market price or cost were expected to change. Alternatively, it might be that the price could only be worked out through a complicated and time-consuming process. If parties want to enter a contract quickly, then it might seem logical to them to enter an agreement that leaves the time-consuming things to be worked out later. Now, the legal problem that can result is a straightforward one. If important things are missed out (to be addressed at a later stage), it might be taken to indicate that the parties did not really intend to enter a contract at that stage. Instead, they will be considered to still be negotiating and simply have an *agreement to agree*. We will see that such an *agreement to agree* is not a contract, and so it is not legally enforceable.

4.4.1 Incomplete Agreements as *Agreements to Agree*

A key decision on incomplete agreements is from the House of Lords case of *May and Butcher Ltd v The King* [1934] 2 KB 17n. After the First World War, the UK Government had a lot of spare equipment left over. The Disposals Board was set up to sell this equipment on. The case concerned an agreement between May and Butcher (the buyer) and the Disposals Board, for the sale of tent equipment (what was referred to as 'tentage'). Under the agreement, the Board agreed to sell all of its stock of tentage to the buyer. The agreement stated that the prices and dates of payment would be 'agreed upon from time to time' between the parties as the 'old tentage become available'. The term concerning price was the main issue in question. But the terms also included an arbitration clause which stated that 'all disputes with reference to or arising out of this agreement will be submitted to arbitration'.

arbitration

is the process where a dispute is settled by a third party rather than the court system.

When the parties were unable to agree a price, the Board said it was no longer bound by the agreement. The buyers then brought an action to enforce the agreement. When the dispute reached the House of Lords, it was held that there was no contract because an important term (the price) still had to be agreed. On that basis, it was simply an agreement to agree. It is useful to look at the reasoning of the lead judgment by Lord Buckmaster.

GUIDED CASE READING 4.1
May and Butcher Ltd v The King [1934] 2 KB 17n

When you read the extracts of the judgment by Lord Buckmaster, try to identify:

- Why the absence of an agreed price meant there was no contract.
- Why the arbitration clause was not effective.

The points that arise for determination are these: Whether or not the terms of the contract were sufficiently defined to constitute a legal binding contract between the parties. The Crown says that the price was never agreed. The [appellant buyers] say first, that if it was not agreed, it would be a reasonable price. Secondly, they say that even if the price was not agreed, the arbitration clause in the contract was intended to cover this very question of price …

My Lords, those being the contentions, it is obvious that the whole matter depends upon the construction of the actual words of the bargain itself …
[The terms between the parties were addressed]

… In my opinion there never was a concluded contract between the parties. It has long been a well recognized principle of contract law that an agreement between two parties to enter into an agreement in which some critical part of the contract matter is left undetermined is no contract at all. It is of course perfectly possible for two people to contract that they will sign a document which contains all the relevant terms, but it is not open to them to agree that they will in the future agree upon a matter which is vital to the arrangement between them and has not yet been determined. It has been argued that as the fixing of the price has broken down, a reasonable price must be assumed. That depends in part upon the terms of the Sale of Goods Act … That provides in s. 8 that 'the price in a contract of sale may be fixed by the contract, or may be left to be fixed in manner thereby agreed, or may be determined by the course of dealing between the parties. Where the price is not determined in accordance with the foregoing provisions the buyer must pay a reasonable price'; while, if the agreement is to sell goods on the terms that the price is to be fixed by the valuation of a third party, and such third party cannot or does not make such valuation, s. 9 says that the agreement is avoided. I find myself quite unable to understand the distinction between an agreement to permit the price to be fixed by a third party and an agreement to permit the price to be fixed in the future by the two parties to the contract themselves. In principle it appears to me that they are one and the same thing …

The next question is about the arbitration clause, and there I entirely agree with the majority of the Court of Appeal and also with Rowlatt J. The clause refers 'disputes with reference to or arising out of this agreement' to arbitration, but until the price has been fixed, the agreement is not there.

The arbitration clause relates to the settlement of whatever may happen when the agreement has been completed and the parties are regularly bound. There is nothing in the arbitration clause to enable a contract to be made which in fact the original bargain has left quite open.

We can see here that the dispute hinges around the interpretation (i.e. the construction) of the two clauses in question.

For Lord Buckmaster there is a crucial distinction to be drawn between two types of agreements about future terms. On the one hand, the parties can contract that they will later adopt a subsequent agreement with all the necessary terms in it. But on the other they cannot simply agree to leave important matters open indefinitely and contract on that basis. Clearly, this case fell into the latter of these camps.

The defendant had argued that where there was no agreement on price, the price would be a 'reasonable' one, relying on s. 8 of the Sale of Goods Act 1893. But the judges were of the view that the proviso of that section only applied where the contract was silent about price. This was not the case here; the parties had made provision concerning price, albeit in a wholly vague way.

Furthermore, Lord Buckmaster was of the view that this case was in effect analogous to the situation referred to in s. 9 of the Act. There, an agreement is voided where a third party is supposed to fix the contract price, but cannot do so. For Lord Buckmaster, there was no real difference between a situation in which a price cannot be fixed by a third party and one in which it cannot be fixed by the two parties to the contract. Since in the former situation the contract is void under s. 9 of the Act, the same should apply in the latter situation as well.

Finally, the issue of the arbitration clause was straightforwardly dealt with. It only applied to disputes between the parties arising from the agreement, but here there was no agreement in the first place because the fundamental question of the price was uncertain.

Viscount Dunedin delivered a detailed judgment that agreed with the approach of Lord Buckmaster. The key principle from the case is that when a 'critical' or 'vital' part of an agreement is to be agreed later (like the price terms), then the agreement is an *agreement to agree*. Such an *agreement to agree* is not a contract and is therefore, unenforceable. Their Lordships were clearly of the view that this had been the status of such agreements in English law historically and they were therefore simply applying a very old principle of the common law.

?!   THINKING POINTS

Would it have made a difference if the parties had performed some of the contract by making and accepting deliveries?

The approach of the House of Lords in *May and Butcher v The King* has been criticised for being too strict in not allowing a reasonable price to be implied. For example, Blanchard J in the New Zealand Court of Appeal case of *Fletcher Challenge Energy Ltd v Electricity Corporation of New Zealand Ltd* [2002] 2 NZLR 433 criticised the decision, stating that there should be a greater focus on the parties' intentions. He was of the view that if it appears that the parties intended to be bound, then the court should try to fill existing gaps if possible. The judge even went so far as to say that he doubted the House of Lords would decide the case in the same way in 2002 as they did at the actual time.

4.4.2 Where the Incomplete Agreement Can Be Made Complete

The approach of the House of the Lords in *May and Butcher* is often compared with the Court of Appeal case of *Foley v Classique Coaches Ltd* [1934] 2 KB 1. Here the claimant (who owned a garage selling petrol) agreed to sell land to the defendant coach company. One of the conditions of the sale was that the coach company had to buy all of its petrol from the claimant seller. The agreement did not refer to a fixed price for the petrol. Instead, it said that it would be supplied 'at a price to be agreed by the parties in writing and from time to time'. In addition, there was an arbitration clause that said: 'If any dispute or difference shall arise on the subject matter or construction of this agreement the same shall be submitted to arbitration…' The sale of the land took place and the parties performed the petrol agreement for three years.

When a dispute arose about the price, the coach company argued that the petrol agreement was not a contract. The Court of Appeal disagreed and held that a contract had been formed.

In the reasoning of Scrutton LJ, the parties must have believed they had a contract because they had been performing it for three years. In addition, the arbitration clause applied to the failure to agree over price. On that basis, it was implied that a reasonable price would be payable.

➔ CROSS-REFERENCE

the position on vague terms is explained at 4.3.

What explains the difference between the decision in *Foley* and the one in *May and Butcher*? Just like the position with vague terms, a court will find it easier to say there is no contract when there has been no performance (an *executory* contract). Likewise, if there has been performance, it is more likely that the gaps will be filled in to reflect the parties' apparent intentions. In *Foley*, there had been continued performance for a fairly lengthy period of time.

But what about the arbitration clause that applied to the agreement of the price in *Foley* but not in *May and Butcher*? Two points could be made here:

■ In *May and Butcher*, the clause could only apply once there was a contract (which there was not because the clause on price was too uncertain). In *Foley*, the court believed there was a contract because there had been continued performance for three years.

■ In *May and Butcher*, the clause referred to 'disputes'. Part of the problem with this was that there was no 'dispute' as such—just a failure to agree. The clause in *Foley* was slightly wider by stating that it applied to 'disputes or differences'. This could apply to failures to agree.

KEY POINTS

Agreements are not required to be complete. Instead, an important term can be left out as long as the agreement includes a mechanism or way to fill the gap later.

We know that an incomplete agreement could be enforceable if it refers to a mechanism to fill in the gaps. But what if the mechanism breaks down for some reason? For example, in *Sudbrook Trading Estate Ltd v Eggleton* [1983] 1 AC 444 the agreement referred to a price to be agreed by a valuer appointed by each party. One party did not appoint a valuer and then claimed the agreement was too uncertain. Lord Fraser explained that if the mechanism in the agreement breaks down, a court could order a different mechanism to be used if the parties' mechanism is 'subsidiary and non-essential' to the agreement. However, where the mechanism is essential to the agreement, then it is not possible for a court to order its own mechanism to be used (*Gillatt v Sky Television Ltd* [2000] 1 All ER (Comm) 461, Court of Appeal).

Ultimately, the effect of an 'agreement to agree' will be settled by reference to the apparent intentions of the parties based on the facts. In *Morris v Swanton Care & Community Ltd* [2018] EWCA Civ 2763 a contract for the sale of shares required a payment of £16m and deferred payments over four years, during which time the seller provided consultancy services. Under the terms of the agreement, after the four years were over, the seller had the option to extend the contract period 'as shall reasonably be agreed'. After four years had passed, however, the request for an extension was rejected, and so the seller brought an action to enforce the extension. Dame Elizabeth Gloster for Court of Appeal decided that the option was simply an agreement to agree. The wording showed an intention to leave the extension to a future agreement. On that basis, there was no enforceable right to have an extension. Likewise, there could be no obligation to negotiate, a point that we now turn to.

4.5 Agreements to Negotiate

Negotiating a contract with a party can be time consuming and costly. In addition, the process has the obvious risk of breaking down so that no contract results. The parties then have to go through the trouble of looking elsewhere. To help manage the risks, parties might enter into an agreement to negotiate, or to negotiate 'in good faith'—a phrase which requires detailed explanation, as we shall see. But are such agreements enforceable as contracts?

On this issue, in *Courtney & Fairbairn Ltd v Tolaini Brothers (Hotels) Ltd* [1975] 1 WLR 297, Lord Denning MR (with whom the rest of the Court of Appeal agreed) stated:

> If the law does not recognise a contract to enter into a contract (when there is a fundamental term yet to be agreed) it seems to me it cannot recognise a contract to negotiate. The reason is because it is too uncertain to have any binding force.

Lord Denning MR indicated that an agreement to negotiate is too uncertain and should be treated the same as an incomplete agreement (by a 'contract to enter into a contract' he meant an 'agreement to agree'). His Lordship then went on to explain the uncertainties associated with an agreement to negotiate:

> No court could estimate the damages because no one can tell whether the negotiations would be successful or would fall through; or if successful, what the result would be. It seems to me that a contract to negotiate, like a contract to enter into a contract, is not a contract known to the law. … [A]n agreement to negotiate should be treated in the same way as an agreement to enter a contract.

The point here is that an agreement to negotiate is too uncertain because negotiations may or may not result in a contract. Consequently, if a party pulls out of negotiations, can the other really claim that it has lost out on a contract or the costs of negotiating? The normal course of negotiations (without any withdrawal) might not result in a contract anyway. For that reason, it cannot be said that one party's withdrawal was the *cause* of loss in any failed negotiation. The loss might have happened even if negotiations had continued. This is similar to when two people start dating. There is no guarantee that it will result in a serious relationship. And so, if one of them stops communicating, can the other really say that such 'ghosting' caused the loss of a serious relationship? After all, things may have fizzled out after a few dates anyway.

4.5.1 Agreements to Negotiate in Good Faith

Another uncertainty that might arise in an agreement to negotiate comes from the fact that in the normal course of a negotiation, each party has the freedom to withdraw. Such a withdrawal is one of a number of possible outcomes from entering into a negotiation. However, in theory, this freedom to withdraw could be limited if an obligation to negotiate 'in good faith' was to be imposed. The possibility of such an obligation being implied was rejected by the House of Lords in *Walford v Miles* [1992] 2 AC 128.

In *Walford v Miles*, the defendants (Mr and Mrs Miles) were selling their photo processing business. The appellants ('the Walfords,' who were brothers) were keen to buy the business and the parties entered an agreement to negotiate. Under this agreement, the Walfords agreed not to withdraw from negotiations. They also agreed to provide evidence from their bank to show they could pay the £2m asking price. In return, the seller (Miles) agreed to deal with the Walfords only, with a view to achieving the sale. This is known as a **lock-in agreement**. In addition, the seller agreed not to negotiate with other potential buyers or consider other offers (a **lock-out agreement**).

'lock-in' agreement
is one in which one party
agrees to only deal with
the other party.

However, the seller continued to negotiate with another party and eventually sold the business to that party. The Walfords then brought an action against the seller for breach of the contract to negotiate. In the action, Walford had claimed £1m. This was because they believed the business was worth £1m more than the asking price. On that basis, they believed the £1m reflected their lost bargain.

'lock-out' agreement
is one in which a party
agrees not to deal with
others.

The Walfords also claimed damages for misrepresentation. This was based on the statement made by Miles that they would not negotiate with anyone else being false. At first instance, the Walfords were awarded £700 for their expenses resulting from the misrepresentation.

➔ CROSS-REFERENCE
The law of
misrepresentation is
explained in Chapter 13.

On the agreement to actually negotiate (the 'lock in' agreement) the Walfords argued that there was an implied duty to negotiate 'in good faith'. This duty was then breached by the sellers because they did not have a *proper reason* for ending negotiations. The judgment of the House of Lords was delivered by Lord Ackner (with whom the other judges agreed).

GUIDED CASE READING 4.2
Walford v Miles [1992] 2 AC 128

When you read the extract of the judgment by Lord Ackner, try to identify:

- Why the duty of good faith was deemed too uncertain.
- Why a duty of faith conflicts with the interests of negotiating parties.

The reason why an agreement to negotiate, like an agreement to agree, is unenforceable, is simply because it lacks the necessary certainty. The same does not apply to an agreement to use best endeavours. This uncertainty is demonstrated in the instant case by the provision which it is said has to be implied in the agreement for the determination of the negotiations. How can a court be expected to decide whether, subjectively, a proper reason existed for the termination of negotiations? The answer suggested depends upon whether the negotiations have been determined 'in good faith'.

The problem for Lord Ackner is that it is impossible to decide what a 'proper reason' would be for ending negotiations. Such a decision would have to be based on an assessment of whether negotiations had been performed in good faith, but this was not an assessment a court could make.

However the concept of a duty to carry on negotiations in good faith is inherently repugnant to the adversarial position of the parties when involved in negotiations. Each party to the negotiations is entitled to pursue his (or her) own interest, so long as he avoids making misrepresentations. To advance that interest he must be entitled, if he thinks it appropriate, to threaten to withdraw from further negotiations or to withdraw in fact, in the hope that the opposite party may seek to reopen the negotiations by offering him improved terms. Counsel for the Walford's, of course, accepts that the agreement upon which he relies does not contain a duty to complete the negotiations. But that still leaves the vital question—how is a vendor ever to know that he is entitled to withdraw from further negotiations? How is the court to police such an 'agreement'? A duty to negotiate in good faith is as unworkable in practice as it is inherently inconsistent with the position of a negotiating party. It is here that the uncertainty lies. In my judgment, while negotiations are in existence either party is entitled to withdraw from those negotiations, at any time and for any reason. There can be thus no obligation to continue to negotiate until there is a 'proper reason' to withdraw. Accordingly, a bare agreement to negotiate has no legal content.

The first reason for this is because a successful negotiation will include the threat of withdrawal—something which is widely recognised and accepted. The parties are adversaries in this sense and there is no reason why they should be expected to look after each other's interests—certainly not above their own. The idea that they should have to act in good faith and only withdraw with proper reason is hence 'repugnant' to common practice. Another way of putting this is that objectively the parties' intentions must be to negotiate in their own interests, rather than in those of the other party.

The second reason is simply that of uncertainty. How does a contracting party know if a reason for withdrawing is a 'proper' one or not? In other words, how does it know if it is acting in good faith? And how can the court know, either?

For these two reasons, an agreement to negotiate can have no legal content. The only possible legal content it could have had was an implied duty to act in good faith, but this did not exist.

KEY POINTS

A duty to negotiate in good faith cannot be implied. The key reasons are that it would be inconsistent with the parties' intentions to act in their own self-interest and the lack of certainty about what 'good faith' might mean.

In the reasoning, Lord Ackner said that the duty could not be implied because parties intend to act in their own interest. The point here is that such an implied duty would not reflect the parties' apparent intentions. The same argument was made more recently by Teare J in *Shaker v Vistajet Group Holdings SA* [2012] EWHC 1329.

In addition, Lord Ackner explained that the duty of good faith was too uncertain to measure or define. It would be too difficult to say when someone has withdrawn for 'proper' reasons and when they have done so in breach of their duty. Back to the dating example, if two people agree to date and *try* to develop a serious relationship it is difficult to identify if they *tried* hard enough.

?! THINKING POINTS

Can you define an obligation to act 'in good faith'? Is it a duty to be honest? A duty to be open and reveal anything important? Is it a duty to be fair and proper and if so, at what point would it be breached?

In explaining the uncertainty of a duty to negotiate in good faith, it was observed that an obligation to use one's 'best endeavours' is not uncertain and can be enforced. This was indeed applied in *Jet2.com v Blackpool Airport Ltd* [2012] EWCA Civ 417. However, the obligation in that case related to how a term of the *contract* was to be performed. It was not an obligation to negotiate an agreement with one's 'best endeavours'.

Lord Ackner's statement about a good faith obligation being uncertain is often criticised. After all, many other civil law jurisdictions (like most of those in the EU) have developed a firm principle of good faith. However, English contract law is markedly different from those in civil law jurisdictions in several important respects, and the general view is that the lack of an implied duty to negotiate in good faith is simply one of them.

4.5.2 Where the Parties *Express* a Duty to Negotiate in Good Faith

In *Walford v Miles* it was clear that a duty of good faith could not be *implied*. It would be inconsistent with the parties' intention to act in their own self-interest and would be too difficult for courts to police. However, what if the parties actually include a term requiring them to negotiate in good faith? Surely then, the obligation reflects their intentions.

The issue was addressed in *Petromec Inc v Petroleo Brasileiro SA Pretrobas* [2005] EWCA Civ 891. Here, the effect of the good faith clause was not essential to the decision. However, Longmore LJ took the opportunity to provide some *obiter* comments. It was observed that, the good faith obligation would be enforceable because it was contained in an *existing* contract. In *Walford*, the agreement to negotiate was all 'subject to contract' (that is, the negotiations were all prior to the existence of a legal relationship, and hence were not a legal relationship in their own right), and the good faith obligation was not expressed, but only purportedly implied.

→ CROSS-REFERENCE
The effect of making agreements 'subject to contract' is explored at 4.6.2.2.

The parties in *Petromec* included an express term imposing a good faith obligation. On this Longmore LJ observed: 'It would be a strong thing to declare unenforceable a clause into which the parties have deliberately and expressly entered…' He went on to say the refusal to allow the term to a have a legal effect '…would be for the law deliberately to defeat the reasonable expectations of honest men'. The point he was making was that the rejection of the duty would have gone against the clear intentions of the parties. In other words, the reasoning in *Walford v Miles*—that the parties must have intended to negotiate in their own self-interest—was turned on its head because here there was an explicit term saying the opposite.

By accepting the existence of the expressed good faith obligation, the only remaining issue for the court was whether it could be enforced in practice. On the facts, it would have been possible to work out the loss caused by a breach of the duty. This was because the duty only applied to the negotiation of a particular known cost to one of the parties. Hence the loss was readily quantifiable. In contrast, the possible loss in *Walford* would have been unknown. After all, the negotiations may or may not have resulted in a contract.

Longmore LJ did acknowledge that the ending of negotiations in bad faith was a difficult concept to define precisely. However, it was felt that such a difficulty should not result in 'blanket unenforceability'. Instead, it was recognised that some forms of conduct would be a more obvious breach of this duty—for example, when a party makes fraudulent statements. If we consider a couple *trying* for a long-term relationship and how we might determine if they are acting in good faith, it would be difficult to work out precisely what they can expect of each other. However, lying and not turning up for dates might be obvious examples of not trying hard enough.

KEY POINTS

Where the parties expressly agree to negotiate in good faith, the courts will try to uphold that obligation where it is possible to do so.

4.5.3 Agreements *Not* to Negotiate with Other Parties

We have already looked at the legal position when parties agree to negotiate with each other. Such 'lock-in' agreements—preventing either party from withdrawing without a 'proper' reason—are not enforceable. But what about an agreement *not* to negotiate with *other* parties (a 'lock-out agreement')?

In *Walford*, the sellers did not just agree to negotiate with the Walfords. They also agreed to end negotiations with other parties and not consider any offers made by them. Such an agreement helps to manage the risks of negotiating. It means that a party will not contract with someone else during negotiations. It's like two people deciding to be exclusive and not date anyone else. It means there is a greater chance of a serious relationship.

In Lord Ackner's judgment in *Walford*, the enforceability of such a 'lock-out' agreement was explained. The first point was that there were 'good commercial reasons' for having such an agreement. On this reference was made to the costs of involved in preparing an offer or even in deciding to make one. Such an agreement helped to guard against the risks of the negotiations being undermined by another party.

The second point was the difference between lock-in and lock-out agreements. Lock-out agreements are not uncertain, as breach can be identified clearly. Such a breach will occur when a party negotiates or contracts with a third party. Identifying such a breach does not rely on the attribution of duty of good faith or a decision about whether a party's conduct was 'proper'.

Ultimately, however, the lock-out agreement in this case was not enforceable because there was no fixed time limit on it. Having a time limit allows the obligation to be measured and certain. This was determined by the Court of Appeal in *Pitt v PHH Asset Management Ltd* [1994] 1 WLR 327. In that case, a 'lock-out agreement', fixed for 14 days, was held to be enforceable.

4.6 Intention to Create Legal Relations

So far, we have looked at cases concerning agreements that are too vague or incomplete. From a practical perspective, they could be too uncertain to be enforced. In addition, the uncertainty could be taken to indicate that the parties did not intend to have a *legal* relationship at that point.

Even if an agreement is complete and certain, however, it still might not be enforceable. This is because of another requirement: it must appear that the parties *intended to enter legal relationship*. By 'legal' relationship, we mean that the parties expected their obligations to be enforceable in law, potentially in a court. As we would expect, this additional requirement of intention is assessed objectively and is based on an assessment of what the facts appear to indicate. However, the requirement is based on two presumptions which apply depending on the type of contract:

- The parties to a social or domestic agreement are *presumed* to have no intention to enter a legal relationship.

- The parties to a commercial agreement are *presumed* to have an intention to enter a legal relationship.

The use of these presumptions make this area of contract law fairly straightforward. But they are only a starting point. As with all presumptions, they can be rebutted based on the facts. As we shall see, it is possible to prove that a social or domestic agreement had the required intention. Likewise, it is possible to prove that a commercial agreement didn't have the required intention. Ultimately, the question of contractual intent is one of fact in every case.

4.6.1 Social and Domestic Agreements

Typically, 'social' and 'domestic' agreements are those made between family members, friends, and those with a personal relationship. It is fair to say that most 'social' agreements are never expected to be legally enforceable. If two friends or family members arrange to meet at the cinema, no one would think that the meeting was a legally enforceable obligation. But social agreements are not just those between friends and family. For example, consider two people that agree to meet using a dating website. They have never met. They may not have had a conversation (except the messages exchanged about meeting). They are not friends, but the social context is the same. It would be very strange if the law could step in to regulate such personal matters. Of course, at the other end of the spectrum there may be very serious promises (with very serious consequences) that are made between those with a personal relationship. For example, a sister might lend her brother a large sum of money to support his business. That's when the question of intention to enter legal relations becomes a real issue.

We have already referred to the presumption against the enforcement of social and domestic agreements. However, it is important to explore where this presumption came from and how it has been applied to different relationships.

4.6.1.1 Agreements between Spouses and Equivalent

Our starting point is *Balfour v Balfour* [1919] 2 KB 571, which is generally thought of as the modern statement on the law's approach to legal relations, although the case law on the subject goes back to the middle ages. The case concerned an agreement between a husband and wife. The husband was stationed abroad as a civil engineer and he took a period of leave to go to England with his wife. When he was due to return, his wife was advised by her doctor to stay in England because of her ill health. The husband then promised to pay his wife £30 a month while he was away. A few months later, they split up and, when the payments stopped, the wife sued the husband on the basis that they had an enforceable agreement. The Court of Appeal held that there was no contract. The main judgment was by Atkin LJ, and it is important to have a closer look at his reasoning.

GUIDED CASE READING 4.3
Balfour v Balfour [1919] 2 KB 571

When you read the extract of the judgment by Atkin LJ try to identify the reasons why domestic agreements are not generally contracts.

The defence to this action on the alleged contract is that the defendant, the husband, entered into no contract with his wife, and for the determination of that it is necessary to remember that there are agreements between parties which do not result in contracts within the meaning of that term in our law. The ordinary example is where two parties agree to take a walk together, or where there is an offer and an acceptance of hospitality. Nobody would suggest in ordinary circumstances that those agreements result in what we know as a contract, and one of the most usual forms of agreement which does not constitute a contract appears to me to be the arrangements which are made between husband and wife. It is quite common, and it is the natural and inevitable result of the relationship of husband and wife, that the two spouses should make arrangements between themselves—agreements such as are in dispute in this action—agreements for allowances, by which the husband agrees that he will pay to his wife a certain sum of money, per week, or per month, or per year, to cover either her own expenses or the necessary expenses of the household and of the children of the marriage, and in which the wife promises either expressly or impliedly to apply the allowance for the purpose for which it is given. To my mind those agreements, or many of them, do not result in contracts at all, and they do not result in contracts even though there may be what as between other parties would constitute consideration for the agreement … [a]nd it constantly happens, I think, that such arrangements made between husband and wife are arrangements in which there are mutual promises, or in which there is consideration … Nevertheless they are not contracts, and they are not contracts because the parties

> The judgment begins by setting out the obvious point that there are many arrangements made socially or domestically which are not legally enforceable simply because nobody expects them to be.

> This naturally extends, in Atkin LJ's view, to arrangements between a husband and wife concerning money matters—the nature of such arrangements is not contractual even though they concern the exchange of money, because nobody expects them to be enforceable. It is worth emphasising that to the modern eye this looks old-fashioned and might well be disputed; this is discussed further in this chapter.

did not intend that they should be attended by legal consequences. To my mind it would be of the worst possible example to hold that agreements such as this resulted in legal obligations which could be enforced in the Courts …

All I can say is that the small Courts of this country would have to be multiplied one hundredfold if these arrangements were held to result in legal obligations. They are not sued upon, not because the parties are reluctant to enforce their legal rights when the agreement is broken, but because the parties, in the inception of the arrangement, never intended that they should be sued upon. Agreements such as these are outside the realm of contracts altogether. The common law does not regulate the form of agreements between spouses. Their promises are not sealed with seals and sealing wax. The consideration that really obtains for them is that natural love and affection which counts for so little in these cold Courts … The only question in this case is whether or not this promise was of such a class or not.

> This reasoning is supplemented by two further reasons, one based in policy and the other in morality. First, Atkin LJ was worried that if such agreements were held to be enforceable it would result in a vast increase in litigation of disputes between husbands and wives—what is often referred to as a 'flood gates' argument. Second, for Atkin LJ there was something distasteful about domestic arrangements, made for love or affection, becoming subject to court rulings.

For the reasons given by my brethren it appears to me to be plainly established that the promise here was not intended by either party to be attended by legal consequences. I think the onus was upon the plaintiff, and the plaintiff has not established any contract. The parties were living together, the wife intending to return. The suggestion is that the husband bound himself to pay 30l. a month under all circumstances, and she bound herself to be satisfied with that sum under all circumstances, and, although she was in ill-health and alone in this country, that out of that sum she undertook to defray the whole of the medical expenses that might fall upon her, whatever might be the development of her illness, and in whatever expenses it might involve her. To my mind neither party contemplated such a result.

> He concludes that when the arrangement was made, neither party intended to be bound. The husband did not intend to be legally bound to give £30 per month to his wife, and the wife did not consider herself bound to use the money for her medical expenses. They came to an agreement out of love or affection, and hence did not think of themselves as having a contract. Therefore, they lacked the necessary intention to enter legal relations.

It is worth emphasising that Atkin LJ's judgment was the only one that was based on lack of intention to create legal relations. Duke LJ indicated that there was no consideration from the wife and Warrington LJ seemed to agree. Atkin's judgment required intention even if there was consideration.

?!   THINKING POINTS

It is fair that agreements like the one in *Balfour* are presumed to be unenforceable?

Balfour concerned a marriage made more than 100 years ago. Today, society is very different. Couples work and may agree to share the responsibility of paying the rent or mortgage. Should such arrangements be thought of in the same way? More importantly, should a husband or wife not be legally entitled to a portion of the other spouses' income if the husband or wife has sacrificed his or her own career for child raising purposes? And what about more minor arrangements among housemates about sharing the costs of food or co-workers in a car-pool agreeing to share the petrol costs?

The *Balfour* case is often cited as authority for the basis of the presumption against the enforcement of social domestic agreements. While it concerned a married couple, the reasoning is equally applicable to all personal relationships. The scope of the presumption was developed further in *Merritt v Merritt* [1970] 1 WLR 1211. It is a case that is often compared with *Balfour* because it was another agreement between a husband and wife.

In *Merritt v Merritt*, a husband left his wife and three children to live with another woman. He promised to pay his wife £40 per month which she would use towards the mortgage. He also promised that once the mortgage was fully paid, he would transfer the house to her. When the mortgage was paid, the husband refused to transfer the house to the wife. Here the Court of Appeal decided that the agreement was enforceable as a contract. The reasoning was explained by Lord Denning MR when he distinguished the case from cases like *Balfour v Balfour*:

> It is altogether different when the parties are not living in amity but are separated, or about to sepa-rate. They then bargain keenly. They do not rely on honourable understandings. They want everything cut and dried. It may safely be presumed that they intend to create legal relations.

The crucial difference between *Balfour* and *Merritt* is the status of the relationships at the time the agreements were made. Because Mr and Mrs Merritt made the agreement after they had separated, it meant there could be an intention to enter legal relations. The fact of separation at the time of the agreement rebutted the presumption against contracts between couples. When couples are about to separate or have separated, they often, as Lord Denning MR rightly pointed out, 'bargain keenly'. In contrast, in *Balfour*, the agreement was supposedly made when the couple were in a friendly relation-ship ('living in amity'). This meant that the presumption of a lack of intention to create legal relations could stand.

The fact that the Balfours split-up so soon after the agreement might of course suggest that things were not quite so amicable at the time the agreement was made. It is possible that a break-up was likely. This, along with the importance of the promise, may be the reason why Lord Upjohn in *Pettitt v Pettitt* [1970] AC 777 referred to *Balfour* and said:

> That case illustrates the well-known doctrine that in their ordinary day-to-day life spouses do not intend to contract in a legally binding sense with one another, though I am bound to confess that in my opinion the facts of that case stretched that doctrine to its limits.

This is as close as a judge will generally come to saying that he or she thinks a prior decision of such long standing as *Balfour v Balfour* was incorrect.

Even if a couple are no longer 'living in amity', an intention will not be found if the agreed obligation is too uncertain, for reasons which we have already explored. In *Merritt v Merritt*, Lord Denning MR made reference to *Gould v Gould* [1970] 1 QB 275. There, following separation, the husband promised £12 a week to the wife 'for as long as he could manage it'. According to Lord Denning MR, this would have been enforceable if it did not have such uncertain language. The uncertain language meant that the parties did not intend to create a legal relationship, even though they had separated. To put it another way, if it was intended to be enforceable, the parties would have used words that created a definite obligation.

One point is left to be added on the subject of contracts created in a marriage, and it concerns so-called 'pre-nuptial' or 'post-nuptial' agreements. This is an exception to the rule of thumb that when a couple is living in amity their agreements are not intended to create legal relationships. In *Radmancher v Granatino* [2010] UKSC 42, the majority of the Supreme Court delivered *obiter* com-ments indicating that pre-nuptial and post-nuptial agreements are contracts. A pre-nuptial agreement is one made by a couple before they marry. It concerns how they will divide their wealth and assets if they ever split up. They have been quite common among celebrities and very wealthy individuals in the US. A 'post-nuptial' agreement is the same but made after the wedding formalities. In *Radmancher* such agreements were viewed as having been made with the intention to be enforceable. However, the Supreme Court also made it clear that it did not really matter because courts can decide how things are divided and override such contracts using powers given to them by applicable legislation.

KEY POINTS

Ordinarily a social and domestic agreement is not legally binding. But if it is certain and shows a clear inten-tion to legally binding, then it should be a contract.

4.6.1.2 Parent and Child Agreements

We have seen that the presumption against domestic contracts was developed in the context of married couples. The principle was applied in the context of a parent and child in *Jones v Padavatton* [1969] 2 All ER 616. In this case, the mother promised to pay her 34-year-old daughter a monthly allowance. In return, the daughter was to leave her well-paid job in Washington DC and go to London to study to become a barrister. For reasons which will become clear, it is also important to point out that the mother and daughter were from Trinidad & Tobago. The agreement was in 1962. In 1964, while the daughter was studying in London, the agreement was changed. The mother bought a house for her daughter to live in rent free. And, instead of an allowance, the daughter could live off the rent paid by her lodgers. Five years after starting the course, the daughter had not completed it. She argued with the mother and then the mother took legal action to take the house. To defend the action, the daughter relied on the agreement she made with her mother. After all, the mother promised she could live there while studying. The key issue was whether there was a contract between the mother and daughter. If there was, then the mother would have been in breach by trying to eject her daughter from the house. The case reached the Court of Appeal, where it was decided that there was no contract. However, the judges adopted a different approach in their reasoning.

Fenton-Atkinson LJ explained that there could not have been an intention to enter legal relations because the agreement was uncertain. First, there was confusion over the allowance. When the original agreement was made, the mother promised 200 dollars but she had in mind British West Indian dollars (equivalent to £42 per month). The daughter expected 200 US dollars (equivalent to £70). When she was paid the smaller amount, she just accepted it. Not only was the amount uncertain, but the daughter never demanded the higher amount as something she was entitled to. That suggested the parties never viewed the agreement as a contract.

Secondly, the housing arrangement was uncertain. Nothing was said about how much of the house the daughter was to occupy. Nothing was said about how much of the rental income the daughter could keep. Also, nothing was said about what was to happen if the rental income was too low. Would the mother make up the difference?

In addition, the daughter's own evidence showed she did not expect a legal relationship. When the mother visited after bringing her action, the daughter refused for hours to let the mother in. She told the court that a 'normal mother doesn't sue her daughter'. Fenton-Atkinson LJ took this as an indication that the daughter never thought that the agreement would be enforceable in court. Instead, it indicated that the daughter treated the agreement as a simple family arrangement.

Dankwerts LJ viewed the agreement as a family arrangement and no different to *Balfour v Balfour*. His Lordship pointed out that the relationship between the parties was good right up until 1967.

Salmon LJ adopted a different approach. Reference was made to the heavy reliance placed on the mother's promise. After all, the daughter had given up a good job in Washington DC on the basis of her mother's financial support. Accordingly, the facts behind the initial agreement rebutted the presumption against domestic agreements. That meant there was a contract. However, nothing was said about how long the daughter had to complete her exams. Salmon LJ said that objectively, it might be implied that she had a reasonable time to complete the exams. But he then decided that the reasonable time must have expired after five years. On that basis, the daughter could not enforce the contract.

Based on the majority reasoning of Dankwerts LJ and Fenton-Atkinson LJ, the presumption had not been rebutted. There was no intention to enter legal relations on the facts, and the uncertainties in the agreement also indicated the lack of sufficient intention to create legal relations.

4.6.1.3 Social Agreements

Beyond agreements between family members, perhaps the best known case on a 'social' agreement is *Simpkins v Pays* [1955] 1 WLR 975. In this case Pays (a grandmother), her granddaughter and a lodger (S) regularly entered a Sunday newspaper fashion competition. On one occasion, they all contributed to the details of the entry but it was in the name of the defendant Pays. They had agreed that if they won they would split the winnings. When Pays received the £750 prize, she refused to split it, claiming the agreement was merely a domestic one. However, it was decided that the agreement was enforceable as a contract.

In his judgment, Sellers J made reference to the presumption against social and domestic agreements:

> It may well be there are many family associations where some sort of rough and ready statement is made which would not, in a proper estimate of the circumstances, establish a contract which was contemplated to have legal consequences, but I do not so find here. I think that in the present case there was a mutuality in the arrangement between the parties. It was not very formal, but certainly it was, in effect, agreed that every week the forecast should go in in the name of the defendant, and that if there was success, no matter who won, all should share equally. It seems to be the implication from, or the interpretation of, what was said that this was in the nature of a very informal syndicate so that they should all get the benefit of success. It would, also be wrong, I think, to say from what was arranged that, because the grand-daughter's forecast was the one which was successful of those submitted by the defendant, the plaintiff and the defendant should receive nothing.

Essentially, the commercial flavour of the agreement rebutted the presumption against social/domestic agreements. This case should be applicable whenever friends and family operate a lottery syndicate as long as it is clear that they agreed to share any winnings.

Another familiar social agreement is where workmates or colleagues agree to be part of a 'car – pool' or simply share the costs of driving to work. There have been cases where the courts have expressed opinions on the enforcement of such agreements. Two cases are commonly cited on this issue. The first is *Coward v Motor Insurers' Bureau* [1963] 1 QB 259. Here, a co-worker agreed to pay towards the costs of petrol in return for an occasional lift to work on his co-worker's motor bike. The two men were killed in an accident arising from the driver's negligence and the passenger's wife was awarded compensation from the driver's representatives. In order to claim the money from the driver's insurer, she was required to prove that there had been a contract between the two men (technically, that the bike had been used for 'hire or reward'). Sellers LJ in the Court of Appeal said that the court would be reluctant to recognise an intention to enter a legal relationship in a situation like this. He referred to uncertainties like holidays, shift changes and overtime as creating uncertainties, not to mention the fact that it was not a regular, daily arrangement but one which the parties merely entered into from time to time. On that basis it would be less likely that a legal relationship was intended.

The *Coward* case is often contrasted with the similar one of *Albert v Motor Insurers' Bureau* [1972] AC 301. There, Lord Cross acknowledged the possibility of such arrangements being legally enforceable. His Lordship said that ultimately, it depends on the facts and whether objectively it could be said that the parties intended a legal relationship.

 THINKING POINTS

Can you identify facts and circumstances that would help to indicate a legal relationship between co-workers sharing costs for a lift to work?

Because the outcome of a case on intention is based on a factual assessment, some decisions are not so clear-cut. A good example is *Hadley v Kemp* [1999] All ER (D) 450 which concerned one of the UK's most well-known bands of the 80's, Spandau Ballet. One of the band members, Gary Kemp, was the composer of the music and lyrics. Around 1981, he made an oral agreement to share the publishing income from Spandau Ballet's songs with the other band members. He paid them until 1988. After the band split, the action brought by the lead singer (Hadley) and the others was for the continued payment of the income. Park J rejected the claim. It was held that on the facts there was no intention for the oral agreement to be legally binding. According to the judge, at the time of the agreement, the band members had much more than a business relationship. They had been school friends and remained close in their band. Furthermore, they formed the band not just to make money but also because they 'loved what they were doing'.

On the facts, a different judge could have decided convincingly that the agreement was a contract. They did have a business relationship, because the band was of course operating commercially. Also, while the members were friends, it is not so hard to accept that the reason why the band members devoted so much to the band was because they would receive the publishing income. In addition, the payments were made consistently for seven years. That being said, if they had wished to be absolutely clear they could have simply had a formal agreement produced by a lawyer with a term expressly indicating that a legal relationship was intended.

4.6.2 Commercial Agreements

Agreements between businesses are presumed to be made with the intention to be legally binding. However, on rare occasions this presumption can be rebutted, on the basis of the facts or the terms of the agreement.

4.6.2.1 The Presumption of an Intention

Ordinarily, agreements between commercial parties are presumed to be made with an intention to enter a legal relationship. The reasons for this are obvious—when commercial parties enter into an agreement they naturally expect to be able to enforce their obligations against each other in a court where necessary. And it is difficult to rebut this presumption. The judicial statement that is often cited to support of this assertion is from *Edwards v Skyways Ltd* [1964] 1 WLR 349. There Megaw J stated:

> In the present case, the subject matter of the agreement is business relations, not social or domestic matters…I accept the propositions …that in a case of this nature the onus is on the party who asserts that no legal effect was intended, and the onus is a heavy one.

The presumption is not just confined to agreements between businesses. It applies equally to any business context, for example, when a business sells to a consumer or when a private sale takes place. In these non-domestic/social agreements, the presumption of a legal relationship is a strong one. It means that we do not see many cases where the intention is disputed in such agreements. When such cases do arise, it must mean that there is something in the facts that is different to an ordinary agreement. A good example is *Esso Petroleum Ltd v Commissioners of Customs & Excise* [1976] 1 WLR 1. This case addressed the status of a promotion where a free gift was promised in return for certain purchases. The actual purchases did not raise any issues but the free gift did.

In this case, Esso had a promotion consisting of a free football World Cup coin (each coin represented a player from the 1970 England squad) given when customers bought 4 gallons of petrol. This was not a case concerning a customer being refused a coin. There was no issue about the legal relationship of the petrol sale. Rather, the problem was that the Customs & Excise Commissioners believed that the coins were subject to tax, which Esso was liable to pay, because they were produced for 'general sale'. The House of Lords held that the coins were not produced for 'general sale' because they were not given in exchange for money directly. Instead, they were given in return for the customer entering into a contract to buy petrol. Technically, no money was being paid for the coins themselves.

Lord Russell and Viscount Dilhorne disagreed; in their opinion, the coins were just a gift. This was based on the fact that the coins did not have much value (Lord Russell likened the value to 3/16ths of a penny). Of course, that did not make a difference to the other judges. This means that a legal relationship should not be ruled out on the basis of how little something is worth.

GUIDED CASE READING 4.4
Esso Petroleum Ltd v Commissioners of Customs & Excise [1976] 1 WLR 1

When you read the extract of the judgment by Lord Simon try to identify:

- why there an intention to enter a legal relationship for the coins;
- the way the contract for the coins would have been formed.

I am, however, my Lords, not prepared to accept that the promotion material put out by Esso was not envisaged by them as creating legal relations between the garage proprietors who adopted it and the motorists who yielded to its blandishments. In the first place, Esso and the garage proprietors put the material out for their commercial advantage, and designed it to attract the custom of motorists. The whole transaction took place in a setting of business relations.

In the second place, it seems to me in general undesirable to allow a commercial promoter to claim that what he has done is a mere puff, not intended to create legal relations (cf *Carlill v Carbolic Smoke Ball Co*). The coins may have been themselves of little intrinsic value; but all the evidence suggests that Esso contemplated that they would be attractive to motorists and that there would be a large commercial advantage to themselves from the scheme, an advantage in which the garage proprietors also would share. Thirdly, I think that authority supports the view that legal relations were envisaged.

[Lord Simon then quoted judges from other cases that stated the presumption of a legal relationship in business matters and business relationships]

I respectfully agree. And I would venture to add that it begs the question to assert that no motorist who bought petrol in consequence of seeing the promotion material prominently displayed in the garage forecourt would be likely to bring an action in the county court if he were refused a coin. He might be a suburban Hampden who was not prepared to forego what he conceived to be his rights or to allow a tradesman to go back on his word.

Believing as I do that Esso envisaged a bargain of some sort between the garage proprietor and the motorist, I must try to analyse the transaction. The analysis that most appeals to me is one of the ways in which Lord Denning MR considered the case ([1975] 1 WLR 406 at 409), namely a collateral contract of the sort described by Lord Moulton in *Heilbut, Symons & Co v Buckleton* ([1913] AC 30 at 47, …):

'… there may be a contract the consideration for which is the making of some other contract. "If you will make such and such a contract I will give you one hundred pounds", is in every sense of the word a complete legal contract. It is collateral to the main contract …'

So here. The law happily matches the reality. The garage proprietor is saying, 'If you will buy four gallons of my petrol, I will give you one of these coins'. None of the reasons which have caused the law to consider advertising or display material as an invitation to treat, rather than an offer, applies here. What the garage proprietor says by his placards is in fact and in law an offer of consideration to the motorist to enter into a contract of sale of petrol. Of course, not every motorist will notice the placard, but nor will every potential offeree of many offers be necessarily conscious that they have been made. However, the motorist who does notice the placard, and in reliance thereon drives in and orders the petrol, is in law doing two things at the same time. First, he is accepting the offer of a coin if he buys four gallons of petrol. Secondly, he is himself offering to buy four gallons of petrol: this offer is accepted by the filling of his tank.

Lord Simon's first reason is that the purpose of the coin gift scheme was to attract motorists' custom—in other words, the overall context was a business one and hence there was a presumption that there was an intention to create legal relations.

The second reason at first glance seems similar to the first. What Lord Simon is making clear here is that while the coins were of little value, they did have an indirect commercial value in that they attracted customers. This applied both to Esso itself and also the individual operators of the various petrol stations involved in the scheme.

The third reason is that while it would be unlikely that a customer would sue to enforce his or her right to a coin if denied one, there would be nothing stopping a very assertive and demanding customer (a 'suburban Hampden') from doing so. This is because the average customer would clearly expect to be entitled to a coin on the basis of there being a promotional scheme (John Hampden was a rebel against Charles I who obstinately refused to give up what he considered to be his legal rights.)

So there was an intention to create legal relations—although ultimately, as we have seen, the court concluded that in the end the coins were not subject to tax because they were not for 'general sale'. Rather, the creation of a contract for the purchasing of petrol was itself the consideration for the contract under which the garage owner was bound to give the customer a coin. The coin was not exchanged for money but for the making of the main contract itself.

The approach adopted in *Esso* was applied by the Court of Appeal in *Bowerman v ABTA* [1996] in relation to a notice displayed in a travel agent store

→ CROSS-REFERENCE
For the facts of *Bowerman v ABTA* see 2.3.2.

 THINKING POINTS

Can you identify any differences between the promotion in *Carlill* and the one in the *Esso* case?

The *Esso Petroleum v Customs and Excise Commissioners* case is one example where on the facts the presumption for commercial relationships might have been rebutted (although ultimately it was not). We now turn to another example in a different context, which is when the agreement contains a term denying any legal relationship.

4.6.2.2 When the Commercial Agreement Has a Term to Deny a Legal Relationship

It is possible for a commercial agreement to rebut the presumption of legal relations using an express term. For example, in *Rose And Frank Co v Crompton Bros Ltd* [1925] AC 445, the agreement had a term stating that it was binding in 'honour' only.

Under the agreement, the claimant was the exclusive agent of Crompton for the sale of Crompton's goods in the US and Canada. So Crompton produced the goods and the (claimant) agent was the one who arranged the orders from buyers. The agreement had a special term that stated the agreement was not intended as a 'legal agreement'. It added that the parties 'honourably pledge themselves' and that it would be carried out with 'mutual loyalty and friendly co-operation'. This was the 'honour clause'. Crompton then terminated the agreement without the required notice. In addition, they refused to carry out orders already placed by the agent. The agent then sued for breach and the question was whether the agreement was legally enforceable.

The House of Lords decided that the agreement could not be treated as a contract because of the honour clause. The existence of this clause meant that the parties had not intended to enter a legal relationship. That meant that the seller, Crompton, was not under any legal obligation to accept orders placed by the agent. That agreement could be ended any time. However, the House of Lords made it clear that a legal relationship did exist for each order that was accepted. So once an order was placed by the agent and accepted by Crompton, there was a legal obligation to complete the order. This reasoning was based on the fact that without that subsidiary obligation, there would be no liability to pay for the goods and no enforceable rights for the buyers concerning the quality and description of the goods.

In commercial agreements, the presumption of a legal relationship is not rebutted easily. In *Edwards v Skyways* [1964] an employer was making employees redundant. As part of the process, they promised to make '*ex gratia*' payments (payments out of goodwill) to the employees being forced to leave. Later, they reneged on this promise on the basis that the payments were expressly made '*ex gratia*' and hence the promise had not been given with the intention to create legal relations. According to Megaw J, the wording used did not exclude the legal enforcement of the payment. Instead, it was simply identifying that there was no pre-existing obligation to make such payments. In other words, it was a payment that was not due under the existing employment contracts which the employees had with the employer. Instead, it was a payment on top of what was required under their existing contracts. But it was still a payment that was agreed with the required intention.

Edwards v Skyways illustrates that the outcome of any dispute on intention may be based on an interpretation of the terms of the agreement. The words used in *Rose and Frank* were clear enough to rebut the presumption of a legal relationship. In contrast, the words used in *Edwards v Skyways* were not sufficient.

The 'honour clause' used in *Rose and Frank* is just one type of term that could rebut the presumption of a legal relationship. An agreement could have the complete range of terms and be certain, but could say it is 'subject to contract' or 'subject to solicitor's advice'. The usual effect is that the agreement will not be legally enforceable because it shows the parties do not intend to contract at that stage (*Winn v Bull* (1877) 7 Ch D 29 and the Court of Appeal case of *Eccles v Bryant and Another* [1947] 2 All ER 865). Agreements 'subject to contract' are the usual practice in property sales like the sale of houses. It means that ordinarily, until the parties complete the exchange of ownership and money, either one can pull-out without a reason.

KEY POINTS

The presumption in commercial agreements can be rebutted by terms expressly stating that the agreement is not legally binding, or sometimes by language indicating that more needs to be done before a contract is formed.

Ultimately, whether there is an intention for a contract to exist is based on what the parties appeared to intend. A draft contract could expressly state that the agreement will be binding only when the parties sign. Ordinarily, that will show an intention to have a binding contract only when the document is signed. However, the circumstances might override that term where it appears that the parties intended for this to happen. This issue was the subject of the dispute in the leading case of *RTS Flexible Systems Ltd v Molkerei Alois Muller GmbH* [2010] UKSC 14. The parties planned to enter a contract on standard industry terms which included a term to the effect that the contract would not be binding until the parties signed. However, the parties did not sign and went ahead with performance. The claimant contractor was paid around 70% of the price from performance before a dispute arose, and then claimed the remaining amount due. On the existence of contracts, Lord Clarke stated:

> 45. The general principles are not in doubt. Whether there is a binding contract between the parties and, if so, upon what terms depends upon what they have agreed. It depends not upon their subjective state of mind, but upon a consideration of what was communicated between them by words or conduct, and whether that leads objectively to a conclusion that they intended to create legal relations and had agreed upon all the terms which they regarded or the law requires as essential for the formation of legally binding relations. Even if certain terms of economic or other significance to the parties have not been finalised, an objective appraisal of their words and conduct may lead to the conclusion that they did not intend agreement of such terms to be a precondition to a concluded and legally binding agreement.

This has become a key statement that we can expect to see in any case concerning disputes over the existence of a contract. It clearly highlights the importance of what the parties' intentions appear to be, based on the circumstances. Lord Clarke went on to observe that an agreement that is 'subject to contract' could be legally binding if the parties appear to agree to waive the requirement later. Whether they have done so depends on the circumstances, 'although the cases show that the court will not lightly so hold'. Hence the conduct of the parties might override their intention to wait for the agreement to be signed, but there needs to be a very strong argument for doing so. Lord Clarke added the following warning about the significance of performance:

> 47. …[I]n a case where a contract is being negotiated subject to contract and work begins before the formal contract is executed, it cannot be said that there will always or even usually be a contract on the terms that were agreed subject to contract. That would be too simplistic and dogmatic an approach. The court should not impose binding contracts on the parties which they have not reached. All will depend upon the circumstances…

Thus if an agreement requires the parties to sign and performance starts before they do so, it does not automatically mean they have a contract—though Lord Clarke did acknowledge that performance 'is plainly a very relevant factor pointing in that direction'. In the *RTS* case, it was held that the conduct of the parties and circumstances showed that they had waived the requirement of signing the agreement and so they already had a contract. A similar approach was adopted in *Anchor 2020 Ltd v Midas Construction Ltd* [2019] EWHC 435 (TCC). There Waksman J held that on the facts, the parties intended to have a contract after one of the parties signed, even though the draft contract required both of them to sign.

Another common example of commercial parties producing an agreement that is not a contract is the use of 'letters of intent'. Often for big projects to commence while the contract is finalised, parties may draft a 'letter of intent' or 'heads of agreement'. These outline obligations and are expected to result in a formal contract later. Such agreements could be unenforceable for uncertainty and classed as an agreement to agree. However, some could be capable of enforcement if they are detailed enough and as a matter of interpretation show an intention to enter legal relations at that stage.

In *ERDC Group v Brunel University* [2006] EWHC 687, Judge Humphrey Lloyd QC explained:

> Letters of intent come in all sorts of forms. Some are merely expressions of hope; others are firmer but make it clear that no legal consequences ensue; others presage a contract and may be tantamount to an agreement 'subject to contract'; others are contracts falling short of the full-blown contract that is contemplated; others are in reality that contract in all but name. There can therefore be no prior assumptions, such as looking to see if words such as 'letter of intent' have or have not been used. The phrase 'letter of intent' is not a term of art. Its meaning and effect depend on the circumstances of each case.

This indicates that when a document describes itself as a letter of intent or equivalent, it does not automatically mean that it will be treated as one. Based on the wording of the letters and the circumstances, the judge decided that the 'letters of intent' in this case were intended to be legally enforceable. On that basis, the documents resulted in a contract.

4.6.2.3 Where the Surrounding Facts Prevent an Intention to Enter a Legal Relationship

It is possible for an agreement between those in business to be made in circumstances that suggest there was no intention to enter a legal relationship. Such an agreement was the subject of *Blue v Ashley* [2017] EWHC 1928 (Comm) and it provides a useful example. It concerned an oral agreement that was made between a billionaire businessman (Ashley) who owned the company Sports Direct, and a former investment banker (Blue) who worked for Ashley as a consultant. They both had a meeting with three others who represented an investment bank. The meeting took place in a pub where they were all drinking alcohol. During a conversation, Ashley said he would pay Blue a bonus of £15m, if Blue managed to increase the share price of sports Direct from £4 to £8. Eventually, when the price increased to £8, Blue claimed the £15m bonus. Ashley refused to pay that figure and so Blue sued. Leggatt J examined the evidence based on the testimony of those present in the pub. It was held that the agreement was not a contract since there could not have been an intention to enter a legal relationship.

The reasoning was detailed and looked at a range of factors that were relevant to intention. These factors were based on the arguments presented and do not represent a legal test. However, it is useful to consider them, because they are an example of how surrounding circumstances might prevent a contract coming into existence between business people.

In the judgment, the first factor was the setting of the agreement. The men were in a pub and had consumed alcohol. Leggatt J observed that this on its own did not mean there was no intention to create a legal relationship. As authority, reference was made to a comment by Coulson J in *MacInnes v Gross* [2017] EWHC 46 (QB). That case featured a conversation in a restaurant and Coulson J stated that a contract can be made anywhere. However, in *Blue v Ashley*, Leggatt J felt that an evening drinking in the pub was an 'unlikely setting' to discuss a bonus when both parties were there to represent Ashley's company in a meeting with others.

The second factor was the purpose of the occasion. The meeting was taking place for business reasons in that it was designed to build a commercial relationship with the three representatives of the investment bank. It was not therefore a social or domestic arrangement, but it was not for the purpose of discussing Blue's pay.

The third factor was the nature and tone of the conversation. It was not consistent with an intention to make a serious offer. The men had been discussing football and then the conversation moved on to how wealthy Ashley would be if the share price went up. The talk of a bonus for Blue was started by one of the bankers who was feeling mischievous. According to Leggatt J, a skilled business person would not be serious about such a bonus based on a figure made up by others who had no knowledge of what Blue was paid.

A fourth factor was a lack of commercial sense. On the face of it, paying for the share price to increase seems like a sound deal. After all, Ashley would have made £1.6 bn from the increase. However, it was more likely that if Ashely intended to give a bonus, it would have been based on a figure that factored-in the £250,000 a year Blue was earning from Ashley. In other words, ten times his salary (£2.5m) would have been an incentive. A bonus of £15m looked like throwing money away. Ordinarily a court will not rescue somebody from a 'bad bargain', but the outlandish figure led Leggatt J to accept that what Ashley said was just banter to emphasise his wealth to the bankers.

A fifth factor was Blue's role in the agreement. The idea that one person could double the share price was deemed 'fanciful' and that no human had such powers.

The sixth factor was the vagueness of the offer. Nothing was said about how long the price had to be at £8; there was no discussion of what Blue was supposed to do in order to get the price up.

Finally, the perceptions of the others at the pub (the investment bankers) were considered. They all saw what was said as some kind of joke. The evidence of Blue's perception based on the conversations that followed also suggested he did not take it seriously until much later. In his conclusion, Leggatt J stated:

> They all thought it was a joke. The fact that Mr Blue has since convinced himself that the offer was a serious one, and that a legally binding agreement was made, shows only that the human capacity for wishful thinking knows few bounds.

Based on these seven factors, no reasonable person would think that a contact was intended and so the agreement was not one. It was a conversation between business people and there was a commercial context. However, based on the circumstances there was no intention for the agreement to be legally binding.

 THINKING POINTS

Could *Blue v Ashley* be explained as a social agreement in which Blue had to prove the legal relationship?

CHAPTER SUMMARY

- To be legally enforceable as a contract the agreement must be *sufficiently* certain and show an intention to enter a legal relationship.
- Agreements can be uncertain because they are vague, or because they are incomplete. This can indicate there was no intention to enter a legal relationship.

- The courts must not rewrite the agreement. They must simply interpret it.
- Previous dealings or performance could mean that an agreement is sufficiently certain, but will not always do so.
- Meaningless terms can be ignored, but an incomplete agreement could be seen as a mere *agreement to agree*.
- If an agreement is incomplete the court may decide that the missing terms are implied, and this is more likely if there has been performance.
- A gap in an incomplete agreement can be filled if the parties have provided a mechanism for doing so, or if the terms can be construed so as to do so.
- An agreement to negotiate (a lock-in agreement) will not be enforceable as a contract. It is not possible to imply an obligation to negotiate in good faith.
- Where the parties *express* a duty to negotiate in good faith it might be possible to enforce it.
- Agreements *not* to negotiate with other parties (lock-out agreements) can be enforceable.
- The parties to a social or domestic agreement are *presumed* to have no intention to enter a legal relationship, but it is possible to rebut this presumption.
- Agreements between businesses are presumed to be made with the intention to be legally binding, but the facts, the interpretation of the terms, or the surrounding circumstances could mean there was no such intention.

KEY CASES

- ☐ *Hillas & Co Ltd v Arcos Ltd* [1932] **All ER Rep 494**—shows how the circumstances can be used to work out what a vague term was intended to mean.
- ☐ *Scammell and Nephew Ltd v Ouston* [1941] **AC 251**—shows that an essential term which is too vague can result in an agreement being found not to have been a contract.
- ☐ *Nicolene Ltd v Simmonds* [1953] **1 QB 543**—provides authority for the removal of meaningless terms that are not essential.
- ☐ *May and Butcher Ltd v R* [1934] **2 KB 17n**—is authority for the effect of an agreement being incomplete, such that it is simply an agreement to agree.
- ☐ *Wells v Devani* [2019] **UKSC 4**—shows how an incomplete or uncertain agreement could be construed to fill in the gaps based on what a reasonable person would have understood the agreement to be.
- ☐ *Foley v Classique Coaches Ltd* [1934] **2 KB 1**—shows that incomplete agreements can be enforceable where they are performed, especially where there is a mechanism provided in the agreement to fill in the gaps.
- ☐ *Walford v Miles* [1992] **1 AC 128**—is authority for lock-in agreements not being enforceable, but lock-out agreements being effective.
- ☐ *Petromec Inc v Petroleo Brasileiro SA Pretrobas* [2005] **EWCA Civ 891** (Longmore LJ)—provides authority for the possibility of enforcing an express duty to negotiate in good faith.
- ☐ *Balfour v Balfour* [1919] **2 KB 571**—represents the modern statement on the intention requirement and the general presumption for social/domestic agreements, including those between spouses.
- ☐ *Merritt v Merritt* [1970] **1 WLR 1211**—provides an example of the presumption between spouses being rebutted.
- ☐ *Jones v Padavatton* [1969] **2 All ER 616**—provides an example of the presumption being applied to a parent/child relationship.
- ☐ *Simpkins v Pays* [1955] **1 WLR 975**—provides an example of the presumption in a social agreement being rebutted.

☐ *Esso Petroleum Ltd v Commissioners of Customs & Excise* [1976] 1 WLR 1—provides authority for the intention to create legal relations being presumed in business and consumer agreements.

☐ *Rose And Frank Co v Crompton Bros Ltd* [1925] AC 445—represents authority for the use of a term in an agreement rebutting the presumption of an intention to enter a legal relationship.

QUESTIONS

1. Dave and Ahmed have been in a long-term relationship for ten years and rent a house together. Dave is the tenant on the rental agreement but Ahmed has always paid towards the rent. Their relationship started to fall apart when Ahmed decided to accept a temporary job as an architect in Bulgaria. To stop the arguing, Ahmed agreed to pay all of Dave's rent while he was away as long as Dave continued to stay in the property and did not move. Months after Ahmed moved to Bulgaria, he met someone else and stopped the making the rental payments for Dave. Can Dave enforce the agreement for the rent to be paid?

2. Evaluate the law relating to agreements used to facilitate negotiations. Should a duty to negotiate in good faith never be implied?

3. Sabrina owns a noodle bar. She enters an agreement with MJH Designs under which they will decorate Sabrina's premises and extend the kitchen area. They leave out the price and timescale in order for them to be worked out later, because Sabrina needs the work to start immediately. Is there a contract between Sabrina and MJH?

4. Describe the extent to which business agreements are presumed to be made with an intention to be legally binding.

For answer guidance to these questions please visit the online resources at www.oup.com/uk/naidoo1e/, where you will also find multiple choice questions to check your understanding of key concepts.

FURTHER READING

Hedley, 'Keeping contract in its place: *Balfour v Balfour* and the enforceability of informal agreements' (1985) 5 OJLS 391.
This is very detailed assessment of domestic agreements. It criticises the concept of the intention to enter a legal relationship as not reflecting the real basis of the decisions.

Leggett, 'Negotiation in good faith: adapting to changing circumstances in contracts and English contract law–Jill Poole Memorial Lecture, Aston University: 19 October 2018' JBL [2019], 2, 104.
This is an approachable and insightful lecture by Leggett LJ concerning aspects of uncertainty and agreements to negotiate in good faith.

Peel, 'Agreements to Negotiate in Good Faith' in Burrows and E Peel (eds), Contract Formation and Parties (2010) OUP at 37.
This provides an excellent assessment and critique of *Walford v Miles*, and provides alternative suggestions.

Consideration and Promissory Estoppel

5

LEARNING OBJECTIVES

By the end of this chapter you should be able to:

- understand what is required for the consideration requirement to be met in different circumstances;
- analyse the cases to reveal how a strict application of consideration can be barrier to reflecting the parties' intentions;
- evaluate the current position on the extent to which a practical benefit from the performance of a contractual duty can be good consideration;
- analyse the development and scope of promissory estoppel as an exception to the consideration rule.

INTRODUCTION

We saw in Chapter 4 that for an agreement to be legally enforceable, there must an intention to enter a legal relationship. This is one of two requirements for an agreement to be legally enforceable. The other requirement is called consideration, and it has a very long history. It is generally required to form a contract, unless the contract is of a certain type called a deed (which is a particularly formal agreement which we need not investigate further beyond the description in 1.1). In its simplest form, consideration is often described as being something of value that is given (or promised) by each party in exchange for the other party's promise or performance. Disputes concerning consideration usually begin by one party claiming that the other is in breach of their contract. The other party then argues that no consideration had been given in return for what they promised to do, and therefore, the agreement is not enforceable.

In a case concerning consideration courts will typically focus on the obligations to be enforced, and then work out if something of value was given (or promised) in return for the performance of those obligations. We will see that sometimes, a strict application of the consideration requirement is a barrier to reflecting the parties' intentions. For that reason, the courts have developed a more relaxed approach in certain circumstances. There is also a limited exception to the requirement for consideration, which is known as promissory estoppel. This is also an important concept which this chapter will explain.

5.1 What is 'Consideration'?

While consideration has been defined in a number of cases, the definition approved by Lord Dunedin in *Dunlop Pneumatic Tyre Co. Ltd v Selfridge & Co. Ltd* [1915] AC 847 is often cited:

> My Lords, I am content to adopt from a work of Sir Frederick Pollock, to which I have often been under obligation, the following words as to consideration: "An act or forbearance of one party, or

the promise thereof, is the price for which the promise of the other is bought, and the promise thus given for value is enforceable" (Pollock on Contracts, 8th ed., p. 175).

This definition is often paraphrased to the effect that consideration is 'the price for the promise'. The idea is that something of value is being offered or given in exchange for the promise made by the other party. The value is described as an act of doing something, or forbearance (not doing something that one has a right to do).

A familiar example is a simple sale of goods. If you offer to buy a pizza for the price listed and a seller accepts, then an agreement exists. Here, you are promising to pay for the pizza. In return, the seller is promising to give you the pizza. In such circumstances, you have promised something of value (the money) in return for the seller's promise. The seller has promised something of value (the pizza) in return for your promise of payment. The result is that both promises are legally enforceable.

In contrast, imagine a chef who, out of kindness, simply offers to give you a pizza and you accept. There is an agreement, but is it legally enforceable? The seller has promised the pizza but you have not promised anything of value in return. Your failure to provide consideration means that the seller's promise will not be enforceable. For a contract to exist in English law there has to be an *exchange* between the parties. If there is nothing of value being provided by one of the parties, then there has been no exchange and the agreement is not enforceable.

KEY POINTS

Generally, promises on their own are not enforceable. They must be 'bought' with something of value (consideration) in order to be enforceable.

5.2 Consideration Does Not Have to Directly Benefit the Promisor

price of the promise
When discussing a particular promise, the party that made the promise is the 'promisor'. The party to whom the promise was made is the 'promisee'.

Consideration is simply the **price of the promise** (i.e. something of value done in return for the promise made). But the action or forbearance which is 'of value' does not have to benefit the promisor. All that is required is that it is requested by him or her. If that is established, the law is satisfied that there was a genuine exchange. To explain, a traditional definition of consideration is useful. It is from Lush J in *Currie* v *Misa* (1875) LR 10 Ex 153 where he observed:

> A valuable consideration, in the sense of the law, may consist either in some right, interest, profit, or benefit accruing to one party, or some forbearance, detriment, loss, or responsibility, given, suffered or undertaken by the other.

So consideration can be either a benefit to the promisor or a disbenefit to the promisee. Both types

→ CROSS-REFERENCE
For the facts of *Carlill* see 2.3.2.

of consideration were present, for example, in *Carlill* v *Carbolic Smokeball Co.* The Court of Appeal acknowledged that the company received the benefit of increased sales by making the advert. In addition, it also noted that Mrs Carlill provided separate consideration in the form of a detriment—the inconvenience of using the smoke ball product as prescribed.

But the forbearance or detriment should be at the request of the promisor. Only then can it be said that there has been an *exchange* by the parties. For example, the advert in *Carlill* stated that £100 would be given to anyone that contracted the flu after taking the time to use the smoke ball as prescribed. Essentially, the detriment of using the smoke ball had been requested by the advert in return for reward if the flu was contracted.

→ CROSS-REFERENCE
For the facts of *Jones v Padavatton* see 4.6.1.2.

The requirement of such a request by the promisor can be illustrated by comparing *Combe v Combe* [1951] 2 KB 215 with *Jones v Padavatton* [1969]. *Combe v Combe* concerned a couple going through a divorce. During the process, the husband promised to pay his wife £100 a year. The wife then chose to not apply to the Divorce Court for maintenance payments (a forbearance of something to which she would be entitled ordinarily). However, the husband's promise did not impliedly or expressly request that the wife forbear from applying to the court. The absence of a request for such forbearance was the main reason why the Court of Appeal agreed that there was no consideration from the wife in exchange for the husband's promise. In contrast, consider *Jones v Padavatton*. By giving up her job in Washington DC, and moving to England to study, the daughter experienced a detriment in relying on the mother's promise of payment. This was done in response to the mother's request in exchange for the promise of an allowance. In other words, it was the price of the promise. As a result, this detriment would have been good consideration. For that reason, the question for the Court of Appeal in that case was whether there had been an intention to enter a legal relationship.

KEY POINTS

Promisee detriment or forbearance will be good consideration only if it was at the request of the promisor.

5.3 Conditional Gifts

It should be emphasised that any request from a promisor must be for the promisee to *actually do something* or *not do something*. In such circumstances, there is an exchange between the parties. In contrast, if the request does not *require* the promisee to do (or not do) something, there will be no consideration from the promisee. The promise, will simply be a gift or at best, a *conditional gift*. Either way, the promise would not be enforceable.

A good example of a promise as a gift is *Re Cory* (1912) 29 TLR 18 (Ch). In this case a YMCA was raising money to build a new hall. It needed to raise £150,000, but had only raised £85,000. At this stage the YMCA did not commit itself to building the hall. They wanted to make sure they could meet their target of £150,000 first, before committing to the build. Cory promised £1050 to the YMCA for the build, and then YMCA subsequently entered into a contract with a construction firm to build the hall. They then claimed the money from Cory's estate when he died, arguing that they had entered into the contract for the build on the basis of being induced to do so by Cory's promise. It was held that the promise of the money was not enforceable because the YMCA had not promised to actually do anything in return for it; it was simply a contribution towards something they were already planning. All Cory did was promise money, but with a condition that it would be used for a particular purpose (the building of the hall)—a different matter from promising money in return for a particular action (or forbearance) So, rather than result in an enforceable promise, the court said there was just a conditional gift and there was no entitlement to the money.

5.4 Past Consideration

The term 'past consideration' is used to describe something of value that was provided *before* the relevant promise was made. Such past consideration will not be good consideration to enforce the *later* promise. This is for the obvious reason that it was not given in exchange for the later promise by definition, because it was provided before that promise was made. Instead, the consideration must be *in return for* or *in response to* the promise. The principle is well established and was one of the reasons why a promise was not enforceable in the early case of *Harford and Gardiner's Case* (1587) 2 Leo. 30. However, it was not until *Eastwood v Kenyon* (1840) 11 Ad & E 438 (QB) and *Roscorla v Thomas* [1842] 3 QB 234 that the past consideration rule was stated and applied authoritatively, in both cases by Lord Denman CJ. The latter of these cases provides a simple example of the rule in action. A sale of a horse had been arranged (the consideration from one party being the horse and from the other being the price). After the sale was agreed, the seller then gave a warranty (i.e. the promise) to the buyer that the horse was 'free from vice'. Once the horse was in the possession of the buyer, it turned out to be ill-tempered and vicious. The buyer sued the seller on the basis that his warranty had been breached. But the court held that there had been no consideration for that promise. Any consideration given supporting the contract had already been exchanged before the subsequent warranty was made. It was therefore not enforceable. Lord Denman CJ summarised the principle succinctly as being that 'the promise must be coextensive with the consideration'.

A more modern example of the past consideration rule in action is the case of *Re McArdle* [1951] Ch 669. Here, Montague McArdle and his wife Marjorie, lived in a house owned by the estate of Montague's father. Marjorie spent £488 pounds decorating and improving the value of the house. Montague then approached his three brothers and his sister with a document addressed to Marjorie. It stated that 'IN CONSIDERATION' for the decorating, they would repay Marjorie £488 from the sale of their father's estate once they inherited it. This document was signed by Montague, his brothers and his sister. When Marjorie was not paid after Montague's father died, she brought an action to enforce the promises made. The Court of Appeal acknowledged that the decorating was something of value. However, it had been done *before* the promises were made by her husband's brothers and sister and so it had not been done in exchange for their promises. On that basis, the decorating was not good consideration. Instead, the act of decorating was simply gratuitous—a free act, as shown by Figure 5.1.

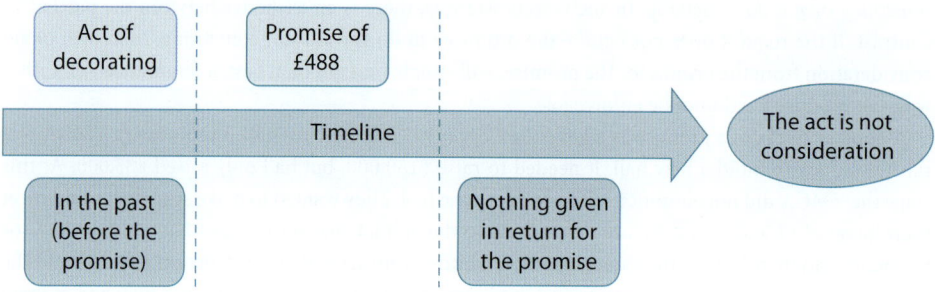

Figure 5.1
Why the decorating in Re McArdle [1951] Ch 669 was 'past consideration'

?!   THINKING POINTS

▪ Based on the facts of *Re McArdle*, can you identify any (non-consideration) reason why in principle the promises of the brothers and sister *should* have been enforceable?
▪ What could have been done to provide consideration for the promises in question?

5.4.1 Past Consideration and Previous Requests

While Lord Denman CJ firmly established the past consideration rule in *Eastwood v Kenyon*, his Lordship also referred to an exception. This exception is where the past act had been requested by the promisor. In support of this exception, the old case of *Lampleigh v Braithwaite* (1615) Hob. 105 was cited as authority.

In that case, Braithwaite had killed a man. He then asked Lampleigh to get him a pardon from the King, and Lampleigh then acted on this request. It involved making journeys at his own expense, and he eventually obtained a pardon for Braithwaite. After this had happened, Braithwaite promised to pay Lampleigh £100 for his efforts (a very significant amount of cash at that time). When Braithwaite failed to pay, Lampleigh sued him. The court observed that Lampleigh's consideration was not past consideration because it was provided in response to a request by the promisor, Braithwaite. The report of *Lampleigh v Braithwaite* provides the following comment by Hobart CJ:

> . . .a meer voluntary courtesie will not have a consideration to uphold an assumpsit. But if that courtesie were moved by a suit or request of the party that gives the **assumpsit**, it will bind; for the promise, though it follows, yet it is not naked, but couples itself with the suit before, and the merits of the party procured by that suit, which is the difference.

assumpsit
was a form of court action, and can also mean a promise.

The statement was made over 400 years ago so the language is archaic, but the principle is simple. It refers to the general rule that a voluntary act (or 'voluntary courtesie') cannot be good consideration. It goes on to say, however, that if the act is done in response to a request (or 'suit'), then the benefit of the act ('the merits of the party procured by that suit') will be good consideration. The promise linked with the request is not lacking consideration, or 'naked'.

It seems that a previous request could be viewed as an implied promise of payment. On that basis, when the request was acted upon, the act was good consideration for the implied promise. The later promise of £100 simply clarified the amount to be paid under the earlier implied promise. That is how the statement by Hobart CJ has been interpreted and applied in later cases like *Re Casey's Patents* [1892] 1 Ch 104, and it is illustrated by Figure 5.2.

In *Re Casey's Patents*, Casey had been managing certain patents for the claimants. The claimants later wrote to Casey saying 'in consideration of your [past] services as practical manager' they would give him a 1/3 share in the patents. These past services had been performed at the request of the claimant. The question was whether the promise of a 1/3 share in the patents was enforceable. The Court of Appeal decided that the past services provided were good consideration to enforce the promise of a share. On this point, Bowen LJ started with a reference to the past consideration rule and the need to try to look beyond it:

> Even if it were true, as some scientific students of law believe, that a past service cannot support a future promise, you must look at the document and see if the promise cannot receive a proper effect in some other way.

The statement then explains how an implied promise of payment (which can be in the form of a request) makes the difference:

> Now, the fact of a past service raises an implication that at the time it was rendered it was to be paid for, and, if it was a service which was to be paid for, when you get in the subsequent document a promise to pay, that promise may be treated either as an admission which evidences or as a positive bargain which fixes the amount of that reasonable remuneration on the faith of which the service was originally rendered.

Looking at the facts in context, it was implied at the time the services were performed, that they would be paid for (the 'remuneration') with a reasonable sum. In response, the services were performed and that was good consideration for that sum. The later promise of a share in the patents was evidence of the amount of the reasonable sum intended.

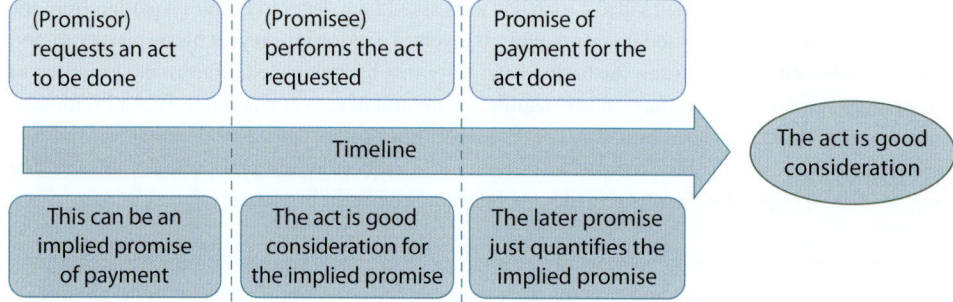

Figure 5.2
How a previous request can get around the past consideration rule

In *Pao On v Lau Yiu Long* [1980] AC 614, Lord Scarman addressed the issue of past consideration and previous requests and helpfully set out some requirements:

> The act must have been at the promisor's request: the parties must have understood that the act was to be remunerated either by a payment or the conferment of some other benefit: and payment, or the conferment of a benefit, must have been legally enforceable had it been promised in advance

So generally, where an act is followed by a promise, the act is past consideration and does not make the promise enforceable. Lord Scarman clarifies that the past act could be good consideration for the future promise if:

- The act was requested by the party making the promise;
- There was an understanding that there would be some of payment in return for the act;
- The promise was of a kind that would ordinarily be legally enforceable.

These authorities make clear that a request (for an act to be done) must result in an *understanding of payment*. If there is such an understanding, the request can be seen as an implied promise of payment. Whether such an understanding of payment arose from the request is as always assessed objectively.

?! THINKING POINTS

What do you think is relevant when seeking to identify if there appears to be an understanding of payment?

In the *Pao On* case, Lord Scarman added:

> It seems clear, therefore, that where the whole agreement is couched in terms of commercial exchange, the courts . . . may be more willing to find that the request carries with it an implied promise to pay.

The point is that in a commercial context it is much easier to establish there was an implied understanding of payment. Likewise, the same can be said where a consumer requests a service from a business. Such an understanding is more likely in a commercial transaction because (objectively) the parties wouldn't expect anything for free. The same can said for parties that are usually paid for their services. An example

KEY POINTS

Where an act is done and then payment is promised, the act can be good consideration if it was in response to a previous request which implied payment would be made.

would be when a window cleaner is approached to clean some windows. Objectively, the window cleaner would expect to do the job for payment and a promisor would know that. So, from an objective perspective, it can be said that payment was implied by the promisor asking for the windows to be cleaned.

5.5 How Much Value Is Needed for Consideration?

So far, we have referred to consideration as being something of value given in return for a promise. But how much value is needed? Does it have to reflect what the promise is worth? Consider a shop that agrees to sell the latest iPhone for £1. Can the shop argue later that its promise to sell is not enforceable because the £1 promised is not enough consideration for the phone worth over £1000? The answer is a simple one. Consideration does not have to represent the market value of what is promised. Instead, consideration needs to be of some value recognised by the law and, of course, £1 is something of value. This distinction between *some value* and *market value* is always made using the legal terms adequate consideration and sufficient consideration. The rule is that consideration must be sufficient, and need not be adequate.

adequate consideration means market value or equivalent (what something is really worth).

It is well established that consideration does not have to be adequate (of market value). All that matters is that a promise is bought with sufficient consideration (*some* value). The point was neatly confirmed in *Mountford v Scott* [1975] Ch 258. This case concerned an option to purchase property worth £10,000 which was secured in return for consideration of £1. The Court of Appeal held that the agreement was enforceable. Cairns LJ explained the denial of consideration

sufficient consideration means some value that the law will recognise.

> . . . [w]ould have been contrary to a mass of English authority to the effect that anything of value, however small the value, is sufficient consideration to support a contract at law

It means it is possible to buy the iPhone for a £1, as long as the seller freely agreed to sell at that price.

5.5.1 The Reasoning behind the Sufficiency Rule

The traditional reasoning is simply that the law will not interfere with a bad bargain freely made. So, if a seller wants to enter into a bad deal and sell something like a £1000 phone for £1, the courts will not interfere. However, the decision by the seller must be freely made. It cannot be the result of duress (e.g. a threat to harm the seller) or a result of fraud. The principle on sufficiency is so well established that it is common for lawyers to advise clients to give or promise £1 as consideration in order to make sure a contract will be enforceable where there would be otherwise be any doubt. This is known as nominal consideration. It is not much, but it is all that is needed for a promise to be enforceable.

➔ CROSS-REFERENCE
For the law relating contracts formed using duress see Chapter 14.]

nominal consideration is used to describe a very small amount that is symbolic or a 'token gesture'.

5.5.2 When Is Value 'Sufficient'?

The fact that consideration has to be of some value that is *recognised by the law* raises an important question: How far will the law go in recognising something's value as being 'sufficient'? In other words, when is something given in return for a promise not considered of any value? *Chappell v Nestle* [1960] AC 87 is useful here. In this case, Chappell owned the copyright for a song called 'Rockin' Shoes'. Nestlé arranged for records of the music to be made and offered them to the public for 1s 6d *plus three wrappers* from their 6d chocolate bars. Under the copyright legislation at the time, if you made recordings of an existing piece of music you had to pay a 6¼% royalty to the copyright holder of 'the ordinary retail selling price'. Nestlé paid royalties to Chappell based on 1s 6d being paid by customers, but Chappell challenged this figure and claimed their copyright had been infringed on the basis that there was no 'ordinary retail selling price'. This was because the wrappers were part of the consideration for the record and hence the transaction was not an 'ordinary retail' one at all. The question for the House of Lords was therefore whether the wrappers were part of the consideration which the customer provided for the record, along with the 1s 6d. By a majority of 3 to 2, the House of Lords held that the wrappers were part of the consideration. It is useful read the relevant majority reasoning by Lord Reid and Lord Somervell. The following is an extract from the relevant part of Lord Reid's judgment:

> It seems to me clear that the main intention of the offer was to induce people interested in this kind of music to buy (or perhaps get others to buy) chocolate which otherwise would not have been bought. It is, of course, true that some wrappers might come from the chocolate which had already been bought or from chocolate which would have been bought without the offer, but that does not seem to me to alter the case. Where there is a large number of transactions - the notice mentions 30,000 records - I do not think we should simply consider an isolated case where it would be impossible to say whether there had been a direct benefit from the acquisition of the wrappers or not.
>
> The requirement that wrappers should be sent was of great importance to the Nestlé Co.; there would have been no point in their simply offering records for 1s. 6d. each. It seems to me quite unrealistic to divorce the buying of the chocolate from the supplying of the records. It is a perfectly good contract if a person accepts an offer to supply goods if he (a) does something of value to the supplier and (b) pays money: the consideration is both (a) and (b). There may have been cases where the acquisition of the wrappers conferred no direct benefit on the Nestlé Co., but there must have been many cases where it did. I do not see why the possibility that in some cases the acquisition of the wrappers did not directly benefit the Nestlé Co. should require us to exclude from consideration the cases where it did. And even where there was no direct benefit from the acquisition of the wrappers there may have been an indirect benefit by way of advertisement.

We can see from Lord Reid's reasoning that the wrappers represented sales (actual sales or potential sales from increased publicity) and that was the point of the promotion. Accordingly, the retail price of the record was not just the 1s 6d sent in to Nestlé, it was also the amount the customer paid for the chocolate. The fact that some of the wrappers might have been from purchases before the promotion did not justify ignoring the many that would have resulted from the promotion. In any case, Nestlé would either benefit directly (from the chocolate sales aimed at securing a record), or indirectly (from the increased sales from the publicity generated). So, while the actual wrappers had no real value Nestlé as a physical item, they represented sales which were clearly of value to them.

We can now turn the relevant extract of Lord Somervell's judgment which represents a wider approach:

> I think they are part of the consideration. They are so described in the offer. "They," the wrappers, "will help you to get smash hit recordings." They are so described in the record itself—"all you have to do to get such new record is to send three wrappers from Nestlé's 6d. milk chocolate bars, together with postal order for 1s. 6d." This is not conclusive but, however described, they are, in my view, in law part of the consideration. It is said that when received, the wrappers are of no value to Nestlé. This I would have thought irrelevant. A contracting party can stipulate for what consideration he chooses. A peppercorn does not cease to be good consideration if it is established that the promisee does not like pepper and will throw away the corn. As the whole object of selling the record, if it was a sale, was to increase the sales of chocolate, it seems to me wrong-not to treat the stipulated evidence of such sales as part of the consideration. For these reasons I would allow the appeal.

Like Lord Reid, Lord Somerville agreed that the wrappers represented consideration because they represented purchases. But Lord Somerville also stated that the wrappers were sufficient consideration because Nestlé asked for them and that technically, they were of some value even if nominal. This was the point he was making by referring to a peppercorn as good consideration. A peppercorn is worth very little, but it is still good consideration if that is what the promisor has asked for in return.

The approach in *Chappell v Nestlé* means that almost anything can be construed as consideration in the right context—even chocolate bar wrappers. But there are limits to what things the courts will recognise as having value. As far back as *Harford and Gardiner's Case* (1587) 2 Leon 30, it was said that a promise of 'love and affection' or friendship was not enough to constitute consideration. This was developed further in *White v Bluett* (1853) 23 LJ Ex 36. In this case, a son had borrowed money from his father. This loan was formalised by the son giving his father a promissory note (a signed note promising to repay the money borrowed). When the father died, the executors used the note to sue the son for the outstanding debt. The son argued that his father had promised to cancel the debt. This promise was in return for the son no longer complaining to his father about his father's plans to divide his estate when he died. The question was whether the son provided consideration in return for the father's promise to cancel the debt. The son had promised to stop complaining to his father. His argument was that since he had a right to complain he was agreeing to deprive himself of something he was entitled to do, and that was something of value sufficient to count as being consideration for the promise to cancel the debt. This was rejected by the court as pushing the notion of value to the point of absurdity. The decisions in *White v Bluett* and *Harford v Gardiner* indicate that there are limits to what the courts will recognise as having value. But it is also worth bearing in mind that in both those cases the purported promises were made in social or domestic contexts, and a modern court may well have decided that there was no intention to create legal relations in either of them. In other words, it may be that the courts in *White v Bluett* and *Harford v Gardiner* were using the mechanism of consideration to avoid giving effect to social agreements, rather than the more modern method, which is to deploy the doctrine of intention to create legal relations.

KEY POINTS

Consideration just has to be of 'some value' rather than equivalent market value.

5.6 Sufficiency: Performance of an Existing Legal Duty

We have seen already that consideration must be of some value to be sufficient. But what if the act is something that the promisee was under a legal obligation to perform anyway? By performing such an obligation, the promisee is simply doing what they had to do notwithstanding the promise from the promisor. The question we need to consider here is whether such performance is of value and therefore sufficient consideration to enforce a promise. After all, if you have to do something anyway due to a legal obligation, are you really providing anything of value in promising to do it for the promisor? You are simply promising to perform an act which you were going to have to do already. We will start with the traditional rule.

5.6.1 The Traditional Rule on the Performance of an Existing Legal Duty

The traditional rule is that the performance of (or a promise to perform) an already-existing legal obligation is not sufficient consideration. This approach is represented by *Collins v Godefroy* (1831) 1 B & Ad 950. Here Godefroy was involved in a civil action. To help support his case, Godefroy had Collins **subpoenaed** by the court to give evidence. This meant that Collins was under a public law obligation to attend and give evidence. The relevant issue was that Godefroy had also promised Collins payment of one guinea a day if he gave evidence accordingly. Having not been paid, Collins brought an action to recover the payment that had been promised. This claim failed and the reason was stated clearly by Lord Tenterden CJ:

subpoena
is a legal document that requires someone to appear in court.

> If it be a duty imposed by law upon a party regularly subpoenaed, to attend from time to time to give his evidence, then a promise to give him any remuneration for loss of time incurred in such attendance is a promise without consideration.

The principle was then applied:

> We think that such a duty is imposed by law; and on consideration. . . of the cases which have been decided on this subject, we are all of opinion that a party cannot maintain an action for compensation for loss of time in attending a trial as a witness.

The promise of payment was hence not enforceable because Collins did not provide consideration in return for it. All Collins did was perform a legal duty—something he was under a legal obligation to do anyway. Such an act was of no value (he would have had to do it without payment, so he was providing nothing in exchange for the promise of money) and was therefore not sufficient consideration.

KEY POINTS

The performance of (or promise to perform) a legal duty is not sufficient consideration.

5.6.2 The Traditional Approach: Performance *beyond* the Existing Legal Duty

What if a promisee has done or (promised to do) *more* than what is required by an existing legal obligation? In such circumstances, the courts have found the existence of sufficient consideration. The case of *Glasbrook Bros Ltd v Glamorgan CC* [1925] AC 270 is a useful illustration. Here, during a miners' strike, a colliery requested a police presence. However, the police felt that it was only necessary to have a mobile force ready to attend the mine if trouble broke out. In response, the colliery agreed to pay the police to provide a force of 70 officers to be stationed on the site. The colliery did not pay and, when sued, it argued that the police had simply performed their existing legal duty, which was to protect the public and private property. On that basis, there was no consideration by the police to enforce the promise of payment. By a majority of 3:2 the House of Lords held that the promise of payment was enforceable.

It was agreed that there would have been no consideration if the police had simply performed their duty to protect the public. That meant two steps needed to be taken. The first was about identifying the legal duty of the police and the second was determining whether the police had gone beyond it.

First, the court held that the police had the freedom to assess the situation and decide what measures were needed to protect the public. In other words, it was for the police to decide what the scope of their legal duty was. It is not for the courts to decide what is needed, as long as the decision by the police has not been made irrationally.

The second step followed on from identifying the duty. Since the police had decided that only a mobile guard was needed, doing so represented their legal duty. That meant providing the stationary guard at the site went beyond their legal duty. By going beyond their legal duty, the police had provided something of value and therefore, sufficient consideration for the promise of payment.

KEY POINTS

If performance (or the promise to perform) goes beyond what is required for the legal duty, then it will be good consideration.

5.6.3 The Limits of the Traditional Approach

The traditional rule on the performance of (or the promise to perform) an existing legal duty is clear from the cases described. However, a strict application of the rule can sometimes lead to unfair or unjust results. For that reason, there are instances of judges going out of their way to find that an existing legal duty has been exceeded in order to find that there has been consideration. In doing so, the relevant judgments serve to highlight the limits of the traditional approach to consideration. In addition, they help to provide a basis for a less restrictive approach to develop.

A useful illustration is the case of *Ward v Byham* [1956] 1 WLR 496 which concerned a legal duty arising from the National Assistance Act 1948. Under section 42, an unmarried mother had a legal duty to 'maintain' her child. The case concerned an agreement between the unmarried parents of a child called Carol. When the parents split up, the father wrote to the mother promising to let her keep the child and also to pay the mother £1 a week. This payment was on the condition that the child was 'well looked after and happy' and that the child was allowed to decide for herself who to live with. The child went to live with the mother and the father paid £1 a week. The payments continued for seven months but stopped when the mother married someone else. She then sued to enforce the promise of £1 a week. In response, the father argued that there had been no consideration for his promise and that the mother had simply performed her existing legal duty under the Act.

All three judges in the Court of Appeal agreed that the promise of payment was enforceable. However, they used different reasoning to come to the same decision. The following majority reasoning was delivered by Morris LJ (with whom Parker LJ agreed):

> [Counsel for the father] submits that there was a duty on the mother to support the child; that no affiliation proceedings were in prospect or were contemplated; and that the effect of the arrangement that followed the letter was that the father was merely agreeing to pay a bounty to the mother. . .the terms of the letter negative those submissions. . .
>
> It seems to me,. . . that the father was saying, in effect: Irrespective of what may be the strict legal position, what I am asking is that you shall prove that Carol will be well looked after and happy, and also that you must agree that Carol is to be allowed to decide for herself whether or not she wishes to come and live with you. If those conditions were fulfilled the father was agreeable to pay. Upon those terms, which in fact became operative, the father agreed to pay £1 a week. In my judgment, there was ample consideration there to be found for his promise, which I think was binding.

Morris LJ's reasoning is straightforward. The father had argued that the mother was merely performing her legal duty and his promise of money had therefore been a 'bounty', meaning it was gratuitous. But the promise had been to keep Carol well looked-after and happy, and to give her the choice of where to live. Since neither of these things were duties arising from the Act, they were outside of the scope of the mother's existing legal duty. Hence there was consideration for the promise of payment.

By relying on the traditional approach, the majority had to draw a fine and strained distinction between 'maintaining' the child and keeping the child 'happy and well looked after'. The former was the duty under the Act. The latter was the promise which the mother had made to the father. If they meant the same thing there would be no consideration for the promise of money, because the mother would just have been promising to perform her legal duty. It was therefore necessary to insist on them being different things. This appears artificial. Worse, it appears to be inconsistent with cases like *White v Bluett*. In *White v Bluett*, not boring someone with complaints was held to have no value, yet according to the majority in *Ward v Byham*, keeping someone happy was of value. It is difficult to see any meaningful difference between keeping someone happy and not boring someone with complaints (i.e. making them unhappy). However, it was the only way to find the existence of consideration using the traditional approach.

We can contrast the reasoning of the majority with the following (minority) reasoning by Denning LJ:

> I approach the case, therefore, on the footing that the mother, in looking after the child, is only doing what she is legally bound to do. Even so, I think that there was sufficient consideration to support the promise. I have always thought that a promise to perform an existing duty, or the performance of it, should be regarded as good consideration, because it is a benefit to the person to whom it is given. Take this very case. It is as much a benefit for the father to have the child looked after by the mother as by a neighbour. If he gets the benefit for which he stipulated, he ought to honour his promise; and he ought not to avoid it by saying that the mother was herself under a duty to maintain the child.

We can see that the minority reasoning by Denning LJ did not adopt the traditional approach. He made it clear that the mother had simply performed her legal duty, but for Denning LJ this did not rule out there being consideration to make the promise binding. Performance of the existing duty of the mother was beneficial to the father and so it was sufficient consideration for the promise for money. Essentially, the father did not have to make the promise of £1 a week, but he chose to do so. He must therefore have seen a benefit to himself in doing so, like having the mother look after the child rather than somebody else, such as a neighbour. Therefore, he was getting something of value, by definition.

Denning LJ's approach challenged the traditional requirement of consideration. It was developed further in Denning LJ's later judgment in *Williams v Williams* [1957] 1 WLR 148.

In this case, a wife left her husband (while remaining married) and at the time, that meant she had no right to financial support from the husband. Instead, she was under a duty to maintain herself. However, the couple signed an agreement under which the husband promised to pay £1, 10s a week. In return, the wife agreed to use the money to maintain herself. She also agreed not to pledge her husband's credit (i.e. not to obtain things on credit in her husband's name, something that was common practice at the time). When the husband stopped paying the agreed sum, the wife sued for the money owed. In response, the husband argued that the wife had provided no consideration because she had a duty to maintain herself and had no legal right to use his name to obtain things on credit. The Court of Appeal decided in favour of the wife on the basis that she had provided consideration.

The majority (Hodson LJ and Morris LJ) said that the wife's legal right to maintenance by her husband was only suspended when they separated. She could offer to return, and if the husband refused to have her back then she would have been entitled to financial assistance from him. So, in return for the husband's promise of payment, she was setting aside her *potential* legal right to be maintained by him. He was therefore benefiting, and hence there was consideration for his promise of money. Denning LJ agreed, but his reasoning was more far-ranging.

His Lordship made it clear that the promisee (the wife) had not gone beyond her own legal duty in return for the promise of money. However, consideration arose from the fact that the husband would have benefited from her performance. If the wife had not made her promise, she might have applied for benefits or used her husband's credit. This would have caused him anxiety and inconvenience, because it would have resulted in inquiries by the National Assistance Board (who dealt with the provision of what we now call 'benefits') or by traders from whom she had bought items on his credit. In other words, in promising her money in return for her maintaining herself, the husband was benefiting in the sense that he was avoiding a lot of trouble. There was therefore consideration for his promise—he was getting something of value. Denning LJ was, in other words, taking a wider and more subjective approach to the meaning of 'value': if a contracting party had promised something, he or she had likely done so for a good reason—i.e. because there was a benefit in it. Since there was a benefit, he or she was getting something of 'value' from the promise, and therefore there was consideration for it making it binding.

Denning LJ's approach was not followed in the other judgments at the time, but his reasoning in *Ward v Byham* and *Williams v Williams* proved influential and, as we shall see, clearly foreshadowed recent developments.

5.7 Performance of an Existing Contractual Obligation Owed to the Promisor

Our earlier discussion concerns the performance of existing legal duties arising from the common law or legislation. We now turn to the performance of existing *contractual* duties—that is, where the parties already have a contract and one party promises to do something more.

5.7.1 The Traditional Rule

The case of *Stilk v Myrick* (1809) 2 Camp 317 is authority for the traditional approach in the context of contractual obligations. Here the claimant was one of 12 crewman on a ship. Under his contract, he would be paid £5 a month for sailing to the Baltic and back again, doing anything necessary on the voyage 'under all emergencies'. When the ship arrived at its port in the Baltic, two of the crew deserted. The ship's master promised to divide the wages of the deserters with the remaining crew in return for them sailing back. On their return, no extra payment was made and so an action was brought. It was held that the promise of extra payment was not enforceable.

The reasoning of the judgment by Lord Ellenborough was based on the absence of consideration from the crew. They were under a contractual duty to do what was needed 'under all emergencies'. The absence of a few crewman was such an emergency. So, in return for the promise of extra wages, all the crew had done was what they were under a contractual obligation to do already. More importantly, the promisor, the master, simply received the performance that he was already entitled to receive *from* the promisee. According to the court, this meant that no consideration was provided. It was acknowledged that if the crew had done more than their contractual duty then there would have been consideration. An example of such consideration being provided is the later case of *Hartley v Ponsonby* (1857) 7 E & B 872.

The facts of *Hartley* were very similar to those in *Stilk* but with one key difference—over half of the crew had deserted (19 out of 36). The ship had sailed from Liverpool to Australia and were contracted to then sail elsewhere if necessary before returning to Liverpool after three years. The desertions took place on arrival in Australia. The master of the ship then issued a written promise to the remaining crewmen of £40 extra if they continued from Australia to Bombay. When the extra money was not paid, the core question was whether the promise to pay was enforceable. Here it was held that the crew were never expected to sail in such dangerous conditions resulting from so many missing crewmen. It was also the case that most of the deserters had been the ablest seamen, and those left were largely inexperienced sailors. Consequently, in agreeing to carry on with the voyage, the remaining crew did more than their contractual duty. On that basis, the crew had provided good consideration to enforce the promise of payment. The difference of course between this case and *Stilk* is that in *Stilk* only two out of 12 crewmen had deserted, and the contract had specifically mentioned 'emergencies'.

5.7.2 The Practical Significance of the Traditional Rule

The traditional rule from *Stilk* v *Myrick* has been approved in cases such as *North Ocean Shipping* v *Hyundai Construction, The Atlantic Baron* [1979] QB 705, though we will see in 5.9 that its application was subsequently refined.

In practical terms, it is a rule that would be relevant when parties agree to change their contract. Such a change is described as a 'variation' of the contract, and is quite common for commercial parties that enter long-term contracts. Circumstances change and then require alterations to the contract. It might be that costs have increased and so one party promises to pay more and then the other agrees. Later, following a dispute, the question for the court is whether the promised variation is enforceable. That is when the rule in *Stilk* would be applied. Often, it would mean that the contract variation was not enforceable because in return, the promisee had simply performed their existing contractual duty. The criticism of the rule is that it often appears to be inconsistent with the parties' intentions. If both the parties seem to have clearly intended that one should, for example, pay more, then why should the court not enforce that promise?

One possible way to avoid the traditional rule would be to simply agree to end the existing contract. Then, the parties could enter a new contract with the new terms. This approach of ending the agreement and starting another was approved by the Court of Appeal in *Compagnie Noga D'Importation et D'Exportation v Abacha (No4)* [2003] EWCA Civ 1100. In practice, however, parties often won't know to end the contract and start another (and if they did, they would know about other ways of providing good consideration.) Moreover, even if they knew to end the contract, the parties might regard that option as being too risky. After all, once a contract is ended, there is nothing to stop one of the parties moving on to a contract with someone else.

KEY POINTS

▪ The traditional rule is that the performance of an existing contractual duty (i.e. doing what the promisee has contracted to do anyway) is not sufficient consideration to enforce a promise.

▪ If, in return for the promise, the promisee goes beyond their existing contractual duty (i.e. doing more than what they have to do) then there will be sufficient consideration.

5.8 Performance of an Existing Contractual Duty Owed to a Third Party

We have seen that under the traditional rule in *Stilk v Myrick*, the performance of a contract by one party is not good consideration to enforce an *additional* promise made by the other party. The party making the additional promise (the promisor) already has a contract with the promisee. In return for the additional promise, the promisee is simply performing what was required under that existing contract. From the perspective of the promisee, they are simply doing what they had to do anyway. From the perspective of the promisor, they are simply receiving the performance that they were entitled to *from that* promisee already.

The promisor's perspective is important and is the basis of a traditional exception: the performance of (or the promise to perform) an existing contractual duty owed to a third party being good consideration for a promise by *another* party. It is useful to consider an example.

An oven producer called (A) has a contract with a restaurant (C) to deliver a new oven within three days for £2000. Then, to make sure it happens, a corporate customer of the restaurant (B) promises to pay (A) £100 to deliver the oven to the restaurant within three days and A agrees. Let us focus on the relationship between the oven producer (A) and the corporate customer (B). B has made a promise of payment, and in return, A is to deliver the oven to the restaurant (C). The problem is that by delivering the oven, A is simply performing an existing contractual duty owed to the restaurant (who is a third party for the purposes of the relationship between A and B). On that basis, could the corporate customer (B) argue that the oven producer (A) did not provide consideration to make the promise of £100 enforceable? After all, (A) is just performing an existing contractual duty (albeit owed to (C)). This is where the traditional exception applies. The performance of an existing contractual duty owed to a third party (the restaurant (C)) is sufficient consideration to enforce a promise made by another party (the corporate customer, (B)), as illustrated by Figure 5.3.

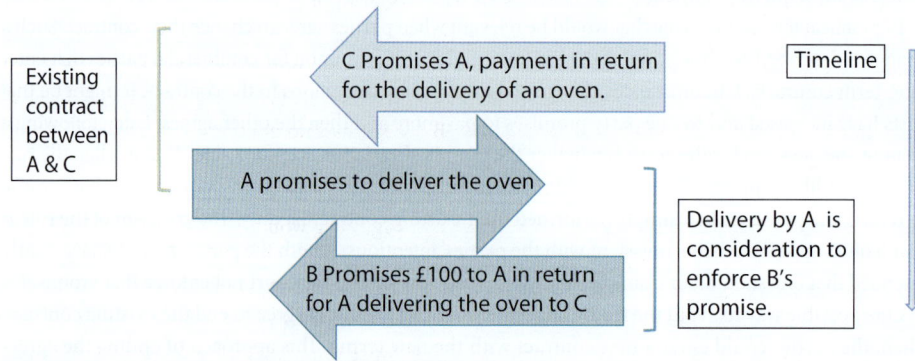

Figure 5.3
Consideration from the performance of a duty owed to a third party

The case law tells us why performance of an existing duty to a third party is of value and therefore, sufficient consideration. By A agreeing to deliver the oven, A has given the promisor (B) an enforceable contractual right for the delivery to take place. That right is enforceable against A and it is a contractual right that did not exist before. That is the key difference between this third party context and the ordinary contractual duty context from *Stilk v Myrick*. There, the promisor received performance that he was entitled to *from* the promisee already. Here, the promisor has received performance that the promisor was not originally entitled to *from* the promisee.

There are two early examples of this type of case on contractual duties owed to a third party. The first is *(Lancelot) Shadwell v (Cayley) Shadwell and Another* (1860) 9 CB (NS) 159. Here an uncle sent a letter to his nephew. In this letter he said he was glad to hear about the nephew's intended marriage to Ellen Nicholl and he recalled that he had promised to assist the nephew 'at starting'. To that end, the uncle promised to pay his nephew an income of £150 a year. This payment was to continue for the rest of the uncle's life unless the nephew's annual income as a barrister reached 600 guineas. When the uncle died, the nephew sued the estate for the arrears (money owed) from not being paid in full. At the time, being engaged to be married was a legally binding contract. The question was whether the nephew provided good consideration to enforce the uncle's promise of payment. All the nephew did was promise to get married to Ellen. However, the nephew already had a contractual duty to Ellen (the third party) to get married. Erle CJ (with whom Keating J agreed) held that the promise by the uncle was enforceable. This was on the basis that the nephew provided consideration by marrying Ellen in return. The uncle was gaining a fresh enforceable right against the nephew in the promise of payment, ensuring that the marriage contract would be performed. Byles J in the minority disagreed on the basis that all the nephew did was perform an existing contractual duty—he already had a marriage contract with Ellen, so he was just promising to do what he was already bound to. All three judges agreed that the uncle had to have requested the marriage to benefit from the promise. The majority inferred the request from the promise itself and the surrounding circumstances.

An early example of a commercial case involving the performance of a contractual duty owed to a third party is *Scotson v Pegg* (1861) 6 H & N 295. Here Scotson had a cargo of coal on board a ship. Pegg promised to unload the cargo at a rate of forty-nine tons per day. In return, Scotson agreed to deliver the coal to Pegg, but suffered losses because Pegg did not unload at the rate promised and caused a delay of five days. Scotson then brought an action against Pegg based on Pegg's promise. To do so, it had to be shown that Scotson provided consideration for Peggs promise to unload at the rate stated. Pegg argued that by delivering the coal to be unloaded, Scotson simply performed a contractual duty owed to another (a third) party. This was based on the fact that before Pegg's promise, Scotson already had a contract with another party (the third party). Under this contract, Scotson had to deliver the coal to the other party or where ever Scotson was told to deliver. The third party had already instructed Scotson to deliver to Pegg. It meant that by allowing Pegg to unload, Scotson was simply performing a contractual duty (owed to a third party).

It was held that this performance was still good consideration to enforce the promise made by Pegg. Pegg's promise (and agreement with Scotson) gave Pegg a benefit. This was because it gave Pegg an enforceable right over Scotson. If Scotson had decided not to deliver coal, Pegg would have had an action against Scotson for non-delivery. Of course, Scotson already had a contractual obligation (with a third party) to deliver to Pegg. But Pegg had no enforceable rights under that contract, since he was not a party to it. In the lead judgment, Martin B observed that ordinarily, Scotson would not have delivered if the third party went bankrupt and did not pay the contract price to Scotson. But following the promise made by Pegg, Pegg would have an enforceable right to that delivery.

While *Scotson v Pegg* is an old case, it was used as authority by the Privy Council in *New Zealand Shipping Co Ltd v A.M. Satterthwaite & Co Ltd, The Eurymedon* [1975] AC 154. In this case, a shipper had a contract with a carrier. Under this contract, the shipper promised to exempt the carrier from liability for damage to the cargo. This exemption also applied to parties employed by the carrier. The carrier contracted with stevedores to unload the cargo. Following some damage to the cargo,

→ CROSS-REFERENCE

For the law relating to the general rule that only parties to a contract can enforce them see Chapter 12 on third party rights.

the stevedores wanted to enforce the exemption of liability promised by the shipper to the carrier (so that they would not have to pay compensation). The question was whether the stevedores had provided consideration for the promise of an exemption of liability. It was argued that there was no consideration because all the stevedores did was what they had to do under their contract with the carrier. On this point Lord Wilberforce observed:

> An agreement to do an act which the promisor is under an existing obligation to a third party to do, may quite well amount to valid consideration and does so in the present case: the promisee obtains the benefit of a direct obligation which he can enforce. This proposition is illustrated and supported by *Scotson v. Pegg* (1861) 6 H. & N. 295 which their Lordships consider to be good law.

Ultimately, therefore, the stevedores had provided consideration allowing them to benefit from the exemption of liability promised by the shipper to the carrier, because in return the shipper was getting an enforceable right against the stevedores to unload the cargo. This passage was then cited with approval by Lord Scarman in the lead judgment of the Privy Council in *Pao On v Lau Yiu Long* [1980] AC 614. This means that the traditional principle from early cases like *Scotson v Pegg* is well now established.

KEY POINTS

The promise to perform an existing contractual duty owed to a third party is good consideration.

5.9 Performance of a Contractual Duty Owed to the Promisor: The Modern Approach

Stilk v Myrick represents the traditional approach to the performance (or promise to perform) of a contractual duty owed to the *promisor*. Such performance is not sufficient consideration to enforce a promise. This is not just because the promisee was simply doing what it had to do anyway. From the perspective of the promisor, they simply receive the performance that they were contractually entitled to receive *from* the promisee anyway. The traditional view was that in such circumstances, there was no extra value going to the promisor. This traditional position continued until the Court of Appeal case of *Williams v Roffey Bros & Nicholls (Contractors) Ltd* [1990] 2 WLR 1153. This case represents a very significant development and it resulted in a major limitation to the principle from *Stilk v Myrick*.

Williams v Roffey concerned an agreement to change the terms of a contract between commercial parties. Roffey had contracted to refurbish a block of 27 flats for a local council. Under this contract, if Roffey failed to complete the work on time, they would be subject to a time penalty clause to the council—meaning in effect they would get much less money for the job overall. To assist, Roffey sub-contracted with Williams for the carpentry work. Williams was to be paid £20,000 in instalments. After some of the work had been completed and Williams had been paid £16,200, Williams encountered financial difficulties. This was mainly a result of Williams underestimating the cost of the work to be done and a failure to supervise his workers adequately. Worried that the carpentry would not be completed, Roffey promised to change their contract. Under this variation, Williams would be paid an extra £10,300. This was to be paid at a rate of £575 as each flat was completed. In return, Williams promised to complete the work *as agreed* under the original contract. Williams completed eight flats but was only paid £1,500. As a result, Williams refused to continue and left. In response, Roffey brought in other carpenters to complete the work. Williams then sued Roffey for a proportion of the extra money that was promised to reflect the eight completed flats. Williams also claimed for a proportion of payment outstanding from the original contract.

Roffey argued that Williams had simply promised to perform an existing contractual duty. After all, in response to the promise of extra money, Williams had promised to complete the work *as agreed* under the original contract. On that basis, Roffey argued there was no consideration for their promise to change the terms and pay the extra money.

The trial judge decided in favour of Williams and then Roffey appealed to the Court of Appeal. The Court of Appeal agreed that Roffey's promise of extra money was enforceable. To reach this conclusion, the Court of Appeal refined the long-standing rule from *Stilk*. In doing so, it was held that Williams' promise to perform his contractual duty gave Roffey a *practical benefit*. That practical benefit was good consideration to enforce Roffey's promise of extra money. The most obvious benefit was the fact that Williams' continued performance would have enabled Roffey to avoid the time penalty clause for late completion. However, we will see from the judgments that there is more to this concept of practical benefit.

GUIDED CASE READING 5.1
Williams v Roffey Bros & Nicholls (Contractors) Ltd [1990] 2 WLR 1153

When you read the extracts of the following judgments, try to identify:

- how the judges interpreted the basis for the established rule from *Stilk* v *Myrick*;
- what the Lord Justices identify as a practical benefit (and therefore sufficient consideration) to Roffey.

We will start with the extract of the judgment by Glidewell LJ:

In his address to us, [Counsel for Roffey] outlined the benefits to his clients, the defendants, which arose from their agreement to pay the additional £10,300 as: (i) seeking to ensure that the plaintiff continued work and did not stop in breach of the subcontract; (ii) avoiding the penalty for delay; and (iii) avoiding the trouble and expense of engaging other people to complete the carpentry work.

However, [Counsel for Roffey] submits that, though his clients may have derived, or hoped to derive, practical benefits from their agreement to pay the 'bonus,' they derived no benefit in law, since the plaintiff was promising to do no more than he was already bound to do by his subcontract, i.e. continue with the carpentry work and complete it on time. Thus there was no consideration for the agreement. [Counsel for Roffey] relies on the principle of law which, traditionally, is based on the decision in *Stilk v. Myrick* (1809) . . .

[The decision and reasoning of *Stilk v Myrick* was addressed]

. . . In *North Ocean Shipping Co. Ltd. v. Hyundai Construction Co. Ltd.* [1979] Q.B. 705, Mocatta J. regarded the general principle of the decision in *Stilk v. Myrick*, as still being good law. He referred to two earlier decisions of this court, dealing with wholly different subjects, in which Denning L.J. sought to escape from the confines of the rule, but was not accompanied in his attempt by the other members of the court . . .

[The judgments from *Ward v. Byham* [1956] were explained]

. . . As I read the judgment of Morris L.J., he and Parker L.J. held that, though in maintaining the child the plaintiff was doing no more than she was obliged to do by law, nevertheless her promise that the child would be well looked after and happy was a practical benefit to the father which amounted to consideration for his promise.

Here, we can see that the dispute basically hinged on whether for consideration there needed to be a 'legal' benefit or just a 'practical' one. Roffey did not dispute that in making the promise to Williams to vary the agreement it was getting certain benefits in practice—escaping the time penalty, keeping Williams doing the work, and avoiding the trouble of getting somebody else to do it. Rather, its argument was that it derived no 'benefit in law', because Williams was undertaking no new legal duty. He was just doing what he was already obliged to.

Next, Glidewell LJ indicates that there were ongoing efforts among the judiciary to liberalise the rule in *Stilk v Myrick*. While Denning LJ had not been wholly successful in doing so, the judgments in *Ward v Byham* and *Williams v Williams* did suggest that consideration could exist where there was a 'practical benefit' to the promisor rather than a legal one.

[The judgments of *Williams v Williams* [1957] were then explained]

There is, however, another legal concept of relatively recent development which is relevant, namely, that of economic duress. Clearly if a subcontractor has agreed to undertake work at a fixed price, and before he has completed the work declines to continue with it unless the contractor agrees to pay an increased price, the subcontractor may be held guilty of securing the contractor's promise by taking unfair advantage of the difficulties he will cause if he does not complete the work. In such a case an agreement to pay an increased price may well be voidable because it was entered into under duress. Thus this concept may provide another answer in law to the question of policy which has troubled the courts since before *Stilk v. Myrick*, and no doubt led at the date of that decision to a rigid adherence to the doctrine of consideration.

This possible application of the concept of economic duress was referred to by Lord Scarman, delivering the judgment of the Judicial Committee of the Privy Council in *Pao On v. Lau Yiu Long* [1980] A.C. 614.

Accordingly, following the view of the majority in *Ward v. Byham* [1956] 1 W.L.R. 496 and of the whole court in *Williams v. Williams* [1957] 1 W.L.R. 148 and that of the Privy Council in *Pao On* [1980] A.C. 614 the present state of the law on this subject can be expressed in the following proposition: (i) if A has entered into a contract with B to do work for, or to supply goods or services to, B in return for payment by B; and (ii) at some stage before A has completely performed his obligations under the contract B has reason to doubt whether A will, or will be able to, complete his side of the bargain; and (iii) B thereupon promises A an additional payment in return for A's promise to perform his contractual obligations on time; and (iv) as a result of giving his promise, B obtains in practice a benefit, or obviates a disbenefit; and (v) B's promise is not given as a result of economic duress or fraud on the part of A; then (vi) the benefit to B is capable of being consideration for B's promise, so that the promise will be legally binding.

As I have said, [Counsel for Roffey] accepts that in the present case by promising to pay the extra £10,300 his client secured benefits. There is no finding, and no suggestion, that in this case the promise was given as a result of fraud or duress. If it be objected that the propositions above contravene the principle in *Stilk v. Myrick*, I answer that in my view they do not; they refine, and limit the application of that principle, but they leave the principle unscathed, e.g. where B secures no benefit by his promise.

It is not in my view surprising that a principle enunciated in relation to the rigours of seafaring life during the Napoleonic wars should be subjected during the succeeding 180 years to a process of refinement and limitation in its application in the present day. It is therefore my opinion that on his findings of fact in the present case, the judge was entitled to hold, as he did, that the defendants' promise to pay the extra £10,300 was supported by valuable consideration, and thus constituted an enforceable agreement.

Another argument in favour of liberalising the rule in Glidewell LJ's view was the development of a doctrine called 'economic duress' in recent years. There is always a danger that a promisor is only promising to change a contract (particularly when it comes to paying more money) because he or she has been given effectively no choice by the promisee. This is thought to have explained the decision in *Stilk v Myrick*: the court in that case had in mind situations in which sailors might extort money from captains when out on voyages. It could very well have been the case that the sailors had arrived at the port in the Baltic and simply said to the captain, 'Pay us more money or we will not complete the voyage'. The captain would have had no choice but to accept. In ruling that such promises would not be enforceable, the court was discouraging such behaviour. In the modern day, it seemed to Glidewell LJ that the doctrine of duress would resolve that problem and there was therefore no need for such a strict approach to be taken to consideration for variation promises.

Glidewell LJ summarised all these recent developments as indicating that the correct question to ask was whether there had been a *practical benefit* to the promisor in making a promise to vary a contract, rather than a *legal* one. If the answer to that question was 'yes', there was consideration for it—although as you will be able to see, it is not quite that simple and other requirements need to be fulfilled.

The apparent departure from *Stilk v Myrick* was, finally, described rather as a 'refinement' of it, although it is difficult now to imagine circumstances in which it will apply, because it will always presumably be possible to find a 'practical benefit' to the promisor whenever a promise is made—otherwise why would the promisor have made it? It is still possible to say that where the promisor secures no benefit whatsoever from a promise there is no consideration for it, but under what circumstances could this be true?

We can now turn to an extract of the judgment by Russell LJ, which provides some useful opinion about the need to modify the traditional rule:

There is no hint in that pleading that the defendants were subjected to any duress to make the agreement or that their promise to pay the extra £10,300 lacked consideration. As the judge found, the plaintiff must have continued work in the belief that he would be paid £575 as he finished each of the 18 uncompleted flats (although the arithmetic is not precisely accurate).

For their part the defendants recorded the new terms in their ledger. Can the defendants now escape liability on the ground that the plaintiff undertook to do no more than he had originally contracted to do although, quite clearly, the defendants, on 9 April 1986, were prepared to make the payment and only declined to do so at a later stage. It would certainly be unconscionable if this were to be their legal entitlement.

. . . [T]he policy of the law in its search to do justice between the parties has developed considerably since the early 19th century when *Stilk v. Myrick*, was decided by Lord Ellenborough C.J. In the late 20th century I do not believe that the rigid approach to the concept of consideration to be found in *Stilk v. Myrick* is either necessary or desirable. Consideration there must still be but, in my judgment, the courts nowadays should be more ready to find its existence so as to reflect the intention of the parties to the contract where the bargaining powers are not unequal and where the finding of consideration reflect the true intention of the parties.

The essence of Russell LJ's view is that effect must be given to the parties' apparent intentions. It certainly seemed as though Roffey had promised extra payment to Williams and that Williams had acted on the assumption he would be paid. It would therefore be 'unconscionable' to decide that there was no enforceable agreement, because that would go against what the parties had clearly intended. This meant that courts should be much looser about the requirement for consideration and should be 'ready to find its existence'—i.e. they should generally find a way for promises between roughly equal parties to be enforceable.

What was the true intention of the parties when they arrived at the agreement . . . The plaintiff had got into financial difficulties. The defendants, through their employee Mr. Cottrell, recognised the price that had been agreed originally with the plaintiff was less than what Mr. Cottrell himself regarded as a reasonable price. There was a desire on Mr. Cottrell's part to retain the services of the plaintiff so that the work could be completed without the need to employ another subcontractor. There was further a need to replace what had hitherto been a haphazard method of payment by a more formalised scheme involving the payment of a specified sum on the completion of each flat. These were all advantages accruing to the defendants which can fairly be said to have been in consideration of their undertaking to pay the additional £10,300. True it was that the plaintiff did not undertake to do any work additional to that which he had originally undertaken to do but the terms upon which he was to carry out the work were varied and, in my judgment, that variation was supported by consideration which a pragmatic approach to the true relationship between the parties readily demonstrates.

He also makes clear that he thinks this to be 'pragmatic'—it was simply enforcing what the two parties had agreed and reflecting the fact that the promisor was getting something out of the new arrangement as well as the promisee.

For my part I wish to make it plain that I do not base my judgment upon any reservation as to the correctness of the law long ago enunciated in *Stilk v. Myrick*. A gratuitous promise, pure and simple, remains unenforceable unless given under seal. But where, as in this case, a party undertakes to make a payment because by so doing it will gain an advantage arising out of the continuing relationship with the promisee the new bargain will not fail for want of consideration.

. . . I too would dismiss this appeal.

Like Glidewell LJ, Russell LJ also suggested that the decision in *Williams v Roffey* did not make *Stilk v Myrick* no longer good law, although, again, it is hard to imagine circumstances in which a 'gratuitous promise, pure and simple' with *no* benefit for the promisor could be made.

We can now turn to the third judgment by Purchase LJ:

The point of some difficulty which arises on this appeal is whether the judge was correct in his conclusion that the agreement reached on 9 April did not fail for lack of consideration because the principle established by the old cases of *Stilk v. Myrick* . . . [and *Harris v Watson* (1791)] . . . I feel I must say at once that, for my part, I would not be prepared to overrule two cases of such veneration involving judgments of judges of such distinction except on the strongest possible grounds since they form a pillar stone of the law of contract which has been observed over the years and is still recognised in principle in recent authority: see the decision of *Stilk v. Myrick* to be found in *North Ocean Shipping Co. Ltd. v. Hyundai Construction Co. Ltd.* [1979] Q.B. 705, 712 per Mocatta J. With respect, I agree with his view of the two judgments

Like Glidewell LJ and Russell LJ, Purchase LJ was at pains to emphasise that *Stilk v Myrick* was still good law and the principle in it held—gratuitous promises to vary contracts for more pay are not enforceable.

by Denning L.J. in *Ward v. Byham* [1956] 1 W.L.R. 496 and *Williams v. Williams* [1957] 1 W.L.R. 148 in concluding that these judgments do not provide a sound basis for avoiding the rule in *Stilk v. Myrick*. Although this rule has been the subject of some criticism it is still clearly recognised in current textbooks of authority: see Chitty on Contracts, 28th ed. (1989) and Cheshire, Fifoot, and Furmston's Law of Contract, 11th ed. (1986) …

In my judgment, therefore, the rule in *Stilk v. Myrick*, remains valid as a matter of principle, namely that a contract not under seal must be supported by consideration. Thus, where the agreement upon which reliance is placed provides that an extra payment is to be made for work to be done by the payee which he is already obliged to perform then unless some other consideration is detected to support the agreement to pay the extra sum that agreement will not be enforceable. The two cases, *Harris v. Watson*, and *Stilk v. Myrick*, involved circumstances of a very special nature, namely the extraordinary conditions existing at the turn of the 18th century under which seamen had to serve their contracts of employment on the high seas. There were strong public policy grounds at that time to protect the master and owners of a ship from being held to ransom by disaffected crews. Thus, the decision that the promise to pay extra wages even in the circumstances established in those cases, was not supported by consideration is readily understandable. Of course, conditions today on the high seas have changed dramatically and it is at least questionable … whether these cases might not well have been decided differently if they were tried today. The modern cases tend to depend more upon the defence of duress in a commercial context rather than lack of consideration for the second agreement. In the present case the question of duress does not arise. The initiative in coming to the agreement of 9 April came from Mr. Cottrell and not from the plaintiff. It would not, therefore, lie in the defendants' mouth to assert a defence of duress. Nevertheless, the court is more ready in the presence of this defence being available in the commercial context to look for mutual advantages which would amount to sufficient consideration to support the second agreement under which the extra money is paid …

It was, however, open to the plaintiff to be in deliberate breach of the contract in order to 'cut his losses' commercially. In normal circumstances the suggestion that a contracting party can rely upon his own breach to establish consideration is distinctly unattractive. In many cases it obviously would be and if there was any element of duress brought upon the other contracting party under the modern development of this branch of the law the proposed breaker of the contract would not benefit. With some hesitation … I consider that the modern approach to the question of consideration would be that where there were benefits derived by each party to a contract of variation even though one party did not suffer a detriment this would not be fatal to the establishing of sufficient consideration to support the agreement. If both parties benefit from an agreement it is not necessary that each also suffers a detriment. In my judgment, on the facts as found by the judge, he was entitled to reach the conclusion that consideration existed and in those circumstances I would not disturb that finding.

However, just like the other judges, Purchase LJ also emphasised that *Stilk v Myrick* had to be understood in its historical context. The decision was made on strong public policy grounds—discouraging extortion. Now that the law provides an alterative resolution in such cases (economic duress) and now that circumstances have changed such that extortion on the high seas is unlikely, there is no need to insist on a strict application of the rule in *Stilk*.

Purchase LJ also mentioned the important caveat that the promise must have been freely given. Williams may very well have informed Roffey that he could no longer do the work and they would have to give him more money or face grave financial consequences. If this had been the case Roffey would have been forced to agree. This could not be allowed—it would be tantamount to saying that a contracting party could provide consideration for a promise for more money by, effectively, refusing to perform his or her duties.

He concludes on the same basis as the other judges—both parties were benefiting (Williams in getting more money; Roffey in avoiding the time penalty and keeping Williams doing the work rather than having to find another carpenter), and hence the promise was enforceable.

THINKING POINTS

Did you agree with Glidewell LJ's interpretation of the majority in *Ward v Byham* (see 5.6.3)?

5.9.1 The Basic Rule Following *Williams v Roffey*

The Court of Appeal went out of its way to say that *Stilk* was not overruled, but instead was just refined. It is often now said that this means the basic rule is that: a promise to perform an existing contractual duty is not consideration for a variation promise (*Stilk*), unless the promise gives the promisor a practical benefit. If it does, then the performance is sufficient consideration.

However, Glidewell LJ stated the legal position and the scope of its application in the following way, which is rather narrower:

(1)   where A has contracted to supply goods or services to B, in return for payment by B; and

(2)   before A completes performance, B doubts A will be able to complete his performance; and

(3)   B then promises A an extra payment. In return, A promises to perform their contractual obligations (i.e. do what they had to do anyway); and

(4)   as a result of promising to make the extra payment, B obtains a 'practical benefit' (or avoids a 'disbenefit'); and

(5)   B's promise of payment was made freely (not a result of fraud or economic duress by A); then

(6)   the benefit to B is sufficient consideration for B's promise to make the extra payment to A. As a result, the promise of extra payment is enforceable.

The first factor refers to contracts for the provision of goods and services. We will see (at 5.10), that the principle cannot apply to promises allowing for the part payment of a larger debt.

Factors (4), (5) and (6) relate to the principle developed in *Williams v Roffey*. The promise to vary the contact (like the promise made by Roffey) must be freely made. In addition, it must result in a practical benefit to the promisor. If it does, then the practical benefit is good consideration and makes the promise enforceable.

In practice, it is likely that a commercial party will only freely promise further payment *because* it will result in a benefit to them. It means that the likely effect of *Williams* v *Roffey* is that it will refine *Stilk* almost out of existence. That being said, it really depends on what is meant by a 'practical benefit' and how easy it is to find one. The easier it is to find a practical benefit, the more limited the traditional rule from *Stilk* becomes. The reasoning used to depart from the traditional rule, and the motive for doing so, are relevant in determining this. They help to understand the scope of what is meant by a 'practical benefit' and, therefore, the scope of *Williams v Roffey* itself.

5.9.2 How Did the Court of Appeal Depart from the Traditional Rule?

We saw that all three Lord Justices viewed *Stilk v Myrick* as a policy decision. They explained that at the time, there must have been a concern that sailors might force their ships' masters to promise to pay them more. This could be done by sailing into the ocean and then refusing to continue or return on time, unless further payment was promised. The possibility of extorting the employer in this way would be encouraged if such promises were enforceable. At the time, there were no rules to protect a contractual party from being extorted in that way. For that reason, a strict approach to consideration was adopted to ensure that such promises would not be enforceable. However, by the time of *Williams v Roffey*, the common law had developed the principle of economic duress. This protects a party if their promises are made as a result of undue financial pressure from the other party. The resulting agreement or variation becomes voidable. According to the judgments in *Williams v Roffey*, this meant there was no longer a need to be so strict with consideration to protect parties. Instead, the application of consideration to freely agreed variations of a contract could be relaxed.

There was no evidence of economic duress in *Williams v Roffey*. All three Lord Justices were of this view because Williams was seen to be in financial difficulty and was approached by Roffey's representative. Williams did not threaten to quit unless he was given more money.

5.9.3　The Need to Depart from the Traditional Rule

The judgments all acknowledge that the traditional rule from *Stilk* had been criticised. The key criticism was that it could have the effect of overlooking the parties' intentions. Under that traditional rule, both parties might have fully intended for a variation to be binding, but it would be unenforceable in the absence of traditional consideration. The result of *Williams v Roffey* is that it allows courts to give effect to the parties' apparent intentions even in the absence of what would traditionally be understood to be consideration.

There are strong arguments in favour of this. In *Williams v Roffey* there were two commercial parties with the same level of bargaining power. They knew what they were agreeing to when the terms were changed. They showed an apparent intention for the variation to be binding. So, why should these intentions be ignored just because the variation lacks something being given in exchange? This approach is more consistent with the way businesses often operate. They frequently make adjustments to their contracts during performance. By recognising such adjustments as enforceable, the decision adopted a commercially pragmatic approach.

5.9.4　A Wide Approach to 'Practical Benefit'

An important issue stemming from this case is what exactly a 'practical benefit' is. In the context of the dispute in *Williams v Roffey* itself, Purchase LJ stated that there had been a clear '*commercial advantage to both sides from a pragmatic point of view*'. So what was the commercial advantage to Roffey? Purchase LJ observed that Williams (like any party to a contract) had the freedom to deliberately breach and '*cut his losses*'. He would be liable in damages for doing so, but the choice was his to make. In other words, the 'practical benefits' hinged on Williams' continued performance of the contract where he might otherwise have stopped. On the payments, Russell LJ referred to the 'haphazard method of payment' in the original contract. He then observed that the new arrangement gave Roffey more control over Williams' performance. This control was a result of linking a fixed sum of money to each completed flat. This was an arrangement that created an incentive for Williams to complete each flat. More generally, in giving Williams an incentive to keep working, Roffey was spared the expense and trouble of finding another carpenter—who may have charged more money anyway.

As a result, the judgments observed that the agreed variation gave Roffey the following practical benefits:

- a better chance of performance by Williams (because he would be able to afford to continue);
- an increased chance of avoiding the penalty clause (because the deadline could be met);
- saved time and trouble of finding another carpenter (because Williams could have decided to quit);
- a more effective system of payments (incentivising the work with payments per flat completed).

There is no clear limit on what a practical benefit is and further cases will reveal different examples. In *Simon Container v EMBA* [1998] 2 Lloyds Rep 429, Judge Raymond Jack QC in the Commercial Court applied the judgment of Glidewell LJ from *Williams v Roffey*. The judge decided that the promisor gained a practical benefit because his promise and resulting successful performance would result in further contracts with the other party. This was the reason for the promise in the first place. By recognising such a benefit, the judge was reflecting the apparent intention of the commercial parties.

It has also been suggested that judges should not focus solely on established practical benefits or what they think should (and should not) be seen as a practical benefit. Instead, they should recognise the benefit that the promisor expected to get, which would be the reason for the promise. On this, Teare J in *Horwood v Land of Leather* [2010] EWHC 546 warned that 'the court should be slow to say that that which a business says is a benefit is not'. This does not mean that every benefit that a business expects in return will be good consideration. However, it is something that the courts should consider, even though it is based on a party's subjective idea of a benefit. Such an approach will be a more accurate reflection of the parties' intentions when they agree to vary the terms of their contract.

KEY POINTS

- The traditional rule from *Stilk v Myrick* has been modified so that a promise to perform an existing contractual duty is good consideration if it gives the promisor a practical benefit.
- The practical benefit is usually found by looking at the reasons for making the promise.

Having explored the case law on the performance of contractual duties, we can move to a related issue concerning the part of payment of debts.

5.10 Part Payment of Debts

There is a well-established rule that a party who owes money (known as a debtor) cannot pay-off the debt by paying less than the amount owed. This rule is often expressed as: part payment does not 'discharge' (i.e. pay-off and end) the debt. The rule has its origins in the ancient law of debt, and goes back to at least *Pinnel's Case* (1602) 5 Co. Rep. 117a. However, the rule has been brought within the general scope of consideration, and that makes sense given the typical circumstances in which the rule would be applied.

An example would be where a debtor owes £1000 and the creditor (the party that is owed money) agrees to wipe out the debt in return for a payment of £800. Essentially, that agreement is a promise by the creditor to end the debt for £800 and not sue for the remaining balance. If the creditor does sue for the remaining £200, the debtor will try to rely on promise made by the creditor. Of course, at that stage, the question is whether consideration was provided in return for the creditor's promise.

?! THINKING POINTS

Why would a creditor promise to allow a debtor to wipe out the debt with less money than the amount owed? For example, if you owed £1000, why might the creditor be willing to wipe out the debt in return for £800?

The leading authority on consideration and the part payment of debts is the House of Lords case of *Foakes v Beer* (1884) 9 App Cas 605. After exploring this case in detail, we can turn to its relationship with the approach adopted in *Williams v Roffey*.

5.10.1 The Leading Case on the Part Payment of Debts (Promises to Accept Less)

In *Foakes v Beer*, following a legal dispute in which a judgment was made against him, Dr Foakes owed £2090 19s to Mrs Beer. In addition, since it was a debt arising from a judgment, she was entitled to interest until the sum had been paid. Dr Foakes wanted time to pay, and so Mrs Beer agreed to allow payment by instalments. Under the agreement, Dr Foakes was to pay £500 immediately and

Mrs Beer 'would not take any proceedings whatever on the said judgment' on the condition that Dr Foakes paid two instalments a year of £150. After the payments were made, Mrs Beer then brought an action for the interest due on the debt. Dr Foakes relied on Mrs Beer's promise not to take further action. The House of Lords held that the promise by Beer 'not to take any proceedings whatsoever' was not enforceable because there was no consideration to enforce it. She was entitled to sue for the interest due on the debt. In other words, a promise to accept less than she was owed (the original judgment debt or 'principal', without interest) was not enforceable without consideration and she was still entitled to the whole debt (the principal plus interest).

It is important to understand the lead judgment by Lord Selborne LC and the near-dissent by Lord Blackburn. We will look at them in turn.

GUIDED CASE READING 5.2
John Weston Foakes v Julia Beer (1884) 9 App Cas 605

When you read the extract of the lead judgment by the Earl of Selbourne LC, try to identify:

- Why there was no consideration.
- The significance of the rule in *Pinnel's Case*.

But the question remains, whether the agreement is capable of being legally enforced. Not being under seal, it cannot be legally enforced against the respondent, unless she received consideration for it from the appellant, . . . What is the consideration? On the face of the agreement none is expressed, except a present payment of £500, on account and in part of the larger debt then due and payable by law under the judgment. The appellant did not contract to pay the future instalments of £150 each, at the times therein mentioned; much less did he give any new security, in the shape of negotiable paper, or in any other form . . .

> Lord Selborne LC here simply makes the point that a promise to accept a lesser sum to discharge the whole debt requires consideration to be enforceable just like any other. And since Dr Foakes had not provided anything to Mrs Beer in return for her promise that she would accept his instalment plan, there was no consideration for it.

The question, therefore, is nakedly raised by this appeal, whether your Lordships are now prepared, not only to overrule, as contrary to law, the doctrine stated by Sir Edward Coke to have been laid down by all the judges of the Common Pleas in *Pinnel's Case* 5 Rep. 117 a. in 1602, and repeated in his note to Littleton, sect. 344 Co. Litt. 212 b, but to treat a prospective agreement, not under seal, for satisfaction of a debt, by a series of payments on account to a total amount less than the whole debt, as binding in law, provided those payments are regularly made . . . The doctrine itself, as laid down by Sir Edward Coke, may have been criticised, as questionable in principle, by some persons whose opinions are entitled to respect, but it has never been judicially overruled; on the contrary I think it has always, since the sixteenth century, been accepted as law. If so, I cannot think that your Lordships would do right, if you were now to reverse, as erroneous, a judgment of the Court of Appeal, proceeding upon a doctrine which has been accepted as part of the law of England for 280 years.

> Lord Selborne LC was of the clear view that, whatever the rights and wrongs of the existing rule, it had to be applied. This was because there was a very old authority for it in the form of *Pinnel's Case*, which even at the time was nearly 300 years old—and seems to have itself been based on principles of even longer standing.

The doctrine, as stated in *Pinnel's* Case, is 'that payment of a lesser sum on the day' (it would of course be the same after the day), 'in satisfaction of a greater, cannot be any satisfaction for the whole, because it appears to the Judges, that by no possibility a lesser sum can be a satisfaction to the plaintiff for a greater sum'. As stated in Coke Littleton, 212 (b), it is, 'where the condition is for payment of £20, the obligor . . . cannot at the time appointed pay a lesser sum in satisfaction of the whole, because it is apparent that a lesser sum of money cannot be a satisfaction of a greater;' . . .

. . . If the question be (as, in the actual state of the law, I think it is), whether consideration is, or is not, given in a case of this kind, by the debtor who

> The Earl of Selbourne LC then explained the rule from *Pinnel's Case*. A smaller debt cannot in itself satisfy a greater one. £19 is of lesser value than £20, so a payment of £19 cannot discharge a debt of £20. Another way of putting this is that if a creditor is owed £20, he is by definition getting less value if he is paid £19 only. Therefore, there can be no consideration making the agreement enforceable because consideration requires something 'of value' in exchange for a promise. It is all very well saying chocolate bar wrappers or peppercorns might constitute 'value' for the purposes of consideration, but it is very hard on its face to see how receiving less money than one is owed can be of greater value than the actual debt.

pays down part of the debt presently due from him, for a promise by the creditor to relinquish, after certain further payments on account, the residue of the debt, I cannot say that I think consideration is given, in the sense in which I have always understood that word as used in our law. It might be (and indeed I think it would be) an improvement in our law, if a release or acquittance of the whole debt, on payment of any sum which the creditor might be content to receive by way of accord and satisfaction (though less than the whole), were held to be, generally, binding, though not under seal; nor should I be unwilling to see equal force given to a prospective agreement, like the present, in writing though not under seal; but I think it impossible, without refinements which practically alter the sense of the word, to treat such a release or acquittance as supported by any new consideration proceeding from the debtor

> However, Lord Selborne LC did suggest that he thought this rule was an unusual one which needed to be revised. If a creditor agrees to accept a lesser sum to discharge a debt, and it appears he or she was giving genuine consent, why should that agreement not be enforceable for want of consideration?

In principle, consideration would be required to enforce Mrs Beer's promise. On the facts there was no consideration since all Dr Foakes did was make a payment and promise to make more until the principal was cleared. According to this judgment, that was not enough for consideration. Dr Foakes was already under an obligation to Mrs Beer to make the full payment. He was in fact not even performing his existing duty. Instead, he was doing less—he was only promising to pay the principal, when he owed the principal together with interest. The absence of consideration from Dr Foakes, or an agreement by deed, meant that the promise by Mrs Beer was not enforceable. In addition, to allow the promise to be enforceable would be inconsistent with the well-established rule from *Pinnel's* case.

We can now turn to the extract of the judgment by Lord Blackburn. His Lordship ultimately agreed with the judgment by the Earl of Selbourne LC. However, we will see that it comes close to being a dissenting judgment.

I think, therefore, that it is necessary to consider the ground on which the Court of Appeal did base their judgment, and to say whether the agreement can be enforced. I construe it as accepting and taking £500 in satisfaction of the whole £2090 19s., subject to the condition that unless the balance of the principal debt was paid by the instalments, the whole might be enforced with interest. If, instead of £500 in money, it had been a horse valued at £500, or a promissory note for £500, the authorities are that it would have been a good satisfaction, but it is said to be otherwise as it was money.

This is a question, I think, of difficulty.

In Coke, Littleton 212 b, Lord Coke says: 'where the condition is for payment of £20, the obligor or feoffor cannot at the time appointed pay a lesser sum in satisfaction of the whole, because it is apparent that a lesser sum of money cannot be a satisfaction of a greater. . . . If the obligor or feoffor pay a lesser sum either before the day or at another place than is limited by the condition, and the obligee or feoffee receiveth it, this is a good satisfaction'.

For this he cites *Pinnel's Case* . . . Lord Coke reports that it was resolved by the whole Court of Common Pleas 'that payment of a lesser sum on the day in satisfaction of a greater cannot be any satisfaction for the whole, because it appears to the judges that by no possibility a lesser sum can be a satisfaction to the plaintiff for a greater sum: but the gift of a horse, hawk, or robe, &c., in satisfaction is good, for it shall be intended that a horse, hawk, or robe, &c., might be more beneficial to the plaintiff than the money, in respect of some circumstance, or otherwise the plaintiff would not have accepted of it in satisfaction...'

[Lord Blackburn referred to the principle from Pinnel's Case and continued]...

This was certainly not necessary for the decision of the case; but though the

> Lord Blackburn here sets out the central (apparent) inconsistency which has plagued this area of law in the eyes of many commentators. This is that English law seems to treat debt obligations in a contradictory way. If Dr Foakes had promised Mrs Beer a horse instead of part of the debt and she had accepted, that would have been an enforceable agreement because there would have been consideration in the form of the horse. It would have been something 'fresh' or additional. Remember that English courts do not concern themselves with market value. A horse might be worth much less than the principal in terms of market price. But if Mrs Beer had accepted it, there would be consideration for the agreement not to enforce the full debt. Yet because Dr Foakes had offered her a sum of money and this was of less value than the principal, her promise in return was not enforceable. What can the justification be for that inconsistency?

> As Lord Blackburn then goes on to make clear, the court in *Pinnel's Case* and its reporter, Lord Coke, were perfectly aware of this inconsistency and indeed appeared to insist on it. A payment of a lesser sum cannot be good consideration for a promise to discharge the entire . . .

resolution of the Court of Common Pleas was only a dictum, it seems to me clear that Lord Coke deliberately adopted the dictum, and the great weight of his authority makes it necessary to be cautious before saying that what he deliberately adopted as law was a mistake, and though I cannot find that in any subsequent case this dictum has been made the ground of the decision . . . yet there certainly are cases in which great judges have treated the dictum in *Pinnel's* Case as good law.

[The judgment referred to some comments from such 'great' judges who regarded the rule from *Pinnel's* case as good law even though it was *obiter dictum*]

. . . After such strong expressions of opinion, I doubt much whether any judge sitting in a Court of the first instance would be justified in treating the question as open. But as this has very seldom, if at all, been the ground of the decision even in a Court of the first instance, and certainly never been the ground of a decision in the Court of Exchequer Chamber, still less in this House, I did think it open in your Lordships' House to reconsider this question. And, notwithstanding the very high authority of Lord Coke, I think it is not the fact that to accept prompt payment of a part only . . . can never be more beneficial than to insist on payment of the whole. And if it be not the fact, it cannot be apparent to the judges.

. . .

What principally weighs with me in thinking that Lord Coke made a mistake of fact is my conviction that all men of business, whether merchants or tradesmen, do every day recognise and act on the ground that prompt payment of a part of their demand may be more beneficial to them than it would be to insist on their rights and enforce payment of the whole. Even where the debtor is perfectly solvent, and sure to pay at last, this often is so. Where the credit of the debtor is doubtful it must be more so. I had persuaded myself that there was no such long-continued action on this dictum as to render it improper in this House to reconsider the question. I had written my reasons for so thinking; but as they were not satisfactory to the other noble and learned Lords who heard the case, I do not now repeat them nor persist in them.

I assent to the judgment proposed, though it is not that which I had originally thought proper.

. . . debt in itself. But if the smaller payment is accompanied by something additional that the creditor values, then there will be consideration for a promise not to enforce a right to the full amount. This could be payment of the lesser sum being made early, or in a different place, or being accompanied by a 'horse, hawk or robe'. In other words, *Pinnel's Case* is quite clear—there can be no consideration in a lesser sum of money in itself, but there can be consideration in a gift which may be of much less value than the principal. This is what the Court in that case decided, and it was what had subsequently been generally accepted as 'good law'.

Lord Blackburn then carefully suggested that since the rule had never the basis of a decision in an appeal court, it was more open for the House of Lords change it on the basis that part payment could be beneficial to a creditor. It could do what a court lower in the hierarchy could not. And he felt it indeed *should* overturn the principle set out in *Pinnel's Case*—because there can be an advantage in a creditor receiving payment of a debt on time even if it is less than he is owed.

He then suggests that this is common sense among businesspeople and that one reason for this is that if a debtor has 'doubtful' credit (i.e. the creditor may be worried the debtor will never be able to pay anything) the creditor will be very happy to get at least some money being paid on time.

However, Lord Blackburn ultimately abandoned this line of reasoning because the other Law Lords were clearly of the view that the rule in *Pinnel's Case* had to remain and be followed. This was, as we have seen, due to it being a rule of very long standing.

KEY POINTS

Part payment of a debt is not sufficient consideration to enforce a promise by a creditor to accept less than the performance due, unless it is accompanied by additional goods or services, or is made in a different place, or earlier than the due date, at the creditor's request.

The rule from *Foakes v Beer* operates in a very similar way to the traditional rule on the performance of an existing contractual duty set out in *Stilk v Myrick*. There, it was said that a promise to perform an existing contractual duty was not good consideration to enforce an additional promise by the other contractual party. But, as we have seen, there will be good consideration if the promisor receives more than the existing contractual duty. Likewise, part payment is not good consideration to enforce a promise from the creditor. But, if the creditor is to receive something that it is not entitled to from the debt (such as payment being made early, in a different place, or with additional goods or services—a 'hawk, horse or robe' or, as shown by *Simantob v Shavleyan* [2019] EWCA Civ 1105, a promise to not rely on a certain defence in court), then there will be good consideration in a part payment for a promise not to enforce a right to the whole. It is clear that there is often a *practical benefit* to the creditor in accepting a part payment of debt. This was acknowledged by Lord Blackburn, who pointed out that a creditor will often see an advantage in a part payment made on time, especially if the debtor has 'doubtful' credit.

Foakes v Beer has attracted a lot of academic criticism because it is said not to recognise the full benefit to the creditor in accepting a lesser sum of money. Worse, it is said to have the potential to produce some very strange results. For example, consider the creditor who is owed £1000 and promises to accept £950 to pay off the entire debt on the due date. We know the payment of £950 on the dute date is not good consideration for the promise to waive the right to the rest. Yet if the creditor agreed to have just £50 but a day earlier than the formal payment date, then there will be good consideration for such a promise. Likewise, if the payment has to be made at a particular place and the creditor wants it at a different place, then the £50 at the different place will be good consideration for the promise to waive the right to the remainder. In fact, £50 on the due date along with a cupcake would be good consideration for such a promise if that is what the creditor has agreed to. Therefore, this legal position can be criticised as being formal and artificial. Instead, the law should focus on the intentions of the parties.

It seems that the rule does serve to protect creditors from being extorted and forced to accept part payment of debts which they are owed. A good example is *D&C Builders Ltd v Rees* [1966] 2 QB 617. Here, following some building work, Mr and Mrs Rees paid £250 to the claimant builders but still owed £483. The claimants had financial difficulties and Mr and Mrs Rees knew it. After ignoring a few requests for the money, Mrs Rees offered to give a cheque for £300 'in full settlement'. The claimant accepted this saying they had no choice in the matter. Now, by accepting the cheque, the claimant was promising not to sue for the remaining balance. When the claimant did sue for the rest of the money, the action was successful. In the Court of Appeal, the majority relied on *Foakes v Beer* to decide that there was no consideration for the promise made by the claimant builder.

D&C Builders shows the use or utility of *Foakes v Beer*. It can protect creditors. That may have been the reasoning behind the rule in *Pinnel's Case* too. That leads us to an obvious question: now that we have the law of economic duress to protect parties in such circumstances, is it time to abandon the rule from *Foakes v Beer*? We can recall that in *Williams v Roffey*, the Court of Appeal severely limited the traditional rule from *Stilk v Myrick*. In doing so, the court relied on the modern doctrine of economic duress. Could the same be done here in relation to the part payment of debts? That is really a question about the relationship between the approach from *Williams v Roffey*, and that of *Foakes v Beer*.

5.10.2 Can the *Williams v Roffey* Approach Apply to the Part Payment of Debts?

The relationship between the decisions in *Williams v Roffey* and *Foakes v Beer* has been addressed by the Court of Appeal in two subsequent cases. The first was *re Selectmove Ltd* [1995] 1 WLR 474. The second was the more recent one of *MWB Business Exchange Centres Ltd v Rock Advertising Ltd* [2016] EWCA Civ 553 (overturned by the Supreme Court in Rock Advertising Ltd v MWB Business Exchange Centres Ltd [2018] UKSC 24).

In *re Selectmove*, Selectmove owed money in unpaid tax and national insurance to the Inland Revenue (which we now call 'HMRC'). Selectmove had a meeting with a representative from the Revenue and the Revenue then brought an action for the full amount due and a winding up petition. A winding up petition is an application to the court to liquidate a company, meaning that its assets are sold to pay its debts. Selectmove argued that the Revenue representative had agreed to accept payment by monthly instalments. This promise by the Revenue to accept instalments meant allowing Selectmove to pay later (paying later was clearly 'doing less' than what Selectmove was under a legal obligation to do). In addition, Selectmove argued that they had provided consideration in the form of a practical benefit.

The Court of Appeal held that there was no agreement between the parties about the instalments. It went on to say that, even if there had been such an agreement, there was no consideration from Selectmove to enforce it. The judgment by Peter Gibson LJ (with whom Stuart-Smith LJ and Balcombe LJ agreed) is a useful demonstration of the relationship between *Williams v Roffey* and *Foakes v Beer*.

GUIDED CASE READING 5.3
re Selectmove Ltd [1995] 1 WLR 474

When you read the extract of the judgment by Peter Gibson LJ try to identify:

- The practical benefit to the Inland Revenue
- Why it was not recognised as consideration

[After explaining why there was no agreement between the company and the Inland Revenue, he turned to the question of consideration]

. . .

The judge held that the case fell within the principle of *Foakes v. Beer* (1884) 9 App.Cas. 605. In that case a judgment debtor and creditor agreed that in consideration of the debtor paying part of the judgment debt and costs immediately and the remainder by instalments the creditor would not take any proceedings on the judgment. The House of Lords held that the agreement was *nudum pactum*, being without consideration, and did not prevent the creditor, after payment of the whole debt and costs, from proceeding to enforce payment of the interest on the judgment. Although their Lordships were unanimous in the result, that case is notable for the powerful speech of Lord Blackburn, who made plain his disagreement with the course the law had taken in and since *Pinnel's Case* (1602) 5 Co.Rep. 117a and which the House of Lords in *Foakes v. Beer*, 9 App.Cas. 605, decided should not be reversed. Lord Blackburn expressed his conviction, at p. 622, that 'all men of business, whether merchants or tradesmen, do every day recognise and act on the ground that prompt payment of a part of their demand may be more beneficial to them than it would be to insist on their rights and enforce payment of the whole'.

The judgment begins by briefly reciting the decision in *Foakes v Beer* and sets the relationship between Selectmove and the Inland Revenue in that context: Selectmove is a debtor and the Revenue is a creditor in the sense that it is owed money. Peter Gibson LJ also makes clear from the beginning that this is a case which brings up the same issue as *Foakes v Beer*—namely, that part payment of a debt is not recognised as good consideration for the discharge of the whole debt. He also suggests he has sympathy with Lord Blackburn's 'powerful' near-dissent in that decision.

Yet it is clear that the House of Lords decided that a practical benefit of that nature is not good consideration in law.

Foakes v. Beer has been followed and applied in numerous cases subsequently, of which I shall mention two. In *Vanbergen v. St. Edmunds Properties Ltd.* [1933] 2 K.B. 223, 231, Lord Hanworth M.R. said:

'It is a well-established principle that a promise to pay a sum which the debtor is already bound by law to pay to the promisee does not afford any consideration to support the contract'.

He then shows that he is bound by precedent: *Foakes v Beer* is a House of Lords decision which has been followed subsequently, and must be seen as good law.

More recently in *D. & C. Builders Ltd. v. Rees* [1966] 2 Q.B. 617 this court also applied *Foakes v. Beer*, Danckwerts L.J. saying, at p. 626, that the case 'settled definitely the rule of law that payment of a lesser sum than the amount of a debt due cannot be a satisfaction of the debt, unless there is some benefit to the creditor added so that there is an accord and satisfaction'.

[Counsel for Selectmove] however submitted that an additional benefit to the revenue was conferred by the agreement in that the revenue stood to derive practical benefits therefrom: it was likely to recover more from not enforcing its debt against the company, which was known to be in financial difficulties, than from putting the company into liquidation. He pointed to the fact that the company did in fact pay its further [tax] liabilities and £7,000 of its arrears. He relied on the decision of this court in *Williams v. Roffey Bros. & Nicholls (Contractors) Ltd.* [1991] 1 Q.B. 1 for the proposition that a promise to perform an existing obligation can amount to good consideration provided that there are practical benefits to the promisee.

[Peter-Gibson LJ then described the facts of *Williams v Roffey* along with the decision and the six factors listed by Glidewell LJ]

...

[Counsel for Selectmove] submitted that, although Glidewell L.J. in terms confined his remarks to a case where B is to do the work for or supply goods or services to A, the same principle must apply where B's obligation is to pay A, and he referred to an article by Adams and Brownsword, 'Contract, Consideration and the Critical Path' (1990) 53 M.L.R. 536, 539–540 which suggests that *Foakes v. Beer*, 9 App.Cas. 605 might need reconsideration. I see the force of the argument, but the difficulty that I feel with it is that, if the principle of *Williams v. Roffey Bros. & Nicholls (Contractors) Ltd.* [1991] 1 Q.B. 1 is to be extended to an obligation to make payment, it would in effect leave the principle in *Foakes v. Beer*, 9 App.Cas. 605 without any application.

When a creditor and a debtor who are at arm's length reach agreement on the payment of the debt by instalments to accommodate the debtor, the creditor will no doubt always see a practical benefit to himself in so doing. In the absence of authority there would be much to be said for the enforceability of such a contract. But that was a matter expressly considered in *Foakes v. Beer* yet held not to constitute good consideration in law. *Foakes v. Beer* was not even referred to in *Williams v. Roffey Bros. & Nicholls (Contractors) Ltd.* [1991] 1 Q.B. 1, and it is in my judgment impossible, consistently with the doctrine of precedent, for this court to extend the principle of *Williams's* case to any circumstances governed by the principle of *Foakes v. Beer*, 9 App. Cas. 605. If that extension is to be made, it must be by the House of Lords or, perhaps even more appropriately, by Parliament after consideration by the Law Commission.

In my judgment, the judge was right to hold that if there was an agreement between the company and the revenue it was unenforceable for want of consideration.

However, he also shows that there is another, more recent, precedent in *Williams v Roffey* which might be relevant. It had been argued that the Inland Revenue was getting a 'practical benefit' in the instalment arrangement with Selectmove, because it did at least allow the Revenue to get something. The choice was between Selectmove paying in instalments or going into liquidation. If Selectmove was liquidated the Revenue might receive little or none of the money owed. If it was kept as a going concern and able to pay in instalments, the Revenue would eventually recoup the outstanding monies. There would thus have been a 'practical benefit' to the Revenue in such an agreement.

The problem for Peter Gibson LJ is that, although he is sympathetic to the idea that the rule in *Williams v Roffey* could be expanded beyond Glidewell LJ's restrictions (i.e. that it only applied in existing contracts where one party was providing goods and services to the other), this would render the decision in *Foakes v Beer* meaningless.

This is because it is always going to be the case that one can discern a 'practical benefit' to the creditor in an agreement of part payment of a debt. If it is a choice between getting some money or none at all, then this is obviously true. But this notion was considered by the House of Lords in *Foakes v Beer*, and the decision in that case was quite clear that such a benefit could not be good consideration for a promise from a creditor to accept less than was owed. Moreover, the decision in *Williams v Roffey* (like that in *Re Selectmove*) was a Court of Appeal decision, whereas *Foakes v Beer* had been a decision of the House of Lords. It would therefore have been impossible for Peter Gibson LJ or the other judges in *Re Selectmove* to undermine it by extending the scope of the rule in *Williams v Roffey* into the arena of debt.

The basic significance of *Selectmove* is that it confirmed the continued application of the traditional rule from *Foakes v Beer*. This means that a creditor can promise to a debtor that part payment of a debt will satisfy the full amount, without that promise being subsequently enforceable. This could be a promise to simply accept less than is owed *per se*, or it could be a promise to accept late payment—which means a lesser amount because of the time value of money but it also means the debtor is doing less than what was required by the obligation. Such a promise might well be a practical benefit to the creditor if the alternative is getting no money at all. However, if no traditional consideration is provided by the debtor, the creditor can take the money paid, and then enforce the original debt. The only way for a debtor to avoid this is by providing consideration, for example, by agreeing to pay the lessor sum earlier; or by paying slightly more than the amount owed (if the promise is to allow late payment).

THINKING POINTS

It is fair that such promises from a creditor to accept less by the due date or to accept the same payments by instalments cannot be enforced at common law?

This creates a difficulty if the desire is to create a unified rule concerning 'practical benefits'. This is because it creates a distinction between two types of obligation: duties to pay money and duties to provide goods or services. *Pinnel's case, Foakes* and *Selectmove* were each concerned with a promise concerning an obligation to pay money owed. *Williams v Roffey* is about an obligation to provide goods or services. The test from that case (set out by Glidewell LJ) refers to the duty to provide goods or services; and in *Selectmove*, Peter-Gibson LJ said that it was not possible to extend *Williams v Roffey* to 'an obligation to make payment'. The obvious criticism is that the same rule should apply to both types of obligation, but instead the law states that a 'practical benefit' is not good consideration for a promise concerning payment obligations, whereas it is good consideration where the promise concerns goods and services.

The distinction is not entirely arbitrary. In *Foakes v Beer*, the promise was to *accept less*. In *Williams v Roffey Bros* the promise was to *pay more*. English law appears to hold that these two circumstances are different. The common criticism is that the distinction is artificial, and that in principle, there is no real difference between these two types of promise.

KEY POINTS

- *Williams v Roffey* applies to promises to do more (in the case, Roffey promised to pay more for the same performance).
- *Foakes v Beer* (as confirmed by *re, Selectmove*) applies to promises to accept less performance (like partial or late payment).

The courts had the opportunity to express an opinion on *Foakes v Beer* and go some way to removing the apparently artificial distinction that has resulted following *Williams v Roffey* and *re Selectmove* in *Rock Advertising Ltd v MWB Business Exchange Services Ltd* [2018] UKSC 24. The contract in the case was a licence agreement that Rock Advertising had to operate on premises managed by MWB. Rock Advertising fell behind on their rental payments. Relying on the terms of the licence, MWB gave notice to end the licence; locked out Rock Advertising from the premises; and sued for the money owed along with damages for breach. Rock Advertising then counter-claimed on the basis that when they fell behind on their payments, they called MWB's credit controller on her mobile who then agreed a payment schedule to pay off the arrears. Essentially, this variation was a promise to allow the licence to continue and for the money owed to be paid late in instalments. MWB argued that any such variation would not be effective because there was what is known as a 'No Oral Modification' clause in the licence. This required any variations to the licence to be agreed in a written document signed by the parties.

At first instance, it was argued that Rock had provided consideration in the form of a practical benefit, but the 'No Oral Modification' clause meant that the variation was not effective. The Court of Appeal's decision focussed on the freedom of the parties and held that they could agree to 'unbind' themselves and vary the contract orally notwithstanding the existence of the 'No Oral Modification' clause (this point was based on the Court of Appeal decision in *Globe Motors Inc v TRW LucasVarity Electric Steering Ltd* [2016] EWCA Civ 396). The Court then decided that the variation was effective because Rock had provided a practical benefit to MWB and therefore, consideration. Essentially,

Foakes v Beer was distinguished because in that case, the debtor had done less than his existing duty by paying late and less than the full amount due. In contrast, it could be said that MWB would benefit from their premises being occupied rather than left empty with no payments coming in. In agreeing to Rock's proposal, they were keeping Rock on as a tenant in a manner which would ensure continued payments indefinitely into the future, with the alternative being to terminate the lease and potentially lose a source of income. So, by agreeing to the payment schedule proposed by Rock, it was said that MWB gained a 'commercial advantage' beyond the payment of the money due. This decision had the effect of using the principle from *Williams v Roffey* to refine the rule from *Foakes v Beer* further.

Unfortunately, in the appeal to the Supreme Court, the opportunity to make a definitive statement on the relationship between *Foakes v Beer* and *Williams v Roffey* was not taken. The Supreme Court overturned the Court of Appeal decision on the basis that the 'No Oral Modification' clause was effective. This meant that the licence had not been varied in the absence of a written and signed variation. That was enough to decide the case. The issue of consideration was addressed briefly by Lord Sumption (with whom Lady Hale, Lord Wilson and Lord Lloyd-Jones agreed). It is useful to read the following relevant comment by Lord Sumption since it is the only comment from the highest court on the issue:

> [18] That makes it unnecessary to deal with consideration. It is also, I think, undesirable to do so. The issue is a difficult one. The only consideration which MWB can be said to have been given for accepting a less advantageous schedule of payments was (i) the prospect that the payments were more likely to be made if they were loaded onto the back end of the contract term, and (ii) the fact that MWB would be less likely to have the premises left vacant on its hands while it sought a new licensee. These were both expectations of practical value, but neither was a contractual entitlement. In *Williams v Roffey Bros & Nicholls (Contractors) Ltd* [1991] 1 QB 1, the Court of Appeal held that an expectation of commercial advantage was good consideration. The problem about this was that practical expectation of benefit was the very thing which the House of Lords held not to be adequate consideration in *Foakes v Beer* (1884) 9 App Cas 605: see in particular p. 622 per Lord Blackburn. There are arguable points of distinction, although the arguments are somewhat forced. A differently constituted Court of Appeal made these points in In re *Selectmove Ltd* [1995] 1 WLR 474, and declined to follow *Williams v Roffey*. The reality is that any decision on this point is likely to involve a re-examination of the decision in *Foakes v Beer*. It is probably ripe for re-examination. But if it is to be overruled or its effect substantially modified, it should be before an enlarged panel of the court and in a case where the decision would be more than obiter dictum.

Lord Sumption noted the only two potential ways in which MWB could be construed to have gained a 'practical benefit' from the new payment schedule. First, it would have more chance of getting at least some money from Rock in the form of future payments, and second, it would mean at least that MWB would receive continued payments and hence a source of income, because Rock would remain as a tenant—which was preferable to the premises simply being empty. But the problem, as Lord Sumption puts it, is that in *Foakes v Beer* the House of Lords had been quite clear that simply getting some money rather than nothing was not good consideration for a promise not to enforce a debt obligation. The creditor had to get some additional advantage rather than simply receive something instead of nothing. However, Lord Sumption (and the other judges in the Supreme Court) declined to make a statement on this issue either way. They preferred not to do so through a panel of only five judges (as was the case in *Rock v MWB*) and, particularly, to do so where the result of the case hinged on the matter rather than here, where it was ultimately irrelevant to the outcome. The dispute in *Rock v MWB* was decided on the 'No Oral Modification' clause point and this meant any statements about consideration would be *obiter* and hence not binding. It was felt that re-examining *Foakes v Beer* with the potential to overrule or change it should be done in a case when the result on that issue would be binding.

The fact that the issue is a 'difficult' one suggests that the Supreme Court wished to wait for a suitable case in which to undertake a detailed and lengthy analysis. But Lord Sumption also said that the decision in *Foakes v Beer* was 'ripe for re-examination', in recognition of the fact that *Williams v Roffey* can only have a truly legitimate basis if its relationship to *Foakes v Beer* is made clear—either through formally modifying or overruling it, or explaining the basis of the difference between promises to pay more and promises to accept less. It is unfortunate that the Supreme Court did not say more, given that it is the first time in the 30 years since *Williams v Roffey* that the highest court have been able to provide a comment on this issue.

> **?!   THINKING POINTS**
>
> What would be the impact of the Supreme Court providing a full re-examination of the cases to state that either *Williams v Roffey* or *Foakes v Beer* should be overruled?

5.11 Promissory Estoppel

Promissory estoppel is a principle that operates as a possible way around the strict consideration requirement from cases such as *Foakes v Beer*. It comes from the case of *Central London Property Trust v High Trees House Ltd* [1947] KB 130 (the 'High Trees' case). The case is often described as Lord Denning's most celebrated case. We will see that Denning J (as he then was) developed promissory estoppel using a great deal of judicial creativity. It resulted in a principle that serves to limit the strict application of the consideration rule. It is important to understand the basics of how the principle was developed, what it does and when it can apply.

→ CROSS-REFERENCE

The role of the equity jurisdiction in contract law was explained at 1.5.2.

Essentially, promissory estoppel is a principle that can prevent a promisor going back on a promise. It was developed from the equity jurisdiction and sits alongside the common law rules that we have covered so far. The scope of the principle is still debated today.

5.11.1 The *High Trees* Case

Our starting point has to be the *High Trees* case itself and the judgment of Denning J. We will then turn to the cases that helped to develop the application of the principle.

The facts of *High Trees* are as follows. In 1937, the claimant landlord leased a block of flats to the defendant (tenant). This lease was for 99 years and had an annual rent of £2500. The tenant would then earn money from letting (renting out) the individual flats to private tenants. However, due to the outbreak of the Second World War and the bombing of London, many people left London. This meant that the tenant was unable to let all of the flats and encountered financial difficulties. So, in 1940 the claimant and defendant agreed to reduce the annual rent to £1250. This enabled the defendant to reduce the rent on the individual flats. Then in 1945, since the war had ended, the claimant took action to enforce the original agreement. The claimant wanted the rent to go back to the original amount of £2500. The claimant also wanted to know if it could claim the money owed from the rent reduction during the war years (the arrears). Denning J decided that the full original rent could resume once the war ended. He also said that the claimant would be *estopped* (legally barred) from claiming the arrears for unpaid rent during the war years (that is, the £1250 per year which had not been paid during the period 1940–1945).

Essentially, the claimant had promised to accept a smaller sum of money (the reduced rent). The defendant had agreed to do so, but provided no consideration. So ordinarily, this would be within the scope of *Foakes v Beer*. It meant that Denning J had to justify his decision not to apply *Foakes v Beer*. Also, a further problem was presented by a principle of common law estoppel from the House of Lords decision in *Jordan v Money* (1854) 5 H. L. C. 185. This ruled-out the application of common law estoppel to promises. Faced with such barriers, we might assume that the judgment would have to be a very long one, with lots of quotes and fine distinctions being made. However, the judgment is short.

GUIDED CASE READING 5.4

Central London Property Trust Ltd v High Trees House Ltd [1947] KB 130

When you read the extract of the judgment by Denning J, try to identify:

■ how Denning J avoids the application of *Foakes v Beer;*
■ the authority for promissory estoppel.

If I were to consider this matter without regard to recent developments in the law, there is no doubt that had the plaintiffs claimed it, they would have been entitled to recover ground rent at the rate of 2,500l. a year from the beginning of the term, since the lease under which it was payable was a lease under seal which, according to the old common law, could not be varied by an agreement by parol (whether in writing or not), but only by deed. Equity, however stepped in, and said that if there has been a variation of a deed by a simple contract (which in the case of a lease required to be in writing would have to be evidenced by writing), the courts may give effect to it as is shown in *Berry v. Berry* [1929] 2 K. B. 316. That equitable doctrine, however, could hardly apply in the present case because the variation here might be said to have been made without consideration. With regard to estoppel, the representation made in relation to reducing the rent, was not a representation of an existing fact. It was a representation, in effect, as to the future, namely, that payment of the rent would not be enforced at the full rate but only at the reduced rate. Such a representation would not give rise to an estoppel, because, as was said in *Jorden v. Money* (1854) 5 H. L. C. 185, a representation as to the future must be embodied as a contract or be nothing.

But what is the position in view of developments in the law in recent years? The law has not been standing still since *Jorden v. Money* (1854) 5 H. L. C. 185. There has been a series of decisions over the last fifty years which, although they are said to be cases of estoppel are not really such. They are cases in which a promise was made which was intended to create legal relations and which, to the knowledge of the person making the promise, was going to be acted on by the person to whom it was made and which was in fact so acted on. In such cases the courts have said that the promise must be honoured. The cases to which I particularly desire to refer are: *Fenner v. Blake* [1900] 1 Q. B. 426, In *re Wickham* (1917) 34 T. L. R. 158, *Re William Porter & Co., Ld.* [1937] 2 All E. R. 361 and *Buttery v. Pickard* [1946] W. N. 25. As I have said they are not cases of estoppel in the strict sense. They are really promises—promises intended to be binding, intended to be acted on, and in fact acted on. *Jorden v. Money* (1854) 5 H. L. C. 185 can be distinguished, because there the promisor made it clear that she did not intend to be legally bound, whereas in the cases to which I refer the proper inference was that the promisor did intend to be bound. In each case the court held the promise to be binding on the party making it, even though under the old common law it might be difficult to find any consideration for it. The courts have not gone so far as to give a cause of action in damages for the breach of such a promise, but they have refused to allow the party making it to act inconsistently with it. It is in that sense, and that sense only, that such a promise gives rise to an estoppel. The decisions are a natural result of the fusion of law and equity: for the cases of *Hughes v. Metropolitan Ry. Co.* (1877) 2 App. Cas. 439, 448, *Birmingham and District Land Co. v. London & North Western Ry. Co.* (1888) 40 Ch. D. 268, 286 and *Salisbury (Marquess) v. Gilmore* [1942] 2 K. B. 38, 51, afford a sufficient basis for saying that a party would not be allowed in equity to go back on such a promise. In my opinion, the time has now come for the validity of such a promise to be recognized.

The basic problem is identified as being one of a lack of consideration. The lease specified a ground rent of £2500 a year, and this had been varied without a benefit to the promisor. In times past an additional problem would have been that an agreement under seal (as this one was) could only be varied by a deed, but this was no longer a requirement thanks to recent developments.

Denning J was clearly of the view that Central London Property Trust, the landlord, would be estopped from enforcing its right to the rent arrears for the period 1940–1945 notwithstanding the lack of consideration for its promise. The problem was that the case of *Jorden v Money* suggested that a promise about the future could not give rise to an estoppel. This meant he had to somehow circumvent that decision.

This was done by holding that *Jorden v Money* was a case in which the promisor did not demonstrate an intention to create legal relations, whereas in other more recent cases courts had begun to hold that if a promisor appeared to intend to be bound by his or her promise, it could be binding even without any apparent consideration. He also managed to circumvent *Foakes v Beer* by placing his solution firmly in equity, discussion of which was absent in that case. This was necessary because of course High Trees House had only payed a lesser sum than the one owed under the lease to Central London Property Trust, which as we have seen would not in itself be enough to discharge the full debt.

The logical consequence, no doubt is that a promise to accept a smaller sum in discharge of a larger sum, if acted upon, is binding notwithstanding the absence of consideration: and if the fusion of law and equity leads to this result, so much the better. That aspect was not considered in *Foakes v. Beer* (1884) 9 App. Cas. 605.

At this time of day however, when law and equity have been joined together for over seventy years, principles must be reconsidered in the light of their combined effect. It is to be noticed that in the Sixth Interim Report of the Law Revision Committee, pars. 35, 40, it is recommended that such a promise as that to which I have referred, should be enforceable in law even though no consideration for it has been given by the promisee. It seems to me that, to the extent I have mentioned that result has now been achieved by the decisions of the courts.

> Denning J here makes clear that he saw himself as seizing an opportunity to make a strong statement on a matter which had been subject to change anyway. The general trend was towards recognising a promise like the one made by Central London Property Trust to High Trees as being binding even in the apparent absence of consideration. Denning J was, in his own eyes, simply confirming this trend.

I am satisfied that a promise such as that to which I have referred is binding and the only question remaining for my consideration is the scope of the promise in the present case. I am satisfied on all the evidence that the promise here was that the ground rent should be reduced to 1,250l. a year as a temporary expedient while the block of flats was not fully, or substantially fully let, owing to the conditions prevailing. That means that the reduction in the rent applied throughout the years down to the end of 1944, but early in 1945 it is plain that the flats were fully let, and, indeed the rents received from them . . . were increased beyond the figure at which it was originally contemplated that they would be let. At all events the rent from them must have been very considerable. I find that the conditions prevailing at the time when the reduction in rent was made, had completely passed away by the early months of 1945. I am satisfied that the promise was understood by all parties only to apply under the conditions prevailing at the time when it was made, namely, when the flats were only partially let, and that it did not extend any further than that. When the flats became fully let, early in 1945, the reduction ceased to apply.

> In principle, then, the promise made by the Trust could be binding in equity—it would be estopped from going back on it. What had to be settled next was the extent of that promise. It had been made as a 'temporary expedient' due to wartime conditions. Denning J held that these conditions ended in early 1945 and the rental market in London was now very strong, so from that point onwards the promise from the Trust ended and the original ground rent of £2,500 a year was from that point owed.

In those circumstances, under the law as I hold it, it seems to me that rent is payable at the full rate for the quarters ending September 29 and December 25, 1945.

> The Trust would have been estopped from claiming the arrears for the period 1940–1945, because the conditions of the estoppel—the war and its effects—continued to prevail during that time. The estoppel naturally ended in early 1945. Alternatively, Denning J also suggested it could simply have been ended by giving notice.

If the case had been one of estoppel, it might be said that in any event the estoppel would cease when the conditions to which the representation applied came to an end, or it also might be said that it would only come to an end on notice. In either case it is only a way of ascertaining what is the scope of the representation. I prefer to apply the principle that a promise intended to be binding, intended to be acted on and in fact acted on, is binding so far as its terms properly apply. Here it was binding as covering the period down to the early part of 1945, and as from that time full rent is payable.

I therefore give judgment for the plaintiff company for the amount claimed.

> He concluded by setting out a principle that he clearly thought was almost common sense; consideration is not necessary where a promise to vary a contract has been made in a way that is intended to be binding, intended to be acted on, and acted on—provided its conditions still apply (such as the war still being in progress).

We can see that Denning J made use of cases from equity to prevent the claimant landlord going back on their promise to accept the smaller sum. But once the reason for the reduction was no longer there (the war ended), the original agreement could continue. However, the key point is that the landlord would be *estopped* from claiming the full amount of rent during the war period. According to Denning J, the principle (which is now known as promissory estoppel) applies when:

- the promise made was intended to be binding;
- the promisor knew the promise would be acted on;
- the promisee acts upon the promise.

On the facts, the promise to reduce the annual rent was intended to be binding. It was expected that the tenant would reduce the rent on the individual flats in response. And finally, the rent on the individual flats was actually reduced.

The reasoning was brief considering the significance of the principle developed. It is useful to explain the reasoning with a wider discussion of the key cases cited.

Denning J argued that he was not bound by *Foakes v Beer*. To justify this, he explained that the House of Lords in that case had not taken into account developments in equity. Reference was made to the 'fusion' of equity and the common law. Previously, these jurisdictions had separate courts and separate principles. However, following the Judicature Acts 1873–75, parties could claim common law and equitable remedies in the same court. In addition, and perhaps more importantly, the courts were meant to consider both common law and equitable principles in their decisions. Denning J then cited cases from the equity jurisdiction that were not considered in *Foakes v Beer*, which he felt should have been. He then went on to develop promissory estoppel.

The key case cited was *Hughes v Metropolitan Railway*. This concerned a clause in a lease which required a tenant to make repairs to the property after having been given notice. The tenant was given notice to perform certain repairs within six months. The parties then started discussions about the sale of the property. When the discussions broke down, the landlord then wanted to take possession of the property because the repairs had not been done within the original six-month period. Based on principles of equity, the House of Lords held that the landlord had impliedly promised that the repairs did not need to be carried out while the discussions were taking place. Essentially, the landlord had waived (set aside) the right to take possession during the discussion period. This meant that even without consideration, the landlord was unable to go back on his implied promise. This principle of equitable waiver is what Denning J developed into promissory estoppel. When Denning J cited *Hughes*, he also cited a page from the case that corresponds with the following passage by Lord Cairns LC ('forfeiture' is when the lease is ended as a result of a breach, because the terms allow that to happen):

> [I]t is the first principle upon which all Courts of Equity proceed, that if parties who have entered into definite and distinct terms involving certain legal results—certain penalties or legal forfeiture— afterwards by their own act or with their own consent enter upon a course of negotiation which has the effect of leading one of the parties to suppose that the strict rights arising under the contract will not be enforced, or will be kept in suspense, or held in abeyance, the person who otherwise might have enforced those rights will not be allowed to enforce them where it would be inequitable having regard to the dealings which have thus taken place between the parties.

In short, if one party can impose a penalty on another because the contract permits it, but that party gives the impression that the right to impose it will be suspended or 'held in abeyance' (i.e. temporarily put on hold or paused), then that right cannot be imposed if it would be inequitable (unfair) to do so. In *Hughes*, the landlord had (impliedly) promised to suspend or interrupt the notice period during the discussions. In effect, the clock had stopped for the notice period during that time. To go back on that was deemed to be inequitable and hence the landlord was estopped from doing so.

Hughes was not considered in *Foakes v Beer* but it is generally accepted that the Law Lords in *Foakes v Beer* must have known about the case. *Hughes* was a House of Lords decision that had taken place only seven years before *Foakes v Beer*. Also, two of the Lords who sat in *Hughes* (Lord Blackburn and Lord Selbourne) also participated in the judgment in *Foakes v Beer*. According to Denning J in *High Trees*, the cases address the same broad principle and *Hughes* should have been considered in *Foakes v Beer*. This meant that he was able to portray his judgment as rectifying a problem.

Another issue for Denning was that in *Jorden v Money*, Lord Cranworth had said that an estoppel could only apply to a representation of existing fact rather than 'a statement of something which the party intends or does not intend to do'. However, the statement in *High Trees* had expressed an intention to allow for a rent reduction (i.e. it was a promise about future payments). Denning J had to therefore find a way to distinguish *Jorden v Money*. He did this by summarising the equity cases as being about 'promises intended to be binding, intended to be acted upon, and [. . .] acted upon'. Since the promise in *Jorden v Money* was not intended to be binding, it was therefore distinguishable. On that rather thin, perhaps even suspicious basis, Denning assumed the freedom to develop a different type of estoppel in equity.

Essentially, the distinction made by Denning J was used to justify the application of equity. This was necessary because the traditional role of equity was to apply in circumstances where the common law didn't. Equity is supposed to prevent injustices resulting from the common law being unable to provide a resolution. The rules from equity were never meant to conflict with the common law. That meant it was necessary to show that promissory estoppel was not conflicting with the common law rule in *Jorden v Money*.

5.11.2 The Development of Promissory Estoppel after *High Trees*

Denning J's decision in *High Trees* has not been overruled and seems to be accepted as an established principle. Subsequent cases have simply developed the requirements for the principle to apply. In doing so, it has become a limited exception to the consideration requirement.

5.11.2.1 A Defence Only

➡ CROSS-REFERENCE
For the facts of *Combe v Combe* see 5.2]

The Court of Appeal in *Combe v Combe* [1951] 2 KB 215 emphasised that promissory estoppel was only available as a defence. In other words, it is only to be used where A sues B as a result of B failing to do something (usually to pay money), having been promised by A that it is not required to do so. When the husband in *Combe v Combe* failed to pay the money promised, the wife sued. Her action relied on estoppel because she had not provided consideration. The question was whether the husband could be estopped from going back on his promise of payment. At first instance, the wife succeeded because the requirements from *High Trees* were satisfied. However, the Court of Appeal (which by then included Denning LJ) held that promissory estoppel could not be used. Denning LJ explained that the principle could be used as a defence to an action only. That meant it could not be a separate cause of action (i.e. it could not be the basis to actually sue someone).

This approach is consistent with the application of promissory estoppel in *High Trees* itself. We can recall that the case, it was the landlord (promisor) who sued the tenant (promisee) for the outstanding rent. The tenant was able to defend the action using promissory estoppel.

The limit to promissory estoppel ensures that it is a limited exception to the consideration requirement rather than being in direct conflict with it. Denning LJ was clear that he felt the principle ought not to be stretched too far 'lest it should be endangered'. The point is that it has a much better chance of survival as a limited exception. His reasoning presumably was that if judges are tempted to 'overreach', the doctrine may end up being overturned entirely by a decision of a higher court.

5.11.2.2 It Must Be Inequitable for the Promisor to Go Back on the Promise

➡ CROSS-REFERENCE
For the facts of *D&C Builders v Rees* see 5.10.1.

Another limitation on promissory estoppel was confirmed in *D&C Builders v Rees* [1966]. Here Mrs Rees had insisted on part payment to pay off the larger amount she owed. By accepting this, the builders effectively promised to take no further action. When they sued for the balance, Rees relied on promissory estoppel as it appeared that the requirements for estoppel were met. However, the Court of Appeal, again led by Lord Denning MR, made clear that there was an additional requirement. According to Lord Denning MR 'the creditor is only barred from his legal rights when it would be inequitable for him to insist upon them'. Since the builders had not freely agreed to the change in price, it was not inequitable to go back on that promise. Sometimes, the case is said to represent a requirement that the *promisee* must not act inequitably. That is because it is clear that Mrs Rees had acted inequitably in forcing the builders to accept the smaller sum. She knew that they were in financial difficulties, and was taking advantage by giving them a 'take it or leave it' ultimatum of a much smaller contract price than that which they were owed. This is implied in the judgments. However, Lord Denning's statement was focussed on the idea that for the promisor to be estopped, it must be inequitable for the *promisor* to go back on the promise.

5.11.2.3 There Must Be a Clear Promise

Woodhouse A.C. Israel Cocoa Ltd SA v Nigerian Produce Marketing Co Ltd [1972] AC 741 is often cited for the requirement that there must be a clear, unequivocal promise. The case involved a potential variation in the currency to be used for payment. However, it was not clear what the variation really consisted of because the language was vague. Lord Hailsham LC in the House of Lords (following the view of Lord Denning MR in the Court of Appeal) was concerned that if the content of the variation was not clear, it could not really be said to be a genuine promise. While the promise must be clear, it does not need to be express—after all, the promise in *Hughes* v *Metropolitan Railway* was implied. This requirement of a clear, unequivocal promise was been applied to refuse an estoppel in *Baird Textiles Holdings Ltd v Marks & Spencer plc* [2001] EWCA Civ 274 and *Kim v Chasewood Park Residents Ltd* [2013] EWCA Civ 239.

5.11.2.4 The Promisee Must Have Altered their Position in Reliance on the Promise

One of the requirements for promissory estoppel from *High Trees* was that the promisee acts on the promise. This is sometimes put as acting in 'reliance' on promise. Over the years there has been debate about the extent of the reliance needed. For example, must the promisee act on the promise to their detriment? In other words, must the promisee suffer or lose something as a result of relying on the promise made? The alternative argument is that the promisee is simply required to have altered its position in response to the promise.

> **?! THINKING POINTS**
>
> ▪ If the promisee is in a worse position from relying on the promise, is it easier to say that it is inequitable for the promisor to go back on the promise?
> ▪ Alternatively, if the promisee is in the same position from relying on the promise, *should* it still be inequitable for the promisor to go back on the promise?

The issue of the extent of the reliance required was addressed by Lord Denning MR in *WJ Alan & Co Ltd v El Nasr Export & Import Co* [1972] 2 QB 189:

> I know that it has been suggested in some quarters that there must be detriment. But I can find no support for it in the authorities cited by the judge. The nearest approach to it is the statement of Viscount Simonds in the *Tool Metal* case [1955] 2 All ER at 660. . . that the other must have been led 'to alter his position', which was adopted by Lord Hodson in *Emmanuel Ayodeji Ajayi v R T Briscoe (Nigeria) Ltd* ([1964] 3 All ER 556 at 559. . .).

This refers to the suggestion of detriment being required and it was then observed that there was no authority for such a requirement. The only requirement was for the promisee to 'alter' their positon. Lord Denning MR then continued:

> But that only means that he must have been led to act differently from what he otherwise would have done. And, if you study the cases in which the doctrine has been applied, you will see that all that is

required is that the one should have 'acted on the belief induced by the other party'. That is how Lord Cohen put it in the *Tool Metal* case ([1955] 2 All ER at 686. . .), and is how I would put it myself.

The comment then explained that 'altering' the position required acting differently than what would been done without the promise. Here, Lord Denning MR himself confirmed the need for the promisee to have 'altered' their positon only. The opinion from Arden LJ in *Collier v P & MJ Wright (Holdings) Ltd* [2007] EWCA Civ 1329 seems to confirm that not much is needed for the promisee to meet the requirement (although her judgment in that case is not binding). Arden LJ referred to *D&C Builders v Rees* and indicated that it was enough for the promisee to have made payments in response to the promise. It will also be remembered that all High Trees House did in response to the promise in *High Trees* was to charge lower rent to tenants and make the annual reduced payment to the Trust, and that was considered enough to have 'acted' on the promise. Table 5.1 summarises the requirement for promissory estoppel.

Table 5.1

A summary of the requirements for promissory estoppel

1	The promise must be clear and unequivocal (whether express or implied)	*Woodhouse A.C. Israel Cocoa Ltd SA v Nigerian Produce Marketing Co Ltd* [1972]
2	The promise must be made with an intention to binding	*Central London Property Trust v High Trees House Ltd* [1947]
3	The promisor must know the promise will be acted upon	*Central London Property Trust v High Trees House Ltd* [1947]
4	The promisee must act upon the promise by altering its position	*WJ Alan & Co Ltd v El Nasr Export & Import Co* [1972]
5	It must be used as a defence only rather than a basis to bring an action	*Combe v Combe* [1951]
6	It must be inequitable for the promisor to go back on the promise	*D&C Builders v Rees* [1966]

5.11.3 The Effect of Promissory Estoppel

One of the key debates over promissory estoppel relates to its effect. Does it merely suspend the legal rights of the promisor or does it extinguish them? In other words, is the right of the promisor to go back on the promise frozen temporarily or wiped out completely? In *High Trees*, Denning J made it clear that the full rent during the war period was not claimable. However, once the war had finished, the entitlement to the full rent could resume. This meant that the rights of the promisor landlord were suspended temporarily. It could also mean that during the period of suspension, the rights were extinguished because the arrears on the full rent were not claimable for that period—they could never be recovered.

The case often cited to support the argument that promissory estoppel only suspends rights is *Tool Metal Manufacturing v Tungsten Electric Co* [1955] 1 WLR 761. The case concerned a licence agreement relating to a patent. Tungsten (the licensee) had to pay a royalty to the patent holder when they made or sold products based on the patent. In addition, they had to pay compensation if they made more than what the licence permitted. In 1942, in response to the war, the appellant (patent holder) agreed to release Tungsten from the compensation obligation. After the war, they claimed the compensation due from the time the war ended. The House of Lords held that the compensation obligation could resume, but only after reasonable notice had been given to the promisee. This is another example of the promisor's future rights being suspended. However, questions arise about what happens if the obligation is a single payment. Would that obligation be extinguished or just delayed? It seems that such a single payment or one off obligation would just be delayed, if that is possible on the facts.

The issue of extinguishing rights has been raised again as a result of the opinions expressed in *Collier v P & MJ Wright (Holdings) Ltd* [2007] EWCA Civ 1329. In this case, Collier and his two business partners had borrowed money from Wright. Wright secured a judgment against them all *jointly* so that they owed £46,000 in total. The debt was to be paid at rate of £600 a month. After around 18 months, it was alleged that Wright promised Collier that if he continued to pay his £200 per month share and paid off a third of the balance, Wright would pursue the other partners for the rest. This meant that Collier would be treated separately rather than a joint debtor. Collier continued to pay £200 per month for a number of years. Following the bankruptcy of the partners, Wright brought an action against Collier for the full balance of the original £46,000 debt.

The Court of Appeal had only to decide if there was a 'genuine triable issue' on promissory estoppel, meaning that it did not have to give a final decision—it just had to decide whether the dispute was one which would require a trial at all. It held that it was, meaning that it was at least arguable that promissory estoppel could be available as a defence to Collier. Arden LJ even said that the there was a real prospect of showing at a trial that Wright's entitlement to the balance was extinguished:

> [40] . . .In all the circumstances, Mr Collier has in my judgment raised a triable issue as to promissory estoppel. . .
>
> [42] The facts of this case demonstrate that, if (1) a debtor offers to pay part only of the amount he owes; (2) the creditor voluntarily accepts that offer, and (3) in reliance on the creditor's acceptance the debtor pays that part of the amount he owes in full, the creditor will, by virtue of the doctrine of promissory estoppel, be bound to accept that sum in full and final satisfaction of the whole debt. For him to resile will of itself be inequitable. In addition, in these circumstances, the promissory estoppel has the effect of extinguishing the creditor's right to the balance of the debt. This part of our law originated in the brilliant *obiter dictum* of Denning J, as he was, in the *High Trees* case. . .

According to Arden LJ, the creditor's right to claim the full balance due was extinguished and so the creditor could not go back on ('resile' from) the promise. This opinion has attracted some criticism. The main criticism is that it means that promissory estoppel would conflict directly with *Foakes v Beer*. Based on *High Trees* itself, it could be assumed that Collier would have to resume payments of £600 a month (as he was jointly liable for the debt). But the creditor (Wright) would be estopped from claiming the balance of £400 a month that was not paid when the partners went bankrupt. Since they were bankrupt and Collier would be protected indefinitely by the estoppel, the creditor would never be able to recover the full balance. It must be emphasised that the case only answered the question of whether the matter was 'triable'. On this issue, Longmore LJ agreed with Arden LJ in principle, but delivered a far more cautious opinion. His Lordship warned that 'agreements which are said to forgo a creditor's rights on a permanent basis should not be too benevolently construed'. In other words, agreements to extinguish the rights of the promisor must not be interpreted too generously and easily in favour of the promisee.

CHAPTER SUMMARY

- English law requires parties to provide 'consideration' in return for their promises (unless the agreement is in the form of a deed) to make them enforceable.
- Consideration is something of value given (or promised) by a party. It is the price of the promise.
- Value given *before* a promise is made is 'past consideration' and is not sufficient.
- If the (past) act was in response to a previous request by the promisor, then it can be good consideration.
- Consideration must be sufficient (of some value) and need not be adequate (market value).

- Nominal value can be sufficient consideration, but not love and affection, or refraining from complaining.
- Performance (or a promise to perform) a legal or contractual obligation is not sufficient consideration, but a promise to do more than what is required is sufficient consideration.
- Performance of an existing contractual duty owed to a third party can be good consideration.
- Performance of an existing contractual duty can be good consideration where it can result in a practical benefit to the promisor, but a practical benefit is not sufficient to enforce a promise to accept less.
- Promissory estoppel operates as a limited exception to the consideration rule, and can apply when its requirements are met.

KEY CASES

- ☐ *Re McArdle* [1951] Ch 669—represents the basic rule on past consideration.
- ☐ *Re Casey's Patents* [1892] 1 Ch 104—confirms a way around the rule on past consideration where there has been a prior request.
- ☐ *Pao On v Lau Yiu Long* [1980] AC 614 (Lord Scarman)—gives an explanation of the requirements for the prior request to prevent a finding that consideration is past.
- ☐ *Chappell v Nestle* [1960] AC 87—shows a wide approach to the meaning of 'sufficient' consideration.
- ☐ *Ward v Byham* [1956] 1 WLR 496—provides authority for the rule on the performance of a legal (public) duty and the basis of the modern approach.
- ☐ *Williams v Roffey Bros & Nicholls (Contractors) Ltd* [1990] 2 WLR 1153—is the major authority on the modern approach to performance of a contractual duty.
- ☐ *Foakes v Beer* (1884) App Cas 605—represents the highest authority on the part payment of debts (promises to accept less).
- ☐ *Re Selectmove* [1995] 1 WLR 474—provides authority on the relationship between the rule in *Williams v Roffey* and the principle in *Foakes v Beer*.
- ☐ *Central London Property Trust v High Trees House Ltd* [1947] KB 130—is the case that introduced promissory estoppel.
- ☐ *Combe v Combe* [1951] 2 KB 215—states a practical limit of promissory estoppel (it cannot be a cause of action).
- ☐ *D&C Builders v Rees* [1966] 2 QB 617—states another practical limit, which is that it must in inequitable for the promisor to go back on the promise.

QUESTIONS

1. Sisko promised £1000 to an app designer called Raj, for creating an app for Sisko's business. This promise was made after Sisko approached Raj and asked her to create the app. At the time no payment was discussed. Is the later promise of £1000 enforceable?

2. Jon bought a hair salon and planned a grand opening for 7th May. He was worried that his decorator Dani might not complete the painting work in time for the grand opening so he promised her an extra £500 to complete the work as agreed. Dani completed the work on time but was never paid the extra money. Can Dani enforce the promise of the extra £500?

3. Is the rule from *Foakes v Beer* 'ripe for re-examination' as Lord Sumption suggested?

4. Should the principle of promissory estoppel be expanded so that it can be a cause of action?

 For answer guidance to these questions please visit the online resources at www .oup.com/uk/naidoo1e/, where you will also find multiple choice questions to check your understanding of key concepts.

FURTHER READING

Chen-Wishart, 'A Bird in the Hand: Consideration and Contract Modification' in Burrows and Peel (eds) Contract Formation and Parties, (2010) OUP.
This chapter provides a clear, in-depth examination of the state of the law relating to the variation of contracts.

Hird & Blair, 'Minding your own business–Williams v Roffey Revisited: Consideration reconsidered' **[1996] JBL 254.**
This is a detailed and clear article following *re, Selectmove*.

Roberts, '*Foakes v Beer*: bloodied, bowed, but still binding authority?' 2018, KLJ 29(3), 344.
A detailed and useful analysis of the law following *Rock Advertising v MWB* [2018].

Senu, 'The last stand: *Foakes v Beer*' LMCLQ 2018, 4(Nov), 552.
An interesting article suggesting a re-examination of *Williams v Roffey*.

PART 2

The Content of the Contract and Performance

The Terms of the Contract

6

LEARNING OBJECTIVES

By the end of this chapter you should be able to:

- explain the different sources and types of terms that can form the obligations in a contract;
- apply the law that allows oral statements to be recognised as terms as well as the law that allows written terms to be incorporated into an oral contract;
- evaluate the principles that are followed by the courts to interpret the meaning of terms;
- understand how terms are implied by legislation as well as by the courts.

INTRODUCTION

In Chapters 2–5 we explored the law relating to *how* contracts are made. In this chapter, our focus is on *what* has been agreed. We know that a contract consists of terms. Such terms can be expressed in writing or in oral statements. In addition, some terms can be implied into a contract by legislation or the courts. As a result, contracts can be in the form of a written document, an oral agreement or even a combination of written terms and oral statements and all three can contain implied terms.

In the context of *what* has been agreed, there are two main types of dispute. One type of dispute relates to the existence of a term that a party claims has been breached. With an oral contract, the defendant might argue that the relevant oral statement did not have the qualities to be a term and so is not part of the contract. A further issue could be the existence of additional printed terms. One party relies on them and the other argues that they are not part of the contract. With a contract made in writing, a party might argue that an oral statement is part of the contractual relationship. A further alternative for either type of contract could be a party arguing that the other is in breach of a term that should be implied into the contract. The other type of dispute over *what* has been agreed relates to the meaning of the terms. In such cases, the meaning of the disputed term will determine whether it has been breached. That requires the courts to interpret the term to reflect the parties' apparent intentions.

In this chapter, we start by exploring the law on express terms. These are terms expressed by the parties in oral statements or in writing. We then turn to the general principles that apply to the interpretation of express terms. Finally, we look at *how* terms can be implied into contracts.

6.1 Express Terms: Oral Contracts

It is easy to think of a contract as a detailed document that is signed by two parties. However, many contracts are made orally. It might be that two parties have negotiated and then agreed to trade based on what was discussed. As consumers, we enter many oral contracts. Typical examples would be: when we hire a taxi or board a bus; when we buy goods in a shop; when we order dinner in a restaurant or drinks at a bar; or when we go to watch a film at a cinema. We might leave with a receipt. That receipt might even have some terms on it. However, it is just evidence of the contract rather than the contract itself.

In addition to statements made by the parties, an oral contract might also include terms implied into it by legislation. Some written terms might accompany an oral contract too. These might be added by being displayed before or at the time of a sale. They might even be on a document signed at the time of a sale.

At this stage, we are concerned with the basic oral contract. These are just as enforceable as a written contract. The only difference is that the parties might well argue about what was said. When they do, it is for a judge to hear what the parties have to say and look at the relevant supporting evidence, if any is available. The judge will then simply decide, on the balance of probabilities, what was agreed. The case then proceeds on that version of the facts. The main legal issue is therefore identifying the terms of the contract.

6.1.1 The Classification of Oral Statements

Before entering the contract, parties may make lots of statements to each other. Some of these pre-contractual statements could be classed as terms of the contract. These would be the statements that appear to show an intention to make a contractual promise. Other statements could be classed as **representations**. These are statements that act as a reason or inducement to enter the contract. Finally, some statements might be just 'puffery', the label given to the kind of sales hype that no one should take seriously.

The classification of statements as terms, representations or puffery has a real *legal* significance:

- A term is part of the contract. If it is breached, the innocent party ought to be entitled to compensation for the resulting loss. Depending on the *type* of term breached, the innocent party might also have the right to end the contract.

- In contrast, if a representation turns out to be false, the action is for misrepresentation. Such an action is based on different rules. The availability of remedies can be more limited compared with an action for breach of contract. Even if a remedy for misrepresentation is possible, it is based on different tests to those used in breach of contract actions. Sometimes, it is possible for a false representation to be established, but not result in a remedy!

A mere puff on its own will not be enough for any legal action. For that reason, our focus is on whether the statements are terms of the contract or just representations. The distinction is a major issue when a party brings an action for breach of contract. By definition, that action is based on a party arguing that a term has been breached. The defendant will then argue that the statement is not a term and is instead, a representation. That would be an obvious argument when, in the circumstances, it is clear that a false representation would not result in a remedy for the claimant. When faced with these arguments, judges have to work out if a statement is a term. The courts have developed some guidance on how to do this.

→ CROSS-REFERENCE
For the methods of incorporating written terms into an oral contract see 6.3.

representation
is a statement that provides a reason to enter the contract but does not contain an obligation like a term does.

→ CROSS-REFERENCE
'Puffery' was explained at 2.3.2.

→ CROSS-REFERENCE
For the law relating to the type of terms and consequences of a breach see Ch. 8.

→ CROSS-REFERENCE
For the law on misrepresentation see Ch. 13.

KEY POINTS

A statement will be a term of the contract if, in the circumstances, it appears that the parties' intended it to be term. If the statement is a term, then a failure to follow it will result in an entitlement to a remedy for breach of contract.

The guidance indicated in the cases tells us what to look for. We know that most parties are not aware of the difference between a term and a representation. So, the real issue is whether a party showed an apparent intention to be contractually responsible for the accuracy of their statement. Such a statement is then classed as a term of the contract.

6.1.2 Guidance on When an Oral Statement is a Term

While the courts have provided some guidance, we need to be a little cautious because of the context of the cases. In many cases, a breach of contract action was the only way for the innocent party to get a remedy. This is because the right to end a contract for misrepresentation is lost easily. In addition, the traditional availability of damages for misrepresentation was extremely limited. As we shall see in the chapter on misrepresentation, a breach of contract action was often the only way for an innocent party to get a remedy prior to 1967. This may have resulted in the judges going out of their way to rule that a statement had become a term of the contract. However, the cases remain as an indication of the methods used by judges to work out if a statement is a term. Here, we will look at the two main ways of identifying an apparent intention for a statement to be a term. First we will address the importance test. We will then turn to the special knowledge test.

6.1.2.1 The Importance of the Statement

A statement could be classed as a term because of its importance to the parties. Here, we are concerned with statements that are crucial to the decision to enter the contract. In other words, the statement is so important that without it having been made, the parties would not have entered into the contract. Also, it is not enough for one party to simply say that the statement had such importance. Instead, an objective approach is adopted. The question to ask is whether it appears that the statement is crucial to both the maker of the statement and the party it is made to. This does not mean that the subject matter of the statement has to be crucially important to both parties. Rather, it means both parties must objectively be said to have understood that the statement was important.

An early is example can be seen from the case of *Bannerman v White* (1861) 10 CB (NS) 844. This concerned the sale of hops. The buyer asked if the hops had been treated with sulphur. He said that if they had, he would not want them, and wouldn't even ask for the price. The seller responded by saying that no sulphur had been used. As a result of the statement, the buyer purchased the hops. He then discovered that a small proportion of the hops had been treated with sulphur and they were all mixed together. Apparently, the seller had acquired a new machine to distribute the sulphur and tested it on five acres out of the 300 acre crop. The buyer then tried to reject the goods and end the contract. In response, the seller sued for the price owed. Erle CJ held that the statement was a term. Essentially, the statement was intended to be contractual because it was obvious that it was of critical importance. It did not particularly matter to the seller that the hops had been treated with sulphur or otherwise. But the seller would have known there would have been no sale if the buyer knew that sulphur had been used—he would have understood the importance of the term on that basis. So by saying that sulphur had not been used, the seller was accepting contractual responsibility for his statement being false.

A statement will not be objectively important if the maker of the statement advises the other party to verify its accuracy. In *Ecay v Godfrey* (1947) 80 Lloyd's Rep 286 a seller of a boat made a statement about its condition. He also suggested that the buyer should have the boat surveyed. As a result, the statement by the seller was held not to have been a term of the contract. Instead, it was a representation. After all, it could not be said that the seller was accepting contractual responsibility for the accuracy of the statement—he was in fact deliberately disavowing such responsibility by suggesting the buyer get a surveyor to look at the boat. On that basis, there was no apparent intention for the statement to be a term.

➡ **CROSS-REFERENCE**

We will see in 6.3.2. that important statements are capable of adding to and even changing the terms of a written contract.

6.1.2.2 Special Knowledge and Skill to Work Out if the Statement is a Term

Where a maker of a statement holds itself out as having special knowledge and skill, the statement is more likely to be held to be a term. Likewise, if the statement is made *to* a party with such special knowledge, then it is more likely that the statement will be held to be a representation. Two key cases illustrate these points.

The first case is *Oscar Chess v Williams* [1957] 1 WLR 370. Here, a private seller (Williams) sold a car to the claimant motor dealer for £290 as a part-exchange deal. The seller said that that car was a 1948 model and confirmed it with the log book. Six months later, the buyer discovered from the manufacturer that the car was in fact a 1939 model. This meant the car was really worth £175. The (car dealer) buyer then brought an action claiming damages for breach of contract. The Court of Appeal decided that the statement about the age of the car was not a term. Instead it was a representation and so the action failed.

The lead judgment for the majority was by Denning LJ. In the judgment Denning LJ identified the main question to answer: was the statement about the year of the vehicle a **warranty** or a representation?

> . . .Lord Moulton made it quite clear, in *Heilbut, Symons & Co v Buckleton* ([1913] AC at p. 51), that "The intention of the parties can only be deduced from the totality of the evidence." The question whether a warranty was intended depends on the conduct of the parties, on their words and behaviour, rather than on their thoughts. . .
>
> It is instructive to take some recent instances to show how the courts have approached this question. When the seller states a fact which is or should be within his own knowledge and of which the buyer is ignorant, intending that the buyer should act on it and he does so, it is easy to infer a warranty; see *Couchman v Hill* ([1947] KB 554), where a farmer stated that a heifer was unserved, and *Harling v Eddy* ([1951] 2 KB 739), where he stated that there was nothing wrong with her. So also if the seller makes a promise about something which is or should be within his own control; see *Birch v Paramount Estates Ltd* ((1956), 16 Estates Gazette 396), decided on 2 October 1956, in this court, where the seller stated that the house would be as good as the show house. If, however, the seller, when he states a fact, makes it clear that he has no knowledge of his own but has got his information elsewhere, and is merely passing it on, it is not so easy to imply a warranty. Such a case was *Routledge v McKay* ([1954] 1 WLR 615), where the seller "stated that a motor cycle combination was a 1942 model, and pointed to the corroboration of that statement to be found in the registration book," and it was held that there was no warranty.
>
> Turning now to the present case, much depends on the precise words that were used. If the seller says: "I believe the car is a 1948 Morris. Here is the registration book to prove it", there is clearly no warranty. It is a statement of belief, not a contractual promise. If, however, the seller says: "I guarantee that it is a 1948 Morris. This is borne out by the registration book, but you need not rely solely on that. I give you my own guarantee that it is", there is clearly a warranty. The seller is making himself contractually responsible, even though the registration book is wrong.
>
> . . .I ask myself: What is the proper inference from the known facts? It must have been obvious to both that the seller had himself no personal knowledge of the year when the car was made. He only became owner after a great number of changes. He must have been relying on the registration book. It is unlikely that such a person would warrant the year of manufacture. The most that he would do would be to state his belief, and then produce the registration book in verification of it. In these circumstances the intelligent bystander would, I suggest, say that the seller did not intend to bind himself so as to warrant that the car was a 1948 model. If the seller was asked to pledge himself to it, he would at once have said "I cannot do that. I have only the log-book to go by, the same as you". . .
>
> . . . It seems to me clear that the plaintiffs, the motor dealers who bought the car, relied on the year stated in the log-book. If they had wished to make sure of it, they could have checked it then and there, by taking the engine number and chassis number and writing to the makers. They did not do so at the time, but only eight months later. They are experts, and, as they did not make that check at the time, I do not think that they should now be allowed to recover against the innocent seller who produced to them all the evidence which he had, namely, the registration book.

warranty

is a type of contractual term. If breached, it results in damages.

This reasoning indicated that the status of a statement is based on the apparent intentions of the parties. It will be a term (what Denning LJ referred to as a 'warranty') if in the circumstances, it appears that a term was intended. The approach adopted showed that a statement might appear to be intended as a term where in the circumstances it is clear that it would be relied upon. That is where the knowledge of the parties comes in. If the maker of the statement appears to have no knowledge of the facts behind their statement, but the other party does, then that other party would not be relying heavily on the statement and both parties would understand this.

On the facts, the maker of the statement (the seller) had no special knowledge and just relied on the log book. The car dealer buyer was aware of that fact. That meant, objectively, the buyer could not have relied heavily on the seller's statement. In such circumstances, it would appear that the seller was not accepting contractual responsibility for the statement. Instead, the seller's statement appeared to be no more than a non-fraudulent misrepresentation.

Denning LJ referred to the fact that the buyer was in a better position to assess the accuracy of the statement. After all, they were motor dealers with expertise in cars. That observation came very close to saying that the buyer was at fault. It was as though Denning LJ was saying that the motor dealer buyer should have known better. This is often criticised because whether the innocent party was at fault should not be relevant to whether a statement is term or a representation.

KEY POINTS

If a maker of a statement appears to have no relevant special knowledge and the other party does, it means the statement is not being relied up heavily and so it is less likely that the statement will be held to be a term.

The *Oscar Chess* case is often compared with the later case of *Dick Bentley Productions Ltd v Harold Smith (Motors) Ltd* [1965] 1 WLR 623. This later case is another example where the knowledge that a party *appeared* to have was relevant to working out intention. Here, the claimant buyer (who was not a car dealer) requested a 'well vetted Bentley' from the defendant seller (a car dealer). The seller said that the car had done 20,000 miles since its gear box had been replaced and engine reconditioned. This figure was based on the speedometer reading rather than a more detailed assessment of the car's history. The buyer discovered a range of faults and that the mileage claim was false. He then brought an action for breach of contract. The trial judge in the County Court found that the mileage figure was more likely to be over 100,000 miles and ruled in favour of the buyer. The question for the Court of Appeal was whether the statement about the mileage was a term, or a representation. It was held that it was actually a term. The main judgment was again from Lord Denning MR (with whom the other judges agreed). The reasoning referred to the principle from *Oscar Chess v Williams* in the following way:

> Looking at the cases once more, as we have done so often, it seems to me that if a representation is made in the course of dealings for a contract for the very purpose of inducing the other party to act upon it, and actually inducing him to act upon it, by entering into the contract, that is *prima facie* ground for inferring that it was intended as a warranty... It is not necessary to speak of it as being collateral. Suffice it that it was intended to be acted upon and was in fact acted on.

→ CROSS-REFERENCE
'Collateral' warranties are explained in 6.2.1.3.

The reference to a statement intended to be acted upon and then acted upon is addressing the role of objective reliance. That in turn shows an intention for the statement to be a term. Lord Denning MR then observed that there was no such reliance in *Oscar Chess v Williams* because of the better knowledge that the buyer had. This was then contrasted with the present case:

> ...Here we have a dealer, Smith, who was in a position to know, or at least to find out, the history of the car. He could get it by writing to the makers. He did not do so. Indeed, it was done later. When

> the history of this car was examined, his statement turned out to be quite wrong. He ought to have known better. There was no reasonable foundation for it.

This comment highlights the fact that the maker of the statement was in a position to know the truth of his statement. It also indicates that this seller was at fault for the false statement. Lord Denning MR then agreed with the statements made by the trial judge:

> He said:
> "I have no hesitation that as a matter of law the statement was a warranty. Mr. Smith stated a fact that should be within his own knowledge. He had jumped to a conclusion and stated it as a fact. A fact that a buyer would act on."
> That is ample foundation for the inference of a warranty.

This confirms that the seller appeared to have special knowledge and that his statements would have been taken seriously and relied upon by the buyer. Therefore, the statement was a term (warranty).

The result was based on the fact that the seller was well placed to know the truth of the statement. This is a result of the seller (the maker of the statement) having special knowledge as a motor dealer. The important point is that objectively, the seller *appeared* to have such knowledge. On that basis, the reasonable buyer would have relied heavily on the statement. In addition, the seller ought to have known that its statements would be relied upon. Almost anybody who buys a second-hand car, after all, will be relying on the statements made by the seller about its history and so on, and any car dealer will know this. As a result, it seems that the seller showed an apparent intention to be contractually responsible for the accuracy of the statement.

?! THINKING POINTS

Is it fair that having special knowledge seems to count against the parties in such a dispute?

Just like in *Oscar Chess*, Lord Denning MR placed a lot of weight on the party with knowledge being at fault. His Lordship even said that the seller 'ought to have known better'. Again, this can be criticised for using fault or negligence in deciding if there is a term, although this is less problematic when the person who has made the statements behaviour is in question (rather than the person to whom the statement is made, as in *Oscar Chess*). That said, the reference to fault would explain a breach of what is called a 'collateral warranty'.

6.1.2.3 Special Knowledge Resulting in a Term Being Held to Have Been a Collateral Warranty

A 'collateral warranty' is a term of the contract, but it is not a promise that appears to guarantee the accuracy of the statement like the term in *Dick Bentley v Smith Motors*. Instead, a collateral warranty is an *implied promise* that the statement was made with reasonable care and skill. Such a term is 'collateral' because it is *about* the statement rather than a promise *in* the statement itself.

The meaning of a 'collateral warranty' was explained directly in *Esso Petroleum Ltd v Mardon* [1976] QB 801. This was another Court of Appeal decision, and it was again led by Lord Denning MR. To illustrate the existence and breach of a 'collateral warranty', it is important to detail the facts.

A large oil company (Esso) had found a site for a new petrol station. Esso's expert (with 40 years of experience) estimated that the petrol bought and sold by the petrol station (the 'throughput') would be 200,000 gallons after two years. On that basis, Esso bought the land and started to build the petrol station. However, the council planning authority refused permission for the petrol pumps to be at the front of the station next to the road. That meant the station had to be built 'back to front' with the pumps not visible from the road. Esso then found a tenant (Mardon) to rent the property and run the petrol station. Without re-assessing the impact of the station being 'back to front', Esso's expert made it clear to Mardon that the throughput was estimated at 200,000 gallons. On the strength of that expert estimate, Mardon entered the tenancy agreement for three years. Unfortunately, after 15 months the throughput was only 78,000 gallons. As a result, Mardon was forced to make losses and incurred expenses in trying to keep the station operational. Eventually, Mardon was unable to pay for the petrol supplied. This prompted Esso to bring an action for possession of the property and the money owed. Mardon then counter-claimed on two alternative grounds relating to the throughput statement. First, there was a breach of a warranty; second, (as an alternative action) there was a negligent mis-statement under the tort of negligence.

The trial judge found there was no breach of a warranty because the statement was not itself a term. This was based on the statement being an estimate rather than a promise or guarantee of the throughput. However, the judge did award damages for negligent mis-statement. The Court of Appeal upheld the negligent mis-statement claim. It also held that the false throughput estimate resulted in a breach of a collateral warranty.

After stating the facts, Lord Denning MR observed that the Misrepresentation Act 1967 could not apply. This was because the statement from Esso's expert was made before the Act came into force. His Lordship then explained the meaning of the breach of a 'collateral warranty' in the following passage:

> Collateral warranty
>
> Ever since *Heilbut, Symons & Co. v. Buckleton* [1913] A.C. 30, we have had to contend with the law as laid down by the House of Lords that an innocent misrepresentation gives no right to damages. In order to escape from that rule, [the claimant] used to allege—I often did it myself—that the misrepresentation was fraudulent, or alternatively a collateral warranty. At the trial we nearly always succeeded on collateral warranty. We had to reckon, of course, with the dictum of Lord Moulton, at p. 47, that "such collateral contracts must from their very nature be rare". But more often than not the court elevated the innocent misrepresentation into a collateral warranty: and thereby did justice—in advance of the Misrepresentation Act 1967. I remember scores of cases of that kind, especially on the sale of a business. A representation as to the profits that had been made in the past was invariably held to be a warranty. Besides that experience, there have been many cases since I have sat in this court where we have readily held a representation—which induces a person to enter into a contract—to be a warranty sounding in damages. I summarised them in *Dick Bentley Productions Ltd. v. Harold Smith (Motors) Ltd.* [1965] 1 W.L.R. 623, 627, . . .
>
> Now I would quite agree with [Counsel for Esso] that it was not a warranty—in this sense—that it did not *guarantee* that the throughput *would* be 200,000 gallons. But, nevertheless, it was a forecast made by a party—Esso—who had special knowledge and skill. It was the yardstick . . . by which they measured the worth of a filling station. They knew the facts. They knew the traffic in the town. They knew the throughput of comparable stations. They had much experience and expertise at their disposal. They were in a much better position than Mr. Mardon to make a forecast. It seems to me that if such a person makes a forecast, intending that the other should act upon it—and he does act upon it, it can well be interpreted as a warranty that the forecast is sound and reliable in the sense that they made it with reasonable care and skill. It is just as if Esso said to Mr. Mardon: "Our forecast of throughput is 200,000 gallons. You can rely upon it as being a sound forecast of what the service station should do. The rent is calculated on that footing." If the forecast turned out to be an unsound forecast such as no person of skill or experience should have made, there is a breach of warranty. . .
>
> In the present case it seems to me that there was a warranty that the forecast was sound, that is, Esso made it with reasonable care and skill. That warranty was broken. Most negligently Esso made a "fatal error" in the forecast they stated to Mr. Mardon, and on which he took the tenancy. For this they are liable in damages.

From the extract, we can see that the term breached was not the actual throughput statement. On the facts, that statement was a representation. It was no guarantee or promise of the actual throughput. Instead, Esso's special knowledge meant there was an implied warranty that reasonable care and skill had been taken in working out the throughput. According to Lord Denning MR, the special knowledge of Esso meant they knew their statement would be relied upon and then it was relied upon. On that basis, the representation was impliedly promising that it had been made with reasonable care and skill. This implied promise (collateral warranty) was breached because the forecast was prepared without care. It should have been re-assessed to factor-in the impact of the pumps being hidden from the road.

KEY POINTS

Even where a statement is a representation, liability for breach of contract can arise if the representation gives rise to a collateral warranty that is breached.

Lord Denning MR also explained the necessity of collateral warranties. Before the Misrepresentation Act 1967, there was no damages remedy for a false but innocently-made representation. For that reason, it was widely acknowledged that courts would look to see if the representation gave rise to a collateral warranty like the one in the case. That way, justice could be done by allowing the innocent party to be compensated for their loss by the damages award for a breach of the collateral warranty.

In the *Esso* case, this award was very different to the award that would have resulted from the statement itself being a term that was breached. The aim of damages for breach of contract is to put the innocent party in the position they would have been in, had the statement been true. So, if the 200,000 gallon throughput statement *was actually* a term, the damages would be the difference between the low profit made, and the profit that *should* have been made from a 200,000 gallon throughput. That would reflect the buyer's lost bargain. In contrast, damages were calculated on the basis of the breach of the collateral warranty, and the reasoning would have been as follows: if the collateral warranty had been true (i.e. the statement was made with reasonable care), then the throughput forecast would have been much lower. The lower forecast would have resulted in the buyer not going ahead with the contract, and so the buyer would not have had incurred expenses or losses from entering the contract. On that basis, the damages (for the breach of the collateral warranty) reflected these expenses and losses.

6.2 Incorporation of Written Terms into Oral Contracts

It is quite common for written terms to be part of an oral contract. Think about when you buy goods in a shop. Essentially it is an oral contract. But, at the point of sale, a term might be displayed on a notice. A familiar example might be a notice saying that you have 30 days to return the goods if you change your mind. When buying from a shop (rather than a distance sale) there is no *legal* right to return goods, just because you have changed your mind. But shops often offer this service to make themselves more attractive to consumers. By displaying the notice, the written term will be incorporated into your oral contract. As a result, you will then have a *contractual* right to return the goods within the 30 days.

There are four ways in which written terms can be incorporated into an oral contract: by signing a document; through giving reasonable notice; through previous dealings and through trade practice. We will explore each of these in turn. Before doing so, we need to address the context of the cases.

→ CROSS-REFERENCE

The law relating to exemption clauses is detailed in Chapter 7.

The cases on the incorporation of terms were developed in the context of exemption clauses. Exemption clauses are terms that exclude or limit the liability of a party in the event of a breach or act of negligence. However, the principles developed apply to the incorporation of terms generally rather than only terms that are exemption clauses.

6.2.1 Incorporation by Signature

In *L'Estrange v F Graucob Ltd* [1934] 2 KB 394 the Court of Appeal made it clear that if you freely sign a document, you are bound by its terms. Even if you don't read the document, you are still bound by it. In this case the claimant agreed to buy a cigarette vending machine for her café from the defendant. The claimant signed a document without reading it. When she discovered that the machine was defective, she brought an action for breach of contract. The defendant seller argued they were not liable because the document signed had an exclusion clause. The clause stated that: 'any express or implied condition, statement, or warranty, statutory or otherwise not stated herein is hereby excluded'. It was held that this clause excluded liability for the defects. It made no difference that the document had not been read.

In his judgment, Scrutton LJ stated the following basic rule:

> When a document containing contractual terms is signed, then, in the absence of fraud, or, I will add, misrepresentation, the party signing it is bound, and it is wholly immaterial whether he has read the document or not.

The reason for this is that signing a document shows an intention to agree to the terms contained in that document.

THINKING POINTS

- Does the decision in *L'Estrange* seem harsh? Consider the clause. Do you think anyone would really agree to pay for goods even if they are completely useless or not even what was ordered?
- Do you think ticking a box on a webpage to agree to the terms should be treated as being equivalent to signing a document?

Today, the type of exclusion clause found in *L'Estrange* would be subject to a test of reasonableness under the Unfair Contract Terms Act 1977, section 7. Such an exclusion clause would be completely ineffective in a consumer contract (s.31, Consumer Rights Act 2015, previously s.6, Unfair Contract Terms Act 1977).

The comment from Scrutton LJ makes it clear that the rule on signing a document is not absolute. The signature must be freely made and it cannot be the result of fraud, or a misrepresentation.

The effect of a signed document that was misrepresented can be seen in *Curtis v Chemical Cleaning and Dyeing Co Ltd* [1951] 1 KB 805. Here, Mrs Curtis took a white satin wedding dress to be cleaned by the defendant. The shop assistant gave Mrs Curtis a document with the heading 'Receipt'. Mrs Curtis was then asked to sign it. Before doing so, Mrs Curtis asked why she had to sign something and the shop assistant then explained that it was because the shop did not accept responsibility for certain specified risks including damage to beads and sequins. However, the exemption on the document was much wider. It excluded liability for all damage caused. Based on the statement about the document, Mrs Curtis signed without reading it and later, when she collected the dress, it was stained. When she complained, the defendant shop tried to rely on the exclusion clause.

The Court of Appeal held that the document had been misrepresented. According to Denning LJ, the clause was only effective to the extent of the misrepresentation. That meant that the clause would only exclude liability for damage to beads and sequins because that is how the document was represented. Since the damage was a stain rather than damage to beads and sequins, the defendant was liable to Mrs Curtis.

KEY POINTS

You are bound by what you sign, but if the meaning of a document has been misrepresented before it is signed, then you are only bound by the version you were told.

6.2.2 Incorporation of Written Terms by Reasonable Notice

Many terms are incorporated into contracts without a signature. Instead, such unsigned terms can be part of the contract if there is *reasonable notice* of the terms. This is an objective standard and it does not matter whether a party actually *knew* of the terms.

For reasonable notice, all we need to do is ask if reasonable steps were taken to give notice of the terms. One way to assess this is to simply ask if the reasonable person would have had notice. An early case on this issue, which is cited by judges as the authority for the reasonable notice requirement, is *Parker v South Eastern Railway* (1877) 2 CPD 416. In this case Mr Parker left his bag in a cloakroom in the defendant's station. He paid the attendant and received a ticket. The front of the ticket had a number, date and opening times. It also said 'see back'. On the back, there was a term limiting the defendant's liability to £10 (a limitation clause). When Mr Parker returned, his bag could not be found. He then brought an action for £24, 10s as the value of the bag. The question was whether the terms on the ticket were part of the contract. Mr Parker had not read the terms, and was not told to do so. The Court of Appeal held that the terms had been incorporated into the contract. The core reasoning on the incorporation of the terms is captured by the following comment by Mellish LJ:

> The railway company, as it seems to me, must be entitled to make some assumptions respecting the person who deposits luggage with them: I think they are entitled to assume that he can read, and that he understands the English language, and that he pays such attention to what he is about as may be reasonably expected from a person in such a transaction as that of depositing luggage in a cloak-room. The railway company must, however, take mankind as they find them, and if what they do is sufficient to inform people in general that the ticket contains conditions, I think that a particular plaintiff ought not to be in a better position than other persons on account of his exceptional ignorance or stupidity or carelessness.

The case shows that the terms were part of the contract because the reasonable person (what the judge referred to as 'people in general') would have had notice. Such a person can read and understand English and would pay attention to the transaction and therefore notice the terms.

KEY POINTS

Actual notice of terms is not required. Instead, *reasonable* notice is enough to incorporate the terms.

On the facts of *Parker*, we might be tempted to wonder why the terms on the ticket were not too late. In other words, it might appear that the contract was formed before the ticket was issued. However, the formation of the contract in *Parker* was explained by Lord Denning MR in *Thornton v Shoe Lane Parking* [1971] 2 QB 163 in the following way:

> We have been referred to the ticket cases of former times from *Parker v. South Eastern Railway Co.* (1877) 2 C.P.D. 416 to *McCutcheon v. David MacBrayne Ltd.* [1964] 1 W.L.R. 125. They were concerned

with railways, steamships and cloakrooms where booking clerks issued tickets to customers who took them away without reading them. In those cases the issue of the ticket was regarded as an offer by the company. If the customer took it and retained it without objection, his act was regarded as an acceptance of the offer: see *Watkins v. Rymill* (1833) 10 Q.B.D. 178, 188 and *Thompson v. London, Midland and Scottish Railway Co.* [1930] 1 K.B. 41, 47.

This observation by Lord Denning MR confirms that the issue of the ticket was an offer which was then accepted by taking it and walking away. Alternatively, the customer could reject the offer by refusing and simply ask the ticket attendant for a refund. That was very different to the formation of a contract involving an automated ticket machine because a customer cannot get their money back once the ticket has been issued.

➡ CROSS-REFERENCE
for the formation of contracts using automatic ticket machines see 3.4.

For reasonable notice there is no need for all of the relevant terms to be seen immediately. It is enough to simply refer to the *existence* of terms. This point was clear from *Thompson v London, Midland and Scottish Railway* [1930] 1 KB 41. Here the train ticket said 'see back'. On the back, it referred to the existence of terms and conditions on the timetables and these timetables were available for sixpence. This approach to referring to the *existence* of terms did not prevent the terms being part of the contract.

The same approach was applied to newspaper scratch cards in *O'Brian v MGN Ltd* [2001] EWCA Civ 1279. The scratch cards simply stated that terms and conditions applied. These terms were not even in the newspaper that issued the cards. Instead, the terms were in previous papers and could be obtained from the newspaper company. That was enough for the terms to be part of the contract. The same would apply to a reference to the full terms being accessible on a website (*Impala Warehousing & Logistics (Shanghai) Ltd v Wanxiang Resources (Singapore) Pte Ltd* [2015] EWHC 811). This method of incorporation is sometimes called 'incorporation by reference'.

The approach towards reasonable notice is based on *reasonable* steps being taken to give notice. In the cases addressed so far, the claimants were expected to read the terms, or the reference to the terms. It follows that if the terms or reference to the terms is not capable of being read, then not enough notice has been given. An example is *Sugar v London, Midland and Scottish Railway* [1941] 1 All ER 172. There a date stamp obscured the reference to terms and conditions. This meant the terms had not been incorporated. The same approach was adopted in *Poseidon Freight Forwarding Co Ltd v Davies Turner Southern Ltd* [1996] 2 Lloyd's Rep. 388. There a faxed page referred to conditions 'on the back' but then the back page did not arrive.

6.2.3 Reasonable Notice and Non-standard Claimants

The requirement of *reasonable* notice means that ordinarily, it does not matter if the claimant was incapable of actually reading the terms. *Thompson v LMS Railway* [1930] 1 KB 41 is the key case on the point. It concerned Mrs Thompson who was given a travel ticket by her niece. This referred to the existence of terms that were on the timetables. Due to the negligence of the defendant train company, Mrs Thompson was injured when stepping off the train and onto the platform. When she claimed damages for the negligence, the train company relied on an exclusion clause in its terms. This clause excluded all liability including liability for personal injury and death (such a clause is no longer enforceable since the Unfair Contract Terms Act 1977, section 2(1); this is now reflected in consumer contracts by s.65, Consumer Rights Act 2015).

In the Court of Appeal, Lord Hanworth MR referred to the fact that Mrs Thompson was unable to read. This was swiftly rejected as something that made no difference. Instead, the judgments focussed on explaining that 'reasonable steps' had been taken to give notice. The point is that it can be assumed that everyone can read and that there is no need to ensure that each person has *actual* notice of the terms. All that is required is that *reasonable* steps are taken. Sankey LJ also observed:

> Supposing again the conditions in the time table were printed in Chinese, so that you could not understand them, there again it probably could not be said you would be bound by the condition.

This is an early indication that reasonable steps would not be reflected by a notice that is expressed in a foreign language only. This is because it is assumed that a reasonable person can read English, but is not required to know other languages.

However, if the party relying on the terms knows that the notice is insufficient for a particular person, then more has to be done for notice to be reasonable. The case of *Geier v Kujawa, Western and Warne Bros (Transport)* [1970] 1 Lloyd's Rep 364 is significant here. It concerned a German chamber maid who spoke very little English. She was being driven from work when the vehicle was involved in an accident. There was an exemption clause displayed on the dashboard. However, the defendant knew that the claimant was not capable of reading the notice without it being translated. On that basis, more had to be done to meet the requirement of reasonable notice.

6.2.4 Reasonable Notice Must Be on a 'Contractual Document'

For reasonable notice, it is often said that the terms must be on a contractual document. That does not mean the terms must be on paper. It just means that terms must be on something that holds itself out as containing terms.

The key case on this requirement is *Chapelton v Barry Urban District Council* [1940] 1 KB 532. The claimant hired some deckchairs on the defendant's beach. The prices were displayed on a notice board next to the pile of deckchairs. It also indicated that customers were to help themselves to the deckchairs and then pay the attendant. The claimant took two chairs and then paid the hire charge. He received two tickets and placed them in his pocket. When he sat on his chair, he fell through the canvass, causing injury. He then brought an action for damages. The defendant tried to rely on a clause on the ticket which excluded liability for personal injury. However, the Court of Appeal held that the ticket was not a contractual document and so its terms were not part of the contract.

The reasoning was based on the idea that the offer by the defendant was on the notice board. That was the 'contractual document' because, it held itself out as having the terms. On that basis, the reasonable person would not expect to find terms on the ticket. Instead, the ticket given later was just a receipt, and was no more than evidence of payment. Slesser LJ also made reference to the wording on the notice. He highlighted that the notice 'respectfully requested' that customers take a ticket and retain it for inspection. That was a further indication that the ticket was just a receipt, rather than something contractual. It gave the impression that having a ticket was for the convenience of the defendant to check how long someone had paid for.

KEY POINTS

For reasonable notice, the relevant term needs to be on whatever holds itself out as having the terms.

6.2.5 Reasonable Notice and Timing

For notice to be reasonable, it must be given *before* or *at the time* the contract is made. If notice is given after the contract is formed, it is too late. This point is illustrated by *Olley v Marlborough*

Court Hotel [1949] 1 KB 532. Here, Mrs Olley and her husband arranged a long-term stay in a hotel. They paid for the first week in advance. Six months into their stay, the claimant's furs, jewellery and some clothes were stolen from their room. The thief had taken the room key from the reception office, but the defendant hotel refused to accept liability for the loss. It relied on the notice on a door inside the bedroom that excluded liability for loss or theft. However, the Court of Appeal held that the terms on the door were too late because the contract was formed before it had been possible to see the notice. On that basis, the exemption clause had not been incorporated into the contract.

The decision was based on the fact that the hotel had not provided notice until after the contract was formed. By then, it was too late. On the facts, Mrs Olley had paid for one week in advance. She then made a second payment after the first week of their stay. If that was a new contract, then arguably, the notice would not have been too late for that second contract. However, Singleton LJ explained that the initial contract was not fixed for a week. Instead, it was for an open period which meant that the later payments were still under the original contract made before entering the room.

 THINKING POINTS

Would the decision have been different if it was not the first time that Mr and Mrs Olley stayed in the hotel?

The case emphasises the need to ensure that notices are displayed prominently before, or at the time of the contract. If the contract is made over the phone, then businesses should refer to terms that exist on their website, or actually state the relevant terms.

The timing issue played an important role in *Thornton v Shoe Lane Parking* [1971] 2 QB 163 which concerned what was a new, automatic multi-storey car park. When Mr Thornton drove to the entrance, there was a notice with the charges. It also stated that cars were parked at the 'owner's risk'. Once the machine issued a ticket, he took it and parked his car. Later, he returned and paid the charge but, before getting into his car, he was injured in an accident. The defendant car park relied on their terms, which excluded liability for all injuries. The terms were on a pillar inside the car park opposite the payment machine. They were also by the ticket office. In addition, the ticket stated that it had been issued subject to the terms displayed. The Court of Appeal ruled that the clause had not been incorporated into the contract because the notice was too late.

The analysis of the contract formation was important to the outcome. The contract formation was based on the final opportunity of the customer to object to the terms. On the facts, once the driver pulled up to the entrance, the driver was committed and the ticket was issued by the machine automatically. On that basis, driving up to the entrance was acceptance. The offer was the notice outside with terms and prices. This meant that the contract was formed *before* the ticket was issued. For that reason, the existence of additional terms that the ticket referred to were not incorporated into the contract.

6.2.6 Really Onerous and Unusual Terms

The requirement of reasonable notice is well established. We know that reasonable steps must be taken to bring the terms to the attention of the other party. Only then is the term incorporated into the contract. However, what is required for 'reasonable steps' to be taken can vary according to the type of term being relied upon. When a term is onerous (i.e. it imposes a very heavy burden) or is unusual, more has to be done to show that reasonable steps were taken. The key statement cited to support this is from *J. Spurling v Bradshaw* [1956] 1 WLR 461 where Denning LJ stated:

> I quite agree that the more unreasonable a clause is, the greater the notice which must be given of it. Some clauses which I have seen would need to be printed in red ink on the face of the document with a red hand pointing to it before the notice could be held to be sufficient.

Later, in *Thornton v Shoe Lane Parking* [1971], Lord Denning MR cited his 'red hand' comment from *Spurling*. However, the building blocks for this approach were laid much earlier in *Parker v South Eastern Railway* (1877) where Bramwell LJ stated:

> It is asked: What if there was some unreasonable condition, as for instance to forfeit £1,000 if the goods were not removed in 48 hours? Would the depositor be bound? I might content myself by asking: Would he be, if he were told 'our conditions are on this ticket,' and he did not read them. In my judgment, he would not be bound in either case. I think there is an implied understanding that there is no condition unreasonable to the knowledge of the party tendering the document and not insisting on its being read. . .

This is an early opinion in favour of requiring a higher degree of notice for 'unreasonable' terms. The comment referred to a term imposing a charge of £1000 for not collecting the item from the cloakroom within 48 hours. Such a term would have been imposing a significant burden on the consumer, and it would be extremely unusual and therefore unexpected. According to Brammell LJ, the standard reasonable notice requirement should only apply when the terms are not unreasonable. Likewise, the Court of Appeal made the point in *Thompson v London, Midland Scottish Railway* [1930]. There Lawrence LJ observed:

> If there were a condition which was unreasonable to the knowledge of the company tendering the ticket I do not think the passenger would be bound.

His Lordship then explained that the term excluding liability for personal injury was not unreasonable!

> Here it cannot be said that the condition in question in this case is an unreasonable one, either from the point of view of the company or from that of the passenger. It is a condition . . . which has existed in respect of excursion trains for upwards of half a century, and is, to my mind, a reasonable condition, which need not have special attention directed to it.

The main case on the incorporation of onerous or unusual terms by notice is *Interfoto Picture Library Ltd v Stiletto Visual Programmes Ltd* [1988] 2 WLR 615. Unlike the previous cases on incorporation by notice, it did not concern an exemption clause.

In *Interfoto*, the defendant company contacted the claimant library with a phone call asking about 1950s pictures on transparencies for use in a presentation. The claimant then posted 47 transparencies along with a delivery note. The note had nine terms and the second term (condition 2) referred to a charge of £5 per day (plus tax) for each transparency that was kept beyond fourteen days. The defendant called the library to say that some of the pictures were of interest and that they would be back in touch. They didn't get in touch and the transparencies were returned almost a month later. So, following condition 2, the claimant sent an invoice demanding payment of £3783.50 (i.e. 47 transparencies at £5 each per day plus tax for two weeks). When this wasn't paid, the claimant brought an action. The Court of Appeal held that condition 2 had not been incorporated into the contract. This was based on the view that more had to be done to give reasonable notice of such an onerous term. On that basis, the defendant just had to pay a reasonable charge for the delay of £3.50 per week for each transparency. As the leading case on the incorporation of onerous or unusual terms, it is useful to read the judgment of Dillon LJ.

GUIDED CASE READING 6.1
Interfoto Picture Library Ltd v Stiletto Visual Programmes Ltd [1988] 2 WLR 615

When you read the extract of the judgment by Dillon LJ, try to identify:

- why not enough was done to give reasonable notice;
- the consequences of insufficient notice in the case.

It has to be said, however, that the holding fee charged by the plaintiffs by condition 2 is extremely high, and in my view exorbitant. The judge held that on a *quantum meruit* a reasonable charge would have been £3.50 per transparency per week, and not £5 per day, and he had evidence before him of the terms charged by some ten other photographic libraries, most of which charged less than £3.50 per week and only one of which charged more (£4 per transparency per week).

> Dillon LJ begins by explaining that the fee charged by the library was significantly higher that the market rate, which is what makes it both 'onerous' (because it is so high) and 'unusual' (because it was very much out of line with the standard in the market).

Quantum meruit

is a Latin term for 'what has been earned', i.e. a reasonable sum for the work done or goods supplied.

... The original telephone call was merely a preliminary inquiry and did not give rise to any contract. But the contract came into existence when the plaintiffs sent the transparencies to the defendants and the defendants, after opening the bag, accepted them by [the defendant's second] phone call to the plaintiffs .... The question is whether condition 2 was a term of that contract.

... The question is therefore whether condition 2 was sufficiently brought to the defendants' attention to make it a term of the contract which was only concluded after the defendants had received, and must have known that they had received the transparencies and the delivery note.

> He then construes the contract as having come into existence when the transparencies were sent to the defendants—this constituted an offer, which the defendants accepted by their phone call to the library saying that some of the pictures were 'of interest'. This meant that condition 2 satisfied the timing requirement—there was an opportunity to see it before acceptance took place.

This sort of question was posed, in relation to printed conditions, in the ticket cases, such as *Parker v. South Eastern Railway Co.* (1877) 2 C.P.D. 416, in the last century. At that stage the printed conditions were looked at as a whole and the question considered by the courts was whether the printed conditions as a whole had been sufficiently drawn to a customer's attention to make the whole set of conditions part of the contract; if so the customer was bound by the printed conditions even though he never read them.

> This meant that the only question was whether reasonable steps had been taken to notify Stiletto of the existence of condition 2. This meant that effectively the test was exactly that of *Parker v SE Railways*, although with a crucial difference.

More recently the question has been discussed whether it is enough to look at a set of printed conditions as a whole. When for instance one condition in a set is particularly onerous does something special need to be done to draw customers' attention to that particular condition? In an obiter dictum in *J. Spurling Ltd. v. Bradshaw* [1956] 1 W.L.R. 461, 466 (cited in Chitty on Contracts, 25th ed. (1983), vol. 1, p. 408) Denning L.J. stated:

'Some clauses which I have seen would need to be printed in red ink on the face of the document with a red hand pointing to it before the notice could be held to be sufficient'.

Then in *Thornton v. Shoe Lane Parking Ltd.* [1971] 2 Q.B. 163 both Lord Denning M.R. and Megaw L.J. held as one of their grounds of decision, as I read their judgments, that where a condition is particularly onerous or unusual the party seeking to enforce it must show that that condition, or an unusual condition of that particular nature, was fairly brought to the notice of the other party. Lord Denning M. R., at pp. 169H–170D, re-stated and applied what he had said in the *Spurling* case, and held that the court should not hold any man bound by such a condition unless it was drawn to his attention in the most explicit way ...

> That crucial difference was that in the modern era the assessment was done for each individual term rather than the terms as a whole. This meant that where one term was especially onerous it needed to be assessed individually to see if reasonable steps had been taken to bring it to the other party's attention. The more onerous the term, the more had to be done to constitute reasonable steps—for instance by printing it in red ink and with a big red hand pointing to it.

Condition 2 of these plaintiffs' conditions is in my judgment a very onerous clause. The defendants could not conceivably have known, if their attention

> The judgment then explained why condition 2 should be classed as onerous—the rate was exorbitant. Perhaps the most significant factor was that it was also so high that it would not have been expected by Stiletto. In this sense it ...

was not drawn to the clause, that the plaintiffs were proposing to charge a 'holding fee' for the retention of the transparencies at such a very high and exorbitant rate.

> ... was 'unusual' as well as 'onerous'. It is the fact that it would not ordinarily be expected that meant something additional had to be done to draw it to Stiletto's attention.

At the time of the ticket cases in the last century it was notorious that people hardly ever troubled to read printed conditions on a ticket or delivery note or similar document. That remains the case now. In the intervening years the printed conditions have tended to become more and more complicated and more and more one-sided in favour of the party who is imposing them, but the other parties, if they notice that there are printed conditions at all, generally still tend to assume that such conditions are only concerned with ancillary matters of form and are not of importance. In the ticket cases the courts held that the common law required that reasonable steps be taken to draw the other parties' attention to the printed conditions or they would not be part of the contract. It is, in my judgment, a logical development of the common law into modern conditions that it should be held, as it was in *Thornton v. Shoe Lane Parking Ltd.* [1971] 2 Q.B. 163, that, if one condition in a set of printed conditions is particularly onerous or unusual, the party seeking to enforce it must show that that particular condition was fairly brought to the attention of the other party.

> Dillan LJ then explained the basic underlying rationale for this: people generally do not carefully read printed terms and conditions and assume them not to be important. This can allow the party relying on printed conditions to 'cheat' and smuggle in very one-sided terms to take advantage of the other party's ignorance. This puts a requirement on a contracting party to make sure that conditions are 'fairly' brought to the attention of the other. This does not mean, again, that a contracting party has a duty to make sure the other party reads a condition. Rather, the duty is to take 'reasonable steps'—a duty which requires more to be satisfied the more onerous or unusual the term is.

In the present case, nothing whatever was done by the plaintiffs to draw the defendants' attention particularly to condition 2; it was merely one of four columns' width of conditions printed across the foot of the delivery note. Consequently condition 2 never, in my judgment, became part of the contract between the parties.

[Bingham LJ delivered a judgment that reflected the same reasoning]

> Since Interfoto had done nothing in particular to bring the condition to Stiletto's attention it had not taken 'reasonable steps' and the condition was not incorporated in to the contract.

The case is quite unusual in having only two judges. Both decided in favour of the defendant. However, they adopted a different approach towards the impact of the onerous term. Dillon LJ said that the onerous term had not been incorporated with the other terms. In contrast, Bingham LJ decided that all of the terms (including the onerous term) had been incorporated. However, the failure to specifically highlight the onerous term meant that it was not enforceable.

Subsequent cases have preferred to say that such terms are not incorporated, rather than incorporated but unenforceable. *AEG (UK) Ltd v Logic Resource Ltd* [1996] CLC 265 provides an example. It concerned a term requiring a buyer to pay for the costs of returning defective goods to the seller. The term was classed as onerous and unusual and so a higher degree of notice was required. It was clear that no additional steps were taken to bring the term to the attention of the buyer. On that basis, the Court of Appeal held that the term was not part of the contract.

KEY POINTS

If the term is onerous or unusual then a higher degree of notice is required for 'reasonable steps' to be held to have been taken.

While the principle from *Interfoto* was a welcome development, there are some uncertainties over its application. One uncertainty is the question about *when* a term is to be classed as 'onerous' or 'unusual'. Different judges can disagree over 'onerousness', as Sir Anthon Evans LJ and Hale LJ did in *O'Brien v MGN Ltd* [2001] EWCA Civ 1279.

Another uncertainty is about the scope of the *Interfoto* principle. Does it apply to signed documents? If it does then it goes some way to reducing the scope for unfairness resulting from the strict rule in *L'Estrange v Graucob*. In *Ocean Chemical Transport Inc v Exnor Craggs Ltd* [2000] 1 All ER (Comm) 519, Evans LJ suggested that *Interfoto* could apply to signed documents in extreme cases. The point wasn't explored in detail because notice of the relevant term had actually been given. More recently, in *Woodeson and another v Credit Suisse (UK) Ltd* [2018] EWCA Civ 1103, Longmore LJ observed:

➜ CROSS-REFERENCE
For L'Estrange v Graucob
see 6.3.1.

> [46] In any event, when the contractual documentation is signed, the *Interfoto* principle has no, or extremely limited, application, see *Peekay v Australia and New Zealand Bank* [2006] EWCA Civ 386, para 43 per Moore-Bick LJ.

However, in *Bates v Post Office Ltd (No 3 Common Issues)* [2019] EWHC 606 (QB), having identified a number of terms as onerous and unusual, Fraser J decided that some of these had been incorporated into the contract because they were on a signed document. While acknowledging the comment from Longmore LJ which does not completely exclude the application of *Interfoto* from signed documents, *L'Estrange v Graucob* was viewed as the binding authority.

➜ CROSS-REFERENCE
For the facts of *Bates v Post Office* see 1.5.3.

6.2.7 Incorporation of Terms by Previous Dealings and Trade Practice

Imagine two parties that enter a contract before reasonable notice of terms can be given. We know that the notice is too late (like it was in *Olley v Marlborough Court Hotel*). But what if they continue to contract in this way? At some point, it might be said that the terms were too late for the previous contract, but are in advance of the next one. In such circumstances, it could be said that the parties have shown an intention to continue on the basis of the terms previously available. On that basis, it could be said that the terms have been incorporated by previous dealings.

This was the approach adopted by Denning LJ in *Spurling v Bradshaw* [1956]. Here the defendant delivered barrels of orange juice to be stored in the claimants' warehouse. After the contract was formed, the defendant received a document containing terms excluding liability for damage or loss of the goods stored. The terms from that document would have been too late for the first contract. However, the same document had been used in their previous transactions. On that basis, Denning LJ acknowledged that for the latest contract, the terms had been incorporated by the parties' previous dealings.

For terms to be incorporated by previous dealings, it is necessary to have a 'consistent' and 'frequent' course of dealings. This was made clear by the House of Lords in *McCutcheon v David MacBrayne Ltd* [1964] 1 WLR 430. Here the claimant asked a relative to ship his car from a Scottish island to the mainland using the defendant shipping service. The relative paid for the car to be shipped and received a receipt. Due to the negligence of the defendant, the ship sank and so the claimant brought an action for the value of the car. The defendant relied on their terms excluding liability. Usually, the defendant would ask customers to sign a document containing the relevant terms. However, on this occasion, they had not done so, but the relative had used the shipping service previously. Sometimes he signed the document, and other times he didn't. The claimant had used the service four times and on all occasions had signed the document. These facts raised the question as to whether the terms on the document could be incorporated from the parties' previous dealings. The House of Lords held that the terms had not been incorporated. Essentially, the House of Lords said that the previous dealings were not sufficiently consistent and frequent.

The same approach was adopted by the Court of Appeal in *Hollier v Rambler Motors (AMC) Ltd* [1972] 2 QB 71. Here the claimant took his car to the defendant garage to be repaired. At the garage, the car was seriously damaged by a fire and so the claimant brought an action for damages. The garage tried to rely on a term excluding liability for damage to vehicles. This exclusion clause was on an invoice that customers would sign when leaving their vehicles. On this occasion, the claimant had not been given anything to sign but he had used the garage three or four times in the previous five years and, on those occasions, he had signed the invoice without reading it. So, one question was whether the term had been incorporated by the previous dealings. The Court of Appeal rejected this argument and decided that the term was not part of the contract. Again, the previous dealings were not sufficiently consistent and frequent. Salmon LJ distinguished this decision from that in *Hardwick Game Farm v Suffolk Agricultural Poultry Producers Association* [1969] 2 AC 31 where the parties had the same sales three or four times a month for three years. That was consistent and frequent enough for a term to be incorporated by previous dealings.

Some industries and sectors operate with the use of certain standard terms. If the use of such terms is well established, it could be said that parties in that sector intend such terms to apply by default when they enter into contracts with each other. In other words, objectively, it appears that the parties understand that the terms would apply (for an example, see the Court of Appeal case of *British Crane Hire Corporation v Ipswich Plant Hire Ltd* [1975] QB 303).

6.3 Oral Statements as Terms That Add to the Written Contract

A formal contract in writing is typical for many dealings between commercial parties. Likewise, consumers also encounter written contracts. There are many examples, but perhaps the more familiar examples would be: a mobile phone contract; a tenancy contract for your accommodation; and an insurance contract for your personal property.

When a contract is written, terms are expressed in the document. But before the written contract is agreed, it is normal for the parties to negotiate. During the negotiations, many statements are made and will then be included in the written contract. Even if the contract is a pre-drafted standard form, statements might be made and agreed before the parties agree to enter the pre-drafted contract. One key issue is the status of oral statements not included in the written contract. Can those statements be treated as terms that are part of the overall contractual relationship along with what has been written?

6.3.1 The Parol Evidence 'Rule'

Whenever there is a discussion of oral statements adding to written terms, reference is made to the so-called 'parol (oral) evidence rule'. Under this rule, evidence outside of the written contract cannot be used to add to, change or contradict what is written. The idea is that when there is a written contract, it is assumed that the parties only intended for the written contract to contain terms. However, so many exceptions to the 'rule' have developed that it is often said that it is not really rule at all. One example is where the parties' apparent intentions indicate that the contract includes things outside of what was written. In such circumstances, the courts will recognise those additional terms. The real effect of the 'rule' is that it indicates who has the burden of proof. The court will focus on what is written unless a party proves there were intended to be other terms. In other words, it tells us that the party claiming the contract includes more than what is written has to prove it.

6.3.2 Collateral Contracts

When there is an apparent intention to treat an oral statement as a contractual promise, it might take the form of a 'collateral contract'. This is a second contract that runs alongside the main written contract. Collectively, the main and collateral contracts then represent the contractual relationship between the parties.

→ CROSS-REFERENCE
Collateral contracts were discussed in the context of auctions in 2.5.2.

A good example is *City And Westminster Properties Ltd v Mudd* [1959] Ch 129. The defendant was a tenant of a shop for five years and had lived in the back office of the premises. When the lease was due for renewal, the new lease had a term stating the shop could be used for the tenant's business purposes only. It specifically excluded using the premises as a place to live. The defendant objected to this. In response, the landlord told the tenant that if he signed the lease, the tenant could continue to live there. On that basis, the defendant tenant agreed to the renewal. Later, the landlord tried to evict the tenant claiming the tenant was in breach of the lease by sleeping in the premises.

Harmon J explained the effect of the statement by the landlord:

> If the defendant's evidence is to be accepted, as I hold it is, it is a case of a promise made to him before the execution of the lease that, if he would execute it in the form put before him, the landlord would not seek to enforce against him personally the covenant about using the property as a shop only. The defendant says that it was in reliance on this promise that he executed the lease and entered on the onerous obligations contained in it. He says, moreover, that but for the promise made he would not have executed the lease, but would have moved to other premises available to him at the time. If these be the facts, there was a clear contract acted upon by the defendant to his detriment and from which the plaintiffs cannot be allowed to resile. . .The promise was that so long as the defendant personally was tenant, so long would the landlords forbear to exercise the rights which they would have if he signed the lease. He did sign the lease on this promise and is therefore entitled to rely on it so long as he is personally in occupation of the shop.

The judgment did not make an express reference to a 'collateral contract' but that is the effect of the statement above. The point here is that there was an important promise made allowing the tenant to live in the premises. In return, the tenant (promisee) provided consideration by acting to his detriment in signing ('executing') the lease. That resulted in an additional contract that could be enforced. If the landlord then went back on the promise ('resiled'), the landlord would be in breach.

KEY POINTS

The use of a collateral contract will allow an oral statement to contradict or add to what is written.

The same approach was adopted by Lord Denning MR in *J.Evans & Son (Portsmouth) v Andrea Merzario Ltd* [1976] 1 WLR 1078. This case concerned the transportation of the claimant's machinery by sea. Because the machinery could rust, the claimant wanted the machinery to be carried below deck. So, the defendant arranging the transport gave an oral assurance that the machinery would be transported in a container, below deck. However, due to an error, the machinery was carried in a container on the deck of the ship and it fell overboard. The oral assurance to keep the goods below deck was not in the written carriage contract. The question for the court was whether the oral assurance could be enforced by the claimant. Lord Denning MR held the only reason why the carriage contract came into existence was because the assurance had been made. This made the assurance enforceable as a separate contract that existed alongside the main one.

6.3.3 Where the Contract Is Both Oral and in Writing

In some circumstances, it is possible for parties to show there was an intention for a contact to be a combination of both oral and written terms. On that basis, the oral statements can be enforced even though they are not in the written contract. This was the approach of Roskill LJ in *Evans v Andrea Merzario* who referred to the parol evidence rule and then explained that why that 'doctrine' did not apply:

> But that doctrine, as it seems to me, has little or no application where one is not concerned with a contract in writing. . . but with a contract which, as I think, was partly oral, partly in writing, and partly by conduct. In such a case the court does not require to have recourse to lawyer's devices such as collateral oral warranty in order to seek to adduce evidence which would not otherwise be admissible.

According to Roskill LJ, in the circumstances, there was no need to rely on the mechanism of a collateral contract to put forward and rely on ('adduce') the oral statement. He stressed that there was a need to look at all of the evidence holistically:

> The court is entitled to look at and should look at all the evidence from start to finish in order to see what the bargain was that was struck between the parties. That is what we have done in this case and what, with great respect, I think the judge did not do in the course of his judgment. . . one should look at the totality of the evidence.

The wider evidence beyond the written document showed an intention for the contract to be both written and oral. Roskill LJ then set out the facts showing why the oral statement was part of the overall contract:

> The defendants gave such a promise, which to my mind against this background plainly amounted to an enforceable contractual promise. In those circumstances it seems to me that the contract was this: "If we continue to give you our business, you will ensure that those goods in containers are shipped under deck"; and the defendants agreed that this would be so. Thus there was a breach of that contract by the defendants when this container was shipped on deck.

This judgment (like that Lord Denning MR) recognised the importance of the oral statement. It was the very basis for agreeing to have the machinery transported. But Roskill LJ preferred to say the statement meant there was an intention for the contract to be both oral and in writing. So according to Roskill LJ, instead of forming a separate (collateral) contract, the statement was simply an oral term that sat in the same contract along with the written terms.

KEY POINTS

The circumstances might show an intention for an oral statement to be a term along with the terms on a document.

6.3.4 'Entire Agreement' Clauses

There is a well-established way to prevent oral statements being contractual. The written contract could have a term stating that the written document represents the entire agreement. Such a term excludes the possibility of an oral statement being a term. In effect, this expresses an intention for the parol evidence rule to apply. The case of *Inntrepreneur Pub Co v East Crown Ltd* [2000] 2 Lloyds Rep 611 is often cited as authority. The case concerned a tied pub, which meant it had to buy its beer from the claimant. When the claimant tried to enforce this obligation, the defendant argued that there had been a collateral promise that he would be released from the tie-in after a certain date. Lightman J held that the oral statement could not be a term. The reasoning was based on the entire agreement clause in the written contract. It showed there had been an intention to exclude oral statements and provide more certainty over the content of the contract.

A basic entire agreement clause can exclude oral statements as terms. However, it would not prevent liability for misrepresentations (*Barclays Bank plc v Unicredit Bank AG* [2014] EWCA Civ 302). This is because a basic 'entire agreement' clause only stops the oral statements being contractual as terms. To exclude liability for false representations, more specific wording is needed. Even then, such an exclusion clause could be challenged using legislation that limits the use of exemption clauses.

→ CROSS-REFERENCE

The use and enforcement of Exemption clauses are explored in Chapter 7.

KEY POINTS

An 'entire agreement clause' in a contract will prevent anything outside of the document being part of the contract.

In the context of distance sales to consumers like those completed on-line, over the phone or by mail order, a rule was introduced by the Consumer Rights Act 2015. Under section 12, certain pre-contract information, like information about the main characteristics of the goods, will be classed as terms.

6.4 The Interpretation of Express Terms

Most commercial cases involve a dispute about the meaning of the terms. The terms are then interpreted by the courts. Over the past 20 years, the judicial approach to interpretation has become increasingly significant. This is a result of judges making statements about principles that shape their approach to interpretation. It is a large area of contract law, but here we focus on the main points. Our starting point is the need for terms to be interpreted.

6.4.1 The Need for Terms to Be Interpreted

With a written contract, the terms agreed by the parties are there to see. These terms are an expression of the parties' apparent intentions, and it is for the courts to apply these intentions. The problem is that parties often argue about what those terms mean. This might be because the meaning of the terms is not very clear. They might have been written by business people rather than lawyers, but even lawyers can draft terms in a fairly vague way. This is often the case when the clients are keen to enter a contract quickly. It is difficult to be clear and detailed enough to cover all eventualities when the drafting is being done rapidly. And the parties may indeed decide that they can start with a basic set of terms and negotiate the niceties as time goes on while the contract is being performed. Even when the terms are detailed and clear, there is often scope for a party to question the meaning of them later. The problem is that it is almost impossible to produce the perfect 'bullet-proof' contract, one in which lawyers cannot find 'holes'.

Following a dispute, lawyers will always try to find a different meaning for the term alleged to have been breached. This is why in practice so many commercial cases require the courts to interpret the contract. This means that, when drafting a contract, it is important to know the principles of interpretation the courts are using to work out what was intended. In *Rainy Sky SA v Kookmin Bank* [2011] UKSC 50, Lord Clarke stated the essence of these principles, which is:

> [T]o determine what the parties meant by the language used, which involves ascertaining what a reasonable person would have understood the parties to have meant.

But, of course, this requires further explanation.

6.4.2 The Traditional Approach to Interpretation

Traditionally, the courts have focussed on the words in the contractual document only. This is known as the 'four corners approach'. The case of *Lovell and Christmas Ltd v Wall* (1911) 104 LT is often cited as authority for this approach because of an influential statement by Cozens-Hardy MR. The idea was that the court would interpret the contract based on what was stated within the four corners of the document. This meant that evidence outside of the document (known as extraneous evidence), like the context or purpose of the contract, would not be used. The result was a more literal approach to interpretation because it was focussed on the grammatical meaning of the words. The clear advantage to this approach is that it provides certainty. The parties can rely on the natural meaning of the words. The same can be said for third parties (i.e. parties outside the contract) that might be relying on the terms of the contract for their own dealings.

The problem with the 'four corners approach' is that it ignores the wider context of the contract. Context can be very important. For example, consider the act of a car that flashes its lights at another. Is it a warning? Is it to say 'thank you'? It is a sign of 'giving way'? Is it a hostile response? Knowing the context of the lights being flashed will help you have a better idea of what it meant to those involved. The same can be said for contracts. The wider context can give us a better understanding of what the parties appeared to intend.

6.4.3 The Modern 'Contextual' Approach to Interpretation

The case law shows a clear trend away from the traditional approach. The current approach includes the wider context and purpose of the terms so that the interpretation reflects 'commercial common sense'. But the broad aim of the interpretation is the same. It is still an objective assessment to reflect what the parties appeared to have intended. That means the focus remains on what a reasonable person in the same circumstances must have intended. It is just that this assessment is done by making use of a wider range of information, rather than just the words used.

KEY POINTS

The modern 'contextual' approach to interpretation makes use of background facts outside of the document. The aim is to ensure that the interpretation reflects 'commercial common sense'.

The modern contextual approach is based on (the now famous judgment) of Lord Hoffman in *Investors Compensation Scheme Ltd v West Bromwich Building Society* [1998] 1 WLR 896 (*ICS*). The facts help to understand the impact of the contextual approach. It started with private elderly investors who had received negligent investment advice. As a result, they had claims against building societies, financial advisors and lawyers. It would not have been efficient for all of these elderly investors to sue their individual advisers. Also, the advisers could have made the cases last so long that the investors might not ever have seen their compensation in their lifetimes. This possibility also increased the chances of them settling for a lot less so as to avoid the stress and risk of not succeeding in time. So instead, to compensate the investors, an Investors Compensation Scheme was set up by a government body. To qualify, the investors had to assign to the scheme their rights to make claims against those liable for their negligent advice. The idea was that the investors would be compensated by the scheme. The scheme would then recover the money paid out with actions for damages against those liable for the advice.

The assignment contract (between the investors and the Scheme) did not assign all claims to the Scheme. One of the terms said that investors retained rights for:

> 'Any claim (whether sounding in rescission for undue influence or otherwise).'

→ CROSS-REFERENCE

For the law on undue influence see Chapter 15.

'Rescission' is the remedy of making the contract void, which is very different to a damages remedy. It can be available when a contract results from a misrepresentation or pressure from a relationship of trust (undue influence). The key issue in the *ICS* case was the meaning of the term. Based on the wording, the defendant building society argued that the Scheme had no right to sue them for damages. After all, the plain wording of the term said that the investors *retained* the rights to '*any claim*'. If the rights to 'any claim' were retained by the investors, then the Scheme would not have been assigned the rights to claim damages from those liable for the advice.

The House of Lords looked beyond the wording to the context of the assignment contract. It was held that the term really meant investors retained rights to:

> '*any claim sounding in rescission (whether for undue influence or otherwise)*.'

This was a serious change. It meant that the investors had assigned to the Scheme their right to claim damages from the building society. The investors could then only seek rescission to end their contract with the building society.

The interpretation by the House of Lords did not reflect the ordinary meaning of the words used. But it made sense in context. After all, the compensation from the scheme was intended to be *instead* of individual damages claims by investors.

The point can be illustrated by a promotion in a pizzeria. The term in *ICS* was equivalent to a promotion that says '*free pizza (whether the toppings are vegetarian or otherwise)*'. In effect, this was changed to '*Free pizza toppings (whether vegetarian or otherwise)*'. That second version is very different and more limited. But it could be said that the plain wording of the first promotion does not make much commercial sense. The pizzeria exists to sell pizzas and a make a profit. Would a reasonable person think they were giving all pizzas away for free?

6.4.4 Lord Hoffman's Principles of Interpretation

To achieve the result in *ICS*, Lord Hoffman made his famous statement on the principles of interpretation:

> My Lords, I will say at once that I prefer the approach of the judge. But I think I should preface my explanation of my reasons with some general remarks about the principles by which contractual documents are nowadays construed. I do not think that the fundamental change which has overtaken this branch of the law, particularly as a result of the speeches of Lord Wilberforce in *Prenn v. Simmonds* [1971] 1 W.L.R. 1381, 1384–1386 and *Reardon Smith Line Ltd. v. Yngvar Hansen-Tangen* [1976] 1 W.L.R. 989, is always sufficiently appreciated. The result has been, subject to one important exception, to assimilate the way in which such documents are interpreted by judges to the common sense principles by which any serious utterance would be interpreted in ordinary life. Almost all the old intellectual baggage of 'legal' interpretation has been discarded. The principles may be summarised as follows.
>
> (1) Interpretation is the ascertainment of the meaning which the document would convey to a reasonable person having all the background knowledge which would reasonably have been available to the parties in the situation in which they were at the time of the contract.
>
> (2) The background was famously referred to by Lord Wilberforce as the "matrix of fact," but this phrase is, if anything, an understated description of what the background may include. Subject to the requirement that it should have been reasonably available to the parties and to the exception to be mentioned next, it includes absolutely anything which would have affected the way in which the language of the document would have been understood by a reasonable man.
>
> (3) The law excludes from the admissible background the previous negotiations of the parties and their declarations of subjective intent. They are admissible only in an action for rectification. The law makes this distinction for reasons of practical policy and, in this respect only, legal interpretation differs from the way we would interpret utterances in ordinary life. The boundaries of this exception are in some respects unclear. But this is not the occasion on which to explore them.

(4) The meaning which a document (or any other utterance) would convey to a reasonable man is not the same thing as the meaning of its words. The meaning of words is a matter of dictionaries and grammars; the meaning of the document is what the parties using those words against the relevant background would reasonably have been understood to mean. The background may not merely enable the reasonable man to choose between the possible meanings of words which are ambiguous but even (as occasionally happens in ordinary life) to conclude that the parties must, for whatever reason, have used the wrong words or syntax: see *Mannai Investments Co. Ltd. v. Eagle Star Life Assurance Co. Ltd.* [1997] A.C. 749.

(5) The "rule" that words should be given their "natural and ordinary meaning" reflects the common sense proposition that we do not easily accept that people have made linguistic mistakes, particularly in formal documents. On the other hand, if one would nevertheless conclude from the background that something must have gone wrong with the language, the law does not require judges to attribute to the parties an intention which they plainly could not have had. Lord Diplock made this point more vigorously when he said in *Antaios Compania Naviera S.A. v. Salen Rederierna A.B.* [1985] A.C. 191, 201:

"if detailed semantic and syntactical analysis of words in a commercial contract is going to lead to a conclusion that flouts business commonsense, it must be made to yield to business commonsense."

A basic summary to the principles can be expressed in the following way:

1. The meaning is based on how a reasonable person with the relevant background knowledge would understand the contract.

2. The 'background' includes all facts this reasonable person could have known.

3. Evidence of previous negotiations cannot be used as background.

4. The literal meaning of the words used is not the same as what would be understood by a reasonable person with the background context.

5. It can't be assumed that there's a mistake in the language. But, if the meaning does not reflect commercial common sense, then an alternative meaning should apply.

6.4.5 Assessment of the Principles

The statement by Lord Hoffman has had a significant impact in cases. It has been cited so much that the case is now one of the most cited contract cases ever. The overall principle has been welcomed. However, its scope has resulted in a lot of debate. The common criticism is that it creates potential for uncertainty because so many things make up the wider background or 'matrix of fact'. That being said, it becomes less of a problem as more senior judges continue to comment on it and provide more guidance.

6.4.5.1 The Approach Could Represent a Judicial Re-writing of the Contract

In the case, Lord Lloyd delivered a detailed dissenting judgment. His Lordship felt there was no rule of interpretation allowing words inside brackets to be taken outside of the brackets to create the opposite effect. It was made clear that the approach of Lord Hoffman for the majority was too 'creative'. The approach crossed the line from purposive interpretation to rewriting the contract. According to Lord Lloyd, the natural meaning of the words should have been applied.

It is important to appreciate that the interpretation was not a result of the term being ambiguous and therefore capable of different meanings. The wording was clear. However, the House of Lords decided that the natural meaning of the words alone meant something had gone wrong with the language. On that basis, the term was interpreted to reflect commercial common sense—i.e. to reflect what would have been intended by the reasonable person knowing the factual background.

6.4.5.2 The Scope of the 'Matrix of Facts' or Background

The first principle has become the starting point for interpreting contracts and has not been challenged. However, the second principle has caused debate. There Lord Hoffman referred to 'absolutely anything' that could affect how a reasonable person would understand the contract. This was actually explained by Lord Hoffman in *Bank of Credit and Commerce International SA v Ali* [2001] UKHL 8.

After referring to the statement from the *ICS* case Lord Hoffman added:

> [39] I did not think it necessary to emphasise that I meant anything which a reasonable man would have regarded as *relevant*. I was merely saying that there is no conceptual limit to what can be regarded as background. It is not, for example, confined to the factual background but can include the state of the law (as in cases in which one takes into account that the parties are unlikely to have intended to agree to something unlawful or legally ineffective) or proved common assumptions which were in fact quite mistaken. But the primary source for understanding what the parties meant is their language interpreted in accordance with conventional usage: "we do not easily accept that people have made linguistic mistakes, particularly in formal documents". I was certainly not encouraging a trawl through "background" which could not have made a reasonable person think that the parties must have departed from conventional usage.

The point here is that, by saying that the background could include 'absolutely anything', he only meant that it could include things beyond facts about the purpose of the contract. For example, the legal background could be relevant. So, in a contract for the sale of alcohol, it can be assumed the parties did not intend to sell alcohol to under 18's. Lord Hoffman was careful to point out that the background facts are those relevant to what was intended by the contract. In other words, facts the reasonable person would have used to work out the commercial purpose of the contract.

6.4.5.3 The Exclusion of Previous Negotiations

Lord Hoffman's third principle excluding the use of previous negotiations also led to a lot of debate. The exclusion goes back to *Prenn v Simmonds* [1971] 1 WLR 1381. There Lord Wilberforce explained that using previous negotiations is not helpful. A lot gets said and it is only the contract that reflects what was agreed. However, since the *ICS* case, some professors (McLauchlan, 'Contract Interpretation: What is it About?' (2009) 31:5 Sydney Law Review 5) and even some judges (Lord Nicholls, 'My Kingdom for a Horse: The Meaning of Words' (2005) 121 LQR 577) have criticised the rule against using negotiations as part of the wider background. This was an issue in *Chartbrook Ltd v Persimmon Homes Ltd* [2009] UKHL 38. There Lord Hoffman (with whom the other Law Lords agreed) applied an interpretation based on 'commercial common sense'. Their Lordships also made some *obiter* comments about the use of previous negotiations. Lord Hoffman observed that negotiations are usually 'drenched in subjectivity', but could contain something relevant to what the parties intended. However, the rule excluding the use of negotiations for interpretation was upheld. This was done for practical reasons, both for the courts and lawyers advising clients—materials arising in negotiations can be vast.

6.4.5.4 The Difficulty Defining 'Commercial Common Sense'

Lord Hoffman's principles of interpretation help to define the contextual approach to reflect commercial common sense. While references to 'commercial common sense' feature in so many cases, it is not a concept with defined limits. As a result, judges will not always agree on what it means. On this point, the following warning by Neuberger LJ in *Skanska Rashleigh Weatherfoil Ltd v Somerfield Stores Ltd* [2006] EWCA Civ 1732 is often cited:

> Judges are not always the most commercially-minded, let alone the most commercially experienced, of people, and should, I think, avoid arrogating to themselves overconfidently the role of arbiter of commercial reasonableness or likelihood.

Even in *ICS* itself, there was disagreement over whether the term reflected commercial common sense. According to Lord Hoffman, the idea of the Scheme providing compensation and then not being able to recoup the loss with a claim made no commercial sense at all. In contrast, Lord Lloyd stated that it made commercial sense. After all, some investors would have been *under*-compensated by the Scheme and so a damages claim against the building society would have been useful to them. In addition, the Scheme would have had claims against the negligent solicitors anyway. It meant they could recoup some of the compensation payment costs. The fact they did not have rights to all the possible damages actions was just a bad deal on their part.

Returning to the pizzeria example, it could be said that the promotion would result in a serious loss. However, the pizzeria would still make money from the sale of drinks and desserts. It might be a bad deal, but can it be said that it makes no commercial sense?

THINKING POINTS

Is it right to assume that parties intend for their contracts to reflect commercial common sense?

6.4.6 The Application of the Contextual Approach to Reflect 'Commercial Common Sense'

The current, modern approach requires contracts to be interpreted with reference to the background facts. The aim is to reflect a meaning that would have been intended in everyday life based on commercial common sense. Certainly, when the terms are capable of different meanings, the court can adopt the one that reflects commercial common sense. In *Rainy Sky SA v Kookmin Bank* [2011], Lord Clarke for the Supreme Court provided some further guidance on this point. It was said that when there are two meanings, the court can simply go with the one that reflects commercial common sense. There is no need to show that the other interpretation would lead to absurd results.

The more controversial issue is the application of the contextual interpretation where the natural meaning of the words is clear. This is what was done in *ICS* itself. The House of Lords provided an interpretation to reflect its own understanding of commercial common sense. This was not done because the term had different meanings. Instead, it was simply felt that something had gone wrong with the wording. This is accepted, but there is a fine line between giving effect to 'commercial common sense' and simply rescuing a party from a bad deal which it has entered into. In *Skanska Rashleigh Weatherfoil Ltd v Somerfield Stores Ltd* [2006] EWCA Civ 1732, Neuberger LJ gave a warning about questioning the parties' wording too easily:

> 21. ...However, it seems to me right to emphasise that the surrounding circumstances and commercial common sense do not represent a licence to the court to re-write a contract merely because its terms seem somewhat unexpected, a little unreasonable, or not commercially very wise. The contract will contain the words the parties have chosen to use in order to identify their contractual rights and obligations...

22. Particularly in these circumstances, it seems to me that the court must be careful before departing from the natural meaning of the provision in the contract merely because it may conflict with its notions of commercial common sense of what the parties may, must or should have thought or intended...Furthermore, sometimes it is plainly justified to depart from the primary meaning of words and given them what might, on the face of it, appear to be a strained meaning, for instance where the primary meaning of the words leads to a plainly ridiculous or unreasonable result.

The comments by Neuberger LJ echo Lord Hoffman's fifth principle from *ICS* and aims to encourage judges to be more cautious. The point is that a contract could simply be the result of a bad deal for one party. That should not be taken as an indication that something has gone wrong with the wording. This point was expanded on by Lord Neuberger PSC in the Supreme Court case of *Arnold v Britton* [2015] UKSC 36.

The case was about a number of leases for holiday chalets. The leases had a term requiring the lessee to pay an annual service charge for repairs and maintenance. Generally among the leases, the clear wording referred to a charge of £90 increasing by 10% a year. Over a long period, this resulted in a very high charge. One of the examples given by Lord Neuberger is a good illustration. The example was that a lease granted in 1980 would have a service charge of £2500 in 2015. By 2072, it would have increased to £550,000! The lessees argued that the term made no sense. The charge would greatly exceed any possible cost of repairs and maintenance. However, the majority of the Supreme Court were not prepared to assume that something had gone wrong with the wording. On that basis, the court decided that the wording had to be given its natural meaning. Lord Neuberger took the opportunity to say more on the principles of interpretation to be applied:

GUIDED CASE READING 6.2
Arnold v Britton [2015] UKSC 36

When reading the guidance by Lord Neuberger, for each factor addressed:

- try to identify the reason for it being stated;
- try to identify the effect of the factor being stated (how it applies).

[17] First, the reliance placed in some cases on commercial common sense and surrounding circumstances (eg in *Chartbrook* [2009] AC 1101, paras 16–26) should not be invoked to undervalue the importance of the language of the provision which is to be construed. The exercise of interpreting a provision involves identifying what the parties meant through the eyes of a reasonable reader, and, save perhaps in a very unusual case, that meaning is most obviously to be gleaned from the language of the provision. Unlike commercial common sense and the surrounding circumstances, the parties have control over the language they use in a contract. And, again save perhaps in a very unusual case, the parties must have been specifically focussing on the issue covered by the provision when agreeing the wording of that provision.

> Lord Neuberger's starting point was the wording. He made the obvious point that a contract is an agreement voluntarily made and drafted by the parties and so they determine what the wording is. By contrast, they do not control the 'background' or what is considered 'commercial common sense' by others. This means their wording has to be the most important consideration.

[18] Secondly, when it comes to considering the centrally relevant words to be interpreted, I accept that the less clear they are, or, to put it another way, the worse their drafting, the more ready the court can properly be to depart from their natural meaning. That is simply the obverse of the sensible proposition that the clearer the natural meaning the more difficult it is to justify departing from it. However, that does not justify the court embarking on an exercise of searching for, let alone constructing, drafting infelicities in order to facilitate a departure from the natural meaning. If there is a specific error in the drafting, it may often have no relevance to the issue of interpretation which the court has to resolve.

> By extension, the wording may simply be unclear or vague, such that the court has to depart from their natural meaning. That is not the same thing, though, as using a lack of clarity as an excuse to depart from the words' natural meaning where it is not absolutely necessary.

[19] The third point I should mention is that commercial common sense is not to be invoked retrospectively. The mere fact that a contractual arrangement, if interpreted according to its natural language, has worked out badly, or even disastrously, for one of the parties is not a reason for departing from the natural language. Commercial common sense is only relevant to the extent of how matters would or could have been perceived by the parties, or by reasonable people in the position of the parties, as at the date that the contract was made. Judicial observations such as those of Lord Reid in *Wickman Machine Tools Sales Ltd v L Schuler AG* [1974] AC 235, 251 and Lord Diplock in *Antaios Cia Naviera SA v Salen Rederierna AB (The Antaios)* [1985] AC 191, 201, quoted by Lord Carnwath JSC at para 110, have to be read and applied bearing that important point in mind.

> Lord Neuberger then shifted his focus to the notion of 'commercial common sense'. His Lordship stressed that in order to prevent any danger that this could be used to rescue a contracting party from a bad bargain, the only relevant question was what 'commercial common sense' would have meant to reasonable people in the positions of the parties at the time of contracting (not afterwards when any disastrous effect had become clear).

[20] Fourthly, while commercial common sense is a very important factor to take into account when interpreting a contract, a court should be very slow to reject the natural meaning of a provision as correct simply because it appears to be a very imprudent term for one of the parties to have agreed, even ignoring the benefit of wisdom of hindsight. The purpose of interpretation is to identify what the parties have agreed, not what the court thinks that they should have agreed. Experience shows that it is by no means unknown for people to enter into arrangements which are ill-advised, even ignoring the benefit of wisdom of hindsight, and it is not the function of a court when interpreting an agreement to relieve a party from the consequences of his imprudence or poor advice. Accordingly, when interpreting a contract a judge should avoid re-writing it in an attempt to assist an unwise party or to penalise an astute party.

> His Lordship then made the related point that the role of the court is not to save a contracting party from its own foolishness. Moreover, it is not to prevent a contracting party from being 'astute' and profiting from a good bargain, which is what might happen in the attempt to rescue the other party from a bad one.

[21] The fifth point concerns the facts known to the parties. When interpreting a contractual provision, one can only take into account facts or circumstances which existed at the time that the contract was made, and which were known or reasonably available to both parties. Given that a contract is a bilateral, or synallagmatic, arrangement involving both parties, it cannot be right, when interpreting a contractual provision, to take into account a fact or circumstance known only to one of the parties.

> On the other hand, an important caveat to this point is that the court is not to only take into account a fact which only one of the parties knows about, because a contract is what *both* parties have agreed. So it must represent that agreement.

[22] Sixthly, in some cases, an event subsequently occurs which was plainly not intended or contemplated by the parties, judging from the language of their contract. In such a case, if it is clear what the parties would have intended, the court will give effect to that intention. An example of such a case is *Aberdeen City Council v Stewart Milne Group Ltd* 2012 SCLR 114, where the court concluded that 'any . . . approach' other than that which was adopted 'would defeat the parties' clear objectives', but the conclusion was based on what the parties 'had in mind when they entered into' the contract: see paras 21 and 22.

> Lord Neuberger's final point brings up another reason why a court may need to engage in the interpretation of terms: the parties may have had a clear agreement but a new situation may have arisen which they had not expected and not made provision for. It could be that careful interpretation of the contract in such a circumstance could make the parties' apparent intentions clear. This is a different exercise to the implication of terms.

The guidance by Lord Neuberger can be summarised in the following way:

1. Judges should not be too eager to avoid giving effect to the natural meaning of the words. After all, the parties had control over the wording and so it is likely to reflect what was intended.

2. If the words are unclear and the contract badly drafted, the court is less likely to follow the natural meaning of the words. Instead, an interpretation based in commercial common sense could be applied.

3. Commercial common sense should be understood from the perspective of the time the contract was created.

4. It is not for the courts to rescue a party from making a bad deal. Bad deals (or bad bargains) happen and result in very one-sided contracts. This does not mean the wording has gone wrong or that the contract makes no sense.

5. The relevant facts are those that could have been known by a reasonable person in the position of each party, not just one or the other.

6. If things happen after creation of the contract that the parties did not prepare for, if it is clear what the parties would have intended to do, then that intention can be given effect.

The factors stated by Lord Neuberger encourage a great deal of caution but also aimed to promote more certainty.

Based on the factors explained by Lord Neuberger, the majority agreed that the term should be given its natural meaning. It could be said that the 10% increase was aimed at covering the increase in costs resulting from inflation. By way of background, prices generally go up each year, as measured by the inflation rate. This means the same amount of money buys less over time. Inflation of no more than 2% each year is the target throughout the EU. That figure would mean that each year our money is worth 2% less than it was previously. But in the 1970s, inflation peaked at 25% because of an increase in the price of oil. Even in the 1980's inflation went to 8%. The point is that a 10% increase each year made sense in the 1970's when it was put in the original leases.

In *Arnold v Britton*, it could not be said that something had gone wrong with the wording. Instead, the contract had simply become a very bad bargain over time. Table 6.1 summarises the main principles of interpretation.

Table 6.1

A summary of the main principles of interpretation

Courts work out the meaning of contracts using the background facts.	*ICS* (Lord Hoffman); *Arnold v Britton* (Lord Neuberger)
Background facts are those available to the reasonable person in the position of the parties.	*ICS* (Lord Hoffman) *BCCI v Ali* (Lord Hoffman)
Interpretation is based on what the parties could have known at the time of contracting.	*ICS* (Lord Hoffman); *Arnold v Britton* (Lord Neuberger)
Statements made in pre-contract negotiations are excluded.	*ICS* (Lord Hoffman) *Chartbook Persimmon Homes* (Lord Hoffman)
When the words are ambiguous, the court can simply apply the meaning that reflects commercial common sense (based on the background).	*Rainy Sky v Kookmin Bank* (Lord Clarke)
If the wording is clear it is likely that the parties intended it. But if it makes no commercial sense, the court may decide that something went wrong with the wording.	*ICS* (Lord Hoffman)
The fact there is a bad bargain for one party does not mean something went wrong with the wording.	*Arnold v Britton* (Lord Neuberger)
If something has gone wrong with the wording, the court can apply a meaning that reflects commercial common sense.	*ICS* (Lord Hoffman);

The modern contextual approach to interpretation can be seen as a welcome development. It provides flexibility and can allow for a fairer result than a strict reliance on the text. However, it results in some uncertainty for those with a contract as well as for lawyers advising on contracts. A key problem is knowing when a court will decide whether or not something has gone wrong with the wording. This difficulty is highlighted by the fact that different views were expressed in the same cases. For example, in *Chartbrook v Persimmon Homes*, the Court of Appeal held that the relevant words were clear and applied their natural meaning. In contrast, the House of Lords decided that the words made no sense and were 'arbitrary and irrational'. Likewise, in *Rainy Sky v Kookmin Bank*, the majority decision in the Court of Appeal applied the natural meaning of the words, but the Supreme Court said that the terms made no sense. There are many examples like this, and many examples of judges in the same court expressing different opinions. That being said, the statements made by the Supreme Court *Arnold v Britton* were aimed at addressing this uncertainty. They were intended to serve as a reminder to judges to be more cautious before deciding to set aside the natural meaning of the words.

The judgment by Lord Neuberger in *Arnold v Britton* had the aim of providing more certainty by encouraging more caution. However, it raises the question as to whether it represents a step back from the modern contextual approach encouraged by Lord Hoffman in *ICS* and subsequently by Lord Clarke for the Supreme Court in *Rainy Sky v Kookmin Bank* [2011] UKSC 50. This issue was addressed by Lord Hodge for the Supreme Court in *Wood v Capita Insurance Services Ltd* [2017] UKSC 24. Lord Hodge made it clear the opinion expressed was not adding further principles of interpretation since there were so many already. After briefly addressing the key cases Lord Hodge stated:

12.   ...To my mind once one has read the language in dispute and the relevant parts of the contract that provide its context, it does not matter whether the more detailed analysis commences with the factual background and the implications of rival constructions or a close examination of the relevant language in the contract, so long as the court balances the indications given by each.

13.   Textualism and contextualism are not conflicting paradigms in a battle for exclusive occupation of the field of contractual interpretation. Rather, the lawyer and the judge, when interpreting any contract, can use them as tools to ascertain the objective meaning of the language which the parties have chosen to express their agreement. The extent to which each tool will assist the court in its task will vary according to the circumstances of the particular agreement or agreements. Some agreements may be successfully interpreted principally by textual analysis, for example because of their sophistication and complexity and because they have been negotiated and prepared with the assistance of skilled professionals. The correct interpretation of other contracts may be achieved by a greater emphasis on the factual matrix, for example because of their informality, brevity or the absence of skilled professional assistance. But negotiators of complex formal contracts may often not achieve a logical and coherent text because of, for example, the conflicting aims of the parties, failures of communication, differing drafting practices, or deadlines which require the parties to compromise in order to reach agreement. There may often therefore be provisions in a detailed professionally drawn contract which lack clarity and the lawyer or judge in interpreting such provisions may be particularly helped by considering the factual matrix and the purpose of similar provisions in contracts of the same type. The iterative process, of which Lord Mance JSC spoke in *Sigma Finance Corpn* [2010] 1 All ER 571, para 12, assists the lawyer or judge to ascertain the objective meaning of disputed provisions.

14.   On the approach to contractual interpretation, the *Rainy Sky* and Arnold cases were saying the same thing.

15.   The recent history of the common law of contractual interpretation is one of continuity rather than change.

The statement by Lord Hodge is a significant one. The aim was to show that *ICS* and the cases that followed had adopted the same approach, but it was just that there were different issues raised by the contracts in those cases. Generally, the courts should make use of the facts and that will include the wording as well as the background, but it is for the court to balance the weight of what is indicated by all of this. For example, where the wording of a complex contract is clear and drafted by experts, there will be no need to consider the context. Alternatively, a complex contract could be made by experts which is nevertheless unclear due to other factors. The wider context would be of more use then. Likewise, the interpretation of other contracts which are made informally or without expertise may need extensive recourse to the context.

Accordingly, the interpretation model or 'paradigm' of focussing on the wording (textualism), or the wider context (contextualism) were not in conflict. They were portrayed as tools to use where necessary. The development of the contextual approach was described as a natural progression of the common law in line with commercial expectations. The extent to which this statement inspires more certainty and less disputes remains to be seen.

THINKING POINTS

Is the point made by Lord Hodge an indication that the Supreme Court is retreating from the development introduced in *ICS*?

6.5 Implied Terms

So far, we have focussed on express terms, including oral ones, and we then looked at how express terms in a written contract are interpreted. We now turn to the law relating to implied terms. These are terms that are not expressed by the parties. They are not written into a contract and they are not stated orally by the parties. Instead, they are unexpressed terms that are simply assumed to be part of the contract and they are just as enforceable as the express terms. Terms can be implied into the contract by legislation; by the courts or case law; or by custom and trade usage and we will address each method in turn.

6.5.1 Terms Implied by Legislation

We often come across written contracts and notices that become part of our contracts. However, it is terms implied by legislation that are more frequently the source of the rights and obligations in our everyday contracts. Think of when you buy goods in a shop, a business website or from a vending machine. You don't have a written contract detailing all of your rights or the seller's obligations. Yet we all know that if the goods are defective, we can get a refund or alternative remedies like a replacement or a repair. That is because the defect is a breach of the contract. But that means a term has been breached, so where is it? For consumers, the Consumer Rights Act 2015 implies a term that goods sold will be of satisfactory quality. That term is implied in all contracts when consumers buy from a trader or business. Before the Act came into force, the same implied term came from the Sale of Goods Act 1979. A defect will usually breach the implied term, and that is the basis for having a remedy from the seller. It is the same when we receive a sub-standard or defective service. We have a remedy when the service has been provided in such a way that it breaches an implied term from the relevant legislation.

In this section we look at the main implied terms from the sale of goods legislation as examples (there are many other areas in which terms are implied by legislation, but the sale of goods is the area in which this is most straightforward to understand). Their application is often based on the vast case law that interprets them, but, for our purposes, we just need to know of the existence of some implied terms for the purposes of illustration. Our concern is with implied terms as a source of contractual terms. These sit alongside the oral statements that are terms as well as those that are written, either in a notice or a contractual document.

6.5.2 Implied Terms in Contracts for the Sale of Goods

Originally, the common law approach to sales reflected the principle '*caveat emptor*' (let the buyer beware). This meant that buyers bought at their own risk. If they wanted the goods to be free from defects, they had to make that a term of the contract. The common law then developed some implied terms, for example on the quality of the goods sold. These were then reproduced in the Sale of Goods Act 1893, which codified the common law. The Act was then replaced by the Sale of Goods Act 1979. Originally, this Act had rules that applied to some or all types of sales contracts (e.g. between private parties; consumers and businesses; and commercial sales like those between businesses). However, the law relating to consumer sales was recently re-formulated in the Consumer Rights Act 2015 (CRA 2015). That leaves the Sale of Goods Act to apply to contracts between businesses and in some instances, private sales.

→ CROSS-REFERENCE
The law relating to the limitation and exclusion of the liability from the implied terms is discussed at 7.6.3 and 7.7.2.

It is fair to say that such implied terms are *imposed* by law and, in consumer contracts, the obligations from such implied terms cannot be excluded or limited. In contrast, in contracts between businesses, it is possible for an exemption clause to limit or exclude implied terms. However this freedom is limited. To be effective, such an exemption clause has to meet the test found in the legislation on exemption clauses.

6.5.2.1 Implied Terms from the Sale of Goods Act 1979

Section 12 of the Act implies a term about the title to goods:

> 12(1) In a contract of sale, other than one to which subsection (3) below applies, there is an implied term on the part of the seller that in the case of a sale he has a right to sell the goods, and in the case of an agreement to sell he will have such a right at the time when the property is to pass...

This implies a term that the seller has the right to sell the goods. So, if a seller does not have the right to sell the goods, there is a breach of this implied term. Its remaining sub-sections provide further details. This implied term applies to contracts between businesses and those between private parties.

Section 13 of the Act implies a term relating goods sold by description:

> (1) Where there is a contract for the sale of goods by description, there is an implied term that the goods will correspond with the description.
>
> (1A) As regards England and Wales and Northern Ireland, the term implied by subsection (1) above is a condition.
>
> (2) If the sale is by sample as well as by description it is not sufficient that the bulk of the goods corresponds with the sample if the goods do not also correspond with the description.
>
> (3) A sale of goods is not prevented from being a sale by description by reason only that, being exposed for sale or hire, they are selected by the buyer.

This also applies to contracts between businesses as well as to private sales and sales that are *by* description. An obvious example is when you buy goods without actually seeing them—such as on the internet or over the telephone. Your choice is based on a description. But the implied term also applies in a wider context than these examples—it can also apply where a purchaser selects goods that he or she has seen if they are also accompanied by a description. In addition, goods can describe themselves. The case law shows that it only applies to descriptions that go to the identity of the goods and it does not relate to descriptions about quality (*Ashington Piggeries Ltd v Christopher Hill Ltd* [1972] AC 441). So, a punctured balloon is still a balloon and if sold there will not be a breach of an implied term under s. 13 (although it almost certainly will under s. 14). Also, it must appear that the buyer relied on the description—in other words, that the decision to buy was not based on the buyer's own inspection of the goods (*Harlingdon & Leinster Enterprises Ltd v Christopher Hull Fine Art Ltd* [1991] 1 QB 564).

Section 14 of the Act implies a term relating to the quality of the goods and their fitness for a particular purpose:

> 14 Implied terms about quality or fitness.
>
> > (2) Where the seller sells goods in the course of a business, there is an implied term that the goods supplied under the contract are of satisfactory quality.

This is the quality obligation. The sale of a punctured balloon will be in breach of this obligation. The wording indicates that it applies only to sales carried out in the 'course of a business'. This phrase was given a wide definition in *Stevenson v Rogers* [1999] QB 1028 to even include 'one off' sales by a business. Section 14 therefore does not apply to sales by a private party like those on online market places.

> (2A) For the purposes of this Act, goods are of satisfactory quality if they meet the standard that a reasonable person would regard as satisfactory, taking account of any description of the goods, the price (if relevant) and all the other relevant circumstances.

This refers to the standard expected. It is not based on the quality expected by a reasonable buyer or seller. Instead, it is a combination of both. The subsection refers to external criteria such as the goods' description, price and so on. The next sub-section refers to internal criteria—i.e. details about the actual goods that could be relevant to whether they meet the standard expected:

> (2B) For the purposes of this Act, the quality of goods includes their state and condition and the following (among others) are in appropriate cases aspects of the quality of goods—
>
> > (a) fitness for all the purposes for which goods of the kind in question are commonly supplied,
> >
> > (b) appearance and finish,
> >
> > (c) freedom from minor defects,
> >
> > (d) safety, and
> >
> > (e) durability.

The next subsection sets out circumstances in which the quality obligation will not be breached:

> (2C) The term implied by subsection (2) above does not extend to any matter making the quality of goods unsatisfactory—
>
> > (a) which is specifically drawn to the buyer's attention before the contract is made,
> >
> > (b) where the buyer examines the goods before the contract is made, which that examination ought to reveal, or
> >
> > (c) in the case of a contract for sale by sample, which would have been apparent on a reasonable examination of the sample.

Sub-section (3) of s. 14 is the source of the implied term that goods sold will be fit for a particular purpose. The obvious example is where a buyer indicates that the goods are to be used for a specified purpose. If they don't meet that requirement, the term is breached. In addition, it can apply where the goods have an obvious purpose that they are unable to fulfil. An example would be a balloon that cannot be inflated. Inflating it is its obvious and only real purpose, so there is no need for the buyer to bring that purpose to the attention of the seller.

> (3) Where the seller sells goods in the course of a business and the buyer, expressly or by implication, makes known—
>
> > (a) to the seller, or
> >
> > (b) . . .

> any particular purpose for which the goods are being bought, there is an implied term that the goods supplied under the contract are reasonably fit for that purpose, whether or not that is a purpose for which such goods are commonly supplied, except where the circumstances show that the buyer does not rely, or that it is unreasonable for him to rely, on the skill or judgment of the seller

Section 15 implies a term where a sale is being made by sample to the effect that the goods will be of the same quality as the sample provided:

> 15 Sale by sample.
>
> (1) A contract of sale is a contract for sale by sample where there is an express or implied term to that effect in the contract.
>
> (2) In the case of a contract for sale by sample there is an implied term—
>
>   (a) that the bulk will correspond with the sample in quality;
>
>   . . . . . .
>
>   (c) that the goods will be free from any defect, making their quality unsatisfactory, which would not be apparent on reasonable examination of the sample.

6.5.2.2 The Terms Implied by the Consumer Rights Act 2015

The implied terms in the Sale of Goods Act 1979 originally applied to consumer contracts too. However, these implied terms in consumer contracts are now found in the CRA 2015. The CRA 2015 applies to contracts between a trader and a consumer as defined by section 2 of the Act:

> (2) "Trader" means a person acting for purposes relating to that person's trade, business, craft, or profession, whether acting personally or through another person acting in the trader's name or on the trader's behalf.
>
> (3) "Consumer" means an individual acting for purposes that are wholly or mainly outside that individual's trade, business, craft, or profession.

Sub-section (5) sets out a limit on auction sales. It states that it is not a consumer sale if a person buys second hand goods at an auction.

Essentially, the CRA implied terms replicate those from the Sale of Goods Act 1979. The wording has been changed slightly in places to be clearer for consumers. However, with one exception, the substance of the implied terms is the same as the corresponding terms from the Sale of Goods Act 1979. On that basis, there is no need to detail the CRA implied terms, Instead. we can refer to Table 6.2 indicating the sections in the CRA that correspond with the implied terms from the Sale of Goods Act.

Table 6.2
The sections of the Sale of Goods Act 1979 and Consumer Rights Act 2015 that imply terms into sales contracts

Implied term	Sale of Goods Act 1979	Consumer Rights Act 2015
The seller has a right to sell	Section 12	Section 17
Sale by description, goods must correspond with the description	Section 13	Section 11
The goods must be of satisfactory quality	Section 14 (2)	Section 9
The goods must be fit for a particular purpose	Section 14 (3)	Section 10
In a sale by sample, the goods sold must correspond with the sample	Section 15	Section 13

While the CRA implied terms replicate the substance of those in the Sale of Goods Act 1979, there is one exception. It is in relation to the quality obligation. The CRA gives an additional external factor of public statements from sellers or producers. Such statements in advertising and labelling sit along with the other external criteria of price and description. This public statement factor was added to comply with EU legislation on consumer protection (Directive 99/44 on Consumer Sales and Associated Guarantees).

The real significance of the public statements factor is that it includes public statements that are just from producers—i.e. statements that have in no way been passed on by the seller. So these statements are relevant in assessing the quality expected from the seller, even though the seller may have nothing to do with the statement in question. The public statements factor is added to the CRA 2015 by the following sub-sections of section 9:

(5) The relevant circumstances mentioned in subsection (2)(c) include any public statement about the specific characteristics of the goods made by the trader, the producer or any representative of the trader or the producer.

(6) That includes, in particular, any public statement made in advertising or labelling.

(7) But a public statement is not a relevant circumstance for the purposes of subsection (2)(c) if the trader shows that—

(a) when the contract was made, the trader was not, and could not reasonably have been, aware of the statement,

(b) before the contract was made, the statement had been publicly withdrawn or, to the extent that it contained anything which was incorrect or misleading, it had been publicly corrected, or

(c) the consumer's decision to contract for the goods could not have been influenced by the statement.

6.5.3 Terms Implied by the Courts

The courts have the ability to imply terms into contracts. These implied terms are generally divided into two separate categories. There are:

- 'terms implied in fact,' and
- 'terms implied in law'.

Terms implied in fact are those that are implied based on the particular facts of a given case. As a result, such an implied term is a 'one-off' based on the apparent intentions of the parties. In contrast, terms implied in law are imposed by the courts in all contracts of a particular type (e.g. employment contracts; tenancy agreements, etc.) and are not based on the facts or the parties' intentions. They are really imposed because the court thinks that the term should be present in a certain type of contract. Lord Steyn in *Equitable Life Assurance Society v Hyman* [2002] 1 AC 408 preferred to label these categories of implied term differently. He described terms implied in fact as '*ad hoc* gap fillers'. ('*Ad hoc*' is Latin to refer to something being done as and when it is necessary). He described terms implied in law as 'standardised. . . general default rules'. These labels are helpful because they capture the effect of the different types of term implied by the courts.

6.5.4 Terms Implied in Fact (Ad Hoc Gap Fillers)

Terms are implied in fact when the court has to fill an obvious gap in a particular contract. This is done based on the facts of the case and is supposed to give effect to what the parties are presumed to have intended. There are two traditional tests for implying a term in this way.

6.5.4.1 The 'Business Efficacy' Test

The first test arises from the Court of Appeal case of *The Moorcock* (1889) 14 PD 64. The case concerned an agreement for cargo from a steamship (The Moorcock) to be unloaded. This was to take place at the defendant's wharf with a jetty that extended into the River Thames. Both parties knew the river was tidal and that the steamship was to rest on the riverbed when the tide was low. Unfortunately, the underside of the Moorcock was damaged by the state of the riverbed because the defendant had not taken steps to ensure that the area was safe. The claimant then brought an action for breach of contract. The issue was that there was no term in the agreement requiring the defendant to take reasonable care to ensure that the area was safe. Consequently, the question for the court was whether such a term was implied. The Court of Appeal agreed that such a term was implied and so the defendant was in breach.

Bowen LJ explained the basis of the implied term:

> An implied warranty, or as it is called a covenant in law, as distinguished from an express contract or express warranty, really is in every instance founded on the presumed intention of the parties and upon reason. It is the implication which the law draws from what must obviously have been the intention of the parties, an implication which the law draws with the object of giving efficacy to the transaction and preventing such a failure of consideration as cannot have been within the contemplation of either of the parties. . .

Payment was being made for allowing the cargo to be unloaded rather than just for using the wharf. But the unloading could only be done if the ship was moored at the jetty. On that basis, it was decided that objectively, the parties intended for the ship to be moored in a safe place. Bowen LJ refers to the implied term as giving 'efficacy' to the contract (i.e. it made the contract workable from a business perspective). The point is that without the term, the contract would not be workable or make business sense. After all, why would you unload a ship where it is not safe? And, if you offer a jetty for unloading, you know that customers would expect it to be safe and would not want to use it if it was not.

The implied term was based on the parties' intentions. In addition, it was to give 'efficacy' to the contract. Those factors serve to limit the implied term to that particular contract, which is why we say it is an implied term in fact, because it is based on the facts of that particular case.

Subsequent cases have made clear that the business efficacy test requires the implied term to be necessary. In *Reigate v Union Manufacturing Co (Ramsbottom) Ltd* [1918] 1 KB 592, Scrutton LJ observed that '[a] term can only be implied if it is necessary in the business sense to give efficacy to the contract'. By that it is meant the contract is not workable or makes no commercial sense without the term.

6.5.4.2 The 'Officious Bystander' Test

The other test for implying a term in fact (based on the parties' intentions) is from *Shirlaw v Southern Foundries* (1926) Ltd [1939] 2 KB 206.

MacKinnon LJ examined the approach adopted in *The Moorcock*. He noted that it had been cited a lot in order to urge courts to imply a term and he wished to put forward a different test for implying a term in order to reflect the parties' intentions:

> For my part, I think that there is a test that may be at least as useful as [the business efficacy test]. If I may quote from an essay which I wrote some years ago, I then said: "Prima facie that which in any contract is left to be implied and need not be expressed is something so obvious that it goes without

saying; so that, if, while the parties were making their bargain, an officious bystander were to suggest some express provision for it in their agreement, they would testily suppress him with a common 'Oh, of course!'"

This has become known as the 'officious bystander test'. The point being emphasised by the test is that the term needs to be really obvious to both parties—so obvious, indeed, that they did not feel the need to make it explicit and simply assumed it was part of their agreement. In that sense, the term will reflect the unexpressed intentions of both parties.

Both the 'business efficacy test' and the 'officious bystander test' achieve essentially the same thing. They allow a term to be implied based on the apparent intentions of the parties to a particular contract. It is not enough for it be just reasonable, or desirable to imply the term. One of many examples is a comment from *Equitable Life Assurance Society v Hyman* [2002] 1 AC 408, in which Lord Steyn said:

> The legal test for the implication of such a term is a standard of strict necessity. The idea is that the implied term must be 'essential to give effect to the reasonable expectation of the parties.

Of course, given that both methods reflect the parties' intentions, such terms can be excluded by the express wording of the contract. If previous drafts of the contract contained the relevant term which was deleted by in the final version, it might appear that the parties intended to exclude such a term. However, in *Bou-Simon v BGC Brokers LP* [2018] EWCA 1525, Asplin LJ expressed an *obiter* comment suggesting that such evidence was relevant only if it was necessary to construe the express terms (rather than when implying a term). Even then, it would only be relevant to the construction or interpretation of the contract if it was part of the surrounding circumstances rather than evidence of previous negotiations. In contrast Singh LJ preferred a wider approach tentatively suggesting that the fact that a term was deleted could be relevant when deciding if the term should be implied. It was also acknowledged that a detailed examination would be needed to determine the point.

?! **THINKING POINTS**

Should evidence of deleted terms in previous drafts be relevant to whether or not a term is implied?

6.5.5 Are the Tests for Implying Terms in Fact (Ad Hoc Gap Fillers) Really about Interpretation?

An attempt to redefine the rules in this area was made by Lord Hoffman in the Privy Council case of *Attorney-General of Belize v Belize Telecom Ltd* [2009] UKPC 10. Here, the rules of a company (in its articles of association) stated that a special director could be appointed by a special shareholder (someone with a certain amount and type of shares). The rules also said that only the special shareholder could remove the special director. The question concerned what was to happen if there was no longer a special shareholder. Was it implied that the special director would have to step down? The Privy Council held that such a term was implied.

Lord Hoffman gave the judgment for the court and attempted to place the law on implied terms on a different conceptual footing. The judgment was on the company articles of association (addressed as 'the instrument') but it was made clear the same approach applied to contracts. On the process of implying terms, Lord Hoffman stated:

> [19] The proposition that the implication of a term is an exercise in the construction of the instrument as a whole is not only a matter of logic (since a court has no power to alter what the instrument means) but also well supported by authority...
>
> [21] It follows that in every case in which it is said that some provision ought to be implied in an instrument, the question for the court is whether such a provision would spell out in express words what the instrument, read against the relevant background, would reasonably be understood to mean...[T]his question can be reformulated in various ways which a court may find helpful in providing an answer—the implied term must "go without saying", it must be "necessary to give business efficacy to the contract" and so on—but these are not in the [Privy Council's] opinion to be treated as different or additional tests. There is only one question: is that what the instrument, read as a whole against the relevant background, would reasonably be understood to mean?

According to Lord Hoffman (with whom all of the other judges agreed) the traditional tests were really about the interpretation of the contract. For both tests, the court was to read the contract as a whole against the relevant background. Based on that, the court could give effect to what would have been understood by the parties. The case was cited by other judges, but it did attract a lot of criticism. In its widest form, Lord Hoffman's judgment was basing the implication of terms in fact on his principles of interpretation set out in the *ICS* case. However, the Supreme Court has since clarified the position.

In *Marks and Spencer plc v BNP Paribas Securities Services Trust Company (Jersey) Ltd* [2015] UKSC 72 the Supreme Court made clear that Lord Hoffman's judgment in *Attorney-General of Belize* had not changed the position of the traditional tests. The case concerned a lease. Under the terms, Marks & Spencer paid a quarter of its annual rent to the defendant landlord in advance. Marks & Spencer then ended the agreement, which it was entitled to do using a 'break clause' in the lease. But it wanted the return of the balance of the rent paid. Nothing in the lease referred to the repayment of advance rent and so was argued that it should be an implied term. The Supreme Court held that the term was not implied, primarily because the lease was very detailed and had been drafted by experts. The terms covered a range of possible things that could happen and, since nothing was included regarding repayment on ending the contract, it was felt that this had not been intended by the parties.

Lord Neuberger PSC (with whom Lord Hodge and Lord Sumption agreed) made it clear that Lord Hoffman's judgment in the *Belize Telecom* case did not change the business efficacy or officious bystander tests:

> [26] I accept that both (i) construing the words which the parties have used in their contract and (ii) implying terms into the contract, involve determining the scope and meaning of the contract. However, Lord Hoffmann's analysis in *Belize Telecom* could obscure the fact that construing the words used and implying additional words are different processes governed by different rules.

Here Lord Neuberger was stating that the process for interpreting express terms is separate from that of implying terms. Later, it was observed that Lord Hoffman's judgment was open to a number of interpretations, some of which are not correct in law. On that basis, Lord Neuberger buried the controversy represented by the *Belize Telecom* judgment. This was done by stating that Lord Hoffman's observations:

> [31] ...should henceforth be treated as a characteristically inspired discussion rather than authoritative guidance on the law of implied terms.

This part of the Lord Neuberger's judgment represents a form of damage limitation. It firmly casts away the perceived impact of *Belize Telecom* on implied terms, and leaves the traditional tests intact.

The idea is that express terms should be interpreted. Then, after that exercise if the result remains unclear, a court can explore the application of the tests to imply a term. This is logical because the express terms might be read to exclude any implied term.

6.5.6 Recent Guidance on the Application of the Traditional Tests

During the detailed judgment in the *Marks and Spencer* case, Lord Neuberger conducted an analysis of the traditional business efficacy and officious bystander tests and the many leading cases that supported them. This included guidance on the tests provided by Lord Simon in *BP Refinery (Westernport) Pty Ltd v President, Councillors and Ratepayers of the Shire of Hastings* (1977) 52 ALJR 20, and that provided by Sir Thomas Bingham MR in *Philips Electronique Grand Public SA v British Sky Broadcasting Ltd* [1995] EMLR 472, and as Bingham LJ in the *The APJ Priti* [1987] 2 Lloyd's Rep 37. Lord Neuberger then put these together with some additional observations:

> [21] If one approaches the question by reference to what the parties would have agreed, one is not strictly concerned with the hypothetical answer of the actual parties, but with that of notional reasonable people in the position of the parties at the time at which they were contracting. Secondly, a term should not be implied into a detailed commercial contract merely because it appears fair or merely because one considers that the parties would have agreed it if it had been suggested to them. Those are necessary but not sufficient grounds for including a term. However, and thirdly, it is questionable whether Lord Simon's first requirement, reasonableness and equitableness, will usually, if ever, add anything: if a term satisfies the other requirements, it is hard to think that it would not be reasonable and equitable. Fourthly, as Lord Hoffmann I think suggested in *Attorney General of Belize v Belize Telecom Ltd* [2009] 1 WLR 1988, para 27, although Lord Simon's requirements are otherwise cumulative, I would accept that business necessity and obviousness, his second and third requirements, can be alternatives in the sense that only one of them needs to be satisfied, although I suspect that in practice it would be a rare case where only one of those two requirements would be satisfied. Fifthly, if one approaches the issue by reference to the officious bystander, it is "vital to formulate the question to be posed by [him] with the utmost care", to quote from Lewison, The Interpretation of Contracts 5th ed. (2011), para 6.09. Sixthly, necessity for business efficacy involves a value judgment. It is rightly common ground on this appeal that the test is not one of "absolute necessity", not least because the necessity is judged by reference to business efficacy. It may well be that a more helpful way of putting Lord Simon's second requirement is, as suggested by Lord Sumption in argument, that a term can only be implied if, without the term, the contract would lack commercial or practical coherence.

The guidance from Lord Neuberger can be summarised in the following way:

1. The courts should focus on what the reasonable person in the parties' position would have agreed.

2. A higher standard is required for detailed commercial contracts. The expectation is that the parties to such contracts have made the agreement with care and that therefore an additional term should not be applied unless it is absolutely necessary.

3. There is no separate requirement for the implied term to be reasonable and equitable. If a term is obvious and necessary then it will by definition be reasonable and equitable.

4. Technically the implied term should be necessary *or* obvious but in practice a term which is necessary will be obvious and vice versa.

5. Care must be taken to make sure the 'officious bystander' is asking the right question. It will be remembered that the officious bystander is imagined to be suggesting a term to the parties. The court must be very careful to make sure this imaginary suggestion is so obvious it goes without saying.

6. A term does not have to be absolutely essential in order to be 'necessary'. Even in the *Moorcock*, the contract to unload could exist without the implied term. It's just that it would not make any business sense and would not reflect parties' apparent intentions. So, by 'necessary' the judges mean necessary to give effect to the parties' intentions.

→ CROSS-REFERENCE

For the facts of *Wells v Devani* see 4.3.2.

The possibility of implying a term into an uncertain agreement to make it a contract was addressed in *Wells v Devani* [2019] UKSC 4. Lord Kitchen had already dealt with the dispute through the interpretation of the contract. However, the trial judge had implied a term instead—something which the Court of Appeal had rejected. Lord Kitchen therefore took the opportunity to express an opinion on whether a term could have been implied (had the case not been resolved using interpretation). On this point, he agreed with the trial judge. A term indicating payment on completion of the sale could have been implied to give the contract business efficacy or 'practical and commercial coherence'. Without the term, there would be no obligation to pay the agent, and this would have been inconsistent with their relationship. While his Lordship acknowledged that some agreements might be too uncertain to be contracts, he made clear that a court could imply terms in order to make an uncertain agreement certain enough to be a contract, as long as the requirements for implying a term are met. If an implied term is so obvious that it 'goes without saying' or is necessary to give business efficacy to the agreement, then there is no reason to refuse to imply such a term. The point was that had the dispute not been resolved through interpretation, the Supreme Court could have achieved the same result with an implied term.

The second point of the guidance expressed by Lord Neuberger was significant to the outcome of *Bou-Simon v BGC Borkers LP* [2018] EWCA Civ 1525. It concerned a loan to an employee who then left the claimant firm. The firm argued that it should be implied that the loan would be payable in full if the employee ever left. The Court of Appeal rejected the approach of the trial judge and held that there was no basis to imply such a term. Aspin LJ observed that the judge had implied the term based on the merits of doing so as the facts appeared during the dispute. Instead, following the guidance by Lord Neuberger, the assessment should have been made as the facts were known at the time the agreement was made. In addition, again based on the judgment by Lord Neuberger, the decision about implying a term should have been made only after construing the express terms. The approach of the trial judge had appeared to do the opposite and construe the contract so as to fit the implied term. Based on circumstances at the time of the contract, and with a view to commercial common sense, Aspin LJ made it clear that the implied term was not so obvious that it went without saying. In addition, it was not necessary for business efficacy. The contract 'would not lack commercial or practical coherence' without it.

6.5.7 Implied Terms in Law (Standardised General Default Rules)

These are terms implied by the courts in any contract of a certain type, such as an employment contract or tenancy agreement, by virtue of the contract being of that type. However, such terms can be expressly excluded or modified by the terms of the contract. That is why Lord Steyn described such terms as 'standardised implied terms' or 'general default rules' (*Equitable life v Hyman* [2002] 1 AC 408). They are implied as a default into all contracts of a particular type but the parties can contract out of them.

In contrast to terms that are one-off gap fillers, terms implied in law are not based on the parties' intentions. But if they do not exist to give effect to the parties' intentions, then what is their basis?

The key cases that developed the use of this type of implied term were not entirely clear about this. It seems from later cases that such terms are really based on policy considerations. That is, certain types of contract ought to have certain terms because of wider societal ramifications.

The main case cited as the basis for such implied terms is *Liverpool City Council v Irwin* [1977] AC 239. The case concerned tenancy agreements in a block of flats. The claimant landlord, the local authority, controlled the communal areas and facilities in a particular block of council flats, such as the rubbish chutes, lifts, staircases, and lights. These were badly in need of repair and so the tenants (including the defendant) refused to pay their rent. When the landlord sued, the tenants argued that the landlord was in breach of contract because of the poor state of the communal areas. There was no term in the contract that put the landlord under an obligation to repair the communal areas—indeed, there were no written obligations for the landlord whatsoever. However, the tenants argued that such a term should be implied. The majority of the Court of Appeal held that such a term was not necessary to make the contract workable, using the test from *The Moorcock* discussed earlier.

However, Lord Denning MR's dissenting judgment adopted a different approach. The judgment goes through a range of earlier cases in the attempt to show that terms are really implied by the courts when it is *reasonable* to do so. On that basis Lord Denning MR said there was an implied term to the effect that the landlord would take reasonable care to ensure that the communal areas were safe and fit for use. Then, on the facts, he held that the tenants had not shown that the landlord had breached the term. Following an appeal, the House of Lords held that the term was implied in all tenancy agreements but that it had not been breached. The important element of the case was the reasoning of the House of Lords in deciding that the term was implied, and that was set out in the main judgment by Lord Wilberforce.

GUIDED CASE READING 6.3
Liverpool City Council v Irwin [1977] AC 239

When you read the extract of the judgment by Lord Wilberforce, try to identify:

- The basis for implying the term.
- How this method of implying a term is different to implying a term for business efficacy.

[Reference was made to terms implied by custom and terms implied as a necessary incident based on the *Moorcock*]

... There is a third variety of implication, that which I think Lord Denning M.R. favours, or at least did favour in this case, and that is the implication of reasonable terms. But though I agree with many of his instances, which in fact fall under one or other of the preceding heads, I cannot go so far as to endorse his principle; indeed, it seems to me, with respect, to extend a long, and undesirable, way beyond sound authority.

...

My Lords, ... it is necessary to define what test is to be applied, and I do not find this difficult. In my opinion such obligation should be read into the contract as the nature of the contract itself implicitly requires, no more, no less: a test, in other words, of necessity. The relationship accepted by the corporation is that of landlord and tenant: the tenant accepts obligations accordingly, in relation inter alia to the stairs, the lifts and the chutes. All these are not just facilities, or conveniences provided at discretion: they are essentials of the tenancy without which life in the dwellings, as a tenant, is not possible. To leave the landlord free of contractual obligation as regards these matters, and subject only to administrative or political pressure, is, in my opinion, inconsistent totally with the nature of this relationship.

Lord Wilberforce begins by making it obvious that he considered Lord Denning MR's approach, which was based on the reasonableness of the term to be implied, to be a step too far. (This was one of a number of occasions when Lord Denning MR's judgments in the Court of Appeal were considered to have gone too far by the House of Lords.)

He then rooted the implication of terms in law firmly in necessity rather than reasonableness (much like the 'business efficacy' test from *The Moorcock*). A landlord has certain obligations to tenants of a block of flats which it owns, because without them the tenancy will not be possible. For example, a tenant cannot realistically live in a block of flats if the lifts and rubbish chutes are not usable.

The subject matter of the lease (high rise blocks) and the relationship created by the tenancy demand, of their nature, some contractual obligation on the landlord.

I do not think that this approach involves any innovation as regards the law of contract. The necessity to have regard to the inherent nature of a contract and of the relationship thereby established was stated in this House in *Lister v. Romford Ice and Cold Storage Co. Ltd.* [1957] A.C. 555. That was a case between master and servant and of a search for an 'implied term'. Viscount Simonds, at p. 579, makes a clear distinction between a search for an implied term such as might be necessary to give 'business efficacy' to the particular contract and a search, based on wider considerations, for such a term as the nature of the contract might call for, or as a legal incident of this kind of contract....

It remains to define the standard. My Lords, if, as I think, the test of the existence of the term is necessity the standard must surely not exceed what is necessary having regard to the circumstances. To imply an absolute obligation to repair would go beyond what is a necessary legal incident and would indeed be unreasonable. An obligation to take reasonable care to keep in reasonable repair and usability is what fits the requirements of the case. Such a definition involves—and I think rightly—recognition that the tenants themselves have their responsibilities. What it is reasonable to expect of a landlord has a clear relation to what a reasonable set of tenants should do for themselves.

...

My Lords, it will be seen that I have reached exactly the same conclusion as that of Lord Denning M.R., with most of whose thinking I respectfully agree. I must only differ from the passage in which, more adventurously, he suggests that the courts have power to introduce into contracts any terms they think reasonable or to anticipate legislative recommendations of the Law Commission. A just result can be reached, if I am right, by a less dangerous route.

> However, this is not exactly the same as the test from *The Moorcock*, because it is not contingent only on the particular facts of a given case, but on the nature of the contract in general. An obligation to keep the common areas of a block of flats in good repair is held by all landlords as a 'legal incident' of their relationships with tenants, and so its implication is not contingent on the particular facts of just one case.

> Of course, having established that a term is supposed to be implied, it still remains to determine what the term actually is. Lord Wilberforce was of the view that, while a landlord has a duty to keep common areas in a block of flats in good repair, this obligation is not absolute. Tenants also have responsibilities, and if they do absolutely nothing to keep the property in decent repair then it is hardly right to hold the landlord responsible. This means that the landlord has a duty to take 'reasonable care' to keep the property in 'reasonable repair'.

> Lord Wilberforce ended by justifying his reasoning on the basis that it could achieve a similar result as Lord Denning MR's in this particular case without going down the 'dangerous' route of allowing courts to insert terms into contracts at will just because they think it is reasonable to do so. Clearly, this would give judges a huge remit and considerably greater power. It would give them license to in effect rewrite contracts as they see fit,

KEY POINTS

Courts should not imply terms just because it is reasonable to do so. A higher standard of 'necessity' is used.

6.5.8 The Basis of Terms Implied in Law

Liverpool v Irwin does not give us a clear idea about why such terms are implied. Implying a term as a 'necessary legal incident' of a certain type of contract does not tell us about what factors are to be considered. Viscount Simonds in *Lister* was cited, and reference was made to 'wider considerations'. But the meaning of that phrase is hardly clear.

In *Scally v Southern Health and Social Services Board* [1992] 1 AC 294, the House of Lords implied a term in certain types of employment contract. The term required the employer to inform the employees of certain benefits (improved pension rights) they were entitled to. According to Lord Bridge (with whom the other judges agreed), such a term was not necessary enough for the contract to have 'business efficacy' because, after all, an employment contract can still be performed if the employer does not inform the employee about changes to pension rights. Rather, it was implied as a 'necessary incident' to such contracts. A similar approach was adopted by the House of Lords in *Mahmood v Bank of Credit and Commerce International SA* [1998] AC 20. Here a term was implied in employment contracts to the effect that the employer will not operate a corrupt or dishonest business so as to undermine trust and confidence between employer and employee. The bank in the case was in breach of this term by acting fraudulently and ultimately destroying the reputations of its employees.

The basis for implying a term as a necessary incident of the contract was addressed in more detail by the Court of Appeal in *Crossley v Faithful & Gould Holdings Ltd* [2004] EWCA Civ 293. Here Dyson LJ (with whom the other judges agreed) acknowledged that the previous cases referred to 'necessity'. But he then explained:

> It seems to me that, rather than focus on the elusive concept of necessity, it is better to recognise that, to some extent at least, the existence and scope of standardised implied terms raise questions of reasonableness, fairness and the balancing of competing policy considerations: see Peden [2001] LQR 459, 467–475.

Rather than focus on necessity, in other words, the real bases are reasonableness, fairness and policy factors. Judges have generally avoided openly basing their decisions on policy. The main reason is that it is seen as going beyond their function. After all, it is for Parliament to make the law and for government to determine policy. Yet it is difficult to say that it is wrong to imply terms using this method. Dyson LJ cited the influential work of Professor Peden that skilfully unpacks the law on implied terms. Some policy factors identified by Professor Peden are the existence of liability in negligence anyway, which the implied terms make contractual; and implied terms being based on an analogy with implied terms from legislation. In such instances, the judges are not really 'making the law' by devising a completely new rule when they decide a term is implied. Professor Pedon also referred to wider fairness-orientated factors like which party is in the better position to insure against the loss and the wider social impact of the implied term. This analysis helps to make more sense out of the exercise of terms being implied in law as 'general default rules'.

6.5.9 Terms Implied by Local Custom or Trade Usage

It is well established that terms can be implied by a custom or trade usage. The existence of this type of implied term was acknowledged by Lord Wilberforce in *Liverpool v Irwin*. An early case on terms being implied by custom is *Hutton v Warren* (1836) 1 M & W 466. Here a local trade custom meant that a tenant was under an obligation to farm according to a certain method. In addition, the tenant was entitled to an allowance for seeds and labour used while farming. In his judgment, Parke B referred to a requirement for a term to be implied by custom. It was stated that the custom must be a 'known' usage. This does not require the parties to actually know of the custom. Instead, an objective perspective is adopted. On that basis, the question to ask is whether the reasonable person in the position of the parties would have known of the custom.

More detail on the knowledge requirement was provided in *Cunliffe-Owen v Teather & Greenwood* [1967] 3 All ER 561. There, the court explained that for a custom to be 'known' it must be 'notorious', 'clearly established' and 'reasonable'. The court also added that it must be recognised as binding.

CHAPTER SUMMARY

- Oral statements can form the terms of a contact, if they are important enough. Otherwise they are at best representations.
- Reliance on a statement can result in it being a term, and so the knowledge of the parties is relevant.
- Written terms can be added to an oral contract by signing a document, by providing reasonable notice of the terms or by a consistent and frequent course of dealing.
- For notice to have been reasonably provided, the terms must be sufficiently noticeable before or at the time the contract is made, and on a 'document' that holds itself out as having terms. The more onerous or unusual a term, the more is required for reasonable notice to be given.
- Oral statements can add to written terms, either because a contract is intended to be written and oral, or because the statement results in a collateral contract.
- The courts will construe the terms based on their wording but, where appropriate, will use the wider context to give effect to commercial common sense.
- Terms can be implied from legislation. The terms provided by the Sale of Goods Act 1979 are good examples.
- Courts can imply terms as one-off gap fillers (terms implied in fact). This is where the term is necessary to give the contract business efficacy, or when the term can be objectively said to have been obvious to the parties.
- Express terms should be construed first before the courts consider implying a term.
- Terms can be implied as standardised general default rules (implied terms in law). The basis for implying a term in law was once said to be necessity but can now be said to be reasonableness, policy considerations and fairness.
- Terms can also can also be implied by custom or usage.

KEY CASES

- ☐ *Dick Bentley v Smith Motors* [1965] 1 WLR 623—shows how oral statements can be terms based on the knowledge of the parties and the resulting reliance on the term.
- ☐ *Esso Petroleum Ltd v Mardon* [1976] QB 801—authority for collateral warranties resulting from statements that are not promissory.
- ☐ *L'Estrange v F Graucob Ltd* [1934] 2 KB 394—represents the basic rule incorporating written terms into an oral contract by signing a document.
- ☐ *Parker v South Eastern Railway* (1877) 2 CPD 416—this is the original authority on incorporation of written terms by reasonable notice.
- ☐ *Interfoto Picture Library v Stiletto Visual Programmes Ltd* [1989] QB 433—authority for the rule that a higher degree of notice is required for onerous or unusual terms.
- ☐ *J.Evans & Son (Portsmouth) v Andrea Merzario Ltd* [1976] 1 WLR 1078—the judgments show the ways an oral statement can be incorporated alongside the written terms of a contract.
- ☐ *Investors Compensation Scheme Ltd v West Bromwich Building Society* [1998] 1 WLR 898—firmly established the contextual approach to interpretation.
- ☐ *Arnold v Britton* [2015] UKSC 36—provides guidance on the application of the contextual approach to interpretation.
- ☐ *Wood v Capita Insurance Services Ltd* [2017] UKSC 24—provides further clarification on the use of the contextual approach to interpretation.
- ☐ *The Moorcock* (1889) 14 PD 64—original authority for the courts to imply terms to realise business efficacy.

☐ *Shirlaw v Southern Foundries* **(1926) 2 KB 206**—original authority for the courts to imply terms using the officious bystander test.

☐ *Attorney-General of Belize v Belize Telecom Ltd* **[2009] UKPC 10**—significant for Lord Hoffman's controversial position on the implication of terms in fact being about the construction of the contract.

☐ *Marks and Spencer plc v BNP Paribas Securities Services Trust Company (Jersey) Ltd* **[2015] UKSC 72**—rejection of any purported change brought about by the *Belize Telecom* case and confirmation of the difference between the processes of construction and implying terms.

☐ *Liverpool City Council v Irwin* **[1977] AC 239**—leading authority on the courts implying terms as a necessary incident to a certain type of contract.

QUESTIONS

1. During negotiations for the purchase of 2000 PC tablets, Gamer Phones Ltd told the seller that if the software was not included there was no way they would go ahead with the purchase. The seller then stated that the software was included. Gamer Phones Ltd agreed to the sale, but the tablets were delivered without software. There is nothing in the written contract about the supply of software. Advise Gamer Phones Ltd.

2. Agnieszka rented two additional tanning booths for her salon for two months for £100 a month per item. She returned them to the supplier after the summer, a month late. She has been charged an extra £2400. The supplier's website contains the terms, and in small print there is a reference to a charge of £1200 per item for every month past the return date. Advise Agnieszka as to whether the term is part of her contract.

3. Do the 'business efficacy' and 'officious bystander' tests amount to the same thing?

4. Evaluate the extent to which the principles of interpretation introduced by Lord Hoffman in the *Investors Compensation Scheme Case* represent an improvement.

 For answer guidance to these questions please visit the online resources at www .oup.com/uk/naidoo1e/, where you will also find multiple choice questions to check your understanding of key concepts.

FURTHER READING

Andrews, 'Interpretation of contracts and "commercial common sense": do not overplay this useful criterion,' CLJ [2017], 76(1), 36.
A long and detailed assessment of the contextual approach to interpretation which unpacks the concept of commercial common sense.

Goh, 'Lost but found again: the traditional tests for implied terms in fact: *Marks & Spencer Plc v BNP Paribas Securities Services Trust Company (Jersey) Ltd*' JBL [2016], 3, 231.
A useful case note on the impact and significance of the relevant Supreme Court case.

McLauchlan, 'Continuity, not change, in contract interpretation?' LQR (2017) 133(Oct) 546.
An excellent, short case note on *Wood v Capita* addressing how the traditional textual and modern contextual approaches to interpretation are to be balanced.

Sumption, 'A Question of Taste: The Supreme Court and the Interpretation of Contracts', available from the Supreme Court website, https://www.supremecourt.uk/docs/speech-170508.pdf
This is from a lecture delivered by Lord Sumption JSC. It addresses the development of the contextual approach to interpretation and how the Supreme Court has limited its scope, indicating a slight retreat. It is short, very clear and provides a useful insight into the issue.

7

Exemption Clauses and Unfair Terms

LEARNING OUTCOMES

By the end of this chapter you should be able to:

- understand the extent to which the common law and legislation control the use of exemption clauses and other unfair terms;
- understand how such terms might also be controlled using concepts of fairness;
- apply the test of reasonableness from the Unfair Contract Terms Act 1977 to exemption clauses used between businesses;
- assess the scope and application of the test of fairness from the Consumer Rights Act 2015.

INTRODUCTION

Exemption clauses are terms that either exclude or limit the liability of a party, and we came across a number of examples in the cases addressed at 6.2. The law relating to the use of such clauses is a mixture of rules found in both the common law and legislation. The common law rules apply to all contracts. In addition, the Unfair Contract Terms Act 1977 applies to the use of exemption clauses in contracts between two businesses. For consumers, the Consumer Rights Act 2015 provides wider protection from unfair terms including exemption clauses.

Before we can examine *how* such terms are controlled, we must know *why* there is a need to control them. The practical context of exemption clauses is simple. One party will be in breach and so the other will seek compensation for the loss caused by the breach. The party in breach will then defend the action by relying on an exemption clause. The dispute is then about whether or not the clause can be relied upon. As we will see, the circumstances in which terms might be assessed for being 'unfair' can be wider than this. Typically, a business will take action against a consumer following the consumer's failure to perform an obligation, which will then prompt the consumer to challenge the obligation as based on an unfair term.

7.1 The Need to Control Exemption Clauses and Unfair Terms

In order to assess the effectiveness of the controls on exemption clauses and unfair terms, it is important to understand why such controls are needed. To do this, we need to consider the effects of such terms as well as the common law basis for allowing them to be effective in the first place.

7.1.1 The Effect of Exemption Clauses and Unfair Terms

An exemption clause either excludes or limits the liability of a party, for example, liability for a breach of contract or liability for an act of negligence. The clause might have wording aimed at excluding all liability (an exclusion clause) or, alternatively, it could limit the liability to specific amount of money (a limitation clause). Beyond straightforward exclusion and limitation clauses, there are clauses that achieve a similar objective, but in a different way. One example is a term allowing a party to change a contractual obligation. Consider a term allowing a travel agent to swap your booked hotel for a different hotel. Ordinarily, such a change would be a breach. However, such a change would not be a breach if a term allows for the change to take place. So rather than excluding liability for such a breach, the term prevents the liability arising in the first place. While there is a difference from a legal perspective, in practice the agent has achieved the same thing. The term allows for making the change without having to compensate the other party.

In assessing the effect of exemption clauses and equivalent terms, it is important to bear in mind that the law will have generally imposed liability for a good reason. If an exemption clause is effective, which is to say, if it excludes the relevant liability, then it will serve to undermine that good reason. This is one reason why exemption clauses are subject to legal controls. Another is that an exemption clause will typically mean that the innocent party will lose what would otherwise be a right to damages, and could even mean that it loses its right end the contract. This leaves such clauses open to abuse because they can be imposed by a large business on a weaker party who does not understand the law or who has no choice but to contract with the larger business on whatever terms they offer. Consumers and small businesses are the obvious examples of parties in such a weaker negotiating position. This is another reason for subjecting the use of exemption clauses to legal controls.

This does not however mean that the use of exemption clauses is always a problem. In fact, exemption clauses are essential tools for commercial parties. Consider a contract with obligations that are very difficult to perform or carry real risks of failure. Such risks can be managed by the parties with the use of exemption clauses. This means that both parties can avoid any unexpected claims by limiting or excluding liability. As a tool for allowing parties to agree between themselves who has responsibility for certain risks, exemption clauses are also very useful. In addition, a party might be happy to agree to the existence of an exemption clause in a contract in return for a significant discount on the contract price. In which case, the contract with its exemption clauses might be seen by both parties as a good deal.

Beyond exemption clauses, other types of terms are recognised as being unfair in consumer contracts. A term is unfair in those circumstances where it is very one-sided in imposing a burden on a consumer, of the type that a consumer would not ordinarily agree to. There are many examples, but a couple of relatable examples are enough at this stage. First, consider a term that applies to the early cancellation of a service. If it imposes a charge that is so high it does not bear any relation to loss caused by the cancellation, it is likely to be an unfair term. Another example is a term that makes the contract renew automatically. If the term gives an unreasonably short period of time to refuse the renewal, it is likely to be an unfair term. Just like with many exemption clauses, the use of unfair terms is often the result of a large business imposing them on a consumer. Alternatively it might simply be that the true nature of the term is disguised, that it is difficult to understand, or that it is in a location where it is difficult to see.

7.1.2 The Common Law Basis for the Use of Exemption Clauses and Unfair Terms

The use of exemption clauses and unfair terms results from the traditional freedom of contract principle and is perhaps the most extreme result of such freedom. In theory, if a party does not want to agree to such terms, they should negotiate a better deal. Alternatively, it could shop around elsewhere for

➜ CROSS-REFERENCE

For the discussion and wider context of freedom of contract see 1.6.1.

better terms. That possibility should then encourage businesses to use more balanced terms. However, the reality is often very different. Parties are often unequal in terms of bargaining strength, i.e. their ability to negotiate. For example, one party might be in such a strong position in the market that it is in a position to dictate terms, leaving weaker parties with no ability to negotiate and no alternative but to accept.

The position is a lot worse when we consider the use of 'standard form' terms in consumer contracts. These are pre-drafted terms that businesses use to enter contracts with consumers. They might be found on standard notices, displays boards, tickets or websites. Even today, consumers often assume that there cannot be anything wrong with the terms presented to them. There is a perception that if the terms are being used, they have been pre-approved and are completely lawful. In many cases, that could be an accurate assumption but it might be that such terms have not yet been challenged using legislation.

In the days before such legislation, the problem of exemption clauses being justified by freedom of contract was well recognised. The problem was explained neatly by Lord Reid in *Suisse Atlantique SA v Rotterdamsche Kolen Centrale NV* [1967] 1 AC 361. He observed that often consumers do not have time to read standard form terms. If they do take the time to read the terms, they would probably not understand them. Those that do understand the terms and object to them will be told to 'take it or leave it'. The few that decide to leave it and go elsewhere will then find others using the same terms. The point was that freedom of contract is supposed to involve some choice or scope for negotiation. Since such a choice is unlikely in reality for consumers, Lord Reid viewed the use of exemption clauses in standard form contracts as 'objectionable'. This opinion is representative of the judicial views that resulted in the courts developing limited ways to control the application of exemption clauses. However, as we shall see, the common law methods for controlling such clauses came to be seen as inadequate, meaning that there was a need for legislation to control their use.

KEY POINTS

The use of exclusion clauses is justified by the principle of freedom of contract, but the exercise of choice was not always possible in the real world.

7.2 Two Types of Unfairness

Before we examine the legal control of exemption clauses and unfair terms, it will be useful to establish a basic understanding of two different types of unfairness. This will then enable us to be more detailed when evaluating how protective the law is.

7.2.1 Procedural Unfairness

This relates to the *way* in which a term in a contract is agreed. Procedural fairness is achieved when terms are clear and noticeable so that it can be said that the other party ought to have known exactly what they were agreeing to. In other words, where the terms are readily noticeable or prominent, and easy enough to understand, it can be said that the other party was able to enter into the contract in an informed and procedurally fair way. If on the other hand important terms are hidden in small print, or are not distinguishable from the less important terms, or if the terms are presented in such a way that there is not enough time for them to be read, then it might be said that the other party did not have the opportunity to give genuinely informed consent. In addition, where terms are not clear or noticeable, this might be an indication that the party relying on them is trying to trick or take advantage of the other.

7.2.2 Substantive Fairness

This relates to the weight of the obligation imposed. Consider a contract that is one-sided because it imposes a significant (or 'heavy') obligation on a consumer. Exclusion clauses are an obvious example because they take might rights away and cause an imbalance between the parties' rights. By imposing such a burden, a term could be unfair 'in substance'.

It is important to protect consumers from such terms because the protection from procedural unfairness may not be enough. Let us assume that a one-sided term like an exclusion clause is very prominent. Perhaps the trader specifically points to it. Let us also assume that it is very easy to understand. Perhaps it goes beyond stating the liability excluded and actually explains the consequences with examples. There can be no complaint about procedural unfairness there. Consumers that are unwilling to agree to such a term could choose to go elsewhere. However, if it is a standard term used by all traders, consumers would have no real choice. They will know and understand the term but would be forced to accept it or go simply go without. That will clearly be a problem when the item to be purchased is essential. That is why it is important to control the substance of terms as well as the procedure by which they become part of the contract.

We can now examine how protective the common law and legislative measures are by identifying to what extent these two types of fairness are achieved.

7.3 Common Law Controls: Rules on the Incorporation of Terms

Before specific legislative controls were introduced, judges developed various methods for preventing unfairness arising through the use of standard form contracts. One key method has been the use of the rules on how terms are incorporated into a contract. We need to address how the incorporation rules were used to achieve a degree of fairness before turning to the effectiveness of this method.

➜ CROSS-REFERENCE
For the detailed the rules on incorporation see 6.2.

7.3.1 The Rules on Incorporation of Terms as a Means to Control Unfairness

The rules on incorporation apply to all types of terms but they were developed in the context of exemption clauses. Judges used these rules to protect parties from unfair exemption clauses where it was possible to do so. Perhaps the most obvious example is the line of cases in which an exemption clause on a ticket or notice was relied upon.

We know from *Parker v South Eastern Railway Co* (1877) that when terms are not signed, they are part of the contract if reasonable notice of their existence has been given to the other party. We also know from *Olley v Marlborough Court Hotel* [1949] that reasonable notice must have been given before or at the time of entering the contract. And we know from *Chapleton v Barry UDC* [1949] that the terms must be on what is regarded as a 'contractual document', meaning a place in which one might reasonably expect to find the terms. Finally, we also know that a higher degree of notice is needed to satisfy the requirement of reasonableness when the terms are very onerous or unusual. This means such terms need to be given more prominence. That principle is based on Lord Denning MR's 'red hand' comment from *Spurling Ltd v Bradshaw* [1956] and *Thornton v Shoe Lane Parking* [1971]. Building on these cases, the Court of Appeal later held that a very onerous and unusual term had not been incorporated into a contract in *Interfoto Picture Library Ltd v Stiletto* Visual Programmes Ltd [1989]. This approach to the incorporation of terms can be seen as a way of promoting more fairness in contract terms. This was confirmed by Bingham LJ's judgment in that case.

➜ CROSS-REFERENCE
For the facts of *Interfoto* v *Stiletto* [1989] see 6.2.6.

GUIDED CASE READING 7.1

Interfoto Picture Library Ltd v Stiletto Visual Programmes Ltd [1989] 2 WLR 615

When you read the extracts from the judgment of Bingham LJ, try to identify:

- the reasons why the requirement of reasonable notice is not just about offer and acceptance but is also about protection from unfairness;
- the type of unfairness that Bingham LJ argues is controlled by the reasonable notice requirement.

In many civil law systems, and perhaps in most legal systems outside the common law world, the law of obligations recognises and enforces an over-riding principle that in making and carrying out contracts parties should act in good faith. This does not simply mean that they should not deceive each other, a principle which any legal system must recognise; its effect is perhaps most aptly conveyed by such metaphorical colloquialisms as 'play-ing fair', 'coming clean' or 'putting one's cards face upwards on the table'. It is in essence a principle of fair and open dealing. In such a forum it might, I think, be held on the facts of this case that the plaintiffs were under a duty in all fairness to draw the defendants' attention specifically to the high price payable if the transparencies were not returned in time and, when the 14 days had expired, to point out to the defendants the high cost of continued failure to return them.

> Bingham LJ started by explaining the duty of good faith that exists in other jurisdictions, and noting that the English common law was unusual in not explicitly recognising that such a duty exists.

English law has, characteristically, committed itself to no such overriding principle but has developed piecemeal solutions in response to demonstrat-ed problems of unfairness. Many examples could be given. Thus equity has intervened to strike down unconscionable bargains. Parliament has stepped in to regulate the imposition of exemption clauses and the form of certain hire-purchase agreements. The common law also has made its contribution, by holding that certain classes of contract require the utmost good faith, by treating as irrecoverable what purport to be agreed estimates of damage but are in truth a disguised penalty for breach, and in many other ways.

> He then—a little obliquely—suggested that the term in question in this dispute would have been ruled out as contrary to such a 'duty of good faith' if the contract had been created in a different jurisdiction.

The well-known cases on sufficiency of notice are in my view properly to be read in this context. At one level they are concerned with a question of pure contractual analysis, whether one party has done enough to give the other notice of the incorporation of a term in the contract. At another level they are concerned with a somewhat different question, whether it would in all the circumstances be fair (or reasonable) to hold a party bound by any conditions or by a particular condition of an unusual and stringent nature.

> But this was not to suggest that English law does not achieve the same result indirectly. Unlike in other legal systems, it has no over-riding duty of good faith, but it has many 'smaller' doctrines which, taken together, amount to the same thing. According to Bing-ham LJ, the cases on reasonable notice for the incorporation of terms had to be understood as a facet of this.

[Reference was made judgment s from *Parker v. South Eastern Railway Co.* (1877) that confirmed the reasonable notice requirement]

> Bingham LJ then related the incorporation rule of reasonable notice to the regulation of unfairness.

. . .

Both Mellish L.J. and Baggallay L.J. were, as it seems to me distinguishing the case in which it would be fair to hold a party bound from the case in which it would not. But this approach is made more explicit in the strongly worded judgment of Bramwell L.J . . .:

. . . It is asked: What if there was some unreasonable condition, as for instance to forfeit £1,000 if the goods were not removed in 48 hours? Would the depositor be bound? I might content myself by asking: Would he be, if he were told 'our conditions are on this ticket,' and he did not read them. In my judgment, he would not be bound in either case. I think there is an implied understanding that there is no condition unreasonable to the knowledge of

> This was evidenced by the various cases cited, which demonstrated that judges were keenly aware that the rules regarding incorporation of terms had been created with specific refer-ence to 'fair dealing'.

the party tendering the document and not insisting on its being read—no condition not relevant to the matter in hand . . .

This is not a simple contractual analysis whether an offer has been made and accepted . . . These authoritative passages appear to base the law very firmly on consideration of what is fair in all the circumstances.

[Reference was made to the 'red hand' comment from Denning LJ in *Spurling Ltd. v. Bradshaw* [1956]]

Here, therefore, is made explicit what Bramwell L.J. had perhaps foreshadowed, that what would be good notice of one condition would not be notice of another. The reason is that the more outlandish the clause the greater the notice which the other party, if he is to be bound must in all fairness be given.

[Comments from Lord Reid and Lord Pierce in *McCutcheon v. David MacBrayne Ltd.* [1964] and Lord Denning MR from *Thornton v. Shoe Lane Parking Ltd* [1971] were cited]

Additional comments were cited to show that incorporation is not about offer and acceptance but also fairness.

. . . Here again, as it seems to me, one finds reference to a concept of fair dealing that has very little to do with a conventional analysis of offer and acceptance.

The tendency of the English authorities has, I think, been to look at the nature of the transaction in question and the character of the parties to it; to consider what notice the party alleged to be bound was given of the particular condition said to bind him; and to resolve whether in all the circumstances it is fair to hold him bound by the condition in question. This may yield a result not very different from the civil law principle of good faith, at any rate so far as the formation of the contract is concerned.

He closed in re-emphasising that the common law position was 'not very different' from that in other jurisdictions, but just achieved the result indirectly through the means of rules concerning incorporation.

This judgment has been cited with approval in many cases since. It confirmed the need for the common law to control unfairness in contract terms. In addition, it confirmed that the incorporation requirement of reasonable notice has always been aimed at limiting such unfairness. Clearly, the reasonable notice requirement is about the *way* the terms are presented and so it is concerned with procedural unfairness. But it is also clear that the requirement of reasonable notice is not just about whether the terms should have been noticed, and it has a substantive element too. This is because the weight of the obligation being imposed—that is, the term's substance—is treated as a factor determining how much must be done to fulfil the reasonable notice requirement. In other words, if the term is substantively unfair, then more has to be done to make the agreement to the terms more procedurally fair. Bingham LJ's confirmation that the incorporation rule reflected a principle of fairness was supported by previous cases. It was reflected in the judicial views expressed as early as *Parker v SE Railway* (1877) and has then featured in other decisions since. As a result, we have a clear judicial statement in support of the view that the incorporation rules can serve a protective purpose. That protection then contributes to the controls on exemption clauses and other unfair terms. However, in order to test the adequacy of this protection, we need to establish the limits of the incorporation rules.

?!   THINKING POINTS

What type of fairness is given effect by the rules on incorporation?

7.3.2 The Limits of the Incorporation Rules

The problem with the incorporation rules is that they are limited in terms of their application and scope. The actual standard of the notice required is low. For example, with unsigned documents the consumer just needs to be capable of knowing of the existence of terms. It does not generally matter whether the terms are in plain language and decent sized print, or are well structured and cross-referenced. It does not matter if in practice there is no time to read and understand them. Such terms are part of the contract if in the circumstances, the reasonable person should have known about the term. Such a low standard does not even require any thought about whether a reasonable person would have agreed to the terms.

Of course, in the case of unsigned documents, a higher standard of notice is required when the terms are onerous or unusual. This means that such terms have to be given more prominence. However, this would not apply to terms excluding liability for negligence causing financial loss or damage to property because such terms are not seen as onerous or unusual. A recent example is *Goodlife Foods Ltd v Hall Fire Protection Ltd* [2018] EWCA Civ 1371 which concerned a contract between two large businesses for the installation of a fire suppression system. The 22 terms, given on a quote, included a clause excluding liability for losses resulting from the system not working. Such loss would have been damage caused by fire, the one event the system was meant to prevent. Coulson LJ agreed with the trial judge that such a clause was not onerous or unusual and so it had been incorporated into the contract by just giving 'ordinary' reasonable notice. This is not a particular problem if the two parties are businesses with adequate legal advice, but it might be a problem for a consumer, or where both parties are businesses but one is much smaller or does not have the wherewithal to obtain legal advice.

Even where special prominence is provided, there is an obvious limit to the protection provided. Consider the use of standard terms. Any special prominence of the terms would allow a consumer to know about the terms. It is then the consumer's choice to enter the contract or go elsewhere. However, if the same terms exist everywhere, then just knowing about the term does not help. The consumer has no real choice if the same terms are found elsewhere. In such circumstances, the consumer, as the weaker party, needs specific protection from terms that impose a heavy burden.

KEY POINTS

The protection provided by the rules on incorporation is limited because giving terms prominence does not necessarily mean that the other party has a realistic alternative but to agree, and because courts have tended to take a fairly relaxed approach to what is 'onerous or unusual'.

7.4 Common Law Controls: The 'Contra Proferentem' Principle of Interpretation

Another way for the common law to control exemption clauses was through the interpretation of the term. Before any legislation was introduced, this common law method was very important. In fact, it was the only way to limit the application of exemption clauses that were part of a contract. When such a term was part of the contract, the next step was to examine its meaning. It would be argued that the exemption clause did not actually cover the particular breach or loss suffered. It would then be for the court to interpret the exemption clause. In doing this, a judge would deliberately interpret the clause against the party relying on it. This is known as the 'contra proferentem' principle. 'Contra' is Latin for 'against'. *'Proferentem'* is a reference to the party that put the term in (i.e. the party that proffered it). Essentially the court would see if the clause was ambiguous, i.e. by having different meanings. If it did, then the court would apply the meaning that worked against the party relying on the clause. That is how the principle works and it means that a strict approach is adopted to the interpretation of exemption clauses.

We will first look at some examples of this approach to controlling exemption clauses. We will then be in a better position to understand the significance of the *contra proferentem* principle today. We will see that the continuing significance of the principle is in question for two reasons. First, there is the potential impact of the legislation on exemption clauses. Secondly, there is the potential impact of Lord Hoffman's restatement of the principles of interpretation.

7.4.1 The Application of the *Contra Proferentem* Principle

When interpreting an exemption clause, the courts demonstrated a strict approach to the wording. A good example of this is *Andrews Bros (Bournemouth) Ltd v Singer & Co Ltd* [1934] 1 KB 17. In the case, the claimant motor dealer entered a contract to buy 'new Singer cars' from the defendant car maker. The defendant delivered a Singer car but it had been driven around 550 miles already. That prompted the buyer to claim there was a breach of contract because the car was not new. The defendant then tried to rely on an exemption clause which stated that 'all conditions, warranties and liabilities implied by statute, common law or otherwise are excluded'. Such a clause seems to exclude liability for everything. However, the Court of Appeal, led by Scrutton LJ, held that the defendant was still liable for breach. This was on the basis that 'new Singer cars' was an express term of the contract. According to the Court of Appeal, the clause only excluded liability that was *implied* rather than liability from an express term. It is almost certain that the defendant car maker intended to exclude all possible liability to the buyer but a strict reading of the words did not reflect this.

7.4.2 Guidance on the Exclusion of Liability in Negligence

Many cases feature a clause that tries to exclude liability in a fairly general way. For example, many disputed exemption clauses have excluded liability 'howsoever caused'. We might legitimately think that such a clause covers all liability. However, the courts have used such general wording to identify different meanings. Is it excluding the liability for failing to perform a contractual obligation? That would be liability for breach of contract only. Alternatively, does the clause also exclude liability caused by acts of negligence? That could be liability for negligent acts under the contract or liability under the tort of negligence. With such different meanings the *contra proferentem* principle is given effect by the court simply adopting whatever narrow meaning is available. This will have the effect of limiting the scope of the clause so that it excludes only one type of liability, leaving the remaining liability as a basis for the innocent party to bring an action. Usually, under this approach, liability in negligence would be taken outside of the clause, making the party in breach liable in negligence. This is done on the basis that the contractual liability is more immediate, because it is a contract that has been created. For that reason, it is assumed that the generic reference to 'liability' in a clause is intended to mean liability in contract for breach. That benefits the innocent party because of the compensation available in the tort of negligence. Usually that compensation will be a lot more than the compensation resulting from a contract claim. Consequently, the exclusion of liability in negligence has been an important aspect of the cases on the *contra proferentem* principle.

Guidance on the exclusion of negligence was provided in *Canada Steamship Lines v The King* [1952] AC 192. In the case, Lord Morton, who delivered the judgment for the Privy Council, helpfully stated the principle as follows:

> (1) If the clause contains language which expressly exempts the person in whose favour it is made (hereafter called "the proferens") from the consequence of the negligence of his own servants, [A party's 'Servants' are the people contracted to work for that party] effect must be given to that provision. . .
>
> (2) If there is no express reference to negligence, the court must consider whether the words used are wide enough, in their ordinary meaning, to cover negligence on the part of the servants of the proferens. If a doubt arises at this point, it must be resolved against the proferens. . .
>
> (3) If the words used are wide enough for the above purpose, the court must then consider whether "the head of damage may be based on some ground other than that of negligence", to quote again Lord Greene in the *Alderslade* case. . .The "other ground" must not be so fanciful or remote that the proferens cannot be supposed to have desired protection against it; but subject to this qualification, which is no doubt to be implied from Lord Greene's words, the existence of a possible head of damage other than that of negligence is fatal to the proferens even if the words used are *prima facie* wide enough to cover negligence on the part of his servants.

This guidance was cited in many cases dealing with the interpretation of exclusion clauses. It can be summarised in the following way:

1. If the wording actually says that it excludes liability in negligence, then it should be allowed to do so.

2. If the wording does not actually refer to negligence, the court has to decide if the wording is wide enough to cover negligence. If there is any doubt, then the clause will not cover negligence.

3. The words might be wide enough to cover liability in negligence. If they are, the court should look to see if there are also other possible types of liability that could have been intended to be covered by the clause. An example is liability for breach of contract. If there is another type of liability, then the clause covers that liability rather than negligence. The idea is that in such circumstances, if the parties had intended for negligence to be covered by the clause, they would have said so.

An example of Lord Morton's second and third principles can be seen in the case of *White v John Warwick* [1953] 1 WLR 1285. The claimant had hired a cycle from the defendant to carry and deliver newspapers. During use the seat tilted forward, causing the claimant to fall off and injure his leg. When the claimant sued, the defendant relied on a clause in the hire contract which stated: 'Nothing in this agreement shall render the owners liable for any personal injuries to the riders of the machines hired. . .'

The Court of Appeal observed that the clause did not expressly refer to the exclusion of liability in negligence. The wording was a lot wider. It then decided that hiring a cycle could give rise to two types of liability. There could be strict liability (i.e. breach of contract) from supplying a defective product. And, in addition, there could be liability under the tort of negligence where the supplier fails to take reasonable care. On that basis, the clause was read to exclude the contractual liability only. This meant that if negligence by the cycle supplier had been established, it would have been liable in negligence.

In his judgment. Denning LJ referred the approach to be adopted with such exclusion clauses:

> In this type of case two principles are well settled. The first is that if a person desires to exempt himself from a liability which the common law imposes on him, he can only do so by a contract freely and deliberately entered into by the injured party in words that are clear beyond the possibility of misunderstanding. The second is: if there are two possible heads of liability on the part of defendant,

one for negligence, and the other a strict liability, an exemption clause will be construed, so far as possible, as exempting the defendant only from his strict liability and not as relieving him from his liability for negligence.

Denning LJ's points are consistent with the principles stated by Lord Morton in the *Canada Steamship* case.

7.4.3 What if the Only Possible Liability Is for Negligence?

If the only possible liability is for negligence then the clause has to cover it provided that the wording appears to do so. This point was addressed in *Alderslade v Hendon Laundry* [1945] KB 189. Here the claimant left ten large Irish linen handkerchiefs at the defendant laundry to be cleaned. The handkerchiefs were then lost by the laundry. The claimant brought a contract action for £5 to cover the cost of replacing the items and, in response, the laundry relied on the following limitation clause: 'The maximum amount allowed for lost or damaged articles is twenty times the charge made for laundering.' That figure would have been just over a tenth of the £5 claim. The clause clearly did not specify that it covered liability for negligent acts. However, the Court of Appeal held that it had to be interpreted as covering negligence, for the reasons explained below, and on that basis, the claim was limited by the clause.

In the lead judgment, Lord Greene MR referred to the previous cases relied upon by the laundry and observed:

> The effect those authorities can I think be stated as follows: where the head of damage in respect of which limitation of liability is sought to be imposed by such a clause is one which rests on negligence and nothing else, the clause must be construed as extending to that head of damage, because it would otherwise lack subject-matter.

Lord Green MR then referred to circumstances in which there is liability other than negligence:

> Where, on the other hand, the head of damage may be based on some other ground than that of negligence, the general principle is that the clause must be confined in its application to loss occurring through that other cause, to the exclusion of loss arising through negligence. The reason is that if a contracting party wishes in such a case to limit his liability in respect of negligence, he must do so in clear terms in the absence of which the clause is construed as relating to a liability not based on negligence. . . In the present case all that we know about the goods is that they are lost. There seems to me to be no case of lost goods in respect of which it would be necessary to limit liability, unless it be a case where the goods are lost by negligence.

What was important was that the clause referred to liability for 'loss' or 'damage'. Lord Green MR made clear that the transaction itself could give rise to different forms of contractual liability, one that is strict and another based on negligent acts. However, the strict liability would only extend to cover things like a failure to wash the items. Liability for 'loss' or 'damage' could only arise from an act of negligence, and on that basis the clause had to cover acts of negligence. This was the only meaning the clause could have—otherwise, it would serve no purpose or function. As a result, the case represents a limit to the *contra proferentem* principle.

KEY POINTS

A clause excluding liability clearly shows an intention to exclude some kind of liability. If there is only one type of liability then the clause should be given the effect of excluding that liability.

→ CROSS-REFERENCE
For the facts of *Hollier v Rambler Motors* in the context of the incorporation rules see 6.2.7.

A very extreme application of the *contra proferentem* principle was demonstrated by *Hollier v Rambler Motors* [1972] 2 QB 71. Mr Hollier's car was taken to a garage for a repair and the car was damaged by a fire caused by the negligence of the garage. The garage tried to rely on the following exclusion clause: 'The company is not responsible for damage caused by fire to customers' cars on the premises. Customers' cars are driven by staff at owners' risk'.

We can recall that the Court of Appeal held that this exclusion clause had not been incorporated into the contract. However, in the lead judgment Salmon LJ took the opportunity to consider the scope of the exclusion clause.

GUIDED CASE READING 7.2

Hollier v Rambler Motors (AMC) Ltd [1972] 2 QB 71

When reading the extracts of Salmon LJ try to identify:

- why Salmon LJ did not like clauses of this type
- how Salmon LJ justified making a distinction between the causes of the fire covered by the clause.

. . . It is well settled that a clause excluding liability for negligence should make its meaning plain on its face to any ordinarily literate and sensible person. The easiest way of doing that, of course, is to state expressly that the garage, tradesman or merchant, as the case may be, will not be responsible for any damage caused by his own negligence. No doubt merchants, tradesmen, garage proprietors and the like are a little shy of writing in an exclusion clause quite so bluntly as that. Clearly it would not tend to attract customers, and might even put many off. I am not saying that an exclusion clause cannot be effective to exclude negligence unless it does so expressly, but in order for the clause to be effective the language should be so plain that it clearly bears that meaning. I do not think that defendants should be allowed to shelter behind language which might lull the customer into a false sense of security by letting him think—unless perhaps he happens to be a lawyer—that he would have redress against the man with whom he was dealing for any damage which he, the customer, might suffer by the negligence of that person.

Salmon LJ frames the issue from the perspective of a business inserting such a clause in a contract. While a clause excluding liability for negligence should make that meaning plain, Salmon LJ recognised that businesses might not want to use the word 'negligence' specifically, for fear of scaring away customers. This was permissible in the sense that a clause could still exclude liability in negligence without using that word. However, it was still necessary to make the effect of the clause clear.

[Reference was made to cases where liability for negligence was excluded without express reference to 'negligence']

. . . It seems to me that in *Rutter v. Palmer*, although the word 'negligence' was never used in the exemption clause, the exemption clause would have conveyed to any ordinary, literate and sensible person that the garage in that case was inserting a clause in the contract which excluded their liability for the negligence of their drivers. The clause being considered in that case—and it was without any doubt incorporated in the contract—was: 'Customers' cars are driven by your staff at customers' sole risk'. Any ordinary man knows that when a car is damaged it is not infrequently damaged because the driver has driven it negligently. He also knows, I suppose, that if he sends it to a garage and a driver in the employ of the garage takes the car on the road for some purpose in connection with the work which the customer has entrusted the garage to do, the garage could not conceivably be liable for the car being damaged in an accident unless the driver was at fault. It follows that no sensible man could have thought that the words in that case had any meaning except that the garage would not be liable for the negligence of their own drivers. That is a typical case where, on the construction of the clause in question, the meaning for which the defendant was there contending was the obvious meaning of the clause.

An example was *Rutter v Palmer*, where a clause excluding liability for a garage owner stating that 'customers' cars are driven. . .at customers' sole risk' was held to exclude liability in negligence because anybody would understand that the only way the garage could be liable for a customer's car being damaged in an accident was if it had been driven negligently. (If it were to be damaged any other way, for instance in an accident caused by another driver, the garage would not be liable anyway.) So excluding negligence liability was the only meaning the clause could have.

[Alderslade v Hendon Laundry was cited and explained]

... Again, this was a case where negligence was not expressly excluded. The question was: what do the words mean? I have no doubt that they would mean to the ordinary housewife who was sending her washing to the laundry that, if the goods were lost or damaged in the course of being washed through the negligence of the laundry, the laundry would not be liable for more than 20 times the charge made for the laundering. I say that for this reason. It is, I think, obvious that when a laundry loses or damages goods it is almost invariably because there has been some neglect or default on the part of the laundry; ... I think that the ordinary sensible housewife, or indeed anyone else who sends washing to the laundry, who saw that clause must have appreciated that almost always goods are lost or damaged because of the laundry's negligence, and therefore this clause could apply only to limit the liability of the laundry, when they were in fault or negligent.

> This was exactly the sort of reasoning which we have already seen being developed in *Alderslade v Hendon Laundry.*

... In those two cases, any ordinary man or woman reading the conditions would have known that all that was being excluded was the negligence of the laundry, in the one case, and the garage, in the other. But here I think the ordinary man or woman would be equally surprised and horrified to learn that if the garage was so negligent that a fire was caused which damaged their car, they would be without remedy because of the words in the condition. I can quite understand that the ordinary man or woman would consider that, because of these words, the mere fact that there was a fire would not make the garage liable. Fires can occur from a large variety of causes, only one of which is negligence on the part of the occupier of the premises, and that is by no means the most frequent cause. The ordinary man would I think say to himself: 'Well, what they are telling me is that if there is a fire due to any cause other than their own negligence they are not responsible for it.' To my mind, if the defendants were seeking to exclude their responsibility for a fire caused by their own negligence, they ought to have done so in far plainer language than the language here used.

> The crucial distinction between those case and this one was the fact that here the clause was being deployed in an attempt to escape liability for the result of a fire. While a reasonable person would understand the clauses in *Rutter* and *Alderslade* as only being able to exclude negligence liability, the opposite would be true here: fires can happen because of a number of reasons, not just due to negligence. A reasonable person would have understood the clause as excluding liability for a purely accidental fire— not one which the garage would have caused. Indeed, a reasonable person would be 'horrified' if the clause had the effect of excluding liability for a fire which the garage had negligently caused.

The clauses in *Alderslade* and *Ritter* were seen as relating to only one possible cause of the loss or damage. That one cause was negligence and so the clauses had to cover it. This meant a customer reading the clauses in those cases would assume that liability for negligence was covered by the clauses. In contrast, there could be fires caused by negligence and those not resulting from negligence. The clause was therefore capable of different meanings: did it cover liability caused by any fire or were fires caused by negligence outside the clause? Salmon LJ believed ordinary customers would be surprised to learn that the clause covered liability for fires caused by the negligence of the garage. Consequently, the clause did not cover fires caused by negligence; that is how it would be read by ordinary customers.

The assessment of the clause in *Hollier* can be criticised for going to too far with the *contra proferentem* rule. This is based on the argument that the case represents an example of judges going out of their way to find different meanings in a clause that is expressed clearly. That is something that the courts should not do (*Direct Travel v McGeown* [2003] EWCA Civ 1606).

?! THINKING POINTS

Could it be said that the interpretation adopted by Salmon LJ reflects what the parties appeared to intend?

7.4.4 A Less Strict Approach for Limitation Clauses

Limitation clauses allow for liability to exist, but only limit the extent of the liability. This means that the impact of a such a clause is not as harsh as an exclusion clause, and it is more likely to be seen simply as an agreed tool to allocate risk. On that basis, the *contra proferentem* principle is not as strict with limitation clauses. The point was authoritatively stated in *Ailsa Craig Fishing Co Ltd v Malvern Fishing Co Ltd* [1983] 1 WLR 964, where a security company (Securicor) had contracted to provide security for a fishing boat harbour. While anchored, the claimant's boat sunk after it made contact with the defendant's boat. The trial judge found that the loss was a result of a breach of contract and negligence by Securicor and awarded £55,000 in compensation However, this award was disputed because Securicor had a limitation clause limiting their liability to £1000. The clause was upheld by the House of Lords, and on interpreting limitation clauses Lord Wilberforce stated:

> The relevant words must be given, if possible, their natural, plain meaning. Clauses of limitation are not regarded by the courts with the same hostility as clauses of exclusion; this is because they must be related to other contractual terms, in particular to the risks to which the defending party may be exposed, the remuneration which he receives and possibly also the opportunity of the other party to insure.

Likewise, Lord Fraser observed:

> There are later authorities which lay down very strict principles to be applied when considering the effect of clauses of exclusion or of indemnity: see particularly the Privy Council case of *Canada Steamship Lines Ltd v R* [1952] . . ., where Lord Morton, . . . summarised the principles. . . . In my opinion these principles are not applicable in their full rigour when considering the effect of conditions merely limiting liability.

Further support for a more relaxed approach towards limitation clauses was provided by Lord Bridge in *George Mitchell (Chesterhall) Ltd v Finney Lock Seeds Ltd* [1983] 2 AC 803. There Lord Bridge approved of the comments expressed by Lord Wilberforce and Lord Fraser from the *Ailsa Craig Fishing* case. However, while a less strict approach is favoured for limitation clauses generally, it should not apply to all limitation clauses. Some clauses might limit liability to such a small amount that it makes them equivalent to exclusion clauses and in such cases there would be a strong argument that the clause should be treated as an exclusion clause. For example, there is little material difference between a limitation clause which limits liability to £50, say, and one which excludes it entirely.

7.4.5 The Limits of the *Contra Proferentem* Principle

The obvious limit to this judicial approach is that it relies on the clause being ambiguous. The idea is that if the clause is capable of different meanings, then there is something to interpret. It follows that if the meaning of the clause is clear, then there is nothing to interpret. The case of *Photo Productions Ltd v Securicor Transport Ltd [1980] AC 827* is a good example of this limitation. The defendant security company had a contract to provide a night time security patrol for the claimant's factory. One of the security guards deliberately started a small fire which spread and destroyed a significant part of the factory. When sued, the defendant relied on the following exclusion clause:

> "Under no circumstances shall the company be responsible for any injurious act or default of any employee of the company unless such act or default could have been foreseen and avoided by the exercise of due diligence on the part of the company as his employer. . ."

The House of Lords held that the clause operated to exclude the liability of the defendant security company. Lord Wilberforce, delivering the lead judgment, explained that the meaning of the clause was clear enough to exclude liability for both negligent and deliberate acts. The case thus represents an extreme example of what can be achieved using an exclusion clause that demonstrates a clear intention and where there is therefore no ambiguity. However, while the fact that the contract was between two large businesses was not raised in the judgment, it is likely that this was also relevant. The wording was clear enough for these businesses to know that the relevant liability was being excluded, because they would have had legal advice as to the clause's meaning and presumably negotiated it. This might not have been the case if the party relying on the clause had been significantly bigger than the other, or had a much stronger bargaining position.

The limiting of the *contra proferentem* principle to situations where there is ambiguity has an impact on the level of protection provided. It might mean that businesses express specific terms more clearly, and such an approach should be encouraged. However, it does not prevent the use of small print or terms being expressed in complex language that consumers would not understand. We must also remember that in many contracts there are lots of terms. Consumers will generally not have time to read all the terms in a contract even if everything in it is clear. Furthermore, where consumers can read and understand the language in which a term is expressed, it might still be difficult for them to assess the relevant risks. For an example, consider a term that excludes liability for defective goods. It would be difficult for a consumer to work out the likelihood of the seller's goods being defective. The consumer might even mistakenly assume that it means the seller cannot be sued but still has to provide a remedy.

Then there is the other problem emphasised by Lord Reid in the *Suisse Atlantique* case. Even where a consumer objects to an exemption clause, they might still be told that they can 'take it, or leave it', and when they go to other sellers find those same sellers relying on effectively the same clause. This will leave them with no alternative but to agree if they want whatever the product is, which is clearly a problem where that product is essential. The common law principles provide no solution to this problem. More specifically, the common law methods did not provide adequate protection from terms that imposed unfair obligations.

7.4.6 The Impact of Legislation Controlling Exemption Clauses

At one point, the rules on incorporation and the principle of *contra proferentem* were the only ways parties could be protected from exemption clauses. However, legislative control was introduced by the Unfair Contract Terms Act 1977. Essentially, this Act made certain exemption clauses ineffective. In addition, it also gave judges the power to assess the reasonableness of exemption clauses and terms achieving the same objectives. We will examine the application of the Act in detail later, but at this stage, we need only to understand the impact of the Act on the common law controls.

Lord Denning MR, in his final case, addressed the issue in the Court of Appeal judgment for *George Mitchell v Finney lock Seeds*. This was done with a colourful account of the judicial response to exemptions clauses. He started by describing a 'bleak winter' of contractual freedom with harsh exclusion clauses. He then identified the existence of a 'secret weapon' in the form of *contra proferentem* interpretation. This was where judges strained the meaning of words in order to be protective. Lord Denning then spoke of a 'spring' of law reform development and the 'summer' represented by the Unfair Contract Terms Act 1977. With reference to exemption clauses after the Act, he then stated: 'We should no longer have to go through all kinds of gymnastic contortions to get around them'. Lord Denning's comments were approved by Lord Bridge and Lord Diplock in the appeal to the House of Lords. Lord Diplock captured the point neatly by observing:

> [T]he Unfair Contract Terms Act 1977, had removed from judges the temptation to resort to the device of ascribing to words appearing in exemption clauses a tortured meaning so as to avoid giving effect to an exclusion or limitation of liability when the judge thought that in the circumstances to do so would be unfair.

The point is that following the Act, there was no longer a need for judges to go out of their way to find different meanings within exemption clauses. In other words, there was no longer a need to stretch the language used in order to be protective of a weaker party. While the *contra proferentem* principle remained as an additional tool for judges, there was no need to push it to its limits.

Beyond the Act, another relevant development has been the modern contextual approach to contract interpretation. This could also limit the application of the *contra proferentem* principle, and so that is our next issue.

7.4.7 The Modern Contextual Approach to Interpretation and the *Contra Proferentem* Principle

➡ CROSS-REFERENCE

For the facts and judgment of the *ICS* case see 6.4.

The application of the *contra proferentem* principle and the guidance from Lord Morton in the *Canada Steamship* case was put in doubt following the *Investors Compensation Scheme (ICS)* case. We can recall that in *ICS*, Lord Hoffman introduced new principles of interpretation and, in doing so, he observed that 'almost all the old intellectual baggage' of (legal) interpretation has been discarded. The question is whether the *contra proferentem* principle was part of that 'baggage'. Lord Hoffman's principles of interpretation were based on construing the contract as a whole. In doing so, judges should consider the wider factual matrix to reflect commercial common sense. The idea is that taking such an approach will give effect to the parties' apparent intentions more accurately. Arguably, this could be inconsistent with the *contra proferentem* principle, which is about interpreting the words strictly against the party relying on the clause. We have seen that under the strict approach, a clause excluding 'all liability' could be interpreted to exclude liability in contract but not negligence. In contrast, under the *ICS* approach, the same term could be taken to mean that all liability is, indeed, excluded. Such an interpretation could even be seen as reflecting commercial common sense.

The potential conflict between the different approaches to interpretation present an obvious need for some clarity. In *Bank of Credit and Commerce International SA v Ali* [2001] UKHL 8, Lord Hoffman took the opportunity to clarify what he meant by 'old intellectual baggage' back in *ICS*. In his judgment, Lord Hoffman cited Lord Denning MR's account of the development of the law relating to exemption clauses from the *George Mitchell* case. Lord Hoffman then explained:

> 60. My Lords, the lesson which I would draw from the development of the rules for construing exemption clauses is that the judicial creativity, bordering on judicial legislation, which the application of that doctrine involved is a desperate remedy, to be invoked only if it is necessary to remedy a widespread injustice. Otherwise there is much to be said for giving effect to what on ordinary principles of construction the parties agreed. . .

This clarification suggests that the *contra proferentem* principle should be reserved for more extreme cases, as a last resort. Lord Hoffman then added:

> 62. The disappearance of artificial rules for the construction of exemption clauses seems to me in accordance with the general trend in matters of construction, which has been to try to assimilate judicial techniques of construction to those which would be used by a reasonable speaker of the language in the interpretation of any serious utterance in ordinary life.

The comments by Lord Hoffman here suggest that the *contra proferentem* principle was part of what he had described as the 'baggage' of legal interpretation. At the very least, they make clear that the more creative and extreme application of the traditional principle is no longer appropriate. This clarification was strictly *obiter* and part of a dissenting judgment. However, since it is clarifying what was meant in a judgment for the majority in *ICS*, the opinion does carry weight.

In terms of the practical significance of Lord Hoffman's clarification, it would be quite extreme to treat it as overruling the cases on the *contra proferentem* principle because the case law is so well established. For that reason, we would expect a more direct statement overruling them expressly if that was the intention. Instead, it is more likely that the courts will continue to apply the *contra proferentem* principle, but judges will only do so when the *natural* meaning of the words results in different meanings.

Furthermore, in *HIH Casualty and General Insurance Ltd v Chase Manhattan Bank* [2003] UKHL 6, the principles put by Lord Morton in the *Canada Steamship* case were described by the House of Lords as guidance rather than a strict code. They remained useful but should not be applied like a statute. Instead, clauses should be interpreted with a view to the wider commercial context of the contract.

More recently, the continuing relevance of the *contra proferentem* principle was addressed in *Transocean Drilling UK Ltd v Providence Resources plc* [2016] EWCA Civ 372. There, Moore-Bick LJ for the Court of Appeal observed that it remained proper to use the principle when the wording is one-sided and 'genuinely ambiguous'. He added that the principle does not apply when the words are clear or when a clause 'favours the parties equally', particularly when the parties have the same bargaining strength. This means that the application of the *contra proferentem* principle does appear to have been limited by the *ICS* development, but that it has not entirely disappeared.

KEY POINTS

- Judges are now less reliant on *contra proferentem* interpretation as a way to protect a weaker party because of the protection provided by legislation.
- When a *contra proferentem* interpretation is made, it should be based on the natural meaning of the words rather than a strained interpretation designed to find an ambiguity.

7.4.8 The Principle of Fundamental Breach

Any account of the common law controls would not be complete without a brief mention of the principle of fundamental breach. It was developed by Lord Denning MR in *Harbutt's Plasticine Ltd v Wayne Tank and Pump Co Ltd* [1970] 1 QB 447. Under this principle, parties could not exclude liability for a fundamental breach. Such a breach would be one relating to the main performance of the contract (in other words, a breach of a condition). According to Lord Denning MR, such a breach would allow the contract to end, and a clause excluding liability for such a breach should not be effective. However, this principle of fundamental breach was rather short-lived and was specifically overruled by the House of Lords in the *Photo Productions* case.

Having explored the application of the common law controls and the extent of the protection reflected by them, we can turn to the legislative controls.

7.5 Introduction to the Legislative Controls of Exemption Clauses and Other Unfair Terms

To address the problem of exemption clauses and unfair terms generally, we now have legislation that runs alongside the common law rules, as detailed in Figure 7.1. Currently, this consists of the Unfair Contract Terms Act 1977 (UTCA) and the Consumer Rights Act 2015 (CRA). The relevant rules from the CRA 2015 actually implement an EU directive on unfair terms. A directive is a type of EU legislation and, once in force, member states have to take steps to ensure that the provisions of the directive are part of their national law. To do so, the UK would often pass legislation in the form of a statutory instrument that either stands alone or amends an existing Act.

The directive was originally implemented in the UK by the Unfair Terms in Consumer Contracts Regulations 1994 which were amended slightly in 1999. Essentially, the Regulations simply copied the wording of the directive. The problem was that the legal position on exemption clauses in consumer contracts was then a little confusing. Such clauses could be challenged under both the Regulations and UCTA because at the time, UCTA applied to all both consumer contracts and those between businesses. However, the problem of such an overlap no longer exists because the Regulations on unfair terms and the application of UCTA to consumers have been replaced by Part 2 of the CRA 2015. Since the CRA is an Act of Parliament, it will continue to apply irrespective of the UK no longer being a member of the EU.

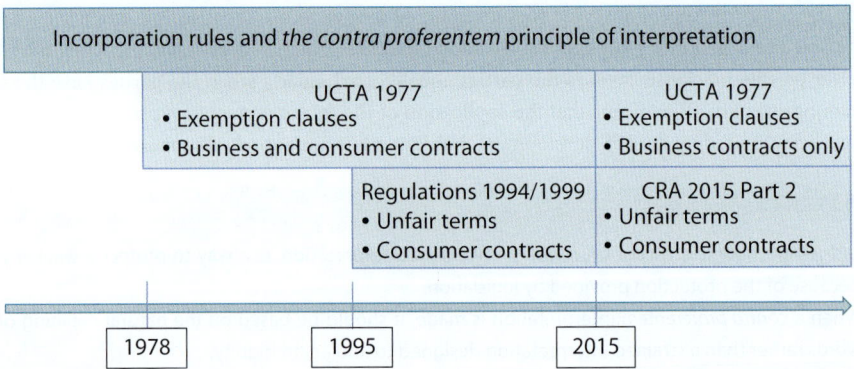

Figure 7.1
The development of the controls on exemption clauses and unfair terms

While the Regulations were replaced by the CRA, the case law under the Regulations remains applicable for the CRA. This is because a lot of the wording and tests are the same. In addition, the CRA reflects changes to the wording used in the Regulations and such changes are better understood with a view to the case law developed from the Regulations. We will first explore the application of UCTA and then turn to the CRA.

7.6 The Unfair Contract Terms Act 1977

UCTA seems rather ordinary compared with the consumer legislation that followed but, at the time, it represented a major change. Essentially, by providing some control of exemption clauses, it represented a legislative restriction on contractual freedom. Originally it also applied to consumer contracts and made a range of exemption clauses in such contracts ineffective. This type of protection for consumers continues, but it is now found in the CRA.

UCTA places controls on the use of certain terms between businesses, not just in contracts but also in notices. Either it makes them ineffective, or it makes them subject to a test of reasonableness. At this stage it is useful to know that these restrictions are in sections 2–7 and that is why sections on other matters like the scope of the Act make references to sections 2–7.

7.6.1 The Scope of the Act: The Type of Terms Covered

Contrary to what the title suggests, the Act does not apply to all 'unfair terms'. Instead, it only covers exemption clauses and terms with an equivalent effect. We know that exemption clauses either exclude or limit the liability of a business, but in section 13, the Act defines this to include a little more:

Section 13 Varieties of exemption clause.

(1) To the extent that this Part of this Act prevents the exclusion or restriction of any liability it also prevents—

(a) making the liability or its enforcement subject to restrictive or onerous conditions;

(b) excluding or restricting any right or remedy in respect of the liability, or subjecting a person to any prejudice in consequence of his pursuing any such right or remedy;

(c) excluding or restricting rules of evidence or procedure;

and (to that extent) sections 2, 6 and 7 also prevent excluding or restricting liability by reference to terms and notices which exclude or restrict the relevant obligation or duty.

(2) But an agreement in writing to submit present or future differences to arbitration is not to be treated under this Part of this Act as excluding or restricting any liability.

A restriction within (a) would be something like a term that says a claim must be made within a certain limited period. It would also include a term that requires claims to be in a certain way that would be difficult for the innocent party to perform.

Point (b) covers the typical exemption clause or clauses that create restrictions on how the innocent party uses their legal rights, and point (c) can also be understood as an aspect of this. Finally, a term committing the parties to arbitration for disputes is also technically a limit on the legal rights of a party. However, it is a useful and convenient method of resolving disputes, and one that is to be encouraged, so for that reason under subsection 2 arbitration is expressly separated from the restrictions covered by the Act.

A very useful function is performed by section 13 (1)(c). We will see that the Act restricts clauses that exempt liability in negligence. The definition of negligence refers to liability for a breach of a duty of care, so what if a clause actually removes the duty of care? Technically, this would mean that there is no breach in the first place to exempt. Essentially, such a clause removes the obligation to take reasonable care entirely, so that there would be no breach to be liable for. The point was raised in *Smith v Eric S Bush (a firm)* [1990] 1 AC 831, where the contract stated that a property valuation was being done without any responsibility for its accuracy. Lord Templeman made it clear that such a clause was within UCTA even though it was not excluding liability. This point was based on section 13 (1)(c) which refers to clauses covered by the Act and, specifically, clauses restricting an obligation or duty. Without this, it would be possible to circumvent the protection from UCTA through the use of a very open 'back door'.

Finally, it is clear that the Act applies not only to contract terms, but also to notices. A 'notice' is defined in section 14 as including:

> ...[a]n announcement, whether or not in writing, and any other communication or pretended communication...

It is natural to think of notices as being those displayed in noticeboards and tickets. However, the definition is wider under the Act, and covers notices expressed in ways other than in writing.

7.6.2 The Scope of the Act: The Type of Liability Covered

The type of liability is addressed by sections 1(3) and (4):

> 1 Scope of Part I
>
> ...
>
> (3) In the case of both contract and tort, sections 2 to 7 apply (except where the contrary is stated in section 6(4)) only to business liability, that is liability for breach of obligations or duties arising—
>
>   (a) from things done or to be done by a person in the course of a business (whether his own business or another's); or
>
>   (b) from the occupation of premises used for business purposes of the occupier...
>
> (4) In relation to any breach of duty or obligation, it is, immaterial for any purpose of this Part of this Act whether the breach was inadvertent or intentional, or whether liability for it arises directly or vicariously.

Since the Act applies to business liability only, it has no application to contracts between private parties.

It refers to liability that is direct and also vicarious. As a result, the Act covers clauses exempting liability for the direct actions of the business but also the liability the law imposes on business for the actions of others. An example would be liability arising from the conduct of employees.

A 'business' is defined in section 14 as:

> ...[I]ncluding a profession, activities of any government department or local or public authority.

This definition would exclude charities. Parties that fall outside the scope of a 'business' fall outside of the Act and in such circumstances, the common law controls would have an important role to play.

There are some contracts that are specifically excluded from the controls in sections 2–7. These are listed at the back of the Act in Schedule 1 which defines the scope of the controls in sections 2, 3, and 7:

> 1. Sections 2 and 3 of this Act do not extend to—
>
>   (a) any contract of insurance (including a contract to pay an annuity on human life);
>
>   (b) any contract so far as it relates to the creation or transfer of an interest in land, or to the termination of such an interest, whether by extinction, merger, surrender, forfeiture or otherwise;
>
>   (c) any contract so far as it relates to the creation or transfer of a right or interest in any patent, trade mark, copyright or design right, registered design, technical or commercial information or other intellectual property, or relates to the termination of any such right or interest;

(d) any contract so far as it relates—

    (i) to the formation or dissolution of a company (which means any body corporate or unincorporated association and includes a partnership), or

    (ii) to its constitution or the rights or obligations of its corporators or members;

(e) any contract so far as it relates to the creation or transfer of securities or of any right or interest in securities.

Also, there is a defined exclusion of international contracts to supply in section 26.

7.6.3 The Controls in Place by the Act

The controls found in the Act apply to different types of liability, such as liability in negligence and liability in contract. Before explaining the control of these in more detail, we need to see how the Act defines negligence.

7.6.3.1 The Scope of Liability in Negligence under the Act

The first of the controls addressed by the Act relates to clauses that limit or exclude liability for negligence. 'Negligence' is defined in section 1 as:

> Section 1:
>
> (1) For the purposes of this Part of this Act, "negligence" means the breach—
>
> (a) of any obligation, arising from the express or implied terms of a contract, to take reasonable care or exercise reasonable skill in the performance of the contract;
>
> (b) of any common law duty to take reasonable care or exercise reasonable skill (but not any stricter duty);
>
> (c) of the common duty of care imposed by the Occupiers' Liability Act 1957...

The point here is that negligence does not only mean liability in negligence under the tort of negligence. It also includes liability arising from contractual terms that impose an obligation to perform with reasonable care and skill. Such a term is only breached if the performing party is negligent. In other words, it is a term that requires a party to perform contractual obligations without being negligent. Furthermore, it applies to liability arising from the Occupiers Liability Act 1957. That Act creates specific liability with respect to lawful visitors that are harmed when on the property of another.

The control of clauses excluding or limiting liability in negligence is stated in section 2. How it is treated depends on the type of loss that results from the negligence covered by the clause.

7.6.3.2 The Control of Clauses Excluding or Limiting for Negligence

> Section 2:
>
> 2 Negligence liability.
>
> (1) A person cannot by reference to any contract term or to a notice given to persons generally or to particular persons exclude or restrict his liability for death or personal injury resulting from negligence.
>
> (2) In the case of other loss or damage, a person cannot so exclude or restrict his liability for negligence except in so far as the term or notice satisfies the requirement of reasonableness.
>
> (3) Where a contract term or notice purports to exclude or restrict liability for negligence a person's agreement to or awareness of it is not of itself to be taken as indicating his voluntary acceptance of any risk.

Section 2 indicates that terms excluding or limiting liability for death or personal injury caused by negligence are wholly ineffective. This would cover, for example, a term excluding liability for death or injury caused by breach of the implied term as to reasonable care and skill in a service contract.

→ CROSS-REFERENCE

For the facts of *Thompson v London Midland Scottish Railway* [1930] see 6.2.3.

Clearly, the term in *Thompson v London Midland Scottish Railway Co* [1930] could not be effective now. The treatment of such clauses seems to be based on policy. The idea is that it is always wrong to allow a party to limit or exclude liability for such a serious type of loss. Section 14 defines 'personal injury' and it states that the term includes: 'any disease and any impairment of physical or mental condition'.

Losses other than death or personal injury are covered by section 2(2). Such losses would include things like liability for damage to goods or financial losses. Such clauses are not ineffective and, instead, they are to be assessed by a judge who will decide if the term is fair and reasonable.

Section 2 (3) is necessary so that the protection provided by section 2(1) and 2(2) is not undermined. These sub-sections prevent or restrict liability in negligence being the subject of an exemption clause. However, if it can be said that agreement to the clause means that the risk of negligence was voluntarily assumed, this would mean there would be no liability in negligence to exclude. A finding of such a voluntary assumption would then circumvent the protection intended by the Act. Sub-section (3) thus serves to close what would otherwise be a gap in the protection provided by section 2.

7.6.3.3 Liability for Breach of Contract

Section 3 addresses terms that limit or exclude liability for breaching contractual obligations. Here, we are concerned with the strict liability imposed by the contract rather than the contractual obligations to act with reasonable care and skill. Such obligations are fault-based and therefore fall within negligence covered by section 2.

> Section 3 Liability arising in contract.
>
> (1) This section applies as between contracting parties where one of them deals on the other's written standard terms of business.
>
> (2) As against that party, the other cannot by reference to any contract term—
>
>   (a) when himself in breach of contract, exclude or restrict any liability of his in respect of the breach; or
>
>   (b) claim to be entitled—
>
>   (i) to render a contractual performance substantially different from that which was reasonably expected of him, or
>
>   (ii) in respect of the whole or any part of his contractual obligation, to render no performance at all,
>
> except in so far as (in any of the cases mentioned above in this subsection) the contract term satisfies the requirement of reasonableness.

This section applies to:

- terms that limit or exclude liability for breach of an express term;
- terms that allow a party to be excused from performing their obligations. And,
- terms allowing a party to change their obligations so that performance is different to what is stated in the contract.

The first type of clause is one that simply limits or excludes liability for a breach. The second refers to a type of clause that achieves the same effect as the first type. Rather than excluding or limiting liability for a breach, a business might try to give itself a right to not perform an obligation. This would mean that there is no breach from a failure to perform, and therefore no liability, which would achieve the aim of an exemption clause without the use of one.

Terms that allow a party to change its performance are another type of term equivalent to an exemption clause. An example is where a food producer agrees to supply a consignment of egg salad sandwiches and then supplies cheese sandwiches instead. Ordinarily that would be a breach, but if there is a term stating that the supplier reserves the right to change the type of sandwich then there would be no breach. Another example would be where a business contracts for a training session in a city location. There could be a term in the contract allowing for the training provider to change the location, and it might then swap the session to a rural location. In both examples, there would be a breach in the absence of the term allowing for the change to be made. On that basis, the term might have an effect equivalent to that of an exemption clause and so that is why such terms are included in the Act.

All three types of terms can be controlled by a judge assessing whether they are reasonable. However, there is a limit to section 3. It only applies to terms when a party 'deals on the other's written standard terms of business'. Some parties will have pre-drafted terms that they always trade with. In contrast, if the parties negotiate the terms for that particular contract, then it is not a case of 'standard terms'. But what if there are pre-drafted standard terms along with some that were negotiated?

The judgment in *Watford Electronics Ltd v Sanderson CFL Ltd* [2000] All ER (Direct) 1145 concerns the issue of 'standard' terms. Judge Thornton QC addressed the argument that standard terms had not been used because they had been amended with an additional clause. One question was whether this meant that the contract was outside of section 3. On this issue, Judge Thornton QC referred to the test to be applied by citing Lord Dunpark in the Scottish case of *McCrone v Boots Farm Sales Ltd* [1981] SLT 103 who stated:

> It is, in my opinion, wide enough to include any contract, whether wholly written or partly oral, which includes a set of fixed terms or conditions which both relies, without material variation, to contracts of the questioning kind.

Judge Thornton QC then applied this to the term that had been added, which created an obligation for a party to use their 'best endeavours'. He observed it was a narrow obligation and 'insubstantial' as it did not affect any of the other standard terms. This meant that the standard terms had only been 'insubstantially and immaterially varied' and so they remained as 'standard terms'.

The approach taken by the judge here shows that the real issue is the extent to which the standard terms have been changed. If there is a change that is 'material' and 'substantial' then the terms can be viewed as having been negotiated and are no longer 'standard'. They will then fall outside section 3. Of course, whether a change is sufficiently 'material' is a question of degree on the facts. Judges do not adopt a strict and narrow approach allowing any amendment to take the contract outside section 3. Instead, they will look at the contract as a whole and determine if enough of it reflects the usual terms used by the party.

7.6.3.4 Exemption Clauses in Sales Contracts

Section 3 is concerned with general contract liability for a breach of an express term. In contrast, sections 6 and 7 relate to liability implied by legislation. Section 6 has controls relating to implied terms in sales and hire purchase contracts and section 7 has the same controls for other contracts that have terms implied by legislation—for example, contracts for services.

Section 6 provides:

> 6 Sale and hire purchase.
>
> (1) Liability for breach of the obligations arising from—
>
>   (a) section 12 of the Sale of Goods Act 1979 (seller's implied undertakings as to title, etc.);
>
>   (b) section 8 of the Supply of Goods (Implied Terms) Act 1973 (the corresponding thing in relation to hire-purchase),
>
> cannot be excluded or restricted by reference to any contract term.

(1A) Liability for breach of the obligations arising from—

(a) section 13, 14 or 15 of the 1979 Act (seller's implied undertakings as to conformity of goods with description or sample, or as to their quality or fitness for a particular purpose);

(b) section 9, 10 or 11 of the 1973 Act (the corresponding things in relation to hire purchase), cannot be excluded or restricted by reference to a contract term except in so far as the term satisfies the requirement of reasonableness.

Under section 6, terms that exclude or limit liability from the implied term relating to the title of the goods are ineffective. Liability from other implied terms like those relating to sale by description and quality can be the subject of an exemption clause. However, such clauses are subject to the test of reasonableness. That has always been the case under UCTA in relation to contracts between businesses. In contrast, when the original version of UCTA also applied to consumer contracts, exemption clauses relating to these implied terms were not permitted in such contracts. We will see that this protection has continued under CRA 2015.

Section 7 applies to contracts other than those for the sale of goods or hire purchase where ownership or possession is transferred. As expected, it adopts the same approach as section 6.

7.6.4 The UCTA 'Reasonableness Test'

From what we have addressed so far, it is clear that some exemption clauses are ineffective and the majority are subject to the test of reasonableness. This means that certain terms can be challenged in court and it is then for the trial judge to assess whether the term is fair and reasonable. If it is, the term can be relied upon. If it is not held to be reasonable then it cannot be relied upon in that contract.

The general test of reasonableness is set out in section 11(1) UCTA which says that:

(1) In relation to a contract term, the requirement of reasonableness for the purposes of this Part of this Act, . . . is that the term shall have been a fair and reasonable one to be included having regard to the circumstances which were, or ought reasonably to have been, known to or in the contemplation of the parties when the contract was made.

(2) In determining for the purposes of section 6 or 7 above whether a contract term satisfies the requirement of reasonableness, regard shall be had in particular to the matters specified in Schedule 2 to this Act; but this subsection does not prevent the court or arbitrator from holding, in accordance with any rule of law, that a term which purports to exclude or restrict any relevant liability is not a term of the contract.

(3) In relation to a notice (not being a notice having contractual effect), the requirement of reasonableness under this Act is that it should be fair and reasonable to allow reliance on it, having regard to all the circumstances obtaining when the liability arose or (but for the notice) would have arisen.

(4) Where by reference to a contract term or notice a person seeks to restrict liability to a specified sum of money, and the question arises (under this or any other Act) whether the term or notice satisfies the requirement of reasonableness, regard shall be had in particular (but without prejudice to subsection (2) above in the case of contract terms) to—

(a) the resources which he could expect to be available to him for the purpose of meeting the liability should it arise; and

(b) how far it was open to him to cover himself by insurance.

(5) It is for those claiming that a contract term or notice satisfies the requirement of reasonableness to show that it does.

Under s.11(1), a clause is reasonable if, in the circumstances, it is reasonable! It sounds rather circular but the wording serves a purpose. The emphasis is on the *circumstances*. This makes the assessment one that is based on the surrounding facts of a particular case, and not the wording of the clause in the abstract. The assessment looks at a range of matters and balances them against each other. As a result, it is very difficult to predict what the result will be in any given case. Some aspects of the term might be reasonable, and others might not be. Since it is based on all relevant circumstances, it is possible for the same exemption clause to be unreasonable in one contract, but reasonable in another.

KEY POINTS

The reasonableness test means that a clause might be unreasonable in one contract but reasonable in another.

A finding of unreasonableness just means that the clause is not enforceable in that particular contract. It means that a finding of unreasonableness does not stop the continued use of the clause. The same clause in the same type of contract but between different parties might well be reasonable in one contract and unreasonable in another. In fact, the same reasonable clause in a contract with identical terms between the same parties, might be unreasonable where the contract was entered in different circumstances.

According to the wording of section 11(1), the reasonableness has to be to be assessed with a view to time of contracting. It means that if later background facts make the clause unreasonable or more reasonable, those facts have to be ignored.

7.6.4.1 Scope to appeal Against a Decision on Reasonableness

Since the assessment is based on the facts, higher courts will be reluctant to set aside a decision of a trial judge. The idea is that the trial judge would have the benefit of assessing the original testimony and other evidence during the trial 'first hand'. For that reason, appeal courts will only interfere with the outcome of the reasonableness test where the trial judge has 'proceeded upon some erroneous principles or was plainly or obviously wrong' (Lord Bridge in *George Mitchell (Chesterhall) Ltd v Finney Lock Seeds Ltd* [1983] 2 AC 803).

7.6.4.2 Prescribed Factors to Consider When Clauses Relate to the Statutory Implied Terms

Section 11(2) applies to the clauses covered by sections 6 and 7. These apply to exemption clauses concerning liability arising from the statutory implied terms. When assessing the reasonableness of such terms, judges have to consider the relevant factors listed in Schedule 2 of the Act (addressed at 7.6.5).

7.6.4.3 Non-contractual Notices

Subsection (3) reflects a slightly different approach for notices containing an exemption clause. It is concerned with notices that are not contractual, like a notice that excludes (common law) negligence. The assessment of reasonableness is based on the time that liability would have arisen.

7.6.4.4 Prescribed Factors to Consider When Assessing Limitation Clauses

Subsection (4) is an additional requirement for judges when assessing limitation clauses. These are not are harsh as exclusion clauses and are seen as a fairer way for commercial parties to manage their risks. For that reason, the judge has to take into account the fact that one party might be in a better position to insure against a particular loss. If that is the innocent party, then this might justify the limitation clause in favour of the other party. The same is true of the resources of the parties. A party with fewer resources, like one that has a lot less income, will have a greater need to manage the risks of liability. On that basis, such a party would be in a better position to justify a limitation clause.

7.6.4.5 The Special Rule on Proof

Finally, subsection (5) makes it clear that the party relying on the exemption clause has to prove it is reasonable. In practice, both parties would put forward arguments relating to the reasonableness of the clause. However, from the judge's perspective, the question is whether the party relying on the clause has done enough to prove it is reasonable.

7.6.5 Factors to Consider from Schedule 2

Schedule 2 lists factors that are relevant to exemption clauses aimed at the obligations implied by legislation (the sections 6 and 7 clauses). It does not mean judges are limited to the factors in Schedule 2 only, it just means that their assessment must consider the Schedule 2 factors along with any other relevant facts.

It is also important to appreciate that some of the factors listed in Schedule 2 can be relevant generally to the assessment of any clause (not just those in sections 6 and 7). The case of *Smith v Eric Bush* [1990] 1 AC 831 provides a useful example of the point. In that case, Lord Griffiths provided some guidance on factors that should always be relevant to the reasonableness of a clause. The factors listed were based on Schedule 2. However, the clause in that case did not concern liability arising from any terms implied by legislation. Instead, it concerned a clause removing the duty to perform an accurate survey of property. Essentially, it was a disclaimer that was equivalent to a term excluding liability for negligence and, on the facts, it was held to be unreasonable. The guidance provided by Lord Griffiths is useful, and is the only guidance on reasonableness from the House Lords. We will now examine this guidance alongside our discussion of each schedule 2 factor in turn. Our starting point is schedule 2 itself.

Schedule 2 lists the following relevant factors:

(a) the strength of the bargaining positions of the parties relative to each other, taking into account (among other things) alternative means by which the customer's requirements could have been met;

(b) whether the customer received an inducement to agree to the term, or in accepting it had an opportunity of entering into a similar contract with other persons, but without having a similar term;

(c) whether the customer knew or ought reasonably to have known of the existence and the extent of the term (having regard, among other things, to any custom of the trade and any previous course of dealing between the parties);

(d) where the term excludes or restricts any relevant liability if some condition was not complied with, whether it was reasonable at the time of the contract to expect that compliance with that condition would be practicable;

(e) whether the goods were manufactured, processed or adapted to the special order of the customer.

We will now address each of them in turn.

7.6.5.1 Bargaining Strength

This is a significant part of any assessment of reasonableness. It can reveal how much choice a party had when agreeing to the exemption clause. Where there is equality of bargaining (negotiating) strength it will count in favour of the clause being reasonable, a point that was made in cases such as *RW Green Ltd v Cade Bros Farm* [1978] 1 Lloyd's Rep 602; *Monarch Airlines Ltd v London Luton Airport Ltd* [1997] CLC 698 and *Watford Electronics Ltd v Sanderson CFL Ltd* [2001] EWCA Civ 317. More recently, bargaining strength was a significant factor in *Goodlife Foods Ltd v Hall Fire Protection Ltd* [2018] EWCA Civ 1371. As we have seen, Hall Fire designed and installed a fire protection system in Goodlife's factory. When there was a fire, the system failed and that resulted in serious damage. Goodlife then sued in negligence and Hall Fire sought to rely on a wide exclusion clause in the contractual document. The clause was held to be reasonable on a number of important grounds. One of these was that the parties had the same bargaining strength based on their turnover. The lead judgment by Coulson LJ supported the view from previous cases that large businesses of equal strength can look after themselves. Essentially, they are in the best position to determine what is fair between themselves.

?!   THINKING POINTS

Is the turnover of a business a useful indication of their bargaining strength? What other factors should be relevant?

Of course, in some cases one party will be in a much stronger position to negotiate and set the terms and that will then count against an exemption clause put in by that party being reasonable. Such an imbalance was an important factor in the decision to class the clauses unreasonable in both *St Albans City and District Council v International Computers Ltd* [1995] FSR 686 and *Motours Ltd v Euroball (West Kent) Ltd* [2003] EWHC 614. In the *St Albans* case, Scott-Baker J observed that the defendant relying on the clause was a wholly owned subsidiary of a business with a turnover of over a £1bn. In contrast, the claimant was a local Council with much less resources and experience in negotiating commercial contracts. According to the judge, the Council was in a better negotiating position than an individual buying from a motor dealer but they were still the weaker party. In *Motours*, Judge Bowers observed that the defendant relying on the exemption clause was a large, multi-million pound provider of telephone services. In contrast, the claimant was a small travel agency with a turnover of £125,000.

When Lord Griffiths in *Smith v Eric Bush* listed the factors that would always be relevant, his Lordship started with bargaining strength. The point was expressed in the following way:

1. Were the parties of equal bargaining power. If the court is dealing with a one-off situation between parties of equal bargaining power the requirement of reasonableness would be more easily discharged than in a case such as the present where the disclaimer is imposed upon the purchaser who has no effective power to object.

The buyer in the case was a consumer which is why, if the case took place today, the term would be assessed under the CRA. It was clear to Lord Griffiths that a consumer could not renegotiate the terms. There was a clear inequality in the ability to negotiate and so that made the clause more unreasonable.

7.6.5.2 Alternatives and Inducement

Paragraph (b) of Schedule 2 refers to the relevance of choices or alternatives which were (or were not) available. Generally, a term is less likely to be reasonable if the business relying on the clause or a competitor did not offer a reasonable alternative. Without any reasonable alternatives for the other party, their choice is not as freely made as it could be. What counts as an alternative might be a term that does not exclude as much, or any liability. This might mean that the contract price is higher but with less risk associated with it. Again, the existence of such an alternative indicates a choice to make a calculated risk. For example, the inducement of a lower price in return for accepting restrictions on the liability of the other party is very different to the position where a term is actually imposed on a party with no choice or *quid pro quo*.

Goodlife Foods provides a useful example. Here, the last paragraph of an exclusion clause stated that the liability could be reinstated, but with a higher price to cover the cost of insurance of that liability. This was an 'important consideration' and made the exclusion clause more reasonable.

7.6.5.3 Where the Exemption Ought to Have Been Known

This factor concerns procedural fairness. The idea is that if a party challenging the clause should have known about the clause then that will make the clause more reasonable. It might be known from previous dealings or because it is used in a particular industry or sector. However, it does need to be balanced against the other factors. For example, a well-known clause is less reasonable where there is absolutely no alternative.

It seems likely that the extent of the knowledge and understanding expected for 'knowledge' under Schedule 2 should be greater than the level required under the incorporation rules. The commercial case of *Britvic Soft Drinks v Messer* [2002] EWCA Civ 548, provides some support for this. Mance LJ cited the trial judge who stated that since the terms applied to all buyers, it meant the buyer could be taken as having knowledge of the terms and their effect. Mance LJ added that para (c) does not put someone who actually knows of the terms in the same position as someone who ought to have known of the existence of the terms:

> It seems to me legitimate to consider and take into account the actual extent of knowledge of a party, however much he or it may, under ordinary contractual principles, have become contractually bound by the particular term(s).

Ordinarily, it would be easy to assume that para. (c) of schedule 2 simply reflects the common law standard of reasonable notice. However, Mance LJ explained that the standard of knowledge under para. (c) was not as low. Instead, to make the clause more reasonable, the level of knowledge that the party has or should have should be greater than simply having been given reasonable notice. Consider a term expressed in small print or unclear language. It might still be incorporated by reasonable notice if it was available. However, the same terms might not be sufficiently noticeable to inform the application of the reasonableness test.

7.6.5.4 Where the Exemption Relates to Liability for the Performance of a Difficult Task

Paragraph (d) concerns an exemption being conditional on some kind of requirement or performance. In principle, if at the time of creating the contract the task was very difficult with a high risk of failure, an exemption of liability for it might be more reasonable. It might be that a seller or supplier has promised a certain level of quality. Alternatively, the seller may have promised to carry out a repair or replacement. However, it might be that specialist workmanship is necessary to carry out the task and that the sources for a replacement are severely limited. In such cases, an exemption clause might be more reasonable. This factor was considered and applied by Lord Griffiths, *Smith v Bush*, in the following way:

> 3. How difficult is the task being undertaken for which liability is being excluded. When a very difficult or dangerous undertaking is involved there may be a high risk of failure which would certainly be a pointer towards the reasonableness of excluding liability as a condition of doing the work. A valuation, on the other hand, should present no difficulty if the work is undertaken with reasonable skill and care.

> It is only defects which are observable by a careful visual examination that have to be taken into account and I cannot see that it places any unreasonable burden on the valuer to require him to accept responsibility for the fairly elementary degree of skill and care involved in observing, following-up and reporting on such defects. Surely it is work at the lower end of the surveyor's field of professional expertise.

The point here is that if a task is relatively easy and risk-free, then that is going to be a factor in favour of the clause being unreasonable. The process of surveying a property was 'elementary' based on observations and was seen as a simple and routine task. Consequently, this meant it was less reasonable to exclude liability for such a service.

7.6.5.5 Goods Made to the Order of the Buyer

The final Schedule 2 point concerns special goods made to the order of the buyer. That is where the buyer provides the specifications and requirements for goods to the seller. Producing goods in this way exposes the seller to a range of risks as they have to rely on the requirements given. Such specifications might even result in the goods performing badly if the buyer has made an error. This means that an exemption might be more reasonable to allow the seller to manage the liability resulting from such risks.

7.6.5.6 Additional Factors That Should Always Be Relevant

In addition to the factors covered in Schedule 2, there are other factors that Lord Griffiths felt should always be relevant. The first is the practical consequences of the reasonableness decision. The other was the availability of insurance. Both are related and it is useful to read the points made by Lord Griffiths along with how they related to the facts of *Smith v Bush*:

> . . .What are the practical consequences of the decision on the question of reasonableness. This must involve the sums of money potentially at stake and the ability of the parties to bear the loss involved, which, in its turn, raises the question of insurance. There was once a time when it was considered improper even to mention the possible existence of insurance cover in a lawsuit. But those days are long past. Everyone knows that all prudent, professional men carry insurance, and the availability and cost of insurance must be a relevant factor when considering which of two parties should be required to bear the risk of a loss.

Lord Griffiths then applied this 'insurance' factor:

> We are dealing in this case with a loss which will be limited to the value of a modest house and against which it can be expected that the surveyor will be insured. Bearing the loss will be unlikely to cause significant hardship if it has to be borne by the surveyor but it is, on the other hand, quite possible that it will be a financial catastrophe for the purchaser who may be left with a valueless house and no money to buy another.

This discussion of who is in the best position to insure is particularly useful. The point is that the role of insurance cannot be ignored. Exemption clauses are about accepting or avoiding risks. When the reasonableness of one is assessed, those risks are clearly relevant. It follows that if those risks can be protected by insurance, then insurance has to be a factor that is relevant generally. This issue of insurance was another important factor in *Goodlife Foods*. According to Coulson LJ, Goodlife Foods was in the best position to insure since they had full knowledge of the risks they were presented with. That then supported the reasonableness of the clause.

In *Smith v Eric Bush*, Lord Griffiths considered the related issue of what he called the 'practical consequences' of a finding of reasonableness or unreasonableness. This involved looking at the sums of money involved for both parties and the impact upon them of allowing or not allowing the clause. He felt that making the surveyor liable would not lead to a flood of claims because such claims would only result from a negligent survey and such negligence should be exceptional rather than routine. In addition, it was felt that such liability would simply result in a small increase in the cost of insurance for surveyors. That in turn would result in a corresponding increase in the fees they charge which would spread the costs resulting from the absence of the exclusion clause. Such a result was preferable over the alternative of making individuals suffer the huge losses resulting from negligent advice. With that in mind, this factor reflects an element of substantive fairness. The guidance from Lord Griffiths on this factor is also a good illustration of the assessment being based on the circumstances rather than the term taken in the abstract. It even addressed the fact that in some cases the potential liability might be so significant that it would be uninsurable. Such circumstances would provide a justification for an exemption clause. Of course, that justification would need to be weighed against any other relevant factors.

In *Smith v Bush*, the loss from negligent advice had the potential to be significant. That then contributed to the clause being unreasonable. Likewise, where a large loss could result from a breach of contract, that fact might then count against use of the clause. This point was acknowledged in *St Albans City and District Council v International Computers Ltd*, where the local Council was considered to have been less capable of bearing a large loss for a defective computer system. The defective programme resulted in the Council suffering losses of just over £1.3m. The potential for such a significant loss at the time of contracting was one of the factors resulting in a decision that the limitation clause was unreasonable. In contrast, consider other commercial circumstances where a clause excludes liability for significant consequential losses. Such a clause might be more reasonable where the liability for direct losses (rather than consequential losses) is accepted and not limited. That was the approach adopted in *SAM Business Systems v Hedley & Co* [2002] EWHC 2733.

Ultimately, the test of reasonableness is based on the balancing all relevant factors. It is particularly important to appreciate that exemption clauses can be extremely useful in commercial contracts. Well-informed parties can openly work out who bears the risks and then price the contract accordingly. In that context, the Act can work to reflect contractual freedom when genuine choices are made. It seems that such genuine choices are assumed when the parties are large and with a fairly equal level of bargaining strength. In that context, the courts have limited the role of UCTA.

 THINKING POINTS

Are small businesses adequately protected by UCTA or should they be protected from unfair terms beyond exemption clauses?

7.7 Consumer Protection from Unfair Terms: The Consumer Rights Act 2015

As explained at 7.5, an EU directive (Directive 93/13 EEC on unfair terms in consumer contracts) required consumers to be protected from unfair terms. This was introduced into UK law by a statutory instrument in the form of the Unfair Terms in Consumer Contracts Regulations 1994, which was then replaced in 1999. The protection provided by the Regulations represented a major improvement for consumers. Essentially, a wide range of terms could be challenged and taken out of use. Part of the reform also allowed government regulatory bodies like the old Office for Fair Trading (now the Competition and Markets Authority) to take action against, and challenge the use of, unfair terms. As a result, thousands of unfair terms are no longer in use.

The 1999 Regulations applied until the Consumer Rights Act 2015 came into force. While the Regulations have been repealed, the case law remains relevant because the provisions in question are now in the CRA; Part 2 of the Act contains all the rules relating to unfair terms in consumer contracts. It is also worth pointing out that since the CRA provisions give effect to the minimum rights contained in an EU directive, the case law from the Court of Justice of the EU also used to apply, as it did with respect to the old Regulations. Following the UK withdrawal from the EU, at the very least, the EU law that applied before the date of withdrawal continues to apply. That is as a result of the EU Withdrawal Act 2018, which effectively incorporated existing EU law into UK law at the time the UK left the EU so as to preserve certainty.

The protections in the CRA are provided in three different ways, as explained in Figure 7.2:

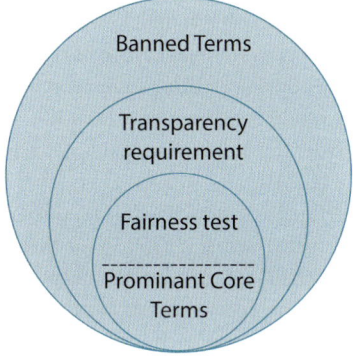

- First, certain terms are banned.
- Second, other terms are subject to a test of fairness. However, the fairness test does not apply to 'core terms' that are transparent and sufficiently prominent. Such core terms are those that set the price, or define what is being supplied.
- Third, there is a general requirement that all terms are 'transparent'. This requires all terms to be in clear language.

Figure 7.2
The ways the CRA provides protection from unfair terms

The drafting of the CRA provided a useful opportunity to improve the protection from unfair terms. Such improvements were based on the criticism of the previous regime that applied to consumers found in UCTA and the Regulations. The most obvious improvement is the fact that the rules are now found in a single source of legislation. The problem of consumers being protected by two separate and overlapping sets of rules (UCTA and the Regulations) no longer exists. Other specific instances of the CRA improving the position for consumers will be addressed as we explore the CRA. We start with the scope, in particular what is required for a consumer contract and notice. We will then examine how the Act provides protection and the extent of that protection.

7.7.1 Scope: Consumer Contracts and Notices

The CRA applies to consumer contracts and notices that appear to be aimed at consumers. This is all defined in section 61:

61 Contracts and notices covered by this Part

(1) This Part applies to a contract between a trader and a consumer.

(2) This does not include a contract of employment or apprenticeship.

(3) A contract to which this Part applies is referred to in this Part as a "consumer contract".

(4) This Part applies to a notice to the extent that it—

    (a) relates to rights or obligations as between a trader and a consumer, or

    (b) purports to exclude or restrict a trader's liability to a consumer.

(5) This does not include a notice relating to rights, obligations or liabilities as between an employer and an employee.

(6) It does not matter for the purposes of subsection (4) whether the notice is expressed to apply to a consumer, as long as it is reasonable to assume it is intended to be seen or heard by a consumer.

(7) A notice to which this Part applies is referred to in this Part as a "consumer notice".

(8) In this section "notice" includes an announcement, whether or not in writing, and any other communication or purported communication.

The section makes it clear that it does not apply to employment contracts. Such contracts are entered into by individuals but the employee is not a 'consumer' in such a contract.

Section 2 of the Act provides definitions. A consumer is 'an individual acting for purposes that are wholly or mainly outside that individual's trade, business, craft or profession' (s.2(3)). As it requires the consumer to be an 'individual' this means that a company or partnership cannot be a 'consumer'. A sole trader like a window cleaner could be an individual, but that person would have to be contracting for a purpose mainly outside their trade. So, a window cleaner buying cleaning equipment would not be a consumer. However, a window cleaner buying lunch would be a consumer, even if it is to have during a lunch break between cleaning windows. If the trader thinks an individual is not acting mainly outside a trade, the trader is the one that has to prove it (s.2(4)).

The consumer has to be in a contract with a 'trader', who is defined as 'a person acting for purposes relating to that person's trade, business, craft or profession, whether acting personally or through another person acting in the trader's name or on the trader's behalf' (s.2(2)). For the purposes of the Act, the word 'business' includes the activities of any government department or local or public authority (s.2(7)). Part 2 of the Act clearly applies to notices, and a wide approach is adopted to how the notice is communicated. It can be the typical written notice but it could be oral or other communications that form part of the contract.

7.7.2 Ineffective Terms

The CRA makes certain terms ineffective and therefore unenforceable. One type of ineffective term is a clause that excludes or limits liability arising from a term implied by the Act. For example, take the implied term that goods supplied must be of satisfactory quality. That implied term is from section 9 of the CRA and cannot be restricted by the trader. The same approach is adopted for the other implied terms. The idea is that such implied terms are important social rights for consumers and so such rights should not be restricted in any way. This is simply continuing the approach that was adopted back when UCTA applied to consumers. Likewise, as a matter of policy, liability for death and personal injury cannot be restricted. Specifically, a trader cannot exclude or limit the liability from:

- terms implied into contracts for the sale of goods (s.31);
- terms implied into contracts for the supply of services (s.57);
- terms implied Contracts for the sale of digital content (s.47);
- negligence for death or personal injury (s.65).

7.7.3 Unfair Terms

This is where the scope of the protection for consumers is much wider than it was under UCTA. The CRA (based on the Directive, like the previous Regulations) controls much more than exemption clauses. It applies to unfair terms generally. Exemption clauses are capable of being an example of an unfair term but the wider scope means that it is possible to control terms that impose a significant imbalance in the rights or obligations of consumers, rather than just exemption clauses. According to

Lord Bingham, such unfair terms are those '. . .imposing on the consumer . . .a disadvantageous burden or risk or duty' (*Director-General v First National Bank plc* [2001] UKHL 52).

Examples of terms deemed to be unfair by the Competition and Markets Authority include:

- Terms that allow traders to increase the price after the contract but before performance (e.g. before goods or services are actually delivered).

- Terms requiring the consumer to pay in full for building work before it even begins. This can be unfair because it means that the consumer is not in a position to withhold payment if the work turns out to be defective or not done at all.

- Exclusion clauses that are too wide, such as one that makes a service entirely at the risk of the consumer.

- Terms that impose excessive notice periods in order to cancel a service.

- Terms that allow a business to cancel membership without a refund.

There are many more examples but at this stage the point is that we are concerned with a wide range of terms. To assist, Schedule 2 of the CRA (based on the Directive) has a long 'grey' list of the type of terms that may be regarded as unfair. In other words, it describes the type of terms that are presumed to be unfair, which then acts as useful guidance. The list is non-exhaustive, so that terms that are not included can still be unfair.

7.7.4 The Effect of a Term Being 'Unfair'

➔ **CROSS-REFERENCE**
The 'grey' list from Schedule 2 of the CRA can be viewed in our online resource centre.

On the requirement for terms to be fair and the test to be applied, we need to turn to section 62 of the CRA. It starts with the effect an unfair term has on the contract:

> 62 Requirement for contract terms and notices to be fair
>
> (1) An unfair term of a consumer contract is not binding on the consumer.
>
> (2) An unfair consumer notice is not binding on the consumer.
>
> (3) This does not prevent the consumer from relying on the term or notice if the consumer chooses to do so.

This makes it clear that unfair terms are not binding on the consumer. That means such terms are ineffective, which was always the case under the 1999 Regulations. According to the Court of Justice in C-118/17, *Dunai v ERSTE Bank Hungary Zrt* [2019], if the term is unfair and therefore ineffective, it is treated as if it never existed. That means the consumer is restored to the position they should have been in if the term had not been included. That should then allow for a restitutionary claim for any money paid or for losses resulting from the term.

Following a finding of an unfair term, the contract usually remains in effect and so it is not ended simply because there is an unfair term. However, if the contract cannot continue without the unfair term because of its importance to the contract then the contract will be ended (*Dunai v ERSTE Bank Hungary Zrt*).

The section then continues with the test of fairness to be applied:

> (4) A term is unfair if, contrary to the requirement of good faith, it causes a significant imbalance in the parties' rights and obligations under the contract to the detriment of the consumer.
>
> (5) Whether a term is fair is to be determined-
>
> (a) taking into account the nature of the subject matter of the contract, and
>
> (b) by reference to all the circumstances existing when the term was agreed and to all of the other terms of the contract or of any other contract on which it depends.

The same test of fairness and relevant considerations are then repeated for notices in sub-sections 6 and 7.

While notices would have been covered previously, the CRA is clearer about the rights of consumers. By making such an express reference to notices, consumers can point to it, and traders have no room to argue that notices are not included.

7.7.5 The Meaning and Application of the Fairness Test

The test of fairness in s.62 (4) is the same as the one contained in the Directive and the Regulations. That means the case law on the meaning of the test remains applicable under the CRA. The test of fairness has three elements. The relevant term must:

- be contrary to the requirement of good faith;
- cause a significant imbalance in the parties' rights and obligations;
- be to the detriment of the consumer.

The last element simply makes clear that it is only terms which make the consumer suffer a disadvantage (rather than a trader) that are of concern. The requirement for a disadvantage is satisfied easily and can simply mean that there is an obligation imposed by the term, a point made by Lord Steyn in *Director General of Fair Trading v First National Bank* [2001] UKHL 52. In contrast, the first two elements have been the subject of academic debate and judicial comments.

On the surface, it might appear that the 'good faith' and 'imbalance' elements are separate components. After all, good faith is about openness and fair dealing commonly associated with being 'up-front' with information rather than making it difficult to find. With that in mind, it could be taken to refer to the way the contract was created (or the way the notice was communicated). For that reason, the good faith requirement certainly concerns procedural fairness. The 'imbalance' element appears to be about the weight of the obligations and how one-sided they are. In that context, the 'imbalance' element would reflect substantive fairness. However, Lord Steyn in *Director General of Fair Trading v First National Bank* [2001] made it clear that there was some overlap between the two aspects of the test:

> [36] . . .The twin requirements of good faith and significant imbalance will in practice be determinative . . . Good faith imports, as Lord Bingham of Cornhill has observed in his opinion, the notion of open and fair dealing: see also *Interfoto Picture Library Ltd v Stiletto Visual Programmes Ltd* [1989] QB 433. And helpfully the commentary to Lando & Beale, Principles of European Contract Law, Parts I and II. . . .explains that the purpose of the provision of good faith and fair dealing is "to enforce community standards of decency, fairness and reasonableness. . . The examples given in Schedule 3 convincingly demonstrate that the argument of the bank that good faith is predominantly concerned with procedural defects in negotiating procedures cannot be sustained. Any purely procedural or even predominantly procedural interpretation of the requirement of good faith must be rejected.

Lord Steyn then turned to comment on 'significant imbalance':

> [37] That brings me to the element of significant imbalance. It has been pointed out by Hugh Collins that the test "of a significant imbalance of the obligations obviously directs attention to the substantive unfairness of the contract": "Good Faith in European Contract Law" (1994) 14 Oxford Journal of Legal Studies 229, 249. It is however, also right to say that there is a large area of overlap between the concepts of good faith and significant imbalance.

The point is that the good faith and imbalance elements should not be seen as reflecting separate considerations of unfairness, as such a clear divide would undermine the level of protection for consumers. Consider a term that is procedurally fair but imposes an outrageous obligation. It might be very prominent and expressed using clear words. It might even be specifically pointed out by a trader to the consumer. The problem is that, if it is used by all traders, there is no real choice for the consumer. The term would impose a significant imbalance but would not be contrary to good faith and, on that basis, it would not be classed as an unfair term if a significant imbalance and bad faith were both necessary and separate requirements. In contrast, if good faith features aspects of both procedural and substantive fairness, then the term in question could be unfair. On that basis, recognising some overlap should allow for more flexibility and a wider range of protection.

KEY POINTS

It is important for the good faith element of the fairness test to not be about procedural fairness only. It must include an aspect of substantive fairness.

Not many cases concerning the fairness test reach the appeal courts but the cases that do then set a standard for the trial judges. The most recent significant case is *ParkingEye Ltd v Beavis* [2015] UKSC 67 where the Supreme Court was faced with a challenge to a notice imposing parking fees. In the case, Mr Beavis went to a retail park and parked in a car park. The notices indicated that parking was free for the first two hours, but after that, a fee of £85 had to be paid. Mr Beavis returned to his car after three hours and when he was charged the £85 fee, he refused to pay, claiming the charge was an unfair term. The Supreme Court held that the charge was not an unfair term, but the real significance of the case, as it pertains to consumer rights, comes from the way in which the Supreme Court defined the tests for 'good faith' and 'significant imbalance'. The way these tests were then applied provides us with further guidance. It is useful to consider the key aspects of the joint judgment by Lord Neuberger P and Lord Sumption (with whom Lord Carnwath, Lord Clarke and Lord Hodge agreed). Lord Mance also delivered a judgment in favour of ParkingEye.

GUIDED CASE READING 7.3

Cavendish Square Holding BV v El Makdessi; ParkingEye Ltd v Beavis [2015] UKSC 67

When reading the extract, try to identify:

- the questions to ask when deciding if a term is contrary to good faith and if there is a 'significant imbalance'.
- the way the Advocate-General in the *Aziz* case applied the tests in her Opinion before the Court of Justice.

105 . . . The effect of the Regulations was considered by the House of Lords in *Director General of Fair Trading v First National Bank plc* [2002] 1 AC 481. But it is sufficient now to refer to *Aziz v Caixa d'Estalvis de Catalunya, Tarragona i Manresa* (Case C-415/11) [2013] 3 CMLR 89, which is the leading case on the topic in the Court of Justice of the European Union. Aziz was a reference from a Spanish court seeking guidance on the criteria for determining the fairness of three provisions in a loan agreement. They provided for (i) the acceleration of the repayment schedule in the event of the borrower's default, (ii) the charging of default interest, and (iii) the unilateral certification by the lender of the amount due for the purpose of legal proceedings. The judgment of the Court of Justice is authority for the following propositions:

Here we see the importance of the case law of the Court of Justice of the EU (CJEU) in these matters. Since the Regulations derived from EU law, it was the most recent relevant decision of the CJEU which was most authoritative.

The test of 'significant imbalance' and 'good faith' in article 3 of the Directive (regulation 5(1) of the 1999 Regulations) 'merely defines in a general way the factors that render unfair a contractual term that has not been individually negotiated' (para 67). A significant element of judgment is left to the national court, to exercise in the light of the circumstances of each case.

The question whether there is a 'significant imbalance in the parties' rights' depends mainly on whether the consumer is being deprived of an advantage which he would enjoy under national law in the absence of the contractual provision (paras 68, 75). In other words, this element of the test is concerned with provisions derogating from the legal position of the consumer under national law.

However, a provision derogating from the legal position of the consumer under national law will not necessarily be treated as unfair. The imbalance must arise 'contrary to the requirements of good faith'. That will depend on 'whether the seller or supplier, dealing fairly and equitably with the consumer, could reasonably assume that the consumer would have agreed to such a term in individual contract negotiations' (para 69).

The national court is required by article 4 of the Directive (regulation 6(1) of the 1999 Regulations) to take account of, among other things, the nature of the goods or services supplied under the contract. This includes the significance, purpose and practical effect of the term in question, and whether it is 'appropriate for securing the attainment of the objectives pursued by it in the member state concerned and does not go beyond what is necessary to achieve them' (paras 71–74). In the case of a provision whose operation is conditional upon the consumer's breach of another term of the contract, it is necessary to assess the importance of the latter term in the contractual relationship.

106. In its judgment, the Court of Justice drew heavily on the opinion of Advocate General Kokott, specifically endorsing her analysis at a number of points. That analysis, which is in the nature of things more expansive than the court's, repays careful study. In the Advocate General's view, the requirement that the 'significant imbalance' should be contrary to good faith was included in order to limit the Directive's inroads into the principle of freedom of contract. '[I]t is recognised,' she said, 'that in many cases parties have a legitimate interest in organising their contractual relations in a manner which derogates from the [rules of national law]' (para AG73). In determining whether the seller could reasonably assume that the consumer would have agreed to the relevant term in a negotiation, it is important to consider a number of matters. These include 'whether such contractual terms are common, that is to say they are used regularly in legal relations in similar contracts, or are surprising, whether there is an objective reason for the term and whether, despite the shift in the contractual balance in favour of the user of the term in relation to the substance of the term in question, the consumer is not left without protection' (para AG75).

Advocate General Kokott returned to the question of legitimate interest when addressing default interest. She observed that a provision requiring the payment upon default of a sum exceeding the damage caused, may be justified if it serves to encourage compliance with the borrower's obligations: 'If default interest is intended merely as flat-rate compensation for damage caused by default, a default interest rate will be substantially excessive if it is much higher than the accepted actual damage caused by default. It is clear,

---

The first element of the CJEU's understanding of what was meant by 'significant balance' and 'good faith' was that national courts (obviously in this case meaning English courts) had considerable discretion in defining the meaning of those phrases for themselves.

But, be that as it may, the CJEU nonetheless went on to provide some further guidance. On the 'significant imbalance' point, the CJEU felt that this had to mean that the consumer would end up being deprived of default rights in national law as a result of the application of the term.

But on its own this would not make a term unfair; it was also necessary that the term was contrary to good faith—in other words, the CJEU was re-emphasising that both a 'significant imbalance' and contrariness to good faith were requirements for a term to be unfair. A term might cause an imbalance but still be fair if the seller had dealt fairly with the consumer and it could be reasonably assumed that he or she would have agreed anyway if given the chance to negotiate. Good faith then is not just about how clear the term is, but about whether the consumer would have agreed—in other words, it encompasses both procedural and substantive fairness.

Finally, also relevant was what might in effect be called proportionality. If a term went beyond what would be necessary to secure whatever it was that the term was designed to achieve, then it may be unfair (because, it is implied, this would be disproportionate).

In the opinion of the Advocate General in *Aziz*, there was good reason for insisting on it being proved that a term both causes a significant imbalance *and* is contrary to good faith before it can be declared unfair. This was freedom of contract—there should be nothing stopping the parties from agreeing on something imbalanced if it is done in good faith.

however, that a high default interest rate motivates the debtor not to default on his contractual obligations and to rectify quickly any default which has already occurred. If default interest under national law is intended to encourage observance of the agreement and thus the maintenance of payment behaviour, it should be regarded as unfair only if it is much higher than is necessary to achieve that aim' (para AG87). Finally, the Advocate General observes that the impact of a term alleged to be unfair must be examined broadly and from both sides. Provisions favouring the lender may indirectly serve the interest of the borrower also, for example by making loans more readily available (para AG94).

> The Advocate General's opinion also emphasised proportionality, again without using that term directly. There is nothing unfair about a term in a contract designed to deter breach, if the way it does so is proportionate to that aim and does not go beyond it.

In assessing unfairness, the Directive (Art 4(1)) and the CRA (S.62.(5)) refer to relevant factors such as the nature of the goods or services under the contract and the surrounding circumstances. According to AG Kokott, such factors includes:

- The practical effect of the term;
- Whether the term reflects a legitimate interest;
- Whether the term goes beyond what is necessary to achieve that objective.

It is clear that the application of the fairness test is based on the surrounding facts. Different terms relating to different services or goods will involve different factors to consider. However, the application of the test by the Supreme Court in *ParkingEye* is instructive. It provides an idea about the level of detail we can expect from the assessment of fairness. In addition, an awareness of the application of the test helps us when we have to formulate arguments about the fairness of a term. A good example of this process can be seen from the way the application of the test by AG Kokott in *Aziz* was used by way of analogy to support the objectives of the charge in *ParkingEye*. Likewise, we could expect first instance judges to refer to the approach of the Supreme Court to inform their decisions.

The application resulted in the term not being unfair. On the significant imbalance point, it was observed that the term did not take away rights, but it did put Mr Beavis in a worse position than under national law. Without the agreement, he would have been liable to the landowner for trespass for the value of the small parking space for the time it was used. Apparently, that liability would have been much less than the parking fine of £85. On that basis, it was agreed that there was a significant imbalance. However, the term could be unfair only if the imbalance was contrary to good faith. That left good faith as the main issue.

On the good faith point, the judgment led by recognising that there was a legitimate interest in imposing the charge. This legitimate interest issue was within the factors relevant to the assessment of fairness in Art 4(1) of the Directive and, therefore, s.62 (5) CRA. According to the judgment, the imbalance 'did not arise "contrary to good faith", because ParkingEye and the landlord. . .had a legitimate interest in imposing the liability. . .'

On the legitimate interest issue, it was observed that the charge was in place to induce shoppers to leave the shopping centre car park within two hours. In other words, it was to motivate consumer behaviour so as to result in a continual 'flow' of customers in and out of the carpark, which would allow new customers to get spaces. This would be good for consumers as a group, and also for the shops in the shopping centre, of course, because it would increase their footfall. This approach was similar to the application by AG Kokott in *Aziz* where the increased rate of interest on the loan had the objective of motivating the debtor to pay off the debt quickly. This was seen as a legitimate interest of the business model. In relation to the proportionality of the parking charge, the judgment felt that it did not go beyond what was necessary to protect the legitimate interest. Another relevant consideration here was that ParkingEye's only source of revenue was the penalty charges in question. The existence of these charges was what allowed the business to operate as a going concern and to manage an otherwise free car park. The charge, in other words, was designed to protect a legitimate interest inasmuch as it was the basis for ParkingEye's entire business model. And as far as the Supreme Court was concerned, it was not disproportionate to that aim.

The next issue was the main question concerning good faith—whether a consumer would agree to such a term. According to the judgment, the reasonable motorist would indeed have agreed to it. The first reason for this concerned procedural fairness. The terms were clear and prominent. There were twenty notices displaying them in the car park and there was no pressure to accept the terms. A motorist who objected could simply leave and park elsewhere without any charge being imposed by ParkingEye. The second reason concerned substantive fairness. Motorists were receiving two hours of free parking in a convenient location. In return, they had to accept the risk of a fine for overstaying. Such a charge was viewed as a normal feature of parking. Motorists would benefit by having spaces to park in rather than have the car park full with long-staying commuters and they would also be able to park for free for two hours. A related point was the fact that the risk of paying was in the control of the motorist. According to the judgment, all they needed to avoid the charge was a watch to tell the time.

Lord Toulson delivered the only dissenting judgment. His view was that ParkingEye had not done enough to prove that the reasonable motorist would agree to the term. One reason was that the charge operated unfairly because it was a flat rate that was the same whether a motorist overstayed by a minute or an hour. The majority rejected this on the basis that it was a common practice ensuring that motorists would understand that such time limits are strict. Of course, familiarity and common practice do not mean that the motorist would necessarily agree to the term given the choice. Lord Toulson also felt that the charge was excessively high, comparing it to the state pension which at the time was £115 a week. He thought that would again have influenced the decision of the consumer if there was a hypothetical opportunity to negotiate.

A further important point made by Lord Toulson was that circumstances might be outside the motorist's control. The car could break down, or there could be unexpected delays such as abnormal queues inside the shops or congestion leaving the car park. No allowance was made for exceptions in the terms, and so a reasonable motorist would be less likely to agree in a hypothetical negotiation. The majority judgment disagreed, mainly on the basis that there was an appeals procedure providing some protection in such special circumstances. Likewise, the Code of Practice of the British Parking Association sets standards for parking operators, which also includes a reasonable grace period at the end of the time limit. The point was that the terms had also to be viewed in the light of the regulatory framework that applied.

> ### ?! THINKING POINTS
>
> Following ParkingEye, what arguments could a consumer rely on to challenge the charge for overstaying in a car park as an unfair term?

7.7.6 The Transparency Requirement

The CRA continues the requirement that all terms must be transparent (s.68(1)).

> **68 Requirement for transparency**
>
> (1) A trader must ensure that a written term of a consumer contract, or a consumer notice in writing, is transparent.
> (2) A consumer notice is transparent for the purposes of subsection (1) if it is expressed in plain and intelligible language and it is legible.

The requirement means that terms have to be in 'plain, intelligible language' and 'legible'. According to the guidance from the UK Competition & Markets Authority (the 'CMA'), it is not enough for the terms to be legible and clear. They also have to be expressed in a way that consumers can understand and which allows them to make informed choices. This means that terms should not be in legal jargon and should be expressed in short sentences. In some cases, that will require the text to be well structured and cross-referenced. In addition, there should be no 'small print'. A further requirement is that the terms should be available for viewing by the consumer so as to allow him or her to become familiar with the terms. That point is consistent with recital 20 in the preamble of the Directive on unfair terms.

The transparency requirement under the Directive only refers to the terms being in 'plain, intelligible language'. This was most recently interpreted by the Court of Justice in Case C-26/13, *Kásler v OTP Jelzálogbank Zrt* [2014]. The Court held that it is not enough for the term to be 'grammatically intelligible to the consumer'. It also requires that there is enough content for the average consumer to 'evaluate, on the basis of clear, intelligible criteria, the economic consequences' of the term. In addition, the consumer should be able to understand the reason for the term being used, and its relationship with the other terms. The same point was made and applied by the Court of Justice in Case C-186/16, *Andriciuc v Banca Românească SA*, [2017]. This means that the requirement is not just a matter of presentation. It also creates a duty to provide an explanation. It follows that this interpretation applies to the identical wording used in the CRA.

The CRA version of the transparency requirement represents a slight improvement from the previous Regulations. This is because it adds that the terms must be 'legible'. Such a requirement should include the need to have an appropriate font size, colour and print quality. The courts could have assumed this anyway, particularly in view of the understanding required by *Kásler v OTP Jelzálogbank Zrt*. The real benefit is that consumers can point to the actual expression of the requirement in the CRA so that the requirement cannot be disputed by a trader.

The transparency requirement is expressed in a distinct section and that might appear to suggest that it is a freestanding requirement for all terms. However, the CMA guidance indicates that failing to meet the requirement does not make the term ineffective independently of the fairness test. The test would still need to be applied, but a total failure of transparency would inform the question of good faith. According to the CMA, a regulator has the power to stop the use of a term or notice if it fails to meet the transparency requirement and this reflects explanatory note 329 of the CRA. It states that public bodies can enforce the requirement under other provisions like the Part 8 of the Enterprise Act 2002 where the term would harm the collective interests of consumers.

Also, on the point of transparency (i.e. how clear the terms are) the CRA continues a provision on terms having different meanings.

> Section 69. . .
> Contract terms that may have different meanings
>
> (1) If a term in a consumer contract, or a consumer notice, could have different meanings, the meaning that is most favourable to the consumer is to prevail.

That must sound familiar. It of course echoes the *contra proferentem* approach. Again, this is not new, but it is important because consumers can point to it when a trader disagrees with the meaning of an ambiguous term or notice.

7.7.7 Terms Excluded from the Fairness Assessment

Following the Directive (and just like the Regulations) the CRA continues to exclude certain terms from the fairness test. To date, this exclusion has been one of the most controversial aspects of the law on unfair terms. Section 64 states:

> (1) A term of a consumer contract may not be assessed for fairness under section 62 to the extent that—
>
>   (a) it specifies the main subject matter of the contract, or
>
>   (b) the assessment is of the appropriateness of the price payable under the contract by comparison with the goods, digital content or services supplied under it.

Terms defining the price or subject matter of the contact are known as 'core terms'. The idea is that when buying, consumers always have two things in mind: what is being bought and the price to be paid. Of course, the scope of these exclusions is very important. If they are defined narrowly then more terms can be challenged using the fairness test. We can address each of the core terms in turn.

7.7.7.1 Terms Defining the Subject Matter of the Contract

Put simply, terms defining the 'subject matter of the contract' are terms that define what the trader is supplying. Such terms were more formally defined by the Court of Justice in both *Kásler v OTP Jelzálogbank Zrt.* and *Andriciuc v Banca Românească SA*. Accordingly, these are terms that 'lay down the essential obligations of the contract and, as such characterise it'. The rulings then added that such terms are not 'ancillary to those that define the very essence of the contractual relationship'. Whether such a term fits within the exclusion is a matter of interpretation. An example of a narrow interpretation is the approach adopted in *Office of Fair Trading v Ashbourne Management Services Ltd* [2011] EWHC 1237. The case concerned gym memberships imposing minimum membership periods ranging from one to three years. The term required the members to continue paying for the remaining membership period even if they chose to leave. One of the arguments was that these terms defined the services being supplied and so they could not be assessed for fairness. Kitchen J rejected this argument and held that the terms were unfair in relation to minimum periods beyond a year. The assessment was performed on the basis that the terms did not define the subject matter of the contract. According to Kitchen J, the assessment was not about the facilities available, or even the length of the minimum period. Instead, the assessment related to the consequences of early termination. This narrow approach is consistent with the consumer protection goals of the legislation.

7.7.7.2 Assessment of the Appropriateness of the Price

The Regulations following the Directive expressed this exclusion with slightly different wording by referring to the 'adequacy of the price'. The change to 'appropriateness' makes no difference to the meaning. In fact, the Supreme Court has defined 'adequacy' as being about the appropriateness of the price (*OFT v Abbey National and Others* [2009] UKSC 6). However, the language is thought to be more consumer-friendly in that it is less 'legal' and more understandable.

The justification for the exclusion of testing the fairness of terms specifying price is that market forces usually control prices. Typically, traders compete on price. Low prices attract consumers and high prices can put them off, the existence of price comparison websites reflecting this. In contrast, market forces do not control other terms because consumers are unlikely to be thinking about them when deciding who to buy from. It would also be highly undesirable from a free market perspective to have judges becoming involved in determining whether prices are fair—indeed, that would strike against the very basis of freedom of contract.

 THINKING POINTS

Should the courts have the power to control prices where they are much higher than the market norm?

The difficulty is that lots of terms can be said to relate to payment and it is fairly easy to raise the argument that a given term should benefit from the exclusion. A more specific problem is that it is not clear whether a term *about* payment is excluded from *any* assessment of fairness, or if it just means that an assessment of whether the amount charged is fair is excluded.

The main controversy has been about terms relating to bank charges. Banks were keen to protect the money they made from overdraft charges. One argument was that such charges were not covered by the test of fairness because they represented the price of the service. In the *First National Bank* case, the House of Lords said that the exclusion from the fairness test regarding price should be interpreted narrowly, and this meant that the term disputed in the case could be assessed for fairness. The term applied to consumers that failed to keep up with their loan repayments. Interest was charged on the outstanding amount even after a court had ordered repayment. Such interest charges were not seen as the price of the loan but, instead, as secondary default terms. Rather than relating to the actual performance of the contract, the terms only applied once there was a breach. The House of Lords held that the term was not unfair, but the term was capable of being assessed.

On the exclusion of terms concerning price and subject matter from the assessment of fairness (at the time, the exclusion was in Regulation 3(2)) Lord Bingham observed:

> [12] In agreement with the judge and the Court of Appeal, I do not accept the bank's submission on this issue. The Regulations, as Professor Sir Guenter Treitel QC has aptly observed (Treitel The Law of Contract, 10th ed. (1999), p. 248), "are not intended to operate as a mechanism of quality or price control" and regulation 3(2) is of "crucial importance in recognising the parties' freedom of contract with respect to the essential features of their bargain": p. 249. But there is an important "distinction between the term or terms which express the substance of the bargain and 'incidental' (if important) terms which surround them": Chitty on Contracts, 28th ed. (1999), vol 1, ch 15 "Unfair Terms in Consumer Contracts", p. 747, para 15–025.

Lord Bingham then framed it in the context of the objectives behind the legislation:

> The object of the Regulations and the Directive is to protect consumers against the inclusion of unfair and prejudicial terms in standard-form contracts into which they enter, and that object would plainly be frustrated if regulation 3(2)(b) were so broadly interpreted as to cover any terms other than those falling squarely within it.

The term was then later described by Lord Bingham as an 'ancillary provision and not one concerned with the adequacy of the bank's remuneration as against the services supplied'.

Clearly, Lord Bingham was concerned that if the core term exclusion was interpreted widely, then too many terms would fall outside the test. On the facts, it was felt that the term was a secondary one and not relating to the price of the service, even though it was a source of revenue. This is consistent with the reasoning behind the core terms exclusion. The term in question was not one that would be at the front of a consumer's mind when joining the bank.

The problem faced with the core terms exclusion, as we have already mentioned, is that almost everything in a contract can be related to the price. Lord Steyn addressed this point in his judgment in the *First National Bank* case:

> Similarly, regulation 3(2)(b) dealing with "the adequacy of the price or remuneration" must be given a restrictive interpretation. After all, in a broad sense all terms of the contract are in some way related to the price or remuneration. That is not what is intended. Even price escalation clauses have been treated by the Director as subject to the fairness provision: see Susan Bright 20 LS 331, 345, and 349. It would be a gaping hole in the system if such clauses were not subject to the fairness requirement. For these further reasons I would reject the argument of the bank that regulation 3(2), and in particular 3(2)(b), take clause 8 outside the scope of the Regulations.

He emphasised the need for a restrictive interpretation of the core terms exclusion. If a wide approach was adopted then many terms would be outside of the legislation, and this would be inconsistent with what was intended.

The most recent Supreme Court case on the core terms exception is *OFT v Abbey National and Others* [2009] UKSC 6. It concerned a challenge to bank charges for unauthorised overdrafts on the basis that they were high and did not bear a relation to the costs to banks. The Court of Appeal (*Abbey National and others v OFT* [2009] EWCA Civ. 116) had decided that the exclusion from the fairness test only applied to charges that arose in the due performance of the contract, such as the main price being charged under the contract. In the context of a bank account, it would relate to any standing charge and the interest charged. However, it would not apply to charges which only occur where the consumer exceeded their overdraft limit. According to the Court of Appeal, this made the term on charges a secondary term, like the one from *First National Bank*, which meant that bank charges were not exempt from the test of fairness. However, the Supreme Court overturned this decision. It held that the price exclusion covered charges that were made in exchange for the services provided by the bank. Surprisingly, no distinction was made between the charges for unauthorised overdrafts, which only some consumers would have to pay, and the revenue always made from having the consumer's money. Instead, it was stated that payments due under the performance of the contract would be within the exception.

The Supreme Court was influenced by the way the charges were used to provide the package of services by the bank. The judgments explained how the charges on overdrafts in effect paid for the free accounts for those in credit. It turned out that around 30% of customers (around 12 million of them) were paying charges for being overdrawn. This amounted to 50% of bank revenue. Lord Walker acknowledged the observation by Lord Mance during the presentations by counsel wherein he observed that the banks were engaged in a kind of 'reverse Robin Hood exercise'. They were using the money to pay for 'free-if-in-credit' banking to 70% (around 42million) of their customers. In effect, the poorer customers were subsidising the accounts of those in credit!

The result was disappointing to consumer activists because it reflected an approach that was not protective of consumers. It was the result of very literal approach, one that made a very fine distinction between the overdraft charge and the interest charge in *First National Bank*. The overdraft charge was seen as the price of the overdraft service that the consumer has chosen to use. In contrast, the charge in *First National Bank* was a result of being in breach of the payment terms. Ultimately, the charges were understood to be the price for the overall package of services provided. The fact that they would only apply in certain secondary circumstances (e.g. in the event of a failure to stay in credit) did not make a difference. Of course, if the term had been assessed for fairness, it could have resulted in the end of 'free-in-credit' banking. That would certainly have been seen as an unfair result to the 42 million in credit and enjoying their free banking.

The price exclusion was addressed more recently by the Court of Justice in *Kásler v OTP Jelzálogbank Zrt.* It concerned a loan made by a Hungarian Bank. The amount owed and the repayments were calculated using a strong foreign currency, the Swiss Franc. The problem was that the amount owed was based on the buying rate of the bank, whereas the terms allowed for the repayments to be based on the bank's selling rate, which was much higher. The term allowing for the selling rate to be used was challenged and so the bank argued that the term was about the adequacy of the price (and hence should be excluded from any assessment of fairness). Here, the ruling indicated that the price exclusion applied to an assessment of the price/quality ratio of the service or goods supplied. This meant the same terms could be assessed for fairness if the assessment related to other issues, like the repayment being based on the bank's selling rate. Likewise, the same might be said of the timing of the repayment. The approach taken here by the Court of Justice was more protective of consumers than the approach adopted by the Supreme Court in *OFT v Abbey National*. Furthermore, in *Kásler v OTP Jelzálogbank Zrt.* the Court of Justice cited the Advocate-General's opinion on the basis of the price exclusion. It observed that it was there because there was no 'legal scale or criterion' that could 'guide such a review'. This shows that the main basis for the exclusion in the eyes of the CJEU is the absence of guidance on how to judge the fairness of the price paid. That suggests that a very narrow approach to the price exception should be adopted, arguably narrower than the approach of the Supreme Court. For example, it should only apply if an assessment of fairness will require a decision on whether the consumer is paying too much. It remains to be seen if this approach will be adopted by UK courts.

7.7.8 The Terms Must Also Be 'Transparent and Prominent' for the Core Terms Exclusion to Work

The CRA response to the *Abbey National* case is an attempt at an improvement. The exclusion has always required the terms on price and subject matter to be in plain, intelligible language. This meant that terms defining the price or subject matter could always be assessed where they were not transparent. However, section 64 adds a little more:

> (2) Subsection (1) excludes a term from an assessment under section 62 only if it is transparent and prominent.
>
> (3) A term is transparent for the purposes of this Part if it is expressed in plain and intelligible language and (in the case of a written term) is legible.
>
> (4) A term is prominent for the purposes of this section if it is brought to the consumer's attention in such a way that an average consumer would be aware of the term.
>
> (5) In subsection (4) "average consumer" means a consumer who is reasonably well-informed, observant and circumspect.

The CRA requires the core terms to be transparent and also 'prominent' enough for the average consumer to be aware of them. Only then can the term be excluded from the assessment. We know that one justification for the price being outside the test of fairness is that consumers will almost always be well aware of the price they are paying for something. However, the approach in *Abbey National* made overdraft charges part of the price, when consumers were not likely to direct their minds to such terms when joining a bank. The aim of the CRA wording is clear. By requiring prominence, it means that at the very least consumers will not be exposed to unfair surprises. That covers the potential procedural unfairness element. Of course (as stated at 7.2.2), knowing of an unfair term does not help if all alternative traders use the term. It is also likely that the need for 'prominence' is within the standard, original concept of transparency, given the way it was defined in *Kásler v OTP Jelzálogbank Zrt*. However, the express reference to prominence might help to avoid disputes when a relevant term is obviously not prominent. If a bank does not make such terms sufficiently prominent, then the terms imposing the charges will not benefit from the exclusion and a court will then be able to assess the fairness of such terms.

7.7.9 Improved Scope under the CRA

Following the Directive, the old Regulations did not apply to terms that had been individually negotiated. The argument was that the real problem was terms that had been pre-drafted by the trader and in which the consumer had no input. In other words, the reasoning was that if the consumer had been able influence the terms, then why would a term be unfair? However, one problem is that even if a consumer has had some input, they are still likely to be in a much weaker position than the trader. Also, there was some evidence of traders carrying out a kind of 'fake' negotiation with the end result always being the trader's standard terms anyway. Even if this conduct would not have been accepted by a court, it will often be enough to dissuade a consumer from challenging a term. This requirement for non-negotiated terms was not brought forward to the CRA and so the fairness assessment can apply even to terms that have been discussed and 'negotiated'.

7.7.10 Enforcement Using Preventative Controls

Preventative control was another major advance from the Regulations which is continued by the CRA. It means that public bodies such as the CMA and local authority trading standards departments can go to court and obtain injunctions. These injunctions actually prevent the use of an unfair term. These powers were introduced because controls of this type were required by the Directive. They are particularly important because while consumers can take action under CRA, it is unlikely that they would do so. This would mean that the protection intended by the legislation would not find its full effect and the behaviour of traders would not change. Schedule 3 of the CRA has a list of bodies which have the power to take action against traders. The CMA is the most important, like a lead body. Others are specific regulatory bodies for utilities such as gas, water and rail services, right through to the Consumers' Association and the Information Commissioner.

The importance of this preventative control cannot be over-emphasised. UCTA does not actually make it unlawful to use exemption clauses or specify that businesses could in some way be prevented from using such terms. Under UCTA, a term in a contract can only be held unreasonable in a particular set of circumstances and, therefore, ineffective. A term cannot be held to be invalid *per se* (unless it excludes liability for death or personal injury). There is therefore no power for a court under UCTA to void a term entirely so that cannot be used against others in the future. Another advantage of all the CMA's (and previously, the OFT's) work is that it has provided a public database allowing businesses to see how to comply with the law. This also makes it much easier for consumers to realise when an unfair term is being used against them.

Section of 71 of the CRA introduces a further improvement relating to enforcement. Under this section, where a case relates to a term of a consumer contract, the court *must* consider the fairness of the term (as long as it has sufficient factual information to do so). This obligation on the court applies automatically, i.e. it applies even if none of the parties have raised the fairness of the term as an issue.

CHAPTER SUMMARY

- The use of exemption clauses and other unfair terms is justified by freedom of contract and good business practice.
- Common law controls at best achieve a low level of fairness:

  - The incorporation rules require reasonable notice, with more having to be done for onerous or unusual terms to fulfil this requirement. But the requirement is satisfied easily.
  - The *contra proferentem* principle of strict interpretation is only effective if the clause has more than one meaning.

- UCTA apples to exemption clauses between businesses. Most clauses are subject to a test of reasonableness.
- Schedule 2 refers to some factors relevant to the assessment of a term's reasonableness. They are useful generally but must be considered when the liability is from statutory implied terms.
- Courts are reluctant to intervene when a contract is between large businesses of equal bargaining power.
- The Consumer Rights Act Part 2 protects consumers from unfair terms.

■ A term is unfair if it causes a significant imbalance to the detriment of the consumer that is contrary to good faith.

   ■ A significant imbalance is where a term puts the consumer in a worse position than he or she is in under national law.

   ■ Good faith is assessed by asking if the average consumer would have agreed to the term. That is balanced against any legitimate interest in having the term.

■ Core terms defining what is supplied or the price to be paid are excluded from the test of fairness.

■ The way the Supreme Court applied the price exclusion in relation to bank charges is controversial and arguably too wide.

KEY CASES

☐ *Interfoto Picture Library v Stiletto Visual Programme Ltd* [1989] QB 433—reviewed the reasonable notice requirement and set a higher standard for onerous and unusual terms.

☐ *Hollier v Rambler Motors [1972] 2 QB 71*—represents the most extreme application of the *contra proferentem* principle.

☐ *Smith v Eric S Bush (a firm) [1990] 1 AC 831*—useful guidance on the application of the factors relevant to reasonableness.

☐ *ParkingEye v Beavis* [2015] UKSC 67—confirms how the elements of the fairness test are to be applied.

☐ *Office of Fair Trading v Abbey National* [2009] UKSC 6—shows how the UK courts will apply the 'core terms' exclusion from the fairness test.

QUESTIONS

1. 'The "core terms exclusion" from the test of unfairness is outmoded, and we should now recognise that the law should have a role in controlling unfair pricing.' Critically discuss.

2. 'Small businesses need more protection than is available to them currently from the effects of unfair terms.' Critically discuss.

3. Cloud Pleaser Ltd orders 1000 units of vaping devices from UberPuff Ltd. Most of the devices are supplied with defective batteries. Following this breach, Cloud Pleaser Ltd demands compensation but Uberpuff Ltd relies on a clause in the delivery note excluding all liability for defects. Advise on the arguments that could be used to challenge the clause.

4. Ahmed and Dave booked a night in the Hotel Majestic for £150. They overslept and left at 11.30am. The Hotel demanded an extra £100 because the terms on their booking form state that 'check out' time is 10.30, after which a further £100 is payable. Advise on the arguments that could be used to challenge the term using CRA 2015.

 For answer guidance to these questions please visit the online resources at www .oup.com/uk/naidoo1e/, where you will also find multiple choice questions to check your understanding of key concepts.

FURTHER READING

Adams & Brownsword, 'The Unfair Contract Terms Act: A decade of discretion' (1988) 104 LQR 94.
An early review of the application of UCTA covering the key cases that laid the foundation for the current approach of the courts.

Davies, 'Bank charges in the Supreme Court' CLJ [2010] 69(1), 21–4.
A useful case note criticising the approach of the Supreme Court in *OFT v Abbey National*.

Peel, 'Contra-Proferentem revisited' LQR (2017) 133 LQR 6.
A case note exploring some recent cases on the interpretation of exemptions clauses.

Willett, 'Re-theorising consumer law' CLJ [2018] 77(1), 179–210.
This is very clear, detailed conceptual analysis of consumer law including unfair terms in the wider context. It proposes a new ethical framework based on consumer need.

Willett, 'Fairness in Consumer Contracts: The Case of Unfair Terms' (Ashgate 2007).
A clear monograph exploring concepts of fairness and how the law should reflect them.

Competition and Markets Authority guidance documents on unfair terms: https://www.gov.uk/government/publications/unfair-contract-terms-cma37

Breach and Termination of the Contract

8

LEARNING OBJECTIVES

By the end of this chapter you should be able to:

- explain what is meant by a breach of contract and how terms can be breached depending on the performance required;
- apply the options available to the innocent party when the other either refuses to perform, or performs in a seriously defective way;
- analyse the type of term breached to determine if the defective performance is serious enough to end the contract;
- evaluate the two different approaches used to assess if the breach is serious enough to end the contract.

INTRODUCTION

In Chapters 6 and 7 we examined where the terms of a contract can come from; how they might be interpreted; and how they might be challenged. Since the terms represent obligations of the parties, where such an obligation is not followed, we say there has been a breach of the contract.

In this chapter, we examine the law relating to breach of contract and how breach can end a contract. We will see that when a term is breached, it does not end the contract automatically. Instead, the breach will entitle the innocent party to compensation for losses caused by the breach. In addition, the breach *might* allow the innocent party to choose to end the contract. We will see that such an option is often determined by the type of term breached or the seriousness of the breach. This means that a typical dispute following an obvious breach will be about whether the innocent party can end the contract. Before we can explore *when* a breach can result in the contract ending, however, we need to briefly look at *how* a party can breach an obligation. That is based on whether the obligation is due to be performed; the type of obligation; and the standard of performance that it requires.

8.1 Performance and When It Is Required

Once the parties have performed their obligations as required by the terms, the contract has been completed (discharged). At any time before that point, the parties can agree to end the contract. Such an agreement would be enforceable as long as consideration was provided. However, if the obligations are not performed as required by the terms, then there is a breach of the contract. Sometimes such a breach is obvious, but often parties argue about whether or not a breach has occurred.

→ CROSS-REFERENCE

For the law relating to the requirement of consideration see Chapter 5.

Such a disagreement can take place even when a party has refused to pay for the other party's performance. Not performing an obligation, like not paying, would seem like an obvious breach, but whether it is will depend on how the contract is construed.

Often, the obligations of the parties are concurrent, so that they are due to be performed at the same time. An example is the ordinary sale of goods. Money is due at the same time as title to the goods is transferred. An example is under the Sale of Goods Act 1979, section 28. This makes the seller's duty to deliver goods and the buyer's duty to accept and pay for them as concurrent obligations. But where a lump sum is to be paid on the completion of work, the payment might not be due until the work has been completed. Typical disputes concern whether there has been enough performance to activate the obligation to pay something. We will explore this issue briefly first, before turning to the different types of obligations. In doing so, we will be describing the law relating to *how* a contract is breached. Once that has been completed, we can then turn to the law that applies *when* there is a breach.

8.1.1 Entire Obligations

It is possible for a contract to indicate an intention for one party to *fully* perform their obligations *before* the other has an obligation to pay anything. In such a case, a refusal to pay before the completion of performance will not be a breach. Instead, it will be said that the obligation to pay did not arise at that stage. The case that is commonly used to illustrate this point is *Cutter v Powell* (1756) 6 TR 320. It concerned a contract requiring Mr Cutter to work on a ship sailing from Jamaica to Liverpool. He was to be paid 30 guineas 'provided [that] he proceeds, continues and does his duty as second mate in the said ship from hence to the port of Liverpool'. Halfway into the voyage, Cutter died. His widow then claimed for a proportion of the promised wages to reflect the work Cutter had done. The Court of Kings Bench held that no wages were payable because Cutter's obligation was 'entire'. In other words, based on the wording of the obligation, which implied that Cutter's duties were to be performed for the entire voyage until its end, no wages would be payable because Cutter's performance was made incomplete by his death. Today, the same facts would raise arguments about the contract being frustrated. However, *Cutter v Powell* predates the law of frustration. The outcome of the case was that the employer was not in breach for its failure to pay, because that obligation did not arise until there was full performance by Cutter.

➡ CROSS-REFERENCE

For the law of frustration see Chapter 16.

The same approach to entire obligations was adopted in *Sumpter v Hedges* [1898] 1 QB 673. This case concerned a builder who had a contract to build some properties. During performance, the builder ran out of money and could not continue, and so the building was incomplete. The other party then completed the work. The builder's claim to have payment for the work that he had performed was rejected because the builder's obligation was construed as entire and had not been performed in its entirety. Since payment under the contract did not fall due until he had completed all of the building work, and he had not done this, he was entitled to none of the payment. The logic of entire obligations was helpfully expressed by Jessel MR in *re Hall & Barker* (1878) 9 Ch. D 538, stating:

> If a man engages to carry a box of cigars from London to Birmingham, it is an entire contract, and he cannot throw the cigars out of the carriage half-way there, and ask for half the money; or if a shoemaker agrees to make a pair of shoes, he cannot offer you one shoe, and ask you to pay one half the price.

Cutter v Powell and *Sumpter v Hedges* can be seen as cases concerning contracts equivalent to those requiring delivery of the box of cigars or the making of the pair of shoes.

KEY POINTS

Some obligations can be construed as 'entire', and in those circumstances the other party's obligation does not become due until the entire obligation is completed.

8.1.2 Substantial Performance

The harshness of the entire obligations rule is softened by the principle of substantive performance. A key case here is *Hoenig v Isaacs* [1952] 2 All ER 176. Hoenig contracted to decorate Isaac's flat for £750. Regarding payment, the contract stated 'net cash as the work proceeds; balance on completion'. Hoenig had received £300 as the work progressed, but when he completed the job and asked for the balance, Isaacs refused to pay the full amount and instead paid only £100 because there were some defects. The Court of Appeal found in favour of Hoenig and awarded the outstanding £350, minus £55 to cover the cost of correcting the defects. On the facts, the failure to pay was a breach because the obligation to pay had been activated. While there had been some minor defects, the work had been in effect completed. This means that although performance was not absolutely complete in the sense of being precisely what had been agreed, and therefore there had been a breach of a term of the contract to do what was promised, the proper remedy was damages calculated to cover the cost of making the defects good. Isaacs had not been entitled to refuse to pay the balance and thus his own obligations under the contract had been breached.

According to the Court of Appeal, Hoenig's obligations had been *substantially* performed and he was therefore entitled to the contract price minus a deduction for the defects. On this point, Lord Denning MR explained that parties are free to make their obligations entire using express wording. However, when courts construe contracts, they do 'lean against' construing obligations as entire if it means that a party gets no payment just because of a few defects.

The line between substantial performance and performance that falls short depends on the facts. In *Bolton v Mahadeva* [1972] 1 WLR 1009 a heating system was to be fitted by Bolton for a price of £560. Once installed, the system proved to be defective, with some of the rooms in the house being much colder than they should have been. There were also dangerous fumes emitted from the boiler. It all required £175 to correct and, on the facts, it was held that Bolton's performance had not been enough to constitute substantial performance. That meant he was not entitled to the price minus an amount to correct the defects (as Hoenig had been), and the defendant was not in breach for refusing to pay anything. The case is often contrasted with *H Dakin & Co v Lee* [1916] 1 KB 566. This case concerned a contract for the claimant to perform certain repairs on Lee's house. The repairs did not comply with the specifications stated in relation to some of the work, but these failures could be corrected fairly easily and were not serious. On that basis, the Court of Appeal held that there had been substantial performance and so the claimant was entitled to payment minus the cost of correcting the defects.

The factual distinction between the cases concerns the degree of performance. In *Bolton* the work was only partially done, as the system was not even functioning. In contrast, in *Dakin*, the work was completed but was defective. It can be likened to the difference between only producing one shoe in a contract to make a pair of shoes, and producing both shoes but failing to provide laces. In *Dakin*, Cozens-Hardy MR added:

> Take a contract for a lump sum to decorate a house; the contract provides that there shall be three coats of oil paint, but in one of the rooms only two coats of paint are put on. Can anybody seriously say that under these circumstances the building owner could go and occupy the house and take the benefit of all the decorations which had been done in the other rooms without paying a penny for all the work done by the builder, just because only two coats of paint had been put on in one room where there ought to have been three?

This comment emphasises that one of the main considerations of the courts is to prevent a party getting something for nothing. They have shown themselves reluctant to allow a party to rely on a technical defect to avoid paying anything when the defect can be corrected easily and that party will then have all of the benefits of performance.

KEY POINTS

Substantial performance might be enough to activate the other party's obligation to pay. This usually happens where performance is complete but is of poor quality.

8.1.3 Severable (Divisible) Obligations

Some obligations of a party can be construed as a number of separate obligations to perform, where the completion of each one can result in a requirement to make a payment. The case of *Regent OHG Aisestadt und Barig v Francesco of Jermyn Street* [1981] 3 All ER 327 contains a useful example of obligations being severable. The claimant made men's clothing and agreed to sell 62 suits and 48 jackets to the defendants for their shop. A number of deliveries were made but due to a shortage of cloth, one instalment was one suit short. The defendant responded by rejecting all of the suits and ending the contract. The claimant then had to sell the suits elsewhere at a lower price, and so sued the defendant for the loss suffered. Mustill J held that the defendant was in breach by ending the contract. Essentially, each instalment was severable (divisible) so that it was a separate obligation each time. This meant that while one short delivery was a breach, it did not entitle the defendant buyer to end the contract and reject all of the complete instalments. Instead, the buyer could have rejected the instalment that was missing a suit and then claimed damages. Again, whether a contract is divisible is determined by the terms and the way they are construed. It is often possible in complicated commercial contracts, and it has also been said that it would be 'unusual' for construction contracts to be entire (*Smales v Lea* [2011] EWCA Civ 1325).

KEY POINTS

Some obligations can be construed as severable so that they are split into parts. The other party's obligations are then activated as each part is performed.

So far, we have seen that in some circumstances non-performance of an obligation will not be considered to be a breach where performance was contingent on the other party having completed its own obligations. However, we have also seen that it is often the case that an obligation to make a payment will arise even where the other party has not perfectly completed its own obligations, but only substantially performed them. In addition, we have seen that obligations can be construed as being 'severable', which means that they are divided into a number of separate duties, the completion of each one resulting in turn in an obligation to make a payment.

8.2 Types of Contractual Obligation

Where obligations have been performed, but imperfectly, whether there has been a breach or not will be determined by the *type* of obligation. The obligations could be 'strict', or alternatively, they could be 'fault-based'. We will address this distinction briefly in order to establish *how* a term can be breached.

8.2.1 Strict Liability Obligations

strict liability
refers to liability that occurs irrespective of the negligence or intention of a party in breach.

Generally, contractual obligations are 'strict'. That means they have to be performed as required by the contract. A party cannot defend their failure by saying they performed with reasonable care. Instead, obligations must be performed to the letter. If they are not, they will be held to have been breached. For that reason, contractual obligations are generally said to give rise to **strict liability**.

An extreme example of this type of liability can be seen in the case of *Arcos Ltd v Ronassan & Son* [1933] AC 470. It concerned a contract for wooden staves to be used to make cement barrels. The contract specified that each piece of wood had to be half an inch thick. It turned out that only 5% of the wood met this requirement. The rest of the wood was ever so slightly thicker, most at 9/16 of an inch. While this meant most of the staves were only 1/16th of an inch thicker than the contract specification, and could still be used for making cement barrels, the buyer wanted to reject the delivery and end the contract. At the time of the delivery, the market price for the wood had fallen. This gave the buyer a good financial reason to end the contract. By doing so, it could avoid any requirement to accept the consignment of wood or make a payment, and it could then renegotiate a lower contract price or buy from another supplier at a lower rate. Even with the very slight deviation in the thickness of the staves from the contract specification, the House of Lords held that there was a breach of the contract, the kind that would allow for termination. In the judgment for the House, Lord Atkin explained why:

> It was contended that in all commercial contracts the question was whether there was a "substantial" compliance with the contract: there always must be some margin: and it is for the tribunal of fact to determine whether the margin is exceeded or not. I cannot agree. If the written contract specifies conditions of weight, measurement and the like, those conditions must be complied with. A ton does not mean about a ton, or a yard about a yard. Still less when you descend to minute measurements does ½ inch mean about ½ inch. If the seller wants a margin he must and in my experience does stipulate for it. Of course by recognized trade usage particular figures may be given a different meaning, as in a baker's dozen; or there may be even incorporated a definite margin more or less: but there is no evidence or finding of such a usage in the present case.
>
> No doubt there may be microscopic deviations which business men and therefore lawyers will ignore.

The statement in the extract is a clear reflection of how strict contractual obligations are. Even though the wood could be used for the purpose intended, there was still a breach. The contract is the expression of the parties' intentions and the intended specification was not met. While this strict approach can appear harsh, it is of course open to the parties to say so in the terms if they wish for there to be a margin for error or flexibility. It is also worth adding that Lord Atkin did acknowledge the scope for 'microscopic deviations', and there have been cases in which truly trivial imperfections have been treated as 'trifles' without any consequence. In *Shipton, Anderson & Co v Weil Brox & Co* [1912] 1 KB 574, for example, a contract was made for the sale of 4,500 tons of wheat. The contact permitted a deviation of 10% from the agreed weight, but the seller shipped 4,950 tons and 55lbs (that is, exceeding the maximum permitted deviation by 55lbs). Here the High Court held that there was no breach because the deviation had no commercial significance (it amounted to an excess of 0.000496%).

 THINKING POINTS

Is it an abuse of contract law to end a contract using a technical breach when the goods can still be used for their intended purpose?

A common criticism of a case like *Arcos* is that it encourages economic opportunism. This is because innocent parties can rely minor deviations to escape a contract for the sale of goods even though there is really nothing wrong with the goods in question. By doing so, they are free to find a better deal elsewhere. For that reason, in *Reardon Smith Line v Yngvar Hansen-Tangen* [1976] 1 WLR 989, Lord Wilberforce described cases like *Arcos* as 'excessively technical' and in need of a 'fresh examination'.

The reason why this is of particular concern in the context of the sale of goods is that a breach of many of the terms implied by the Sales of Goods Act 1979 (s.13 on sale by description; s.14 on quality and fitness; and s.15 sale by sample) allow for the innocent party to reject the goods and end the contract without payment. This was the case, for instance, in *Arcos*—the staves did not match their description, which was a breach of an implied term under s.13 of the Sale of Goods Act 1893, the forerunner of the 1979 Act of the same name. This is what had entitled the buyer to reject the consignment entirely. As an attempt to prevent contracting parties gaining an advantage in this way, section 15 A was added to the Act in 1995. It refers to circumstances when a 'breach is so slight that it would be unreasonable' to end the contract. In such circumstances, the innocent party can only be awarded damages. The same approach is adopted when the wrong amount is delivered. Under Section 30(2A) (also added in 1995), the buyer cannot end the contract where the 'shortfall or, . . . excess is so slight that it would be unreasonable for him to do so'.

8.2.2 Fault-based Obligations

→ CROSS-REFERENCE

For the facts and discussion of *Liverpool CC v Irwin* [1977] see 6.5.7.

While obligations in contracts generally give rise to strict liability, some are fault-based. Put simply, they require performance to be done with reasonable care. We have already seen an example of such a term in *Liverpool CC v Irwin*. There, the House of Lords implied a term as a general default rule in tenancy agreements. But the term was not strict and absolute. Instead, it simply required the landlord to take reasonable care to ensure the communal areas were fit and safe. It meant that if the areas were not fit or safe, there would be no breach if the landlord had taken reasonable care to perform the obligation. That obligation would have been breached only if there was fault or negligence by the landlord. Such a fault would be where the landlord had acted below the standard expected of a reasonable landlord.

Even some implied terms from legislation can be fault-based. An example is the Consumer Rights Act 2015, section 49. It applies to contracts for a service, and states:

> (1) every contract to supply a service is to be treated as including a term that the trader must perform the service with reasonable care and skill.

For service contracts between businesses, an equivalent implied term can be found in the Supply of Goods and Service Act 1982, s.13.

We enter contracts for services all the time. Examples include things like taking a suit or dress to be dry cleaned; a PC repair; or simply getting a haircut. At the very least, such services must be provided with reasonable care and skill. Of course, your contract may have express terms (written or oral) that create a strict obligation. An example would be where the dry cleaner agrees to actually remove a stain, or where the hairstylist promises that your hair will be a certain colour or style. With such a strict obligation, there is a breach if the trader fails to deliver what was agreed. The fact that the performance was done with a reasonable level of care and skill will not be a defence. However, in the absence of such strict express terms, the term implied by the legislation is the default.

KEY POINTS

- A breach of contract results from a failure to perform an obligation.
- Whether there has been a failure to perform will depend on the standard of performance required, i.e. whether it is strict or fault-based.

8.3 The Practical Effect of 'Ending a Contract' Following a Breach

→ CROSS-REFERENCE

The law on compensatory damages is explored in Chapter 9.

Following a breach, the innocent party is entitled to damages to compensate him or her for the loss caused. In addition, the breach might allow the innocent party to end the contract. It might seem a little strange that there is *contractual* right to damages even when the contract has ended. We might question how if it has ended, a party can then rely on it for damages. And how can the other party rely on exclusion clauses from the ended contract to avoid paying damages? The answer lies in the effect of ending the contract. On this point, the following comment from Lord Wilberforce in *Photo Productions v Securicor* [1980] is useful:

→ CROSS-REFERENCE
For the facts and decision of *Photo Productions v Securicor* [1980] see 7.4.5.

> . . .[W]hen in the context of a breach of contract one speaks of "termination," what is meant is no more than that the innocent party or, in some cases, both parties, are excused from further performance. Damages, in such cases, are then claimed under the contract, so what reason in principle can there be for disregarding what the contract itself says about damages – whether it **liquidates** them, or limits them, or excludes them?

liquidated damages clause
is a term that fixes a sum to be paid as damages based on a pre-estimate of the potential loss that could be caused. In describing the effect of such a clause, it can be said that it 'liquidates' the damages.

This shows that when we talk of ending a contract (or 'termination'), we only mean that the parties are released from their remaining obligations. In effect, the requirement for contractual performance ceases. On that basis, the contract is not completely wiped clean, as if it had never existed. Instead, the parties can still rely on terms like those excluding or limiting damages. Likewise, if they have a term concerning the use of arbitration in a dispute, they can rely on it. However, the requirement for actual performance of the contract has come to an end. In the case cited above, Lord Diplock provided a more detailed, conceptual explanation:

> Every failure to perform a primary obligation is a breach of contract. The secondary obligation on the part of the contract breaker to which it gives rise by implication of the common law is to pay monetary compensation to the other party for the loss sustained by him in consequence of the breach; but, with two exceptions, the primary obligations of both parties so far as they have not yet been fully performed remain unchanged. This secondary obligation to pay compensation (damages) for non-performance of primary obligations I will call the "general secondary obligation." It applies in the cases of the two exceptions as well.
>
> The exceptions are: (1) Where the event resulting from the failure by one party to perform a primary obligation has the effect of depriving the other party of substantially the whole benefit which it was the intention of the parties that he should obtain from the contract, the party not in default may elect to put an end to all primary obligations of both parties remaining unperformed. . .(2) Where the contracting parties have agreed, whether by express words or by implication of law, that any failure by one party to perform a particular primary obligation. . ., irrespective of the gravity of the event that has in fact resulted from the breach, shall entitle the other party to elect to put an end to all primary obligations of both parties remaining unperformed. . .
>
> Where such an election is made (a) there is substituted by implication of law for the primary obligations of the party in default which remain unperformed a secondary obligation to pay monetary compensation to the other party for the loss sustained by him in consequence of their non-performance in the future. . . and (b) the unperformed primary obligations of that other party are discharged. This secondary obligation is additional to the general secondary obligation; I will call it "the anticipatory secondary obligation."

Lord Diplock turned to situations in which the innocent party (the 'party not in default') chooses ('elects') to end the contract. On this there were two points to be made. The first point was that the obligations the parties agree to *perform* are primary obligations. When a primary obligation is breached, a secondary obligation from the common law allows the innocent party (the party 'not in default') to obtain damages. Such a secondary obligation may also allow the innocent party to choose ('elect') to end the contract. By doing so, it simply releases both parties from any further performance of their primary obligations. His Lordship also mentioned the circumstances in which a breach would allow for a contract to end; namely where the breach is serious enough to prevent the innocent party getting the benefit contracted for. Typically, such a breach happens when a party refuses to perform the contract entirely; where performance is so bad that the innocent party is effectively deprived of any of the material benefit contracted for; or where the parties have agreed that a certain breach will allow the contract to end. That can be done with express words, or because the term breached is so important.

The second point made by Lord Diplock was that even the most serious breach does not end the contract automatically. It simply results in the innocent party having a choice to continue with performance or end it. In other words, the innocent party has the option to end the contract or allow it to continue.

From what has been covered so far, we can summarise the effect of a breach in the following way:

- The innocent party is entitled to damages (based on a secondary obligation).
- If the breach is serious enough, the innocent party has a choice: either end the contract or continue.
- A breach could be serious enough because of the type of term breached or the consequences of the breach.
- Following a choice to end the contract, the parties are released from further (future) performance of their primary obligations.

8.4 Making the Choice to Continue or End the Contract

A breach might be of a type that *allows* the innocent party to end the contract. Such a breach results in a choice, often referred to as an 'election'. The innocent party can elect to continue, or to end the contract. The exercise of this choice or election can have very serious consequences. First, the choice to continue means that both parties must continue to perform their obligations. If the innocent party is then in breach later, reference to the previous breach will not matter. It will not excuse the later breach by that party.

When the innocent party chooses to continue, the innocent party is 'affirming' the contract. Such affirmation must be communicated in a way that is clear enough to show an intention to continue. Likewise, the choice of ending the contract must also be communicated in a 'clear and unequivocal' way (Lord Steyn in *Vitol v SA v Norelf Ltd* [1996] AC 800). Such a requirement allows the innocent party to avoid affirming or terminating the contract by accident and hence to keep the potential for performance open if desired. Consider a breach (like a refusal to continue performance). The first reaction of the innocent party might be to contact the guilty party. In doing so, the innocent party might ask the guilty party to rethink their refusal. The innocent party might want to see if the other party will change its mind and honour their contract. Such entirely sensible contact by the innocent party should not be taken either as an affirmation or termination of the contract (*Yukong Line Ltd of Korea v Rendsberg Investments Corporation of Liberia* [1996] 2 Lloyd's Rep 604).

The choice by the innocent party is an important decision, one that requires some thought and advice. This is recognised by the courts in allowing a period time for the innocent party to make the choice. In *Stocznia Gdanska SA v Latvian Shipping Company (No 3)* [2002] EWCA Civ 889, Rix LJ observed:

repudiation

is a reference to a breach that allows for the contract to end.

[87] In my judgment, there is of course a middle ground between acceptance of **repudiation** and affirmation of the contract, and that is the period when the innocent party is making up his mind what to do. If he does nothing for too long, there may come a time when the law will treat him as having affirmed. If he maintains the contract in being for the moment, while reserving his right to treat it as repudiated if his contract partner persists in his repudiation, then he has not yet elected.

The point here is that the innocent party does not have to make a decision immediately. Instead, that party has some time to assess their options. Doing nothing for too long could amount to an affirmation of the contract because it might be deemed to have shown an intention to continue. However, if the innocent party has reserved its right to end the contract (in other words has indicated that ending the contract is being considered and remains a possibility) then the delay will not amount to affirmation. The period of time for making the choice to end the contract or continue will vary on the facts of each case. This point was emphasised by Rix LJ subsequently in *Force India Formula One Team Ltd v Etihad Airways PJSC* [2010] EWCA Civ 1051. There it was explained that some cases '*may be more or less complex and call for more or less urgency*'.

In *Stocznia Gdanska SA v Latvian Shipping Company (No 3)* [2002] Rix LJ added the following warning about taking time to decide whether to continue or end the contract:

> 87 . . .As long as the contract remains alive, the innocent party runs the risk that a merely **anticipatory repudiatory breach**, a thing "writ in water" until acceptance, can be overtaken by another event which prejudices the innocent party's rights under the contract—such as frustration or even his own breach. He also runs the risk, if that is the right word, that the party in repudiation will resume performance of the contract and thus end any continuing right in the innocent party to elect to accept the former repudiation as terminating the contract.

anticipatory repudiatory breach is refusal to perform before the performance is meant to start.

This warns that whatever the period, the contract is not frozen or suspended. It continues to run, and so the innocent party runs the risk of being in breach of its own obligations. Also, the contract remains at the risk of being ended by a rule of law like the principle of frustration. That is where performance has become impossible through no fault of the parties. If that happens, the innocent party will lose the right to damages for breach.

→ **CROSS-REFERENCE**
For the law relating to frustration see Chapter 16.

A good illustration of the risk of frustration is *Avery v Bowden* (1855) 5 El & Bl 714. Here a ship was chartered to collect goods from Odessa. When it arrived, the goods were not available to be loaded. That was a breach by the defendant, who gave the excuse that war was imminent between Russia and Great Britain. However, the claimant remained at the port (hence affirming the contract) for 45 days waiting for confirmation of the declaration of war. Then the Crimean war eventually started. This meant that performing the contract would now be illegal (because it would have constituted trading with the enemy). That meant the contract was ended by what we now refer to as 'frustration' (although English law did not use this term at that time). As a result, the claimant lost the opportunity to get damages for the original breach.

We know that if the contract continues, there is also the risk of the innocent party being in breach. If such a breach happens, it is clear that the earlier breach by the other party cannot be used to justify it (*Fercometal SARL v Mediterranean Shipping Co. SA, The Simona* [1989] AC 788).

KEY POINTS

Following a breach that allows for termination, the innocent party can take some time to decide and enter discussions before doing so. However, there are risks because the contract is running until it is ended.

8.5 Ending the Contract Following a Refusal to Perform

An obvious way to breach a contract is to simply refuse to perform it. Such a refusal is a 'repudiatory breach', meaning the innocent party can elect to end the contract. This could happen at any time when a party is meant to be performing a contract. An example would be a producer with a contract to make weekly deliveries of clothes for twelve months. In the third month, the producer might decide to stop the deliveries. Perhaps the producer has found a more profitable buyer. Alternatively, perhaps the producer has taken on too much work and can no longer produce enough for the contract. Whatever the reason, if the producer no longer wishes to make the weekly deliveries, the refusal to deliver will be a repudiatory breach.

Refusal to perform could also take place *before* the performance is due to start under the contract. Such a refusal is known as an 'anticipatory' repudiation or breach. For an example, let us go back to the clothing producer with the contract to make weekly deliveries. A month before the first delivery is due, the producer calls the buyer. The producer says that the clothes will not be delivered at all. This refusal to perform is *before* performance was meant to happen.

When a party knows that it cannot start performance, it makes sense to tell the other party. Doing so might reduce the loss suffered by the innocent party. For example, the innocent party might have time to find a replacement to contract with. As a result of this, any damages award to be paid by the party in breach could be reduced. But irrespective of how the innocent party learns of the refusal, once it is clear that the other party is refusing to perform, the innocent party will be entitled to end the contract or affirm it.

8.5.1 The Rights of the Innocent Party Following Refusal to Perform

We know that a refusal to perform is a repudiatory breach. We also know that when there is a repudiatory breach, the innocent party can elect to affirm the contract, or end it. Affirmation may seem a strange choice where the breach was a refusal to perform. It would mean that the contract would continue even though one party had no intention to perform. In practice, this option is only realistic for the innocent party if continuing does not require the party in breach to cooperate. If it is possible for the innocent party to perform its own obligations completely without the cooperation of the party in breach, it can affirm the contract, perform its obligations, and then sue for the outstanding price due under the contract. Such action will be for a debt rather than damages for loss caused by a breach.

An extreme example of such an affirmation following refusal to perform is found in *White & Carter (Councils) Ltd v McGregor* [1962] AC 413. This was a Scottish case, but the principles on which the decision was based hold true in both English and Scottish law. The claimants were advertising agents. Their main business was to supply bins to local councils to be used in the streets. They were not paid by the councils. Instead, they made their money by advertising businesses on the bins. They entered a contract to advertise the defendant's garage. This contract was entered into by a sales representative of the garage. However, the owner of the garage did not approve, and sought immediately to end the contract by sending the claimants a letter. So, on the same day as the contract was created, the defendant then attempted to end it. Essentially, that was a refusal to perform and hence an anticipatory breach. In response, the (innocent) claimants opted to affirm the contract. The contract was for a three year period. It stipulated that fees were payable weekly, and that if any payment of four weeks was in arrears, the whole payment for the full three years would then become payable. The claimants thus advertised the garage on their bins and, when the defendant failed to make a payment during that period, sued for the whole payment for three years which they were entitled to under the contract. The defendant garage argued that the claimants' decision to affirm had been unreasonable. It was only prepared to pay for the appellant's lost profit, rather than the full price. In summary, the claimants advertiser could have allowed the contract to end when the defendant wrote them his letter. It could have then sued for damages to compensate for losses caused by the breach. Instead, it chose to advertise for a month and then sue for the price for three years when the defendant failed to pay, which was obviously a much a higher amount than what could have been claimed in damages.

By a majority of 3:2, the House of Lords held that the innocent party (the claimant advertisers) had the choice. They could accept the breach and end the contract. Alternatively, they could continue with the contract and then claim the contract price. The leading judgment was delivered by Lord Reid and its importance requires us to explore it detail.

GUIDED CASE READING 8.1

White & Carter (Councils) Ltd v McGregor [1962] AC 413

When you read the following extract, try to identify:

◾ why Lord Reid believed there was no duty to stop the advertiser increasing its loss;

◾ the requirement that limits the innocent party's choice to continue with the contract;

◾ the practical reason that could limit the innocent party's choice to continue.

The general rule cannot be in doubt. It was settled in Scotland at least as early as 1848 and it has been authoritatively stated time and again in both Scotland and England. If one party to a contract repudiates it in the sense of making it clear to the other party that he refuses or will refuse to carry out his part of the contract, the other party, the innocent party, has an option. He may accept that repudiation and sue for damages for breach of contract, whether or not the time for performance has come; or he may if he chooses disregard or refuse to accept it and then the contract remains in full effect.

. . .

I need not refer to the numerous authorities. They are not disputed by the respondent but he points out that in all of them the party who refused to accept the repudiation had no active duties under the contract. The innocent party's option is generally said to be to wait until the date of performance and then to claim damages estimated as at that date. There is no case in which it is said that he may, in face of the repudiation, go on and incur useless expense in performing the contract and then claim the contract price. The option, it is argued, is merely as to the date as at which damages are to be assessed.

Developing this argument, the respondent points out that in most cases the innocent party cannot complete the contract himself without the other party doing, allowing or accepting something, and that it is purely fortuitous that the appellants can do so in this case. In most cases by refusing co-operation the party in breach can compel the innocent party to restrict his claim to damages. Then it was said that, even where the innocent party can complete the contract without such co-operation, it is against the public interest that he should be allowed to do so. An example was developed in argument. A company might engage an expert to go abroad and prepare an elaborate report and then repudiate the contract before anything was done. To allow such an expert then to waste thousands of pounds in preparing the report cannot be right if a much smaller sum of damages would give him full compensation for his loss. It would merely enable the expert to extort a settlement giving him far more than reasonable compensation.

[Reference was then made to the decision of the First Division in *Langford & Co. Ltd. v. Dutch* [1952] S.C. 15. There an advertiser agreed to show a film for a year. Following a refusal by the other party, the advertiser continued and then sued for the contract price. However, the court held that the advertiser was not entitled to affirm and continue. Lord Reid then turned to explain the decision]

. . . We must now decide whether that case was rightly decided. In my judgment it was not. It could only be supported on one or other of two grounds. It might be said that, because in most cases the circumstances are such that an innocent party is unable to complete the contract and earn the contract price without the assent or co-operation of the other party, therefore in cases

Lord Reid begins by making the position of English (and Scottish) law clear, and indeed insists on its clarity. The innocent party has two options—to accept the repudiation, or to reject it so that the contract continues. The garage's argument was that this 'choice' was really just a way of measuring damages. The innocent party could choose repudiation, which would result in one calculation of damages assessed at the point of discharge, or affirmation, which would result in the contract continuing to the date of intended performance, with this providing a different calculation of damages. The latter did not mean literally performing the contract and wasting money and then demanding compensation for it. None of the cases, according to the garage's counsel, were of that type.

This was supported, in the garage's view, by the basic realities of contracting. In almost all cases the innocent party does not really have the choice to go ahead with performance and then claim damages, as the advertiser was doing here. Most of the time this course of action would not be available because it would usually require the cooperation of the party refusing to perform. Reference was then made to the garage's argument that it was not in the 'public interest' to allow the innocent party to affirm and continue as it would encourage the wastage of money on useless performance.

Lord Reid then rejected the application of *Langford v Dutch*, which on its face appeared to be very similar to the instant case. The decision in that case could only have been justified in his view on two grounds. The first was easily dealt with. This was the argument . . .

where he can do so he should not be allowed to do so. I can see no justification for that.

The other ground would be that there is some general equitable principle or element of public policy which requires this limitation of the contractual rights of the innocent party. It may well be that, if it can be shown that a person has no legitimate interest, financial or otherwise, in performing the contract rather than claiming damages, he ought not to be allowed to saddle the other party with an additional burden with no benefit to himself. If a party has no interest to enforce a stipulation, he cannot in general enforce it: so it might be said that, if a party has no interest to insist on a particular remedy, he ought not to be allowed to insist on it. And, just as a party is not allowed to enforce a penalty, so he ought not to be allowed to penalise the other party by taking one course when another is equally advantageous to him. If I may revert to the example which I gave of a company engaging an expert to prepare an elaborate report and then repudiating before anything was done, it might be that the company could show that the expert had no substantial or legitimate interest in carrying out the work rather than accepting damages: I would think that the *de minimis* principle would apply in determining whether his interest was substantial, and that he might have a legitimate interest other than an immediate financial interest ... Here the respondent did not set out to prove that the appellants had no legitimate interest in completing the contract and claiming the contract price rather than claiming damages; there is nothing in the findings of fact to support such a case, and it seems improbable that any such case could have been proved. It is, in my judgment, impossible to say that the appellants should be deprived of their right to claim the contract price merely because the benefit to them, as against claiming damages and re-letting their advertising space, might be small in comparison with the loss to the respondent: that is the most that could be said in favour of the respondent. Parliament has on many occasions relieved parties from certain kinds of improvident or oppressive contracts, but the common law can only do that in very limited circumstances. Accordingly, I am unable to avoid the conclusion that this appeal must be allowed ...

> ... that because in most cases the innocent party would not be in a position to complete the contract and earn the price as the advertisers had done here, it should not be permitted to ever happen. Clearly, there was no logical justification for that argument. The second argument, however, had more weight: there were sound reasons to limit the rights of an innocent party to affirm a contract and continue to perform, for instance if it was being done just to punish the other party for breach.

> This meant, in short, that there might be a requirement for the innocent party to have had a legitimate interest in affirming the contract and continuing to perform. On this requirement, the garage had not proven the absence of a legitimate interest on the facts.

> However, here there was no sense in which the innocent party did not have a legitimate interest in affirming and continuing its own performance—even if it would result in extensive losses for the one in breach.

Lord Reid focussed on the options of the innocent party following the refusal to perform. The option to affirm is a well-established right of the innocent party. However, it is limited by two factors. First, exercising the option to affirm would not be realistic if continuing the contract would require the refusing party (the party in breach) to perform in some way. Ordinarily, the party in breach cannot be forced to perform. The only exception is when a court grants the remedy of specific performance (known as 'specific implement' in Scotland). That is a remedy at the discretion for the court and a separate issue. However, on the facts, affirming did not require the party in breach to do anything. That meant continuing was factually possible.

?! THINKING POINTS

Would it have been fairer to only allow damages for the advertiser's lost profit?

The second limit to continuing the contract was rather vague. Lord Reid stated that the innocent party cannot affirm if it has no 'legitimate interest' in doing so. It is for the party in breach to prove that the innocent party had no legitimate interest in continuing. Of course, in this case the garage would not have known to make such an argument.

The obvious difficulty is the question of what is meant by a 'legitimate interest'. Lord Reid referred to it as being 'financial or otherwise', which is not particularly clear. It was also stated that the innocent party 'ought not to be allowed to saddle the other party with an additional burden with no benefit to himself', which suggests that there is no legitimate interest when there is no benefit to the innocent party in allowing the contract to continue. But that still leaves uncertainty about what is classed as beneficial. It also raises the question of why an innocent party would allow a contract to continue if it saw no benefit in doing so.

The dissenting judges (Lord Keith and Lord Morton) referred to what is known as the duty to mitigate losses. This is a well-established principle in damages claims. The innocent party can claim for losses resulting from a breach. However, it cannot increase the claim by unreasonably increasing its own losses beforehand, and nor can it claim for losses that would have been avoided if it had acted reasonably after the breach. Allowing a party to unreasonably increase its losses would unfairly punish the party in breach. The duty to mitigate also has an economic basis. It discourages the wasting of resources involved in a party not taking steps to reduce its loss. The dissenting judges felt the same duty applied in the case. In doing so, they were implicitly deciding that there was no difference between a claim for damages (where the duty to mitigate applies) and a claim for the contract price following an anticipatory breach.

> **CROSS-REFERENCE**
> The duty to mitigate is detailed in 10.4.

In not applying the duty to mitigate, the majority were indicating that the action for the price (following performance) was conceptually different to an action for damages (following the breach). Perhaps the most obvious difference is that the action for a price is fixed by the contract (in *White & Carter*, for instance, this was the price for the full three years of advertising) In contrast, an action for damages is for compensation for losses suffered. With the latter there is a need to put limits on compensation for loss suffered because it is not fixed. As a result, claims are limited to the losses that were quite likely to result from the breach, with all other losses being too 'remote'. A further limit is the duty to mitigate. In an action for the price, these limits are unnecessary because the contract already stipulates what the price is. Since the claimant will have been denied that price by the breach, the remedy is straightforward: the price stipulated in the contract.

> **CROSS-REFERENCE**
> The rules of remoteness are detailed in Chapter 10.3.

The decision in *White & Carter* has been heavily criticised (see, for example, Liu, 'The White & Carter principle: a restatement (2011) MLR 171). Criticisms are generally levelled at the inefficiency (and wastage) in allowing the innocent party to affirm rather than simply requiring an action for damages. In addition, the meaning of 'legitimate interest' was not defined in the judgment, and this has therefore been the source of some uncertainty, both for lawyers and business people.

8.5.2 The Legitimate Interest in Continuing the Contract

Following *White & Carter*, parties in breach have argued that the innocent party had no 'legitimate interest' in affirming the contract. This has meant that judges have had to try and define what this phrase means. *Clea Shipping Corporation v Bulk Oil International Ltd, The Alaskan Trader* [1983] 2 Lloyd's Rep 645 provides a useful description of the way the requirement for the innocent party to have a 'legitimate interest' in affirming has been applied.

The case concerned a time-charter for a ship for two years with a **charterparty agreement**. After a year, the ship needed serious repairs. The charterers stated that they no longer needed the ship, repudiating the contract. However, the owner wished the charterparty to continue and so repaired the ship over a number of months. The ship was then made available fully staffed for the charterer. But the charterer made no use of the ship, on the basis that the owner's failure to keep the ship seaworthy had itself been a breach that had entitled the charterer to repudiate the contract. The charterer had paid the hire fee and so subsequently then brought an action to recover it through arbitration. The arbitrator held that while the owner had breached the contract by failing to keep the ship seaworthy, this was not a repudiatory breach and hence the charterers had not been entitled to terminate the contract. Their termination itself constituted a breach. However, the arbitrator also held that the owner had had no legitimate interest in affirming the contract and continuing performance, and that it ought to have

charterparty agreement
is a contract for the hire of a ship and its crew for a defined period (a time charter) or to go to a certain place (a voyage charter). The contract is between the charterer (i.e. the hirer) and the ship owner.

accepted the termination and claimed damages for the breach. In the Commercial court of the Queen's Bench Division, Lloyd J held that the decision of the arbitrator had to be followed. According to Lloyd J, that decision could not be interfered with, unless it was one no reasonable arbitrator could have made. However, he then discussed how judges had defined and applied the test of 'legitimate interest', stating:

> Whether one takes Lord Reid's language, which was adopted by Orr and Browne LJJ in *The Puerto Buitrago*, or Lord Denning MR's language in that case ('in all reason'), or Kerr J's language in *The Odenfeld* ('wholly unreasonable . . . quite unrealistic, unreasonable and untenable), there comes a point at which the court will cease, on general equitable principles, to allow the innocent party to enforce his contract according to its strict legal terms. How one defines that point is obviously a matter of some difficulty, for it involves drawing a line between conduct which is merely unreasonable (see per Lord Reid in *White & Carter v McGregor*. . ., criticising the Lord President in *Langford & Co Ltd v Dutch* . . .) and conduct which is wholly unreasonable (see per Kerr J in *The Odenfeld* [1978] 2 Lloyd's Rep 357 at 374). But however difficult it may be to define the point, that there is such a point seems to me to have been accepted both by the Court of Appeal in *The Puerto Buitrago* and by Kerr J in *The Odenfeld*.

The comments from Lloyd J show that there are different terms used to define when there is no 'legitimate interest' in affirming a contract after a repudiatory breach. Judges have indicated that there is no legitimate interest to continue the contract when it would be 'unreasonable' and 'wholly unreasonable' to do so. Such terms are not very helpful and do not provide certainty over when the option to continue is not available. Lloyd J went on to refer to 'extreme' cases where the right to continue would be limited. Again, it is not very instructive. But it does tell us that the limit to affirmation is exceptional rather than routine. In other words, in most cases following a breach, the innocent party will have the freedom to continue with the contract (as long as that can be done without the cooperation of the party in breach). However, there will be special cases where the courts will limit the right to continue by identifying that there was no legitimate interest in doing so.

 THINKING POINTS

Is there any reason why judges have not provided a clearer definition of 'legitimate interest' beyond 'reasonableness'?

In *Ocean Marine Navigation Ltd v Koch Carbon Inc., The Dynamic* [2003] EWHC 1936 (Comm) Simon J provided a summary to explain the line of decisions on the *White & Carter* principle:

> 23. These cases establish the following exception to the general rule that the innocent party has an option whether or not to accept a repudiation:
>
> i) The burden is on the contract-breaker to show that the innocent party has no legitimate interest in performing the contract rather than claiming damages.
>
> ii) This burden is not discharged merely by showing that the benefit to the other party is small in comparison to the loss to the contract breaker.
>
> iii) The exception to the general rule applies only in extreme cases: where damages would be an adequate remedy and where an election to keep the contract alive would be unreasonable.

This indicates that there is no legitimate interest in affirming if damages would be adequate as a remedy and continuing with the contract would be unreasonable. It is for the party in breach to prove that these requirements are met. That task is not completed (discharged) just by showing that continuing would result in a minor benefit to the innocent party compared with the loss it would suffer through breach. Just like Lloyd J's decision in *The Alaskan Trader*, it is only in extreme cases where the choice to continue the contract will be limited. This approach is aimed at providing some certainty through stating a rule that ordinarily applies, but allowing some flexibility to depart from it in extreme cases.

The same approach is reflected in *Isabella Shipowner SA v Shagang Shipping Co. Ltd, The Aquafaith* [2012] EWCA 1077 (Comm). In the judgment, Cooke J commented that continuing the contract would have to be 'beyond all reason' and 'perverse' for there to be no legitimate interest in doing so. The comment does not provide a clear test. But, the standard reflected is a high one. Again, it means that the right to affirm will only be limited in exceptional cases.

The *White & Carter* principle and the right to continue was applied to a tenancy agreement in *Reichman v Beverage* [2006] EWCA Civ 1659. The contract was a five year lease for a solicitors' practice. Around half-way through the lease, the practice closed and the tenant (solicitors) no longer needed the property. On that basis, the tenant stopped paying the rent. The landlord then sued for the outstanding payments for the entire remainder of the lease. Essentially, the tenant was in breach and the landlord wished to affirm the contract. The landlord had not tried to find another tenant. In fact, it was reported that the landlord had even turned down a possible replacement tenant. The tenant (solicitors) therefore argued that there was no legitimate interest in continuing the contract and, on that basis, the landlord should have simply accepted the breach and sued for damages. The Court of Appeal held that the landlord was entitled to affirm the contract and sue for the price as it had done.

Lloyd LJ (with whom Rix LJ and Auld LJ agreed) explained that there was a legitimate interest in continuing the contract because there was no clear right to damages. Under the law on tenancy agreements, there is no clear right to damages from the tenant in breach. On that basis, it was not unreasonable for the landlord to claim the price rather than risk a claim for damages. In addition, the tenant could have sublet the property or found another tenant. Accordingly, there was nothing unreasonable about the landlord expecting the tenant to do that. Clearly, the availability of a damages claim is relevant to the legitimate interest issue. The obvious criticism of the case is that the Court of Appeal could have taken this as an opportunity to clarify the law relating to a damages claim resulting from a breach of a tenancy agreement. It could have held that a landlord in such a case is entitled to damages. That would have then led to a more detailed assessment of the right to continue following a breach.

Unfortunately, the concept of legitimate interest from *White & Carter* has not been defined any further. It means that the scope of the limit on the ability to affirm the contract remains uncertain.

KEY POINTS

- Ordinarily, following a breach that allows the contract to end, the innocent party can choose to end the contract or continue (where the cooperation of the party in breach is not needed).
- The right to continue will not apply if there is no legitimate interest in continuing and if damages are adequate as remedy.
- There is no legitimate interest in the exceptional cases where it would be wholly unreasonable to continue.

8.5.3 Acceptance of an Anticipatory Repudiatory Breach

So far, we have explored the law concerning the choice of an innocent party to affirm a contract after a repudiatory breach. Of course, the innocent party also has the option to accept the breach. In doing so, the contract (i.e. its primary obligations) will come to an end. The party in breach will then be liable for damages. The question of whether the innocent party has to wait for the date of performance before claiming damages was addressed in *Hochster v De La Tour* (1853) 22 LJQB 455. Here the claimant contracted to be a courier for the defendant from 1st June. On 11th May, the defendant told the claimant his services would not be needed. So, on 22nd May the claimant brought an action for damages. The defendant argued this action could not be carried out until the 1st June (the date for performance to start) because it was only at that point that there would have been an actual breach. The court disagreed, and held that an action could be brought before the specified date for performance.

The case is an early indication of the rights an innocent party has following an anticipatory repudiatory breach. The innocent party can end the contract and claim damages following the refusal to perform. There is no need to wait for the date when performance was due to start. If this was not the case, the contract would remain until the date when performance was meant to start. This would result in the innocent party having to continue to prepare for performance of the contract. Often, that would involve expenses and effort. It is far more efficient to allow the innocent party to move on, once there is an anticipatory repudiatory breach.

8.6 Ending the Contract Following Seriously Defective Performance

We know that when an obligation has not been performed, this is classed as a breach. In principle, the innocent party will then have a right to claim damages. Whether the innocent party can also choose to end the contract is a different matter. To have that option, the breach must be classed as a repudiation of the contract (a repudiatory breach). Whether the breach is repudiatory is based on the seriousness of the breach. We will see that there are two ways to identify if a breach is serious enough:

- One way is to focus on the term breached. If it is a really important term, then any breach of it would be serious. We will see that such important terms are called 'conditions'. If on the other hand the term is not vital to the contract's continuation, then it is called a 'warranty' and the breach of it will not be classed as repudiatory.

- Alternatively, the focus could be on the actual consequences of the breach. If the consequences are really serious, then the breach is serious enough to end the contract.

Whatever approach is adopted, it is important for the law to be clear on the matter. Parties need the certainty of knowing *when* a breach gives the right to end the contract. Consider the position of an innocent party following a breach. The innocent party might think it is serious enough to end the contract. On that basis, the innocent party might then accept the breach and say that the contract has been ended. However, if there was no right to end the contract, the innocent party would then be liable for wrongful repudiation. Essentially, by ending the contract, the innocent party would be in breach for a refusal to perform. Such a risk means that the decision to end a contract should be made carefully. Of course, the risk to the innocent party is based on how clear the law is. The clearer the law is about the right to end the contract, the less risk there is in seeking to exercise the right.

We will see that there are various ways to identify a breach that allows for the contract to end. The key cases are about a breach that takes place during the performance of the contract. However, the same principles can apply to an anticipatory breach. That would be the case if, before performance is due to start, a party indicates that a term will not be followed. It is not a refusal to perform the contract. Instead, it is just that performance will be different to what was agreed. A right to damages exists at that point. However, the right to end the contract will be based on the importance of the term or the consequences flowing from the breach. In principle, that assessment would be the same as the one made following a breach during performance.

8.6.1 The Traditional Classification Approach

We know that a serious breach will be repudiatory. Such a breach will allow the innocent party to end the contract. To determine if a breach is serious enough, the traditional case law focussed on the type (or classification) of the term breached. Originally, terms were classified as either 'conditions' or 'warranties:'

- **Conditions** are the really important terms. These are often described as going to the 'root of the contract'. In other words, they are the essential obligations that form the basis of the contract.

- **Warranties** are the other obligations that are not so important. They are often described as 'peripheral' or secondary and do not carry out the basis of the contact.

Generally, a breach of a condition is classed as a repudiatory breach. It does not matter if it is only a small breach of the term. The idea is that a 'condition' is so important that *any* breach of it will allow the innocent party to end the contract.

conditions
are the terms imposing the essential obligations that form the basis of the contract.

warranties
are terms that impose secondary obligations that do not carry out the basis of the contract.

KEY POINTS

Generally, *any* breach of a condition will allow the contract to end.

The basic distinction between conditions and warranties is often demonstrated by contrasting two early cases. The first is *Poussard v Spiers and Pond* (1876) 1 QBD 410. It concerned a singer employed to perform a lead role in an opera for three months. She missed the first week of the show as a result of illness and during that time an alternative performer was used. When the singer returned to perform, she was told she was not needed. Essentially, her employer ended her contract and the singer then brought an action for breach. Blackburn J for the court held that the failure to perform on the first week was a breach of a condition. As a result, the other party was entitled to end the contract. The reason for this was that the opening night would have been very important. On that basis, the obligation to perform from the start date 'went to the root of the matter' and hence had been a condition. Its breach enabled the employer to end the contract.

The other contrasting case is *Bettini v Gye* (1876) 1 QBD 183 which was decided a few months earlier than *Poussard*. It concerned a singer who was contracted to perform for a season. The terms specified that the singer had to attend 'without fail' six days before show. This was to allow for rehearsals. The singer turned up less than six days before the show and so his contract was ended. Blackburn J for the court held that the employer was in breach for wrongfully ending the contract. The reasoning was that the term breached did not go to the root of the contract. It concerned rehearsals, which were a secondary obligation. Rehearsals are important, but the main purpose of the contract was to carry out the actual performances and hence the term breached was only a warranty. On that basis, the employer would have had a right to damages only.

8.6.2 When Is a Term Classed as a 'Condition' in Advance?

There are various ways in which a term can be pre-classified as a condition. This is useful, because knowing that a term is a condition means that an innocent party should know when there is a right to end the contract. That should then enable the innocent party to avoid the risk of being liable for wrongful repudiation. We will address the ways terms can be classed as conditions in order of priority as reflected in the key cases. We will then assess the extent to which the classification of terms provides certainty for the innocent party.

8.6.2.1 Legislation Imposing Conditions

➡ CROSS-REFERENCE

For examples of terms implied by the Sale of Goods Act 1979 see 6.5.2.1.

It is possible for legislation to classify certain terms as conditions. There are various examples but a familiar one is the implied terms following the sale of goods. We have already established that the Sale of Goods Act 1979 implies terms into (non-consumer) contracts for the sale of goods. Consider the term that goods sold must be of satisfactory quality (section 14(2)) and the implied term on goods being fit for a purpose (s.14(3)). Under section 14(6) '. . . *the terms implied by subsections (2) and (3) above are conditions*'. Such an express classification of the terms means that a breach can result in the contract being ended. The same can be seen in section 13 which applies to a sale by description. Section 13 (1A) states that the term implied is a 'condition'.

Ordinarily, any breach of these (and other) implied conditions would allow the buyer to end the contract. This is described as rejection (i.e. a refusal to accept the goods). Any payment is refunded and damages can be claimed. It was of course this which allowed the buyer in *Arcos v Ronaasen* to reject the shipment of barrel staves, as described earlier. However, this right to end the contract is now subject to section 15A. This refers to circumstances in which the breach of the implied condition is so 'slight' that it is unreasonable to reject the goods. In such situations 'the breach is not to be treated as a breach of condition but may be treated as a breach of warranty'. In such case, damages would be claimable, but the buyer would have no right to reject the goods entirely. The inclusion of s.15A in 1995 does add an element of uncertainty. This is because it cannot be said that *any* breach of the implied terms would allow for the contract to end. However, section 15A is there to prevent a party relying on a technical breach to escape a contract. Knowing its purpose serves to help to define its application, although it is possible for a breach to be on the borderline between being sufficiently 'slight', and not being sufficiently 'slight'. That point will then be argued by the parties on the facts.

➡ CROSS-REFERENCE

For the rights of consumers to end a contract following a breach see 8.9.

8.6.2.2 Judicial Precedent Making a Term a Condition

Sometimes there is precedent that makes certain terms a condition. There are many examples in various types of contracts. A good example of a term being classified as a condition as result of precedent is found in *Maredelanto Compania Naviera SA. v Bergbau-Handel GmbH. (The Mihalis Angelos)* [1971] 1 QB 164.

The case concerned a charterparty agreement. One of the terms specified when the owner of the ship would make it available to be loaded. It said that the ship would be 'expected ready to load . . . about July 1, 1965'. This term is known as an 'expected ready to load' clause. The Court of Appeal confirmed that such a term was a condition. As a result, all ordinary 'expected ready to load' clauses will be treated as conditions.

Megaw LJ, Edmond-Davis LJ and Lord Denning MR delivered consistent judgments on the point. However, the approach of Megaw LJ is particularly useful. It was more detailed on the wider issue of conditions existing as a result of precedent. Having concluded that the term would be a condition, Megaw LJ went on to explain four reasons for doing so:

> . . .I reach that conclusion for four interrelated reasons.
>
> First, it tends towards certainty in the law. One of the essential elements of law is some measure of uniformity. One of the important elements of the law is predictability. At any rate in commercial law, there are obvious and substantial advantages in having, where possible, a firm and definite rule for a particular class of legal relationship: for example, as here, the legal categorisation of a particular, definable type of contractual clause in common use.
>
> It is surely much better, both for shipowners and charterers (and, incidentally, for their advisers), when a contractual obligation of this nature is under consideration, and still more when they are faced with the necessity for an urgent decision as to the effects of a suspected breach of it, to be able to say categorically: "If a breach is proved, then the charterer can put an end to the contract", rather than that they should be left to ponder whether or not the courts would be likely, in the particular case, when the evidence has been heard, to decide that in the particular circumstances the breach

was or was not such as "to go to the root of the contract". Where justice does not require greater flexibility, there is everything to be said for, and nothing against, a degree of rigidity in legal principle.

Second, it would, in my opinion, only be in the rarest case, if ever, that a shipowner could legitimately feel that he had suffered an injustice by reason of the law having given to a charterer the right to put an end to the contract because of the breach by the shipowner of a clause such as this. If a shipowner has chosen to assert contractually, but dishonestly or without reasonable grounds, that he expects his vessel to be ready to load on such-and-such a date, wherein does the grievance lie?

Third, it is, as Mocatta J. held, clearly established by authority binding on this court that where a clause "expected ready to load" is included in a contract for the sale of goods to be carried by sea, that clause is a condition in the sense that any breach of it enables the buyer to reject the goods without having to show that the dishonest or unreasonable expectation of the seller has in fact been prejudicial to the buyer.

The judgment of Bankes L.J., in which Warrington L.J. and Atkin L.J. concurred, in *Finnish Government v. H. Ford & Co. Ltd.* (1921) 6 L1.L.Rep.188 is in point. The clause there was "Steamers expected ready to load February and/or March 1920." Bankes L.J. said, at p. 189: "I come to the conclusion . . . that this clause is one containing a contract. It is a contract which is in its nature a condition. . . ." That authority is not only binding on this court, but is, I think, completely and desirably in conformity with the line of cases which have decided—and the law in that respect is now accepted as being beyond dispute—that a statement in a contract of sale as to the loading period is a condition in the sense which I have indicated. If the contract says "loading to be during July," the buyer can reject the goods if the loading was not complete until midday on August 1. He is not limited to claiming damages; he is not obliged to show that he has suffered any damage.

It would, in my judgment, produce an undesirable anomaly in our commercial law if such a clause—"expected ready to load"—were to be held to have a materially different legal effect where it is contained in a charterparty from that which it has when it is contained in a sale of goods contract. . .

The fourth reason why I think that the clause should be regarded as being a condition when it is found in a charterparty is that that view was the view of Scrutton L.J. so expressed in his capacity as the author of Scrutton on Charterparties. . .

The reasoning is an illustration of how a term could be a condition as a matter of precedent. A key basis of this precedent was the need for commercial certainty. The innocent party will be able to treat the contract as at an end if an 'expected ready to load' clause has been breached, and then make other arrangements to meet the demands of related contracts. The same practical advantage forms the basis of the term being a condition in sale of goods contracts. Treating the same term as a condition in charterparty agreements makes the status of the term consistent. That need for consistency was then an additional factor, and it was even said that the sale of goods cases were binding on the court. Holding that such a term was a condition was also consistent with the apparent intentions of charterers and shipowners. The conduct resulting in the breach would by definition be dishonest or negligent such that a shipowner could hardly complain about the contract ending. The fourth reason was the authority of the leading text on charterparties which supported such terms being classified as conditions. These factors may well be relied upon to classify other terms as conditions in other common types of contract. In some cases, other additional factors might also be relevant.

8.6.2.3 *The Intentions of the Parties*

If it appears that the parties intended for a term to be a condition, then in principle, it should be classed as one. *Lombard North Central plc v Butterworth* [1987] 1 QB 527 concerned a five year hire-purchase agreement for a computer. The rental was based on four payments of £584 each year. Clause 2 of the contract stated that for each payment, time was 'of the essence' of the contract. When the sixth payment was delayed, the claimant finance company repossessed the computer and sold it elsewhere. In effect, it had treated the breach of Clause 2 as repudiatory. The Court of Appeal held that the claimant had been entitled to end the contract. The main basis for this was the fact that payment on time was 'of the essence'. That showed an intention to treat the obligation as a condition.

Mustill LJ provided some useful guidance in the reasoning:

> 4. It is possible by express provision in the contract to make a term a condition, even if it would not be so in the absence of such a provision.
>
> 5. A stipulation that time is of the essence, in relation to a particular contractual term, denotes that timely performance is a condition of the contract. The consequence is that delay in performance is treated as going to the root of the contract, without regard to the magnitude of the breach.
>
> 6. It follows that where a promisor fails to give timely performance of an obligation in respect of which time is expressly stated to be of the essence, the injured party may elect to terminate and recover damages in respect of the promisor's outstanding obligations, without regard to the magnitude of the breach.

The guidance makes it clear that the parties can make a term a condition. The obvious effect is that any breach of such a term allows for the innocent party to end the contract. The parties can make a term a condition by showing a clear intention for it to be one. It does not matter that ordinarily, the term would not have been a condition automatically. According to Mustill LJ, saying time 'is of the essence' was enough to make the time of performance a condition. The parties had indicated that the obligation was of crucial importance. In doing so, they had showed an intention for a breach of that term to end the contract. It follows that the term was intended to be a condition.

The intention for a term to be a condition must be clear and consistent with the other terms. The obvious way of expressing such an intention is in the wording of the contract. A term could be described as a 'condition'. It might go further, explicitly stating that any breach of the term can result in the contract ending. However, such an intention needs to be very clear when the contract is read as whole, and the mere use of the word 'condition' in itself may not be enough to render a term a condition. This is because, as we shall see in *Schuler AG v Wickman Machine Tool Sales* [1974], the word 'condition' is often used simply to refer to contractual terms in general (as in the commonly-encountered phrase 'Terms and Conditions').

This important limit to the use of the word 'condition' was shown by the majority of the House of Lords in *Schuler AG v Wickman Machine Tool Sales* [1974] AC 235. The case concerned a contract between a manufacturer in Germany (Schuler) and a UK company (Wickman). Under the contract, Wickman was made the only seller of Schuler's goods in the UK. This arrangement was for four and half years. Clause 7(b) of the contract said 'it shall be a condition of this agreement that. . .' Wickman visit six car manufacturers each week to get orders. Based on the length of the contract, that obligation would result in 1400 visits. Wickman was in breach of this obligation. Since the obligation breached was labelled as a 'condition', Schuler ended the contract. The key issue in the case was the status of Clause 7(b). Was it intended to be a real (legal) condition? If it was, it would mean that *any* breach of it would allow for Schuler to end the contract. To help understand the reasoning, it is useful to know that Clause 11 referred to a right to end the contract following a 'material breach'. It said that following a 'material breach', the innocent party could request in writing that the breach be corrected. If it was not corrected in 60 days, the innocent party could then end the contract.

The majority of the House of Lords (4–1) held that Schuler was not entitled to end the contract. According to the majority, the parties could not have intended that any breach of Clause 7(b) would allow for the contract to end. In other words, the parties could not have intended to treat Clause 7(b) as a real (legal) condition. It is useful to explore the reasoning of the lead judgment by Lord Reid and then contrast it with the reasoning of the minority judgment by Lord Wilberforce.

GUIDED CASE READING 8.2

Schuler AG v Wickman Machine Tool Sales [1974] AC 235

When you read the extract of the judgment by Lord Reid, try to identify:

- the significance of referring to a term as a 'condition'
- why the wording of clause 7(b) was not enough to show an intention for it to be a legal condition

Schuler maintains that the word 'condition' has now acquired a precise legal meaning; that, particularly since the enactment of the Sale of Goods Act 1893, its recognised meaning in English law is a term of a contract any breach of which by one party gives to the other party an immediate right to rescind the whole contract. Undoubtedly the word is frequently used in that sense. There may, indeed, be some presumption that in a formal legal document it has that meaning. But it is frequently used with a less stringent meaning. One is familiar with printed 'conditions of sale' incorporated into a contract and with the words 'For conditions see back' printed on a ticket. There it simply means that the 'conditions' are terms of the contract.

In the ordinary use of the English language 'condition' has many meanings, some of which have nothing to do with agreements. In connection with an agreement it may mean a pre-condition: something which must happen or be done before the agreement can take effect. Or it may mean some state of affairs which must continue to exist if the agreement is to remain in force.

The legal meaning on which Schuler relies is, I think, one which would not occur to a layman; a condition in that sense is not something which has an automatic effect. It is a term the breach of which by one party gives to the other an option either to terminate the contract or to let the contract proceed and, if he so desires, sue for damages for the breach.

> Lord Reid acknowledged that the word 'condition' now had a fixed legal meaning in English law, but also made clear that he though the social context needed to be taken into account: the word 'condition' is also used more loosely to simply mean 'a term of a contract' (such as in the phrase 'terms and conditions). It also has various meanings in everyday English. It would be overly legalistic, in other words, to insist that the use of the word 'condition' by definition referred to its strict legal meaning. So it was still open for the court to decide that this 'condition' was in fact not one in the technical legal sense.

Sometimes a breach of a term gives that option to the aggrieved party because it is of a fundamental character going to the root of the contract, sometimes it gives that option because the parties have chosen to stipulate that it shall have that effect. Blackburn J. said in *Bettini v. Gye* (1876) 1 Q.B.D. 183, 187: 'Parties may think some matter, apparently of very little importance, essential; and if they sufficiently express an intention to make the literal fulfilment of such a thing a condition precedent, it will be one; . . .'

> A term could become a 'condition' in the legal sense in two ways. It could be that the term went 'to the root' of the contract. Or it could be that the parties have stipulated that they want the term to be a condition.

In the present case it is not contended that Wickman's failures to make visits amounted in themselves to fundamental breaches. What is contended is that the terms of clause 7 'sufficiently express an intention' to make any breach, however small, of the obligation to make visits a condition so that any breach shall entitle Schuler to rescind the whole contract if they so desire.

Schuler maintains that the use of the word 'condition' is in itself enough to establish this intention. No doubt some words used by lawyers do have a rigid inflexible meaning. But we must remember that we are seeking to discover intention as disclosed by the contract as a whole. Use of the word 'condition' is an indication—even a strong indication—of such an intention but it is by no means conclusive.

> Here, the term in question certainly was not in the former category—a failure to comply with it might mean simply making 1399 out of 1400 visits, which would hardly 'go to the root of the contract'. Instead, the term in question could only be a condition if the parties had intended it to be so. Use of the word 'condition' was indicative of intent but not decisive. Other factors had to be taken into account.

The fact that a particular construction leads to a very unreasonable result must be a relevant consideration. The more unreasonable the result the more unlikely it is that the parties can have intended it, and if they do intend it the more necessary it is that they shall make that intention abundantly clear.

Clause 7 (b) requires that over a long period each of the six firms shall be visited every week by one or other of two named representatives. It makes no provision for Wickman being entitled to substitute others even on the death or retirement of one of the named representatives. Even if one could imply some right to do this, it makes no provision for both representatives being ill during a particular week. And it makes no provision for the possibility that one or other of the firms may tell Wickman that they cannot receive Wickman's representative during a particular week. So if the parties gave any thought to the matter at all they must have realised the probability that in a few cases out of the 1,400 required visits a visit as stipulated would be impossible. But if Schuler's contention is right, failure to make even one visit entitle them to terminate the contract however blameless Wickman might be.

This is so unreasonable that it must make me search for some other possible meaning of the contract. If none can be found then Wickman must suffer the consequences. But only if that is the only possible interpretation.

If I have to construe clause 7 standing by itself then I do find difficulty in reaching any other interpretation. But if clause 7 must be read with clause 11 the difficulty disappears. The word 'condition' would make any breach of clause 7 (b), however excusable, a material breach. That would then entitle Schuler to give notice under clause 11 (a) (i) requiring the breach to be remedied. . .

In my view, that is a possible and reasonable construction of the contract and I would therefore adopt it. The contract is so obscure that I can have no confidence that this is its true meaning but for the reasons which I have given I think that it is the preferable construction. It follows that Schuler was not entitled to rescind the contract as it purported to do.

> One of these factors had to be reasonableness. Would it have been reasonable in the circumstances for the parties to have made the term a condition? Here, the answer would have to have been 'no', because it may have meant the termination of the contract simply for a failure of Wickman's sales representative to make one out of 1,400 visits. On its own this was not enough for Lord Reid to say the parties had not intended the clause to be a condition.

> But another factor to be taken into account was the context of the clause in question, and here that context made clear that the clause had not been intended to be a condition, because there was another clause (11) in the contract providing a method for remedying its breach.

> So while the contract was very unclear, Lord Reid was of the view that the only realistic interpretation of it was that clause 7 was not a condition.

It is clear that the use of the word 'condition' can be an *indication* that a term is a (legal) condition. However, the use of the word is not conclusive.

The majority held that clause 7 was not intended to be a legal condition. If it was such a condition, then *any* breach would allow for the contract to end. Even one failed visit out of 1400 would be such a breach, whatever the reason. If Wickman's representatives were ill, or if they were not allowed by the car manufacturers to visit, there would still be such a breach. According to Lord Reid, the parties could not have intended to allow for the contract to end so easily. Treating the obligation as a legal condition would lead to an 'unreasonable' result.

It was stated that the more 'unreasonable' the result, the less likely it would be that the parties intended it. The other majority judges used more colourful language. Lord Morris referred to results that would be 'utterly fantastic'. Lord Simon referred to 'absurd results' and Lord Kilbrandon referred to 'grotesque consequences'. On that basis, (from an objective perspective) the term was not intended as a legal condition. Instead, it was just a reference to the term being important enough for its breach to potentially be a 'material breach', that is one that activated clause 11.

The interpretation of 'condition' given in this case was said to be justified further because of Clause 11. Clause 11 suggested a result other than an immediate right to the end the contract. Accordingly, the contract itself was capable of different interpretations and certainly did not show clear intention for Clause 7 to give an immediate right to terminate in the case of breach.

The approach of the majority could be questioned on the basis that Clause 7 was the only term to use the word 'condition'. That might be taken to indicate that the special legal meaning was intended rather than an ordinary meaning of describing an obligation. Also, the contract was written by commercial parties. Perhaps the legal meaning was intended, however unreasonable that might be.

It could be argued that opening the usage of the word up to interpretation might cause some uncertainty for contractual parties who wish to use the word in its legal sense.

Another argument against the majority approach concerns Clause 11. We can recall that clause 11 allowed for 60 days for a material breach to be corrected before ending the contract. On the facts, we might question if Clause 11 really did apply to the breach. After all, a failure to make a number of visits each week cannot be corrected without a time-machine. Something like a failure to deliver goods would work well for Clause 11. The party in breach could then correct the breach by actually delivering the goods. But in the context of the obligation in question, it is difficult to imagine how Clause 11 would have been of any use. Consequently, could it really have been used to cast doubt on the meaning of 'condition' in clause 7?

Lord Wilberforce delivered a powerful dissenting judgment. This highlights the basis for giving the word 'condition' its legal meaning:

> ...Does clause 7 (b) amount to a "condition" or a "term"? (to call it an important or material term adds, with all respect, nothing but some intellectual assuagement). My Lords, I am clear in my own mind that it is a condition, but your Lordships take the contrary view. On a matter of construction of a particular document, to develop the reasons for a minority opinion serves no purpose. I am all the more happy to refrain from so doing because the judgments of Mocatta J., Stephenson L.J., and indeed of Edmund Davies L.J., on construction, give me complete satisfaction and I could in any case add little of value to their reasons. I would only add that, for my part, to call the clause arbitrary, capricious or fantastic, or to introduce as a test of its validity the ubiquitous reasonable man (I do not know whether he is English or German) is to assume, contrary to the evidence, that both parties to this contract adopted a standard of easygoing tolerance rather than one of aggressive, insistent punctuality and efficiency. This is not an assumption I am prepared to make, nor do I think myself entitled to impose the former standard upon the parties if their words indicate, as they plainly do, the latter. I note finally, that the result of treating the clause, so careful and specific in its requirements, as a term is, in effect, to deprive the appellants of any remedy in respect of admitted and by no means minimal breaches.

Lord Wilberforce's powerful dissent reflects the need for commercial certainty. It suggests that questioning the meaning of words because they might result in unreasonable consequences results in uncertainty. Essentially the parties will have to look beyond the wording used and consider reasonableness to determine if they can end the contract. In addition, interpreting the word 'condition' with reference to the reasonable person raises further uncertainty. What are the standards of this reasonable person? While Lord Wilberforce's comment about not knowing whether the reasonable man is English or German is amusing, but it makes the serious point that the standard of 'reasonableness' is not fixed but highly variable. He also charged the majority of unrealistically reflecting a standard of 'easy-going tolerance' rather than the approach of commercial parties intending to act in their own interests.

?! THINKING POINTS

How would the outcome of this case influence the drafting of contracts (i.e. what does it encourage parties to do)?

The case of *Schuler v Wickman* can be taken to show that while using the word 'condition' is an indication of the intended status of a term, it is not conclusive. The more unreasonable the consequence of giving a term the status of a condition, the less likely it is that such a status was intended. The existence of Clause 11 gave a justification for an alternative interpretation of Clause 7. But even if there was no Clause 11, it is possible that the result would have been the same if the case had been decided today. After all, Lord Hoffman's principles of interpretation from the *ICS* case would be

→ CROSS-REFERENCE
For Lord Hoffman's principles of interpretation see 6.4.4.

relevant. That is, if clear wording does not reflect 'commercial common sense', it might be interpreted differently. Alternatively, if the case had been decided today, the result might be that nothing had gone wrong with the wording and that it was just a bad bargain. Such an alternative would be consistent with Lord Wilberforce's dissenting judgment.

The significance of interpretation is made clear by *Rice (Trading as 'Garden Guardian') v Great Yarmouth Borough Council* [2000] All ER (D) 902. Here the Court of Appeal adopted a restrictive approach to a term allowing the contract to end following a breach. This was done to reflect 'commercial common sense'. The claimant had two contracts with the defendant Council to maintain the Council's sports pitches, gardens and parks. Clause 23.2.1 in the contracts stated that the Council could end the contract following any breach by the other party. In response to some breaches, the Council gave notice to end both contracts. The claimant then brought an action for damages on the basis that the Council had not right to end the contracts. The question for the Court of Appeal was whether the parties intended for the contracts to end following *any* breach of *any* obligation. It was held that such an interpretation of the contract could not have been intended. On that basis, the claimant was entitled to damages.

Hale LJ delivered the judgment for the Court of Appeal. Reference was made to the argument of the Council that the wording of the term should be applied literally. That would have then enabled the Council to terminate following any breach. The judgment then cited Lord Wilberforce from *Bunge Corporation v Tradax Export SA* [1981] 1 WLR 711 who observed:

> [I]t is open to the parties to agree that, as regards a particular obligation, any breach shall entitle the party not in default to treat the contract as repudiated.

This was a starting point. The parties can agree on the consequences that will flow from a breach of a term. Hale LJ then contrasted this comment by Lord Wilberforce with the following observation by Lord Diplock in *Antaios Compania SA v Salen Rederiern* [1985] AC 191:

> . . .[I]f detailed semantic and syntactical analysis of words in a commercial contract is going to lead to a conclusion that flouts business commonsense, it must yield to business commonsense. . .

Hale LJ considered that allowing the Council to end the contract following any breach of any term at any time 'flies in the face of commercial common sense', because a very minor breach would be visited with the same 'draconian' consequences as a major one.

Clearly the terms of a contract are an expression of the parties' intentions. The approach of the Court of Appeal was to question the natural meaning of the words used. The *ICS* case was not cited by the court. However, it is clear that the approach adopted echoes Lord Hoffman's principles of interpretation. The use of the general termination clause did not make sense given that the obligations varied so much. The claimant had a wide range of obligations such as mowing lawns, planting flowers and trimming bushes, and the seriousness of a breach of these obligations could vary considerably. As a result, it could not have been intended for the all of the obligations in the contract to have the effect of a condition.

The case could be criticised for creating some uncertainty; after all, the wording was clear. The result is that to ensure the right to termination following a breach, the terms need to be specific. An example would be a term that refers to the breach of a specific obligation, (rather than 'any' obligation) resulting in a right to end the contract. With that in mind, the judgment encourages more openness when drafting contracts. Parties can still control their right to end the contract, but need to be very clear about it in their terms.

 THINKING POINTS

If a contract specifies that for all obligations, any breach will result in one party having the right to end the contract, do you think it is likely that other party would agree to it?

8.7 Ending the Contract Based on the *Effect* of the Breach: Innominate Terms

Traditionally, terms were classed as conditions and warranties. However, as mentioned earlier, a third category of **innominate term** has been recognised. The idea is that some terms are too complicated to classify as a condition or warranty just from an interpretation of the contract. Such innominate terms are capable of being breached in a very serious way. Equally, such terms are capable of only being subject to a minor breach.

> **innominate term** means a 'term with no name', i.e. not a condition or warranty.

KEY POINTS

Innominate terms are those that cannot be pre-classified based on the wording of the contract. This is because they could go to the root of the contract, but equally could be deemed secondary and minor.

We will see that a breach of an innominate term can allow the contract to be ended. Whether it does is based on the seriousness of the actual breach. This type of term was recognised by Diplock LJ in *Hongkong Fir Shipping v Kawasaki Kisen Kaisha* [1962] 2 QB 26. Later, this type of term received the label of 'innominate term', although it has also attracted the label of 'intermediate term'. What this type of term is, and the way it operates, can be seen from the facts and reasoning in that case.

The case concerned a charterparty agreement. Under this contact, a ship was hired for two years. One of the terms placed an obligation on the owner of the ship that the ship would be 'in every way fitted for ordinary cargo service'. This is known as a 'seaworthiness clause'. It requires the ship to be in a good enough state to carry cargo. However, the ship had an old engine and inefficient engine room staff, and suffered a breakdown on its first voyage. It had to be taken in for repairs, which took in total 20 weeks. During this period the defendant charterer attempted to end the contract, because it did not think that the vessel could be made seaworthy in good time. Once the repairs were finished, however there was still well over a year and a half remaining on the contract, and the claimant owner then sued the charterer for wrongful repudiation of the contract. That there had been a breach of the seaworthiness clause was not in dispute. The parties' disagreement was about whether its breach had entitled the charterers to repudiate the contract.

The Court of Appeal held that the term was too complex to classify as a either a condition or warranty. There was no relevant statute or binding precedent, and the intentions of the parties were not clear. In addition, the term was capable of being subject to a very serious breach (going to the root of the contract) but at the same time, a breach could have had trivial consequences. As Upjohn LJ observed, the seaworthiness clause would be breached: 'if a nail is missing from one of the timbers of a wooden vessel, or if proper medical supplies or two anchors are not on board at the time of sailing'. This could hardly be said to go 'to the root of the contract'. But equally, the clause might be breached by problems preventing the ship from carrying the cargo for the whole duration of the charterparty, in which case clearly the breach could be said to go 'to the root of the contract'. For these reasons, the Court of Appeal were unable to class the term as a condition or a warranty. Instead, the focus was on the actual consequences of the breach. Based on the consequences, Diplock LJ (along with the other judges) agreed that the breach was not sufficient to allow the charterers to end the contract. While it had caused delays, the ship would still be operable and fit to carry cargo for well over half of the duration of the charterparty. The charterers were therefore entitled to damages only. The approach adopted represented a very significant development and it is important to have a closer look at the main judgment by Diplock LJ.

GUIDED CASE READING 8.3

Hongkong Fir Shipping Ltd v Kawasaki Kisen Kaisha Ltd [1962] 2 QB 26

When you read the relevant extract of the judgment by Diplock LJ, try to identify:

- the basis for recognising 'innominate terms'
- the test to be applied when a term is innominate

[Diplock LJ referred to terms being viewed as conditions or warranties and continued]

Lawyers tend to speak of this classification as if it were comprehensive, partly for the historical reasons which I have already mentioned and partly because Parliament itself adopted it in the Sale of Goods Act, 1893, as respects a number of implied terms in contracts for the sale of goods and has in that Act used the expressions 'condition' and 'warranty' in that meaning. But it is by no means true of contractual undertakings in general at common law.

No doubt there are many simple contractual undertakings, sometimes express but more often because of their very simplicity ('It goes without saying') to be implied, of which it can be predicated that every breach of such an undertaking must give rise to an event which will deprive the party not in default of substantially the whole benefit which it was intended that he should obtain from the contract. And such a stipulation, unless the parties have agreed that breach of it shall not entitle the non-defaulting party to treat the contract as repudiated, is a 'condition'. So too there may be other simple contractual undertakings of which it can be predicated that no breach can give rise to an event which will deprive the party not in default of substantially the whole benefit which it was intended that he should obtain from the contract; and such a stipulation, unless the parties have agreed that breach of it shall entitle the non-defaulting party to treat the contract as repudiated, is a 'warranty'.

There are, however, many contractual undertakings of a more complex character which cannot be categorised as being 'conditions' or 'warranties' . . . Of such undertakings all that can be predicated is that some breaches will and others will not give rise to an event which will deprive the party not in default of substantially the whole benefit which it was intended that he should obtain from the contract; and the legal consequences of a breach of such an undertaking, unless provided for expressly in the contract, depend upon the nature of the event to which the breach gives rise and do not follow automatically from a prior classification of the undertaking as a 'condition' or a 'warranty'. . . .

. . . [T]he shipowners' undertaking to tender a seaworthy ship has, as a result of numerous decisions as to what can amount to 'unseaworthiness,' become one of the most complex of contractual undertakings. It embraces obligations with respect to every part of the hull and machinery, stores and equipment and the crew itself. It can be broken by the presence of trivial defects easily and rapidly remediable as well as by defects which must inevitably result in a total loss of the vessel.

Consequently the problem in this case is, in my view, neither solved nor soluble by debating whether the shipowner's express or implied undertaking to tender a seaworthy ship is a 'condition' or a 'warranty'. . . .

What the judge had to do . . . was to look at the events which had occurred as a result of the breach at the time at which the charterers purported to rescind

Diplock LJ noted that it was common for lawyers to divide terms starkly into 'conditions' and 'warranties' and acknowledged that there are some circumstances in which this makes sense. There are some terms the breach of which would clearly deprive the innocent party of most or all of the benefit it had contracted for. And there are some for which this clearly is not true. That is the basis for the division of terms into 'conditions' and 'warranties'.

However, there were many other terms for which this rigid classification could not apply. This was often because the term in question could be breached in a variety of ways, some serious and some not. This would mean the consequences of breach would not be clear until the breach actually took place.

The term in question here was exactly of that type. The breach of a 'seaworthiness' clause might simply mean a trivial defect, such as a missing piece of equipment, but it might also mean the sinking of the ship. So, in some circumstances its breach would look like that of a warranty, and in others like that of a condition.

the charterparty and to decide whether the occurrence of those events deprived the charterers of substantially the whole benefit which it was the intention of the parties as expressed in the charterparty that the charterers should obtain from the further performance of their own contractual undertakings ...

The question which the judge had to ask himself was, as he rightly decided, whether or not at the date when the charterers purported to rescind the contract, ... the delay which had already occurred as a result of the incompetence of the engine room staff, and the delay which was likely to occur in repairing the engines of the vessel and the conduct of the shipowners by that date in taking steps to remedy these two matters, were, when taken together, such as to deprive the charterers of substantially the whole benefit which it was the intention of the parties they should obtain from further use of the vessel under the charterparty.

> So, what the judge had to do with such a term was look at what had happened as a result of the breach and base his decision on that. If the breach deprived the innocent party of substantially the whole benefit of the contract then it could be treated as equivalent to a breach of a condition. But if it did not, then it could be equivalent to a breach of a warranty.

The question in the case was whether the breach could entitle the innocent party to end the contract. Traditionally, that would be based on the classification of the term breached. That classification would be done by statute, precedent or the parties' intentions based on the importance of the term. The importance of the term (i.e. whether it goes to the root of the contract) would be assessed by looking back to the time of entering the contract. However, the seaworthiness clause was too complicated to be classified in that way. When viewed at the time of contracting, it would have been capable of resulting in serious consequences following a breach. However, a breach of it would also have been capable of resulting in very minor consequences. For that reason, with such a term, Diplock LJ confirmed that the rights following a breach are based on the actual consequences of that breach.

If the actual consequences resulting from the breach are serious enough, then the innocent party can end the contract. The question to ask was whether the breach deprived the innocent party substantially of the benefit intended by the contract. If the answer was 'yes' then the effect of the breach would be equivalent to a breach of condition and would entitle the innocent party to terminate. If the answer was 'no' then the breach would be equivalent to a breach of warranty and so the innocent party would be entitled to damages only.

This question is really asking if the actual breach was so serious that it is no longer possible to get the performance contracted for. This is not assessed in an absolute strict way because of the use of the word 'substantially'. Instead, we decide whether the innocent party can still get most of the performance contracted for. On the facts, the charterer was only deprived of four months out of a 24-month contract. According to the trial judge and Court of Appeal, having 20 months remaining meant the breach was not serious enough. The charterer had not been deprived of 'substantially the whole benefit intended'. This represents a 'consequential' approach of focussing on the consequences of the breach to determine if the contract can be ended.

KEY POINTS

- Innominate terms are those that are too complicated to pre-classify as a condition or warranty.
- A breach of an innominate term will allow for the contract to end if it deprived the innocent party substantially of the intended benefit of the contract.

8.7.1 Guidance to Assess the Seriousness of a Breach

The obvious criticism of the consequential approach from *Hongkong Fir* is that it causes some uncertainty for commercial parties. If terms are pre-classified, or the remedies following a breach are predetermined, this should mean that the parties know their rights following any breach. The *Hongkong Fir* approach relies on assessing the consequences of the breach and working out if the effects are serious enough. Sometimes that answer will be obvious, but borderline cases will be difficult to deal with. That being said, the classification approach has uncertainties too where there is disagreement about the classification and the right to end the contract.

Some of the uncertainty about assessing the seriousness of the breach was addressed in *Ampurius Nu Homes Holdings Ltd v Telford Homes (Creekside) Ltd* [2013] EWCA Civ 577. There the Court of Appeal provided some guidance on how to determine if a breach is serious enough to satisfy the *Hongkong Fir* test. When applying the test, Lewison LJ referred to the following relevant factors:

> [52] . . .How much of the intended benefit under the contract has the injured party already received? Can the injured party be adequately compensated by an award of damages? Is the breach likely to be repeated? Will the guilty party resume compliance with his obligations? Has the breach fundamentally changed the value of future performance of the guilty party's outstanding obligations?

Of course, it goes without saying that the more guidance that is provided by the courts, the better it is for commercial certainty.

8.7.2 Proportionality Resulting from *Hongkong Fir*

The approach of focussing on the effects of the breach rather than a classification of terms has its advantages. It means that the remedy (i.e. damages only or ending the contract with damages) will always be proportionate to the actual breach. So, a serious breach could result in the contract ending but a minor breach would not. That seems fair.

A useful example of this advantage of proportionality and its wider effects is *Cehave NV v Bremer Handelsgesellschaft GmbH (The Hansa Nord)* [1976] QB 44. Here the term breached was seen as an innominate term that failed to satisfy the *Hongkong Fir* test.

The case concerned a contract for the sale of citrus pulp pellets in 'good condition' for £100,000. The cargo arrived in Rotterdam partially damaged, so the buyer ended the contract partially on the basis that the requirement that the pellets be in 'good condition' was a condition of the contract. (It also had other grounds for doing so which need not interest us here.) The entire cargo was then sold by the order of a Dutch court to a third party. From there, it was sold in its entirety to the original buyer for £30,000. The original buyer then used the entire cargo of pellets for their original purpose to feed cattle. The buyer was clearly taking advantage of the fact that there had been a decline in the market value of the pellets between the time of making the contract and delivery. It was using a technicality to escape from its initial obligation to pay £100,000 in order to take advantage of the favourable market conditions.

The Court of Appeal held that the term requiring the goods to be in 'good condition' was an innominate term. This was on the basis that a breach could be minor or very serious. The Court then applied the *Hongkong Fir* test. It was held that the breach did not deprive the buyer substantially of the benefit intended. After all, the buyer could still use the goods as intended and indeed still used the entire cargo for that purpose. On that basis, the breach was not serious enough for the contract to end.

This case shows a crucial advantage of the consequential approach. It works to prevent parties cashing-in on a technical breach to escape the contract for a better deal (what can be called 'economic opportunism').

8.7.3 The Consequential Approach before *Hongkong Fir*

Hongkong Fir is cited as a case that recognised a new type of term. This new type of term allowed for the contract to end depending on the effects of the breach. However, sometimes, judges had previously adopted this approach anyway. When called upon to classify a term as a condition or warranty, some judges did not focus on how important the term appeared to be at the time of contracting.

Instead, they classified the term based on the effects of the breach. The point was commented upon by Lord Denning MR in *Mihalis Angelos* [1971], in which he referred to the traditional division of conditions and warranties and observed:

> It would be a mistake, however, to look upon that division as exhaustive. There are many terms of many contracts which cannot be fitted into either category. In such cases the courts, for nigh on 200 years, have not asked themselves: was the term a condition or warranty? But rather: was the breach such as to go to the root of the contract? If it was, then the other party is entitled, at his election, to treat himself as discharged from any further performance. That is made clear by the judgment of Lord Mansfield in *Boone v. Eyre* (1777) 1 Hy.Bl. 273; and by the speech of Lord Blackburn in *Mersey Steel & Iron Co. v. Naylor, Benzon & Co.* (1884) 9 App.Cas. 434, 443–444; and the notes to *Cutter v. Powell* (1795) 6 Term Rep. 320 (2 Smith's Leading Cases, 13th ed. (1929), pp. 16–18). The case of *Hongkong Fir Shipping Co. Ltd. v. Kawasaki Kisen Kaisha Ltd.* [1962] 2 Q.B. 26 is a useful reminder of this large category.

The earlier decision of *Aerial Advertising Co v Batchelor Peas (Manchester) Ltd* [1938] 2 All ER 788 is a good example. Here, Aerial Advertising contracted to promote Batchelor Peas using a banner towed by a small aeroplane. A term of the contract required the pilot to call Batchelor Peas each day to have the route approved. On one occasion, the pilot did not get the route approved. It was Armistice Day 1937 and the plane flew over the crowded main square in Salford during the two minutes' silence towing a banner saying 'Eat Batchelor Peas'. Understandably, this was not well-received by the public. It resulted in a great deal of hostility towards Batchelor Peas. In response, Batchelor Peas ended the contract, and so Aerial Advertising sued for wrongful repudiation. The question was whether the breach was one that allowed for termination, i.e. was the relevant term a condition? The court held that the term was a condition and so the contract could be ended. However, the term could hardly have been said to have been one going to the root of the contract. It was a term that if breached, could have no consequences at all, or it could have serious consequences like it did in the case. To then classify the term as a condition suggests that the judge really focussed on the effects of the breach to determine the classification.

8.8 A Classification or Consequential Approach?

The traditional approach was based on the classification of the term breached. Following a breach, the contract could be ended if the term could be classed as a condition. Such a classification has always been based on assessing the term as it appeared at the time of contracting. In contrast, *Hongkong Fir* represents a consequential approach. The remedy is based on the actual consequences of the breach. One uncertainty following *Hongkong Fir* was whether the new approach replaced the traditional approach to classification or was simply an option to explore when the term could not be classified.

Key cases like *The Hansa Nord* and the House of Lords case of *Bunge Corporation New York v Tradax Export SA* [1981] 1 WLR 711 show that the classification approach remains. However, it is supplemented by the consequential approach. In *The Hansa Nord*, Lord Denning MR and Roskill LJ found the term breached was an innominate term. But in doing so, they indicated that the term could not be a condition and there was no authority or apparent intention for it to be a condition. Likewise, in *Bunge Corporation*, Lord Wilberforce, Lord Roskill and Lord Scarman all appreciated the flexibility offered by assessing terms as innominate. However, they all indicated that this was not a starting point for terms in general. The House of Lords found that the term breached was a condition. This was based on there being an implied intention for the term to be one. Reference was made to its importance as concerning the time of performance. The fact that the parties would benefit from the certainty of treating it as a condition was very influential too. As a result, the contract could be ended following its breach.

Certainly, if a term is classed as a condition by statute or by a binding precedent, then it will be a condition. This is because a court will have to apply such authority. Where no such authority exists, the courts should consider the parties' intentions before treating the term as innominate. This is consistent with the following observation made by Hamblen LJ in *Grand China Logistics Holding (group) Co Ltd v Spar Shipping AS* [2016] EWCA Civ 982:

> [92] The modern English law approach to the classification of contractual terms is that a term is innominate unless it is clear that it is intended to be a condition or a warranty - see, for example, *Cehave N.V. v Bremer Handelgesellschaft* (*The Hansa Nord*) [1976] QB 44 at p. 70H–71B (Roskill LJ); *Bremer v Vanden* [1978] 2 Lloyd's Rep. 109 at p. 113 (Lord Wilberforce); *Bunge v Tradax* at p. 715H–716A (Lord Wilberforce), at p. 717G–H (Lord Scarman) and at p. 727E (Lord Roskill). As Lord Scarman stated at p. 717:
> "Unless the contract makes it clear, either by express provision or by necessary implication arising from its nature, purpose, and circumstances. . . that a particular stipulation is a condition or only a warranty, it is an innominate term, the remedy for a breach of which depends upon the nature, consequences, and effect of the breach."

The comment cites authority from the key cases to indicate that a term is innominate if there is no apparent intention for it be a condition or warranty. In other words, if there appears to be an intention for the term to be a condition or a warranty, then it will be one. However, if there appears to be no such intention, then the term is an innominate one and the right to end the contract will be determined by the seriousness of the actual breach.

From the cases, it seems that when a term is breached, we should first determine whether the term is classified as a condition or warranty by statute, precedent or the parties' intentions. If it cannot be so classified, then the next step is to treat it as an innominate term and apply the *Hongkong Fir* test. This can be viewed as a four-step process, as shown in Figure 8.1.

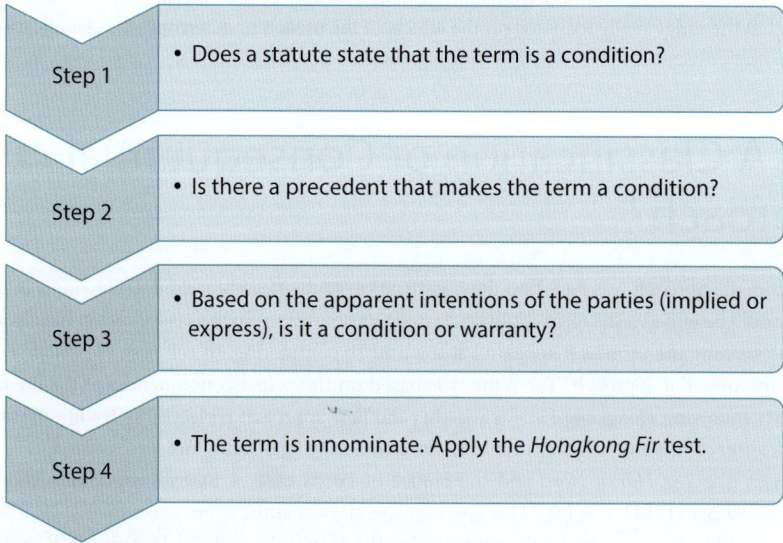

Figure 8.1
The process to decide whether there is a right to end the contract following defective performance

8.9 The Right to End the Contract from Legislation

So far, we have seen three ways a contract can end following a breach. It can end where the breach is a refusal to perform; where the term breached was a condition; and where the breach of an innominate term satisfies the *Hongkong Fir* test. A fourth way a contract can end following a breach is simply where legislation allows it. In this category we are not concerned with legislation making a term a condition. Instead, we are concerned with legislation that provides a direct right to end the contract following a breach. The main example of such legislation is the Consumer Rights Act 2015.

The Consumer Rights Act 2015 'includes' terms relating to quality, fitness for purpose, and description in consumer sales contracts. However, unlike the Sale of Goods Act 1979, which applies to contracts between businesses, the terms from the CRA 2015 are not expressly classed as 'conditions'. This approach of not explicitly making such terms conditions is for two reasons. First, the language of the CRA 2015 avoids legal terminology as far as it is possible. This reflects the aim of ensuring that its provisions are transparent and accessible for consumers. In other words, the Act was drafted to be more understandable. The second reason for not classifying the terms as conditions is that there is simply no need to do so. This is because the remedies following a breach of these terms are listed as non-excludable rights for the consumer. Consequently, the type of term has no role in dictating the remedy, and so there is no need to label them as either conditions or warranties.

In the list of remedies, the consumer has a 'short-time right to reject' the goods. In effect, this is really a short-term right to end the contract. Alternatively, the consumer can choose a repair or replacement of the goods.

If a term included by the CRA 2015 is breached, the right reject the goods and end the contract lasts up to 30 days after the sale (s.22(3)). This means that the consumer can return the goods for a refund following such a breach. If the consumer requests or agrees for repairs to be made during that 30 day period, the period 'stops running' to resume again after the repairs are completed. However, there is a minimum of 7 days given to inspect the repair once it is done (s.22(7)), meaning that the period in which there is a short-term right to reject may be extended beyond 30 days. During that time the short-term right to end the contract remains. After the period (or extended period) of 30 days in which there is a 'short term right to reject' following a breach, the only remedies are repair, replacement, or a price reduction. If these are impossible, disproportionate, or impose significant inconvenience on the consumer, then there is a final right to end the contract.

Under the Consumer Rights Act 2015, there is a right to end the contract following late delivery of goods. Section 28 gives the seller 30 days to deliver. After that, the contract can be ended. If under the contract the delivery was urgent, the 30 day period does not apply. For example, consider a wedding cake that is to be delivered on a wedding day. Failure to deliver the cake on time will mean the contract can be ended straight away. If the contract is ended, then s.28 (9) becomes relevant. It says the buyer can claim back 'all payments made under the contract'. Section 28 (13) also refers to the possibility of the consumer having additional remedies. This is there so that it is not assumed that damages are excluded. Damages may be available and will be based on ordinary contract principles.

➡ CROSS-REFERENCE
For the rules on compensatory damages see Chapter 9.

CHAPTER SUMMARY

- Some obligations are construed as 'entire' so that only completed performance by one party activates the obligation to pay.

- Substantial performance might be enough to activate the other party's obligations in such circumstances.

- If the obligations are severable, it means payment will be required for each of the separate obligations performed.

- Generally, contractual obligations are 'strict' so that a party cannot defend their failure to perform by saying they did so with reasonable care or had no intention to breach.

- Some obligations will be fault-based so that there is a breach only after a failure to take reasonable care.

- Following a breach, the innocent party is entitled to damages.

- If the breach is serious enough, the innocent party has a choice to terminate the contract or affirm it.

- Following a choice to end the contract, the parties are released from their primary obligations.

- The right to affirm will not apply if there is no legitimate interest in continuing and if damages are adequate as a remedy.

- The right to terminate following defective performance arises when there is a breach of a condition.

- A term can be classed as a condition by legislation, precedent or the parties' intentions.

- Labelling a term as a condition is an indication of intention but is not conclusive.

- If a term cannot be pre-classified as a condition or warranty it is treated as innominate.

- A breach of an innominate term will allow for termination if the consequences deprive the innocent party substantially of the benefit intended.

KEY CASES

- ☐ *Cutter v Powell* (1756) 6 TR 320—this is the authority for entire obligations.

- ☐ *H Dakin & Co v Lee* [1916] 1 KB—this represents an example of substantial performance activating the obligation to pay.

- ☐ *Regent OHG Aisestadt und Barig v Francesco of Jermyn Street* [1981] 3 All ER 327—this is a useful example of obligations being severable.

- ☐ *White & Carter (Councils) Ltd v McGregor* [1962] AC 413—this provides the rule whereby a party can continue the contract following a refusal to perform by the other party.

- ☐ *Maredelanto Compania Naviera SA. v Bergbau-Handel GmbH. (The Mihalis Angelos)* [1971] 1 QB 164—this is an example of a term being a condition as a matter of binding precedent.

- ☐ *Schuler AG v Wickman Machine Tool Sales* [1974] AC 235—this is an authority for the use of the parties' intentions to decide if a term is a condition.

- ☐ *Rice (Trading as 'Garden Guardian') v Great Yarmouth Borough Council* [2000] All ER (D) 902—this is an authority for the effect of termination clauses and whether they show an intention to end the contract following a breach.

- ☐ *Hongkong Fir Shipping v Kawasaki Kisen Kaisha* [1962] 2 QB 26—this is an authority for the classification of terms as 'innominate' and the consequential approach that applies.

- ☐ *Bunge Corporation New York v Tradax Export SA* [1981] 1 WLR 711—this is an authority for the classification approach being supplemented by the consequential approach rather than being replaced by it.

QUESTIONS

1. Cloud Pleaser Ltd (CP Ltd) contracted with Vape Distribution Ltd (VD Ltd) for the delivery of 3000 units of vape liquid per month for one year. One of the terms stated that CP Ltd must approve the source of the products. Two months into the contract, VD Ltd did not seek approval for its latest source. A month later, CP Ltd was the subject of serious negative comments on social media platforms because it was revealed that CP Ltd's vape liquid was sourced from a factory that uses child labour. Having suffered a serious loss of sales CP Ltd would like to be advised as to whether it has the right to end its contract with VD Ltd.

2. Analyse the extent to which an innocent party can continue with a contract following a refusal to perform by the other party.

3. Critically evaluate the extent to which an innocent party can end a contract following defective performance of the other party which results in a breach.

 For answer guidance to these questions please visit the online resources at www .oup.com/uk/naidoo1e/, where you will also find multiple choice questions to check your understanding of key concepts.

FURTHER READING

Andrews, 'Breach of contract: a plea for clarity and discipline' (2018) 134 LQR 117.
A long article providing detailed criticism of the case law on breach and anticipatory breach.

Ezeoke, 'Assessing seriousness in repudiatory breach of innominate terms' [2017] JBL 198.
This provides a detailed examination of the *Hongkong Fir* test together with some suggestions.

Liu, 'The White & Carter principle: a restatement' (2011) 74(2) MLR 171.
A leading assessment of *White & Carter v McGregor* and the 'legitimate interest' test.

PART 3

Enforcement of the Contract

Remedies Part I: Compensatory Damages Following a Breach

9

LEARNING OBJECTIVES

By the end of this chapter you should be able to:

- assess the different ways that compensatory damages can be worked out;
- apply the principles relating to loss that is claimable;
- identify the kinds of loss (resulting from a breach) that can be compensated by damages;
- evaluate the principles and reasoning that influence whether the type of loss is claimable.

INTRODUCTION

We saw in Chapter 8 that following a breach of a term, the innocent party has a right to damages. Such damages are aimed at compensating the innocent party for any losses it has suffered that were caused by the breach. However, it cannot expect to receive whatever amount of money it demands and it will usually be faced with a dispute about which losses are claimable. For example, we know that lost profits should be claimable, but what about compensation to cover the costs of correcting a breach? Beyond financial losses, is it possible to claim for injured feelings, harm to reputation or even loss of enjoyment or disappointment?

In this chapter, we will examine the detailed rules about the *types* of loss that are claimable. We will start with the compensatory purpose of damages. We then examine the types of losses that are claimable in damages. We will then see how the courts have developed rules for recognising a wider range of losses. The law that applies to factors limiting the award of damages is addressed in Chapter 10. We then turn to the non-compensatory remedies in Chapter 11.

9.1 The Action for Damages

Following a breach, the innocent party has a right to compensatory damages, but there is no obligation to claim such damages. The innocent party is free to accept the losses suffered. If the innocent party has performed its obligations, but has not been paid, it could bring an action for the price due. Such an action is very different to an action for damages because it is really about a fixed debt that is owed. An example of such an action is the one in *White & Carter v McGregor*. In contrast, a damages action is not for the money due under the contract. Instead, a damages claim is based on the loss suffered as a result of the breach.

It is easy to imagine that all disputes and damages claims are argued in formal court proceedings. However, most cases are settled either informally or by using a method of Alternative Dispute Resolution (ADR). There are many different forms of ADR but the main forms include mediation

→ CROSS-REFERENCE

For the detail and judgment of *White & Carter v McGregor* [1962] see 8.5.1.

and arbitration. Mediation is where the parties negotiate with the help of a mediator and agree on an outcome. Arbitration is a more adversarial process where a third party, appointed by one party or both, decides the outcome of the dispute. Often the parties will have agreed to resolve any dispute through ADR by putting an arbitration or mediation clause in the contract. ADR is generally less time-consuming than litigation, so the parties can move on quickly after a breach. The other obvious advantage is that the parties will avoid the legal costs associated with a court action. They will also have more control over what amount of money is to be paid. Under the Civil Procedure Rules which govern the court process, where a party refuses to take part in ADR, they run the risk of this being factored into the decision made by the court on the allocation of costs. Under Part 1.4(2) (e) of the Civil Procedure Rules there is a duty placed on courts to actively encourage ADR, though it cannot be imposed on the parties (*Halsey v Milton Keynes General NHS Trust* [2004] EWCA Civ 576). Courts have interpreted this to mean they should 'encourage' ADR by making it clear to parties to a dispute that they will bear the costs of court action even if they are victorious when they have unreasonably refused ADR.

Where contract rights are being enforced, it needs to be done within set time limits. Sections 5 and 8 of the Limitation Act 1980 indicate that for a breach of a simple contract (a contact other than a deed), the time limit is six years from the date of the breach. For a breach of a Deed, the limit is twelve years.

Whether it is a court action or action using ADR, it is important for the innocent party to know what they have a right to claim. Likewise, it is important for the party in breach to know their potential liability. While the case law does not indicate precisely how much can be claimed in any given circumstance, it does provide guidance on the types of losses that are recoverable, and that is the main content of this Chapter. Furthermore, as we will see in Chapter 10, there is guidance on how the claims can be limited and reduced.

9.2 The Aim of Damages Following a Breach

Following a breach, the innocent party is entitled to compensatory damages. That means damages are intended to make up for any losses caused by the breach. This compensatory aim is very important, particularly when there is no loss arising from the breach. If a breach causes no loss to the innocent party, then there is nothing to compensate. In such circumstances, there is only a right to **nominal damages**. To award anything more would only serve to punish the party in breach. That has never been the aim of damages in contract law. A breach of contract is not a civil wrong. Parties are not disciplined for breaching a contract and so damages cannot be award to punish a party for the breach (*Addis v Gramophone Co. Ltd* [1909] AC 488).

nominal damages are a 'token gesture' for amounts like a few pounds.

This firm rule against punitive damages means that parties have the freedom to choose to breach their contracts where it makes good business sense to do so. That would be where the liability for the breach will be outweighed by the profit gained from contracting with someone else. This is known as an 'efficient breach', which is always an option because damages do not penalise parties for the way they breach their contracts. Instead, the courts focus on the loss caused by the breach and aim to ensure the damages compensate the innocent party for the loss suffered.

A reminder of this traditional approach in which damages are only compensatory was emphasised in *Ruxley Electronics and Construction Ltd v Forsyth* [1996] AC 344. There Lord Lloyd stated:

> It is first necessary to ascertain the loss the plaintiff has suffered by reason of the breach. If he has suffered no loss, as sometimes happens, he can recover no more that nominal damages. For the object of damages is always to compensate the plaintiff, not to punish the defendant.

Knowing that damages for a breach are compensatory helps us to know if a claim is worth making. But on its own, it does not tell us how the damages are worked out. For that, we need to know what loss the innocent party is to be compensated for. This point was addressed in *Robinson v Harman* (1848) 1 Exch 350. There, Baron Parke made the following statement:

> The rule of the common law is that where a party sustains loss by reason of a breach of contract, he is, so far as money can do it to be placed in the same situation, with respect to damages, as if the contract had been performed.

This comment by Parke B is about the general aim of damages in contract law and is commonly cited in cases dealing with damages. The point being made is that damages awards in contract are based on what the contract *should* have given the innocent party.

KEY POINTS

The aim of damages for breach is to put the innocent party into the financial position they would have been in, had the contract been performed.

This aim tells us about the loss that is compensated for: the bargain (or deal) that would have resulted from the contract being performed. The same principle was explained more recently, in *Farley v Skinner* [2001] UKHL 49 where Lord Scott observed:

> The basic principle of damages for breach of contract is that the injured party is entitled, so far as money can do it, to be put in the position he would have been in if the contractual obligation has been properly performed. He is entitled, that is to say, to the benefit of his bargain.

This means that damages should put the innocent party in the position that they (objectively) expected to be in following performance. For that reason, it is generally said that such damages reflect the innocent party's 'expectation interest'. The expectation interest was identified in a leading article by Fuller and Perdue, 'The Reliance Interest in Contract Damages' (1937) 46 Yale LJ 52. This is based on damages reflecting the benefit expected (hence the name) from the performance of the contract. If the benefit expected from performance is prevented by a breach, then that is the loss. On that basis, the damages compensate for that loss, as shown by Figure 9.1. In more recent years, some commentators have preferred the 'performance interest' as a more accurate term to use (e.g. Friedmann in 'The Performance Interest in Contract Damages' (1995) 111 LQR 628). However, the terms 'expectation interest' and 'performance interest' are generally used to mean the same thing.

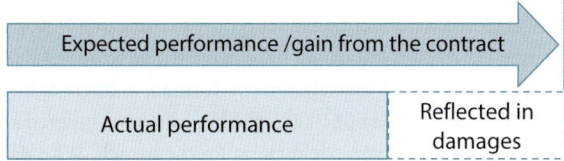

Figure 9.1
The aim of damages following a breach

9.3 Identifying the Expectation (Performance) Loss

The idea of putting the innocent party financially in the position it would have been in if the contract had been performed seems quite abstract. The same can be said when we hear that damages protect the expectation (or performance) interest. However, these concepts are not so abstract when we consider *how* the relevant loss is identified. Of course, the loss suffered from not having full performance of a contract will vary and it really depends on what performance was contracted for. That being said, we can identify three typical ways of identifying the relevant expectation (performance) loss. One way is to claim for consequential losses. Another is a claim for the difference in value and the third is the cost of correcting the breach.

9.3.1 Consequential Losses

One way of working out the losses arising from a breach is the lost profit measure. Sometimes a party expects the performance of the contract to result in profits being made. If the breach results in a reduction or loss of such profits, then that is the loss for which compensation has to be given.

Consider the following example. You own a pizzeria and need a new oven urgently. You call a seller of industrial ovens in the morning to order a new oven. During the call, you make it clear that the oven is needed urgently. You say that you cannot operate as a business without it. You even have table bookings for the evening. In response, the seller agrees to have the new oven delivered and installed by 6pm that day. You now have a contract for the oven to be installed by 6pm. In breach, the oven does not arrive. Your calls are ignored and then, finally, it arrives two days later. What is the loss resulting from the breach? You contracted for an oven, and now you have one. However, it was delivered late and so the pizzeria has not been able to operate for two days. It has therefore suffered a loss of revenue as a result of the breach by the seller. In principle, you should then be entitled to any profit the pizzeria would have made, had the contract been performed. Such profit is within your expectation (or performance) interest because of what was said when the contract was made. You will recall that at that stage, it was made clear that the pizzeria could not operate without the oven (which should ensure that the lost profit was sufficiently foreseeable at the time of the contract and not too remote to be claimed).

→ CROSS-REFERENCE

For the detailed rules on remoteness see 10.3.

9.3.2 The Difference in Value

Another way of working out the loss arising from a breach is the 'difference in value' measure. This is a claim based on the value of what the claimant should have got from performance of the contract. That figure is then compared with the value of what the claimant party actually got. The difference is the loss suffered. Therefore, it is the basis of the compensatory damages.

Let us return to the pizzeria with a different transaction. You have paid £3000 for a fridge that is normally £3500. You chose that particular fridge because the discount made it a good bargain for you. However, the model that arrives is a different one that is only worth £2500—a breach of contract. Had the contract been performed correctly, you would have had a fridge worth £3500. Consequently, having a fridge worth £3500 represents your expectation (performance) interest. Instead, what you got is worth £1000 less. That difference in value of £1000 is the loss you have suffered and it represents your lost bargain. It is therefore, the amount you could claim for the breach. With damages of £1000, you are now in the same (financial) position that you contracted to be in. You have a fridge worth £2500 plus a further £1000. That adds up to the £3500 value that you contracted for.

The same approach can be adopted even if the seller's breach was serious enough to allow for termination. This is the case in the previous scenario. Since the fridge that has arrived is a different model to the one that was ordered, the seller has breached an implied condition under s. 13 of the

Sale of Goods Act 1979 (goods sold will meet their description). You could therefore return the fridge and your money will be refunded. You could then sue for the amount you need to put yourself in the position you should have been in had the contract been performed. You should have had a fridge worth £3500. You have paid £3000 for it and that is how much money you will be refunded. That means you need an extra £500 to reflect your expectation (performance) interest. That is the amount you would need to buy the same fridge from a different seller. The same also applies if you contracted for the fridge and the seller refused to deliver it. Your loss is £500 (which would be claimable above the refunded amount).

9.3.3 The Cost of Cure (i.e. the Cost of Repair)

The other typical way of working out the loss arising from a breach is the 'cost of cure' measure. Many cases refer it as damages for 'reinstatement'. Put simply, it is the cost of physically correcting the breach. An example of that would be the cost of repair to correct any defects. This measure might be appropriate where the correct fridge is sent to the pizzeria, but it is defective. If it is repaired, then you will have what you contracted for. You would be in the position you should have been in, had the contract been performed correctly. So, the cost of the repairs is the loss that can be claimed in damages.

Ordinarily, the claimant has a choice between the cost of cure and the difference in value measures. Damages cannot reflect both. After all, each measure compensates for the same kind of loss. If both were available, the claimant would be over-compensated. Consider the pizzeria example again. If the oven delivered was defective, you would be entitled to the cost of cure (i.e. the cost of repair) as described earlier. You could not then very well claim for the difference in value between what you actually received and what you should have received, because the repairs to the fridge, for which you have been compensated, will have eliminated any difference in value between those two things.

A major issue with the cost of cure measure relates to its availability. It will not be available where it is disproportionate, even if there is no difference in value. The key case here is *Ruxley Electronics and Construction Ltd v Forsyth* [1996] 1 AC 344.

Ruxley concerned a consumer contract. Mr Forsyth wanted a swimming pool installed in his garden. He entered into a contract with Ruxley for the pool to be built for £17,797.40. Under the final terms, the pool was to be 7ft 6 inches at the deep end. It was later discovered that the finished pool was only 6ft 9 inches at the deep end (9 inches/22.8 cm less than it should have been). The failure to build the pool to the correct depth was a breach. However, neither available method for assessing the loss seemed suitable. On the one hand, although the pool was slightly shallower than it should have been, the court held that there was no difference in the value of Mr Forsyth's property as a result—its commercial value, whether 7ft 6 inches deep or 6ft 9 inches, was the same. Using the 'difference in value' measure would therefore result in no damages being awarded.

At the other extreme, correcting the breach (i.e. using the cost of cure measure) would have required the removal of what was built and a new replacement pool being built in its place. The cost of such a correction (or reinstatement) would have been £21,560—far in excess of the original contract price. When Forsyth refused to pay the outstanding balance, Ruxley sued for the remaining price due. Forsyth then counterclaimed for breach. Since there was no difference in value, Forsyth naturally wanted the cost of reinstatement.

At first instance, the judge refused to award the cost of reinstatement. First of all, it was felt that such an award was disproportionate to the loss suffered. The pool could still be used as a pool and it was even deep enough for diving. That was because according to official guidelines, the minimum depth for diving is 5ft 2. The judge also refused the award for a second reason. He did not believe that Forsyth intended to have the pool rebuilt anyway. Instead, he awarded £2,500 to Forsyth for 'loss of amenity'. That is like an award for loss of enjoyment or personal disappointment. Forsyth then appealed and a majority in the Court of Appeal awarded the cost of reinstatement (£21,560). In the lead judgment, Staughton LJ held that the difference in value measure should not be used, because it would result in no damages being awarded but Forsyth had clearly suffered a loss. And since the cost of cure was the only alternative, it therefore had to be used. Moreover, if it were the case that a builder could get away with paying no damages for breaching a contract if there was no difference in value between what was bargained for and what was performed, it would result in builders (naturally) taking a shoddy approach to fulfilling precise contract specifications. In addition, whether Forsyth intended to have the pool rebuilt or not was in his view irrelevant. However, the House of Lords overturned that decision and upheld the approach of the trial judge.

The lead judgments were by Lord Jauncey and Lord Lloyd. The other Lords approved their reasoning on the key issues. We will take closer look at the approach adopted by Lord Lloyd because of the authority used in support.

GUIDED CASE READING 9.1
Ruxley Electronics and Construction Ltd v Forsyth [1996] 1 AC 344

When you read the extracts of the judgment by Lord Lloyd try to identify:

- why the damages for reinstatement was rejected
- the test to be applied when claiming damages for reinstatement

[After detailing the facts and then the decisions of the previous courts, Lord Lloyd referred to the aim of damages as being compensation for loss rather than to punish the breaching party, citing by Parke B in *Robinson v Harman*]

In building cases, the **pecuniary loss** is almost always measured in one of two ways; either the difference in value of the work done or the cost of reinstatement. Where the cost of reinstatement is less than the difference in value, the measure of damages will invariably be the cost of reinstatement. By claiming the difference in value the plaintiff would be failing to take reasonable steps to mitigate his loss. In many ordinary cases, too, where reinstatement presents no special problem, the cost of reinstatement will be the obvious measure of damages, even where there is little or no difference in value, or where the difference in value is hard to assess. This is why it is often said that the cost of reinstatement is the ordinary measure of damages for defective performance under a building contract.

pecuniary loss
means financial loss.

> Lord Lloyd here sets out the general rule that the cost of reinstatement (or the cost of cure) is the preferred option in construction cases—and indeed in most ordinary cases, though for different reasons.

But it is not the only measure of damages. Sometimes it is the other way round. This was first made clear in the celebrated judgment of Cardozo J. giving the majority opinion in the Court of Appeals of New York in *Jacob & Youngs v. Kent*, 129 N.E. 889.

In that case the building owner specified that the plumbing should be carried out with galvanized piping of 'Reading manufacture'. By an oversight, the builder used piping of a different manufacture. The plaintiff builder sued for the balance of his account. The defendant, as in the instant case, counter-claimed the cost of replacing the pipe work even though it would have meant demolishing a substantial part of the completed structure, at great expense. Cardozo J. pointed out, at p. 891, that there is 'no general license to install whatever, in the builder's judgment, may be regarded as "just as good." ' But he went on to consider the measure of damages in the following paragraph:

> However, this is a general principle and does not have to hold true in all cases. There might be valid reasons for using difference in value as the measure of loss, and one example is the case from New York referred to here, which has some similarities with *Ruxley*. Here, again, a minor departure was made from specifications, with no material reduction in value.

'[2] In the circumstances of this case, we think the measure of the allowance is not the cost of replacement, which would be great, but the difference in value, which would be either nominal or nothing . . . It is true that in most cases the cost of replacement is the measure. . .. The owner is entitled to the money which will permit him to complete, unless the cost of completion is grossly and unfairly out of proportion to the good to be attained. When that is true, the measure is the difference in value. Specifications call, let us say, for a foundation built of granite quarried in Vermont. On the completion of the

> In his judgment on that case, the famous US jurist Cardozo J made clear that while he did not wish to give builders license to do anything they liked as long as there was no difference in value to what was received, minor departures from specifications which resulted in no reduction of value could not justify awarding the cost of reconstruction as damages.

building, the owner learns that through the blunder of a sub-contractor part of the foundation has been built of granite of the same quality quarried in New Hampshire. The measure of allowance is not the cost of reconstruction. There may be omissions of that which could not afterwards be supplied exactly as called for by the contract without taking down the building to its foundations, and at the same time the omission may not affect the value of the building for use or otherwise, except so slightly as to be hardly appreciable.'

Cardozo J.'s judgment is important, because it establishes two principles, which I believe to be correct, and which are directly relevant to the present case; first, the cost of reinstatement is not the appropriate measure of damages if the expenditure would be out of all proportion to the benefit to be obtained, and, secondly, the appropriate measure of damages in such a case is the difference in value, even though it would result in a nominal award.

[Some additional authority for the same point was then addressed. One was *Bellgrove v. Eldridge*, 90 C.L.R. 613 from the High Court of Australia. The other was a judgment from the House of Lords in *East Ham Corporation v. Bernard Sunley & Sons Ltd.* [1966] A.C. 406. There Lord Cohen allowed reinstatement damages because it was not unreasonable to do so].

One other very recent authority may be mentioned, although it is currently subject to appeal to your Lordships' House. In *Darlington Borough Council v. Wiltshier Northern Ltd.* [1995] 1 W.L.R. 68, 79, Steyn L.J. said:

'in the case of a building contract, the *prima facie* rule is cost of cure, i.e. the cost of remedying the defect: *East Ham Corporation v. Bernard Sunley & Sons Ltd.* [1966] A.C. 406. But where the cost of remedying the defects involves expense out of all proportion to the benefit which could accrue from it, the court is entitled to adopt the alternative measure of difference of the value of the works . . .'

. . .

If the court takes the view that it would be unreasonable for the plaintiff to insist on reinstatement, as where, for example, the expense of the work involved would be out of all proportion to the benefit to be obtained, then the plaintiff will be confined to the difference in value. If the judge had assessed the difference in value in the present case at, say, £5,000, I have little doubt that the Court of Appeal would have taken that figure rather than £21,560. The difficulty arises because the judge has, in the light of the expert evidence, assessed the difference in value as nil. But that cannot make reasonable what he has found to be unreasonable.

. . .

Intention

I fully accept that the courts are not normally concerned with what a plaintiff does with his damages. But it does not follow that intention is not relevant to reasonableness, at least in those cases where the plaintiff does not intend to reinstate. Suppose in the present case Mr. Forsyth had died, and the action had been continued by his executors. Is it to be supposed that they would be able to recover the cost of reinstatement, even though they intended to put the property on the market without delay?

There is, as Staughton L.J. observed, a good deal of authority to the effect that intention may be relevant to a claim for damages based on cost of reinstatement. The clearest decisions on the point are those of Sir Robert Megarry V.-C. in *Tito v. Waddell* (No. 2) [1977] Ch. 106, and Oliver J. in *Radford v. De Froberville* [1977] 1 W.L.R. 1262 . . .

The effect of this, according to Lord Lloyd, was that the cost of reinstatement should not be used where it would result in disproportionate sums being awarded, and in those cases difference in value was the more acceptable measure. This was supported by other authorities, which imply that the cost of reinstatement should not be used where it would be unreasonable to do so. The statement by Steyn LJ in *Darlington Borough Council v Wiltshier Northern* seems to suggest in particular that where the cost of remedying any defects would be disproportionate this would quality as being 'unreasonable'.

The problem is that the court in *Ruxley* was faced with a decision between an unreasonable result (achieved through applying the cost of cure measure) and one in which the claimant got nothing at all (the effect of using the difference in value measure). But Lord Lloyd was clear that just because the difference in value measure would result in only nominal damages did not justify leaping to the disproportionate effect of applying the cost of cure measure. In other words, the cost of cure measure should definitely be avoided in these circumstances.

The judgment then turned to the next key issue, which was whether it was relevant that Forsyth apparently had no intention to actually use his damages award to rebuild the swimming pool. The general rule is that the court has no interest in what the innocent party intends to do with damages awarded after a breach. It can spend the money as it sees fit. However, the absence of an intention to use the award to rebuild is relevant to the reasonableness of making the award. Lord Lloyd cited some authorities in support of this.

In the present case the judge found as a fact that Mr. Forsyth's stated intention of rebuilding the pool would not persist for long after the litigation had been concluded. In these circumstances it would be 'mere pretence' to say that the cost of rebuilding the pool is the loss which he has in fact suffered. This is the critical distinction between the present case, and the example given by Staughton L.J. of a man who has had his watch stolen. In the latter case, the plaintiff is entitled to recover the value of the watch, because that is the true measure of his loss. He can do what he wants with the damages. But if, as the judge found, Mr. Forsyth had no intention of rebuilding the pool, he has lost nothing except the difference in value, if any.

...

Does Mr. Forsyth's undertaking to spend any damages which he may receive on rebuilding the pool make any difference? Clearly not. He cannot be allowed to create a loss, which does not exist, in order to punish the defendants for their breach of contract. The basic rule of damages, to which exemplary damages are the only exception, is that they are compensatory not punitive.

Forsyth clearly had no intention of using his award to rebuild the pool and this made the cost of cure measure a 'pretence'—no cure would take place. Staughton LJ in the Court of Appeal had used the illustration of a stolen watch—if somebody has a watch stolen he or she is entitled to the value of the watch (because that is what was lost) but the money can be used for any purpose. As Lord Lloyd pointed out, though, if Forsyth was not going to rebuild the pool he would have lost nothing—he would still have a perfectly functional pool. He is therefore entirely unlike the person with the stolen watch.

Lord Lloyd concluded by making an argument based on the underlying principle of contract damages—that they are to compensate rather than punish. Forsyth was simply 'creating' a loss by seizing on a minor defect in order to make the appellants suffer for the breach, and this could not be allowed. To award him the cost of cure would be to overcompensate him for his loss.

In summary, where the breach of a construction contract—and presumably of any contract in general—causes physical damage or defects, the cost of cure (or reinstatement) will be the normal award, but only if it is reasonable to use that measure. This means that the amount awarded is not disproportionate to the loss suffered, and that the innocent party actually intends to use the money to remedy the defect(s) in question. The high cost was therefore not the main reason for the decision in *Ruxley*. The emphasis was on it being disproportionate to the loss suffered. The contract was for a usable pool and the one that was built was usable. It was even safe for diving, though such a use was not specified in the contract. It was slightly too shallow. But this had no material effect on its value. An award of £21,000 would therefore far outweigh Forsyth's loss, and could not be sensibly called compensation.

 THINKING POINTS

If the pool was built to only 4ft deep, what difference would that have made?

Generally speaking, courts do not require a damages award to be spent in a certain way. With that in mind, why was Forsyth's intention about rebuilding the pool such a big issue? The trial judge had not believed that Forsyth wanted damages to actually correct the breach. The House of Lords made use of that conclusion. However, their Lordships did not use Forsyth's intention as a basis to refuse damages. Instead, it was relevant to the question of whether there was any loss suffered. If Forsyth had no intention to rebuild the pool, it showed he was satisfied with the pool being 6ft 9. Therefore, awarding him the cost of reinstatement would simply have the effect of punishing the builders for their breach, and contract damages are not awarded to punish a party for their breach. That might lead us to wonder what would have happened if Forsyth had rebuilt the pool and then claimed damages. On that basis, reinstatement damages could have been less unreasonable. That being said, on its own it might not have been enough to justify reinstatement. After all, a claimant is required to show that he or she has behaved reasonably to mitigate his or her losses after a breach, and rebuilding the pool in the circumstances would hardly seem to satisfy this requirement.

THINKING POINTS

- Should the intention of the claimant regarding correcting the breach be relevant?
- Should it make a difference if the claimant repairs the defect and then makes a claim?

Ultimately the House of Lords ratified the trial judge's 'loss of amenity' award. The pool builders never challenged the award. Instead, in the House of Lords, it was Forsyth's Counsel who argued that the award had no legal basis. Lord Lloyd noted the reason behind this tactical move. If the loss of amenity award had no basis, then the court would be left with two choices. It could award the difference in value, which was nothing. Alternatively, it could award the full cost of reinstatement. The point is that Forsyth's counsel was hoping to box the House of Lords into an 'all or nothing' choice, and thus making it go for the cost of reinstatement (rather than nothing). However, Lord Lloyd, implied that even if there had been no basis for a loss of amenity award, it would have made no difference—insisting on the cost of reinstatement would still be unreasonable. That is, he would have preferred to have given nothing at all rather than far too much.

→ CROSS-REFERENCE
For the discussion of the legal basis of the loss of amenity award see 9.7.2.

A common criticism of *Ruxley* is that it might allow a party to deliver less performance than it should. A party could 'cut corners' provided the cost of reinstatement is going to be disproportionate to the loss suffered. They would only be liable for loss of amenity and even that claim might be rejected. In that sense, the approach taken in *Ruxley* does not protect the expectation (performance) interest fully. Alternatively, it can be argued that the need to protect the expectation (performance) interest is not the only objective in awarding damages. The damages should not also over-compensate the innocent party, which would effectively punish the party in breach. These objectives have to be balanced against each other.

As expected, later cases have applied the approach from *Ruxley*. The case of *Birse Construction Ltd v Eastern Telegraph Co. Ltd* [2004] EWHC 2512 is a good example. It concerned a contract for the construction of a building. When it was complete, there were some defects but, instead of trying to repair the defects, the building was put up sale by the owner. The price was the same as it would have been without the defects which indicated there was no difference in value arising from the defects. When the builder claimed the money owned, the owner counterclaimed for breach. The judge observed that ordinarily, the measure is the cost of repair. However, following *Ruxley*, the use of that measure has to be reasonable. Since the building was being sold, there was no intention to repair it. And since the value was the same, it would be sold without any loss. On that basis, such an award would have been out of proportion with the loss and so awarding the cost of repair was considered unreasonable. The judge also rejected the loss of amenity claim. Again, that was because no steps were taken to correct the defects. This indicated that the owner had not really suffered any loss of amenity. Since there was no difference in value, the owner was awarded nominal damages of £2.

A similar approach was adopted in *Harrison v Shepard Homes Ltd* [2011] EWHC 1811. The case concerned some houses that were built with a slight defect in their foundations that caused some of them to crack slightly. The expert evidence showed that the cracks were cosmetic and there was no real risk of the buildings moving or being unstable. The owners claimed the cost of repair, which meant the cost of replacing the foundations. This claim was rejected as unreasonable because the effects were so minor. Essentially, the cost of repair was disproportionate to any resulting benefit. Also, the judge pointed out that the owners would simply sell the properties and use the money to buy better homes. On that basis, the difference (the reduction) in value was awarded.

KEY POINTS

- The cost of reinstatement is the usual measure of damages. However, it will not be awarded where it would be unreasonable to do so.
- The cost of reinstatement could be unreasonable where the cost of reinstatement would be disproportionate to the loss suffered.
- The absence of an intention to repair would make it more unlikely that the cost of reinstatement measure would be seen as reasonable where it indicates that no loss was suffered.

9.4 Expenses Claims—Compensation for Reliance on the Contract

The aim of damages is to compensate the claimant for any loss suffered as a result of the breach—that is, to put the claimant in the position it should have been in had the contract been performed. Another way of putting it is that the aim is to protect the claimant's expectation (performance) interest. However, sometimes it is too difficult to work out the value of the expectation (performance) interest. It might be that the claimant could have made a lot of money from performance. Equally, it might be that the claimant could have made very little from performance. In such circumstances, an alternative measure would be preferred. The courts have allowed innocent parties to choose to recover their wasted expenses. These are the costs incurred from relying on the contract. For that reason, traditionally, such an award has been classed as protecting the 'reliance interest'. The key difference is that, in this case, damages are to compensate for wasted expenditure rather than expected loss. Such an award puts the claimant *back* in the position they were in before the contract was made. These expenses are losses, and so the award is still compensating for loss.

9.4.1 The Basis for Allowing Damages for Wasted Expenditure

The traditional case on damages for wasted expenditure is *Anglia Television Ltd v Reed* [1972] 1 QB 60. Here the TV company planned to make a TV film. In preparation for the film, some money was spent on designs, props, and fees for staff. The company then contracted with the actor Robert Reed for the lead role. Further expenses were paid but a few days later, Reed pulled out of the project. This refusal to perform was an obvious breach. The company was unable to find a replacement for the role and had to abandon the film. Ordinarily, a claim for damages would reflect the performance interest. That would be the lost profit expected from the film. The problem was that such a loss was impossible to assess. Any figure claimed would be too speculative because it would depend on the success of the film. While a TV film will not be a success or flop to the extent that a cinematic release can be, it is still very difficult to predict in advance how much money one will make. So instead, the company claimed the £2750 in expenses it had wasted. That figure was for all of the expenses used on the film project. It included expenses incurred both before and after the formation of the contract with Reed. Reed argued that he should only be liable for expenses incurred once he had entered the contract.

The judgment of the Court of Appeal was by Lord Denning MR (with whom the other judges agreed). In allowing the total claim to succeed, Lord Denning MR stated some principles about such claims.

> It seems to me that a plaintiff in such a case as this has an election: he can either claim for loss of profits; or for his wasted expenditure. But he must elect between them. He cannot claim both. If he has not suffered any loss of profits—or if he cannot prove what his profits would have been—he can

claim in the alternative the expenditure which has been thrown away, that is, wasted, by reason of the breach. That is shown by *Cullinane v. British "Rema" Manufacturing Co. Ltd.* [1954] 1 Q.B. 292, 303, 308.

If the plaintiff claims the wasted expenditure, he is not limited to the expenditure incurred after the contract was concluded. He can claim also the expenditure incurred before the contract, provided that it was such as would reasonably be in the contemplation of the parties as likely to be wasted if the contract was broken. Applying that principle here, it is plain that, when Mr. Reed entered into this contract, he must have known perfectly well that much expenditure had already been incurred on director's fees and the like. He must have contemplated—or, at any rate, it is reasonably to be imputed to him—that if he broke his contract, all that expenditure would be wasted, whether or not it was incurred before or after the contract. He must pay damages for all the expenditure so wasted and thrown away. This view is supported by the recent decision of Brightman J. in *Lloyd v. Stanbury* [1971] 1 W.L.R. 535. There was a contract for the sale of land. In anticipation of the contract—and before it was concluded—the purchaser went to much expense in moving a caravan to the site and in getting his furniture there. The seller afterwards entered into a contract to sell the land to the purchaser, but afterwards broke his contract. The land had not increased in value, so the purchaser could not claim for any loss of profit. But Brightman J. held, at p. 547, that he could recover the cost of moving the caravan and furniture, because it was "within the contemplation of the parties when the contract was signed". That decision is in accord with the correct principle, namely, that wasted expenditure can be recovered when it is wasted by reason of the defendant's breach of contract. It is true that, if the defendant had never entered into the contract, he would not be liable, and the expenditure would have been incurred by the plaintiff without redress; but, the defendant having made his contract and broken it, it does not lie in his mouth to say he is not liable, when it was because of his breach that the expenditure has been wasted.

The judgment indicates that ordinarily, a claimant has a choice between two types of compensation. The claim can be for wasted expenditure or for the loss of performance (i.e. the lost bargain like lost profits). The claimant cannot have both the wasted expenditure and damages for the lost bargain. This is because if the contract had been performed, the expenditure would have been lost anyway. The difference is it would have been made up and covered by profits. On that basis, if a court awards the amount to be made from performance and the expenses incurred, the claimant would be overcompensated. It would be like receiving goods contracted for but without paying anything. Clearly that would put the claimant in a much better position than that expected from performance.

KEY POINTS

Ordinarily, the claimant has a choice to claim for the lost bargain *or* the wasted expenditure resulting from the breach.

The wasted expenditure is not limited to the amount spent after the contract was entered into. It can cover expenditure paid before the contract too. What matters is that the expenditure was wasted as a result of the breach. In *Reed*, the company paid for a number of things in preparation for the filming. The contract with Reed was then made. Clearly this previous expenditure was not in response to (or a result of) the contract with Reed. However, the breach of Reed's contract resulted in all the expenditure being wasted because it was not possible to find another actor in time. This means that the award for wasted expenses is not based on the costs resulting from the making of the contract. Instead, it is based on the losses resulting from the breach.

At the time of contracting, the wasted expenditure must be foreseeable to the defendant. Alternatively, it must be objectively foreseeable, i.e. foreseen by the reasonable person in the defendant's position. This is the justification for imposing liability on the party in breach. The making of the contract might not have caused the relevant expenses. However, Reed knew (or should have known) the film could be abandoned as a result of his refusal. This meant that when he entered into the contract, he appeared to be accepting the risks of causing such losses. That, in turn, provides a justification for imposing that loss on Reed following his breach.

9.4.2 When Wasted Expenditure Cannot Be Claimed: The Problem with Bad Bargains

Ordinarily, a claimant will have the choice of compensation for wasted expenditure (the reliance measure) or the expectation (performance) loss. However, the choice is not unrestricted. The award of wasted expenditure is not available where the contract was a bad bargain for the claimant. Such a bad bargain is where the benefit expected was going to be too low to cover the expenditure. These bad deals can happen, and when they do the innocent party might be very relieved to see the contract breached by the other party. It might mean that the breach will allow it to avoid what could have been a more serious loss. However, in these circumstances lost performance damages would be of no use. After all, had the contract been performed, there would not have been a profit. In such circumstances, a claim for wasted expenditure would seem like a good idea. That way, in theory, the losses arising from relying on the contract would be recoverable in damages. However, the courts have been clear that such a claim for expenditure will not be allowed. The reason for this is simple. Such damages would put the claimant in a *better* position than if the contract had been performed. In other words, it would not be compensating for losses caused by the breach, and instead, it would be compensating for the loss caused by making a bad deal, as shown by Figure 9.2.

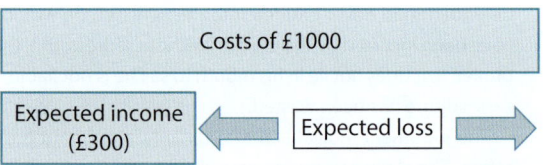

> If the contract was performed, the claimant would suffer a £700 loss. If the costs were awarded, the claimant would suffer no loss.

> Costs of £1000

> Expected income (£300)　←　Expected loss　→

Figure 9.2
A claim for expenses following a bad bargain

The authorities for the limits on wasted expenditure claims start with *C & P Haulage v Middleton* [1983] 1 WLR 1461. Here the defendant tenant rented a garage from which to run his business. The contract was renewable every six months. The tenant spent money on making the property suitable for his use. That involved having an electricity supply installed and having a wall built and certain equipment installed. However, the contract contained an important term about any fixtures installed (e.g. equipment installed in the property). It stated that if the contract ended, all fixtures would become owned by the claimant landlord. The dispute arose because the claimant landlord instructed the defendant to leave the property. This was done ten weeks before the contract was due to end and was a breach. In response, the defendant left and was given permission by the Council to run his business from his garage at home. That meant he could continue trading but with the added bonus of not having to pay rent. In such circumstances, the profit made was more than what it would have been had the contract been performed. In other words, the breach did not cause any lost profit. When the tenant was sued for some outstanding rent, he counterclaimed for his money spend on the property. The question was whether the tenant was entitled to be compensated for that expenditure.

The Court of Appeal confirmed that the tenant was not entitled to his expenditure. It was observed that had the contract been performed, it would have ended in ten weeks. At that point, under the contract, the fixtures would have been owned by the landlord anyway. So, compensating for the tenant's expenditure would have put him in a better position than if the contract had been performed. On this, Ackner LJ made the following observation:

> It is not the function of the courts where there is a breach of contract knowingly, as this would be the case, to put a plaintiff in a better financial position that if the contract had been properly performed.

On that basis, the tenant was awarded nominal damages of £10.

KEY POINTS

Wasted expenditure will not be awarded if it puts the claimant in a position that is better than if the contract had been performed.

The significance of the *C & P Haulage* case was made clear by Teare J in *Omak Maritime Ltd v Mamola Challenger Shipping Ltd* [2010] EWHC 2026 (Comm). It concerned a long-term charterparty agreement (the hire of a ship and crew). The charterer ended the contract and was in breach for doing so. At the time, the standard market rate for the hire of ships was much more than the contract rate. In fact, the market rate was around $7500 a day more. That allowed the ship owner to enter a new contract with another charterer and make more money. This meant that there would have been no lost profit resulting from the breach. For that reason, following the breach, the shipowner claimed for the cost of preparing the ship for the charterparty. The claim was rejected by Teare J and his judgment explained the limits of expenditure claims:

> [42] I consider that the weight of authority strongly suggests that reliance losses are a species of expectation losses and that they are neither,. . ."fundamentally different" nor awarded on a different "juridical basis of claim". That they are a species of expectation losses is supported by the decision of the Court of Appeal in *C & P Haulage v Middleton* and by very persuasive authorities in the United States, Canada and Australia.
>
> . . .
>
> [44] It seems to me that the expectation loss analysis does provide a rational and sensible explanation for the award of damages in wasted expenditure cases. The expenditure which is sought to be recovered is incurred in expectation that the contract will be performed. It therefore appears to me to be rational to have regard to the position that the Claimant would have been in had the contract been performed.
>
> [45] If there were an independent principle pursuant to which expenditure incurred in expectation of the performance of a contract was recoverable without regard to what the position would have been had the contract been performed the Defendant would in effect underwrite the Claimant's decision to enter the contract. If the contract was unwise from his point of view, because his expenses were likely to exceed any gross profit, it is difficult to understand why the Defendant should pay damages in an amount equal to that expenditure. His breach has not caused that loss. The Claimant's expenditure should only be recoverable where the likely gross profit would at least cover that expenditure.

The judgment confirmed that usually a claimant can choose the wasted expenditure or the amount reflecting lost performance. However, wasted expenditure cannot be awarded where the claimant has made a bad a bargain. That is where the profit expected from the contract would not cover the expenses. The reasoning was based on two key factors.

First, if the profit would be less than the expenses, the award of expenditure has a strange result. It would put the claimant in a position that would be better than if the contract had been performed. In effect, it does not compensate for loss caused by the breach. Instead, it would cover the loss caused by making a bad deal. That is what Teare J meant by saying that the award would be 'underwriting' the claimant's bad decision.

Secondly, the limit applied to wasted expenditure claims has to have a conceptual basis. It cannot apply just because it is fair to the party in breach. That is why Teare J said that such claims are simply another way of compensating for lost performance. It is expected that such costs would be covered by the performance. When that is prevented by a breach, the award is made. If the costs would not have been covered by performance in the first place, then it follows that there is no need for an award of damages. Put more simply, ordinarily the profits gained from a contract will cover expenses, and so ordinarily, the expectation measure (which compensates for lost profit) will automatically include compensation for wasted expenses. It is only where the expected profits are impossible to assess that it becomes necessary to consider the wasted expenses in their own right. This suggests that the so-called 'expectation' and 'reliance' measures have basically the same conceptual basis.

9.5 Damages for a Lost Chance

Following a breach, the innocent party might suffer loss that is difficult to assess or value. Such a loss should still be claimable. What matters is that there has been loss as a result of the breach. As long as it is clear that a loss has been suffered, the courts will figure out its value. This includes circumstances in which there has been a loss of a chance or opportunity—such as a competition or auction. In such a contract, it is not certain that the chance would have resulted in the innocent party gaining something. But what is certain, it is that the innocent party has been deprived of an actual chance to gain something.

The case of *Chaplin v Hicks* [1911] 2 KB 786 is the key authority on loss of chance claims. Here, a beauty competition had been held and the claimant had got through to an advanced stage in which there were only 50 performers left. These were each to be interviewed and, after the interview, 12 of them would be given a job in a theatre. Chaplin was selected for interview but was notified of this too late, in breach of contract, causing her to miss it. She then brought an action for her loss. She could not sue for the lost income she would have made in the theatre because she could not prove that she would have been one of the twelve selected. For that reason, the breach did not result in the income being lost. However, she had lost a *chance* of getting the income, and at first instance damages were awarded on that basis. The award was determined by a jury and the Court of Appeal then upheld that decision. Vaughan-Williams LJ explained the why the award could be made:

> It was said that the plaintiff's chance of winning a prize turned on such a number of contingencies that it was impossible for any one, even after arriving at the conclusion that the plaintiff had lost her opportunity by the breach, to say that there was any assessable value of that loss. . . I am unable to agree with that contention. I agree that the presence of all the contingencies upon which the gaining of the prize might depend makes the calculation not only difficult but incapable of being carried out with certainty or precision. The proposition is that, whenever the contingencies on which the result depends are numerous and difficult to deal with, it is impossible to recover any damages for the loss of the chance or opportunity of winning the prize. . . .I do not agree with the contention that, if certainty is impossible of attainment, the damages for a breach of contract are unassessable. . . I only wish to deny with emphasis that, because precision cannot be arrived at, the jury has no function in the assessment of damages.
>
> . . .In the case of a breach of a contract for the delivery of goods the damages are usually supplied by the fact of there being a market in which similar goods can be immediately bought, and the difference between the contract price and the price given for the substituted goods in the open market is the measure of damages; that rule has been always recognized. Sometimes, however, there is no market for the particular class of goods; but no one has ever suggested that, because there is no market, there are no damages. In such a case the jury must do the best they can, and it may be that the amount of their verdict will really be a matter of guesswork. But the fact that damages cannot be assessed with certainty does not relieve the wrong-doer of the necessity of paying damages for his breach of contract. . .It is true that no market can be said to exist. None of the fifty competitors could have gone into the market and sold her right; her right was a personal right and incapable of transfer. But a jury might well take the view that such a right, if it could have been transferred, would have been of such a value that every one would recognize that a good price could be obtained for it. . .The jury came to the conclusion that the taking away from the plaintiff of the opportunity of competition . . . deprived the plaintiff of something which had a monetary value

On the facts, it was clear Chaplin had lost the chance of being one of the twelve selected. Vaughan-Williams LJ made it clear that if the loss is difficult to quantify as an amount of money, damages can still be awarded. Reference was made to the sale of goods where the difference in value award is based on the difference between the contract price and market price. Where there is no market price, damages are still awarded even if it involves 'guesswork'. In this case, it was for the jury to work out the value of the loss. If that was not allowed, the claimant would not be compensated for her lost opportunity resulting from the breach. The jury in the court awarded compensation of £100, which was a lot of money back then. It reflected the jury's assessment of the value of the interview and the chance it represented.

?! THINKING POINTS

Is it fair to make the defendant pay damages when the value of the loss is so uncertain? Would it have been more unfair to the claimant if no award had been made?

The scope and operation of the principles in *Chaplin* were addressed in *Allied Maples Group Ltd v Simmons and Simmonds* [1995] 4 All ER 907. There, a breach by the defendant solicitors had caused a loss of a chance. A number of arguments were raised in defence. One of these questioned when a loss of a chance should result in damages. They argued that the chance should be one that had at least a 50% likelihood of success. This was rejected by the Court of Appeal. According to Stuart-Smith LJ, the chance needs to be a 'substantial rather than a speculative one'. In other words, all that is needed is a clear lost opportunity. However, it is likely that the probability of success will be relevant to the amount awarded.

Another argument concerned the type of chance that can result in damages. In *Chaplin*, the chance was for something that could be beneficial. In the reasoning of *Chaplin*, Vaughan-Williams LJ referred to the 'valuable right' that was lost. In contrast, in *Allied Maples* the chance lost was the chance to avoid a liability. On that basis, the defendants argued that it was different and not supported by *Chaplin*. Again, the Court of Appeal rejected this argument. Stuart-Smith LJ observed that 'there is no difference in principle between the chance of gaining a benefit and the chance of avoiding a liability'.

9.6 Damages for Non-financial Loss

We already know that financial losses are claimable. Typically, such losses come in the form of lost profit, the difference in value, or the cost of repair. The financial loss could even be wasted expenditure or a lost chance. However, it is possible for a breach to cause a loss that is not financial. Consider the enjoyment you might expect to result from performance. If a breach prevents such enjoyment, can you claim damages to reflect that loss of enjoyment? Likewise, what if a breach causes harm to your reputation; or even physical or psychological harm? Over the years, the courts have had to deal with such claims. These are generally referred to as claims for 'non-financial' or 'non-pecuniary' losses.

9.6.1 Damages for Pain and Suffering

Defective consumer goods are the most obvious example of a breach that could cause pain and suffering. When goods are defective, that is a breach of the term concerning quality included in consumer contracts. Such a defect might make the goods dangerous so that the buyer or user is injured by the goods. An example would be a mobile phone battery that overheats and burns in your pocket. This would cause financial loss in terms of the money spent. It would also cause financial loss

→ CROSS-REFERENCE
For the discussion of implied terms and terms included in consumer contracts see 6.5.2.

from the physical damage to your clothes. Such a breach could also cause pain and suffering. In the context of consumer goods, it is clear that damages can be awarded for pain and suffering resulting from a breach.

Such a category of claimable loss is clear from *Godley v Perry* [1960] 1 All ER 36. In this case a six-year-old boy had bought a plastic catapult from a newsagent. Due to a defect, the catapult broke during normal use and, as a result, the boy lost an eye. Edmond Davis J in the High Court awarded £2500 in damages following the breach. In those days, the award represented a considerable sum (enough to buy a house). According to the judge, the award was for the loss of an eye, the pain and suffering, and the discomfort of having to remove an artificial eye each day. The award was not itemised any further and so it is not clear how much of the award was for pain and suffering. However, it is clear that such a type of loss is claimable as damages following a breach of contract.

9.6.2 Damages for Physical Inconvenience

A breach of contract could directly cause the innocent party to experience physical inconvenience. When such a loss results, it is possible to claim damages.

In *Bailey v Bullock* [1950] 2 All ER 1167, the claimant owned a house which was let to tenants. He then planned to move in with his family. To do so, the claimant instructed the defendant, a solicitor, to end the tenancy. Unfortunately, the solicitor failed to take steps to end the tenancy. This meant that the claimant and his wife had to stay with his in-laws where they had to share a small bedroom with their child. When sued, the defendant accepted there had been a breach of contract. The issue in the case concerned damages and what loss was claimable. Barry J in the High Court awarded £300 for *physical* discomfort and inconvenience which was a direct result of the breach. Barry J also made clear that the award was not compensation for any loss of status or embarrassment suffered by the claimant. Likewise, it was not for annoyance or mental distress.

Another example that is often cited is *Hobbs v London & South Western Railway* (1875) LR 10 QB 111. In breach of contract, the defendant railway company took the claimant and his family to the wrong station. This meant they had to walk five miles in the rain. The subsequent claim resulted in the four judges of the Divisional Court awarding £8 as compensation for physical inconvenience and discomfort. The loss was a result of the defendant not performing their contractual obligations.

9.6.3 Damages for Harm to Reputation

It is possible for a contract to be breached in such a way that it harms the reputation of the innocent party. A damages claim for such harm was made in *Addis v Gramophone* [1909] AC 488. The claimant in this case had been wrongfully dismissed from his job as a manager. Under the contract, the employer could end it by giving six months' notice. Usually, such a notice period means that you work and get paid as normal until the end of the period. However, in this case, once the notice had been given, the employer hired a replacement manager. This meant that the claimant was unable to earn an income during the notice period. For that reason, the employer was liable for breach. The claimant sought to recover his lost income of £15 a week plus the commission he could have earned. More importantly, he wanted extra damages to reflect the harsh and humiliating way the contract was breached. He argued that it had hurt his feelings and harmed his reputation. The House of Lords allowed the standard claim for his lost income. However, it did not allow damages for the injured feelings or harmed reputation. The judgment by Lord Atkinson focussed on the claim for the non-financial loss and explained why it had to fail:

> I have been unable to find any case decided in this country in which any countenance is given to the notion that a dismissed employee can recover in the shape of exemplary damages for illegal dismissal, in effect damages for defamation, for it amounts to that. . .

I have always understood that damages for breach of contract were in the nature of compensation, not punishment. . .

In many other cases of breach of contract there may be circumstances of malice, fraud, defamation, or violence, which would sustain an action of tort as an alternative remedy to an action for breach of contract. If one should select the former mode of redress, he may, no doubt, recover exemplary damages, or what is sometimes styled vindictive damages; but if he should choose to seek redress in the form of an action for breach of contract. . .One of these consequences is, I think, this: that he is to be paid adequate compensation in money for the loss of that which he would have received had his contract been kept, and no more.

I can conceive nothing more objectionable and embarrassing in litigation than trying in effect an action of libel or slander as a matter of aggravation in an action for illegal dismissal, the defendant being permitted, as he must in justice be permitted, to traverse the defamatory sense, rely on privilege, or raise every point which he could raise in an independent action brought for the alleged libel or slander itself.

In my opinion, exemplary damages ought not to be, and are not according to any true principle of law, recoverable in such an action as the present, and the sums awarded to the plaintiff should therefore be decreased by the amount at which they have been estimated, and credit for that item should not be allowed in his account.

The claim for harmed reputation and injured feelings was rejected. According to the House of Lords, such losses go beyond the compensatory aim of damages in contract. Allowing such an award would punish the defendant for the way the contract was breached. The point is that damages in contract are supposed to be for the consequences of the breach itself. The damages are not for the consequences of the *manner* of the breach.

The same point was made by the House of Lords in *Johnson v Unisys Ltd* [2001] UKHL 13. There the manner of the breach had caused a nervous breakdown. However, no award was made because the breakdown was not a result of the breach. Instead it was a result of the *way* the contract was breached. The reason for this distinction is that if damages were awarded for the *way* in which a contract is breached (in addition to the actual breach) this creates a further obligation. It means if a party breaches a contract, it has to be done in a nice way to avoid further liability. This does not reflect the expectations of commercial parties and would be impossible to assess. In addition, such an obligation to be nice (when breaching the contract), would not usually be a term of the contract. The award of such damages would therefore not put the innocent party in the position it would have been had the contract been performed. Instead, such damages would simply punish the party in breach for its behaviour.

KEY POINTS

Damages are for the loss resulting from the actual breach rather than the way the contract was breached.

Lord Atkinson made it very clear that contract law is not the place for damages for harmed reputation. Such a loss should be remedied by the tort of defamation. That is the area of law that protects our reputations. If the claim in the case had been successful, it would have allowed for a defamation claim through the back door. In fact, Lord Atkinson appeared to express irritation at the attempt to claim such damages in contract.

The *Addis* case makes it clear that damages cannot be claimed for harmed reputation based on the manner of the breach. That is an ordinary rule for contracts, but what if the actual breach results in a harmed reputation that causes financial loss? Such a financial loss should be claimable depending on the contract. For example, it will be possible to make such a claim where the contract aims to improve a party's reputation. If a breach then causes harm to the innocent party's reputation, that claim should be successful. Essentially, it would be framed as a consequential financial loss resulting from the breach. *Ariel Advertising v Batchelor Peas* is an example of this. The breach caused a loss of sales because the public boycotted the innocent party. The claim was not for a harmed reputation resulting from the *way* the contract was breached. It was for a financial loss caused by the breach itself.

➜ CROSS-REFERENCE

For the facts of *Ariel Advertising v Batchelor Peas* [1938] see 8.7.3.

A similar distinction was made by the House of Lords in *Malik v Bank of Credit and Commerce International* [1998] AC 20. The claimants were former employees of BCCI. This bank collapsed due to serious fraud by the bank's controllers which had been well publicised in the media. Following the collapse of the bank, the claimants (who had nothing to do with the fraud) were made redundant. Like many others, they found they could not get a job in another bank. This difficulty was a result of their past association with the BCCI. Essentially, the fraud had harmed the reputation of the employees. The claimants then brought an action against the BCCI. They argued that the fraud was a breach of their employment contracts with the bank. That breach then caused financial loss because it made it harder to get another job.

The House of Lords allowed the claim and upheld the award of damages. In doing so, a distinction had to be made between damages for harmed reputation and the award made in the case. The judgment by Lord Steyn is useful on this point.

GUIDED CASE READING 9.2
Malik v Bank of Credit and Commerce International [1998] AC 20

When you read the extracts from the judgment by Lord Steyn, try to identify:

▪ how a distinction was made between the claims in this case and the rejected claim in *Addis;*
▪ why it was necessary to recognise an implied term of trust and confidence in the contract.

. . .

The employer's primary case is based on a formulation of the implied term that has been applied at first instance and in the Court of Appeal. It imposes reciprocal duties on the employer and employee . . .. For convenience I will set out the term again. It is expressed to impose an obligation that the employer shall not—

'without reasonable and proper cause, conduct itself in a manner calculated and likely to destroy or seriously damage the relationship of confidence and trust between employer and employee'.

[Academic and judicial authority for the implied term was explained]

The evolution of the implied term of trust and confidence is a fact. It has not yet been indorsed by your Lordships' House. It has proved a workable principle in practice. It has not been the subject of adverse criticism in any decided cases and it has been welcomed in academic writings. I regard the emergence of the implied obligation of mutual trust and confidence as a sound development.

. . .

It is arguable that these relatively senior bank employees may be able to establish as a matter of fact that the corruption associated in the public mind, and in the minds of prospective employers, with the bank may have undermined their employment prospects. They may conceivably be able to prove that in the financial services industry they were regarded as potentially tarnished and therefore undesirable employees to recruit. In that way these particular employees may be able to sustain their assertions of fact that they have suffered financial loss.

. . .

[It was then explained that the fraud by the bank was a breach of the implied term owed to their employees. Lord Steyn continued]

In considering the availability of the remedy of damages it is important to bear in mind that the employees claim damages for financial loss.

> First, it had to be established that there was an implied term in the contracts of employment to the effect that neither employer nor employee would act in such a way as to damage the relationship of confidence and trust between them. This was easily done, because it had already been settled that such a term was implied in employment contracts by lower courts to widespread acceptance. The House of Lords here simply had to affirm this.

> It then fell to the court to decide if that term had been breached and if it had resulted in a financial loss—and ultimately the answer to both these questions was determined to be 'yes'.

That is the issue. It will be recalled that the Court of Appeal decided the case against the employees on the basis that there is a positive rule debarring the recovery of damages in contract for injury to an existing reputation, and that in truth the two employees were claiming damages for injury to their previously existing reputations. For this conclusion the Court of Appeal relied on three decided cases, namely *Addis v Gramophone Co Ltd* [1909] AC 488, [1908–10] All ER Rep 1, *Withers v General Theatre Corp Ltd* [1933] 2 KB 536, [1933] All ER Rep 385 and *O'Laoire v Jackel International Ltd (No 2)* [1991] ICR 718 . . .

The true *ratio decidendi* of the House of Lords decision in *Addis v Gramophone Co Ltd* has long been debated. Some have understood it as authority for the proposition that an employee may not recover damages even for pecuniary loss caused by a breach of contract of the employer which damages the employment prospects of an employee. If *Addis's* case establishes such a rule it is an inroad on traditional principles of contract law. And any such restrictive rule has been criticised by distinguished writers: see Treitel An Outline of the Law of Contract (9th edn, 1995) p. 893 and Burrows Remedies for Torts and Breach of Contract (2nd edn, 1994) pp. 221–225. Moreover, it has been pointed out that Addis's case was decided in 1909 before the development of modern employment law, and long before the evolution of the implied mutual obligation of trust and confidence. Nevertheless, it is necessary to take a closer look at *Addis's* case so far as it affects the issues in this case . . .

[The facts and decisions of Addis were explained]

I would accept, however, that Lord Loreburn LC and the other Law Lords in the majority apparently thought they were applying a special rule applicable to awards of damages for wrongful dismissal. It is, however, far from clear how far the ratio of *Addis's* case extends. It certainly enunciated the principle that an employee cannot recover exemplary or aggravated damages for wrongful dismissal. That is still sound law. The actual decision is only concerned with wrongful dismissal. It is therefore arguable that as a matter of precedent the *ratio* is so restricted. But it seems to me unrealistic not to acknowledge that *Addis's* case is authority for a wider principle. There is a common proposition in the speeches of the majority. That proposition is that damages for breach of contract may only be awarded for breach of contract, and not for loss caused by the manner of the breach. No Law Lord said that an employee may not recover financial loss for damage to his employment prospects caused by a breach of contract. And no Law Lord said that in breach of contract cases compensation for loss of reputation can never be awarded, or that it can only be awarded in cases falling in certain defined categories. *Addis's* case simply decided that the loss of reputation in that particular case could not be compensated because it was not caused by a breach of contract: see Nelson Enonchong 'Contract Damages for Injury to Reputation' (1996) 59 MLR 592 at 596. So analysed *Addis's* case does not bar the claims put forward in the present case . . .

. . .

. . . [T]he present case . . . is based not on the manner of a wrongful dismissal but on a breach of contract which is separate from and independent of the termination of the contract of employment. In my judgment therefore the authorities relied on by Morritt LJ do not on analysis support his conclusion.

The issue is that the decision in *Addis v Gramophone* appears to suggest that an employee cannot recover damages caused by a breach of contract on the part of the employer which harms the employee's reputation. The remedy in those circumstances should, according to the decision in *Addis*, be pursued through the tort of defamation. However, *Addis* is an old case and preceded the development of both modern employment law and the relevant implied term.

Lord Steyn solved the problem by clarifying the real *ratio* of *Addis*. In his view, the effect of the decision in that case was that damages for breach of contract cannot be awarded for the manner of the breach. That did not mean that no employees could ever recover financial losses for damage to their job prospects caused by a breach of contract.

Therefore, *Addis* could be distinguished: it concerned damages sought for the manner of the breach, whereas in the present case the damages were for losses which were a consequence of the breach.

Moreover, the fact that in appropriate cases damages may in principle be awarded for loss of reputation caused by breach of contract is illustrated by a number of cases which Morritt LJ discussed: *Aerial Advertising Co v Batchelors Peas Ltd (Manchester)* [1938] 2 All ER 788, *Foaminol Laboratories Ltd v British Artid Plastics Ltd* [1941] 2 All ER 393 and *Anglo-Continental Holidays Ltd v Typaldos Lines (London) Ltd* [1967] 2 Lloyd's Rep 61. But, unlike Morritt LJ, I regard these cases not as exceptions but as the application of ordinary principles of contract law. Moreover, it is clear that a supplier who delivers contaminated meat to a trader can be sued for loss of commercial reputation involving loss of trade: see *Cointax v Myham & Son* [1913] 2 KB 220 and *GKN Centrax Gears Ltd v Matbro Ltd* [1976] 2 Lloyd's Rep 555. Rhetorically, one may ask, why may a bank manager not sue for loss of professional reputation, if it causes financial loss flowing from a breach of the contract of employment? The speeches of the majority of the House of Lords in *Spring v Guardian Assurance plc* [1994] 3 All ER 129, . . . are also instructive. In that case the majority held that a former employee could recover damages for financial loss which he suffered as a result of his employer's negligent preparation of a reference. The reference affected his reputation. The majority considered that, if the reference had been given while the plaintiff was still employed, his claim could have been brought in contract. On that hypothesis he could have sued in contract for damage to his reputation. The *dicta* in *Spring v Guardian Assurance* show that there is no rule preventing the recovery of damages for injury to reputation where that injury is caused by a breach of contract. The principled position is as follows. Provided that a relevant breach of contract can be established, and the requirements of causation, remoteness and mitigation can be satisfied, there is no good reason why in the field of employment law recovery of financial loss in respect of damage to reputation caused by breach of contract is necessarily excluded . . .

Lord Steyn went on to make clear that it was in fact well established in precedent that if a loss of commercial reputation resulted from a breach, compensation could be given. There was no real difference between a trader whose commercial reputation has been ruined by a supplier delivering contaminated meat, and a banker whose commercial reputation had been ruined by a previous employer having engaged in serious fraud. In both circumstances a term had been breached and a loss suffered as a result. This was in fact 'ordinary principles of contract law' at work.

All of this meant that there was no reason why Malik and the other claimants should not receive compensation for their harmed employment prospects, as this was a result of the breach of the relevant implied term (and not the manner of any breach).

KEY POINTS

If the actual breach (rather than the manner of the breach) harms the reputation of the innocent party, which in turn causes financial loss, damages for that loss are recoverable.

The House of Lords decision in *Malik v BCCI* resulted in over 300 claims by former employees. Such claims will always have problems relating to proof. For example, the claimant has to prove that there was a sufficient disadvantage in the labour market. In addition, it would have to be proven that such a disadvantage was a result of the term breached. In some cases, these factors will be very difficult to satisfy. The later claim in *BCCI v Ali (No.3)* [2002] EWCA Civ 82 is a good example.

The former employees argued that their past association with the bank had caused financial loss. However, the Court of Appeal disagreed and held that the claimants had failed to prove that their failure to get a job was caused by their past association with the bank. This difficulty was anticipated by the House of Lords in *Malik v BCCI*. There, Lord Steyn commented on the problem of causation towards the end of his judgment. In addition, Lord Nicholls warned:

Finally, although the implied term that the business will not be conducted dishonestly is a term which avails all employees, proof of consequential handicap in the labour market may well be much more difficult for some classes of employees than others.

Lord Nicholls then went on to provide an example:

> An employer seeking to employ a messenger, for instance, might be wholly unconcerned by an applicant's former employment in a dishonest business, whereas he might take a different view if he were seeking a senior executive.

The point is that the fraud was a breach of contract. That breach is capable of imposing a stigma on former employees. Other banks might not employ them because they have worked for a fraudulent bank. However, such a stigma or harmed reputation would not apply to every former employee. For many, being formerly employed by a fraudulent bank would have no impact on their job prospects.

9.7 Damages for Loss of Enjoyment (and Other Types of Mental Distress)

Another important issue in damages concerns claims for different types of mental distress like loss of enjoyment. It is not difficult to imagine that a breach could result in such distress or loss of enjoyment. Likewise, a breach could result in injured feelings, upset, disappointment and so on. Similarly, a breach could result in anxiety and stress. We can quibble over the meaning of each of these words—anxiety, for example, sounds far more severe than disappointment. But essentially, all of these terms are simply different grades of the same thing, which is generally described as 'mental distress'. For that reason, it is important that we don't assign too much weight to the language used to describe these losses. Whichever form of this type of loss is being claimed, the same precedents and principles are applied. The question is, to what extent can you claim for such a loss following a breach?

In *Addis v Gramophone*, the claimant sought damages for his harmed reputation. In addition, the claimant wanted damages for his injured feelings and distress. Just like with the harmed reputation, the House of Lords rejected the claim for injured feelings. We know now that the case really excludes damages to compensate for the *manner* of the breach. However, previously, the case was given a wider significance. It represented a general rule against damages for non-financial losses like mental distress and upset. That remains the default principle, but an exception has developed.

The leading case on this exception is *Farley v Skinner* [2001] UKHL 49. This was a decision by the House of Lords, but before we turn to that case, it is useful to address the cases leading to it. Doing so helps to develop a more detailed understanding of the significance of the *Farley* case.

9.7.1 The Development of the Exception Allowing Damages for Types of Mental Distress

The initial major step was taken by Lord Denning MR in *Jarvis v Swan Tours* [1973] QB 233. The claimant was a solicitor. He booked a Christmas skiing holiday for £63.45 with the defendant. The brochure described the holiday as a 'house party'. This included a 'yodeller evening' and 'welcome party', 'afternoon tea and cakes' and a resident host. Unfortunately, the holiday was a disaster. There were no full sized skis. In relation to the house party, there were only 13 guests in the first week. In the second week, there were no other guests. The host spoke very little English. The afternoon tea and cakes turned out to be dry nut cake and crisps. In addition, the yodeller was a local man who performed a few songs in his work clothes. Having been so disappointed with the holiday, the claimant sued for breach. In doing so, he sought a refund of the price of the holiday. In addition, he claimed his lost salary for the two weeks he took off work (£93.27). The trial judge held there was a breach, but refused to award the lost income. Instead, the judge awarded half the cost of the holiday (£31.72) on the basis that the claimant had received half a holiday. More importantly, in the Court of Appeal, the award was increased to £125 (around £1885 in today's money). This increase was to reflect the loss of enjoyment promised.

After detailing the facts Lord Denning MR turned to the issue of damages.

What is the right way of assessing damages? It has often been said that on a breach of contract damages cannot be given for mental distress. Thus in *Hamlin v Great Northern Railway Co* ((1856) 1 H & N 408 at 411) Pollock CB said that damages cannot be given 'for the disappointment of mind occasioned by the breach of contract'. And in *Hobbs v London & South Western Railway Co* ((1875) LR 10 QB 111 at 122, [1874–80] All ER Rep 458 at 463) Mellor J said that

"for the mere inconvenience, such as annoyance and loss of temper, or vexation, or for being disappointed in a particular thing which you have set your mind upon, without real physical inconvenience resulting, you cannot recover damages."

The courts in those days only allowed the plaintiff to recover damages if he suffered physical inconvenience, such as, having to walk five miles home, as in *Hobbs's* case; or to live in an overcrowded house: see *Bailey v Bullock*. . .

I think that those limitations are out of date. In a proper case damages for mental distress can be recovered in contract, just as damages for shock can be recovered in tort. One such case is a contract for a holiday, or any other contract to provide entertainment and enjoyment. If the contracting party breaks his contract, damages can be given for the disappointment, the distress, the upset and frustration caused by the breach. I know that it is difficult to assess in terms of money, but it is no more difficult than the assessment which the courts have to make every day in personal injury cases for loss of amenities. Take the present case. Mr Jarvis has only a fortnight's holiday in the year. He books it far ahead, and looks forward to it all that time. He ought to be compensated for the loss of it.

. . .Here, Mr Jarvis's fortnight's winter holiday has been a grave disappointment. It is true that he was conveyed to Switzerland and back and had meals and bed in the hotel. But that is not what he went for. He went to enjoy himself with all the facilities which the defendants said he would have. He is entitled to damages for the lack of those facilities, and for his loss of enjoyment. . .

A similar case occurred in 1951. It was *Stedman v Swan's Tours*. A holiday-maker was awarded damages because he did not get the bedroom and the accommodation which he was promised. The county court judge awarded him £13 15s. This court increased it to £50.

I think the judge was in error in taking the sum paid for the holiday, £63·45, and halving it. The right measure of damages is to compensate him for the loss of entertainment and enjoyment which he was promised, and which he did not get. Looking at the matter quite broadly, I think the damages in this case should be the sum of £125. I would allow the appeal accordingly.

The decision by Lord Denning MR was a significant step away from the traditional approach. A lot of importance was placed on the type of contract. It was one in which 'entertainment and enjoyment' was contracted for. This was part of the expectation or performance interest and so its loss had to be compensated.

Holiday contracts clearly fit within this category of contract. However, there are many contracts that will not. An example can be seen from *Alexander v Rolls Royce Motor Cars* [1996] RTR 95. Here the car company did not repair a car in breach of contract. The Court of Appeal rejected a claim for damages for loss of enjoyment or distress, which the claimant had made on the basis that he enjoyed driving his car and had bought it for prestige purposes. This was because a contract for repairing a car was not of a type having an important purpose of providing enjoyment or freedom from distress.

?!   **THINKING POINTS**

Beyond holidays, what other contracts are entered to gain enjoyment, entertainment, or freedom from distress?

Assuming the contract is of the 'right' kind, the next important question is what triggers a right to additional damages for non-financial loss. In *Jarvis*, the damages were not awarded just because the claimant was disappointed with the holiday. It was clear that the disappointment (or distress) must result from a breach. Such an approach is consistent with the rule that damages awards compensate for loss resulting from a breach.

The case represented an improved level of consumer protection, certainly in the context of holiday purchases. Today, consumer holidays are protected by The Package Travel and Linked Travel Arrangement Regulations 2018 (implementing the EU Package Travel Directive 2015) and is an update and significant improvement of the original The Package Travel, Package Holidays and Package Tours Regulations 1992 (again based on EU law). However, the legislation only applies to package holidays and equivalent arrangements. It means that the approach from Jarvis remains relevant to holidays beyond the scope of the legislation but also to contracts that are for enjoyment, but do not involve a holiday.

At first instance, Jarvis was not awarded his lost income. That was correct because his lost income was not a consequence of the breach. Had the contract been performed, he still would have lost his salary. Instead, the amount awarded at first instance was the basic financial loss award. Jarvis had half a holiday and so he was awarded the difference in value between what he got and what he should have got. The Court of Appeal went further by awarding extra damages for loss of enjoyment. The total amount happened to be the difference in value, plus the same amount Jarvis would have earned—which is surely not just a coincidence. But such lost income is strictly speaking irrelevant in calculating the value of the loss. The 'coincidence' of the figures is not based on legal principle. It is simply the effect of the Court of Appeal making an award that maintained fidelity to what the judge at first instance had awarded.

Lord Denning MR did observe that claims for loss of enjoyment (or equivalent) would be difficult to calculate. This difficulty was not a barrier to such a claim since the same difficulty arises in personal injury cases in tort. The point was that calculating the loss of enjoyment would be no more difficult than calculating damages to reflect the limited use of a leg or severe pain resulting from the negligence of the defendant in a tort claim.

In principle, the extra amount awarded for loss of enjoyment is consistent with the basic aim of contract damages. We can recall that the innocent party is to be put in the position they contracted for. Jarvis received half a holiday and so he was compensated for the half he didn't get. In addition, according to Lord Denning MR, Jarvis contracted for enjoyment and entertainment. Since a breach deprived him of that, the Court compensated him for that loss. More accurately, the claimant was compensated by recognising both the financial and non-financial expectations arising from the contract. This put Jarvis in the position he should have been in had the contract been performed.

One thing that really stands out in Lord Denning MR's judgment is the absence of authority. Here, we have a judgment that is developing an exception to the traditional rule. For such a task, more detailed legal reasoning would generally be expected. However, setting aside the absence of authority, the judgment of Lord Denning MR was well received. It was frequently cited in subsequent cases to justify damages awarded for loss of enjoyment.

The principle developed in *Jarvis* was explained by Bingham LJ in *Watts v Morrow* [1991] 1 WLR 1421. First, the basic rule against such damages for non-financial loss was addressed:

> A contract-breaker is not in general liable for any distress, frustration, anxiety, displeasure, vexation, tension or aggravation which his breach of contract may cause to the innocent party. This rule is not, I think, founded on the assumption that such reactions are not foreseeable, which they surely are or may be, but on considerations of policy.
>
> But the rule is not absolute. Where the very object of a contract is to provide pleasure, relaxation, peace of mind or freedom from molestation, damages will be awarded if the fruit of the contract is not provided or if the contrary result is procured instead. If the law did not cater for this exceptional category of case it would be defective...

> In cases not falling within this exceptional category, damages are in my view recoverable for phys-
> ical inconvenience and discomfort caused by the breach and mental suffering directly related to that
> inconvenience and discomfort.

There were three important points made in the comments by Bingham LJ:

First, as a general rule, claims for losses like loss of enjoyment or mental distress are not allowed. There are policy reasons for restricting such awards. The reference to policy was not explained, but it is likely to mean two things. There is a desire to prevent a flood of cases from arising and causing legal uncertainty—i.e. cases where all claimants seek damages for disappointment following any and every breach of a contract. And there is a need to protect judges from having to engage too much in subjective decision-making, which would be necessary in assessing whether a given claimant was 'distressed' (as this obviously varies from person to person and case to case).

Secondly, damages for such losses can be awarded in certain exceptional circumstances. This is where the enjoyment or pleasure is 'the very object' of the contract. In other words, the non-financial expectation (like enjoyment) must appear to be the whole point of the contract. We will see that this requirement has since been modified and refined in *Farley v Skinner* [2001], but the point remains that the general rule is non-recovery of non-financial losses except for certain contracts.

The third point relates to an additional exception relating to traditional damages for physical inconvenience or discomfort. When this can be claimed, it is possible to include damages for mental distress or disappointment. To do so, the mental distress (or disappointment) must be shown to have been caused by the inconvenience (or discomfort)—rather than the breach itself. Again, allowing the damages for loss like disappointment here would not cause any particular problems. After all, the claim for physical inconvenience must be established first.

This additional exception was applied in *Watts v Morrow*. The case concerned a couple interested in buying a house. They hired a surveyor to inspect the house. This was to confirm its value and identify any faults. The surveyor's report said that any of the defects could be dealt with using ordinary maintenance. However, once the couple had bought the property, it turned out there were serious problems. These required repairs costing £33,961. The couple then sued for breach of contract and were awarded the cost of the repairs. In addition, the judge awarded the couple £4000 each for distress and inconvenience. The Court of Appeal disagreed with the award. It felt that the contract was not the type where freedom from distress was the 'very object' of the contract. Its object had really been to assess the value of the property. However, the Court did allow £750 each for inconvenience *including* any distress resulting from that inconvenience.

9.7.2 Loss of Enjoyment and the 'Pleasurable Amenity' Award in the *Ruxley* Case

➔ **CROSS-REFERENCE**

For the facts and decision in *Ruxley Electronics v Forsyth* [1996] see 9.3.3.

The type of damages awarded in *Jarvis* can be used to explain the loss of amenity award in *Ruxley Electronics v Forsyth* [1996]. You will recall that, in breach, the pool was not the correct depth and, following a claim, the first instance judge awarded £2500 for loss of 'pleasurable amenity'. The award was not disputed in the House of Lords and so it was upheld. However, Lord Lloyd expressed an opinion on the legal basis of the award:

> *Addis v Gramophone Co Ltd* established the general rule that in claims for breach of contract, the plaintiff cannot recover damages for his injured feelings. But the rule, like most rules, is subject to exceptions. One of the well-established exceptions is when the object of the contract is to afford pleasure, as, for example, where the plaintiff has booked a holiday with a tour operator. If the tour operator is in breach of contract by failing to provide what the contract called for, the plaintiff may recover damages for his disappointment (see *Jarvis v Swans Tours Ltd* ... [1973] QB 233 and *Jackson v Horizon Holidays Ltd* ... [1975] 1 WLR 1468).

> This was, as I understand it, the principle which Judge Diamond applied in the present case. He took the view that the contract was one 'for the provision of a pleasurable amenity'. In the event, Mr Forsyth's pleasure was not so great as it would have been if the swimming pool had been 7ft 6in deep. This was a view which the judge was entitled to take. If it involves a further inroad on the rule in *Addis v Gramophone Co Ltd* then so be it. But I prefer to regard it as a logical application or adaptation of the existing exception to a new situation

The starting point was the general rule against damages for injured feelings. Reference was then made to the exception of contracts that have enjoyment as their objective, like holiday contracts. Lord Lloyd then turned to the pleasurable amenity award and made clear he preferred to treat it as a 'logical application or adaptation' of existing rules to a new situation.

The problem with the first instance award in *Ruxley* was that the judge simply awarded damages for what he called the loss of pleasurable amenity. This was to ensure that Forsyth received some compensation for the breach. However, it was not firmly founded on the principle from *Jarvis*. That is why Lord Lloyd attempted to put it on that footing. In principle, we can see how the award for loss of pleasurable amenity can be consistent with loss of enjoyment. It seems very much like the same thing—it is all about lost pleasure arising from a breach of contract, whether the breach related to a defective swimming pool or unsatisfactory holiday.

The only difficulty is that (at the time) *Jarvis* damages had a limited application. The non-financial loss (such as lost enjoyment) had to relate to the 'very object' of the contract. In the case of a contract for a pool, enjoyment would appear to be *an* objective, but it would not be the *only* objective. At best it would be one of a number of objectives along with the objective of increasing the value of the property. The point is that loss of pleasurable amenity seems no different to loss of enjoyment, but the actual award for it in *Ruxley* was not consistent with the requirements for such an award.

Of course, Lord Lloyd could just have decided that the loss of pleasurable amenity was a new exception to the general rule. However, instead he attempted to broaden the principle established in *Jarvis*, and on this Lord Mustill also provided a helpful observation:

> But these remedies are not exhaustive, for the law must cater for those occasions where the value of the promise to the promisee exceeds the financial enhancement of his position which full performance will secure. This excess, often referred to in the literature as the "consumer surplus" (see for example the valuable discussion by Harris, Ogus and Phillips (1979) 95 LQR 581) is usually incapable of precise valuation in terms of money, exactly because it represents a personal, subjective and non-monetary gain. Nevertheless, where it exists the law should recognise it and compensate the promisee if the misperformance takes it away.

Here Lord Mustill gave recognition of the importance of non-financial value to consumers. We know that when something is bought, we gain something of value. We have paid for it and so it is worth something. If it turns out to be worth less because of a breach, then we have suffered financial loss. That loss can be awarded as compensation. At that point we are no longer financially worse off as a result of the breach. But does that really protect our expectation (performance) interest fully? In other words, does that compensation really put us in the position we should have been in?

The point is that with many purchases, consumers expect to gain something beyond financial value. That might be something like enjoyment or freedom from distress. This value beyond financial gain is the 'consumer surplus value' and is explained by Figure 9.3. If damages were to be awarded for that too, then that would represent complete protection of the expectation (or performance) interest. This is how Lord Mustill explained the loss of pleasurable amenity award, but it also provides a basis for awards for non-financial losses like loss of enjoyment (or mental distress) generally.

The actual value of the consumer surplus in any given situation is subjective and personal. However, its existence is capable of being assessed objectively. When someone books a holiday, they will have an expectation of enjoyment or freedom from distress. Such an expectation is obvious from an objective perspective. That means the other party should reasonably be aware of that expectation. It is then not

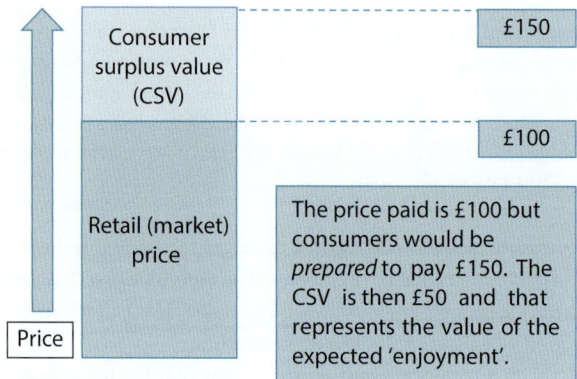

Figure 9.3
How the value of the consumer surplus is calculated

unfair to make a party pay for the loss of such an expectation resulting from a breach. The amount to be awarded will be difficult to calculate precisely but, as we have seen, this is should not prevent damages being awarded in principle. Essentially, the consumer surplus value can be calculated by speculating about the amount a consumer would have paid for the contract above the market price. For example, consider a consumer who pays £200 for an air balloon experience. They might have been prepared to pay even more because of the enjoyment expected, but obviously only paid £200 because that was the cost of the ticket. Perhaps the consumer would have been prepared to pay £300, but got a good deal. The extra £100 represents their consumer surplus. That £100 sum is clearly a subjective figure and is speculative. This means that allowing damages on this basis will result in sellers entering contracts without having an idea about how much a breach could cost. But courts have ultimately decided that this is a problem worth having in order to better reflect the realities of consumer expectations and contracting.

9.7.3 The Current Position on Loss of Enjoyment (Mental Distress) Damages

This area was subjected to a detailed assessment by the House of Lords in *Farley v Skinner* [2001] UKHL 49. In doing so, the court developed the rules further. The case represents the current position of the law and so it is the primary case on damages for this type of loss.

Farley v Skinner was another case concerning a contract to survey a property. Mr Farley was thinking of buying a large countryside property called Riverside House 15 miles away from Gatwick Airport. It had a swimming pool, a tennis court, an orchard, a paddock, a croquet lawn and a stream running through it. Mr Farley hoped it would be the ideal place to enjoy his retirement. Before buying, he employed the defendant surveyor to assess the value and quality of the property. Mr Farley was particularly concerned about the possibility of aircraft noise because he wanted peace and tranquillity. For that reason, he instructed the surveyor to assess the potential for aircraft noise. He even said that he did not want a house under a flight path. When the surveyor report was completed, it stated that it was not likely that the property would suffer greatly from the noise of aeroplanes. On that basis, Farley went ahead with the purchase. He later discovered that the property was badly affected by aeroplane noise. It turned out that Riverside House was near to a navigation beacon. That was where aeroplanes would fly in circles above each other when waiting for permission to land. This practice is known as 'stacking' and the surveyor had been negligent in not discovering it. Such negligence amounted to a breach so Farley remained at the property and sued for breach of contract.

At first instance, he was awarded £10,000 for 'discomfort' resulting from the breach. However, the Court of Appeal held that the award was contrary to established principle. Enjoyment or peace of mind here was not the 'very object of the contract'. Instead, the very object of the contract was the assessment of the property's condition and value. The House of Lords then upheld the award of the trial judge. In doing so, it developed the law on non-financial loss and it is useful to examine the judgment by Lord Steyn (with whom Lord Brown –Wilkinson and Lord Scott agreed).

GUIDED CASE READING 9.3
Farley v Skinner [2001] UKHL 49

The following extract is useful because it refers to a wide range of earlier cases. In doing so, we can see a range of scenarios raising the issue of damages for different degrees of mental distress. When reading the extract try to identify:

- how Lord Steyn modifies the rules from *Watts v Morrow*;
- the difference between *Farley v Skinner* and the contract in *Watts v Morrow*.

[18] It is necessary to examine the case on a correct characterisation of the Plaintiff's claim. Stuart-Smith LJ [2000] Lloyd's Rep PN 516, at 521, thought that the obligation undertaken by the surveyor was 'one relatively minor aspect of the overall instructions'. . . . But the Court of Appeal's characterisation of the case was not correct. The Plaintiff made it crystal clear to the surveyor that the impact of aircraft noise was a matter of importance to him. Unless he obtained reassuring information from the surveyor he would not have bought the property. That is the tenor of the evidence. It is also what the judge found. The case must be approached on the basis that the surveyor's obligation to investigate aircraft noise was a major or important part of the contract between him and the Plaintiff. It is also important to note that, unlike in *Addis v Gramophone Co Ltd* [1909] AC 488, the Plaintiff's claim is not for injured feelings caused by the breach of contract. Rather it is a claim for damages flowing from the surveyor's failure to investigate and report, thereby depriving the buyer of the chance of making an informed choice whether or not to buy resulting in mental distress and disappointment.

> Lord Steyn begins by straight away making clear that the contract must have peace of mind or enjoyment as a 'major or important' purpose (rather than being its 'very object' as Bingham LJ had put it in *Watts v Morrow*) in order for non-financial losses to be recoverable.

> He also makes clear that this is not a case of somebody suffering hurt feelings because of a breach, but rather an actual loss—that is, the capacity to make an informed choice—which resulted in loss of enjoyment or disappointment.

[19] The broader legal context of *Watts v Morrow* must be borne in mind. The exceptional category of cases where the very object of a contract is to provide pleasure, relaxation, peace of mind or freedom from molestation is not the product of Victorian contract theory but the result of evolutionary developments in case law from the 1970s. Several decided cases informed the description given by Bingham LJ of this category. The first was the decision of the sheriff court in *Diesen v Samson* 1971 SLT (Sh Ct) 49. A photographer failed to turn up at a wedding, thereby leaving the couple without a photographic record of an important and happy day. The bride was awarded damages for her distress and disappointment. In the celebrated case of *Jarvis v Swans Tours Ltd* [1973] 1 QB 233, . . . the plaintiff recovered damages for mental distress flowing from a disastrous holiday resulting from a travel agent's negligent representations: compare also *Jackson v Horizon Holidays Ltd* . . . [1975] 1 WLR 1468. In *Heywood v Wellers (a firm)* [1976] QB 446, . . . the plaintiff instructed solicitors to bring proceedings to restrain a man from molesting her. The solicitors negligently failed to take appropriate action with the result that the molestation continued. The Court of Appeal allowed the plaintiff damages for mental distress and upset. While apparently not cited in *Watts v Morrow*, *Jackson v Chrysler Acceptances Ltd* [1978] RTR 474 was

> He then described the development of the principle that non-financial losses should be recoverable where the contract is to provide pleasure or peace of mind, noting that the law had developed doctrinally since the 1970s in the appellate courts, and that it was already a fact of life in the lower courts that this kind of damages was routinely awarded. One implication is that practice in the lower courts may have preceded the evolution of the concept in the higher ones. Another is that since the doctrine was of recent development, there was no reason why it could not be further refined or clarified.

decided before *Watts v Morrow*. In Jackson's case the claim was for damages in respect of a motor car which did not meet the implied condition of merchantability in s 14 of the Sale of Goods Act 1893. The buyer communicated to the seller that one of his reasons for buying the car was a forthcoming touring holiday in France. Problems with the car spoilt the holiday. The disappointment of a spoilt holiday was a substantial element in the award sanctioned by the Court of Appeal.

[20] . . . I am satisfied that in the real life of our lower courts non-pecuniary damages are regularly awarded on the basis that the defendant's breach of contract deprived the plaintiff of the very object of the contract, *viz* pleasure, relaxation, and peace of mind. The cases arise in diverse contractual contexts, e g the supply of a wedding dress or double glazing, hire purchase transactions, landlord and tenant, building contracts, and engagements of estate agents and solicitors. The awards in such cases seem modest. For my part what happens on the ground casts no doubt on the utility of the developments since the 1970s in regard to the award of non-pecuniary damages in the exceptional categories. But the problem persists of the precise scope of the exceptional category of case involving awards of non-pecuniary damages for breach of contract where the very object of the contract was to ensure a party's pleasure, relaxation or peace of mind.

> However, with all of this said, it remained the case that this was a fairly recent development in the law and it was still not quite clear when exactly this type of damages could be awarded. Did it have to be when the contract had as its 'very object' pleasure, relaxation, or peace of mind, and what precisely did this mean?

[21] An important development for this branch of the law was *Ruxley Electronics and Construction Ltd v Forsyth* [1996] AC 344 . . . Lord Mustill and Lord Lloyd . . . justified the award in carefully reasoned judgments which carried the approval of four of the Law Lords. It is sufficient for present purposes to mention that for Lord Mustill, . . . at p. 360, the principle of *pacta sunt servanda* would be eroded if the law did not take account of the fact that the consumer often demands specifications which, although not of economic value, have value to him. This is sometimes called the 'consumer surplus' . . . I am satisfied that the principles enunciated in *Ruxley's* case in support of the award of £2,500 for a breach of respect of the provision of a pleasurable amenity have been authoritatively established . . .

> Clearly, in *Ruxley v Forsyth* the very object was not pleasure, relaxation or peace of mind if 'very object' meant the *sole* object. While pleasure and relaxation are important aims of a contract to build a swimming pool, other factors are relevant—the value of the property, for instance. But this did not undermine the reasoning in *Ruxley* that Mr Forsyth should be compensated for his lost amenity. This suggested that damages for non-financial losses could be awarded when pleasure, relaxation, peace of mind and so on were not the 'very object' of the contract, but rather an important object of it.

[22] Counsel for the surveyor advanced three separate arguments each of which he said was sufficient to defeat the Plaintiff's claim. First, he submitted that even if a major or important part of the contract was to give pleasure, relaxation and peace of mind, that was not enough. It is an indispensable requirement that the object of the entire contract must be of this type . . .

[23] The first argument fastened onto a narrow reading of the words 'the very object of [the] contract' as employed by Bingham LJ in *Watts v Morrow* [1991] 1 WLR 1421, 1445. Cases where a major or important part of the contract was to secure pleasure, relaxation and peace of mind were not under consideration in *Watts v Morrow*. It is difficult to see what the principled justification for such a limitation might be. After all, in 1978 the Court of Appeal allowed such a claim in *Jackson v Chrysler Acceptances Ltd* in circumstances where a spoiled holiday was only one object of the contract. Counsel was, however, assisted by the decision of the Court of Appeal in *Knott and another v Bolton and others* (1995) 45 Con LR 127, (1995) 11 Const LJ 375 which in the present case the Court of Appeal treated as binding on it. In *Knott v Bolton* an architect was asked to design a wide staircase for a gallery and impressive entrance hall. He failed to do so. The plaintiff spent money in improving the staircase to some extent and he recovered the cost of the changes. The plaintiff also claimed damages for disappointment and distress in the lack of an

> This made it easy to deal with the first and main argument put by Skinner's counsel, which was that the main object of the contract was to value the property, rather than to investigate aircraft noise to ensure Farley had pleasure and relaxation, and on that basis the 'very object' of the contract had not been frustrated. Lord Steyn drew on *Ruxley* to make clear that the correct question is whether pleasure, relaxation, peace of mind, etc., was an important purpose of the contract—not whether it was its 'very object'. He did this by reference to *Knott v Bolton*, making clear that he thought that case had been wrongly decided—there was no reason, if the owners of the house had not received the pleasure which they had contracted for in receiving an impressive staircase, why they should not be compensated.

impressive staircase. In agreement with the trial judge the Court of Appeal disallowed this part of his claim. Reliance was placed on the dicta of Bingham LJ in *Watts v Morrow* [1991] 1 WLR 1422, 1445.

[24] Interpreting the dicta of Bingham LJ in *Watts v Morrow* narrowly, the Court of Appeal in *Knott v Bolton* ruled that the central object of the contract was to design a house, not to provide pleasure to the occupiers of the house. It is important, however, to note that *Knott v Bolton* was decided a few months before the decision of the House in *Ruxley Electronics and Construction Ltd v Forsyth*. In any event, the technicality of the reasoning in *Knott v Bolton*, and therefore in the Court of Appeal judgments in the present case, is apparent. It is obvious, and conceded, that if an architect is employed only to design a staircase, or a surveyor is employed only to investigate aircraft noise, the breach of such a distinct obligation may result in an award of non-pecuniary damages. Logically the same must be the case if the architect or surveyor, . . . concludes a separate contract, separately remunerated, in respect of the design of a staircase or the investigation of aircraft noise. If this is so the distinction drawn in *Knott v Bolton* and in the present case is a matter of form and not substance. David Capper, 'Damages for Distress and Disappointment—The Limits of *Watts v Morrow*' (2000) 116 LQR 553, 556 has persuasively argued:

> 'A ruling that intangible interests only qualify for legal protection where they are the "very object of the contract" is tantamount to a ruling that contracts where these interests are merely important, but not the central object of the contract, are in part unenforceable. It is very difficult to see what policy objection there can be to parties to a contract agreeing that these interests are to be protected via contracts where the central object is something else. If the defendant is unwilling to accept this responsibility he or she can say so and either no contract will be made or one will be made but including a disclaimer.'

There is no reason in principle or policy why the scope of recovery in the exceptional category should depend on the object of the contract as ascertained from all its constituent parts. It is sufficient if a major or important object of the contract is to give pleasure, relaxation or peace of mind. In my view *Knott v Bolton* was wrongly decided and should be overruled. To the extent that the majority in the Court of Appeal relied on *Knott v Bolton* their decision was wrong.

> This was also supported by academic commentators—Capper, for instance, pointing out that there did not appear to be any sensible reason why the loss of an intangible interest (meaning enjoyment, peace of mind, etc.) should not be compensated when it was an important reason for the contract existing if it was not the *main* reason for it existing.

> This meant that *Knott* should be overruled and that the principle from *Jarvis* should be extended to cases where an intangible interest was an 'important object' of the contract—not its 'very object'.

KEY POINTS

Loss of enjoyment (and equivalent mental distress) can be claimed where it is a major or important object of the contract.

The change gives the availability of such damages a wider scope. After all, there are far more contracts where enjoyment is an important object than its 'very object'. The wider scope enabled Mr Farley to be entitled to damages for the type of mental distress experienced. It also clarifies the loss of pleasurable amenity award in *Ruxley*. Enjoyment of the pool was not the 'very object' of the building contract. But it could be seen as an important object of it.

On the application to the facts, the instruction to the surveyor was significant. It specifically required the surveyor to assess the potential disturbance from aeroplane noise. That meant there was a contractual obligation to report on the noise. This made the need for peace and freedom from distress an *important* object of the contract. In contrast, in *Watts v Morrow*, there was not such contractual obligation. For that reason, freedom from distress was not even an important object of the contract.

The reason for supporting the change was based on the status of the exception. This was not a long-standing rule 'set in stone'. It was an exception that had fairly recently evolved. Bingham LJ's summary of the exception from *Watts v Morrow* was seen as *obiter*. It was not viewed as a fixed rule. Furthermore, there were already cases in which damages for distress had been awarded when enjoyment was not the very object of the contract. One was from the Court of Appeal, the other was *Ruxley*.

This more relaxed approach was applied in *Hamilton v David & Snape* [2003] EWHC 3147. Here solicitors failed in breach of contract to take steps to prevent an ex-husband taking his child out of the UK. Neuberger J awarded £25,000 for the financial loss and £20,000 for mental distress resulting from the breach. The main object of that contract was the care and protection of the child. But the judge agreed an important aim of the contract was to give the mother peace of mind over the status of her child.

The case of *Herrmann v Withers LLP* [2012] EWHC 1492 provides another example. It concerned the purchase of a house. The buyer's solicitor wrongly indicated that there would be a right to use a nearby garden. Following this breach, Newey J awarded £2000. This was based on pleasure and peace of mind from the garden being an important object of the contract. The award was a lot less than the £50,000 claimed for the loss, to keep the award 'modest'. That was consistent with the final comments of Lord Steyn in *Farley*. Lord Scott also delivered the same warning in the case about the need to prevent the awards being too high.

9.7.4 Damages for Mental Distress Caused by Physical Inconvenience or Discomfort

The second exception from *Watts v Morrow*, regarding damages for mental distress caused by physical inconvenience arising from a breach was also explored in *Farley* by Lord Scott. This type of award was on a much stronger footing, as it had a fairly long pedigree. Cases like *Bailey v Bullock* and *Hobbs v London & South Western Railway Co* are usually cited as authority. Indeed, these cases were the basis of the damages award in *Watts v Morrow*. In *Farley*, Lord Scott also confirmed that if the inconvenience causes a form of mental distress, then that can result in damages too. In his judgment, inconvenience and real discomfort were set forth as an alternative basis of the award:

> If the cause is no more than disappointment that the contractual obligation has been broken, damages are not recoverable even if the disappointment has led to a complete mental breakdown. But, if the cause of the inconvenience or discomfort is a sensory (sight, touch, hearing, smell etc.) experience, damages can, subject to the remoteness rule, be recovered.

→ CROSS-REFERENCE

For the facts of *Bailey v Bullock* [1950] and *Hobbs v S.W Railway* (1875) see 9.6.2.

→ CROSS-REFERENCE

For the rules on remoteness see 10.3.

Lord Scott was emphasising the cause of the disappointment or mental distress. If they result from physical inconvenience arising from a breach, damages can be awarded for the disappointment or mental distress. There is no need to show that the mental element was an important object of the contract. It just needs to flow from the inconvenience and satisfy the remoteness rule, which generally applies to all types of damages in contract law. Table 9.1 summarises the availability of damages.

Table 9.1

The availability of damages for non-financial loss

Type of loss	Claimable?	Authority
Pain and suffering	Yes, as a consequence of a breach.	*Godley v Perry* [1960]
Physical inconvenience	Yes, as a consequence of a breach.	*Bailey v Bullock* [1950]
Harmed reputation and injured feeling from the manner of the breach?	No. It is not a consequence of the actual breach and would be punitive.	*Addis v Gramophone* [1909]
Harmed reputation (resulting from a breach)	Yes, indirectly (i.e. only if it results in financial loss).	*Malik v BCCI* [1998]
Loss of enjoyment/mental distress	Yes, if freedom from distress/enjoyment is an important object of the contract.	*Farley v Skinner* [2001]

9.7.5 Controlling the Size of the Awards for Mental Distress

Usually, damages for financial loss are not difficult to work out. The same cannot be said for damages for mental distress like disappointment or loss of enjoyment. A judge could be guided by the consumer surplus value. The problem is that it is subjective and will vary. Of course, difficulty in working out the amount of an award is not a reason to refuse it. We can recall Lord Denning MR in *Jarvis* making precisely that point. Mental distress will be difficult to assess but no more than damages for pain and suffering. In addition, mental distress awards are common in other areas of law. The tort of negligence is perhaps the most obvious example. So, potential difficulties in calculating an award should not be seen as a problem. However, a real concern is the size of the award. In particular, courts have shown a desire not to let claims get 'out of control.' For that reason, the House of Lords in *Ruxley* warned about keeping the awards within sensible limits. On this point, Lord Steyn in *Farley* stated:

> [28] In the surveyor's written case it was submitted that the award of £10,000 was excessive. . . I have to say that the size of the award appears to be at the very top end of what could possibly be regarded as appropriate damages. Like Bingham LJ in *Watts v Morrow*, at 1445H, I consider that awards in this area should be restrained and modest. It is important that logical and beneficial developments in this corner of the law should not contribute to the creation of a society bent on litigation.

The same warning was made by Lord Scott. In making it, the judges were providing guidance to lawyers and County Court judges. If the awards were too large, they would become an incentive to sue. Parties would be encouraged to claim for a breach in the hope of 'cashing in' on the damages award. Of course, it is important to compensate for loss. However, large awards could result in exaggerated claims like those common in consumer insurance. This need to limit the awards is therefore based on reasons of policy—that is, to prevent the development of a US-style litigation culture. In other words, the UK courts do not want to encourage the development of a society that wants to sue for everything. In doing so, it should prevent a flood of less-deserving and potentially frivolous cases.

Another factor relevant to the size of the award is the need for consistency. The point was made in in *Milner v Carnival plc* [2010] EWCA Civ 389. Permission for the appeal was granted in the hope of gaining guidance on damages awards for holidays. The case concerned luxury world cruise for around 106 days. The cost of the cruise for the claimant couple was just over £59,000. For that, they were promised such luxury and star treatment that it would be the experience of a lifetime. However, the couple experienced noise and vibrations in their cabin. It meant they were unable to sleep well during the voyage. After 28 days, the couple left the voyage at Hawaii and made their own way back to the UK. Following their complaints, the couple accepted a refund of £48,270. However, they sued claiming for the reduction in value, wasted expenditure and, distress and disappointment. The trial judge awarded damages, but much less than the amounts claimed. The Court of Appeal reduced the awards further.

The lead judgment was by Ward LJ with whom the other judges agreed. Ward LJ considered the size of the awards made in earlier holiday cases on the basis of their comparative monetary value. The judge also made it clear that it was important to consider 'comparable' awards from other areas of law. Reference was made to awards made in personal injury cases for psychiatric harm. In addition, claims for injured feelings in sex and race discrimination cases as well damages for bereavement were considered. It resulted in Mr Milner being awarded £4000 and Mrs Milner £4500 for inconvenience and distress. A further £3500 was awarded to reflect the reduction in value.

KEY POINTS

Awards in contract for mental distress should be in line with those in other areas of law. That is a guiding factor in quantifying the award, along with the need to avoid excessive sums being awarded.

The award in *Milner* covered financial loss, physical inconvenience and mental distress. It is important that the losses claimed do not overlap and are kept distinct. Otherwise, a claimant would be over-compensated.

 THINKING POINTS

Should disappointment and inconvenience be compared to injured feelings from discrimination and psychiatric injury in tort?

9.7.6 No Mental Distress from Commercial Contracts

The cases we have considered so far are consumer cases, but what if the innocent party is a business? Can that business claim for mental distress and loss of enjoyment? Well it is hard to imagine a company being distressed or upset. But the same cannot be said for a person in business. A good example of the approach which the courts have taken to this kind of scenario is *Hayes v James & Charles Dodd* [1990] 2 All ER 815.

In this case, the claimants wanted a garage for their car repair business. When negotiating for the lease, the defendant solicitors said there was access through land at the back. This was essential because the front access was through a narrow tunnel. The claimants entered the lease and then discovered that the access at the back was blocked. As a result, after a year they were forced to close the business. They then sued for breach and at first instance were awarded damages for their wasted expenditure. More importantly, they were awarded £1500 each for mental distress in the form of 'anguish and vexation'.

In the Court of Appeal, Staughton LJ rejected the damages award for mental distress. In doing so, he cited comments from Kerr LJ in *Perry v Sidney Phillips & Son (a firm)* [1982] 1 WLR 1297 and Dillon LJ in *Bliss v South East Thames Regional Health Authority* [1987] ICR 700. Based on these comments, it was observed that even if such loss was likely, it was not to be compensated through an award of damages. Staughton LJ explained that 'as a matter of policy' such claims were limited to certain contracts—those in which freedom from distress are an important object of the contract, as we have seen. The present case, however, concerned 'commercial activity with a view to profit'. In his judgment, Staughton LJ stated:

> Like the judge, I consider that the English courts should be wary or adopting what he called 'the United States practice of huge awards'. Damages awarded for negligence or want of skill, whether against professional men or anyone else, must provide fair compensation, but no more than that. And I would not view with enthusiasm the prospect that every shipowner in the Commercial Court, having successfully claimed for unpaid freight or demurrage, would be able to add a claim for mental distress suffered while he was waiting for his money.

These are statements of policy. They encourage caution regarding the size of awards. And Staughton LJ adopts a clear stance against commercial parties claiming for mental distress. Such a policy statement will act as a barrier to such claims from commercial contracts. In addition, courts have continued to emphasise that freedom from a type of mental distress has to be important object of the contract in order to receive an award on that basis. That alone will be a sufficient barrier in relation to commercial contracts. Furthermore, as Staughton LJ indicated, disappointment and distress can be expected as an ordinary part of being in business. On this Lord Cooke in *Johnson v Gore Wood & (a firm)* [2002] 2 AC 1, 49 observed:

> Contract-breaking is treated as an incident of commercial life which players in the game are expected to meet with mental fortitude.

This statement reflects the fact that mental well-being, enjoyment, relaxation and so on are not an expectation for commercial contractors. Such contracts are aimed at making profits. Consequently, the awards of damages for types mental distress like loss of enjoyment will be limited to consumer contracts.

CHAPTER SUMMARY

- Ordinarily, damages for breach of contract are to compensate for the loss caused by the breach rather than to punish the party in breach.
- Compensatory damages reflect the expectation/performance interest of the innocent party.
- The use of the cost of repair/reinstatement measure is not permitted if it would be unreasonable, for example where it would be wholly out of proportion to the benefit to be gained. It would also be unreasonable where the innocent party has no intention to repair because that indicates no loss was suffered.
- Expenses or reliance claims are permitted as they still compensate for loss, unless the contract was a bad bargain.
- Damages for loss of chance can be awarded where the breach prevents the chance promised under the contract.
- Damages can be awarded for non-financial loss like pain and suffering, and physical inconvenience that result from a breach.
- Damages for injured feelings and harmed reputation resulting from the way the contract was breached are not permitted.
- Damages for harmed reputation resulting from the actual breach can be awarded where the claim is framed as a financial loss.
- Damages for types of mental distress can be awarded where the freedom from such a loss is at least, an important object of the contract.
- Damages for loss of enjoyment can be explained as reflecting the consumer surplus value of the contract.
- Damages for loss of enjoyment are kept within reasonable limits as a matter of policy.
- It is not possible for businesses to claim damages for mental distress.

KEY CASES

- ☐ *Robinson v Harman* (1848) 1 Exch 350—is the main authority for the aim of damages in contract.
- ☐ *Ruxley Electronics and Construction Ltd v Forsyth* [1996] 1 AC 344—represents the rule on the availability of damages for the cost of repair/reinstatement.
- ☐ *Anglia Television Ltd v Reed* [1972] 1 QB 60—is the authority for damages for wasted expenditure.
- ☐ *C & P Haulage v Middleton* [1983] 1 WLR 1461—provides authority for wasted expenditure claims being rejected where the contract reflects a bad bargain.
- ☐ *Chaplin v Hicks* [1911] 2 KB 786—shows it is possible to claim damages to reflect the loss of a chance due under a contract.
- ☐ *Addis v Gramophone* [1909] AC 488—is a significant authority that rules-out damages for loss resulting from the way a contract is breached (rather than resulting from the actual breach).
- ☐ *Malik v Bank of Credit and Commerce International* [1998] AC 20—shows that damages for harmed reputation are possible (indirectly) if the loss is framed as financial loss resulting from the breach.

☐ *Jarvis v Swan Tours* [1973] QB 233—established the early principle allowing damages for loss of enjoyment (mental distress).

☐ *Farley v Skinner* [2001] UKHL 49—is the leading authority on damages for mental distress generally, following a breach.

☐ *Hayes v James & Charles Dodd* [1990] 2 All ER 815—is the first clear authority that rules-out mental distress damages in business contracts.

QUESTIONS

1. Bodgit Builders Ltd contracts to build a garage for Aaliyah at a price of £5000. The contract specifies that the garage is to be 7m long. However, when the building is completed, it is only 6m 70cm long. Aaliyah wants to claim £4000 in damages, which is the amount required to correct the breach of contract. There is no difference in value between the garage that was built and the garage specified in the contract. Advise Aaliyah.

2. Critically evaluate the principle that damages for lost enjoyment or peace of mind arising from a breach are only available when one of those intangible benefits was an important purpose of the contract.

3. Should the decision in *Addis* be re-examined in light of more recent developments?

 For answer guidance to these questions please visit the online resources at www.oup .com/uk/naidoo1e/, where you will also find multiple choice questions to check your understanding of key concepts.

FURTHER READING

McKendrick & Graham, 'The sky's the limit: contractual damages for non pecuniary loss' LMCLQ [2002] 161.
This is a leading extended case note on *Farley v Skinner*. It presents some useful opinions in an accessible way.

Mullen, 'Damages for breach of contract: quantifying the lost consumer surplus' OJLS (2016), 36(1), 83.
This is a detailed and 'heavy-weight' article on the consumer surplus value and how it could be applied with more accuracy.

Phang, 'The crumbling edifice? The award of contractual damages for mental distress' JBL [2003] JBL 341.
A clear and detailed assessment of the cases on damages for harmed reputation which suggests an alternative approach.

Phang, 'Subjectivity, objectivity and policy–contractual damages in the House of Lords' [1996] JBL 362.
A clear and detailed conceptual assessment of whether damages should be based on the difference in value or the cost of reinstatement.

Rowan, 'Cost of Cure Damages and the Relevance of the injured Promisee's Intention to Cure' (2017) 76(3) CLJ, 616..
This is an excellent, detailed assessment of the cases on the cost of reinstatement which observes that they appear to conflict on the significance of the innocent party's intention to use the damages award to correct the breach.

Remedies Part II: Principles That Can Limit the Damages Awarded Following a Breach

10

LEARNING OBJECTIVES

By the end of this chapter you should be able to:

- apply the principles of causation, contributory negligence, mitigation and remoteness
- analyse the aim of the principles limiting damages awards
- evaluate the development and application of the remoteness rules
- understand the conceptual basis of the remoteness rules

INTRODUCTION

In the previous chapter, we saw how the aim of damages following a breach is compensatory and how that aim is reflected in the categories of claimable loss. Our next stage is to address the factors that a defendant might rely on to limit a damages claim.

We will start with the principle of causation. The idea here is that the breach must have caused the loss. A related issue is the limited application of contributory negligence. Where relevant, damages can be reduced to reflect any fault on the part of the innocent claimant. Both of these factors, as we shall see, are of fairly minor importance. The main limiting factor is the principle of remoteness. This is by far the most significant and interesting in terms of the case law. It is a principle that limits liability to the risks the party in breach appeared to accept. Finally, we look at the duty to mitigate losses. This requires the innocent party to take reasonable steps to reduce (and not unreasonably increase) the loss suffered after a breach.

Depending on the facts, disputes can involve any or all of these limitations. Where possible, the party in breach will argue that their breach did not cause some or all of the loss. Likewise, they will argue that some or all of the loss suffered was too unlikely at the time of contracting and is therefore too remote. Even if the breach caused the loss and the loss was not too remote, it might be argued that the damages should be reduced because the innocent party did not mitigate their losses.

10.1 Causation

We know a breach of contract can result in the innocent party suffering a range of losses. However, for a loss to be claimable, the breach must have been its actual cause. The same general requirement exists for damages claims in other areas, like those in tort. The requirement seems very obvious. After all, where the loss is caused by something other than the breach, then surely the claimant should not claim damages from the party in breach. However, closer examination of this issue reveals why there are arguments and therefore cases concerning causation. Take a typical example of a contract to provide advice for the purchase of a business. Let us assume that negligent advice to buy the business amounts to a breach. Following negligent advice, if the buyer suffers losses, we would assume that the advisor would be liable. However, it might be possible to prove that the same decision to buy would have been made anyway, even if the advice had been given correctly, i.e. without negligence. In such circumstances, it could be argued that the breach was not the cause of the loss. It would have happened anyway. That was the approach adopted by the Court of Appeal in *Levicom International Holdings BV v Linklaters (A firm)* [2010] EWCA Civ 494.

10.1.1 The 'But For' Test

Causation hinges on whether the breach *caused* the loss and that is based on an assessment of the facts. On a simple level, this assessment is a 'but for' test. This just involves asking whether, 'but for' the breach, the loss would have been suffered. If the loss would have happened anyway, the breach was not the factual cause. While early cases in tort and contract use this test, it is often criticised as vague and imprecise. But one thing the test can do is reveal that there is no causal link between the breach and the loss. In other words, the test can enable a court to rule out the possibility of the loss being caused by the breach.

The more obvious limit of the 'but for' test is that it does not necessarily identify the cause of the loss. So, you could apply the test and find that the loss would not have happened 'but for' the breach. The problem is that such a result does not always mean that the breach was the *direct* cause of the loss. Instead, it might have been the result of a subsequent intervening act known as a *novus actus interveniens*. The breach might have provided the opportunity for the subsequent intervening act to take place, but that is not necessarily the same thing as saying the breach caused the loss. This issue requires some detailed explanation.

novus actus interveniens is a Latin term to describe a new intervening act that is the real cause of the loss.

10.1.2 Intervening Acts

The most obvious intervening act would be an act by a third party. The case that is often cited on this issue is *Stansbie v Trowman* [1948] 2 KB 48. However, it is not a case in which the third party was deemed to have intervened. Instead, it shows that the action of a third party might not break the chain of causation. In this case, a decorator was left alone to decorate a house. He then went to buy some wall paper leaving the door lock on its latch so it could be opened by turning the handle. He was away for around 1 hour 45 minutes. During that time, a thief took the opportunity to enter and steal some jewellery and clothes. The home owner then claimed the value of the items from the decorator. It was argued that leaving the door unlocked was a breach that resulted in the loss. It could be said that 'but for' the breach, there would have been no loss. In response, the decorator argued that the loss resulted from an intervening act by a third party. The Court of Appeal disagreed and found the decorator liable.

To find the decorator liable, the court identified a contractual obligation to take reasonable care. In particular, this included keeping the house secure, and that duty had been breached. Of course, it was the thief that had taken the items. However, the duty to take reasonable care had been there to prevent precisely what happened. On that basis, the theft was not an intervening act and did not break the chain of causation, leaving the decorator liable for the loss.

Unreasonable conduct by the claimant is another intervening act that can break the chain of causation. The authority often cited for this is *Lambert v Lewis* [1982] AC 225. It concerned a farmer who bought a defective towing hitch. The defect meant there was a breach of the sale of goods contract between the farmer and the seller. However, the farmer continued to use it to link his Land Rover to a trailer. One day during use the hitch gave way and the trailer detached. It then crashed into car, killing one person and injuring another. One of the actions brought by the injured party was against the farmer. The farmer then brought an action for breach of contract against the seller of the hitch. On the facts, the House of Lords held that the conduct of the farmer was an intervening act. He knew the hitch was defective and continued to use it. That meant the farmer was liable in negligence. In addition, the seller was not liable to the farmer for the loss, as it was not caused by a breach.

10.2 Contributory Negligence

The conduct of the innocent party might well be an intervening act, like in *Lambert v Lewis*. That would make the innocent party's actions the real cause of the loss rather than the breach by the other party. However, it is possible for the innocent party to be partially responsible for the loss but not for its actions to be classed as an intervening act. Instead, the actions of the party in breach could be the cause of the loss, but the innocent claimant could be partly at fault. In such circumstances, the party in breach will be liable to the claimant, but there could be a reduction in the damages award to reflect the degree of fault on the part of the claimant.

Reductions in damages for contributory negligence are common in the tort of negligence and are based on the Contributory Negligence Act 1945. For an example in the negligence context, consider a negligent driver that hits a cyclist. The driver will be liable in damages for the resulting injuries. But if the cyclist was not wearing a helmet, this would likely raise an issue of contributory negligence. It could be argued that the absence of a helmet contributed to the cyclist's injuries. If the absence of a helmet meant that the cyclist was partly at fault for his or her injuries, then there would be a reduction in the damages awarded. For our purposes, the question is whether the Contributory Negligence Act 1945 applies to damages for breach of contract.

Section 1 of the Act indicates that it applies where damage is the 'fault' of the claimant or the 'fault' of another party. Fault is then defined as acts or omissions (i.e. a failure to act) that would give rise to liability in tort. The problem is that sometimes, a breach of contract can also give rise to liability in tort. This is known as concurrent liability and is more often seen when a contract obligation is fault –based, requiring a party to take reasonable care. Their failure to do so would be a breach of the contract. Alternatively, the same failure might be enough to bring an action under the tort of negligence. Consider a garage that repairs a flat tyre on a car. The repair is then performed negligently. Perhaps the interior side wall of the tyre was too damaged to make the tyre safe for a repair. Consequently, while the customer is driving, the tyre bursts and causes a crash resulting in damage to the car and a head injury. The garage would be liable for breach of contract but, as an alternative, the garage could also be liable in the tort of negligence. In such circumstances, if the customer was partly at fault for the extent of the injury, the garage would argue for a contributory negligence reduction. For example, perhaps the air bag did not inflate and the on-board computer indicates that the airbag warning light had been ignored for weeks. In such a case, could the customer avoid the reduction by relying on a breach of contract claim?

This reduction for contributory negligence in contract was discussed by Hoffman J in *Forsikringsaktieselskapet Vesta v Butcher* [1986] 2 All ER 488. There it was stated that where there is concurrent liability, a reduction for contributory negligence can also be made where the damages are for breach of contract. This approach can be explained as necessary to prevent claimants avoiding a reduction simply by choosing to frame their legal action in contract rather tort. That explains why Hoffman J also said that the reduction could not apply where the term breached was based on strict liability. In addition, it was said that the reduction would not apply to fault-based contractual obligations that do not give rise to liability in tort that is independent of the contract.

➔ CROSS-REFERENCE

For the discussion of strict liability see 8.2.1.

The opinion of Hoffman J favouring the reduction in contract cases with concurrent liability was approved when the case reached the Court of Appeal ([1988] 2 All ER 43). It was also adopted by the Court of Appeal in *Trebor Bassett Holdings Ltd and the Cadbury UK Partnership v ADT Fire and Security plc* [2012] EWCA Civ 1158. In *Barclays Bank plc v Fairclough Building Ltd* [1995] QB 214, the Court of Appeal confirmed that there cannot be a reduction for contributory negligence when the obligation breached is a strict one. This all means that in practice, the application of contributory negligence to damages for breach of contract will be very limited.

?!   THINKING POINTS

Does the exclusion of contributory negligence from strict obligations mean that the claimant can be over-compensated?

10.3 Remoteness of the Loss Claimed

Even if the loss is a type that is claimable and was caused by the breach, there is an additional and very significant potential limitation. For damages to be claimable, the losses in question cannot have been too 'remote' from the breach. We will see that the operation of this requirement can be a major limit to any claim for losses resulting from a breach. To appreciate when losses are too remote, a detailed assessment of the case law is required. However, at this stage, it is useful to have a basic idea of the remoteness principle and why it is needed.

10.3.1 The Need for the Remoteness Principle

Essentially, losses are too remote if (back when the contract was entered) their occurring as a result of the breach was unlikely or unforeseeable. The whole point is to ensure that the party in breach is only liable for the losses whose risks they appeared to accept by entering the contract. Without a remoteness rule, a party in breach would be liable for all loss resulting from the breach. This would include losses that the party in breach could never have known about. That is hardly fair. In fact, entering a contract would be a very risky thing to do if a party in breach could be sued for every loss caused by a breach. The fact that a limit is placed on how much can be claimed might seem equally unfair to the innocent party. However, the innocent party is in control of the situation because it is in a position to tell the other party about any and all relevant information about the contract. At the time of contracting, if a potential loss for Party A does not appear to be an obvious consequence of a potential breach by Party B, it can be made obvious simply by Party A telling Party B about it. A simpler way of putting this is that Party A has the responsibility to make Party B aware of the potential consequences of breach where they are not obvious.

The need for a remoteness principle can be illustrated with an extreme example. Imagine a student who earns some extra money as an independent bicycle courier. The student is hired to take a small parcel to deliver directly to a business person in a building across the city. Successful delivery is a contractual obligation. On the way, the student is hits a large pot-hole in the road and comes off the bike. The parcel lands in the middle of the road and is crushed by a bus. The sender that hired the student is then informed about how the parcel was destroyed. In response, the student is told that the parcel was a revolutionary prototype for a new microchip. It was going to a buyer who was paying £10 bn, if it arrived on time. On these facts, the breach has caused the sender to suffer a loss of £10bn. Should the student be liable for that loss? The packaging used and collection process was the same for any ordinary small parcel to be delivered by a cycle courier. At the time the job was agreed, a reasonable person in the same position as the student would have had no idea that a breach could cause such a loss. This is where the remoteness principle is relevant. At the time of the contract, causing such a loss would have been so unlikely that the loss will be too remote. After all, it can expected that such a high value item would be transported using a more secure method. Classing such a loss as too remote would not be unfair on the innocent sender because the sender could have told the student of the parcel's value and the importance of it being delivered on time. It would then be clear to the student that such a loss would be a likely consequence of failure to deliver. At that point there would be choices. The student could choose to not accept such a risk personally by arranging for insurance cover. Alternatively, liability could be limited to a small amount by using an exemption clause in the contract. Another option would be to simply refuse the job.

KEY POINTS

The remoteness rule limits liability to reflect the risk of loss that appeared to be accepted at the time of entering the contract.

10.3.2 The Basic Remoteness Test

This basic test is known as the *reasonable contemplation* test. 'Contemplation' means foreseeing or predicting something. In this context, 'reasonable' means 'objective'. The question to ask is whether the loss was within the 'reasonable contemplation' of the parties at the time they entered the contract. We can see that the test operates by looking back to when the parties made the contract. Back then, could they have foreseen or predicted that a future breach could cause such a loss? This is done from an objective perspective based on the facts available to the parties. It means we are not concerned with what the parties actually knew. Instead, the test is about what a reasonable person in the position of the parties *should* have known.

Put simply, the test asks if the parties were capable of knowing that a future breach could result in the relevant loss. If the loss could have been reasonably foreseen, this means that the parties knew there was a risk of a breach causing such a loss. By going ahead with the contract, it can be said that the parties then accepted the risk of causing such losses. Therefore, if a breach results in that loss, then the party in breach can be fairly made liable for it. If the loss could not have been foreseen sufficiently at that time of contracting, then the loss is *too remote* to result in damages.

KEY POINTS

The basic (general) remoteness test asks if the loss was within the reasonable contemplation of the parties at the time of contracting.

The cases on remoteness have never really questioned the need for a remoteness rule or the basic test. Instead, the key issue has been how probable or likely the contemplated loss needs to be. We know that the loss must be of a type and extent that the parties could (objectively) foresee. The problem is that there are different degrees of probability. There are things that have no chance of happening. Beyond that, we can foresee things as having a slight chance of happening. At the other extreme, we can foresee things as an absolute certainty. In the context of remoteness, the degree of likelihood or foresight required is a very important issue and we will see that when we explore the development of the basic test.

10.3.3 The Development of the 'Reasonable Contemplation' Test

The first key case on remoteness to address is *Hadley v Baxendale* (1854) 9 Exch 341. It is still cited by judges as representing the basic reasonable contemplation test. In other words, it is cited as authority for a remoteness rule based on what parties could have foreseen when contracting.

However, we will see that later cases have shaped how likely the loss has to be in order not to be too remote.

The claimant in *Hadley v Baxendale* owned a flour mill. One day, the steam engine that powered the mill had a broken crankshaft. To get a new one that fit, the owner had to send the broken one to be used as a pattern. To do so, the claimant mill contracted for the defendant courier (trading as Pickford & Sons) to deliver the item. When the defendant had collected the item, it waited a week before delivering it. This delay resulted in a serious cost to the claimant. Without a new crankshaft, it could not operate the mill, and this resulted in lost profit. Since the delay was a breach, the claimant sought damages of £300, which was a large sum back then. However, the Court of Exchequer held that the lost profit was too remote.

The lead judgment was by Baron Alderson who stated the rule to be applied. It was said that following a breach, damages should be:

> . . .[S]uch as may fairly and reasonably be considered as either arising naturally, ie, according to the usual course of things, from such breach of contract itself, or such as may reasonably be supposed to have been in the contemplation of both parties at the time they made the contract as the probable result of the breach of it.

This statement indicates that damages must be for loss that would appear to be 'naturally arising from the usual course of things' or sufficiently foreseeable as the consequence of a breach. The judgment then referred to unusual or special losses that the parties have told each other about:

> If special circumstances under which the contract was actually made were communicated by the plaintiffs to the defendants, and thus known to both parties, the damages resulting from the breach of such a contract which they would reasonably contemplate would be the amount of injury which would ordinarily follow from a breach of contract under the special circumstances so known and communicated.

This refers to losses that are ordinarily not objectively contemplated (i.e. losses arising from special circumstances). Such losses are recoverable in damages if they were communicated as a possibility at the time of contracting. Finally, on this point, Alderson B referred to circumstances in which a party in breach has not been told about the possibility of special circumstances:

> But, on the other hand, if these special circumstances were wholly unknown to the party breaking the contract, he, at the most, could only be supposed to have had in his contemplation the amount of injury which would arise generally, and in the real multitude of cases not affected by any special circumstances, from such a breach of contract.

Losses arising from special circumstances (unusual losses) cannot be claimed in damages where those circumstances were not made known to the party in breach at the time of contracting—the breaching party can only be liable for what could be expected to be losses which would arise 'generally' from such a breach.

The principles outlined were then applied. Anderson B considered what the defendant delivery business might have known when they entered the contract. They knew the item was a broken crankshaft. They knew the claimant was the owner of the mill. But they did not know the mill could not operate while the broken crankshaft was away for repairs. In fact, it would have been fair at the time the contract was made to assume that the mill would have a spare crankshaft. For that reason, the lost revenue for the mill was not within their reasonable contemplation. The loss did not flow 'naturally' from the breach. That made it a special loss which had not been communicated to the defendant as a possibility. For that reason, the lost profit was too remote and could not be claimed.

According to Alderson B, the loss will appear to be 'contemplated' in the following circumstances:

- where the loss arises naturally from the contract being breached (i.e. it is obvious as a possibility); or,
- where any special loss (i.e. not arising naturally) was communicated to the other party, meaning it was brought within their contemplation.

10.3.4 The Standard of Contemplation—How Foreseeable Does the Loss Have to Be?

The reasonable contemplation test remains. However, the circumstances required to satisfy it have changed. The first main change was made by the Court of Appeal in *Victoria Laundry (Windsor) Ltd v Newman Industries Ltd* [1949] 2 KB 528. The claimant laundry agreed to buy a larger boiler from the defendant. The idea was that with a larger boiler, they could expand their business. The defendant knew that the boiler was needed immediately, but delayed delivery for five months. This delay was a result of the boiler being damaged when it was dismantled for delivery. The delay was a breach and so the claimant sued to recover the resulting lost profit. There were two categories of lost profit claimed. There was the £16 per week that could have been made from extra customers. In addition, there was a claim for £262 per week. This reflected the profit expected from a dyeing contract with a Government department that supplied the military, which the laundry could now not perform because it had no suitable boiler.

The Court of Appeal held that the first claim of £16 could succeed. However, the lost profit from the Government contract was too remote.

In the judgment for the Court, Asquith LJ referred to Alderson B's judgment from the *Hadley* case. It was observed that two principles arose from that case. The first applied to natural loss. This was described by Asquith LJ as the 'ordinary and obvious' losses flowing from a breach. The second applied to special losses. Asquith LJ then applied these two principles together as a single rule with the same basic object: at the time of the contract was made the loss had to be 'reasonably foreseeable as liable to result from the breach'. The language he used has been criticised, as we shall see shortly, but for the time being we will examine the basis for his judgment.

By 'reasonably foreseeable' the judgment meant the loss had to be objectively foreseeable. The standard of foresight was addressed too. It had to be foreseen as 'liable to result'. This was explained by Asquith LJ as 'likely'; a 'serious possibility;' 'on the cards' and a 'real danger' of happening. Objectively, the loss could appear to be likely in its own right simply by virtue of being obvious. Alternatively, it could be made more likely because of what the parties had told each other. As illustrated by Figure 10.1, if the likelihood of the loss resulting is low, then more information has to be communicated about it for it to be claimable.

This shows how the single rule works. As the likelihood of the loss occurring reduces, the amount of information to be communicated about the potential loss must increase for the loss not to be too remote.

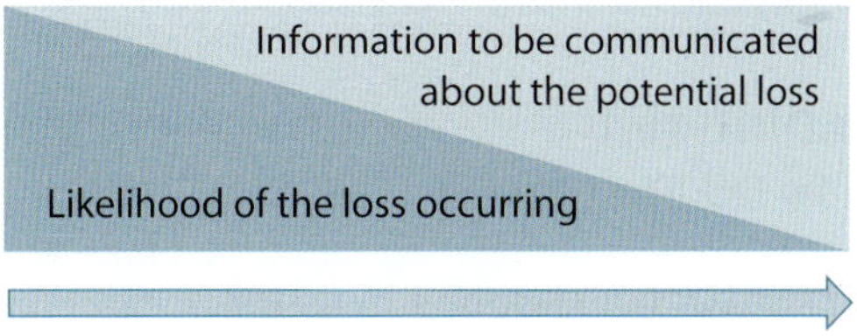

Information to be communicated about the potential loss

Likelihood of the loss occurring

Figure 10.1
The operation of a single remoteness test

The application of the rule was straightforward. Asquith LJ made reference to the large expensive boiler being bought by a laundry business. It was obvious it would be used to heat water for washing and dyeing. Equally, it was obvious that it was bought for a business. It was argued that it might have just been needed as a spare boiler (like in *Hadley v Baxendale*). That argument was rejected by Asquith LJ on the grounds that the defendants had been told that the boiler was needed urgently. Ultimately, it all meant that the ordinary lost profit appeared as a sufficiently foreseeable result of the breach. However, the profit from the special contract was not so likely. The defendant had no reason to know about the possibility of such a loss. The claimant had not mentioned the Government contract at the time of contracting. Consequently, that loss of £262 per week was too remote. That might seem unfair to the claimant. However, all the claimant had to have done to avoid this result was to have told the defendant about the Government contract at the time of contracting.

10.3.5 The Loss Has to Be 'Quite Likely' or a 'Serious Possibility'

The issue of how likely the loss became the subject of debate. It was discussed in detail by the House of Lords in *Koufos v C. Czarnikow Ltd, The Heron II* [1969] 1 AC 350. We can recall that Asquith LJ in *Victoria Laundry* said the loss had to be 'reasonable foreseeable' as 'liable to result'. Other phases were used too. By the time of the *Heron II*, the remoteness test for the tort of negligence had been established. That was done by the Privy Council in *Overseas Tankship (UK) Ltd v Morts Dock & Engineering co Ltd, The Wagon Mound (No 1)* [1961] 1 AC 388. There it was made clear that for negligence, the loss just has to be 'reasonably foreseeable'. So in the *Heron II*, the House of Lords considered the question of whether there should be a difference between the remoteness tests for contract and the tort of negligence, and whether it was appropriate to use the language of 'reasonable foreseeability' (as opposed to 'reasonable contemplation').

In *The Heron II*, the defendant ship owner contracted to carry the claimant's sugar to Basrah. The defendant knew there was a sugar market at Basrah. It also knew that the claimant was a sugar trader. The defendant did not know for certain that the claimant planned to sell its sugar on arrival. However, given the circumstances, such a plan to sell was not unlikely. In breach, the defendants stopped at some additional ports. The resulting delay meant the sugar arrived 9 days late and, by then, the market price of sugar had fallen. It meant the claimant made £4183 less that it would have done if the sugar had arrived on time. This lost profit was then claimed from the defendant ship owner. The House of Lords discussed how likely the loss that is objectively foreseen has to be in order for damages to be awarded. It decided that a higher degree of likeliness was required than the one used in tort. On the facts, this was satisfied and so all of the Lords agreed the loss was not too remote. On that basis, it was recoverable. It is a difficult case to be absolutely clear about, because all five of the Lords gave lengthy and detailed judgments and these are not always easily reconciled with each other. With that said, the lead judgment was by Lord Reid and we shall concentrate on his comments.

GUIDED CASE READING 10.1
Koufos v C. Czarnikow Ltd, The Heron II [1969] 1 AC 350
••

When you read the extract from Lord Reid's judgment, try to identify:

■ why the remoteness test in contract should be stricter than the one in the tort of negligence.
■ how foreseeable the loss has be so that it is not too remote.

So the question for decision is whether a plaintiff can recover as damages for breach of contract a loss of a kind which the defendant, when he made the contract, ought to have realised was not unlikely to result from a breach of contract causing delay in delivery. I use the words 'not unlikely' as denoting a	Lord Reid makes clear that 'not unlikely' means less than an even chance for a particular reason. The ship owner would have easily contemplated that the sugar was to be sold and hence that …

degree of probability considerably less than an even chance but nevertheless not very unusual and easily foreseeable.

[reference was made to the *Hadley v Baxondale* and the test from Alderson B]

. . . The crucial question is whether, on the information available to the defendant when the contract was made, he should, or the reasonable man in his position would, have realised that such loss was sufficiently likely to result from the breach of contract to make it proper to hold that the loss flowed naturally from the breach or that loss of that kind should have been within his contemplation.

The modern rule of tort is quite different and it imposes a much wider liability. The defendant will be liable for any type of damage which is reasonably foreseeable as liable to happen even in the most unusual case, unless the risk is so small that a reasonable man would in the whole circumstances feel justified in neglecting it. And there is good reason for the difference. In contract, if one party wishes to protect himself against a risk which to the other party would appear unusual, he can direct the other party's attention to it before the contract is made, and I need not stop to consider in what circumstances the other party will then be held to have accepted responsibility in that event. But in tort there is no opportunity for the injured party to protect himself in that way, and the tortfeasor cannot reasonably complain if he has to pay for some very unusual but nevertheless foreseeable damage which results from his wrongdoing. I have no doubt that today a tortfeasor would be held liable for a type of damage as unlikely as was the stoppage of Hadley's Mill for lack of a crankshaft: to anyone with the knowledge the carrier had that may have seemed unlikely but the chance of it happening would have been seen to be far from negligible. But it does not at all follow that *Hadley v. Baxendale* would today be differently decided.

. . .

But then it has been said that the liability of defendants has been further extended by *Victoria Laundry (Windsor) Ltd. v. Newman Industries Ltd.* I do not think so . . .

It appears to me that this was well justified on the earlier authorities. It was certainly not unlikely on the information which the defendants had when making the contract that delay in delivering the boiler would result in loss of business: indeed it would seem that that was more than an even chance . . .

But what is said to create a 'landmark' is the statement of principles by Asquith L.J. This does to some extent go beyond the older authorities and in so far as it does so, I do not agree with it. In paragraph (2) it is said that the plaintiff is entitled to recover 'such part of the loss actually resulting as was at the time of the contract reasonably foreseeable as liable to result from the breach'. To bring in reasonable foreseeability appears to me to be confusing measure of damages in contract with measure of damages in tort. A great many extremely unlikely results are reasonably foreseeable: it is true that Lord Asquith may have meant foreseeable as a likely result, and if that is all he meant I would not object further than to say that I think that the phrase is liable to be misunderstood. For the same reason I would take exception to the phrase 'liable to result' in paragraph (5). Liable is a very vague word but I think that one would usually say that when a person foresees a very improbable result he foresees that it is liable to happen.

. . . a delay would affect the price (because prices in an open market will fluctuate). However, not being experts in the sugar trade, they would have had no way of predicting whether a late delivery would have resulted in a higher or lower price for the sugar. In other words, there was a 50/50 chance that the sugar's price would be negatively affected by late delivery. Therefore, if 'not unlikely' meant 'better than an even chance', the sugar merchants would have escaped liability.

He then re-states Alderson B's test and uses that to frame his judgment, making it clear that the essence of the rule is sound.

Lord Reid then sets out the reason why the test in contract is different to that in tort. It is important to bear in mind that this case was being decided less than ten years after the Privy Council's decision in *The Wagon Mound*, and so this issue was still fresh. His point is that in contract the claimant will have had the opportunity to let the defendant know about special circumstances in advance, which would have allowed the defendant to price the possibility of loss into the contract accordingly. It therefore isn't fair to award a claimant damages for losses in special circumstances which the defendant did not reasonably contemplate and which were not made known to him or her. This is not the case with tort, where there is no opportunity for the victim to protect himself or herself in advance, and where therefore the law should provide more protection.

Lord Reid then sought to clarify the decision in *Victoria Laundry*. He was particularly keen that in contract the phrase 'reasonable foreseeability' should be avoided, so as not to confuse the tests in contract and tort. The point is that something can be 'foreseeable' without being very likely, meaning that it is not a very suitable term to use in the contract case, where the emphasis is on something being quite likely. The same was true of 'liable to result', which he felt could include something very improbable but foreseeable, along with 'on the cards' or 'a real danger'.

I agree with the first half of paragraph (6). For the best part of a century it has not been required that the defendant could have foreseen that a breach of contract must necessarily result in the loss which has occurred. But I cannot agree with the second half of that paragraph. It has never been held to be sufficient in contract that the loss was foreseeable as 'a serious possibility' or 'a real danger' or as being 'on the cards'.

?! THINKING POINTS

If something is a 'serious possibility' does it really sound less likely than something that is 'quite likely' or 'not unlikely'?

All of the Law Lords were clear that the remoteness test is an objective one. It is not necessary for the defendant to have actually foreseen the likelihood of loss. Instead, we have to ask what a reasonable person in the same circumstances at the time of contracting would have contemplated as a quite likely (or not unlikely) result of a breach.

It was agreed that *Victoria Laundry* was decided correctly. The problem was with the language used by Asquith LJ when applying the remoteness test. Lord Reid felt too many outcomes are 'on the cards'; 'liable to result'; a 'serious possibility' or a 'real danger' of happening. For that reason, he preferred to use 'quite likely' or 'not unlikely'. This was to represent a degree of foresight or likelihood that is less than an even chance, but not so low as to cover usual consequences.

The other judges agreed that 'on the cards' suggested a degree of likelihood that was too low. However, they expressed different opinions on the other phrases. For example, Lord Upjohn felt that a 'serious possibility' or 'real danger' did indeed represent a higher degree of likelihood. Lord Pearce also supported this language. Lord Hodson felt that 'liable to result' was fine. In the application, Lord Morris referred to the loss being 'likely' and 'liable to result'. However, Lord Morris also indicated that the actual language was not significant—in the end none of these phrases is very precise.

Whatever the preferences of the Lords, it is clear they meant broadly the same thing. They were referring to a likelihood that was below an even chance but higher than the test used in tort. They also had to ensure that their preferred test would reflect the result in *Hadley v Baxendale*. That was because *Hadley* was seen as the key authority on basic remoteness.

The language preferred by Lord Reid might well seem as vague as the other phrases. However, the later cases have tended to adopt the approach of Lord Reid. Even in *Farley v Skinner*, their Lordships referred to the loss as being 'quite likely' and 'not unlikely'.

KEY POINTS

- *The remoteness test from The Heron II: at the time of the contract, the loss from a potential breach must been (objectively) contemplated as quite likely or not unlikely.*
- The contract remoteness test is stricter than the one in tort because parties to a contract have the opportunity to communicate the potential loss to each other when entering the contract.

It was important to address the degree of likelihood of the loss because of what was said by Asquith LJ. The parties suggested that it covered loss that only had a slight chance of resulting. This was partly a result of Asquith LJ referring to 'reasonably foreseeable' losses. As Figure 10.2 illustrates, that was the relaxed test used in tort. It would mean a wider range of loss would fall within it, making the remoteness test easy to satisfy. The Lords agreed that Asquith LJ intended a stricter standard for contract. This standard would limit losses more than the rule used in tort.

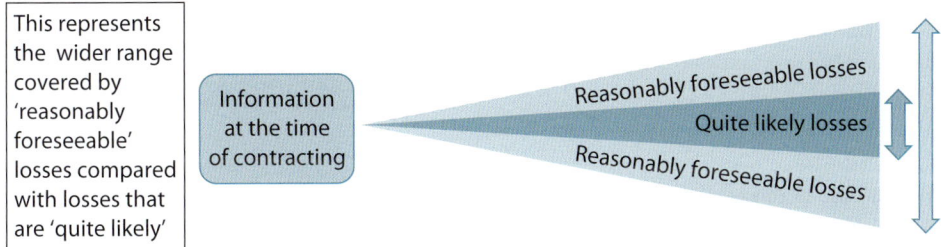

This represents the wider range covered by 'reasonably foreseeable' losses compared with losses that are 'quite likely'

Figure 10.2
'Reasonably foreseeable' losses and 'quite likely' losses

10.3.6 Remoteness Where a Breach Results in Physical Damage

So far, the cases on remoteness have been concerned with lost profits. Clearly this a type of financial loss. Likewise, financial loss can arise from physical damage. An example would be a breach that causes damage to an item of property. The innocent party could then claim for the difference in value or the cost of repair to reflect the financial loss suffered. However, physical damage raises issues when put in the context of the remoteness rule. These issues were addressed by the Court of Appeal in *Parsons (Livestock) Ltd v Uttley Ingham & Co Ltd* [1978] 1 QB 791.

The claimants in *Parsons* were pig farmers. They ordered an animal feed hopper for £275 to store their pignuts. The contract included the installation of the hopper. During installation, the defendant neglected to unseal the ventilation lid. This caused the pignuts to become mouldy. After eating these pignuts, many pigs became ill with *E coli* and 254 of them died. The defective installation was a clear breach of the contract and so the claimant brought an action for the loss of the pigs. The claim consisted of the value of the pigs and the lost profit from sales totalling over £36,000. In response, the defendant argued that the loss was too remote. This was based on the fact that ordinarily, mouldy nuts would not be fatal to pigs. The *E coli* suffered was a rare disease and such consequences had been too unlikely. On that basis, they argued that only damage to the feed had been contemplated as a likely result of the breach. For that reason, the defendant argued that they should be liable only for the cost of another bag of pig nuts (£18).

The trial judge upheld the farmer's claim, as did the Court of Appeal. In doing so, the Court of Appeal held that the loss was not too remote but adopted different approaches to reach the same outcome. Lord Denning MR delivered the first judgment, and the other was by Scarman LJ (with whom Orr LJ agreed) and so the judgment by Lord Denning MR represents the minority reasoning. However, it is important to understand the approach it represents in contrast to the majority reasoning.

GUIDED CASE READING 10.2
H Parsons (Livestock) Ltd v Uttley Ingham & Co Ltd [1978] 1 QB 791

When you read the extracts of the judgment by Lord Denning MR, try to identify:

- why Lord Denning MR did not apply the remoteness test from *The Heron II*;
- the remoteness test that Lord Denning MR did apply.

> . . .
>
> In *C. Czarnikow Ltd. v. Koufos* [1969] A.C. 350 the House of Lords said that, in remoteness of damage, there is a difference between contract and tort. In the case of a breach of contract, the court has to consider whether the

consequences were of such a kind that a reasonable man, at the time of making the contract, would contemplate them as being of a very substantial degree of probability.

[Reference was made to the different phrases used by the Lords to describe the degree of foresight]

In the case of a tort, the court has to consider whether the consequences were of such a kind that a reasonable man, at the time of the tort committed, would foresee them as being of a much lower degree of probability . . .

I find it difficult to apply those principles universally to all cases of contract or to all cases of tort: and to draw a distinction between what a man 'contemplates' and what he 'foresees'. I soon begin to get out of my depth. I cannot swim in this sea of semantic exercises—to say nothing of the different degrees of probability—especially when the cause of action can be laid either in contract or in tort. I am swept under by the conflicting currents. I go back with relief to the distinction drawn in legal theory by Professors Hart and Honoré in their book Causation in the Law (1959), at pp. 281–287. They distinguish between those cases in contract in which a man has suffered no damage to person or property, but only economic loss, such as loss of profit . . ., and those in which he claims damages for an injury . . . or damage actually done to his property . . .

[Tort cases were cited to show a distinction between pure financial loss and physical damage]

It seems to me that in the law of contract, too, a similar distinction is emerging. It is between loss of profit consequent on a breach of contract and physical damage consequent on it.

Loss of profit cases

I would suggest as a solution that in the former class of case—loss of profit cases—the defaulting party is only liable for the consequences if they are such as, at the time of the contract, he ought reasonably to have contemplated as a serious possibility or real danger . . .

Physical damage cases

In the second class of case—the physical injury or expense case—the defaulting party is liable for any loss or expense which he ought reasonably to have foreseen at the time of the breach as a possible consequence, even if it was only a slight possibility . . . you must ask: ought he reasonably to have foreseen, at the time of the breach, that something of this kind might happen in consequence of it? This is the test which has been applied in cases of tort ever since The Wagon Mound cases [1961] A.C. 388 and [1967] 1 A.C. 617. But there is a long line of cases which support a like test in cases of contract.

. . .

Each suffers like damage. The test of remoteness is, and should be, the same in both . . .

. . . [I]n some cases the makers of the hoppers supply them direct to the pig farmer under a contract with him, but in others they supply them through an intermediate dealer . . . in one case the pig farmer can sue the manufacturer in contract. In the other in tort. The test of remoteness should be the same. It should be the test in tort.

Applied to this case, it means that the makers of the hopper are liable for the death of the pigs. They ought reasonably to have foreseen that, if the mouldy pignuts were fed to the pigs, there was a possibility that they might become ill. Not a serious possibility. Nor a real danger. But still a slight possibility.

Lord Denning here summarises the judgments in The Heron II as they concern remoteness—i.e. that the test in contract is different to that in tort, and requires the loss to have been of a much higher likelihood.

He then, as was often the case in his judgments, attempted to innovate. His argument is in effect that the difference is not between contract and tort, but between cases in which there has only been economic loss and those in which there has been either injury or damage to property. This distinction cuts across both contract and tort.

So, where the loss is purely economic—that is, where it concerns lost profit—the test is basically that contained in The Heron II. But where the loss is physical (whether injury or damage to property) the test is the one from The Wagon Mound. It so happens that the former is a contract case and the latter is a tort one, but the two tests would cut across both areas of law.

This is more rational and fair in Lord Denning MR's view, because it means that the measure of damages will be the same whether somebody sues in contract or tort where the loss is effectively the same.

On that basis the makers were liable for the illness suffered by the pigs. They suffered from diarrhoea at the beginning. This triggered off the deadly E. coli. That was a far worse illness than could then be foreseen. But that does not lessen this liability. The type or kind of damage was foreseeable even though the extent of it was not: see *Hughes v. Lord Advocate* [1963] A.C. 837.

So here, where the damage was physical, the correct test was the one set forth in *The Wagon Mound*. The illness to the pigs was a slight possibility which was 'foreseeable' and therefore the loss was recoverable.

?! THINKING POINTS

If the death of the pigs had been quite likely or a serious possibility following a potential breach, would the farmers have entered the contract in the first place?

There is a lot of merit in making a distinction between financial and physical loss. Typically, physical damage also results in liability in the tort of negligence. That meant the farmers could have sued for the breach of contract or for the same loss in negligence. According to Denning, the same loss is suffered and so the same remoteness test should apply. After all, why limit the contract action with a strict test when the tort action is available anyway?

In terms of application, illness was a reasonably foreseeable consequence of a breach (i.e. a slight possibility). That was enough for the loss to be claimable. It did not matter that the rare disease and death that followed was not foreseeable.

The majority reasoning was represented by the judgment of Scarman LJ. This judgment also allowed the claim and did so on the basis that the loss was not too remote. However, a different approach was adopted. While this approach was less radical than Denning's, it does represent a further development. But like many judgments, it is delivered as a 'clarification' of the existing law:

> I differ from him only to this extent: the cases do not, in my judgment, support a distinction in law between loss of profit and physical damage. Neither do I think it necessary to develop the law judicially by drawing such a distinction. Of course (and this is a reason for refusing to draw the distinction in law) the type of consequence - loss of profit or market or physical injury - will always be an important matter of fact in determining whether in all the circumstances the loss or injury was of a type which the parties could reasonably be supposed to have in contemplation.
>
> [After discussing some of the key cases, the judgment returned to the trial judge's findings.]
>
> He was saying, in effect, that the parties to this contract must have appreciated that, if, as happened in the event, the hopper, unventilated, proved not to be suitable for the storage of pignuts to be fed to the plaintiffs' pigs, it was not unlikely there was a serious possibility that the pigs would become ill. . .
>
> I would agree with McGregor on Damages, 13th ed. (1972), pp. 131–132 that
>
> ". . . in contract as in tort, it should suffice that, if physical injury or damage is within the contemplation of the parties, recovery is not to be limited because the degree of physical injury or damage could not have been anticipated."
>
> . . .It is enough [that] physical injury must have been a serious possibility. . .
>
> It does not matter, in my judgment, if they thought that the chance of physical injury, loss of profit, loss of market, or other loss as the case may be, was slight, or that the odds were against it, provided they contemplated as a serious possibility the type of consequence, not necessarily the specific consequence, that ensued upon breach.

Scarman LJ did not adopt a distinction between physical and financial loss. He felt that such a distinction was not supported by the cases. Instead, in his view the same test for contract should apply whatever the loss. It has to appear as a serious possibility at time of contracting. However, on that point he diluted the test. He 'clarified' that only the *type* of loss had to be a serious possibility. The precise extent of the loss and actual damage suffered does not have be within the contemplation of the parties. That approach allowed for the loss to be claimable.

In terms of application, some illness was a serious possibility of a defective food storage unit. That was enough for the loss to be claimable. Again, it did not matter that the extent of loss suffered was not within the parties' contemplation.

KEY POINTS

For all loss from a breach the same rule applies. It must be possible to say that the *type* of loss could be (objectively) contemplated as a serious possibility (or quite likely) at the time of contracting.

The approach of the majority reasoning could be criticised as not reflecting the previous law. Consider this test in the context of *Victoria Laundry*. We could say that lost profit appeared as a serious possibility of a breach when contracting and that there is no need for it to be shown that the parties contemplated the extent or seriousness of the lost profit. Such an approach raises the obvious question as to why the profit from the Government contract was too remote. That is, the majority approach in *Parsons* focussed on the 'type' of loss. Pigs getting ill was the same type of loss as the death of the pigs from E.coli. It was just that the death was a more serious consequence of that *type* of loss. If that is the case, can it be said that the special profit lost in *Victoria Laundry* was just a more serious consequence of the same *type* of loss as the daily profit?

Alternatively, it could be said that there is no inconsistency at all between the majority approach of Scarman LJ and the result in *Victoria Laundry*. In *Brown v KMR Services Ltd* [1995] 4 All ER 598, Stuart-Smith LJ referred to the losses in *Victoria Laundry* and said:

> I accept that difficulty in practice may arise in categorisation of loss into types or kinds, especially where financial loss is involved. But I do not see any difficulty in holding that loss of ordinary business profits is different in kind from that flowing from a particular contract which gives rise to very high profits, the existence of which is unknown to the other contracting party who therefore does not accept the risk of such loss occurring.

According to the comment by Stuart-Smith LJ, the focus on the *type* of loss can be applied to the result in *Victoria Laundry*. The lost profit from the special contract was a different *type* of loss to the ordinary daily profit.

 THINKING POINTS

Do you agree that the lost profit from the special contract was different in *type*?

In *Brown v KMR Services*, the Court of Appeal applied the approach of the majority in *Parsons*. In this case, the claimant had suffered financial losses. This loss was not a result of physical damage. On the facts, the defendant could have been liable for breach of contract and negligence. It was held that the *type* of loss had to be a serious possibility (i.e. 'quite likely' or 'not unlikely'). However, following *Parsons*, the actual extent of the loss suffered did not have to be within the contemplation of the parties. Interestingly, the contract remoteness test was applied to the liability in both contract and negligence. The same was done more recently in *Wellesley Partners LLP v Withers LLP* [2015] EWCA Civ 1146. On this approach in *Wellesley Partners*, Floyd LJ stated:

> . . . I am persuaded that where, as in the present case, contractual and tortious duties to take care in carrying out instructions exist side by side, the test for recoverability of damage for economic loss should be the same, and should be the contractual one.

The logic for this approach was then explained:

> The basis for the formulation on the remoteness test adopted in contract is that the parties have the opportunity to draw special circumstances to each other's attention at the time of formation of the contract.

This reasoning is based on the point made by Lord Reid in the *Heron II*. In contract, only loss that is a serious possibility (or quite likely) is claimable. That is because the parties have the opportunity to tell each other about the possible losses that could arise. Usually in negligence such communication is not possible. However, when there is an action in negligence between contractual parties, such communication is possible. So, even though it is a negligence action, the stricter contract remoteness rule applies.

10.3.7 The Knowledge That the Parties Can Expect to Have

The remoteness rule requires the loss to be within the reasonable contemplation of the party in breach. Now, the operation of such a test is based on what the guilty party should have known. For example, should the party in breach have known that such a loss was quite likely? That knowledge could come from a number of sources. Such sources would include the surrounding circumstances and the context of the contract. In addition, we know that information communicated by the innocent party would be highly relevant. But even with relevant factors like these, we have to wonder how much knowledge the party in breach is assumed to have anyway.

The extent to which the party in breach is deemed to know of the processes of the other party was addressed in *Balfour Beatty (Construction) Ltd v Scottish Power plc* [1994] SLT 807. The House of Lords said there was no general rule that parties are presumed to know about each other's business practices. However, the simpler the activity, the easier it would be to infer knowledge of the activity. In this case, the construction company was building an aqueduct and needed a continuous pour of cement. This pour was interrupted by a power supply failure caused by the defendant's equipment. Consequently, the cement hardened before more could be added. This meant that all of it had to be destroyed and the process started all over again. The House of Lords said that the defendant electricity company could not have known about the defendant's work processes and therefore the need for a continuous pour. Furthermore, they could not have known that if the pour was interrupted, everything would have to be demolished and restarted. As a result, the defendant was not liable for the cost of the demolition and rebuilding.

10.3.8 Intention as the Conceptual Basis of Remoteness

The most significant recent development comes from *Transfield Shipping Inc v Mercator Shipping Inc (The Achilleas)* [2008] UKHL 48. One initial difficulty with the judgments was that there was no clear majority approach. This made it unclear what the resulting precedent was. However, since then, judges in later cases have tried to make sense of the judgments. In doing so, the significance of the case has become clearer. It is useful to have a detailed account of the case facts.

The Achilleas concerned a charterparty contract (where a ship and crew are hired for a certain time period or a particular voyage). In the case, the charterer returned the ship nine days late. This late return was a clear breach. In terms of the resulting loss, the shipowner had arranged for another party to charter the ship. This is known as a 'follow-on charter'. It was a lucrative contract and required the shipowner to deliver the ship to the new charterer by a certain date. However, because the shipowner received the ship late, it could not be delivered to the new charterer in time. Consequently, the shipowner had to renegotiate its contract with the new charterer. By then, the market rate for hire had fallen from $39,500 to $31,500 a day. To the shipowner, that represented a loss of $1,364,584. This amount was based on losing $8000 a day for the entire length of the follow-on charter. It was this total loss that was claimed from the defendant charterer as a consequence of their nine day delay. In contrast, the defendant charterer argued that their liability was only $158,301. That was the difference between the rate in their contract and the higher market rate over the nine days. Importantly, this was the liability that was commonly understood in the shipping industry as resulting from a late return. Basically, it represents the profit a shipowner generally loses when a ship is returned late. The charterer is expected to pay for the additional time at the contract rate. If the market rate is higher, then that increase should be included too. That way, in theory, the shipowner would not suffer a loss. Essentially, the charterer wanted to compensate for losses suffered for the duration of the delay. However, the shipowner claimed for the loss suffered for the duration of the follow-on charter.

The arbitrators and trial judge held that the claim by the shipowner was not too remote. The Court of Appeal agreed. The reasoning was based on the fact that it was *quite likely* there would be a follow-on charter. On that basis, it should have been contemplated that such a loss could result. However, the House of Lords disagreed and held that the charterer was only liable for the $158,301. The rest of the loss relating to the follow-on charter was too remote. The judgment of Lord Hoffman is very significant and so it is important to take a closer look.

GUIDED CASE READING 10.3
Transfield Shipping Inc v Mercator Shipping Inc (The Achilleas) [2008] UKHL 48

When you read the extracts from the judgment of Lord Hoffman, try to identify:

▪ the conceptual basis of the remoteness that is recognised;
▪ the reasons behind that conceptual basis and its impact on the application of the remoteness test.

[Reference was made to the dissenting arbitrator who agreed with the majority that the loss would have been very likely, but (unlike the majority) he held that the loss claimed was still too remote].

[6] . . . But he said that a reasonable man in the position of the charterers would not have understood that he was assuming liability for the risk of the type of loss in question. The general understanding in the shipping market was that liability was restricted to the difference between the market rate and the charter rate for the overrun period and 'any departure from this rule [is] likely to give rise to a real risk of serious commercial uncertainty which the industry as a whole would regard as undesirable'.

. . .

[9] . . . The case therefore raises a fundamental point of principle in the law of contractual damages: is the rule that a party may recover losses which were foreseeable ('not unlikely') an external rule of law, imposed upon the parties to every contract . . . or is it a *prima facie* assumption about what the parties may be taken to have intended, no doubt applicable in the great majority of cases but capable of rebuttal in cases in which the context, surrounding circumstances or general understanding in the relevant market shows that a party would not reasonably have been regarded as assuming responsibility for such losses?

[10] . . . There is no case in which the question now in issue has been raised. But that in itself may be significant. This cannot have been the first time that freight rates have been volatile. There must have been previous cases in which late redelivery caused the loss of a profitable following fixture. But there is no reported case in which such a claim has been made . . . Instead,

Lord Hoffman begins by making clear where the difficulty arises. The loss of the follow-on charter was 'very likely' in the views of the arbitrators and it therefore easily met the requirement of being 'quite likely'. However, it was commonly accepted in the shipping industry that in these circumstances the only recoverable loss was for the duration of a delay, and not for follow-on charters. So was the correct approach to award damages for losses which were 'not unlikely' (or 'quite likely') *per se*, or to award damages for losses based on the contemplation of the parties given the expectations in the industry and other background circumstances?

there has been a uniform series of *dicta* over many years in which judges have said or assumed that the damages for late delivery are the difference between the charter rate and the market rate . . .

[Reference was then made to cases and the leading books on charterparty agreements to support the point. Lord Hoffman then referred to the views of leading professors from their publications.]

[11] . . . They show that there is a good deal of support in the authorities and academic writings for the proposition that the extent of a party's liability for damages is founded upon the interpretation of the particular contract; not upon the interpretation of any particular language in the contract, but (as in the case of an implied term) upon the interpretation of the contract as a whole, construed in its commercial setting . . . I agree that cases of departure from the ordinary foreseeability rule based on individual circumstances will be unusual, but limitations on the extent of liability in particular types of contract arising out of general expectations in certain markets, such as banking and shipping, are likely to be more common. There is, I think, an analogy with the distinction which Lord Cross of Chelsea drew in *Liverpool City Council v Irwin* [1977] AC 239, 257–258, . . . between terms implied into all contracts of a certain type and the implication of a term into a particular contract.

[12] It seems to me logical to found liability for damages upon the intention of the parties (objectively ascertained) because all contractual liability is voluntarily undertaken. It must be in principle wrong to hold someone liable for risks for which the people entering into such a contract in their particular market, would not reasonably be considered to have undertaken.

[13] The view which the parties take of the responsibilities and risks they are undertaking will determine the other terms of the contract and in particular the price is paid. Anyone asked to assume a large and unpredictable risk will require some premium in exchange . . .

. . .

[21] It is generally accepted that a contracting party will be liable for damages for losses which are unforeseeably large, if loss of that type or kind fell within one or other of the rules in *Hadley v Baxendale* . . . That is generally an inclusive principle: if losses of that type are foreseeable, damages will include compensation for those losses, however large. But . . . it may also be an exclusive principle and that a party may not be liable for foreseeable losses because they are not of the type or kind for which he can be treated as having assumed responsibility.

> Lord Hoffman was of the view that the correct approach was the latter of these—i.e. that the contract had to be understood in its commercial setting. To be recoverable a loss had to be in the reasonable contemplation of the parties at the time of making the contract, taking the contract within its commercial setting and in light of expectations in that setting.

> However, Lord Hoffman then introduced another consideration into the mix had the breaching party assumed 'responsibility' for the loss or the 'risk' of it occurring? He appeared to suggest that in certain circumstances it did not matter whether a loss was foreseeable (or in the contemplation of the parties) but whether the breaching party had 'assumed responsibility'.

Lord Hope adopted a similar approach to Lord Hoffman. In contrast, Lord Rodger and Baroness Hale gave judgments that were much closer to the traditional approach set forth in *Hadley v Baxendale* and *The Heron II*. Lord Walker then said that he agreed with the reasoning of Lords Hoffman, Hope *and* Rodger! That makes it difficult to work out the precedent set by the case.

10.3.8.1 *The Significance of* The Achilleas

In terms of the significance of the case, the approach of Lord Hoffman and Lord Hope represents a development of the conceptual basis of the remoteness rule and its application. However, it does not replace the test from *The Heron II* that interpreted *Hadley v Baxendale*. It is more accurate to say that the test in *The Heron II* allows us to establish whether a party has assumed responsibility for a loss (that is, if the loss is in the contemplation of the parties as the probable result of the breach, then it can be said that the breaching party was assuming responsibility for it, or the risk of it happening). But the commercial context, such as expectations in the relevant market (if there is one), could also be relevant.

KEY POINTS

■ *The test from The Heron II continues to apply, but it is now seen as the primary means for identifying the risk of loss accepted by the parties.*

■ *In exceptional cases, other strong evidence of such an intention might displace the outcome of the The Heron II test.*

Technically the loss claimed was a quite likely (a serious possibility) and that was the outcome of the arbitration. But at the same time, the defendant charterer could not have intended to be responsible for that loss. This was based on the general understanding in the shipping industry. In that market, it was commonly assumed that a delay would result in extra payment. That payment would be the contract rate for the extra days. In addition, the difference in the contract and a higher market rate would be paid.

The result was that the loss claimed was too remote. This was because the defendant could not have intended to accept responsibility for it, irrespective of its likelihood. To achieve this, Lord Hoffman had to show that remoteness was really based on the parties' intentions, as shown by Figure 10.3. Lord Hoffman aimed to ensure that the approach did not change everything. For that reason, it was said that ordinarily, the *The Heron II* test would be a strong enough indication of intention. However, in certain markets, there could be a strong understanding that there was no such intention. Examples of such markets included the shipping industry and banking sector.

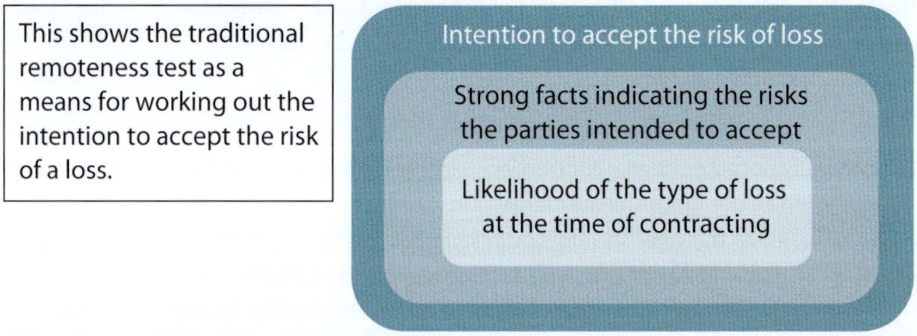

> This shows the traditional remoteness test as a means for working out the intention to accept the risk of a loss.

> **Intention to accept the risk of loss**
>
> Strong facts indicating the risks the parties intended to accept
>
> Likelihood of the type of loss at the time of contracting

Figure 10.3
Remoteness and the intention to accept the risk

10.3.8.2 The Reasoning of Lords Hoffman and Hope

The judgments of Lord Hoffman and Lord Hope concerned the basis for the remoteness rule. Traditionally, the remoteness test seemed to be treated as rule of law, rather than a reflection of the parties' intentions. Under such a rule of law, loss could be claimed if it should have been contemplated as quite likely. However, in these judgments, remoteness was understood to be based on the parties' intentions. It was shown that such an approach could explain the test from *The Heron II*. After all, that test would be satisfied when the loss appeared to be quite likely when the contract was created. By entering the contract, the defendant would be showing the apparent intention to accept the risks of foreseeable losses. But that is only one assumption that can be made about the intentions of the defendant. Other factors or circumstances could be relevant. These could show that there was in fact no intention to accept the risk. For example, in the relevant market or industry, it may be understood that the loss in question cannot be claimed. Such an understanding is then part of the circumstances relevant to working out the parties' intentions. It is part of the general context of the contract to be taken into consideration when working out if the defendant accepted the risk of the loss.

All of this was to make a clear point. Lord Hoffman wanted to treat the remoteness rule as being based on the parties' intentions. The point was that by doing so, it would not be inconsistent with or undermine existing case law.

THINKING POINTS

Does this approach by Lord Hoffman echo his contextual approach to interpretation?

➜ CROSS-REFERENCE
For a detailed discussion of the contextual approach to interpretation see 6.4.3.

Lord Hoffman put forward more reasons to justify basing remoteness on the parties' intentions. First, he pointed out that the type of loss claimed in the case could not be very unusual. Other ship owners must have suffered it too at some point, yet the claim itself had not been argued in a case before. This was attributed to the fact that it was accepted in the sector that the extra days are paid for at the contract rate or the higher market rate. That then covers the loss suffered by the ship owner. The point is that the general understanding in the shipping industry was supported by evidence from the case law.

Lord Hoffman said that it was logical for a defendant to be liable only for the risks which they can be said to have accepted. Contract liability is all about liability that is *voluntarily* accepted. Likewise, it would be unfair to impose liability for risks that have not been accepted. On that point, it was observed that the risks accepted would be reflected in the price paid. Parties accepting higher risks would charge more. A remoteness principle based on a strict rule of law would not reflect this, but one based on the parties' intentions would.

Similarly, implied terms are imposed by the courts. These can be implied in law so that they apply to all contracts of a certain type. When that is done, it is not based on intentions but instead, on grounds of policy and fairness. But even when that is done, the obligation imposed is aimed to be consistent with the commercial context. In doing so, it is consistent with the general expectations parties should have in that market.

➜ CROSS-REFERENCE
For the discussion of implied terms in law see 6.5.7.

Lord Rodger and Baroness Hale applied the traditional *Heron II* test. In doing so, they concluded that the loss was too remote. The problem is that it is difficult to see why the loss was not contemplated as a likely possibility. On the facts, such a loss would have been obvious. Furthermore, the arbitrators concluded that the loss was very likely and therefore, sufficiently contemplated.

10.3.8.3 *The Case Law Following* The Achilleas

Given the different reasoning adopted, there was no clear majority reasoning. That resulted in some uncertainty over the practical impact of the case. It is then for later cases to provide some guidance. The approach represented by *The Achelleas* was not followed by the Singapore Court of Appeal in *MFM Restaurants Pte Ltd v Fish & Co Restaurants Pte Ltd* [2010] SGCA 36. This was on the basis that it was not strictly binding there. It was felt that the assumption of the risk was already incorporated into the standard *Heron II* test. Of course, in England and Wales, the approach of Lord Hoffman cannot be set aside so easily.

In *Supershield Ltd v Siemens Building Technologies FE Ltd* [2010] EWCA Civ 7, Toulson LJ (with whom the other Lord Justices agreed) provided some guidance. The traditional remoteness test was viewed as a policy rule. However, it was felt that an interpretation of the contract or commercial context could override the policy rule. Accordingly, a loss that is within the parties' contemplation might still be too remote if it is shown that the risk of it happening could not have been accepted. That was the result in the *Achilleas* itself. Likewise, even if the loss is not within the parties' contemplation, there could still be liability. That would be where the circumstances show that the risks of the loss were accepted anyway. That was the approach adopted in the *Supershield*.

An interpretation of *The Achilleas* was provided by Hamblen J in *Sylvia Shipping Co Ltd v Progress Bulk Carriers Ltd (The Sylvia)* [2010] EWHC 542 (Comm). There, it was observed that the traditional test would be enough for the majority of cases. However, there could be 'unusual' cases like the *Achilleas*. In such cases, the courts will also look at the context and market to see if there was an acceptance of the relevant risks. Hamblen J went on to say that these would be 'rare' cases. Such cases would be those where the traditional test could result in 'unquantifiable, unpredictable, uncontrollable or disproportionate liability'. Furthermore, it would include cases where there is clear evidence that the liability would be inconsistent with 'market understanding and expectations'. This approach was echoed by Sir David Keene in the Court of Appeal case of *John Grimes Partnership Ltd v Gubbins* [2013] EWCA Civ 37.

At this stage, it appears that the *Heron II* test will continue to decide the remoteness rule. It reflects an intention to accept the risk of the loss. However, strong evidence against such an intention could mean that there is no liability for the loss. Ultimately, this approach gives judges the flexibility to ensure that the outcome reflects commercial common sense.

10.4 The Duty of Mitigation

So far we have seen that a damages claim could be limited by the principles of causation, contributory negligence and remoteness. A further limit that could be relied upon by a defendant is the duty to mitigate the loss.

➡ CROSS-REFERENCE

Mitigation was a key issue in *White & Carter v McGregor* [1962], discussed at 8.5.1.

A claimant will want to be compensated for all of the loss suffered as a result of a breach. But in some cases, the claimant might have been able to prevent the full loss being suffered. Alternatively, the claimant's own conduct might have increased the loss suffered. In such circumstances, the question is whether the claimant is still entitled to be compensated for all of the loss. That is where the duty to mitigate is relevant. It is a duty not to increase the loss and to minimise it where it is reasonable to do so.

As an example, consider a standard, basic hotel that has allowed itself to be overbooked. A pre-booked customer goes to check-in only to be told that there is no longer a room available. That is a breach. The customer would be entitled to damages to cover the extra amount needed to pay for a room in an alternative hotel. But this has to be reasonable. So if the customer responds by checking into an expensive luxury hotel, then it could be said that the customer has unreasonably increased the loss resulting from the breach.

The duty to mitigate is defined by a range of cases which reveal it has two aspects. The first is that the loss has to be minimised where it is reasonable to do so. The example often cited is *Payzu v Saunders* [1919] 2 KB 581. This concerned a contract for silk to be delivered over nine months. Payment was to be made each month after delivery. After one payment, the seller refused to continue unless the payments were made 'cash on delivery'. This was a clear breach and the buyer refused to comply. They then sued for the difference between the contract price and the market price. At this stage, the market price of the silk had increased significantly. The court held the buyer was not entitled to such compensation. The reason was simply that the buyer should have agreed to pay on delivery and then sued for any associated losses (if any). By not doing so, the buyer had not taken reasonable steps to reduce its loss. The decision has been criticised because it meant that the supplier could then sell the goods elsewhere and benefit from the increased market price (Bridge, 'Mitigation of Damages in Contract and the Meaning of Avoidable loss' (1989) 105 LQR 398).

Mitigation requires *reasonable* steps to reduce the loss rather than absolute steps. In some cases, the innocent claimant could be capable of reducing the loss, but it would not be reasonable for it to do so because of the consequences that might result. An example that is often cited is *James Finlay & Co v NV Kwik Hoo Handel Maatschappij* [1929] 1 KB 400. The case concerned a contract for sugar to be shipped over three months, the latest to be shipped in September. The cargo was actually loaded and shipped in October. However, the transferrable ownership document (the bill of lading) incorrectly stated that the cargo was shipped in September. The claimant did not know about the error, and entered contracts with sub-buyers for the sale of the cargo. These contracts with the sub-buyers stated that the bill of lading was 'conclusive evidence' of the shipment date. The sub-buyers eventually refused to accept the cargo because the bill of lading was not accurate. The claimant buyer was then forced to sell the sugar at an auction for less than the market price. They then sued the seller, and the seller argued that the loss should have been mitigated by the claimant simply enforcing the contracts for the sub-sales. After all, the contracts did state that the bill of lading was 'conclusive evidence' of the shipment date. The Court of Appeal disagreed and held that it would have been unreasonable for the claimant to insist on enforcement of the sub-contracts. If they had (knowing that the bill of lading was inaccurate) it would have served to harm the claimant's business reputation. Thus the claimant had acted reasonably.

The other aspect of the duty is that the loss must not be unreasonably increased. This really depends on the circumstances. A useful example is *Banco de Portugal v Waterlow & Sons Ltd* [1932] AC 452. Here a breach by the defendant, which was a printer printing money for the claimant, resulted in lots of unauthorised money being put into circulation. To control the damage and protect the currency, the claimant issuing bank decided to replace any unauthorised money with authorised currency. It then claimed the cost of doing so from the defendant. The defendants denied that they were liable for the loss. They argued that the loss was caused by the bank's own decision to replace the unauthorised money. On that basis, the defendants felt they were only liable for the cost of making more bank notes. The House of Lords held that the defendant was liable for the all of the loss claimed. The judgments referred to the duty to mitigate and explained that the action taken by the bank was reasonable even though it had resulted in a greater loss. Consequently, on the facts, although the loss had been increased by the bank, it had not been unreasonably increased. So the duty does not create an absolute obligation not to increase the losses suffered. Instead, losses must not be unreasonably increased.

KEY POINTS

The duty to mitigate requires the claimant to:

▦ *take reasonable steps to reduce the loss; and*
▦ not *unreasonably* increase the loss.

CHAPTER SUMMARY

■ The loss claimed must have been caused by the breach rather than an intervening act.

■ The 'but for' test is used to rule out breach as the cause of the loss, but cannot in itself identify the cause.

■ Where there is concurrent liability in contract and negligence, it is possible for damages to be reduced for contributory negligence.

■ The defendant is only liable for losses that are not too remote. The test for remoteness is the reasonable contemplation test.

■ The standard of contemplation is that at the time of the contract, the loss must have been a 'quite likely' or ('not unlikely') result of a potential breach.

■ For physical loss, only the *type* of loss has to be (objectively) foreseen as quite likely; the severity of the loss does not have to have been foreseen.

■ The remoteness test is the primary means to identify the risks that the parties intended to accept by entering the contract.

■ Since the remoteness test is the indication of the parties' intentions, other strong evidence of intentions might be used to contradict the outcome of the remoteness test.

■ Finally, the innocent claimant is under a duty to mitigate the loss suffered by taking reasonable steps to reduce it or by not unreasonably increasing it.

KEY CASES

☐ *Lambert v Lewis* **[1982] AC 225**—an authority on causation and unreasonable conduct breaking the chain of causation.

☐ *Forsikringsaktieselskapet Vesta v Butcher* **[1986] 2 All ER 488**—the authority on the availability of a reduction in damages for contributory negligence that is always cited, even by higher courts.

☐ *Hadley v Baxendale* **(1854) 9 Exch 341**—the traditional authority for the basic remoteness rule. Whatever developments take place, judges make sure that it is consistent with this case.

☐ *Victoria Laundry (Windsor) Ltd v Newman Industries Ltd* **[1949] 2 KB 528**—delivered the remoteness rule as a single test of reasonably foreseeable losses. Again, when judges develop the remoteness rule, they aim to be consistent with the outcome of this case.

☐ *Koufos v C. Czarnikow Ltd, The Heron II* **[1969] 1 AC 350**—the leading authority on the standard of likelihood required for the remoteness test.

☐ *Parsons (Livestock) Ltd v Uttley Ingham & Co Ltd* **[1978] 1 QB 791**—authority for the remoteness rule for loss caused by physical damage or injury.

☐ *Transfield Shipping Inc v Mercator Shipping Inc (The Achilleas)* **[2008] UKHL 48**—the most recent significant case that recognised the intention basis of the remoteness rule as opposed to it being a rule of law.

☐ *Banco de Portugal v Waterlow & Sons Ltd* **[1932] AC 452**—a House of Lords authority on the claimant's duty to mitigate their loss.

QUESTIONS

1. Nigella owns a luxury car hire business and placed an order for an addition ten Bentley Continental GT's from Gordon, a dealer of nearly new cars. Nigella makes it clear that she needs the cars by the end of May because she has bookings for the cars, and Gordon agrees. The delivery of the cars is delayed so they arrived two weeks late. This means that Nigella was unable to fulfil the bookings made for those weeks. One of these bookings was to supply the cars to a 'grime' artist 'Normsy' for his latest music video, which would have earned Nigella a further £100,000. Advise Nigella as to losses that she should be able to claim for.

2. 'The various limitations on damages claims by the innocent party mean that the law ends up treating the breaching party too leniently.' Discuss.

3. 'The decision of the House of Lords in *The Achilleas* was an undesirable development in the law.' Discuss.

 For answer guidance to these questions please visit the online resources at www .oup.com/uk/naidoo1e/, where you will also find multiple choice questions to check your understanding of key concepts.

FURTHER READING

Bridge, 'Mitigation of Damages in Contract and the Meaning of Avoidable Loss' (1989) 105 LQR 389.
This is a leading article on mitigation and provides some excellent criticism of the cases.

Kramer, 'The new test of remoteness in contract' (2009) 125 LQR, 408.
A significant case note on *The Achilleas* which provides useful criticism and the views on the importance of interpretation.

Lord Hoffmann, 'The Achilleas: custom and practice or foreseeability?' Edin. LR 2010, 14(1).
This provides a very interesting and approachable account of the House of Lord's development of remoteness in *The Achilleas*. An essential read.

Peel, 'Remoteness re-visited' (2009) 125 LQR, 6.
Another important case note on *The Achilleas* that provides useful criticism of the two approaches adopted by the judgments.

Robertson, 'The Basis of the Remoteness Rule in Contract' (2008) 28 Legal Studies 172.
This is one of the 'heavyweight' articles cited by Lord Hoffman in *The Achilleas*. It provides a very detailed critique of basing remoteness on the parties' intentions.

11 Remedies Part III: Non-compensatory Remedies

LEARNING OBJECTIVES

By the end of this chapter you should be able to:

- explain the requirements for the remedies (associated with contracts) beyond ordinary compensatory damages;
- apply the rules governing the availability of these remedies including the validity of clauses that fix the damages to be awarded following a breach;
- assess the development and availability of restitutionary (gain-based) damages following a breach;
- evaluate the case law on damages based on a fee that might have been negotiated to release the defendant from the obligation breached (negotiating damages).

INTRODUCTION

In the previous two chapters, we looked at compensatory damages and the principles that can limit such awards. Such damages are the standard remedy following a breach. However, there are also some alternative, exceptional remedies that could be available to an innocent party. Generally, they can only be used when an award of compensatory damages would for some reason not be adequate or is unavailable.

We start with specific performance and injunctions. Both remedies were developed in equity rather than the common law. This means that their application is largely discretionary and so we will look at the factors that could be relevant to the exercise of that discretion. We then turn briefly to the remedy of restitution for unjust enrichment. While this is a different area of law, it can provide a remedy where there was thought to have been a contract but it turns out there wasn't one. In certain circumstances, it could also provide a remedy following a breach. A basic grasp of this area will also help to understand the very exceptional 'restitution for a wrong' remedy. This remedy is a genuine departure from the traditional compensatory approach. It is one of the more exciting aspects of contract law because it is so controversial. Our final two issues are also controversial and equally exciting, and have been clarified by recent decisions by the Supreme Court. The first of these relates to the remedy of negotiating damages. The other issue relates to agreed damages clauses and the extent to which they are unenforceable as penalties.

11.1 Specific Performance

Specific performance is a court order instructing a party to perform the contract. Failure to follow such an order can be serious. It can amount to a contempt of court, resulting in fines and possible imprisonment.

The remedy is exceptional. It was developed through equity and now serves as a supplement to the common law. The remedy remains available at the discretion of the courts. So, unlike damages, there is no legal right to specific performance. With that in mind, its availability can be a little uncertain. However, over the years, the case law has developed some rules and relevant factors regarding its application. These help to give us a better idea about whether such a remedy is likely to be granted. Here we address some of these rules and factors.

11.1.1 Damages Must Be Inadequate

We know that an award of compensatory damages is the usual remedy following a breach. Specific performance is not a remedy that is chosen as an alternative to damages. Instead, it is only a possibility when damages would be inadequate. By 'inadequate' we don't mean that the amount will not be enough. After all, damages are based on the loss suffered. Instead, damages are inadequate where the award does not protect the innocent party's expectation (performance) interest.

Damages might not protect the expectation interest for a range of reasons, but we can focus on some typical examples. The most obvious is when there is a contract for something that is unique. Consider a contract for the sale of JK Rowling's first draft of the first *Harry Potter* book. Likewise, consider a contract for footwear that Usain Bolt actually wore in the 100m final at the London Olympics. Both contracts are for the sale of a unique item. Crucially, this means that there is no available market for such goods. If the seller decides to sell to someone else, there is a breach. But damages would not help the innocent party. That is because damages for breach of a sales of goods contract are meant to enable the innocent party to purchase goods elsewhere. In doing so, the buyer would be in the position they should have been in, had the contract been performed. Clearly, that is not possible with the first draft of the first *Harry Potter* book or Usain Bolt's shoes. In those cases, damages would not protect the buyer's performance interest.

While specific performance is exceptional, it is addressed in legislation. Section 52 of the Sale of Goods Act 1979 makes reference to specific performance as a possible remedy. That applies to commercial contracts. Basically, it confirms that the remedy is available in relation to the sale of particular (as opposed to generic) goods. For consumers, the Consumer Rights Act 2015, s.58 refers to the power of the courts to order specific performance. But in either case, the basic requirements from the case law apply.

Even if the goods are not unique, it still might be possible to show that damages are inadequate. The real issue is whether there is, in practice, an available market. The case often cited for this point is *Sky Petroleum Ltd v VIP Petroleum Ltd* [1974] 1 WLR 576. It concerned a ten-year agreement for the supply of petrol and diesel, and the defendant supplier wanted to end the contract. However, at the time, there was a global oil shortage. Oil and its products were not unique, but it would not have been possible for the claimant to obtain oil elsewhere before going out of business. For that reason, a mandatory injunction was granted to ensure performance. This type of injunction had the same effect as specific performance by stopping the supplier ending the contract. It was chosen because unlike specific performance, it is available at an interim (or initial) hearing. Such mandatory injunctions are only available when damages are inadequate. The point then, is that damages could be inadequate when the available market is not commercially realistic even if the goods being sold are generic, like oil.

Specific performance is more common in relation to contracts for the sale of land or a house. This is because each such property is seen as unique. That even applies where a house is on an estate with houses of the same type from the same builder. This position is well established in law, but is not without criticism.

Damages could be inadequate where it is impossible to quantify the loss suffered. That might be because the loss is too speculative. The point was mentioned by the House of Lords in *Co-operative Insurance Society Ltd v Argyll Stores Ltd* [1998] AC 1.

Ordinarily, specific performance will not be needed when the obligation is the payment of money. In such circumstances, damages should be adequate. However, where the obligation to pay is not enforceable, it could then justify specific performance. The key example is *Beswick v Beswick* [1968] AC 58. Here an uncle sold his business to his nephew. Under the terms the nephew had to make weekly payments of £6 10s to the uncle. More importantly, on the uncle's death, weekly payments of £5 had to be made to the uncle's widow. After the uncle's death, the widow was not paid. At the time, it was well established that only a party to a contract could enforce it. The widow was not a contractual party, but the uncle's estate was, and so the estate could enforce the contract. The problem was that the estate was only entitled to nominal damages because the estate had suffered no loss. Instead, the loss was suffered by the widow only. Consequently, the House of Lords ordered specific performance for the estate.

→ CROSS-REFERENCE
For the law relating to the rights of parties outside of a contract see Chapter 12.

11.1.2 The Discretion of the Court

Even if damages are inadequate, specific performance can still be refused (*Co-operative Insurance Society Ltd v Argyll Stores Ltd* [1998]) because, after all, the application of the remedy should also be fair and just, given that it originates in equity. That can be determined by assessing the consequences of the remedy based on the facts. The important point here is that this assessment should be made in view of *all* the relevant facts. The award of the remedy might well be fair for the claimant, but that needs to be balanced against any resulting unfairness to the defendant. A number of relevant and related factors have been revealed by the case law.

In some cases, an award of specific performance could result in the defendant suffering hardship. If that is greater than the loss to the claimant, the remedy might not be ordered. The key example here is *Patel v Ali* [1984] Ch 283. The defendant seller contracted to sell her house. The sale was delayed and so four years on, the buyer sought specific performance. However, during the period of delay, the seller's circumstances had changed significantly. She had suffered from cancer and had her leg removed. She had two additional children and her husband became bankrupt and was imprisoned. As a result, the seller was dependent on the help of friends and family nearby. The court held that specific performance would result in 'hardship amounting to injustice'. On that basis, damages were awarded. In his decision, the judge emphasised that the hardship was a result of unexpected changes of circumstances. Financial difficulties on their own would not ordinarily be enough.

Oppression of the defendant is a factor based on the same reasoning as hardship. In certain contracts, it is accepted that specific performance would be oppressive. The key example is a contract of employment or personal service. The idea of forcing someone to work for someone else conflicts with principles of personal freedom and liberty. In fact, specific performance as a means of forcing a person to work for another is now prohibited under the Trade Union and Labour Relations (consolidation) Act 1992, s.236.

A number of factors were relevant to the refusal of specific performance in *Co-operative Insurance Society Ltd v Argyll Stores Ltd* [1998]. The contract was a sub-lease granted by the claimant to the defendant. It was for the largest unit of a new shopping centre. The defendant agreed to run their supermarket there for 35 years. The presence of such a shop was important for the claimant because it would attract lots of customers. In turn, that would benefit the smaller businesses in the centre. With 20 years remaining on the lease, the defendant notified the claimant that they were closing the shop. This decision was based on the shop not making enough money. The claimant then sought specific performance for the defendant to continue leasing the shop for the remaining 20 years. The House of Lords recognised that damages would be inadequate. This was based on it being too difficult to assess the claimant's loss over such a long period of time. In particular, it would have been too speculative to work out what the financial impact would have been on the smaller businesses in the shopping centre. However, this was still not enough to justify the order of specific performance. It would be too oppressive to force the defendant to continue in a failing business for 20 years. It would also have been disproportionate to the loss arising from the breach.

The need for constant supervision has also developed as a well-recognised reason to refuse the remedy. It is based on avoiding the risk of continuing litigation to enforce the remedy. Consequently, the courts prefer to allow the remedy when the obligation to be performed is a single one-off act, such as transferring ownership of something. This was another reason for the decision in the *Argyll Stores case*. If the remedy had been granted, it would have required supervision for 20 years. This does not mean that specific performance will not be available whenever the obligation is a long one. What matters is the potential to have to keep enforcing the obligation. That really depends on how simple the obligation is. *Wolverhampton Corporation v Emmons* [1901] KB 515 concerned a contract for the building of houses. Specific performance was ordered for the builders to complete the houses. Such an obligation will take some time to perform, however the builder's obligation was well defined because they had to follow detailed plans. That meant a dispute over compliance with the court order was unlikely.

Another factor that could be relevant to the exercise of the discretion relates to mutuality. The idea is that in equity, both parties should be entitled to performance, not just one of them. Traditionally, the claimant could have the remedy if it would have been available to both parties (*Flight v Bolland* (1828) 4 Russ 298). This has been developed in *Price v Strange* [1978] Ch 337. Essentially, the remedy can be allowed if the defendant would have an adequate remedy for a future breach by the claimant. Such a requirement can provide fairness to the defendant by not exposing them to hardship.

KEY POINTS

- ▦ Unlike damages, there is no right to specific performance; instead it is discretionary.
- ▦ For specific performance, damages must be inadequate to protect the expectation interest.

11.2 Performance-based Remedies in Consumer Contracts

The Consumer Rights Act 2015 has special rules on remedies following a breach. These rules are in sections 19 to 23 and are presented in a hierarchical structure. At the top of the hierarchy are the first tier remedies of remedies of repair and replacement. These are followed by the possibility of the second tier remedies, price reduction and a final right to reject (i.e. end the contract for a refund). This hierarchy of remedies was not an innovation from the UK. Instead, it reflects Directive 99/44 EC from EU law. Originally, the remedies were added to the Sale of Goods Act 1979 in 2003 before being carried over to the CRA 2015, so that they are embedded firmly into UK law. These performance-based remedies reflect the tradition of civil law jurisdictions from the EU. Such rights for consumers throughout the EU represent an enhanced level of consumer protection. A detailed assessment is better placed in more specialist books on consumer law and sales law, but it is useful to provide a brief overview.

Clearly, repair, replacement and price reduction are performance-based remedies. They keep the contract alive through performance by the trader. Following a breach, consumers can rely on this hierarchy of performance-based remedies by opting for repair or replacement. Alternatively, they can exercise a short-term right to end the contract by rejecting the goods and claiming a refund and possibly damages. If the short-term right to reject is not available, then the hierarchy of remedies would be the only source of a remedy.

The consumer can insist on repair or replacement as long as these are not impossible. These are to be carried out within a reasonable time without significant inconvenience for the consumer. In addition, the seller bears the costs, for example the costs of postage, labour and material. Also, if both remedies are possible, but one is disproportionate to the other, then the disproportionate remedy is not an option. A remedy is disproportionate if it imposes unreasonable costs on the seller based on the price paid; the significance of the breach; and whether the remedy would cause significant inconvenience on the consumer.

➡ CROSS-REFERENCE
For the discussion of the short-term right to reject see 8.6.2.1.

The important point is that the proportionality comparison is between repair and replacement, rather the remaining 'second tier' remedies. This means that if repair is impossible, then the consumer can insist on replacement, irrespective of the cost. An extreme example can be seen from the (EU) Court of Justice ruling in C-65/09, *Gebr Weber v Jurgen Wittmer* [2011]. It concerned the sale of polished tiles for EUR 1,382.27. Around two thirds were laid in the consumer's house before a variation in the shading was noticed. That was a breach of the quality obligation. An expert confirmed that the shading was a result of micro brush marks which could not be removed. At first instance, it was held that the only remedy was the complete replacement of the tiles at a cost of EUR 5830.57. That covered the cost of removing the defective tiles and laying the equivalent amount of new tiles. The Court of Justice upheld this approach, only adding that the seller's payment for the cost of replacement could be limited to a proportionate amount. That figure was for the national court to determine, based on the circumstances, which the court had done.

The consumer can move to the second tier options in three circumstances. One is where both repair and replacement are both impossible. Another is where there has been a failed repair or replacement. The final circumstance is where those remedies have not been provided within a reasonable time and without significant inconvenience to the consumer. In the second tier of remedies, price reduction would reflect the difference in value and keep the contract alive. If the consumer chooses the final right to reject then there might be a reduction in the refund to reflect the consumer's beneficial use of the goods. It should be emphasised that such a deduction is for *use* rather than to reflect a reduction in the market value of the goods. In some cases, defects might make goods completely unusable so that there is no basis for the deduction. In addition, the CRA 2015 introduced a rule that no deduction for beneficial use can be made in the first six months, unless the purchase was of a motor vehicle.

KEY POINTS

Under the CRA 2015, following a breach, consumers are entitled to performance-based remedies such as repair and replacement. Where these are not available, consumers are entitled to a price reduction or an end to the contract.

11.3 Injunctions

An injunction is another equitable remedy. From a basic, general perspective, an injunction is an order to stop someone doing something. As an order from the court the penalties for breaching an injunction are the same as those for specific performance.

Injunctions can be available in many areas of law. In contract, injunctions are used to stop a party doing something they promised *not* to do. Such a promise is a negative obligation. An example would be where a café is under a contractual obligation to not have outside seating. If it looks like such a facility is going to be introduced, an injunction might be sought to prevent it. This may be better than waiting for the breach and then claiming damages, which would mean the outside seating would remain.

There are two types of injunction:

- *Prohibitory* injunctions are used to stop a breach by enforcing a particular negative obligation. This would be the type of injunction used to stop the café introducing an outside seated area.

- *Mandatory* injunctions are used after the breach. Such an injunction requires a party to correct or reverse the effect of the breach. So, if the outside seated area is introduced, the remedy would require its removal.

As a remedy from equity, injunctions are ordered at the discretion of the court. In the case of mandatory injunctions, they are generally reserved for more extreme cases. Also, the same requirements concerning orders for specific performance apply to an order for a mandatory injunction.

In contrast, prohibitory injunctions are not as restricted. The requirements relevant to specific performance and mandatory injunctions do not apply, and here the courts are more willing to exercise their discretion to enforce an obligation. A common example is where a business stops a worker revealing information they promised to keep confidential, where clearly waiting for the breach and then suing for damages would be useless because by that time the confidential information would already have been revealed. They are also used in actions concerning the economic tort of inducement to breach a contract. That is an action to stop someone taking steps to get a party to breach an existing contract.

11.3.1 Contracts for Personal Services

The courts will not allow an injunction to be used to achieve the effect of specific performance in cases of contracts for personal services or employment contracts. That being said, the distinction within the cases can be a fine one. This can be illustrated with the two cases that follow.

The first case on this point is *Lumney v Wagner* (1852) 1 De GM & G 604. The defendant performer had agreed to sing at the claimant's theatre for three months. She also agreed not to perform in other theatres without the claimant's permission. In breach, she arranged to sing at other venues. The claimant then sought an injunction preventing her from doing so, and it was granted. In a strict sense, this remedy was not forcing the defendant to work for the claimant. It just meant she could not perform in other theatres during that period. In theory, she could have had a completely different job elsewhere without breaching the injunction. On that basis, the granting of the injunction was not equivalent to ordering specific performance of her contract. The obvious criticism is that it is unrealistic to expect a professional singer to take a different job. It could be said that in reality, the injunction would have had an effect equivalent to ordering specific performance.

The other case of *Warner Bros Inc. v Nelson* [1937] 1 KB 209 is more extreme. It concerned Bette Davis, who was a very famous US actress at the time. In her contract with Warner Bros, she agreed not to star in films made by other companies for three years. This obligation was enforced with an injunction. The same criticism as before applies. Was it realistic to assume that such an actress would take a different job? The effect was to lock her into her employment with Warner Bros and this was more extreme because of her status and the long period of the obligation.

In contrast, a more nuanced approach was adopted in *Page One Records Ltd v Britton* [1968] 1 WLR 157. It concerned a rock band called 'The Troggs'. They were famous at the time both in the UK and US. Following a contract dispute with their manager, an injunction was sought to prevent them working with a new manager. However, this was rejected because the band could not continue without a manager. That meant the injunction would force them to work with their current manager, which would be oppressive. The same approach was adopted in *Warren v Mendy* [1989] 1 WLR 853. This concerned a contract between a boxer and his manager. The injunction was sought to prevent the boxer working with the defendant, a new manager. The injunction was refused because the effect would have been to force the boxer to remain with his manager, and that decision was upheld by Court of Appeal.

The courts in *Page One Records* and *Warren* were more willing to consider the context and did not simply assume that any job would do. They showed an awareness that it might be oppressive to order a prohibitory injunction preventing an employee breaching an employment contract if there were no realistic employment prospects elsewhere.

KEY POINTS

▪ Injunctions are an order from the court to stop a party doing something.
▪ Injunctions are not to be granted to achieve the effect equivalent to specific performance so as to evade the restrictions applied to specific performance in personal services contracts.

11.3.2 Commercial Contracts

In contrast to the cases on personal services, a stricter approach is applied to commercial contracts. This was demonstrated in *LauritzenCool AB v Lady Navigation Inc* [2005] EWCA Civ 579. It concerned a charterparty agreement for two ships. The owners wanted to end the agreement to free the ships for other contracts. The Court of Appeal granted an injunction to prevent the ships being used elsewhere. In doing so, the court acknowledged that realistically, the owners would have to continue the charterparty. However, the court made a distinction in relation to the type of contract. It was not a personal contract, or equivalent to one. It did not undermine or restrict the personal liberty of an individual.

11.4 Restitution for an Unjust Enrichment

We have already seen in 1.5.3 that the law of contract is part of the wider private law of obligations that also includes tort and unjust enrichment. The key feature of the law of unjust enrichment is that the remedy is *not* based on the loss suffered. Instead it is based on reversing the *benefit* gained by the other party. This means that principles of remoteness and mitigation do not apply. They are only relevant when assessing a claimant's *loss* and to work out how much of that loss the party in breach should be responsible for.

According to Lord Steyn in *Banque Financière de la Cité v Parc (Battersea) Ltd* [1999] AC 221, unjust enrichment is based on the following requirements:

- A party receives a benefit (they were enriched)
- The enrichment was at the expense of the claimant
- It is unjust for the enriched party to keep the benefit

These requirements are not concerned with a contract. However, actions for unjust enrichment can be relevant to parties that have *had* a contract or where parties expected to have a contract. It is in these narrow contexts that we need to consider restitution as a possible remedy. Such a remedy could result in the return of a payment made. Alternatively, it could mean that payment is awarded for the value of goods of services provided.

→ CROSS-REFERENCE
For the discussion of damages liability as secondary obligations see 8.3.

→ CROSS-REFERENCE
The law on mistake is the subject of Chapter 17.

→ CROSS-REFERENCE
The certainty requirement was explained at 4.2–4.5.

→ CROSS-REFERENCE
Misrepresentation is the subject of Chapter 13. Chapters 14 explains illegitimate threats and pressure under the heading of Duress; and Chapter 15 details Undue influence.

11.4.1 A Contract Cannot Exist between the Parties

If a contract exists, then it is not possible to rely on unjust enrichment. Instead, the contract governs the rights of the parties. Either the contract dictates the outcome with its actual express terms, or the contract's secondary obligations on compensatory damages will apply. But sometimes a contract is void from the start. An example might be a contract that was made as a result of a mistake of fact. A typical example is where a contract is made about a thing that no longer exists at the time. Likewise, the same can be said when an agreement is too uncertain to be a contract. When a contract is void from the start, there are no rights or obligations to be enforced. If any money is paid, then it is an unjust enrichment claim that is used to recover it. The same can be said where it is decided that there never was a contract. Likewise, the parties might have made payments on the basis of a contract that they expect to enter. If they did not get around to entering the contract, an unjust enrichment claim might be possible to recover money paid.

In addition, some contracts can become void (i.e. where a party has the right to make the contract void). That may be where it is made following a misrepresentation. The same applies when a contract is entered as a result of illegitimate threats or pressure.

Finally, we have seen in Chapter 8 that a contract can come to an end following a repudiatory breach. When that happens, there is a secondary contractual obligation to pay damages. However, in certain circumstances, the innocent party might be able to rely on an unjust enrichment claim as an alternative to a contract action for breach. When available, an action based on unjust enrichment will allow for the return of any money paid. This is quite controversial. The contract is over, but the secondary obligation from the contract to pay damages only is still there. It then seems strange to ignore the liability from that secondary obligation and rely on unjust enrichment. However, the scope for an unjust enrichment claim in a 'contract' context is extremely limited. The key limitation is that there must be what is called 'a total failure of consideration'. That is our next point to consider.

11.4.2 There Must Be a Total Failure of Consideration

In contract law, 'consideration' can be the promise of a benefit. But in the context of unjust enrichment actions, 'consideration' has a different meaning. The word is used to refer to the basis for giving a benefit to someone else. On this, a comment by Viscount Simon LC in *Fibrosa SA v Fairbairn Lawson Combe Barbour Ltd* [1943] AC 32 is often cited. There, the following point was observed:

> [I]t is, generally speaking, not the promise which is referred to as the consideration, but the performance of the promise.

We know that a *promise* of value is enough to create the contract. But for a restitutionary remedy, *performance* of the promise is the issue. The defendant must not have provided any performance due under the contract. That is what makes any benefit (or enrichment) 'unjust'.

Where the defendant has provided some of the performance, there is a partial failure of consideration. Such a partial failure is not enough to get back any payments made, and the correct remedy is damages. The traditional case often cited for this point is *Whincup v Hughes* (1871) LR 6 CP 78. To work out if the failure of consideration is total, the courts focus on the performance contracted for.

In *Fibrosa v Fairbairn*, a buyer paid in advance for machinery to be made and delivered. Before delivery could take place, war broke out. The buyer was based in what had become enemy territory. That meant performance would have been illegal. The House of Lords confirmed that the contract had come to an end. More importantly, it was held that there was a total failure of consideration. On that basis, the buyer was entitled to the return of the payment. The basis of the contract was the delivery of the machinery. That was the performance the seller was to provide. The fact that the seller had to manufacture the machinery did not matter. There was still a total failure because it was a contract for a sale. That required ownership to be transferred and this had not happened—the buyer had received absolutely nothing which it had bargained for.

The requirement of a total failure of consideration was further defined by House of Lords in *Stocznia Gdanska SA v Latvian Shipping Co* [1998] 1 WLR 574. Here shipbuilders contracted to build a number of refrigeration ships. Under the terms, the buyer had to pay in instalments. The second payment was due after a certain stage of construction. When the buyer didn't pay, the builders sued. In response, the buyer argued there had been a total failure of consideration. This was based on not having ownership of the ships contracted for. Based on the terms, the House of Lords held that there had not been a total failure.

On the total failure of consideration point, Lord Goff made some important observations (the reference to 'property' in the following comment means ownership):

> I start from the position that failure of consideration does not depend upon the question whether the promisee has or has not received anything under the contract like, for example, the property in the ships being built under contracts 1 and 2 in the present case. Indeed, if that were so, in cases in which

the promisor undertakes to do work or render services which confer no direct benefit on the promisee, for example where he undertakes to paint the promisee's daughter's house, no consideration would ever be furnished for the promisee's payment. In truth, the test is not whether the promisee has received a specific benefit, but rather whether the promisor has performed any part of the contractual duties in respect of which the payment is due.

According to the statement, for a total failure of consideration we do not look at what has been received from performance. Instead, the focus is on whether an obligation from the contract has been performed. Knowing that means the courts have to interpret the contract to identify the performance required from the obligations. In the case itself, the contract was not seen as a simple contract of sale. Instead, it was a contract to design and build the ships and then transfer them to the buyer. This was supported further by the instalment payments. The second instalment corresponded with a stage of construction. That meant there had been some performance as required under the contract.

11.4.3 The Advantage of Restitution over Compensatory Damages

When possible, a claim based on unjust enrichment has a real advantage over a claim for breach. This is where the innocent claimant has entered into a bad bargain. Consider a Pizzeria that contracts to buy a new scooter for deliveries. The contract price of the scooter is £2000. The buyer pays the £2000 in advance but it is not delivered. To make matters worse, it is discovered that the market price for the scooter has fallen to £1500. If the buyer sues for compensatory damages, the claim would be for £1500. That will be enough to buy an alternative scooter elsewhere. Such an award would then place the buyer in the position they would have been in, had the contract been performed. In that position, the buyer would have a scooter at a cost of £2000 (as intended originally under the contract). Alternatively, if the restitutionary remedy for unjust enrichment was the basis for the claim, the buyer would be able to receive a refund of the £2000 paid. They could then buy the alternative scooter for £1500, and still have another £500 left over. Essentially, the buyer would thereby escape the consequences of making a bad deal.

THINKING POINTS

→ CROSS-REFERENCE
For the limits of reliance damages see 9.4.2.

Is it fair that a party can escape a bad bargain with a restitutionary remedy (when available) but not with reliance damages for expenses?

Being able to escape a bad bargain might seem unfair to the party in breach. That party might argue that the contractual remedy should apply. On the other hand, the party in breach has failed to engage with the contract in not supplying the scooter at all. On that basis, perhaps it can be said that the party in breach ought not to be entitled to rely on remedies from the contract, as they have ignored it. Whether that is enough to justify the approach taken in the cases is debatable.

KEY POINTS

■ Restitution for unjust enrichment can apply when a contract is void or never came into existence. Otherwise, the remedy of damages from the contract should apply.

■ There has to be a total failure of consideration. A partial failure will not allow for restitution.

11.4.4 Getting Paid for Services or Goods Provided

Restitution as a remedy for unjust enrichment does not only apply to enrichment resulting from a payment. A party can be enriched by receiving goods or services that they have not paid for. We will briefly address the remedy in this context.

11.4.4.1 The Quantum Meruit Remedy

A *quantum meruit* is another restitutionary remedy and is also the subject of intense debate. However, for our purposes, we just need to appreciate the basics.

The remedy is an award of a reasonable sum for work done. Consider a party that provides goods or services that had been requested, though not as a result of a contractual obligation. Where no payment is made in return, the performing party would seek a *quantum meruit*, meaning a reasonable sum in respect of the service or goods provided. In the context of goods supplied the remedy is properly called a *quantum valebat*. The same rules apply, however, and the term *quantum meruit* is generally used to cover both.

Just like restitution for money paid, a *quantum meruit* can be sought where there is no contract or when a contract is voided. In addition, it could be sought when a contract has ended—for example when a contract has been discharged and goods or services have changed hands ancillary to performance of it.

11.4.4.2 Availability of a Quantum Meruit

A *quantum meruit* award might be the only remedy where there is no contract. A typical example of this is *British Steel Corporation v Cleveland Bridge & Engineering Co* [1984]. We can recall that the parties expected to enter into a contract. On that basis, the claimant started manufacturing parts. Unfortunately, the parties could not agree on the terms and so no contract was made. On the facts, both parties objectively expected the work to be paid for. The solution was to award the claimant a *quantum meruit* for the work done, meaning a reasonable sum for the cost of the parts which had been sent.

The same can apply where a contract is void. When it is, there are no contractual rights to enforce *Rover International Ltd v Cannon Film Sales* [1989] 1 WLR 912. A *quantum meruit* could then be available as a remedy.

Where there is a breach of contract, a *quantum meruit* is also an option. For the remedy to be available, the contract must have been ended. It is useful where only some performance has been provided before the contract ends. Usually, the contract price to be paid is based on full performance. In such circumstances, the claim for a *quantum meruit* would be used to be paid for the work done.

> ➔ CROSS-REFERENCE
>
> For the basic facts of the *British Steel Corporation v Cleveland Bridge & Engineering Co* [1984] see 4.3.2.

11.4.2.3 Assessment of the Amount to Be Awarded

The amount to be awarded will be a reasonable amount for the work done. This is assessed objectively. It will be the amount a reasonable person would have expected to pay (*Benedetti v Sawiris* [2012] UKSC 50). Clearly, the market price for the work done will be the most important factor here. But it is important to appreciate that the amount of the award is also contingent on the gain or benefit given to the defendant. It is not based on the claimant's cost of providing the service. It follows that a price stated in a contract should not necessarily limit or dictate the amount of the *quantum meruit* award. This is especially so when there is a voided contract or where there was never a contract in the first place (since the contract price in those circumstances obviously has no binding effect). However, where a contract is terminated for breach, the contract price may still be used to set the award. That was the opinion of Cook J in *Taylor v Motobility Finance Ltd* [2004] EWHC 2619 (Comm). This is useful in circumstances in which a claimant may end up being better off than if the contract had been performed because of the court finding that the *quantum meruit* is higher than the contract price.

11.5 Restitution for a Wrong: The Account of Profits Award

In some cases, following a breach, the innocent party might not have suffered any loss at all. In such cases the effect of the traditional contract damages rule would mean that there is nothing to be compensated for. Ordinarily, there would be an award of nominal damages which takes the form of a token amount to reflect that the claimant has won the dispute. In the circumstances, any substantial award would not be compensatory. Instead, such an award would simply punish the other party for their breach, and we already know that contract damages are not aimed to punish the party in breach (*Addis v Gramophone*).

→ **CROSS-REFERENCE**

For the discussion of *Addis v Gramophone* [1909] see 9.6.3.

> **?! THINKING POINTS**
>
> ▪ Does it seem fair that if there is no loss, no damages will be awarded?
> ▪ What if the party in breach made a huge profit from that breach?

Of course, it is possible that the party in breach has made a profit from it. In fact, the potential to profit might have been the reason for breaching the contract. If the breach causes no loss, the party in breach would not have to pay compensatory damages as a general rule, while at the same time enjoying the profit made from the breach. Such circumstances raise an important question. Should the innocent party be awarded some or all of the profit enjoyed by the party in breach? If so, on what legal basis could such an award be made?

We have already seen that restitutionary remedies take away the gain given to one party. It is important to appreciate that the reason for this is that the gain has come at the expense of the innocent claimant. That party might be claiming the return of a payment. Alternatively, they might seek payment for goods or a service. In such circumstances, something (money, goods, or services) has been *subtracted* from one party to benefit another and this is the justification for it being awarded as a remedy. In contrast, when we talk about claiming the profit made from a breach, we are talking about a benefit which the breaching party gained but that did not come at the expense of the claimant. To award the claimant such a benefit would require therefore an extension of the restitutionary remedies and this has been an issue in a number of cases.

11.5.1 The Traditional (General) Rule on the Account of Profits Claim

Our starting point is the traditional position on claiming the profit from a breach. This position was addressed directly in *Surrey County Council v Bredero Homes* [1993] 1 WLR 1361. Before addressing this position, it is useful to look at the facts of the case. These facts provide a good example of our basic context of a breach that results in no actual loss to the innocent party, but does result in the other party gaining a profit.

Surrey County Council sold land to the defendant, a property developer. The idea was that the developer would then build houses on the land to sell. Put simply, under the agreement, the developer could only build according to the existing planning permission which permitted the building of 72 houses as a maximum. In breach of this agreement, the developer built an additional five houses. This was done having secured new planning permission from the district authority. The Council then sued the developer for breach. On the facts, the Council had not suffered any actual loss as a result of the breach, but the developer had profited from their breach. That profit was from having five additional houses to sell. On that basis, the Council wanted some or all of the profit made by the developer. The claim was rejected by the Court of Appeal who awarded nominal damages of £2 because no loss had been suffered.

KEY POINTS

The general rule is that if a party profits from their breach, the innocent party has no right to claim that profit.

Given the established compensatory basis for contract damages, we might wonder why the Council even dared to make such a claim. Of course, there had to be some sort of legal basis to support their argument. That legal basis was *Wrotham Park Estate Co v Parkside Homes Ltd* [1974] WLR 798, a case concerning an infringement of property rights. It is important to understand this earlier case because of the attention and significance that it attracted later.

In the case, a developer bought some land. This land was subject to a **restrictive covenant**. The restrictive covenant required any building development to follow a certain layout. However, the developer built houses in a way that breached the restrictive covenant. The claimant had the right to enforce the covenant and so they sought a mandatory injunction.

> **restrictive covenant**
> is a limit on the *use* of land and is legally enforceable. It continues to apply even when land is sold.

As a matter of policy, Brightman J refused to grant the injunction because it would have resulted in houses being demolished. The judge then turned to the possibility of damages and, from the language used, he was keen to make an award. Brightman J said the defendant had 'invaded the plaintiffs' rights in order to reap a financial profit'. Furthermore, the defendant should not have 'undisturbed possession of the fruits of their wrong-doing'. The problem was that the claimant had suffered no loss. The breach had not even reduced the value of their neighbouring land. That meant that there was no scope for traditional compensatory damages. However, Brightman J acknowledged that the defendants expected to make £50,000 profit. On that basis, the claimant was awarded 5% of the profit (£2500). The basis for the figure is important. It reflected a reasonable amount the claimant might have negotiated to release the restriction in the covenant. Crucially, it was a figure based on the profit made from the defendant's wrongdoing.

The claimant in *Wrotham Park* did not have a contract with the defendant. Instead, it was about the enforcement of property rights. However, the damages were awarded in lieu of (i.e. instead of) an injunction. When that is done, it is supposed to be on the same basis as damages at common law. That was a point confirmed later in *Johnson v Agnew* [1980] AC 367. With that in mind, could the *Wrotham Park* award be treated as damages at common law for a breach of contract? That issue was addressed directly by the Court of Appeal in *Surrey v Bredero Homes*.

In *Bredero Homes*, Dillon LJ stated that *Wrotham Park* was about the interference with property rights. Infringing the restrictive covenant was likened to trespass to land in tort. There you can get damages, even though there is no loss caused by a party entering your land. This makes tort a better analogy than contract law. In addition, he observed that the award in *Wrotham Park* was damages in lieu of an injunction. In contrast, the Council in *Bredero Homes* had not applied for an injunction, so there was nothing that they could be said to be claiming damages 'instead of'.

In *Bredero Homes*, Steyn LJ regarded the award in *Wrotham Park* as restitutionary, and made some important statements about restitution-based remedies following a breach:

> The introduction of restitutionary remedies to deprive cynical contract breakers of the fruits of their breaches of contract will lead to greater uncertainty in the assessment of damages in commercial and consumer disputes. It is of paramount importance that the way in which disputes are likely to be resolved by the courts must be readily predictable. Given the premise that the aggrieved party has suffered no loss, is such a dramatic extension of restitutionary remedies justified in order confer a windfall in each case on the aggrieved party? I think not. In any event such a widespread availability of restitutionary remedies will have a tendency to discourage economic activity in relevant situations. In a range of cases such liability would fall on underwriters who have insured relevant liability

> risks. Inevitably underwriters would have to be compensated for the new species of potential claims. Insurance premiums would have to go up. That, too, is a consequence which mitigates against the proposed extension. The recognition of the proposed extension will in my view not serve the public interest. It is sound policy to guard against extending the protection of the law of obligations too widely. For these substantive and policy reasons I regard it as undesirable that the range of restitutionary remedies should be extended in the way in which we have been invited to do so.

In other words, where Dillon LJ gave robust legal reasons for rejecting the intrusion of *Wrotham Park* damages into contract law, Steyn LJ rooted his objections in policy; it was not only difficult to justify doctrinally, but also undesirable to award *Wrotham Park* damages in contract cases.

The *Bredero Homes* case represents the traditional rejection of (and general rule against) awarding the profit from a breach and the use of *Wrotham Park* to do so. However, we will see that the approach of the Court of Appeal is not absolute. There have been some instances where damages have been based on the profit gained from the breach.

11.5.2 The Very Exceptional Account of Profits Award

The account of profits award (sometimes described as 'disgorgement') results in the profits obtained from the breach being awarded to the innocent party. Such an award is not compensatory, because it is not based on the loss which the innocent party has suffered. Instead, such an award is a deterrent to discourage parties from acting in a certain way, and it serves effectively to punish the party in breach. The use of such a remedy is therefore inconsistent with ordinary contract principles. However, controversially, the House of Lords permitted such an award in *Attorney-General v Blake* [2001] 1 AC 268.

11.5.2.1 The Development Introduced by Attorney-General v Blake [2001]

The House of Lords developed a very limited exception to the rules on damages for breach of contract in *Attorney-General v Blake*. The case concerned an action against George Blake, a former UK spy. In the 1950s he passed secret information to the Soviet Union. As a result, in 1961 he was convicted of treason, but in 1966 he escaped from prison and fled to Moscow. Then, in 1989 he wrote his autobiography. It was published in the UK and so the UK Government brought an action against Blake for the remaining £90,000 due to be paid by his publisher. Essentially, the Government wanted Blake to hand over the profits obtained from his wrongdoing.

The established claim for profit following a breach of confidence was not an option because the information in the book was already in the public domain. For that reason, the Government initially relied on breach of a fiduciary duty. This claim, which was based in equity, was rejected at first instance and in the Court of Appeal because there was no such breach. The main reason was that there is no fiduciary duty owed to an employer by a *former* employee. Consequently, in the appeal to the House of Lords, the Attorney-General for the Government focussed on Blake's breach of contract. Essentially, Blake signed a contract when he joined the UK intelligence services. In this contract, he agreed not to publish any official information gained from his job. The problem was that since the Government had suffered no financial loss from the breach, there was no scope for a standard (compensatory) damages award. However, the House of Lords (by a majority of four to one) allowed the claim for the profit as the remedy for the breach. This award was treated as a special or exceptional remedy and so the reasoning adopted by the House of Lords is both very interesting and important.

The lead judgment was by Lord Nicholls. It referred to examples where damages are based on the benefit obtained from wrongdoing. These included torts like trespass to land and unlawful interference of goods. Reference was also made to areas of law where an account of profits is a standard remedy. Infringement of intellectual property like copyright was one of these examples. Others included actions for breach of confidence and breach of a fiduciary duty in equity. The judgment then referred to the usual circumstances where damages would be inadequate. Examples of the use of injunctions and specific performance were then provided to show the typical alternatives where damages would be inadequate. It was then observed that such alternatives are not always available. It is from that point that we will explore the judgment.

GUIDED CASE READING 11.1
Attorney-General v Blake (Jonathan Cape Ltd Third Party) [2001] 1 AC 268

When reading the extracts of the lead judgment by Lord Nicholls, try to identify:

- the reasons for the exceptional remedy being granted;
- how the future use of the remedy was limited;
- the legal basis for the exception.

An instance of this nature occurred in *Wrotham Park Estate Co Ltd v Parkside Homes Ltd* [1974] . . . The judge considered that if the plaintiffs were given a nominal sum, or no sum, justice would manifestly not have been done. He assessed the damages at 5% of the developer's anticipated profit . . .

[After acknowledging that *Wrotham Park* was about property rights rather than contract rights, Lord Nicholls stated that there was no reason why contract rights should attract a 'lesser degree of remedy'. The facts and decision of *Surrey v Bredero* were then explained.]

This is a difficult decision. It has attracted criticism from academic commentators and also in judgments of Sir Thomas Bingham MR and Millett LJ in *Jaggard v Sawyer* [1995] 1 WLR 269. I need not pursue the detailed criticisms. In the *Bredero* case Dillon LJ himself noted . . ., that had the covenant been worded differently, there could have been provision for payment of an increased price if a further planning permission were forthcoming. That would have been enforceable. But, according to the *Bredero* decision, a covenant not to erect any further houses without permission, intended to achieve the same result, may be breached with impunity. That would be a sorry reflection on the law. Suffice to say, in so far as the *Bredero* decision is inconsistent with the approach adopted in the *Wrotham Park* case, the latter approach is to be preferred.

> Lord Nicholls here makes clear that he disapproves of the decision in *Bredero*, chiefly on the grounds of justice: He does this not because he intends to apply *Wrotham Park* directly in the instant case, but because he wants to make the wider point that contract damages ought not to be confined to recovery of financial loss alone.

The *Wrotham Park* case, therefore, still shines, rather as a solitary beacon, showing that in contract as well as tort damages are not always narrowly confined to recoupment of financial loss. In a suitable case damages for breach of contract may be measured by the benefit gained by the wrongdoer from the breach.

[Reference was then made to some examples of awards that appeared to have an equivalent effect to an account of profits.]

There is a light sprinkling of cases where courts have made orders having the same effect as an order for an account of profits, but the courts seem always to have attached a different label . . .

These cases illustrate that circumstances do arise when the just response to a breach of contract is that the wrongdoer should not be permitted to retain any profit from the breach. In these cases the courts have reached the desired result by straining existing concepts . . .

> This was confirmed by a 'light sprinkling' of cases which seemed to amount to awarding an account of profits—again, chiefly in the interests of justice.

. . . Remedies are the law's response to a wrong (or, more precisely, to a cause of action). When, exceptionally, a just response to a breach of contract so requires, the court should be able to grant the discretionary remedy of requiring a defendant to account to the plaintiff for the benefits he has received from his breach of contract.

[Examples of damages based on the gain from wrongdoing were then stated.]

When the circumstances require, damages are measured by reference to the benefit obtained by the wrongdoer. . . . Breach of confidence is an instance of this. If confidential information is wrongfully divulged in breach of a non-disclosure agreement, it would be nothing short of sophistry to say that an account of profits may be ordered in respect of the equitable wrong but not in respect of the breach of contract which governs the relationship between the parties.

. . .

The main argument against the availability of an account of profits as a remedy for breach of contract is that the circumstances where this remedy may be granted will be uncertain . . . I do not think these fears are well founded. I see no reason why, *in practice*, the availability of the remedy of an account of profits need disturb settled expectations in the commercial or consumer world. An account of profits will be appropriate only in exceptional circumstances . . . No fixed rules can be prescribed. The court will have regard to all the circumstances . . . A useful general guide, although not exhaustive, is whether the plaintiff had a legitimate interest in preventing the defendant's profit-making activity and, hence, in depriving him of his profit. It would be difficult, and unwise, to attempt to be more specific.

[The Court of Appeal judgment by Lord Woolf MR was discussed to reject a wider approach that was suggested.]

The present case is exceptional. The context is employment as a member of the security and intelligence services . . .

. . .

The Crown had and has a legitimate interest in preventing Blake profiting from the disclosure of official information, whether classified or not, while a member of the service and thereafter . . . . Undermining the willingness of prospective informers to co-operate with the services, or undermining the morale and trust between members of the services when engaged on secret and dangerous operations, would jeopardise the effectiveness of the service. An absolute rule against disclosure, visible to all, makes good sense.

In considering what would be a just response to a breach of Blake's undertaking the court has to take these considerations into account. The undertaking, if not a fiduciary obligation, was closely akin to a fiduciary obligation, where an account of profits is a standard remedy in the event of breach. Had the information which Blake has now disclosed still been confidential, an account of profits would have been ordered, almost as a matter of course. In the special circumstances of the intelligence services, the same conclusion should follow even though the information is no longer confidential. That would be a just response to the breach . . .

This was also the case in other circumstances such as a breach of confidence where the account of profits remedy would be routinely applied. To insist on a difference between equity and contract in this way was to put an entirely artificial border between the two— i.e. to engage in 'sophistry'.

Lord Nicholls then dismissed what he called the 'main' argument against using an account of profits as a contractual remedy, which was that it would introduce uncertainty— although it must be said that he then rather undermines this argument by observing that 'no fixed rules' could be prescribed!

The main principle in his view was that this was an exceptional case, in which the government had a legitimate interest in effect in punishing Blake—that is, it had a legitimate interest in discouraging behaviour of the sort he had engaged in.

Reference was also made to the breach being very close to a breach of a fiduciary obligation for which an account of profits is the usual remedy.

In terms of legal principle, the decision in *Blake* was ground-breaking. It allowed for an account of profits to be made as a remedy for a breach of contract. Clearly, this was not a compensatory remedy. It was not even an award to release a restriction from a contract. Instead, it was simply stripping the party in breach of their profit. The effect was to punish Blake and discourage others from committing the same kind of breach. Previously, no such remedy was possible in contract.

The practical significance of the award is limited by the fact that its application is exceptional. The following key requirements can be said to emerge from the judgment:

- The account of profits is only available where all other remedies are inadequate.

- Even then, the innocent party needs a 'legitimate interest' in taking away the profit gained.

- A further limit was linked to the type of obligation breached. The obligation breached should be equivalent to a breach of a fiduciary duty or breach of confidence.

The first requirement is straight-forward enough. As a remedy, account of profits is a last resort.

The second requirement of a 'legitimate interest' is difficult to define. It could be the same as the requirement for an injunction. Alternatively, it could incorporate policy considerations. Lord Nicholls referred to the importance of intelligence workers not revealing information gained on the job. In particular, there was the need to protect the interests of other workers and informants.

As for the third requirement, Blake's breach was said to be closely related to a breach of a fiduciary duty or more specifically, a breach of confidence. An account of profit is a typical remedy following a breach of confidence. That close relationship or similarity was used to further justify the award. It was said that, had the information been confidential at the time of the breach, there would have been an account of profits for breach of confidence. While the information was not confidential, on the facts, the UK Government had a legitimate interest in not having such information being revealed by past employees. According to Lord Nicholls, it meant such content in the future needed to be protected, and the award given was a way to achieve it.

It was also stated that the following reasons on their own would not be enough to justify the new remedy:

- The breach was cynical or deliberate;

- The breach enabled the party in breach to make more money by contracting with another party;

- By entering another contract, the party in breach was unable to perform the original one.

The requirements and guidance suggested that the remedy from *Blake* would be highly exceptional. Ordinarily, the standard rules on compensatory damages would apply. There will still be cases where the innocent party gets nominal damages, even if the other party profited from the breach. In some exceptional cases, the equitable remedies of an injunction or specific performance will be available. Beyond that, it might be possible to have an account of profits if all else fails to do justice in the given case.

This also means that the remedy should not undermine the principle of an 'efficient breach'. Just as it was before the *Blake* case, it is permissible for a party to breach a contract to secure a better deal elsewhere. They just have to compensate the innocent party for the resulting loss if there is any.

11.5.2.2 The Reliance on Wrotham Park in Blake

Reference was made to other non-contract examples where damages are not compensatory. This was to show that in principle, such damages are possible and exist already as a response to wrongdoing. The next step was to bring such damages into the contract context.

The *Wrotham Park* case was very significant. At its core, it concerned the infringement of property rights. But the idea of such damages reflecting what would hypothetically have been negotiated could have an application in contract. If it did, it would of course represent a departure from the traditional role of damages in contract. But the *Bredero Homes* decision by the Court of Appeal had effectively excluded the application of *Wrotham Park* to contracts.

This prompted Lord Nicholls to disapprove of the way *Bredero Homes* limited *Wrotham Park*. That in turn resurrected *Wrotham Park* and it was treated as representing a remedy applicable to contracts. In the judgment, *Wrotham Park* was described as a 'solitary beacon' for damages being measured by the gain. But this in turn became a 'green light' to depart from traditional compensatory damages.

Crucially, *Wrotham Park* was taken as a foundation for the account of profit remedy. After all, both awards were based on the gain obtained from the breach rather than the loss suffered. It is just that the account of profit remedy is for all of the gains obtained by breach, not just a reasonable part of it. In that context, the *Blake* award had the appearance of being an extension of *Wrotham Park*. It follows that the *Wrotham Park* award was being classed as a type of restitutionary remedy.

11.5.2.3 The Judicial Response to Blake

Lord Nicholls said that the remedy in *Blake* would not result in commercial uncertainty. This was based on the remedy being very exceptional. In fact, the requirements from *Blake* are so strict, it is difficult to see how it could apply to a commercial contract. However, shortly after *Blake*, the remedy was indeed applied in a commercial context.

Esso Petroleum Co. Ltd v Niad Ltd [2001] All ER (D) 324 concerned an agreement between commercial parties. It involved the fuel supplier Esso, and the defendant petrol station selling Esso fuel. Esso had a scheme called 'Pricewatch' and Niad agreed to participate. It required participating petrol stations to report on the prices charged by competitors. Esso would then set a price to match the competitors. In return, Esso provided financial support to the petrol stations in the scheme. That support was in the form of a discounted supply of fuel. However, on four occasions Niad did not reduce his prices as the scheme required. Esso then took action for breach of contract but the traditional award of compensatory damages was not possible. This was due to Esso being unable to show how many sales they lost following a breach by a single station. As a result, by relying on *Blake*, Esso sought an account of profits. In other words, they claimed the profit Niad had made as a result of his breach.

Morritt V-C allowed the award. According to the judge, the case was exceptional because other remedies were inadequate. In addition, the loss caused could not be worked out. The judge also agreed that the breach could undermine the entire Pricewatch scheme. After all, Esso's scheme had been advertised to the public to attract customers. It would have the opposite effect if it was not put into effect by the retailers. On that basis, it was also then said that Esso had a 'legitimate interest' in claiming the profit made.

 THINKING POINTS

Should the *Blake* award have been made in *Esso v Niad*?

Esso v Niad attracted a great deal of criticism for its account of profits award. It is generally thought that the circumstances were not sufficiently exceptional. The approach to 'legitimate interest' was a lot wider than that suggested in *Blake*. The term breached was clearly important, but in many commercial contracts, important terms are breached. It was hardly exceptional in that sense. Also, the obligation breached was not 'akin' to a breach of confidence or fiduciary duty. It appears that the award was made just because no other remedies would have been adequate.

Later, the account of profits award was sought in *Experience Hendrix LLC v PPX Enterprises Inc.* [2003] EWCA Civ 323. That particular claim was rejected by Mance LJ, explaining some factors that made the claim in *Blake* so exceptional:

- *Blake* concerned issues of national security. There was a need to stop spies profiting from a breach of their secrecy obligations and to protect informants.
- Blake's breach attracted a large profit only because of his notoriety resulting from the breach.
- The obligation breached was based on special trust and confidence equivalent to a fiduciary obligation.

This observation by Mance LJ has the effect of limiting the account of profits to very special facts. The need for the obligation to be akin to a fiduciary obligation is important here. Its re-emphasis since *Blake* supports it as an essential requirement. The point is that commercial obligations are generally unlikely to meet this requirement. The relationship of self-interest for profit is inconsistent with a fiduciary obligation. That then should serve to keep *Blake* out of commercial disputes.

The requirement was echoed by Hildyard J in *CF Partners (UK) LLP v Barclays Bank plc* [2014] EWHC 3049. There Hildyard J referred to the choice between damages and an account of profits and stated:

> 1172. The choice is likely to depend on whether the rights of the claimant are of a particularly powerful kind and/or such that his interest in full performance is particularly strong; and on whether those rights are asserted in an ordinary commercial context ("where a degree of self-seeking and ruthless behaviour is expected and accepted to a degree") or in the context of a relationship of special trust, such as was the case on *Blake* itself or such as in a fiduciary relationship (where "self-seeking behaviour is required to be reined in on the grounds that special obligations…have been assumed…", and there is an enhanced importance of deterring abusive behaviour).

It seems that *Esso* took place within an ordinary commercial context where an account of profits should not be permitted. However, while *Esso* did not put into effect the factors listed by Mance LJ, the Court of Appeal in *Hendrix* did not disapprove of it exactly. Instead, Mance LJ simply distinguished it from *Hendrix*. It was observed that in *Esso*, the breach went to the 'root' of the promotion. It would have made it appear untrue and a device to mislead customers. That just meant that the claimant in *Hendrix* could not rely on *Esso* to obtain an account of profits. Since *Esso*, courts have been very cautious with claims for an account of profits. The consistent trend has been for the courts to say that the claim is not exceptional enough. This is clear from the *Hendrix* case. It is also reflected by the first instance decisions of *Vercoe v Rutland Fund Management Ltd* [2010] EWHC 424 and *One Step (Support) Ltd v Morris-Garner* [2014] EWHC 2213; and *CF Partners (UK) v Barclays Bank*. While the remedy remains a possibility, we will see in 11.7 that the Supreme Court decision in *Morris-Garner v One-Step (Support) Ltd* [2018] UKSC 20 casts a shadow over the legal basis of the award in *Blake*. It was not overruled or even re-examined. However, by taking away a significant part of the award's legal basis, the likelihood of such a claim being successful has been severely reduced.

KEY POINTS

A claim for an account of profits is so exceptional that it should only remain for facts equivalent to those in *Blake*.

11.6 Negotiating Damages

The revival of *Wrotham Park* in *Blake* had a further consequence for damages following a breach. Essentially, *Blake* lifted the barrier that had kept *Wrotham Park* outside of the contract context. In doing so, it opened the possibility of claims for the type of damages actually awarded in *Wrotham Park*. We can recall that in *Wrotham Park*, the defendant infringed the land restriction and the court awarded damages instead of an injunction. Importantly, the award was based on the amount of money that could have been negotiated to lift the restriction on the land. This was valued at 5% of the defendant's expected profit. Such an award has attracted labels such as damages for a 'lost bargaining opportunity', 'Wrotham Park damages', 'hypothetical bargain damages' and 'negotiating damages'. We will look at a useful example of the application of the award in the context of a contract, before turning to the wider issues raised by the award.

➜ CROSS-REFERENCE
For the facts and decision of *Wrotham Park Estate Co v Parkside Homes Ltd* [1974] see 11.5.1.

11.6.1 The Application of Negotiating Damages Following *Blake*

A significant example of an award based on *Wrotham Park* is *Experience Hendrix LLC v PPX Enterprises Inc* [2003] EWCA Civ 323. The case concerned early music recordings by the rock and guitar legend, Jimmy Hendrix. The Hendrix estate had an agreement with the record company defendant. The record company breached this agreement by using certain recordings which it had promised not to use. On the facts, the estate had suffered no loss because it had never intended to publish the recordings itself. However, the record company made a significant profit from the breach. Mance LJ delivered the main judgment, which referred to *Blake* supporting the *Wrotham Park* award. It resulted in the estate being awarded a third of the profit. This award reflected the amount that could have been negotiated to allow the recordings to be used. In addition, an injunction was granted in relation to the use of the music in the future. The *Wrotham Park* 'negotiating damages' award was also applied to commercial contracts in *Force India Formula One Team Ltd v Aerolab SRL* [2013] EWCA Civ 780 and *Pell Frischmann Engineering Ltd v Bow Valley Iran Ltd* [2009] UKPC 45.

One problem with the application of the award has been its availability. The courts have not been clear on when a claimant would be entitled to such an award. Was it an alternative to other awards or a last resort? Even then, would there be a right to such an award or was it at the discretion of the courts? A further problem was that the size of the award would be difficult to predict. That in turn, causes uncertainty. An example is *Lane v O'Brien Homes* [2004] EWHC 303 which had facts similar to *Wrotham Park*. However, the judge awarded 50% of the profit (compared with the 5% in *Wrotham Park*). That was deemed to be the amount that might have been negotiated to release the property restriction. This is often cited to indicate how unpredictable the awards generated by this remedy can be.

11.6.2 The Background Issue on the Basis of the Award

The most significant issue arising from negotiating damages relates to the basis of the award. It has been a very contentious issue and a full account is better left for further reading, of which there is plenty. However, it is important to examine the basic arguments concerning the basis of the award to understand how the issue was settled by the Supreme Court in *Morris-Garner v One-Step (Support) Ltd* [2018].

There are arguments to suggest that the *Wrotham Park* award was restitutionary. That was the view of Steyn LJ in *Surrey v Bedero* and appeared to be reflected by the approach of Mance LJ in *Hendrix*. Such a view would also be consistent with the House of Lords decision in *Blake* which relied on *Wrotham Park*. In *Blake*, the account of profits was not actually described as restitutionary, but it was clearly a remedy of that type in that it took *all* of the profit away. Furthermore, in the absence of loss, there was no chance of it being compensatory. As a type of restitution for a wrong, the award in *Wrotham Park* could be seen as a partial account of profits at one end of the spectrum, with the full account of profits at the other end. That appeared to be how it was viewed in *Hendrix*. Likewise, in *Force India Formula One Team Ltd v Aerolab SRL* [2013] the Court of Appeal approved of the award being based on what could have been negotiated to allow restricted information to be used. However, the sum was based on how much it would have cost to get the information from elsewhere. Essentially, that figure represented the value of the gain to the defendant rather than any loss suffered by the claimant. Again, such an approach represents a restitutionary (gain-based) approach.

The potential restitutionary basis can be contrasted with a more conventional compensatory basis. Consider *Wrotham Park* itself. The defendant ignored the property restriction and made a profit. The claimant was then awarded the sum that could have been negotiated by the claimant to release the defendant from the property restriction. Such damages could be conceptualised as compensating for the lost opportunity to negotiate a fee. In a contract context, this would be achieved by awarding the sum that could have been demanded for allowing the defendant to be released from the obligation that they breached. That sum represents the 'loss' suffered by the claimant. This was the view of both Sir Thomas Bingham and Millett LJ in the Court of Appeal case of *Jaggard v Sawyer* [1995] 1 WLR 269.

Furthermore, a compensatory basis for the award was implied by *Pell Frischmann Engineering Ltd v Bow Valley Iran Ltd* [2009]. Following a breach of confidentiality clauses in a joint venture agreement, the Privy Council allowed a *Wrotham Park* award of $2.5m. That was the amount that might have been negotiated to relax the obligation breached. The fact that the party in breach only made £1.8m from the breach did not matter. This means that the award was not based on the gain of the defendant. If it was, then it would have been less than or equal to the profit obtained.

It is important to appreciate the special nature of the compensatory basis described in the cases that applied *Wrotham Park*. The compensatory basis for 'negotiating damages' was very different to the traditional compensatory damages ordinarily awarded for a breach. We saw in Chapter 9 that damages are awarded for the actual loss caused by the breach. In contrast, negotiating damages (as defined by the early cases) do not compensate for actual loss caused by the breach. Instead, they compensate for the lost opportunity to negotiate a fee to release the defendant from the obligation they breached. In other words (if viewed as compensatory), the damages are for the loss resulting from not having made an alternative contract, rather than the loss suffered from the breach of the actual contract. We will see that more recently, the Supreme Court has clarified the position on negotiating damages to be more in line with traditional compensatory damages.

A key criticism of the compensatory basis for *Wrotham Park* damages is the artificiality of the hypothetical negotiation it is based on. The idea is that the innocent party has missed out on the fee that could have been negotiated. However, it is possible that the innocent party would never have negotiated. Take *Wrotham Park* itself, for example. The claimant insisted it would not have been willing to relax the restriction, a point observed by Brightman J in the case. Yet damages were based on the loss suffered from not being able to negotiate a fee to relax the restriction. This is what Steyn LJ described as a 'fiction' in *Surrey v Bredero* and why Mance LJ in *Hendrix* did not view the award as compensatory. According to Mance LJ, the Hendrix estate would never have consented to the release of the recordings, even for a fee. It was indeed for that reason that the breach by the record company had caused them no financial loss—they would never have released the recordings and so would never have made any money that way themselves. Accordingly, that meant the award in the case could not have been compensatory.

KEY POINTS

- *Blake* opened the door to allow negotiating damages to apply to breach of contract.
- For years, the basis of the award was debatable and the cases were inconsistent. The award was considered capable of having a restitutionary basis, or alternatively, a compensatory basis.

11.6.3 The Compensatory Basis and Availability of the Award

Recently, the compensatory basis of 'negotiating damages' as well as the availability of the award was confirmed by the Supreme Court in *Morris-Garner v One-Step (Support) Ltd* [2018] UKSC 20. This was the first time the highest court had the opportunity to address the issue of negotiating damages and try to settle the issues raised over the years.

The facts were very straightforward. The claimants, One-Step, were a business that helped young people following their time in the care system. The defendants (Karen Morris-Garner and Andrea Morris-Garner) initially worked for One-Step. One was a director of One-Step, the other was a manager. They both decided to leave and they entered a three-year contract with One-Step on doing so. Under the contact, the Morris-Garners promised not to compete with One-Step or approach any of One-Step's clients. Also, they agreed to keep certain information about One-Step confidential. Unknown to One-Step at the time, the Morris-Garners had already set up a competing business called Positive Living Ltd. This new business went on to trade for three years before being sold for almost £12.8m. In contrast, One-Step suffered a serious fall in their revenue.

One-Step then brought an action against the Morris-Garners for breach. According to One-Step's expert, the resulting loss of business could be estimated at £3.4m to £4.4m, but this was difficult to prove. Rather than claim such losses, they argued that they should be entitled to an account of profits or negotiating damages. According to their expert's findings, the fee to release the Morris-Garners from the contractual restrictions would have been between £5.3m and £6.3m. At first instance the claim for an account of profits was rejected, but the judge agreed that negotiating damages was an appropriate award. The Court of Appeal upheld this decision, and then the defendants appealed to the Supreme Court. The Supreme Court clarified the availability and basis of negotiating damages. Consequently, it was held that the negotiating damages were not available. Instead, on the facts, the damages should be based on the financial loss caused by the breach, even though the full extent would have been difficult to calculate. It is important to take a closer look at the main judgment delivered by Lord Reed (with whom Lady Hale, Lord Wilson and Lord Carnwath agreed).

The judgment started by acknowledging a real lack of clarity on the availability and theoretical basis of *Wrotham Park* damages. Therefore, the judgment aimed to solve these issues. The term '*Wrotham Park* damages' was rejected in preference of 'negotiating damages'; *Wrotham Park* as a case was described as being no longer significant and of 'little more than historical interest'. Lord Reed then went on to deliver an in-depth assessment of the relevant case law. This was done using the following categories: cases on 'user damages'; cases on damages instead of an injunction under Lord Cairns' Act; and finally, the cases before and after *Blake* where negotiating damages were awarded. The very important points come from the conclusions, the summary of the conclusive points, and the application. We will address the extracts corresponding with these important issues in turn.

11.6.3.1 The Operation of the Compensatory Basis

Our first issue from the judgment of Lord Reed is the compensatory basis of negotiating damages. Here, we will see how the damages are compensatory along with how that fits with ordinary damages principles:

> Conclusions
>
> [91] The use of an imaginary negotiation can give the impression that negotiation damages are fundamentally incompatible with the compensatory purpose of an award of contractual damages. Damages for breach of contract depend on considering the outcome if the contract had been performed, whereas an award based on a hypothetical release fee depends on considering the outcome if the contract had not been performed but had been replaced by a different contract. That impression of fundamental incompatibility is, however, potentially misleading. There are certain circumstances in which the loss for which compensation is due is the economic value of the right which has been breached, considered as an asset. The imaginary negotiation is merely a tool for arriving at that value. The real question is as to the circumstances in which that value constitutes the measure of the claimant's loss.
>
> [92] As the foregoing discussion has demonstrated, such circumstances can exist in cases where the breach of contract results in the loss of a valuable asset created or protected by the right which was infringed, as for example in cases concerned with the breach of a restrictive covenant over land, an intellectual property agreement or a confidentiality agreement. . . The claimant has in substance been deprived of a valuable asset, and his loss can therefore be measured by determining the economic value of the asset in question. The defendant has taken something for nothing, for which the claimant was entitled to require payment.
>
> . . .

[94] It is not easy to see how, in circumstances other than those of the kind described in paras 91-93, a hypothetical release fee might be the measure of the claimant's loss. It would be going too far, however, to say that it is only in those circumstances that evidence of a hypothetical release fee can be relevant to the assessment of damages. If, for example, in other circumstances, the parties had been negotiating the release of an obligation prior to its breach, the valuations which the parties had placed on the release fee, adjusted if need be to reflect any changes in circumstances, might be relevant to support, or to undermine, a subsequent quantification of the losses claimed to have resulted from the breach. It would be a matter for the judge to decide whether, in the particular circumstances, evidence of a hypothetical release fee was relevant and, if so, what weight to place upon it. However, the hypothetical release fee would not itself be a quantification of the loss caused by a breach of contract, other than in circumstances of the kind described in paras 91–93 above.

The extract explains that negotiating damages are compensatory. The appearance of incompatibility with the traditional understanding of contract damages was attributed to the way negotiating damages had been viewed. They had been seen as damages for the loss of a fee that could have been demanded from an alternative contract. That is very different to ordinary damages for actual loss caused by a breach of the actual contract.

Lord Reed then explained why negotiating damages were consistent with traditional damages awards. The loss that has been suffered is that of a valuable asset, of which the breach deprives the innocent party. One example of this would be a contract about the copyright in music. If the defendant is not meant to release the music but does so (in breach of the contract), the rights holder has suffered a loss in the value of the copyright. Ordinary damages principles would then allow for compensation to reflect that loss. According to Lord Reed, a reference to what could have been demanded as fee (to allow for such a use of the rights) is simply evidence towards working out the value of the loss. Importantly, the loss is actual loss resulting from a breach of the actual contract. Such an approach puts negotiating damages following a breach on the same footing as ordinary (traditional) compensatory damages for breach.

KEY POINTS

- Awards classed as negotiating damages (*Wrotham Park* damages) are compensation for actual loss caused by the breach.
- The fee that could have been negotiated simply goes towards the evidence of the value of the loss.

The judgment also indicated that while the hypothetical fee would not normally be the loss caused by a breach, it might be in some cases. The example given was circumstances in which the parties were actually negotiating a fee to release one party from a contractual obligation. This example was based on the facts of *Pell Frischmann Engineering Ltd v Bow Valley Iran Ltd* [2009]. Such a fee on its own might well reflect the value of the loss, but it is for the trial judge to determine based on the circumstances.

With negotiating damages being confirmed as compensatory, we have to wonder about the impact of the decision in *Morris-Garner* on *Blake*. We can recall that *Blake* allowed for an account of profits. Such a restitution for a wrong was largely based on an extension to the damages award from *Wrotham Park*. That award was viewed as gain-based and, therefore, restitutionary. With a compensatory basis for negotiating damages confirmed, the main authority relied upon for the remedy in *Blake* has been removed. In *Morris-Garner*, Lord Reed did refer to *Blake* as a case that caused uncertainty. The reasoning of Lord Nicholls was politely contradicted, but Lord Reed also made it clear that *Blake* was not about a claim for negotiating damages. On that basis, it was said that the 'soundness of that decision is not an issue in this appeal'.

This all means that *Blake* continues to provide limited authority for an account of profits remedy for a breach of contract. That was acknowledged as such in Lord Reed's summary of conclusions. Consequently, *Blake* should now be seen as a *sui generis* principle (i.e. an autonomous principle distinct from negotiating damages and the ordinary damages principles).

sui generis is Latin for 'of its own kind' and is used to describe legal principles that stand alone from general principles.

> **?!**   **THINKING POINTS**
>
> By removing the restitutionary basis of *Wrotham Park*, Lord Reed undermined the basis of *Blake*. With that in mind, why didn't the Supreme Court simply overrule *Blake*?

11.6.3.2 Negotiating Damages as 'User' Damages

Lord Reed's summary of conclusions was based on an analysis of the case law made earlier in the judgment. The first two points in this summary relate to 'user damages:'

> [95] The foregoing discussion leads to the following conclusions:
>
> (1) Damages assessed by reference to the value of the use wrongfully made of property (sometimes termed "user damages") are readily awarded at common law for the invasion of rights to tangible moveable or immoveable property (by detinue, conversion or trespass). The rationale of such awards is that the person who makes wrongful use of property, where its use is commercially valuable, prevents the owner from exercising a valuable right to control its use, and should therefore compensate him for the loss of the value of the exercise of that right. He takes something for nothing, for which the owner was entitled to require payment.
>
> (2) Damages are also available on a similar basis for patent infringement and breaches of other intellectual property rights.

'User damages' are an established instance where a hypothetical fee is awarded to the party whose rights were infringed. The context relates to rights to be enforced with an action for trespass, conversion or detinue (the wrongful interference with goods). It also applies to intellectual property rights. It is important to appreciate that in this context, we are not concerned with a breach of contract. Instead, this category relates to a direct infringement of property rights.

11.6.3.3 Negotiating Damages in Lieu of an Injunction or Specific Performance

The next range of points in the summary related to the award of damages in lieu of an injunction or specific performance:

> [95] ...
>
> (3) Damages can be awarded under Lord Cairns' Act in substitution for specific performance or an injunction, where the court had jurisdiction to entertain an application for such relief at the time when the proceedings were commenced. Such damages are a monetary substitute for what is lost by the withholding of such relief.
>
> (4) One possible method of quantifying damages under this head is on the basis of the economic value of the right which the court has declined to enforce, and which it has consequently rendered worthless. Such a valuation can be arrived at by reference to the amount which the claimant might reasonably have demanded as a quid pro quo for the relaxation of the obligation in question. The rationale is that, since the withholding of specific relief has the same practical effect as requiring the claimant to permit the infringement of his rights, his loss can be measured by reference to the economic value of such permission.
>
> (5) That is not, however, the only approach to assessing damages under Lord Cairns' Act. It is for the court to judge what method of quantification, in the circumstances of the case before it, will give a fair equivalent for what is lost by the refusal of the injunction.

Damages can be awarded where a court does not grant an injunction or specific performance. That was the context of the award in *Wrotham Park*. The damages award reflects the loss suffered from not having the equitable remedy available. It was said that such a loss could be measured by reference to the hypothetical fee for releasing the infringing party from the relevant restriction. Such a figure could reflect the value of what was lost by allowing the infringement. But again, it is for the judge to determine how the damages are to be worked out based on the circumstances.

11.6.3.4 Negotiating Damages within the Context of the Principles Concerning Ordinary Damages (for Breach)

In the summary of conclusions, this point started with reference to damages for the loss caused by the breach under ordinary (or traditional) damages principles:

> [95] . . .
>
> (6) Common law damages for breach of contract are intended to compensate the claimant for loss or damage resulting from the non-performance of the obligation in question. They are therefore normally based on the difference between the effect of performance and non-performance upon the claimant's situation.
>
> (7) Where damages are sought at common law for breach of contract, it is for the claimant to establish that a loss has been incurred, in the sense that he is in a less favourable situation, either economically or in some other respect, than he would have been in if the contract had been performed.
>
> (8) Where the breach of a contractual obligation has caused the claimant to suffer economic loss, that loss should be measured or estimated as accurately and reliably as the nature of the case permits. The law is tolerant of imprecision where the loss is incapable of precise measurement, and there are also a variety of legal principles which can assist the claimant in cases where there is a paucity of evidence.
>
> (9) Where the claimant's interest in the performance of a contract is purely economic, and he cannot establish that any economic loss has resulted from its breach, the normal inference is that he has not suffered any loss. In that event, he cannot be awarded more than nominal damages.

Lord Reed started with the basic compensatory aim of the award and how the loss is usually determined. It is for the claimant to show the loss that has or will be suffered. The important point is the reference to the accuracy and precision of identifying such loss. Lord Reed indicated that while the loss needs to be measured as accurately as possible, it does not need to be precise. The point being made might sound obvious, but it needs to be appreciated with the background of claims for negotiating damages.

There have been cases where there was no actual loss resulting from a breach, and the absence of such a loss was a basis for the negotiating damages award. Likewise, the negotiating damages award has been used when the loss was difficult to estimate accurately. With that in mind, Lord Reed was making it clear that if loss is simply difficult to estimate, it is still capable of being reflected in a damages award under ordinary principles. It appears that this confirmation serves two related purposes. First, it is aimed at taking away an assumed basis for negotiating damages. Secondly, it is to show that an ordinary damages remedy is possible in circumstances where the negotiating damages are no longer available following *Morris-Garner* itself. Essentially, it limited negotiating damages to claims for the loss of a *valuable* asset. Where the breach has not resulted in the loss of a *valuable* asset, the imprecision of the estimated loss should not prevent a claim under ordinary damages principles. The further point was a reminder that if no loss has been suffered, the award is nominal damages. Again, this clarification serves to address the problem of parties claiming negotiating damages just because they have suffered no loss resulting from the breach.

The remaining points were that:

(10) Negotiating damages can be awarded for breach of contract where the loss suffered by the claimant is appropriately measured by reference to the economic value of the right which has been breached, considered as an asset. That may be the position where the breach of contract results in the loss of a valuable asset created or protected by the right which was infringed. The rationale is that the claimant has in substance been deprived of a valuable asset, and his loss can therefore be measured by determining the economic value of the right in question, considered as an asset. The defendant has taken something for nothing, for which the claimant was entitled to require payment.

(11) Common law damages for breach of contract cannot be awarded merely for the purpose of depriving the defendant of profits made as a result of the breach, other than in exceptional circumstances, following *Attorney General v Blake*.

(12) Common law damages for breach of contract are not a matter of discretion. They are claimed as of right, and they are awarded or refused on the basis of legal principle.

These last few points confirmed that negotiating damages fall within ordinary contract damages principles. Such an award is only available for breach when it has resulted in loss. That loss must be the loss of a *valuable asset*. The innocent party will then seek damages to be compensated for the value of that loss. As we have already seen, the value of that loss might well be influenced by the fee that could have been negotiated to release the other party from the obligation that they breached. It was also pointed out that an account of profits is only available on the exceptional grounds stated in *Blake*. Finally, the award is based on a right to damages arising from legal principles, rather than discretion exercised by the judge. This is consistent with negotiating damages being in the existing framework of ordinary contract damages.

Essentially, the judgment provided a clear indication as to the compensatory basis of what has been seen as negotiating damages. In the context of breach of contract, 'negotiating damages' are really just 'damages' assessed in a different way. The fee that could have been negotiated to release the defendant is taken into account simply to help determine the value of the lost asset. The fee itself is not the loss suffered. Rather, it is the value of the lost asset that is the consequence of a breach, just like lost profits would be in many cases.

 THINKING POINTS

Given the need for the loss of a valuable asset and the role of the potential fee that could have been negotiated, does this approach get around the criticism about the artificiality of awarding negotiating damages where the innocent party would never have negotiated?

11.6.3.5 The Availability of Negotiating Damages Following a Breach

The final part of the judgment was the application of the principles. It is useful to read this application because it helps to give us a better idea of the availability of negotiating damages:

The present case

[96] Applying these conclusions to the present case, it is apparent that neither the judge nor the Court of Appeal applied an approach which can now be regarded as correct. The judge was mistaken in considering that the claimant had a right to elect how its damages should be assessed.

He was mistaken in supposing that the difficulty of quantifying its financial loss, such as it was, justified the abandonment of any attempt to quantify it, and the award instead of a remedy which could not be regarded as compensatory in any meaningful sense.

[97] The Court of Appeal was mistaken in treating the deliberate nature of the breach, or the difficulty of establishing precisely the consequent financial loss, or the claimant's interest in preventing the defendants' profit-making activities, as justifying the award of a monetary remedy which was not compensatory. The idea that damages based on a hypothetical release fee are available whenever that is a just response, that being a matter to be decided by the judge on a broad brush basis, is also mistaken. The basis on which damages are awarded cannot be a matter for the discretion of the primary judge.

[98] This is a case brought by a commercial entity whose only interest in the defendants' performance of their obligations under the covenants was commercial. Indeed, a restrictive covenant which went beyond what was necessary for the reasonable protection of the claimant's commercial interests would have been unenforceable. The substance of the claimant's case is that it suffered financial loss as a result of the defendants' breach of contract. The effect of the breach of contract was to expose the claimant's business to competition which would otherwise have been avoided. The natural result of that competition was a loss of profits and possibly of goodwill. The loss is difficult to quantify, and some elements of it may be inherently incapable of precise measurement. Nevertheless, it is a familiar type of loss, for which damages are frequently awarded. It is possible to quantify it in a conventional manner, as is demonstrated by Mr Hine's report.

[99] The case is not one where the breach of contract has resulted in the loss of a valuable asset created or protected by the right which was infringed. Considered in isolation, the first defendant's breach of the confidentiality covenant might have been considered to be of that character, but in reality the claimant's loss is the cumulative result of breaches of a number of obligations, of which the non-compete and non-solicitation covenants have been treated as the most significant, as explained in para 17 above.

Previous cases like *Hendrix* had showed that non-compensatory damages could be awarded as a 'just response' if the loss was difficult to estimate, if the breach was deliberate and there was an interest in preventing the defendant from profiting from it. The *Morris-Garner* case signals an end to that approach.

The application by Lord Reed commenced by making it clear that claimants do not have a choice of how damages are to be worked out (i.e. consequential loss or loss of a fee). Damages are for the consequential loss caused by the breach. In this case, this would have meant the lost profit and loss of goodwill (i.e. the value of the business's reputation) which would have been difficult to quantify. But this difficulty was not a reason to focus on a different measure or allow the claimant to opt for that alternative measure. Instead, the only measure was the loss suffered. It was just that in some cases, the loss will be of a valuable asset that has been taken as a result of the breach, and that will be where so-called 'negotiating damages' are awarded. *Morris-Garner* was not one of those cases.

Lord Reed also observed that the breach of the confidentiality obligation could also have meant the loss of a valuable asset. However, ultimately it was less significant than the accumulation of other breaches of various obligations. Consequently, the loss was driven by the more significant contractual obligations breached, and these had caused a loss of profit and goodwill that should have been compensated through an 'ordinary' damages award.

The approach of the Supreme Court tells us that the focus is on the loss caused by the breach. That will vary from case to case. It might be that the loss amounts to that of a valuable asset and in such cases that value should be awarded. Alternatively, there might be the more standard loss of profit. There might even be a combination of both. Whatever it is, it is a matter for the judge to determine. Judges do not have the power to simply award non-compensatory damages.

?! THINKING POINTS

What would the outcome be if there was lost profit in the form of loss of business but also, at the same time, loss of a valuable asset?

So far, it is clear from the previous extracts that the fee that could have been negotiated is only relevant insofar as it allows one to calculate the value of the lost 'valuable asset'. The analysis then raises an obvious question about *which* obligations relate to a valuable asset. The point was addressed towards the start of the conclusion:

> [93] It might be objected that there is a sense in which any contractual right can be described as an asset, or indeed as property. In the present context, however, what is important is that the contractual right is of such a kind that its breach can result in an identifiable loss equivalent to the economic value of the right, considered as an asset, even in the absence of any pecuniary losses which are measurable in the ordinary way. That is something which is true of some contractual rights, such as a right to control the use of land, intellectual property or confidential information, but by no means of all. For example, the breach of a non-compete obligation may cause the claimant to suffer pecuniary loss resulting from the wrongful competition, such as a loss of profits and goodwill, which is measurable by conventional means, but in the absence of such loss, it is difficult to see how there could be any other loss.

Lord Reed here acknowledges that any contractual right might be argued to be, or to protect, a valuable asset. He appeared here to draw a distinction between 'conventional' losses such as lost profits, which are not necessarily connected with an underlying tangible or intangible asset, and something like a right to control land, intellectual property or confidential information, which has an actual economic value and which could be the subject of a transaction. A non-compete clause (like the one in the instant case) did not protect a valuable asset in this sense. Its breach only amounted to loss of profit and goodwill which could be assessed under traditional damages rules.

It is fair to say that the judgment could have done more to define 'valuable asset' (on this see Burrows (2018) 134 LQR 515). It seems that subsequent disputes in this area of damages might focus on the line between rights concerning valuable assets and those which do not. However, the major points of debate have been clarified by the *Morris-Garner* case.

KEY POINTS

- A damages award is available as of right because such an award is compensation for actual losses caused by a breach.
- By definition, therefore, an alternative award cannot be available just because there was no loss. No loss means just that: there was no loss. That results in nominal damages.
- By definition also, therefore, an alternative award cannot be available just because the *loss* caused by the breach is difficult to work out.

11.7 Agreed Damages and Penalty Clauses

An alternative remedy for a breach is one that has been agreed by the parties. They could have a term stating that a certain sum is payable as compensation following a certain breach. Such a term is known as a 'liquidated damages clause' if it is not penalising the party in breach. However, if the clause is classed as a penalty clause, meaning it serves to penalise a party for their breach, then it will be unenforceable. The rules that apply to distinguish between acceptable (liquidated) damages clauses and unacceptable penalties have been very contentious. In fact, the very power of the courts to override the parties' intentions to strike down certain agreed damages clauses as penalties is itself contentious. In this section we will explore the basic issues raised when parties put a term in their agreement so as to fix the damages in the event of a breach.

KEY POINTS

Terms that agree in advance on the damages to be paid following a breach could either be enforceable as a liquidated damages clause, or unenforceable as a penalty clause.

11.7.1 The Benefit of Agreeing Damages

A term fixing the amount of damages in advance is very useful because it gives the parties more certainty over the risks they are taking by entering the contract. They know how much will be payable following a breach. We have seen from Chapters 9 and 10 that damages claims can be complicated. Furthermore, the parties will avoid the costs and time-consuming process of a damages action if they have specified their intentions in the form of a liquidated damages clause.

11.7.2 The Impact of Rules Restricting Agreed Damages

The benefits of agreeing damages at the time of contracting is all simple enough in principle. The problem is that the courts have developed rules to strike down clauses that serve to penalise a party for their breach. Such clauses are called penalty clauses and are unenforceable. This is clearly a restriction on freedom of contract because it means courts are effectively overriding the expression of the parties' intentions. Such interference has been justified by the fact that damages are not meant to penalise a party for being breach. It is then consistent for the same requirement to apply to agreed damages clauses. A related point is that if the sum in a clause is so high that it is penal, then it could be said that it is just a bad bargain. If so, then to some extent, having rules on agreed damages challenges the courts' established approach of not interfering with a bad bargain freely made.

?! THINKING POINTS

> Between commercial parties whose contracts are negotiated by lawyers, in principle, should it matter if the agreed damages clause is really a penalty for being in breach?

If an agreed damages clause is classed as a penalty clause, then the innocent party would have to rely on a damages action to secure compensation in a dispute following a breach. Such an outcome might well be preferred by a party in breach. An obvious example would be when the breach has caused a small amount of loss, but the agreed damages clause requires a far more significant payment. In such circumstances, the party in breach has a clear incentive to challenge the agreed damages clause as a penalty.

11.7.3 The Traditional Rules

The main issue on agreed damages is the distinction between the enforceable liquidated damages clause, and the unenforceable penalty clause. The rules on identifying penalty clauses came from Lord Dunedin's judgment in *Dunlop Pneumatic Tyre Co Ltd v New Garage and Motor co Ltd* [1915] AC 79.

These rules were routinely applied for 100 years until the highest court had the opportunity to review them in the joined case of *Cavendish Square Holdings BV v Makdessi, ParkingEye Ltd v Beavis* [2015] UKSC 67. It is important to have a basic account of the traditional rule before turning to the changes made by the Supreme Court.

Dunlop v New Garage concerned the enforcement of the terms restricting the resale of Dunlop's tyres and other components. Like all of Dunlop's customers, New Garage (a dealer) had agreed to three main restrictions on their freedom. First, they could not resell Dunlop components below Dunlop's list price. Secondly, they could not sell to traders who Dunlop had stopped supplying. Finally, traders could not export Dunlop components without consent. Under the terms of the agreement, if any of these obligations were breached, Dunlop would be entitled to £5 'by way of liquidated damages and not as a penalty' for each item resold in breach. It was expected that if tyres were sold below Dunlop's minimum price, other trade customers would have to buy alternative components in order to compete, and that would result in Dunlop losing customers. Following a breach, New Garage challenged the term as a penalty. The House of Lords held that the term under dispute was indeed a liquidated damages clause rather than a penalty. The £5 per breach was seen as a genuine pre-estimate of the potential loss. The full extent of the potential loss at the occurrence of every breach would have been difficult to work out, but the clause was a principled attempt to provide a method of compensation agreed in advance. On that basis, the clause was effective.

The judgment by Lord Dunedin provided the guidance for distinguishing between a liquidated damages clause and a penalty clause. It started with the following three propositions based on the existing case law:

1. Use of the terms 'penalty or liquidated damages' does not indicate the true status of the clause. It is for the court to assess the clause to determine what it really is.

2. A penalty is a payment *in terrorem* (it operates as a threat or deterrent) whereas liquidated damages are based on a genuine pre-estimate of the loss arising from the breach.

3. The status of the clause is based on a construction of the contract.

These points indicate a basic distinction between the types of agreed damages terms. Liquidated damages clauses are based on a genuine pre-estimate of losses arising from the breach. In contrast, penalties operate as a threat to hold a party to their obligations. In other words, they are terms that operate as a deterrent (we will see that this point on penalties has been changed by the Supreme Court in *Makdessi*). The courts are concerned with the substance of the clause and how it operates, rather than its form or label, and that substance is determined through construction of the contract.

The guidance then went on to provide some tests to assist with the construction of the contract, tests that would be 'helpful, or even conclusive'. These are the factors that have formed the traditional test:

4   ...

   (a) It will be held to be penalty if the sum stipulated for is extravagant and unconscionable in amount in comparison with the greatest loss that could conceivably be proved to have followed from the breach.

   (b) It will be held to be a penalty if the breach consists only in not paying a sum of money, and the sum stipulated is a sum greater than the sum which ought to have been paid. . .

   (c) There is a presumption (but no more) that it is penalty when "a single lump sum is made payable by way of compensation, on the occurrence of one or more or all of several events, some of which may occasion serious and others but trifling damage." . . .

On the other hand:

   (d) It is no obstacle to the sum stipulated being a genuine pre-estimate of damage, that the consequences of the breach are such as to make precise pre-estimation almost an impossibility. On the contrary, that is just the situation when it is probable that pre-estimated damage was the true bargain between the parties.

The points listed as 4 (a)–(d) represent the core of the traditional test. If we take (a), the question is whether the amount in the clause is unreasonably high compared with the maximum loss that could have been expected to result. Such a sum is certainly not a genuine pre-estimate of loss.

The second factor (b) relates to a breach of an obligation to pay money. If the amount in the clause is more than what should have been paid, then it would be a penalty under this guidance. With a payment obligation, there is nothing to estimate in terms of loss. The potential loss is the money not paid. If the clause requires more, then it must be because it is acting as a deterrent to breach by penalising a party for being in breach.

The third point (c) is another situation expected to result in a clause operating as a penalty. If the same sum is payable for breaches irrespective of their seriousness, it can hardly be said that it was based on a genuine pre-estimate of loss. In *Dunlop*, the same £5 per breach applied to all three obligations. However, it could not be said that the loss from a breach of any of those obligations would never reach that level.

The final point addresses the argument that there cannot be a genuine pre-estimate if it is near impossible to foresee the potential loss. According to the House of Lords, the fact that a loss is very difficult or almost impossible to predict in advance is something that goes in favour of the clause being by way of liquidated damages rather than a penalty.

KEY POINTS

- Under the traditional test, liquidated damages clauses were based on a genuine pre-estimate of the loss.
- In contrast, penalties were not a genuine pre-estimate and operated as a deterrent to hold a party to their obligations.

The guidance from Lord Dunedin was clearly based on the idea that a liquidated damages clause is a genuine pre-estimate of the loss arising from the potential breach. If it appeared to be a genuine pre-estimate, then the clause would stand. That basic point remains an important consideration today following the recent review by the Supreme Court in *Makdessi*.

However, the general approach represented by these tests have been criticised over the years. This criticism was captured by in the main joint judgment by Lord Neuberger and Lord Sumption in *Makdessi*. They considered it to be 'unfortunate' that the guidance had 'achieved the status of a quasi-statutory code' in the case law that followed and had come to be applied inflexibly. They even called the traditional approach 'an ancient, haphazardly constructed edifice which has not weathered well'. This was a reference to wider tests that had been developed over the years, such as whether there was a commercial justification for the clause (*Lordsvale Finance plc v Bank of Zambia* [1996] QB 752 and *Murray v Leisureplay plc [2005]* EWCA Civ 936). *Makdessi* provided an opportunity to expand the traditional approach and make it less rigid.

11.7.4 The Approach Following *Cavendish Square Holdings v Makdessi* [2015]

In *Makdessi*, the Supreme Court explained what triggers the penalty clause rules, the test that should be applied and the rationale or basis for the rules. In this case, Makdessi agreed to sell his majority shares in a company to Cavendish. The price, which included goodwill (i.e. the value of the business's reputation), was to be paid in instalments. The parties were commercially experienced, of equal bargaining power, and their lawyers spent months negotiating the terms. These terms included a restriction on Makdessi competing with the company in future, in order to protect the value of its goodwill. In addition, there were two terms that stated the consequences of a breach of this restriction. Under the term 'cl 5.1', following a breach of the restriction, Makdessi would not be entitled to the final two payment instalments. Also, under 'cl 5.6', following the same breach, Cavendish would be entitled to the remaining shares at a price that excluded the value of the goodwill. That price would have been a lot lower than the price including the value of the goodwill. Following a breach, Cavendish tried to enforce clauses 5.1 and 5.6 but Makdessi challenged them as penalties. Following the review of the law on liquidated damages and penalties, the Supreme Court upheld the terms.

➜ CROSS-REFERENCE
For the facts of *ParkingEye* [2015] see 7.7.5.

We have already seen the facts of *ParkingEye v Beavis* in the context of unfair terms. The Supreme Court held that the parking charge was not an unfair term. In addition to challenging the fairness of the charge, Beavis also challenged the charge as a penalty. This challenge was also dismissed by the Supreme Court. The reasoning for this was based on the development of the rules on penalties in *Makdessi*. That means our focus will be on the judgments relating to *Makdessi*.

11.7.4.1 The Jurisdiction to Review a Clause

The Supreme Court confirmed that the starting point was the jurisdiction to review a clause. This point was established by the previous cases. The joint judgment by Lord Neuberger and Lord Sumption (with whom Lord Carnwath agreed) explained the position in the following way:

> [13] ... The penalty rule regulates only the remedies available for breach of a party's primary obligations, not the primary obligations themselves. ..
>
> [14]. This means that in some cases the application of the penalty rule may depend on how the relevant obligation is framed in the instrument, ie whether as a conditional primary obligation or a secondary obligation providing a contractual alternative to damages at law. Thus, where a contract contains an obligation on one party to perform an act, and also provides that, if he does not perform it, he will pay the other party a specified sum of money, the obligation to pay the specified sum is a secondary obligation which is capable of being a penalty; but if the contract does not impose (expressly or impliedly) an obligation to perform the act, but simply provides that, if one party does not perform, he will pay the other party a specified sum, the obligation to pay the specified sum is a conditional primary obligation and cannot be a penalty.

➜ CROSS-REFERENCE
For the discussion of damages as a secondary obligation see 8.3.

We already know that the obligation to pay damages is a secondary obligation. Likewise, an agreed damages clause must operate as a secondary obligation in order for it to be capable of being assessed. Primary obligations are those that must be performed which either require a party to do (or not do) something. Failure to follow the obligation is a breach. If the breach triggers the payment, that payment is a secondary obligation. This is contrasted with 'conditional primary obligations'. Under such an obligation, if the condition is not met, then the price changes. In other words, it is possible for a purported agreed damages clause to really be a price adjustment clause. For an example, consider a term stating that if a pizza is not delivered within an hour, the pizza will be half price. Failure to get the pizza delivered within the hour is not a breach. But the failure to meet the condition means that a discount is applied. The term in that case would be a primary obligation—in other words, it would be a price adjustment clause. That is very different to an agreed obligation for the delivery to take place by a certain time. A failure to perform that would be a breach. Any payment or discount resulting would be the result of a secondary obligation, equivalent to damages.

KEY POINTS

The damages clause must be secondary obligation in order for the courts to be able to assess it to see if it is a penalty.

Sometimes, the distinction between agreed damages and a price adjustment clause can be difficult to make. It requires an interpretation of the contract. Furthermore, it is possible for there to be a conditional primary obligation even where not meeting that condition happens to be a breach. That was a point acknowledged by the Supreme Court. In the case, Lords Neuberger, Sumption and Carnwath held that cl. 5.1 was a price adjustment clause and part of the primary obligations rather than being a secondary obligation. Essentially the value of the price reduced (by two payments) if a primary condition was not met. The fact that not meeting the condition would have also been a breach did not make a difference. Lords Hodge, Toulson and Clarke said that there was a 'strong argument' for such an approach to the damages clause, but went on to assess the clause as a secondary (damages) clause. Lord Mance did not express a view on the point. The majority found that cl. 5.6 was a secondary obligation and could be assessed.

The fact that there was no unanimous view on whether the clauses could be assessed shows that it can be difficult to assess whether the jurisdiction of the court applies. This means that going forward, there will be some uncertainty over whether a court will assess a clause. That being said, any resulting uncertainty will not have a major impact in practice because of the approach taken towards the assessment of a clause when the jurisdiction does apply. This is because the test for identifying a penalty was relaxed to a point where it would be difficult to class any agreed damages as a penalty.

11.7.4.2 Validity of an Agreed Damages Clause

If a clause is assessable, then the next step is to actually assess its enforceability and determine if it is a penalty or not. After reviewing the case law, Lord Neuberger and Lord Sumption (with whom Lord Carnwath agreed) explained why the assessment of agreed damages clauses had to change:

> [31] In our opinion, the law relating to penalties has become the prisoner of artificial categorisation, itself the result of unsatisfactory distinctions: between a penalty and genuine pre-estimate of loss, and between a genuine pre-estimate of loss and a deterrent. These distinctions originate in an over-literal reading of Lord Dunedin's four tests and a tendency to treat them as almost immutable rules of general application which exhaust the field. . .The real question when a contractual provision is challenged as a penalty is whether it is penal, not whether it is a pre-estimate of loss. These are not natural opposites or mutually exclusive categories. A damages clause may be neither or both. The fact that the clause is not a pre-estimate of loss does not therefore, at any rate without more, mean that it is penal. To describe it as a deterrent (or, to use the Latin equivalent, *in terrorem*) does not add anything. A deterrent provision in a contract is simply one species of provision designed to influence the conduct of the party potentially affected. It is no different in this respect from a contractual inducement. Neither is it inherently penal or contrary to the policy of the law. The question whether it is enforceable should depend on whether the means by which the contracting party's conduct is to be influenced are "unconscionable" or (which will usually amount to the same thing) "extravagant" by reference to some norm.

The problem of the traditional guidelines was that they had come to be applied inflexibly. Under such an approach, if the clause was not a pre-estimate then it was assumed to be penal. Their Lordships preferred a more holistic approach based on an overarching question about whether the clause is penal. In other words, even if a clause is not a pre-estimate of loss, this should not be taken to mean that it is definitely penal. Likewise, if a clause operates as a deterrent, this does not necessarily mean it is penal. Rather, in broad terms, the court should be concerned about whether the influence from a clause is achieved in an 'unconscionable' (or extravagant) way so that it is penal. The need to prevent penalty clauses of this nature from being enforceable was the basis of the jurisdiction.

KEY POINTS

A clause will not be penal just because it is not a pre-estimate of loss or because it acts as a deterrent.

The joint lead judgment then went on to formulate how that 'real' or overarching question is to be answered. In other words, the judgment provided a test to decide the issue:

> [32] The true test is whether the impugned provision is a secondary obligation which imposes a detriment on the contract-breaker out of all proportion to any legitimate interest of the innocent party in the enforcement of the primary obligation. The innocent party can have no proper interest in simply punishing the defaulter. His interest is in performance or in some appropriate alternative to performance. In the case of a straightforward damages clause, that interest will rarely extend beyond compensation for the breach, and we therefore expect that Lord Dunedin's four tests would usually be perfectly adequate to determine its validity. But compensation is not necessarily the only legitimate interest that the innocent party may have in the performance of the defaulter's primary obligations. This was recognised in the early days of the penalty rule, when it was still the creature of equity... And it is recognised in the more recent decisions about commercial justification...

The test is based on establishing whether the clause is designed to protect the legitimate interest of the innocent party (as opposed to penalising breach, which is by definition not legitimate). In the case of a straightforward damages clause, the legitimate interest would be to have compensation for the breach. In other cases, the legitimate interest might go beyond compensation—for example, deterrence.

 THINKING POINTS

Given the criticism of 'legitimate interest' in the context of breach and electing to continue the contract, does the use of the phrase 'legitimate interest' undermine certainty?

For straightforward agreed damages clauses, Lord Dunedin's test should be adequate. It will certainly allow a court to determine that a clause is enforceable as a liquidated damages clause. However, where an agreed damages clause is clearly not a pre-estimate of loss, like the clauses in *Makdessi*, it is necessary to consider the extent of the innocent party's legitimate interest. The next step is then to assess whether the detriment (i.e. the consequences of the clause being effective, like the sum it stipulates should be paid) is disproportionate to the protection of that legitimate interest. If it is so disproportionate that it becomes unconscionable or extravagant, then it will be a penalty and hence unenforceable. These steps to be taken to assess an agreed damages clause are summarised in Figure 11.1.

KEY POINTS

A damages clause which applies following a breach and imposes a detriment that is out of all proportion to the protection of a legitimate interest of the innocent party, will be unenforceable as a penalty.

In *Makdessi*, the cl.5.1 reflected a desire to protect a legitimate interest beyond compensation. There was a legitimate interest in ensuring that the price to be paid for shares reflected their value. That value was heavily influenced by the goodwill of the company, and that goodwill would be maintained by the obligations being followed. Protection of the same interest applied to cl.5.6, which aligned the price of the shares with their value in the absence of goodwill. The clauses did serve as a deterrent, but this was not objectionable, as the overriding aim was not to punish *Makdessi*. Furthermore, the parties were experienced commercially and negotiated over months on an equal basis using specialist lawyers. Accordingly, the Court indicated that there was a 'strong initial presumption' that the parties had effectively indicated the legitimacy of the interest which the terms were designed to protect.

On the next step of the analysis, it was held that the clauses were not out of proportion to the aim of protecting the legitimate interests of Cavendish. The same approach was adopted to the challenge to the charge in *ParkingEye*. There was a legitimate interest beyond compensation—i.e. a need to deter overstaying as well as to make money in carrying out the management of the car park. In addition, the charge was not disproportionate to such an interest, especially when compared to the charges imposed by council car parks for overstaying.

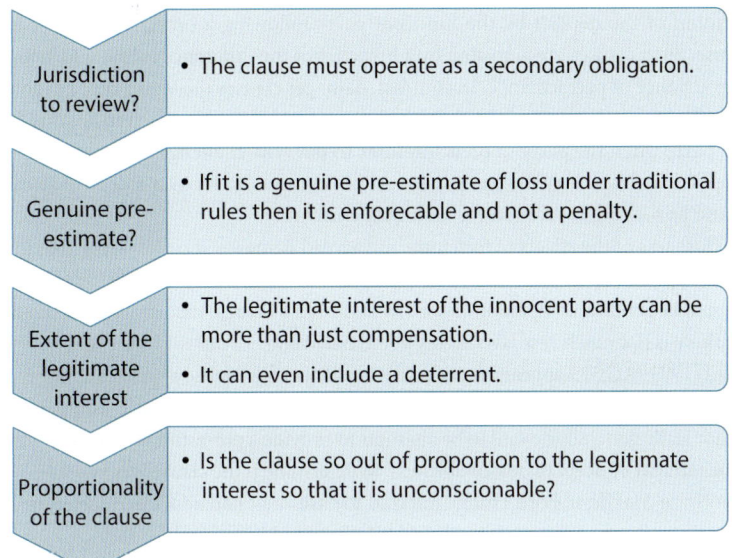

Figure 11.1
The process to be adopted when a clause is challenged as a penalty

11.7.4.3 The Significance of Makdessi

The *Makdessi* case is very significant because it was the first time the highest court had the opportunity to review the area and make changes. The practical significance is that the protective bar is set quite low so that many more clauses will be enforceable, rather than classed as penalties. In other words, the modified approach makes it much harder to find that an agreed damages clause is a penalty.

Genuine pre-estimates will be enforceable as such clauses would reflect the standard interest of being compensated for losses. The assessment of the legitimate interest is more important when the clause is not a pre-estimate. In such a case, it might be found that the legitimate interest goes beyond being compensated. The clause will be enforceable in these circumstances unless it is completely out of proportion with those wider interests.

There is a strong presumption that there is such a wider legitimate interest when parties contract on an equal footing. That means it is even less likely that a penalty will exist between large commercial parties. The clause must then be disproportionate to the protection of whatever legitimate interest is being pursued for it to be said that the clauses are unconscionable or extravagant as penalties.

Looking ahead, it is possible that there will be some uncertainty over what fits within the definition of a 'legitimate interest' in each case. Likewise, there might some flexibility in the courts' assessment of what is proportionate. What we can say is that it does seem that the Supreme Court has retained its power to intervene when a damages clause is unconscionable, but at the same time the penalty rule has been relaxed to a point where successful challenges will be limited to exceptional cases.

11.7.5 Forfeiture Clauses as Penalties

forfeiture clause

requires a payment in advance of performance and allows the innocent party to keep it following a breach.

So far, we have addressed the basic legal position on penalty clauses. However, it is important to mention a related term known as a **forfeiture clause**. While the name will not be familiar, their use in transactions might be. Consider a transaction where a party has to pay an initial deposit (as opposed to part-payment) and will not get it back following a breach. That process is achieved with a forfeiture clause. The party in breach forfeits the deposit in the event of the breach. The effect of such a clause (i.e. the retention of the deposit by the innocent party following a breach) is similar to an agreed damages clause. Such clauses are activated by a breach, but the difference is that a forfeiture relates to a sum paid in advance of performance. In contrast, damages clauses relate to a sum payable on breach. That means different actions are involved. Agreed damages clauses are raised in actions for breach by the innocent party when the party in breach refuses to pay. The challenge to the clause as a penalty is then relied upon as a defence by the party in breach. In contrast, to recover a deposit already paid, the claimant would be seeking restitution for an unjust enrichment.

Given the closeness of the effects of forfeiture and agreed damages, it makes sense that the same penalty rule would apply to forfeiture clauses. For example, if the amount deposited is significant and could never be taken to be genuine compensation for any loss from a breach, then arguably it should be treated as a penalty. There is not much case law on this point, but *Workers Trust and Merchant Bank Ltd v Dojap Investment Ltd* [1993] AC 573 appears as authority for the penalty clause approach to apply to forfeiture clauses. Here the Privy Council held that a forfeiture clause was unenforceable as a penalty. However, deposits cannot really generally be said to be attempts to provide a pre-estimate of loss. On that basis, the court used the familiar concept of 'reasonableness' to determine if the clause was penal.

More recently, in *Makdessi*, Lord Hodge referred to cases that had addressed forfeiture, including a case from the Hong Kong Court of Appeal, and briefly stated:

> [238] ... (a) a deposit which is not reasonable as earnest money may be challenged as a penalty and (b) where the stipulated deposit exceeds the percentage set by long established practice the vendor must show special circumstances to justify that deposit if it is not to be treated as an unenforceable penalty.

This shows that the actual penalty rule does not apply to forfeiture. But there is a standard to be met in order for a forfeiture clause to be enforceable. It relies on reasonableness in the sense that the deposit should be 'reasonable as earnest money'. This is a term in property law, which means that a deposit is reasonable. Reasonableness can be determined by the circumstances, but clearly the market norm is a key factor.

CHAPTER SUMMARY

- Specific performance and injunctions are remedies from equity and can be available following a breach. Such remedies are awarded at the discretion of the court and only when damages would be inadequate.

- The Consumer Rights Act 2015 gives consumers the right to performance-based remedies of repair, replacement or price reduction.

- Restitution for an unjust enrichment can apply when the contract is void; where was no contract; and where there was a total failure of consideration.

- Damages for a breach are compensatory, so that an innocent party is generally not entitled to the profit made by a party in breach.

■ An account of profits reflects a form of restitution for a wrong and is a highly exceptional remedy for a breach. It was applied as a remedy for a breach in *Attorney-General v Blake*. To do so, the reasoning relied on *Wrotham Park* as a case featuring a restitutionary remedy.

■ The reliance on *Wrotham Park* in *Blake* opened the door for negotiating damages to be available for a breach of contract. However, there was uncertainty as to the basis of the award, i.e. whether it was restitutionary or compensatory.

■ The Supreme Court in *Morris-Garner v One-Step* confirmed that negotiating damages are compensation for the loss of a valuable asset. The hypothetical fee that could have been negotiated is just evidence towards the value of that lost asset.

■ For negotiating damages to be awarded, it must be shown that the loss was of a valuable asset. If the loss was something else like profits, then that is the loss to claim for, irrespective of the difficulty of calculating it.

■ If there is no loss, then nominal damages are awarded.

■ An alternative to compensatory damages is the enforcement of an agreed damages clause.

■ Traditionally, these would be enforceable as a liquidated damages clause if they were a genuine pre-estimate of the loss. If the sum was much larger, the clause would be operating as a deterrent and would be unenforceable as a penalty.

■ The traditional approach was liberalised by the Supreme Court in *Makdessi*. It is now much harder to class a clause as a penalty, but the power remains for the courts to do so.

■ Under *Makdessi*, a clause will only be a penalty if it is so out of proportion with the protection of the legitimate interest that the innocent party has in the clause that the clause is unconscionable.

KEY CASES

☐ *Co-operative Insurance Society Ltd v Argyll Stores Ltd* [1998] AC 1—a leading case on the granting of specific performance.

☐ *Warren v Mendy* [1989] 1 WLR 853—a useful authority on the refusal to grant injunctions in personal services contracts where this would force one party to work for another (something that specific performance cannot be used for).

☐ *Stocznia Gdanska SA v Latvian Shipping Co* [1998] 1 WLR 574—this case concerned the concept of a 'total failure of consideration', the requirement for restitution for unjust enrichment in the contract context.

☐ *Surrey County Council v Bredero Homes* [1993] 1 WLR 1361—while the reasoning has been the subject of criticism, this case still represents an example of the normal rule against restitutionary remedies for a breach when no loss has been suffered.

☐ *Wrotham Park Estate Co v Parkside Homes Ltd* [1974] WLR 798—this is no longer a case to cite as authority in the contract context, but it is important to know it as the initial basis for negotiating damages, and a key authority for the account of profits award in *Blake*.

☐ *Attorney-General v Blake* [2001] 1 AC 268—this is the controversial case that allowed for the awarding of an account of profits following a breach. It represents a highly exceptional principle.

☐ *Morris-Garner v One-Step (Support) Ltd* [2018] UKSC 20—A very important case in which the Supreme Court sought to clarify the basis of negotiating damages and the availability of the award.

☐ *Dunlop Pneumatic Tyre Co Ltd v New Garage and Motor co Ltd* [1915] AC 79—The judgment of Lord Dunedin represents the much-criticised traditional approach to liquidated damages clauses and penalty clauses.

☐ *Cavendish Square Holdings BV v Makdessi, ParkingEye Ltd v Beavis* [2015] UKSC 67—The very important case from the Supreme Court that represents the new approach to penalty clauses.

QUESTIONS

1. A new night club called 'Phatz' entered a contract with the local council to lease premises and park-ing facilities. One of the terms allows Phatz to advertise using a sky beam but only up to 11.30 pm. In breach, the sky beam is used regularly all night long because it attracts more customers. The continued use of the sky beam has not resulted in financial loss to the council.

   Advise the council on the following matters:

   (a) The steps that the council can take to stop the use of the Sky beam after 11.30pm.

   (b) The extent to which the council will be entitled to damages for the breach.

2. The approach adopted by the Supreme Court in *Morris-Garner v One-Step* [2018] resolved the prob-lems associated with negotiating damages. Critically discuss.

3. The approach taken by the Supreme Court in *Cavendish Square Holdings v Makdessi* [2015] repre-sents an improvement to the law relating to penalty clauses. Critically discuss.

For answer guidance to these questions please visit the online resources at www .oup.com/uk/naidoo1e/, where you will also find multiple choice questions to check your understanding of key concepts.

FURTHER READING

Bartscherer, 'Two steps forward, one step back: One Step (Support) Ltd v Morris-Garner and Another' MLR (2019), 82(2), 367.
This is a useful extended case note on *Morris-Garner* which also contrasts the majority judgment with the dissenting judgment of Lord Sumption.

Burrows, 'One step forward?' LQR (2018), 134, 515.
This is a shorter case note on *Morris-Garner*, with useful views from a leading authority.

Conte, 'The penalty rule revisited' LQR (2016), 132, 382.
This is a case note on Makdessi that provides some useful criticism of using the category of secondary obligations for the jurisdiction to apply.

Morgan, 'The penalty clause doctrine: unlovable but untouchable' CLJ (2016), 75(1), 11.
This is an excellent, short case note on *Makdessi* with criticism throughout.

Rowan, 'The "legitimate interest in performance" in the law on penalties' CLJ (2019), 78(1), 148.
This is a clear, very detailed assessment of the meaning of 'legitimate interest' in determining the scope of the new approach to penalty clauses.

Third Party Rights (the Doctrine of Privity)

12

LEARNING OBJECTIVES

By the end of this chapter you should be able to:

- understand the basic principle behind the rule against contracts being enforced by third parties
- critique the traditional rule against giving third parties rights of enforcement
- apply the legislation that creates an exception and allows for third party rights of enforcement
- understand and assess the methods developed by the courts to provide a remedy for third parties

INTRODUCTION

Contracts are legally enforceable agreements between two parties. However, many contracts are made to benefit someone else. As a result, the legal position of parties outside of the contract (known as 'third parties') is a very important issue. Because they are outside of the contract and not privy to it, the law relating to their position is commonly described as 'privity'.

This chapter is about the doctrine of privity of contract. That means it is about the rights and obligations of third parties. The starting point is the basic common law rule of privity. At common law, third parties have no general right to enforce contracts made by others. Likewise, contracts made by others cannot impose obligations on third parties. This is a fairly straightforward principle and is based on sound reasons, but in practice privity has become a complex area. The existence of the rule resulted in a range of clever devices being developed to get around it, all of which are of commercial importance. And the rule against parties enforcing contracts made by others in particular was also severely criticised over the years for various reasons which we will examine. The basis for such criticism resulted in some partial exceptions being developed in the case law, and ultimately in a statute—namely the Contracts (Rights of Third Parties) Act 1999. This complicates matters further, because the Act only applies in certain circumstances and its application can be excluded by the terms of the contract. So there will be circumstances in which the common law exceptions and devices remain relevant, and they must therefore be studied alongside it.

12.1 Third Parties and the Context of Disputes

When we hear about third parties and contracts made by others, it can all appear quite abstract. For that reason, it is useful at this stage to have a basic understanding of the main types of dispute that can raise an issue of privity. While these disputes are typically commercial, we can appreciate the main issues raised with the use of more relatable examples.

Consider a kind student that decides to treat his parents to a special dinner. The student goes to a fancy restaurant, books a table for his parents in their names and pays in advance. The parents turn up to the restaurant and wait to be seated, only to be told that there are no tables left for them. Ordinarily, the restaurant will be in breach of its contract with the student and the parents are just third parties. They are outside the contract and not privy to it. But key issues can arise in this restaurant example, and these are the issues that can arise with privity disputes generally:

- Can a third party enforce a contract made by others?
- Can a third party rely on a defence from a contract made by others?
- Can a party to a contract enforce it against a third party?
- Can a party to a contract rely on a defence from the contract when sued by a third party?

The first two issues concern the third party's ability to benefit from a contract made by others. The remaining two issues concern obligations being imposed on a third party by a contract made by others. We can take these in turn using our restaurant example.

The first issue is perhaps the most obvious. Can the parents enforce the contract made between the student and the restaurant? When the contract was made, it was clear that the parents were to receive the benefit that the student contracted for. It might seem logical for the restaurant to be liable to them for their loss, but then, they are not a party to the contract. Likewise, if the student sued the restaurant, could the claim include not only the financial loss suffered by the student (i.e. the money paid) but also any losses suffered by the parents resulting from the breach? It might be argued that since the parents are not a contractual party, their loss cannot be claimed by the student.

The second issue about the third party relying on a defence from the contract could arise when exemption clauses are used. For example, the standard terms of the restaurant agreed by the student might state that there is no liability for glasses that are accidently damaged by customers. Imagine that the parents had accidently smashed two expensive champagne flutes while waiting to be seated. If the restaurant sued them for the cost of the glasses, could the parents rely on the exemption clause? Alternatively, could the restaurant argue that since the parents are a third party, they cannot benefit from the terms of a contract to which they had not agreed?

The third issue about a party to a contract enforcing it against a third party can be illustrated if we amend the initial facts of our example. Perhaps the student only paid a deposit for the booking and agreed to pay the rest the following day but never did. In such circumstances, could the restaurant demand the outstanding balance from the parents? If it did, it would be trying to enforce the contractual right owed by the student against his third party parents.

The fourth issue concerns a contractual party relying on a defence from the contract when sued by a third party. In our example, perhaps the terms agreed by the student included an exemption clause in favour of the restaurant. The clause excluded liability for the loss of coats and bags stored in the cloakroom. Following the theft of the parents' coats, if they sued the restaurant for negligence, could the restaurant rely on the clause? Alternatively, it might be argued that the clause should only be effective against those that agreed to it—in this case the student.

We will see from the cases that these issues can arise in a wide range of other contexts. But at this stage, we can see from these illustrations how the position of a third party can raise legal issues and be the subject of a dispute. Such disputes have a long history in contract law. In exploring the law of privity, our starting point is the development of the general privity rule against third party rights.

12.2 The Development of the Doctrine of Privity

The case often cited as the modern origin of the privity doctrine is *Tweddle v Atkinson* (1861) 1 B & S 393. This concerned a contract between the fathers of a couple who were about to get married. In the contract, Tweddle's father promised to give £100 to his son. In return, Mr Guy (who was the father of

Tweddle's fiancé), promised to give £200 to his future son-in-law, Tweddle. The contract even stated that Tweddle had the 'full power' to sue either father for the money promised. Unfortunately, the fiancé's father, Mr Guy died before making the payment. That prompted Tweddle to claim the £200 from the executor of Mr Guy's estate. There was no evidence to suggest that Mr Guy had changed his mind about paying and so the executer could assume that, had Mr Guy been alive, he would have paid the money. However, executors are only authorised to make payments from an estate to cover the estate's liability for legally enforceable obligations. The executer did not pay Tweddle, and so Tweddle brought an action for the £200. A key question for the court was whether Tweddle could enforce the contract between his father and Mr Guy. The Queen's Bench Court decided that Tweddle had no right to enforce the contract.

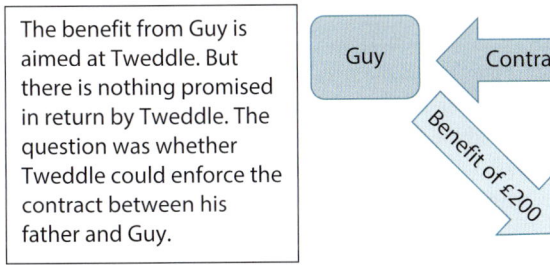

The benefit from Guy is aimed at Tweddle. But there is nothing promised in return by Tweddle. The question was whether Tweddle could enforce the contract between his father and Guy.

Figure 12.1
The contractual relationship in *Tweddle v Atkinson* (1861)

In the reasoning, Wightman J observed:

> [N]o stranger to the consideration can take advantage of a contract, although made for his benefit.

The judgment of Crompton J explained the reason for the decision in the following way:

> The modern cases . . . shew that the consideration must move from the party entitled to sue upon the contract. It would be a monstrous proposition to say that a person was a party to the contract for the purpose of suing upon it for his own advantage, and not a party to it for the purpose of being sued.

The reasoning shows that the court based their 'privity rule' on consideration. Since Tweddle had not provided consideration for the promise of payment, as illustrated by Figure 12.1, he was not a party to any contract with Guy for the £200. On that basis, he could not enforce the contract. The court made a clear link between consideration and privity, but it could be said that the two rules are separate. After all, consideration is about identifying *which* promises are enforceable. In contrast, a privity rule is about *who* can enforce a contract.

According to Crompton J, if a party has the benefit of enforcing a contract, it should be possible for the contract to be enforced against that party too. In the case, the claimant was trying to enforce the contract for his benefit. However, the contract imposed no obligations or duties on that claimant. The idea of the claimant having an enforceable benefit without any obligation was described as 'monstrous'. But what is so bad about having an enforceable benefit without an obligation? Yes, it is one sided, but it is difficult to see a practical reason for supporting such a hostile response to the idea. Of course, contracts are based on the theory of an exchange between the parties, but that is a theoretical principle rather than a practical one. Yet it seems to be so important that it can override the need to reflect the parties' intentions. We can recall that the contract was made for the benefit of Tweddle. It even stated that Tweddle had the 'full power' to enforce the contract. However, the court did not give effect to that clear intention. Irrespective of the intention expressed in the contract, the claimant could not enforce it without being a party to it.

➡ CROSS-REFERENCE
For the discussion of the basic requirement of consideration see 5.1–5.2.

The judgments in *Tweddle* put a clear focus on consideration. That can be taken to suggest that the case does not represent an independent rule on privity, but it did lay the foundations for it.

12.2.1 The Independent Doctrine of Privity

The later House of Lords case of *Dunlop Pneumatic Tyre Co Ltd v Selfridge & Co Ltd* [1915] AC 847 is treated as confirming a privity doctrine that is separate from the requirement for consideration to move from the promisee.

In this case, Dunlop, the tyre manufacturer, sold tyres to a trade buyer called Dew & co. Under the sales contract, Dew & Co had to agree not to resell the tyres below Dunlop's list price. If they did, they would have to pay Dunlop a penalty of £5 for each tyre sold below the list price. This type of obligation is known as a 'resale-price maintenance' clause. In addition, Dew & co promised to impose the same resale price maintenance clause on any traders they resold the tyres to.

Dew then resold tyres to a retailer, Selfridge, using terms including the resale price maintenance obligation. The case arose because Selfridge resold the tyres to customers for less than the list price. Dunlop then sued Selfridge for an amount based on £5 per tyre. Selfridge was subject to the price maintenance obligation from the contract with their own seller, Dew. The question was whether Dunlop could enforce that obligation.

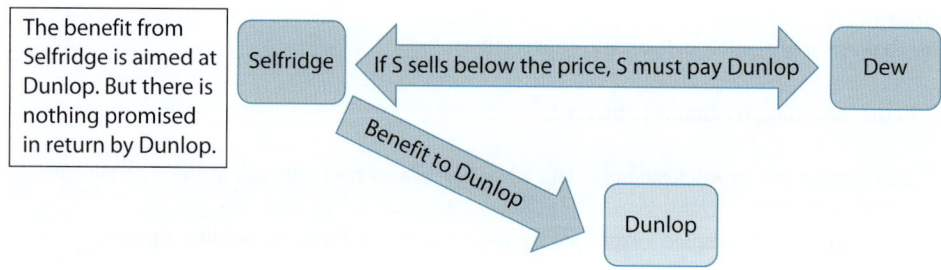

Figure 12.2

The contractual relationship in *Dunlop v Selfridge* [1915]

One of the arguments made by Dunlop was that Dew was acting as an agent of Dunlop when they sold tyres to Selfridge. Following the Court of Appeal, the House of Lords, decided that Dunlop could not enforce the obligation owed by Selfridge. The most relevant and significant judgments were delivered by Viscount Haldane and Lord Dunedin. We will look at both in turn, starting with Viscount Haldane LC who stated:

> My Lords, in the law of England certain principles are fundamental. One is that only a person who is a party to a contract can sue on it. Our law knows nothing of a *jus quaesitum tertio* arising by way of contract. . . . A second principle is that if a person with whom a contract not under seal has been made is to be able to enforce it consideration must have been given by him to the promisor or to some other person at the promisor's request. These two principles are not recognized in the same fashion by the jurisprudence of certain Continental countries or of Scotland, but here they are well established. A third proposition is that a **principal** not named in the contract may sue upon it if the promisee really contracted as his agent. But again, in order to entitle him so to sue, he must have given consideration either personally or through the promisee, acting as his agent in giving it.
>
> My Lords, in the case before us, I am of opinion that the consideration, the allowance of what was in reality part of the discount to which Messrs. Dew, the promisees, were entitled as between

jus quaesitum tertio
is a Latin reference to third party rights.

principal
is the label given to the person represented by an agent. So, an agent acts on behalf of its principal.

themselves and the appellants, was to be given by Messrs. Dew on their own account, and was not in substance, any more than in form, an allowance made by the appellants. . .

No doubt it was provided as part of these terms that the appellants should acquire certain rights, but these rights appear on the face of the contract as *jura quaesita tertio*, which the appellants could not enforce. Moreover, even if this difficulty can be got over by regarding the appellants as the principals of Messrs. Dew in stipulating for the rights in question, the only consideration disclosed by the contract is one given by Messrs. Dew, not as their agents, but as principals acting on their own account.

We can see here that the main reason for Viscount Haldane's decision was that there was no consideration moving from Dunlop for the promise made by Selfridge. That was his chief focus. However, he also said that a contract can only be enforced by a party to it. This was an expression of the privity rule. That is, he was identifying the existence of a privity doctrine separate from the requirement for consideration.

The other significant judgment on this issue was given by Lord Dunedin:

My Lords, I confess that this case is to my mind apt to nip any budding affection which one might have had for the doctrine of consideration. For the effect of that doctrine in the present case is to make it possible for a person to snap his fingers at a bargain deliberately made, a bargain not in itself unfair, and which the person seeking to enforce it has a legitimate interest to enforce. Notwithstanding these considerations I cannot say that I have ever had any doubt that the judgment of the Court of Appeal was right.

My Lords, I am content to adopt from a work of Sir Frederick Pollock, to which I have often been under obligation, the following words as to consideration: "An act or forbearance of one party, or the promise thereof, is the price for which the promise of the other is bought, and the promise thus given for value is enforceable." (Pollock on Contracts, 8th ed., p. 175.)

Now the agreement sued on is an agreement which on the face of it is an agreement between Dew and Selfridge. But speaking for myself, I should have no difficulty in the circumstances of this case in holding it proved that the agreement was truly made by Dew as agent for Dunlop, or in other words that Dunlop was the undisclosed principal, and as such can sue on the agreement. None the less, in order to enforce it he must show consideration, as above defined, moving from Dunlop to Selfridge.

In the circumstances, how can he do so? The agreement in question is not an agreement for sale. It is only collateral to an agreement for sale; but that agreement for sale is an agreement entirely between Dew and Selfridge. The tyres, the property in which upon the bargain is transferred to Selfridge, were the property of Dew, not of Dunlop, for Dew under his agreement with Dunlop held these tyres as proprietor, and not as agent. What then did Dunlop do, or forbear to do, in a question with Selfridge? The answer must be, nothing. . .

To my mind, this ends the case.

Lord Dunedin also therefore based his decision on consideration—under the original contract with Dunlop, Dew acquired ownership of the tyres and then transferred them to Selfridge in return for money. This meant that Dunlop had not provided consideration to Selfridge (because it had not provided Selfridge with any benefit, nor indeed anything at all, as shown by Figure 12.2) and on that basis it could not enforce any rights against Selfridge.

While the decision by Lord Dunedin was based on consideration, however, it did not ignore the privity rule. According to his judgment, privity was not an issue because it was felt that Dew acted as Dunlop's agent. On that basis, the privity rule was not actually applied. However, the existence of an independent privity rule was the reason why it was necessary to mention the agency relationship. Without such a relationship, the privity rule would have been another reason to prevent Dunlop enforcing the contract.

KEY POINTS

The judgments by Viscount Haldane LC and Lord Dunedin represent authority for a privity rule that operates independently from consideration.

At first glance, the consideration and privity rules appear to achieving the same thing. However, the rule that consideration must move from the promisee really identifies *which* promises are enforceable. In contrast, the privity rule identifies *who* can enforce a promise. For an example, take the promise by Mr Guy in *Tweddle v Atkinson*. That was supported with consideration moving from the other party to the contract (Tweddle's father). Likewise, the same can be said about the promise by Selfridge. It was enforceable because there would have been consideration moving from Dew. This means that both of the relevant promises in *Dunlop v Selfridge* and *Tweddle v Atkinson* were enforceable in principle. It is just that they could not be enforced by the claimant in the respective cases, because neither of them was a party to the contract. Such a restriction is a result of the privity rule, which determines *who* can enforce a contract.

KEY POINTS

- Consideration identifies *which* promises are enforceable.
- Privity identifies *who* can enforce the promises.

12.2.2 The Application of the Doctrine of Privity to Exemption Clauses

The cases following *Dunlop v Selfridge* cited Viscount Haldane LC and applied a separate privity doctrine independent of the requirement for consideration. The House of Lords, for example, confirmed the existence of a separate privity doctrine to exemption clauses in *Scruttons Ltd v Midland Silicones Ltd* [1962] AC 446. In this case, a cargo owner arranged for a shipping company (a carrier) to deliver a cargo of chemicals. The contract limited the carrier's liability for damaging the cargo to $500. The carrier contracted with stevedores (stevedores are businesses that are used to unload cargo from ships) and their contract stated that the stevedores would have the benefit of the limitation clause. When unloading, the cargo was damaged. The cargo owner then brought an action for negligence against the defendant stevedores. The question for the court was whether the stevedores could rely on the limitation clause which was in the contract between the cargo owner and the carrier.

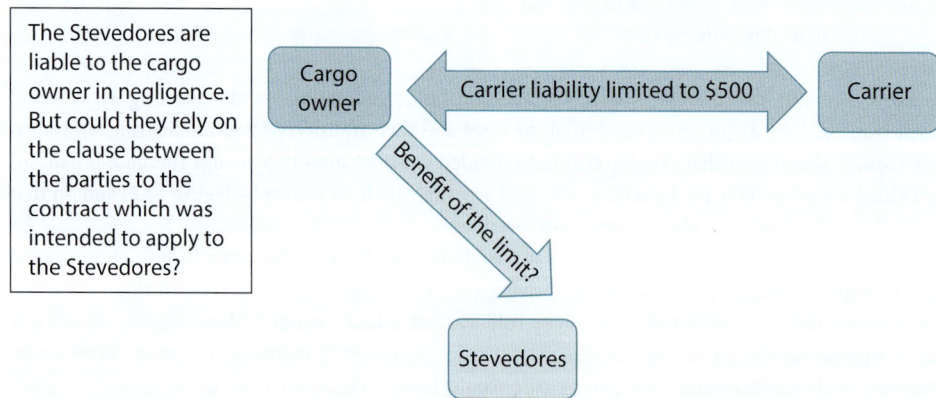

Figure 12.3
The contractual relationship in *Scruttons Ltd v Midland Silicones Ltd* [1962]

The House of Lords confirmed that the defendant stevedores could not rely on a defence from a contract to which it was not a party. It is useful to look at the judgment by Lord Reid who explained the reasoning in the following way:

> In considering the various arguments for the appellants I think it is necessary to have in mind certain established principles of the English law of contract. Although I may regret it, I find it impossible to deny the existence of the general rule that a stranger to a contract cannot in a question with either of the contracting parties take advantage of provisions of the contract, even where it is clear from the contract that some provision in it was intended to benefit him. That rule appears to have been crystallised a century ago in *Tweddle v Atkinson* and finally established in this House in *Dunlop Pneumatic Tyre Co Ltd v Selfridge & Co Ltd*. There are, it is true, certain well-established exceptions to that rule—though I am not sure that they are really exceptions and do not arise from other principles. But none of these in any way touches the present case.
>
> The actual words used by Viscount Haldane LC in the *Dunlop case* ([1915] AC at p. 853) were made the basis of an argument that, although a stranger to a contract may not be able to sue for any benefit under it, he can rely on the contract as a defence if one of the parties to it sues him in breach of his contractual obligation—that he can use the contract as a shield though not as a sword. I can find no justification for that. If the other contracting party can prevent the breach of contract well and good, but if he cannot I do not see how the stranger can. As was said in *Tweddle v Atkinson* ((1861), 1 B & S at p. 398) the stranger cannot "take advantage" from the contract.

The key reasoning was based on the application of the privity doctrine. The stevedores were not privy to the contract between the carrier and cargo owner and were therefore strangers to it. On that basis, the stevedores could not rely on the limitation clause within it, as shown by Figure 12.3. Only the carrier could rely on the clause if they damaged the cargo and it did not matter that the carrier happened to have hired the stevedores to unload the cargo.

?! THINKING POINTS

In principle, did the Stevedores really deserve to have the protection of the clause? Was such protection even intended by the cargo owner?

Lord Reid seems to indicate that the doctrine of privity was too well-established to set aside or refine. It was applied as a separate rule and determined the outcome without any reference to the requirement for consideration.

The case also shows the scope of the doctrine of privity. Previous cases had shown that a contract could not be enforced by a third party. In other words, such a stranger to a contract could not rely on it to bring an action. The *Scruttons* case goes further. It shows that when sued by a party to a contract, a third party cannot rely on that contract to *defend* the action. The point is that the doctrine of privity does not only apply to positive rights from a contract. It also prevents a third party relying on negative rights from the contract.

KEY POINTS

The doctrine of privity also prevents a third party from relying a defence from the contract made by others.

Interestingly, while Lord Reid applied the privity rule, it was with 'regret'. This attitude towards the doctrine of privity was typical of many judges at the time. By then, the rule had been exposed to a great deal of criticism.

12.3 The Basis for Criticising the Doctrine of Privity

The fact that the doctrine of privity had resulted in criticism should not be a surprise, because we know that legislation was eventually passed to improve the legal position. However, it is useful to appreciate the main general criticisms because it helps provide a context for subsequent developments.

The main criticism of the doctrine of privity was that its application could go against the parties' intentions. A contract could show a clear intention for it to be enforced by a third party. However, the rule would prevent the third party from enforcing the contract. That was the position in *Tweddle v Atkinson*.

The other main criticism was about resulting unfairness. Consider a promise made in a contract to benefit a third party. The third party might then act in reliance on that promise. For example, it might pay for things or line up sales based on the existence of the promise. The privity rule could then result in even further losses for the third party beyond simply not having what was promised.

The privity rule can therefore have the effect that the party who has actually suffered a loss cannot sue, but a party which has suffered no loss can. Think, for example, of *Dunlop v Selfridge*, where Dunlop, which had suffered what was in effect a loss, could not sue. However Dew, which had not been harmed by Selfridge's breach, could sue. In turn this means that in most cases damages for breach will be nominal, because the party suing will not have suffered a loss. It is the third party that has suffered the loss. This also has the undesirable consequence that a party can be in breach but with no real liability in damages. That in turn presents a further criticism. A party could breach a contract, seek a better profit elsewhere and not have to compensate for the loss caused.

➡ CROSS-REFERENCE

For the compensatory aim of damages see 9.1.

12.4 Reasons for the Doctrine of Privity

It is important to appreciate that there are some good reasons for having a doctrine of privity.

The first is that contract law is based on the idea of an exchange of value between the parties. It results in a contract that can be described in law as a bargain. The result is that each party owes or owed something to the other. Without the privity rule, a party to a contract could owe an obligation to a third party with no obligation being imposed on that third party in return. Does this really matter? Well, it does help identify precisely who can enforce a contract.

An example from the Law Commission (Consultation Paper 121, Privity of Contract (1991) at 2.19) is a contract between a road building business and the government department responsible for roads. Under the contract, the government department pays for a motorway to be built. Such a motorway would be a huge benefit to those in the area relying on it. Without the privity rule, could the general public relying on the road sue the road building company for a delay or failure to complete the work? In other words, privity prevents indeterminate and unpredictable claims from the very wide class of people who might be 'third parties' to a contract.

A second justification is that privity prevents obligations from being imposed on third parties by others. Imagine an agreement between two colleagues that makes it a duty for a third colleague to buy milk to stock their communal fridge each day. Privity protects that third colleague, as a 'stranger' to the contract, because the doctrine has the effect that the only people with enforceable rights and obligations arising from a contract are those who are privy to it.

Perhaps another justification is that privity is not the real problem. It has been argued that the real problem and source of injustice lies in the rules on damages. Ordinarily, a party is only entitled to damages for their own losses. If that rule was relaxed, it could allow the innocent party after a breach of contract to recover losses caused to a third party if it was obvious that the contract intended to benefit that third party. This would simply be using damages to protect the innocent party's expectation interest, which in this case would mean providing a benefit to a third party.

12.5 Judicial Views on Privity and the Need for Legislative Reform

Nevertheless, over the years and from a very early stage, the doctrine of privity has been exposed to a lot of criticism. Many judges expressed their dissatisfaction with its effects. Often, the rule operated as an unwanted restriction on what the judges could decide. In *Darlington Borough Council v Wiltshier Northern Ltd* [1995] 1 WLR 68, Steyn LJ addressed the criticism and the need for reform.

GUIDED CASE READING 12.1
Darlington Borough Council v Wiltshier Northern Ltd [1995] 1 WLR 68

The extract from Steyn LJ's judgment is a useful summary of the need for reform. When reading try to identify:

- the reasons to reform the privity rule;
- the judicial criticism;
- Steyn LJ's view on the likelihood of legislative change at the time;
- why it would have been difficult for the courts to change the rule.

The case for recognising a contract for the benefit of a third party is simple and straightforward. The autonomy of the will of the parties should be respected. The law of contract should give effect to the reasonable expectations of contracting parties. Principle certainly requires that a burden should not be imposed on a third party without his consent. But there is no doctrinal, logical or policy reason why the law should deny effectiveness to a contract for the benefit of a third party where that is the expressed intention of the parties. Moreover, often the parties, and particularly third parties, organise their affairs on the faith of the contract. They rely on the contract. It is therefore unjust to deny effectiveness to such a contract. I will not struggle further with the point since nobody seriously asserts the contrary; but see a valuable article by Jack Beatson, . . . 'Reforming the Law of Contracts for the Benefit of Third Parties: a Second Bite at the Cherry' (1992) 45 C.L.P. 1.

> Steyn LJ sets about making a comprehensive condemnation of the doctrine of privity. He begins with a principle—that the law should give effect to contracting parties' intentions as much as possible. Moreover, it should attempt to do justice, and this will be undermined where a third party has organised its affairs in expectation that a contract will benefit it. Likewise, while it would be wrong to impose an obligation on a third party without their consent, there was no reason why it should be deprived of a benefit intended by the parties.

The genesis of the privity rule is suspect. It is attributed to *Tweddle v. Atkinson* (1861) B. & S. 393. It is more realistic to say that the rule originated in the misunderstanding of *Tweddle v. Atkinson* . . . [this was then supported by academic authority]. While the privity rule was barely tolerable in Victorian England, it has been recognised for half a century that it has no place in our more complex commercial world. Indeed, as early as 1915, in *Dunlop Pneumatic Tyre Co. Ltd. v. Selfridge & Co. Ltd.* [1915] A.C. 847, 855, when the House of Lords restated the privity rule, Lord Dunedin observed in a dissenting speech that the rule made 'it possible for a person to snap his fingers at a bargain deliberately made, a bargain not in itself unfair, and which the person seeking to enforce it has a legitimate interest to enforce.'

> He then extends his critique to the doctrinal origins of the privity rule, arguing that it is based on a misunderstanding of the decision in *Tweddle v Atkinson*, and moves on to the practical argument that privity is artificial and outdated.

. . . While the rigidity of the doctrine of consideration has been greatly reduced in modern times, the doctrine of privity of contract persists in all its artificial technicality.

In 1937 the Law Revision Committee in its Sixth Report (Cmd. 5449, para. 41–48) proposed the recognition of a right of a third party to enforce the contract which by its express terms purports to confer a benefit directly on him . . . Lord Scarman, who as a former chairman of the Law Commission usually favoured legislative rather than judicial reform where radical change was involved, reminded the House that it might be necessary to review all the cases which 'stand guard over this unjust rule:' *Woodar Investment Development Ltd. v. Wimpey Construction U.K. Ltd.* [1980] 1 W.L.R. 277, . . . In 1981 Dillon J. described the rule as 'a blot on our law and most unjust:' *Forster v. Silvermere Golf and Equestrian Centre* (1981) 125 S.J. 397. In 1983 Lord Diplock described the rule as 'an anachronistic shortcoming that has for many years been regarded as a reproach to English private law:' *Swain v. The Law Society* [1983] 1 A.C. 598, . . .

> He then summarises the various criticisms of the doctrine that had been made by judges and academics, and concludes with the concern that privity might even make the UK economy uncompetitive with those of other EU Member States.

But as important as judicial condemnations of the privity rule is the fact that distinguished academic lawyers have found no redeeming virtues in it: see, for example, Markesinis (1987) 103 L.Q.R. 354; Reynolds (1989) 105 L.Q.R. 1; Beatson (1992) 44 C.L.P. 1 and Adams and Brownsword (1993) 56 M.L.R. 722. And we do well to remember that the civil law legal systems of other members of the European Union recognise such contracts. That our legal system lacks such flexibility is a disadvantage in the single market . . .

In 1991 the Law Commission revisited this corner of the law. In cautious language appropriate to a consultation paper the Law Commission has expressed the provisional recommendation that "there should be a (statutory) reform of the law to allow third parties to enforce contractual provisions made in their favour" . . . No doubt there will be a report by the Law Commission in the not too distant future recommending the abolition of the privity of contract rule by statute. What will then happen in regard to the proposal for legislation? The answer is really quite simple: probably nothing will happen.

But on this occasion I can understand the inaction of Parliament. There is a respectable argument that it is the type of reform which is best achieved by the courts working out sensible solutions on a case by case basis, e.g. in regard to the exact point of time when the third party is vested with enforceable contractual rights . . . But that requires the door to be opened by the House of Lords reviewing the major cases which are thought to have entrenched the rule of privity of contract. Unfortunately, there will be few opportunities for the House of Lords to do so . . .

> However, he then concluded the judgment on a pessimistic note by suggesting that the Law Commission's recommendations on reforming the doctrine of privity were unlikely to come to fruition (alluding to the fact that there was unlikely to be space made in the legislative timetable for reform of an area of law that was completely obscure to the voting public). He therefore put his hopes on the judiciary making the necessary changes while acknowledging the slim chance of the House of Lords having the opportunity to do so. This was because it was unlikely that the representatives of a claimant would ever argue before the House of Lords that privity should be re-examined; instead they would rely on technical attempts to circumvent or exploit it.

Not long after the *Darlington Borough Council case*, the Law Commission reported their recommendations for reform. The report resulted in the Contracts (Rights of Third Parties) Act 1999, our next issue to explore.

12.6 Ways around the Privity Rule: The Contracts (Rights of Third Parties) Act 1999

The Contracts (Rights of Third Parties) Act 1999 is the major exception to the privity rule. Before the Act, the courts recognised a number of ways to avoid the effects of privity. It is important to appreciate that the exceptions developed by the courts remain useful in circumstances where the Act cannot apply. The 1999 Act is aimed at providing a solution to the privity problem. Essentially, the focus is on allowing third parties to enforce a contract. We will have a look at the aim, requirements, scope and operation of the Act.

12.6.1 The Aim of the 1999 Act

The Act does not abolish the traditional doctrine of privity. Instead, it provides a significant exception to it. It does not impose a rule that third parties must be able to enforce a contract. Instead, it is aimed at giving effect to the parties' intentions. If they show that a third party is to have enforceable rights, the Act allows for it. In some circumstances, the Act presumes there was such an intention, but it is only a presumption. The parties could rebut it by showing an intention to prevent any enforceable third party rights. This broad aim of the Act reflects the fact that it was drafted to deal with the problem that third parties had no rights, even though the parties had intended to provide them.

The Act operates to allow a third party to enforce a promise in a contract without providing any consideration. All that matters is that the promise is of the kind that would be enforceable by a contractual party—for example, where the promisee has provided consideration. This means that a promise which is unenforceable between the parties to a contract cannot suddenly become enforceable by a third party.

12.6.2 The Test for Enforcement by a Third Party

The relevant test for enforcement is in section 1. This lists the requirements to be met for the third party to have an enforceable right. It is useful to read the entire section and then consider the individual aspects in turn.

1 **Right of third party to enforce contractual term.**

   (1) Subject to the provisions of this Act, a person who is not a party to a contract (a "third party") may in his own right enforce a term of the contract if—

      (a) the contract expressly provides that he may, or

      (b) subject to subsection (2), the term purports to confer a benefit on him.

   (2) Subsection (1)(b) does not apply if on a proper construction of the contract it appears that the parties did not intend the term to be enforceable by the third party.

   (3) The third party must be expressly identified in the contract by name, as a member of a class or as answering a particular description but need not be in existence when the contract is entered into.

   (4) This section does not confer a right on a third party to enforce a term of a contract otherwise than subject to and in accordance with any other relevant terms of the contract.

   (5) For the purpose of exercising his right to enforce a term of the contract, there shall be available to the third party any remedy that would have been available to him in an action for breach of contract if he had been a party to the contract (and the rules relating to damages, injunctions, specific performance and other relief shall apply accordingly).

   (6) Where a term of a contract excludes or limits liability in relation to any matter references in this Act to the third party enforcing the term shall be construed as references to his availing himself of the exclusion or limitation.

   (7) In this Act, in relation to a term of a contract which is enforceable by a third party—

   "the promisor" means the party to the contract against whom the term is enforceable by the third party, and

   "the promisee" means the party to the contract by whom the term is enforceable against the promisor.

12.6.2.1 The Classification of the Parties

We have been focussed on the issue of a third party enforcing rights under the contract. We should remind ourselves that such rights are being enforced against a party to the contract. That party is the promisor because it is their obligation (from their promise) that is being enforced. The other party to the contract is the promisee. This helpful classification of the parties is confirmed in s.1(7) and allows the Act to distinguish easily between the parties to the contract.

12.6.2.2 Third Party Enforcement Must Have Been Intended

Section 1 (1) is concerned with the source of a third party's enforcement rights. Section 1 (1) (a) refers to contracts that expressly state that the third party has a right of enforcement. In such circumstances, the Act allows the third party to enforce the rights stated in the contract. This sub-section resolves the problem seen in *Tweddle v Atkinson*. When s.1 (1) (a) applies, the third party will need to prove that the contract expressly allows for third party enforcement.

12.6.2.3 The Presumption of an Intention to Allow for Third Party Enforcement

Some contracts intend to give a benefit to a third party, but don't actually refer to third party enforcement. Such contracts would not be covered by s.1 (1) (a). Instead, they will be a matter for s.1 (1) (b).

Section 1 (1) (b) is wider than s.1 (1) (a) and has two elements. It applies when a contract 'purports to confer a benefit' on a third party. That is the first element. With such a contract, it is presumed that the parties intended to allow the third party to enforce it.

One issue with s.1 (1) (b) has been about the language used. The term '*purports* to confer a benefit' could simply mean that the contract has to be beneficial to a third party. Alternatively, it could mean that the benefit has to be *a* purpose of the contract or even the *only* purpose. On this issue Lindsay J in *Prudential Assurance Co Ltd v Ayres* [2007] EWHC 775 (Ch) observed:

> There is within s.1(2) (b) no requirement that the benefit on the third party shall be the predominant purpose or intent behind the term or that it denies the applicability of section 1 (1) (b) if a benefit is conferred on someone other than the third party.

Accordingly, the benefit to the third party does not have to the main purpose of the contract. The comment by Lindsay J was developed further in *Dolphin Maritime & Aviation Services Ltd v Sveriges Angfartygs Assurans Forening, The Swedish Club* [2009] EWHC 716 (Comm). On this issue Christopher Clarke J stated:

> A contract does not purport to confer a benefit on a third party simply because the position of that third party will be improved if the contract is performed. The reference in the section to the term purporting to "confer" a benefit seems to me to connote that the language used by the parties shows that one of the purposes of their bargain (rather than one of its incidental effects if performed) was to benefit the third party.

This means that 'purport to confer a benefit' requires the benefit to be *a* purpose of the contract and so it does not have to be the only purpose. Such a wide approach ensures that the effectiveness of the Act is not unnecessarily restricted.

12.6.2.4 Rebutting the s.1(1)(b) Presumption

The aim of s.1 (1)(b) is to create a presumption of third-party enforcement being intended. The presumption arises when a contract 'purports to confer' a benefit on a third party, but there is a second part of s.1 (1)(b). The presumption can be rebutted, and this is addressed by s.1(2).

Section 1(2) refers to circumstances in which a contract shows that third party enforcement was *not* intended. In such circumstances, the presumption of enforceable rights will be rebutted. In a dispute, the presumption works in favour of the third party. It is then for the promisor to prove that third party enforcement was not intended. To do so, the promisor would have to rely on the wording of the contract, or as s.1(2) puts it, 'the proper construction of the contract'. 'Proper construction' suggests it would be wrong to interpret the contract against the promisor. Instead, a meaning should be applied that reflects the context.

To rely on s.1(2) and rebut the presumption, it is not enough to show that the contract is simply silent on the issue of third party enforcement. That point was made in the first reported case on the Act, *Nisshin Shipping Co. Ltd v Cleaves & Co. Ltd* [2003] EWHC 2602 (Comm). The case concerned a broker who had arranged for a number of charterparty agreements for a shipowner. Under the terms of each agreement, the broker was entitled to a commission of 1% for its services. Each charterparty agreement also had an arbitration clause. The dispute arose when the shipowner refused to make a payment. The broker then tried to enforce the arbitration. Of course, the brokers were not a party to any of the charterparty agreements, but Colman J allowed the brokers to enforce the contract under dispute. Essentially, the clause did impliedly 'purport to confer a benefit' on the brokers. As a result, an intention to allow enforcement by the brokers was presumed. The contract did not have to show an actual intention to allow enforcement by the broker. What mattered was that the contract did not rule out an intention for such enforcement. This meant the presumption in favour of third party enforcement was not rebutted.

12.6.2.5 Identification of the Third Party

Section 1(3) requires the contract to expressly identify the third party. This can be done by stating the name of the third party. Alternatively, the contract can refer to the class the third party is a member of, or the description the third party has to fit. This will show that the parties intended enforcement by a particular third party or type of third party. This requirement gets around the problem stated by the Law Commission about the building of a road, which we referred to earlier. While the new motorway would be for the benefit of road users, it would be strange to allow them to have enforceable rights against the business. Under the Act, if the road users are not in a class or type specified in the contract, they would have no right of enforcement.

The requirement in s.1(3) is does not specify that the third party has to know about the contract. This point was demonstrated in *Charity Commission v Framjee* [2014] EWHC 2507 (Ch). The case concerned a website set up to receive donations for various charities. The donations would then be passed to the relevant charity. The court confirmed that each donation was a contract between the donor and the trust body behind the website. On the facts, this gave an enforceable right to the relevant charities to ensure they received the actual donations. After all, the contracts in question all aimed to provide a particular charity with a benefit. The fact that the charity would have been unaware of these contracts at the time they were formed was not an issue.

The s.1(3) requirement can restrict the application of the Act and can have unfortunate consequences. For example, the type of third party to benefit might be really obvious and, accordingly, left unexpressed, but in these circumstances according to the Act no enforceable right is given. *Avraamides v Colwill* [2006] EWCA Civ 1533 provides a good example. The claimants (Mr and Mrs Avraamides) employed a bathroom business to refurbish their two bathrooms. The work was defective and on that basis the bathroom business would have been liable to the claimants for the breach. However, by the time action was brought, the bathroom business had been sold. The contract between the new owner and seller of the business contained an important clause. The first part stated that the new owner had to 'complete outstanding customer orders taking into account any deposits paid by customers'. The second part said the owner had to 'pay any liabilities properly incurred' by the business.

Based on the second part of this clause, the claimants argued that the new owner was liable to them. They did not have a contract with the new owner so the key issue was whether they could enforce the liabilities clause. That clause was in the contract between the new owner and the seller. That made the claimants a third party to the contract. Since they stood to benefit from the contract, they argued that they could enforce it under s.1 (1) (b). The claimant was successful at first instance. However, the Court of Appeal held that the Act did not apply to give them a right of enforcement.

Waller LJ gave the main judgment. On whether the wording of the clause was enough to identify the type of third party Waller LJ stated:

> [16] . . .
>
> [I]n my view there is nothing . . . which limits "liabilities properly incurred" to liabilities to customers. On any natural reading liabilities to suppliers or for telephone bills or whatever would seem to come within the compass of liabilities properly incurred.
>
> [17] . . . By s 1(3) of the 1999 Act "The third party must be expressly identified in the contract by name, as a member of a class or as answering a particular description . . .". The second part of the [clause] simply does not identify any third party or class of third parties.

His Lordship then considered whether the claimant could be saved by the Act and observed:

> [19] The answer I am afraid is that s 1(3), by use of the word "express", simply does not allow a process of construction or implication. I considered whether it would be possible for [counsel for the claimants] to rely on the fact that "customers" are identified in the contract as beneficiaries of the first part of [the clause], even if liabilities in the second part includes persons other than customers. Could he submit that even though others are included within the liabilities under the second part, "customers" as a class are identified and that is sufficient. The difficulty is that the section is concerned with the benefit conferred on a third party, and with the identification of that person. The benefit from the obligation to pay liabilities properly incurred would benefit third parties but of a large number of unidentified classes.

With a great deal of sympathy, the Court of Appeal felt limited by the wording of the Act. It is not enough for the third party to benefit to be identifiable from the circumstances. The party must be identifiable at the very least from a description that has been expressed in the contract. There was an express reference to 'customers' in the first part of the clause. However, that could not be taken to mean that the second part was a reference to liabilities to customers. This is because these liabilities could be owed to any class of party, customers being just one type.

?! THINKING POINTS

Given the purpose of the limit, rather than seek to identify 'customers' as a class, could the Court have simply accepted a class made up of those that the business was liable to?

It could be said that the claimant deserved to enforce the clause. It might be fairly assumed that the Act was meant to protect such a party. Unfortunately, the wording of the Act was a barrier to such protection.

12.6.2.6 The Benefit of the Contract for the Third Party

Section 1 recognises rights for third parties. However, the enforcement of the benefit must be consistent with what the contract says. Section 1 (4) indicates that the benefit can be limited by other terms of the contract. That is consistent with the idea that the third party should be entitled to the benefit *intended* by the contract. It means that the third party does not somehow end up in a better position than the parties to the contract. Likewise, the third party is bound by any exemption clauses that apply between the contractual parties (s.1(6)). It may seem like an obvious point, but by virtue of this being clear in the Act, disputes resulting from any uncertainty on the point will not arise. The Act also refers to rights relating to the enforcement of the contract. Section 1(5) makes it clear that the remedies that a contractual party usually has in relation to a breach will be available to the third party. Examples of such remedies would be a damages claim, injunctions and specific performance.

12.6.3 Rules on the Parties Changing or Ending the Contract

Ordinarily, parties to a contract have the freedom to make changes to the terms. The parties can even agree to end the contract. Such freedom can undermine the position of a third party. In fact, s.1 of the Act would be of little use if the parties had an unrestricted freedom to change the terms intended to benefit the third party. Likewise, the same can be said about the parties being able to remove the benefit by ending the contract. For that reason, section 2 of the Act has some rules on changing and ending the contract. It places the following limit on the parties:

➡ CROSS-REFERENCE

For the discussion consideration and the variation of the contract see 5.9.

> 2   **Variation and rescission of contract**
>
> (1) Subject to the provisions of this section, where a third party has a right under section 1 to enforce a term of the contract, the parties to the contract may not, by agreement, rescind the contract, or vary it in such a way as to extinguish or alter his entitlement under that right, without his consent if—
>
> (a) the third party has communicated his assent to the term to the promisor,
>
> (b) the promisor is aware that the third party has relied on the term, or
>
> (c) the promisor can reasonably be expected to have foreseen that the third party would rely on the term and the third party has in fact relied on it.

The section refers to circumstances in which the parties will not be able to change the benefit or end the contract. If these circumstances prevail, it will not mean that the contract can never be changed or ended. Instead, it means that the consent of the third party will be required.

Section 2(1) applies when the third party has a right to enforce the contract from section 1. The basic default position is that the parties have the freedom to change or end the contract. It is just that in the following three circumstances, consent from the third party is required:

12.6.3.1 Third Party Assent to the Benefit from the Contract

Consent from the third party is required if the third party has assented to the term already. Such assent must be communicated to the promisor and there is some clarification on the meaning of 'assent' in s.2(2):

> (2) The assent referred to in subsection (1)(a)—
>
> (a) may be by words or conduct, and
>
> (b) if sent to the promisor by post or other means, shall not be regarded as communicated to the promisor until received by him.

It follows that the assent does not have to be formal and in writing. It can be an oral statement. In addition, the communication requirement means that it must be received, and it is assumed that the standard rules on communication of acceptance will apply. This means the communication must be capable of being read or heard by the promisor. The language of s.2(2)(b) makes clear that the postal rule does not apply because the assent must be received.

➡ CROSS-REFERENCE

For the rules on communication of acceptance see 3.2–3.3.

12.6.3.2 Reliance by the Third Party

Section 2(1) (b) and (c) are concerned with third party reliance on the benefit of the contract. Reliance is a familiar concept in contract law. Generally, it is understood to require a party to act on the promise or rights. The Act refers to 'reliance' rather than 'detrimental reliance' and so it is not necessary for the third party to suffer loss as a result of its reliance. Instead, at the most, the third party needs to have altered its position. By doing so, there will be evidence of the reliance. Under s.2(1)(b), terms regarding the benefit cannot be changed (or the contract ended) if the promisor knows that there has been such reliance. Likewise, the same limit applies if, in the circumstances, reliance is reasonably foreseeable to the promisor.

12.6.3.3 The Basis for the Limits

It must be emphasised that ordinarily the parties to the contract retain their freedom to make changes. Section 2 is simply there to limit the parties' freedom when it is justified to do so. Protecting the objective expectations of the third party is not on its own enough. If it was, then changes to a contract by its parties would never be allowed by the Act. But those expectations become real when there has been assent or actual reliance or where reliance is a fair possibility. In short, it seems that the limits are there to protect the *actual* (which is to say, realistic) expectations of the third party.

Section 2 (3) allows for the parties to avoid the limits in s.2(1):

> (3) Subsection (1) is subject to any express term of the contract under which—
>
> (a) the parties to the contract may by agreement rescind or vary the contract without the consent of the third party, or
>
> (b) the consent of the third party is required in circumstances specified in the contract instead of those set out in subsection (1)(a) to (c).

The limits in s.2(1) operate by requiring the consent of the third party for any changes. Section 2(3) allows for the parties to take away or limit the need for consent. All they have to do is make this clear in the contract. Essentially, by doing so, the parties retain the freedom to change or end the contract. Again, this is consistent with balancing the need for contractual freedom and the actual expectations of the third party. If the contract actually says that the benefit can be changed without consent, then the third party's expectations cannot be disappointed. After all, the third party would know from the outset that the benefit could be changed. It's like going to the zoo having been told beforehand that the lions are shy and might be hiding. You are aware of the possibility of not seeing them. Your expectations have to factor-in that possibility. Not seeing the lions is then consistent with your expectations.

12.6.4 Defences and 'Set-Offs' for the Promisor

The Act allows a third party to enforce rights against a promisor. When that is the case, the promisor is as liable to the third party as they would have been to the other contractual party (the promisee). It follows that the promisor should have the same defences against the third party as they would in an action by the promisee. This is covered by section 3 in the following way:

> 3   Defences etc. available to promisor
>
> (1) Subsections (2) to (5) apply where, in reliance on section 1, proceedings for the enforcement of a term of a contract are brought by a third party.
>
> (2) The promisor shall have available to him by way of defence or set-off any matter that—
>
> (a) arises from or in connection with the contract and is relevant to the term, and
>
> (b) would have been available to him by way of defence or set-off if the proceedings had been brought by the promisee.

(3) The promisor shall also have available to him by way of defence or set-off any matter if—

    (a) an express term of the contract provides for it to be available to him in proceedings brought by the third party, and

    (b) it would have been available to him by way of defence or set-off if the proceedings had been brought by the promisee.

(4) The promisor shall also have available to him—

    (a) by way of defence or set-off any matter, and

    (b) by way of counterclaim any matter not arising from the contract, that would have been available to him by way of defence or set-off or, as the case may be, by way of counterclaim against the third party if the third party had been a party to the contract.

(5) Subsections (2) and (4) are subject to any express term of the contract as to the matters that are not to be available to the promisor by way of defence, set-off or counterclaim.

The common example of s.3 is when the contract results from some wrongdoing by the promisee. Such wrongdoing could be in the form of a misrepresentation. If the promisee later sued to enforce the contract, the (innocent) promisor would rely on wrongdoing by the promisee as a defence. Likewise, the same defences are permitted against third party enforcement. Again, this means that the third party does not acquire better rights than the promisee.

12.6.5 Protecting the Promisor from Double Liability

With so much being said about third party enforcement, it might be easy to overlook the rights of the promisee. The promisee has the ability to enforce obligations against the promisor. As a result, the promisor has two parties that they could be liable to. This means there needs to be some rules to prevent overlapping claims.

Section 4 indicates that the third-party rights do not prevent enforcement of any terms by the promisee. After all, the promisee is a party to the contract. Section 5 then goes on to prevent the promisor being liable twice for the third party's loss:

5 **Protection of promisor from double liability**

Where under section 1 a term of a contract is enforceable by a third party, and the promisee has recovered from the promisor a sum in respect of—

    (a) the third party's loss in respect of the term, or

    (b) the expense to the promisee of making good to the third party the default of the promisor,then, in any proceedings brought in reliance on that section by the third party, the court or arbitral tribunal shall reduce any award to the third party to such extent as it thinks appropriate to take account of the sum recovered by the promisee.

Section 5 refers to circumstances in which the promisee has been awarded damages for the third party already. After that, if the third party makes a claim, the court can take into account the amount awarded to the promisee. However, if the promisee does recover damages for the third party's loss, the Act does not make the promisee hand over the award to the third party. This concerns the remedy for the promisee and is an issue outside of the Act and a matter for common law rules.

12.6.6 Exemption Clauses

Perhaps the most controversial aspect of the Act is the way it treats third parties in relation to exemption clauses. It stands out because it is one area where the third party is not treated like a promisee.

→ CROSS-REFERENCE
For the discussion of the
effect of s.2(2) UTCA 1977
see 7.6.3.

Section 7(2) refers to challenges to unreasonable terms under s.2(2) of the Unfair Contract Terms Act 1977. According to s.7(2) of the 1999 Act, third parties cannot use s.2(2) of UCTA to challenge an exemption clause in the contract. Furthermore, section 7(4) states that the third party is not a contracting party for purposes of other legislation. That also prevents a third party relying on UCTA, because UCTA only applies between 'contracting parties' (s.3, UCTA 1977). Likewise, the same limit applies in relation to consumer contracts under part 2 of the Consumer Rights Act 2015. The right to challenge the fairness of terms is between the consumer and trader only.

The practical effect is straightforward. The third party cannot challenge the fairness or reasonableness of a term in the contract. Only the promisee is able to do so. This rule allows the parties to have the freedom to work out the rights of the third party, and that is its justification. If the third party could challenge the reasonableness or fairness of the terms, this would mean the third party could alter the benefits it is entitled to under the contract.

12.6.7 Scope: Contracts to Which the Act Does Not Apply

The Act has a list of contracts that fall beyond the scope of the Act. These exclusions are detailed in section 6. It refers to employment contracts as well as negotiable instruments like bills of exchange. Also, the Act does not apply to certain contracts of carriage including the carriage of goods by sea. However, the exclusion of contracts for the carriage of goods by sea does have one important exception. The section allows third parties to have the benefit of exemption clauses in such contracts. That point will be dealt with further in 12.7.2.

12.7 Ways around the Privity Rule: Common Law Developments

The 1999 Act is the main exception to the privity rule and allows for enforcement by a third party. As indicated already, a number of other ways of getting around the privity rule had been developed already by the courts. These developments remain relevant, particularly in circumstances where the Act cannot apply.

The ways around the privity rule can be divided into two categories:

- Exceptions allowing the third party to enforce a contract
- Exceptions allowing the promisee to enforce their own contract for a third party

12.7.1 The Use of a Collateral Contract

This is a device that can result in the third party having a contract with a promisor, as a result of a different contract. The case that is often cited for this device is *Shankin Pier v Detel Products Ltd* [1952] 2 KB 854. The defendant was a manufacturer of paint. The claimant was the owner of a pier that wanted to have the pier painted. During discussions with the owner of a pier, the defendant manufacturer (Detel) stated that the paint would last seven to ten years. On that basis, the pier owner contracted with painters, instructing them to buy and use Detel's paint. The paint only lasted a few months and so the pier owner sued the manufacturer. The manufacturer argued that the pier owner was a third party. After all, the manufacturer sold their product to the painters which meant a contract existed between the painters and Detel. According to Detel, it followed that the pier owner was a stranger to the contract for the sale of paint. This status of the claimant as a third party to that contact was correct. However, McNair J held that there was a separate collateral contract between the pier owner and the manufacturer. Essentially, the manufacturer made a promise to the pier owner. In return, the pier owner instructed the painters to buy the paint from the manufacturer. In doing so, the pier owner had provided consideration for the promise about the quality of the paint. The resulting contract had been breached and so the pier owner was entitled to damages.

The existence of a collateral contract meant that the pier owner had the right to sue the manufacturer. This means that strictly speaking this was not a real exception to the privity rule—the pier owner was still a stranger to the contract for the sale of the paint, but had a separate contract with the manufacturer giving rise to obligations in the ordinary way. However, the use of collateral contracts is a way of avoiding the privity problem.

At common law, manufacturers do not have a contractual relationship with consumers. Instead, the manufacturer just has a contract with the party that it supplies. However, under the Consumer Rights Act 2015 (following the EU directive on consumer sales and associated Guarantees 99/44 EC) a manufacturer's guarantee results in a contractual relationship between the manufacture and consumer buyers for the purpose of enforcing the guarantee.

12.7.2 Agency

An agent is a party authorised to act on behalf of another, their principal. Many commercial contracts involve agents acting for a principal. In a simple context, this results in a situation involving three parties: the principal, the agent and the other party dealing with the agent. The principal would have a contract with the agent and the agent would have a contract with the other party. That might look like there is no contractual relationship between the principle and other party. But the agent is acting on behalf of the principal. On that basis, there is really a contract between the principal and the other party. This means that the principal can enforce the contract, even though it was entered into by the agent.

Even back in *Dunlop v Selfridge*, the House of Lords had to respond to an argument based on agency. In that case Dunlop was a stranger to the contract between Dew and Selfridge. But if Dew had been acting as an agent for Dunlop, then there would have been a contract between Dunlop and Selfridge. However, the court acknowledged that there was no such agency relationship. Dew was not acting on behalf of Dunlop. That was clear from the fact that Dew actually owned the goods to be sold. This meant that the consideration was moving from Dew in their own capacity rather than from Dew on behalf of Dunlop.

➡ CROSS-REFERENCE
For the facts of *Dunlop v Selfridge* see 12.2.1.

Agency is a very well-established and significant area of commercial contract law. Although the detail of the area is beyond this book, it is worth briefly explaining how it can be used to get around the doctrine of privity.

In *Scruttons v Midland Silicones*, the stevedores could not to rely on an exemption clause from the contract between the cargo owner and carrier. However, Lord Reid did provide some guidance on how agency could have provided a solution:

➡ CROSS-REFERENCE
For the facts of *Scruttons v Midland Silicones* see 12.2.2.

> I can see a possibility of success of the agency argument if (first) the bill of lading makes it clear that the stevedore is intended to be protected by the provisions in it which limit liability, (secondly) the bill of lading makes it clear that the carrier, in addition to contracting for these provisions on his own behalf, should apply to the stevedore, (thirdly) the carrier has authority from the stevedore to do that, or perhaps later ratification by the stevedore would suffice, and (fourthly) that any difficulties about consideration moving from the stevedore were overcome.

Lord Reid then observed that no such conditions had been met in the case. In particular, the contract between the cargo owner and carrier did not extend the exemption clause to the stevedores. As we can expect, the judgment prompted parties to draft their shipping contracts to reflect Lord Reid's guidance. Such a contract was the subject of a dispute in *New Zealand Shipping Co Ltd v AM Satterthwait & Co Ltd, The Eurymedon* [1975] AC 154.

The Eurymedon concerned a contract to carry cargo by sea. The contract between the cargo owner (the shipper) and the carrier had an exemption clause. This excluded the carrier from all liability for claims made a year after delivery. That meant the carrier could only be liable for loss if the action was brought within a year after delivery. Another term of the contract stated that the exemption applied to the carriers' servants, agents and independent contractors. The carrier hired the defendant stevedores for the unloading. Following some damage, the cargo owner brought an action against the stevedores in negligence. Since the legal action was a year after delivery, the stevedores wanted to rely on the exemption. That was understandable since the contract between the cargo owner and carrier stated that the clause applied to those employed by the carrier. It was held that the stevedores could rely on the clause. In doing so, the Privy Council recognised a contractual relationship between the cargo owner and the stevedores.

GUIDED CASE READING 12.2
New Zealand Shipping Co Ltd v AM Satterthwait & Co Ltd, The Eurymedon [1975] AC 154

When you read the extracts of the judgment by Lord Wilberforce, try to identify:

▪ how the contract between the stevedores and the cargo owner was formed;
▪ the consideration provided by the stevedores.

. . . The starting point, in discussion of this question, is provided by the House of Lords decision in *Midland Silicones Ltd. v. Scruttons Ltd.* [1962] A.C. 446. There is no need to question or even to qualify that case in so far as it affirms the general proposition that a contract between two parties cannot be sued on by a third person even though the contract is expressed to be for his benefit . . . But *Midland Silicones* left open the case where one of the parties contracts as agent for the third person: in particular Lord Reid's speech spelt out, in four propositions, the prerequisites for the validity of such an agency contract . . .

> Lord Wilberforce is clear from the outset that he is going to base his judgment on agency, which Lord Reid had 'left open' as a possible avenue in *Midland Silicones* as a way to circumvent privity.

. . .

Clause 1 of the bill of lading, whatever the defects in its drafting, is clear in its relevant terms. The carrier, on his own account, stipulates for certain exemptions . . . which discharges the carrier from all liability for loss or damage unless suit is brought within one year after delivery. In addition to these stipulations on his own account, the carrier as agent for, . . . independent contractors stipulates for the same exemptions.

. . .

The carrier was, indisputably, authorised by the appellant to contract as its agent for the purposes of clause 1. All of this is quite straightforward and was accepted by all the judges in New Zealand. The only question was, and is, the fourth question presented by Lord Reid, namely that of consideration. It was on this point that the Court of Appeal differed from Beattie J., holding that it had not been shown that any consideration for the shipper's promise as to exemption moved from the promisee, i.e. the appellant company.

> This allowed him to conceptualise the carriers as taking on the role of an agent for the stevedores. The carriers acted as the stevedores' agent and in doing so made a contract between the shipper and the stevedores, from the which the latter could benefit.

. . . There is possibly more than one way of analysing this business transaction into the necessary components; that which their Lordships would accept is to say that the bill of lading brought into existence a bargain initially unilateral but capable of becoming mutual, between the shipper and the appellant, made through the carrier as agent. This became a full contract when the appellant performed services by discharging the goods. The performance of these services for the benefit of the shipper was the consideration for the agreement by the shipper that the appellant should have the benefit of the exemptions and limitations contained in the bill of lading.

> This was because there was a contractual relationship between the shipper and the stevedores arising from the fact that the stevedores were acting to benefit the shipper by unloading the cargo; this provided consideration in return for being able to enforce the exemption clause.

... In their Lordships' opinion, consideration may quite well be provided by the appellant, as suggested, even though (or if) it was already under an obligation to discharge to the carrier ... An agreement to do an act which the promisor is under an existing obligation to a third party to do, may quite well amount to valid consideration and does so in the present case: the promisee obtains the benefit of a direct obligation which he can enforce. This proposition is illustrated and supported by *Scotson v. Pegg* (1861) 6 H. & N. 295 which their Lordships consider to be good law.

Technically the stevedores were just performing an existing contractual duty owed to a third party, i.e. the carrier, but it was already long established that this could fulfil the requirement for consideration for a promise, as established in *Scotson v Pegg*.

→ **CROSS-REFERENCE**
For the facts of *Scotson v Pegg* (1861) see 5.8.

The stevedores were able to rely on the clause stated in the contract between the cargo owner and carrier. This was possible because the clause resulted in a contract between the stevedores and the cargo owner.

Essentially, the clause was an offer for a unilateral contract like the one in *Carlill v Carbolic Smoke Ball Co*. In the circumstances, it made sense to treat the offer as a promise for an act. It could not be a promise for a promise (which results in a bilateral contract). That was because the stevedores would not have been promising anything for the cargo owner. Instead, their promise to unload was actually made to the carrier.

→ **CROSS-REFERENCE**
For the facts of *Carlill v Carbolic Smoke Ball Co* [1893] see 2.3.2.

The cargo owner's offer for a unilateral contract had been made to the carrier. However, the carrier was regarded as an agent of the stevedores. That meant the offer was really made to the stevedores via the carrier. The stevedores accepted the offer by the act of unloading. Such acceptance through performance was the same thing as Mrs Carlill using the smoke ball. In addition, the performance by the stevedores was also good consideration to enforce the promise made by the offeror.

Of course, the stevedores had been hired by the carrier to unload. That meant the stevedores already had a contractual duty to unload, owed to a third party. For that reason, Lord Wilberforce referred to *Scotson v Pegg*. There it was held that the performance of a contractual duty owed to one party is good consideration for a promise made by someone else. The reasoning is based on the fact that the promisor (i.e. the cargo owner) gains the right to sue another party (i.e. the stevedores). This all meant that the stevedores had a separate contract with the cargo owner.

The approach adopted by Lord Wilberforce for the Privy Council is an exception to the privity rule. It is based on agency and the use of a collateral contract. It has been criticised as artificial, but on the other hand, it is commercially convenient. It makes the terms of the carriage contract workable. It also reflects the bargain made between the carrier and the cargo owner because the existence of the exemption clause would have been balanced by a lower price charged by the carrier.

The approach from the *Eurymedon* was then approved by the Privy Council in cases such as *Port Jackson Stevedoring Pty Ltd v Salmond & Spraggon Pty (Australia) Ltd, New York Star* [1981] 1 WLR 138 and *The Mahkutai* [1996] AC 650. It was also approved by the House of Lords in *Homburg Houtimport BV v Agrosin Private Ltd, The Starsin* [2003] UKHL 12. However, it seems that the *Eurymedon* approach is limited by the agency requirement. For that reason, it has been difficult to expand its application beyond shipping contracts.

Southern Water Authority v Carey [1985] 2 All ER 1077 concerned building contracts with similar facts to the *Eurymedon*. Here, the water company contracted with a builder to construct a sewage works. Under the terms, liability for defects could only last until 12 months after completing the work. So, after 12 months, such liability was excluded. This exemption clause applied to the builder as the main contractor. It also stated that it applied to any sub-contractors, servants or agents of main contractor. The contract also said that the builder was also contracting on behalf of its sub-contractors, agents and servants.

Over 12 months after completion, the water company sued one of the sub-contractors in negligence. The sub-contractor then sought to rely on the exemption clause. It was held that the *Eurymedon* approach could not apply and so the sub-contractor was a stranger to the contract. That meant the clause could not be relied upon by the sub-contractor. The court applied the requirements stated by

Lord Reid in the *Scruttons* case. All of these were satisfied except the third requirement. The main contractor had to have the authority to act as an agent for the sub-contractor. Such authority had to be in place at the time of the contract. On the facts, no such authority was in place at that time. In addition, the principal had to be identifiable at the time of the contract. Again, on the facts, the main contractor did have the principal in mind for the job, but that was not enough. The point is that the party to the main contract has to be an authorised agent of a principal at the time contracting. That technical requirement limits the scope of the *Eurymedon* approach.

12.7.3 Assignment of the Contract Benefit to the Third Party

Another way around the traditional privity rule is assignment. This is where a party to a contract passes on (assigns) their contractual rights to a different party. Such an assignment of rights would mean that the third party steps into the shoes of the party that assigned the rights. It is like handing the gaming control pad to someone else to finish the game, and is often done in relation to debts. The creditor who is owed money might simply sell the debt to someone else. The rights to the debt are then assigned to the new party. This means that the one that owes the money (the debtor) has to pay the new creditor.

The assignment requires a contract of assignment between the party giving up the rights (the assignor) and the party receiving the rights (the assignee). Under the rules relating to assignment, there are some limits:

■ Only the benefit of a contact can be assigned. That point was emphasised by Lord Brown-Wilkinson in the House of Lords case of *Linden Gardens Trust Ltd v Lenesta Sludge Disposals Ltd* [1994] 1 AC 85. It means that obligations or burdens cannot be assigned.

■ The assignment cannot be done where the contract is for a personal service. The point is that the assignment needs to make no difference to the other party to the contract. The performance of a personal service, if that benefit was assigned to a new assignee, would become different to what was agreed.

■ *Linden Gardens* also indicates that an assignment is not effective if the contract stipulates that assignments are not allowed. For that reason, some commercial contracts have a term that prevents any assignment of the rights under the contract. That is particularly useful if *who* you are in a contract with is important. Alternatively, some commercial contracts have specific limits on the type of party that could be an assignee. In doing so, it ensures that an assignee (as the new contractual party) meets certain financial standards or qualities.

Assignment is a good way of getting around the privity rule. However, it does mean that the assignor, as an original contractual party, falls out of the picture. Essentially, that party loses the right to enforce the contract.

12.7.4 The Creation of a Trust for the Benefit of a Third Party

Another established way to get around the privity rule is the creation of a trust. Before addressing how a trust can be used as way around the privity rule, we need to appreciate briefly what a trust is, and how they work.

Trusts were developed in equity and have a range of applications. One example you might have heard of is a 'trust fund'. That is something that wealthy people might set up for their children. It requires a contract that shows a clear intention to set up a trust. This contract or trust document is between the original owner of the property or funds, and some trustees. Once set up, the trustees are technically the legal owners of the fund or property. However, the *use* of the fund or property is reserved for another party called the 'beneficiary'. Essentially, the trustees own the fund or property, but on behalf of the beneficiary. Such a beneficiary has clear rights in equity over whatever is held on trust for them. In fact, equity recognises a beneficiary as the 'beneficial owner'. This status means the beneficiary can enforce their rights against the trustees. They can also enforce rights against other parties that secure an interest in whatever is held on trust. That can be done in a number of ways. The beneficiary can require the trustee to take action. Alternatively, the beneficiary can take action, but in the trustees' name.

In our context, a trust can be used to get around the privity rule because the rights arising from a contract are a type of personal property. This means that the benefit of a contractual obligation can be owned. On that basis, it is possible to hold a contractual promise on trust for a beneficiary. Such a trust is known as 'trust of a promise' and was shown in *Les Affréteurs Réunis Société Anonyme v Leopold Walford (London) Ltd* [1919] AC 801. Put simply, two parties could enter a contract—perhaps it is goods in return for a series of payments. The parties could agree for the right to those payments to be held on trust for a third party beneficiary. It would mean that the third party beneficiary would be able to enforce those rights if the payments stopped. An important point here is that with a trust, there is no need for the beneficiary to provide consideration. For this to be done, there has to be an express intention by the parties to set up a trust (*Re, Schebsman* [1944] Ch 83). If this done, the trust cannot be changed or ended without the consent of the third party beneficiary. A more recent example is *Nisshin Shipping Co Ltd v Cleaves & Co Ltd* [2003] EWHC 2602 (Comm) which concerned a contract between a charterer and shipowner. The contract expressly created a trust under which a broker would be paid a commission by the shipowner. The Commercial Court accepted that the obligation to pay was enforceable by the charterer as a trustee. In addition, it was also stated that the broker would be able to enforce the contract directly under the 1999 Act.

The 1999 Act does provide a more convenient alternative to the creation of a trust. However, it should be appreciated that a trust of a promise can be more advantageous to the beneficiary. Essentially, a trust cannot be changed or ended by the parties without the consent of the beneficiary. In contrast, in certain circumstances, it is possible for the contractual parties to change or end the benefit to the third party under section 2 of the 1999 Act.

12.7.5 Law of Tort

In certain circumstances, the law of tort provides further ways around privity. It could be used by a third party to get the benefit of a contract made by others. In addition, tort can be used to impose an obligation on a third party.

The benefit of a contract could be enforced by a third party using the tort of negligence. The key case here is *White v Jones* [1995] 2 AC 207. It concerned a contractual relationship between a law firm and an elderly client. After a family dispute, the client had a will drawn up to ensure that his daughters did not inherit anything on his death. However, he later changed his mind and instructed the firm to write a new will. Under this new will, the daughters were to inherit £9000 each. Unfortunately, the firm failed to produce the new will before the client died. This meant the daughters were cut out of the inheritance and so they sued the law firm and relevant lawyer in negligence. By a majority of 3:2, the House of Lords upheld the decision of the Court of Appeal and allowed the claim.

The case is a very significant one and is analysed in depth by the large books on tort law and journal articles. For our purposes, it is simply an example of how tort has been used to get around the privity rule. The inheritance was a benefit from a contract and was intended to be given to a third party. The third party was able to bring an action in negligence to enforce the benefit. The action was possible on the basis that the solicitors owed a duty of care to the third party daughters. That duty was then breached by their negligent failure to carry out the instructions of the client. It was also significant that there was no other remedy for the breach. The estate of the client would not have been awarded damages because it had suffered no loss. Instead, the resulting loss was suffered by the third party daughters. If it was possible for the contractual party (the estate in the name of the deceased father) to claim compensation for the breach, then the third party daughters would not have had a claim.

Usually, in negligence, the claimant is compensated to be placed back in the position before the negligent act took place. By awarding the inheritance, the damages reflected the contract measure. It placed the claimants in the position they would have been in had the contract been performed. In doing so, the award protected the expectation interest of the client. Again, this seems to be exceptional and based on the unique loss resulting from the failure to produce the will.

The approach in negligence does have some further limits. First, there has to be a negligent act or failure to act. *White v Jones* was seen as a case of a negligent failure to act. If it was simply a case of a refusal to perform then there would have been a breach of contract but that would not provide the basis of a claim by a third party because there would have been no negligence. A further limit relates to the terms of the contract. Liability for negligently preparing a will could be the subject of an exemption clause. If it is, then subject to the fairness test from the Consumer Rights Act 2015, the exclusion would be effective.

The law of tort can also be used to impose an obligation on third parties. Essentially, tort can protect the operation of a contract. If someone wrongly interferes with contractual rights, then they can be liable in tort. Such wrongful interference takes place when someone causes a contractual party to be in breach. This intentional *inducement to breach* can result in damages or an injunction to stop the interference.

The early authority on this tort is *Lumley v Gye* (1853) 3 E & B 114. Here Lumley had contracted for an opera singer to perform exclusively at his theatre. This meant that for the period stated in the contract, she could not sing for a different theatre. The defendant, Gye, then convinced the singer to perform at his theatre for more money. In agreeing to do so, the singer had breached her contract. Lumley was able to obtain an injunction to stop the singer performing elsewhere. However, she then left the jurisdiction. Lumley then sued Gye and was awarded damages. The relevant point here is that a contract between two parties resulted in an obligation being imposed on a third party. Put simply, the contract had a term preventing the singer singing elsewhere. The application of the tort meant there was a restriction on the third party, Gye. He was committing a tort (inducement to breach) by convincing the singer to leave and work for him. Without the contract, Gye would have been free to contract with the singer. However, the tort protecting the contract served to restrict what Gye could do lawfully.

The approach in *Lumley v Gye* was approved and explained by Lord Hoffman in *OBG Ltd v Allen* [2007] UKHL 21. While there are not many appeal cases on this tort, it happens to be used frequently as the basis for injunction applications which are not reported. Sports governing bodies often rely on this tort to secure an injunction to stop the resale of their tickets. They make sure the terms of the contract on the ticket do not allow for resale. When ticket touts buy such tickets and then resell them for considerably more, an action can be brought for intentionally inducing a breach of the original contract of sale.

12.8 Legislative Exceptions to the Privity Rule

In addition to the common law developments, various exceptions to the privity rule have been introduced by legislation. They apply to very specialised areas of law. We do not need to explore these in detail, but we can just acknowledge them as examples of legislative exceptions. Some examples that are often cited relate to insurance:

- The Married Women's Property Act 1882 allows a spouse or children of a life insurance policy holder to enforce rights from the policy.
- The Road Traffic Act 1988 has some rules on the enforcement of motor insurance policies. When an insured driver causes loss to a third party, that party can sue the insurer directly.

■ There is also an exception that applies when goods are shipped. The Carriage of Goods by Sea Act 1992 allows a party that is entitled to the goods to sue the carrier where the carrier is liable for damage. This is an exception because the original contract of carriage is between the shipper (original owner) and the carrier.

Another common example relates to consumer package holidays and equivalent linked travel arrangements. The Package Travel and Linked Travel Arrangement Regulations 2018 (implementing the EU Package Travel Directive 2015) is an update of the original Package Travel, Package Holidays and Package Tours Regulations 1992 (again based on EU law). This legislation allows consumers booked on the relevant type of holidays to enforce the contract against travel companies even where the contract is made on their behalf.

12.9 Enforcement by a Contractual Party for the Benefit of a Third Party

There are a few ways in which a party to a contract can enforce a benefit intended for a third party. One way of doing so is through the remedy of specific performance. The other way is through a damages claim. Each of these are addressed in turn.

12.9.1 Specific Performance

The remedy of specific performance from equity might be a way around the privity rule. Where possible, it could allow a third party to have the benefit intended by the contract. The key example here is the House of Lords case of *Beswick v Beswick* [1968] AC 58. The contract was between uncle Beswick and his nephew, John. The uncle agreed to sell his coal business to John. In return, John agreed to pay £6 10s a week to the uncle. That payment had to carry on for the rest of uncle's life. Furthermore, it was agreed that if the uncle died, the nephew had to pay £5 a week to the uncle's widow for the rest of her life. The nephew made the payments to the uncle but when the uncle died, the nephew only made one payment to the widow. The contract between the uncle and nephew was partly for her benefit, so she took action to enforce it.

In allowing the widow's claim, the House of Lords had to deal with two problems. First, the privity problem. The widow was not a party to the contract. This meant that, as a third party, she could not enforce the contract. However, she was also the administrator of the uncle's estate. So, on behalf of the estate in the name of the uncle, she could enforce the contact. That led to the other problem. The estate had suffered no loss. It was the widow that was owed the money, not the estate. This meant the estate would be entitled to nominal damages only. For that reason, the House of Lords granted the estate an order for specific performance. Consequently, the nephew had to carry out his agreed obligation of payment to the widow.

Their Lordships were very critical of the privity rule, and it is clear that they were keen to find a suitable remedy. Lord Pearce observed:

> The condition as to payment of an annuity to the widow personally was valid. The estate (though not the widow personally) can enforce it. Why should the estate be barred from exercising its full contractual rights merely because in doing so it secures justice for the widow who, by a mechanical defect of our law, is unable to assert her own rights? Such a principle would be repugnant to justice and fulfil no other object than that of aiding the wrongdoer. I can find no ground on which such a principle should exist.

→ CROSS-REFERENCE
For the discussion of specific performance as a remedy see 11.1.

We can recall that specific performance is a remedy that can be granted when damages would be inadequate. Where it is granted, the innocent party can make the party in breach perform. Where the obligation was intended to benefit a third party, the third party then receives that benefit from the performance.

12.9.2 Damages That Also Reflect the Loss Suffered by the Third Party

The general rule is that a party claiming damages can only do so in relation to the loss suffered by that party. In other words, a loss suffered by others ordinarily cannot be claimed by the innocent party to the contract. However, some exceptions have been developed by the courts and we will address these in turn.

12.9.2.1 The Exception for Consumer Contracts Made to Benefit Others

It is easy to imagine contracts that we enter for ourselves along with others. A typical example would be a holiday where one person contracts for their family. Following a breach and loss suffered by the entire family, would the holiday company be liable to all the family members? The strict privity rule would mean that only the member of the family that entered the contact can sue. Moreover, that contractual party would be compensated for their own loss only because the traditional rule on damages only allows a claimant to have damages for losses they have suffered. Such a strict approach to damages would create a legal 'black hole'. It would mean that the party in breach could cause loss to others but would not be liable for such losses. This position was addressed by the Court of Appeal in *Jackson v Horizon Holidays Ltd* [1975] 1 WLR 1468.

In the case, Mr Jackson booked a holiday in Sri Lanka for himself, his wife, and their three-year-old twins. Under the original terms, the hotel was to be luxury accommodation with a range of facilities and quality meals. However, the contract was changed because the hotel was still being built. In a letter to change the contract, the holiday company referred to an alternative resort hotel. This was to be a luxury hotel with a swimming pool, mini golf course, a private bath in each room and even a beauty salon. In return for accepting the change to the hotel, the holiday price was reduced from £1432 to £1200.

Unfortunately, when the family arrived, the hotel was far from luxurious. It had none of facilities listed. The children's room had stinking black mildew and fungus on the walls. That meant the family had to all sleep in the same room. There was no toilet paper; the bed sheets were dirty and the food was awful. Essentially, it was a disaster holiday and a clear breach of the contract. After two weeks they managed to move to the original hotel which was better, even with the building work taking place.

When sued, the defendant holiday company accepted that they were in breach. By this time, it was clear that damages could be awarded for loss of bargain and disappointment (mental distress) as result of the Court of Appeal decision in *Jarvis v Swan Tours* [1973]. However, the dispute was about the award of damages made by the trial judge who awarded £1100. This award and its basis was the key issue. The judge said he could not make an award for disappointment and distress of the family members. He went on to say that his award could reflect the impact of the family's distress on the claimant. This award was challenged for being too much, and for being wrong in principle. It was argued that the damages should only reflect the loss to Mr Jackson personally as the only party to the contract.

The Court of Appeal rejected the appeal and upheld the award by the trial judge but recognised a new basis for it. It was held that the damages could also reflect the actual loss suffered by the family members.

The main reasoning was delivered by Lord Denning MR in a typically clear way and (again, typically) with very little authority:

> We have had an interesting discussion as to the legal position when one person makes a contract for the benefit of a party. In this case it was a husband making a contract for the benefit of himself, his wife and children. Other cases readily come to mind. A host makes a contract with a restaurant for a dinner for himself and his friends. The vicar makes a contract for a coach trip for the choir. In all these cases there is only one person who makes the contract. It is the husband, the host or the vicar, as the case may be. Sometimes he pays the whole price himself. Occasionally he may get a contribution from the others. But in any case it is he who makes the contract. It would be a fiction to say that the contract was made by all the family, or all the guests, or all the choir, and that he was only an agent for them. Take this very case. It would be absurd to say that the twins of three years old were parties to the contract or that the father was making the contract on their behalf as if they were principals. . .It would equally be a mistake to say that in any of these instances there was a trust. The transaction bears no resemblance to a trust. There was no trust fund and no trust property. No, the real truth is that in each instance, the father, the host or the vicar, was making a contract himself for the benefit of the whole party. In short, a contract by one for the benefit of third persons.
>
> What is the position when such a contract is broken? At present the law says that the only one who can sue is the one who made the contract. None of the rest of the party can sue, even though the contract was made for their benefit. But when that one does sue, what damages can he recover? Is he limited to his own loss? Or can he recover for the others? Suppose the holiday firm puts the family into a hotel which is only half built and the visitors have to sleep on the floor? Or suppose the restaurant is fully booked and the guests have to go away, hungry and angry, having spent so much on fares to get there? Or suppose the coach leaves the choir stranded halfway and they have to hire cars to get home? None of them individually can sue. Only the father, the host or the vicar can sue. He can, of course, recover his own damages. But can he not recover for the others? I think he can. The case comes within the principle stated by Lush L.J. in *Lloyd's v. Harper* (1880) 16 Ch.D. 290, 321:
>
> > "I consider it to be an established rule of law that where a contract is made with A for the benefit of B, A can sue on the contract for the benefit of B, and recover all that B could have recovered if the contract had been made with B himself."
>
> It has been suggested that Lush L.J. was thinking of a contract in which A was trustee for B. But I do not think so. He was a common lawyer speaking of common law. His words were quoted with considerable approval by Lord Pearce in *Beswick v. Beswick* [1968] A.C. 58, 88. I have myself often quoted them. I think they should be accepted as correct, at any rate so long as the law forbids the third persons themselves from suing for damages. It is the only way in which a just result can be achieved. Take the instance I have put. The guests ought to recover from the restaurant their wasted fares. The choir ought to recover the cost of hiring the taxis home. There is no one to recover for them except the one who made the contract for their benefit. He should be able to recover the expense to which he has been put, and pay it over to them. Once recovered, it will be money had and received to their use. (They might even, if desired, be joined as plaintiffs). If he can recover for the expense, he should also be able to recover for the discomfort, vexation and upset which the whole party have suffered by reason of the breach of contract, recompensing them accordingly out of what he recovers.
>
> Applying the principles to this case, I think that the figure of £1,100 was about right. It would, I think, have been excessive if it had been awarded only for the damage suffered by Mr. Jackson himself. But when extended to his wife and children, I do not think it is excessive.

The contract was viewed as one made for the family as a whole. In a strict sense, Lord Denning MR did not change the privity rule. That would be the case if the family could *enforce* the contract. Instead, the focus was on the related rule that limits the awards to loss suffered by contractual party. In the circumstances, this would produce an unjust result. It would leave third party family members without compensation, even where they have suffered expenses and losses following a breach. To remove this injustice, the contracting party can recover damages to reflect the loss suffered by the third parties.

The approach adopted in the case is certainly convenient and does seems fair. After all, the contract was for the benefit of Mr Jackson and also his family. Part of the expectation contracted for was his own and that of the family. Following a breach, the family suffered loss. Surely, that loss represents performance that was contracted for, but not delivered. The passage quoted from Lush LJ seems crucial to the outcome. It is the only authority cited that appears to allow for this wider approach to damages. We will see that the reliance on that quote has been met with some clear disapproval.

The principle developed by Lord Denning MR in *Jackson* received the disapproval of the House of Lords in *Woodar Investments v Wimpey Construction* [1980] 1 WLR 277. The case was about the sale of land. Under the contract, the defendant buyer agreed to pay £850,000 to the seller. In addition, the buyer agreed to pay £150,000 to a third party (Transworld Trade Ltd). The buyer then exercised a termination clause to end the contract. In response, the seller brought an action for breach. The claim was for the seller's own loss but also for the £150,000 loss suffered by the third party. The Court of Appeal allowed for the damages claims, relying on the decision in *Jackson*. In contrast, the House of Lords held that there was no breach. On that basis, there could be no damages claim. However, the court went on to discuss the £150,000 claim for the third party. In doing so, what was said on damages was *obiter* only, but while it is not binding, it is highly persuasive. It is useful to examine the relevant part of the judgment by Lord Wilberforce:

> The second issue in this appeal is one of damages. Both courts below have allowed Woodar to recover substantial damages in respect of condition 1 under which £150,000 was payable by Wimpey to Transworld Trade Ltd on completion. On the view which I take of the repudiation issue, this question does not require decision, but in view of the unsatisfactory state in which the law would be if the Court of Appeal's decision were to stand I must add three observations:
>
> 1. The majority of the Court of Appeal followed, in the case of Goff LJ with expressed reluctance, its previous decision in *Jackson v Horizon Holidays Ltd*. I am not prepared to dissent from the actual decision in that case. It may be supported either as a broad decision on the measure of damages (per James LJ) or possibly as an example of a type of contract, examples of which are persons contracting for family holidays, ordering meals in restaurants for a party, hiring a taxi for a group, calling for special treatment. As I suggested in *New Zealand Shipping Co Ltd v A M Satterthwaite & Co Ltd* (. . .[1975] AC 154 at 167), there are many situations of daily life which do not fit neatly into conceptual analysis, but which require some flexibility in the law of contract. *Jackson's* case may well be one.
>
>   I cannot agree with the basis on which Lord Denning MR put his decision in that case. The extract on which he relied from the judgment of Lush LJ in *Lloyd's v Harper* ((1880) 16 Ch D 290 at 321) was part of a passage in which Lush LJ was stating as an 'established rule of law' that an agent (sc. an insurance broker) may sue on a contract made by him on behalf of the principal (sc. the assured) if the contract gives him such a right, and it no authority for the proposition required in *Jackson's* case, still less for the proposition required here, that, if Woodar made a contract for a sum of money to be paid to Transworld, Woodar can, without showing that it has itself suffered loss or that Woodar was agent or trustee for Transworld, sue for damages for non-payment of that sum. That would certainly not be an established rule of law, nor was it quoted as such authority by Lord Pearce in *Beswick v Beswick*.
>
> 2. Assuming that Jackson's case was correctly decided (as above), it does not carry the present case, where the factual situation is quite different. I respectfully think therefore that the Court of Appeal need not, and should not have followed it.
>
> 3. Whether in a situation such as the present, *viz* where it is not shown that Woodar was agent or trustee for Transworld, or that Woodar itself sustained any loss, Woodar can recover any damages at all, or any but nominal damages, against Wimpey, and on what principle, is, in my opinion, a question of great doubt and difficulty, no doubt open in this House, but one on which I prefer to reserve my opinion.

Lord Wilberforce chose to address the damages issue because the legal position represented by the Court of Appeal judgments was so unsatisfactory. The first observation begins by approving of the result in *Jackson*. The principle from *Jackson* is accepted even if does not fit the general rules. However, Lord Denning MR's reliance on the quote by Lush LJ was questioned. The second observation distinguishes the facts of *Woodar* from those in *Jackson* and the third observation doubts if the seller would have been entitled to damages beyond their own loss.

The other judges delivered opinions that were consistent with what that of Lord Wilberforce. Lord Scarman especially took the opportunity to emphasise how inadequate the law was, even going so far as to say that the House of Lords should reconsider the privity rule entirely. These comments were also approved by some of the other Lords.

The main point from the opinion in *Woodar* was that *Jackson* did not represent a general rule. On that basis, a party could not *generally* receive damages for a loss suffered by a third party. This was a point that was illustrated by *Beswick v Beswick*.

The Law Lords all rejected Lord Denning MR's reliance on the statement by Lush LJ. However, they also felt that the decision in *Jackson* was acceptable. With that in mind, it is difficult to see what the legal basis for the *Jackson* decision really is. The principle from *Jackson* is generally viewed as an exceptional category of case. This perspective is based on the comments by Lord Wilberforce. The category effectively covers consumer cases only, for example, package holidays, meals in a restaurant, or the hiring of a taxi. The existence of this class of exceptions can be justified because with such group activities, consumers might not have the choice to contract separately. Even where they do have such an opportunity, they would not think it was important.

KEY POINTS

In certain consumer contracts intended to benefit third parties, the innocent party to the contract can claim damages to reflect the losses suffered by the third parties.

Where there is no payment in advance, it is possible that in some cases each member of the group will have a contract with the provider. For example, consider two people that go to a restaurant. It might have been booked by one of them. They might have decided that one would pay for the meal rather than split the cost. However, both would have a contract with the restaurant. That is because by ordering, each customer is impliedly promising to pay in return for being served. The restaurant is impliedly promising to serve in return for payment. That was the conclusion of Tucker J in *Lockett v Charles* [1938] 4 All ER 170. There, a husband paid the bill for the food ordered for himself, and by his wife. That did not prevent the wife's contract claim for the poor quality food. The same would apply when a group orders or 'flags-down' a taxi; or when a couple check-in to a hotel. In contrast, for the circumstances where there is only one party that has the contract, *Jackson* has a limited role. It could allow the damages to reflect the third party's loss.

12.9.2.2 Transferred Loss (The 'Albazero Exception')

Since the *Woodar* case, the courts have maintained a *general* rule against the recovery of damages for third parties. However, they have developed a further exception that applies to the transfer of property from one party to another.

The first key case on this was *Linden Gardens Trust v Lenesta Sludge Disposals* [1994] AC 85. Here, the defendant construction company agreed to redevelop a building for the claimant property company. As planned, after the work was done, the property was then sold to a buyer for the market value. The seller did try to assign to the buyer their contractual rights against the builder. Unfortunately the assignment was not valid. Later, the buyer discovered that the building work was defective, and that is where the privity problem arose. The buyer could not sue the builder for compensation for the defects because there was no contract between them. The property company that had sold the building was a party to the contract, but had suffered no loss. After all, they had sold the building for the full market value.

The House of Lords allowed the property company to claim damages to reflect the loss suffered by the third party buyer. Such a claim (like the one in *Jackson*) is an exception to the general rule. Allowing the claim for damages meant that the legal 'black hole' was avoided. To do otherwise would have meant that the builders would not have been liable to compensate anyone for the losses caused. They could breach their contracts at their leisure!

The reasoning by Lord Brown-Wilkinson was based on authority developed from shipping contracts. The key case cited was *The Albazero* [1977] AC 774 and in particular the judgment of Lord Diplock, which was based on the old case of *Dunlop v Lambert* (1839). Lord Diplock explained the basis of an exception that is referred to as the '*Albazero* exception' or 'transferred loss exception'. This exception allows the original seller (the shipper of goods) to claim for losses resulting from the carrier damaging the cargo even when the loss is suffered by a third party buyer. The contractual relationships are illustrated in Figure 12.4.

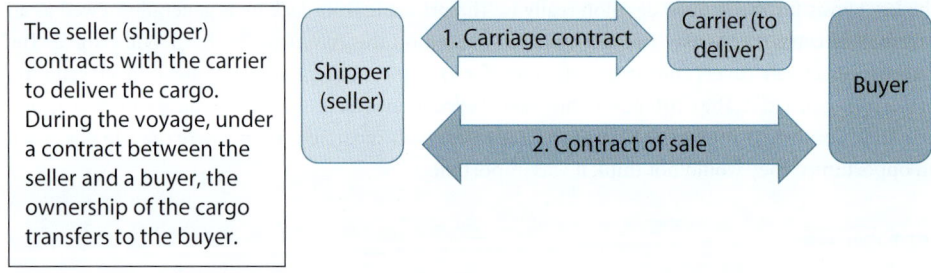

Figure 12.4
The basic contractual relationships in *The Albazero* [1977]

If the breach (damage) happens before ownership passes, there is no problem. The seller (the shipper) can sue the carrier and recover damages because the seller has suffered a loss resulting from a breach of their contract with the carrier. However, if the breach happens after ownership has passed, then it causes a loss to the buyer. But that buyer does not have a contract with the carrier. Under the ordinary rules, the seller would only be entitled to nominal damages since the seller would have suffered no loss.

According to Lord Diplock in *The Albazero*, the rationale for the exception is that the carrier will know that the ownership of the goods will transfer during transit. As a result, it is foreseeable that their breaches could cause loss to a subsequent owner. For that reason, it is assumed that the original owner enters the contract for themselves (as owner) but also on behalf of anyone that is going to be an owner during transit or when the goods arrive. On that basis, the carrier can be liable to the shipper for losses suffered by the subsequent (third party) owner.

In *Linden Gardens*, this shipping exception was applied to a construction contract by Lord Brown-Wilkinson (with whom the other Lords agreed) who explained:

> In my judgment the present case falls within the rationale of the exceptions to the general rule that a plaintiff can only recover damages for his own loss. The contract was for a large development of property which, to the knowledge of both [contractual parties], was going to be occupied, and possibly purchased, by third parties. . .Therefore it could be foreseen that damage caused by a breach would cause loss to a later owner and not merely to the original contracting party. . .
>
> In such a case, it seems to me proper, as in the case of the carriage of goods. . ., to treat the parties as having entered into the contract on the footing that [the original owner and contracting party] would be entitled to enforce contractual rights for the benefit of those who suffered from defective performance. . .

Essentially, the builder would have known that the building was to be owned or used by another party later. Therefore, the other party contracts on the understanding that they can sue for the loss suffered by a new buyer. Essentially, the claimant party (the property company) claimed the third party's (the buyer's) losses were 'transferred losses' of the property company.

The transferred loss exception as extended by Lord Browne-Wilkinson to contracts beyond shipping, was applied by the Court of Appeal in *Darlington Borough Council v Wiltshire Northern Ltd* [1995] 1 WLR 68. In the case, the claimant Council wanted a recreation centre to be built on their land. Ideally, they would have borrowed money and then entered a contract with a building company. However, because of the restrictions on local authority borrowing, they had to adopt a different approach. They arranged for a company called MG to contract with the defendant builders to build the centre. The Council would then reimburse the money paid out by MG. In return, MG would then assign to the Council, their contractual rights to sue the builders for defects.

The work was done and, as arranged, MG assigned their rights to the Council. Later the Council found defects in the work and then brought an action under the contract against the builder. Under the law on assignment, a party can only assign the rights it actually has. It cannot assign *better* rights than those which it has. That principle was a key factor in the builders' defence. They accepted that before the assignment, MG could have sued, but they questioned if MG could have recovered damages. After all, MG would have suffered no loss because MG was not to be the owner or intended user of the centre. For that reason, it was argued that MG should only be awarded nominal damages. It followed that, after the assignment, the Council would only be entitled to nominal damages too.

The Court of Appeal allowed the Council's damages claim. Essentially, MG would have been able to claim damages for the Council's loss using the transferred loss exception. Therefore, that right to damages had been assigned to the Council.

The important point here is how the Court of Appeal applied the exception. By doing so, the scope of the exception was extended slightly. Consider the facts of *Darlington Council*. The Council was the third party. This third party did not *become* the owner of the property after the contract. Instead, the Council was always the owner of the property. It means that a party to a contract can recover loss for a third party that has always owned the property.

KEY POINTS

- In *Linden Gardens*, the party to the contract could claim for the loss suffered by a third party who had the property transferred to them.
- In *Darlington Council*, the party to the contract could claim the loss suffered by a third party who had always owned the property.

The approach in *Darlington Council* is consistent with the approach of Lord Browne-Wilkinson in *Linden Gardens*. After all, it would have been known all along that any loss caused would be suffered by the Council. In applying the transferred loss exception in *Darlington Council*, Steyn LJ acknowledged that it was 'a very conservative and limited extension'. Such an extension was necessary so that there could be a damages award for the loss caused by a breach.

?! THINKING POINTS

Can you identify transactions beyond construction and shipping where it might be argued that the reasoning of the transferred loss exception should be applied to allow a claim for the loss suffered by a third party?

The House of Lords had a further opportunity to reconsider the transferred loss exception in *Alfred McAlpine Construction Ltd v Panatown Ltd* [2001] 1 AC 518. Panatown contracted with the defendant builders to construct some buildings. The buildings were to be on land owned by UIPL Ltd. This third party would be the one that would suffer loss resulting from defects in the construction. For that reason, there was a 'Duty of Care Deed' between UIPL and the builders. Under that deed, the builders would owe a duty of care to UIPL meaning that the builders could be liable to UIPL for any loss caused by their negligence. Unfortunately, there were defects and delays in construction. The loss was suffered by UIPL and not Panatown but they agreed Panatown would sue on the contract for the loss suffered by UIPL. The action failed at first instance but in the Court of Appeal the *Albazero* exception was applied and so damages were awarded for UIPL's loss. However, the House of Lords held that Panatown could not be awarded damages. According to the majority, the transferred loss exception could not apply because UIPL already had a direct action against the builders from the duty of care deed. Essentially, the transferred loss exception is necessary to avoid a legal 'black hole' where damages cannot be claimed for loss caused by a breach. According to the majority, in this case, there was no 'black hole' to avoid. On this point Lord Millett observed:

> [T]he function of the rule was to escape the undesirable consequences of the privity rule, and does not apply where it is not needed.

The *Panatown* case is not without its criticism. The deed gave the third party a direct action, but it was an inferior action to the one in contract. It concerned losses arising from negligence, and negligence would have to be proven. However, the existence of the deed could be taken to show that a contract claim on behalf of the third party was not intended. Lord Clyde addressed the argument about the rights of the deed being different to a contract action. He stated in response that even if the remedies 'do not absolutely coincide, the express provision of the direct remedy for the third party is fatal'.

More recently, the transferred loss exception was the basis of an argument in *Swynson Ltd v Lowick Rose LLP* [2017] UKSC 32. Before lending money to a third party, EMSL, the claimant Swynson contracted with the defendant accountants Lowick. Under this contract, the accountants were to produce a report about EMSL's financial position to inform Swynson's decision to grant the loan. Relying on the report, Swynson provided the loan. Unfortunately, the report was negligently prepared and that was made clear when EMSL proved to struggle financially even after the loan was granted. The owner of Swynson (Mr Hunt) became the controlling shareholder of EMSL and then, in his own personal capacity, paid off the loans it owed to Swynson. Since a company has its own legal personality and is separate to its shareholders, Mr Hunt's action was done as a third party to the contract between Swynson and the accountants. Since Mr Hunt could not sue the accountants for the loss he had suffered in paying EMSL's debt, Swynson as the contractual party sued for breach, claiming £16.1m. One of their arguments was that while they had suffered no loss (the loan had been repaid), Hunt's losses were transferred losses of Swynson.

The argument was unanimously rejected by the Supreme Court. Put simply, the contract between Swynson and the accountants was not aimed at benefiting a type of third party (for example, one that refinances the debts of EMSL). On the transferred loss exception, Lord Sumption (with whom Lord Neuberger P, Lord Clarke and Lord Hodge agreed) cited *Panatown* emphasising that the exception was 'driven by legal necessity' to avoid a 'legal black hole'. The exception for transferred loss was defined by Lord Sumption in the following way:

> [14] The principle of transferred loss is a limited exception to the general rule that a claimant can recover only loss which he has himself suffered. It applies where the known object of a transaction is to benefit a third party or a class of persons to which a third party belongs and the anticipated effect of a breach of duty will be to cause loss to that third party. It has hitherto been recognised only in cases where the third party suffers loss as the intended transferee of the property affected by the breach.

On the facts, 'the known object' of the contract was not to benefit a third party. Also, it could not be said that a breach would cause loss to a third party or type of third party. The exception had only ever been applied where a third party suffered loss following property being transferred. When Lord Mance described the exception, he also made reference to property under the contract being 'transferred to or occupied by a third party'. That inclusion of 'occupied' covers the Court of Appeal application in *Darlington Council*. The other judgment by Lord Neuberger P described the transferred loss exception in the following way:

> [w]here (a) at the time of making the contract with A, B would reasonably have anticipated that A would transfer the property to a person such as C and that that person would suffer loss if B breached the contract, so that the contract can be seen as having been entered into by B partly for C's benefit, and (b) there is nothing in the contract or the surrounding circumstances which negatives the conclusion that the principle should apply.

The requirements for the transferred loss exception can be summarised in the following way:

- It is known that the contract is to benefit a third party (or class of third party)
- It must be anticipated that a breach will cause loss to that third party
- The loss would arise from having property or occupation of property being transferred
- The third party cannot have a direct right of action for the same loss
- There is nothing to indicate that the parties did not intend for the exception to apply

12.9.2.3 The Wider Exception for Transferred Loss

In *Linden Gardens*, Lord Griffiths preferred a wider transferred loss exception. His Lordship referred to the standard 'narrow' exception (i.e. based on property rights being transferred) and then explained:

> I cannot accept that in a contract of this nature, namely for work, labour and the supply of materials, the recovery of more than nominal damages for breach of contract is dependent upon the plaintiff having a proprietary interest in the subject matter of the contract at the date of breach.

Lord Griffiths went on to provide an everyday example to show the need for a wider approach:

> In everyday life contracts for work and labour are constantly being placed by those who have no proprietary interest in the subject matter of the contract. To take a common example, the matrimonial home is owned by the wife and the couple's remaining assets are owned by the husband and he is the sole earner. The house requires a new roof and the husband places a contract with a builder to carry out the work. The husband is not acting as agent for his wife, he makes the contract as principal because only he can pay for it.

The example then turned to the breach and loss suffered to explain why the contractual party should have damages:

> The builder fails to replace the roof properly and the husband has to call in and pay another builder to complete the work. Is it to be said that the husband has suffered no damage because he does not own the property? Such a result would in my view be absurd and the answer is that the husband has suffered loss because he did not receive the bargain for which he had contracted with the first builder and the measure of damages is the cost of securing the performance of that bargain by completing the roof repairs properly by the second builder.

This is a much wider approach than the one based on Lord Browne-Wilkinson's judgment from the same case, and not just because it applies even when there is no property transfer. It is much wider because the award would not be based on the actual loss to the third party, nor would it be based on expecting a third party to suffer loss. Likewise, it would not be based on an understanding of a potential claim on behalf of the third party. Instead, it would be about claiming damages because the innocent party has not received the performance contracted for. Such an award simply protects the performance interest of the innocent contractual party. It then results in the damages award needed to get the performance contracted for. In Lord Griffiths' example, the damages would be for the cost of correcting the faults on the roof. That would then leave the contracting party with what they contracted to get, i.e. a repaired roof.

In *Linden Gardens* itself, the other Lords did not apply the approach of Lord Griffiths, but they did show their sympathy and understanding towards it. Later, in *Darlington*, Steyn LJ approved the wider approach of Lord Griffiths. Furthermore, in *Panatown*, the dissenting judgments of Lord Millett and Lord Goff both supported and applied the wider approach.

In *Swynson v Lowick* [2017], Lord Mance observed that there was 'much to be said for the broader principle' stated by Lord Griffiths. But of course, even this wider approach would have made no difference in the case. All three judgments recognised that Swynson's performance interest at the time of the contract would never have included a benefit to a third party like Mr Hunt.

The opinions that have endorsed the wider approach by Lord Griffiths over the years suggest that in theory there is some scope for it to be developed further. That being said, there is less pressure to do so given the effects of the 1999 Act. If there is a clear aim for a contract to benefit a third party, the Act should apply. If such an aim is not present, it is difficult to see how the transferred loss exception would apply, since it requires the contract to have the aim of benefiting a third party. However, even if there is such an aim, there might be residual scope for the transferred loss exception to apply. An example might be where the Act's requirement for an *express* identification of the class of third party to benefit is not satisfied. It might be that the transferred loss exception could apply where the type of third party is unexpressed but is so obvious that it is implied.

➔ CROSS-REFERENCE

For the discussion of the identification requirement see 12.6.2.5.

CHAPTER SUMMARY

- Under the general privity rule, a third party cannot enforce a contract. Only the parties to the contract can do so.
- The privity rule also prevents a third party relying on a contract to defend an action (e.g. the third party cannot rely on an exemption clause from the contract).
- The rule was heavily criticised, the main criticisms being:
  - the rule ignored the intentions of the parties;
  - it would result in unfairness where the third party acted in reliance on the contract;
  - where the third party suffers loss, the parties would not be awarded compensation.
- The only real justifications were the need to prevent parties being exposed to indeterminate claims from unknown third parties, and the need to prevent obligations being imposed on third parties, but the rule was applied to go beyond these risks.
- The main exception is the 1999 Act, which allows for third parties to have enforceable rights. There are some basic requirements for the Act to apply:
  - Third party enforcement must have been intended;
  - The third party must be identified, whether as a particular party or class of party.
- The ability of the parties to amend or end the contract giving rights to a third party is limited.
- At common law, before the Act, various devices were developed to evade the effect of the privity rule. They remain in use where the Act cannot apply.
- Key examples of the common law exceptions include: the use of a collateral contract, agency, assignment, trusts, and the law of tort.

- There some exceptions to the privity rule in various pieces of legislation.
- A party to a contract could enforce the benefit intended by the contract using remedies such as specific performance, and certain damages claims.
- Damages claims by a contractual party can reflect the loss suffered by a third party in certain consumer contracts. While the reasoning behind this is very suspect, the courts have accepted it.
- There is a further limited exception for damages to reflect transferred loss in relation to contracts transferring property interests.
- There is scope for a wider exception based on the comments by Lord Griffiths in *Linden Gardens* but this has not yet been developed.

KEY CASES

- ☐ *Dunlop Pneumatic Tyre Co Ltd v Selfridge & Co Ltd* [1915] **AC 847**—authority for the established privity rule operating independently of consideration.
- ☐ *Scruttons Ltd v Midland Silicones Ltd* [1962] **AC 446**—confirmed that third parties could not rely on exemption clauses from the contract to defend an action.
- ☐ *Darlington Borough Council v Wiltshier Northern Ltd* [1995] **1 WLR 68**—useful for an exception to the privity rule but is also the most detailed judicial account of the criticism of privity and the need for reform.
- ☐ *Avraamides v Colwill* [2006] **EWCA Civ 1533**—highlights a limit of the 1999 Act in relation to the need for the third party or class of third party to be identifiable from an express description.
- ☐ *Shankin Pier v Detel Products Ltd* [1952] **2 KB 854**—represents the use of a collateral contract to get around the privity rule.
- ☐ *New Zealand Shipping Co Ltd v AM Satterthwait & Co Ltd, The Eurymedon* [1975] **AC 154**—provides authority on the use of agency to get around the privity rule.
- ☐ *Les Affréteurs Réunis Société Anonyme v Leopold Walford (London) Ltd* [1919] **AC 801**—authority on the use of trusts to get around the privity rule.
- ☐ *White v Jones* [1995] **2 AC 207**—shows how in some instances the law of tort could provide a remedy for a third party following a breach.
- ☐ *Beswick v Beswick* [1968] **AC 58**—shows how an order of specific performance by a contractual party could enable a third party to benefit from the contract.
- ☐ *Jackson v Horizon Holidays Ltd* [1975] **1 WLR 1468**—the authority allowing a party to claim for the losses suffered by a third party in limited circumstances.
- ☐ *Woodar Investments v Wimpey Construction* [1980] **1 WLR 277**—contains important comments to help to define the scope of the exception represented by *Jackson*.
- ☐ *Linden Gardens Trust v Lenesta Sludge Disposals* [1994] **AC 85**—authority for the extension of the transferred loss exception to contracts for the transfer of property in general.
- ☐ *Alfred McAlpine Construction Ltd v Panatown Ltd* [2001] **1 AC 518**—provides a limit to the transferred loss exception.
- ☐ *Swynson Ltd v Lowick Rose LLP* [2017] **UKSC 32**—Provides further guidance on the application of the transferred loss exception.

QUESTIONS

1. 'The common law exceptions alone were sufficient to get around the doctrine of privity.' Critically discuss.
2. 'The Contracts (Rights of Third Parties) Act 1999 provides a satisfactory resolution to a longstanding problem in the common law.' Critically discuss.

3. As a gift before leaving to explore the rainforests in South America, Devon purchased a one-year subscription to GameStream (an unlimited streaming service for console games) for his sister Lucy. It cost £200, which Devon paid up front. Devon arranged this subscription though Entertainment Supermarket Ltd. Two weeks after Devon left, Lucy attempted to download a game and discovered that GameStream has suspended its service because of technical problems. Advise Lucy as to how she might secure a remedy from Entertainment Supermarket.

 For answer guidance to these questions please visit the online resources at www .oup.com/uk/naidoo1e/, where you will also find multiple choice questions to check your understanding of key concepts.

FURTHER READING

Coote, 'The performance interest, *Panatown*, and the problem of loss' (2001) 117 LQR 81.
Provides a detailed examination of the *Panatown* case and its impact on the exception for damages claims reflecting the loss suffered by a third party.

Law Commission (Law Com No 242) 'Privity of Contract: Contracts for the Benefit of Third Parties' (1996) https://www.lawcom.gov.uk/project/privity-of-contract-contracts-for-the-benefit-of-third-parties/
This is the report that followed the consultation document and proposed the provision of the Act. It provides a clear account of the common law and the limits of the rules developed by the courts, as well as the basis for, and intended application of, the Act.

MacMillan, 'A birthday present for Lord Denning: the Contracts (Rights of Third Parties) Act 1999' (2000) MLR 63(5), 721.
A detailed, clear analysis of the 1999 Act, its background and application.

Stevens, 'The Contracts (Rights of Third Parties) Act 1999' (2004) 120 LQR 292.
A very detailed and critical assessment of the Act and the problems with the privity rule that underpinned the need for the reform.

Trotter, 'Reconsidering transferred loss' MLR (2019), 82(4), 727.
A useful extended note on *Swynson Ltd v Lowick Rose LLP*, the most recent authority on the transferred loss exception.

PART 4

Factors That Can End the Contract

13

Misrepresentation

LEARNING OBJECTIVES

By the end of this chapter you should be able to:

- apply the basic requirements for establishing that there has been an actionable misrepresentation;
- explain the remedy of rescission and identify the circumstances when it is not available;
- evaluate the different types of claims that can be made for damages;
- explain the role and application of the more recent rules for consumers;
- analyse the extent to which an exemption clause can cover liability for misrepresentation.

INTRODUCTION

It is easy to imagine a party making various statements to encourage another party to enter a contract. If any of those statements turn out to be false, the innocent party might want to escape from the contract because they were misled into entering it. The law allows an innocent party to do this: if a party has entered into a contract after being misled, he or she cannot be said to have genuinely consented to it, because their consent was impaired by the false statements. They can therefore get out of the agreement. As a result, misrepresentations are known as a 'vitiating factor' because they represent a defect in the way the contract was made.

This is a straightforward concept, but the law has, surprisingly, had problems dealing with it. This is primarily because the wrongdoing, in the form of false statements, takes place *before* the parties enter the contract and have the effect of making the contract voidable because it was not a true agreement. The remedies, therefore, cannot come from the contract itself. Instead, the rules on misrepresentation and relevant rights emerge from a mixture of common law torts, legislation, equity and unjust enrichment.

This chapter explains the law relating to the requirements and remedies for misrepresentation. The rules that we cover developed originally in the context of all types of contracts. However, more recent legislation has introduced some specific protection for consumers. Consequently, the common law rules and older legislation that we cover are now more applicable to non-consumer contracts, i.e. contracts between businesses and those between private parties. We start by addressing the kind of false statements that can result in a remedy. Next, we address the common law and legislative remedies that could be available to the innocent party. We then turn to the impact of the more recent consumer legislation, before finally examining the extent to which an exemption clause could cover liability for misrepresentation.

13.1 An *Actionable* Misrepresentation

→ CROSS-REFERENCE

For the distinction between terms and representations see 6.1.1.

representor
is a party making a representation. A 'representee' is a party to whom a representation is made.

Before entering a contract, there might be negotiations during which various statements are made. These statements could be oral, or expressed on paper or in an electronic way like an email, text or website. We have seen that some such statements could be classed as terms of the contract, which could be the basis of a breach of contract action. Alternatively, statements about certain facts might be classed as representations. When such representations are false, they are known as misrepresentations and could result in a remedy for the innocent **representee**.

It is well established that for a misrepresentation to result in a remedy, the false representation must be *actionable*. An actionable misrepresentation can be defined as an untrue statement of fact that induces a party to enter a contract. We can break down the requirements of an actionable misrepresentation in the following way:

- There has to be a false representation about an existing or past fact:
  - not puffery;
  - not an opinion;
  - not a statement about a future intention;
  - not an abstract statement of law.
- The statement must have induced the innocent party to enter the contract.

The requirements will be explained in turn. Each has some case law that serves to define its scope.

13.1.1 Puffery and Sales Hype

→ CROSS-REFERENCE

For the discussion of 'puffery' in the context of adverts see 2.3.2.

We have seen that puffery is the term used to describe a certain type of 'sales hype.' It relates to the kind of statements that no reasonable person would take seriously, like an obvious gimmick such as 'Red Bull gives you wings'. Alternatively, it could be a statement that cannot be verified objectively, such as a drink that 'refreshes parts others cannot reach'. It was made clear at an early stage, in the case of *Dimmock v Hallett* (1866) 2 Ch App 21, that such statements are not actionable. In this case, land was described as 'fertile and improvable,' a statement that was held to be mere sales talk and puffery. The words 'fertile and improvable' were treated as vague, non-specific and subjective. On that basis, the description was not enough to qualify as a false statement of *fact*.

13.1.2 Statements of Opinion

The starting point on opinions is that they are not normally actionable. They are just statements of belief rather than statements of fact—as long as the opinion actually *appears* to be nothing more than an opinion. It is easy to imagine a representor making a statement which includes words like 'I think'; 'I believe' or even 'in my opinion' to indicate an opinion is being expressed. But the test for this must be an objective one, taking into account the wider context of the statement being made.

The key authority on the basic rule is *Bisset v Wilkinson* [1927] AC 177 which concerned land being sold for sheep farming. The seller told the buyer that the land could hold 2000 sheep. Once the contract was made, the buyer discovered that the statement was false. In response, he wanted to end the contract on the basis that he had entered it after a misrepresentation. However, the seller was not a sheep farmer. In addition, the field had never been used for sheep. That meant his statement could only have been speculative—i.e. a matter of belief or opinion. More importantly, the buyer was aware of this. It meant that the statement would have *appeared* to be nothing more than an opinion to the buyer. For that reason, he could only be expected to have treated the statement as an opinion rather than an actionable statement of fact.

KEY POINTS

Ordinarily, an opinion is not a statement of fact.

However, an apparent statement of opinion or belief can imply that the person making the statement has a factual basis for that opinion or belief, and in those circumstances the statement may be treated as being one of fact. This is illustrated by *Smith v Land and House Property* (1884) 28 Ch D 7 where a landlord was selling property that was being rented by a tenant. The landlord stated that the tenant was a 'most desirable tenant'. In itself that sounds like a statement of opinion. However, landlords are in a position to know the truth about their tenants. Their apparent opinions about a tenant will therefore implicitly have a factual basis. So when it was discovered later that the tenant was behind with the rent, the statement was held to have been a misrepresentation. The reasoning was explained by Bowen LJ in the Court of Appeal:

> In a case where the facts are equally well known to both parties, what one of them says to the other is frequently nothing but an expression of opinion . . . But if the facts are not equally well known to both sides, then a statement of opinion by one who knows the facts best involves very often a statement of a material fact, for he impliedly states that he knows facts which justify his opinion.

In making the statement, the landlord was implying that he had a factual justification for his opinion, because he was in a position to know the truth and the buyer was not.

 THINKING POINTS

Does this seem harsh? What if the landlord does not actually know the facts behind the statement?

In some cases, an opinion could concern something that cannot have a factual basis. For example, consider a forecast by an expert. Such an opinion will be informed by special knowledge and skill rather than actual existing facts. However, such an opinion can still result in a representation that is actionable.

The key case on this point is *Esso Petroleum v Mardon* [1976] QB 801. It concerned a petrol station to be built by Esso. Their expert, who had around 40 years of experience, had estimated the amount of fuel the station was expected to sell (the throughput). He gave a figure of 200,000–250,000 gallons a year after the first two years, which was based on the fuel pumps being positioned so as to face the road. However, the local authority did not grant planning permission for the pumps to face the road, and so they were located at the back of the station and could only be accessed by a side street. Mardon was interviewed as a potential tenant to run the petrol station. During discussions, Esso's expert stated the same estimate of throughput. While this sounded very high, Mardon relied on the expert and entered the tenancy contract. Unfortunately, business was very slow and the throughput was only 78,000 gallons.

When Esso sued for the outstanding rent and payment for petrol, Mardon counter-claimed. One of the arguments raised was that the throughput statement was a misrepresentation. On that argument, Lord Denning MR made reference to the special knowledge and skill of Esso. When they had expressed their estimate, they had also implicitly made a further representation that their estimate was made with reasonable care and skill. Since the estimate was a negligent one (i.e. made without reasonable care and skill), Esso were liable.

It is important to appreciate that the liability for the statement was based on the *way* the statement was made, rather than the statement itself. Yes, the statement was not accurate, and it had not been made with reasonable care and skill. However, it was the (implied) representation that the statement had been made with reasonable care and skill that was false, and it was that which resulted in the liability for misrepresentation. This approach applies whenever a statement is made by someone with special knowledge and skill, but having such skill and knowledge is not enough. What really matters is the *appearance* of special knowledge and skill. Esso held itself out as having such special knowledge and skill. Crucially, if they did not have such knowledge, they could have said so.

KEY POINTS

An opinion by an expert might be actionable where the maker of the statement impliedly represents that the opinion was made with reasonable care and skill. If it then emerges that the statement was not made with reasonable care and skill, the implied representation is a false statement of fact.

A further issue regarding statements of opinions relates to statements worded as opinions, but not believed by the person stating them. In other words, a person might lie about what their opinion is. In such a case, the representor can still be liable, because it is assumed that when a statement is made, the representor impliedly represents that they are being honest. If they are not being honest, they have made an actionable misrepresentation. This point is developed further in 13.1.3.

13.1.3 Statements about Future Intentions

Parties often make statements about what they will do in the future. For example, sellers of a hair salon might say that they will not open a competing salon nearby. Such statements could be classed as a promise and might be important enough to be incorporated as a term of the contract. If such a statement is not a term, it will be a representation. However, such statements about future intentions are generally not actionable. This is because when made, such statements are not statements of fact. Instead, they are statements about something that may or may not happen in the future.

Inntrepreneur Pub Co (CPC) Ltd v Sweeney [2002] EWHC 1060 (Ch) is a useful illustration of the rule on statements of future intention. During negotiations for a tenancy of a pub, the landlord pub company predicted that the tenant would be released from a beer tie-in. That tie-in required the tenant to sell the beer provided by the landlord only. The prediction was simply a statement of intention. It was honestly made too, because at the time, there was a policy to release all pubs from the tie-in. The tenant entered the contract, and later the landlord refused to release him from the tie-in. In the case, Park J held that there was no actionable misrepresentation; the statement had simply been an honest representation as to future intention.

KEY POINTS

Generally, a statement of future intention is not a statement of existing fact and therefore will not actionable.

The *Inntrepreneur Pub v Sweeney* case is an example of a simple statement of future intention, but what if the representor was lying? For example, what if the statement of future intention was made to deceive the representee? The courts are keen to discourage fraud and, for that reason, the courts have a mechanism to allow for such statements to result in liability, and this was recognised in *Edgington v Fitzmaurice* (1885) 29 ChD 459. It concerned statements in a company prospectus that any investment would be used to expand the company. This was a statement of intention, but it was not an honest one. It could be shown that the directors never intended to use the investment in that way. The claimant brought an action for fraudulent misrepresentation under the tort of deceit. This action was successful and was also upheld by the Court of Appeal.

In the judgment by Bowen LJ, the basis of the actionable misrepresentation was stated in the following way:

> A mere suggestion of possible purposes to which a portion of the money might be applied would not have formed a basis for an action of deceit. There must be a mis-statement of an existing fact; but the state of a man's mind is as much a fact as the state of his digestion. It is true that it is very difficult to prove what the state of a man's mind at a particular time is, but if it can be ascertained it is as much a fact as anything else. A misrepresentation as to the state of a man's mind is therefore a misstatement of fact.

What is important is the mechanism adopted by Bowen LJ. The actual false statement alone was not actionable—after all, it was not a statement about an *existing* fact. Instead, at the time that the statement is made, the maker of the statement represents that it is an honest one. It is like having a label on their head which says 'I honestly believe what I'm saying'. That is the representation. It is about the status of the representor's mind. Such a representation (of being honest) is a representation of existing fact. It is then for the innocent party to prove that the representor was not being honest. If this can be proven, then it means there has been an actionable misrepresentation about the state of the representor's mind at the time. The quote from Bowen LJ was cited with approval in *Al Khudairi v Abbey Brokers Ltd* [2010] EWHC 1486 (Ch) indicating it remains an important principle.

In practice, the operation of the mechanism stated by Bowen LJ would be very straightforward. If a statement of intention is proven to be fraudulent, then there will be a fraudulent misrepresentation. As long as the remaining requirement of inducement is met, the misrepresentation will be actionable.

The mechanism for fraudulent statements of intent should apply equally to a fraudulent statements worded as opinion. When an opinion is made, the maker represents that the opinion was an honest one. If it can be proven to be dishonest, then it could be actionable as a misrepresentation as to the state of the representor's mind. In some cases, it would be difficult to prove such dishonesty, but in other cases, it might not be so difficult. Consider *Bisset v Wilkinson*, the statement was not actionable because it was an honest opinion. The evidence showed that seller did not know the facts behind the statement and the buyer would have been aware of that. In contrast, if a surveyor had previously explained to the seller that there was no way the field could hold 2000 sheep, the testimony from the surveyor would be evidence towards showing that the seller was being dishonest.

KEY POINTS

- Ordinarily a statement as to future intention is not actionable because it is not about an *existing* fact.
- If that statement was fraudulent, then the representor has made a misrepresentation as to their state of mind, which is an existing fact.

13.1.4 Abstract Statements of Law

At one point, it was assumed that false statements about the law were never actionable. The idea was that the law ought to be known by both parties and so a false statement about the law will have no influence over the other party. However, it is now clear that a misrepresentation about the way the law *applies* can be actionable, even if abstract statements about the content of the law are still considered not to be factual. The distinction is based on *Kleinwort Benson Ltd v Lincoln City Council* [1999] 2 AC 349. Essentially, the House of Lords addressed an unjust enrichment claim following a mistake about the law. It said that a mistake about the way the law applied could result in a remedy. The same approach was then adopted in relation to misrepresentation in *Pankhania v Hackney London Borough Council* [2002] EWHC 323 (Ch). It concerned the sale of property being rented by a car parking business. The seller said that the business was a 'contractual licensee'. On that basis, the seller added that

→ **CROSS-REFERENCE**

For the examination of the law on mistake see Chapter 17.

the occupation of the business could be ended with a three-month notice period. After entering the contract, the buyer discovered that the statement was not correct. In fact, under the relevant legislation, the tenancy could not be ended so easily. The court held that the statement was actionable and upheld the buyer's claim because there had been a false statement made about *how* the law *applied* to a particular set of circumstances. It was not a false *abstract* statement about the content of the law.

The distinction between these types of statement can be illustrated with an example. Consider the following statement: 'new businesses will never need planning permission to operate'. This is a false statement but it is not actionable because it is an *abstract* statement of law. It is not related to a given set of facts. In contrast, consider negotiations about the sale of premises where the seller says: 'for your business to operate on the property, there is no need for planning permission'. The statement is about *how* the law *applies* to the actual circumstances rather than an abstract statement of law.

KEY POINTS

An abstract statement of law is not a statement of fact, but a statement about how the law applies is a statement of existing fact.

13.2 Misrepresentation from a Failure to Reveal Facts

We know that a false *statement* can be actionable. But what if you know information that is bound to be important to the other party? Perhaps it is so important that if revealed, the other party would refuse to enter a contract. Let us assume you are not asked any questions that require you to reveal the information. You enter the contract and then the other party discovers the information you kept to yourself. The other party might feel misled by your silence. In such circumstances, can they treat your silence as a misrepresentation? In doing so, they would be arguing that you had an obligation to disclose material facts (i.e. an obligation to reveal important information) before contracting.

Generally, a party is under no duty to reveal material facts. This general approach is well established from early cases like *Keates v Earl of Cadogan* (1851) 10 CB 591 and *Fletcher v Krell (1873) 42 LJQB 55*. In *Keates*, a landlord was under no duty to reveal that a property was unfit to live in. *Fletcher* concerned a lady appointed as a governess. She was under no duty to reveal that she had been divorced. A more recent example of the rule can be seen in *Sykes v Taylor-Rose* [2004] EWCA Civ 299. This concerned the sale of a house. During negotiations, the seller did not reveal that a murder had taken place in the house. This failure to reveal the murder was not an actionable misrepresentation. The idea is that generally, if you are silent, you are not making a representation. It is for the other party to ask questions. The resulting answers are then statements that could be actionable if they are false.

The *general* rule on silence is a starting point. It is not an *absolute* rule and so there will be circumstances where the general rule does not apply. These can be seen in cases where remaining silent has resulted in liability. We will address each of the main 'exceptions' in turn below.

13.2.1 Representations by Conduct

A party might remain silent about an issue and not say anything about it. At the same time, their conduct or actions might create a certain impression. If this is a false impression, it could amount to a misrepresentation.

An early case on representations by conduct is *R v Barnard* (1837) 7 Car & P 784. The defendant, wearing an Oxford undergraduate gown, obtained boot-straps on credit from a shop. At the time, it was common for some shops to give credit to Oxford students. The defendant was found guilty of obtaining goods by false pretences. He had never made a statement about being a student at Oxford. However, by dressing up as one, he had made a representation that he was an Oxford student. The case was about a criminal offence but it is always taken to indicate how conduct could result in a misrepresentation.

The same approach was applied to a misrepresentation claim in *Spice Girls Ltd v Aprilia World Service* [2002] EWCA Civ 15. The case concerned a pop group that enjoyed world-wide fame from the late 1990's. They introduced the concept of 'girl power' and were highly marketable. The defendant company (AWS) agreed to sponsor a European tour. In addition, they agreed to pay fees in return for being allowed to produce and sell Spice Girl themed motor scooters. The logos and images for the scooters also featured all of the Spice Girls. Before finalising the contract, all five Spice Girls had participated in a photoshoot for AWS in connection with the promotion of the scooters. But what they did not reveal to AWS at the time was that they all already knew that one member, Geri Halliwell, had expressed an intention to leave the group. Later, after the contract had been made, Geri then quit, and AWS sued on the basis that they had only entered into the contract because there were five Spice Girls, each with their own personality and brand. AWS argued that they had wasted expenditure on photos, logos and so on for one member who was now no longer in the group. The court held that the Spice Girls' overall conduct amounted to a representation that the group had five members and would continue to do so—i.e. that none of the group had an expressed intention to quit. This created a false impression for AWS. As a result, the group was liable for misrepresentation.

13.2.2 Where Defects Are Deliberately Hidden

If one party deliberately conceals defects in goods it is selling to another, then it can result in an actionable misrepresentation even though there has been no 'statement' made as such. The case of *Schneider v Heath* (1813) 3 Camp 506 is a good example. It concerned the sale of a ship 'to be taken with all faults'. However, the seller kept the ship constantly afloat to hide the bottom of the hull. This was to conceal the fact that the keel was broken and that the underside had been eaten by worms. The action for misrepresentation was allowed but the judgment given by Mansfield CJ was not very detailed. It is likely that the liability was influenced by the court's aim of discouraging fraud. Furthermore, this was not an example of a seller failing to volunteer important facts. Rather, he had taken positive action to hide the defects. By presenting the ship, he was in effect making a representation to the effect that there were no defects being deliberately hidden. The action taken to hide the defects meant that this representation was false.

13.2.3 Half-true Statements

A half-true statement is a representation that is technically true but would be false if the full facts were revealed at the time. Consider the sale of a cycle repair shop on a university campus. The seller says it is the only place for cycle repairs on the campus. Technically, that statement might be true. However, what if at the time, the seller already knew that the Student's Union was about launch its own cycle repair service? Such a fact suddenly makes the original statement so misleading that it leads to a conclusion that is almost opposite to the truth, and this makes it potentially actionable.

An early authority on this point is *Dimmock v Hallett* (1866) 2 Ch App 21 which concerned the sale of a large estate. The auctioneer indicated that the farms on the estate were being rented by tenants. He even referred to the rental income from two of the tenancies. At the time, the statement was technically true. The farms on the estate did indeed have these paying tenants. However, at the time of the statement, both of the tenants had already given notice to end their tenancies. While the statement was technically true, it was clearly misleading in the light of the full facts.

The Court of Appeal held that the statement was calculated to mislead and was an actionable misrepresentation.

The case can be explained in another way. By making the statement, there was a representation that it was a full and complete statement, when in fact it was so incomplete that it could be considered to be false.

KEY POINTS

Generally, there is no duty to reveal facts. It is okay to be silent. But if you do make a representation, it needs to be a full and complete one so that it is not misleading.

13.2.4 True Statements That Become False by the Time the Contract Is Entered

During negotiations, a statement could be true at the time it was made. By true we mean it was full and complete and not in any way misleading. However, some time might pass between the negotiation and the making of the contract. By the time the contract is actually in effect, the statement might have become false. Consider the sale of the cycle repair shop. The seller says that it is the only place to have a cycle repaired on campus, and in this example, the statement was true and complete at the time. A month later, the sale takes place. It is then discovered that a week before the sale, the seller was informed that the Student's Union was launching its cycle repair service. The seller's statement was true and complete at the time it was made, but become false later, before the contract became effective. Failure to give notice of that change means that the statement might result in an actionable misrepresentation.

The main case on such statements is *With v O'Flanagan* [1936] Ch 575 which concerned the sale of a doctor's practice. During negotiations in January, the seller stated that the practice was making £2000 a year, which was true at the time. However, by the time the sale was concluded, in May, the income had fallen to £5 a week. This was because in the weeks leading to the signing of the contract, the defendant doctor had fallen ill. In his absence, the practice had been run by a temporary doctor and it had lost many patients. After the contract was signed, the buyer discovered that the income was much lower than £2000 a year. He then sought to end the contract for misrepresentation. Essentially, it was argued that the seller's failure to correct the earlier statement was actionable and the Court of Appeal agreed.

The reasoning of Lord Wright MR addressed the source of the principle relied upon:

> I take the law to be as it was stated by Fry J. in *Davies v. London and Provincial Marine Insurance Co.* 8 Ch. D. 469 where it is perhaps most fully expressed . . . "Again, in ordinary contracts the duty may arise from circumstances which occur during the negotiation. Thus, for instance, if one of the negotiating parties has made a statement which is false in fact, but which he believes to be true and which is material to the contract, and during the course of the negotiation he discovers the falsity of that statement, he is under an obligation to correct his erroneous statement; although if he had said nothing he very likely might have been entitled to hold his tongue throughout." Then he adds what was material in that case and what is material in this case: "So, again, if a statement has been made which is true at the time, but which during the course of the negotiations becomes untrue, then the person who knows that it has become untrue is under an obligation to disclose to the other the change of circumstances."

In other words, there is a duty to correct a true statement if becomes false before the contract comes into effect.

Lord Wright MR then explained the basis for this approach by citing the comments of Lord Cranworth from *Smith v Kay* (1859) 7 HL Cas. 750:

> . . . He says of a representation made in negotiation some time before the date of a contract: "It is a continuing representation. The representation does not end for ever when the representation is once made; it continues on.

This indicates that the duty to reveal exists in this situation because the representations are continuing. They are not final just because they have been expressed. They remain live right up to when the contract becomes enforceable. That is because the representee can expect the statement to remain true; their decision to enter into the contract at a particular date would reasonably have been contingent on the facts remaining as originally represented.

The other key judgment in *With v O' Flanagan* was by Romer LJ. This agreed with Lord Wright MR and summarised the legal position in the following way:

> If A. with a view to inducing B. to enter into a contract makes a representation as to a material fact, then if at a later date and before the contract is actually entered into, owing to a change of circumstances, the representation then made would to the knowledge of A. be untrue and B. subsequently enters into the contract in ignorance of that change of circumstances and relying upon that representation, A. cannot hold B. to the bargain.

Romer LJ made a clear reference to the fact that the maker of the statement must *know* that it had become false. Lord Wright MR also indicated that the duty to reveal applies only when the representor discovers the truth.

THINKING POINTS

If the maker of a statement later has a reason to doubt its accuracy, should that doubt be revealed? Alternatively, should the rule only apply if there is actual knowledge of the statement being false?

However, it is not clear if *actual* knowledge of the change in accuracy is needed. It could be argued that if the representor *ought* to have known had they taken more care (i.e. if they had constructive knowledge) then that might be sufficient. This could be supported with the fact that since 1963, the courts have recognised negligent misrepresentation. The point is that it could be argued that the failure to correct a false statement could result from negligence and be actionable.

The difference between the 'changed circumstances' situation and half-truths can be explained in the following way:

- In the half-truth' situation, the statement is true at the time it is made, but serves to conceal other relevant information that would make the statement false.

- By contrast, in the 'changed circumstances' (*With v O' Flanagan*) situation the statement is completely true when made, but is made untrue by a later change in circumstances which comes to the representor's attention (before the contract becomes effective.).

The representation by conduct in *Spice Girls v Aprilia* was also treated as a continuing representation. From the outset, the group had represented themselves as group of five, none of whom had a declared intention to quit, to AWS. Before entering the contract, one of the Spice Girls (Geri) had told the others that she planned to leave after the tour. After entering the contract, Geri left the group and AWS then discovered that the other members had known Geri was leaving before the contract was entered into. The court cited *With v O'Flanagan* to say that the representation of the group consisting of five members, none of whom had a declared intention to quit, was continuing. More specifically, it was a representation that they expected to be a five during the contract period. When Geri had revealed she was going to leave, that fact should have been revealed before the contract commenced.

KEY POINTS

If a representation becomes false to the knowledge of the representor, the representor has an obligation to correct it.

13.2.5 Special Contracts with a Duty to Reveal Facts

There are some special contracts that require a party to reveal important facts before contracting. Such an obligation can be described as a positive duty to reveal material facts. Here we address two examples, one from traditional insurance contracts, the other relating to fiduciary relationships.

13.2.5.1 Contracts *Uberrimae Fidei (of 'Utmost Good Faith')*.

The most common traditional example of such contracts is insurance. Here, the proposer (i.e. the customer who is asking to be insured) was under a duty to reveal all important facts to the insurance company. This was so that the company could make a realistic assessment of the risk and set the price. This duty to disclose was an obligation arising out of the good faith duty stated in the Marine Insurance Act 1906. The duty was controversial because proposers did not always know which facts to reveal, and in particular consumers struggled with the obligation because it was difficult to know what facts an insurer would want to know. The obligation was serious because of the consequence of breaching the duty. Under the Act, the insurer could end the contract from the start as if it never existed. The problem was that in practice, the failure to reveal all important facts would only be discovered following an insurance claim, and this would then leave the claimant to bear the loss. However, this position is no longer such a problem for consumers following the Consumer Insurance Act 2012, which does not require the positive disclosure of material facts. Instead, the insurer asks questions and the consumer needs to respond accurately. Untrue statements result in a range of remedies based on the seriousness of the false statement so that the remedies are now more proportionate to a breach. The position relating to commercial insurance contracts has improved too. It is now found in the Insurance Act 2015. The good faith obligation is defined in clearer way. In addition, the consequences of a breach are more proportionate.

13.2.5.2 Fiduciary Relationships

Some contracts are between parties that have a fiduciary relationship. It is said that such relationships are based on trust and confidence. Examples would be contracts between a solicitor and client; between an agent and their principal; or between those in a business partnership agreement. Again, in such special contracts, there is a duty to reveal material facts.

13.3 The Requirement of Inducement

For a false representation to be actionable, it must have induced the representee to enter the contract. Essentially, this requirement of inducement is concerned with effect of the statement or failure to reveal facts. It is often seen as a matter of causation and it is always the claimant representee that has the burden of proving inducement based on the facts (*BV Netherlands Industrie Van Eiprodukten v Rembrandt Enterprises, Inc* [2019] EWCA Civ 596). It is also well established that for inducement to be proved the false representation does not have to have been the only reason for entering into the contract (*Edgington v Fitzmaurice* (1885) 29 Ch D 459). Instead, it is sufficient for that representation to be *a* reason for entering into the contract. We will see that the case law shows that in proving inducement, there is a distinction between fraudulent representations and those that were not fraudulent but were simply negligently or innocently made.

In *Raiffeisen Zentral Bank of Osterreich AG v Royal Bank of Scotland* [2010] EWHC 1392 (Comm), Christopher Clarke J summarised the case law on inducement for non-fraudulent misrepresentations to show that the false statement had to be a 'real and substantive cause' in the 'but for' sense. Generally, the claimant representee will need to prove that but for the misrepresentation, they would not have entered the contract on the terms that they did. If they would have entered the contract anyway, then the statement would not be actionable. An example is *Smith v Chadwick* (1884) 9 App Cas 187, where the claimant representee bought shares in a company and later sought to end the contract on the grounds of misrepresentation. He relied on a number of false statements from the company prospectus and one of these was that Mr Grieve MP was a member of the Board of Directors. However, in court, the claimant admitted that the statement had not influenced him when he bought the shares. On that basis, there was no inducement and so that particular representation was not actionable.

→ CROSS-REFERENCE
For the discussion of the 'but for' test in the context of breach see 10.1.1.

Since the statement does not have to be the only reason for entering into the contract, it means that the misrepresentation does not have to be the only 'but for' cause. Consider the sale of a classic car where the seller falsely states that it was a 1960 model. The buyer might well prove that but for the statement about the age of the car, the buyer would not have paid £30,000. That would satisfy the inducement requirement even though the buyer would also not have paid that amount if the engine had not been reconditioned.

The 'but for' test does not require the representee to prove that the contract would not have been entered into had the truth been revealed (*Raiffeisen Zentral Bank of Osterreich AG v Royal Bank of Scotland*). Such an approach would be too generous to the representee and would allow a successful claim even when a representee did not actually consider, notice or even understand the false representation before entering the contract. Consider a buyer who, among other things, was falsely told that certain products were sugar-free. Let us assume that the buyer did not notice the representation and it played no part in the decision to enter into the contract. Clearly the representation did not operate as a reason to enter into the contract. If the court were then to ask if the contract would have been created had the seller said that the products contained sugar, the buyer might well say that the contract would not have been created. If inducement could be established in this way, misrepresentations would be actionable even where the actual false representation played no part in the decision to enter into the contract on the terms agreed. For that reason, the representee must show that 'but for' having been materially induced by the misrepresentation, it would not have entered into the contract on the terms that it did.

While it is the representee that has the burden of proving inducement, the courts have shown that with certain statements, inducement could be inferred from the facts. In *Haywood v Zurich Insurance Co Plc* [2016] UKSC 48, Lord Clarke indicated that a 'material' statement can result in an inference of fact that there was inducement, adding that the inference was particularly strong when the statement is fraudulent. A statement would be material where it is so important that a reasonable person would have been induced. However, this is only an inference and it is just part of the wider facts that are balanced in the assessment of inducement.

In the context of a fraudulent statement, the representee continues to have the burden of proving inducement, but the requirement is easier to satisfy in order to discourage fraud. In *BV Netherlands Industrie Van Eiprodukten v Rembrandt Enterprises, Inc* [2019], Longmore LJ examined the cases on inducement and explained that it is for the representee to prove they were 'materially influenced' by the fraudulent statement by showing it was 'actively present to his mind' at the time. Furthermore, Longmore LJ referred to fraudulent statements that are intended to be acted upon. Such statements give rise to an evidential presumption of fact that the statement was an inducement and, crucially, such a presumption is 'very difficult to rebut'. While the inducement requirement is not as strict in the context of fraudulent statements, Longmore LJ made it clear that it is not enough for the representee to show that they 'might' have acted differently as a result of the fraudulent statement.

KEY POINTS

- For inducement, the statement does not have to be the only reason for entering into the contract.
- If a statement is so important that it would have induced a reasonable person, then inducement might be inferred from the facts, but it is part of the overall assessment of those facts.
- To prove inducement following a non-fraudulent representation, it must be shown to be a 'but for' cause.
- For fraudulent representations, the representee must have been 'materially influenced' by the statement, i.e. that it was actively present in their mind.

13.3.1 Where the Representee Does Not Believe the Statement

If the representee did not believe a statement, then it might seem logical to question if it as capable of being an inducement. However, it is now clear that if a statement was not believed by a representee, it is still possible to class it as an inducement. The point was addressed by the Supreme Court in *Hayward v Zurich Insurance Company plc* which concerned a fraudulent insurance claim and the financial settlement contract agreed by the parties. The insurer settled the claim, even though they suspected that the statements in the claim were false. They agreed to settle because they felt that a judge might still be convinced by the false statements. According to the Supreme Court, those statements could still be an inducement.

The lead judgment was by Lord Clarke. After referring to the requirements for fraudulent misrepresentation, the following point was observed:

[18] . . . To my mind it is not necessary, as a matter of law, to prove that the representee believed that the representation was true. In my opinion there is no clear authority to the contrary. However, that is not to say that the representee's state of mind may not be relevant to the issue of inducement. Indeed, it may be very relevant. For example, if the representee does not believe that the representation is true, he may have serious difficulty in establishing that he was induced to enter into the contract or that he has suffered loss as a result.

[19] A person in the position of the employer or its insurer may have suspicions as to whether the representation is true. It may even be strongly of the view that it is not true. However, the question in a case like this is not what view the employer or its insurer takes but what view the court may take in due course.

This is just such a case, as the judge correctly perceived. As he put it, the employer and its advisers must take into account the possibility that Mr Hayward would be believed by the judge at the trial. That is because the views of the judge will determine the amount of damages awarded . . .

[23] I am not persuaded that the authorities lead to any other conclusion. As stated above, the ingredients of the tort of deceit are not in dispute subject to one question, which is whether a claimant alleging deceit must show that he believed the misrepresentation. In my opinion the answer is no . . .

[32] . . . As I see it, the representee's reasonable belief as to whether the misrepresentation is true cannot be a necessary ingredient of the test, because the representee may well settle on the basis that, at any rate in a context such as the present, he thinks that the representation will be believed by the judge.

The reasoning was based on the need to assess inducement on the facts of the case. For the fraudulent misrepresentation, it did not matter that the statement was not believed by the representee. What mattered was that the statement appeared to influence the insurer in some way. On the facts, the false statements did indeed influence the insurer. It did not believe the statements, but it felt that judges would, and on that basis entered into the settlement agreement. That meant the statements had indeed induced the insurer to enter into the contract.

13.3.2 Where the Representee Has the Accuracy of the Statement Checked before Entering the Contract

Following a false representation, the representee might not enter into the contract immediately. Instead, the representee might hire an expert to assess the accuracy of the representation. Consider the sale of a business. The seller inaccurately says that over the previous year, the average turnover was £50,000 per month. The buyer then hires an accountant to assess the business accounts. The accountant is careless and confirms the turnover as £50,000 per month and in response the buyer enters into the contract and buys the business. It is then discovered that the average turnover was really only £25,000. In such circumstances, it would look like the false statement was not an inducement. Instead, it could be argued that the buyer was induced by the accountant's assessment rather than the seller's false representation. In fact, we might be led to ask, if the seller's representation was really an inducement, then why have it verified by an expert?

The same argument would arise when the representee chooses to check the accuracy of the statement personally. After doing so, if the representee then enters the contract, it might appear that the representee was induced by their own examination and not the original statement.

The issue of a representee seeking verification of a statement was addressed in *Attwood v Small* (1838) 6 Cl & Fin 232, which concerned the sale of a mine. The seller made some false (but non-fraudulent) statements about how much money could be made from the mine. The buyer then hired a third party expert to inspect the mine to verify the statements. The expert then confirmed that the statements were true. In response, the buyer entered into the contract and then discovered later that the statements were false. This led to an action to end the contract for misrepresentation. The House of Lords held that the statements did not induce the buyer to enter into the contract and so they were not actionable. Instead, the buyer had been induced to enter into the contract by the third party inspection.

The decision in *Attwood v Small* meant that the buyer could not end the contract. Also, back then, damages were not available for non-fraudulent statements. However, the buyer might have had a damages claim under the contract with the expert. Today, the expert could also be liable to the buyer in the tort of negligence. That would be useful where there is no contract between them. The liability would be for the expert's negligently prepared statement confirming what the seller had said. Such an action for negligent misstatement has been possible since the House of Lords case of *Hedley Byrne v Heller* [1964] AC 465.

➔ CROSS-REFERENCE
For the discussion of negligent mis-statement under the tort of negligence see 13.8.1.

The approach in *Attwood v Small* should be treated with some caution for two reasons. First, we know that the false statement does not have to be the only reason to enter the contract. It can be one of a number of reasons, which is a point established clearly in the later case of *Edgington v Fitzmaurice*. For that reason, *Attwood v Small* can be seen as a case illustrating what happens if the representee relies on the third party examination *only*.

The second reason is that inducement is a question of fact. It is for the claimant to show that the original representation was an inducement. Of course, that will be more difficult when a third party is used to verify the statement. However, it might be possible to show that the representation remained an inducement. The point here is that *Attwood v Small* should not be used to rule out the possibility of inducement completely.

Attwood v Small was in the context of a third party verifying a statement made. However, it is generally assumed that it also applies to circumstances in which the representee verifies the statement made. Again, this should not be taken to mean that there can never be inducement in such a case. Instead, if the representee performs its own examination, it will just be more difficult to prove that the original statement was an inducement.

The representation in *Attwood v Small* was not fraudulent, however the statement in *Pearson & Son Ltd v Dublin Corporation* [1907] AC 351 was a fraudulent one. There, the House of Lords expressed an *obiter* comment about fraudulent representations. Their Lordships indicated that such statements will be actionable even if the representee has assessed the accuracy of the statement. In this case, the representor made a fraudulent statement but the contract had a clause stating that the representee was relying on its own inspection. It even said the representee was not in any way relying on statements made in negotiations. This meant that by signing the contract, the representee was agreeing that it was induced by its own examination only. However, the House of Lords held that the statement was still actionable on the basis that one cannot contract out of fraud. But it followed that even without the relevant clause in the contract, any verification made by the representee in these circumstances would not have prevented inducement. It was also clear that House of Lords wanted to discourage fraud by ensuring that the representor did not benefit from the fraud.

The approach towards fraudulent statements being verified was addressed in *Morris v Jones* [2002] EWCA Civ 1790. It concerned a contract for a lease and a fraudulent statement about the condition of the property. The representee received three surveyor's reports suggesting that the representation was not accurate. After entering the contract, the representee sought to end it for misrepresentation and the Court of Appeal decided in favour of the representee. The Court cited *Edgington v Fitzmaurice* and held that the original statement was still an inducement. It did not matter that there were other reasons for entering the contract. With this result, there was no need to rely on the comments made in the *Pearson Corp* case. It means the *obiter* comment about representees testing the accuracy of a fraudulent statement from the *Pearson Corp* case remain as *obiter*.

KEY POINTS

- Where a statement is not believed by the representee, it still might be possible to prove inducement.
- If the statement was verified by the representee or a third party for the representee, inducement is far less likely unless the statement was fraudulent.

13.3.3 Where the Representee Does Not Take the Opportunity to Verify a Statement

During negotiations, the representee might be given the chance to verify the accuracy of a statement made by the representor but fail to take that opportunity. In such circumstances, it might seem that the representee was not induced by the statement. Instead, it might appear that they were induced by their own failure to take the chance to verify the statement. However, it is clear that in such circumstances, the representee remains induced by the original statement.

The key case on the issue is *Redgrave v Hurd* (1881) 20 ChD 1 which concerned the sale of a partnership in a solicitors' practice along with a house. During an interview, the seller stated the income of the practice. On the evidence, the trial judge (Fry J) decided that the seller stated the income as £300 (or £300–£400) a year. However, the accounts showed that the practice made less than £200 per year. When questioned about it, the seller told the buyer that the additional money was from other business. He then offered the paperwork which was supposed to confirm this extra income. However, the buyer did not take the opportunity to check this paperwork. Had he done so, he would have discovered that the extra income was only five to six pounds per year. The buyer then agreed to buy the property and the partnership. Later, after discovering the statement of extra income was false, the buyer refused to complete the purchase. This prompted the seller to sue for specific performance to force the purchase. The buyer then counter-claimed on the basis that the statement about the income was a misrepresentation. The Court of Appeal made it clear that even though the buyer had been given the chance to discover the truth, this did not prevent inducement. As a result, the misrepresentation was actionable and so the contract could be rescinded.

The lead judgment by Sir George Jessel MR described the principle of equity to be applied:

> One way of putting the case was, "A man is not to be allowed to get a benefit from a statement which he now admits to be false. He is not to be allowed to say, for the purpose of civil jurisdiction, that when he made it he did not know it to be false; he ought to have found that out before he made it." The other way of putting it was this: "Even assuming that moral fraud must be shewn in order to set aside a contract, you have it where a man, having obtained a beneficial contract by a statement which he now knows to be false, insists upon keeping that contract. To do so is a moral delinquency: no man ought to seek to take advantage of his own false statements." The rule in equity was settled, and it does not matter on which of the two grounds it was rested. If a man is induced to enter into a contract by a false representation it is not a sufficient answer to him to say, "If you had used due diligence you would have found out that the statement was untrue. You had the means afforded you of discovering its falsity, and did not choose to avail yourself of them." I take it to be a settled doctrine of equity . . .

The reasoning establishes two principles that determined the outcome of the case:

- A party cannot benefit from its own false statements that have resulted in a contract.
- A representor cannot keep the contract alive by arguing that the other party should have been more careful.

KEY POINTS

If a representee is given the opportunity to verify a statement but does not take it, the statement can still be an inducement.

It could be said that the decision in *Redgrave* does not encourage parties to look after themselves. After all, the buyer could have protected himself by looking at the papers offered. In not doing so, he was partly to blame for his loss. However, allowing the seller to keep the contract would have been a worse outcome. Doing so would have allowed the seller to benefit from his own false statement.

Nowadays, the same decision on rescinding the contract would be made. That would reflect the principles stated by Sir George Jessel MR. However, if a representee is partly at fault, it might affect a separate claim for damages. If the facts of *Redgrave* happened today, the representee would also claim damages for negligent misrepresentation. However, under the Law Reform (Contributory Negligence) Act 1945, an award of damages can be reduced to reflect the representee's degree of fault. Such partial fault would be where a reasonable person would have taken the opportunity to verify the statement. Where it was reasonable to rely on the statement (rather than take the opportunity to verify it) the damages will not be reduced.

?! THINKING POINTS

Consider the date of the case and the fact that the representor was a solicitor. Was it reasonable for the buyer to rely on the statement and not take the opportunity to verify?

13.4 The Basic Remedy of Rescission

The basic remedy is rescission, which has its origins in equity and can be available for vitiating factors generally, including misrepresentation. Rescission as a remedy can be likened to the idea of tearing up the contract as if it did not take place. It is very different to terminating a contract following a breach for the following reasons:

- Termination for breach can only end a contract prospectively. That means the primary obligations no longer *continue*, but it is not as if they never existed.

- Rescission operates retrospectively. Essentially, all rights and obligations are wiped out from the start as though they never existed. The logic here is that the contract should never have come into being, because the innocent representee was misled and so its consent was spoilt (vitiated).

13.4.1 The Effect of Rescission

The effect of rescission is mutual restitution. It means that the parties are put back into their pre-contractual position, for example, the thing bought is returned to one party, and the money paid is returned to the other. However, if there is no rescission, the contract continues like any other contract. That is why it is said that an actionable misrepresentation makes a contract **voidable** rather than void.

voidable contract
is still valid but it can be made void (or avoided) by the innocent party.

Technically, after an actionable misrepresentation, the contract continues as normal. The rights and obligations continue in effect until the innocent party chooses to rescind the contract. If that happens, the contract is made void. In the light of this effect, rescission can be a very powerful remedy when it is available. That point is reinforced by the fact that it is an 'all or nothing' remedy. The courts have not restricted an innocent party to partial rescission in any case. Instead, if an innocent party is allowed to rescind a contract, it is the whole contract, a point that was confirmed by the Court of Appeal in *TSB Bank plc v Camfield* [1995] 1 WLR 430.

Mutual restitution is usually straightforward, with the parties being restored to their pre-contractual positions. Of course, during the time the contract was alive, the innocent party might have made other payments under the contract. Restitution suggests that the innocent party will be reimbursed for such payments. Such a reimbursement is called an *indemnity payment*. However, the courts have made a distinction between the types of payments that can be remedied with an indemnity payment. Payments required *by the contract* can be returned, but no other losses are recoverable as the consequence of rescission. Instead, they should be the subject of a damages claim (if one is permitted).

The distinction between payments that can be returned as an indemnity payment comes from *Whittington v Seale-Hayne* (1900) 82 LT 49. This case concerned a lease contract for a farm which was entered into following statements about the good condition of the property. Unfortunately, after entering into the contract, it became clear that the statements were false. The condition was so bad that repairs were needed. Even the water supply was poisonous, which resulted in the death of some of the tenant's poultry. The innocent representee (the tenant) then sought to rescind the contract. He also claimed an indemnity for his losses and for any payments made during his time as a tenant. The idea was that such an indemnity would restore his pre-contractual position.

Farwell J confirmed that the contract could be rescinded. It was then held that an indemnity covered losses arising from contractual obligations only. That included the rent paid and the cost of repairs required by the contract. However, the medical costs for the poultry and the loss of poultry could not be claimed as indemnities. Clearly these were losses suffered as a result of entering into the contract but they were not a result of performing obligations under it. The judge made it clear that such losses could only be the subject of a separate damages claim. At the time, such damages were only available for fraudulent misrepresentation, but on the facts the false representations had not been fraudulent.

- An actionable misrepresentation can result in the contract being voidable.
- When it is rendered void by the innocent party choosing to rescind, the parties' pre-contract position should be restored.
- Rescission will only allow for the return of payments required to be made by the contract.

13.4.2 How a Contract Can Be Rescinded

To rescind, the innocent party (the representee) must communicate an intention to rescind, which essentially means giving notice to the representor. Usually, giving notice is straightforward—the representee could simply tell the other party orally or in writing. The contract is then treated as having been rescinded from that point of notice. Of course, it might be that the representor has disappeared and cannot be found. A typical example would be where a fraudulent statement is made by a criminal to acquire goods before hiding from the police. In such circumstances, a strict requirement for the innocent party to actually communicate an intention to rescind would seem unfair. That very problem was addressed in *Car and Universal Finance v Caldwell* [1965] 1 QB 525.

The case was about the sale of a car by Caldwell (the representee). A fraudster bought the car from him using a cheque which was subsequently dishonoured by the bank (in other words, the cheque 'bounced'). The seller then attempted to rescind on the basis that the fraudster had made a false representation about having the money to support the cheque, but he could not find the fraudster. Instead, the seller did the next best thing by informing the police and by asking the Automobile Association for help. The fraudster sold the car and it was eventually sold to an innocent third party (Car & Universal Finance). The question was whether the third party had a good title to the car. If they did, the original seller (Caldwell) would have no claim for the return of the car. Instead, he would just be entitled to payment from the fraudster. Such a claim would be worthless since the fraudster had disappeared. Alternatively, if the third party did not have a good title to the car, Caldwell would be able to reclaim it. The third party would then have a contract claim against the fraudster.

We can recall that until a contract is rescinded, it operates like a normal contract. The rights and obligations from the contract continue to be enforceable. That means the title to goods acquired under a (voidable) contract can be sold on. However, once rescission takes place, the buyer no longer has a good title to pass on. Essentially it is all about timing, and that was the issue in this case.

Caldwell brought an action to recover the car from the innocent third party and the Court of Appeal upheld the claim. On the facts, Caldwell had done enough to rescind the contract between himself and the fraudster. He could not contact the fraudster, but notifying the police and the Automobile Association had been enough as the next best thing. Crucially, this rescission came before the fraudster had sold the car, as illustrated by Figure 13.1. That meant the fraudster did not hold the title (ownership) to the car at the time he re-sold it. Consequently, the third party (Car & Universal Finance) had never acquired the title to the car, and so the original owner (Caldwell) could recover it.

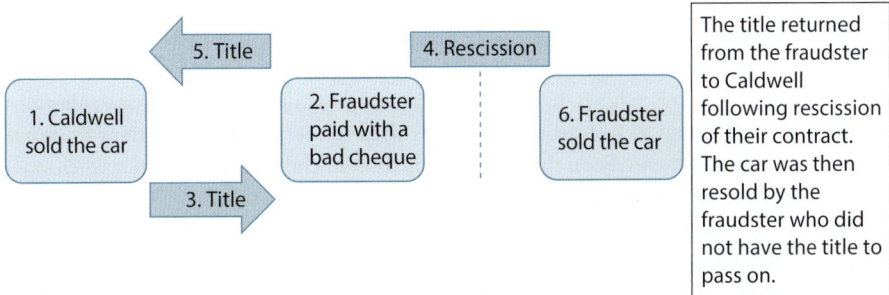

Figure 13.1
The timing of rescission in *Car & Universal Finance v Caldwell* [1965]

13.5 How the Right to Rescind Can Be Lost

In certain circumstances, the innocent party will lose the right to rescind. Such circumstances are referred to as 'bars' to rescission. Essentially, the innocent party is prevented or 'barred' from rescinding, and these bars are defined in Table 13.1. When that happens, the contract simply continues like any other normal (valid) contract. We will address the 'bars' to rescission in turn.

Table 13.1
The four traditional bars to rescission

Affirmation	When the innocent party shows an intention to carry on and not rescind.
Lapse of time	When here the innocent party takes too long to rescind.
Impossibility of restitution	When it is not possible to restore the parties to their original position.
Supervening third party rights	When the rights of an innocent third party prevent rescission.

Whether any bars apply depends on the individual facts of a case. We need to address the main case law on each bar and this will also allow us to understand the scope of their application.

13.5.1 Affirmation of the Contract

Affirmation will take place where an innocent party indicates that the contract should continue. After doing so, the right to rescind is lost. The innocent representee cannot then decide to end the contract because of the misrepresentation. If they do, it will be a breach of the contract. This bar balances the position between the parties. The right to rescind resulted from the innocent party being misled. Likewise, it is also misleading to affirm a contract and then rely on the original misrepresentation to end it.

Clearly, it is important to know how a contract can be affirmed. Essentially, the innocent party has to *show* an intention to carry on with the contract—something that can be done expressly by implication through conduct. What matters is that objectively there was a clear apparent intention to continue. For that to happen, the innocent party must also *appear* to know of the misrepresentation. After all, if it looks like you do not even know about the false statement, how can you appear to affirm?

Consider the sale of a doughnut shop on campus and a misrepresentation about there being no other source of doughnuts on campus. Following the sale, the representee buyer discovers that the Students' Union is selling doughnuts. In response, the representee then posts on their Facebook page indicating that they have a wider range of doughnuts than the Students' Union and it will be introducing a delivery service to the halls of residence. This response shows knowledge of the seller's misrepresentation. It also shows that the representee buyer is affirming the contract; after all, the buyer has not tried to end it. Instead, the buyer has tried to carry on and take steps to compete. The representee cannot then rely on the misrepresentation to end the contract later when it turns out these steps have not been successful.

The case of *Long v Lloyd* [1958] 1 WLR 753 is often cited as the key case on affirmation. It concerned the sale of a lorry following the seller's false but non-fraudulent statement about the lorry being in 'exceptional condition'. On its first journey, a number of faults were discovered. The dynamo did not work, there was leaking oil seal, and a cracked wheel. The representee (buyer) then complained to the seller and, in response, the seller agreed to pay half the cost of repairs. The buyer agreed and repairs were done. The lorry was then used for a second journey and more faults were found. When an expert inspected the lorry, it was described as unroadworthy. The buyer then wanted to end the contract and return the lorry. The Court of Appeal upheld the previous decision that the buyer was barred from rescinding because his conduct appeared to affirm the contract.

After explaining how rescission can be available for innocent misrepresentation, Pearce LJ turned to affirmation point:

> On the following day the plaintiff, knowing all that he did about the condition and performance of the lorry, dispatched it, driven by his brother, on a business trip to Middlesbrough. That step, at all events, appears to us to have amounted, in all the circumstances of the case, to a final acceptance of the lorry by the plaintiff for better or for worse, and to have conclusively extinguished any right of rescission remaining to the plaintiff after completion of the sale.

The judgment shows that the buyer's decision to send the lorry on another long journey indicated affirmation of the contract. The decision might seem a little harsh on the (representee) buyer, who was left without a remedy. However, the buyer was claiming rescission following the misrepresentation only after having agreed to repairs and going on a second journey. That conduct would have indicated to any reasonable representor that he was not ending the contract following the misrepresentation.

It should be emphasised that each case will be different, as it all depends on what can be reasonably inferred from the innocent party's conduct. For example, the innocent party might complain about the misrepresentation but then might carry on while waiting for a response about the complaint. In such circumstances, such conduct might not be considered enough for affirmation (*Edwards v Ashik* [2014] EWHC 2454 (Ch)).

Affirmation is based on acknowledging that the innocent party accepts the wrongdoing. If there have been several misrepresentations, however, the affirmation might relate to some but not all. The point is that affirmation could be based on one false statement. However, rescission might be possible on the basis of a different statement. This may be possible where the conduct affirming the contract shows that the representee had no knowledge of the other false statements.

KEY POINTS

Rescission will not be an option where the innocent representee has shown an intention to continue with the contract after discovering the misrepresentation.

13.5.2 Lapse of Time

The right to rescind does not last indefinitely. Instead, it can be lost by a lapse of time, and the period allowed for rescission will depend on the facts of each case. Whatever period is allowed, it is important to appreciate the rules on *when* the time period starts. We will always know when the innocent representee attempts to rescind, but it is not possible to identify the period of time that has lapsed without knowing when the 'clock starts ticking'.

It is well established that the time starts depending on the type of misrepresentation:

- **Fraudulent misrepresentation**: The time starts from the time at which the innocent representee discovers the fraud. Also, the time period itself is not used as a bar. Instead, the time period is used to indicate affirmation. So, once the fraud is discovered, a failure to end the contract will eventually indicate affirmation. For that reason, lapse of time is not an independent bar to rescission when the misrepresentation is fraudulent.

- **Negligent misrepresentations**: The time starts from the time at which the misrepresentation is or should have been discovered. It is not linked to affirmation, but is based on it being inequitable to grant rescission after a lengthy period of time.

- **Innocent misrepresentations**: The time starts from the point at which the contract comes into effect. Lapse of time is also not linked with affirmation here. If the representee takes too long, rescission will not be possible where it would be inequitable to grant it.

The traditional position on lapse of time following a non-fraudulent misrepresentation is from *Leaf v International Galleries* [1950] 2 KB 86 which, until recently, was considered to be a leading case. It is useful to explain this position so we can appreciate the extent to which matters have changed.

The case concerned the sale of a painting where the seller represented that it was by the famous artist, Constable. Five years after the sale, the (representee) buyer tried to sell the painting at an auction. At that point, he was advised that it was not a Constable painting. Since the original statement had been a non-fraudulent (innocent) misrepresentation, the time available for rescission was held to have started from the date of the contract. That meant at least five years had passed before any attempt to rescind. The Court of Appeal held that the lapse of time here meant the buyer was barred from rescinding.

The basic rule from the case is that after a 'reasonable period of time', the right to rescind is lost. The main reasoning was by Denning LJ and was based on the approach that applies to rejecting goods following a breach of a condition. Such a rejection is the way a contract for the sale of goods is terminated following a breach. According to the judgment, rejection was classed as a more 'potent' or serious remedy than rescission. On that basis, if rejection for breach would not be available, then the innocent party surely ought not to be able to end the contact using a weaker remedy of rescission. This relates to the position of the representor, in that its position should not be worse than the one that would result following a breach of a condition. The right to reject would be lost if the buyer appears to have 'accepted' the goods. 'Accepted' here basically means that the buyer has indicated that the goods are fine. Such an indication can be inferred following a failure to reject within a 'reasonable period of time'.

The reasonable period for acceptance was defined as the time that should be needed to inspect the goods to discover any faults. According to Denning LJ, a 'few days' was enough, based on the facts. In other words, the innocent party is given the time needed to discover the misrepresentation. The immediate response should then be to communicate an intention to rescind.

More recently, in *Salt v Stratstone Specialist Ltd* [2015] EWCA Civ 745 the lapse of time bar was developed further. The case concerned the sale of a car described by the seller as 'brand new'. During the first year, various defects emerged and the seller arranged for some of these to be repaired. Eventually, a year after the purchase, the buyer wanted to reject the car. This was on the basis of a breach of the quality obligation from the Sale of Goods Act 1979, which applied to consumer sales at the time. A legal dispute then followed during which documents were revealed showing the true background of the car. While it had not been registered before the sale, the car sold had not been 'brand new' and, at the time of the sale, it had in fact been two years old. In addition, it had been involved in an accident and had been repaired. In the light of this information, the buyer relied on misrepresentation to rescind the contract. At that stage, three years had passed since the sale. However, the Court of Appeal upheld the previous decision, recognising that in principle rescission remained a possible remedy.

On this issue, Longmore LJ referred to the reasoning from *Leaf v international Galleries* and stated:

[34] It must, moreover, be remembered that *Leaf* was decided well before the Misrepresentation Act was passed. It must be doubtful whether since the enactment of s 1 it is still good law that a representor should be in no worse position than if the representation had become a term of the contract, particularly if the representor takes no steps to prove that he was not negligent.

[35] In all the circumstances, it does not seem to me that lapse of time on its own can be a bar to rescission in this case. As [the first instance judge] pointed out, the ground on which rescission became available only became known to Mr Salt on disclosure of documents. Most of the subsequent delay has been due to the litigation process and Stratstone's wrongful refusal to take the car back and return the price.

This reasoning casts some doubt on *Leaf v International Galleries*. Longmore LJ referred to the Misrepresentation Act 1967. This came after *Leaf v International Galleries*. Section 1 says that rescission is an option where the misrepresentation has become a term of the contract. This was used to question whether the availability of termination (rejection) for breach should influence rescission. The point was that the legislation does not place a higher priority on breach. In other words, it does not assign a greater importance to remedies following a breach. Longmore LJ used this as a basis for a suggestion on the availability of rescission. According to the judgment, it was likely that the right to reject had not been lost. However, Longmore LJ added that rescission should be available even if the right to terminate for breach is not available.

When Longmore LJ considered the issue of lapse [at para. 35], it was based on the time at which the misrepresentation was discovered. The rest of the delay had been due to the conduct of the seller.

In the other judgment, Roth J made a more specific comments indicating how the time period is worked out for negligent misrepresentation. Time starts when the misrepresentation *should* have been discovered.

On the lapse of time bar, Longmore LJ had said that it was not 'on its own' a bar in this case. The meaning of this statement was explained by Roth J as follows:

[43] As Longmore LJ has explained, rescission for misrepresentation is an equitable remedy . . ., an objection to rescission must therefore rest on an equitable basis. Accordingly, it is something of a misnomer to say that rescission may be barred by lapse of time. It is only the lapse of a reasonable time such that it would be inequitable in all the circumstances to grant rescission which constitutes a bar to the remedy.

The point is that the bar to rescission does not rest solely on the time period that has passed. Instead, the relevant consideration is whether it would be unfair to grant rescission in view of the time that has passed. The decision will then be based on the facts of the case.

KEY POINTS

Following the discovering of a fraudulent misrepresentation, a lapse of time might be evidence of the representee affirming the contract.

For non-fraudulent misrepresentations, lapse of time will influence a wider question as to whether it is unfair to allow rescission.

13.5.3 Where 'Restitution' Is Not Possible

Restitution means that the parties are restored to their pre-contract position, a remedy the cases refer to using the Latin term *restitution in integrum*. Therefore, in a contract for the sale of goods, the buyer returns the goods and the seller returns the payment. Of course, sometimes, absolute restitution is impossible. It might be that what has been bought has changed. That could be because the goods are now damaged, destroyed or even consumed. Some goods perish naturally, and food is a good example. Consider a contract relating to the sale of a building. It could have been badly damaged.

restitution in integrum
is a Latin term to describe the restoration of the original position.

Alternatively, it could have changed so much that it is no longer what was sold. In these circumstances, the representor will argue that restitution is impossible. To allow rescission could also seem unfair to the representor. For example, the innocent party may have already had some benefit from the contract. To then refund all the money would seem too generous and would mean they have had something for nothing. For that reason, the impossibility bar serves to prevent the unjust enrichment of the innocent party. That was a point observed in *Halpern v Halpern* [2006] EWHC 1728 (Comm). There, Carnwath LJ cited Treitel's *Law of Contract*, stating:

> the essential point is that the representee should not be unjustly enriched at the representor's expense; that the representor should not be prejudiced is a secondary consideration.

Then there is the position of the innocent party. If strict restitution of the original position is required, it could be unfair to the innocent party. Often the misrepresentation is only discoverable from the use of goods, but goods often change in some way after use. At the very least, they could be worth slightly less. It would seem harsh for the innocent party to be locked into a contract following such a minor change, especially since the contract was entered into as a result of a misrepresentation. The point is that there are good reasons on both sides for the impossibility bar to be applied with some flexibility.

The courts showed early signs of a more flexible approach in *Erlanger v New Sombrero Phosphate Co* (1878) 3 App Cas 1218. This case concerned a contract for the sale of a phosphate mine. Following the sale, the mine was then worked, which meant that some of its content had been extracted and sold. The buyer then claimed to rescind the contract following a breach of a fiduciary duty. Such an action has its origins in equity, just like the remedy of rescission. Since some of the mine had been worked, strict restitution was not exactly possible, but the court allowed rescission. That meant the buyer had the money returned and the partially worked mine was returned to the seller, but that was not all. In addition, the buyer had to account for the profit made from working the mine. On this point, Lord Blackburn observed:

> [Equity could] . . . take accounts of profits, and make allowance for deterioration. And I think the practice has always been for a Court of Equity to give this relief whenever . . . it can do what is practically just, though it cannot restore the parties precisely to the state they were in before the contract.

Such an account of profit meant the buyer was not unjustly enriched. Likewise, the seller's original financial position was restored. This was an outcome based on what was '*practically just*'.

The approach of accounting for the benefit gained is often described as 'counter-restitution'. It was explained and applied more recently in *Salt v Stratstone* [2015]. As well as lapse of time, the seller argued that restitution was impossible on two grounds. The first ground was that the car had been registered and so it was different to the unregistered car sold. Longmore LJ rejected this argument outright because otherwise it would be impossible to rescind whenever a car is falsely described as new. According to Longmore LJ, '*registration is a legal concept which does not change the physical entity that a car is*'.

The second ground was that the returned car would be worth a lot less because the value of new cars depreciates significantly over the first year. In addition, the car had done 15,000 miles which made it different in terms of wear and tear, but that 15,000 miles also represented use or 'enjoyment' which the buyer had got out of the car. In response, Longmore LJ cited a range of judicial comments from previous cases, in particular, the comments of Lord Blackburn from *Erlanger* and Carnwath LJ from *Halpern* were cited. Longmore LJ then observed:

> [22] But neither depreciation [nor] intermittent enjoyment should, in my view, be regarded as reasons for saying restitution is impossible. It has always been the case that a court of equity, contemplating rescission, could order an account and/or an inquiry to determine the terms on which restitution should be made, see Chitty, Contracts, 31st edition . . . and Cartwright, Misrepresentation, Mistake and Non-Disclosure (. . . 2012) . . .

➡ **CROSS-REFERENCE**

For the facts of *Salt v Stratstone* [2015] see 13.5.2.

[30] … Rescission is *prima facie* available if "practical justice" can be done. If "practical justice" requires a representor to be compensated for depreciation, it is for the representor so to assert and prove; likewise if the representor asserts that use of the car is to be taken into account, which may well be difficult if the car was as "troublesome" (to use Judge Harris's words) as this Cadillac was. The absence of evidence about depreciation or the value of the use of the car should not operate to the disadvantage of the representee who should never have been put in the position of having a troublesome old car rather than a brand new one.

The case does more than just confirm that there is flexibility in how the parties' original position can be restored. Instead, it encourages courts to make use of that flexibility to allow rescission to be a more realistic possibility.

 THINKING POINTS

While the approach of Longmore LJ might be said to make for greater fairness, could it also result in greater uncertainty?

Longmore LJ cited the cases demonstrating flexibility in relation to the impossibility bar. The key feature was Lord Blackburn's reference to the need for equity to reflect what is 'practically just'. This was taken as a basis for the application of impossibility bar. Consequently, some changes, depreciation, and even use, should not prevent rescission. Instead, such factors can be accounted for with what is essentially compensation to the representor.

The application of this flexibility resulted in the buyer receiving all of the money paid. This was because the seller had not proven that it should have been paid for the depreciation or beneficial use of the car. Of course, the seller did not make a case for such a payment because it relied on rescission being barred.

KEY POINTS

Rescission can be barred by impossibility, but a flexible approach is taken to identify such impossibility based on what is 'practically just'.

13.5.4 Third Party Rights Preventing Restitution

The effect of rescission is mutual restitution. In the context of goods, the money is returned to one party and the goods returned to the other party. But what if, before rescission is sought, the goods have been sold on? If those goods are now owned by someone else (a third party), they cannot be returned and, consequently, rescission will not be possible. Such third party rights would seem to be another example of a reason for restitution being impossible, and hence to fall under that bar. However, over the years, judges have tended to list third party rights as a separate fourth bar to rescission. The most recent example of that was Longmore LJ in *Salt v Stratstone*.

For a third party to own the goods, it is not simply a matter of the goods having been sold to that party. To be the new owner in law, the third party has to be a *bona fida* purchaser for value. Buying with value is a reference to consideration, whereas '*bona fide*' is a reference to the purchase being made in good faith. In other words, when buying the goods, the third party did not know of the misrepresentation. Following such a purchase, the third party will own the goods. At that point, the original owner would have no claim over the goods and, without a claim to the goods, rescission cannot take place.

A third party can acquire ownership after a misrepresentation because of two things. First, a misrepresentation only makes a contract voidable; and, when a contract is voidable (but not yet rescinded) the parties still have their rights arising from it. These rights include the right of ownership of the goods. The owner therefore has the right to sell the goods and pass on title/ownership as long as this happens before there has been notice of rescission. Secondly, when sold to a good faith buyer for value, that third party buyer becomes the new owner.

The main example of this kind of situation is *Lewis v Averay* [1972] 1 QB 198. Lewis advertised his car for sale and a fraudster then bought the car using a cheque with a false name. At the very least, this was a misrepresentation about the fraudster's ability to pay. Obviously, the cheque turned out to be useless and could not be cashed. Before the fraud was discovered, the fraudster sold the car to Averay and so the original owner brought an action to recover the car from him. To do so, Lewis had to rescind the contract with the fraudster. However, it was held that rescission was barred because Averay had become the new owner already. On that basis, Averay was entitled to keep the car.

Clearly, Averay's ownership was determined by the timing. He was the innocent third party buyer and bought the car *before* the original owner thought to rescind the contract with the fraudster. Consequently, at the time of the resale, the fraudster had ownership from the voidable contract (with the original owner) and such ownership could then be transferred. The timing and resulting consequences were different to *Car & universal Finance v Caldwell*. There, the original contract was rescinded *before* the resale to a *bona fide* purchaser.

→ CROSS-REFERENCE
The use of a false name can raise the question about whether there has been a mistake as to identity. For the law relating to such a mistake see 17.4.2.

→ CROSS-REFERENCE
For the facts of Car & Universal Finance [1965] see 13.4.2.

KEY POINTS

Following a misrepresentation, if the goods sold are owned by a third party, rescission is not possible. This usually happens where the goods are resold to a third party *before* the original owner has attempted to rescind.

In both *Lewis v Averay* and *Car v Universal Finance v Caldwell*, there were two innocent parties. There was the innocent original owner and the innocent third party. In such a situation, both innocent parties would want the goods, because the alternative is to sue the fraudster. Of course, that is usually a pointless action because the fraudster will be hard to find. Faced with two innocent parties, the outcome is based on the timing. The question to ask is simple: was the original contract still voidable at the time of the later resale? If it was, then the ownership could be passed on by the fraudster.

?!   THINKING POINTS

Would it be fairer for the innocent parties to split the value of the goods? Are there any potential practical problems associated with such an alternative?

13.5.5 Where Rescission Is Refused under the Misrepresentation Act 1967

So far, we have looked at the bars to rescission. These represent circumstances in which the innocent representee loses the right to rescind. When the bars do not apply, the right to rescind exists, but even where it does exist, the courts might have the power to refuse it.

The power to refuse rescission is from Section 2(2) of the Misrepresentation Act 1967. The entirety of section 2 concerns damages. Section 2(1) refers to damages for negligent misrepresentation. Section 2(2) is about damages being awarded instead of rescission. Our focus here is on the decision of the court to refuse rescission and award damages instead. The sub-section is actually expressed as one long sentence, but for convenience, we will view it in stages:

Subsection 2 starts with reference to its scope:

→ CROSS-REFERENCE

For the measure and availability of damages under s.2(2) see 13.10.

> (2) Where a person has entered into a contract after a misrepresentation has been made to him otherwise than fraudulently, and he would be entitled, by reason of the misrepresentation, to rescind the contract, . . .

The scope for s.2(2) is limited to non-fraudulent misrepresentations such as those made negligently or innocently. The sub-section goes on to define the court's ability to refuse rescission:

> . . . then, if it is claimed, in any proceedings arising out of the contract, that the contract ought to be or has been rescinded, the court or arbitrator may declare the contract subsisting and award damages in lieu of rescission, . . .

This refers to a power of the court to keep the contract alive and award damages instead of rescission. Finally, subsection 2 provides the basis or grounds for awarding damages instead of rescission:

> . . . if of opinion that it would be equitable to do so, having regard to the nature of the misrepresentation and the loss that would be caused by it if the contract were upheld, as well as to the loss that rescission would cause to the other party.

This means that judges can exercise the power to refuse rescission and award damages instead to achieve a fair outcome. In doing so, the judge has to consider the factors listed, which include the effect on each party.

The first factor is the nature of the misrepresentation and was the subject of *obiter* comments in *William Sindell plc v Cambridgeshire County Council* [1994] 1 WLR 1016. The case concerned the sale of land to build houses on. The defendant seller stated that they did not know of any rights or limits that might affect the use of the land. The land was then bought for £5m, but 18 months later there was a fall in property prices which resulted in the land being worth around £2m. The claimant builders then discovered a sewer under the land. That meant they could not build on a strip running across it. Naturally, the purchaser wanted to escape the contract (i.e. rescind it) because it was now worth £3m less than its original value. One of the key arguments was based on the misrepresentation about knowing of rights or limits on the use of the land. Ultimately, this point failed because it was held that the seller's statement was true. However, the Court of Appeal provided guidance on the exercise of the discretion under s.2(2).

Hoffman LJ said the first factor was about the importance of the misrepresentation to the transaction. On this, the statement in the case was classed as relatively minor. It would have cost £18,000 to correct the property to reflect the misrepresentation. That cost was minor given that the sale was for £5m.

The remaining factors concern the interests of the parties. The innocent representee would want to end the contract (because the land was now of considerably less value than it was when purchased), whereas the representor would want the contract to continue (because rescission would mean returning the purchase price). The judge has to then consider the two other factors from the sub-section. One factor is the loss to be suffered by the representee if the contract continues. That factor is then compared with the loss to the representor if rescission was allowed.

According to Hoffman LJ, s.2(2) assumes that the representee's 'loss' would be reflected in a damages award. Furthermore, the representor's loss from losing the contract would be the loss of the bargain. That then reveals the appropriate question to ask: is it fair to force the representee to continue the contract with compensation, or is it fairer to take away the representor's bargain?

According to Hoffman LJ, in this case, rescission would have required the seller to return £8m (the £5m plus interest) for land now worth £2m. For that reason, it was said that *if* there was a right to rescind, damages would have been awarded instead. The reason for the s.2(2) power was explained by Hoffman LJ as follows:

> ...The Law Reform Committee Report makes it clear that s.2(2) was enacted because it was thought that it might be a hardship to the representor to be deprived of the whole benefit of the bargain on account of a minor misrepresentation ...

The point is that a minor misrepresentation would cause loss to the innocent representee, but as a minor statement, it might be fairer to compensate for the loss rather than allow rescission. The alternative would be to impose greater losses on the representor by taking away what was gained from the deal. Such losses might well be out of proportion to the effect of the statement.

Consider the sale of a vaping lounge for £500,000. The seller innocently states that it is fully equipped to provide wi-fi throughout, a statement which turns out to be a misrepresentation. It might cost just £100 to set up the wi-fi, and so it would disproportionate to allow the buyer to end the contract. The seller would have to return the price, i.e. £500,000, a lot of which may be profit from the deal. It would be better or fairer to simply require the seller to pay £100 in damages for the wi-fi to be installed.

?! THINKING POINTS

Ordinarily, by continuing the contract, the innocent party would have compensation for loss caused by the false statement. With that in mind, why would the innocent party still want to rescind?

The power in s.2(2) will also enable a court to prevent the representee from escaping a bad bargain. This was also clearly in the judges' minds in *William Sindell*. Through reasons completely separate from the false statement, something bought, such as property, may not be worth as much as it appeared to be when it was originally purchased. Alongside compensation for losses caused by the misrepresentation, the representee may well then want to escape the greater loss resulting from the bad bargain. Likewise, the same would apply where the bargain is 'bad' because there are better deals elsewhere. For example, the value of property bought may be the same as it was, but there is a superior property on sale elsewhere for the same price. In these sorts of circumstances, s.2(2) will prevent the innocent representee relying on a minor, technical misrepresentation to escape from the contract. Instead, the innocent party can be compensated for the loss caused by the misrepresentation only, but the contract will remain.

13.6 Introduction to Damages for Misrepresentation

Rescission is the basic remedy following an actionable misrepresentation, and it applies to all types of misrepresentation. Of course, it can be barred. Alternatively, in some circumstances, it can be refused by the judge.

As a separate remedy, damages are available for fraudulent and negligent misrepresentations. Such damages will serve to compensate the innocent party for losses caused by entering into the contract. There is no right to such compensation following a mere innocent misrepresentation, although a judge can award damages instead of rescission. That can happen when a misrepresentation is negligent or innocent under the 1967 Act, as we have seen. In that limited context, it can be said that it is possible to have damages for an innocent misrepresentation.

In this section, we look at the damages remedy for each type of misrepresentation. For each type, it is important to know how the damages award is measured; the relevant remoteness rule that applies to limit the award; and anything that can reduce the amount to be awarded. We will see that the amount of damages awarded will depend on the type of misrepresentation. From the common law, there is the traditional fraudulent misrepresentation claim under the tort of deceit. Originally, this was the only ground for damages, with the common law alternative of innocent misrepresentation resulting in the possibility of rescission only. Then, in 1963, negligent mis-statement under the tort of negligence was recognised. The Misrepresentation 1967 Act then introduced another version of negligent misrepresentation. In addition, the Act introduced the possibility of innocent misrepresentation resulting in damages instead of rescission.

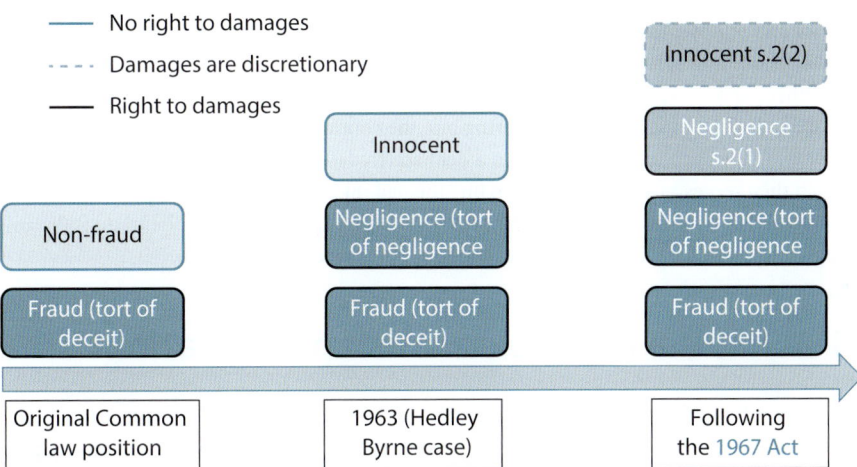

Figure 13.2
The basis, development, and availability of damages for misrepresentation

Damages arising from each of these types of misrepresentation will vary. There are variations in the way damages are measured as well as different remoteness rules. On a practical level there are different procedural aspects to the respective claims. One example is about proof, and who has to prove what. Another issue is about when damages can be reduced to reflect the innocent party's degree of fault. We will see that such variations are very important because, in practice, the representee will choose what claim to rely on. A fraudulent misrepresentation does not necessarily mean that the representee claimant must bring an action for fraudulent misrepresentation. Likewise, following a negligent statement, the representee does not necessarily have to bring a claim for negligent misrepresentation. Instead, the representee will bring the claim that suits the circumstances and reflects their objectives in seeking damages.

Consider the example of a fraudulent misrepresentation. When that happens, the representee could claim damages for negligent misrepresentation. That might seem strange, but we need to appreciate the broader connection between the types of false statement. The types represent different levels of seriousness and wrongdoing. It means the fraudulent statement (like a deliberate lie) will certainly be enough for a negligence action. Such a negligence action is based on a statement being made with no reasonable grounds for believing it and we will see there are some good reasons for such a strategy. In contrast, we will see some advantages in relying on an action for fraud rather than an action for other types of misrepresentation.

We start with fraudulent misrepresentation and will explore it with some detail. Such detail is necessary to provide a foundation and a point of comparison to the other types of claim.

13.7 Fraudulent Misrepresentation

This action might not be the obvious first choice for a claimant because it is very difficult to prove and can be an expensive action. However, we will see that in certain circumstances it could be the best claim to make. Usually, that is the case because of the potentially serious limits that apply to the other types of claim.

Fraudulent misrepresentation is an action based on the tort of deceit. This common law tort covers fraud generally, and that includes losses from fraudulent misrepresentations. It means that the damages for fraud are based on the tort of deceit rather than in contract. The fact that the action is not based on the contract is significant. It means there is no need for a contractual relationship between the representor and representee. For that reason, the representee can claim against a fraudulent third party. That will be useful when a third party fraudulently induced the representee to enter into a contract with another party.

Consider the sale of a nail salon. Before entering into the contract, the buyer decides to contact the seller's accountant. The accountant then makes a deliberately false statement about the value of the business which then serves as an inducement to buy the nail salon. The resulting contract is between the buyer and seller. The seller is of course, completely innocent. However, when the fraud is discovered, the buyer can claim damages from the accountant if the fraud can be proven.

13.7.1 What Is a Fraudulent Misrepresentation?

The definition of a fraudulent misrepresentation is from the House of Lords case of *Derry v Peek* (1889) 14 App Cas 337. The case concerned a tram company and a statement in their company prospectus. They indicated that their trams had the right to use steam power, whereas others were just horse powered. This representation was not accurate because, while steam power could be used, it required permission from the Board of Trade (which the representor assumed was merely a formality). The representee bought shares in the company based on this statement. When the company applied to use steam power, the application was rejected and, later, the company went into liquidation. The representee then relied on fraudulent misrepresentation against the directors. The House of Lords held that the statement was not fraudulent because, on the evidence, there was no dishonesty; the company had believed that permission was just a formality. On that basis, the false statement was one that had been made without reasonable care, but this fell short of the definition of fraud.

In arriving at this decision, Lord Herschell cited a number of previous judicial statements about fraudulent misrepresentation. Based on these statements, the judgment went on define a fraudulent misrepresentation in the following way:

> First, in order to sustain an action of deceit, there must be proof of fraud, and nothing short of that will suffice. Secondly, fraud is proved when it is shewn that a false representation has been made (1) knowingly, or (2) without belief in its truth, or (3) recklessly, careless whether it be true or false. Although I have treated the second and third as distinct cases, I think the third is but an instance of the second, for one who makes a statement under such circumstances can have no real belief in the

truth of what he states. To prevent a false statement being fraudulent, there must, I think, always be an honest belief in its truth. And this probably covers the whole ground, for one who knowingly alleges that which is false, has obviously no such honest belief. Thirdly, if fraud be proved, the motive of the person guilty of it is immaterial. It matters not that there was no intention to cheat or injure the person to whom the statement was made.

This idea of fraud was then contrasted with statements that we would now call negligent. These were referred to as statements made with a lack of care or having no reasonable grounds:

In my opinion making a false statement through want of care falls far short of, and is a very different thing from, fraud, and the same may be said of a false representation honestly believed though on insufficient grounds . . .

Lord Herschell also addressed another type of fraud. This is where a representor deliberately turns a blind eye to the facts revealing the truth:

. . . if I thought that a person making a false statement had shut his eyes to the facts, or purposely abstained from inquiring into them, I should hold that honest belief was absent, and that he was just as fraudulent as if he had knowingly stated that which was false.

This case is the leading one on the definition of fraudulent misrepresentation. It is always cited when a court has to decide if a statement was fraudulent. The test is applied objectively based on what the representor appeared to know. In *Versloot Dredging BV v HDI Gerling Industrie Versicherung AG (The DC Merwestone)* [2013] EWHC 1666 (Comm) Popplewell J confirmed that there is no separate requirement of dishonest intent because the dishonesty is established by meeting the definition provided by Lord Herschell, which includes 'having no real belief' in the statement's truth. The judgments of the Court of Appeal and Supreme Court that followed did not question the approach adopted by Popplewell J.

In *Derry v Peek*, Lord Herschell was very clear about the difference between fraud and what is now called negligence. However, the distinction was raised much later in *Thomas Witter Ltd v TBP industries Ltd* [1996] 2 All ER 573, where the scope of the third category of '*recklessly careless whether it be true*,' was questioned. First, it has the word 'careless,' and negligence is a failure to take reasonable care. Secondly, 'reckless' is ordinarily seen as another word for careless. In response, Jacob J took the opportunity to expand on the difference between recklessness for fraud, and mere negligence.

Jacob J explained recklessness for fraud as being where a party indicates that a statement is true even though that party had no idea if the statement is true or not. That has an aspect of dishonesty, which is what fraudulent misrepresentation is about. In contrast, a negligent statement is made with no reasonable grounds for believing it to be true, but it is a statement that the representor appears to believe as having been true at the time. With such negligent statements, it can be said that the representor ought to have known the truth by being more careful. Put another way, a reasonable person would have been more careful, for example, by performing some checks to find support for the statement before making it.

13.7.2 The Assessment of Damages

The damages award for fraud is very different to the award for breach for contract. Damages under the tort of deceit are assessed in a very generous way. This is because such an assessment is not just compensatory; it is also designed to discourage fraud.

The key case on the way such damages are measured is *Doyle v Olby (Ironmongers) Ltd* [1969] 2 QB 158. This case concerned the sale of a shop, where the seller had falsely stated that all of the sales were 'over the counter'—meaning sales were made in the shop. The truth was that over half of the sales were from the seller travelling around two days a week to get orders. After buying the business, the buyer suffered serious losses and then brought an action for fraudulent misrepresentation. The trial judge awarded £1500, which reflected the difference in value or, alternatively, the amount to cover the cost of a traveller. Either way, it was the contract measure of damages and was aimed at putting the buyer in the position he would have been in had the statement been true. On appeal, the award was changed to £5500.

In the lead judgment, Lord Denning MR explained the basis of the larger award.

> In so doing, he treated the representation as if it were a contractual promise, that is, as if there were a contractual term to the effect "The trade is all over the counter. There is no need to employ a traveller." I think it was the wrong measure. Damages for fraud and conspiracy are assessed differently from damages for breach of contract.
>
> . . .
>
> On principle the distinction seems to be this: in contract, the defendant has made a promise and broken it. The object of damages is to put the plaintiff in as good a position, as far as money can do it, as if the promise had been performed. In fraud, the defendant has been guilty of a deliberate wrong by inducing the plaintiff to act to his detriment. The object of damages is to compensate the plaintiff for all the loss he has suffered, so far, again, as money can do it. In contract, the damages are limited to what may reasonably be supposed to have been in the contemplation of the parties. In fraud, they are not so limited. The defendant is bound to make reparation for all the actual damages directly flowing from the fraudulent inducement. The person who has been defrauded is entitled to say;
>
> "I would not have entered into this bargain at all but for your representation. Owing to your fraud, I have not only lost all the money I paid you, but, what is more, I have been put to a large amount of extra expense as well and suffered this or that extra damages."
>
> All such damages can be recovered: and it does not lie in the mouth of the fraudulent person to say that they could not reasonably have been foreseen. For instance, in this very case Mr. Doyle has not only lost the money which he paid for the business, which he would never have done if there had been no fraud: he put all that money in and lost it; but also he has been put to expense and loss in trying to run a business which has turned out to be a disaster for him. He is entitled to damages for all his loss, subject, of course to giving credit for any benefit that he has received.

The contract measure of damages was firmly rejected. It is not enough for the representee to be put in the position it would have been in had the statement been true. Rather, they are to be compensated for all the losses suffered as a result of entering into the contract. In other words, the contract measure compensates for *expectation* loss, whereas the fraud measure compensates for *reliance* losses—those which arose from relying on the statement. In the case, those losses included all of the money paid for the business and all related expenses. From the resulting figure, the court deducted any money gained, like the proceeds from reselling the business.

→ CROSS-REFERENCE
for the discussion of the remoteness rule for breach of contract see 10.3.

The remoteness rule for fraud is a very generous one. The fraudulent defendant is liable for *all direct loss*, so unlike the contract test, the award is not limited by what was contemplated at the time. Likewise, damages are not limited to reasonably foreseeable losses like in the tort of negligence. Instead, for fraud, damages are assessed irrespective of foreseeability. Such a generous remoteness rule is justified by the need to discourage fraud. On this point in *Smith New Court Ltd v Scrimgeour Vickers (Asset Management) Ltd* [1997] AC 254, Lord Steyn observed:

> . . . Such a policy of imposing more stringent remedies on an intentional wrongdoer serves two purposes. First it serves a deterrent purpose in discouraging fraud . . . Secondly, as between the fraudster and the innocent party, moral considerations militate in favour of requiring the fraudster to bear the risk of misfortunes directly caused by his fraud.

In addition, it is only fair that the victim of fraud should not have to bear any of the losses caused. That means all of the loss should be on the fraudulent representor.

■ The measure of damages for fraud is based on losses incurred from relying on the statement.

■ The remoteness rule is generous, because damages cover all losses, irrespective of foreseeability.

13.7.3 The Point in Time to Assess the Loss Suffered

The overall approach adopted in *Doyle v Olby* was approved by the House of Lords in *Smith New Court Ltd v Scrimgeour Vickers (Asset Management) Ltd* [1997] AC 254. A key issue in the case was the point in time that the loss was to be assessed. The case concerned the sale of shares in a company called Farranti. Following a fraudulent misrepresentation by the seller (a bank), the shares were bought for around £23m. A few months passed and then the shares unexpectedly suffered a huge loss in value as a result of Farrenti being the victim of serious fraud. The innocent (representee) buyer then had to sell their shares for around £11m, and so they brought an action for fraudulent misrepresentation against the seller.

The Court of Appeal assessed the loss at the time of the sale. At that time, the buyer had paid around £1.2m above the true value of the shares. On that basis, the buyer was awarded that amount. However, the House of Lords disagreed and decided that the time of the assessment is not always the time of the contract coming into effect. What mattered was that the representee was compensated for all loss suffered. On that basis, the representee was entitled to the difference between the price paid and the £11m.

The lead judgment cited *Doyle v Olby* with approval. Lord Brown-Wilkinson also stated some principles to be followed when awarding damages for fraudulent misrepresentation:

> In sum, in my judgment the following principles apply in assessing the damages payable where the plaintiff has been induced by a fraudulent misrepresentation to buy property:
>
> 1. The defendant is bound to make reparation for all the damage directly flowing from the transaction;
>
> 2. Although such damage need not have been foreseeable, it must have been directly caused by the transaction;
>
> 3. In assessing such damage, the plaintiff is entitled to recover by way of damages the full price paid by him, but he must give credit for any benefits which he has received as a result of the transaction;
>
> 4. As a general rule, the benefits received by him include the market value of the property acquired as at the date of acquisition; but such general rule is not to be inflexibly applied where to do so would prevent him obtaining full compensation for the wrong suffered;
>
> 5. Although the circumstances in which the general rule should not apply cannot be comprehensively stated, it will normally not apply where either (a) the misrepresentation has continued to operate after the date of the acquisition of the asset so as to induce the plaintiff to retain the asset or (b) the circumstances of the case are such that the plaintiff is, by reason of the fraud, locked into the property.
>
> 6. In addition, the plaintiff is entitled to recover consequential losses caused by the transaction;
>
> 7. The plaintiff must take all reasonable steps to mitigate his loss once he has discovered the fraud.

The actual time at which the loss is to be assessed was addressed at points (4) and (5). Generally, it is the date of the contract. However, that does not apply where it means the innocent party would not be compensated fully for the loss suffered. In some cases, the loss would have to be assessed based on a later date. Lord Brown-Wilkinson then explained when that would be the case. For example, the fraud may have induced the innocent party to hold on to the thing bought. In addition, the fraud might mean that the innocent party is 'locked' into the thing bought. In such circumstances, the innocent party is unable to, and is not expected to, resell earlier.

KEY POINTS

A flexible approach is adopted to the date of the assessment of loss to ensure that the innocent party is compensated fully.

13.7.4 Claims for Lost Profits

Doyle v Olby concerned the sale of a business following a fraudulent misrepresentation. The direct losses were claimed and awarded. However, the representee did not claim for the profits that could have been made. Such a claim is possible, but we have to remember that the claim is in the tort of deceit. That means the damages are based on the reliance measure and so any lost profit claimed has to be a result of entering into the contract. It is not based on the profit that would have been made had the statement been true. The approach to such a claim can be seen from *East v Maurer* [1991] 1 WLR 461.

East v Maurer concerned the sale of a hair salon. The seller was an internationally experienced, popular hair dresser who had two salons in Bournemouth and decided to sell one. During negotiations with the (claimant) buyer, the seller made a fraudulent statement. He said that he would not be working at the other salon except in emergencies. To be more convincing, he added that he planned to open a salon in Switzerland. After buying the business, the number of customers fell significantly. It turned out that the seller was working full-time at the other local salon. Eventually, the representee sold the business for a lot less than she had paid and then brought an action for fraudulent misrepresentation. The judge awarded the price paid for the salon minus the sum received from the resale. In addition, he awarded damages to reflect business expenses, trading losses and even disappointment and inconvenience. Finally, the judge awarded £15,000 in lost profits which was the amount of profit the buyer could have expected to make from the business if the seller had not been competing with it at his remaining salon. The seller then appealed against the lost profit award.

In the lead judgment of the Court of Appeal, Beldam LJ agreed that a loss of profit was a direct loss suffered but disagreed with the way the award had been calculated. It was observed that the £15,000 profit was what the buyer had expected to make from the business for the time she had it. In other words, it was the amount that should have been earned if the seller's representation had been true. Such a measure was recognised as the traditional expectation measure from contract law (i.e. the loss of bargain). Instead, lost profit had to be assessed to reflect the loss suffered from relying on the statement (i.e. the reliance measure). Had the statement not been made, the buyer would have bought a different salon for a similar value. The buyer would have then made profits from that business. According to Beldam LJ, it was the profit from this alternative (hypothetical) business that the buyer had lost and, on that basis, the lost profit was reduced to £10,000.

13.7.5 The Duty of the Innocent Party to Mitigate the Loss

→ CROSS-REFERENCE
On the duty to mitigate in breach of contract claims see 10.4.

In *Doyle v Olby*, Lord Denning MR acknowledged the duty of the claimant to mitigate the loss:

> There is nothing to be taken off in mitigation: for there is nothing more that he could have done to reduce his loss. He did all that he could reasonably be expected to do.

The duty to mitigate is relevant because the claim is for loss suffered rather than an action for the agreed price or a debt. This means the innocent party has to act reasonably to reduce the loss. Likewise, the loss ought not to be unreasonably increased. A failure to follow the duty to mitigate would limit the loss that can be reflected in damages.

Lord Brown-Wilkinson expanded on the duty in the *Smith New Court* case stating:

> Finally, it must be emphasised that the principle in *Doyle v. Olby*, strict though it is, still requires the plaintiff to mitigate his loss once he is aware of the fraud. So long as he is not aware of the fraud, no question of a duty to mitigate can arise. But once the fraud has been discovered, if the plaintiff is not locked into the asset and the fraud has ceased to operate on his mind, a failure to take reasonable steps to sell the property may constitute a failure to mitigate his loss requiring him to bring the value of the property into account as at the date when he discovered the fraud or shortly thereafter.

The point here is that the duty to mitigate applies when fraud is discovered. If the duty is not followed, the loss is assessed at the date of discovering the fraud, and hence before the loss was increased.

The approach to mitigation was followed by the Court of Appeal in *Downs v Chappell* [1997] WLR 426. This case concerned the sale of a bookshop for £120,000 after the seller made a fraudulent misrepresentation about the profit being made. Sometime after the sale, the representee (buyer) discovered the fraud and decided to sell the business. Initially, the representee rejected two offers of £76,000, hoping for a better price, but eventually the business was sold for £60,000. The representee then claimed the difference between the price he paid and the lower price he sold the bookshop for. However, the Court of Appeal awarded less as it was felt that when the fraud was discovered, the offers to buy should have been accepted. On the representee's decision to reject the initial offers, Hobhouse LJ observed:

> . . . it was their choice, freely made, and they cannot hold the defendants responsible if the choice has turned out to have been commercially unwise. They were no longer acting under the influence of the defendants' representations.

On that basis, the award was based on the difference between the price paid and the offers rejected. This approach means that after buying something, if a fraudulent misrepresentation is discovered, it is better to accept the first reasonable offer. Otherwise, one might be seen as not having acted reasonably to reduce one's loss.

13.7.6 Contributory Negligence

Contributory negligence happens when the representee is partly at fault for the loss. Where the liability is for loss caused by negligence, the Contributory Negligence Act 1945 applies. The Act allows for the damages to be reduced in order to reflect the degree of fault on the part of the claimant. We can recall that the Act may also apply to damages for breach of contract in certain circumstances.

→ CROSS-REFERENCE
For the discussion of contributory negligence and its application to damages following a breach see 10.2.

In cases of fraud, no such deduction is made. The point was made by Mummery J in *Alliance and Leicester Building Society v Edgestop Ltd* [1993] 1 WLR 1462. It was further confirmed directly by the House of Lords in *Standard Chartered Bank v Pakistan National Shipping Corporation (No2)* [2002] UKHL 43. The reasoning was based on two factors. Firstly, it did not matter if the representee could have discovered the truth before entering the contract. This point was clear from early cases like *Edgington v Fitzmaurice* and *Redgrave v Hurd*, and is justified on policy grounds to discourage fraud.

The second factor related to the interpretation of the Act. Essentially, it was said that the Act did not apply to all common law claims. Instead, it only applies to losses caused by 'fault'. Such 'fault' is defined in the Act as negligence. On that basis, the reduction from the Act could not apply to claims based on fraud.

13.8 Negligent Mis-statement (under the Tort of Negligence)

The case of *Donoghue v Stevenson* [1932] AC 562 famously recognised a general principle of negligence in tort. Under the principle, a negligent party is not liable to just anyone. Instead, that party can only be liable to anyone to whom they owe a *duty of care*. In the early days, the test for a duty of care was a simple one; such a duty was owed to anyone that could be harmed as a reasonably foreseeable consequence of the negligent act. Consequently, as in the case of *Donoghue v Stevenson*, a manufacturer owes a duty of care to the final consumer because, objectively, a consumer can be harmed by its negligence. Since that landmark case, the test has developed additional requirements. The tort of negligence is a huge area of law that developed very quickly but here, we are concerned with its application to negligently-made false statements.

13.8.1 The Recognition of Mis-statement under the Tort of Negligence

Initially, the tort of negligence applied to acts of negligence causing physical harm. However, it was extended to negligently-made false statements causing financial loss in *Hedley Byrne & Co Ltd v Heller & Partners Ltd* [1964] AC 465. The relevant point for our purposes is that such statements can give rise to the formation of contracts. The facts of the case provide a helpful example.

The claiments (Hedley) were advertising agents and a customer, Easipower Ltd, placed an order for TV and newspaper advertising. Before booking advertising space, Hedley wanted to check that Easipower had the ability to pay. To do so, they instructed their bank to get a report from Easipower's bank, Heller. Heller sent a letter which said 'without responsibility', Easipower were good for business. Relying on that statement, Hedley booked and paid for advertising space, the idea being that Easipower would then pay Hedley later. However, before paying the outstanding £17,000 they owed, Easipower went into liquidation and so Hedley sued Heller in the tort of negligence for the loss suffered—arguing that Heller's statement that Easipower was good for business had been negligently made.

The claim was based on the loss resulting from Heller's negligent statement. Since the case was about an extension to the tort of negligence, it is not surprising that it got to the House of Lords. In terms of the decision, Heller was not liable. That was because the statement was made 'without responsibility'. Such a disclaimer served as an exemption clause, excluding liability. However, the real significance of the case is to do with the scope of negligence. The House of Lords confirmed that the tort of negligence applied to negligent statements.

Lord Morris explained concisely the basis of the liability for negligent statements:

> . . . I consider that it follows and that it should now be regarded as settled that if someone possessed of a special skill undertakes, quite irrespective of contract, to apply that skill for the assistance of another person who relies upon such skill, a duty of care will arise. The fact that the service is to be given by means of or by the instrumentality of words can make no difference. Furthermore, if in a sphere in which a person is so placed that others could reasonably rely upon his judgment or his skill or upon his ability to make careful inquiry, a person takes it upon himself to give information or advice to, or allows his information or advice to be passed on to, another person who, as he knows or should know, will place reliance upon it, then a duty of care will arise.
>
> . . . [T]he bank . . ., by the words which they employed, effectively disclaimed any assumption of a duty of care. They stated that they only responded to the inquiry on the basis that their reply was without responsibility. If the inquirers chose to receive and act upon the reply they cannot disregard the definite terms upon which it was given . . . the words employed were apt to exclude any liability for negligence.

The case confirmed that the tort of negligence could apply to statements causing financial loss. For liability, a duty of care has to be established between the two parties. A duty of care can arise where:

- The maker of a statement has special knowledge or skill;

- Objectively, the statement would be relied upon by the other party (meaning that the other party would reasonably rely on it);

- It is reasonably foreseeable (to the representor) that its statement will be relied upon by the other party;

- And, arising from later cases, an assumption of responsibility (*White v Jones* [1995] 2 AC 207; *Henderson v Merritt Syndicates Ltd* [1995] 2 AC 145 and *Spring v Guardian Assurance plc* [1995] 2 AC 296).

The next question is simply whether that duty of care has been breached. A negligently prepared statement will be sufficient for a breach.

On the facts, Heller would have owed such a duty of care to Hedley and this would have been breached by the negligent statement. However, there was no liability because of the disclaimer. That served to prevent the duty of care having been assumed by Heller.

This extension of negligence has resulted in the evolution of a large area of law mainly because of a key function of this liability. It does not rely on a contractual relationship between the claimant and defendant. Instead, all that is required is a duty of care to be owed by the representor to the party relying on them. This means that, following a negligent misstatement, the *Hedley Byrne* principle is the only option for damages if the parties do not have a contract. It is this principle that imposes liability on a referee who negligently writes a job reference that results in a loss to an employer who relied on it, for example.

13.8.2 Liability in Negligence between Contractual Parties

The *Hedley Byrne* principle can also apply between parties that go on to enter a contract and so the liability can apply to a representor's pre-contractual statements to a representee. This was confirmed by the Court of Appeal in *Esso v Mardon* where Lord Denning MR explored negligence as an alternative claim for damages. On the existence of a duty of care between the contractual parties, Lord Denning MR observed:

> → CROSS-REFERENCE
> For the facts of *Esso v Mardon* [1976] see 13.1.2.

> It seems to me that *Hedley Byrne*, properly understood, covers this particular proposition: If a man, who has or professes to have special knowledge or skill, makes a representation by virtue thereof to another - be it advice, information or opinion - with the intention of inducing him to enter into a contract with him, he is under a duty to use reasonable care to see that the representation is correct, and that the advice, information or opinion is reliable.

The judgment then addressed how the duty would be breached:

> If he negligently gives unsound advice or misleading information or expresses an erroneous opinion, and thereby induces the other aide into a contract with him, he is liable in damages.

While *Hedley Byrne* can apply to contractual parties, it is no longer the only option following a negligent misrepresentation. Instead, when there is a contract between the parties, the representee can rely on the Misrepresentation Act 1967. The Act did not apply in *Esso* because the facts took place before the Act was in force. We will see that the Act has significant advantages for the innocent party. Under the Act, the damages award is more generous and, in addition, it is easier for the innocent party to establish liability.

With a claim based on the tort of negligence, the representee has to prove what is required, so it is for the representee to show that the duty of care existed. In addition, the representee has to prove there was negligence, which means proving that the statement was made without reasonable care. Usually that requires proof that the statement was not based on reasonable grounds and, in practice, this is difficult to provide.

13.8.3 The Assessment of Damages

Just like the tort of deceit, damages for negligence are based on the reliance measure, so the damages will be to compensate for losses caused by relying on the statement.

While the same reliance measure applies, the actual award in negligence will be limited in comparison to one arising from a claim in the tort of deceit. This is a result of the remoteness rule that applies to negligence generally, from *The Wagon Mound* [1961]. The negligent party is only liable for losses that were *reasonably foreseeable* at the time of making the statement. This test is not as strict as the one that applies to breach of contract claims but it is certainly more limited than the remoteness test for fraud. Liability for fraud is for all direct losses irrespective of foreseeability, whereas in negligence, losses that were not reasonably foreseeable cannot be claimed.

A further potential limit on damages for negligence is from the application of the contributory negligence principle. The Contributory Negligence Act 1945 was drafted to apply to claims in negligence. As a result, if the representee is partly at fault for their loss, damages will be reduced to reflect that degree of fault.

13.9 Negligent Misrepresentation under the Misrepresentation Act 1967

The 1967 Act is one of the shortest Acts of Parliament that you will come across, but we will see that the meaning of its key provisions has been the source of intense debate. The main feature of the Act is that it introduced its own version of negligent misrepresentation. It was not a response to the House of Lords decision in *Hedley Byrne*, since the origins of the Act were in the Law Reform Committee Report 1962, issued a year before the judgments in the case were delivered. Instead, the Act sits somewhat awkwardly alongside the decision in *Hedley Byrne*, providing another category of what is often called 'negligent misrepresentation'.

Our starting point is section 2 (1) of the Act, which states:

> 2   Damages for misrepresentation.
>
> (1) Where a person has entered into a contract after a misrepresentation has been made to him by another party thereto and as a result thereof he has suffered loss, then, if the person making the misrepresentation would be liable to damages in respect thereof had the misrepresentation been made fraudulently, that person shall be so liable notwithstanding that the misrepresentation was not made fraudulently, unless he proves that he had reasonable ground to believe and did believe up to the time the contract was made the facts represented were true.

The language could be a lot clearer. The fact that it is expressed as one sentence does not help either. It is useful to summarise the subsection as having four key points before exploring it is more detail:

■ Regarding its scope, it applies to the parties to a contract only.

■ It defines negligent misrepresentation as a false statement that is honest, but made with no reasonable grounds for believing it to be true.

- It reverses the burden of proof. It says it is for the maker of the statement to prove they were not negligent.
- On damages, the representor is liable as if he made the statement fraudulently, even though the statement was negligent.

13.9.1 Application to Contractual Parties

The sub-section applies to statements that took place between the two parties to a contract. This means the Act cannot be used following a negligent misrepresentation by a third party. This point was confirmed in *Taberna Europe CDO II plc v Selskabet af 1 September 2008 A/S (formerly Roskilde Bank A/S)* [2016] EWCA Civ 1262. We can recall that liability under the tort of negligence arises from a duty of care, and it does not rely on there being a contractual relationship. Consequently, just like in *Hedley Byrne* itself, the tort of negligence remains as a crucial potential avenue of claim against third parties. This is why the law relating to the *Hedley Byrne* principle continued to develop so much after the Act.

13.9.2 Negligent Misrepresentation Defined

We can see that there is no direct reference to 'negligence' in section 2. However, the application to negligence is clear when the sub-section is read as a whole. The liability is for a misrepresentation that is honest but made with no reasonable grounds for believing it. This is consistent with the comments made by Lord Herschall in *Derry v Peek* that referred to what became known as negligence.

→ CROSS-REFERENCE
For the comments by Lord Hershell see 13.7.1.

13.9.3 The Reversed Burden of Proof

This third point is very significant. The representee does not have to go through the trouble of proving negligence. Instead, the burden is on the representor, who has to prove that the statement was not negligent. To do so, the representor has to prove there were reasonable grounds for believing the statement made. This means that the representee has to prove that an actionable statement was made, but, after that, it is assumed that the statement was negligent. This approach is justified by the fact that it will be the representor who has access to all the facts relevant to the statement. That party is in a better position to disprove negligence than the representee is in to prove negligence. Negligence is disproved by showing reasonable grounds for making the statement. If that can be done, there is no liability under s.2(1).

   Disproving negligence can be a difficult task. The point is well illustrated by *Howard Marine and Dredging Co Ltd v Ogden & Sons (Excavations) Ltd* [1978] QB 574. This case concerned the hire of barges to move clay. The claimant barge owner made a misrepresentation about the how much the barges could carry. It was said that they could carry 1600 tonnes and this figure was based on the capacity stated in the Lloyd's Register. Lord Denning MR in his judgment referred to this register as the shipping industry 'bible'. However, the entry in the register was not correct and the barges could really only carry around 1055 tonnes. That was the figure indicated in the documents of the barges, written in German, but the representor preferred to rely on the Lloyd's Register. Six months after the contract, the defendant representee was sued for outstanding hire charges. The defendant then counter-claimed partly relying on s.2(1) of the Act. It was then for the claimant representor to prove reasonable grounds for having made the statement. On this issue, the majority of the Court of Appeal held that the representor had not shown reasonable grounds for making the statement. It was not enough to have relied on the register and ignored the other documents available. The dissenting judgment was by Lord Denning MR, who felt that the register was so important that it was reasonable to rely on it. In contrast, the majority felt it was not reasonable to rely on the register when the representor had documents indicating the truth. On that basis, reasonable grounds for making the statement had not been demonstrated. Following s.2(1) of the Act, this meant the representor was liable even though no actual negligence had been proven; it was just that it could not be disproven.

The case shows how difficult it can be for the maker of the statement to disprove negligence. In fact, for the majority, Bridge LJ expressed doubt as to whether the facts would have been enough to prove liability for negligence in tort. However, the court was compelled to conclude that the representor had made his statement negligently because of the way the burden of proof shifted as a result of the wording of the Act.

13.9.4 The Assessment of Damages under s.2(1): Measure and Remoteness

The final important point from s.2(1) relates to the way the damages award is to be measured and this aspect has been controversial. It says that the representor is liable as if the statement had been fraudulent. But the precise meaning of the sentence has been the subject of debate and severe criticism almost from the moment the Act was passed. The big questions raised by the wording were as follows:

- Does it mean the damages will be exactly the same as those for fraud? That would include the generous remoteness rule applied to losses resulting from fraud. Alternatively;

- is the wording used in s.2(1) simply a reference to the tort (reliance measure) rather than the contract (expectation) measure? If so, that would allow for the consistent tort of negligence remoteness rule to apply.

The leading case confirming the meaning of s.2(1) on damages is *Royscott Trust Ltd v Rogerson* [1991] 2 QB 297. The case concerned a finance agreement for the sale of a car. A customer agreed to buy a car and paid a deposit but the remaining amount was to be paid on hire purchase terms. That required the (motor dealer) seller to contract with the (claimant) finance company. This meant the finance company paid the seller the remaining balance for the car and, in return, the company would own the car and be repaid with instalments by the customer.

The customer paid some instalments and then wrongfully sold the car. The finance company then brought an action for the resulting loss. One of the grounds was misrepresentation by the seller brought under s.2(1) of the Act. It was based on the seller misrepresenting the amount of the deposit paid and price agreed with the customer. The finance company argued that if the true figures had been known, they would not have entered the finance agreement.

The judge held that the seller was liable for the misrepresentation. However, he only awarded the extra amount of money the finance company paid as a result of the misrepresentation. The finance company then appealed on the basis of the award. It was argued that the award did not reflect their real loss and, instead, they wanted the outstanding amount due for the car since they no longer had the car to recall and sell. The seller argued that this loss was too remote, because the customer failing to pay would be reasonably foreseeable whereas the loss from the (wrongful) sale by the customer was not foreseeable. That then meant the Court of Appeal had to decide on the measure of damages from s.2(1). If the full fraud measure applied, then the award could cover all losses irrespective of foreseeability. The Court of Appeal delivered a detailed judgment referring to the leading published views on s.2(1), but held that the fraud measure did indeed apply to s.2(1). That meant the seller was liable for all of the loss suffered by the finance company as a result of its reliance on the misrepresentation.

GUIDED CASE READING 13.1
Royscott Trust Ltd v Rogerson [1991] 2 QB 297

When reading the extracts of the judgment by Balcombe LJ, try to identify:

- the basis of the views expressed by academic commentators;
- the reason why Balcombe LJ decided the fraud measure had to apply.

. . . However, there is now a number of decisions which make it clear that the tortious measure of damages is the true one. Most of these decisions are at first instance and will be found in Chitty on Contracts, 26th ed. (1989), . . ., and in McGregor on Damages, 15th ed. (1988), . . . One at least, *Chesneau v. Interhome Ltd.* (1983) . . . is a decision of this court. The claim was one under section 2(1) of the Act of 1967 and the appeal concerned the assessment of damages.

. . .

In view of the wording of the subsection it is difficult to see how the measure of damages under it could be other than the tortious measure and, . . . that is now generally accepted. . . .

> At the outset Balcombe LJ made clear that the approach was definitely tortious in the sense that it was a reliance measure rather than the (contract) expectation measure. That at least got him half way, but the important question was whether the result was analogous to the tort of negligence or fraud.

The first main issue before us was: accepting that the tortious measure is the right measure, is it the measure where the tort is that of fraudulent misrepresentation, or is it the measure where the tort is negligence at common law? . . . In my judgment the wording of the subsection is clear: the person making the innocent misrepresentation shall be 'so liable,' i.e. liable to damages as if the representation had been made fraudulently. . . . This was the conclusion to which Walton J. came in *F. & B. Entertainments Ltd. v. Leisure Enterprises Ltd. (1976)* . . . See also the decision of Sir Douglas Frank Q.C., sitting as a High Court judge, *in McNally v. Welltrade International Ltd.* [1978] . . . In each of these cases the judge held that the basis for the assessment of damages under section 2(1) of the Act of 1967 is that established in *Doyle v. Olby* . . . This is also the effect of the judgment of Eveleigh L.J. in *Chesneau v. Interhome Ltd* . . . 'By "so liable" I take it to mean liable as he would be if the misrepresentation had been made fraudulently.'

> The answer to this, in his view, was clearly fraud, because the wording of the Act could not really be interpreted any other way. And this was supported by existing case law.

. . .

In Treitel, The Law of Contract, 7th ed. (1987), p. 278, he says: 'Where the action is brought under section 2(1) of the Misrepresentation Act, one possible view is that the deceit rule will be applied by virtue of the fiction of fraud. But the preferable view is that the severity of the deceit rule can only be justified in cases of actual fraud and that remoteness under section 2(1) should depend, as in actions based on negligence, on the test of foreseeability'.

The only authority cited in support of the 'preferable' view is *Shepheard v. Broome* [1904] A.C . . ., a case under section 38 of the Companies Act 1867, which provided that in certain circumstances a company director, although not in fact fraudulent, should be 'deemed to be fraudulent'. As Lord Lindley said, at p. 346: 'To be compelled by Act of Parliament to treat an honest man as if he were fraudulent is at all times painful,' but he went on to say:

'but the repugnance which is naturally felt against being compelled to do so will not justify your Lordships in refusing to hold the appellant responsible for acts for which an Act of Parliament clearly declares he is to be held liable'.

> The problem was that academic opinion was firmly to the contrary. While there was very little justification for it in the case law, most reaction to the Act had considered treating a negligent misrepresentor as though he had been fraudulent to be too harsh. However, the only case law that really spoke to this point was an old company law case which seemed to suggest that a statute must be interpreted literally even when it appears to impose the burden of fraud on somebody who has not actually behaved fraudulently. In other words, the wording of the Act had to be strictly applied even if it had a 'repugnant' outcome.

...

It seems to me that that case, far from supporting Professor Treitel's view, is authority for the proposition that we must follow the literal wording of section 2(1), even though that has the effect of treating, so far as the measure of damages is concerned, an innocent person as if he were fraudulent.

Chitty on Contracts, 26th ed. (1989), vol. 1, p. 293, para. 439, says: 'it is doubtful whether the rule that the plaintiff may recover even unforeseeable losses suffered as the result of fraud would be applied; it is an exceptional rule which is probably justified only in cases of actual fraud'.

No authority is cited in support of that proposition save a reference to the passage in Professor Treitel's book cited above.

Professor Furmston in Cheshire, Fifoot and Furmston's Law of Contract, 11th ed. (1986), p. 286, says: '...Though it would be quixotic to defend the drafting of the section, it is suggested that there is no such "fiction of fraud" since the section does not say that a negligent misrepresentor shall be treated for all purposes as if he were fraudulent. No doubt the wording seeks to incorporate by reference some of the rules relating to fraud but, for instance, nothing in the wording of the subsection requires the measure of damages for deceit to be applied to the statutory action'.

With all respect to the various learned authors whose works I have cited above, it seems to me that to suggest that a different measure of damage applies to an action for innocent misrepresentation under the section than that which applies to an action for fraudulent misrepresentation (deceit) at common law is to ignore the plain words of the subsection and is inconsistent with the cases to which I have referred.

> All of this meant that the 'plain' meaning of the section had to be given effect, and that meant the 'fiction of fraud' was the correct way to measure the damages.

Essentially, the Court of Appeal confirmed the following points about section 2(1) damages:

- The award is for loss caused by *entering* the contract. This is the reliance measure from tort.
- Liability is for all direct losses because it is based on the remoteness rule from the tort of deceit.

Because he cited academic commentary and dealt with the opinions of those scholars carefully and successfully, the decision of Balcombe LJ was well-reasoned and effectively put an end to the arguments about the meaning of s.2(1). The 'fiction of fraud' may indeed be a fiction but it is deemed to be what the Act seeks to achieve.

KEY POINTS

- Damages under section 2(1) of the Misrepresentation Act are based on the reliance measure used in tort.
- The generous remoteness rule from the tort of deceit applies to s.2(1).

The decision in *Royscot v Rogerson* continues to represent how s.2(1) should be applied. However, the decision did result in a lot of criticism. This was even acknowledged in *Smith New Court Securities* where Lord Steyn referred to s.2(1) and observed:

> ...the rather loose wording of the statute compels the court to treat a person who was morally innocent as if he was guilty of fraud...

He then made reference to an article by Professor Hooley ((1991) 107 LQR 547) which suggested that Parliament should change the wording because the Act treated 'an honest but foolish man as if he *were dishonest'*. However, the issue of damages under s.2(1) was not an issue in the case and so for that reason, Lord Steyn chose not to doubt the correctness of the decision in *Royscot*. Likewise, in *Yam Seng Pte Ltd v International Trade Corporation Ltd* [2013] EWHC 111, Leggatt J indicated that *Royscot* represented the legal position and must be applied until it is overruled.

 THINKING POINTS

Is it fair that under section 2(1) a representor who cannot disprove negligence has the same liability as someone who acted fraudulently? Is there any justification for such an approach?

13.9.5 Contributory Negligence

We know that there are circumstances where the representee is partly at fault for their loss. The facts of *Redgrave v Hurd* are a good example. The representee was given the opportunity to discover the truth, but did not take it. If such a case happened today, it would be argued that the damages should be reduced to reflect that degree of fault.

> ➔ CROSS-REFERENCE
> For the facts and discussion of Redgrave v Hurd (1881) see 13.3.3.

Initially, there was some uncertainty about whether such a reduction could apply under s.2(1). Since *Royscot* confirmed that s.2(1) of the 1967 Act was indeed based on a 'fiction of fraud,' it might then be assumed that s.2(1) would adopt the same approach to contributory negligence. We can recall that in fraud cases, no reduction in damages is made to reflect the fault of the representee. However, in *Gran Gelato Ltd v Richcliff (group) Ltd* [1992] Ch 560, no such assumption was made. Instead, it was held that damages under s.2(1) could be reduced for contributory negligence.

In the judgment, Sir Donald Nicholls V-C stated:

> It would be very odd if contributory negligence were available as a defence to a claim for damages based on a breach of a duty to take care [i.e. the tort of negligence] in and about the making of a representation, but not available to a claim for damages under the 1967 Act in respect of the same representation.

The common criticism of this view is an obvious one. The approach is inconsistent with the wider principle from *Royscot*. Yes, *Royscot* was about the measure and remoteness rules, but the whole point of the judgment hinged on negligent misrepresentations being treated as fraudulent misrepresentations under s. 2(1) of the Act. However, for the purpose of contributory negligence, the tort of negligence approach applies.

KEY POINTS

Damages under s.2(1) can be reduced for contributory negligence.

13.10 Damages in Lieu of Rescission and Innocent Misrepresentations

The final possible category of damages for misrepresentation is from section 2(2) of the 1967 Act. It will be recalled that s.2(2) is about damages instead of rescission. This applies to 'non-fraudulent' misrepresentations, which means it applies to two types of misrepresentation between parties to a contract. First, it applies to negligent misrepresentations, meaning those where the representor has failed to

> ➔ CROSS-REFERENCE
> For the wording of s.2(2) and its function see 13.5.5.

prove reasonable grounds for believing the statement. Section 2(3) prevents the claimant being over-compensated by stating that damages under 2(2) must be taken into account when assessing the award under s.2(1). The point here is that the representee might well be entitled to damages under s.2(1), but at the same time, a judge might refuse to allow rescission, and award damages instead of rescission. In such a case, the award of damages instead of rescission under s.2(2) should be taken into account when awarding damages under s.2(1) for the loss caused by relying on the negligent misrepresentation.

Second, s.2(2) also applies to innocent misrepresentations. That is where the representor has managed to prove it had reasonable grounds for believing the statement. Section 2(2) is the only way to get damages following an innocent misrepresentation. We have already seen that:

- Section 2(2) damages are only available instead of rescission.
- The decision to make the award is at the discretion of the judge.

When the discretion is exercised, the innocent party is denied the remedy of rescission and gets damages instead. That is simple enough. However, there are some further issues about s.2(2) that we need to address. First, we need to consider *when* the judge has the power to award damages under s.2(2). The second issue concerns the measure of damages under s.2(2).

13.10.1 When Does the Judge Have the Power to Award Damages?

It is obvious from the wording of s.2(2) that damages are awarded instead of rescission, but this wording can have two possible meanings. It could mean that a court can award damages when the right to rescind the contract has been lost, perhaps because a bar to rescission applies. The logic here is that the damages award ensures that a remedy is provided to the representee. Alternatively, the wording could mean that damages are only available if the right to rescind actually exists. In other words, there is a power to swap one remedy for the other only. This would be a more literal interpretation of the wording and would mean that the courts would have no power to award damages where rescission has been barred. In such circumstances, the representee would then be left with no remedy at all.

There was some initial uncertainty about which approach should be adopted, but the matter was settled more recently by Longmore LJ in *Salt v Stratstone* [2015].

→ **CROSS-REFERENCE**

For the facts of *Salt v Stratstone* [2015] see 13.5.2.

GUIDED CASE READING 13.2
Salt v Stratstone [2015]

The extracts of the judgment by Longmore LJ refers to the approach adopted in the previous first instance cases. Try to identify:

- the cases showing a preference for the more literal approach;
- the reasoning of the judge who preferred to allow damages where there was no right to rescind;
- why that reasoning was rejected.

[15] This raises the much discussed question whether s 2(2) is available at all if there is a bar to rescission; it is a question on which there is a conflict of authority at first instance. In *Alton House Garages (Bromley) Ltd v Monk* (1981) (unreported) Cantley J decided that, if rescission was barred, damages were not available; Mustill J seems to have assumed that this was the position in *Atlantis Lines and Navigation Co Inc v Hallam Ltd* [1983] 1 Lloyds Rep 188 . . .

Jacob J adopted the contrary view in *Thomas Witter Ltd v TBP Industries Ltd* [1996] 2 All ER 573 . . ., after Mr David Foxton of counsel, with commendable industry, unearthed a statement from the Solicitor General (Sir Dingle

Longmore LJ first carried out a wide-ranging survey of the cases on this point, mainly to demonstrate that there was apparently no unified approach. In some cases, a literal approach had been adopted: if rescission was unavailable, nor were damages. In others, the approach had been to use damages *because* rescission was unavailable. Clearly, the law needed to be clarified by a higher court, and this was going to be the job of the Court of Appeal.

Foot) during the passing of the Act through Parliament which assumed that unavailability of rescission would not prevent damages. As Professor Hugh Beale points out in his note on the case ((1995) 111 LQR 385), however, Sir Dingle's statement was not wholly free from ambiguity which was perhaps not wholly surprising since he rose to speak at 3.17am when the House of Commons had been sitting since the previous morning.

[16] Subsequently . . . Humphrey Lloyd QC sitting in the Technology and Construction Court in *Floods v Shand Construction* [2000] BRL 81 refused to follow *Thomas Witter* on the basis that the literal meaning of the statute was too clear. So did . . . Raymond Jack QC (as he then was) sitting as a High Court Judge in *Government of Zanzibar v British Aerospace Ltd* [2000] 1 WLR 2333, ... Mr R Tedd QC sitting as a Deputy Judge of the Chancery Division followed these last two decisions in *Pankhania v London Borough of Hackney* [2002] EWHC 2441 (Ch) rather than continuing a potentially endless chain of judicial reconsideration of the same point at first instance.

[17] The point appears to be open at the level of the Court of Appeal. The words of the statute are *'if it is claimed . . . that the contract ought to be or has been rescinded the court . . . may declare the contract subsisting and award damages in lieu of rescission'.* No doubt a claimant can be said to make a claim even if he is subsequently held not to be entitled to do so. But the

words *'in lieu of rescission'* must, in my view, carry with them the implication that rescission is available (or was available at the time the contract was rescinded). If it is not (or was not available in law) because e.g. the contract has been affirmed, third party rights have intervened, an excessive time has elapsed or restitution has become impossible, rescission is not available and damages cannot be said to be awarded 'in lieu of rescission'.

Perhaps surprisingly, Longmore LJ then came down on the literal side of the fence: if rescission is not available, nor are damages. This is because of the use of the words 'in lieu', which he felt could only mean something along the lines of a substitute: the swapping of one for another. This is surprising at first blush but it is consistent with the purpose of s. 2 (2), which is to prevent rescission from having an unjust outcome by awarding damages instead. In other words, it is there to protect the representor from the potentially harsh outcome of rescission (bearing in mind that this will only really be relevant where the representation has been made innocently).

KEY POINTS

A judge only has the power to award damages instead of rescission if the innocent party actually has the right to rescind.

13.10.2 The Measure of Damages under s.2(2)

The measure of s.2(2) damages is not entirely certain from the wording of the section. However, this was a further point discussed by Hoffman LJ in *William Sindell Plc v Cambridgeshire County Council* [1994]. In that case, it was decided that there had not been a misrepresentation and so the discussion of damages was therefore *obiter*. While not binding, the persuasive force in this instance is very strong given the status of Hoffman LJ in the field of contract law.

→ CROSS-REFERENCE
For the facts of *William Sindell v Cambridgeshire County Council* [1994] see 13.5.5.

Hoffman LJ explained that the s.2(2) measure would be different to the s.2(1) measure. Three reasons were then given to support this opinion:

First, section 2(1) provides for damages to be awarded to a person who "has entered into a contract after a misrepresentation has been made to him by another party and as a result thereof"—sc. of having entered into the contract—"he has suffered loss." In contrast, section 2(2) speaks of "the loss which would be caused by it"—sc. the misrepresentation—"if the contract were upheld." In my view, section 2(1) is concerned with the damage flowing from having entered into the contract, while section 2(2) is concerned with damage caused by the property not being what it was represented to be.

Secondly, section 2(3) contemplates that damages under section 2(2) may be less than damages under section 2(1) and should be taken into account when assessing damages under the latter sub-section. This only makes sense if the measure of damages may be different.

Thirdly, the Law Reform Committee report makes it clear that section 2(2) was enacted because it was thought that it might be a hardship to the representor to be deprived of the whole benefit of the bargain on account of a minor misrepresentation. It could not possibly have intended the damages in lieu to be assessed on a principle which would invariably have the same effect.

The Law Reform Committee drew attention to the anomaly which already existed by which a minor misrepresentation gave rise to a right of rescission whereas a warranty in the same terms would have grounded no more than a claim for modest damages. It said that this anomaly would be exaggerated if its recommendation for abolition of the bar on rescission after completion were to be implemented. I think that section 2(2) was intended to give the court a power to eliminate this anomaly by upholding the contract and compensating the plaintiff for the loss he has suffered on account of the property not having been what it was represented to be. In other words, damages under section 2(2) should never exceed the sum which would have been awarded if the representation had been a warranty.

The significance of the opinion from Hoffman LJ is straightforward. Damages under s.2(2) are to reflect the difference in value. The aim is to put the representee in the position it would have been in had the statement been true. It is not damages based on the consequential loss caused by relying on the false statement. In the context of the facts of the case, if damages were awarded, the amount could not reflect the later fall in the value of the property since such a drop in value was unrelated to the truth of the representation. Instead, if a damages award was made under s.2(2), it would cover the cost of moving the sewer.

The reasoning was based on three factors. The first related to the wording. The Act refers to loss caused by the misrepresentation. It does not refer to loss caused by entering into the contract.

The second factor was s.2(3). That sub-section makes sense if s.2(2) damages are different to those under 2(1) because s.2(3) expects the award under 2(2) to be less. At the very least, it expects s.2(2) damages to be different.

The final factor was the purpose of s.2(2), derived from the Law Reform report leading to the Act, which addressed an inconsistency in the old law. This was that a very minor innocent misrepresentation could have serious consequences, i.e. the rescission of the contract. Yet the same statement, were it to be held to have been incorporated as a warranty in the contract, would result only in loss of bargain (expectation) damages. It followed that s.2(2) damages should be limited and more aligned with a breach of warranty award. Table 13.2 summarises the rules on damages for misrepresentation.

Table 13.2

A comparison of the rules on damages for misrepresentation

	Fraud (tort of deceit)	Negligence (tort of negligence)	Negligence (s.2(1) Misrepresentation Act 1967)	Innocent (s.2(2) of the Act—damages in lieu of rescission)
Burden of proof	Representee (claimant)	Representee (claimant)	Representor (defendant)	Representor (defendant)
Damages measure	Reliance loss based on the contract not having been made	Reliance loss based on the contract not having been made	As for fraud	Expectation measure—as if the statement had been true
Remoteness limit	All direct loss irrespective of foreseeability	Reasonably foreseeable loss only	As for fraud	Likely to be reasonably foreseeable loss
Contributory negligence reduction	Does not apply	Does apply	Does apply	Does apply
Who can be liable to the claimant?	Contractual parties and third parties	Contractual parties and third parties	Contractual parties	Contractual parties

Can you identify any reasons why an action under the tort of deceit would be preferred over an action under s.2(1)?

13.11 Misrepresentation and Consumer Contracts

Traditionally, the rules on liability and remedies for misrepresentation applied to all types of contracts. However, there has been a fairly recent change in relation to consumer contracts. As stated in the chapter introduction, the relevant rights for consumers now derive from legislation. This means that the rules we have covered so far apply to both commercial contracts (i.e. contracts between businesses and to private sales (i.e. contracts between private parties). Here we address the basic rules and remedies for consumers arising from that legislation.

The rights applicable to consumers arise from the Consumer Protection from Unfair Trading Regulations 2008 (the 2008 Regulations). The 2008 Regulations impose obligations on traders and initially these obligations resulted in criminal liability enforced by public bodies like Trading Standards. However, the 2008 Regulations were amended by the Consumer Protection (Amendment) Regulations 2014, which extended the Regulations 2008 to allow for private enforcement by consumers.

The 2008 Regulations do not apply specifically to misrepresentations. Instead, liability is for unfair commercial practices. A 'commercial practice' is defined in Regulation 2 as:

> . . . any act, omission, course of conduct, representation or commercial communication (including advertising and marketing) by a trader, which is directly connected with the promotion, sale or supply of a product to or from consumers, whether occurring before, during or after a commercial transaction (if any) in relation to a product.

Regulation 3 refers to circumstances in which such practices will be unfair and that includes cases where the practice is misleading. It is in this context that misrepresentations are covered. Interestingly, Regulation 3 it is not confined to pre-contractual practices but also covers practices made after a contract was created. These could be statements relating to the remedies available following a breach and things relating to the aftersales care process.

It should be noted that for consumers, there is only liability for a misleading *action* (Regulation 27B) and so consumers cannot rely on the 2008 Regulations for a failure to act. Consequently, issues of non-disclosure would be outside the Regulations and so the traditional common law rules would have to be relied upon in those circumstances. That being said, there might not be a difference in practice. Strictly speaking, while a non-disclosure will not be a misleading *action*, disputes which will typically arise will involve half-truths, failures to notify changes in circumstances, or indeed misrepresentation through conduct, all of which will likely qualify as being actions.

Regulation 5 (2) describes when a practice in the form of an action is misleading:

> (a) if it contains false information and is therefore untruthful in relation to any of the matters in paragraph (4) or if it or its overall presentation in any way deceives or is likely to deceive the average consumer in relation to any of the matters in that paragraph, even if the information is factually correct; and
>
> (b) it causes or is likely to cause the average consumer to take a transactional decision he would not have taken otherwise.

→ CROSS-REFERENCE
For the common law rules on non-disclosure as a misrepresentation see 13.2.

False statements are clearly covered as well as correct but misleading statements. The requirement in (b) is important because it is the Regulations' version of inducement. It is an objective test based on the 'average consumer'. Such an average consumer is 'reasonably well informed, observant and circumspect' (Regulation 2). The idea is that the practice has to be capable of affecting the decision-making of the average consumer. This standard should be more protective that the common law notion of the 'reasonable person'. Of course, some consumers might be influenced by a practice even when the average consumer might not be. However, Regulation 2 deals with consumers that are considered to be vulnerable due to things like their mental state, physical state and age. Such consumers can be within the 'average consumer' standard if such consumers can be reasonably foreseen to be contracted with by the trader.

→ CROSS-REFERENCE
The EU concept of 'average consumer' was addressed in 7.7.8. in relation to unfair terms.

13.11.1 Remedies Following Liability for an Unfair Practice

Following an unfair practice, consumers are entitled to a remedy. The new Part 4 of the 2008 Regulations introduces the following remedies to Regulation 27:

- The consumer can 'unwind' the contract;
- The contract could continue but with a discount for the consumer;
- The consumer can claim damages.

When Regulations 27E-H refer to 'unwinding' of the contract, it means the contract is ended. It is like rescission in that the money is returned and the goods are returned. Regulation 27E provides for refunds following a sale to a consumer. Where the goods cannot be returned in their original state, the refund is based on the market value of the goods. For this remedy, the consumer has to indicate that the goods are being rejected within 90 days of receiving the goods.

The discount is an alternative remedy to unwinding the contract. The idea is that the consumer choses to continue with the contract but with a discount. Discounts are dealt with in Regulation 27I and are based on the seriousness of the practice. For example, a minor unfair practice results in a 25% discount. At the other extreme, a very serious practice results in a 100% discount.

Regulation 27J provides the remedy of damages. This is in addition to the other remedies. Damages here are not awarded to reflect the difference between the price and market value, since the other remedies largely cover that type of loss. What it does cover is resulting financial loss as well a range of non-financial losses. This Regulation specifically refers to the suffering of '*alarm, distress or physical inconvenience or discomfort which the consumer would not have suffered if the prohibited practice in question had not taken place*'. This range of losses is wider than what can be claimed from the Misrepresentation Act 1967, but the Regulation states that the loss must have been reasonably foreseeable at the time of the practice. That is less generous than s.2(1) of the Misrepresentation Act because there is no such remoteness limit under that Act, but it is more generous than the remoteness rule that applies to damages for a breach of contract.

→ CROSS-REFERENCE
For the remoteness rules on damages for breach see 10.3.5.

Regulation 27J also lists circumstances in which a damages award is not available. An example would be where the trader proves that the practice was a mistake or an accident. Another example is where the trader proves that the practice was attributable to a third party or information given to the trader by a third party. There is also a wider factor on the list, which is that damages are not available where 'the trader took all reasonable precautions and exercised all due diligence to avoid the occurrence of the prohibited practice'. Essentially, these circumstances work as trader defences in relation to damages. By proving any of these, the trader is showing that they are not at fault. Put another way, it is this aspect of Regulation 27J that links the practice in this area closer to a form of negligence. This seems similar to s.2(1) of the Misrepresentation Act 1967, where damages are available unless the trader proves they had reasonable grounds for making the statement.

13.11.2 Removal of Damages under s.2(1) of the Misrepresentation Act

The reform made one crucial change to the Misrepresentation Act 1967. Section 2(4) was added to the 1967 Act, and this states:

> This section does not entitle a person to be paid damages in respect of a misrepresentation if the person has a right to redress under Part 4A of the Consumer Protection from Unfair Trading Regulations 2008 (SI 2008/1277) in respect of the conduct constituting the misrepresentation.

If a remedy is possible under the 2008 Regulations, in other words, then the consumer cannot rely on s.2(1). The context is important. The rights arising from the 2008 Regulations are not in addition to those provided by the 1967 Act. A consumer cannot choose s.2(1) of the Act as an alternative. Instead, section 2(1) will only be an option if there is no remedy available under the 2008 Regulations.

The new limit to the scope of s.2(1) has the potential to represent a reduction in consumer protection given that there are circumstances when damages are not available under the 2008 Regulations. In such circumstances, unwinding or a discount will be available and so damages under s.2(1) of the 1967 Act will not be an option. Even if damages were possible under the 2008 Regulations, such damages are likely to be much less than those under s.2(1).

We can recall the severe criticism of s.2(1)'s 'fiction of fraud'. With that in mind, perhaps it can be said that the reform helps to correct the problem because damages under the 2008 Regulations are limited to reasonably foreseeable losses—the same remoteness rule that applies to the tort of negligence. However, at present, the reform results in a new inconsistency. A statement to a business in a commercial contract will result in generous damages based on the fraud measure. Yet, the same statement in a consumer contract will result in a more limited award meaning that businesses enjoy a greater level of protection than consumers.

The amendment to s.2(1) is only relevant to s.2(1) damages and so consumers can still rely on common law negligence or fraud. These actions remain as available alternatives to the 2008 Regulations. Regulation 27L prevents a double recovery stating that damages under the 2008 Regulations cannot be claimed if there has been an award at common law. Likewise, if there has been an award under the 2008 Regulations, then an award at common law is not available.

13.12 Exemption Clauses and Misrepresentation

So far, we have looked at the liability for misrepresentations and the possible remedies. Such liability presents a clear risk for a party that has made representations. We know that parties like to control risks in their contracts and they do so with the use of exemption clauses. Since a misrepresentation can result in liability, it is another risk that a party might seek to control. For that reason, parties sometimes try to exclude or limit liability for misrepresentations using an exemption clause, but the freedom to do so is limited by common law rules as well as legislation.

The common law restriction is from the House of Lords case of *Pearson v Dublin Corporation* [1907]. There it was made clear that a party cannot exempt liability for their own fraudulent statements. Clearly there is a good policy reason for not allowing such clauses to be effective. Almost a hundred years later, the House of Lords sought to clarify the extent of this rule in *HIH Casualty & General Insurance v Chase Manhattan Bank* [2003] UKHL 6, which confirmed the rule from *Pearson*. However, it was stated in the judgments in that case that a party could exempt liability for fraudulent statements made by their agents. This is because that would not be a situation in which a representor is exempting liability for their own fraud, but rather one in which they are exempting liability for something they might not have control over. Furthermore, this would not result in a fraudulent party benefiting from their dishonesty and the fraudulent agents would still be liable for their fraud. However, any exemption clause would have to be worded clearly so as to exempt liability for fraudulent statements made by agents.

In addition to imposing liability, the Misrepresentation Act 1967 always included a provision on exemption clauses, which is detailed in section 3 of the Act. This was then amended by the Unfair Contract Terms Act 1977. More recently, it was amended so as to refer to the Consumer Rights Act 2015.

The wording of section 3 of the Misrepresentation is as follows:

> 3. Avoidance of provision excluding liability for misrepresentation.
>
> (1) If a contract contains a term which would exclude or restrict—
>
> (a) any liability to which a party to a contract may be subject by reason of any misrepresentation made by him before the contract was made; or
>
> (b) any remedy available to another party to the contract by reason of such a misrepresentation, that term shall be of no effect except in so far as it satisfies the requirement of reasonableness as stated in section 11(1) of the Unfair Contract Terms Act 1977; and it is for those claiming that the term satisfies that requirement to show that it does.
>
> (2) This section does not apply to a term in a consumer contract within the meaning of Part 2 of the Consumer Rights Act 2015 (but see the provision made about such contracts in section 62 of that Act)

→ CROSS-REFERENCE

For the discussion of UCTA 1977 and the reasonableness test see 7.6.4.

Section 3(1)(b) refers to terms exempting liability or remedies. It makes such clauses subject to the test of reasonableness from UCTA 1977. Under S.11(1) UCTA 1977, the reasonableness of the term is based on the time the contract was entered. Of course, this approach to the exemption clauses applies only to contracts between businesses.

There are two issues concerning the scope of s.3 that have been the subject of some debate and discussion. The first is about how to approach general exemption clauses which appear to exempt liability for all types of misrepresentations.

The second issue is about more indirect ways of exempting liability through 'entire agreement clauses' and 'no reliance clauses'. We will address each of these issues in turn.

13.12.1 Exemption Clauses Covering All Types of Misrepresentation

In *Thomas Witter Ltd v TBP industries Ltd [1996] 2 All ER 573*, Jacob J observed that a term exempting liability for fraud would be unreasonable. The judge then considered clauses that attempt to exempt liability for misrepresentation generally. Such clauses would be attempting to exempt all types of misrepresentation, which would of course also include liability for fraud. For that reason, Jacob J felt that such a general clause would be unreasonable too. This would mean the whole clause would fail. Jacob J felt it was not possible to say a clause was unreasonable because it attempted to cover fraud, but then allow it to remain effective so as to exempt liability in negligence.

The opposite view was expressed by Raymond Jack QC in the *Government of Zanzibar v British Aerospace Ltd [2000]* 1 WLR 2333. According to that judge, such a general clause would not be rejected outright as a whole. Instead, it would be only be ruled out to the extent that it covered fraud. The rest of the clause, i.e. its application to negligence, could be assessed separately. This approach was favoured by Gloster J in *Six Continental Hotels Inc v Event Hotels GmbH [2006] EWHC 2317*.

13.12.2 The Issue of 'Entire Agreement' and 'Non-reliance' Clauses

'Entire agreement' clauses are used to ensure that the contract consists of the written document only. Essentially, under such a clause, any pre-contractual statements are not to be classed as terms of the contract. Such clauses do not deny the existence of any representations made, or even try to negative any reliance on representations. This means that entire agreement clauses do not seek to restrict liability for misrepresentation and, for that reason, Lightman J in *Inntrepreneur Pub v East Crown* [2000] stated that s.3 would not apply to the assessment of such clauses. The same approach was taken in the opinion of Rix LJ in *AXA Sun Life Services v Campbell Martin* [2011] EWCA Civ 133. Of course, such a clause could be worded to also exclude liability for misrepresentation, but in that case, the clause would be subject to s.3.

KEY POINTS

Ordinarily, since an entire agreement clause just prevents representations being terms, they do not restrict liability for misrepresentation. On that basis they are outside of the scope of s. 3 of the Misrepresentation Act 1967.

The issue of 'non-reliance' clauses has inspired a great deal of debate. These clauses indicate that one party has not relied on any statements or representations made by the other. We know that for an actionable misrepresentation, there has to be some reliance on the statement and that is reflected by the inducement requirement. Consequently, by agreeing to such a clause, the representee might be making a future misrepresentation claim impossible. For that reason, in *Inntrepreneur*, Lightman J stated that 'non-reliance' clauses will be subject to s.3. Essentially, such clauses would operate to prevent liability for representations arising in the first place, and in so doing they would indirectly exclude liability for misrepresentation. Likewise, in *Government of Zanzibar v British Aerospace (Lancaster House) Ltd* [2000] 1 WLR 2333, Judge Raymond Jack QC observed:

> A term which negates a reliance which in fact existed is a term which excludes a liability which the representor would otherwise be subject to by reason of the misrepresentation. If that were wrong, it would mean that section 3 could always be defeated by including an appropriate non-reliance clause in the contract, however unreasonable that might be.

This approach was also favoured by Christopher Clarke J in *Raiffeisen Zentralbank Osterreich AG v Royal Bank of Scotland Plc* [2010] EWHC 1392 (Comm), who stated:

> [315]　. . . to tell the man in the street that the car you are selling him is perfect and then agree that the basis of your contract is that no representations have been made or relied on, may be nothing more than an attempt retrospectively to alter the character and effect of what has gone before, and in substance an attempt to exclude or restrict liability.

The point was that by making representations but then agreeing there was no reliance on them would have the effect of excluding liability for them. During the judgment, Christopher Clarke J also cited two examples from Toulson J from *IFE Fund SA v Goldman Sachs International* [2006] EWHC 2887 (Comm), stating:

> [292]　He gave the example of the seller of a car who says to a buyer "I have serviced the car since it was new, it has had only one owner and the clock reading is accurate". Such statements would be representations and would remain so even if the seller had added the words "but those statements are not statements on which you can rely".

[293] By contrast, if the seller of the car said "The clock reading is 20,000 miles, but I have no knowledge whether the reading is true or false" the position would be different because the qualifying words could not fairly be regarded as an attempt to exclude liability for a false representation arising from the first half of the sentence.

In the first example, the statements are clear representations that would be relied upon as reasons for entering into the contract. If false, these statements should be capable of resulting in a remedy for misrepresentation. To then qualify the statements by saying that they cannot be relied upon would be an attempt to prevent inducement and effectively exclude liability for misrepresentation. In contrast, in the second example, the statement is one that cannot be relied upon in the first place and which makes this clear to the representee, and so there is nothing in the statement that attempts to exclude liability. The distinction is a fine one that was approved in the Court of Appeal by Lewison LJ in *First Tower Trustees v CDS (Superstores International Ltd* [2018] EWCA Civ 1396.

In contrast, Court of Appeal cases such as *Watford Electronics Ltd v Sanderson CFL Ltd* [2001] EWCA Civ 317 (Chadwick LJ) and *Peekay Intermark Ltd v Australia and New Zealand Banking Group Ltd* [2006] EWCA Civ 386 (Moore-Bick LJ) have been used to argue that non-reliance clauses can fall outside of the scope of section 3. The approach taken in these judgments indicated that on agreeing to a non-reliance clause, a party will then be estopped from claiming later that there was reliance on a statement.

The status of non-reliance clauses was settled more recently by the Court of Appeal in *First Tower Trustees Ltd v CDS (Superstores International) Ltd* [2018] EWCA Civ 1396. The appellants were the landlords of a warehouse property. The respondent, who traded under the retail name 'The Range', had entered a lease to occupy part of the building. In the period up to the point of contracting, the landlords knew that the property was contaminated with asbestos to such an extent that it could not be entered. Before entering into the contract, the respondents had asked the landlord about the existence of dangerous substances or environmental problems within the relevant part of the property. The solicitors for the landlords had simply responded that they did not know of any such problems but that the 'buyer must satisfy itself'. They did add that they would notify the respondents if they had information that made their statements inaccurate. Before the contract was formed, the agents of the landlord received reports indicating that the property was contaminated and could not be entered. This information was not passed on to the respondents, who then entered into the lease contract.

At first instance, the statements about there being no dangerous substances were held to be misrepresentations. This finding was not in dispute and, instead, the focus of the case was clause 5.8 of the lease, which stated: 'the tenant acknowledges that this lease has not been entered into in reliance wholly or partly on any statement or representation made by or on behalf of the landlord'. The question was whether this was simply defining the basis of the contract, i.e. the extent of the primary obligations, or whether it was in effect excluding liability for misrepresentation. If it was excluding such liability, then following s. 3 of the Misrepresentation Act 1967, the clause would be subject to the test of reasonableness from UCTA 1977. The first instance judge held that the term was excluding such liability. Furthermore, based on the test from UCTA, the clause was unreasonable. On that basis, an award of £1.4m plus interest was made for the loss resulting from the misrepresentation under s.2(1) of the Misrepresentation Act. In the appeal that followed, the Court of Appeal upheld the first instance decision and provided clear guidance on s.3 of the Misrepresentation Act and its application to no-reliance clauses. It is useful to read the reasoning in the judgments by Lewison LJ and Leggatt LJ. Sir Colin Rimer agreed with both.

We will begin with Lewison LJ, who stated:

[41] . . . Absent clause 5.8, I consider that the position is clear. The landlords would have been liable for misrepresentation. The only reason why they may not be is the existence of clause 5.8. On the face of it, therefore, clause 5.8 is a contract term which would exclude liability for misrepresentation.

[After approving of the examples from Toulson J that were cited by Christopher Clarke J in *IFE Fund SA v Goldman Sachs International*, Lewison LJ continued:]

[47] It is now firmly established at this level in the judicial hierarchy that parties can bind themselves by contract to accept a particular state of affairs even if they know that state of affairs to be untrue. This is a particular form of estoppel which has been given the label "contractual estoppel." . . . Aikens LJ put the point thus in *Springwell Navigation Corp v JP Morgan Chase Bank* [2010] EWCA Civ 1221; [2010] 2 CLC 705 at [143]: . . . .

[48] He concluded on this point at [144]:

"So, in principle and always depending on the precise construction of the contractual wording, I would say that A and B can agree that A has made no precontract representations to B about the quality or nature of a financial instrument that A is selling to B."

[49] However, as Aikens LJ recognised . . ., the position at common law is not the end of the inquiry. There remains for consideration whether there is a "statute to the contrary". Whether section 3 of the 1967 is such a statute is a question, not of the interpretation of the contract, but of the interpretation of the statute. The fact that clause 5.8 of the lease operates as a contractual estoppel does not prevent consideration of this question; not least because section 3 is expressly directed at contract terms.

[reference was made to statements by Bridge LJ in *Cremdean Properties v Nash* [1977] 2 EGLR 80 and Judge Raymond Jack QC in *Government of Zanzibar v British Aerospace (Lancaster House) Ltd* [2000] 1 WLR 2333 favouring the non-reliance clauses being subject to section 3 of the misrepresentation Act 1967 and continued:]

54. We were pressed with the decision of this court in *Watford Electronics* . . . . The contract in that case contained a clause (clause 7.3) which limited liability for indirect losses. It also contained an entire agreement clause (clause 14) that stated:

"... no statement or representations made by either party have been relied upon by the other in agreeing to enter into the Contract."

[A passage from Chadwick LJ in *Watford Electronics* was cited and then Lewison LJ continued:]

56. What is critical to an understanding of this part of the judgment is that Chadwick LJ was not considering whether the non-reliance clause (clause 14) was or was not an exclusion clause. What he was considering was the construction of the completely different clause in the contract (clause 7.3) which limited liability for indirect loss arising out of negligence or otherwise. The question was whether that clause was intended to capture liability for pre-contractual misrepresentation. It was in that context that he held it was bizarre to attribute to them in clause 7.3 an intention to exclude a liability which they must have thought could never arise. He was not considering whether section 3 applied to clause 14.

67. I would hold, therefore, that a clause which simply states (as clause 12.1 of the agreement for lease and clause 5.8 of the lease do) "that this lease has not been entered into in reliance wholly or partly on any statement or representation made by or on behalf of the landlord" is a contract term which would have the effect of excluding liability for misrepresentation; and consequently is subject to the test of reasonableness. . . .

Lewison LJ indicated that the effect of clause 5.8 was to exclude liability for misrepresentation because, without the clause, there would be no question about the landlord being liable. This approach was consistent with the comments by Toulson J and Christopher Clarke J from previous cases. It was also recognised that parties are free to agree on a state of affairs. They can agree on the basis they are entering the contract, and that can include whether there have been any representations. Permitting such an approach is justified by freedom of contract; it can then result in a contractual estoppel whereby the parties are prevented from denying that state of affairs exists. This had been acknowledged previously by Aikens LJ in *Springwell Navigation*. However, crucially, Aikens LJ had recognised that such an approach was the common law position only, and that a further question arises as to whether what has been agreed is consistent with legislation. That is where section 3 of the Misrepresentation Act would be relevant. If the effect of the agreed clause is to exempt liability for misrepresentation, then the clause is subject to the reasonableness test from UCTA and a party cannot rely on contractual estoppel to prevent this. This does not mean that the contractual estoppel is pointless. It can be relied upon between the parties on all other matters where doing so is not contrary to legislation.

In *Watford Electronics*, Chadwick LJ explained that if the parties agreed there was no reliance on any representations, then it was not possible to say that the parties had intended to exclude liability for misrepresentations. This was because it would be bizarre for them to agree to exclude liability that they assumed would not exist in the first place. This point was distinguished by Lewison LJ, who explained that Chadwick LJ was commenting on a clause that limited liability for indirect loss. Chadwick LJ was not discussing the effect of a non-reliance clause and the context of liability for misrepresentation.

The judgment by Leggatt LJ is useful for clarifying the policy context of the 1967 Act:

> [94] ... Where a duty is imposed by law and not because it is a term of a contract agreed between the parties, the distinction between a contract term which excludes liability and one which prevents liability from arising by giving rise to a contractual estoppel is a distinction without a difference ...
>
> [95] Section 2(1) of the Misrepresentation Act 1967 creates a statutory tort, ... The liability arises by operation of law independently of what the parties have agreed. If, as in the present case, all the elements necessary to give rise to liability in damages under section 2(1) have in fact been proved but a term of the contract prevents the claim from succeeding because it contains an agreement that no reliance has been placed on the representation, the term is excluding liability which would exist in the absence of the term.
>
> [Reference was made to the idea of lawyers drafting terms to prevent the liability for misrepresentation arising in the first place]
>
> ... No rational legislator could have intended that the need for a contract term to satisfy a test of reasonableness could be avoided simply by felicity in drafting the contract term.
>
> [96] The decision to make section 3 applicable to all contracts induced by misrepresentation, ... is readily understandable. The importance which English law attaches to the freedom of parties to contract on whatever terms they choose depends crucially on the assumption that their consent to the terms of the contract has been obtained fairly. That is not the case where one party's consent has been induced by a misrepresentation made by the other contracting party. Misrepresentation is a paradigm "vitiating factor" which undermines the validity of a contract. This does not mean that a party cannot choose to give up the right to complain that its consent to the terms of the contract was obtained by misrepresentation. But in so far as a contract term is said to have removed that right, a control mechanism is needed to ensure that this term was a fair and reasonable one to include. That, at all events, is the policy which Parliament has thought it right to adopt. It is the duty of the courts to uphold and not to subvert that policy choice.

He effectively said that there was no difference between a clause exempting liability for misrepresentation and one that simply prevented the liability arising. The effect of two such clauses would be the same. But if lawyers could simply draft their contracts to prevent reliance, it would allow for liability for misrepresentation to be prevented without being tested for reasonableness. Such a way around section 3 could never have been intended by Parliament. Leggatt LJ acknowledged that freedom of contract allows parties to choose the terms of their contract, so ultimately, they can choose to set aside liability for misrepresentation, but the decision to do so must be fair and reasonable, and that is the policy behind section 3. It is not for the parties to set aside that policy.

KEY POINTS

- Non-reliance clauses prevent liability for misrepresentation in the first place and are therefore subject to section 3 of the 1967 Act.
- Agreeing to a state of affairs, like that there has been no reliance on a statement, will give rise to a contractual estoppel (at common law) preventing parties claiming a different state of affairs existed. That will apply between the parties, except in relation to challenging the reasonableness of a term preventing liability for misrepresentation.

13.12.3 Exemption Clauses in Consumer Contracts

Section 3(2) sets out the approach adopted for consumer contracts. Such clauses are covered by s.62 of the Consumer Rights Act 2015. Clauses within this section of the CRA 2015 are subject to the test of fairness.

'Entire agreement' and 'non reliance' clauses are not an issue in consumer contracts. All terms (except the 'core' terms) can be challenged under the fairness test. The assessment of such terms is not restricted to exemption clauses like s.3 of the 1967 Act.

→ CROSS-REFERENCE
For the test of fairness see 7.7.5.

CHAPTER SUMMARY

- Not all false representations result in liability for misrepresentation, only those that are *actionable*.
- Honest opinions are generally not actionable. False opinions can result in liability where the representor appears to know the facts behind the opinion; where the opinion is not honest; or where there is a representation that a statement has been made with reasonable care and skill where in fact it has not been.
- Forecasts and statements about the future are generally not actionable unless they are not honestly made.
- There is no general duty to reveal material facts. However, if a representation is made, it must be full and complete and remain full and complete until the contract is entered into.
- The false statement must be an inducement to enter into the contract. Such inducement can be presumed using an objective test.
- Where the representee tested the accuracy of the statement or had a third party do so then inducement is less likely.
- Where the representee did not take the opportunity to verify a statement there is still inducement.
- The basic remedy following an actionable misrepresentation is rescission. The effect is mutual restitution and the representee has to communicate their intention to rescind, or do the next best thing when communication is not possible.
- Rescission can be barred by lapse of time; affirmation of the contract; when restitution is not substantially possible; and supervening third party rights.
- Under s.2(2) of the Misrepresentation Act 1967, it is sometimes possible for a judge to exercise their discretion to refuse rescission and award damages instead.

- Damages are available at common law under the tort of deceit where the statement was deliberately false or where the representor was reckless as to whether it was true.

- Under the tort of deceit, damages are for all loss arising from relying on the false statement. The remoteness rule is generous, allowing for all such losses to be recovered irrespective of foresight.

- Since *Hedley Byrne v Heller*, damages are also available for negligent misstatement under the tort of negligence. This is limited to reasonably foreseeable losses only. There has to be a duty of care owed by the representor, but there is no need for a contractual relationship.

- S.2(1) of the Misrepresentation Act 1967 introduced its own version of negligent misrepresentation that applies between parties that have a contract.

- Under s2(1) there is liability for damages if the representor cannot disprove negligence by showing he or she had reasonable grounds for making the statement.

- The measure of damages and remoteness rule are the same as those used in the tort of deceit.

- Unlike under the tort of deceit, the damages under the tort of negligence and s.2(1) can be reduced for contributory negligence.

- Where damages are awarded under s.2(2) instead of rescission, the contract (i.e. expectation) measure applies.

- The power to award such damages in lieu of rescission only exists if the representee was actually entitled to rescind at the time.

- Following the Consumer Protection (Amendment) Regulations 2014, misrepresentation in consumer contracts is now largely governed by the Consumer Protection from Unfair Trading Regulations 2008.

- Terms cannot exempt liability for a fraudulent misrepresentation.

- Under Section 3 of the 1967 Act, terms that do attempt to exempt liability for non-fraudulent misrepresentations are subject to the test of reasonableness from the Unfair Contract Terms Act 1977.

- Section 3 will also apply to terms that prevent liability for misrepresentation in the first place like non-reliance clauses.

KEY CASES

- ☐ *Esso Petroleum v Mardon* **[1976] QB 801**—A useful authority on the liability of an expert opinion as well as the application of negligent misstatement under the tort of negligence to parties with a contractual relationship.

- ☐ *With v O'Flanagan* **[1936] Ch 575**—the key case on representations continuing until the contract is entered into, which imposes an obligation on a representor to correct statements that become false later.

- ☐ *BV Netherlands Industrie Van Eiprodukten v Rembrandt Enterprises, Inc* **[2019] EWCA Civ 596**—The judgment of Longmore LJ provides a very useful analysis of the inducement requirement in the context of fraudulent misrepresentations.

- ☐ *Salt v Stratstone Specialist Ltd* **[2015] EWCA Civ 745**—the judgment of Longmore LJ provides useful guidance on the application of the remedy of rescission as well the availability of damages in lieu of rescission under s.2(2) of the Misrepresentation Act 1967.

- ☐ *Derry v Peek* **(1889) 14 App Cas 337**—this remains the key case for the definition of a fraudulent misrepresentation.

- ☐ *Smith New Court Ltd v Scrimgeour Vickers (Asset Management) Ltd* **[1997] AC 254**—a leading authority on damages for fraudulent misrepresentation.

- *Hedley Byrne & Co Ltd v Heller & Partners Ltd* [1964] **AC 465**—this is significant for its recognition that the tort of negligence applies to negligently made false statements, though the test to be applied has been developed by later cases.

- *Royscott Trust Ltd v Rogerson* [1991] **2 QB 297**—While it has been criticised, it remains the key authority on the damages award to be made under s.2(1) of the Misrepresentation Act 1967.

- *William Sindell plc v Cambridgeshire County Council* [1994] **1 WLR 1016**—the judgment of Hoffman LJ provides important guidance on the exercise of discretion under s.2(2) of the Misrepresentation Act 1967 and the measure of damages.

- *First Tower Trustees v CDS (Superstores International* **Ltd** [2018] **EWCA Civ 1396**—this is the latest case on the exclusion of liability for misrepresentation and specifically the use of non-reliance clauses.

QUESTIONS

1. Ikra told Tyrese that she was thinking of selling her trampoline centre. She told Tyrese that the business was making profits of £200,000 a year and offered the accounts to confirm the figure. Tyrese did not bother to read the accounts because Ikra had an expensive sports car and he knew that the centre was busy, having been a customer himself. Ikra also stated that the business had a licence to sell alcohol so the profits could be increased by installing a bar.

   Two months later, when Tyrese bought the business, he discovered that the profits were only £100,000 a year. In addition, he has been told by the council that the alcohol licence was being revoked and that notice of this had been sent to Ikra a month before the sale took place.

   Advise Tyrese.

2. There is now no reason for bringing a claim in fraud for misrepresentation, since a claim brought under s. 2 (1) of the Misrepresentation Act 1967 will be just as good if not better. Critically discuss.

3. Critically assess the extent to which a contract can be rescinded following an actionable misrepresentation.

 For answer guidance to these questions please visit the online resources at www .oup.com/uk/naidoo1e/, where you will also find multiple choice questions to check your understanding of key concepts.

FURTHER READING

Atiyah & Treitel, 'Misrepresentation Act 1967' MLR (1967) 30, 369.
The first detailed assessment of the Act and a key journal article by two of the most significant contract scholars. It was cited by Balcombe LJ in *Royscot v Rogerson*.

Hooley, 'Damages and the Misrepresentation Act 1967' LQR 107 (1991) 547.
A short case note providing useful criticism of *Royscot v Rogerson*. It was cited by Lord Steyn in *Smith New Court Ltd v Scrimgeour Vickers (Asset Management) Ltd*.

Loi, 'Pre-contractual misrepresentations: mistaken belief induced by mis-statements' JBL [2017] 7, 598.
An excellent case note on the Supreme Court's approach in *Hayward v Zurich Insurance* towards inducement when the representee knows that a statement is false.

Turner, 'Rescission and damages "in lieu" thereof under the Misrepresentation Act 1967' LQR 132 (2016), 388.

This is a useful note on *Salt v Stratstone* and the approach taken by Longmore LJ on the availability of damages under s.2(2) of the Misrepresentation Act 1967.

The Law Commission and The Scottish Law Commission: Consumer redress for misleading and aggressive practices (Law Com no 332)(Scot Law com no 226). https://www.lawcom.gov.uk/ project/consumer-redress-for-misleading-and-aggressive-practices/

This is the report that led to the Consumer Protection (Amendment) Regulations 2014, which amended the Consumer Protection from Unfair Trading Regulations 2008.

14

Duress

LEARNING OBJECTIVES

By the end of this chapter you should be able to:

- understand the basic requirements for a duress action and the remedies available;
- explain how the concept developed, what types of pressure it covers and the effect that pressure has to have in order for an agreement to be voided;
- assess and evaluate the uncertainties resulting from the cases;
- apply the rules to a given set of facts.

INTRODUCTION

The word 'duress' is associated with a threat that forces someone to do something. It is not difficult to imagine this in a context of contracts. The typical hypothetical example would be a party that signs a contract at gunpoint. We know that the choice between entering the contract or taking a bullet to the head is no real choice at all. Entering a contact under duress in this fashion means that the consent to the contract was impaired by the wrongdoing. This means that duress is another *vitiating factor*, like misrepresentation, and therefore it results in the contract being voidable.

→ **CROSS-REFERENCE**
For the significance of a voidable contract see 13.4.1.

In this chapter we examine the law relating to contracts made as a result of duress. We start with the role of the law and the shape of the area, which provides a brief overview of the development of the duress principle. We then turn to the initial categories of duress, and with each we explore the principles arising from the case law and the scope of the duress principle in those contexts. Of these categories, economic duress and lawful act duress are the most recent to have evolved, and they are particularly interesting because they continue to be the subject of judicial and academic debate. Our final issue concerns the remedies for duress, and a key issue here is the question of whether duress can result in a claim for damages.

14.1 The General Role of the Law on Duress

In the context of contracts, duress means improper pressure exerted to secure a contract. This is easily identified where somebody is signing at gunpoint. The victim is consenting to the contract but the absence of a real choice means that the consent is impaired and not given freely. However, it is important to appreciate that duress is about much more than pressure that impairs or limits the ability to consent freely. We all regularly experience a range of pressures that might make us feel that we have no choice but to enter into a contract. You might need petrol during a motorway journey and feel forced to accept the high prices of the closest petrol station. However, such pressure will not amount to duress. For duress, the pressure has to be *illegitimate*, which means it has to be classed as improper. The point was observed jointly by Lord Wilberforce and Lord Simon in *Barton v Armstrong* [1976] AC 104:

> ...[F]or in life, including the life of commerce and finance, many acts are done under pressure, sometimes overwhelming pressure, so that one can say that the actor had no choice but to act. Absence of choice in this sense does not negate consent in law: for this the pressure must be one of a kind which the law does not regard as legitimate.

Essentially, the law on duress is not based on impaired consent only, but is also concerned with the pressure having been exercised through wrongdoing. In that wider context, the law on duress can appear related to the area of contract law known as undue influence, an area which is covered in the next chapter. Broadly, both duress and undue influence provide remedies when consent has been impaired by wrongdoing. Both concern pressure, but duress is about pressure arising from a threat whereas undue influence is about pressure arising from a relationship in which one party has a position of dominance and influence over another. There is even scope for a little overlap between these areas, but undue influence developed out of equity and has its own rules and tests. On that basis, addressing these areas in separate chapters allows us to maintain a more effective focus on the different issues raised.

14.2 Background and the Shape of Common Law Duress

Duress is one of the more recent areas of contract law to have developed, with the bulk of this development having taken place from the 1970s onwards. That might seem long ago, but in view of the long history of common law contract, duress is considered a relatively new area. While it is now well established, the precise scope continues to be debated, and there is even a little uncertainty over the tests to be applied.

To have a good understanding of duress, it is important to understand its development. Originally, duress was limited to threats of death or physical harm (known as duress of the person). Then, the courts extended duress to include threats of financial harm (known as economic duress). At the same time, the courts also clarified that duress could apply to a threat to damage property (duress of goods). This meant that duress could apply in three contexts and that gave rise to the three types or categories of duress. However, throughout the cases in all of these contexts, the courts have based duress on the presence of two key factors. One factor is the legitimacy or wrongfulness of the pressure imposed. The other factor is the effect of the pressure on the victim.

Duress as a principle can be defined on the basis of these two factors. The definition accepted by the courts was given by Lord Hoffman for the Privy Council in *R v Attorney-General of England and Wales* [2003] UKPC 22. This was done by citing Lord Scarman from an earlier House of Lords case:

> [15] In *Universe Tankships Inc of Monrovia v International Transport Workers Federation* [1983]...Lord Scarman said that there were two elements in the wrong of duress. One was pressure amounting to a compulsion of the will of the victim and the second was the legitimacy of the pressure.

This indicates that for duress, the following requirements must be satisfied:

- The pressure must be 'illegitimate' and;
- result in a 'compulsion of will'.

These two factors reflect the fact that duress extends beyond the original three categories and so duress is not limited to threats of personal harm, damage to goods or financial harm. Instead, what matters is the legitimacy of the pressure exerted by the threat, and its effect. Consequently, while duress developed in the context of the three particular categories listed above, it is not confined to them. Essentially, these categories can just be thought of as more obvious examples of the types of pressures that can induce a contract, but there may be others. Consider the threat of private nude photos being posted online (which is a criminal offence under the Criminal Justice and Courts Act 2015, s.33). It is easy to imagine it would be enough to induce a party to enter into a contract. It would certainly be a stretch to say that such a threat amounted to economic duress, duress to goods or physical harm. Likewise, there would be many other threats that would not fit neatly into the original duress categories. Such limits call for an approach that focusses on principle rather than categorisation, and indeed such a principle-based approach was taken by the Privy Council in *R v Attorney General*. As we shall see, the court also made clear in its decision in that case that such an approach had always been implicit.

In taking this more principled approach, we might think that we can ignore the categories of duress and instead focus on the application of the two key factors alone. However, the categories remain significant because the tests to be applied can be slightly different, depending on the category of duress. Furthermore, there are some uncertainties associated with the category of economic duress and so it has to be singled out for special treatment. Finally, the categories may retain some significance because *R v Attorney General* is a Privy Council case and so it is not strictly binding on English courts. Until the approach adopted in that case is confirmed by the Supreme Court, there will always be some room for doubt about the use of a wider, principled approach. With all of this in mind, we will discuss duress using the three categories in turn.

Duress in contract developed out of threats to do something unlawful. That would be where a legal rule or enforceable rights are infringed. Key examples would be a criminal offence; a tort; or even a breach a contract. However, such unlawfulness was never a separate requirement and instead the courts have looked for 'illegitimate' pressure which is just a way of indicating wrongdoing. It just so happened that, generally, threats of *unlawful* action would be classed as 'illegitimate'. We will see that this might not be absolute, particularly in the context of economic duress.

We then have the more recent recognition of 'lawful-act duress'. The idea here is that a threat of lawful action could be 'illegitimate'. An example of such a threat would be the act of reporting someone for driving without insurance. The act of reporting such a matter is *lawful*, but using the threat of doing so to secure a contract is likely to be considered to be illegitimate pressure. When faced with a threat of *lawful* action, the question of its legitimacy takes into consideration other factors. For that reason, we will address threats of lawful action as a separate category of duress.

14.3 Duress of the Person

The earliest recognised form of duress is a threat to harm a person, and the case that is cited most often for this is *Barton v Armstrong* [1976] AC 104, from Australia. If you read the facts from the judgments, it reads like the plot from a gangster film. There was even reference to a suspected hitman, called Vijonivic, from the former Yugoslavia. As entertaining as the case is, it is cited because it was decided by the Privy Council and hence is highly authoritative.

The facts are straightforward and resulted from the hostile business relationship between the parties. Barton (the claimant) was the managing director of a company and Armstrong (the defendant) was the company chairman. Both wanted the other out of the business and, eventually, Barton agreed to pay-off and buy the shares from Armstrong. However, he later sought to end that agreement, arguing it had been made as a result of threats to his life and that of his family. The trial judge accepted that Armstrong had indeed threatened to murder Barton, but felt that this was not the main reason for his agreement to the terms. Instead, the main reason for agreeing to the terms appeared to have been commercial, as it was the means for taking over and saving the company. The Court of Appeal of New South Wales agreed, but the majority of the Privy Council found in favour of Barton.

The Privy Council observed that for duress the pressure must be illegitimate and that the threat to harm another would be illegitimate. They then focussed on the effect of the threat which is really the significant point from the case. It concerned the extent to which the illegitimate pressure has to be the cause of the victim's action. On that point, Lord Cross for the majority referred to the basis duress shares with fraudulent misrepresentation:

> There is an obvious analogy between setting aside a disposition for duress . . . and setting it aside for fraud. In each case—to quote the words of Holmes J. in *Fairbanks v. Snow* (1887) 13 N.E. Reporter 596,. . .—"the party has been subjected to an improper motive for action." . . .Had Armstrong made a fraudulent misrepresentation to Barton for the purpose of inducing him to execute the deed . . ., the answer to the problem which has arisen would have been clear. If it were established that Barton did not allow the representation to affect his judgment then he could not make it a ground for relief. . .If on the other hand Barton relied on the misrepresentation Armstrong could not have defeated his claim to relief by showing that there were other more weighty causes which contributed to his decision. . ., for in this field the court does not allow an examination into the relative importance of contributory causes.
>
> . . .Their Lordships think that the same rule should apply in cases of duress and that if Armstrong's threats were "a" reason for Barton's executing the deed he is entitled to relief even though he might well have entered into the contract if Armstrong had uttered no threats to induce him to do so.

Put simply, the threat just has to have been 'a' reason for entering into the contract. It does not have to have been the only reason, or even a significant reason. The case sets a low standard to satisfy by showing that it would not matter if the contract would have been entered into even without a threat. In practice, it is difficult to imagine such a threat not being 'a' reason for entering a contract. Of course, the victim could actually admit that the threat played no part in their decision, but in the absence of doing so, it might as well be assumed that such a threat will have been a reason for entering a contract in any given duress of the person case.

In the main judgment, the burden of proof was also addressed. Lord Cross observed that Barton had proven the threats had been made and it was then for Armstrong to disprove that the threats were a reason for Barton's agreement. In other words, it was for Armstrong to prove the threats had no effect on Barton's decision.

KEY POINTS

- For duress, the pressure must be 'illegitimate'. The pressure arising from a threat to harm a person is illegitimate.
- For threats to harm a person, the illegitimate pressure just has to be 'a' reason for entering the contract. That is enough for it to result in a 'compulsion of will'.

14.4 Duress of Goods or Property

It is easy to imagine that a threat to goods or property could compel someone to enter into a contract. Consider a threat of having your car tyres 'slashed' or the windows of your house smashed. Such threats might well be enough for you to agree to a transaction of some kind. Likewise, consider a threat to wipe the memory of your phone unless you pay the repairer more money. Such a threat could have a real impact on your decision to pay. The potential effect of the pressure arising from such threats is obvious, but the courts were initially slow to recognise duress beyond threats to harm or kill a person.

For a long time, it seemed that threats relating to goods or property did not amount to duress, a position that was a result of *Skeate v Beale* (1841) 11 Ad & E 983. In this case, the claimant landlord believed he was owed £19 10s by the defendant tenant. For that reason, the landlord unlawfully took possession of £20 worth of the tenant's goods and then threatened to sell them unless he was paid. In response, the tenant agreed to pay, and gave £3 7s 6d as part payment to have the goods back, but he did not pay the remaining amount of £16 2s 6d. As a result, the landlord brought an action to enforce the agreement and the tenant's main defence was that the agreement was a result of duress of goods. This defence was rejected by the court. Lord Denman CJ acknowledged duress to the person would prevent a party acting freely but that duress of goods would not have the same effect. It was stated that the tenant could have used his legal rights to bring an action for the goods rather than enter into the agreement with the landlord.

Lord Denman CJ did acknowledge that if the full £20 was actually paid, the outcome might have been different. On such alternative facts, if there was no right to the full £20, the tenant could claim it back. Such an alternative is reflected by the old case of *Astley v Reynolds* (1731) 2 Str 915, a case which was not cited by Lord Denman CJ, but which did feature in the argument for the tenant's defence.

In *Astley v Reynolds*, the claimant **pawned** a plate in return for £20. At the time, nothing was said about interest payments and three years later the claimant returned with the £20. The defendant refused to return the plate unless he was also given £10 as interest, an amount way above any standard interest rate. To get his plate back, the claimant paid the money, but then brought an action to recover the amount paid beyond the normal rate of interest. It was an established action for 'money had and received,' an action that might now be called an unjust enrichment claim. The important point is that Holt CJ allowed the recovery of the money on the basis of duress of goods.

pawning
is process where you leave goods with a pawn broker as security for loan. If not paid by a certain date, the pawn broker can sell the goods.

In both of these cases there had been the same type of pressure. However, the distinction appeared to be that in *Astley*, the action was for money actually paid. In contrast, in *Skeate* there was an agreement to pay (i.e. an executory contract, one that was not yet performed). Such a distinction seems artificial, but it is based on the use of the old 'money had and received' claim. But whatever the reason for the distinction, in *Skeate*, the court declined to end the contract for duress to property. That was then taken as authority that duress was confined to threats to the person.

Following the later recognition of economic duress, *Skeate v Beale* must now be said to have not been good law. Indeed, that was the opinion in *Occidental Worldwide Investment Corporation v Skibs A/S Avanti (The Siboen and The Sibotre)* [1976] 1 Lloyd's Rep. 293. In the judgment, Kerr J referred to an agreement following an immediate threat of goods being damaged and gave the example of a threat to slash a valuable painting. Kerr J then observed that he did not think such an agreement would be upheld. The comment from Kerr J was not essential to the decision and is classed as *obiter*, but the point was supported further in *Dimskal Shipping Co SA v International Transport Workers Federation (The Evia Luck)* [1991] 3 WLR 875. In this case, Lord Goff referred to *Skeate* as limiting duress to threats to the person. After citing cases recognising economic duress, he concluded that the limitation represented by *Skeate* had been 'discarded'.

At this stage there is no case that formally overrules *Skeate*. However, we have judicial opinion indicating that it no longer represents the legal position. In fact, we will see that the principle of duress has been expanded so much that it is bound to cover threats to property. All that this needed is sufficient illegitimate pressure, and the threat does not have to be directed to a particular category, like a person or goods.

In the context of duress to a person, we know the pressure needs to be 'a' reason for entering into the contract. Such a causal link is enough to satisfy the requirement for a compulsion of will. In contrast, the causation requirement for duress to goods is uncertain, as there has been no judicial statement directly on the point. We will see in 14.5 that for economic duress a stricter standard of causation is required to show compulsion, and it is likely that the same approach would apply to duress of goods.

14.5 Economic Duress

Economic duress was recognised in English law in the 1970s and it concerns agreements resulting from illegitimate commercial pressure. Typically, this relates to the renegotiation of contracts, where one party threatens to breach a contract unless new terms are agreed. In such circumstances, the other party might be pressured into agreeing to the new terms from the fear of suffering serious financial loss. For an example, consider a business that has a contract to supply milk to a supermarket chain. Months into the contract, the supermarket chain demands that the price of the milk be reduced by 20%, and threatens to end the contract and use an alternative supplier unless the reduction is agreed. Following such a threat, the supplier would be concerned about losing a lot of profit from the contract, but losing the supermarket contract could result in the supplier breaching its other contracts, like those with other dairy farmers used to fulfil the large orders. Of course, following a breach by the supermarket, the supplier could sue the supermarket for damages and could even reduce their losses by finding another supermarket to supply. However, by then, the milk supplier might have gone out of business, and so, in such circumstances, the supplier would be faced with a difficult choice. One option would be to agree to the change and accept the resulting drop in profit. Another option would be to face the greater loss caused by the supermarket contract ending. It is not difficult to see that the supplier might agree to the new terms to avoid the greater loss. Such a choice would not have been a freely made one, but is instead a result of the financial pressure arising from the threat to breach. The supplier would then later seek to recover the money due under the original contract. Such a claim would be based on arguing that the new terms resulted from economic duress.

Before economic duress was recognised, the court's options were very limited. The only protective tool at their disposal was the traditional consideration rule. Consider the case of *Stilk v Myrick*. The promise of extra wages was not enforceable because, in return, all the crew had done was promise what they had to do anyway and so their performance was deemed to be of no additional value. Such an approach to consideration is often viewed as reflecting a policy objective of protecting parties like the ship's master from being extorted. It meant a crew would not be able to benefit by forcing a ship's master to pay them more.

➡ CROSS-REFERENCE

For the discussion of *Stilk v Myrick* (1809) see 5.7.1.

The policy objective in *Stilk v Myrick* was acknowledged by the Court of Appeal in *Williams v Roffey*. We can recall that in that case, the Court of Appeal relaxed the consideration requirement and preferred to rely on the recently developed principle of economic duress to protect parties from extortion. This meant that if the new terms were agreed freely, the consideration could be found in the practical benefit to the promisor arising from the promisee agreeing to perform its contractual duty. If the new terms were not agreed freely (i.e. as the result of illegitimate pressure), the promisor could challenge the new terms by relying on economic duress.

➡ CROSS-REFERENCE

For the discussion of *Williams v Roffey* [1990] see 5.9.

The use of economic duress to protect parties from extortion makes a great a deal of sense. To appreciate this point, we only have to look at the obvious limits of consideration. It can only provide protection for a victim (the promisor) when there is no consideration. Consider the milk supplier agreeing to the 20% discount following a threat of a breach. Traditionally, that promise would not be enforceable where there is nothing given in return for the promise of allowing the discount. In such circumstances, the traditional consideration rule would work to protect the milk supplier. But what if the supermarket demanded the discount in return for £100 of supermarket vouchers? The vouchers would be good consideration for the variation of the contract and the fact that they would be worth very little would be irrelevant. After all, consideration has to be sufficient (i.e. of some value) and does not have to be adequate (i.e. it need not be of fair market value). In these circumstances, the consideration rule cannot really be relied upon to make unfairly renegotiated terms unenforceable, because it is so easily circumvented. It is much better to rely on the duress principle, which focusses on the pressure and its effect.

➡ CROSS-REFERENCE

For the discussion of adequacy and sufficiency of consideration see 5.5.

While duress requires illegitimate pressure, there is a strict standard that applies in the context of economic duress. Clearly, commercial pressure is normal in business and even very intense commercial pressure can be expected. Not every deal made is a 'win' for both parties and, often, a party enters into a contract on bad terms because they are unable to negotiate better terms. Such a one-sided contract could be formed with no wrongdoing at all. Consider a business that is desperate for money to survive. It might have no option but to accept a loan with a very high rate of interest. The decision to accept such a loan would be induced by a high level of commercial pressure but, at the same time, there will have been no wrongdoing by the lender *per se*. To distinguish between pressure which amounts to economic duress and ordinary commercial pressure, the courts focus on legitimacy. If the pressure is deemed to be illegitimate, then it could amount to economic duress.

KEY POINTS

- The consideration rule is not enough to protect a party from being forced to agree to vary their contract terms.
- When a party relies on economic duress, the counter argument is that their decision resulted from ordinary (legitimate) commercial pressure, and so the distinction between these two things is important.

At this stage, we can turn to the key cases on economic duress that show the development of the principle. In addition, some aspects of these cases added to the development of duress generally. We will start with the cases that confirmed that duress extends to economic duress. At the same time, we will identify the requirements for economic duress and how they are satisfied.

Our starting point is when economic pressure can be illegitimate for duress purposes. We will then turn to cases that provide guidance on the 'compulsion of will' requirement. This division of issues is just for convenience and helps us to know what cases are more significant for each duress requirement.

14.5.1 Illegitimate Pressure Arising from a Threat to Breach

In most cases, the main difficulty has been to identify whether a particular example of financial or commercial pressure was illegitimate. The common law was slow to recognise economic duress, and the first case to do so was *Occidental Worldwide Investment Corporation v Skibs A/S Avanti, The Siboen and The Sibotre* [1976] 1 Lloyd's Rep. 293, which concerned two charterparty agreements. They were renegotiated so that the charterer would pay less each month. After agreeing to the change, the owners later withdrew their ships and so the charterer sued for breach. In response, the owners argued that the new terms had been agreed as a result of duress. The duress argument failed, but only on the facts. Kerr J held that the owners acted under 'great pressure' but it was still acceptable commercial pressure.

In the judgment, Kerr J expressed an opinion about the scope of duress. The judge acknowledged that duress is not confined to threats to harm a person. It could be much wider and cover threats to damage property. More importantly, the opinion acknowledged that a threat to breach a contract could result in duress. No reference was made to the term 'economic duress', but that is what was in effect being recognised.

The Siboen and The Sibotre was a first instance decision. In addition, the comments from Kerr J were *obiter* and there was not even a finding of duress on the facts. However, other cases built on the wider scope of duress, and the first case to apply the opinion of Kerr J and actually find economic duress was *North Ocean Shipping Co Ltd v Hyundai Construction Co Ltd, The Atlantic Baron* [1979] QB 705.

The *Atlantic Baron* case is a good example of economic duress arising from a threat to breach. The case concerned a ship building contract. Under the terms, a ship building yard agreed to build an oil tanker for a price of $30,950,000 paid in five instalments. During performance, the value of the US dollar fell by 10% and so, in response, the yard demanded an extra 10% be added to the price, and threatened to end the contract unless the increase was agreed. The problem was that the prospective owners had already arranged a lucrative contract with the oil giant Shell. Under this contract, Shell was to take use of the tanker once it was complete, and the owner did not want to lose this lucrative contract or, worse, be liable to Shell. This pressure led to the owner agreeing to the new price and they then increased their payments. Eight months after the tanker was delivered, the owner sued for the return of the extra money paid. The claim relied on two key points: first, that there had been no consideration for their promise to pay more, and, second, that their agreement had been made as a result of duress.

Mocatta J held that the yard had provided consideration for the promise to increase payments. This was a result of the yard increasing its payment security to reflect the increase. More importantly, Mocatta J found that there had been economic duress on the facts, but that the owner could not rescind the amendment to the contract. Essentially, they had affirmed the contract by taking too long to claim.

After dealing with the consideration point, Mocatta J turned to the duress argument. Reference was made to the rejection of *Skeate v Beale* by Kerr J in *The Siboen and The Sibotre*. Mocatta J then made a statement on the scope of duress:

> First, I do not take the view that the recovery of money paid under duress other than to the person is necessarily limited to duress to goods falling within one of the categories hitherto established by the English cases. . .Secondly, from this it follows that the compulsion may take the form of "economic duress" if the necessary facts are proved. A threat to break a contract may amount to such "economic duress." Thirdly, if there has been such a form of duress leading to a contract for consideration, I think that contract is a voidable one which can be avoided and the excess money paid under it recovered.
>
> I think the facts found in this case do establish that the agreement to increase the price by 10 per cent. . . . was caused by what may be called "economic duress." The Yard were adamant in insisting on the increased price without having any legal justification for so doing and the owners realised that the Yard would not accept anything other than an unqualified agreement to the increase. The owners might have claimed damages in arbitration against the Yard with all the inherent unavoidable uncertainties of litigation, but in view of the position of the Yard *vis-à-vis* their relations with Shell it would be unreasonable to hold that this is the course they should have taken: see *Astley v. Reynolds*. . . The owners made a very reasonable offer of arbitration coupled with security for any award in the Yard's favour that might be made, but this was refused. They then made their agreement, which can truly I think be said to have been made under compulsion, by the telex of June 28 without prejudice to their rights. I do not consider the Yard's ignorance of the Shell charter material. It may well be that had they known of it they would have been even more exigent.
>
> . . .[W]hat is said in Chitty on Contracts, 24th ed. . . ., to which both counsel referred me, is relevant, namely, that a contract entered into under duress is voidable and not void:
>
> ". . . consequently a person who has entered into a contract under duress, may either affirm or avoid such contract after the duress has ceased . . . if, after escaping from the duress, he takes no steps to set aside the transaction, he may be found to have affirmed it."
>
> . . .
>
> The owners were, therefore, free from the duress on November 27, 1974, and took no action by way of protest or otherwise between their important telex of June 28, 1973, and their formal claim for the return of the excess 10 per cent. paid of July 30, 1975, when they nominated their arbitrator. . . [T]he final payments were made without any qualification and were followed by a delay until July 31, 1975, before the owners put forward their claim, the correct inference to draw, . . . is that the action and inaction of the owners can only be regarded as an affirmation of the . . . agreement to pay the additional 10 per cent.

The judgment represents the first finding of economic duress, and so it confirmed the extension to the traditional doctrine of duress. The duress arose from a threat to breach a contract, and while there was no reference to 'illegitimate pressure', we know that the legitimacy of any threat is important. In fact, it was even highlighted by the Privy Council in *Barton v Armstrong*. The point is that a threat to breach a contract can be classed as illegitimate pressure given that a breach of contract is technically unlawful—it is a failure to complete a legally enforceable duty. For that reason, a threat to breach is a threat of unlawful action, and such unlawfulness should mean that the pressure is illegitimate.

?! THINKING POINTS

On the facts, why was there no economic duress in *Williams v Roffey* [1990]?

The judgment of Mocatta J also confirmed the effect of duress. It makes the contract voidable, not void. This works because the victim has intentionally consented; it is just that the consent was not freely given and was impaired. So just like a misrepresentation, duress results in an enforceable contract which the victim has the chance to rescind later. The bars to rescission also apply and prevented a remedy in this particular case. On the facts, once the owners were free from the duress, they took eight months to complain and they had made the full final payment. These facts meant that the contract had been affirmed by the owners. This means that in practice, once a victim is free from the pressure, it is important to challenge the agreement as early as possible.

The extension of duress to economic duress became well-established and was confirmed by the Privy Council in *Pao On v Lau Yiu Long* [1980] AC 614. It was then confirmed by the House of Lords in *Universe Tankships of Monrovia v International Transport Workers Federation* [1983] 1 AC 366.

The Atlantic Baron suggests that the pressure arising from a threat to breach is illegitimate in itself. However, some judges have appeared to prefer a more flexible approach. In *DSND Subsea Ltd v Petroleum Geo Services Ltd* [2000] Dyson J listed the factors relevant to whether pressure is illegitimate. Within the list, reference was made to whether the threatened breach was in good or bad faith. Later, in *Huyton SA v Peter Cremer GmbH & Co* [1999] CLC 230, Mance J referred to compromises made in good faith, indicating that the courts would be reluctant to interfere in such cases. Crucially, he said that good faith would not 'always' be a defence where there was a threat of unlawful action. That comment implies that good faith *might* be a defence sometimes. Clearly, this would make the assessment of legitimacy more flexible, but, at the same time, it would make it less certain. More recently, in the Court of Appeal case of *Times Travel (UK) LTD v Pakistan International Airlines Corporation* [2019] EWCA Civ 828, David Richards LJ (with whom the other Lord Justices agreed) considered illegitimate pressure resulting from a threat to breach and observed:

> Lord Scarman's observation that the threat of unlawful action will be treated as illegitimate, whatever the demand, holds good for the commission or threat of a tort or similar wrong or an offence. It will also be true of many, perhaps most, threats of a breach of contract, but academic writers are nearly unanimous in thinking that there may be some threats of breach of contract which will not be treated as illegitimate: see Chitty on Contracts (33rd ed. 2018) at paras 8-038–8-045, Goff & Jones: The Law of Unjust Enrichment (9th ed. 2016) at 10-61-10-63, Burrows: The Law of Restitution (3rd ed. 2011) at pp. 267–275. It was also the view of Dyson J in *DSND Subsea Ltd v Petroleum Geo-Services ASA* [2000] BLR 530 at [134].

This comment by David Richards LJ acknowledges that leading academic commentators believe that a threat to breach should not *always* make the resulting pressure illegitimate. So far, the cases involving a threat to breach have indicated that the threat to breach was itself enough for the pressure to qualify as illegitimate. However, it appears that in an appropriate case, it may be worth arguing that the threat to breach was in good faith and so the pressure should not be classed as illegitimate. The success of such an argument remains to be tested in a case, but there is academic and some judicial support for such an approach.

With all of that said, in the *Times Travel* case, David Richards LJ also made it clear that Dyson J's reference to whether the threat was in good or bad faith should not be taken as '*general or freestanding touchstones of illegitimate pressure*'. In other words, in the context of economic duress generally, the threat having been made in bad faith is not a general requirement. Likewise, the making of a threat in good faith will not in itself prevent a finding of duress.

14.5.2 Threat of Unlawful Industrial Action

So far, we have seen how illegitimate pressure can arise from a threat to breach. However, it was not long before it was argued that the threat of industrial action could result in economic duress. Industrial action is typically done by employees represented by a trade union. Following a dispute with employers, the employees as union members might strike, i.e. refuse to work, and protest. Another common form of action is simply working strictly to the contract requirements, and doing no more.

The key case concerning industrial action and economic duress is *Universe Tankships of Monrovia v International Transport Workers Federation* [1983] 1 AC 366. In the case, the claimant's ship was unable to leave a port because industrial action by the defendant union resulted in the ship being 'black listed'. That meant the harbour workers would not use their towboats (tugs) to tow the ship out of the harbour. This unavailability of the ship was very costly for the claimant and so they negotiated with the union, who demanded payments to allow the ship to leave. They wanted $80,000 back-pay for the crew along with a contribution of $6,480 to their workers' welfare fund. The claimant agreed and paid, but then brought an action to recover the money paid to the welfare fund on the basis that it was paid under economic duress. The majority of the House of Lords upheld the claim, which meant that the money paid was recoverable.

Lord Diplock delivered the lead judgment for the majority in which there was a lot of discussion about the lawfulness of the union's action. This was not done in order to work out the legitimacy of the threat and whether there had been economic duress, since economic duress was conceded by the union. The key issue was whether the Trade Union and Labour Relations Act 1974 prevented the remedy of recovering the money paid. The majority held that the Act allowed action relating to the terms and conditions of employment, but it did not cover action relating to the welfare fund, and so the Act did not prevent that payment being recovered. This meant that the case really hinged on the scope of the Act rather than whether there had been economic duress. However, the dispute raised the question of whether the lawfulness of a demand could determine the legitimacy of the resulting pressure and the judgments discussed the matter as a result.

The minority judgments linked the lawfulness of the demand with the legitimacy of the pressure. According to Lord Scarman, the demand for the welfare fund payment was protected under the Act as it was within the wider scope of 'terms and conditions of employment'. On that basis, the demand for the payment was legitimate pressure *per se* and therefore not economic duress.

Lord Diplock could also have linked the legitimacy of the pressure with the lawfulness of the demand, and the fact that he did not do so should not rule out such a link being made. In fact, the later opinion of Lord Goff in *Dimskal Shipping Co SA v International Transport Workers Federation (The Evia Luck)* [1991] 3 WLR 875 supports the use of such a link. In *The Evia Luck*, Lord Goff referred to the approach taken by Lord Diplock in *The Universe Tankships case*, stating:

> It is enough to state that, by parity of reasoning, not only may an action of restitution be rejected as inconsistent with the policy of a statute such as that under consideration in [*The Universe Tankships case*], but in my opinion a claim that a contract is voidable for duress by reason of pressure legitimised by such a statute may likewise be rejected on the same ground.

In other words, if the demand made in *The Universe Tankships* was not made lawful by legislation, the pressure would be classed as illegitimate. However, this is not the same thing as saying that the pressure arising from a threat of *lawful action* will always be legitimate. We will at 14.6 that a threat of lawful action can still amount to duress. The possibility of such lawful act duress was even acknowledged in the judgment by Lord Scarman in *The Universe Tankships case*.

→ CROSS-REFERENCE

For the discussion of lawful act duress see 14.6.

Overall, in this context of legitimacy, *The Universe Tankships case* shows that economic duress does not just arise from a threat to breach a contract. Such a threat is just one way of creating illegitimate pressure. The threat of industrial action can be another source of illegitimate pressure resulting in economic duress, particularly where it is not made lawful by legislation.

14.5.3 Compulsion of Will: The Old Strict Requirement of an Overborn Will

Shortly after *The Atlantic Baron*, economic duress was discussed by the Privy Council in *Pao On v Lau Yiu Long* [1980]. Under the main agreement, the claimant sold their business to the defendant. Payment was in the form of 4.2 million shares in the defendant's company, and these had a market value $2.43 each. Under the terms of the agreement, the claimant had to wait a year before selling 60% of the shares. This was an important requirement, because the sale of large amounts of the shares would devalue them, so that the defendant's shares in their own company would be worth less. But the restriction on selling created a risk for the claimant because it was possible that their shares might have devalued by the time they were allowed to sell. To address this concern, the parties made a second agreement.

In the second agreement, the defendant would buy back the claimant's shares after a year for $2.43 each. The claimant then realised that this was a bad deal, because share prices can go up as well as down. The claimants then demanded that the second agreement be replaced by a guarantee. Under this guarantee, the claimant would simply be compensated for any fall in the value of the shares, and, crucially, the claimants said they would not go ahead with the main agreement unless this guarantee was agreed. At that point, the defendant could have sued for breach, but they felt that such an action would have a negative impact on the company. They then agreed to replace the second agreement with the guarantee. Later, the share price fell to $0.35 and when the claimant tried to enforce the guarantee the defendant refused. One of their arguments was that the guarantee was a result of economic duress.

The Privy Council held that there was commercial pressure. However, it was not a case of economic duress. The defendant simply weighed the risks and made a commercial decision. There was the risk of loss from no deal going ahead and that risk of loss was deemed to be bigger than the risk of the share prices falling later.

Lord Scarman delivered the judgment for the Privy Council:

> Duress, whatever form it takes, is a coercion of the will so as to vitiate consent. Their Lordships agree with the observation of Kerr J. in *Occidental Worldwide Investment Corporation v. Skibs A/S Avanti* [1976] . . . that in a contractual situation commercial pressure is not enough. There must be present some factor "which could in law be regarded as a coercion of his will so as to vitiate his consent." This conception is in line with what was said in this Board's decision in *Barton v. Armstrong* [1976] . . . by Lord Wilberforce and Lord Simon . . . In determining whether there was a coercion of will such that there was no true consent, it is material to inquire whether the person alleged to have been coerced did or did not protest; whether, at the time he was allegedly coerced into making the contract, he did or did not have an alternative course open to him such as an adequate legal remedy; whether he was independently advised; and whether after entering the contract he took steps to avoid it. All these matters are, . . . relevant in determining whether he acted voluntarily or not.
>
> In the present case there is unanimity amongst the judges below that there was no coercion of the first defendant's will. In the Court of Appeal the trial judge's finding . . . that the first defendant considered the matter thoroughly, chose to avoid litigation, and formed the opinion that the risk

in giving the guarantee was more apparent than real was upheld. In short, there was commercial pressure, but no coercion.

It is doubtful, however, whether at common law any duress other than duress to the person sufficed to render a contract voidable . . . Recently two English judges have recognised that commercial pressure may constitute duress the pressure of which can render a contract voidable: Kerr J. in [*The Siboen and The Sibotre*] . . . and Mocatta J. in [*The Atlantic Baron*]. Both stressed that the pressure must be such that the victim's consent to the contract was not a voluntary act on his part. In their Lordships' view, there is nothing contrary to principle in recognising economic duress as a factor which may render a contract voidable, provided always that the basis of such recognition is that it must amount to a coercion of will, which vitiates consent. It must be shown that the payment made or the contract entered into was not a voluntary act.

 THINKING POINTS

Why was there economic duress in the *Atlantic Baron* but not in *Pao On*?

The cases so far illustrate the difficult distinction judges have to make. In any given case, the pressure might be classed as economic duress, or it might simply be acceptable commercial pressure. In the *Atlantic Baron*, the owner had to decide between losing a contact with Shell and simply paying the extra 10%. Suing the yard was not an option, as the delay would have resulted in the owner not having the tanker ready for Shell. In *Pao On*, the choices were not so absolute. Not buying the claimant's business and suing the claimant for breach could make the company look less successful, as though it was struggling, and that in turn could have resulted in its share price falling. Alternatively, the guarantee was not all bad. At the time, it was felt that the shares would increase in value and there was only a small risk of having to pay on the guarantee. That takes us to the basic essence of duress: the victim has a choice, but it is really about taking the lesser of two evils. In *Pao On*, the options were not really 'evil' enough. It was more like choosing a Hawaiian pizza over a painfully-hot chilli pizza rather than having to choose the hot chilli pizza over the option of starving.

Lord Scarman did not refer to the 'legitimacy' of the pressure. However, perhaps there was no need to do so since the defendant could not show the required level of compulsion anyway.

On showing the necessary compulsion, reference was made to the following relevant factors such as: did the victim object? Was there legal advice? What alternatives were open to the victim? And, did the victim act quickly to avoid the agreement? These factors should not be treated as essential requirements for duress. They are simply facts that might go towards evidence of compulsion. The major significance of the case comes from the language used. Duress was defined as a 'coercion of will so as to vitiate consent'. It was then said that it has to be shown that the payment or contract 'was not a voluntary act'.

The language of the Privy Council suggested that the victim's will had to be 'overborn'. It required the pressure to take over the victim and thus forcing that party to agree. This approach became known as the 'overborn will theory' and was severely criticised in an article by Professor Atiyah (1982) 98 LQR 197. Here it was argued that duress does not take over and make the victim act involuntarily. Instead, the victim acts intentionally in the knowledge of what they are agreeing to and with their consent being given consciously. However, their consent is not genuinely free.

Consider the following example. You are told to sell your PC Tablet for £1 or else your fingers will be broken. When you go ahead and sell it for a £1, you are well aware of doing so. You have acted voluntarily and intentionally agreed. It is not as though you become a mindless automaton. The real issue is that you have not agreed freely, because your agreement came as a result of having no real alternative. Such an approach is consistent with the effect of duress on a contract. Just like misrepresentation, we know that duress results in a voidable contract because the victim has consented in an impaired way. In contrast, the 'overborn will' requirement would suggest there was no consent and that should result in there being no contract—i.e. a contract that is treated as being void from the start.

KEY POINTS

- The 'overborne will' requirement is not consistent with cases finding duress from a voluntary decision to agree.
- In addition, it is also not consistent with duress resulting in a voidable contract.

14.5.4 Rejection of 'Overborn Will' Requirement

Not long after *Pao On*, in *The Universe Tankships case* [1983] the House of Lords sought to clarify the law on duress. After citing *Barton v Armstrong* and *Pao On*, Lord Scarman took the opportunity to state the requirements for duress and clarify the basis of the action:

> The authorities upon which these two cases were based reveal two elements in the wrong of duress; (1) pressure amounting to compulsion of the will of the victim; and (2) the illegitimacy of the pressure exerted. . .Compulsion is variously described in the authorities as coercion or the vitiation of consent. The classic case of duress is, however, not the lack of will to submit but the victim's intentional submission arising from the realisation that there is no other practical choice open to him. . .This is the thread of principle which links the early law of duress (threat to life or limb) with later developments when the law came also to recognise as duress first the threat to property and now the threat to a man's business or trade.

This shows that the victim's will does not have to be overborn by the pressure. Instead, what matters is that the victim had no reasonable alternatives. This applies to the general principle of duress and is not limited to a particular context.

For the majority, Lord Diplock expressed a consistent view when explaining the basis of duress. This began by saying that it was not about pressure overbearing the will of the victim:

> It is not that the party seeking to avoid the contract which he has entered into with another party, or to recover money that he has paid to another party in response to a demand, did not know the nature or the precise terms of the contract at the time when he entered into it or did not understand the purpose for which the payment was demanded.

Lord Diplock then explained the basis for duress in the following way:

> The rationale is that his apparent consent was induced by pressure exercised upon him by that other party which the law does not regard as legitimate, with the consequence that the consent is treated in law as revocable. . .

This makes it clear that duress is not based on a party's total failure to actually consent. Instead, it is about the party's 'apparent consent' being induced by illegitimate pressure.

Later, in *The Evia Luck* [1993], Lord Goff acknowledged that a 'coercion of will' had been suggested as a basis of duress. The judgment then referred to the criticism of this by leading scholars and observed that it was unhelpful to refer to a claimant's will being coerced. It is now accepted that duress is not based on the victim's will being taken over or overborn and, instead, there is a requirement of a 'compulsion of will'. Such a requirement is taken to mean that the victim voluntarily chooses to agree, because it was the only realistic choice following wrongful pressure. Of course, that does not tell us precisely how to satisfy the requirement of compulsion.

14.5.5 Compulsion of Will: No Practical Alternative and Causation

If the illegitimate pressure is *the* cause of the victim's action, it can be said that it resulted in a compulsion of will. An obvious way to evidence such a cause is to identify that there was no practical alternative available to the victim. Logically, compulsion seems linked with causation and having no practical alternative. Having no practical alternative would surely be evidence supporting compulsion and, likewise, evidence of the pressure being the cause of a decision would go towards establishing compulsion too.

A good basic example of the requirements for economic duress and a finding of no practical alternative is *Atlas Express Ltd v Kafco (Importers v Distributers) Ltd* [1989] 1 QB 833. Kafco was a small company that imported basket products. They had a profitable contract supplying the products to a long-established national retail chain called Woolworths. Kafco had contracted with Atlas Express to deliver the products to the Woolworths stores, but when Atlas Express started deliveries, they realised that they had underestimated their costs. For that reason, they demanded more money from Kafco and threatened to stop deliveries unless they were paid more. Kafco then agreed because they did not want to lose their contract with Woolworths. Later, when Atlas Express sued to recover the new rate, Kafco challenged the rate on the basis of economic duress.

In the Commercial Court, Tucker J held that the agreement to amend the rate was voidable for economic duress. The pressure was illegitimate because the threat to breach was a threat of unlawful action. On the facts, Kafco had no practical alternative and so that was the compulsion of will. It would have been very difficult, if not impossible to find another carrier to meet the delivery schedule at such short notice. Furthermore, suing for breach would not have protected Kafco from losing their contract with Woolworths and, in addition, they would have been liable to Woolworths for breach.

The case shows that the basic requirements are:

- illegitimate pressure, resulting in;
- a compulsion of will because;
- there is no other practical alternative.

In *B & S Contracts and Designs Ltd v Victor Green publications* [1984] ICR 419, there was a finding of economic duress and, again, the compulsion of will was based on there being no practical alternative. The case concerned an implied threat to not perform a contractual obligation unless payment was made. The Court of Appeal found that under the contract such non-performance would be a breach. As such, it was a threat of unlawful action and that was then taken to result in illegitimate pressure. According to Griffiths LJ, the pressure put the victim in an 'impossible position' and he 'had no alternative but to pay'. Kerr LJ agreed with the other judgments and explained the point:

> It appears from the authorities that it will only constitute duress if the consequences of a refusal would be serious and immediate so that there is no reasonable alternative open, such as by legal redress, obtaining an injunction, etc. I think that this is implicit in the authorities to which we have been referred, of which the most recent one is [*The Universe Tankships case*].
>
> . . . [T]here was no other practical choice open to the defendants in the present case, and accordingly I agree that this is a case where money has been paid under duress, which was accordingly recoverable by the defendants provided they acted promptly as they did . . .

In the reasoning, no other reference was made to anything else relating to compulsion. There was no reference to how the pressure *caused* the payment and so it seemed that having no practical alternative was enough to show compulsion.

In contrast, the role of causation (i.e. the extent to which the pressure must cause the victim to act) has featured as an issue in some cases. One of these was *The Evia Luck*, where Lord Goff referred to causation when defining economic duress. After citing *The Siboen and The Sibotre*, *The Atlantic Baron* and *Pao On*, Lord Goff observed:

> …[I]t is now accepted that economic pressure may be sufficient to amount to duress for this purpose, provided at least that the economic pressure may be characterised as illegitimate and has constituted a significant cause inducing the plaintiff to enter into the relevant contract.

Here Lord Goff referred to the pressure being a 'significant cause'. We can contrast this with the approach to threats to harm a person. In *Barton v Armstrong*, it was enough for the pressure to have been 'a' cause to show the required level of compulsion. However, Lord Goff suggests a higher level of causation is needed for economic duress. This distinction was explained by Mance J in *Huyton SA v Peter Cremer GmbH & Co* [1999] CLC 230:

> The use of the phrase 'a significant cause' by Lord Goff in *The Evia Luck*, … suggests that this relaxed view of causation in the special context of duress to the person cannot prevail in the less serious context of economic duress. The minimum basic test of subjective causation in economic duress ought, it appears to me, to be a 'but for' test. The illegitimate pressure must have been such as actually caused the making of the agreement, in the sense that it would not otherwise have been made either at all or, at least, in the terms in which it was made. In that sense, the pressure must have been decisive or clinching. There may of course be cases where a common-sense relaxation, even of a but for requirement is necessary, for example in the event of an agreement induced by two concurrent causes, each otherwise sufficient to ground a claim of relief, in circumstances where each alone would have induced the agreement, so that it could not be said that, but for either, the agreement would not have been made. On the other hand, it also seems clear that the application of a simple 'but for' test of subjective causation … could lead too readily to relief being granted. It would not, for example, cater for the obvious possibility that, although the innocent party would never have acted as he did, but for the illegitimate pressure, he nevertheless had a real choice and could, if he had wished, equally well have resisted the pressure and, for example, pursued alternative legal redress. …
>
> …It is not necessary to go so far as to say that it is an inflexible third essential ingredient of economic duress that there should be no or no practical alternative course open to the innocent party. But it seems, as I have already indicated, self-evident that relief may not be appropriate, if an innocent party decides, as a matter of choice, not to pursue an alternative remedy which any and possibly some other reasonable persons in his circumstances would have pursued.

The extract of the judgment by Mance J indicates that for a compulsion of will the pressure has to cause the victim to act. For duress of the person, the pressure just has to be 'a' reason. For economic duress, it needs to be *the* cause and, to establish that, the 'but for' test should be applied. The question to ask would be: but for the pressure, would the victim have agreed to the terms? Such a test represents a higher standard of causation to that used for duress to the person. The different standard appears to be based on the seriousness of the illegitimate pressure. If such pressure is very serious, like a threat to kill, then it is easy to show compulsion just from the pressure being 'a' reason. In contrast, when such pressure is less serious (like financial pressure), more has to be done to show compulsion.

The causation test cannot be as strict where there are two different causes of illegitimate pressure which in themselves would both have been enough to qualify as economic duress. Otherwise each cause would cancel the other out. If the person would not have entered into an agreement 'but for' Pressure A, then Pressure B cannot logically be said to have been the 'but for' pressure. But the same will also be true in reverse if Pressure B would in its own right have been the 'but for' pressure.

Mance J also acknowledged that the 'but for' test was insufficient on its own. The point was that it could be satisfied even when the victim had a practical alternative. For that reason, having no practical alternative is a specific requirement for economic duress. It is not simply evidence of compulsion or the pressure having been a cause. It was not described as an absolute or 'inflexible' requirement, but it is clearly a general requirement.

Subsequent cases have confirmed the significance of showing no practical alternative, and *DSND Subsea Ltd v Petroleum Geo-Services ASA* [2000] BLR 530 is one of these. In this case, Dyson J listed the requirements for economic duress, and the 'lack of a practical choice for the victim' was a separate third requirement. The other requirements were illegitimate pressure and the pressure being a significant cause. Later, in *Kolmar Group AG v Traxpo Enterprises Pty Ltd* [2010] EWHC 113, Christopher Clarke J summarised the requirements and rules for economic duress:

> [92] . . . I agree, that the authorities (summarised in Goff & Jones, The Law of Restitution (17th ed.) 10-025 to 10-51 and Chitty on Contracts (30th ed.) 7-014 – 7-055; and in *DSND Subsea Ltd v Petroleum Geo Services ASA* [2000] BLR para 131) establish the following principles:
>
> (i) Economic pressure can amount to duress, provided it may be characterised as illegitimate and has constituted a "but for" cause inducing the Claimant to enter into the relevant contract or to make a payment. See Mance J in *SL Huyton SA v Peter Cremer GmbH & Co* [1999] . . .
>
> (ii) a threat to break a contract will generally be regarded as illegitimate, particularly where the Defendant must know that it would be in breach of contract if the threat were implemented;
>
> (iii) it is relevant to consider whether the Claimant had a "real choice" or "realistic alternative" and could, if it had wished, equally well have resisted the pressure and, for example, pursued practical and effective legal redress. If there was no reasonable alternative, that may be very strong evidence in support of a conclusion that the victim of the duress was in fact influenced by the threat.
>
> (iv) the presence, or absence, of protest, may be of some relevance when considering whether the threat had coercive effect. But, even the total absence of protest does not mean that the payment was voluntary.

These points indicate that for the relevant 'compulsion' of will:

- The pressure should be the 'but for' cause (unless there are several pressures, any of which would have been sufficient in its own right);
- no practical alternative for the victim will be very strong evidence of the compulsion, and;
- evidence of the victim protesting (i.e. initially disagreeing with the new terms) could be relevant, but is not essential.

The points made by Christopher Clarke J serve as very useful guidance for establishing the compulsion of will required for economic duress. It is aimed at summarising the requirements developed in previous cases. It was already well established that pressure from a threat to breach is generally illegitimate. On the issues of compulsion, the judgment also mentioned the 'but for' cause which is consistent with what Mance J explained in *Huyton*, rather than the 'significant cause', which had been used in other cases. This difference in language could mean:

- The causation standard for demonstrating compulsion is either the 'but for' cause or a 'significant cause'. These are applied inconsistently, and so the legal position is not ideal and needs to be clarified by the appeal courts directly.
- Alternatively, the difference in language could simply reflect the fact that the level of causation needed can vary. The variation could be based on the seriousness (i.e. the level of illegitimacy) of the economic pressure. That would be consistent with the tests being different for duress to the person and economic duress.

More recently, in *Sheikh Tahnoon Bin Saeed Bin Shakhboot Al Nehayan v Ioannis Kent* [2018] EWHC 333 (Comm), Leggatt LJ addressed causation for economic duress. He showed a preference for the 'but for' test, based on the comment by Christopher Clarke J in *Kolmar*. He also made reference to the significance of there being no practical alternative for the victim. Leggatt LJ observed that Christopher Clarke J had viewed it as very strong evidence of compulsion, but not as an essential requirement. Likewise, he did not consider the absence of a practical alternative to be essential.

KEY POINTS

The recent cases from the Commercial Court do not take the absence of a practical alternative to be essential to prove duress. Instead, it is very strong evidence of compulsion. What seems to matter is that the pressure was the 'but for' cause (and, of course, that it was illegitimate).

14.6 Lawful Act Duress

So far, the categories of duress we have covered relate to threats to do something unlawful, such as threats to harm a person or property and threats to breach a contract. The same can be said for industrial action beyond what is permitted by legislation. It is the unlawfulness of the threatened action that makes the pressure illegitimate. The recognition of economic duress showed that duress was not limited to threats of harm and this widening of the scope of duress inspired a lot of debate about pressure arising from lawful acts, or threats to carry out lawful acts.

The key issue is the illegitimacy of the pressure. Consider a threat to do something that is not unlawful. A typical example would be a threat to accurately reveal that a person has been having an affair. Understandably, this could compel a two-timing 'love rat' to enter into a contract. Since the action threatened would not be unlawful, in what circumstances can it be classed as illegitimate? That is the main issue and has been the subject of recent judicial and academic debate. A secondary issue is the requirement of compulsion. As with the previous section, we will address these issues of illegitimacy and compulsion in turn.

14.6.1 Illegitimate Pressure from a Threat of Lawful Action

The possibility of lawful act duress was recognised at a fairly early stage. In *The Universe Tankships case* [1983], Lord Scarman started with a reference to the traditional position and then addressed lawful act duress:

> The origin of the doctrine of duress in threats to life or limb, or to property, suggests strongly that the law regards the threat of unlawful action as illegitimate, whatever the demand. Duress can, of course, exist even if the threat is one of lawful action: whether it does so depends upon the nature of the demand. Blackmail is often a demand supported by a threat to do what is lawful, e.g. to report criminal conduct to the police. In many cases, therefore, *"What [one] has to justify is not the threat, but the demand . . ."*: see per Lord Atkin in *Thorne v. Motor Trade Association* [1937] A.C. 797, 806.

In short, the pressure from a threat of lawful action can be illegitimate, and this all depends on the demand that accompanies the threat. This approach is not controversial and in fact, it would be highly controversial if only threats of unlawful action counted for duress, because a threat of lawful action can result in pressure that is just as powerful. The real problem and potential for controversy comes from the assessment of the demand. Where the demand combined with the threat amounts to blackmail, and is therefore a criminal office, there is no doubt that the pressure will be classed as illegitimate. However, there is uncertainty when the demand combined with the threat does not amount to a crime or a tort. For that reason, it is useful to examine briefly what things the courts will look at to determine if the demand makes the pressure illegitimate.

THINKING POINTS

What factors *should* be considered in deciding whether a demand makes pressure illegitimate?

For a demand to make pressure illegitimate, we could expect it to be improper in some way. The obvious suggestion would be that the demand has to be unfair or made in bad faith. Or perhaps it has to be morally wrong in some way. That is our first issue. The second issue is whether it is a good idea for the courts to assess the demand in the first place. Both issues were addressed by Steyn LJ in *CTN Cash and Carry v Gallaher Ltd* [1994] 4 All ER 714. Here the defendant was the only supplier of some leading brands of cigarettes. It delivered a cargo of cigarettes to the wrong warehouse and the goods were stolen, so the buyer did not pay. The supplier mistakenly thought that the goods were the responsibility of the buyer at the time of the theft and so demanded the payment of £17,000. The supplier believed in good faith that this sum was due and threatened to end the buyer's line of credit unless payment was made. This was a threat of lawful action because the terms of the contract gave the supplier the discretion to end the credit facility. The buyer then paid the money but later claimed its return on the basis of economic duress. In the Court of Appeal, the claim was rejected because the pressure was not illegitimate.

The lead judgment by Steyn LJ explained the issues raised by extending duress to cover a threat of lawful action as well as such threats of lawful action being made in good faith.

GUIDED READING 14.1
CTN Cash and Carry v Gallaher Ltd [1994] 4 All ER 714

When reading the short extract below, try to identify:

■ why it is important for the courts to recognise lawful act duress but why problems will result from doing so;
■ the extent to which Steyn LJ strikes a satisfactory balance in addressing the problems resulting from lawful act duress.

. . . The defendants exerted commercial pressure on the plaintiffs in order to obtain payment of a sum which they *bona fide* considered due to them. The defendants' motive in threatening withdrawal of credit facilities was commercial self-interest in obtaining a sum that they considered due to them.

. . .

I also readily accept that the fact that the defendants have used lawful means does not by itself remove the case from the scope of the doctrine of economic duress. Professor Birks, in An Introduction to the Law of Restitution (1989) p. 177, lucidly explains:

'Can lawful pressures also count? This is a difficult question, because, if the answer is that they can, the only viable basis for discriminating between acceptable and unacceptable pressures is not positive law but social morality. In other words, the judges must say what pressures (though lawful outside the restitutionary context) are improper as contrary to prevailing standards. That makes the judges, not the law or the legislature, the arbiters of social evaluation.'

It had been established that the supplier genuinely believed it was entitled to the money demanded, and were only acting in commercial self-interest, which is not something the law discourages.

However, Steyn LJ wanted to make clear that lawful action should be capable of amounting to duress. The problem was that in deciding the legitimacy of the lawful action, judges would have to determine and apply standards of social morality. That is not the role of a judge in a modern democracy, and it will also result in uncertainty and arbitrary decision-making.

On the other hand, if the answer is that lawful pressures are always exempt, those who devise outrageous but technically lawful means of compulsion must always escape restitution until the legislature declares the abuse unlawful. It is tolerably clear that, at least where they can be confident of a general consensus in favour of their evaluation, the courts are willing to apply a standard of impropriety rather than technical unlawfulness.

[After turning to some authority, the judgment continued.]

. . . [I]t seems to me that an extension capable of covering the present case, involving 'lawful act duress' in a commercial context in pursuit of a *bona fide* claim, would be a radical one with far-reaching implications.

It would introduce a substantial and undesirable element of uncertainty in the commercial bargaining process. Moreover, it will often enable *bona fide* settled accounts to be reopened when parties to commercial dealings fall out. The aim of our commercial law ought to be to encourage fair dealing between parties. But it is a mistake for the law to set its sights too highly when the critical inquiry is not whether the conduct is lawful but whether it is morally or socially unacceptable. That is the inquiry in which we are engaged. In my view there are policy considerations which militate against ruling that the defendants obtained payment of the disputed invoice by duress.

Outside the field of protected relationships, and in a purely commercial context, it might be a relatively rare case in which 'lawful act duress' can be established. And it might be particularly difficult to establish duress if the defendant *bona fide* considered that his demand was valid. In this complex and changing branch of the law I deliberately refrain from saying 'never'. But as the law stands, I am satisfied that the defendants' conduct in this case did not amount to duress.

> But against this has to be balanced the need to avoid the undesirable situation that anybody could exert any pressure, no matter how egregious, as long as it was technically lawful.

> Steyn LJ was therefore aware of the need to strike a balance between these two dangers, but his judgment ultimately erred on the side of avoiding judges becoming arbiters of social morality. It was better to make things as certain as possible—i.e. to keep matters rooted in positive law if possible and perhaps only recognise lawful act duress when the demand is not made in good faith. The alternative would be to open the door to litigation whenever one party felt another had 'got one over' on it.

> This meant that while fair dealing was important, the law should not as a general rule base its outcomes on what was morally or socially acceptable rather than *lawful*. Put another way, in the context of commercial disputes generally, illegitimate pressure should mean a threat to act unlawfully.

> In summary, 'lawful act duress' would be rare. In a purely commercial context like this one, almost any instance of lawful pressure (applied in good faith) will be considered to be acting in commercial self-interest and hence legitimate. But, of course, there might be exceptions.

Overall, the judgment made it clear that lawful act duress would be difficult to establish in an agreement between commercial parties. Furthermore, it will be very unlikely and 'rare' in circumstances where a demand is believed to have been made in good faith.

?! THINKING POINTS

Why should cases in the commercial context be treated differently to non-commercial cases like those between a consumer and business or private employee and employer?

More recently, in the *Times Travel* case, David Richards LJ analysed the significance of *CTN Cash and Carry*. Times Travel were one of a number of agents that sold flight tickets for Pakistan Airlines, and in the case of Times Travel, their business was almost exclusively the sale of these tickets. The airline had failed to pay the commission that their agents were entitled to under their contracts. Following demands and claims for payments, the airline ended these agency agreements, which was something that they were entitled to do under those contracts. They then offered their agents new contracts, but on terms that required such agents to waive their rights to their unpaid commissions. Essentially, this meant that the airline's existing agents had to agree to set aside their claims to the money owed by the airline. Times Travel agreed to the new contract in order to survive, but later sought to recover the unpaid commission, claiming that the agreement had resulted from economic duress. The first instance judge held there was lawful act duress and found in favour of Times Travel. However, the Court of Appeal, led by David Richards LJ, overturned the decision on the basis that there had been no duress. It was a case of a threat of lawful action with a demand that was made in good faith but was objectively unreasonable. David Richards LJ explained the significance of *CTN Cash and Carry* in the following way:

> 62. In my view, *CTN Cash and Carry v Gallagher* can be taken to establish that where A uses lawful pressure to induce B to concede a demand to which A does not *bona fide* believe itself to be entitled, B's agreement is voidable on grounds of economic duress. It cannot be taken to establish that if A genuinely but unreasonably believes the demand to be well-founded, the same result follows. While it may be that Nicholls LJ would have favoured that outcome, it runs counter to the judgment of Steyn LJ. . .

CTN Cash and Carry was then mapped on to the context of the *Times Travel* case:

> 70. In the light of what I take to be the effect of the decision of this court in *CTN Cash and Carry*, the critical issue for the purposes of this case is whether economic duress can, in a commercial context, arise where lawful acts or threats are made by A in support of a demand which A genuinely believes he is entitled to make. If that belief is reasonably, as well as genuinely, held, I can see no basis on which a plea of economic duress could succeed and it would, in any event, be contrary to the decision in *CTN Cash and Carry*. But, what is the position if the belief, though genuine, is unreasonable?

After providing a detailed examination of the cases on lawful act duress since *CTN Cash and Carry v Gallagher*, David Richards LJ concluded:

> 72. There is little or no support in the other authorities for the extension of lawful act duress in a commercial context to cover a demand which is made in good faith but unreasonably.

The approach adopted here is consistent with the limits of lawful act duress that were explained by Steyn LJ in *CTN Cash and Carry*. It means that any attempt to find duress in a threat of lawful action with combined with a demand made in good faith (i.e. made in the genuine belief of being entitled to make the demand) is likely to fail. Even if the demand is objectively unreasonable, it will still not be enough for duress if it has been made in good faith in this sense.

KEY POINTS

■ Lawful act duress is possible. The legitimacy of the pressure is based on the demand.

■ In a purely commercial context, lawful act economic duress will be difficult to establish because it is normal and acceptable for parties to act in their own commercial self-interest.

■ In a purely commercial context, a claim of duress following a threat of lawful action made in good faith has little or no chance of success, even if the demand was objectively unreasonable.

In the cases so far, lawful act duress was argued unsuccessfully. In contrast, *Akai Holdings Ltd (Liquidators) v Ting* [2010] UKPC 21 might be a case where such duress was established. Akai was a company run by a corrupt Mr Ting. When it went into liquidation, the liquidators wanted a scheme in place to fund the liquidation and pay the debts. This involved the company's shares being transferred to a third party. The scheme could only operate with shareholder approval, and it had a deadline. Mr Ting controlled two companies that had shares in Akai. He objected to the scheme and had a right to do so because of the way the scheme was structured. This meant the scheme could not operate. However, his objections were supported using forged and false evidence.

With time running out, the liquidators entered into an agreement with Mr Ting. Under its terms, Mr Ting would no longer object to the scheme and, in return, the liquidators would not take any legal action against Mr Ting. Three years later, the Hong Kong Commercial Crime Bureau found evidence of Mr Ting's serious misuse of Akai company money. It was alleged that he misused over HK$400m through false accounting, and it was clear that his objections were really designed to prevent an investigation being conducted into his misuse of company money. The liquidators then wanted to bring an action against Mr Ting. To do so, they argued that the agreement to take no action against him should be rescinded because it had been made under duress. The Privy Council agreed that the agreement was a result of duress and allowed for rescission.

The relevant point here is that Mr Ting's objection to the scheme was not itself unlawful, because he was a shareholder in Akai Holdings Ltd and shareholders had the right to object. That meant the threat to continue objecting resulted in pressure from a lawful act which induced the liquidators to enter the subsequent agreement. Lord Saville delivered the judgment for the Privy Council and decided that the pressure exerted was illegitimate. To support this, reference was made to Mr Ting's use of forged and false documents to support his objection. In other words, there was unlawful conduct involved in creating the pressure. In addition, Mr Ting was not objecting in good faith; the agreement had indeed been made in order to stop him acting in bad faith. Finally, the whole point of objecting was to prevent an investigation into Mr Ting's false accounting. In stating that the pressure was illegitimate, Lord Saville said it was a result of 'unconscionable conduct'.

Compulsion was not assessed in detail. The liquidators had to choose between abandoning the liquidation or entering into the agreement, and so according to the Privy Council they had had no practical alternative.

The duress claim was a few years after the agreement. On this, Lord Saville said that on the facts the agreement had not been affirmed by the delay, but it is not entirely clear why this was so.

The case could be seen as a lawful act duress case. Mr Ting's threat to continue objecting was lawful. He demanded that no legal action be taken against him and that demand was technically lawful too. However, the demand was certainly not made in good faith like the demand in *CTN Cash and Carry*. Instead, Mr Ting's demand was based on improper and immoral motives, because it was to designed to avoid liability for his hidden financial wrongdoing.

It does look like pressure will be illegitimate where it results from conduct that is obviously improper and in bad faith. In other words, the point by Professor Birks which was cited by Steyn LJ in *CTN* was being put into effect here. This approach was confirmed in *Progress Bulk Carriers Ltd v Tube City IMS LLC* [2012] EWHC 273 (Comm). In this case, Cooke J acknowledged that lawful act duress would be highly unusual in a commercial context. The judge then made reference to Steyn LJ's judgment in *CTN Cash and Carry* and the view of Professor Birks that he had cited, stating: 'the courts are willing to apply a standard of impropriety rather than technical lawfulness'. Of course, it is important to remember that the point by Professor Birks (cited by Steyn LJ) was in the context of when there is a clear 'consensus in favour' of the pressure being illegitimate so as to not cause any uncertainty.

More recently, the law on lawful act duress was reviewed in two cases. The first was *Al Nehayan v Kent* [2018] EWHC 333 (Comm), featuring Leggatt LJ, who had just been promoted to the Court of Appeal before delivering the judgment. The second case was *Times Travel (UK) Ltd v Pakistan International Airlines Corporation* [2019] EWCA Civ 828 in the Court of Appeal. It is useful to look at these cases in turn.

In *Al Nehayan v Kent*, the parties were business partners who had started a few companies with the claimant as the primary investor, putting in around €31m. When the business started struggling, the claimant decided to pull out, and that prompted the parties to enter into two agreements. The first was a framework agreement to de-merge the relevant companies, which included obligations on the defendant to make certain payments. The second agreement was a promissory note under which the defendant would pay back €5.4m in instalments.

Later, the claimant brought an action claiming over €15m due under the agreements, and the defendant argued that the agreements had resulted from duress. The claimant had threatened to block a particular deal unless the agreements were made. This deal involved a huge investment into the defendant's company and it was the only remaining way for the defendant to rescue his company. In addition, Leggatt LJ observed that there had been no commercial justification for the demand for €5.2m. All of this was said to make the demands illegitimate. However, the finding of duress was ultimately based on threats of unlawful action, specifically duress to the person.

While the case was decided on the basis of threats of unlawful action, Leggatt LJ did suggest a test for lawful act duress. He surveyed the previous cases on lawful act duress, and then observed:

> [187]　. . . For this purpose it is appropriate to take account of the legitimacy of the demand and to judge the propriety of the defendant's conduct by reference not simply to what is lawful but to basic minimum standards of acceptable behaviour. To the complaint that this makes the law uncertain, I would give two replies. First, as the authorities have emphasised, the standard of unconscionability is a high one and it is only in cases where the demand made and means used to reinforce it are completely indefensible that the courts will intervene. Second, no apology is needed for intervening in such cases, as the enforcement of basic norms of commerce and of fair and honest dealing is an essential function of a system of commercial law. As Mance J said in *Huyton SA v Peter Cremer GmbH & Co* [1999] 1 Lloyd's Rep 620 . . . "The law has frequently to form judgments regarding inequitability or unconscionability, giving effect in doing so to the reasonable expectations of honest persons. It is the law's function to discriminate, where discrimination is appropriate, between different factual situations . . ."
>
> [188]　It does seem to me, however, that the test suggested in Chitty on Contracts could be made more precise by transposing into objective requirements the elements of the offence of blackmail. On this basis a demand coupled with a threat to commit a lawful act will be regarded as illegitimate if (a) the defendant has no reasonable grounds for making the demand and (b) the threat would not be considered by reasonable and honest people to be a proper means of reinforcing the demand.

According to these *obiter* comments, even if the conduct or demand is lawful, it can still be illegitimate if objectively it is unreasonable and improper. Ordinarily, such an approach would be criticised for being based on a given judge's own understanding of these terms which, in turn, would cause uncertainty. However, Leggatt LJ made clear that he considered it necessary for courts to retain the power to intervene in exceptional cases where conduct and the demand made are 'completely indefensible'.

We can contrast the views of Leggatt LJ here with those expressed in the *Times Travel* case. In that case, David Richards LJ for the Court of Appeal commented specifically on the detailed opinion expressed by Leggatt LJ. This was necessary because the opinion of Leggatt LJ had been made in the context of supporting the trial judge decision in *Times Travel*, a decision that the Court of Appeal overturned. After analysing the cases and citing the views of leading scholars, David Richard LJ responded in the following way:

> 101.　I do not agree with all that Leggatt LJ said on this issue. First, as regards the discussion of *CTN Cash and Carry* and other cases at [182], I have already made clear my disagreement with an analysis of Steyn LJ's judgment that sees his reference to whether conduct is morally or socially acceptable as extending the concept of lawful act duress beyond the case of the demand made in bad faith. Other authorities are cited by Leggatt LJ for their references to unconscionability but that is the language of equity where unconscionable conduct has a well-understood meaning that, in the absence of protected relationships, does not embrace the use of lawful means for *bona fide* purposes.
>
> 102.　. . . In particular, I find it difficult to see why the use of lawful means in pursuit of a *bona fide* demand should contravene such basic standards. Leggatt LJ refers to the standard of unconscionability being a high one and that the courts will intervene only in cases where the demand

made, and the means used, are "completely indefensible" and where intervention is needed to enforce "basic norms of commerce and fair and honest dealing". Expressed in these general terms, it is difficult to disagree with these sentiments, but the difficulty and uncertainty comes in applying them to particular cases.

These contrasting approaches show that there is still debate and uncertainty remaining about lawful act duress. As things stand, the Court of Appeal has expressed disagreement with the wider principle of lawful act duress favoured by Leggatt LJ. This is because of the risk of uncertainty that it will carry when trying to apply it.

14.6.2 'Illegitimacy' for Lawful Act Duress outside of the Commercial Context

The judgment of Steyn LJ in *CTN Cash & Carry* made a range of statements that were applied to lawful act duress generally. However, when he turned to the limits of lawful act duress, he did so purely in respect of the commercial context. Lawful act duress outside the commercial context was an issue for the Privy Council in *R v Attorney-General* [2003] UKPC 22.

It is useful to address some background facts leading to the dispute in *R v Attorney-General*. In the Gulf War of 1991, a patrol from the famous SAS Regiment (the UK's elite Special Forces) was deployed behind enemy lines. On their return, one member of the patrol wrote a book which detailed his experiences and the operation. At the time it was published, the book was very controversial, because up to that point, SAS operations had been kept entirely secret. In response, the Ministry of Defence decided to prevent such information being made public in the future, and had SAS members sign confidentiality agreements. Under the terms of these agreements, members would not be permitted to reveal anything about their experiences. This obligation applied both during their employment as well as after their military careers ended.

The case concerned another member of the SAS patrol, referred to as R, who was from New Zealand by origin. He returned to New Zealand and secured a deal to produce a book about the mission. In response, the Attorney-General sought an injunction, but the court refused grant it; instead, it ordered R to hand over any profits and pay damages.

R then challenged the agreement. One of his arguments was that it had been obtained by duress. This was based on the fact that the SAS had told its members to sign or be 'returned to unit'. Essentially, if they did not sign, they would be thrown out of the elite SAS and returned to their previous (standard) army unit. Such an action would normally be a punishment resulting from a disciplinary offence, or from not being good enough. This meant that it was seen as a humiliating demotion. The fact that the SAS had a discretion to 'return to unit' anyway meant that their threat was one of lawful action.

The Privy Council assessed the legitimacy of the pressure and held that there had been no duress. The majority judgment was delivered by Lord Hoffman.

GUIDED READING 14.2
'R' v Her Majesty's Attorney-General for England and Wales [2003] UKPC 22

Below is a full extract of the judgment on the duress argument. Try to identify:

- what was said about the compulsion of will on the facts; and
- why the demand did not make the pressure legitimate.

[15] In *Universe Tankships Inc of Monrovia v International Transport Workers Federation* [1983] 1 AC 366, 400, . . . Lord Scarman said that there were two elements in the wrong of duress. One was pressure amounting to compulsion of the will of the victim and the second was the illegitimacy of the pressure. R says that to offer him the alternative of being returned to unit, which was regarded in the SAS as a public humiliation, was compulsion of his will. It left him no practical alternative. Their Lordships are content to assume that this

> Lord Hoffman accepted that there had been compulsion of the will, which satisfied the first element of Lord Scarman's description of duress in *Universe Tankships*.

was the case. But, as Lord Wilberforce and Lord Simon of Glaisdale said in *Barton v Armstrong* [1976] AC 104, 121:

'in life ... many acts are done under pressure, sometimes overwhelming pressure, so that one can say that the actor had no choice but to act. Absence of choice in this sense does not negate consent in law: for this the pressure must be one of a kind which the law does not regard as legitimate.'

[16] The legitimacy of the pressure must be examined from two aspects: first, the nature of the pressure and secondly, the nature of the demand which the pressure is applied to support: see Lord Scarman in the *Universe Tankships case*, at p. 401. Generally speaking, the threat of any form of unlawful action will be regarded as illegitimate. On the other hand, that fact that the threat is lawful does not necessarily make the pressure legitimate. As Lord Atkin said in *Thorne v Motor Trade Association* [1937] AC 797, 806:

'The ordinary blackmailer normally threatens to do what he has a perfect right to do – namely, communicate some compromising conduct to a person whose knowledge is likely to affect the person threatened ... What he has to justify is not the threat, but the demand of money.'

[17] In this case, the threat was lawful. Although return to unit was not ordinarily used except on grounds of delinquency or unsuitability and was perceived by members of the SAS as a severe penalty, there is no doubt that the Crown was entitled at its discretion to transfer any member of the SAS to another unit. Furthermore, the judge found, in para 123:

'The MOD could not be criticised for its motivation in introducing the contracts. They were introduced because of the concerns about the increasing number of unauthorised disclosures by former UKSF personnel and the concern that those disclosures were threatening the security of operations and personnel and were undermining the effectiveness and employability of the UKSF. Those are legitimate concerns for the MOD to have.'

[18] It would follow that the MOD was reasonably entitled to regard anyone unwilling to accept the obligation of confidentiality as unsuitable for the SAS. Thus the threat was lawful and the demand supported by the threat could be justified. But the judge held that the demand was unlawful because it exceeded the powers of the Crown over a serviceman under military law. It was an attempt to restrict his freedom of expression after he had left the service and was no longer subject to military discipline.

[19] The judge's reasoning was that R had signed the contract because he had been ordered to do so. The MOD could not give a serviceman an order which, as a matter of military law, he was obliged to obey after he had left the service and therefore it was an abuse of power for the MOD to try to extend the temporal reach of its orders by ordering the serviceman to sign a contract which could be enforced after he had left.

[20] If R had signed the contract because as a matter of military law he had been obliged to do so, their Lordships would see much force in this reasoning. But they agree with the Court of Appeal that this was not the case. There was no order in the sense of a command which created an obligation to obey under military law. Instead, R was faced with a choice which may have constituted 'overwhelming pressure' but was not an exercise by the MOD of its legal powers over him. The legitimacy of the pressure therefore falls to be examined by normal criteria and as neither of the courts in New Zealand considered either the threat to be unlawful or the demand unreasonable, it follows that the contract was not obtained by duress.

The case, then, would hinge on the second element set out by Lord Scarman, which was the legitimacy of the pressure. This in turn led to two further considerations—the nature of the pressure and the nature of the demand made. As Lord Hoffman makes clear, this will very often be determined through establishing whether the threatened action was lawful or unlawful, but not always. While a threat of unlawful action is illegitimate, a threat of lawful action is not necessarily legitimate.

Here, the threat was not unlawful—it was a threat to exercise a power which the Crown definitely had. This meant that the legitimacy of the pressure would be determined by the demand. And, on this point, he agreed with the trial judge that the demand was entirely reasonable in its context.

There was, however, an added complication, which was that the trial judge had ultimately decided the matter on the basis of excess of powers. He had conceptualised the situation as one in which R had been *ordered* to sign a contract which would be enforceable even after leaving the armed services (when rightly he would no longer be subject to such orders).

But for Lord Hoffman this had not been the case. There may have been pressure put on R to sign the agreement but he had not been commanded to do so, and could have refused to sign and still serve in the armed forces. In other words, there had been legitimate pressure put on him to comply with a legitimate demand—not an order. If he had been ordered to sign then it would have been an excess of powers, seeking to bind him effectively for life through a military command, and that would have been unlawful and hence illegitimate.

It could be said that the language used by Lord Hoffman (describing the MOD's demand as 'justified' and 'reasonable') went beyond the wording of *CTN Cash & Carry*, which had only required 'good faith'. After all, a demand can be made in good faith—that is, in the genuine belief of the entitlement to make it—but still be unreasonable or unjustified from an objective perspective. The fact that the wording in *R v Attorney-General* is different might then be taken to suggest that a threat of lawful action made in good faith but which is objectively unreasonable could be enough to establish duress outside of commercial relationships.

In the *Times Travel* case, David Richards LJ examined the judgment of Lord Hoffman and explained:

> 75. The reference to the demand not being unreasonable does not introduce a new basis for economic duress in a commercial context. First, of course, it was not a commercial case. Second, it involved the exercise of powers to which public law considerations applied. The MOD did not enjoy an unfettered, absolute right to transfer soldiers out of the SAS. A threat to do so in support of an unjustified demand would, as Lord Hoffman said at [18], be unlawful. In order for the threat to be lawful, the demand had to be reasonably made, which was held to be by the Privy Council.

This implies that there is scope for non-commercial lawful act duress to be wider than in the commercial context, with the former being based on the 'reasonableness' of the demand, and the latter with the requirement only that it needs to have been made in good faith and not necessarily reasonably.

From the judgment of Lord Hoffman, the following general points can be made:

- Duress requires (1) illegitimate pressure amounting to (2) a compulsion of will.

  It is not based on set categories of threats. The case did not concern a threat to kill or physically harm. No threat had been made to property or financial interests. Yes, R might well have suffered a fall in income, but that was never mentioned in the case. Instead, the only source of compulsion was the need to avoid public humiliation.

- Generally, pressure from threats of unlawful action will be illegitimate.

In the specific context of (non-commercial) lawful act duress:

- A justified and reasonable demand will not result in the pressure being illegitimate.
- If the demand is unlawful, the pressure will be illegitimate.

14.6.3 Compulsion of Will from a Threat of Lawful Action

The cases on lawful act duress are focussed heavily on the issue of legitimacy and the requirements for compulsion have not been explored with the same level of detail.

In *Al Nehayan v Kent*, Leggatt LJ adopted the 'but for' causation test for economic duress. In doing so, he cited with approval the comments made by Christopher Clarke J in *Kolmar*. From this discussion, it does seem that economic duress has the same requirements for compulsion whether the action threatened is lawful or not. The same point applies in relation to the absence of a practical alternative. Just as with economic duress, it is very strong evidence of compulsion but it is not an essential requirement.

The position with lawful act duress that is not economic is less certain. In *R v Attorney General* there was no separate assessment of causation. However, it was accepted that there was no practical alternative for R, and that was enough to establish compulsion. If the pressure is the 'but for' cause and there is no practical alternative, that will be enough for compulsion. Whether any less will do is not entirely clear.

Of course, the point made by Mance J in *Huyton* should be useful here. Mance LJ compared the causation requirements for economic duress and threats of harm. Economic pressure is less serious than duress of the person. It is not intrinsically as illegitimate. On that basis, economic pressure has to have a greater causal effect. Likewise, the same could be said for (non-economic) pressure from a threat of lawful action. Such pressure is intrinsically not as illegitimate as a threat of unlawful action, and on that basis, it requires more to show it was the cause for compulsion to be established.

14.7 Remedies for Duress

It is clear from the many cases above that duress results in a voidable contract. That means the contract is valid but can be rescinded by the victim, which is the same basic remedy for misrepresentation. Likewise, the same bars to rescission apply. Following rescission, restitution can result, enabling the victim to claim back the benefit given to the other party as a result of the duress.

→ CROSS-REFERENCE
For the discussion of the bars to rescission see 13.5.

Whether damages can result from duress depends on the circumstances. If the act of duress is a tort then it would be an independent source of damages. The question of duress as a tort has been the subject of some judicial opinion.

In the *Universe Tankships case* [1983] Lord Scarman delivered a dissenting judgment on the legitimacy of the pressure. But he also addressed the issue of duress as a tort in the following way:

> It is, I think, already established law . . . that duress, if proved, not only renders voidable a transaction into which a person has entered under its compulsion but is actionable as a tort, if it causes damage or loss. . .

This suggests duress could be a tort, because duress is wrongdoing that could result in losses being suffered by the victim. Such losses would be particularly important to recover where the right to rescind the contract has been lost. In such circumstances, if no established tort has been committed, there would be no remedy for the victim.

Of course, the duress might well involve the commission of an established tort, for example the conduct might have involved a trespass to the person. In such circumstances, damages can be awarded based on the tort committed rather than for duress. An analysis of the relevant torts is beyond the scope of this book but it is important to acknowledge the way in which the courts have linked torts to conduct amounting to duress.

The reliance on an established tort that coincides with the conduct amounting to duress is what Lord Diplock had recognised in *The Universe Tankships case* [1983] by stating:

> The use of economic duress to induce another person to part with property or money is not a tort per se: the form that the duress takes may, or may not, be tortious.

This opinion is consistent the observation by Lord Goff in *The Evia Luck* [1992]:

> . . .conduct does not have to be tortious to constitute duress for the purpose of English law.

The point being made is that duress can be found even if no tort has been committed. That suggests that duress is not itself a tort. If it is not a tort, then it cannot be an independent source of damages.

Should duress be an independent tort? Are there any problems with defining the scope of such a suggested tort?

The issue was discussed by Leggatt LJ in *Al Nehayan v Kent* and he favoured the approach of Lord Diplock. That meant damages would only be available if the conduct coincidently resulted in an established tort being committed. Based on the facts, damages were permitted under the tort of intimidation, which was favoured over creating a tort of duress. To support this, Leggatt LJ cited a comment from Sales J from *Investec Bank (Channel Islands) Ltd v The Retail Group plc* [2009] EWHC 476 (Ch), who observed:

The primary object of a plea of economic duress in relation to a contract is to avoid the contract, which is a legal consequence significantly different from establishing a cause of action in damages. So far as a cause of action in damages is to be made out, I can see no proper basis in principle why it should be on any basis other than a pleading of facts and matters sufficient to establish a cause of action for the tort of intimidation.

The observation by Sales J rejects the idea of duress being a basis for damages. Instead, it favours the use of established torts to support a damages claim in a duress case.

Leggatt LJ then briefly explored the tort of intimidation which was established by the House of Lords in *Rookes v Barnard* [1964] AC 1129. According to Leggatt LJ, the House of Lords confirmed that the tort did not cover threats to commit a crime or a tort only, but also covered threats to breach a contract. The essential requirements for the tort of intimidation were stated by Longmore LJ in *Berezovsky v Abramovich* [2011] EWCA Civ 153 and were summarised by Leggatt LJ as:

(i) a threat by the defendant to do something unlawful or "illegitimate"; (ii) the threat must be intended to coerce the claimant to take or refrain from taking some course of action; (iii) the threat must in fact coerce the claimant to take such action; (iv) loss or damage must be incurred by the claimant as a result.

Leggatt LJ then explained why blackmail could fit within the tort of intimidation and, on that basis, why damages could be awarded on the basis of the tort of intimidation.

Al Nehayan v Kent confirms that duress is not a distinct tort. This means a party cannot claim damages just because there has been duress. However, a party can claim damages on the basis of another tort, if, along the way, one was committed. The tort of intimidation is a distinct tort and has its requirements that must be met to establish liability. Of course, the approach of Leggatt LJ was to confirm the wide scope of intimidation, and so parties have more scope to argue for damages on that basis.

A final point on remedies relates to the position of consumers. The act of duress can amount to an unfair commercial practice under the Consumer Protection from Unfair Trading Practices Regulations 2008. Furthermore, one of the remedies under the 2008 Regulations is damages. The application of the 2008 Regulations means that the common law of duress is less relevant to consumer contracts. We will examine the relevant context of the Regulations in the next chapter, which is about undue influence. It is left until that stage because the Regulations apply to conduct including both duress and undue influence. This means a better understanding and appreciation of the Regulations will be gained if undue influence is covered first.

CHAPTER SUMMARY

■ For duress, there must be 'illegitimate' pressure resulting in a 'compulsion of will'.

■ Since duress impairs consent, it is a vitiating factor that results in a voidable contract. The victim may then be able to rescind it.

■ Generally, threats of unlawful action result in illegitimate pressure.

■ The difficulty with economic duress is in making a distinction between ordinary commercial pressure and illegitimate commercial pressure.

■ Pressure from a threat to breach is usually classed as illegitimate. There is opinion to suggest a threat to breach made in good faith should not always result in illegitimate pressure.

■ With a threat of lawful action, the legitimacy of the pressure is based on the demand.

■ In a purely commercial context, lawful act (economic) duress will be difficult to establish. If the demand is made in good faith, there is little or no chance of duress being established, even if the demand was unreasonable.

■ Lawful act duress outside of the commercial context appears to be possible where the demand is unreasonable and not justified.

■ For a compulsion of will (causation) the effect of the pressure varies according to the seriousness of the threat. On that basis, threats to harm a person just need to be 'a' reason for entering the contract. For economic loss and lawful act duress, however, the threat must be the 'but for' cause, and there is stronger evidence of compulsion where there was no practical alternative.

■ Duress is not an independent tort and so a victim is not entitled to damages. However, damages could be available under an established tort if the conduct involves the commission of such a tort.

KEY CASES

☐ *Barton v Armstrong* [1976] **AC 104**—represents the main authority on duress to the person and as a case from the Privy Council, it often features in cases as the source of the general tests for duress.

☐ *R v Attorney-General of England and Wales* [2003] **UKPC 22**—The latest higher authority on duress as a Privy Council case. It provides the general test for duress, showing a principle-led approach to duress rather than it being limited to set categories. The case also represents the approach taken for non-commercial lawful act duress.

☐ *North Ocean Shipping Co Ltd v Hyundai Construction Co Ltd, The Atlantic Baron* [1979] **QB 705**—the first case to find economic duress on the facts, and hence often cited in economic duress cases.

☐ *Universe Tankships of Monrovia v International Transport Workers Federation* [1983] **1 AC 366**—often cited for the test by Lord Scarman as well as for confirmation that compulsion does not require an overborn will. The case is also the authority on economic duress arising from a threat of strike action.

☐ *DSND Subsea Ltd v Petroleum Geo-Services ASA* [2000] **BLR 530**—The first instance decision of Dyson J is used to support the role of good faith in determining if pressure is legitimate for the purposes of economic duress.

☐ *Kolmar Group AG v Traxpo Enterprises Pty Ltd* [2010] **EWHC 113**—A first instance decision of Christopher Clarke J that surveyed the case law and confirmed both the 'but for' test for economic duress and that the absence of a practical alternative is good evidence of compulsion but not a separate requirement.

☐ *CTN Cash and Carry v Gallaher Ltd* [1994] **4 All ER 714**—Here Steyn LJ confirmed the existence of lawful act duress as well as its scope in relation to commercial contracts: that it is highly unlikely that there will be duress from a threat of lawful action made in good faith. As the first Court of Appeal case on the matter it continues to be cited because it is so authoritative and thorough.

- *Times Travel (UK) Ltd v Pakistan International Airlines Corporation* [2019] **EWCA Civ 828**—the most recent case on lawful act duress and the second case on the matter from the Court of Appeal. Trial judges will be citing the detailed analysis of David Richards LJ until the issue is addressed by the Supreme Court.

- *Al Nehayan v Kent* [2018] **EWHC 333 (Comm)**—Another significant case on lawful act duress. Some points are superseded by *Times Travel* but the remaining *obiter* from Leggatt LJ on the scope of the area is very influential.

QUESTIONS

1. Pressure from threats of lawful action should never be described as illegitimate, because there is nothing illegitimate about abiding by the law. Critically discuss.

2. The victim having no practical alternative is a more sensible and clear requirement than 'compulsion of the will'. Critically discuss.

3. Relu is the owner of a successful gym and operates his business in rented property owned by Ella's company. Having seen the success of Relu's gym, Ella demands a 30% increase in the rental payments, and in return she offers to provide free wifi in the building. When Relu refuses, Ella threatens to end the tenancy by relying on a term in their agreement that allows her to terminate with 30 days' notice. Relu reluctantly agrees because there are no alternative premises in the area for his business to continue. Advise Relu.

 For answer guidance to these questions please visit the online resources at www .oup.com/uk/naidoo1e/, where you will also find multiple choice questions to check your understanding of key concepts.

FURTHER READING

Davies & Day, '"Lawful act" duress' LQR (2018) 134, 5.
A case note providing a concise but detailed analysis of the first instance decision in *Times Travel*, and was cited by Leggatt LJ in *Al Nehayan v Kent*.

Macdonald, 'Duress by threatened breach of contract' [1989] JBL 460.
A detailed but clear article on the development of economic duress following *Atlas Express v Kafco*.

Mckendrick, 'The Further Travails of Duress' in Burrows and Rodger (eds), Mapping the law: Essays in Memory of Peter Birks (OUP) 2006.
This is detailed assessment of the cases on duress and supports the idea of the pressure from threats to breach always being illegitimate.

Smith, 'Contracting under pressure: a theory of duress' CLJ (1997), 56(2), 343.
A long, detailed and useful examination of duress and the theoretical underpinnings based on impaired consent and wrongdoing.

15 Undue Influence, Unconscionability, and Equality of Bargaining Power

LEARNING OBJECTIVES

By the end of this chapter you should be able to:

- discuss the key cases on undue influence and apply the principles to a given set of facts
- explain the development of undue influence and define its scope
- demonstrate a basic understanding of unconscionability and the attempts made to establish a wider inequality of bargaining power principle
- understand the use and scope of the recent legislation that applies to consumers and traders

INTRODUCTION

While duress concerns pressure arising from a threat, undue influence is largely about pressure and influence arising from a relationship. It is easy to imagine a one-sided relationship where one party has a significant amount of influence over the decisions of another. It might be that a stronger (influencing) party is in a dominant or superior position over another. Likewise, it could be that a weaker (dependant) party is extremely vulnerable and relies heavily on another. The existence of such a relationship of influence is not necessarily a problem. However, if the weaker party makes a gift or enters a contract as a result of the influence being exploited, it raises a question as to whether their consent was impaired. It might turn out that they made a free and informed decision, but alternatively their decision could have been made under a 'mental fog' of influence. Undue influence is therefore a *vitiating factor* like duress and misrepresentation which could then result in a voidable contract and therefore rescission.

This chapter begins with the basic role of the law on undue influence before moving to the substantive case law. The case law is divided into three categories, which are based on the different ways of proving undue influence. The first relates to what is known as 'actual undue influence', which is where a complainant proves undue influence (the weaker party or victim is referred to as the 'complainant' to be consistent with the language of the courts). The second is where undue influence between two parties can be *presumed* from the circumstances. The third category has been a major problem in modern cases and it involves undue influence coming from a third party. Typically, this third category of case features a wife who, as a result of undue influence from her husband, enters a contract with a bank to allow the matrimonial home to be used as security for a loan for the husband's business. Following the substantive law on undue influence, we turn to the wider issues that complete the 'bigger picture'. The first of these is the area often referred to as 'unconscionability', which is about the exploitation of weakness. The second is the attempt to create a wider 'inequality of bargaining power' principle. Finally, we look at the Consumer Protection from Unfair Trading Practices Regulations 2008, which can cover conduct otherwise classed as duress, undue influence and harassment.

15.1 The Uncertain Basis of Undue Influence

The law of undue influence has its origins in equity and developed to fill the gap in the common law resulting from duress being limited to threats of physical harm. Given that undue influence was recognised in the 1800s, it is surprising that its basis has not been defined in a clear and definitive way. This uncertainty was highlighted in the leading House of Lords case of *Royal Bank of Scotland v Etridge and others (No 2)* [2001] UKHL 44, where Lord Nicholls observed:

> [11] ... Several expressions have been used in an endeavour to encapsulate the essence: trust and confidence, reliance, dependence or vulnerability on the one hand and ascendancy, domination or control on the other. None of these descriptions is perfect. None is all embracing. Each has its proper place.

Whatever description is used, in broad terms it can be said that undue influence is about one party having influence over the decisions of another. If such influence is used to secure a transaction, it can then mean that the weaker party has not freely consented. Beyond this, the theoretical basis of undue influence has been the subject of academic debate. In the context of presumed undue influence, Birks & Chin ('On the Nature of Undue Influence' in Beatson & Friedmann (eds) Good Faith and Fault in Contract Law (OUP, 1995)) raised two possible alternatives:

(1) A 'claimant-sided' approach where influence becomes undue because there was too much influence from 'excessive' or 'morbid dependency'. This does not require positive acts of wrongdoing or abuse on the part of the defendant.

(2) A 'defendant-sided' approach where influence becomes undue because it has been exploited or abused by the defendant. This approach bases undue influence on the wrongdoing or exploitation by the defendant.

From these alternatives, Birks & Chin argued that the law on undue influence reflected a 'claimant-sided' approach. In contrast, Professor Bigwood advanced a sophisticated argument in favour of a defendant-sided basis. It also recognised that where a defendant simply fails to ensure the complainant consented freely this could be a form of passive wrongdoing (Bigwood, Undue Influence: 'impaired consent' or 'wicked exploitation'? OJLS (1996), 16(3) 503).

The case law does not help because the judicial comments are mixed, with some focussing on consent and others referring to the additional factor of abuse of influence or wrongdoing. For the claimant-sided approach, support is found in cases where undue influence was presumed even though there was no positive act of wrongdoing by the defendant (e.g. *Allcard v Skinner* (1887) 36 Ch.D 145). Subsequent support of the claimant-sided approach can be found in *Pesticcio v Huet* [2004] EWCA Civ 372, in which Mummery LJ stated:

> 20. ...Although undue influence is sometimes described as an "equitable wrong" or even a species of equitable fraud, the basis of the court's intervention is not the commission of a dishonest or wrongful act by the defendant, but that, as a matter of public policy, the presumed influence arising from the relationship of trust and confidence should not operate to disadvantage of the victim, if the transaction is not satisfactorily explained by ordinary motives... A transaction may be set aside by the court, even though the actions and conduct of the person who benefits from it could not be criticised as wrongful.

This clear position on there being no requirement for wrongdoing was supported by Auld LJ in *Macklin v Dowsett* [2004] EWCA Civ 904 who referred to the authorities from the Court of Appeal and stated:

> [The cases] underlined the rationale of the doctrine of undue influence as the protection of the vulnerable in dealings with their property and also the lack of the need to show misconduct on the part of the transferee.

However, a 'claimant-sided' approach to undue influence cannot be said to be the prevailing view, because a lot of subsequent cases appear to refer to the wrongdoing of the defendant influencer. Such cases include the leading case of *Etridge*, where Lord Nicholls observed:

> 6. . . .Undue influence is one of the grounds of relief developed by the courts of equity as a court of conscience. The objective is to ensure that the influence of one person over another is not abused. . .
>
> 7 . . .Equity extended the reach of the law to other unacceptable forms of persuasion. The law will investigate the manner in which the intention to enter into the transaction was secured. . .If the means used is regarded as an exercise of improper or "undue" influence, and hence unacceptable, whenever the consent thus procured ought not fairly be treated as the expression of a person's free will.

Lord Nicholls refers to abuse of influence, and his comments support the idea of finding some wrongful conduct. Similar language can be found in the judgment by Lord Hoffman in *R v Attorney-General* [2003] UKPC 22. In addition, Lord Millett referred to the need for abuse and victimisation in *National Commercial Bank (Jamaica) Ltd v Hew* [2003] UKPC 51 but there are many more examples reflecting a defendant-sided basis and so the weight of the cases favours the need for there to have been wrongdoing by the defendant.

In contrast to the conventional debate, Chen-Wishart rejects the binary choice between impaired consent and wrongdoing. As an alternative, she puts forward a convincing theory based on the type of relationship between the parties (Chen-Wishart, 'Undue Influence: Beyond impaired consent and Wrong Doing, Towards a Relational Analysis' in Borrows and Rodger (eds), Mapping the Law: Essays in Memory of Peter Birks (OUP, 2006)).

The ongoing debate and inconsistent judicial comments show us that the theoretical basis of undue influence is uncertain. However, the wide tests developed by the courts to find a presumption of undue influence have been used consistently, with some flexibility in their application. The uncertainty over the *basis* of undue influence simply means that there is uncertainty over what the tests reflect or represent.

15.2 Actual Undue Influence

The existence of this category might seem strange. After all, this chapter is about the law of undue influence, so why is only part of it called 'actual' undue influence? The answer comes from the development of the law on undue influence. In the earliest cases, the complainant would have to prove that the transaction resulted from such influence. Later, in the important case of *Allcard v Skinner* (1887) 36 Ch.D 145, presumed undue influence was established, which meant that in certain circumstances undue influence would be presumed without direct proof. Having two approaches meant there was a need to distinguish between them and that is why we have two categories, called 'actual undue influence' and 'presumed undue influence'.

In practice, these are not separate claims; both involve an innocent party alleging undue influence. The practical significance of the distinction is that each has different proof requirements. Actual undue influence describes a situation in which the innocent party simply has direct proof of undue influence. In contrast, undue influence can be presumed following a transaction that is 'out of the ordinary' between parties that have a relationship of influence.

In the leading case of *Royal Bank of Scotland v Etridge and others (No 2)* [2001] UKHL 44, Lord Nicholls described actual undue influence as covering 'overt acts of improper pressure or coercion such as unlawful threats'. That sounds like duress, and there is a reason for that. It was developed at a time when duress only covered threats of physical harm, and the idea was that equity would provide a remedy where the common law could not. Of course, we know that duress was eventually extended and that it now covers threats amounting to illegitimate pressure resulting in a compulsion of will. With that in mind, there is now some overlap between the actual undue influence and duress. The point was acknowledged by the House of Lords in *Etridge*.

A good example of such an overlap is the case of *Williams v Bayley* (1866) LR 1 HL 200. Here a son forged his father's signature on documents to get money from a bank. When the bank discovered the fraud, the bank indicated that it would not prosecute the son, if the father paid the son's debts. The father agreed and granted a mortgage over his business as security for the money to be paid. When the father did not pay, the bank sued. In the House of Lords, it was confirmed that the agreement to take on the son's debt had resulted from undue influence and so consequently the agreement was set aside. Now that duress is wide enough to cover such facts, this case now resembles a duress case more closely than an undue influence one.

Such an overlap does not mean that actual undue influence is no longer relevant because undue influence is wide enough to apply to facts falling short of duress. A good example is the case of *Bank of Credit and Commerce International SA v Aboody* [1990] 1 QB 923. This concerned a mortgage signed by a wife so that her husband could have money for his business. At the age of 17 she was the subject of an arranged marriage to a husband who was 20 years older. She was dominated by her abusive husband and she would sign whatever he told her to. For the disputed transaction, he said her signature had to be witnessed at the bank, but in fact she was required to receive advice from a solicitor at the bank about the risks of signing. During her personal meeting, the husband burst in uninvited and was rude and overbearing. He shouted at the solicitor, telling him to let her sign. At this point the wife broke down into tears and signed the document, apparently in order to stop the row. The events that had taken place on that day were enough for the Court of Appeal to find actual undue influence.

Unfortunately, Mrs Aboody was not entitled to a remedy because there was no 'manifest disadvantage' in the transaction. This was a requirement which was later rejected by the House of Lords in *CIBC Mortgages v Pitt* [1994] AC 200. However, the case is a good example of *actual* undue influence on facts falling short of duress. There was no threat made by the husband *per se*. Instead, it was just that Mrs Aboody was pressured into signing without freely considering her own interests.

In modern practice, cases on actual undue influence are rare. Most cases rely on presumed undue influence because it is often easier to establish. But where the complainant is in a relationship where in the circumstances no presumption can be made, the only option would be to rely on proving actual undue influence.

15.3 Presumed Undue Influence

Most of the law on undue influence is concerned with presumed undue influence. As stated previously, there is no need for direct proof of undue influence here, and instead it is presumed from the parties' relationship and the relevant transaction.

A relationship of influence can be established in two different ways:

- some relationships are presumed to be ones of influence, so the complainant could show they are in a 'protected relationship' with the defendant. An example of such a relationship is the religious leader/disciple. Other examples are addressed below;

- alternatively, the complainant could prove the existence of a relationship of influence. That could be because the facts show the relationship was based on trust and confidence or some form of domination or control.

The next stage is to consider if the influence was used (or abused). That is based on the type of transaction in question. If it is one that is out of the ordinary for the relationship, it suggests the *use of* influence and, if that is the case, then *undue* influence will be *presumed*. It is then for the defendant to rebut the presumption by showing that the decision was freely made. A relevant factor is whether the complainant had independent legal advice before the transaction. If such advice was received, it will help to show that the decision was freely made.

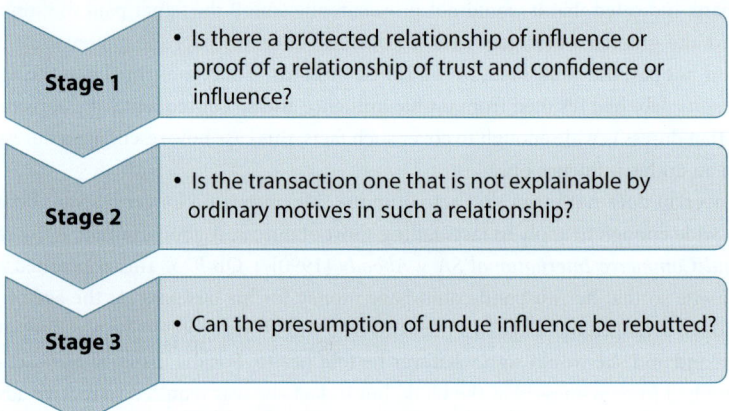

Figure 15.1
The process for establishing presumed undue influence

We will begin with the first stage. To do so, we need to address the law relating to protected relationships, before turning to the position for other relationships. Once that stage is complete, we will move on to the second stage, about the use of influence. Finally, we will address the issues relating to the presumption of undue influence being rebutted.

15.4 Presumed Undue Influence: Protected (Special) Relationships

The courts have determined that influence can certainly be presumed from the following relationships: religious leader and disciple; solicitor and client; doctor and patient; parent and child; trustee and beneficiary. There is no controversy over the status of these relationships. The position was explained in *Etridge* where Lord Nicholls stated:

[18] . . . The law has adopted a sternly protective attitude towards certain types of relationship in which one party acquires influence over another who is vulnerable and dependent and where, moreover, substantial gifts by the influenced or vulnerable person are not normally to be expected. Examples of relationships within this special class are parent and child, guardian and ward, trustee and beneficiary, solicitor and client, and medical adviser and patient. In these cases the law presumes, irrebuttably, that one party had influence over the other. The complainant need not prove he actually reposed trust and confidence in the other party. It is sufficient for him to prove the existence of the type of relationship.

The comment by Lord Nicholls confirms that there are certain relationships that have a special status because they are presumed to be based on influence. Furthermore, it makes clear that the presumption of influence in such relationships is *irrebuttable*. It means as a legal rule that in such relationships there is influence and this cannot be disputed.

The reason why there is protection for these relationships is that, by definition, they are relationships of trust and confidence, a point that was explained further by Nourse LJ in *Goldsworthy v Brickell* [1987] Ch 378:

. . .[D]octors and solicitors are trusted and confided in by their patients and clients to give them conscientious and disinterested advice on matters which profoundly affect, in the one case their physical and mental, and in the other their material, well-being. It is natural to presume that out of that trust and confidence grows influence.

The point is that a relationship of trust and confidence results in influence. Typically, one party is in a superior position and provides guidance to the other party who has an expectation of guidance to rely on. This also explains why the marriage relationship is not included as a protected relationship. This position on marriage was confirmed in *Howes v Bishop* [1909] 2 KB 390 and approved by the House of Lords in *Barclays Bank v O'Brien* [1994] 1 AC 180 as well as in *Etridge* and subsequently *Dailey v Dailey* [2003] UKPC 65. Yes, of course, we can assume spouses trust each other and will have confidence in each other. However, the starting point is that spouses are equals, and it would be strange if the law *presumed* that a married couple were not equal partners in their relationship. That being said, we will see that in some cases involving marriage a relationship of influence can be proven.

Allcard v Skinner (1887) is treated as a key case as it confirmed undue influence could be presumed. It concerned a gift, but the same principles apply for contracts. In the case, Allcard was introduced to a religious order called the Sisters of the Poor and became a nun in their convent. Skinner was the leader of the convent, with the title of Lady Superior, who was to be treated as 'the voice of God'. As a nun, Allcard had to take a vow of poverty, which required her to hand over her inherited wealth to be used to help the poor. She also took a vow of obedience, and one of the rules was that a nun could not get advice from an outside source unless approved by the Lady Superior. After eight years, Allcard left the convent and then, six years later, she sought to recover the unspent money.

The Court of Appeal allowed for undue influence to be presumed, but her action failed because of her delay. She had been free from the influence for some time and so, by waiting six years, her action was barred by laches. She should have brought her action as soon as it appeared she was free from the influence of the religious order.

laches
is a Latin term referring to the delay in making the claim. Put simply, it is lapse of time.

GUIDED CASE READING 15.1
Allcard v Skinner (1887) 36 Ch.D 145

When reading the extract of the judgment by Lindley LJ, try to identify:

- the basis for presuming undue influence. Did the influencer act in a wrongful or improper way?
- The test to be applied and;
- the reasons why it could not be shown that the decision was freely made.

The result of the evidence convinces me that no pressure, except the inevitable pressure of the vows and rules, was brought to bear on the Plaintiff; that no deception was practised upon her; that no unfair advantage was taken of her; that none of her money was obtained or applied for any purpose other than the legitimate objects of the sisterhood . . .

. . .

> Lindley LJ makes clear from the outset that he did not think on the facts that the claimant ultimately would have had a case if she had been required to prove undue influence. But because of the nature of the relationship between her and the defendant, this was not necessary.

The doctrine relied upon by the Appellant is the doctrine of undue influence expounded and enforced in *Huguenin v. Baseley* (1807) 14 Ves 273 and other cases of that class. These cases may be subdivided into two groups, which, however, often overlap.

First, there are the cases in which there has been some unfair and improper conduct, some coercion from outside, some overreaching, some form of cheating, and generally, though not always, some personal advantage obtained by a donee placed in some close and confidential relation to the donor . . .

The second group consists of cases in which the position of the donor to the donee has been such that it has been the duty of the donee to advise the donor, or even to manage his property for him. In such cases the Court throws upon the donee the burden of proving that he has not abused his position, and of proving that the gift made to him has not been brought about by any undue influence on his part. In this class of cases it has been considered necessary to shew that the donor had independent advice, and was removed from the influence of the donee when the gift to him was made . . . This principle has been constantly recognised and acted upon in subsequent cases, but in all of them, as in *Huguenin v. Baseley* . . . itself, it was the duty of the donee to advise and take care of the donor . . .

> He first describes the cases on undue influence as falling into two groups, which as will be obvious, basically reproduce the distinction between what we now call 'actual undue influence' and 'presumed undue influence'. In the latter category it was necessary to show that the person receiving the gift had received independent advice, which meant that he or she was no longer under the influence of the donor.

Rhodes v. Bate Law Rep.1 Ch. 252. was determined on the same principle as *Huguenin v. Baseley*, the Court having come to the conclusion that the relation of the defendant to the plaintiff was really that of a solicitor to his client.

. . .

Courts of Equity have never set aside gifts on the ground of the folly, imprudence, or want of foresight on the part of donors . . . On the other hand, to protect people from being forced, tricked or misled in any way by others into parting with their property is one of the most legitimate objects of all laws . . .

> He then explained the reason for the principle existing—which is not to protect people in general from their own mistakes or lack of foresight, but to prevent them being forced or tricked.

As no Court has ever attempted to define undue influence, which includes one of its many varieties. The undue influence which Courts of Equity endeavour to defeat is the undue influence of one person over another; not the influence of enthusiasm on the enthusiast who is carried away by it, unless indeed such enthusiasm is itself the result of external undue influence. But the influence of one mind over another is very subtle, and of all influences religious influence is the most dangerous and the most powerful, and to counteract it Courts of Equity have gone very far. They [the courts] have not shrunk from setting aside gifts made to persons in a position to exercise undue influence over the donors, although there has been no proof of the actual exercise of such influence; and the Courts have done this . . . to protect persons from the exercise of such influence under circumstances which

> Next, he explained the basis of the notion of presumed undue influence, which is that the law attempts to protect people from 'subtle' but 'powerful' influences, like that of a religious leader, in which it would be impossible to prove actual undue influence. This meant that this was a case of such undue influence. Therefore, it was not strictly speaking relevant that Lindley LJ could not find evidence of undue influence—it was presumed.

render proof of it impossible. The Courts have required proof of its non- exercise, and, failing that proof, have set aside gifts otherwise unimpeachable. In this particular case I cannot find any proof that any gift made by the Plaintiff was the result of any actual exercise of power or influence on the part of the lady superior . . . apart from the influence necessarily incidental to their position in the sisterhood. . . .

[The] rule against consulting externs, that rule in my judgment turns the scale against the Defendant. In the face of that rule the gifts made to the sisterhood cannot be supported in the absence of proof that the Plaintiff could have obtained independent advice if she wished for it, and that she knew that she would have been allowed to obtain such advice . . . I doubt whether the gifts could have been supported if such proof had been given, unless there was also proof that she was free to act on the advice which might be given to her . . . The gifts cannot be supported without proof of more freedom in fact than the Plaintiff can be supposed to have actually enjoyed.

> In effect, the fact that in circumstances like this undue influence was presumed meant that the defendant would have had to rebut the presumption, probably by proving the claimant had had independent advice. Since she had not, and since the rules of the Sisterhood indeed forbade it, it is likely that the claimant would have been able to recover the money had she not been barred by her delay.

Where a gift is made to a person standing in a confidential relation to the donor, the Court will not set aside the gift if of a small amount simply on the ground that the donor had no independent advice. In such a case, some proof of the exercise of the influence of the donee must be given. The mere existence of such influence is not enough in such a case . . . But if the gift is so large as not to be reasonably accounted for on the ground of friendship, relationship, charity, or other ordinary motives on which ordinary men act, the burden is upon the donee to support the gift.

> He closed by making clear that if the gift is small, then there should be proof of the use of influence. However, such a use of influence is presumed when the gift is so large that it cannot be explained by ordinary motives, i.e. it is out of the ordinary.

Cotton LJ adopted the same detailed approach as Lindley LJ whereas the judgment of Bowen LJ agreed, but was less detailed.

The closing remarks from the previous extract show that influence on its own is not an issue. It was made clear that the law intervenes when there is a gift so large that cannot be explained by ordinary motives. That is also the test that was approved by the House of Lords later in the leading case *Etridge*. It requires a transaction that is not normal for the type of relationship, and that then gives rise to a presumption of *undue* influence. We will explore that second stage of presumed undue influence in more detail below.

 THINKING POINTS

There was no 'wrongful' conduct by the Lady Superior. But could it be said that there was wrongful conduct in not permitting or encouraging external advice? More broadly, could it be wrongful to accept gifts without first making sure the decision is free from influence?

Importantly, there was no need in Lindley LJ's view for there to have been any wrongdoing by the influencer. In fact, both Lindley LJ and Cotton LJ were clear that the Lady Superior had not acted in a way that was obviously wrongful. Instead the focus was on the absence of a freely made decision.

Once undue influence is presumed, it is for the defendant to rebut the presumption by proving that the decision was freely made. Implicit in the judgment is that the availability of independent advice will be crucial in this, but it would not be enough if such advice could not be acted on. That would have been a problem for the Lady Superior if she had indeed been called to rebut the presumption, since the rules of her Sisterhood prohibited outside advice. That meant the defendant would have had no realistic way of showing the gift was freely made. Fortunately for her, this ultimately did not affect the outcome of the case.

KEY POINTS

In a 'protected relationship,' influence exists as a matter of law because by definition such relationships are based on trust and confidence.

15.5 Presumed Undue Influence: All Other Relationships

Outside of the protected relationships, undue influence can still be presumed. This aspect of presumed undue influence was explained in *Etridge* by Lord Nicholls in the following way:

> 14. Proof that the complainant placed trust and confidence in the other party in relation to the management of the complainant's financial affairs, coupled with a transaction which calls for explanation, will normally be sufficient, failing satisfactory evidence to the contrary, to discharge the burden of proof. On proof of these two matters the stage is set for the court to infer that, in the absence of a satisfactory explanation, the transaction can only have been procured by undue influence. In other words, proof of these two facts is *prima facie* evidence that the defendant abused the influence he acquired in the parties' relationship. He preferred his own interests. He did not behave fairly to the other. So the evidential burden then shifts to him. It is for him to produce evidence to counter the inference which otherwise should be drawn.

The statement by Lord Nicholls represents the established case law in this area. For the presumption to apply, the claimant must prove:

- there was a relationship of trust and confidence (or influence generally); and,
- the transaction was one that was out of the ordinary and therefore calls for an explanation.

With both elements established, undue influence is presumed. Then, as with protected relationships, it is for the defendant to rebut the presumption.

Generally, most cases refer to the complainant having developed a relationship of trust and confidence with the defendant, and that was the language used by Lord Nicholls in the previous statement. However, sometimes it is not a relationship of trust and confidence that is established to have been present. Instead, it is a relationship of control or dominance by one party over the other. A good example is the context of spouses. Sometimes, judges have said that a wife had trust and confidence in the husband over financial matters. In other cases, their emphasis has been on the fact that the husband has been controlling and dominant. It means that the courts often appear to be looking for trust and confidence and use those words in their judgments. However, in reality, what they are really looking for is a relationship that suggests one party has influence over the other, wherever that influence comes from.

It is useful to look at some key examples of such influence being proven. Obviously, each case turns on its own facts and what can be proven in the circumstances, but the facts and reasoning in the judgments help us to know what to look for. Remember, these are relationships that are not ordinarily based on trust and confidence (or influence), so when the claim is successful, it is because the relationship has crossed over into one of influence. The following headings do not represent an exact science, but may help to categorise the cases.

15.5.1 Trust and Confidence Arising from Vulnerability and Reliance on Advice

Ordinarily, there is no relationship of trust and confidence between a bank and a client, a point that was emphasised by the House of Lords in *Natwest v Morgan* [1985] AC 686. The reasoning was explained by Nourse LJ in *Goldsworthy v Brickell* [1987]:

> . . .[A] banker, being a person having a pre-existing and conflicting interest in any loan transaction with a customer, cannot ordinarily be trusted and confided in so as to come under a duty to take care of the customer and give him disinterested advice.

Just like in a buyer/seller relationship, the parties in a bank/client relationship are looking out for their own interests. However, a relationship of trust and confidence between a bank and a client can still be established in the right circumstances and a good example of this is *Lloyds v Bundy* [1975] QB 326.

In this case Mr Bundy, an old farmer, agreed to guarantee his son's business overdraft. This required the farmer to use his house as security for the debt, which was done by granting a charge over the property for the bank. The bank then allowed the son to increase his debt. This prompted the son and the bank's new assistant manager to visit Bundy at his house, where the assistant manager explained the bank was prepared to allow the son's debt to continue. To do so, the bank needed to increase the guarantee and charge over Bundy's property to £11,000. Pre-drafted forms were then handed over and signed. Later, the son's business stopped trading, so the bank took action to evict Bundy and sell his property. Following a challenge to the transaction, the Court of Appeal held that the increased charge and guarantee could be ended for undue influence.

The guarantee and the charge had initially been for £1,500. At the request of the bank and the son, this had then been increased by £5,000. At that time, the son and the previous assistant manager had visited the farmer and left the forms for him to sign once he had legal advice. His solicitor had advised that £5000 was the most he should guarantee, as it represented half the value of his house, which was his only asset. He had then agreed to the increase and these earlier transactions were not disputed.

The majority reasoning was based on the judgment of Sir Eric Sachs. Reference was made to the facts from the trial where the assistant manager said that he thought Bundy was relying on him for advice on the transaction. Bundy said he had always trusted the original assistant manager. According to the judgment, the new manager had inherited that trust, which had built up over many years. The point was addressed before turning to the significance of the reliance:

> It is, of course, plain . . . the bank would derive benefit from the signature, that there was a conflict of interest as between the bank and Mr. Bundy, that the bank gave him advice, that he relied on that advice, and that the bank knew of the reliance. The further question is whether on the evidence concerning the matters already recited there was also established that element of confidentiality which has been discussed. In my judgment it is thus established.
>
> . . .
>
> The situation was thus one which to any reasonably sensible person, who gave it but a moment's thought, cried aloud Mr. Bundy's need for careful independent advice. Over and above the need any man has for counsel when asked to risk his last penny on even an apparently reasonable project, was the need here for informed advice as to whether there was any real chance of the company's affairs becoming viable if the documents were signed. If not, there arose questions such as, what is the use of taking the risk of becoming penniless without benefiting anyone but the bank? . . .
>
> . . .
>
> . . .[N]othing in this judgment affects the duties of a bank in the normal case where it is obtaining a guarantee, and in accordance with standard practice explains to the person about to sign its legal effect and the sums involved. . . When, however, a bank, as in the present case, goes further and advises on more general matters germane to the wisdom of the transaction, that indicates that it may - not necessarily must - be crossing the line into the area of confidentiality so that the court may then have to examine all the facts including, of course, the history leading up to the transaction, to ascertain whether or not that line has, as here, been crossed.

According to the judgment, the facts gave rise to a relationship of trust and confidence. Bundy had relied on the bank for advice on the merits of the transaction and the bank knew they were being relied upon. That resulted in the bank being in breach of their duty by advising on something they had a financial interest in. Furthermore, the bank did not advise on the need for independent legal advice, which was made worse by the fact that they knew Bundy had a solicitor who had been used just months before for advice on the previous guarantee to the bank.

?! THINKING POINTS

The deal was done at the farmer's house. Is that another indication of the crossing the line into another relationship?

The reasoning did not directly link the home visits to the relationship of influence, but it could have been used to suggest that the relationship was beyond the ordinary bank/client relationship. In addition, with the transaction having taken place at the home, there was no opportunity for Bundy to get independent advice.

In terms of the transaction, Bundy was risking his only asset, yet the transaction was for the benefit of the bank. It provided security for the debts they had allowed the son to build up and that was then taken as an indication that it was a transaction calling for an explanation.

The same approach to vulnerability and reliance was adopted in *Goodchild v Bradbury* [2006] EWCA Civ 1868 which concerned the transfer of land by an elderly and vulnerable great-uncle to his great nephew. The Court of Appeal agreed that a relationship of trust and confidence had developed, with the great-nephew being in a position of dominance. That finding, along with a transaction that could not be explained by ordinary motives, then resulted in a presumption of undue influence.

15.5.2 Trust and Confidence Arising from Physical Dependence and Reliance

It is not difficult to imagine a relationship of influence developing between a vulnerable party and a carer or helper, and one such case is *Goldsworthy v Brickell*. Mr Goldsworthy was an 85-year-old farmer who lived on his own. His farm was in a run-down condition and making losses. After a loss of cattle, Goldsworthy asked Brickell, a neighbouring farmer, for advice. Brickell then provided assistance to Goldsworthy over a five-month period, for instance by placing his own employees to work on Goldsworthy's farm and even providing someone to do the washing and cleaning at Goldsworthy's farmhouse as well his shopping. All of this was without any cost to Goldsworthy. After a few months, Brickell was effectively running the farm for Goldsworthy, and then Brickell was granted a tenancy for the farm. He was also granted an option to buy the property on the death of Goldsworthy. This transaction was the issue in the case, because the terms were so unfavourable to Goldsworthy.

The Court of Appeal held that the transaction could be set aside for undue influence. Nourse LJ agreed with the trial judge finding that:

> ... [T]he defendant had become a business adviser of the plaintiff and had been entrusted with the management of his farming business and some at least of his personal affairs and everyday needs.

Essentially, a relationship of trust and confidence had developed from Goldsworthy's physical dependence and reliance on Brickell, and that was enough to show influence. In addition, it was said that there was no need to show there had been a dominating influence. The transaction was then treated as one that called for an explanation.

A similar case is *Hammond v Osborn* [2002] EWCA Civ 885, which involved an elderly man who gave most of his wealth to his carer. A relationship of trust and confidence was proven on the facts, which resulted from the physical and emotional dependence. Along with the nature of the transaction, undue influence was presumed. The Court of Appeal also emphasised that there was no need to prove there had been wrongdoing by the carer, citing *Allcard v Skinner* as authority.

15.5.3 Trust and Confidence Indicated by the Transaction

A more controversial approach was adopted in *Credit Lyonnais Bank Nederland NV v Burch* [1997] 1 All ER 144. This concerned an employer who owned a travel company and a junior employee, Helen Burch. She was close to her employer, and looked up to him as a successful businessman. She often served as a babysitter for his children in the evenings and weekends and would even accompany the family on their holidays to Italy. When the business was in financial trouble, the employer approached Burch and asked her to use her flat to provide security for the business overdraft. That involved granting a charge over the flat in favour of the bank. Later, the bank sought possession of the flat and Burch argued that her agreement was a result of undue influence. The trial judge had no problem finding a relationship of trust and confidence and, coupled with the nature of the transaction, this resulted in a presumption of undue influence. That presumption could not be rebutted since there had been no independent legal advice.

The Court of Appeal agreed and upheld the decision to set aside the transaction. However, the approach of Millett LJ was slightly different and has attracted some criticism. Millett LJ described the transaction as 'excessively onerous' and one that 'shocks the conscience of the court'. Essentially, Burch was risking her home and even bankruptcy for a business she had no financial interest in. Millett LJ then stated:

> . . . [A] relationship like that of employer and junior employee which is easily capable of developing into a relationship of trust and confidence, the nature of the transaction may be sufficient to justify the inference that such a development has taken place; and where the transaction is so extravagantly improvident that it is virtually inexplicable on any other basis, the inference will be readily drawn. . .

Millett LJ used the nature of the transaction to find the relationship of influence and set it aside. This suggests that the transaction was so outrageous and unfair that it could only be explained by the existence of a relationship of trust and confidence. The criticism is that this means a judge just needs to find a transaction highly unfair in order to set it aside, and that is not the approach of the previous cases. Instead, the transaction should be separate to the question of the relationship, which is certainly the approach described later by the House of Lords in *Etridge*.

THINKING POINTS

Should it matter that the transaction was used to determine the relationship? Would it mean that undue influence goes beyond procedural fairness to reflect substantive fairness?

→ CROSS-REFERENCE
On the types of fairness see, 7.2.

The approach taken by Millett LJ does add some flexibility. And a suspect transaction must surely still be part of the factual background of the case. It may even be that judges in other cases have used the transaction to help infer the existence of the relevant relationship but have simply refrained from saying so explicitly in their judgments. A similar approach was adopted in *Sheikh v Malik* [2018]

EWHC 972 (Ch), where Fancourt J suggested that the greater the benefit conferred by the transaction, the more likely it is that there was trust and confidence.

15.5.4 A Relationship of Trust and Confidence Arising from Being Part of an Institutional Hierarchy

→ CROSS-REFERENCE
For the facts of *R v Attorney-General for England Wales* see 14.6.2.

Being within an institutional hierarchy can be a relevant consideration when identifying whether there is a relationship of trust and confidence. The key example is *R v Attorney-General for England Wales* [2003]. As an alternative to duress, the claimant in that case argued that the contract had resulted from undue influence. The Privy Council acknowledged that there could be a relationship of influence in these circumstances and the basis for this was explained by Lord Hoffman:

> [24] In the present case it is said that the military hierarchy, the strong regimental pride which R shared and his personal admiration for his commanding officer created a relationship in which the Army as an institution or the commanding officer as an individual were able to exercise influence over him. Their Lordships are content to assume that this was the case.

However, the majority held that there was nothing to make the influence *undue*. The transaction could be explained by ordinary motives in that relationship, and so the claim failed because the second ingredient was missing.

Lord Scott dissented on the undue influence point, citing *Allcard v Skinner* to support a presumption of influence. Lord Scott then stated:

> [41] Are these principles ones that should be applied to the contract in the present case? I think they are. The appellant was not, of course, an unworldly man in a secluded religious order. He was a soldier in a highly trained and efficient fighting unit. The essence of efficiency in a military unit is obedience to orders. The Armed Services operate on a hierarchical basis. Each rank looks to the rank or ranks above for direction and, having received that direction, is expected to comply with it. . .. It has become a music-hall joke for a sergeant-major to say to the troops under him "I want three volunteers; you, you and you". The hierarchical culture of the Armed Services and the deference and obedience to senior officers . . . which is part of that culture are the essential background to the circumstances in which the appellant was asked to sign the contract. . .
>
> . . .
>
> [45] In my opinion, the relationship between the appellant and his senior officers and the circumstances, as found by the judge. . .produced a classic "relationship" case in which undue influence should be presumed.

That view was not shared by the other judges, who maintained that trust and confidence or influence had to be proven in these circumstances. However, in the context of such an institutional hierarchy, the judgments do suggest it would not take much to establish such proof.

15.5.5 Trust and Confidence: Love and Affection and Reliance on Financial Matters

When a couple are in a relationship of love and affection it is not difficult to imagine one party experiencing a 'mental fog' from such a strong emotional tie. For that reason, it is possible to prove the existence of a relationship of trust and confidence.

An example is *Leeder v Stevens* [2005] EWCA Civ 50 which concerned a married man and the complainant he was having a long-term affair with. According to the evidence, they had been in a 'loving' relationship for ten years. The transaction related to the complainant's house, which was worth £70,000 and was her only asset. At the suggestion of the defendant, she transferred half of the house to him and, in return, he paid off her remaining mortgage of just £5,000.

Following a dispute over the transaction, it was set aside by the Court of Appeal because the complainant had proved there was a relationship of trust and confidence. Jacob LJ observed that the relationship had a long past and the complainant expected it to continue and eventually lead to marriage. Reference was also made to the fact that she had let the defendant pass on advice from his solicitor rather than get the advice directly herself. This meant it was not a relationship 'at arm's-length' and indicated trust and confidence in the defendant. The transaction was then deemed to be one that called for an explanation because it was so disadvantageous.

Most of the modern cases on undue influence concern this type of relationship. Often, there is a wife seeking to set aside a contract resulting from undue influence exerted by the husband. We have established that marriage is not a protected category, so what is it that tends to reveal there is a relationship of trust and confidence between a husband and wife? In the cases, it has tended to be that the wife has always deferred all financial matters to the husband. That has then been taken to indicate trust and confidence in financial matters. Added to this is the pressure from the emotional, sexual and financial ties between them. The relationship between spouses was addressed in *Etridge*, where Lord Scott suggested that the traditional assumption against a marriage being one of presumed influence should be reconsidered:

> [159] . . . For my part, I would assume in every case in which a wife and husband are living together that there is a reciprocal trust and confidence between them. In the fairly common circumstance that the financial and business decisions of the family are primarily taken by the husband, I would assume that the wife would have trust and confidence in his ability to do so and would support his decisions. I would not expect evidence to be necessary to establish the existence of that trust and confidence. I would expect evidence to be necessary to demonstrate its absence.

Lord Scott's view is not the prevailing one, but it is true that evidence of one spouse having the role over the financial matters is generally enough to show that there was trust and confidence in financial matters. But it is important to appreciate the bigger picture here. Proving trust and confidence might be straightforward for spouses but that does not mean it is easy to prove *undue* influence. Trust and confidence (or some other form of influence) is just one requirement. For *undue* influence, as we have seen, the transaction also has to be one that calls for an explanation. We will see at 15.6 that it can be very difficult to prove this second requirement in the context of spouses.

KEY POINTS

- Love and affection between a couple can result in a relationship of trust and confidence and therefore influence.
- It might be easy for spouses to prove trust and confidence in financial matters. However, it is very difficult to prove that any given transaction is suspect and calls for an explanation.

15.6 Presuming Undue Influence: The Transaction Must Call for an Explanation

So far, we have considered how influence can be established. Either it is presumed from the relationship or proven on the facts. But, for presumed undue influence, that is just the first stage. The second stage is to prove the transaction was one calling for an explanation. While we have seen this basic requirement in operation in some of the cases, it is important to examine it in more detail because doing so helps to establish a better understanding of what to look for.

In *Allcard v Skinner*, Lindley LJ clearly stated that influence on its own was not enough and that something else was needed for a presumption of undue influence. This, he suggested, was a gift so large that it could not be explained by ordinary motives in that relationship, and that became the second ingredient for the presumption undue influence. Such a transaction indicates a real risk that the influence in question has been used. However, it is important to appreciate the limit represented by the requirement. Consider a transaction made whilst under a mental fog of influence. If that transaction appears ordinary for the type of relationship in question because it is a kind of transaction that is often made in the absence of the exertion of any influence in such a relationships, there is no basis to suggest the *use* of the influence.

This second ingredient helps define the scope of the law because it indicates the distinction between everyday influence and *undue* influence. The point was addressed in *Etridge*, where Lord Nicholls addressed a range of relationships based on trust and confidence where influence is expected, and then added:

> 24. . . .The law would out of touch with everyday life if the presumption [of undue influence] were to apply to every Christmas or birthday gift by a child to a parent, or to an agreement whereby a client or patient agrees to be responsible for the reasonable fees of his legal or medical adviser. The law would be rightly open to ridicule, for transactions such as these are unexceptionable. They do not suggest that something may be amiss.

Transactions often happen between parties where one has influence over another and usually the law rightfully has no interest in them. However, when a transaction is one that is not normally expected between such parties, it will be one which 'calls for an explanation' and it is in these circumstances that a court will interest itself in a transaction.

15.6.1 The Old Requirement of a Manifest Disadvantage

This second ingredient was given an interpretation by the House of Lords in *National Westminster Bank Plc v Morgan* [1985] AC 686. There, Lord Scarman said that it required there to have been a sufficiently serious disadvantage to the complainant. On that basis the rule became that the presumption could only apply if the transaction was a 'manifest disadvantage' to the complainant. The requirement was controversial because if there was some benefit to the complainant, the presumption of undue influence would be ruled out on the grounds of there being no manifest disadvantage. And it did not matter that the complainant was risking their only asset, like a house.

The controversial 'manifest disadvantage' requirement was finally set aside in *Etridge*. According to Lord Nicholls' judgment in that case, the requirement had tended not to be applied as Lord Scarman had intended and as such, it had caused problems and confusion for the courts. The key example was vulnerable wives. Marriage does not result in a presumption of influence, as we have seen, but it is open for a spouse to prove a relationship of trust and confidence in the other. Lord Nicholls referred to the example of a wife agreeing to use the marital home to finance the debts of her husband's business. In a narrow sense, the wife risks everything and gains nothing and it is a manifest disadvantage to her on that basis. But in a wider sense, if the business is a source of family income, the wife might have a reason to assist, and then it could not realistically be said to have been a manifest disadvantage to her. This made the requirement difficult to apply.

The solution was to simply go back to the test stated by Lindley LJ in *Allcard v Skinner*. Consequently, there is no longer need to establish a manifest disadvantage for the complainant, and instead, in the words of Lord Nicholls, the courts simply look for 'a transaction that is not readily explicable by the relationship of the parties'. In other words, the transaction calls for an explanation because it is out of the ordinary for parties in such a relationship. It means what we are looking for are facts that raise a suspicion or show something is amiss. When that requirement is met, the presumption of undue influence can apply. Lord Hobhouse in *Etridge* gave an example of a solicitor who buys a client's property at a low price.

Following *Etridge*, there is no longer a formal requirement of a 'manifest disadvantage' to the complainant but that does not mean that a resulting disadvantage is no longer relevant. It will be part of the evidence to show the existence of the second ingredient. As Lewison J explained in *Thompson v Foy* [2009] EWHC 1076 (Ch), a disadvantage is no longer a distinct requirement. But it is still useful as evidence towards there having been an abuse of influence. It means that the more disadvantageous the transaction, the more likely it is that it calls for an explanation. However, we will see that this does not apply in the same way for relationships based on love and affection.

15.6.2 The Difficulty in Dealing with Spouses

Between spouses, the transaction having been disadvantageous is less useful in proving that it is one that 'calls for an explanation'. This is because there is a general perception in society that there are good reasons why a spouse or partner might enter into a disadvantageous transaction with the other. The significance of this was explained in *Etridge* in the context of wives using their houses to guarantee security for the debts of their husbands' businesses. And the same applies to couples generally, not just married couples. On this Lord Nicholls stated:

> 30. I return to husband and wife cases. I do not think that, *in the ordinary course*, a guarantee of the character I have mentioned is to be regarded as a transaction which, failing proof to the contrary, is explicable only on the basis that it has been procured by the exercise of undue influence by the husband. Wives frequently enter into such transactions. There are good and sufficient reasons why they are willing to do so, despite the risks involved for them and their families. They may be enthusiastic. They may not. They may be less optimistic than their husbands about the prospects of the husbands' businesses. They may be anxious, perhaps exceedingly so. But this is a far cry from saying that such transactions as a class are to be regarded as prima facie evidence of the exercise of undue influence by husbands.
>
> 31. I have emphasised the phrase 'in the ordinary course'. There will be cases where a wife's signature of a guarantee or a charge of her share in the matrimonial home does call for explanation. Nothing I have said above is directed at such a case.
>
> 32. I add a cautionary note... Statements or conduct by a husband which do not pass beyond the bounds of what may be expected of a reasonable husband in the circumstances should not, without more, be castigated as undue influence. Similarly, when a husband is forecasting the future of his business, and expressing his hopes or fears, a degree of **hyperbole** may be only natural. Courts should not too readily treat such exaggerations as misstatements.
>
> 33. Inaccurate explanations of a proposed transaction are a different matter. So are cases where a husband, in whom a wife has reposed trust and confidence for the management of their financial affairs, prefers his interests to hers and makes a choice for both of them on that footing. Such a husband abuses the influence he has. He fails to discharge the obligation of candour and fairness he owes a wife who is looking to him to make the major financial decisions.

hyperbole
refers to exaggerated statements not to be taken seriously or literally.

Lord Scott also made a comment that expanded on this 'cautionary note:'

> 160. There are, of course, cases where a husband does abuse that trust and confidence. He may do so by expressions of quite unjustified over-optimistic enthusiasm about the prospects of success of his business enterprises. He may do so by positive misrepresentation of his business intentions, or of the nature of the security he is asking his wife to grant his creditors, or of some

other material matter. He may do so by subjecting her to excessive pressure, emotional black-mail or bullying in order to persuade her to sign. . .

Both Lord Nicholls (with whom the other Lords agreed) and Lord Scott felt the need to provide guidance on the issue. The central point was that it was fairly normal for a wife to agree to the house being used as security for the husband's business. On its face this will be a risky transaction and can be classed as disadvantageous to the wife, because if the debts are not paid, the bank can sell the house to get its money. On its own, however, that risk does not mean the transaction 'calls for an explanation' because it can be explained by ordinary motives of people in such a relationship. The practical consequences of this are potentially serious. A complainant could prove trust and confidence in financial matters but the transaction may still not be enough for the second ingredient needed to presume undue influence. This approach has been criticised for overlooking the inequality in power within heterosexual relationships that has been normalised in society. According to such critiques, the law as it stands serves to make it harder for a wife to show that a transaction was not justified by ordinary motives (Auchmuty, 'The Rhetoric of Equality and the Problem of Heterosexuality' in Mulcahy & Wheeler (eds), 'Feminist Perspectives on Contract law' Glasshouse Press (2005)).

Where there is a positive act of wrongdoing the position would be different. Examples include false statements, pressure to sign or domination. Even the deliberate failure of a husband to reveal to his wife that he was having an affair at the time he asked her to enter into the transaction could be sufficient wrongdoing (*Hewett v First Plus Financial Group Plc* [2010] EWCA Civ 312). The point is that where there is sufficient wrongdoing, the transaction will not be explicable in terms of ordinary motives in such a relationship. The circumstances would then suggest that the consent was obtained by the *use* of influence. However, as Lord Nicholls was at pains to point out, in looking at what was said and done, the courts should be realistic. It is accepted that the spouse with the business might exaggerate their potential to be successful, but where conduct or statements (or omissions) are misleading or unjustified, then that is when the line is crossed.

KEY POINTS

Where there is a relationship of love and affection, a disadvantage arising from an agreement to use the house as security for a spouse or partners' business debts is not enough. The facts have to be examined to see if there is something else that suggests the possible use of influence.

Essentially, what this boils down to is that some transactions can be explained by motives inspired by love and affection. Of course, some couples may no longer have such an emotional bond but even then, there would be nothing unusual about them supporting each other, especially where it is to protect a marriage. Such support could result from loyalty, a high degree of commitment or simply conceding to the perception of what society expects. Likewise, it could be motivated by the fact that the two parties' financial position is so closely connected. This means the transaction on its own may not raise any suspicion, and so more is needed to suggest that influence was exercised.

?! THINKING POINTS

The transaction in *Leeder v Stevens* between a man and his 'other woman' suggested the use of influence. However, a wife providing security for the husband's business debt does not on its own suggest the use of influence. Is that an inconsistency? Or, is there a difference between a spouse and someone that has a long-term loving relationship? And is there a greater difference still between a marriage and a clandestine relationship?

The reference by the judges to wrongdoing by a husband (or equivalent) should be taken in its context. It does not mean such wrongdoing is always needed for undue influence generally; after all, that level of wrongful conduct was not required in *Allcard*. However, that case concerned religious influence, which was described as the 'most powerful' and 'dangerous' level of influence. In contrast, the influence arising from trust and confidence between a couple is not as severe and, therefore, it seems that more by way of wrongdoing is needed in that context.

Further guidance can be taken from *R v Attorney-General* [2003]. There, the Privy Council recognised the high level of influence exercised within the institutional hierarchy but Lord Hoffman (for the majority) found that the transaction did not call for an explanation. It could be explained by the relationship rather than by the use of influence. Essentially, the confidentiality agreement was seen as a reasonable or ordinary request with almost 97% of the members that voted being in favour of such an agreement. In applying the requirement for the second ingredient, Lord Hoffman stated:

> [24]   . . . The reason why R signed the agreement was because, at the time, he wished to continue to be a member of the SAS. If facing him with such a choice was not illegitimate for the purposes of duress, their Lordships do not think that it could have been an unfair exploitation of a relationship which consisted in his being a member of the SAS. . .

This means that the transaction was explicable without the exercise of influence, just like a spouse securing debts of the other's business. With that in mind, a higher level of wrongdoing would have been needed for the transaction to be explained by the use of influence—for example, the level of wrongdoing that would serve to have made the pressure illegitimate for the duress claim. This underscores how different issues are being balanced for the presumption of undue influence. *Allcard* featured one of the highest levels of influence and such a large transaction that it was out of the ordinary for that type of relationship. However, there was no obvious wrongdoing and, at best, it could be said that the Lady Superior failed to take steps to ensure the transaction was freely made. In R's case, there was also a high level of influence and no advice offered but the transaction was treated as reasonable and explainable. In that sense, it was just like a risk taken by one spouse to support the other. Consequently, for the whole transaction to be one that suggests the *use* of influence, more obvious wrongdoing was needed.

→ **CROSS-REFERENCE**
For the discussion of the type of threat being used to determine what is needed for a compulsion of will in a duress action see 14.5.5. and 14.6.3.

15.6.3 The Absence of Legal Advice

The courts have sometimes treated the absence of legal advice as a fact suggesting the *use* of influence. In *Allcard v Skinner* the gift was large and, in addition, there was no opportunity for independent legal advice. That was more than enough to say that the transaction could not be explained by ordinary motives. Where a complainant has been actually deprived of the opportunity for legal advice, as in *Allcard v Skinner*, it could raise an even stronger concern over the transaction. However, in *R v Attorney-General* [2003], Lord Hoffman explained that the absence of legal advice does not necessarily mean that the transaction resulted from the use of influence:

> 23.   The absence of independent legal advice may or may not be a relevant matter according to the circumstances. It is not necessarily an unfair exploitation of a relationship for one party to enter into a transaction with the other without ensuring that he has obtained independent legal advice.
>
> . . .
>
> 27.   . . . Here it is important to note that R does not allege that he did not understand the implications of what he was being asked to do. The contract was in simple terms and the explanatory memorandum even plainer. . . . [W]hen he saw the actual contract he knew what it meant.

> 28. In these circumstances, their Lordships do not think that the absence of legal advice affected the fairness of the transaction. The most that R can say is that a lawyer might have advised him to reflect upon the matter and, as in fact he changed his mind within a fairly short time after signing, that might have led to his not signing at all. But that is a decision which he could have made without a lawyer's advice.

According to Lord Hoffman, the contract was clear and understandable. That meant an informed decision could be made without advice—such advice would have made no difference. It was clear that R signed because he wanted to stay in the SAS. He did not sign as a result of influence.

In addition, Lord Hoffman observed that the undue influence claim was contradicted by the duress claim. It was recalled that R argued the *threat* of being returned to unit was the only reason for signing. That was inconsistent with R's argument that he signed as a result of influence arising from trust and confidence. Again, it was a fact that supported the idea that the transaction could be explained without the use or abuse of influence.

KEY POINTS

The transaction must be one that suggests the use of influence. That is where it is not explained by ordinary motives expected in that relationship. We then say that the transaction 'calls for an explanation'.

Relevant factors suggesting the *use* of influence are usually combined in some way:

- a very large gift or one that risks the complainant's only asset;
- a transaction that was disadvantageous to the complainant;
- wrongful conduct like misleading statements, pressure, or emotional blackmail;
- unavailability of independent legal advice.

15.7 Rebutting the Presumption of Undue Influence

Now that we have looked at the two ingredients required for a presumption of undue influence we can turn to the third stage, where the evidential burden shifts to the influencer. That party must prove that the transaction was *freely made* by the complainant. On this issue, the Court of Appeal in *Allcard v Skinner* referred to the need for independent legal advice and this has given rise to a lot of judicial discussion. It is easy to jump to the conclusion that the presumption is rebutted by showing such advice was given, but we need to be more careful.

Even in *Allcard v Skinner*, it was stated that the availability of advice was not enough if it could not be acted upon. The point is that the presumption is rebutted by showing the transaction was *freely made*. If the complainant received independent legal advice, it at least shows that the decision was informed, but an informed decision does not mean it was free from influence. The significance of the availability independent legal advice was detailed in *Etridge*. On that point Lord Nicholls observed:

> 20. Proof that the complainant received advice from a third party before entering into the impugned transaction is one of the matters a court takes into account when weighing all the evidence. The weight, or importance, to be attached to such advice depends on all the circumstances. In the normal course, advice from a solicitor or other outside adviser can be expected to bring home to a complainant a proper understanding of what he or she is about to do. But a person may understand fully the implications of a proposed transaction, for instance, a substantial gift, and yet still be acting under the undue influence of another. Proof of outside advice does not, of itself, necessarily show that the subsequent completion of the transaction was free from the exercise

of undue influence. Whether it will be proper to infer that outside advice had an emancipating effect, so that the transaction was not brought about by the exercise of undue influence, is a question of fact to be decided having regard to all the evidence in the case.

In *R v Attorney-General* [2003], Lord Hoffman expressed the same point:

23. . . .[T]he transaction may be such as to give rise to an inference of undue influence even if the induced party was advised by an independent lawyer and understood the legal implications of what he was doing.

The comments show that it is for the defendant (influencer) to show that the decision was freely made, and a large part of that can be achieved by showing that the complainant had received legal advice. But a person can still be acting on the influence even after having been advised. For that reason, advice having been given is just part of the evidence helping show that the decision was freely made. Of course, where there is a presumption of undue influence, the absence of advice is significant because it can make it extremely difficult to prove the decision was freely made. A good example is *Allcard v Skinner*, where the unavailability of advice meant that there was really no chance of rebutting the presumption (although the claim ultimately failed for other reasons).

KEY POINTS

Independent advice does not necessarily result in a freely made decision. It depends on the level or degree of the potential undue influence. If it is very strong, advice would have less of an impact.

15.8 Situations Involving Three Parties

So far, we have looked at actual undue influence and presumed undue influence. The focus has been on how the existence of these types of undue influence can be established. Here, we examine cases of undue influence which involve three parties: the influencer, the complainant and a bank. This is a recently-developed area and the cases are a fascinating read, and are a good example of judicial innovation resolving a specific problem. At a wider level, the rules developed are significant from social and economic perspectives.

15.8.1 The Background and Issues

It is useful for us to start with an outline of the context. Most of the cases concern what has become a typical scenario, where a wife enters a contract to allow the matrimonial home to be used as security to finance her husband's business. It usually begins with the husband's business not doing very well. He then needs a loan or an increased overdraft from the bank. The bank will agree, but only if there is security (or collateral) for the debt. The idea is that if the repayments are not made, the bank needs a way to get back the money owed. Typically, the only asset of value is the matrimonial home, so the bank will want to use the home as security for the debt. That involves a charge over the property being granted to the bank. Just like with a mortgage, if the repayments are not made, the bank will take possession of the house and sell it. In order for the charge to be granted, the wife must also consent, because she has an enforceable interest in the property. Without her consent, she can block the bank's attempt so possess the house later and so, in such circumstances, the house will not be good security for the debt. To ensure that it is good security, the bank will require the wife to sign a document agreeing to the bank's legal interest in the house. The wife then signs, but only as a result of pressure or undue influence by the husband. Later, the husband's business does not keep up the repayments, which then prompts the bank to seek possession of the house. The wife then challenges the bank's right to do so by arguing that she signed the documents as a result of undue influence by her husband.

This typical scenario has arisen in a very significant number of cases and formed the basis of the eight appeals in the leading case of *Etridge*. (A notable exception is *Barclays Bank v Rivett* [1999] 1 FLR 730, in which the Court of Appeal agreed that the undue influence of a wife over her husband could be presumed on the facts.) The social significance of the case arises from the fact that this sort of transaction is common. For most small businesses, the only way to secure finance is with the family home. That leads us to the economic significance of the case. Such transactions allow for businesses to exist and grow. Consequently, the economy as a whole benefits by having more businesses trading and more employment.

Having addressed the basic factual context and its wider significance, we can turn to the legal significance of the case. These transactions create an unusual problem because the undue influence is not exerted by a party to the relevant contract. Instead, it is typically exerted by the husband, who is outside the relevant contract between the bank and the wife. For the purposes of the transaction, the husband is then a 'third party'.

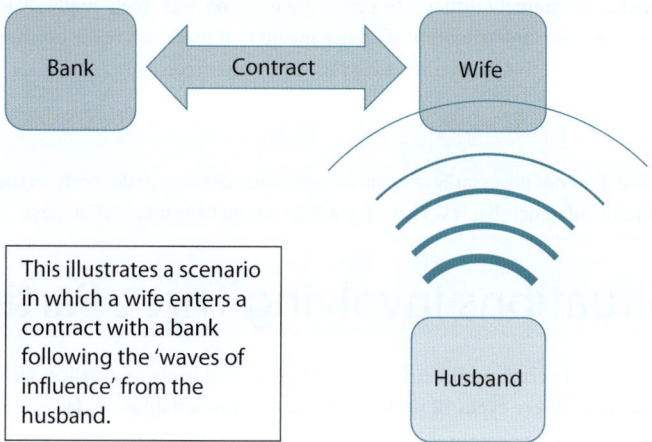

This illustrates a scenario in which a wife enters a contract with a bank following the 'waves of influence' from the husband.

Figure 15.2
The contractual relationship in the cases with three parties

On the face of it, the contract is between two innocent parties. The wrongdoing is by someone outside the contract. But what should the law do? First of all, there is a policy balance that must be struck, which was explained by Lord Brown-Wilkinson in *Barclays Bank v O'Brien* [1994] in the following way:

> It is easy to allow sympathy for the wife who is threatened with the loss of her home at the suit of a rich bank to obscure an important public interest *viz.,* the need to ensure that the wealth currently tied up in the matrimonial home does not become economically sterile. If the rights secured to wives by the law renders vulnerable loans granted on the security of matrimonial homes, institutions will be unwilling to accept such security, thereby reducing the flow of loan capital to business enterprises. It is therefore essential that a law designed to protect the vulnerable does not render the matrimonial home unacceptable as security to financial institutions.

The point made by Lord Brown-Wilkinson is extremely important. It captures the policy objectives that the law should reflect:

- Vulnerable parties, like the wives in the cases, need protection and should be allowed to end the relevant contracts.

■ At the same time, if banks cannot rely on matrimonial homes as security, they will stop lending where the only security available is the home, and that means small businesses and the wider economy would suffer.

The same point was emphasised Lord Nicholls in *Etridge*, who referred to the wide increase in homeownership and the fact that 95% of businesses were small businesses that would rely on using the matrimonial home as security for a loan. Furthermore, these businesses accounted for nearly a third of all employment.

Whatever solution the law devises, it needs to reflect these policy objectives. The basic solution was originally provided by Lord Brown-Wilkinson in *O'Brien*. The case introduced a mechanism to meet the key objectives and was an impressive and significant development. By examining that decision first, we will then be able to see how the balance was improved by the House of Lords in *Etridge*.

15.8.2 The Basic Mechanism—Constructive Notice

To appreciate the logic of the mechanism introduced, we need to briefly consider the position of the parties and the resulting dilemma. It could be said that it is unfair for the wife to be locked into the contract since she has not freely consented. On the other hand, the bank has not done anything wrong and so it could be said that it is unfair to take the contract away from the bank.

We can now contrast this with a scenario with slightly different facts, in which the bank actually knew of the undue influence from the husband. In other words, the bank knew the wife did not freely consent, but went ahead anyway. In such circumstances, it is no longer unfair for the bank to lose the contract since it could be said that the bank entered the contract at its own risk and could hardly complain as a result. We could even say that the bank is no longer an innocent party in those circumstances and was partly at fault. In such a case, there is no legal dilemma between harming two innocent parties. Of course, in reality a bank would never go ahead with such a transaction but the logic of this situation can be applied to the real-world problem.

Consider the original scenario with another slight difference. This time the bank does not know of the undue influence, but the warning signs are there indicating a possibility of undue influence. We can then say that the bank *should* have known of the undue influence had it been more careful and made enquiries. In that situation, the bank is still partly at fault. It did not have actual notice of undue influence but it ought to have known, had it taken more care. This means the bank had **constructive notice** of the potential undue influence. Since we can identify some fault on the part of the bank, there is no dilemma of choosing between two completely innocent parties and, again, it would not be unfair to end their contract. It is this reasoning that was introduced by Lord Brown-Wilkinson in *O'Brien*.

O'Brien was really concerned with a misrepresentation by a husband to his wife about how much of the house was being used as security for a loan. He said it covered £60,000 when in fact it was for £130,000. However, the mechanism used by the House of Lords was applicable equally to undue influence, as both concern free consent to a contract between spouses. Lord Brown-Wilkinson stated that the bank was 'on inquiry' of the risk of misrepresentation (or undue influence) where (1) the transaction was not to the financial advantage of the wife; and (2) there was a real risk that the husband had committed a wrong that would allow the wife to end the transaction. These circumstances were in effect 'alarm bells' alerting the bank that something might be wrong. The bank should in such circumstances take reasonable steps to ensure that the wife knows the risks and is told to get independent advice. Without taking such steps, the bank would have 'constructive notice' of the wrongful conduct. The bank could not then complain if the wife enforced her right to end the transaction.

The constructive notice mechanism was not just limited to wives. Lord Brown-Wilkinson emphasised it was based on emotional pressure from living together and, therefore, the same protection rightly applied to all cohabiting couples, same-sex or otherwise. All that was needed was for the bank

constructive notice is judge-made notice rather than actual notice. It arises when a party would have had notice, had they been more careful.

to know that they were living together. This was further clarified by the Court of Appeal in *Massey v Midland Bank Plc* [1995] 1 All ER 929, where Steyn LJ observed that cohabitation was not essential. It was enough for the bank to know that the parties were in a relationship.

The transactions addressed so far have been for the benefit of one party. *CIBC Morgtages v Pitt* [1994] 1 AC 200 featured a joint loan for joint purposes and, on that basis, Lord Brown-Wilkinson held that the bank would not be 'on inquiry'. It was suggested however that the position would be different if the bank knew the loan was for the husband's purposes.

→ CROSS-REFERENCE
For the facts of *Burch* see 15.5.3.

The mechanism from *O'Brien* was applied outside of what is not ordinarily a loving or sexual relationship in *Burch* [1997] which concerned an employer and his junior employee. In that case, the Court of Appeal confirmed the presumption of undue influence and set aside the transaction with the bank because the bank knew of facts that suggested a relationship of trust and confidence.

15.8.3 The Development of Constructive Notice from *Etridge*

While the mechanism from *O'Brien* was a major improvement, it was not enough to prevent the wave of similar cases that followed. Of these, the appeals in *Etridge* reached the House of Lords, which provided the opportunity to develop the mechanism by introducing more certainty and simplicity. Three of the Lords provided guidance for the banks, but we will focus on the version by Lord Nicholls, since that judgment was approved by the other two Law Lords:

> 82. . . . But the law does not regard sexual relationships as standing in some special category of their own so far as undue influence is concerned. Sexual relationships are no more than one type of relationship in which an individual may acquire influence over another individual. . . . What is appropriate for sexual relationships ought, in principle, to be appropriate also for other relationships where trust and confidence are likely to exist.
>
> . . .
>
> 84. The crucially important question raised by this wider application of the *O'Brien* principle concerns the circumstances which will put a bank on inquiry. . .[A] bank cannot be expected to probe the emotional relationship between two individuals, whoever they may be. Nor is it desirable that a bank should attempt this. . .[T]he test of what puts a bank on inquiry should be simple, clear and easy to apply in widely varying circumstances.
>
> . . .
>
> 87. . . .[I]f a bank is not to be required to evaluate the extent to which its customer has influence over a proposed guarantor, the only practical way forward is to regard banks as 'put on inquiry' in every case where the relationship between the **surety** and the debtor is non-commercial.
>
> 88. Different considerations apply where the relationship between the debtor and guarantor is commercial, as where a guarantor is being paid a fee, or a company is guaranteeing the debts of another company in the same group. Those engaged in business can be regarded as capable of looking after themselves and understanding the risks involved in the giving of guarantees.

surety
is a reference to a party that is providing the security for the loan.

Essentially, Lord Nicholls widened the scope of the mechanism from *O'Brien* and in doing so created more certainty for the banks and for the law. The bank is simply on inquiry when the relationship between the party giving security and the one benefiting is non-commercial. Such a non-commercial relationship is enough for the 'alarm bells' to be ringing. Parties in a commercial relationship, on the other hand, are expected to have the knowhow to look after themselves. Of course, there might be uncertainty when a wife is a shareholder or even a director of the company to benefit. That might seem to concern a relationship that is both commercial and non-commercial. Lord Nicholls addressed that type of situation earlier in the judgment:

49. Less clear-cut is the case where the wife becomes surety for the debts of a company whose shares are held by her and her husband. Her shareholding may be nominal, or she may have a minority shareholding or an equal shareholding with her husband. In my view the bank is put on inquiry in such cases, even when the wife is a director or secretary of the company. Such cases cannot be equated with joint loans. The shareholding interests, and the identity of the directors, are not a reliable guide to the identity of the persons who actually have the conduct of the company's business.

It was important to address this point because, increasingly, spouses are directors of businesses and, as Lord Nicholls pointed out, this is not usually a good indication of where power lies with respect to the company; a spouse who is a director or shareholder may still be under influence of the other. This point from Lord Nicholls was applied in *Syndicate Bank v Dansingani* [2019] EWHC 3439 (Ch). The case concerned a wife who was a director and joint shareholder of a company with her husband. She had no real role in the running of the business and the bank ought to have known that because it had dealings with the husband only. The guarantee from the wife to support the finance from the bank had been secured using a faxed document, and at no point was she instructed to get legal advice. In the circumstances, having established, trust and confidence in her husband over financial matters, the court set aside the wife's guarantee.

15.8.4 Reasonable Steps for the Bank to Take to Avoid Constructive Notice

Banks knew from *O'Brien* that if reasonable steps were not taken to ensure a spouse was aware of the risks and had independent advice, they were fixed with constructive notice and were then vulnerable to the rights of the complainant. Given the importance of this, there was a need for guidance on the 'reasonable steps' banks should take to ensure their transactions are safe. On this issue, Lord Nicholls started with the general basic requirement for reasonable steps to be taken:

50. . . .For the future a bank satisfies these requirements if it insists that the wife attend a private meeting with a representative of the bank at which she is told of the extent of her liability as surety, warned of the risk she is running and urged to take independent legal advice. In exceptional cases the bank, to be safe, has to insist that the wife is separately advised.

. . .

54 . . .This does not wholly eliminate the risk of undue influence or misrepresentation. But it does mean that a wife enters into a transaction with her eyes open so far as the basic elements of the transaction are concerned.

The guidance acknowledged the banks' response to *O'Brien*. They did not want the responsibility of advising the wife and did not like the risks associated with disputes about what was said. Instead, they adopted a practice of instructing wives in such circumstances to get advice from a solicitor. The banks then relied on confirmation from the solicitor that the documents and risks were explained. On that basis, Lord Nicholls provided detailed guidance on that practice of using a solicitor.

The guidance can be summarised as follows:

- ▪ The bank should explain the purpose of seeing the solicitor. That includes the fact that the bank will rely on the confirmation given by the solicitor to protect the transaction.
- ▪ The bank should contact the wife directly to check the name of the solicitor she intends to use. She should be told that it is okay to use the husband's solicitor or one already acting for the couple. The wife should also be asked if she prefers a different solicitor.

- The bank should send the solicitor all of the relevant information. That must include information on things like the terms of the transaction and the husband's current debt.

- If the bank suspects the wife has been misled or is not acting freely, the bank should tell the solicitor along with its reasons.

- The bank can proceed on confirmation from the solicitor that appropriate advice was given.

- If the bank knows the wife did not receive advice, it enters the transaction at its own risk. The same can be said if it *should have known* advice was not received. This indicates that a bank should only go ahead following confirmation from the solicitor that appropriate advice was given.

15.8.5 Guidance for Solicitors

With banks relying so much on advice provided by solicitors, Lord Nicholls wanted to give guidance on their role. He expressed concern about the quality of advice in some cases, even describing some as 'disturbing'. It was said that the cause might have been that solicitors did not understand what was required, and so his guidance on advice represented a 'core minimum' of requirements to be met. This guidance can be summarised in the following way:

The basis of the meeting: The purpose of the meeting and the fact that the bank will rely on it to protect their transaction will need to be explained. The solicitor would need the wife to confirm that she is instructing the solicitor to act for her.

The quality of the meeting: The meeting should be face to face without the husband (or party to benefit) and it should be in non-technical language so it is understandable. Solicitors should make sure they have all the information they need from the bank. Without that information, they should not confirm to the bank that advice was given.

Independence of the advice: In principle, it is acceptable for the solicitor to also represent the bank or even the husband. However, the solicitor must be acting for the wife and only in her interests. If the solicitor thinks there is a risk of a conflict of interest, then they should not continue with the wife.

The advice should cover the following matters:
(a) The aim and effect of the bank documents

  The solicitor should explain that the wife could lose her home; that her home might be her only asset; and that she could face bankruptcy.

(b) The seriousness of the risks—the wife's liability and financial means

  That includes the amount of money involved; the liability being guaranteed and the effect of the terms and in particular, how the bank could increase it and change the terms without her. The wife's financial position is important too. She should understand her financial means and the value of her property. They should discuss what other assets she can use for repayments if the business fails.

(c) Make it clear that the wife has a choice

  The wife should know that it is her decision to make. To explain her choice, she and the solicitor will need to discuss the husband's financial position, how much the business owes and its current overdraft.

(d) The solicitor should check that the wife wants to go ahead

  This involves asking if she consents to the solicitor writing to the bank confirming what has been explained. The point is that such confirmation to the bank should only be given with the wife's authority. Also, the solicitor should check if the wife wants him or her to negotiate terms with the bank. Those terms might include the order that assets will be taken away or even the amount the wife is to be liable for.

The primary aim is to ensure that the solicitor's advice is effective, and not just a formality, so that it ensures that the wife (or equivalent party) understands the transaction. It also serves to protect solicitors. If they follow the guidance, they will not be liable to the wife in damages for negligent misstatement or for breach of contract.

→ CROSS-REFERENCE

For the rules on liability for negligent misstatement see 13.8.1.

KEY POINTS

- The bank's contract is safe and cannot be challenged for undue influence if the bank follows the steps outlined by Lord Nicholls.
- The guidance does not require the bank to have confirmation of a freely made decision. Instead, the aim is to ensure that the wife (or equivalent party) knows what they are getting into.

The guidance is focussed firmly on ensuring that the wife (or equivalent party) has a complete understanding of the transaction. Of course, a clear understanding of a transaction is not the same as entering into one freely, and so it can be said that the guidance aims to *inform* the wife rather than ensure free consent. On that basis, the guidance does not prevent the use of undue influence to secure the transaction. This was justified on the basis most people would be outraged if faced with the kind of questions that could be used to identify undue influence. In addition, it is unlikely that solicitors are equipped to carry out that kind of exercise and, even if they did, it would result in greater legal costs. These factors were then put in the context of the widened scope for putting banks on inquiry. It was felt that anything more than confirmation of appropriate advice would be disproportionate. It would impose a heavy burden on a wider range of customers in order to protect a small minority that *might* have been wronged.

The only reference to a higher level of protection was in the context of a solicitor. Lord Nicholls referred to cases where it is 'glaringly obvious' the wife has been 'grievously wronged'. In such circumstances, the solicitor should not act further. Such circumstances were not defined but the comment provides a further layer of protection as it goes further than just requiring that the party providing the security be informed.

The guidance is extremely useful because it allows for the wife to be informed while at the same time enabling the bank to know how to protect its transactions. It does the same thing for solicitors, who now know that if they follow the core minimum guidance, then they are not at risk of a failure in their duty to their client.

Essentially, the guidance provides the certainty of a division of responsibility and therefore liability. Consider the bank. If it gets the confirmation of appropriate advice, it knows its transaction is secure. If the wife was badly advised by the solicitor, it is not the bank's problem (unless it should have known about the bad advice). If the repayments are not made, the bank can take the house. The wife's only available remedy would be from a damages claim against the solicitor for the bad advice. Where a solicitor has followed the core requirements, he or she will not be liable to the wife.

?! THINKING POINTS

Following the guidance in *Etridge*, the wife (or equivalent) will know the risks, but might still enter into a contract as a result of undue influence. Should the law be more protective?

15.9 Remedies for Undue Influence

Just like with duress, there is no tort of undue influence and so a complainant cannot rely on undue influence alone to claim damages for losses suffered as a result. Of course, there might have been wrongful conduct that happens to breach a tort like harassment or intimidation, but otherwise the remedy is rescission. That means the usual bars to rescission apply. In *Etridge*, Lord Scott referred to this basic remedy in the following way:

→ CROSS-REFERENCE
For the basic effect of a
voidable contract and
rescission see 13.4.1.

> [144] . . . If contractual consent has been procured by undue influence or misrepresentation for which a party to the contract is responsible, the other party, the victim, is entitled, subject to the usual defences of change of position, affirmation, delay etc, to avoid the contract.

Just like the cases on duress and misrepresentation, the courts have shown some flexibility in the application of this remedy. The case often cited is *Cheese v Thomas* [1994] 1 WLR 124, which concerned an 85-year-old complainant and his great-nephew. They agreed to buy an £83,000 house to share, with the complainant contributing £43,000 towards the purchase. The defendant nephew put in £40,000 using a mortgage on the property. The defendant failed to keep up his payments, but by then the market price had fallen and so the house was only sold for £55,000. The complainant relied on undue influence and the presumption was accepted on the facts, but the appropriate remedy was a problem. Ordinarily, the complainant would get back the money paid, but making the defendant pay all of the £43,000 was deemed to be too harsh. It would have meant that he absorbed all of the £28,000 loss resulting from the fall in price. Instead, the Court of Appeal approved of the loss being shared proportionately. This seemed to fit within the 'change of position' addressed in the statement by Lord Scott.

15.10 Exploitation of Weakness, Unconscionability, and Inequality of Bargaining Power

Having examined the law relating to undue influence, we can now turn to an overview of some remaining principles relevant to the wider values reflected by the concept of undue influence. Undue influence (just like duress) focusses on the way the contract is created and so it can be said to be protective of procedural fairness. The fact that a contract is very one-sided is not a basis for undue influence, so where undue influence is established, the contract can be set aside even if there is no disadvantage to the complainant. Where the transaction results in a serious disadvantage to the complainant it is just part of the evidence to suggest there has been a *use* of influence.

While undue influence reflects a level of procedural fairness, there are some cases based in equity that reflect a level of protection going beyond procedural fairness. These are cases where the contract was set aside because it was an 'unconscionable bargain'. The term 'unconscionability' has not been given a legal definition by the courts, but it refers to a contract that a person of good conscience would not make. Such contracts are morally unacceptable because there has been an exploitation of weakness which has also resulted in a very one-sided and unfair contract. The point is that in such cases, fairness in substance also becomes a consideration for the court.

Early cases show the courts protecting young people that were in line to inherit a fortune on the death of a relative. These are often called the 'expectant heir' cases. Expectant heirs were vulnerable to unscrupulous or 'shady' money lenders who, knowing that the heir was soon to inherit vast wealth, would exploit his naivety for profit. One example is *Earl of Aylesford v Morris* (1873) 8 Ch App 484, which concerned a 21-year-old who was in line to inherit his father's estate. Having built up some debts, he agreed to a loan with an interest rate of 60% without getting any independent advice. Later, the contract was set aside on the basis that he would repay with an interest rate of 5%. Essentially, it was felt that the lender had taken advantage of the young claimant.

Another line of cases concerned weakness in the sense of being 'poor and ignorant'. In *Fry v Lane* (1888) 40 Ch D 312, the complainant was a laundryman earning just £1 a week. He entered a contract to sell an interest he was due to inherit for £170, when it was actually worth £475. This transaction was set aside because the buyer had taken advantage of the complainant. In his reasoning, Kay J referred to the following points:

- Fry was 'poor and ignorant' (this represents a type of weakness);
- There was no independent advice (this shows room for exploitation);
- The purchase was at a 'considerable undervalue' (representing an unfair deal).

These factors were applied in *Cresswell v Potter* [1978] 1WLR 255. The complainant was a Post Office telephonist and in her divorce settlement agreement, she transferred her half of the matrimonial home to her ex-husband. In return, she was freed from any liability under the mortgage but, in reality, this freedom was not worth much at all. The judge indicated that she was getting virtually nothing in return for her share. Later, the house was sold for a much higher price than it was purchased. The claimant challenged the agreement so that she could then be entitled to half of the profit and, Megarry J allowed the original agreement to be set aside, using the factors from *Fry v Lane*.

Unconscionability has been applied in some cases, and discussed in others. Generally, the cases suggest a need for the following:

- A transaction that is so disadvantageous that it is unfair to the complainant;
- The complaint has some vulnerability or weakness that has been exploited;
- The resulting transaction was overreaching and oppressive.

Throughout, the principle has been treated as exceptional and its precise application has not been determined clearly. It requires exploitation that goes beyond just being a 'bad bargain' and into the realm of being morally improper (*Alec Lobb (Garages) Ltd v Total Oil Ltd* [1985] 1 WLR 173). The transaction should be one that is 'overreaching and oppressive' (*Strydom v Vendside Ltd* [2009] EWHC 2130). In other words, it should be a transaction that 'shocks the conscience of the court' (*Portman Building Society v Dusangh* [2000] 2 All ER (Comm) 221). The problem is that it is not really possible to work out when these requirements will be met. It might be this uncertainty that has meant that the principle is hardly used in practice and that, instead, complainants try to rely on other actions like undue influence where the facts allow it. In contrast, a wider principle of unconscionability using a less strict test has been recognised in Singapore (*Bom v Bok* [2018] SGCA 83) and in Australia (*Commercial Bank of Australia Ltd v Amadio* (1983) 151 CLR 447).

While cases concerning actions based on unconscionability are exceptional, sometimes in cases based on an action for duress or undue influence unconscionability is added as an additional argument (an example being *Libyan Investment Authority v Goldman Sachs* [2016] EWHC 2530 (Ch), in which the unconscionability claim was rejected because the undue influence claim failed). The principle of unconscionability itself has been the subject of academic debate, with some commentators arguing that presumed undue influence should be within a wider principle based on unconscionability (for example, Capper, 'Undue Influence and Unconscionability: A Rationalisation' (1998) 114 LQR 479). However, some disagree and argue that undue influence should a distinct category in its own right (for example Bigwood, 'Exploitative contracts' OUP, 2003). The fact that undue influence is concerned with procedural fairness whereas unconscionability is also concerned with substantive fairness means that both of these principles arising from equity raise different concerns (Enonchong, 'The modern English doctrine of unconscionability', (2018) Journal of Contract Law, 34, (3), 211).

15.11 Lord Denning's Principle of Inequality of Bargaining Power

Another remaining point to address is based on the judgment of Lord Denning MR in *Lloyds v Bundy*, which attempted to introduce a wide principle of 'inequality of bargaining power' and which was later rejected. This principle was aimed at pulling duress, undue influence and the unconscionability cases together under one umbrella principle. It is another example of Lord

Denning's infamous 'innovations' in the law of contract and, for that reason, it is useful to read parts of his judgment:

> There are cases in our books in which the courts will set aside a contract, or a transfer of property, when the parties have not met on equal terms - when the one is so strong in bargaining power and the other so weak - that, as a matter of common fairness, it is not right that the strong should be allowed to push the weak to the wall.
>
> [Lord Denning MR then referred to cases on duress, undue influence, unconscionable bargains and 'salvage' (which relates to ships) and continued]
>
> Gathering all together, I would suggest that through all these instances there runs a single thread. They rest on "inequality of bargaining power." By virtue of it, the English law gives relief to one who, without independent advice, enters into a contract upon terms which are very unfair or transfers property for a consideration which is grossly inadequate, when his bargaining power is grievously impaired by reason of his own needs or desires, or by his own ignorance or infirmity, coupled with undue influences or pressures brought to bear on him by or for the benefit of the other. When I use the word "undue" I do not mean to suggest that the principle depends on proof of any wrongdoing. The one who stipulates for an unfair advantage may be moved solely by his own self-interest, unconscious of the distress he is bringing to the other. I have also avoided any reference to the will of the one being "dominated" or "overcome" by the other. One who is in extreme need may knowingly consent to a most improvident bargain, solely to relieve the straits in which he finds himself.

This inequality of bargaining power principle represented a very significant potential change. It was not based on wrongdoing or dominance but rather on the protection of weaker parties from very bad bargains made in certain circumstances. Such an approach would represent a ground-breaking level of protection for weaker and vulnerable parties. It gave rise to a great deal of debate, with some being in favour, and many against. A key criticism was that it would lead to uncertainty. Parties enjoying a high level of bargaining power would not know if any of their agreements were secure, or open to challenge. For example, how would such a party know in advance that a deal was bad enough to represent 'grossly inadequate' consideration? Likewise, the point relating to procedural fairness concerning 'pressures' and 'impairment' of bargaining power are not clear.

At the very least, Lord Denning's principle may ultimately have been developed and shaped by later cases. However, any chance of that was ended by the House of Lords case of *Natwest v Morgan* [1985] in which Lord Scarman rejected the principle directly. He made clear that it could not be the basis of undue influence since the basis of that area was already well established. In addition, he pointed out that Parliament has passed legislation in various forms to address the inequality of bargaining power. Examples of such legislation were cited and included the Consumer Credit Act 1974 and legislation implying terms like the Supply of Goods and Service Act 1982. According to Lord Scarman, it was for Parliament to decide if more protection is needed. While Lord Scarman's reasons have continued to be criticised, the inequality of bargaining power principle has never been adopted by a court. In *Credit Lyonnaise v Burch* [1997] the judgment of Millett LJ came close to giving effect to Lord Denning's approach but the judgment could also be explained using established principles. As for further protection from legislation, consumers can now rely on the Consumer Protection from Unfair Trading Practices Regulations 2008, and the relevant basics of these Regulations are explained at 15.12.

➡ **CROSS-REFERENCE**
For the discussion of *Burch* see 15.5.3.

15.12 The Consumer Protection from Unfair Trading Practices Regulations 2008

➡ **CROSS-REFERENCE**
For the discussion of the application of the Regulations to misleading practices see 13.11.

The Regulations apply to practices of traders which are unfair to consumers. We have already addressed the general scope of the Regulations in the context of misleading practices. Our concern here relates to the Regulations' control of 'aggressive practices'. Such aggressive practices can involve duress and undue influence. As a result, the Regulations represent an alternative means to securing a remedy where the complainant is a consumer.

The relevant provision is Regulation 7. It starts by defining an aggressive practice:

> 7 (1) A commercial practice is aggressive if, in its factual context, taking account of all of its features and circumstances—
>
> (a) it significantly impairs or is likely significantly to impair the average consumer's freedom of choice or conduct in relation to the product concerned through the use of harassment, coercion or undue influence; and
>
> (b) it thereby causes or is likely to cause him to take a transactional decision he would not have taken otherwise.

It then provides the factors to be considered to identify the use of such a practice:

> (2) In determining whether a commercial practice uses harassment, coercion or undue influence account shall be taken of—
>
> (a) its timing, location, nature or persistence;
>
> (b) the use of threatening or abusive language or behaviour;
>
> (c) the exploitation by the trader of any specific misfortune or circumstance of such gravity as to impair the consumer's judgment, of which the trader is aware, to influence the consumer's decision with regard to the product;
>
> (d) any onerous or disproportionate non-contractual barrier imposed by the trader where a consumer wishes to exercise rights under the contract, including rights to terminate a contract or to switch to another product or another trader; and
>
> (e) any threat to take any action which cannot legally be taken.

Regulation 7 then goes on to define coercion and undue influence:

> (3) In this regulation—
>
> (a) "coercion" includes the use of physical force; and
>
> (b) "undue influence" means exploiting a position of power in relation to the consumer so as to apply pressure, even without using or threatening to use physical force, in a way which significantly limits the consumer's ability to make an informed decision.

The aim is to protect consumers from high-pressure sales (or purchases). The effect of such pressure is simple; it can limit the ability of the consumer to make a decision freely.

The three basic elements of an 'aggressive commercial practice' under Regulation 7 are therefore as follows:

- It applies to traders using harassment, coercion (including physical force) or undue influence.
- The practices are those that impair (or are likely to impair) the average consumer's 'freedom of choice' or conduct; and
- The average consumer makes (or is likely to make) a different decision as a result of the practice.

The reference to the 'average consumer' reflects an objective approach, like the use of the 'reasonable person'. The average consumer is an EU concept that the UK has made use of in the Consumer Rights Act 2015. We can recall that the average consumer is 'reasonably well-informed, observant and circumspect'.

It is useful to look at the key aspects of the three elements of Regulation 7 in more detail. Take harassment and coercion. They include both physical and psychological pressure and are intended to be wider than common law duress. In fact, we will see that a wider range of pressure is covered, not just pressure that is classed as illegitimate.

Undue influence is defined in a way that appears wide too. It refers to a 'position of power' being exploited which goes beyond relationships of trust and confidence to cover persuasion that exploits a weakness. The position of power could simply be a result of a trader having control over the consumer's goods and what is now the Competition and Markets Authority provided an example in their guidance on the Regulations. It concerns a mechanic who does more work on a car than what was agreed and then refuses to return the car without full payment being made. The position of power comes from knowing that the consumer needs the car and will not simply walk away. At common law, we would probably class this as an example of duress of goods.

The reference to coercion, undue influence and harassment is not meant to result in practices fitting neatly into these as individual categories. Instead, it is better to treat all three as representing a single category because there is so much scope for overlap. In fact, some examples provided by the Competition and Markets Authority are treated as a combination of coercion, undue influence and/or harassment depending on the factual background and what was said. It is useful to consider some of these examples and how they make use of the Regulation 7(2) factors to be considered.

- One example features a funeral parlour and a consumer who lost a relative recently. The staff pressure the consumer into buying an expensive coffin by suggesting that a cheaper product would bring shame and embarrassment on the family. This example reflects the exploitation of misfortune and timing. It is said to represent coercion, or undue influence, or both.

- The typical example of 'significant impairment' is the salesperson who comes to a consumer's house and ignores their requests to leave. The salesperson could stay for such a long time that eventually the consumer feels pressured into entering into a contract. This could be coercion, harassment, or both, and clearly timing and location are relevant considerations here.

- Consider a doorstep trader insisting on immediate payment who then insists on driving the consumer to the cashpoint. According to the CMA, that could be undue influence or coercion depending on what was said. Such a scenario brings in issues about the nature of the practice, its timing and location.

- Timing and location will be factors raised by late night calls or calls at inconvenient locations like at work. Such conduct could constitute harassment, coercion or undue influence, or even all three.

- The scope of the Regulation is widened as a result of its covering the 'exploitation of a specific misfortune or circumstance'. This can cover a trader taking advantage of an emotional concern that impairs the consumer's decision-making. This might be about a disability, body image or appearance. Such a concern might be a source of shame or embarrassment that a salesperson could exploit. The Schedule of the Regulations even includes the trader manufacturing concern, such as by suggesting that his or her job is on the line to play on the sympathies of a prospective purchaser.

The examples show that Regulation 7 covers a range of pressure and influence extending beyond the traditional case law. However, it only applies in the context of a trader and a consumer. In addition, it does not apply to mortgages, charges and certain leases.

Just like with the position for misleading practices, liability for aggressive practices is subject to the due diligence defence. This covers practices beyond the control of the trader or those arising by accident. The defence also covers traders where they have taken reasonable precautions and exercised due diligence to avoid the offence. Such a defence seems appropriate to misleading statements because what is expressed often relies on different sources of information. However, it is difficult to see how this defence could operate in the context of coercion, undue influence or harassment.

Following an infringement of this Regulation, the consumer is entitled to a remedy. These are detailed in the new Part 4A of the Regulations. We can recall that these remedies include unwinding the contract, a discount, and damages.

→ CROSS-REFERENCE
For the remedies available from the Regulations see 13.11.1.

CHAPTER SUMMARY

- The conceptual basis of undue influence is uncertain. While it has been argued that it is based on impaired consent (i.e. that it is claimant-sided) the weight of the cases suggests an approach based on wrongdoing (i.e. that it is defendant-sided).

- Actual undue influence describes the situation when the innocent party simply has direct proof of undue influence.

- For presumed undue influence there must be a relationship of influence (from a 'protected' relationship or from such influence being proven) and a transaction that is not explainable by ordinary motives in that relationship.

- The presumption of undue influence can be rebutted where it is shown that the decision was freely made.

- A relationship of influence can be presumed where it is based on trust and confidence. Trust and confidence has been shown to exist based on the following factors:

  - vulnerability and reliance on advice
  - physical dependence and reliance
  - an unconscionable transaction
  - being part of an institutional hierarchy
  - love and affection and reliance on financial matters, particularly between spouses

- While it is possible for a relationship of influence to exist between spouses, it will be difficult to show that a transaction is one that is not explained by ordinary motives in that relationship.

- A presumption of undue influence can be rebutted by showing that the transaction was freely made. If the complainant received legal advice, this will help to rebut that presumption.

- Where property has been used as security by the complainant to support a loan to a third party, the bank is 'on inquiry' of potential undue influence where the complainant and party to benefit are in a non-commercial relationship.

- When a bank has been put 'on inquiry', it must take reasonable steps to ensure the transaction is being freely made. This requires the bank to tell the party providing the security to get legal advice and present confirmation that the advice was given.

- If the bank takes the relevant reasonable steps, the transaction is secure. If it fails to take such steps, the transaction is at risk.

- Solicitors should follow the guidance provided by Lord Nicholls to avoid being liable to the complainant.

- Undue influence results in the contract being voidable, and so it can be rescinded by the complainant as long as the bars to rescission do not apply.

- A transaction can be set aside by the court where it is unconscionable (i.e. where it 'shocks the conscience' of the court). There is an ongoing debate about whether undue influence should be part of the wider unconscionability principle.

- More broadly, Lord Denning MR suggested placing undue influence, duress and unconscionability within a wider inequality of bargaining power principle, but this never received judicial support.

- The Consumer Protection from Unfair Trading Practices Regulations 2008 apply between consumers and traders. The Regulations provide remedies for conduct that includes duress and undue influence.

KEY CASES

☐ *Royal Bank of Scotland v Etridge and others (No 2) (2001)* **UKHL 44**—the leading case on undue influence generally, as it the latest binding case on the subject from the highest court. It confirmed the tests to be applied for presumed undue influence and the approach taken to constructive notice.

☐ *Allcard v Skinner* **(1887) 36 Ch.D 145**—a leading case on undue influence. As the first appeal case that confirmed presumed undue influence, all subsequent cases aim to be consistent with the principles stated in the judgments.

☐ *Bank of Credit and Commerce International SA v Aboody* **[1990] 1 QB 923**—a useful example of actual undue influence.

☐ *Barclays Bank v O'Brien* **[1994] 1 AC 180**—a significant House of Lords case in which Lord Browne-Wilkinson introduced the constructive notice solution to cases involving three parties.

☐ *Natwest v Morgan* **[1985] AC 686**—an early House of Lords case on undue influence in which Lord Scarman introduced the much-criticised requirement of manifest disadvantage (which was later rejected in *Etridge*).

☐ *Lloyds v Bundy* **[1975] QB 326**—represents an example of the bank/client relationship crossing into one of trust and confidence. This was also the case in which Lord Denning MR proposed an overarching principle of equality of bargaining power.

☐ *Hammond v Osborn* **[2002] EWCA Civ 885**—an example of trust and confidence arising from physical dependence, and also of a presumption of undue influence arising in the absence of a positive act of wrongdoing.

☐ *Credit Lyonnais Bank Nederland NV v Burch* **[1997] 1 All ER 144**—an example of presumed undue influence between employer and employee, which is significant for the judgment of Millett LJ, who found trust and confidence from the transaction being unconscionable.

☐ *R v Attorney-General for England Wales* **[2003] UKPC 22**—a Privy Council decision confirming that trust and confidence might arise from an institutional hierarchy.

☐ *Leeder v Stevens* **[2005] EWCA Civ 50**—an example of trust and confidence arising from a relationship of love and affection.

☐ *Cresswell v Potter* **[1978] 1WLR 255**—provides a more up-to-date test for unconscionability which was supported in *Alec Lobb (Garages) Ltd v Total Oil Ltd* [1985] 1 WLR 173.

QUESTIONS

1. Evaluate the extent to which the law protects wives (or equivalent) from the abuse of influence by their husbands (or equivalent).

2. Explain the extent to which *Royal Bank of Scotland v Etridge [2001]* clarified the law on undue influence.

3. Abi has been in a long-term relationship with Beena and they own a flat together. Abi wants to use the flat as security for a loan to enable her to open a coffee shop. She then tells Beena to go to the bank and sign a document. Realising that Beena is not keen on the idea, Abi tells Beena that if she really loved her, she would agree. The bank tells Beena about the transaction and about the requirement for her to get legal advice. Beena then visits a solicitor (Cheryl) who Abi was using to help set up her business. During the meeting, at which Abi was present, Beena is told of the risks. Cheryl then sends a letter to the bank explaining that Beena understands the risks but will do anything to keep Abi happy. After Beena signs the document, the bank provides the loan. Following Abi's failure to meet the repayments, the bank seeks possession of the flat. Advise Beena.

 For answer guidance to these questions please visit the online resources at www.oup.com/uk/naidoo1e/, where you will also find multiple choice questions to check your understanding of key concepts.

FURTHER READING

Auchmuty, 'The Rhetoric of Equality and the Problem of Heterosexuality' in Mulcahy & Wheeler (eds), 'Feminist Perspectives on Contract law' Glasshouse Press (2005)).
An excellent socio-legal assessment of *Etridge* that reveals how the protection is limited in the context of heterosexual relationships.

Bigwood, 'Undue Influence: impaired consent or wicked exploitation'? (1996) OJLS, 16(3) 503.
A shorter but significant assessment of undue influence arguing that it is based on the abuse performed by the stronger party rather than the consent of the weaker party.

Chen-Wishart, 'Undue Influence: Beyond impaired consent and Wrong Doing, Towards a Relational Analysis' in Borrows and Rodger (eds), Mapping the Law: Essays in Memory of Peter Birks (OUP, 2006).
This is a detailed introduction to a new theory underpinning the basis of undue influence.

Moore, 'Why does Lord Denning's lead balloon intrigue us still? The prospects of finding a unifying principle for duress, undue influence and unconscionability' (2018) 134 LQR 257.
A clear and detailed assessment relating to the possibility of aligning duress, undue influence and unconscionability as suggested by Lord Denning in *Lloyds v Bundy*.

16 Frustration of the Contract

LEARNING OBJECTIVES

By the end of this chapter you should be able to:

- understand the basis of the frustration principle and the requirements for its application;
- appreciate the importance of parties using terms to allocate the risks of impossibility of performance;
- assess and evaluate the financial consequences of frustration at common law and under the applicable legislation;
- apply the rules to a given set of facts.

INTRODUCTION

It is possible for an unexpected event to take place that would make the performance of a contract completely different to what both parties intended. It might be that the event made performance physically impossible or illegal. Alternatively, perhaps the contract was based on a state of affairs that no longer exists as a result of the event. In such circumstances, it might be that the event has 'frustrated' the contract so that the contract is ended automatically. In practice, this will be held to have taken place when one party brings an action claiming damages for breach following the other party's failure to perform. The other party will then defend the action by arguing that the contract was frustrated. Whether a given event was enough to frustrate a contract depends on the circumstances. In practice, the doctrine of frustration has a very limited scope and so its application is exceptional. However, recent events have illustrated its continuing relevance. These include the UK's leaving of the European Union, which has already given rise to at least one case in which frustration was pleaded, and the COVID-19 outbreak of 2020, which also has the potential to result in many frustrated contracts which have become no longer possible to perform as intended.

In this chapter we will begin with the background and basis of the frustration principle before turning to the ways in which a contract can be frustrated. We then address the factors limiting the scope of the principle. Finally, we examine the effects of a frustrated contract, which includes limited 'restitutionary' financial adjustments between the parties based on specific legislation. We will see that unlike misrepresentation, duress and influence, frustration is not about remedying wrongdoing. But nor it is about providing a fair distribution of the loss in response to unexpected risks. Rather, the law seeks to prevent one party unfairly benefiting from an unforeseen windfall at the expense of the other in the aftermath of a frustrating event.

16.1 The Development of the Frustration Principle

It is important to survey the development of the frustration principle because this will help us to understand why it is needed as well as its legal basis. We will start with the common law's original position before the principle of frustration was recognised.

16.1.1 The Original Approach: 'Absolute Contracts'

The early position on contract performance was very strict. If a party did not perform its obligations, it would be in breach, even where performance was impossible. On that basis, absolute performance was required and so the early approach is described as being based on 'absolute contracts'. It sounds like a harsh rule, but the idea was that if the parties wanted flexibility, it was open to them to add terms to provide it. The case that is always cited for this early approach is *Paradine v Jane* (1646) Aleyn 26 where a landlord sued a tenant for outstanding rent. The tenant argued that the land was occupied by an enemy army (during the English civil war) and, for that reason, he could not access and use the land. This defence was rejected by the court because there was a contractual obligation to pay rent. If the tenant wanted to be excused from the rent in certain circumstances, he should have put a term in the contract allowing for that. Since there was no such term in the contract, the tenant was liable for the outstanding rent.

16.1.2 The Origin and Basis of Frustration

The early position on absolute contracts was challenged successfully in the landmark case of *Taylor v Caldwell* (1863) 3 B & S 826. The contract was for the hire of a music hall and its gardens to allow concerts to take place on four specified nights during the summer. Unfortunately, the hall was destroyed by a fire before the first night. The claimant hirer then brought an action for breach (because the owner of the hall had failed in its obligation to provide the hall for the concerts) to recover £58, which reflected the money spent on printing and advertising in advance of the concert dates. However, Blackburn J rejected the claim on the basis that performance had become impossible, which then released the parties from the contract.

The reasoning of the judgment mainly relied on civil law (Roman law) in which it was implied that a party would be released from an obligation where the subject matter perished through no fault of that party. In addition, some English cases were cited to support the result, in particular English authority on contracts for personal services. In such cases, the death of the service provider appeared to end the contract, and so the executors of the service provider's estate would not be liable for breach in those circumstances. One such case was *Hall v Wright* (1859) E.B. & E. 746 where Crompton J stated:

> Where a contract depends upon personal skill, and the act of God renders it impossible, as, for instance, in the case of a painter employed to paint a picture, who is struck blind, it may be that the performance might be excused.

This comment along with others were then cited by Blackburn J in *Taylor v Caldwell* who then observed:

> It seems in these cases, the only ground on which the parties or their executors can be excused from the consequences of the breach of the contract is that from the nature of the contract there is an implied condition of the continued existence of the contractor, and, perhaps, in the case of the painter of his sight . . .

> The principle seems to us to be that in contracts in which the performance depends on the continued existence of a given person or thing, a condition is implied that the impossibility of performance arising from the perishing of the person or thing shall excuse performance. In none of these cases is the promise in words other than positive, nor is there any express stipulation that the destruction of the person or thing shall excuse the performance; that excuse is implied in law, because from the nature of the contract it is apparent that the parties contracted on the basis of the continued existence.

The case introduced what has become the doctrine of frustration into English law. Blackburn J cited a range of specific examples of when impossibility excuses the parties from performance of the contract and, by identifying a basis for these cases, it was then possible to identify a general doctrine. This doctrine, in his original conception of it, excuses the parties where they are not at fault for the impossibility of performance. But when looking at this case it is important to appreciate that even then 'impossibility' was an ambiguous word, being in part based on how the relevant obligation is interpreted. For example, what if the hall in *Taylor v Caldwell* was not destroyed and instead there was simply a new local rule limiting the capacity of the hall to 20 people? In such a case, the contract would still be performable; it is just that the event would be smaller than what Taylor had expected. Moreover, it could be argued that performance had not become in the *strictest sense* impossible—perhaps the concerts could have gone ahead in the ruin of the hall, or perhaps the hall could have been rebuilt.

The reference to the impossibility being no fault of the parties is also important. If the fire was due to the fault of the owner (Caldwell) then he would have been liable for breach. It means that as a rule, for a contract to be frustrated the event cannot be due to the fault of either party. This, as we shall see, is also a somewhat ambiguous principle and has led to some difficulties in future cases.

The parties in *Taylor v Caldwell* both relied on the existence of the music hall, and that factor represents another rule: there must be frustration of the objectives of *both* parties. Such objectives are those indicated by the contract. In formal terms, the courts say there must be frustration of the 'common adventure' which means it is not enough for the objectives of just one party to have become impossible. For an example, imagine if the contract terms in *Taylor v Caldwell* referred to the use of the land only, but Taylor agreed because he planned to use the land as a venue for a concert. Arguably, the fire would only frustrate Taylor's objectives rather than that of both parties because, in that example, only one of the parties, not both, were not relying on the existence of the music hall. Again, this, as we shall see, has been a further point of difficulty in the development of the law.

➡ CROSS-REFERENCE

For the discussion of implied terms *in fact* see 6.5.4.

A final important point to emphasise about the judgment of Blackburn J was that the principle of frustration was in his view based on the existence of an implied term in fact to the effect that performance of the contract was contingent on the continued existence of the music hall; it was implied that if the hall did not exist (through no fault of either party) the contract would be ended. It follows that where there is no reliance on the existence of something, the contract would be absolute and, of course, if the contract actually makes an obligation absolute, then it will be. While the overall effect of frustration remains, however, we will see that it is no longer based on this reasoning.

Blackburn J did not refer to 'frustration' or describe the contract as 'frustrated'. That label was introduced in later cases by other judges. Also, nothing was really said about the financial consequences of the contract ending. In *Taylor v Caldwell*, the operation of the doctrine meant there was no liability for breach, but nothing was said about what would happen if there was money paid in advance. The financial adjustments to be made were developed later by the courts and then by legislation.

16.1.3 The Legal Basis of Frustration

The rules from *Taylor v Caldwell* have been applied and shaped by later cases which we will address below. However, one significant aspect that has been changed is the basis of frustration. Initially, frustration was a result of an implied term in fact, as we have seen, but this was the subject of debate and criticism because it was so artificial. The problem was that for there to be an implied term in fact, the term must be one that would have been really obvious to the parties when entering the contract. In the frustration context, the term would apply when an obligation became impossible to perform, in which case it would then release the parties by ending the contract. However, such an obligation would not necessarily have been obvious to *both* parties. In many cases, it is not certain what both parties would have agreed if such a term was mentioned to them. In fact, there were cases where the test for implying a term would not have been satisfied yet the contract was still frustrated, and where this was seen as the right outcome. For these reasons, the basis of frustration was changed in the House of Lords case of *Davis v Fareham UDC* [1956] AC 696. It is one of the most important cases on frustration and it is usually cited in judgments of frustration cases. We will address the case in its factual context later because at this stage our focus is on the basis of frustration.

In *Davies v Fareham*, Lord Reid and Lord Radcliffe stated that they considered the implied term basis to be artificial. Lord Reid referred to some cases with frustrated contracts where the result in the cases was sound, but in which to say at the time of contracting that *both* parties would have agreed to the existence of the relevant implied term appeared far-fetched. On one example, Lord Reid observed:

> I cannot think that a reasonable man in the position of the seaman in *Horlock v. Beal* [1916] 1 A.C. 486 would readily have agreed that the wages payable to his wife should stop if his ship was caught in Germany at the outbreak of war, . . .
>
> I may be allowed to note an example of the artificiality of the theory of an implied term given by Lord Sands in *James Scott & Sons Ltd. v. Del Sel* [1922] S.C. 592, 597: "A tiger has escaped from a travelling menagerie. The milkgirl fails to deliver the milk. Possibly the milkman may be exonerated from any breach of contract; but, even so, it would seem hardly reasonable to base that exoneration on the ground that 'tiger days excepted' must be held as if written into the milk contract."
>
> . . .
>
> It appears to me that frustration depends, at least in most cases, not on adding any implied term, but on the true construction of the terms which are in the contract read in light of the nature of the contract and of the relevant surrounding circumstances when the contract was made.

Lord Radcliffe adopted the same approach and stated the principle underlying frustration in the following way:

> . . . [F]rustration occurs whenever the law recognizes that without default of either party a contractual obligation has become incapable of being performed because the circumstances in which performance is called for would render it a thing radically different from that which was undertaken by the contract. *Non haec in foedera veni*. It was not this that I promised to do.

Lord Radcliffe also warned that frustration 'is not to be lightly invoked as the dissolvent of a contract' in order to emphasise that the scope of frustration should be limited.

The statement by Lord Radcliffe is regarded as the test for frustration and represents the 'construction theory' as its basis. The idea is that the contract is to be construed (interpreted) and that exercise in 'construction' will determine what performance was required by the contract. That should then be compared with what performance would be, following the event. The question to ask is whether performance has become 'radically different' from what was agreed. If it is radically different, then performance is not what the parties consented to and the contract is ended by frustration. Essentially the operation of frustration in ending the contract is based on a rule of law rather the parties' intentions, much like the traditional consideration rule. This approach of construction rather than that of an implied term was subsequently approved in a range of cases but, in particular, by Lord Hailsham and Lord Roskill in *National Carriers Ltd v Panalpina (Northern) Ltd* [1981] AC 675 as well as Lord Phillips MR in *Great Peace Shipping Ltd v Tsavliris Salvage (International) Ltd* [2002] EWCA Civ 1407.

→ CROSS-REFERENCE
For the principles of
interpretation see 6.4.

To determine what performance was required, the principles relating to interpretation could be relevant. However, it has been acknowledged that what is now a wider approach should be adopted. In *Edwinton Commercial Corporation v. Tsavliris Russ (Worldwide Salvage and Towage) Ltd*, (*The 'Sea Angel'*), Rix LJ referred to the relevance of:

> ... [T]he parties' knowledge, expectations, assumptions and contemplations, in particular as to risk, as at the time of the contract, at any rate so far as these can be ascribed mutually and objectively ...

These factors can go beyond what is permitted under the principles of interpretation developed more recently, a point that was addressed by Marcus Smith J in *Canary Wharf (BP4) T1 Limited v European Medicines Agency* [2019] EWHC 335 (Ch). After citing the above comment from Rix LJ with approval, he observed that the factors mentioned by Rix LJ could arise out of previous negotiations and expressions of subjective intent, which are considerations outside of the principles of interpretation. For that reason, Marcus Smith J suggested that the construction theory fell short of being an adequate theoretical basis for frustration. Instead, the judge preferred to incorporate the additional factors mentioned by Rix LJ in order to create what he described as the 'radical difference theory' of frustration. This still requires the construction of the contract but with regard to a wider range of factors that are not ordinarily associated with the exercise of construction. Whether this distinction is supported in later cases remains to be seen, but it does appear more accurate following developments in the way contracts are construed.

Of course, what is (or is not) 'radically different' is a question of degree. It does not require literal impossibility or illegality. But it does go far beyond mere increased price or inconvenience, which has also been emphasised repeatedly in the case law, as we shall see. It might be more accurate to say that it requires *performance as it was originally intended* to be impossible, even if strictly speaking the parties can still do something.

The approach adopted in *Davis v Fareham* means that some care is needed when relying on the early cases. The point was made by Lord Roskill in *Pioneer Shipping Ltd v BTP Tioxide Ltd (The Nema)* [1982] AC 724. In that case, Lord Roskill referred to the previous statement by Lord Radcliffe (from *Davies v Fareham*) and then observed:

> It should therefore be unnecessary in future cases, where issues of frustration of contracts arise, to search back among the many earlier decisions in this branch of the law when the doctrine was in its comparative infancy. The question in these cases is not whether one case resembles another, but whether applying Lord Radcliffe's enunciation of the doctrine, the facts of the particular case under consideration do or do not justify the invocation of the doctrine always remembering that the doctrine is not lightly to be invoked to relieve contracting parties of the normal consequences of imprudent commercial bargains.

The comment shows that setting the doctrine of frustration on a different basis does not make the old cases useless. Instead, they must be read in the light of the approach confirmed by Lord Radcliffe in *Davis v Fareham*.

The last part of Lord Roskill's comment is very important. Frustration should not allow parties to escape the 'normal consequences of imprudent *commercial* bargains'. This is based on many previous cases and it is important because it represents a policy factor in the application of frustration.

KEY POINTS

■ Frustration is no longer based on an implied term. Instead, it is based on a rule of law. The question is whether performance is 'radically different' to what was agreed based on a true construction of the contract.

■ Frustration is narrow and exceptional, i.e. it is not to be lightly invoked.

■ Frustration must not be used to allow parties to escape a bad commercial deal. This is an important policy factor.

16.1.4 The Basic Requirements for Frustration

The requirements for frustration have been developed in a number of cases, mainly from the House of Lords. The resulting principles were summarised in *J. Lauritzen AS v Wijsmuller BV (The Super Servant Two)* [1990] 1 Lloyds Rep 1. There, Bingham LJ stated five key propositions about frustration. These were said to be 'established by the highest authority' and 'not open to question' and so they are usually cited by first instances judges dealing with disputes over frustration. It is useful to lead with these propositions before looking at the key cases so we can appreciate the wider context of the cases and the principles being applied. The propositions by Bingham LJ can be summarised in the following way:

1. Frustration was developed to reduce the harsh consequences and injustice of absolute contracts by providing a 'reasonable and fair' solution.

2. Because frustration has the effect of ending the contract and releasing the parties from the obligations, its application should be limited.

3. Frustration operates automatically so it does not rely on the parties' wishes.

4. The frustrating event must be an 'outside event' beyond the control of the parties.

5. The party relying on the frustration must not be at fault for the 'frustrating' event.

We will discuss the bases of these propositions, their scope and examples in more detail as we proceed through the chapter, starting with the grounds for frustration.

16.2 The Grounds for Frustration

We know that frustration requires an unexpected event which makes performance 'radically different' from what was agreed. This means that it can be said that the contract is no longer performable as it was originally intended. In identifying whether there is such a radical difference, the cases have indicated that there are three main grounds for a contract to be frustrated:

- physical impossibility resulting from destruction or unavailability of the subject matter of the contract, encompassing literal destruction, death and illness, failure of a specific source of goods, and so on;

- supervening illegality, i.e. where performance has become illegal after the contract was created;

- frustration of a common purpose, i.e. where the contract was for a purpose which no longer exists.

Generally, cases fall into one of these grounds and we will detail each one in turn, before we address the factors limiting frustration.

16.2.1 Physical Impossibility

Destruction of the subject matter of the contract, death and illness, unavailability and a failure of a source can all make performance of the contract (as originally intended) physically impossible. We will examine the case law on these in turn.

16.2.1.1 Destruction of the Subject Matter of the Contract

Destruction of the thing the contract is about is perhaps the easiest scenario to understand. As with all cases, the contract must be construed so as to identify the *agreed* performance. That performance might rely on the existence of something, and if that thing is destroyed, it is possible for the contract to be frustrated. Of course, the other requirements have to be met too.

The most obvious example of destruction is *Taylor v Caldwell*. The contract assumed the exist-ence of the music hall and its destruction then meant the contract was impossible to perform as originally intended. Since that destruction was through no fault of the parties, the contract was frustrated. This case is also a good illustration of what 'impossibility' really means. On the facts the contract was not just for the music hall, it was for the *use* of the hall *and* the gardens. Since the gardens remained fine and could have been used, it was not absolutely *impossible* for the parties to perform the contract, albeit in a very different way to that intended. They could, for instance, have had the concert in a marquee, or even in the ruined hall. The point is that this would have been radically different from what the parties originally intended—it was not impossible to per-form the contract *per se*, but it was impossible to perform it as it had been envisaged at the time it was made.

This common law ground for frustration has been codified in the Sale of Goods Act 1979, s.7 which applies to the sale of 'specific goods'. Specific goods are defined in s.61 of the Act as goods that are identified and agreed upon at the time of the contract. Under s.7, if such goods perish through no fault of the parties before the risk (i.e. the legal responsibility) passes to the buyer, the contract is frustrated.

The reference to 'specific goods' is important because it is that aspect which makes performance of the contract radically different if the goods no longer exist. Often when we select items in a shop we are buying specific goods. Consider the purchase of footwear that we inspect, try on and then have them taken to the till. We are offering to purchase that particular set of footwear rather than others in stock. Likewise, when we buy on-line, we could select a unique product like a limited-edition product with a special code or one that was owned and signed by a celebrity. In such a transaction, the contract is for specific goods and if those goods are destroyed before delivery or are no longer obtainable for some other reason then, the contract cannot be performed as originally intended. In contrast, con-sider the standard on-line purchase of footwear based on a description, size and image. Any of the corresponding footwear in the warehouse will do to perform the sale. Following the order, the seller might select a particular box containing footwear matching the order which is then destroyed before delivery. Such a contract is still performable as originally intended because the seller can simply select another corresponding item to carry out the contract.

In practice, s. 7 is relied upon by a seller and, when a dispute arises, it is usually about whether the seller was at fault. Alternatively, the dispute would be about whether the legal responsibility for the goods had already passed to the buyer before they perished.

Overall, the basic question is simply whether the contract is still performable as originally intended and has not become 'radically different'.

16.2.1.2 Death and Serious Illness or Incapacity

The death of a party will not necessarily make performance of the contract radically different because it all depends on what the contract required. Contracts involving a personal service can be frustrated following death, illness or incapacity. Typically, we focus on the service provider not being able to perform, but the same rule should also, in principle, apply to the person receiving the service. What matters is the construction of the contract; the question to ask is whether what was agreed can still be performed as intended. Some contracts specify that a particular person will do something using their special skills, for example, a particular chef to cater for a function. On the death of that chef, the chef's estate will not be liable. That was the reasoning drawn from *Taylor v Caldwell*, using *Hall v Wright* as authority. Even a commercial contract might rely on the skill of another person, with examples including the skill relating to expert opinion on a valuation; a design and building skill; or even the ability to negotiate. Ultimately, whether the contract remains performable as intended or not will be dictated by the terms and how they are construed. If a business is to provide a personal service by a particular employee, following their death the contract might remain performable as intended by other employees depending on how the obligation is interpreted. It might be that a reference to a particular employee or individual being the one to perform is worded in such a way that performance under the contract can be by that person only. Their death would then frustrate the contract because obviously performance would then be radically different to what was intended—it would have to be done by another person entirely. Alternatively, the reference to a particular person could simply identify who the business has decided to allocate the work to. As such, the reference to a particular person would be for businesses efficiency and administrative purposes or even to simply enable the customer to know who to expect. In such a case, another person from the business could perform the contract in the same way and so there would be no frustration following the death of the person named.

Incapacity is the term used to cover serious illness, injury or disability and it is clear that such incapacity is capable of resulting in a frustrated contract. A key example is *Condor v Barron Knights Ltd* [1966] 1 WLR 87, which concerned a sixteen-year-old drummer who had a contract to perform with a pop group. The contract required him to perform seven days a week but during a performance he collapsed. He was then admitted to a hospital for a few days and then, on medical advice, was told he would only be able to work for four nights a week. In response, the group ended his contract, and so he claimed damages for breach. It was held that the dismissal of the claimant drummer was not a breach because the contract had been frustrated. Essentially, the contract required the claimant to work seven days a week and, through no fault of the parties, such performance of the contract was no longer possible.

The same approach can apply where the person *receiving* a service is incapacitated where it is clear from the contract that the service is *for* a particular person. In addition, the incapacity must make it impossible for the contract to be performed. *Parker v Arther Murray Inc.* (1973) 295 NE 2d 487 is a useful example and, while it is a US case, there is no reason why it the same approach cannot be adopted in English law. Here, the claimant booked a course of dancing lessons which were paid for in advance. However, during the course he was seriously injured in a car accident after which he was no longer able to dance. He then claimed the return of his advance payment and the defendant refused because the contract said it was 'non-cancellable'. On appeal, the Illinois court construed the contract and held that it had become impossible to perform as intended. It was said that the term preventing cancellation was never intended to override the rules on impossibility.

Ultimately, the question is whether the incapacity means the contract cannot be performed as originally intended, which depends on the construction of the contract. In *Blankley v Central Manchester and Manchester Children's University Hospitals NHS Trust* [2015] EWCA Civ 18, the appellant was the victim of medical negligence resulting in brain damage. To claim compensation, she entered a conditional fee arrangement with a law firm which meant that the fee would be paid out of any damages awarded. However, her condition meant that she temporarily lost her capacity to instruct the firm, which then resulted in the Court of Protection appointing a deputy to act for her (the Court of Protection has powers from the Mental Capacity Act 2005 so that judges can make decisions for those that lack the mental ability to make decisions). The work of the firm continued and they succeeded in obtaining a settlement but then the victim disputed the firm's bill. The core of her argument was that the contract with the firm was frustrated by her incapacity because under the contract she was under an obligation to instruct the law firm. The Court of Appeal found in favour of the firm and rejected the frustration argument because performance had not become *radically different* from what was intended under the contract. The contract was performable on behalf of the defendant victim and, according to Richards LJ, it was a like a company instructing a solicitor. If the board of directors resigns, there is no one to instruct the solicitors until the new board is appointed, but that would not change the nature of the contract so as to frustrate it. Also, the incapacity fluctuated, which meant that any delay caused by it was expected to be temporary. Throughout the judgment, Richards LJ emphasised two well established principles of frustration. First, that frustration must not be lightly invoked, and secondly, frustration must be kept within narrow limits.

?! **THINKING POINTS**

If through no fault of your own you are involved in an accident and can no longer exercise for a year, can you think of any reasons why your one-year gym membership would not be frustrated?

16.2.1.3 Unavailability

A contract could be frustrated if a particular thing required for performance is no longer available. Many cases on unavailability involve a charterparty agreement where the ship is seized or detained by a government during the hire period. This is analogous to 'destruction' because, although the ship still exists, it cannot be obtained to perform the contract. Cases during the two world wars often involved ships that had been requisitioned by the state, effectively placing the ship under its control for a certain period. The same can apply to goods that are requisitioned by a government. Likewise, a contract to provide a service might be frustrated if one of the parties is conscripted and is therefore legally required to join the military. Again, that was done in the UK during the world wars.

Where the unavailability is permanent the matter is relatively straightforward. Temporary unavailability raises much more scope for argument because in those circumstances the subject matter of the contract is unavailable but will become available at some point. In such circumstances, it might be said that the contract is still performable as originally intended. Of course, this depends on the facts surrounding the unavailability and the meaning of the obligations agreed. For example, frustration might be more obvious where the contract says performance must be at a particular time. The unavailability would then clearly make those terms impossible to perform. The case of *Gamerco SA v ICM/Fair Warning (Agency) Ltd* [1995] WLR 1226 provides a useful illustration.

The contract in *Gamerco* was between a music promotor and the company representing the legendary 80's rock band, Guns & Roses. The claimant promotor agreed to arrange a concert at a particular stadium in Spain. However, five days before the concert was due to take place the stadium was declared unsafe by the local public authority and so the stadium permit was withdrawn, essentially making it unavailable. The promotor claimed the return of their advance payment on the ground that the contract was frustrated. In response, the band's agent argued that the promotor was liable for breach in failing to arrange the concert at the stadium. The High Court held that the promotor was not in breach and, instead, the contract was frustrated. Through no fault of the parties, the contract could not be performed as intended due to the unavailability of the stadium at that particular date. It might be that the stadium would have been available in the future for the concert after having been made safe and being once again licensed for performances, but by then it would have been too late and the tour would have moved on.

When there is no essential start date, it becomes more difficult to identify unavailability. Without an essential start date, the parties might actually expect the contract to start without delay. However, what really matters is what the contract requires rather than what is in the minds of the parties. If there is no strict start date, the contract might still indicate that is must start quickly—for example, it might say that 'time is of the essence'. If so, the delay that could result from the unavailability might be enough to make performance radically different to what was intended.

The key case here is *Jackson v Union Marine Insurance Co Ltd.* (1874) L.R. 10 C.P. 125 which was about a charterparty agreement. Under the terms, the shipowner was required by charterers to 'proceed with all dispatch' from Liverpool to Newport (Wales) to load rails and then sail to San Francisco. On 3rd January 1872, one day out of Liverpool, the ship ran aground. It would not be repaired until August 1872 and so the charterers withdrew from the contract and, on 16th February 1872, they chartered another ship. The issue was whether the charterers were in breach or whether the contract had been frustrated. The majority of the Court of Exchequer Chamber (equivalent to what is now the Court of Appeal) held that the charterparty had been frustrated by the unavailability.

The key reasoning was from Bramwell B. The judgment explained that the intended voyage was no longer possible:

> I understand that the jury have found that the voyage the parties contemplated had become impossible; that a voyage undertaken after the ship was sufficiently repaired would have been a different voyage, not, indeed, different as to the ports of loading and discharge, but different as a different adventure, - a voyage for which at the time of the charter the plaintiff had not in intention engaged the ship, nor the charterers the cargo; a voyage as different as though it had been described as intended to be a spring voyage, while the one after the repair would be an autumn voyage . . .
>
> The question turns on the construction and effect of the charter. By it the vessel is to sail to Newport with all possible dispatch, . . . It is said this constitutes the only agreement as to time, and, provided all possible dispatch is used, it matters not when she arrives at Newport. I am of a different opinion. If this charterparty be read as a charter for a definite voyage or adventure, then it follows that there is necessarily an implied condition that the ship shall arrive at Newport in time for it. Thus, if a ship was chartered to go from Newport to St. Michael's in terms in time for the fruit season, and take coals out and bring fruit home, it would follow, . . . that, if she did not get to Newport in time to get to St. Michael's for the fruit season, the charterer would not be bound to load at Newport, though she had used all possible dispatch to get there, . . .
>
> . . . [T]he shipowner undertook to use all possible dispatch to arrive at the port of loading, and also agreed that the ship should arrive there "at such a time that in a commercial sense the commercial speculation entered into by the shipowner and charterers should not be at an end, but in existence." That latter agreement is also a condition precedent. Not arriving at such a time puts an end to the contract; . . .

The agreement did not have a date for the ship to arrive at Newport and it did not state when the voyage had to be completed. On that basis it might seem that a delay, even of seven months, would not result in performance being radically different to what was intended. However, what counts as performance is based on the meaning (i.e. construction) of the contract. The need for 'all possible dispatch' suggested time was important. It followed that an extensive delay would mean that performance would then be radically different.

However, even without the term specifying 'all possible dispatch', it is likely that the decision would have been the same, because the reasoning focussed on the fact that there was a planned voyage, i.e. to load from one place and deliver to another. From that, the parties could not have intended for it to happen at some random point in the future because that would not have made commercial sense. The contract was a 'voyage charterparty' which means the ship was hired to go from a specified place to another, and therefore, there was a reason for such a journey. Without specific dates, it may have been easy to say that the voyage could happen at any time, but does that mean the voyage could commence in ten years? We know that would not make sense because the goods to be loaded would not be waiting indefinitely, nor would any buyer. Market prices would have changed and the intended use of the goods might well have changed. It would be like a pizza being ordered in the evening which can only be delivered the following morning. The point is that, in this case, there was a commercial objective behind the agreement, which implied that the voyage had to take place within an acceptable period. The unavailability of the ship for a few days or even weeks might not have been a problem *per se*, but the potential delay was so long that performance represented a different voyage to what had been intended.

A different issue is raised when there is no specific voyage, as is the case when there is a time charterparty. In such a contract, the ship is not hired to go to a particular place, and instead is hired for a defined period. In these cases, the focus is on how much of the contract period is interrupted by the unavailability. At some point, the unavailability will be so long that it can be said that performance as originally intended is not possible, but this can be difficult in cases when the length of the interruption is not known. In such cases, the courts can only focus on how long they expect the unavailability to last, and a good example is *Tamplin Steamship Co v Anglo-Mexican Petroleum Products Co* [1916] 2 AC 397.

In *Tamplin*, a tanker was chartered from December 1912 for five years but, in February 1915, the UK Government requisitioned the tanker as a wartime measure. At the time of the requisition there was almost three years left on the contract and, at the time of the trial, there were still 19 months to go. The charterers were willing to continue the contract by paying the hire charges (known as 'agreed freight') but the shipowners claimed the contract had been frustrated. Such a consequence would have meant that the shipowners were entitled to government compensation since the requisitioned tanker would not be available for hire. The House of Lords by a majority of 3-2 held that the contract was not frustrated. Two of the Lords felt that the event was covered by a clause in the contract. Lord Loreburn who delivered the majority judgment felt that the potential delay was not sufficiently serious. This was because it was generally assumed that the war would not last much longer.

?!   THINKING POINTS

Consider the actions of the shipowners. Did they act reasonably or in good faith by claiming the contract was frustrated in order to claim the government compensation? Could it be said that the majority did not want to allow the shipowners to benefit from economic opportunism?

Unavailability during a war was also the issue in the later case of *Morgan v Manser* [1948] 1 KB 184. It concerned a comedian (Charlie Chester Manser) who entered a ten-year contract with his manager in 1938. Under this contract, the manager would be paid a commission based on Manser's earnings. In 1940, as a result the Second World War, Manser was conscripted. After the war, Morgan sued Manser because the comedian had taken on engagements without permission. It was held that the contract was frustrated in 1940 and the reasoning was based on the idea that it was likely that Manser would have to remain in the army for quite some time. Of course, by the time of the case, the period of unavailability was known, but it had not been at the time. The court had to cast itself back to the time of the event and then ask if the contract was performable after the conscription, given what was known at that time. It could be said that the court had the benefit of hindsight in the case because it was known how long the comedian's unavailability for the contract actually lasted. However, even if that fact was set aside, it was plainly the case at the time of the event that it was generally expected that the war would last for many years.

KEY POINTS

Impossibility from temporary unavailability of the thing contracted for can only frustrate the contract if the period of unavailability (expected following the event) takes up enough of the remaining contract period.

16.2.1.4 *Failure of a Particular Source or Method*

Some contracts are about something that has to come from a particular place or source. If (through no fault of the parties) such a source is no longer available, the contract might be frustrated. This was the position in *Howell v Coupland* (1876) 1 QBD 258 which concerned a contract for 200 tons of potatoes grown on land owned by the seller. Through no fault of the seller, the crop was destroyed by a disease which meant only 80 tons could be delivered. The buyer then sought damages for breach but the Court of Appeal confirmed that the contract had been frustrated.

The failure of a source can also arise simply from the subject matter not being accessible. Consider a contract for a particular crop of olives from a specified farm in Sicily and then the crop becoming no longer accessible because the land is surrounded by lava from Mount Etna. In such a case, the seller might successfully argue that the contract has been frustrated because the source of the olives was specified in the contract. If no source was specified for the Sicilian olives, the contract would still be performable as intended because they could be sourced from any other farm or supplier. In such a case, the contract cannot be frustrated.

This point is also illustrated by *Blackburn Bobbin Co Ltd v T W Allen & Sons* [1918] 2 KB 467. The case concerned a contract for the sale of Finland silver birch timber. The seller, who was based in Hull, did not stock the wood and would normally get their supply shipped direct from Finland. However, when war broke out, German war ships occupied the sea so that no ships could leave Finland. This made it impossible to source the timber direct from Finland. The question was whether the contract had been frustrated. The Court of Appeal confirmed that the contract had not been frustrated and so the seller was liable for breach. The reasoning was very clear. The seller intended to source the timber direct from Finland but the contract had no such requirement. That meant the Finland silver birch could have been supplied from stock in the UK or elsewhere and so the fact that war prevented the timber coming from Finland did not make the contract impossible to perform as originally intended.

The seller argued that it was implied that the sale would be based on the seller's usual method but this was rejected by Pickford LJ, stating:

> The sellers in this case agreed to deliver the timber free on rail at Hull, and it was no concern of the buyers as to how the sellers intended to get the timber there.

The comment confirmed that no source of the timber was assumed by the contract. Instead, it was just an assumption of one party, the seller. On this Pickford LJ observed:

> To dissolve the contract the matter relied on must be something which both parties had in their minds when they entered into the contract, such for instance as the existence of the music-hall in *Taylor v. Caldwell* . . ., or the continuance of the vessel in readiness to perform the contract, as in *Jackson v. Union Marine Insurance Co* . . .

The point is that frustration is about whether the contract was performable as intended, rather than the objectives held by *one* of the parties. Remember, the contract represents the intentions of *both* parties. If both parties had intended the timber to be shipped direct from Finland, then frustration might have been possible, because in such circumstances, the contract would not have been performable.

The rule applied in *Blackburn Bobbin Co* is often expressed as a requirement for frustration of the 'common adventure', i.e. the objectives that the parties have in common, which therefore represents the contract. The approach adopted in *Blackburn Bobbin Co* was applied more recently in *CTI Group Inc v Transclear SA, The Mary Nour* [2008] EWCA Civ 856 where the claimant buyer contracted for cement to be delivered to Mexico. The defendant seller was unable to deliver due to the seller's supplier being pressured by a Mexican cement cartel to withdraw their supply. The Court of Appeal held that the sales contract was not frustrated, and one of the key reasons was that the contract did not rely on the seller using a particular supplier. On that basis, the seller was liable for breach of contract in failing to supply the cement from somewhere else.

KEY POINTS

A failure of a source of the thing contracted for will only frustrate a contract if, under the contract, both parties were relying on that particular source.

16.3 Illegality

If a contract becomes illegal to perform, then it is capable of being frustrated for the obvious reason that performance will certainly be radically different to what was intended, having become unlawful. As before, the question to ask is whether the contract is performable as intended and that depends on the facts and the construction of the contract. For example, it is possible for performance to be illegal without frustrating the contract, as illustrated by the case of *Cricklewood Property and Investment Trust Ltd v Leighton's Investment Trust, Ltd* [1945] AC 221. The contract was a building lease and, following the outbreak of war, temporary legal restrictions were imposed on building. The House of Lords confirmed that the lease was not frustrated because, however long the restrictions would last, it would have been a fraction of the 99-year lease. On that basis, the contract was deemed to be performable as intended, though performance had to be delayed.

Ordinarily frustration is about preventing unjust enrichment following unexpected events preventing performance. However, with illegality, there is an additional policy factor: ensuring the relevant law is observed. That point was stated by Professor Treitel (in his book 'Frustration and Force Majeure', 2nd ed. (2002) Sweet & Maxwell) which was cited by Beatson J in *Islamic Republic of Iran Shipping Lines v Steamship Mutual Underwriting Association (Bermuda) Ltd* [2010] EWHC 2661 (Comm). It is this policy interest that can prevent the parties relying on a term to exclude frustration (*Ertel Bieber & Co v Rio Tinto Co Ltd* [1918] AC 260).

Major cases relate to war time periods where performance would amount to trading with the enemy. The case often cited for this is *Avery v Bowden* (1856) 6 El. & Bl. 972 which concerned a ship that had to load goods at Odessa, which was part of the Russian Empire. The outbreak of the Crimean war, between Russia and an alliance which included Great Britain, meant that performance was illegal, as it would have been classed as trading with the enemy. On that basis, the contract was frustrated. Likewise, the same approach was adopted in *Fibrosa v Fairbairn Ltd* [1943] AC 32. The contract was for machinery to be built in England and delivered to a port in Poland. As a result of the Second World War, German troops occupied Poland and the country became enemy territory. Consequently, performance of the contract became unlawful and the contract was frustrated.

Illegality does not just come about when trading at a time of war. There are many other situations in which a contract can become illegal to perform. An example would be where one country imposes economic sanctions on another so that it becomes illegal to trade with anyone in that country without government approval. That was the issue in the *Islamic Republic of Iran Shipping Lines* [2010] case. Using the Counter-Terrorism Act 2008, trade restrictions were imposed on Iran, but the disputed insurance contract was not frustrated. Essentially, on the facts, performance of the relevant obligation had not become unlawful.

Beyond hostile relations between nations, performance can still become unlawful. Consider a contract to build on some land in the countryside. Environmental legislation might then be passed protecting the land from being built on. A recent example in this vein, illustrating the strict approach to illegality and frustration generally is *Canary Wharf (BP4) T1 Limited v European Medicines Agency* [2019] EWHC 335 (Ch). It concerned a 25-year lease agreed in 2014 which enabled the defendant EMA to secure premises from the claimant landlord. The EMA had been set up under EU law as the EU agency responsible for approving and supervising medicines in the EU. Under such rules, the EMA had its headquarters in London, and this was in property that the landlord developed to suit the EMA under an earlier agreement to enter a lease. Following the Brexit referendum, the EMA sent a letter to the landlord stating that, if Brexit occurred, they would treat the lease as frustrated because the agency had to be based in an EU Member State. Later, the EU passed legislation in the form of Regulation 2018/1718 which stated that, in 2019, the EMA would relocate to Amsterdam. The landlord disagreed and brought an action to clarify whether Brexit could frustrate the lease.

The EMA's main argument for frustration was based on illegality on the basis that they were legally required to move to Amsterdam and that, under EU rules, the EMA did not have the power or capacity to pay rent in London. In a detailed judgment, Marcus Smith J rejected this argument on the basis that, while the EMA did have to relocate, they did have the power to deal with property based in a non-EU country and the lease even gave the EMA the ability to sub-lease or assign the lease to another party. The judge added that even if the EMA did not have powers under EU law to pay for the rent, it would not frustrate the contract because it would not make performance illegal under English law. This additional observation is relevant to the scope of illegality for frustration and illustrates that contractual performance has to become illegal in the place of performance (in this case England) for frustration to operate. Consequently, while the EMA was under a legal obligation to relocate, that was not enough to make performance illegal for frustration. We will address the remaining aspects of the case under the relevant headings below. The EMA was granted leave for an appeal but withdrew the appeal in July 2019 and instead, sublet the premises in accordance with the terms of the lease.

16.4 Impossibility of a Common (Shared) Purpose

So far, we have addressed physical and legal issues. The third ground for frustration relates to the underlying purpose of the contract. In this context the obligations stated in the contract remain perfectly performable, without any changes at all, but it is just that the whole point of the contract is no longer possible to achieve. Essentially, it is where an event destroys 'some basic though tacit assumption on which the parties have contracted' (Asquith LJ in *Parkinson v Commissioners of Works* [1949] 2 KB 632). The emphasis here should be on the reference to the 'parties'. We are not dealing with the unexpressed assumption or unexpressed purpose of one party. Instead, it is that of *both* parties, so it can be said that it was represented by the contract.

The key case is *Krell v Henry* [1903] 2 KB 740 and its facts provide us with an example. It was one of the many 'coronation cases' resulting from Edward VII being ill on the day of his coronation. The facts of *Krell v Henry* are straightforward. The defendant, Henry, saw an advert in a window of a flat in Pall Mall which was on a planned procession route to celebrate the coronation. The advert indicated that rooms were being let with windows overlooking the procession route for the planned two dates. Henry then arranged by letter to hire the rooms for the two days (daytime only). He enclosed a deposit of £25 with the remaining £50 being due on arrival. However, the entire event was cancelled when Edward VII became ill with appendicitis. As a result, Henry did not pay the remaining £50 and so the owner of the rooms (Krell) sued for the outstanding balance.

The Court of Appeal held that the cancellation of the procession had frustrated the contract. Based on the common law at the time, it meant Henry lost his deposit but did not have to pay the £50. The main significance of the case lies in the basis for frustration. Performance had to be impossible through no fault of the parties and had to result from an unexpected event. Krell argued that the contract had simply been for the hire of rooms and, on that basis, it was still performable. Henry argued that the foundation of the contract had disappeared; it was a contract for a view of the procession and, therefore, it was clearly no longer performable. Vaughan Williams LJ delivered the lead judgment (Romer LJ and Stirling LJ delivered concurring judgments).

GUIDED READING 16.1
Krell v Henry [1903] 2 KB 740

The extract of the lead judgment by Vaughan-Williams LJ forms the basis of frustration of the common purpose. Try to identify:

- how the frustration principle was extended to cover the purpose of the contract;
- why the purpose became the foundation of the contract i.e. why it was a contract for a view of the event.

> . . . I do not think that the principle of the civil law as introduced into the English law is limited to cases in which the event causing the impossibility of performance is the destruction or non-existence of some thing which is the subject-matter of the contract or of some condition or state of things expressly specified as a condition of it. I think that you first have to ascertain,

not necessarily from the terms of the contract, but, if required, from necessary inferences, drawn from surrounding circumstances recognised by both contracting parties, what is the substance of the contract, and then to ask the question whether that substantial contract needs for its foundation the assumption of the existence of a particular state of things. If it does, this will limit the operation of the general words, and in such case, if the contract becomes impossible of performance by reason of the non-existence of the state of things assumed by both contracting parties as the foundation of the contract, there will be no breach of the contract thus limited . . . In my judgment the use of the rooms was let and taken for the purpose of seeing the Royal procession. It was not a demise of the rooms, or even an agreement to let and take the rooms. It is a licence to use rooms for a particular purpose and none other. And in my judgment the taking place of those processions on the days proclaimed along the proclaimed route, which passed 56A, Pall Mall, was regarded by both contracting parties as the foundation of the contract;

and I think that it cannot reasonably be supposed to have been in the contemplation of the contracting parties, when the contract was made, that the coronation would not be held on the proclaimed days, or the processions not take place on those days along the proclaimed route; and I think that the words imposing on the defendant the obligation to accept and pay for the use of the rooms for the named days, although general and unconditional, were not used with reference to the possibility of the particular contingency which afterwards occurred. It was suggested in the course of the argument that if the occurrence, on the proclaimed days, of the coronation and the procession in this case were the foundation of the contract, . . . it would follow that if a cabman was engaged to take some one to Epsom on Derby Day at a suitable enhanced price for such a journey, say 10l., both parties to the contract would be discharged in the contingency of the race at Epsom for some reason becoming impossible; but I do not think this follows, for I do not think that in the cab case the happening of the race would be the foundation of the contract. No doubt the purpose of the engager would be to go to see the Derby, and the price would be proportionately high; but the cab had no special qualifications for the purpose which led to the selection of the cab for this particular occasion. Any other cab would have done as well.

Moreover, I think that, under the cab contract, the hirer, even if the race went off, could have said, 'Drive me to Epsom; I will pay you the agreed sum; you have nothing to do with the purpose for which I hired the cab,' and that if the cabman refused he would have been guilty of a breach of contract, there being nothing to qualify his promise to drive the hirer to Epsom on a particular day. Whereas in the case of the coronation, there is not merely the purpose of the hirer to see the coronation procession, but it is the coronation procession and the relative position of the rooms which is the basis of the contract as much for the lessor as the hirer; and I think that if the King, before the coronation day and after the contract, had died, the hirer could not have insisted on having the rooms on the days named. It could not in the cab case be reasonably said that seeing the Derby race was the foundation of the contract, as it was of the licence in this case. Whereas in the present case, where the rooms were offered and taken, by reason of their peculiar suitability from the position of the rooms for a view of the coronation procession, surely the view of the coronation procession was the foundation of the contract, which is a very different thing from the purpose of the man who engaged the cab—namely, to see the race—being

Here, although Vaughan-Williams LJ still couched things in terms of 'impossibility', we can clearly see a more modern understanding of frustration emerging in which what really matters is not 'destruction' of the subject matter *per se*, but rather the non-existence of a particular 'state of things'. This could be, for instance, a functioning music hall, but it could equally be a law or simply a set of circumstances. That was the case here—the contract was contingent on the procession taking place and would not have come into existence otherwise. (Where Vaughan-Williams LJ uses the term 'the principle of the civil law' here, he is referring to frustration, which was originally a civil law concept, as we have seen.)

The crucial point here was that the contract would not have been created were it not for this procession and the viewing of it. That was its whole 'common' purpose for both parties.

This was different to the example of a taxi driver being hired to take somebody to Epsom on Derby Day and the event being cancelled. In those circumstances the customer would have had the purpose of going to see the Derby, but the taxi driver would simply have been hiring his taxi out as normal. In other words, such a contract would not have a 'common purpose' and the customer would still owe the money for the trip.

What reinforced this was imagining if the situation were to be reversed. If in the taxi driver example the customer had said to the taxi driver that he still wished to go to Epsom despite the Derby not taking place, the taxi driver would hardly be in a position to refuse. The contract would still have had to have been performed. This reinforced the point that the purposes of the two parties in that example would have been different. The opposite was true of Krell and Henry's arrangement. If the shoe was on the other foot and Henry had been insisting to have the hire of the rooms even in the absence of the procession, Krell would not have been obliged to provide them. This is because their purpose in creating the contract was a common one—to lease the rooms, or provide the lease of the rooms, respectively, for the objective of watching the procession.

held to be the foundation of the contract. Each case must be judged by its own circumstances. In each case one must ask oneself, first, what, having regard to all the circumstances, was the foundation of the contract? Secondly, was the performance of the contract prevented? Thirdly, was the event which prevented the performance of the contract of such a character that it cannot reasonably be said to have been in the contemplation of the parties at the date of the contract? If all these questions are answered in the affirmative (as I think they should be in this case), I think both parties are discharged from further performance of the contract.

Vaughan-Williams LJ summarised the position accordingly—the assessment was based on what the foundation of the contract was, whether its performance was prevented, and whether the parties could have predicted it. In other words, frustration is much wider than just cases of 'destruction' of the subject matter or supervening illegality.

The case is significant because it shows that frustration is not limited to the parties' reliance on the existence of something stated in the contract. Instead, the shared (common) purpose can be the essential foundation of the contract and if that purpose disappears or becomes meaningless, as for instance with a cancelled procession, the contract might be frustrated.

The development represented by the case appeared to be achieved without difficulty. It was based on a wide approach to what the parties objectively view as the foundation of the contract. It was well established that frustration could result when the contract actually refers to something, for example, a concert hall, a particular ship for a set voyage or even a person to perform. The Court of Appeal felt that the same should apply when parties rely on the existence of a state of affairs not expressed in the contract. In practice, the difficulty is in finding or identifying the unexpressed foundation of the contract.

The unexpressed foundation of the contract is based on the parties' apparent intentions and so we have to look at what the surrounding facts suggest. In *Krell v Henry*, reference was made to the price, which at the time was a significant amount of money. There was the location of the flat, its view, and the dates of hire, which were the same as the procession. In addition, the hire was for the daytime only, and that was specifically mentioned in the advert. These surrounding circumstances could be used to show what the parties must have intended. According to the Court of Appeal, it meant the parties relied on the procession happening as the basis of the contract. In other words, it was not a contract for the hire of a room but was instead, a contract to view the procession, much like a ticket to see a band perform.

?! THINKING POINTS

Could it be said that the contract in *Krell* was just the hire of the facilities for the *chance* to see the procession?

The obvious problem is the difficulty in defining the limits of the principle arising from the case. Vaughan Williams LJ aimed to do so with the cab to Epsom example. It was clear that if the Derby was cancelled, such a contract would not be frustrated. Travelling to watch the races would not be the foundation of the contract and would be the purpose of the passenger only. It would not be the objective of both parties to make it the foundation of the contract and so, even with an inflated price, it would simply be a contract from one place to another that remains performable, independently of the race.

The difficulty is in the distinction between the cab example and the rooms to watch the procession. It was said that the cab did not have 'special qualifications' unlike the room, and that any cab would have done. The fact that it was Derby day and the price was inflated was not enough, so therefore such facts would not amount to 'special qualifications'. That leads us to wonder what is required for such 'special qualifications'. Remember, we are looking for facts that indicate the foundation of the contract without the contract actually stating it. It seems that the key to this might lie in the fact that, without a view of the procession, there would not have been a market to let the rooms for the daytime. There simply would not have been any parties interested in entering into such a contract. But a market for taxis exists universally, and people take taxis to all manner of places for all manner of reasons, all the time.

KEY POINTS

Frustration of the purpose of the contract is very exceptional and must be based on an assumption that would have been made by *both* parties as to the foundation of the contract.

→ CROSS-REFERENCE

For the facts of *Canary Wharf v European Medicines Agency* [2019] see 16.3.

The cab to Epson example from *Krell v Henry* was discussed by Marcus Smith J in *Canary Wharf v European Medicines Agency* [2019]. He made the obvious point that the inflated price of the cab would be a result of the high demand and limited supply of cabs on that day. The driver would not be concerned with the purpose of the journey, just like the passenger would not be concerned with the identity of the driver, so that any cab would do. Marcus Smith J went further. He expanded the example to one in which a cab is being hired on the same day, and to go to the same location, but for a different purpose, such as to visit a relative living in Epson. The price would remain high because of market forces on that day and, if the race was then cancelled, the market price would fall to the normal rate, but the purpose of the contract would not be undermined. Likewise, if the relative was unavailable but the races went ahead, the passenger would still be held to the contract. In contrast, the contract in *Krell v Henry* was based on the procession taking place, as it was essentially the buying and selling of a room with a view of the procession, not just any room. Marcus Smith J also observed that the case would have been different if the room was a hotel room charging a high price because of the rooms being in high demand due to the coronation; in such circumstances the hotel room would be like the cab.

The judgment in *Krell v Henry* made it clear that each case has to be assessed on its own facts, but the cab example does not help determine when the principle will apply. It only really tells us when it will *not*. This makes the scope and application of the case principle somewhat uncertain. However, that uncertainty is not a pressing issue because the case is viewed as exceptional. The courts have been reluctant to apply it and they have been clear about not wanting to expand it. In fact, Lord Wright warned against doing so in *Maritime National Fish Ltd v Ocean Trawlers Ltd* [1935] AC 524.

Krell v Henry is usually contrasted with another 'coronation case', *Herne Bay Steamboat v Hutton* [1903] 2 KB 683. This case was considered around the same time as *Krell* and the judgment, which featured the same judges, was delivered a few days before *Krell*. The case concerned the hire of a steamship for the coronation dates. The contract referred to two purposes, one was for Hutton to take passengers to watch the new King review the naval fleet at Spithead, off the coast of Kent. The other purpose was to take the passengers on a tour of the fleet for the day. The total cost was £250, which was an inflated price, with £50 to be paid in advance. Hutton paid the £50, but when the King's attendance was cancelled, Hutton refused to pay the balance. The claimant then brought an action for non-payment and the Court of Appeal held that the contract was not frustrated and, therefore, Hutton was in breach for non-payment and was liable in damages.

GUIDED READING 16.2
Herne Bay Steamboat v Hutton [1903] 2 KB 683

The extracts below feature all three judgments. When reading try to:

- identify the different reasoning used by the Lord Justices; and
- how the contract was different to the one in *Krell*.

Vaughan-Williams LJ:

. . . Mr. Hutton, in hiring this vessel, had two objects in view: first, of taking people to see the naval review, and, secondly, of taking them round the fleet. Those, no doubt, were the purposes of Mr. Hutton, but it does not seem to me that because, as it is said, those purposes became impossible, it would be a very legitimate inference that the happening of the naval review was contemplated by both parties as the basis and foundation of this contract, so as to bring the case within the doctrine of *Taylor v. Caldwell* . . . On the contrary, when the contract is properly regarded, I think the purpose of Mr. Hutton, whether of seeing the naval review or of going round the fleet with a party of paying guests, does not lay the foundation of the contract within the authorities.

> We can clearly see here that the reason why the contract was not frustrated in this case was because Herne Bay Steamboats were simply a commercial outfit hiring boats to paying customers and would be doing so whether or not the naval review was taking place.

. . . I will content myself with saying this, that I see nothing that makes this contract differ from a case where, for instance, a person has engaged a brake to take himself and a party to Epsom to see the races there, but for some reason or other, such as the spread of an infectious disease, the races are postponed. In such a case it could not be said that he could be relieved of his bargain. So in the present case it is sufficient to say that the happening of the naval review was not the foundation of the contract.

> In other words, it was a 'taxi to Epsom' sort of scenario, rather than one like the contract in *Krell v Henry*. The naval review taking place was not the foundation of the contract because that was not a purpose the two parties had in common.

Romer LJ:

In my opinion, as my Lord has said, it is a contract for the hiring of a ship by the defendant for a certain voyage, though having, no doubt, a special object, namely, to see the naval review and the fleet; but it appears to me that the object was a matter with which the defendant, as hirer of the ship, was alone concerned, and not the plaintiffs, the owners of the ship.

> Romer LJ made a similar point; the defendant may have wanted to see the naval review but the plaintiff (claimant) was entering into the contract for ordinary commercial purposes.

. . .

In the present case, with regard to the suggestion that there was something in the stipulation that the plaintiffs were to have the right on their part of placing ten persons on board, which would change the nature of the hiring, I need only say that there is nothing in that provision to lead the Court to treat the transaction otherwise than as an ordinary case of hiring a vessel: it does not make it in any sense a joint speculation or anything of that sort. The stipulation that the owners are 'to have the right of ten persons above crew, &c., on board' only amounts to this, that in the eye of the law the defendant as the hirer of the ship licenses the owner to send ten persons on board.

> This was not altered by the fact that the contract stipulated that Hutton could have an extra ten people on board—this was just a stipulation that any passenger might make when hiring a vessel (just like somebody would reserve a certain number of seats at a restaurant for a meal).

The view I have expressed with regard to the general effect of the contract before us is borne out by the following considerations. The ship (as a ship) had nothing particular to do with the review or the fleet except as a convenient carrier of passengers to see it: any other ship suitable for carrying passen-

> He also referred to the taxi example, and spelled it out: here the boat was analogous to the cab taking a person to Epsom. Any other ship would have done, and the ship would have been hired to any other set of passengers who had no intention of watching the naval review. There was no common foundation for both parties.

gers would have done equally as well. Just as in the case of

the hire of a cab or other vehicle, although the object of the hirer might be stated, that statement would not make the object any the less a matter for the hirer alone, and would not directly affect the person who was letting out the vehicle for hire. In the present case I may point out that it cannot be said that by reason of the failure to hold the naval review there was a total failure of consideration. That cannot be so. Nor is there anything like a total destruction of the subject-matter of the contract. It follows that, in my

opinion, so far as the plaintiffs are concerned, the objects of the passengers on this voyage with regard to sight-seeing do not form the subject-matter or essence of this contract. With regard to the one contention of fact on which the defendant relied, namely, that the plaintiffs, the owners of the ship, had on their part put themselves in the position of not having been able to carry out the contract, and so repudiated it, I can only say that the defendant has not proved his case.

Stirling LJ:

It seems to me that the reference in the contract to the naval review is easily explained; it was inserted in order to define more exactly the nature of the voyage, and I am unable to treat it as being such a reference as to constitute the naval review the foundation of the contract so as to entitle either party to the benefit of the doctrine in *Taylor v. Caldwell* . . . I come to this conclusion the more readily because the object of the voyage is not limited to the naval review, but also extends to a cruise round the fleet. The fleet was there, and passengers might have been found willing to go round it. It is true that in the event which happened the object of the voyage became limited, but, in my opinion, that was the risk of the defendant whose venture the taking the passengers was.

> Stirling LJ also added the significant point that, while the object of the voyage had become 'limited' by the cancellation of the naval review, the passenger had another purpose—the tour of the fleet—which could still take place, because the fleet were still there. Put in more modern language, performance of the contract may have been different to what Hutton had intended, but certainly not radically different. Even if the 'common purpose' argument had succeeded, then, the contract would probably still not have been frustrated.

An important issue raised by the case is the distinction between it and *Krell v Henry*. There was, and is, a lot of debate about why the contract was frustrated in *Krell v Henry* but not in *Herne Bay v Hutton*. Even those who agree with the decisions raise serious questions over the reasoning used. Stirling LJ's judgment is the simplest and also the most easy to agree with. He simply identified two purposes for the contract (seeing the naval review take place and taking a tour of the fleet) and concluded that since only one could not take place (the naval review) the contract was still performable as intended for the large part and hence should not be frustrated. The reasoning of the other judges is much more convoluted.

 THINKING POINTS

Based on the reasoning adopted in *Herne Bay v Hutton*, would the contract have been frustrated if the fleet had sailed away?

Professor Brownsword (Brownsword, 'Henry's lost spectacle and Hutton's lost speculation' (1985) 129 SJ 860) put forward a useful distinction to explain the two cases. He boiled the matter down to the basic difference that Hutton's contract was a commercial venture. It was about making a profit from passengers, and he had suffered the commercial disappointment of not being able to make the money he hoped for. In contrast, Henry was a consumer and his only interest was in viewing the procession. More importantly, Krell would have known that anyone hiring the room would be doing so only for that unique event. This distinction is significant in light of the policy statement of Lord Roskill in the *Nema*. Frustration cannot allow a party to escape the 'consequences of an imprudent *commercial* bargain'. Denying frustration of the ship hire is consistent with this policy aim. In contrast, Henry's disappointment was that of a consumer. Recognising frustration in such a contract would not undermine the overall policy. With that suggested distinction in mind, it could be said that the court was less willing to allow the ship hire to be frustrated because it was a commercial contract, whereas in *Krell* the court had no such reluctance because the contract was between private individuals.

In *Canary Wharf v European Medicines Agency*, Marcus Smith J observed that in *Herne Bay v Hutton* and the cab to Epson example, the parties paid more as a result of market forces at the time and that they both reflect instances of making bad bargains. It was said that if the price to be paid was reduced following the cancellation of the event, neither party could complain. However, in *Krell v Henry*, if the price to be paid was significantly reduced, the purpose of the contract would still be compromised by the cancellation.

Frustration of purpose was also argued by the EMA in *Canary Wharf v European Medicines Agency*. On this point the judge observed that while the premises were built to suit the EMA, having a permanent headquarters in London for 25 years was not the *common* purpose of the lease. The parties had different purposes with the EMA wanting bespoke premises, flexibility in the terms and the lowest rent. In contrast, the landlord wanted long-term cash at the highest rate and was willing to develop the property to secure such a contract. Furthermore, the EMA had a detailed right to sublet or assign the lease so that the landlord would be no worse off if the EMA left. The existence of such a contractual right indicated that the risk of leaving had been accepted by the EMA and meant there was no common purpose beyond what was stated in the lease.

Physical destruction / unavailability of the subject matter	Supervening illegality	Frustration of a common purpose
• **Destruction:** *Taylor v Caldwell* (1863)	• *Avery v Bowden* (1856)	• *Krell v Henry* [1903]
• **Death /incapacity:** *Condor v Barron Knights* [1966]	• *Fibrosa v Fairnbairn* [1943]	• *Herne Bay Steamship v Hutton* [1903]
• **Unavailability:** *Jackson v Union Marine Insurance* (1874) *Tamplin v Anglo-Mexican Petrolium* [1916]	• *Canary Wharf v European Medicines Agency* [2019]	• *Canary Wharf v European Medicines Agency* [2019]
• **Failure of a source:** *Blackburn Bobbin Co v TW Allen & Son* [1918]		

Figure 16.1
The grounds for frustration with the corresponding key cases

16.5 Limits to the Application of the Frustration Principle

So far, we have addressed the grounds for frustration. Our next step is to consider the factors that serve to limit the scope for a contract to be frustrated, which we will examine in turn. Our starting point concerns circumstances in which performance becomes more difficult or more expensive than expected.

16.5.1 Greater Expense or Difficulty

It is easy to imagine the main obligation of a contracting party becoming far more difficult or far more expensive that what was expected. In such a case, we would understand why that party might want to get out of the contract. However, it is clear from the case law that even if the difficulty or expense was a result of an unexpected event beyond the control of the parties, this would not be enough to frustrate the contract. Such an approach is consistent with not allowing a party to use frustration to escape a bad bargain, but also with the point that what is required for frustration is for performance to have become radically different to what was intended. Greater expense or difficulty is not 'radical difference'.

The case of *Davis v Fareham UDC* is not just significant for establishing the basis for frustration. It is also the major authority on this type of limitation on the scope of the principle. The facts are useful in illustrating the point.

Davies contracted to build 78 houses for the defendant Council for which Davis would be paid a fixed sum of £92,425. This work was to be completed in eight months, but actually took 22 months. The delay was due to a range of factors outside of the control of the parties, such as a shortage of workers and building materials which had arisen due to the chaotic state of the post-war economy. On completion, Davis was paid the fixed sum due under the contract, but the problem was that the delay had meant that the work cost Davis an additional £17,651. To recover this amount, Davies argued that the events causing the delay had frustrated the contract, and so it should be entitled to be paid for the work done. This *quantum meruit* claim would have then covered the actual full cost of the houses.

The House of Lords rejected the claim on the basis that the contract had not been frustrated. It is useful to look at the reasoning of the judgment of Lord Radcliffe:

> . . . it is not hardship or inconvenience or material loss itself which calls the principle of frustration into play. There must be as well such a change in the significance of the obligation that the thing undertaken would, if performed, be a different thing from that contracted for . . .
>
> . . .
>
> All that anyone, arbitrator or court, can do is to study the contract in the light of the circumstances that prevailed at the time when it was made and, having done so, to relate it to the circumstances that are said to have brought about its frustration. It may be a finding of fact that at the time of making the contract both parties anticipated that adequate supplies of labour and material would be available to enable the contract to be completed in the stipulated time. I doubt whether it is but, even if it is, it is no more than to say that when one party stipulated for completion in eight months, and the other party undertook it, each assumed that what was promised could be satisfactorily performed. That is a statement of the obvious that could be made with regard to most contracts. I think that a good deal more than that is needed to form a "basis" for the principle of frustration.
>
> . . .
>
> Two things seem to me to prevent the application of the principle of frustration to this case. One is that the cause of the delay was not any new state of things which the parties could not reasonably be thought to have foreseen. On the contrary, the possibility of enough labour and materials not being

available was before their eyes and could have been the subject of special contractual stipulation. It was not made so. The other thing is that, though timely completion was no doubt important to both sides, it is not right to treat the possibility of delay as having the same significance for each. The owner draws up his conditions in detail, specifies the time within which he requires completion, protects himself both by a penalty clause for time exceeded and by calling for the deposit of a guarantee bond and offers a certain measure of security to a contractor by his escalator clause with regard to wages and prices. In the light of these conditions the contractor makes his tender, and the tender must necessarily take into account the margin of profit that he hopes to obtain upon his adventure and in that any appropriate allowance for the obvious risks of delay. To my mind, it is useless to pretend that the contractor is not at risk if delay does occur, even serious delay. And I think it a misuse of legal terms to call in frustration to get him out of his unfortunate predicament.

The general approach of Lord Radcliffe was simple. The obligation was to build the houses and that obligation was construed by the court as one that could still be performed. Performance was more expensive, inconvenient and required more work but that was not enough to make performance 'radically different'. On the facts, performance was not made completely different to what was contracted for. The obligation to build houses was still performable; it was just more difficult and more expensive than what Davis had planned. The costs and difficulty of building simply related to the objectives of one party and so the cost and difficulty could not be viewed as the foundation or basis of the contract.

A further point related to the foreseeability of the labour and supply shortages. We will address foresight as a separate limit to frustration below, but at this stage the point is that a foreseeable event is something that the parties can plan for through the terms of the contract itself. They could decide how to spread foreseeable losses and who they should fall on. When a contract does not have terms providing for the risks of a foreseeable event, it suggests the parties intended for the loss to lie where it falls. The risk of delay (from supply problems and resulting increased wage payments) were therefore on Davis, and according to Lord Radcliffe these would have been risks factored into the price offered in the tendering process.

KEY POINTS

A contract will not be frustrated just because performance by one party has become more expensive or difficult.

On a higher level, we can contrast *Davis v Fareham* with the consideration case of *Williams v Roffey* in the context of the renegotiation of contracts. Both cases concern a contractor that had under-priced work to be done and sought to renegotiate. The relevant point (observed by Professor McKendrick in *Force Majeure and Frustration of Contract*, 2nd ed. (1995) LLP) is that in *Davis*, the court did not help the contractor to renegotiate the terms even though the under-pricing resulted from something outside of their control. In contrast, in *Williams* the under-pricing was entirely the fault of the contractor, yet the court developed the law to help the contractor with the consequences of the under-pricing. This can be seen as an inconsistency, but both cases do represent a common theme. The decisions in both cases simply uphold what was agreed. In *Williams*, the parties agreed to change the terms and that version of their bargain was then upheld by the court. In *Davis*, neither party actually agreed to change the terms of the contract and the court upheld what had actually been originally agreed. In other words, in both cases the bargain representing the parties' intentions was upheld.

Davis confirms that extra expense or difficulty is not enough for the doctrine of frustration to operate. The point was relevant to a number of cases following the closure of the Suez Canal in 1956. The Suez Canal runs through Egypt from the Mediterranean Sea (Europe) to the Red Sea (East Africa). It was built so that ships could access a short-cut between Europe and Asia. It is now just over 200m wide and around 120 miles long. Without it, ships travelling to and from Asia would have to go on much longer and more dangerous routes around Africa or up along the Arctic Circle above Russia.

→ CROSS-REFERENCE
For the facts and judgments of *Williams v Roffey* [1990] see 5.9.

The problem was that in 1956, Egypt nationalised the Canal to take control of it and keep the revenue generated. This resulted in military action between Egypt and joint forces from the UK, France and Israel, the UK and France having been the Canal's previous owners. Consequently, the canal was closed and blocked off by sunken ships.

One of the significant frustration cases resulting from the closure was *Tsakiroglou & Co Ltd v Noblee Thorl GmbH* [1962] A.C. 93. The contract was for the purchase and delivery of Sudanese groundnuts. The seller was to have them transported from the Port of Sudan (in East Africa) to Hamburg (Germany) and the terms also stated that the cargo was to arrive in November or December 1956. On 2nd November, the Canal was closed to ships, and so the seller did not ship the goods. When the buyer sued for breach, the seller argued that the closure of the Canal had frustrated the contract. The terms of the contract did not specify that the cargo had to be shipped through the Canal. However, the seller argued there was an assumption between the parties that the Canal would be available because that was how goods were transported to Europe from East Africa (and Asia). The buyer argued that there was no such assumption and that performance was possible by shipping the cargo around the cape of Africa. Such a voyage was around 11,137 miles in contrast to delivery via the Canal which was less than half that distance, at approximately 4,386 miles. It meant going around the cape of Africa was far more impractical and expensive for the seller.

The House of Lords held that the contract was not frustrated because performance was still possible by going around the cape of Africa. It was also acknowledged that the longer voyage would not cause the cargo to perish. The fact that the cost of shipping would have doubled was not even argued because of the decision in *Davis v Fareham*, and the correctness of not relying on the extra cost was emphasised by Lord Reid. Extra cost would not make the contract 'radically different' and so, for frustration, other arguments must be relied upon.

The main argument was the unexpressed assumption of using the Canal. This was rejected by the House of Lords. Use of the Canal was not the basis of the contract and was simply how the seller planned to deliver the goods. According to the judgments, the route was not a concern of the buyer, who had contracted only for the goods and documents to be delivered. Viscount Simonds added that frustration 'must be applied within narrow limits' which echoed the same point made by Lord Radcliffe in *Davis*. There Lord Radcliffe had said that 'Frustration is not to be lightly invoked as the dissolvent of a contract'.

?! **THINKING POINTS**

What if the contract required the groundnuts to be carried via the Suez Canal? What if it was for perishable goods that could never last the journey around the Cape?

16.5.2 Fault and Self-induced Impossibility

From the cases so far, we know that the 'impossibility' must be outside the control of the parties and that this has been a consistent requirement from the very start. As such, there are lots of judicial statements to support it. For example, in *Bank Line, Ltd v Arthur Capel & Co* [1919] AC 435 Lord Sumner observed:

> I think it is now well settled that the principle of frustration of an adventure assumes that the frustration arises without blame or fault on either side. Reliance cannot be placed on a self-induced frustration . . .

Even Lord Blackburn referred to frustration as being a result 'caused by something for which neither party was responsible' (*Dahl v. Nelson, Donkin & Co* (1881) 6 App. Cas. 38). That statement was then cited by Lord Sumner in *Hirji Mulji v. Cheong Yue Steamship Co. Ltd* [1926] AC 497. If the purported 'frustrating' event was attributable to the fault of one party and therefore self-induced, then it will not result in a frustrated contact. On that basis, the term 'self-induced frustration' might seem to be a little misleading, because of course by definition, if an event is self-induced it is not a frustrating one, but that is the term that is sometimes used.

Sometimes, by causing the 'impossibility' of performance (as originally intended) a party will be in breach, but that is not always the case. A party could be at fault for the impossibility, but their conduct might still not be enough for a breach. In such a case, where performance is impossible, if the contract is not frustrated then the obligations must be carried out and the subsequent failure to perform will amount to a breach.

The case of *Maritime National Fish Ltd v Ocean Trawlers Ltd* [1935] AC 524 is a good example of self-induced frustration. It concerned a charterparty agreement for a steam trawler (with trawling equipment) named the St Cuthbert. Both parties knew that a licence was needed for such a ship to be used with trawling equipment. The appellant charterer applied for five licences but only three were granted and so they used the three licences for other ships they actually owned. They then tried to return the St. Cuthbert to the respondent owner.

The appellant charterer argued that without the licence, use of the St Cuthbert would be illegal and, therefore, the contract had been frustrated for illegality. The owner then sued for the outstanding hire charges due under the contract. The Privy Council decided in favour of the respondent owner on the basis that there was no frustration and so the appellant was liable for the payments due under the contract. The judgment was delivered by Lord Wright, who cited previous cases to show that the relevant impossibility must be outside the control of the parties. On the facts, the appellant charterers had three out of five licences and chose not to use one of these for the St. Cuthbert. Such conduct was not a breach but it was the cause of the supervening illegality because they could have applied one of the three licences to the St. Cuthbert.

A more extreme example of this limit to frustration is shown by *Laurizen (J) AS v Wijsmuller BV, The Super Servant Two* [1990]. The contract was for an oil drilling rig to be transported using a ship. It was clear that the defendant had only two ships that could perform this task. One ship was the Super Servant One, the other was the Super Servant Two. Even though only one was needed, the contract referred to both but did not indicate which one would be used. The defendant decided to use the Super Servant Two and so the other ship was used for a contract with another party. Before the rig was transported, the Super Servant Two sank. The claimant then argued that the failure to provide the ship was a breach and, in response, the defendant owner argued that the contract had been frustrated. It had no ships to perform it.

The Court of Appeal held that the contract had not been frustrated because the purported frustration resulted from the defendant's choice to use the Super Servant Two. In selecting that ship, the defendant had not breached the contract, and it could not be proved that the Super Servant Two had sunk due to negligence, for absence of evidence. But the choice made by the defendant nevertheless prevented frustration. The result can be seen as a harsh one because, unlike *Maritime National Fish v Ocean Trawlers*, the defendant did not choose which contract to breach. However, a narrow, strict approach was adopted to the decision to select the ship. According to Bingham LJ in the lead judgment, it was:

> . . . [I]nconsistent with the doctrine of frustration as previously understood on high authority that its application should depend on any decision, however reasonable and commercial, of the party seeking to rely on it.

The contract referred to both ships as possibilities. The problem for the defendant was that it would have made no sense to hold back the other ship just in case it was needed. It was a normal commercial decision to allocate one to this contract and the other to another contract. However, as Bingham LJ observed, such factors make no difference. This strict approach is consistent with the point that frustration must not be 'lightly invoked'. In *Canary Wharf v European Medicines Agency* [2019] the illegality argument was rejected because the EMA did have the power to pay for and manage property

→ CROSS-REFERENCE
For the facts of Canary Wharf v European Medicines Agency see 16.3.

outside the EU, but Marcus Smith J added that if performance had been illegal, the illegality would have been self-induced. This was based on the EU Regulation from 2018 that required the EMA to relocate to Amsterdam. According to the judge, the Regulation could have conferred on to the EMA the power to pay for or manage the property following its relocation. Instead, the EU simply chose to use the regulation to order the EMA to move to Amsterdam. *Maritime National Fish v Ocean Trawlers* as well as the *Super Servant Two* were cited as authority for the *obiter* comment.

KEY POINTS

For frustration the impossibility must not be self-induced. That means the event relied upon must not result from the fault or even a decision of either party.

16.5.3 Foreseeability of the Event

A purported frustrating event might be one that was foreseeable. If it was, then we would expect the parties to cover the risks by including a term specifying whether the contract ends or continues, as well as which party bears the loss. If they do not include such terms, it might then be assumed that they intended for the contract to continue if the foreseeable event takes place, and for any consequent loss to lie where it falls. The reality is a little more detailed. Obvious questions arise about how foreseeable the event has to be and whether it has to be foreseen in the contract.

The cases provide some guidance, and our starting point is *Ocean Tramp Tankers Corporation v V/O Sovfracht, The Eugenia* [1964] 2 QB 226, which was another case from the Suez Canal crisis. It concerned a charterparty agreement to carry cargo from the Black Sea to India. Both parties knew that the Suez Canal might be closed but they were unable to agree terms in the contract to deal with it. They did include a 'war clause' in the contract to prevent the charterers taking the ship into a dangerous zone without the consent of the owners. The ship was taken into the Canal during the hostilities and it was trapped because of the sunken ships blocking the Canal. The Court of Appeal confirmed that the trapping of the ship was self-induced because the charterers had ordered the ship into the canal in breach of the 'war clause' in the contract.

The case was decided on the basis of that breach. However, the Court expressed some *obiter* comments about frustration. Lord Denning MR rejected the argument that frustration might be excluded because the risk was foreseeable, stating:

> It has frequently been said that the doctrine of frustration only applies when the new situation is "unforeseen" or "unexpected" or "uncontemplated", as if that were an essential feature. But it is not so. The only thing that is essential is that the parties should have made no provision for it in their contract. The only relevance of it being "unforeseen" is this: If the parties did not foresee anything of the kind happening, you can readily infer they have made no provision for it: whereas, if they did foresee it, you would expect them to make provision for it. But cases have occurred where the parties have foreseen the danger ahead, and yet made no provision for it in the contract. Such was the case in the Spanish Civil War when a ship was let on charter to the republican government. The purpose was to evacuate refugees. The parties foresaw that she might be seized by the nationalists. But they made no provision for it in their contract. Yet, when she was seized, the contract was frustrated, see *W. J. Tatem Ltd. v. Gamboa* [1939] 1 KB 132. So here the parties foresaw that the canal might become impassable: it was the very thing they feared. But they made no provision for it. So there is room for the doctrine to apply if it be a proper case for it.

According to Lord Denning MR, foresight of the relevant event does not prevent frustration. All that matters is that the event was not foreseen by the terms of the contract. Lord Denning's approach appears quite relaxed in that in limiting the effect of foresight it increases the scope for frustration to apply.

That seems inconsistent with the general approach of keeping the principle confined within narrow limits.

The authority relied upon was the Spanish Civil War case of *Tatem v Gamboa*, but that case might not represent the point Lord Denning used it to support. As Lord Denning indicated, in *Tatem* the ship was chartered to evacuate refugees and was then captured. The parties did not include a provision in the contract about the ship being captured even though the possibility was real. In fact, capture was something that would have been readily foreseen, which is why the hire cost was so high at £250 a day. Such high costs reflected the increased risks of capture or destruction. Goddard J held that the contract was frustrated when the ship was seized, and in the reasoning, it was acknowledged that the possibility of the ship being seized was foreseeable to the parties. However, the period of detainment was not foreseeable and this detainment was for the rest of the contract and then for some time after. The point is that Goddard J was not saying that foresight by the parties is irrelevant. Instead, the judgment was based on the gravity or seriousness of the event not being foreseen, and there is some logic to support this. If the parties cannot foresee the seriousness of the event, then how can we say they accepted the risks?

The point also applies to an event that is foreseen by the contract and the House of Lords case of *The Nema* is a good example. Here the potential delay caused by a strike frustrated a charterparty agreement, yet strikes were addressed in the contract terms. The relevant term indicated that no payments would be due during the strike periods; however, it seems that the term did not relate to strikes with a real potential to be lengthy.

This all suggests that as a starting point, a contract will not be frustrated by an event where the event itself was foreseeable, as well as its extent or scale. Some further guidance on this point was provided by Rix LJ in *Edwinton Commercial Corp v Tsavliris Russ (Worldwide Salvage and Towage) Ltd (The 'Sea Angel')*—[2007] EWCA Civ 547. There, reference was made to the views of Professor Treitel from his book, *Frustration and Force Majeure*, and those of the authors of *Chitty on Contract*. Essentially, both of these authorities indicated that frustration should be possible if the event is just objectively foreseeable, but not its extent. They add that if the type and seriousness of the event are foreseeable as likely or a serious possibility, then frustration will not be possible.

In the judgment of *The Sea Angel*, Rix LJ went on to provide the following statement on foresight:

> [127] . . . In a sense, most events are to a greater or lesser degree foreseeable. That does not mean that they cannot lead to frustration. Even events which are not merely foreseen but made the subject of express contractual provision may lead to frustration: as occurs when an event such as a strike, . . . lasts for so long as to go beyond the risk assumed under the contract and to render performance radically different from that contracted for. However, as Treitel shows through his analysis of the cases, and as Chitty summarises, the less that an event, in its type and its impact, is foreseeable, the more likely it is to be a factor which, depending on other factors in the case, may lead on to frustration.

The point here is that foresight is not an automatic exclusion of frustration. What matters is the extent to which it was foreseen (or is foreseeable). It needs to be foreseen or be so foreseeable that it can be said that the parties accepted the risks that could result.

If the contract has terms managing other risks, it might well have an influence on the significance of foresight. An example is *Blankley v Central Manchester and Manchester Children's University Hospitals NHS Trust* [2015] EWCA Civ 18 Following Phillips J at first instance, Richards LJ addressed foresight in his reasoning. The appellant's condition meant that incapacity was likely at some point, but no reference to it was made in the contract. However, the terms did refer to the contract ending following the death of the victim. On that basis, Phillips J inferred that the parties did not intend to end the contract on incapacity. After all, it should have been foreseen as likely, and yet it was not included alongside the term on death; it could therefore be said that if the contract was to end on incapacity, it would have said so.

➜ CROSS-REFERENCE
For the facts of *Blankley v Central Manchester and Manchester Children's University Hospitals NHS Trust* [2015] see 16.2.1.2.

16.6 Force Majeure Clauses

A further limit to frustration is based on the terms used. We know that the parties can decide what should happen following certain foreseeable events. They can add terms that either end the contract or require it to continue if such an event takes place. Essentially, such terms are allocating the risks, but the ability to do so does not mean that the parties' intentions defeat frustration. After all, frustration is an automatic principle that applies irrespective of the parties' wishes (*Hirji Mulji v Cheong Yue Steamship Co Ltd* [1926] AC 497). Instead, the use of such terms can mean that the conditions for frustration are not met. Consider a term stating that the contract continues even if the venue hired for an event has been destroyed. That term then indicates that the parties intended for an alternative venue to be provided following such destruction. In such a case, the destruction would not destroy the basis of the contract because it would remain performable under its own terms.

→ CROSS-REFERENCE

For the regulation of fairness in consumer contracts see 7.7.

Terms managing the risks of impossibility or the effects of events beyond the control of the parties are known as 'force majeure' clauses. In practice, they have become essential terms of pre-drafted standard contracts. In commercial contracts, the basic templates used for drafting often have very long and detailed force majeure clauses. The idea is to cover as much as possible and in doing so, to manage all potential risks. We can often see such clauses in our written consumer contracts.

The widespread use of force majeure clauses is one of the main reasons why the application of frustration is so limited in practice. That being said, the effectiveness of such clauses depends on their scope. Cases often feature contracts with such clauses and the dispute will often hinge on whether the clauses cover the event. If they do not, then frustration becomes a possibility. It can be expected, for example, that force majeure clauses in most commercial contracts will cover the effects of disease or pandemics, but whether any given clause covers the specific consequences of the COVID-19 pandemic remains to be seen.

These clauses therefore need to be drafted well but the problem is that parties do not know the true extent of any foreseeable event until it happens. When an event does happen, it is often argued by one party that the clause was too narrow to cover the event. The use of wide wording might seem like a good idea but the courts have shown that the clauses have to show a clear intention for the particular type of event to be covered.

A useful example for the point is *Metropolitan Water Board v Dick, Kerr & Co Ltd* [1918] AC 119. The respondent agreed to construct a reservoir in six years. A very detailed clause in the contract gave the contractors an extension of time for delays 'howsoever occasioned'. As a result of the war, the Government ordered all construction projects to stop. The House of Lords held that the contract was frustrated because the clause was interpreted to cover temporary difficulties only. According to Lord Finlay LC, the clause did not:

> . . . [C]over the case where the interruption is of such a character and duration that it vitally and fundamentally changes the conditions of the contract and could not possibly have been contemplated of the parties when the contract was made.

This point is consistent with the significance of foresight. The term needs to cover the type and extent of the event in order to show an intention for the contract to continue following the event. This will mean that the parties have allocated the risks between themselves and the contract is performable as they originally intended. If the clause does not cover the event, then the parties have not covered the risks, which then raises the possibility of frustration if the other requirements are satisfied.

KEY POINTS

To be effective, force majeure clauses need to cover the type and extent of the event.

One clear limit on the effectiveness of force majeure clauses is where the performance would amount to trading with the enemy during a war. In *Ertel Bieber and Co v Rio Tinto Co Ltd* [1918] AC 260 the contract was for the supply of cupreous sulphur ore for copper from an English company operating in Spain and a buyer in Germany. The contract had a clause indicating that the obligation to supply would be suspended in the event of strikes or war. However, following the declaration of war between Britain and Germany the House of Lords held that the contract was void on the basis of an established public policy rule against trading with the enemy at a time of war. It is useful to explore the reasons underpinning this policy rule to help determine its scope. Lord Dunedin explained that continued contractual relations between parties in separate belligerent enemy states allows for information to pass which could harm the progress of the war, and also that trading would increase the resources of an enemy, or reduce those of Britain. If the contract term had been allowed to operate it would have suspended the deliveries. That would mean the British seller would hold on to the goods to deliver after the war, and so they would not be readily available for the British war effort. Furthermore, the knowledge that the resources would be delivered after the war would mean that the enemy buyer would not feel constrained by the need to reserve its own stock and would have more freedom to use or sell its own resources. Lord Atkinson added that one of the aims of Britain going to war was to harm the commercial activity of the enemy so as to force them to come to peace. Even if allowing trade to continue would have benefited Britain, that would be for the State to decide rather than an individual. The case shows that as a matter of policy, force majeure clauses cannot keep a contract valid if performance involves trading with an enemy at a time of war. Based on the reasons underpinning the policy, the same restriction should not apply when performance becomes illegal due to other reasons.

Greater expense of difficulty	Self-induced frustration	Foreseeability	Force Majeure clauses
• *Davies v Fareham UDC* [1956] • *Tsakiroglou v Noblee Thorl* [1962]	• *Maritime National Fish v Ocean Trawlers* [1935] • *Laurizen v Wijsmuller (The Super Servant Two)* [1990]	• *Ocean Tramp Tankers v V/O Sovfracht (The Eugenia)* [1964] • *Edwinton commercial Corporation v Tsavliris (The Sea Angel)* [2007]	• *Metropolitan Water Board v Dick, Keer* [1918]

Figure 16.2
The limits to frustration with the corresponding cases

16.7 The Effects of Frustration—the Resulting Remedy

So far, we have looked at the basis of frustration, its grounds and its limits, and so our next step is to explain its effects. We have already seen that frustration releases the parties from their obligations automatically, so that a party cannot be sued for non-performance. This is because it would not be just to require the parties to perform after an event has resulted in performance becoming radically different to what it had been intended. However, it has also long been the view that in order to achieve a truly fair and just solution, it is important for the law to have some rules on when an advanced payment is made or when the other party incurs expenses under the contract before the frustrating event. This is to prevent one party unjustly benefiting at the other party's expense by sheer luck in the aftermath of a frustrating event.

Consider a contract where one party pays a deposit or even a part payment in advance of performance. Following the frustrating event, the contract is over, and so that raises a question about whether such advanced payment should be retained or returned. If it is not returned, it might well be very unfair to the party that paid if it received nothing in return for the payment. Alternatively, the other party might have incurred expenses before the frustrating event and so it might be unfair to take away the advance payment. As an example, imagine a building contract where some payment in advance is made and the building work commences. Following a frustrating event, like the act of building on the land becoming illegal under new legislation, the builder might have outstanding costs and the other party might have received no benefit in return for its advance payment. Clearly, it might be said that for a fair and just solution there is a need for some financial adjustments to be made. The current position on financial adjustments following frustration is covered by an Act of Parliament. However, before we look at this, it is useful to know the common law position because, in so doing, we will be able to understand and evaluate how the law was improved by the Act. In addition, the Act does not apply to every contract and so there is still scope for the common law rules to apply.

16.7.1 The Traditional Common Law Position

The traditional common law position was a simple one. The frustrating event ended the contract and released the parties from any *further* obligations. However, rights accrued before the event took place continued to be enforceable. For example, consider the hiring of a nightclub for a private party. The club requires a deposit of £1000 paid in advance, which is an obligation under the contract. Following the destruction of the club, the contract is frustrated. The £1000 was due to be paid before the frustrating event and so, under the traditional common law position, if no payment had been made, then the club would be entitled to it. If only part of the payment had been, for instance £250, the club would be entitled to the outstanding £750. If the full deposit had been paid, then the club could retain it all.

The traditional common law position was capable of producing some unfair or inconsistent results. The case commonly used to illustrate this unfairness is *Chandler v Webster* [1904] KB 493, which was another 'coronation case'. The contract was for a room to watch the coronation procession, like in *Krell v Henry*, and, under its terms, the full hire of £141.15s was payable in advance. The claimant paid £100 of this. Following the cancellation of the procession and frustration of the contract, the claimant sued for the return of the £100. The Court of Appeal held that the £100 was not recoverable because it was an obligation to be carried out *before* the date of the frustrating event. Moreover, on that basis, the claimant was in fact also liable for the outstanding balance of £41 15s since the obligation to pay the full amount had fallen due before the frustrating event.

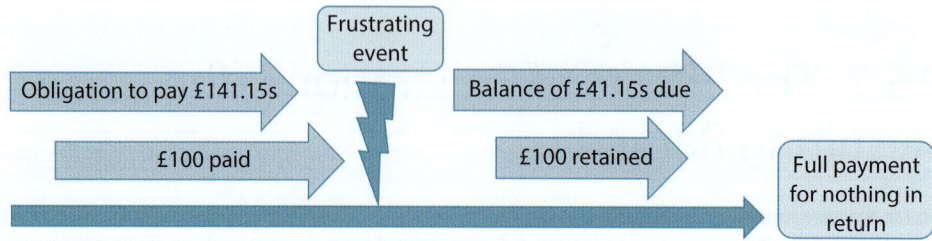

Figure 16.3
The effect of frustration in *Chandler v Webster* [1904]

Essentially, the common law approach meant that Chandler had to pay all the money in return for nothing. The claimant did argue that there had been a total failure of consideration because he received nothing in return for his money. If that had been accepted, it would have been possible to recover the money back as a restitutionary remedy. However, the total failure argument was rejected by the Court because it would mean that the contract was void from the start (void *ab initio*). According to the Court, the contract was a valid one that had become void, whereas a total failure of consideration would have meant that there was never a valid contract in the first place. The result appeared quite harsh toward the claimant and so it attracted criticism.

➜ CROSS-REFERENCE
For the detail on restitution as a remedy see 11.4.

The total failure of consideration point was overruled by the House of Lords in *Fibrosa Spolka Akcyjna v Fairbairn* [1943] AC 32. Fairbairn contracted to build machinery and deliver it to Poland for the buyer, Fibrosa. The price for this was £4800 and one third of the sum (£1600) was payable in advance, but only £1000 was paid. War was then declared before any machinery was delivered and then the port to be used for delivery was occupied by the German army. The agent of Fibrosa then wanted the £1000 back, but Fairbairn refused to pay because of the work it had already done on the machinery. It wanted to keep the £1000 and counter-claimed for the outstanding £600.

Following *Chandler v Webster*, Fairbairn would have been entitled to the full advance payment, meaning it would have kept the £1000 and been awarded the unpaid £600. However, the House of Lords adopted a different approach. It was held that the rule on money due in advance did not apply if the consideration had wholly failed. According to this decision, consideration would wholly fail if the basis for paying no longer existed. Since no machinery had been received, no contractual benefit was gained by the buyer—it had received none of the benefits it was supposed to receive under the contract—and so, following that failure of consideration, the £1000 had to be returned to the buyer, Fibrosa.

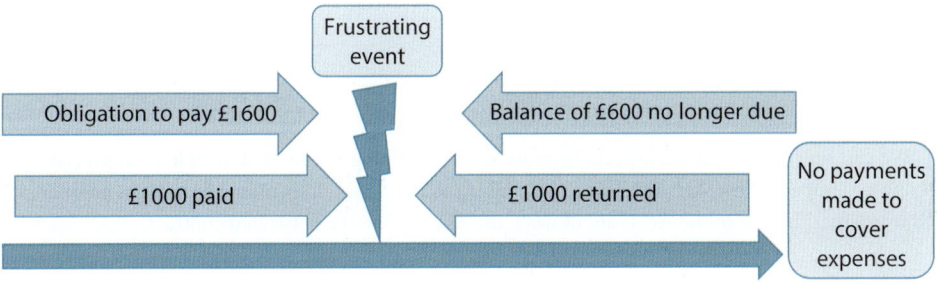

Figure 16.4
The effect of frustration in *Fibrosa v Fairbairn* [1943]

Understandably, the *Fibrosa* case attracted criticism for its unfair result since Fairbairn had worked on producing the machinery and incurred expenses. With that in mind, it is not difficult to see the imbalance. The producer (Fairbairn) was left out of pocket whereas the buyer (Fibrosa) experienced no loss at all. It could be said that *Fibrosa* represents a change, but not an improvement. It simply switched the burden of frustration from one party to the other. In addition, the *Fibrosa* approach to a total failure of consideration is limited, because if the contract was partially performed (like the buyer receiving a small part of the machinery ordered, no matter how inexpensive), then there could be no total failure of consideration.

An early example of another extreme effect of frustration is *Appleby v Myers* (1867) LR 2 CP 651. Here the contract was for the building of machinery on the buyer's property and its subsequent maintenance. Payment was due on completion and, when the machinery was almost complete, the whole property and the machine were destroyed by a fire. The contract was held to have been frustrated and so the claimant sought compensation for the work done before the destruction. The court refused to award any compensation because payment was due at a date after the frustrating event. Since the parties were released from all future obligations, there was no obligation to pay anything. Again, this was a harsh result that imposed all the loss on one party. The position would have been even more unfair if the defendant buyer had somehow benefited from the work done. Then they would have got something for nothing with the seller suffering all of the loss.

16.7.2 The Law Reform (Frustrated Contracts) Act 1943

The Law Reform (Frustrated Contracts) Act 1943 represents the current position and was aimed at providing a fairer outcome following frustration. It is important to emphasise that the aim was not to balance the losses between the parties. Rather, it was to prevent one party gaining benefits at the expense of the other party (in other words, unjust enrichment) through, essentially, fluke. Nor was it a response to the *Fibrosa* case which took place just before the Act came into force. Instead, it was a response to the common law approach as exemplified in *Chandler v Webster*.

The Act is concerned only with the effects of frustration and has no provisions on when a contract is frustrated. It is a very short Act and does not provide a full set of absolute rules. Instead, it gives the courts powers within certain limits to prevent unjust enrichment. The Act is understood more easily by addressing each main provision (sections 1(2) and 1(3)) in turn, along with the corresponding provisions and discussion of the relevant law. To assist further, it is useful to begin with a basic overview of what the Act introduced:

- Money paid in advance is returned, and money payable in advance is no longer payable (s.1(2)).
- However, the court has a discretion to deduct expenses from what was paid or payable (the s.1(2) *proviso*).
- Performance might give a 'valuable benefit' to one party. If it does, the other party could be awarded some payment in return (s.1(3)).

We can now explore these aspects in more detail. In doing so, we will be able to appreciate the scope and impact of the Act. The important part is section 1, which introduced the rules on financial adjustments. The rest of the Act is about *when* the Act applies to a frustrated contract.

16.7.2.1 Money Paid or Payable in Advance

Section 1(2) below contains a rule on money that is paid or payable *before* the frustrating event:

> (2) All sums paid or payable to any party in pursuance of the contract before the time when the parties were so discharged (in this Act referred to as "the time of discharge") shall, in the case of sums so paid, be recoverable from him as money received by him for the use of the party by whom the sums were paid, and, in the case of sums so payable, cease to be so payable:

Section 2(2) goes on to add a *proviso* about expenses incurred by one party that was paid money (or was supposed to have been paid money) before the event.

> Provided that, if the party to whom the sums were so paid or payable incurred expenses before the time of discharge in, or for the purpose of, the performance of the contract, the court may, if it considers it just to do so having regard to all the circumstances of the case, allow him to retain or, as the case may be, recover the whole or any part of the sums so paid or payable, not being an amount in excess of the expenses so incurred.

Section 1(4) provides guidance to a court on what can be classed as 'expenses' for the purposes of s.1(2) (and s.1(3)):

> (4) In estimating, for the purposes of the foregoing provisions of this section, the amount of any expenses incurred by any party to the contract, the court may, without prejudice to the generality of the said provisions, include such sum as appears to be reasonable in respect of overhead expenses and in respect of any work or services performed personally by the said party.

Section 1(5) provides a rule on the significance of insurance when working out if money is to be retained or returned:

> (5) In considering whether any sum ought to be recovered or retained under the foregoing provisions of this section by any party to the contract, the court shall not take into account any sums which have, by reason of the circumstances giving rise to the frustration of the contract, become payable to that party under any contract of insurance unless there was an obligation to insure imposed by an express term of the frustrated contract or by or under any enactment.

Section 1(2) introduces a starting point on money that was paid or payable. If money was paid, then it should be returned. If money was due to be paid, then that obligation ends. This starting point addresses the unfairness resulting from cases like *Chandler v Webster*. If the Act applied to the facts of *Chandler*, the deposit would have been returned and the outstanding amount would not have to have been paid. This prevents one party getting a financial windfall as a result of frustration without doing anything in return.

The s.1(2) *proviso* means that the basic rule in s.1(2) is not absolute, because it is subject to adjustments that a court can make. These adjustments are to reflect the performance expenses incurred by the party that was paid the money (or was meant to have been paid the money). Consider a contract like the one in *Chandler v Webster* but with an extra term requiring the room to be modified for comfortable viewing. That would be an expense for the room owner under the contract. If all of the deposit was then ordered to be returned, the room owner would be out of pocket. Under the *proviso*, the court has the power to allow some of the deposit to be retained in reflection of this. The same applies to money that was not actually paid, but was payable before the event. It is no longer payable but, under the expenses *proviso*, the court could require some payment to cover the expenses of the other party.

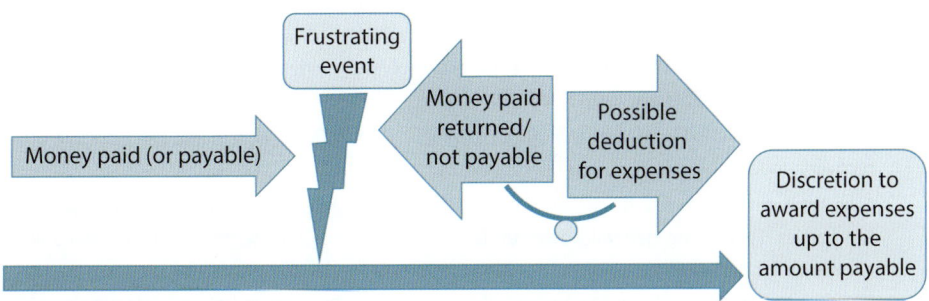

Figure 16.5
The effect of s.1(2) of the Law Reform (Frustrated Contracts) Act 1943

There are two important aspects of the *proviso* on expenses. The first is the clear upper limit or cap on what can be awarded as expenses. The second is that there is no absolute *right* to an expenses payment since the court has a *discretion* to award it. We will explore these aspects in turn.

16.7.2.2 The Limit to the Expenses Award

The amount of any expenses award is limited to the amount paid or payable. Consider *Fibrosa*. £1600 was payable to the seller in advance. If the Act applied, the courts could have allowed the seller to retain money to cover its expenses, but only up to £1600. This limit means that if a party wants any chance of claiming expenses in the event of frustration, it should require a sufficient advance payment. If no money was payable in advance then there is no power for the court to award any amount of money to cover expenses.

16.7.2.3 The Exercise of the Court's Discretion

A party that has incurred expenses in the performance of a contract has no *right* to all or part of the advance payment (or money due in advance) to cover its expenses. Instead, any award of expenses is at the discretion of the court. This is a result of the wording in the *proviso*, which says that the court 'may' award money if 'it considers it just to do so'. It means that where a party does claim for expenses within the limit of what was payable in advance, the court has the power to award all, some or none of the amount claimed. This freedom is based on the circumstances and what the court thinks is fair and reasonable.

There is no presumption on how the courts should exercise their discretion and that was made clear in *Gamerco v ICM* [1995]. While we covered the facts already, we did not address the issues relevant to the Act. The promotor had made an advance payment of $412,000 to the rock band and the band wanted to keep some of that payment to cover their expenses, which were speculated by its agent to have been £50,000. However, based on the circumstances, Garland J allowed for the full advanced payment of $412,000 to be returned to the promoter. This was partly done because the claimant promotor had also lost $450,000 in preparing for the concert, but also because the judge clearly did not think that the £50,000 figure provided by the band's agent was either accurate or justified. That was the result, but the useful part of the judgment concerned the exercise of discretion. The judge considered three ways the discretion could be exercised. These were options presented as theories explored by leading academic commentators who had discussed the Act over the years. Garland J referred to three theories in turn:

> ➡ **CROSS-REFERENCE**
> For the facts of *Gamerco v ICM/Fair Warning (Agency) Ltd* [1995] see 16.3.1.3.

(1) Total retention. This view was advanced by the Law Revision Committee in 1939 (Cmd. 6009) on the questionable ground "that it is reasonable to assume that in stipulating for prepayment the payee intended to protect himself from loss under the contract." As the editor of Chitty on Contracts, 27th ed. (1994)..., (Mr. E. G. McKendrick) comments: "He probably intends to protect himself against the possibility of the other party's insolvency or default in payment." To this, one can add: "and secure his own cash flow."

In *BP Exploration Co. (Libya) Ltd. v Hunt (No. 2)* [1979]... Robert Goff J. considered the principle of recovery under subsections (2) and (3). He said...:

"The Act is not designed to do certain things: (i) It is not designed to apportion the loss between the parties. There is no general power under either section 1(2) or section 1(3) to make any allowance for expenses incurred by the plaintiff (except, under the proviso to section 1(2), to enable him to enforce **pro tanto** payment of a sum payable but unpaid before frustration); and expenses incurred by the defendant are only relevant in so far as they go to reduce the net benefit obtained by him and thereby limit any award to the plaintiff. (ii) It is not concerned to put the parties in the position in which they would have been if the contract had been performed. (iii) It is not concerned to restore the parties to the position they were in before the contract was made.

> **pro tanto**
> is a Latin term meaning 'to that extent'.

A remedy designed to prevent unjust enrichment may not achieve that result; for expenditure may be incurred by either party under the contract which confers no benefit on the other, and in respect of which no remedy is available under the Act."

He then turned to section 1(2) and said:

". . . The allowance for expenses is probably best rationalised as a statutory recognition of the defence of change of position. True, the expenses need not have been incurred by reason of the plaintiff's payments; but they must have been incurred in, or for the purpose of, the performance of the contract under which the plaintiff's payment has been made, and for that reason it is just that they should be brought into account."

I do not derive any specific assistance from the *B.P Exploration Co.* case. There was no question of any change of position as a result of the plaintiffs' advance payment.

(2) Equal division. This was discussed by Professor Treitel in Frustration and Force Majeure, ... There is some attraction in splitting the loss, but what if the losses are very unequal? Professor Treitel considers statutory provisions in Canada and Australia but makes the point that unequal division is unnecessarily rigid and was rejected by the Law Revision Committee in the 1939 report . . . It may well be that one party's expenses are entirely thrown away while the other is left with some realisable or otherwise usable benefit or advantage. Their losses may, as in the present case, be very unequal. Professor Treitel therefore favours the third view.

(3) Broad discretion. It is self-evident that any rigid rule is liable to produce injustice. The words, "if it considers it just to do so having regard to all the circumstances of the case," clearly confer a very broad discretion. Obviously the court must not take into account anything which is not "a circumstance of the case" or fail to take into account anything that is and then exercise its discretion rationally. I see no indication in the Act, the authorities or the relevant literature that the court is obliged to incline towards either total retention or equal division. Its task is to do justice in a situation which the parties had neither contemplated nor provided for, and to mitigate the possible harshness of allowing all loss to lie where it has fallen.

The *proviso* gives a discretion to judges to award expenses with the award being limited to what was payable before the event. However, there was a debate about how this discretion should be exercised. The three main theories were addressed in the judgment: total retention; equal division; and broad discretion. *Gamerco v ICM* was the first case in a higher court on the interpretation of s. 1(2) of the Act, so this was the first opportunity for there to be judicial comment on the point. This might seem strange, given that this was all taking place 50 years after the Act was passed, but this just serves to demonstrate how rarely frustration cases reach the higher courts.

Total retention meant allowing the party who was to be paid in advance to keep it all. The logic here is based on the reason for requiring advance payment. It is usually to cover some sort of costs or reduce the risks in starting performance, and so allowing the full amount to be retained might well reflect the parties' intentions. Equal division might well seem fair. The idea is that by sharing the payment between the parties, they could both bear the loss equally. However, the parties' losses might not be the same. Garland J preferred the third option of a broad discretion to maximise the flexibility to reflect the objectives of the Act.

The reference to the opinion of Goff J in the *BP* case provides some further guidance. It indicates three things that the Act was not intended to do. The Act was not intended to:

■ Spread the losses, because it is the expenses incurred that count, not the loss.

■ Cast the parties to the position they expected to be in following performance.

■ Cast the parties back to the pre-contract position.

It is, as we have already seen, intended to prevent unjust enrichment. The emphasis must therefore be on what the trial judge considers to be just in view of the circumstances and evidence, and this means giving him or her broad discretion.

16.7.2.4 Section 1(3)—Payment for Receiving a 'Valuable Benefit'

Section 1(3) concerns the possibility of a payment being made by a party that has received a 'valuable benefit' from performance of the contract:

> (3) Where any party to the contract has, by reason of anything done by any other party thereto in, or for the purpose of, the performance of the contract, obtained a valuable benefit (other than a payment of money to which the last foregoing subsection applies) before the time of discharge, there shall be recoverable from him by the said other party such sum (if any), not exceeding the value of the said benefit to the party obtaining it, as the court considers just, having regard to all the circumstances of the case and, in particular,—
>
> (a) the amount of any expenses incurred before the time of discharge by the benefited party in, or for the purpose of, the performance of the contract, including any sums paid or payable by him to any other party in pursuance of the contract and retained or recoverable by that party under the last foregoing subsection, and
>
> (b) the effect, in relation to the said benefit, of the circumstances giving rise to the frustration of the contract.

The last subsection of s. 1 is about the valuable benefit under s.1(3). It explains how that could include a benefit to a third party:

> (6) Where any person has assumed obligations under the contract in consideration of the conferring of a benefit by any other party to the contract upon any other person, whether a party to the contract or not, the court may, if in all the circumstances of the case it considers it just to do so, treat for the purposes of subsection (3) of this section any benefit so conferred as a benefit obtained by the person who has assumed the obligations as aforesaid.

According to Goff J in *BP Exploration Co (Libya) v Hunt (No 2)* [1979] 1 WLR 783, the Act's goal of preventing unjust enrichment must also be met in circumstances in which performance by one party gives the other a benefit other than a payment. In the subsequent appeal, the use of the term 'unjust enrichment' was described as unhelpful because it is not actually contained within the Act, but Goff J's approach was nonetheless adopted.

Payment for a valuable benefit is a further consideration beyond the issue of expenses. The point can be illustrated with an example. Consider a builder whose main task under a contract is to build an extension on a restaurant, but who has also agreed to renovate the dining area and kitchen first. Having completed the dining area and kitchen, a change in the law makes building on the land illegal, which then frustrates the contract. The parties would then be released from any further obligations. The builder might have been owed or even paid (under the contract) money *before* the frustrating event. On that basis, the builder will then claim some or all of what was paid or payable to cover expenses from performance like the cost of materials and wages to employees. It is s.1(2) of the Act that will be relied upon to claim for these expenses.

As a separate issue, the restaurant now has a new kitchen and a refurbished dining area. Clearly, the work done is a benefit to the restaurant and it would be unfair for it to keep that benefit and not pay anything for it. The alternative would see it being in effect 'unjustly enriched'. That is where s.1(3) comes in. Section 1(3) refers to circumstances when performance provides a 'valuable benefit' to the other party. When that is the case, the court has the discretion to award a 'just' sum to the party who provided the benefit. This even applies to a valuable benefit given to a third party under the contract (s.1(6)).

The award for giving a valuable benefit is limited to the value of the benefit, which makes sense in the light of the unjust enrichment objectives of the Act. It is important to appreciate that the award for the valuable benefit is discretionary. Judges should consider all the surrounding facts, and two specific factors must be considered. The first is any expense that has been incurred by the party that received the benefit. They might have received something of value and should pay for it, but if they also incurred costs under the contract, those costs should be factored in. The second factor is the effect the frustrating event had on the benefit. It might be that the benefit is of value but no longer of use to the party.

One key issue raised by s.1(3) has been about the meaning of a 'valuable benefit'. Does it apply to something given before the frustrating event that no longer exists afterwards? The Act's focus on unjust enrichment suggests not, but this is by no means straightforward. Consider *Appleby v Myers*. The machinery was destroyed by the event and, on the facts, it was not complete by the time of the event. But if it had been completed and was in use (before payment was due), the buyer would have had the benefit of it up to the point of destruction. Alternatively, it could be said that the valuable benefit should only be one existing after the event. Then there is the type of benefit that s.1(3) refers to. The obvious one is an end product like the new kitchen or refurbished rooms, but could a 'valuable benefit' include something beyond an end product? Taking the facts of *Appleby* again, we know the machinery was destroyed, but if the buyer was to have the same work done again, they will have gained knowledge of the construction process. For example, based on the first (destroyed) attempt, the buyer might be aware of problems to avoid or ways to solve problems encountered. That in turn could mean that the next machine is built a lot faster and therefore at a lower cost and price. Such a financial saving would be beneficial and could even be quantified.

The meaning of a valuable benefit under the Act was explored by Goff J in *BP Exploration Co (Libya) v Hunt (No 2)* [1979] 1 WLR 783. The defendant Mr Hunt owned an 'oil concession' which is the right to search for oil in land, in this case, in Libya. Hunt did not have the resources to search for the oil himself and so he entered into an agreement with the oil company, BP. Under this agreement, Hunt transferred to BP a half share in his oil concession and, in return, BP would make payments in cash and oil as well as cover the costs of searching for the oil (the exploration). Also, if enough oil was discovered, BP would develop the oil field for production and, if oil was being produced, BP would have a greater share of the profits in the early stages. Essentially, the agreement meant that BP took the risk of expenses even if no oil was found. However, if oil was found, then BP would get the bulk of the profit in the early stages. In that sense, it was like a 'no win no fee' arrangement used by personal injury lawyers.

BP's exploration resulted in the discovery of a large quantity of oil. The oil was pumped and sold for four years, when BP's interest in the concession was suddenly nationalised (expropriated) meaning that the government took over BP's share in return for some compensation. Two years later, the same was done with Hunt's share. BP argued that the contract was frustrated and on that basis sought payment for the valuable benefit conferred on Hunt. Goff J determined that the benefit gained by Hunt was worth almost $85m. The claimant BP was then awarded a just sum of $35.5m from Hunt for conferring that benefit on Hunt.

GUIDED READING 16.3
BP Exploration Co (Libya) v Hunt (No 2) [1979] 1 WLR 783

The part of the judgment covering s.1(3) is very long and detailed. Our extract below is selective and refers to the key points only. Remember the context. The defendant has had a benefit so it is the claimant that will claim to be entitled to a 'just sum' in return for that benefit. Typically, such a claim is a result of having incurred costs from performance that led to the benefit.

When reading try to identify:

- any limits to working out the value of the benefit; and
- any limits on how the just sum is worked out.

. . .

(1). *The principle of recovery*

(a) The principle, which is common to both section 1 (2) and (3), and indeed is the fundamental principle underlying the Act itself, is prevention of the unjust enrichment of either party to the contract at the other's expense . . .

Goff J here makes clear that the purpose of the Act is to prevent unjust enrichment, rather than fairly or equally apportioning losses. He also makes clear that the 'valuable benefit' to . . .

[U]nder section 1 (3) the net benefit of the defendant simply provides an upper limit to the award—it does not measure the amount of the award to be made to the plaintiff . . . [T]he net benefit obtained by the defendant from the plaintiff's performance may be more than a just sum payable in respect of such performance, in which event a sum equal to the defendant's net benefit would not be an appropriate sum to award to the plaintiff . . .

. . .

(3) Claims under section 1 (3)

(a) General. . . . In the case of an award under section 1 (3) there are, therefore, two distinct stages—the identification and valuation of the benefit, and the award of the just sum. The amount to be awarded is the just sum, unless the defendant's benefit is less, in which event the award will be limited to the amount of that benefit.

(b) Identification of the defendant's benefit. . . . Now, I am satisfied that it was the intention of the legislature, to be derived from section 1 (3) as a matter of construction, that the benefit should in an appropriate case be identified as the end product of the services. This appears, in my judgment, not only from the fact that section 1 (3) distinguishes between the plaintiff's performance and the defendant's benefit, but also from section 1 (3) (b) which clearly relates to the product of the plaintiff's performance.

Let me take the example of a building contract. Suppose that a contract for work on a building is frustrated by a fire which destroys the building and which, therefore, also destroys a substantial amount of work already done by the plaintiff. . . . [I]n respect of the work he has done, the effect of section 1 (3) (b) will be to reduce the award to nil, because of the effect, in relation to the defendant's benefit, of the circumstances giving rise to the frustration of the contract . . . [T]he subsection therefore contemplates that, in such a case, the benefit is the end product of the plaintiff's services, not the services themselves . . .

(c) Apportioning the benefit. . . . [Where] the defendant has obtained the benefit by reason of work done by both the plaintiff and by himself, the court will have to do its best to apportion that benefit and to decide what proportion is attributable to the work done by the plaintiff. That proportion will then constitute the relevant benefit for the purposes of section 1 (3) of the Act.

(d) Valuing the benefit. . . .

[S]ection 1 (3) (b) makes it plain that the plaintiff is to take the risk of depreciation or destruction by the frustrating event. If the effect of the frustrating event upon the value of the benefit is to be measured, it must surely be measured upon the benefit as at the date of frustration . . .

. . .

Section 1 (3) (*a*) requires the court to have regard to the amount of any expenditure incurred before the time of discharge by the benefited party in, or for the purpose of, the performance of the contract. The question arises—should this matter be taken into account at the stage of valuation of the benefit, or of assessment of the just sum? Take a simple example. Suppose that the defendant's benefit is valued at £150, and that a just sum is assessed at £100, but that there remain to be taken into account defendant's expenses of £75: is the award to be £75 or £25? . . .

[T]he Act as it stands, under section 1 (3) the proper course is to deduct the expenses from the value of the benefit, with the effect that only in so far as they

---

. . . the defendant is not a measurement of the amount to be awarded, but just an upper limit on what the claimant can get.

This means that two calculations need to be made—the valuation of the benefit (so that the judge knows what the upper limit can be) and then the amount to be awarded (which will be capped at that limit).

In calculating the value of the benefit, what mattered in Goff J's view was the 'end product' which the defendant had obtained. This clearly has to be the case if the aim of the Act is to prevent unjust enrichment. Unjust enrichment of the defendant will only be a concern if it is walking away after the frustrating event with something of value at the expense of the other party. In other words, it will only matter where there has been a valuable 'end product' to the defendant.

This did not make apportionment entirely irrelevant, because it might be the case that the benefit was the result of joint work by both parties; this would then necessarily require some attempt to divide the benefit between the parties to figure out the value of the benefit to the defendant, which would then provide the limit on the amount the claimant could recover.

The final main point on the valuation of the benefit is that the assessment has to take place on the basis of the valuation at the time of the frustrating event, because this is how one can establish the effect of the frustrating event.

The next question then, was how to decide on the amount to be awarded—the 'just sum' which the claimant should receive. This had to take into account the expenses of the defendant, but this was not necessarily straightforward, as Goff J's example demonstrates.

reduce the value of the benefit below the amount of the just sum which would otherwise be awarded will they have any practical bearing on the award . . .

(e) Assessment of the just sum. . . . However, under section 1 (3) as it stands, if the defendant's actual benefit is less than the just or reasonable sum which would otherwise be awarded to the plaintiff, the award must be reduced to a sum equal to the amount of the defendant's benefit.

. . .

[T]he defendant will only have been prepared to contract for the goods or services on the basis that he paid no more than the contract consideration, it may be unjust to compel him, by an award under the Act, to pay more than that consideration, or a rateable part of it, in respect of the services or goods he has received . . . [I]t is likely that in most cases this will impose an important limit upon the sum to be awarded—indeed it may well be the most relevant limit to an award under section 1 (3) of the Act.

> The answer to his example, we can take from this, is to deduct the expenses of £75 from the overall value of the benefit of £150, making for an award of £75 to the claimant.

> This will necessarily also mean that if the 'just sum' is more than the defendant's benefit, then it will have to be reduced so as not to exceed the defendant's benefit. This is because it would not be fair to make the defendant pay for more than what was received—again, because this would in effect unjustly enrich the claimant.

The case was the first case to be decided under the Act and remains as the only case to explore s.1(3) in any detail. Goff J's approach to s.1(3) was approved later by the Court of Appeal and House of Lords when the case was appealed, and so even though the appeals took place it is Goff J's first judgment that is always cited. It means that the proper process for a court to adopt is to identify the benefit and its value before working out the just sum to be paid.

The benefit is limited to the end product resulting from the performance and this end product is one that exists after the frustrating event. This means if what is built is destroyed by the frustrating event, there is no end product, even if it was in use before that point. In working out the value of the benefit, it is assessed at the time of the frustrating event rather than before it. If the party with the benefit contributed towards it, then those expenses are deducted from the value. Doing so lowers the upper limit of the potential just sum award.

The sum awarded for giving the benefit is one that is just and reasonable. The cost of the performance will be a relevant factor but the contract price should presumably also be relevant. For example, if the contract price was discounted, then that should be reflected in the just sum. The point here is that if performance was priced at a low level, then the sum should be consistent with that rather than being based on higher market prices.

The requirement of the valuable benefit being an end product has significant consequences. If the benefit does not survive, then there is nothing of value obtained by the defendant and so no award for a just sum can be made. This is because s.1(3) states that the just sum cannot be more than the value of the benefit given. This approach to s.1(3) has been severely criticised because the party claiming the sum might have gone through a lot of expense in performing the contract. To really appreciate this problem, we only have to consider *Appleby v Myers* which would be decided the same way same today under the Act because the machine was destroyed. This argument rests on the assumption that Goff J was incorrect in treating the Act as being based on preventing unjust enrichment rather than the fair apportionment of the loss. If fair apportionment was the basis of the Act, the application of s.1(3) would have been different. It has been said that this unnecessarily limits the options that judges have, but it does have the advantage of providing greater certainty and keeping frustration as very much a last resort. The counter argument is that s1(3) refers to a valuable benefit obtained 'before time of discharge' and that perhaps the Act did therefore intend a wider approach. However, that approach was rejected by Goff J and the judgment was approved in the subsequent appeals.

?! THINKING POINTS

To what extent does the Act fall short of reflecting common law restitution for unjust enrichment?

16.7.2.5 The Remaining Provisions of the Act

Section 2 is about the scope of the Act's application. It refers to its application to contracts frustrated after its commencement date and its application to contracts with the Crown (i.e. the Government) as well as private parties. It is also made clear that the Act applies only where the contract does not provide for its own agreed financial adjustments. Consequently, if the terms refer to what the parties want to happen following frustration, then those intentions are applied rather than the Act. This means the Act is not absolute and does not override the parties' intentions. Of course, it is for the court to construe such terms to determine if they apply to the actual frustrating event. Finally, section 2 specifies some types of contracts that the Act does not apply to. It does not apply to insurance contracts or contracts for the sale of specific goods, where s.7 of the Sale of Goods Act 1979 applies. Also, it does not apply to *voyage* charterparty agreements and other contracts for the carriage of goods by sea.

CHAPTER SUMMARY

- The principle of frustration was developed to address the injustice of the early approach based on absolute contracts.
- Initially, frustration operated on the basis of an implied term but is now based on a wide construction of the contract to determine if performance is radically different to what was intended. The contract is then ended as a rule of law rather than by the parties' intentions.
- Frustration operates automatically irrespective of the parties' intentions and does not operate to allow parties to escape the consequences of a bad bargain.
- Frustration must be the result of an outside event beyond the control of the parties.
- The grounds for frustration represent different circumstances in which performance has become radically different to what was intended:

  - Physical impossibility is a ground for frustration and cases reflect the following categories of such impossibility: destruction of the subject matter of the contract; death or incapacity of a party; unavailability of the subject matter of the contract; and the failure of specific source or method.
  - Supervening illegality can frustrate a contract.
  - Frustration of a common purpose can frustrate a contract. It is even more exceptional as a ground because often the parties have their own different purposes. This ground requires the facts to show a mutual foundation of the contract that is destroyed by the event.

- The application of the frustration principle is limited by a range of factors so that it does not apply in the following circumstances:

  - Where the event simply makes performance more expensive or difficult;
  - Where the event is self-induced by being due to the fault of a party;
  - Where the type of event and its extent was sufficiently foreseeable at the time of entering the contract.
  - Where the consequences of the event are determined by a clause in the contract the risks of the event have been allocated and so the contract cannot be frustrated.

- The common law consequences of frustration could produce unjust results. The parties were released from their future obligations but, initially, their obligations before the event had to be fulfilled. This meant money due before the event was payable.
- Later, if there was a total failure of consideration then there was no obligation to pay any money due before the event. That simply moved the unfairness from one party to the other.

■ The Law Reform (Frustrated Contracts) Act 1943 now applies to determine the consequences of frustration:

■ Money paid (or payable) before the event is returned (or is no longer payable). This is subject to proviso that considers the expenses under the contract of the party paid (or owed advance payment). The court can deduct an amount for such expenses.

■ Where performance results in a 'valuable benefit' to one party, the other party could be awarded some payment in return.

KEY CASES

☐ *BP Exploration Co (Libya) v Hunt (No 2)* **[1979] 1 WLR 783**—the main authority on the application of the 1943 Act and the approach to be adopted when applying s.1(3) on the financial adjustments reflecting a valuable benefit.

☐ *Davis v Fareham UDC* **[1956] AC 696**—one of the most important cases on frustration, always cited by later cases. The judgment of Lord Radcliffe represents the test for frustration as well as the legal basis of the principle. It is also the case to cite for hardship and greater expense being insufficient for frustration.

☐ *Canary Wharf (BP4) T1 Limited v European Medicines Agency* **[2019] EWHC 335 (Ch)**—the latest case on frustration, in which the detailed judgment of Marcus Smith J confirms the current approach to be adopted. It is particularly useful on the grounds of illegality, common purpose and limits such as self-induced frustration.

☐ *Edwinton Commercial Corporation v. Tsavliris Russ (Worldwide Salvage and Towage) Ltd, (The 'Sea Angel')* **[2007] EWCA Civ 547**—the judgment of Rix LJ represents a modern and detailed indication of how to apply the test. It is also a key authority on foresight.

☐ *Gamerco SA v ICM/Fair Warning (Agency) Ltd* **[1995] WLR 1226**—this is the leading authority on the approach to be adopted in relation to the financial adjustments under the s.1(2) of the 1943 Act.

☐ *Herne Bay Steamboat v Hutton* **[1903] 2 KB 683**—As an instance where frustration of purpose was rejected, it appears less important than *Krell v Henry* but the judgment of Vaughan Williams LJ helps to define the limits and application of frustration of the common purpose.

☐ *Krell v Henry* **[1903] 2 KB 740**—this remains the only authority on frustration of a common purpose and so any argument for such frustration will aim to be consistent with the judgment of Vaughan-Williams LJ.

☐ *J. Lauritzen AS v Wijsmuller BV (The Super Servant Two)* **[1990] 1 Lloyds Rep 1**—This is useful for the summary by Bingham LJ of the five key propositions about frustration. It is also a major authority on self-induced frustration.

☐ *Maritime National Fish Ltd v Ocean Trawlers Ltd* **[1935] AC 524**—a major authority on self-induced frustration.

☐ *Pioneer Shipping Ltd v BTP Tioxide Ltd (The Nema)* **[1982] AC 724**—the judgment of Lord Roskill represents authority for the point that frustration must not enable parties to escape bad bargains. It is also a useful authority on the use of *force majeure* clauses.

☐ *Taylor v Caldwell* **(1863) 3 B & S 826**—As the case that established the principle of frustration, the judgment of Blackburn J is usually cited by later cases for consistency. It is also the case for impossibility by destruction of the subject matter.

QUESTIONS

1. Assess the extent to which the application of the principle of frustration is limited and whether these limits are justified.

2. Critically evaluate the extent to which the Law Reform (Frustrated Contracts) Act 1943 provides a satisfactory balance between the parties' interests.

3. RapidBetCasino is an online gambling business. In 2019 they entered into a shirt sponsorship agreement with Nottchester Town Football Club under which RapidBetCasino would pay £3m a year for five years in return for their name to be displayed on the club's football shirts. Recently, following the success of the ban on tobacco advertising, the UK Government has decided to ban all direct and indirect television advertising of gambling businesses. RapidBetCasino now claim that once the legislation is in force, the sponsorship agreement will be frustrated. Advise Nottchester FC.

 For answer guidance to these questions please visit the online resources at www .oup.com/uk/naidoo1e/, where you will also find multiple choice questions to check your understanding of key concepts.

FURTHER READING

Brownsword, 'Henry's lost spectacle and Hutton's lost speculation' (1985) 129 SJ 860.
This is a short, brilliant article exploring the distinction between *Krell v Henry* [1903] and *Herne Bay v Hutton* [1903].

Clark, 'Frustration, restitution and the Law Reform' (Frustrated Contracts) Act 1943 [1996] LMCLQ 170.
A short note on *Gamerco SA v ICM* [1995] which focusses on the financial adjustments following frustration.

Haycroft & Waksman, 'Frustration and restitution' [1984] JBL 207.
This article analyses the application of the Law Reform (Frustrated Contracts) Act 1943 and criticises the approach adopted by Goff J in *BP Exploration v Hunt* [1979] for requiring a valuable benefit in the form of an end product.

Mckendrick, 'Brexit, uncertainty and the doctrine of frustration' JIBLR (2019) 34 (7), 199.
A detailed authoritative case note on *Canary Wharf v European Medicines Agency* [2019].

McKendrick, 'The construction of force majeure clauses and self-induced frustration' [1990] LMCLQ 153.
This is a useful, authoritative short note that provides an assessment of *The Super Servant Two* [1990] and comments on the scope of self-induced frustration.

Mistake

LEARNING OBJECTIVES

By the end of this chapter you should be able to:

- explain and evaluate the development of the law relating to:
  - mistakes preventing the formation of an agreement;
  - agreements resulting from both parties mistakenly relying on the existence of a state of affairs;
- assess and evaluate the tests to be applied;
- apply the rules to a given set of facts;
- understand the related areas of rectification and the defence of *non est factum*

INTRODUCTION

This chapter concerns situations in which one or both parties enter into a contract on the basis of a mistake that is so serious that it negates their consent to a contract; or, it means they did not consent to the agreement in the first place. Following such an 'operative' mistake, the contract will be *void* from the start and therefore treated as though a valid contract *never* existed. This can be contrasted with contracts resulting from duress, undue influence and misrepresentation. Those kinds of pre-contractual wrongdoing result in the contract being voidable (rather than void) because consent appears to have been given, but is compromised because it was not given freely.

We will begin with the general rule, which is based on an objective approach. We then examine the law on mistake as being an exception to that general rule. We start with mistakes that prevent the formation of an agreement. The most significant mistake of this type is known as a 'unilateral mistake', which is where one party appears to have entered the contract on the basis of a mistake. The most extreme example of this is when somebody enters into a contract with somebody who was pretending to be somebody else—that is, a fraudster. Some textbooks cover such formation mistakes in a chapter following agreement. However, since the law of misrepresentation is relevant to mistakes as to identity, it is useful to address such issues of mistake at this later stage, after having had the chance to see how misrepresentation operates.

Our next significant issue is known as 'common mistake', which is where at the time of creating the contract, both parties appear to be making the same mistake about the existence of an essential state of affairs. The principles that apply are linked with frustration and so it is useful for this chapter on mistake to follow the one on the more established doctrine of frustration. We will then address the related remedy of equitable rectification before finally turning to the highly exceptional defence of *non est factum*.

17.1 Introduction to Mistakes Preventing the Formation of an Agreement

The case law has shown that in limited circumstances certain mistakes can prevent the formation of an agreement. In such a case, the absence of an agreement means that there is no valid contract, meaning that what one or both parties thinks is a contract is treated as void from the start. There are some cases that can be categorised as 'mutual mistakes', where the parties are at cross purposes. Essentially each party unknowingly makes a mistake about what the other intends in their offer and acceptance. And there are some cases that can be categorised as 'unilateral mistakes', where one party is making the mistake and the other party either knows or should have known about it. Before examining these two types of mistake, we need to start with the general rule on how the courts determine if an agreement, and therefore a contract, has been formed.

17.2 The 'General Rule'

➜ **CROSS-REFERENCE**
On the objective approach to the parties' intentions see 1.3.

We have seen that when the courts have to decide if an agreement exists, an objective approach is used. This means that the courts are concerned with the parties' *apparent intention* (i.e. what their intention appears to be) rather than their actual intention. This objective approach is the starting point when dealing with mistake, so that, as a general rule, if it looks like the parties made an agreement, then there is one. Ordinarily, the fact that one party actually made a mistake is not enough to deny the existence of an agreement.

The authority for this general approach is the well-known case of *Smith v Hughes* (1871) LR 6 QB 597 which concerned an agreement to sell oats. The seller provided a sample and then the buyer placed an order. When the oats arrived, the buyer refused to accept them because the oats were new and the buyer expected old oats. While the seller never said that the oats would be old, the price was high for new oats, which is why the buyer expected old oats (which were more useful than new ones). The seller then sued for the price and the claim was rejected by the jury at first instance. However, on appeal it was held that the jury was misdirected about the law that applied and so a retrial was ordered. The important points from the appeal came from the statements of the judges about the law that applied. All of the judges found in favour of the seller, and the following part of the judgment by Blackburn J is particularly useful:

> In this case I agree that on the sale of a specific article, unless there be a warranty making it part of the bargain that it possesses some particular quality, the purchaser must take the article he has bought though it does not possess that quality. And I agree that even if the vendor was aware that the purchaser thought that the article possessed that quality, and would not have entered into the contract unless he had so thought, still the purchaser is bound, unless the vendor was guilty of some fraud or deceit upon him and that a mere abstinence from disabusing the purchaser of that impression is not fraud or deceit; for, whatever may be the case in a court of morals, there is no legal obligation on the vendor to inform the purchaser that he is under a mistake, not induced by the act of the vendor. . .
>
> I apprehend that if one of the parties intends to make a contract on one set of terms, and the other intends to make a contract on another set of terms, or, as it is sometimes expressed, if the parties are not *ad idem* there is no contract, unless the circumstances are such as to preclude one of the parties from denying that he has agreed to the terms of the other. The rule of law is that . . . whatever a man's real intention may be, he so conducts himself that a reasonable man would believe that he was assenting to the terms proposed by the other party, and that other party upon that belief enters into the contract with him, the man thus conducting himself would be equally bound as if he had intended to agree to the other party's terms.

ad idem

is short for *'consensus ad idem'*. This is a Latin reference to a 'meeting of the minds' or actually agreeing the same thing.

When one party conducts itself so as suggest it is assenting to a contract, the agreement is valid and binding assuming the other requirements are met. It doesn't matter that the party may be making a mistake about the subject matter of the contract. Even if the other party knows of the mistake there is no obligation to correct it. The only exception is if the mistaken belief was a result of fraud (or some other misrepresentation) but, even then, the contract would only be voidable rather than void, and hence valid until the innocent party rescinds it. That shows how exceptional it is for a contract to be voided following a mistake.

➡ **CROSS-REFERENCE**
For the requirements of rescission and its availability see 13.4–13.5.

In the judgment, Blackburn J recognised that there would be no contract when the parties were at cross-purposes. On that point, reference was made to one party intending to contract on one set of terms and the other on different terms. However, the judgment went on to emphasise that it is the objective assessment that counts. If it *appears* that the parties have made an agreement, then there is one, but if it *appears* they were not in agreement then there is no contract. It does not matter what they were *actually* thinking or intending. Essentially, from an objective perspective the parties in the case had an agreement. The agreement was for oats of any age and that is what the seller supplied. This objective approach promotes commercial certainty so that a party will know if they have a contract by simply relying on what was said and done.

The case of *Smith v Hughes* represents a wide-ranging rule that applies to contract law generally and so it is exceptional for a court to find a contract void for mistake. We can now turn to the relevant exceptions.

KEY POINTS

As a general rule the courts adopt an objective approach to determine what the parties intended, and so it is highly exceptional for a contract to be voided on the basis of a mistake.

17.3 Cross-purposes (Mutual Mistake) Resulting from a Latent Ambiguity

A 'latent' ambiguity is a term that the parties did not know was ambiguous at the start. Such a major term will have different meanings, and so a dispute will arise in which it appears that both parties mistakenly intended to agree to different things. The ambiguity might make it impossible to determine what the parties objectively agreed and so the only option is to say that no contract was formed. The rather vague case of *Raffles v Wichelhaus* (1864) 2 Hurl. & C 906 can be used as an example. It concerned the sale of a cargo of cotton and, under the agreement, the cotton was 'to arrive ex Peerless from Bombay'. In other words, it was to be carried on a ship called the 'Peerless' sailing from Bombay. However, neither party knew that there were two ships named 'Peerless' that sailed from Bombay. One was to sail in October and the other was to sail in December. The claimant seller based the offer on the ship sailing in December. In contrast, the buyer accepted the offer believing the cargo would be on the ship sailing in October. For that reason, the cargo arrived later than when the buyer expected it to, and following their non-payment, the seller claimed the price.

The court found in favour of the buyer but, surprisingly, no reasoning was provided! That has resulted in some uncertainty about the significance of the case. Since the buyer's defence was successful, it appears that the case represents an exception to the general rule. It is often treated as a case about a 'mutual mistake', since both parties were at cross-purposes. Essentially, they intended different things because of the latent ambiguity resulting from two ships having the same name. On that basis, the court's decision could have been based on the fact that it was impossible to objectively identify which ship was intended in the contract. We can contrast the case with *Smith v Hughes* where there was no objective ambiguity and so irrespective of what the parties actually intended, it appeared they entered into a contract for oats of any age.

?!   **THINKING POINTS**

In *Raffles v Wichelhaus*, the seller claimed the price and the buyer defended the action by relying on *its own* mistake resulting from the ambiguity. On that basis, could the case represent a type of unilateral mistake (i.e. a mistake made by one party)?

Raffles is often contrasted with *Scriven Bros v Hindley & Co* [1913] 3 KB 564, where a seller arranged for his bales of hemp and tow to be sold an auction. Both products were used to make fabric, but tow was much cheaper and inferior to hemp. The auction catalogue referred to the bales as two separate lots, which meant each consignment was a separate purchase. However, it did not indicate which one was the tow and which one was the hemp. Also, both lots had the same shipping mark, 'SL'. Before the auction, the buyer inspected the lot containing hemp. He then mistakenly believed both lots were hemp since they had the same shipping mark. During the auction, the buyer made a very high bid for the lot containing tow, believing he was bidding for hemp. When the mistake was discovered, the buyer did not pay and was then sued. It was held that there was no contract because there was no agreement. The reasoning was not entirely clear and has been the subject of interpretation. Under the general rule, there would have been a contract because it appeared that the buyer was buying tow. Since the court found that there was no contract, the case represents an exception. The preferred view is that it is a case of a latent ambiguity, since the content of each lot was ambiguous and could have been hemp or tow. It resulted in the buyer intending to purchase hemp while the auctioneer intended to sell tow. Again, viewed objectively, it could not be said which product the contract related to.

17.4 Unilateral Mistake

A unilateral mistake is where *one* party enters into an agreement on the basis of a serious or funda-mental mistake. Ordinarily, from an objective perspective it would appear that an agreement, and therefore a contract, has been formed. However, if the other party is aware of the mistake (or should have been aware it) then it is possible that no agreement was formed. That would be where it can be said that the mistake had the effect of negating completely the consent of the mistaken party. There are two circumstances where such a unilateral mistake can prevent the formation of an agreement. The first is where one party knows the other has made a mistake about an important term. The second is the major issue of mistake as to identity.

17.4.1 Where One Party Appears to Know the Other Has Made a Mistake about a Term

The position where one party knows that the other has entered the agreement on the basis of a mis-take about an important term was explained in *Shogun Finance v Hudson* [2003] UKHL 62. On that issue Lord Phillips made the following observation:

[123]   . . . If an offeree understands an offer in accordance with its natural meaning and accepts it, the offeror cannot be heard to say that he intended the words of his offer to have a different mean-ing. The contract stands according to the natural meaning of the words used. There is one important exception to this principle. If the offeree knows that the offeror does not intend the terms of the offer to be those that the natural meaning of the words would suggest, he cannot, by purporting to accept the offer, bind the offeror to a contract—*Hartog v Colin and Shields*

[1939] 3 All ER 566; *Smith v Hughes* (1871) LR 6 QB 597. Thus the task of ascertaining whether the parties have reached agreement as to the terms of a contract can involve quite a complex amalgam of the objective and the subjective and involve the application of a principle that bears close comparison with the doctrine of estoppel. Normally, however, the task involves no more than an objective analysis of the words used by the parties. The object of the exercise is to determine what each party intended, or must be deemed to have intended.

This exception to the objective approach makes a great deal of sense. We know the objective approach is there to ensure certainty by enabling parties to know when they have an agreement. However, when a mistake is made about an important term, if the other party knows about the mistake, that other party also knows there was no real agreement. It would be strange if the law allowed that party to enforce the appearance of a contract in such circumstances. Consequently, the other party is not allowed to rely on the appearance of a contract if they knew there was no real agreement.

Since this exception is based on what a party actually knows, it brings in a subjective element which is why it is an exception to the general rule. However, the mistaken party will need to prove that the other party knew of the mistake. To do so, there needs to be evidence and such evidence depends on the facts that exist at the time. That is what Lord Phillips meant by saying that the overall task is no more than an objective analysis. The point is that to prove such subjective knowledge, the courts would need to assess whether the facts *appear* to indicate such knowledge.

KEY POINTS

An exception to the general rule is where one party appears to know the other made a mistake about an important term.

An early indication of the exception can be seen in *Smith v Hughes* itself where Blackburn J indicated that a mistake about a term could mean that the parties did not have an agreement. This was explained in the context of the direction to the jury at the trial stage:

> . . . But I doubt whether the direction would bring to the minds of the jury the distinction between agreeing to take the oats under the belief that they were old, and agreeing to take the oats under the belief that the plaintiff contracted that they were old.
> The difference is the same as that between buying a horse believed to be sound, and buying one believed to be warranted sound; but I doubt if it was made obvious to the jury, and I doubt this the more because I do not see much evidence to justify a finding for the defendant on this latter ground if the word "old" was not used.

The extract of the judgment makes an important distinction based on the intention of the parties in the case. First, the buyer might have *appeared* to simply believe the oats were old and that would not be enough to deny the existence of a contract. Alternatively, the buyer might have believed it was a term of the contract that the oats were old, which would be enough to deny the existence of a contract (if it is proven that the mistaken belief was known by the other party). Of course, the word 'old' was not used by the parties and so it would have been very difficult to prove it was believed to have been a term.

The mistake must be about an important term, so that it can be said that the mistaken party did not really intend to contract on what the terms appeared to indicate. The case often cited for such a unilateral mistake of a term is *Hartog v Colin & Shields* [1939] 3 All ER 566 which was cited by Lord Hobhouse in *Shogun Finance*. The case sets a rule on 'snapping up' an offer where it is obvious the offer contained an error. The case concerned the sale of 30,000 hare skins and the negotiations were in the context of a price per item. However, when the offer to sell was made it was expressed as a price per pound, i.e. by weight, which made the goods considerably cheaper. The buyer then immediately accepted the offer and when the seller refused to deliver, the buyer sued for breach. Singleton J held that there was no contract because the seller had made a mistake and the buyer would have known about it. Of course, an objective approach needs to be taken, but, on the facts, objectively the seller would have appeared to have intended to sell at a price per item since that was the context of the negotiations. The offer of a price based on weight would then *appear* to have been a mistake which the buyer ought to have known about. This meant that objectively the offer did not reflect the apparent intention of the seller.

In a more modern context, *Hartog v Colin & Shields* was applied in *Chwee Kin Keong v Digilandmall. com Pte* [2005] 1 SLR 502. In this case, a laser printer for business use was advertised on the seller's website for $66 when such printers would normally be sold for $3854. This led to almost 800 buyers placing orders for just over 4000 printers, and the website automatically accepted the orders before the seller detected the mistake. When the seller refused to carry out the orders, some of the buyers sued. Following *Hartog v Colin & Shields*, the Singapore Court of Appeal held that the contracts were void for unilateral mistake. Essentially, the mistake was about a term (the price) and, in the circumstances, the buyers would have known that the website pricing was a mistake. They knew the price was too good to be true, but took advantage of it anyway and 'snapped it up' knowing it was a mistake. Of course, if they could not have known of the mistake, there would have been nothing to negate the *appearance* of an intended agreement.

17.4.2 Introduction to Mistake as to the Identity of a Party

➡ CROSS-REFERENCE
For the application of the law on misrepresentation applying to such circumstances see 13.4.2.

We know a mistake about an important term is an exception to the general rule and so it makes sense that the same should apply to a mistake as to *who* the other party really is. The context is important, and should be familiar. It is a scenario in which a fraudster (pretending to be someone else) buys something using a bad cheque or another payment that fails. The fraudster then sells the goods to an innocent party before disappearing with the money. We are left with two innocent parties, the original seller and the innocent buyer, one being entitled to the goods and the other being entitled to claim damages from the fraudster. Of course, the right to claim against such a fraudster is pointless when the fraudster cannot be reached, and so both innocent parties would want the right to the goods.

At the very least, the fraudster would have made a misrepresentation about the payment or their creditworthiness (i.e. their ability to pay). Following such a misrepresentation, a contract still results because the parties intended to make a contract. However, it is a voidable contract and so the innocent seller can rescind it. Until that is done the contract is capable of passing on rights. This means that at any time before rescission, the fraudster can resell and pass on a good title to an innocent buyer. That innocent buyer will then be able to keep the goods. In contrast, if the contract has been rescinded before the resale, the fraudster no longer has title to pass on to an innocent buyer. That is the effect of the *nemo dat rule*. In such circumstances, the original seller is entitled to recover the goods from the innocent buyer.

nemo dat quod non habet

is a Latin term meaning you cannot give what you do not have.

➡ CROSS-REFERENCE
For a diagram of the position when the contract is voidable for misrepresentation see Fig 13.1 in 13.4.2.

Typically, the fraudster acts quickly to resell the goods before disappearing and so it is often too late for the innocent seller to rescind their contract with the fraudster. This is where the law relating to unilateral mistake could be useful for the innocent seller. If the seller's contract with the fraudster is void for mistake, then the timing of the resale is irrelevant. It would mean that the fraudster never had a title to pass on to an innocent buyer. Consequently, the seller would continue to be the owner of the resold goods (as shown in figure 17.1). The key issue is how such a seller can rely on mistake.

Figure 17.1
The basic scenario of goods being sold following a mistake as to identity

17.4.2.1 Case Law Development: Transactions Made Using Written Correspondence

The case law has developed based on a mistake as to the identity of the fraudster where the fraudster has claimed to be someone else. While the seller will argue that they made a mistake as to the identity of the other party, the cases have adopted a very narrow approach. Identity must be a major factor in the transaction, so that it has to be shown that the seller intended *only* to contract with the party that the fraudster pretended to be. This intention needs to appear so strong that it is equivalent to a term. When that is the case, it can be said that there was no agreement and therefore no contract because it will appear that the offer or acceptance was only intended for someone else. When that standard is not met, it is said that the seller simply made a mistake about the fraudster's attributes, in particular the fraudster's creditworthiness. Such a mistake does not prevent a contract because there is still an intention to enter into a contract with the other party. Consequently, the mistake about creditworthiness simply results in a contract being voidable for fraudulent misrepresentation so that it can be rescinded later. But until the contract is rescinded, the fraudulent buyer can pass on a good title to a buyer.

KEY POINTS

- The case law makes a distinction between a mistake as to a party's attributes (when there is just a misrepresentation about the ability to pay) which results in a voidable contract, and when there is a mistake as to identity resulting in a void contract.
- For mistake as to identity, it must appear that the innocent party only intended to contract with the party that the fraudster pretended to be.

The leading case on mistake as to identity is the House of Lords case of *Shogun Finance v Hudson* [2003]. The main significance of that case is that it ruled on the debated points resulting from the earlier cases. To appreciate the judgments in *Shogun Finance*, it is necessary to understand the previous cases, and *Cundy v Lindsay* (1878) 3 App Cas 459 was the leading authority before *Shogan Finance*.

In *Cundy v Lindsay*, Lindsay sold handkerchiefs to a fraudster called Blenkarn. When invoiced, Blenkarn did not pay. He had already sold the goods to various buyers including Cundy who had bought 3000 handkerchiefs. To recover the goods, the seller brought a claim against Cundy under the tort of conversion, arguing that the fraudster never had a title to pass on to the buyer. To support the claim, it was argued that there was no agreement between the seller and the fraudster. It is important to appreciate the facts behind the argument. Blenkarn had sent letters to the seller ordering the goods, which were signed to look like the order was placed by 'Blenkiron & Son'. Also, the letters had a trading address of 37 Wood Street. Blenkiron & Son was a respectable business based at 123 Wood Street. The seller knew of Blenkiron & Son of Wood Street and argued that they had only intended to contract with this Blenkiron & Son. Even the seller's letters and invoices were sent to 'Blenkiron & Son' (albeit at 37 Wood Street). The case reached the House of Lords, where the seller's claim was upheld. That meant the contract with the fraudster was void and, on that basis, the goods could be recovered from the buyer.

Lord Cairns LC explained the result in the following way:

> . . . I ask the question, how is it possible to imagine that in that state of things any contract could have arisen between the Respondents and Blenkarn, the dishonest man? Of him they knew nothing, and of him they never thought. With him they never intended to deal. Their minds never, even for an instant of time rested upon him, and as between him and them there was no consensus of mind which could lead to any agreement or any contract whatever. As between him and them there was merely the one side to a contract, where, in order to produce a contract, two sides would be required.

The same point was explained by Lord Hatherley but with reference to the ownership of the goods:

> The whole case, as represented here is this; from beginning to end the Respondents believed they were dealing with Blenkiron & Co., they made out their invoices to Blenkiron & Co., they supposed they sold to Blenkiron & Co., they never sold in any way to Alfred Blenkarn; and therefore Alfred Blenkarn cannot, by so obtaining the goods, have by possibility made a good title to a purchaser, as against the owners of the goods, who had never in any shape or way parted with the property nor with anything more than the possession of it.

The reasoning was straightforward. There was no contract because it appeared that the seller intended to contract with Blenkiron & Son *only*. The fraudster would have known this since it was the basis of his deception and the address and signature on the fraudster's letter supported this.

The case did not refer to the 'law of mistake' because it predates the recognition of unilateral mistake as a principle. However, the later cases recognise *Cundy* as the basis of the law on unilateral mistake as to identity.

 THINKING POINTS

Would it have made a difference if the fraudster (Blenkarn) had actually paid for the goods?

Later cases served to define the limits of the principle from *Cundy*. We can contrast *Cundy* with the case of *King's Norton Metal Co Ltd v Edridge* (1897) 14 TLR 98. The seller (King's Norton) was a producer of metal products. They received a letter ordering wire from a business called Hallam & Co., and the letter head indicated that Hallam & Co. was a large producer with offices in other countries. The goods were sent to the address on the letter but no payment was made. It then transpired that Hallam & Co did not exist and had been made up by a fraudster called Wallis. Before the fraud was discovered, Wallis sold the goods to Edridge. The seller then sued Edridge for damages under the tort of conversion. In doing so, it was argued that there was no contract between the seller and the fraudster and therefore no title had passed from the seller, due to a mistake as to identity. This argument was based on the seller only intending to contract with Hallam & Co.

The Court of Appeal rejected the seller's claim based on mistake and simply held that the seller's contract was voidable following a fraudulent misrepresentation. Since there was no rescission before the resale to Edridge, the fraudster had passed on a valid title (ownership) to Edridge.

The reasoning was based on the seller's intention. The seller had just intended to contract with whoever wrote the letter. There was no mistake about what party the seller intended to contract with, because Hallam & Co and the fraudster Wallis were the same party. The Court did observe that the case might have been like *Cundy v Lindsay* if Hallam & Co did exist and was separate to the fraudster. It could then be said that the seller had intended to sell to Hallam & Co only, rather than to the fraudster. But on the facts there was no other party, only the author of the letter. For that reason, the court was of the view that the seller had simply made a mistake about the attributes of the fraudster. This meant it was not a mistake about identity; it was simply a mistake concerning the fraudster's ability to pay and his status as representing a large business.

The cases therefore create a distinction between a mistake as to identity and one as to attributes. This is a fine distinction and it is useful to consider it in the context of an example. Imagine a designer with his own line of clothing. He receives a letter ordering a number of formal dresses indicating that payment will to take place after delivery. Most importantly, the letter states that it is from 'Katherine, HRH The Duchess of Cambridge'. Knowing that there is a high demand for everything that the Duchess wears, the designer agrees and sends the dresses along with an invoice addressed to 'Katherine, HRH The Duchess of Cambridge'. Later, it is discovered that the letter was written by a fraudster. If the decision in *Cundy v Lindsay* were to be followed, it would suggest that the designer has entered the contract based on a mistake as to identity because, objectively, it *appears* that he intended to sell the dresses to the Duchess of Cambridge only. This is equivalent to saying that the designer's acceptance was just for the Duchess and not any other potential party, and there would be a sound basis, therefore, to argue that there was never a contract.

In contrast, imagine that the fraudster sends the letter using the name of 'Princess Elsa'. Unaware that there is no such Princess in real life, the designer sends the dresses and the invoice. In this case there has been no mistake as to identity. The Princess does not actually exist, and this means that the designer intended to contract with whoever ordered the dresses. Of course, this was all done on the basis of the buyer being a princess, but that is no different to selling on the basis that a buyer is honest and will pay. The designer is just a victim of a fraudulent misrepresentation by a party that the designer intended to contract with. Essentially, the designer was misled about the buyer's characteristics or attributes. In contrast, if there really was a Princess Elsa (outside of the 'Disney universe'), the position would be different and it could be argued that the designer intended only to contract with that real princess rather than the fraudster.

The distinction made between identity and attributes is not without criticism. It can be a difficult one to make and it could be argued that the scope of mistake should be wider, because a person's name is relevant to their identity. On the other hand, why is a person's identity not an attribute? That would suggest a narrower approach, with all mistaken identity issues being treated as misrepresentations.

17.4.2.2 Case Law Development: Face-to-face Transactions

Cundy v Lindsey and *Kings Norton* did not concern face-to-face transactions. Rather, the parties dealt with each other using letters sent by post. That raises the question as to whether the principle in *Cundy* also applies when the parties agree face to face. For example, a fraudster could enter a shop in order to acquire goods and pay later. Essentially, that would involve convincing the seller to sell the goods on credit. To do so, what if the fraudster pretends to be Prince William? He could be a lookalike, so that he is a convincing imposter. In such a case, the key question would be whether there has been a mistake as to identity. Alternatively, is the contract simply voidable for fraud because the seller was misled about the buyer's attributes?

According to the cases, dealing face to face does make a real difference. There is a presumption that the seller intends to contract with the person in front of them. This is a very strong presumption and applies even when the fraudster pretends to someone else, even if that someone else is well-known.

The series of face-to-face cases starts with *Phillips v Brooks Ltd* [1919] 2 KB 243. The claimant seller had a jewellery shop, and one day a fraudster came in and selected a ring and some pearls to buy. To pay, he wrote a cheque for £3000 and signed it as Sir George Bullough. He said 'You see who I am, I am Sir George Bullough,' and gave an address. The seller then confirmed the address using a directory. The fraudster was allowed to leave with the ring having said he needed it for his wife's birthday, and then pawned the ring for £350. When the seller discovered that the buyer was not Sir George, he sued the pawn broker in conversion for the return of the ring. This was based on the argument that there had been no contract with the fraudster as it arose from a mistake as to his identity. The argument was rejected by the court which held that the contract was not void for mistake and, instead, was voidable for fraud. That meant the fraudster had passed on rights over the ring to the pawn broker. In the judgment, Horridge J, referring to the claimant seller, stated:

> [A]lthough he believed the person to whom he was handing the ring was Sir George Bullough, he in fact contracted to sell and deliver it to the person who came into his shop,

He also referred to the US case of *Edmonds v Merchants' Dispatch Transportation Co* 135 Mass 283, stating:

> The headnote in that case contains two propositions, which I think adequately express my view of the law. They are as follows: "If A., fraudulently assuming the name of a reputable merchant in a certain town, buys, in person, goods of another, the property in the goods passes to A." "If A., representing himself to be a brother of a reputable merchant in a certain town, buying for him, buys, in person, goods of another, the property in the goods does not pass to A."

He then cited Morton CJ from the US case:

> The following expressions used in the judgment of Morton C.J. seem to me to fit the facts in this case: "The minds of the parties met and agreed upon all the terms of the sale, the thing sold, the price and time of payment, the person selling and the person buying. The fact that the seller was induced to sell by fraud of the buyer made the sale voidable, but not void. He could not have supposed that he was selling to any other person; his intention was to sell to the person present, and identified by sight and hearing; it does not defeat the sale because the buyer assumed a false name or practised any other deceit to induce the vendor to sell."

It could be said that the identity of the buyer was important to the seller, because otherwise why did he confirm the address given? However, confirming the address is no different to asking for proof of an ability to pay. According to the judgment, there was an apparent intention to sell to the party physically in the shop and that meant the false name was just a misleading attribute resulting from fraud.

The reasoning appears to narrow the scope of mistake as to identity. The intention is to sell to the party that is standing in front of the seller identified by 'sight and hearing', and so the use of a false name when transacting face to face is just an act of fraud. This appears to make it almost impossible for a contract to be voided for mistake in such circumstances.

 THINKING POINTS

> Should it really matter that a fraudster impersonates someone else in a face-to-face transaction rather than one done over a distance in writing?

Phillips v Brooks draws a line between fraud (i.e. fraudulent misrepresentation) and mistake. We know an act of fraud makes the contract voidable and that was well-established long before any doctrine of mistake was developed. Consider the impact of the court finding a mistake as to identity in *Phillips*. This would have meant no contract was formed, but we would then have to wonder what this would have meant for the scope of fraud. It would have meant there would be one rule applying when a fraudster lies about identity, and another rule when he or she lies about other things. Since both lies are examples of fraud, it would be strange if the outcome was determined by what *type* of lies are being told. On that basis, the finding of fraud and a voidable contract made sense. However, we then arrive at a distinction between contracts made in person (like in *Phillips*) and those made at a distance in writing (like in *Cundy*). Such a distinction is hardly ideal, because it means different rules apply for what is effectively exactly the same fraud (a lie about identity). We will see judicial criticism of the distinction between face-to-face transactions and those using correspondence in writing in the judgments in the *Shogan Finance* case.

Phillips v Brooks is often contrasted with *Ingram v Little* [1961] 1 QB 31, which has similar facts but a different decision. It concerned the sale of a car by three sisters who were approached by a fraudster offering to buy the car using a cheque. The sellers refused, making it clear that the sale was cash only. The fraudster then explained that he was PGM Hutchinson, a successful businessman, and gave an address. One of the sisters then went to the post office and, using a directory, confirmed a PGM Hutchinson at the address. On that basis, the sisters accepted a cheque for the car and then the fraudster sold it to an innocent motor dealer. When the cheque was rejected by the bank, the sisters brought an action in conversion against the innocent buyer. This was based on the argument that they had made no contract with the fraudster because there had been a mistake as to his identity. On the facts, the majority of the Court of Appeal agreed.

Both Sellers LJ and Pearce LJ accepted the presumption from *Phillips v Brooks* about to face-to-face dealing. That presumption meant that, ordinarily, the seller intends to contract with the party physically in front of them, and the name given is just an attribute. This was the position of the sellers when they first discussed the sale of the car. However, the sellers then refused to accept a cheque and accepted it later only after verifying the address and being convinced the fraudster was telling the truth. According to majority, these facts rebutted the general presumption. They felt that, on the facts, the sellers had only intended to direct their offer to the real PGM Hutchinson. This meant there was no contract with the fraudster because the offer could only have been accepted by the real PGM Hutchinson.

The principle or test arising from the decision was stated by Pearce LJ in the following way:

> . . . Each case must be decided on its own facts. The question in such cases is this. Has it been sufficiently shown in the particular circumstances that, contrary to the *prima facie* presumption, a party was not contracting with the physical person to whom he uttered the offer, but with another individual whom (as the other party ought to have understood) he believed to be the physical person present. The answer to that question is a finding of fact.

This statement of law was cited with approval by Phillimore LJ in *Lewis v Averay* [1972], the case in which a fraudster pretended to be a famous Robin Hood actor. Phillimore LJ held that the facts in *Lewis* did not rebut the presumption of an intention to contract with the physically present fraudster. Megaw LJ, in his judgment in the same case, also found in favour of the innocent buyer, since the mistake of the seller was just about the attributes of the fraudster, not his identity. In other words, it 'was simply a mistake as to the creditworthiness of the man who was there present and who described himself as Mr Green'. In contrast, Lord Denning MR, also sitting in *Lews v Averay*, cast some doubt on the way the law was applied in *Ingram*. Lord Denning MR simply said that a mistake as to identity should always make the contract voidable rather than void. This was on the basis that the innocent party who buys from the fraudster has no responsibility for the loss. In contrast, the seller allows the fraudster to have the goods and commit further fraud on the (innocent) buyer.

Ingram v Little can also be criticised for being inconsistent with *Phillips v Brooks*, because in both cases the seller went through the effort of trying to verify the identity of the fraudster, but in the first case the finding was of mistake as to identity, and in the second, it was one of fraudulent misrepresentation. There does not appear to be much justification for this distinction.

In *Ingram*, Devlin LJ also criticised the way in which the law created an imbalance between the two innocent parties. His point was that the innocent buyer's rights are dictated by the intention and conduct of the original seller. This prompted a suggestion that the loss should be divided between the innocent buyer and seller, with the exact apportionment reflecting any fault of either party. This view was considered by The Law Reform Committee, 'Transfer of Title to Chattels' (1966, Cmnd 2598) but was rejected as impractical. For example, where the goods have been resold many times, dividing the loss would be difficult and, in addition, such a rule would cause a great deal of uncertainty. Instead, the Committee recommended that mistakes as to identity should make the contract voidable, just like with fraud—which of course was the basis for Lord Denning MR's later comments in *Lewis v Averay*. However, the recommendations were never adopted and simply remain as suggestions.

→ CROSS-REFERENCE
For the facts and decision of *Lewis v Averay* see 13.5.4.

17.5 The Leading Case on Mistake as to Identity

The highest court did not have the opportunity to review this area of law until *Shogun Finance v Hudson* [2003] UKHL 62. The facts are important because of the arguments that arise from them.

In this case a fraudster had a driving licence belonging to a Mr Durlabh Patel. Using this, he went to a car showroom in Leicester to buy a car. Pretending to be Mr Patel, he entered into a finance agreement in the form of a hire purchase contract. This is where a finance company buys the car and owns it but the customer has the use of the car while paying the finance company the cost plus interest in instalments. Once the cost is fully paid, ownership of the car is transferred to the customer. This finance agreement was with the claimant finance company, and it was entered into after credit checks on the customer were performed. Such checks are routine for finance businesses as a way to verify that the customer has a good record for repaying. Of course, all of this was done under the name of Mr Patel, who happened to have a good credit score. After agreeing the finance, the fraudster drove away in the car and then sold it to an innocent buyer called Hudson. Eventually, the claimant finance company brought an action in conversion against the innocent buyer on the basis that the finance agreement had resulted from a mistake as to identity. This argument was important because of the Hire Purchase Act 1964, governing hire-purchase agreements. Under s.27, an innocent buyer i.e. a good faith buyer for value, could secure a good title to the goods. But if there was never a valid hire purchase agreement, the Act could not apply. By a majority of 3:2, the House of Lords found in favour of the finance company so that the finance agreement was voided for mistake. This meant that the claimant had always had ownership of the car.

The reasoning was based on the law relating to mistake of identity. Most of the Lords expressed their views on the area and there was real disagreement between the majority and minority.

Lord Nicholls (along with Lord Millett) delivered a detailed dissenting judgment. While it does not represent the current legal position, it is useful to read it in summary because it represents a model that could be used to criticise the current position and inform legislative reform, if any takes place in future. Also, the judgment of Lord Nicholls was delivered first and so the lead judgment of the majority by Lord Hobhouse makes reference to it. Consequently, beginning with a summary of the minority judgment of Lord Nicholls, allows for a better understanding of the current position represented by the lead judgment for the majority.

17.5.1 The Approach Adopted by the Minority

The dissenting judgment by Lord Nicholls provides a detailed assessment of the law on mistake as to identity. It addresses the inconsistencies arising in the case law and suggests an alternative approach. One key issue was the distinction between face-to-face transactions and other transactions. The earlier cases presume that the seller intends to contract with the person in front of them but the same does not apply when the transaction is not made in person, like in *Cundy*. This distinction was severely criticised and it was felt that the method of communication should not matter. Furthermore, the distinction becomes even more artificial in the light of more recent forms of communication. Consider a transaction made over the phone. It is not carried out face to face but the innocent seller is actually talking to the fraudster directly. The same problem arises with a video call.

Lord Nicholls suggested that there were two solutions. One option was to overrule the face-to-face cases, which would then eliminate the presumption about intending to deal with the person physically in front of the seller. However, the alternative he (and Lord Millett) preferred was to overrule the old House of Lords case of *Cundy v Lindsay*. That would mean the presumption that a seller intended to deal with the person purporting to be the buyer would apply to all forms of communication, rather than just in face-to-face transactions. He did not make it entirely clear what would be required to rebut that presumption, and in fact it is easy to assume it would never be possible to rebut the presumption. The point was developed further by Lord Millett, who doubted the merits of making this a 'presumption' and suggested that it is really a rule.

This would have meant that there would be a voidable contract, rather than no contract. Such an approach would address the other inconsistency in the cases—namely the one between mistaken identity and fraudulent misrepresentation. The point was that fraud does not negate consent to a contract and so it results in a contract that is voidable. So why should a mistaken identity resulting from fraud be treated differently? Both scenarios make the seller a victim of fraud, yet the consequences are different depending on what the fraud relates to. According to the minority, this distinction was illogical. They also considered it from the perspective of an innocent buyer. Such a buyer is unnecessarily vulnerable and should not be exposed to different amounts of loss based on the type of thing the fraudster happened to have lied about to the original seller. Finally, the previous cases resulted in a distinction between mistakes about identity and those concerning attributes. This was seen as artificial an unnecessarily complicated. The distinction meant in effect that if identity was fundamental then there might never have been a contract. If it was not fundamental, then the contract would be voidable for fraud. The problem is that it is a difficult distinction to apply, and it might be that in some cases creditworthiness is more important than identity *per se*. Indeed, in *Shogun Finance* itself the identity of the person entering the hire purchase agreement did not particularly matter to the finance company except insofar as there was a credit record attached to that identity.

That takes us to the other key point concerning the innocent buyer's position. The rule allowing for mistake to make the contract void really works against the innocent buyer. The innocent buyer's rights in this situation are determined by factors completely outside their control. Consider Hudson in the *Shogun Finance* case, for instance—as far as he knew, he was just buying a car, and paid accordingly. Innocent buyers cannot fairly be said to have taken on a risk of fraud occurring, whereas the original seller definitely can, since it will have sold the goods to somebody on credit without any certainty that the money would ultimately be paid. The fact that the original seller has assumed the risk should really work against the original seller, then, rather than the innocent buyer. But instead the cases make the seller's assumption of risk work against the innocent buyer, resulting in that innocent buyer potentially being inflicted with an order to return goods with no hope of recovering any payment it made to the fraudster.

For these reasons, the dissenting judges felt that the hire purchase contract did exist, and following the fraud it should be voidable rather than void for mistake. Since the seller had not rescinded the contract before the resale, the innocent buyer should have acquired ownership of the car.

KEY POINTS

The approach of the minority (dissenting) judgments:

- Overruled *Cundy v Lindsey* so that the rule on face-to-face transactions would apply to all forms of communication.
- Aligned issues of identity with fraudulent misrepresentation so that there would not be a distinction drawn between attributes and identity.
- Represented an approach that is fairer to the eventual innocent buyer.

17.5.2 The Current Approach (Adopted by the Majority)

The majority of the Lords held that the contract was void for mistake and their judgments represent the current position. We can now turn to the lead judgment of the majority by Lord Hobhouse, with whom Lord Walker and Lord Phillips agreed.

GUIDED READING 17.1
Shogun Finance v Hudson [2003] UKHL 62

When reading the extracts of the judgment by Lord Hobhouse, try to identify:

■ the basis for not treating the transaction as one that was made face to face; and

■ why the identity was so fundamental to the transaction.

[48] It has been suggested that the finance company was willing to do business with anyone, whatever their name. But this is not correct: it was only willing to do business with a person who had identified himself in the way required by the written document so as to enable it to check before it enters into any contractual or other relationship that he meets its credit requirements. Mr Durlabh Patel was such an identified person and met its credit requirements so it was willing to do business with him. If the applicant had been, say, Mr B Patel of Ealing or Mr G Patel of Edgbaston, it would not have been willing to deal with them if they could not be identified or did not meet with its credit requirements. Correctly identifying the customer making the offer is an essential precondition of the willingness of the finance company to deal with that person . . . This is not a case such as that categorised by Sedley LJ ([2002] QB at 846) as the use of a 'simple alias' to disguise the purchaser rather than to deceive the vendor—the situation which resembles that in *King's Norton Metal v Edridge* . . .. But, even then, in a credit agreement it would be useless to use a pseudonym as no actual verifiable person against whom a credit check could be run would have been disclosed and the offer would never be accepted. Mr Durlabh Patel is the sole hirer under this written agreement. No one else acquires any rights under it . . .

> Lord Hobhouse rejected the implication from Lord Nicholl's judgment that the buyer's identity was not particularly important except insofar as there was a credit history attached to it. As far as he was concerned, the opposite was true: the fact that the identity had a credit history meant identity was fundamental to the transaction.

[49] Mr Hudson seeks to escape from this conclusion by saying: 'but the Rogue was the person who came into the dealer's office and negotiated a price with the dealer and signed the form in the presence of the dealer who then witnessed it'. . . . The gist of the argument is that oral evidence may be adduced to contradict the agreement contained in a written document which is the only contract to which the finance company was a party. The agreement is a written agreement with Mr Durlabh Patel. The argument seeks to contradict this and make it an agreement with the Rogue. It is argued that other evidence is always admissible to show who the parties to an agreement are. Thus, if the contents of the document are, without more, insufficient unequivocally to identify the actual individual referred to or if the identification of the party is non-specific, evidence can be given to fill any gap. Where the person signing is also acting as the agent of another, evidence can be adduced of that fact. None of this involves the contradiction of the document: *Young v Schuler* (1883) . . . But it is different where the party is, as here, specifically identified in the document: oral or other extrinsic evidence is not admissible. Further, the Rogue was no one's agent (nor did

> This was reinforced by the fact that the contract was a written one and that it named the purported counterparty as Mr Durlabh Patel. Since this was clearly the case, outside evidence could not be used to contradict it—especially not oral evidence in the form of a conversation had at the dealership between the dealer and the Rogue. In other words, the written agreement, which named Mr Durlabh Patel and was based on it being a contract with that person with that identity and credit history, trumped any other circumstantial indication that the finance company had meant to contract with the person who had physically appeared at the dealership, i.e. the Rogue.

he ever purport to be). The rule that other evidence may not be adduced to contradict the provisions of a contract contained in a written document is fundamental to the mercantile law of this country; the bargain is the document; the certainty of the contract depends on it . . . This rule is one of the great strengths of English commercial law and is one of the main reasons for the international success of English law in preference to laxer systems which do not provide the same certainty. The case of *Hector v Lyons* (1989) 58 P&CR 156 is simply an application of this basic and long established principle. The father was claiming to be able to enforce a contract of sale of land. The father had conducted the negotiations. Woolf LJ said, at pp. 160–161:

'In this case there is no dispute as to who, according to the written contract, are the parties. The son was described in the contract as one of the parties. He does exist and, in so far as there was a contract at all, it was between him and the other party identified in the contract, Mrs Pamela Doris Lyons.'

Browne-Wilkinson VC delivered a judgment to the same effect. On p. 159 he referred to the cases 'entirely concerned with transactions between two individuals face to face entering into oral agreement', saying:

'In my judgment the principle there enunciated has no application to a case such as the present where there is a contract and wholly in writing. There the identity of the vendor and of the purchaser is established by the names of the parties included in the written contract.'

Mr Hudson submitted, as he had to, that this decision was wrong and should be overruled. In my opinion the Court of Appeal's decision was clearly correct and correctly reasoned in accordance with well established principles.

> This is, in effect, the parole evidence rule in action, and Lord Hobhouse provides a robust defence of it here, arguing that it is one of the cornerstones of English contract law that if a written contract names one party or both, then they are the parties to the contract and oral evidence cannot be used to challenge this.

[50] The argument also fails on another ground. There was no *consensus ad idem* between the finance company and the Rogue. Leaving on one side the fact that the Rogue never had any intention himself to contract with the finance company, the hire-purchase 'agreement' to which Mr Hudson pins his argument was one purportedly made by the acceptance by the finance company, by signing the creditor's box in the form, of a written offer by Mr Durlabh Patel to enter into the hire-purchase agreement. This faces Mr Hudson with a dilemma: either the contract created by that acceptance was a contract with Mr Durlabh Patel or there was no *consensus ad idem*, the Rogue having no honest belief or contractual intent whatsoever and the finance company believing that it was accepting an offer by Mr Durlabh Patel. On neither alternative was there a hire-purchase agreement with the Rogue.

> A further, perhaps more straightforwardly understood problem for Hudson was that if indeed it was true that despite the written agreement the finance company had only intended to contract with the person who had appeared at the dealership (which is to say the Rogue) then there was no contract at all, because the parties had had no *consensus ad idem*. The finance company had believed itself to have been accepting an offer with one person when in fact it was somebody else, and the Rogue had had no honest contractual intent at all.

[51] . . . The title to the car was in the finance company. The hirer/debtor under the 'agreement' was Mr Durlabh Patel not the Rogue. The Rogue only comes into the picture because he was the unidentified individual who came into the dealer's office and caused the dealer to sell the motor car to the finance company . . . But the Rogue never had any face-to-face dealings with the finance company; he dealt with it solely by submitting a written document containing an offer and acceptance clause. There is no room for the application of the 'face-to-face' principle between the Rogue and the finance company. Nor was the dealer the agent of the finance company to enter into any contract on behalf of the finance company. The dealer is a mere facilitator serving primarily his own interests.

. . .

[55] But, before I leave this case, I should shortly summarise why the argument of the appellant's counsel was so mistaken. The first reason was that they approached the question as if it was simply a matter of sorting out the common

> And finally the face-to-face presumption could not apply here because the Rogue and finance company had had no face-to-face dealings at all—everything had been done on paper with the car dealership who was not acting as an agent for the finance company.

law authorities relating to the sale of goods. They did not treat it as a matter of applying a statutory exception to the basic common law rule, *nemo dat quod non habet*. Further, they did not analyse the structure of the overall transaction and the consumer credit agreement within it. Accordingly, they misrepresented the role of the dealer, wrongly treating him as the contracting agent of the finance company which he was not. They never analysed the terms of the written document and had no regard at all to the offer and acceptance clause it contained . . . They made submissions which contradicted the express written contract and were therefore contrary to principle and long established English mercantile law. They submitted that *Cundy v Lindsay* . . . was wrongly decided and should be overruled, substituting for it a general rule which, in disregard of the document or documents which constitute the agreement (if any), makes everything depend upon a factual enquiry into extraneous facts not known to both of the parties thus depriving documentary contracts of their certainty. They sought to convert a direct documentary contract with the finance company into a face-to-face oral contract made through the dealer as the contracting agent of the finance company, notwithstanding that the dealer was never such an agent of the finance company. Finally they sought, having by-passed the written contract, to rely upon authorities on oral contracts for the sale of goods, made face to face and where the title to the goods had passed to the 'buyer', notwithstanding that this was a documentary consumer credit transaction not a sale and, on any view, no title had ever passed to R. In the result they have invited a review of those authorities by reference to the particular facts of each of them. They have sought to draw your Lordships into a discussion of the evidential tools, e.g. rebuttable presumptions of fact and the so-called face-to-face 'principle', used by judges in those cases to assist them in making factual decisions . . . notwithstanding that the present case concerns the construction of a written contract. . . .

Inevitably over the course of time there have been decisions on the facts of individual 'mistaken identity' cases which seem now to be inconsistent; the further learned, but ultimately unproductive, discussion of them will warm academic hearts. But what matters is the principles of law. They are clear and sound and need no revision. To cast doubt upon them can only be a disservice to English law. Similarly, to attempt to use this appeal to advocate, on the basis of continental legal systems which are open to cogent criticism, the abandonment of the soundly based *nemo dat quod non habet* rule (statutorily adopted) would be not only improper but even more damaging.

> Lord Hobhouse then levelled something of a broadside at the counsel for Mr Hudson. He provides a litany of criticisms, but these are fairly easily summarised: they had played rather fast and loose with the written contract and looked instead to extraneous facts and oral arrangements. This was precisely the opposite of what he felt should have been their starting point—the written agreement between the parties.

> He closed by reaffirming the importance of the basic rule of *nemo dat quod non habet* (which means basically that a person who does not own property, such as a thief, cannot then confer it on somebody else), arguing that it is a good one and foundational to the English law of contract. He clearly took a dim view of attempts to undermine such fundamental principles through the courts.

The majority were not under any illusion about the state of the case law. They recognised that there were some inconsistencies. For example, in *Ingram v Little* there was a face-to-face transaction and so the presumption applied, yet it was rebutted on the facts—even though these seemed largely similar on their material points to other cases which had gone the other way. But Lord Hobhouse took the view that such inconsistencies did not particularly matter as long as there were consistent principles underlying the case law. *Ingram*, in other words, can just be seen as a bad or erroneous *application* of a sound principle. The suggestion is that there is actually a perfectly good and principled reason for insisting on a distinction between face-to-face transactions and written agreements which name the parties—the latter being treated almost as sacrosanct in English law, because of their certainty.

A further point made by Lord Hobhouse was that the buyer's arguments sought to undermine the *nemo dat* rule, one which is very well established in the common law and incorporated into the Sale of Goods Act. However, this might have been going too far. The minority were not saying that the fraudster could give a title he did not have. Their argument was that this was a hire-purchase agreement and on that basis, title could pass using the exception from the Hire Purchase Act. This cannot really be said to undermine the *nemo dat* rule (and, if it does, the undermining was done by Parliament in passing the Act, not the minority in arguing for it to apply).

The *Shogun Finance* case will continue to be criticised because it maintains the distinction between face-to-face dealings and those that are written. It also favours finance companies and equivalent sellers at the expense of innocent buyers. In other words, it continues to put the risk of the original seller contracting on credit onto the innocent subsequent buyer. This seems unfair, since finance companies run credit checks and have it in their power to be more thorough with their verification of identity, whereas innocent buyers (such as Mr Hudson) may well not have it in their power to do this.

The current position is that the transaction between a seller and fraudster is viewed objectively and the question is whether there is a contract. A mistake as to identity will mean there was no contract, which will have been void from the start. Such a mistake is possible where identity is so fundamental that it is effectively, on the facts, a term. Whether this is so will vary according to the facts of each case. If it is a face-to-face transaction, then there is a strong presumption that the seller intends to contract with the party physically present, whoever that really is. Unless the presumption can be rebutted on the facts, a contract is formed that is voidable for fraud. If the contract is in writing without the parties being present together physically, then it is possible that the identity is important enough and, if it is, the contract will then be void for mistake.

KEY POINTS

- An agreement can be void for mistaken identity if the identity is a fundamental as a term on the facts.
- Having names on a written document could be enough. The use of the names to run credit checks or some other process that the transaction relies on will help.
- In face-to-face dealings without a written document, it is presumed that the 'seller' intends to sell to the party in front of them.
- Whether a phone or video call is treated as face to face remains to be seen.

It can be argued that phone and video calls take place at a distance and should be within *Cundy v Lindsay* rather than the presumption about face-to-face dealings, because the parties are not physically in front of each other. However, *Shogan Finance* appears to put the emphasis firmly on the importance of what is written, with the identity of the parties being an important term. Accordingly, the names on the document show that there was an intention to contract with the person named only. The same might not be said of phone and video calls, which are more likely to indicate an intention to contract with the fraudster appearing on the phone or on screen rather than who the fraudster is pretending to be.

17.6 Introduction to Common Mistake

It is important to keep in mind that a *common* mistake is very different to a *unilateral* mistake. A common mistake is where *both* parties make the *same* mistake at the time that they enter an agreement. They have not disagreed on anything and both intend the same thing, so there is no dispute about the formation of the contract. Instead, the mistake is about an assumption that both parties relied on. For example, both parties might enter into a contract for goods to be transported from one country to another, without knowing that the movement of such goods across a border has been banned. They had assumed that the transportation would be possible, but this was mistaken. It means that the contract (as both parties viewed it) was *never* performable. In such a case, the contract could be void for common mistake, if the strict test applied by the courts were to be satisfied.

We will see that judges have developed similar tests both for common mistake and frustration, but there is a very clear difference between the two principles. Frustration occurs when something happens *after* the contract has been created such that performance becomes radically different from what was intended. With common mistake, performance was already radically different from what was intended at the time the contract was created. The contract was *never* performable as originally envisaged by the parties. This is why common mistake is often referred to as 'initial impossibility' and frustration as 'subsequent impossibility', although it is important to emphasise that neither mistake nor frustration is nowadays accurately described as just being about performance being literally impossible—they are both rather wider than that.

17.7 The Basic Test and Requirements for Common Mistake

The existence of a doctrine of common mistake is now said to have been confirmed by the House of Lords case of *Bell v Lever Bros* [1932] AC 161. At the time the case was decided, there was some doubt about whether it really recognised such a thing as common mistake. However, following further cases, it is now clear that it confirmed its existence. As the only case from the highest court on the issue it is the leading case, and so all cases concerning common mistake will make some reference to *Bell v Lever Bros*. However, the test and its scope have been developed and interpreted by later cases. For that reason, we will consider extracts from *Bell v Lever Bros* only where they have a current application.

The most recent significant case is *Great Peace Shipping v Tsavliris Salvage (International) Ltd (The Great Peace)* [2002] EWCA Civ 1407. In it, Lord Phillips MR for the Court of Appeal clarified the test for common mistake by stating the following requirements:

> [76] ...(i) there must be a common assumption as to the existence of a state of affairs; (ii) there must be no warranty by either party that that state of affairs exists; (iii) the non-existence of the state of affairs must not be attributable to the fault of either party; (iv) the non-existence of the state of affairs must render performance of the contract impossible; (v) the state of affairs may be the existence, or a vital attribute, of the consideration to be provided or circumstances which must subsist if performance of the contractual adventure is to be possible.

These requirements were based on those applied to frustration as well as previous cases on common mistake. If they are met, it means the mistake is operative and the contract will be void. Of course, if the mistake is not operative, it means that the contract is valid and consequently a non-performing party will be in breach.

Requirements (i) and (v) are related. They both refer to the existence of a 'state of affairs' assumed to exist by both parties. It is just that (v) is more detailed. According to (iv), the non-existence of such a 'state of affairs' must then make performance 'impossible'.

Requirements (ii) and (iii) really serve as limits. According to (ii), a party must not have promised that the state of affairs existed. If they did then that party accepted the risks of the state of affairs not existing. Likewise, according to requirement (iii), neither party must be at fault for the state of affairs not existing. We shall consider these requirements in turn and we will see a summary of them in Table 17.1.

17.7.1 The Parties Must Have Assumed That a State of Affairs Existed

A 'common assumption' is simply an assumption that *both* parties make. At the time of contracting they assume the existence of something (i.e. a 'state of affairs'). Such a state of affairs can be fairly wide-ranging, and an obvious example would be assumption about the existence of an item being sold. The real scope is addressed in factor (v) from Lord Phillips MR where reference was made to the existence of the consideration or 'vital attribute of it'. But in addition, it refers to circumstances that would make the 'contractual adventure possible'.

The requirement of a 'common assumption' was considered more recently in *Triple Seven MSN 27251 Ltd v Azman Air Services Ltd* [2018] EWHC 1348 (Comm). The judge, Mr Peter Macdonald Eggers QC, explained that some assumptions are reflected in the contract terms while others will be apparent from the background of the contract. Such assumptions might include the reason for the contract; how practicable performance is going to be; the ability of a party to perform; or the nature and identity of the subject matter of the contract (i.e. the thing being bought or sold). It could even concern the title to goods, or the reason or motive for entering the contract. However, for all of these the assumption needs to be *fundamental*, which means the assumption relied upon must be objectively important or serious.

17.7.2 The Non-existence of the State of Affairs Must Make Performance Impossible or Radically Different

This requirement is very important and goes to the core of common mistake. It is not enough for the state of affairs to simply not exist, and instead more is needed. The non-existence must make the performance 'impossible'. In the judgment of *The Great Peace*, Lord Phillips MR also referred to the 'essence of the obligation' being impossible.

This requirement has been the subject of some criticism because of the reference to impossibility. Such a requirement of impossibility might appear too narrow because we know that it might be possible to perform a contract even though performance will no longer reflect what the parties intended. It could even be said, for instance, that illegality will often not strictly speaking make performance of a contract *impossible*—just unlawful. Use of the word 'impossible' was moreover a change to the language used by Steyn J in *Associated Japanese Bank International Ltd v Credit du Nord SA* [1989] 1 WLR 255, in which he had observed:

> The mistake must render the subject matter of the contract essentially and radically different from the subject matter which the parties believed to exist.

This tied mistake more closely to the language used to describe situations in which frustration applies. This judgment of Steyn J was heavily relied upon in *The Great Peace*, but 'impossibility' was used rather than 'essential and radical difference'. That did result in suggestions of a different approach to common mistake, but in *Kyle Bay Ltd v Underwriters* [2007] EWCA Civ 57, Neuberger LJ observed that both approaches 'may essentially amount to the same thing'. Likewise, Leggatt, J in *Dana Gas PJSC v Dana Gas Sukuk Ltd* [2017] EWHC 2928 (Comm) expressed the same point.

The issue was addressed in the *Triple Seven case* [2018] in which the judgment did not consider the tests to be representing different approaches. It was observed that 'essential and radical difference' is wide and can apply to performance that is technically possible but fails to reflect the commercial purpose of the contract. It was then pointed out that this wider scope is reflected in the requirements from *The Great Peace*, specifically requirement (v), which refers to assumptions about the 'contractual adventure'. On that basis, it can be said that the reference to 'impossibility' was not intended to limit the range of assumptions covered.

In *Triple Seven*, it was also acknowledged that both 'impossibility' and 'essential and radically different' were terms adopted from the law of frustration. What mattered was that performance would always be *fundamentally different* to what was assumed by the parties.

It is clear in any event that performance of the contract must be fundamentally different from what was intended, which will of course include circumstances in which it was impossible, and that means it is necessary to identify what performance actually was expected from the contract. On that point, Lord Phillips MR in *The Great Peace* provided the following guidance:

> [74] … [I]t is necessary to identify what it is that the parties agreed would be performed. This involves looking not only at the express terms, but at any implications that may arise out of the surrounding circumstances. In some cases it will be possible to identify details of the "contractual adventure" which go beyond the terms that are expressly spelt out, in others it will not.

Clearly, the starting point will be the terms of the contract, which will often identify what performance was expected. But the assessment goes beyond express terms and so the expected performance could be implied from the circumstances.

17.7.3 The Risk of the Non-existence Must Not Have Been Accepted by One of the Parties

This factor serves as a real barrier to finding an operative common mistake. If a party *promises* that a state of affairs exists then the mistake cannot be operative and so the contract will not be void. The reason is that such a promise means that the promisor is deemed to have been accepting the risk of being wrong. It can then be said that the parties agreed for that promisor to be liable if that state of affairs did not exist. Likewise, the same can be said if such a promise can be implied from the circumstances. Such an acceptance of risk could be implied on the basis of existing case law, and the Court of Appeal case of *William Sindle v Cambridge CC* [1994] is useful on this point. The Court of Appeal acknowledged a general rule about leases to the effect that, ordinarily, a lessor (the landlord) does not promise (warrant) that the property is fit for a particular use. On that basis, the risk of a mistake about that issue is impliedly accepted by the lessee. All of this is really about how a judge construes the contract and it is the same approach that we saw in relation to frustration. If a party is deemed to have accepted the risk of an event occurring, then it will not be a frustrating event.

→ CROSS-REFERENCE
On the acceptance of the risk of a *later* event preventing performance see 16.5.3–16.6.

An example of the seller appearing to accept such a risk from an implied term is the Australian case of *McRae v Commonwealth Disposals Commission* (1951) 84 CLR 377. In this case, the defendant invited offers to buy the wreck of an oil tanker for salvage, using a tendering process. This wreckage was said to be located on 'Jourmaund Reef'. The defendant contracted with the claimant and then the claimant discovered there was no such place as Jourmaund Reef and asked for a specific location. The defendant gave the information and then the claimant spent a lot of money trying to find the wreck. It then became clear that it did not in fact exist and that the defendant had confused it with another wreck located elsewhere. When the claimant brought an action for breach the defendant relied on common mistake as a defence, arguing that both parties incorrectly assumed the existence of the wreck. In rejecting this argument, the court found in favour of the claimant who was entitled to damages for breach.

The reasoning was based on the construction of the contract. According to the judges, the defendants appeared to impliedly promise that the wreck existed, which then meant that the risk of it not existing had been accepted by the defendants. That was enough to rule out the reliance on mistake, and the approach adopted was then subsequently supported by Lord Phillips MR in *The Great Peace*:

> [75] Just as the doctrine of frustration only applies if the contract contains no provision that covers the situation, the same should be true of common mistake. If, on true construction of the contract, a party warrants that the subject matter of the contract exists, or that it will be possible to perform the contract, there will be no scope to hold the contract void on the ground of common mistake.

This approach demonstrates the importance of the way in which judges construe contracts. It might be obvious from the wording of a term that a party has made a promise about the existence of the subject matter. But even if it is not obvious, such a promise might be apparent from the construction of the contract. If that is the case, it can be said that one party accepted the risk of the non-existence of the state of affairs in question. The likelihood of this was acknowledged by Lord Phillips MR who relied on a comparison with frustration:

> [85] Circumstances where a contract is void as a result of common mistake are likely to be less common than instances of frustration. Supervening events which defeat the contractual adventure will frequently not be the responsibility of either party. Where, however, the parties agree that something shall be done which is impossible at the time of making the agreement, it is much more likely that, on true construction of the agreement, one or other will have undertaken responsibility for the mistaken state of affairs. This may well explain why cases where contracts have been found to be void in consequence of common mistake are few and far between.

The fact that common mistake is more exceptional than frustration shows the limited scope of the doctrine, given how exceptional frustration is. The reason why a common mistake argument has a low likelihood of success is that when contract is created, both parties agree to perform their obligations and, in doing so, it is more likely that they are promising that the circumstances will exist to enable complete performance.

17.7.4 A Party Must Not Be at Fault for the Non-existence of the State of Affairs

This requirement is straight-forward and again it is based on the facts. If a party is at fault for the state of affairs not existing, then the mistake is not operative. Instead, the non-existence was self-induced and results in liability for breach. Again, that is a well-established principle for frustration too. The early authority for this is *McRae v Commonwealth Disposals Commission*. The risk had been accepted in that case but, in addition, the judgment also made clear the defendant was ultimately at fault. After all, the defendant had no reasonable grounds to believe the wreck existed. Consequently, the court stated that the defendant's mistake was self-induced, and so they could not rely on mistake to make the contract void. While the *McRae* case is Australian, it is generally assumed that it represents the position in English law. The approval of the case by the Court of Appeal in *The Great Peace* [2002] supports that view.

17.7.5 Policy and the Need for the Assumption to Be Fundamental

We have already seen that Lord Phillips MR observed in *The Great Peace* that cases on common mistake were '*few and far between*'. One of the reasons given was that contracts are often construed so as to reveal that one party has assumed the risk of the mistake. But, in addition, a restrictive approach has always been adopted, just like it has for unilateral mistake, because there is a need to ensure certainty. If it appears that the parties have created a contract, the courts will be very reluctant to interfere. This point was made by Steyn J in *Associated Japanese Bank*, who referred to the 'respect for the sanctity of contract'. He went on to say that the 'first imperative must be to uphold contractual bargains, not to undermine them'. These statements echo the views expressed by Lord Atkin in *Bell v Lever Bros*, who warned that '. . .it is of paramount importance that contracts should be observed'.

The need for common mistake to be exceptional means that it will not apply to all common assumptions. Likewise, it will not apply every time performance would be different to what the parties intended. Instead, the assumption and difference in performance should be fundamental. For that reason, in *Triple Seven* [2018], MacDonald Eggers QC suggested that the way to approach common mistake consisted of two steps:

> 66. . . . (a) assessing the fundamental nature of the shared assumption to the contract, and (b) comparing the disparity between the assumed state of affairs and the actual state of affairs and analysing whether that disparity is sufficiently fundamental or essential or radical.

We will see that where the common mistake argument has failed, this has been based on failure at one or both of these steps.

KEY POINTS

For common mistake:

- The assumption must be a fundamental one.
- The difference between the performance assumed and the reality must be fundamental, essential or radical.

In the *Triple Seven* judgment the first step, concerning the fundamental nature of the shared assumption, was expanded upon. The assumption must be one without which the parties would not have entered into the contract. However, Macdonald Eggers QC made it clear that on its own, such an assumption or inducement would not necessarily make a shared assumption fundamental. The point was that an assumption or inducement could be necessary for the parties to enter into the contract but still relate to something that is not fundamental or important. Authority for this requirement came from *Bell v Lever Bros* in which Lord Akin addressed some aspects of the assumption for common mistake, stating:

> . . .[T]he sale of a horse or of a picture, it might be said that the fundamental reason for making the contract was the belief of both parties that the horse was sound or the picture an old master, yet in neither case would the condition as I think exist. . .

He added:

> We therefore get a common standard for [common] mistake,. . . Does the state of the new facts destroy the identity of the subject-matter as it was in the original state of facts?

The comment has been taken to indicate that the assumption must be one that, if the truth about it were known, both parties would not have entered into the contract. But, in addition, the non-existence of the state of affairs relating to that assumption must also be total. If both parties assumed a painting was by an old master when it really wasn't, the case would probably end up being dealt with as a breach or a misrepresentation. What would allow mistake to operate, Lord Akin implied, would be the non-existence of the painting in the first place.

17.7.6 Summary of the Requirements for Common Mistake

It is useful to summarise the basic requirements for common mistake. These are outlined in Table 17.1.

Table 17.1

The basic requirements for common mistake

1.	At the time of contracting, there is a shared assumption about a state of affairs existing, when in reality, it did not exist.
2.	The assumption must be fundamental. Showing the parties would not have contracted if they knew the assumption was wrong is necessary but, on its own, this is not enough.
3.	The assumption being wrong has to make the expected performance either impossible or 'radically different' to what was originally intended.
4.	Neither party should be at fault for the assumption being wrong i.e. a party cannot be at fault for the state of affairs not existing.
5.	The contract cannot (expressly or impliedly) put the risk of the assumption being wrong on one of the parties.

17.8 The Juristic (Legal) Basis of Common Mistake

The legal basis of common mistake has been an issue over the years. This issue does not arise with unilateral mistake because that concerns whether or not an agreement exists. If it does not exist then there was never a contract. In contrast, with common mistake there has been an agreement and there is a contract waiting to be performed. Typically, following non-performance, one party sues for breach and the other relies on common mistake to defend the action, arguing that the contact was void from the start. For this to be allowed the common mistake needs some sort of legal basis to operate and make the contract void.

In *Bell v Lever Bros*, the possible basis of common mistake was framed as follows:

> A condition derives its efficacy from the consent of the parties, express or implied. They have agreed, but on what terms. One term may be that unless the facts are or are not of a particular nature, or unless an event has or has not happened, the contract is not to take effect. With regard to future facts such a condition is obviously contractual. Till the event occurs the parties are bound. Thus the condition (the exact terms of which need not here be investigated) that is generally accepted as underlying the principle of the frustration cases is contractual, an implied condition.

The operation of this approach of the contract being conditional was then defined further:

> The proposition does not amount to more than this that, if the contract expressly or impliedly contains a term that a particular assumption is a condition of the contract, the contract is avoided if the assumption is not true.

Lord Atkin suggested that common mistake operated on the basis of there being an implied term. Such an implied term could make a contract conditional on the existence of a particular state of affairs. The extract reminds us that at the time, frustration was also conceptualised as deriving from an implied term and so it made sense to recognise the same basis for common mistake. Both principles are concerned with performance becoming impossible (and later 'radically different'). The only difference is *when* the contract becomes impossible to perform, as we have already seen.

Of course, we know that later the implied term basis for frustration was rejected in favour of a 'rule of law' basis. It follows that common mistake should be based on a rule of law too and that was a point recognised by Lord Phillips MR in *The Great Peace*:

➔ CROSS-REFERENCE
For the development of the legal basis of frustration see 16.1.3.

> [61] . . . Lord Atkin advanced an alternative basis for his test: the implication of a term of the same nature as that which was applied under the doctrine of frustration, as it was then understood. In so doing he adopted the analysis of Scrutton LJ in the Court of Appeal. It seems to us that this was a more solid jurisprudential basis for the test of common mistake that Lord Atkin was proposing. At the time of *Bell v Lever Bros Ltd* [1932] . . .the law of frustration and common mistake had advanced hand in hand on the foundation of a common principle. Thereafter frustration proved a more fertile ground for the development of this principle than common mistake, and consideration of the development of the law of frustration assists with the analysis of the law of common mistake.

Lord Phillips MR charted the development of frustration from its original implied term basis to being based on a rule of law, and then returned to the doctrine of common mistake:

> [73] What do these developments in the law of frustration have to tell us about the law of common mistake? First that the theory of the implied term is as unrealistic when considering common mistake as when considering frustration. Where a fundamental assumption upon which an agreement is founded proves to be mistaken, it is not realistic to ask whether the parties impliedly agreed that in those circumstances the contract would not be binding. The avoidance of a contract on the ground of common mistake results from a rule of law under which, if it transpires that one or both of the parties have agreed to do something which it is impossible to perform, no obligation arises out of that agreement.

These statements show that an implied term basis for common mistake was rejected for artificiality, just as was the case with frustration. It would also, of course, result in an inconsistency if mistake and frustration had alternative bases.

KEY POINTS

Like the principle of frustration, common mistake is based on a rule of law. It does not come from an implied term.

17.9 Types of Common Mistake

There are various ways to categorise the small number of cases on common mistake. Putting the cases in categories makes it easier for us to identify the most relevant ones, or which parts of cases to apply. However, it must be remembered that common mistake operates as a general principle. It applies in a general context rather than to specific types or categories of mistakes. Consequently, it is possible for the principle to apply to a future case falling outside of the categories listed below.

17.9.1 A Mistake about the Existence of the Subject Matter of the Contract

An established category of common mistake is where the subject matter of the contract (i.e. the thing contracted for) no longer exists by the time the contract was entered. An example would be where the parties enter into an agreement concerning the use of a ship that no longer exists. This is often described as *res extincta*. While this type of common mistake is well established, its scope and application are not altogether clear.

res extincta
is a Latin term indicating that something no longer exists.

The case often cited on this category is *Couturier v Hastie* (1856) 5 HL Cas 673. This concerned a contract for the sale of corn being transported on a ship. During the voyage, the corn started to deteriorate and, in response, the ship's master sold the corn before it got worse. None of this was known by the parties by the time they created the contract and, since there was no corn at all, the buyer did not pay. That prompted the seller to sue for the price, arguing that it was the 'adventure' that was being sold. In other words, it was a contract for the shipping documents and insurance relating to the corn and that included the risk of the goods. According to the seller, the transaction concerning the ownership documents and the insurance remained performable. However, this argument was rejected by the House of Lords. The key reasoning was from Lord Cranworth LC, who stated:

> [T]he whole question turns upon the construction of the contract. . .looking to the contract itself alone, it appears to me clearly that what the parties contemplated. . .The contract. . .plainly imports that there was something which was to be sold at the time of the contract, and something to be purchased.

This reasoning was based on the construction of the contract, i.e. the words and the circumstances. According to the court, the contract was for the actual corn rather than rights arising from the documents. Since the corn did not exist at the time of the contract, the buyer was not liable to pay. Interestingly, the court did not refer to mistake as the basis for its decision and there was no mention of mistake in the judgments. Likewise, there was no mention of the contract being void. However, the case is regarded as early authority for common mistake on the existence of the 'subject matter' of the contract. It is generally accepted that (what is now) section 6, Sale of Goods Act 1979, is based on *Couturier v Hastie*. Section 6 states:

> Where there is a contract for the sale of specific goods, and the goods without knowledge of the seller have perished at the time when the contract is made, the contract is void.

This was taken from the original 1893 Sale of Goods Act which was drafted by codifying the common law. As such, the s.6 replicates how *Couturier* was perceived when the original Act was drafted—a point that was observed by Lord Phillips MR in *The Great Peace* case. The result in *McRae* might appear to be inconsistent with this rule. However, it can be said that s.6 is concerned with goods that perish before the contract is made. In contrast, the wreckage in *McRae* did not perish; it simply never existed.

➜ CROSS-REFERENCE
for the facts and decision
of *McRae v Commonwealth
Disposals Commission*
(1951) see 17.7.3.

The reasoning in *Couturier* highlighted the importance of the construction of the contract. The corn or 'subject matter' of the contract did not exist at the time of contracting. However, that would not end the contract automatically—it all depended on what was promised in the contract. It was ultimately determined to be one for goods rather than the documents giving rights over those goods and, therefore, the buyer was not liable to pay. But nothing was said about whether the seller was liable for non-delivery of the goods, and that issue would also depend on the construction of the contract. The question to ask would be whether the seller appeared to accept the risk of the goods not existing. That would be based on the terms and the circumstances. If the terms were construed to expressly or impliedly cover the issue, then that is what would apply.

Of course, in *McRae* the party relying on the mistake had been at fault and, in addition, the terms were interpreted to mean that that party had accepted the risks of the wreck not existing. Today such mistakes about the existence of things are much less likely because of the existence of new methods of communication that did not exist at the time (e.g. communication over the web or phone networks). A seller in the modern day should therefore generally know about their goods having perished before making a contract. According to Professor Atiyah, ('Introduction to Contract law', 5th ed. (1995) Clarendon), having the ability to know if the goods exist means it is more likely that the seller will be impliedly promising that they do. In such a case, the seller will be accepting the risk of the goods not existing.

The non-existence of the subject matter does not have to relate to something that has perished. It is a little wider, so that the category also includes cases where it was impossible for the contract subject matter to exist. An example is *Sheikh Brothers v Ochsner* [1957] AC 136, which concerned a contract for a crop to be harvested from the appellant's land. Under its terms, an average of 50 tons a month would be delivered. However, both parties did not know that it was impossible for such a quantity to be farmed from that land. On the facts, the Privy Council held that the contract was void for common mistake.

Another wider example of non-existence is where the subject matter is based on the contract's purpose. In the related context of frustration, impossibility of a commercial purpose was illustrated using the 'coronation cases'. The same event gave rise to mistake cases too. An example is *Griffith v Brymer* (1903) 19 TLR 434, which was yet another dispute about the hiring of a room to view the King's coronation procession. We can recall that the event was cancelled due to the King being seriously ill. In this case, the contract was created an hour after the decision to operate on the King, and at the time the parties were unaware that the coronation would not take place. This meant the commercial purpose of the contract was *never* performable, and so the contract was set aside. This was a case cited by the Court of Appeal in *The Great Peace* as an early example of what is now common mistake. We know from *Krell v Henry* that the viewing of the coronation would have been the foundation of the contract, so that such a contract would be for the viewing of the procession rather than just the hiring of the room. Essentially, the view of the procession was the subject matter of the contract and since that subject matter could not exist, it could be the basis for common mistake to apply.

→ CROSS-REFERENCE
For the discussion of frustration of the common purpose see 16.4.

17.9.2 Mistake as to Title or Ownership

We know a contract will not be performable if the thing it relates to (the subject matter of the contract) does not exist, but performance of a contract might be radically different to what was intended because of other factors. These factors can be categorised in the same way as the grounds for frustration. Such impossibility or radical difference could be physical, legal or even relate to commercial purpose of the contract. Where that is the case before the contract is made, there is a chance of the contract being void for mistake.

→ CROSS-REFERENCE
For the grounds of frustration see 16.2–16.4.

The case of *Cooper v Phibbs* (1867) LR 2 HL is often treated as an example of 'legal impossibility'. It concerned an agreement for Cooper to buy the lease of a business from Phibbs. Both parties believed Phibbs was the owner. However, unbeknownst to both parties, Cooper was already the owner, and so the House of Lords allowed the contract to be set aside. Lord Atkin in *Bell v Lever Bros* explained *Cooper v Phibbs* as an example of common mistake as to title. But, more broadly, the case can be categorised as one concerning legal impossibility, as it can be said that it is legally impossible to buy something you already own.

17.9.3 Mistakes as to Quality

A significant issue in the law of common mistake relates to mistakes about the quality of the thing contracted for. We will see that there is very little chance of such a claim succeeding but, before doing so, it is important to appreciate what is meant by 'quality' in this context.

A mistake might concern a characteristic of a thing being bought. The usual example is the sale of a painting that the parties mistakenly believe was by a famous artist. The painting exists, but both parties are mistaken about a certain quality of it. This assumption is the 'state of affairs' that does not exist. The question is whether that assumption is enough for the law on mistake to apply.

KEY POINTS

A mistake as to quality is not about how well something performs and whether it is defective. Instead, we are referring to 'a' quality that the parties assumed when contracting.

We know that the chance of the contract being void for mistake is always slim because a restrictive approach is adopted generally so as to protect commercial certainty. But, in addition, mistake as to quality could open the door for the parties to escape a bad bargain, which was also the courts' specific concern with allowing frustration of a common purpose.

The possibility of mistake as to quality was explored by the House of Lords in *Bell v Lever Bros*. As stated earlier, this is the highest authority on mistake. It concerned service contracts Lever Bros had with two of their directors, and one of these directors was the claimant, Bell. The company wanted to end the service contracts of both directors, and to do so, the company contracted to pay Bell £30,000 and the other director £20,000 in compensation. The payments were then made, but later it was discovered that the service contracts could have been ended without compensation. This was because both directors had been involved in activity that conflicted with the interests of the company.

Lever Bros then sued for the return of the money on the basis of fraudulent misrepresentation. When this argument was rejected, the company relied on mistake. The company argued that the payments had been made as a result of a mistaken belief that the directors had a right to be compensated. That was really about the contract being different to what both parties believed it to be. The point was that the contract was supposed to have been one providing for the payment of compensation that the directors *were* entitled to. Instead, it had ended up being a contract for the payment of compensation that they *were not* entitled to. Essentially, there had been a mistake as to a quality of the service contracts. Clearly Lever Bros had made a mistake, but the directors had too and they had negotiated the compensation they believed was due. This mistake argument was rejected by majority of 3:2 in the House of Lords and so the contract was not void. However, the reasoning from the key judgment by Lord Atkin is the source of the principles on common mistake.

On the issue of mistake as to quality Lord Atkin observed:

> Mistake as to quality of the thing contracted for raises more difficult questions. In such a case a mistake will not affect assent unless it is the mistake of both parties, and is as to the existence of some quality which makes the thing without the quality essentially different from the thing as it was believed to be. Of course it may appear that the parties contracted that the article should possess the quality which one or other or both mistakenly believed it to possess. But in such a case there is a contract and the inquiry is a different one, being whether the contract as to quality amounts to a condition or a warranty, a different branch of the law. . .
>
> . . . But, on the whole, I have come to the conclusion that it would be wrong to decide that an agreement to terminate a definite specified contract is void if it turns out that the agreement had already been broken and could have been terminated otherwise. The contract released is the identical contract in both cases, and the party paying for release gets exactly what he bargains for. It seems immaterial that he could have got the same result in another way, or that if he had known the true facts he would not have entered into the bargain. A. buys B.'s horse; he thinks the horse is sound and he pays the price of a sound horse; he would certainly not have bought the horse if he had known as the fact is that the horse is unsound. If B. has made no representation as to soundness and has not contracted that the horse is sound, A. is bound and cannot recover back the price. A. buys a picture from B.; both A. and B. believe it to be the work of an old master, and a high price is paid. It turns out to be a modern copy. A. has no remedy in the absence of representation or warranty. A. agrees to take on a lease or to buy from B. an unfurnished dwelling-house. The house is in fact uninhabitable. A. would never have entered into the bargain if he had known the fact. A. has no remedy, and the position is the same whether B. knew the facts or not, so long as he made no representation or gave no warranty. A. buys a roadside garage business from B. abutting on a public thoroughfare: unknown to A., but known to B., it has already been decided to construct a byepass road which will divert substantially the whole of the traffic from passing A.'s garage. Again A. has no remedy. All these cases involve hardship on A. and benefit B., as most people would say, unjustly. They can be supported on the ground that it is of paramount importance that contracts should be observed, and that if parties honestly comply with the essentials of the formation of contracts—i.e. agree in the same terms on the same subject-matter—they are bound, and must rely on the stipulations of the contract for protection from the effect of facts unknown to them.

This reasoning was shared by the majority. When the contract is for something that does not exist, the contract is essentially different to what the parties consented to. In contrast, the contract in this case was not 'essentially different' to what the parties consented to. It was there to terminate the service contract and the service contract actually existed. The problem was that the parties did not realise the contracts could be ended without compensation, and that was an issue about a quality of the service contract (rather than its existence). The facts were likened to a contract for a horse which stipulates for ownership to be transferred. That objective does not change just because the horse is defective. The same was said about a lease for an uninhabitable house; a garage to be affected by a bypass; and a painting that is modern rather than by an old master. The point was that such quality problems do not mean that the parties failed to consent to the contract. Such a contract is still performable and is not 'essentially different' to what the parties consented to. If anything, the contract is simply a bad bargain.

The judgment by Lord Atkin narrows the scope for mistake relating to a quality. On its own, it could even be said that it rules out the argument completely. However, the two minority judges agreed with the principle of mistake, but not the application by the majority. According to the minority, the mistake had made the contract fundamentally different to what was originally intended. This suggests that in theory, a mistake of quality might make a contract fundamentally different to what was intended. It is just that this was not one such case.

At first instance, Wright J held that the contract was void for common mistake, since both parties contracted on the basis of a false assumption. They both believed the directors were entitled to be compensated. The Court of Appeal and the two dissenting judges of the House of Lords agreed with that approach. According to these judgments, the mistake was fundamental enough. In contrast, the majority did not focus on the importance of the mistake and, instead, they focussed on whether the mistake about a quality made the contract fundamentally different to what was intended.

The obvious criticism is that the majority approach was too restrictive. The mistake was not enough to make the contract 'essentially' or fundamentally different. Both Lever Bros and the directors contracted under the same belief that the directors were entitled to a combined total of £50,000. Apparently, such a resulting contract was not different enough to one in which no compensation was payable. It seems that in either case, the compensation agreement ended the service contracts, which is what it was ultimately created for. In other words, Lever Bros still got something out of the contract, and it did not matter that the service contracts could have been ended in a different way. Essentially, it was just a bad deal. Because of this case, it is difficult to imagine a mistake about quality being enough to make a contract void.

?! THINKING POINTS

Would the decision have been different if the service contracts had been for a fixed term and had already terminated by the time the compensation contracts were entered?

17.9.4 The Application of the Restrictive Approach to Quality

→ CROSS-REFERENCE

For detail of *Leaf v International Galleries* [1950] in the context of misrepresentation see 13.5.2.

The mistake as to quality argument has since featured in a number of cases. We can recall that *Leaf v International Galleries* [1950] concerned the sale of a painting that both parties had mistakenly believed was by the artist Constable. One of the arguments advanced by the buyers was based on common mistake, and was rejected by the Court of Appeal. Denning LJ observed that there was a mistake as to quality, but not about the subject matter of the contract. Both parties entered a contract for the sale of a specific painting and agreed the same terms about the same painting. That was enough for a contract to exist and the authenticity of the painting was not fundamental enough to make a difference. Any remedy would then be based on pre-contractual statements or the terms of the contract. The same can be said about the sale of the car in *Oscar Chess v Williams* [1957].

Clearly, it is very exceptional to succeed in a claim for common mistake as to quality, but it is not impossible. The point is supported by *Associated Japanese Bank (International) Ltd v Credit du Nord SA* [1989] 1 WLR 255. In this case, a businessman sought to raise some money and so he entered into an agreement with the claimant bank. Under this agreement, the bank would buy his packaging machines and then lease them back for him to use. To protect itself, the claimant bank entered into a contract with the defendant bank under which the defendant agreed to act as a guarantor for the lease payments by the businessman. The contract for the guarantee was the subject of the case. The businessman failed to make the payments and then it was discovered that he had been fraudulent and that the machines had never existed. The claimant bank then sought to enforce the guarantee for the outstanding rental payments.

Steyn J held that there was a term making the contract conditional on the machines existing, and that was enough to reject the action by the claimant bank. But he went further and considered the alternative of common mistake. This was not a case about the non-existence of the subject matter of the contract, since the contract was for the guarantee of a debt, and that debt existed. The question was whether the guarantee contract was 'essentially and radically different' because of a mistake made by the parties. According to Steyn J, both parties assumed the debt *related* to the lease of goods that actually existed. On that basis, the guarantee was 'essentially and radically different' to one that was for goods that did *not* exist.

In his reasoning, Steyn J indicated that the case was analogous to those concerning non-existence of a state of affairs. The debt was the subject matter of the contract, but the whole guarantee contract was based on the leased goods actually existing. Such goods would have been the security, so that following non-payment, the claimant bank could recover the money owed from the defendant guarantor, and the defendant guarantor could then cover its loss by taking possession of the goods. This is why the case was deemed to be analogous to those concerning non-existence. This took the contract over the line into being 'essentially and radically different' to what the parties agreed. To that limited extent, the claim based on common mistake as to quality would have been successful.

The most important modern case on common mistake is *Great Peace Shipping v Tsavliris Salvage* [2002] EWCA Civ 1407. This case concerned an argument based on mistake as to a quality, but in it, the Court of Appeal took the opportunity to provide a detailed assessment of the law on common mistake generally.

The facts of the case are straightforward. A ship in the South Indian Ocean was damaged and the defendant salvage company agreed to provide their services to assist. To evacuate the damaged ship, the defendant needed to charter a ship that was nearby, and a list of ships in the area was provided by another organisation. The *Great Peace* was supposed to be 35 miles away from the damaged ship and so the defendant contracted to charter it from its owners. Shortly after, it became apparent that the *Great Peace* was actually 410 miles away. On that basis, the defendant chartered a different ship that was closer and then cancelled the charter of the *Great Peace*. Under the contract for the *Great Peace* there was a cancellation fee of five days' hire, which amounted to $82,500. When the defendants refused to pay, the claimant sued to recover the cancellation fee.

The defendant argued that the contract for the *Great Peace* was void for common mistake. Of course, the chartered ship did exist, but both parties made a mistake about its distance from the damaged ship, and hence a 'quality'. This defence was rejected at first instance and then by Lord Phillips MR delivering the judgment for the Court of Appeal. The relevant extract below from that judgment explains the importance of the construction of the contract and why there is a low likelihood of an argument about mistake as to quality succeeding:

> [82] . . .[A]n allegation that a contract is void for common mistake will often raise important issues of construction. Where it is possible to perform the letter of the contract, but it is alleged that there was a common mistake in relation to a fundamental assumption which renders performance of the essence of the obligation impossible, it will be necessary, by construing the contract in the light of all the material circumstances, to decide whether this is indeed the case. . . .

→ CROSS-REFERENCE
For the facts and decision of *Oscar Chess v Williams* [1957] see 6.2.1.2.

[86] Lord Atkin himself gave no examples of cases where a contract was rendered void because of a mistake as to quality which made "the thing without the quality essentially different from the thing as it was believed to be". He gave a number of examples of mistakes which did not satisfy this test, which served to demonstrate just how narrow he considered the test to be. Indeed this is further demonstrated by the result reached on the facts of *Bell v Lever Bros Ltd* [1932] ...itself. ...

The result in this case

[162] ...It was unquestionably a common assumption of both parties when the contract was concluded that the two vessels were in sufficiently close proximity to enable the Great Peace to carry out the service that she was engaged to perform. Was the distance between the two vessels so great as to confound that assumption and to render the contractual adventure impossible of performance? If so, the defendants would have an arguable case that the contract was void under the principle in *Bell v Lever Bros* ...

165 ...the vessels were considerably further apart than the defendants had believed did not mean that the services that the Great Peace was in a position to provide were essentially different from those which the parties had envisaged when the contract was concluded. The Great Peace would arrive in time to provide several days of escort service. The defendants would have wished the contract to be performed but for the adventitious arrival on the scene of a vessel prepared to perform the same services. The fact that the vessels were further apart than both parties had appreciated did not mean that it was impossible to perform the contractual adventure.

The question was whether the mistake as to a quality was enough to make the contract impossible or 'essentially' different. To work out the performance expected, the court examined the contractual 'adventure' of the *Great Peace* providing assistance and an escort service for the damaged ship. This adventure remained possible even though the *Great Peace* was very far away. It could still arrive and provide a few days of assistance. Lord Phillips MR agreed with the judgment of Toulson J at first instance, which had focussed on the conduct of the defendant charterers. When they had discovered the true location of the *Great Peace* they had not tried to cancel it immediately. Instead, they had secured the alternative, closer ship first. Once that was done, they had then tried to cancel the contract with the *Great Peace*. This conduct showed that the contractual adventure had still been possible and that it was just a better option to use a closer ship. Essentially, the use of the *Great Peace* was just a bad bargain.

We already know that *The Great Peace* case is significant because in it, the Court of Appeal firmly aligned common mistake with frustration so as to clarify its legal basis. In addition, it also reformulated the test for common mistake. But in the context of mistake as to quality, the case confirms and continues the very strict approach adopted in *Bell v Lever Bros*. On that point Lord Phillips MR acknowledged the examples given by Lord Atkin. In those examples, it was clear that, had the real facts been known, the contracts would not have been made, yet that was not enough for a mistake as to quality to be operative. Instead, the mistake has to be so fundamental that it means that performance is impossible or essentially different and it seems highly unlikely that a mistake as to quality will be sufficient for this.

Bell v Lever Bros continues to be the most authoritative case on common mistake since it was decided by the House of Lords, but it is the interpretation from the *Great Peace* that should be applied. However, the *Great Peace* is most notable for what it did in relation to common mistake in equity, and this is our next issue.

17.10 Common Mistake in Equity

In *Bell v Lever Bros* the mistake related to the quality of the subject matter of the contract. It was a very serious mistake and yet the contract was not void. It is hard to imagine a mistake as to quality being more serious and so the case created a real barrier to relying on a mistake as to quality. However, in

Solle v Butcher [1950] 1 KB 671, Denning LJ famously managed to introduce an exception based on the equitable jurisdiction. Its practical significance was that it served as a way around the strict common law approach.

Solle v Butcher concerned the lease of a flat with an agreed rent of £250 a year. However, both parties did not realise that rent control rules applied to the flat, which limited the rent to £140 per year. At best, this was an instance of the parties making a mistake about a quality, and the mistake was nowhere near as serious as the one in *Bell v Lever Bros*. In that case, the difference was between paying nothing and paying £50,000, whereas in *Solle*, the difference was between paying £140 a year or £250 a year. Clearly, the common mistake in *Solle* was not enough to make the contract void, but Denning LJ (with the support of Bucknill LJ) reasoned that the approach adopted in *Bell* only applied at common law. They then held that the equitable jurisdiction could grant rescission following a common mistake, which meant the mistake in effect made the contract voidable. This approach was based on an interpretation of the case law from the equitable jurisdiction. In particular Denning LJ placed a great deal of reliance on the House of Lords case of *Cooper v Phipps* (1867) LR 2 HL 149. The principle was stated in the following way:

> A contract is . . .liable in equity to be set aside if the parties were under a common misapprehension either as to the facts or as to their relative and respective rights, provided that the misapprehension was fundamental and the party seeking to set it aside was not himself at fault.

Later, in *Magee v Pennine Insurance Co Ltd* [1969] 2 QB 507, Lord Denning MR cited the principle again so that *Solle* represented a wider principle of common mistake. It did not sit easily next to the House of Lords decision in *Bell* since it was based on an assumption that the judgments in *Bell* represented the common law position only.

Following *Solle*, there was uncertainty as to the scope of the principle it represented and when it would be applied. Later cases treated mistake in equity as something that could be argued if the contract was not void at common law under the strict standard from *Bell*. In *Solle*, Denning LJ suggested that the principle from equity had always been there, but was just not addressed by the House of Lords in *Bell*. The effect was to distinguish *Solle* from *Bell* so that *Bell* did not have to be followed. In doing this, Denning LJ was said to be simply recognising the full scope of the law on common mistake. Clearly, this was a very bold move on his part and, given the basis of the principle, we might assume that it was short lived. However, the principle remained in place for over 50 years until it was reviewed in *The Great Peace*. This review of mistake in equity is the most significant part of that case.

GUIDED READING 17.2

Great Peace Shipping v Tsavliris Salvage (International) Ltd (The Great Peace) [2002] EWCA Civ 1407

When reading the extract below from the judgment by Lord Phillips MR from *The Great Peace*, try to identify:

- the difficulty resulting from having a different standard for mistake in equity; and
- why *Bell* represents a complete statement on common mistake rather than just at common law.

[98] The following issues fall to be considered in relation to the effect of common mistake in equity. (1) Prior to *Bell v Lever Bros Ltd* was there established a doctrine under which equity permitted rescission of a contract on grounds of common mistake in circumstances where the contract was valid at common law? (2) Could such a doctrine stand with *Bell v Lever Bros Ltd*? (3) Is this court none the less bound to find that such a doctrine exists having regard to *Solle v Butcher* and subsequent decisions?

His comments helpfully begin by listing three questions needing to be answered. These suggest that even if there was an inconsistency between *Bell* and *Solle* it was still possible for the Court of Appeal here to find that the *Solle v Butcher* line of cases could be followed.

[The judgment then assessed *Bell v Lever Bros* along with the cases that pre-dated it including cases based on equity]

[118] These passages demonstrate that the House of Lords in *Bell v Lever Bros* . . . considered that the intervention of equity, as demonstrated in *Cooper v Phibbs* . . ., took place in circumstances where the common law would have ruled the contract void for mistake. We do not find it conceivable that the House of Lords overlooked an equitable right in *Lever Bros* to rescind the agreement, notwithstanding that the agreement was not void for mistake at common law. The jurisprudence established no such right. Lord Atkin's test for common mistake that avoided a contract, while narrow, broadly reflected the circumstances where equity had intervened to excuse performance of a contract assumed to be binding in law.

Lord Phillips MR then explained that the House of Lords in *Bell* had not overlooked equity, as Denning LJ had seemed to imply in *Solle*, and indeed it was not 'conceivable' that the House of Lords would have done so.

[Denning LJ's reasoning in *Solle v Butcher* was then discussed]

[126] Toulson J . . . described this decision by Denning LJ as one which 'sought to outflank *Bell v Lever Bros Ltd* . . .' We think that this was fair comment. It was not realistic to treat the House of Lords in *Bell v Lever Bros Ltd* as oblivious to principles of equity, nor to suggest that 'if it had been considered on equitable grounds the result might have been different'. For the reasons that we have given, we do not consider that *Cooper v Phibbs* . . . demonstrated or established an equitable jurisdiction to grant rescission for common mistake in circumstances that fell short of those in which the common law held a contract void . . ..

This meant that Denning LJ's analysis of *Bell* was simply wrong, although of course the position was stated more politely than that (with Denning LJ's reading of *Bell* described as 'not realistic').

. . .

[130] In *Bell v Lever Bros Ltd* the House of Lords equated the circumstances which rendered a contract void for common mistake with those which discharged the obligations of the parties under the doctrine of frustration. Denning LJ rightly concluded that the facts of *Solle v Butcher* . . . did not amount to such circumstances. The equitable jurisdiction that he then asserted was a significant extension of any jurisdiction exercised up to that point and one that was not readily reconcilable with the result in *Bell v Lever Bros Ltd*.

[153] A number of cases, albeit a small number, in the course of the last 50 years have purported to follow *Solle v Butcher* [1950] . . ., yet none of them defines the test of mistake that gives rise to the equitable jurisdiction to rescind in a manner that distinguishes this from the test of a mistake that renders a contract void in law, as identified in *Bell v Lever Bros Ltd* [1932] . . . This is, perhaps, not surprising, for Denning LJ, the author of the test in *Solle v Butcher*, set *Bell v Lever Bros Ltd* at nought. It is possible to reconcile *Solle v Butcher* and *Magee v Pennine Insurance Co Ltd* [1969] . . . with *Bell v Lever Bros Ltd* only by postulating that there are two categories of mistake, one that renders a contract void at law and one that renders it voidable in equity. Although later cases have proceeded on this basis, it is not possible to identify that proposition in the judgment of any of the three Lords Justices, Denning, Bucknill and Fenton Atkinson, who participated in the majority decisions in the former two cases. Nor, over 50 years, has it proved possible to define satisfactorily two different qualities of mistake, one operating in law and one in equity.

Lord Phillips MR next summarises the problem arising from Denning LJ's judgment in *Solle*, which was to in effect create two categories of mistake—one in law and one in equity, both of which having different outcomes and neither of which being properly defined. This was not a sensible position for the law to be in.

[154] In *Solle v Butcher* Denning LJ identified the requirement of a common misapprehension that was 'fundamental', and that adjective has been used to describe the mistake in those cases which have followed *Solle v Butcher*. We do not find it possible to distinguish, by a process of definition, a mistake which is 'fundamental' from Lord Atkin's mistake as to quality which 'makes the thing [contracted for] essentially different from the thing [that] it was believed to be' . . .

He elaborated on this further by explaining that the failure to define the difference between equitable and common law mistake was based on there being no actual difference between what the common law required for there to have been a common mistake, and Denning LJ's proposal that in equity the requirement was for a 'fundamental' common misapprehension. These were in effect the same thing.

[155] A common factor in *Solle v Butcher* and the cases which have followed it can be identified. The effect of the mistake has been to make the contract a particularly bad bargain for one of the parties. Is there a principle of equity which justifies the court in rescinding a contract where a common mistake has produced this result?

...

[156] Thus the premise of equity's intrusion into the effects of the common law is that the common law rule in question is seen in the particular case to work injustice, and for some reason the common law cannot cure itself. But it is difficult to see how that can apply here. Cases of fraud and misrepresentation, and undue influence, are all catered for under other existing and uncontentious equitable rules. We are only concerned with the question whether relief might be given for common mistake in circumstances wider than those stipulated in *Bell v Lever Bros Ltd* ... But that, surely, is a question as to where the common law should draw the line; not whether, given the common law rule, it needs to be mitigated by application of some other doctrine. The common law has drawn the line in *Bell v Lever Bros Ltd*. The effect of *Solle v Butcher* ... is not to supplement or mitigate the common law: it is to say that *Bell v Lever Bros Ltd* was wrongly decided.

[157] Our conclusion is that it is impossible to reconcile *Solle v Butcher* with *Bell v Lever Bros Ltd*. The jurisdiction asserted in the former case has not developed. It has been a fertile source of academic debate, but in practice it has given rise to a handful of cases that have merely emphasised the confusion of this area of our jurisprudence ..., Toulson J ... has demonstrated the extent of that confusion. If coherence is to be restored to this area of our law, it can only be by declaring that there is no jurisdiction to grant rescission of a contract on the ground of common mistake where that contract is valid and enforceable on ordinary principles of contract law. That is the conclusion of Toulson J. Do the principles of case precedent permit us to endorse it? What is the correct approach where this court concludes that a decision of the Court of Appeal cannot stand with an earlier decision of the House of Lords? There are two decisions which bear on this question ...

[160] We have been in some doubt as to whether this line of authority goes far enough to permit us to hold that *Solle v Butcher* ... is not good law. We are very conscious that we are not only scrutinising the reasoning of Lord Denning MR in *Solle v Butcher* and in *Magee v Pennine Insurance Co Ltd* [1969] ... but are also faced with a number of later decisions in which Lord Denning MR's approach has been approved and followed. Further, a division of this court has made it clear in *West Sussex Properties Ltd v Chichester District Council* 28 June 2000 that they felt bound by *Solle v Butcher*. However, it is to be noticed that while junior counsel in the court below in the *West Sussex Properties* case had sought to challenge the correctness of *Solle v Butcher*, in the Court of Appeal leading counsel accepted that it was good law unless and until overturned by their Lordships' House. In this case we have heard full argument, which has provided what we believe has been the first opportunity in this court for a full and mature consideration of the relation between *Bell v Lever Bros Ltd* and *Solle v Butcher*. In the light of that consideration we can see no way that *Solle v Butcher* can stand with *Bell v Lever Bros Ltd*. In these circumstances we can see no option but so to hold.

More importantly, though, *Solle v Butcher* and the cases following it had allowed mistake to result in contracts being voidable simply on the basis of being bad bargains. This was precisely what the House of Lords had sought to avoid in *Bell v Lever Bros*, so the only way to allow the *Solle* line of cases to remain good law would be to suggest that the basis for the decision in *Bell* had been entirely wrong.

It was in other words impossible to reconcile *Solle* and *Bell*, and the law had to fall down on the side of the latter, partly because it was a House of Lords decision but also because it was in keeping with accepted fundamental principles of common law.

There was some reluctance about this, because it meant in effect overturning a considerable body of cases following on from *Solle v Butcher*—most recently in the year 2000, only two years prior to the *Great Peace*. But it had to be done to make the law clear.

[161]. We can understand why the decision in *Bell v Lever Bros Ltd* did not find favour with Lord Denning MR. An equitable jurisdiction to grant rescission on terms where a common fundamental mistake has induced a contract gives greater flexibility than a doctrine of common law which holds the contract void in such circumstances. Just as the Law Reform (Frustrated Contracts) Act 1943 was needed to temper the effect of the common law doctrine of frustration, so there is scope for legislation to give greater flexibility to our law of mistake than the common law allows.

> The judgment closes by conceding that Denning LJ's approach did at least make for greater flexibility, but it suggested that the appropriate way to achieve this was through legislation rather than judicial innovation. This is a slightly strange comment, because usually legislation is seen as a 'blunt instrument' that must be given flexibility by the courts, but in any event legislation on the matter is very unlikely to be forthcoming.

This part of *The Great Peace* judgment is very significant as it aims to end the approach represented by *Solle v Butcher*. In doing so, it removes the principle of mistake in equity which had been part of the law of mistake for over 50 years.

The importance of the reasoning lies in how the Court of Appeal disposed of mistake in equity. It made clear that the principle from equity applied in the same way as the common law and was not a wider principle, and that there was no likelihood that the House of Lords had overlooked equity cases in *Bell*. This meant that when the House of Lords had stated their principle of common mistake in *Bell*, they had made a complete statement of the law.

It also made the law much clearer. The two tests arising from *Solle* and *Bell* appeared to mean the same thing yet, somehow, rescission could be allowed in equity when the test for making the contract void at common law was not satisfied. This unsatisfactory position was brought to an end.

A third point concerned the role of equity. Traditionally, it applied in circumstances where the common law rules did not apply. The idea was that equity prevented any injustice resulting from the common law being unable to develop so as to provide justice in a given situation. An example would be the rules on undue influence. The common law had no rules to cover the effects of undue influence and the duress principle was too narrow to do so. The same could not be said for common mistake, because the Lords in *Bell* had stated the test to be applied and defined its scope. It was therefore a misuse of equity to extend that scope in *Solle v Butcher*.

The fourth point related to the power of the Court of Appeal in *The Great Peace* to set aside the doctrine of mistake in equity, which had been introduced by the Court of Appeal itself in *Solle*. Court of Appeal decisions are ordinarily binding on future Courts of Appeal. In addition, *Solle* had existed for over 50 years and had been applied by other courts, including the Court of Appeal. According to the judgment in the *Great Peace*, however, those later cases had never provided a detailed assessment of the principle and that meant the Court of Appeal was not clashing head on with its own previous decisions. Instead, the Court described itself as doing something it had not done before, which was to provide a detailed assessment of *Solle*. That detailed assessment revealed that *Solle* was inconsistent with *Bell v Lever Bros* and, since *Bell* was an earlier case from the House of Lords, it should have been followed in *Solle*.

The judgment in *The Great Peace* set out to set aside *Solle v Butcher* and end mistake in equity. This was a difficult task and one that would ordinarily only have been expected of the House of Lords. The fact that it was done with a single judgment means there is less scope to interpret and limit the effect intended. If there had been different judgments, it would have then invited lawyers to focus on any differences in the language used, the issues addressed and not addressed, and so on. Such differences could potentially then have been used to suggest that some aspect of mistake in equity remained. The scope for doing was removed because of there only being a single judgment.

The Great Peace serves to clarify the law and remove the uncertainty that surrounded mistake in equity. It is generally seen as a welcome and sensible change to the law. However, one concern has been that it effectively overruled *Solle* when the outcome of the case did not strictly speaking require it to do so. In other words, the outcome would have been the same even if *Solle* was not set aside, because the mistake would not have been fundamental enough for *Solle* to apply anyway. Also, the mistake about the location of the ship was one that was covered by the terms of the contract. This means that in theory, it could be said that *Solle* was not formally overruled. Consequently, a subsequent Court of Appeal might be able to choose between *Solle* or *The Great Peace*. In reality, such a problem is unlikely given the detailed assessment provided in *The Great Peace* as well as the support it has received. The opinion of Lord Walker in the Supreme Court case of *Pitt v Holt and another; Futter and another v Futter and others* [2013] UKSC 26; *Pitt v Commissioners for HMRC* [2013] UKSC 26 is useful here too. There Lord Walker referred to *The Great Peace* and added that it 'did not follow (and has effectively overruled) *Solle v Butcher*.' Opinions such as that reinforce *The Great Peace* and serve to keep the principle from *Solle v Butcher* buried.

KEY POINTS

The Great Peace has effectively overruled *Solle v Butcher* and ended the more relaxed approach of common mistake in equity.

17.11 Equitable 'Rectification' for Common Mistake

A common mistake about a state of affairs existing at the time of making a contract can, then, result in the contract being void. A separate issue can arise when the parties enter into an agreement which is later put into writing. Such a process is something we might expect of most commercial contracts. Parties negotiate orally and eventually agree, and then want to formalise their agreement. But what if the written version does not reflect what was agreed? In such a case it might be possible to rely on rectification, which is a remedy developed in equity rather than under the common law. Essentially, a party applies to have the written version of a contract corrected so as to reflect what was really agreed, or if there was no prior agreement, then what the parties actually intended. This is a remedy that applies in limited circumstances only because the courts are keen to ensure it is not used just to escape a bad deal. For the purposes of this chapter, we cover the basic essentials only to provide awareness of the remedy.

It is important to appreciate when rectification applies. It is not concerned with mistakes in the initial agreement which remains performable. Instead, rectification is concerned with an error made when what was agreed (or to be agreed) was put in writing. A crude illustration would be two parties appearing to orally agree to, or negotiate to agree, the supply of 'diet cola' but then drawing up a written version of the agreement referring to 'cola'.

The approach to rectification is strict, as illustrated in *Fredrick E Rose (London) Ltd v William H Pim Jnr & Co* [1953] 2 QB 450. In this case, Egyptian buyers asked the claimant to supply 'feveroles'. The claimant did not know what feveroles were, so they asked the defendants. The defendants said 'feveroles' were just horsebeans and so, on that basis, the claimant bought a quantity of horsebeans from the defendant which were then resold to the Egyptian buyers. The Egyptian buyers then claimed damages for breach because 'feveroles' were a specific type of horsebean rather than horsebeans generally. The claimant then sought rectification of their contract with the defendant. They wanted to switch the word 'horsebeans' to the more specific word 'feveroles'. The claimant would then be able to claim damages from the defendant for breach.

The Court of Appeal refused to allow for rectification and overturned the first instance decision. Essentially, the written document reflected what the parties had agreed. Of course, both parties had made a mistake by believing that 'feveroles' meant 'horsebeans'. On that basis, they had made their initial agreement for horsebeans and so, objectively, that was what their agreement appeared to be for. As a result, the written version simply reflected what appeared to have been agreed. On the facts, there had been no common mistake in drafting the written contract. While rectification was refused, the contract was voidable for misrepresentation. However, rescission was barred because the ownership of the beans had passed to the Egyptian buyers.

Later cases like *Joscelyne v Nissen* [1970] 2 QB 86 show that the initial agreement does not have to be a complete agreement and can have some uncertainties. In that case, the Court of Appeal did

→ CROSS-REFERENCE

For the discussion of third party rights as a bar to rescission see 13.5.4.

allow rectification. Useful guidance was also provided by Peter Gibson LJ in *Swainland Builders Ltd v Freehold Properties Ltd* [2002] 2 EGLR, which can be summarised in the following way:

(1) The parties must have a 'common continuing intention' about an issue in the document to be rectified.

(2) While the agreement does not have to be a complete one, there still needs to be an outward expression of an agreement.

(3) The 'common continuing intention' must have continued to the time the document was drafted.

(4) As a result of a mistake, the document does not reflect the common continuing intention.

One contentious issue has been about whether such a 'common continuing intention' should be determined with an objective or subjective assessment. Lord Hoffman, in *Chartbook Ltd v Persimmon Homes* [2009] UKHL 38, expressed a clear *obiter* comment in favour of an objective approach. This certainly made sense in the context of rectifying a written document that was meant to reflect a prior agreement. However, recently in *FSHC Group Holdings Ltd v GLAS Trust Corp Ltd* [2019] EWCA Civ 1361, Leggatt LJ for the Court of Appeal made clear that a subjective assessment applies when the common intention is not in the form of prior agreement. This represents a welcome clarification that is supported by the case law and leading academic commentators.

While the application of rectification is limited in order to ensure that it is not used just to get out of a bad deal, the need for rectification is limited further by the recent principles of interpretation. We can recall that when Lord Hoffman restated the principles of interpreting contracts he also referred to circumstances in which errors have been made in the language of a contract. His comments make clear that judges can interpret contract terms in a way that corrects obvious mistakes so as to enable the contract to reflect commercial common sense. Such an approach was supported by the judgment of Arden LJ in *Cherry Tree Investments Ltd v Landmain Ltd* [2012] EWCA Civ 736 in which Lord Hoffman's principles were described as a form of 'corrective interpretation'.

> **→ CROSS-REFERENCE**
>
> For the discussion of the interpretation principles see 6.4.

Having the wider modern tool of 'corrective interpretation' available raises an obvious question about the need for rectification. Certainly, the scope for corrective interpretation reduces the need to rely on a rectification claim, but it does not replace rectification entirely because of differences between the claims. The main one is that evidence of earlier negotiations cannot be used when interpreting the contract whereas such evidence is relied upon in claims for rectification. Also, consider a mistake resulting in terms not being included in the contract. Those terms cannot be added through interpretation because the judges are only to interpret the terms that are actually in the contract. For that reason, a (corrective) interpretation was not possible in the *Cherry Tree Investments* case.

17.12 The *Non Est Factum* Defence

We now turn to a very limited defence, often referred to as the 'plea of *non est factum*'. It is addressed in this chapter because it relates to a mistake resulting in there being no consent to a contract. The term '*non est factum*' is Latin for 'it is not my deed' and is an old defence from the sixteenth century when contracts were in the form of a deed. It applied when a party was blind or illiterate and therefore unable to know what they had signed, and did so after having been misled. The modern context is wider and the defence is now available as protection not only for the illiterate and blind. It is also worth pointing out that even if the defence is not successful it still might mean that the contract is voidable for fraud.

> **→ CROSS-REFERENCE**
>
> For the discussion of parties being bound by what they sign see 6.2.1.

We know that as a general rule, a party is bound by what they sign because a signature is taken to indicate a clear apparent intention enter into the contract. *Non est factum* can then be described as being a very limited exception to this general rule. In fact, the defence is so limited that it has not been successful since it was defined by the House of Lords in *Saunders v Anglia Building Society* [1971] AC 1004 (often known as *Gallie v Lee*).

The case is the leading authority on *non est factum* and it concerned a 78-year-old widow (Mrs Gallie). She intended to sign over her house to her nephew. This was to be done as a gift so he could use it as security to finance a business with Mr Lee. Lee presented a deed to Gallie for her to sign, but she was unable to read it because she had broken her glasses. For that reason, she asked Lee what the document was and he explained that it was a deed of gift that would gift the house to her nephew. She then signed it and the signature was witnessed by her nephew. In reality, the document was a deed of sale and it actually resulted in the house being sold to Lee who then used it as security for a mortgage. He spent the money for his own purposes and did not make any mortgage repayments, which then prompted the mortgage lender to seek possession of the house. When the lender took action, Gallie relied on the *non est factum* defence. The House of Lords acknowledged the defence and defined its scope but then held that Gallie could not rely on it.

The judgments acknowledged that the defence was originally available for the blind and the illiterate, citing *Thoroughgood's Case* (1582) 2 Co Rep 9b as authority for the point. They then confirmed that the defence was not limited to the blind and illiterate and, instead, it applies to any party not capable of reading or understanding a document they are signing. The case also confirmed the effect of the defence. If successful, it means that there was no consent to the contract and so it will be void.

The judgments in *Gallie v Lee* analysed the old cases on *non est factum* and, in doing so, they set out the following requirements for the defence to operate:

- The signature must result from fraud;
- The content of the document must be fundamentally different to what the innocent party believed it to be;
- The innocent party cannot be at fault.

The first factor is straightforward and should have been satisfied on the facts. Likewise, the third factor was not an issue as there was no fault by Gallie. She was unable to read the document and relied on Lee to explain it. The reason for rejecting the defence was based on the second factor. She knew the contract would remove her interest in the property and also that her nephew planned to use it for a mortgage to finance a venture with Lee. For that reason, the House of Lords felt that the deed was not 'fundamentally different' to what she would have believed it to be.

> ### ?! THINKING POINTS
>
> Do you agree with the decision in against Gallie?
>
> What competing interests was the court trying to balance?

The case shows that a very strict approach is adopted to the defence. In fact, Lord Wilberforce observed that Gallie's argument 'fell short, very far short' of what was needed for it to succeed. The document was different to what she had been led to believe but that difference was not enough to show there was no consent at all. At best, there would have been fraud, and that would have made the contract voidable. Such a remedy would have been of no use, though, because the lender had agreed to the mortgage arrangements before there had been any attempt to rescind the deed.

The strict approach serves to protect third parties relying on a contract. Consider the defendant lender, who was an innocent third party. It lent money to Lee because the signed deed indicated that he owned the property. If the document was void, then the lender would have no security to rely on following non-payment. The point is that in applying the defence, the interests of the victim and innocent third parties have to be balanced against each other.

A further limit is in the third requirement. The victim cannot be at fault, and this could simply mean a failure to take sufficient precautions. The obvious example is signing something without enquiring about its content and effect. Lord Wilberforce made it clear that it is for the party relying on the defence to prove they acted carefully. Lord Pearson gave the example of a person in business who is given a pile of documents by a secretary. The documents are not read and, instead, the business person relies on the secretary to explain the content of the documents. If the secretary has fraudulently slipped in a different document, the business person is at fault. In such circumstances, *non est factum* cannot be relied upon. According Lord Pearson, the business person 'takes the chance of a fraudulent substitution'. Judges, then, will restrict the defence using a strict approach to fault.

Overall, it is clear that the defence does exist, but its application in practice is very narrow and highly exceptional. With such a low likelihood of success, it is better to rely on other principles to escape a contract.

CHAPTER SUMMARY

- The general rule is that objectively, if there appears to be an agreement, then there is one. There are some exceptions for mistakes but the application of them is very limited.
- Such 'operative' mistakes mean that there was no consent to an agreement, or the consent was negated. Either way, the contract is void from the start.
- Some mistakes prevent the formation of an agreement, such as:
  - A cross-purposes mistake resulting from an ambiguity (where both parties intend something different).
  - A unilateral mistake where one party enters an agreement on the basis of a fundamental mistake about a term that the other party knows about; or where there is a mistake as to the identity of one party.
- Mistake as to identity can be operative if it appears that the offer or acceptance was intended for someone else. For that it has to appear that identity was fundamental.
- A mistake about the attributes of one party, such as their ability to pay, will simply result in a contract that is voidable for misrepresentation.
- The cases make a distinction between transactions made through correspondence in writing and those that have been made face to face.
- There is a strong presumption that in face-to-face transactions, a party intends to contract with the person physically in front of them, rather than the person they pretended to be. The presumption is so strong that it seems like a rule.
- The approach adopted can be criticised for failing to protect innocent third parties. Where the mistake is operative, the contract is void even though the seller was partly at fault. It might be fairer for mistakes as to identity to result in a voidable contract.
- A common mistake (the same fundamental mistake by both parties) can negate consent and thereby result in a void contract.
- Common mistake is related to frustration. Frustration takes place when performance of the contract becomes radically different to what was intended due to a supervening event. With common mistake, the contract was impossible or would result in radically different performance from what was envisaged right from the start.
- Just like frustration, a restrictive approach is adopted to prevent a party escaping a bad bargain.
- Recently the requirements were summarised by the Court of Appeal. The Court also confirmed its legal basis as being a rule of law rather than an implied term.
- The mistake has to be so fundamental that it means the performance is impossible or essentially different to what was agreed. It is highly unlikely that a mistake as to quality will be sufficient.
- The Court of Appeal introduced a more relaxed standard of common mistake in equity in the case of *Solle v Butcher* but 50 years later this was effectively overruled, again by the Court of Appeal.

- Equitable rectification is a possible remedy where a written contract does not reflect what had been agreed, or the continuing common intention for the contract.
- The very old defence of *non est factum* remains available but its requirements are so strict so that its use is extremely unlikely.

KEY CASES

☐ *Smith v Hughes* (1871) **LR 6 QB 597**—This is the main authority for the objective approach to contract formation and represents the starting point on mistake issues.

☐ *Chwee Kin Keong v Digilandmall.com Pte* [2005] **1 SLR 502**—The Singapore Court of Appeal in this case applied *Hartog v Colin & Shields* [1939] 3 All ER 566 on the matter of unilateral mistake as to a term. It is not binding on English courts but contains very useful reasoning.

☐ *Cundy v Lindsay* (1878) **3 App Cas 459**—The early House of Lords case on what is now unilateral mistake as to identity. Even the latest case from the House of Lords aimed to be consistent with it.

☐ *King's Norton Metal Co Ltd v Edridge* (1897) **14 TLR 98**—A case identifying a limit to *Cundy*, where the mistake was simply about attributes rather than identity.

☐ *Phillips v Brooks Ltd* [1919] **2 KB 243**—The case that confirmed the distinction between face-to-face transactions and those made through written correspondence. It is also the source of the presumption that in a face-to-face transaction, parties intend to contract with the person physically in front of them.

☐ *Shogun Finance v Hudson* [2005] **UKHL 62**—As the most recent case from the House of Lords on mistake as to identity, it is the leading case on that issue. The detailed analysis confirmed the previous case law and re-emphasised how difficult it is to rebut the presumption applied to face-to-face transactions.

☐ *Bell v Lever Bros* [1932] **AC 161**—As the only case on common mistake from the House of Lords it is the key authority and so all cases on the issue will cite it and aim to be consistent with it. It provides the test to be applied for establishing a mistake as to quality and makes clear that this will be very difficult to pass.

☐ *Great Peace Shipping v Tsavliris Salvage (International) Ltd* (*The Great Peace*) [2002] **EWCA Civ 1407**—The most recent appeal case on common mistake. It provided an interpretation of *Bell v Lever Bros* and formulated that decision into a test. Most notably, it ended the more flexible principle of common mistake in equity.

☐ *Triple Seven MSN 27251 Ltd v Azman Air Services Ltd* [2018] **EWHC 1348 (Comm)**—a recent first instance case on common mistake that skilfully explains and clarifies the tests confirmed in *The Great Peace*.

QUESTIONS

1. 'The current position on mistake as to identity fails to strike an adequate balance between the rights of the innocent seller (who sold goods to a fraudster) and the interests of an innocent third party to whom the goods were resold (by the fraudster).'

   With reference to the case law, assess the accuracy of the statement above.

2. Critically evaluate the extent to which a party can rely on common mistake to render a contract void.

3. Jerzy owns a business producing fancy dress costumes based on films and books. He is visited by a con artist called Kelly Chase who introduces herself as Leeta van Themaat, the Regional Purchasing Manager of Waitbury's, a well-known large supermarket chain. She negotiates the purchase of 1000 costumes from Jerzy's 'Roald Dahl' collection at a total price of £5,000, to be formalised later. Later

that day, an email arrives with an attached Waitbury's contract, with terms indicating that payment will be made within a week of receiving the goods with an invoice. Jerzy signs and returns the document before arranging for delivery to the address of the regional Waitbury's warehouse indicated in the contract. A week after delivering the goods, Jerzy has not received any payment and visits the office at the warehouse only to discover an empty building. He then discovers his goods were sold to a local fancy dress shop. Realising that he has been the victim of fraud, Jerzy now wants his goods returned. Advise Jerzy.

4. (a) Hotel Zheng contracts with Ellen's Patisserie for the weekly supply of 500 cupcakes topped with buttercream made using butter from the famous Dave's Organic Dairy (DOD). Unknown to both parties, DOD ceased trading shortly before the contract was entered. Following Ellen's failure to supply the cupcakes using the 'DOD' buttercream, Hotel Zheng claims damages from Ellen. Advise Ellen.

   (b) Eco-Building is building company specialising in the building of eco-friendly homes. They enter a contract to build 2000 homes for Green holdings on a plot of land recently acquired by Green Holdings. Their negotiations started because of the Government policy of providing Eco-grants to builders. These grants were for £15,000 per house build to pay towards solar panels and air compressor units for heating. Unknown to the parties, two days before signing their contract, the Government formally revokes the building grants. Eco-Building now refuses to carry out the building work because of the unexpected increase in costs. Advise Eco-Building.

 For answer guidance to these questions please visit the online resources at www .oup.com/uk/naidoo1e/, where you will also find multiple choice questions to check your understanding of key concepts.

FURTHER READING

Chandler, Devenney & Poole, 'Common mistake: theoretical justification and remedial inflexibility' [2004] JBL 34.
A clear and long article on the significance of *The Great Peace*. There is a lot of detail on the theoretical basis of common mistake and the article also explores the role of equity.

Hare, 'Identity mistakes: a missed opportunity?' MLR (2004), 67(6), 993.
A clear and detailed critique of *Shogun Finance* that favours the approach taken by the minority.

Macmillan, 'Rogues, Swindlers and Cheats: The Development of Mistake of identity in English Contract Law' (2005) 64(3) CLJ 711.
This is a detailed and long article that explores the historical background of the early cases on mistake as to identity and argues that *Cundy v Lindsey* was influenced by the criminal law.

MacMillan, 'Mistake as to identity clarified?' LQR (2004) 120(Jul), 369.
A useful short case note on *Shogun Finance*.

Morgan, 'Common mistake in contract: rare success and common misapprehensions' (2018) 77(3) CLJ, 559.
A clear extended note on the recent cases arguing common mistake, suggesting that the principle of common mistake should be replaced.

Peel, 'Rectification revisited' LQR (2020), 136, 205.
A clear and short note on the judgment of Leggatt LJ in *FSHC Group Holdings v GLAS Trust Corp*.

Index